UNIVERSITY CASEBOOK SERIES®

FEDERAL INCOME TAXATION

SEVENTH EDITION

DANIEL L. SIMMONS
Professor of Law Emeritus
University of California at Davis

MARTIN J. MCMAHON, JR.
James J. Freeland Eminent Scholar in Taxation
Professor of Law
University of Florida

BRADLEY T. BORDEN
Professor of Law
Brooklyn Law School

DENNIS J. VENTRY, JR.
Professor of Law
University of California at Davis

FOUNDATION
PRESS

University Casebook Series is a trademark registered in the U.S. Patent and Trademark Office.

© 1950, 1953–1955, 1960, 1962, 1972, 1986, 1994, 1998, 2004 FOUNDATION PRESS
© 2008 By THOMSON REUTERS/FOUNDATION PRESS
© 2017 LEG, Inc. d/b/a West Academic
    444 Cedar Street, Suite 700
    St. Paul, MN 55101
    1-877-888-1330

Printed in the United States of America

ISBN: 978-1-60930-264-1

PREFACE

This text deals with fundamental income taxation principles. What is income? What expenditures are deductible? When are income and deduction items properly taken into account? Who is the appropriate taxpayer? This seventh edition is a significant revision of the material in the sixth edition, reflecting new tax legislation enacted since 2008, as well as the important judicial and administrative developments in that time period.

Because the detail and complexity of the Internal Revenue Code and Treasury Regulations continue to increase, this edition, like its predecessors, is selective rather than encyclopedic. Our guiding philosophy in selecting and structuring the materials has been to organize the materials to facilitate selective assignments for a three or four hour basic course that demonstrate the overall structure and policies of federal income taxation and provide in depth analysis of representative important issues. In their entirety the materials provide sufficient scope and depth for a sequence of two or more courses ranging from five to nine hours, depending on whether the courses are at the J.D. or LL.M. level. As a result, it is not possible to cover the entire volume in a single three or four hour course in Basic Federal Income Taxation.

Like its predecessor editions and its companion volumes, FEDERAL INCOME TAXATION OF BUSINESS ORGANIZATIONS, 5TH ED., FEDERAL INCOME TAXATION OF CORPORATIONS 4th ED., AND FEDERAL INCOME TAXATION OF PARTNERSHIPS AND S CORPORATIONS, 5TH ED., this book charts a course between those books that employ primarily textual explanation and those that rely for the most part on cases. Most chapters and sections of chapters are introduced by a textual discussion or outline of the basic issues and structure of the statute governing treatment of the particular item or transaction covered in the chapter or section. Principal cases have been included to illustrate key concepts not governed by a detailed statutory provision, as well as to illustrate how the courts have utilized the technical tools at their disposal. We recognize, however, that detailed statutory rules have come to dominate analysis of certain issues. Accordingly, in a significant number of chapters and sections, the "principal case" is an excerpt from a congressional committee report or an Explanation by the Staff of the Joint Committee on Taxation, which helps the student understand the reasons for the change in the statute as well as providing a road map to assist in mastering the detailed statutory provisions. In many chapters a brief introductory explanation precedes the principal case. This introductory text provides important background information to provide historical or policy context for the principal case. In the DETAILED ANALYSIS which follows the principal cases, we have attempted to provide sufficient discussion of rulings and cases to give an insight into the endless variety of factual situations to which the highly technical provisions of the Internal Revenue Code must be applied. The DETAILED ANALYSIS also provides additional historical background and discussion of sequential amendments to particular provisions of the Code and Regulations necessary to understand the significance of particular provisions. The breadth and detail of the DETAILED ANALYSIS is such that most instructors will wish to assign only portions of it depending on the scope of their particular course. To assist in selective use of DETAILED ANALYSIS, we have tried to arrange the DETAILED ANALYSIS to begin with the general and move to the more specific and technical issues as the outline format progresses.

The Internal Revenue Code and Treasury Regulations are the centerpiece of any course in federal taxation. This volume is intended to be used in conjunction with either a complete set of the Code and Regulations or one of the several available edited versions of the Code and Regulations. The statutory and regulatory references at the head of each topic are not intended to be exhaustive. Rather, they represent only the essential sections of the Code and Regulations that the student must understand to obtain the framework for the cases and materials under the particular topic. We have not undertaken completely to explain the operation of the Code and Regulations in the introductory text and DETAILED ANALYSIS. The student must work with the statute and regulatory material before undertaking the examination of its application in the materials in this volume.

This text is divided into eleven broad Parts and thirty-nine chapters. Most basic tax courses will cover some of the material in most of the principal Parts of the text, but it is unlikely that all of the material in any one Part will be covered. Each chapter is organized in an outline format. This arrangement in both the subdivisions within the chapters and the DETAILED ANALYSIS is intended to facilitate the assignment of only selected portions of the material to provide an overview of some topics, while at the same time providing detailed discussion of complex issues for consideration in advanced courses. The organization of the materials is explained in greater detail in the Instructor's Note, which follows the preface.

As to editorial matters, the statutory references throughout are to the 1986 Code, except where the text expressly indicates otherwise. References in the cases and other primary sources to the 1954 and 1939 Codes and prior statutes have been edited to conform them to the 1986 Code numbering. Generally the practice is to omit the earlier citation and instead refer to the matter as "the former version," or "the predecessor," or to give the current relevant 1986 Code section if there has been no significant change in the statutory language. But if a significant change has occurred, that fact is noted and the prior language is given. In general, references to the Code and Regulations are current as of October 31, 2016. Citations to cases and rulings also are current as of August 31, 2016. Footnotes in cases and materials frequently have been omitted. Where retained the original numbering of the footnotes has been kept so that, in many instances, the footnote numbers within a chapter are not consecutive. Editorial footnotes for cases and materials are so designated and are indicated by an asterisk. References to Tax Court Memorandum decisions are to the number assigned by the Tax Court and not to any particular commercial publication.

We are very grateful to Professor Alice Abreu, our co-author on the fifth edition of the casebook and Professor Gregg Polsky, our co-author on the sixth edition of the casebook, for their enormous contributions to this text, and most of all to the late Paul R. McDaniel, who was the masterful guiding force of every previous edition of this casebook since 1972.

MARTIN J. MCMAHON, JR.
DANIEL L. SIMMONS
BRADLEY T. BORDEN
DENNIS J. VENTRY, JR.

November 1, 2016

Paul R. McDaniel
In Memoriam

This edition of FEDERAL INCOME TAXATION, CASES AND MATERIALS is the first new edition since the death of Paul McDaniel on July 16, 2010. We will miss greatly his intellect, insights, guiding hand, humor, and personal warmth. This text traces its origins back to Volume I of Surrey, Warren, McDaniel & Ault, Federal Income Taxation, published in 1972. Marty McMahon and Dan Simmons were invited to join the team of authors in 1987, after the passing of Stanley Surrey and William Warren, and worked first with both Paul and Hugh Ault and later with Paul and other co-authors on successor volumes and annual supplements for nearly twenty-five years. Brad Borden and Dennis Ventry have been added to the team after Paul's passing.

We have endeavored to carry forward crucial lessons taught to us by Paul about describing the Code, regulations, cases, and rulings. Paul always believed that the purpose of a law school classroom tax textbook was not to completely describe the rules for the students, but rather provide for them a framework for reading the Code and regulations themselves and to provide illustrations of the application of the rules of the Code and regulations that the students could use as tools to answer in class questions beyond those clearly addressed by the Code and regulations. That is a methodology that we have since always aspired to apply, although in the era of constant tax acts and a flood of new complex regulations, it is becoming ever-increasingly more difficult. We will miss Paul greatly, but his indelible mark on this text and much of his remarkable input will be present in every edition to come.

INSTRUCTOR'S NOTE

Basic Philosophy

In preparing this edition of FEDERAL INCOME TAXATION, CASES AND MATERIALS, we have been mindful that the complexity of the Internal Revenue Code and Treasury Regulations make it impossible in a four hour course in basic income taxation to cover all of the fundamental principles in depth. Nevertheless, it is important to acquaint students with the full range of general principles. Each instructor must chose those topics to cover in depth and those topics with respect to which only the general principles will be covered. Any particular instructor may wish to vary the coverage from year to year. Thus, rather than provide a text that dictates the scope and depth of the course, we have prepared a set of materials from which any instructor can draw to fit his or her particular needs.

Our guiding philosophy in selecting and structuring the materials has been to organize the materials to facilitate selective assignments for a three or four hour basic course that demonstrate the overall structure and policies of federal income taxation and provide in depth analysis of representative important issues. In their entirety the materials provide sufficient scope and depth for a sequence of two or more courses ranging from five to nine hours, depending on whether the courses are at the J.D. or LL.M. level. It is not possible to cover the entire volume in a single three or four hour course in Basic Federal Income Taxation.

The book is divided into eleven broad Parts and thirty-nine chapters, which are further subdivided into sections to facilitate selective use to suit the particular courses. Most chapters and sections of chapters are introduced by a textual discussion or outline of the basic issues and structure of the statute governing treatment of the particular item or transaction covered in the chapter or section. Most sections include a principal case (or cases) to illustrate key concepts not governed by a detailed statutory provision or to illustrate how the courts have utilized the technical tools at their disposal. Because detailed statutory rules dominate analysis of certain conceptual issues, in a significant number of sections the "principal case" is an excerpt from a congressional committee report, which helps the student understand the reasons for the change in the statute as well as providing a road map to assist in mastering the detailed statutory provisions.

The DETAILED ANALYSIS that follows the principal cases provides discussion of rulings and cases to give an insight into the endless variety of factual situations to which the highly technical provisions of the Internal Revenue Code must be applied. The DETAILED ANALYSIS also provides important historical background and discussion of sequential amendments to particular provisions of the Code and Regulations necessary to understand the significance of particular provisions. The breadth and detail of the DETAILED ANALYSIS is such that most instructors will wish to assign only portions of it, depending on the scope of their particular course. To assist in selective use of DETAILED ANALYSIS, it is arranged in an outline format that moves from the general to the more specific as the outline format progresses.

In very practical terms, the organization of the book means that the instructor will assign only the introductory material and the principal case for those areas in which he or she wishes to cover only the basic principles. In area where some greater depth of detail is desired, the first one or two divisions of the DETAILED ANALYSIS also will be assigned. In those areas where the instructor wishes to expose the students to the full range of technical details—as worked out in regulations, rulings and court decisions—the entire DETAILED ANALYSIS would be assigned. The text thus provides the desired level of detail the instructor seeks as to any particular topic.

Each of the authors will be willing to share their individual syllabi on request.

Organization

The materials generally have been sequentially organized on a conceptual rather than on a transactional basis.

Part I (Chapter 1) provides an introduction to Federal Income Taxation. It provides an overview of the most important tax policy issues, describes the history of the income tax, explains the tax legislative process and the relevant administrative and judicial processes and authorities, briefly surveys income tax procedure and tax penalties, and ends with a discussion of ethical considerations in tax practice. This is broad background material and although the Chapter is lengthy, we expect that most instructors will assign it in its entirety even though much of the material may not be discussed directly in class.

Part II (Chapters 2–11) covers the definition of gross income, including recognition of gain in basic property transactions. (More complex property transactions are covered in Parts VI, VII, and IX). The organizational theme of the Chapter is that receipts in any form that are not a return to capital ought to be included in the tax base. Chapters 2–4 thus focus on the significance, if any, of the form of or reason for the receipt, while Chapters 6–8 deal with gains from property and investment income, with Chapters 6 and 7 focusing on the return of capital concept, and Chapter 8 focusing on receipts representing a return to capital that are not fully included in the tax base. Chapter 9 (damage awards) and Chapter 10 (cancellation of indebtedness income), emphasize the theoretical idea that consumption ought to be paid for with tax-paid dollars. Part II ends with a discussion of tax expenditure analysis in Chapter 11. Most of this material will be covered in any basic income taxation course. Some sections of chapters, however, might be omitted by instructors who prefer to devote more time to deductions, timing issues, or complex property transactions. To facilitate such omissions, items such as prizes and awards and nonshareholder contributions to capital, for example, are assigned to separate sections that an instructor may elect not to assign.

Part III (Chapters 12–17) covers business deductions and credits. The organizational theme of this part is that the cost of earning receipts ought to be excluded from the tax base. This Part begins by examining the treatment of items that clearly have been incurred in a business or profit-seeking context. Chapter 12 deals primarily with the "ordinary and necessary expense" concept and limitations on the deduction of current profit-seeking expenses, including a section on "tax penalties"—the analog of tax expenditures. Most of the material in this Chapter typically is covered in a basic tax course, although some of the detailed discussion, for example, some of the tax penalties DETAILED ANALYSIS , may be omitted. Chapters 13 through 15 deal with capital expenditures and recovery of basis through depreciation and loss deductions. Most instructors will cover most of the material in these Chapters, although some material and chapter sections, such as the economic analysis of depreciation and the one dealing with natural resources, easily may be omitted. Chapter 16 covers the limitations on the deduction of interest, and Chapter 17 deals with business credits.

Part IV, Chapters 18 through 20, discusses the treatment of expenses that combine both business or profit seeking aspects and personal living expense aspects. These chapters deal with the problem of determining whether an expenditure was incurred for a profit-seeking purpose or a personal purpose. The placement of this material after coverage of unambiguous profit-seeking deductions in Part III, like the placement of Chapters 9 and 10 in Part II, is intended to emphasize the idea that consumption should be purchased with after-tax income. Because all of the sections in Chapter 19 regarding business versus personal expenditures present variations on a common them, many instructors may choose to cover only a few sections in detail, leaving the remaining sections to generalized coverage.

Part V, consisting of Chapters 21 through 23, deals with deductions and credits for personal living expenses and presents issues raised by tax expenditure analysis. Again, we expect that most instructors in basic income taxation courses will elect to cover most of the topics in this Part. However, most instructors in a three or four hour basic course will want to omit portions of the DETAILED ANALYSIS that deal with less commonly encountered issues. Chapter 23 focuses solely on tax expenditures for education. We have collected in one place the discussion of all of these provisions, whether providing an exclusion, deduction, or credit, to provide a more complete context for discussing varied approaches to providing tax incentives for a particular type of activity.

Part VI deals with the characterization of gains and losses from property. We expect that many instructors in basic courses will cover only selected portions of this Part. Chapter 24, which deals comprehensively with the treatment of capital gains, can be covered selectively. For example, an instructor may choose to omit portions of the DETAILED ANALYSIS dealing with section 1221(a)(1), to cover only a few of the several cases dealing with judicial limitations on the definition of capital asset, to cover the "sale or exchange" requirement only at the most elementary level, and to omit entirely some of the more technical aspects of capital gains covered in the latter sections of the Chapter. Chapter 25, dealing with § 1231 assets, depreciation recapture, and the comminution of the recognition of gain and loss on the sale of a going business, is a chapter that can be covered at varying levels of depth in a basis income tax course, or one which, alternatively, might be combined with Parts VII through IX in an advanced income tax course.

Part VII deals with deferred recognition transactions that are unrelated to accounting method issues. Many instructors will want to cover Chapter 26, which deals with § 1031 like-kind exchanges, as a paradigm nonrecognition rule. Chapter 27, which deals with § 1033 involuntary conversions and other miscellaneous nonrecognition rules most likely will be covered only selectively, if at all, in most basic courses.

Part VIII covers timing and other tax accounting issues. Most instructors in basic courses will cover selected portions of Chapters 28 (accounting methods) and 29 (annual accounting), but may wish to omit Chapter 30 (deferred compensation and § 83). Chapters 31 (installment sales) and 32 (original issue discount) also will be covered only selectively in most basic courses. Part VIII, standing alone however, if covered comprehensively, provides sufficient material for a two hour advanced course in tax accounting at either the J.D. or LL.M. level. Parts VI though IX, with some omissions, easily may be combined as the basis for a three hour advanced income taxation course at the J.D. level by instructors who choose to cover Parts I through V (and Part X) comprehensively in a three hour basic federal income taxation course.

Part IX deals with tax motivated transactions. Most of the material is suitable for advanced courses and only selected portions are likely to be covered in a basic course. For example, Chapter 33, dealing with leasing transactions might be omitted entirely. Both Chapter 34, dealing with structural aspects of traditional leveraged tax shelters and the administrative and judicial responses thereto, and Chapter 35, dealing with legislative responses to traditional leveraged tax shelters, probably would be included only selectively in a basic course. Chapter 36, dealing with modern corporate tax shelters and the economic substance doctrine, probably is generally suitable only for an advanced course.

Alternatively, Part IX, combined with Parts VI and VII provides sufficient material for an advanced 2 hour course in taxation of property transactions at either the J.D. or LL.M. level. They also may be combined with the portions of Part VIII relating to tax accounting rules for property transactions in a three hour course covering taxation of property transactions.

Part X covers assignment of income and the taxable unit issues. We expect that most instructors in the basic income tax course will include selected material from Chapter 37 (assignment of income) and will include all of Chapter 38 (taxable unit and divorce), with the exception of the section on the grantor trust rules.

Part XI (Chapter 39) deals with the alternative minimum tax. Many instructors may wish to devote a day to this material to familiarize students generally with the concept and to explore the policy implications of the need for the alternative minimum tax as a way of "capping-off" the basic income tax course.

Class Discussion Problems

Because teachers approach their courses with different objectives and use different techniques for handling the materials, the materials have been designed to be flexible and easily adapted to whatever approach the teacher wishes to adopt—an intensive technical analysis, a problem oriented method, a consideration of the policies that underlie the technical tax structure, or a survey of the principal elements of the federal income tax structure. Although the text itself does not contain sets of questions or problems within the materials, we recognize that many instructors prefer to use a series of problems that students can prepare in advance as significant portion of their class discussion. We have, therefore, provided a separate set of accompanying Class Discussion Problems for this purpose. (We believe that the unique format of a separate volume for the problems facilitates use in the classroom by eliminating the constant turning of pages from the problems to the relevant materials in the text.)

The problems are designed to lead the students through a precise examination of the relevant sections of the Code and Regulations and the leading cases and rulings discussed in the text. Some problems will require students to study and apply the Code and Regulations, while others will require extrapolation or reasoning by analogy from cases and other materials covered in the reading. The problems are coordinated to the Chapters and Sections in the text to which they relate, and within each problem set generally follow the order that the material is covered in the text. Each instructor should chose the problems that he or she wishes to assign to achieve the level of complexity that he or she wants to reach in the course.

TABLE OF CONTENTS

PART VII. DEFERRED RECOGNITION
OF GAIN FROM PROPERTY

PART VIII. TIMING OF INCOME AND DEDUCTIONS

PART XI. ALTERNATIVE MINIMUM TAX

TABLE OF CASES

The principal cases are in bold type.

TABLE OF INTERNAL REVENUE CODE SECTIONS

TABLE OF TREASURY REGULATIONS

TABLE OF RULINGS

FEDERAL INCOME TAXATION

SEVENTH EDITION

PART I

Introduction to Federal Income Taxation

CHAPTER 1

INTRODUCTION

SECTION 1.   AN OVERVIEW OF POLICY ISSUES AND THE CURRENT INCOME TAX

A. SELECTION OF A TAX—GOALS AND CRITERIA

Supreme Court Justice Oliver Wendell Holmes once observed, "Taxes are what we pay for civilized society."[1] Indeed, choices about the nature of the tax system represent a society's decisions about the allocation of the cost of government between and among competing economic and social sectors. Allocating tax burdens requires difficult policy choices that get reduced during the legislative process to ostensibly neutral and highly technical tax provisions in the Internal Revenue Code (the "Code"). For policymakers and experts alike, these choices involve evaluating a number of core objectives, including:

Raising revenue—The fundamental objective of any tax system is to raise adequate revenue for governmental functions.

Supplementing fiscal policy objectives—By reducing or increasing taxes, the economy may be stimulated in times of economic slowdown or dampened in times of inflation.

Affecting income and wealth distribution—A country may seek to reduce the disparities in economic wealth among its people. This goal may be accomplished through the tax system by raising revenue from persons "better off" (those with greater income, wealth, or consumption) in order to distribute the revenue through transfer payments (such as Medicaid, Medicare, or other social welfare programs) or the tax system (such as through tax credits and tax rebates). To a more limited extent, this redistributive goal might be achieved without transfer payments by requiring "better off" citizens to pay more than proportionately greater taxes compared to less well-off citizens even though the public goods purchased with government revenues may provide proportionate benefits to all citizens.

Providing financial assistance to achieve social goals—Special tax provisions may encourage or support socially desirable objectives, such as subsidizing charitable contributions or

---

[1]   Justice Holmes in Compania General de Tabacos de Filipinas v. Collector, 275 U.S. 87, 100 (1927). These words are inscribed on the front of the Internal Revenue Service building in Washington, D.C.

reducing poverty. Such tax provisions are the functional equivalents of direct spending programs.

Achieving economic goals—Special provisions may encourage investment in particular economic activities, such as investment in new machinery and equipment or new technology. These provisions also are the functional equivalents of direct spending programs.

Regulation—By imposing taxes on specific activities deemed undesirable or harmful (including, for example, "sin" taxes on cigarettes and alcohol, or denying deductions for political lobbying activities), the government may achieve effects similar to direct regulation or prohibition of the activity.

Traditionally, tax policymakers and experts have employed three standards for evaluating and implementing the range of policy objectives in designing a tax system and crafting tax legislation: equity, efficiency, and simplicity.

The traditional concept of *equity* in taxation embodies two separate notions, namely *horizontal equity* and *vertical equity*. Horizontal equity reflects the principle that persons similarly situated should pay equal amounts of tax. The choice of a tax base in some sense reflects a judgment about which persons are similarly situated. An income tax, for example, reflects a judgment that people with equal incomes should be taxed equally. Once income has been identified as the preferred tax base, horizontal equity can assist in testing the impact of alternative provisions. Even with agreement on the preferred base, it is not always clear when people are (or are not) similarly situated due to the elusiveness of the concept of income. For instance, two people with equal incomes taxed the same under an income tax might in fact have different levels of wealth or consumption as a result of personal circumstances such as family size, marital status, health, and age.

Meanwhile, vertical equity reflects the principle that differently situated taxpayers should bear different tax burdens. In particular, wealthier persons should bear more of the tax burden than less wealthy persons under the principle of vertical equity. A tax system's rate schedule may reflect this policy judgment with upper-income persons subject to higher tax rates than lower- or middle-income persons. At the same time, defining who is better off may also be reflected in the choice of tax base. An individual with more income than her neighbor might be considered "better off" if the tax system used income as the tax base. On the other hand, the relative tax burdens between these neighbors might be much different if the tax base were based on personal consumption or wealth rather than on income.

These traditional concepts may not have significance independent of underlying value judgments.[2] The role of horizontal equity may be confined to analyzing the propriety of the tax base that has been proposed or chosen, but other considerations may override considerations of horizontal equity. For example, horizontal equity is violated when a particular type of income is exempted, such as interest on state and local bonds, because it reduces the tax burden on the taxpayer realizing income from that source relative to the tax burden of other taxpayers realizing income from taxable (rather than tax-exempt) sources. Similarly, horizontal equity is violated when a deduction is allowed for expenses other than the cost of earning income, such as the deduction for home mortgage interest, which allows taxpayers with a particular consumption pattern (that is, homeownership versus renting) to pay less in tax than other taxpayers with identical economic income but different consumption patterns.

At the same time, the concept of vertical equity has little content apart from the underlying social and economic values that shape the tax system. For example, if income is the tax base, either a proportionate tax or a progressive tax results in higher-income households paying a greater proportion of their income in taxes than other households. But that truism does not answer questions pertaining to *how much more* of the tax burden upper-income households should bear; that is, whether the burden should increase proportionate to income or rise at a faster rate. Moral, social, economic, and philosophical considerations must inform these decisions about what it means to pay one's "fair share" of taxes to support the provision of public goods.

For its part, *efficiency* has two distinct meanings. Efficiency may refer to the market economy's allocation of resources to their most productive use. Any tax—effectively a price increase on the taxed item or activity—has an efficiency cost because it alters the relative values of labor, capital, and leisure, thereby affecting the allocation of resources. The goal is to choose a tax system, consistent with other objectives, that minimizes these efficiency costs on the economic and social behavior that society values, and, as a corollary, to impose efficiency costs on economic and social behavior that society wishes to discourage.

Efficiency can also refer to how government subsidies in the form of tax provisions are in fact received by the intended beneficiaries. For example, the exemption from income taxation for interest on municipal bonds subsidizes state and local governments in the form of reduced interest costs for borrowing. To the extent the subsidy is received by the holders of the bonds rather than state and local governments, the use of the tax system to achieve this nontax goal is inefficient and, ultimately, ineffective. The exemption may also be deemed inefficient if the benefit

---

[2]   See generally, McDaniel and Repetti, Horizontal and Vertical Equity: The Musgrave/Kaplow Exchange, 1 Fla. Tax Rev. 607 (1993).

to some individual taxpayers exceeds the incentive benefit to state and local government. This issue is discussed in Chapter 8, Section 4.

In the context of evaluating a tax system, the concept of *simplicity* also contains several analytical components. For instance, the term simplicity can be used to assess statutory language and how that language facilitates or hampers taxpayer compliance. Just as significantly, it can also refer to how taxation complicates everyday life for taxpayers by forcing them to account for the tax consequences of nearly all transactions. Moreover, simplicity can relate to aspects of tax administration. For example, the ability of a country to administer a particular tax may influence both the choice of the tax base and rate structures, because some types of taxes and rate structures are inherently more complicated to administer than others.

In adopting a tax, a choice must be made among several different possible tax bases. Thus, the tax may be based upon income from all sources, income from wages alone, personal consumption (either by individuals or on a transactional basis), accumulations or transfers of wealth, and accessions of wealth, property, or specific activities or types of transactions. The tax bases are not mutually exclusive and more than one type of tax base will often be adopted within a taxing jurisdiction. There is no single tax base that is *a priori* optimal. Rather, the different effects produced by various tax bases must be considered. One tax base will achieve some broad policy objectives better than others. Thus, if the primary concern is to achieve redistribution of wealth, a tax on wealth will be more effective than a tax on personal consumption. In addition, particular taxes will be felt differently by various elements within society and by different segments in the economy. These differences can be identified by tax experts and flagged for policymakers, but the decision as to which type of tax to adopt will rest on broad philosophical, historical, social, religious, and economic views held throughout the society.

Another fundamental policy question involves the nature of the rate structure. A rate structure may be progressive, proportional, or regressive. As already noted, a progressive income tax subjects higher increments of income to higher rates, such that persons with higher incomes pay a higher percentage in tax than people with lower incomes. Comparatively, a regressive tax (such as a retail sales tax) results in lower-income persons paying a higher percentage of their incomes in tax than people with higher incomes.

Some types of rate structures are more appropriate to one type of tax than to another. A proportional or "flat rate" tax is the most workable rate structure for a retail sales tax or real property taxes, while a progressive rate structure is more administrable for an income tax or other personal taxes, including an indirect consumption tax. Naturally, this choice is governed by the goals sought to be achieved. A progressive income tax, for example, is consistent with the goal of income redistribution, while a retail sales tax is not.

There are additional policy considerations depending upon the type of system that has been adopted. In the context of an income tax these considerations include the definition of the taxable unit, the determination of the taxable period, and selection of rules to administer the tax in a way that is viewed as both efficient and fair by the taxpaying public.

B. THE STRUCTURE OF THE INCOME TAX AND SELECTED POLICY ISSUES

An income tax is composed of several fundamental structural elements. The following material identifies those elements and briefly sets forth the existing statutory rules and policy issues with respect to each element.

(1) THE DEFINITION OF INCOME AND DEFINING THE TAX BASE

(a) General: The Definition of Income

"Income" has been defined by economists and legal scholars in a number of different ways. The most prominent and influential baseline concept of economic income among both economists and legal academics is that articulated nearly 100 years ago by economists Robert Haig and Henry Simons. According to the Haig-Simons definition of income, personal income reflects "the algebraic sum of (1) the market value of rights exercised in consumption and (2) the change in the value of the store of property rights" between two specified periods.[3] Stated simply, the definition considers personal income as the sum of consumption plus the change in value of net assets owned. Personal income, Simons wrote, "connotes, broadly, the exercise of control over the use of society's scarce resources,"[4] while in Haig's words, personal income equated with "the money value of the net accretion to one's economic power between two points of time."[5]

---

[3]   Henry C. Simons, Personal Income Taxation: The Definition of Income as a Problem of Fiscal Policy 50 (University of Chicago Press, 1938). See also Robert M. Haig, "The Concept of Income—Economic and Legal Aspects," in Haig, ed., The Federal Income Tax 7 (Columbia University Press, 1921). The "Haig-Simons" definition of income is more accurately termed the "Schanz-Haig-Simons" definition. According to Simons himself, German economist Georg Schanz articulated an "original and challenging" concept of income, (see Simons supra at 60), which "influenced Simons considerably" (see C. Harry Kahn, Personal Deductions in the Federal Income Tax 121 (NBER Books, 1960). See also Simons supra at 58–99 (treating Schanz prominently in discussing the income concept). Almost no modern treatments of the income concept give Schanz his due. But see J. Clifton Fleming & Robert J. Peroni, Reinvigorating Tax Expenditure Analysis and Its International Dimension, 27 Va. Tax Rev. 437, 450 (2008) (discussing the baseline for traditional tax expenditure analysis as the "Schanz-Haig-Simons" definition of income).

[4]   Simons, supra at 49.

[5]   Haig, supra at 7.

This accretion- and consumption-based concept of income commands a broad income tax base, much broader than the tax base under current law. For example, the Haig-Simons definition of income would tax the economic value of net imputed rental income from owner-occupied housing; that is, the income a homeowner receives from effectively renting the home to himself or herself, net of annual expenses associated with owning the home (such as property taxes paid, mortgage interest paid, depreciation of the structure, etc.).[6] See Chapter 2, Section 3 and Chapter 21, Sections 5.4 & 5.5. Similarly, the Haig-Simons definition of income would tax the value of imputed income from household services; that is, the income "earned" by family members performing household services such as daycare and housecleaning that the taxpayer would otherwise have to satisfy with out-of-pocket, after-tax dollars. See Chapter 38, Section 1.4.

Throughout this book, we will witness numerous deviations from a broad, Haig-Simons definition of income. These deviations result from a combination of administrative, political, economic, and social considerations. They also result in a smaller tax base.

(b) General: Defining the Tax Base

The beginning point for the definition of the tax base is gross income as defined in § 61 of the Code. The sections following § 61 provide detailed rules for the treatment of certain types of income (see §§ 71 to 90) and for specific exclusions of selected receipts from gross income that relieve these receipts from tax (see §§ 101 to 140). Costs of producing income are allowed as deductions by § 162 and subsequent sections, and are thereby subtracted from gross income. Meanwhile, § 262 and succeeding sections disallow or defer deductions for certain expenses, such as expenses that provide a benefit beyond the current taxable year, even though in some instances they represent costs of producing income. For corporations, the subtraction of business expenses from gross income results in "taxable income." But for individuals this computation is an interim step to arrive at adjusted gross income or "AGI." From adjusted gross income taxpayers either subtract a "standard deduction" (defined in § 63(c) and adjusted for inflation) or, alternatively, subtract the sum of certain itemized personal deductions if those deductions exceed the value of the standard deduction. See Chapters 21 and 22. In addition, the taxpayer is allowed to subtract one personal exemption for each member of the family unit (defined in § 151 and adjusted for inflation). The resulting figure is the individual taxpayer's taxable income. These adjustments may be analyzed as an attempt to achieve horizontal equity by adjusting the tax burden for such factors as family size and circumstance.

---

[6]   Simons condemned the failure of the U.S. income tax to account for the economic value of imputed rental income, calling it an "egregious discrimination between renters and homeowners." Simons, supra at 112. "[W]hen property is employed directly in consumption uses," Simons continued "there is the strongest case for recognizing an addition to taxable income." Id

The tax rates set forth in § 1 for individuals are then applied to taxable income to determine the tax imposed. The numerous tax credits available to taxpayers beginning with § 21 can act to further reduce tax owed. After determining final tax liability, the taxpayer files a signed tax return and either remits payment to the Internal Revenue Service (IRS) for tax owed or obtains a refund from the government if the allowable tax credits exceed the tax imposed. The taxpayer is also eligible to receive a refund if the taxpayer does not owe any additional federal income tax in the first instance (that is, any tax in addition to the tax withheld from wages by employers or already otherwise paid to the government such as estimated payments).

A number of difficult policy issues are embedded in the statutory structure implementing the current income tax. For example, although § 61 begins with the sweeping proposition that gross income includes income from whatever source derived, subsequent statutory provisions provide special exclusions from gross income. Some of these provisions are intended to provide financial support for particular kinds of activities or to encourage specific social or economic behavior. A prominent example of these incentive-based provisions is the exclusion from income for interest paid on bonds issued by state and local governments (see Chapter 8, Section 4). In other instances, there may be a problem in defining the scope of the term "gross income" as respects a particular type of receipt or economic benefit. For example, a long-standing problem involves defining which types of non-cash benefits provided to an employee are includible in gross income. In these situations, the statutory language provides a detailed though administrable definition of what is to be included and excluded from the tax base.

In order to reach net income, current costs of producing income generally are deductible whereas expenditures for personal consumption, such as for food, are not. It is thus necessary to classify expenditures as profit-seeking versus personal. But many types of expenditures are not so easily classified, because they contain both profit-seeking and personal aspects. Some provisions in the deduction-granting sections thus draw the necessarily difficult dividing line between the two categories of expenditures. As noted above, other deduction-granting provisions exclude from the tax base certain items of personal costs that would not be deductible under § 262. These special personal deductions, like certain special exclusions from income, are granted to provide relief from hardship or to provide incentives for certain types of activities.

Certain of the tax credits provided to taxpayers help implement the structure of the income tax. For example, the tax credit for withheld income taxes insures that the withholding system is meshed with the taxpayer's obligation to self-assess one's tax liability. Meanwhile, other tax credits facilitate social or economic objectives of the government.

(c) Income from Property

Gross income includes not only income such as salaries, dividends, and interest, but also income from property transactions. The rules dealing with the costs of acquiring property and gains and losses from property transactions require further explanation.

Capital versus Ordinary Expenditures. Not all profit-seeking expenditures are deductible when made. Because income generally refers to changes in net worth, expenditures which merely convert one asset into another do not result in a loss meriting deduction from the tax base. Suppose, for example, that a taxpayer purchases stock for $10,000 cash. No change in net worth has occurred; one asset—cash—has been converted into another asset—stock. Section 263 provides that these "capital expenditures" are not currently deductible, but the line between capital expenditures and currently deductible expenditures is not always easy to draw.

Return of Capital. Because only net gains and losses are to be taken into account, if stock purchased for $10,000 is sold for $12,000, the taxpayer receives $2,000 of additional gross income. The other $10,000 represents a return of the taxpayer's capital. Thus, taxpayers must keep track of their investments in various assets in order to compute gain or loss correctly. This investment to the extent not previously deducted is generally referred to as "basis."

Realization and Recognition. Perhaps the most significant difference between the Haig-Simons definition of income and the current federal income tax definition is the treatment of gains and losses from the increase or decrease in the value of property. Although such accrued gains and losses are clearly income or loss under the Haig-Simons definition, they are generally not accounted for under the federal income tax until a sale or other "realization" event has occurred. For example, if a taxpayer purchases stock for $10,000 that increases in value to $12,000 by the end of the year, there is no addition to gross income for that year under the federal income tax. Even realized gains are not accounted for if a specific provision states that the gain or loss shall not be recognized. The realization and recognition requirements have been justified as eliminating the need for periodic valuation of assets and for avoiding potential problems of liquidity (that is, being forced to pay tax on an asset's appreciation even though the taxpayer has not converted that appreciation to cash). Nevertheless, deferring these gains and losses adds significant complexity to the tax system, while deferring built-in gains provides substantial economic benefits to holders of property. Unrealized and unrecognized gains and losses represent alterations in net worth to the same extent as other items of income or loss.

Depreciation. A problem results from the decision not to account for accrued gains and losses with respect to wasting assets used in a profit-seeking activity (often referred to as depreciable property). Here, unlike an investment in stock, it is known that the asset will lose all of its value (other than scrap value) over time. Economic depreciation is the estimate of the annual decline in value of depreciable property and it represents an appropriate deduction under an income tax. As the cost of the asset is deducted through depreciation, the unrecovered investment in the property for tax purposes (i.e., basis) is reduced. As discussed in Chapter 14, Section 1, depreciation deductions permitted under the tax laws greatly exceed economic depreciation. Sections 167, 168, and 197 are the principal provisions governing the depreciation deduction.

Capital Gains and Losses. While § 61 includes in gross income all gains derived from dealings in property, the federal income tax gives preferential treatment to property gains that qualify as "capital gains." Currently the preference is provided by a number of "maximum rates" on several different categories of property, sorted by the kind of property and the length of time that taxpayers hold the property before sale. The most significant preferential rate—known as "long-term" capital gains—reduces the rate of tax to 20 percent for income otherwise in the 39.6 percent bracket, 15 percent for income otherwise in the 25 percent or higher bracket (but below the 39.6 percent bracket), and zero for income otherwise in the 10 or 15 percent bracket (see Chapter 24). The existence of these preferential rates causes substantial complexity and gives rise to numerous taxpayer schemes to convert ordinary income into capital gain. Such conversion can be accomplished by a variety of techniques that are discussed in the material throughout this book.

Indexing Assets and Liabilities to Inflation. There are a number of items in the tax base that are affected by inflation. Nevertheless, the United States historically has imposed its tax on a nominal dollar basis and has not indexed the basis of assets for inflation. Thus, if a taxpayer purchases an asset in Year 1 for $100 and holds it for one year, selling it for $110, and the inflation rate for the year was 10 percent, the taxpayer has experienced no gain in "real" terms (that is, in inflation-adjusted terms) However, because the tax is imposed on nominal dollars, the taxpayer realizes a gain of $10 and pays tax accordingly. As will be discussed, an adjustment for inflation creates considerable complexity, but it is also necessary if the tax is to be imposed on real rather than nominal income. Equally important, taxpayers engaged in debt transactions are also affected by inflation. During a period of inflation, debtors will realize gains as they repay debt with deflated dollars, while lenders will realize corresponding losses. Indexing the tax base for inflation thus requires indexing debts as well as the cost of assets.

(2) ESTABLISHING THE RATE STRUCTURE

Section 1 of the Code specifies the rates of tax applied to brackets of individual income. The rates of tax rise with income, thus establishing a progressive rate structure. Section 1 provides seven marginal tax brackets: 10 percent, 15 percent, 25 percent, 28 percent, 33 percent, 35 percent, and 39.6 percent. See I.R.C. § 1(a) and (i). The upper and lower parameters of each bracket are statutorily specified in terms of 2002 dollars, and are adjusted annually for inflation (see § 1(i)(1)(C)). The actual, inflation-adjusted dollar range for each bracket is announced annually in an IRS Revenue Procedure. For the publication corresponding to tax year 2016, see Rev. Proc. 2015–53; 2015–44 I.R.B. 615.

The rates specified in § 1 are marginal tax rates, that is, they are the rates applied to the highest dollar of taxable income of the taxpayer. In 2016, a single individual with taxable income of $415,051 was subject to the top marginal rate of 39.6 percent. However, the entire $415,051 in taxable income was not taxed at 39.6 percent. Instead, only the taxpayer's last dollar earned was taxed at 39.6 percent, because the top rate bracket only applied to taxable income "*over* $415,050. The remaining taxable income was taxed at the respective rates for the preceding six brackets: 10 percent for the first $9,275 in taxable income, 15 percent for taxable income from $9,276 to $37,650, 25 percent for taxable income from $37,651 to $91,150, and so on. Thus, while this taxpayer could be said to be "in" the 39.6 percent bracket, only one of the taxpayer's dollars got taxed at 39.6 percent. Consequently, the taxpayer's tax bill was considerably lower than if the taxpayer paid 39.6 percent in tax on the entire $415,051 of taxable income: $120,530.14 (corresponding to a 29 percent effective tax rate on total taxable income) versus $164,360.19 (corresponding to a 39.6 percent effective rate).

Beyond these computational details of the rate structure, there are numerous policy issues to consider, including the following:

Progressivity. The progressive rate structure has been subjected to various criticisms over the years.[7] Some of these criticisms have spawned proposals for an alternative, single-rate structure—popularly called a "flat tax"—that would apply a proportionate rate above a specified exemption level. Nonetheless, the progressive income tax has long represented the consensus view of what is considered a "fair" distribution of the tax burden. Indeed, the progressive income tax has been the centerpiece of distributive justice in U.S. fiscal policy for more than 100 years. The progressive tax rate is not intended to redistribute wealth, but is a statement about the allocation of the cost of government among greater and lesser income levels. One theoretical justification for progressive rates is that a marginal dollar is more important to low-income taxpayers than it is to high-income taxpayers, with the latter group more able to satisfy desires for high levels of consumption. In addition, the progressive rate structure of the federal income tax helps achieve overall proportionality in the distribution of taxes, because it counteracts the effect of regressive taxes at both the federal level (e.g.,

---

[7]   Compare Blum and Kalven, The Uneasy Case for Progressive Taxation (1953) with McMahon and Abreu, Winner-Take-All-Markets: Easing the Case For Progressive Taxation, 4 Fla. Tax Rev. 1 (1998).

Social Security taxes and excise taxes) and state level (e.g., sales taxes, gasoline taxes, and cigarette taxes).

Determining the Point at Which Positive Rates Begin. In establishing a rate structure, it has generally been thought desirable to provide a certain amount of income that is subject to a zero rate of tax, thus permitting taxpayers a tax-free base level of income with which to meet the necessities of life. That amount, coupled with the personal exemptions for additional family members, provides family units of different sizes and compositions with varying levels of untaxed income. Since 1969, Congress has attempted to insure that the amount of income which different family units receive free of tax has corresponded to the poverty level so that those families with incomes below the poverty level do not incur income tax liability. The enactment of various personal tax credits, such as the Earned Income Credit and Child Tax Credit (see Chapter 22, Section 2.A.) has reinforced this goal.

Indexing for Inflation. The rate structure is also affected by inflation. A taxpayer whose income rises only with the level of inflation, for example, can move into a higher tax bracket due to a wage increase even though there has been no increase in the taxpayer's wages in "real" dollar terms (that is, in terms of accounting for the purchasing power of a dollar today versus the purchasing power of a dollar at some point in the past). Until 1985, the federal income tax brackets were not indexed for inflation. Beginning in 1986, Congress indexed tax brackets and personal exemptions, ensuring that taxpayers move into higher tax brackets only as a result of increases in real income.

(3) DEFINING THE TAXABLE UNIT

The definition of the taxable unit adds another fundamental element to the income tax. Here the issues arise in terms of whether a husband and wife should be treated as a single taxpaying unit, whether children should be included in the taxable unit of the family, and whether various legal entities such as corporations, partnerships, and trusts should be taxed separately from their "owners." See Chapter 38.

The tax rate schedules in § 1 of the Code treat married couples as a single taxpaying unit. Until 1987, the income derived by minor children, whether from wages or from trusts created by members of the family, was taxed entirely independently of the income of the parents. Treating children as separate taxable units created incentives to shift income from parents to children in order to enable that income to be taxed at the bottom of the rate schedule applicable to the child. Aggregate family taxes could thus be reduced without a significant shift in the overall economic circumstances of the family. Between 1987 and 2005, investment income of children under the age of 14 was taxed at the higher of the child's own tax rate or the rate that would apply if the income were taxed to the parents (although children still reported their income on a separate return). Congress extended this rule to apply to children under the age of 18, as well as to full-time students over age 17 but under age 24 (see § 1(g)). All earned income of children, whatever age, and investment income of persons age 18 or over (except full-time students) is taxed at the individual rate applicable to that person.

A corporation is usually treated as a taxpayer separate from its shareholders, but a partnership is generally treated as a conduit so that tax is imposed directly on individual partners. For its part, a trust is treated as a separate taxpayer in some cases, while in others either the creator of the trust or its beneficiary is taxed on the trust's income.

(4) DETERMINING THE TAXABLE PERIOD AND THE TAXABLE INCOME FOR THAT PERIOD

The taxable period for computing income is one year, typically the calendar year for individuals. The rules for assigning items of income and deduction to the proper tax year are set forth in § 441 and subsequent sections. Taxpayers are generally permitted to choose their accounting method for computing income. The cash receipts and disbursements method and the accrual method are the two most commonly used methods. Under the cash method, income is reported in the year actually received and deductions are claimed in the year actually paid. Under the accrual method, income is reported in the year all events have occurred that establish the right to be paid and the amount can be determined with reasonable accuracy; deductions generally are allowed when all events have occurred that establish the liability and the amount can be determined with reasonable accuracy, although in many cases actual payment is required. Most individuals use the cash method although the accrual method is required for certain business activities because of the distortion that would arise under the cash method. Most corporations are required to use the accrual method.

The concept of income as an increase in net worth suggests the use of the accrual method, because individual's net worth can increase without the receipt of cash or its equivalent. Yet the cash method is much simpler to use and comports with the way most individuals account for income and expense. Many of the issues in this area arise from the conflict between these two competing considerations; that is, accurate measurement of increases/decreases in wealth versus ease of use. Other complications arise because the accrual method itself leads to distortions if a future right or liability is taken into account at its nominal dollar value rather than its present value, without taking into account a discount to reflect the time value of money.

A number of the tax rules for assigning income to taxable periods apply to all taxpayers regardless of the accounting method used. For example, the nondeductibility of capital expenditures and the requirement that only realized and recognized gains be included in gross income apply to all taxpayers. The question of which rules ought to depend upon the accounting method selected by the taxpayer is a subject of continuing debate.

(5) OTHER KEY CONCEPTS

(a) Timing

A number of Code provisions allow taxpayers to claim accelerated deductions or to defer taking income into account. Provisions allowing accelerated deductions permit taxpayers to claim deductions in a period earlier than they otherwise would be permitted under rules designed to measure income accurately. An immediate deduction for equipment and machinery along with accelerated depreciation are the most common examples of this type of deduction. A similar effect can be achieved by deferring income from the taxable period in which it is earned until a later period. The treatment of qualified employee retirement plans is an example of this type of provision. By accelerating deductions or deferring income, the taxpayer pays a lower tax in the current period than otherwise would be due. The taxpayer typically will pay that amount of tax in a later period but, in the meantime, has the use of the taxes foregone for the current period. In effect, the government has granted the taxpayer an interest-free loan, which the taxpayer can use and invest until the tax is due in a subsequent period.

The ability to accelerate deductions to a year earlier than that required under normal income tax principles or to defer income to a period later than the period in which it is economically earned is a perennial issue in tax reform, especially in periods of high interest rates. It is essential to understand the concept of the time value of money since many of the transactions that will be considered in the following materials are structured to maximize that value. Suppose that a taxpayer receives an item of income in Year 1 on which a tax of $100 is incurred. Suppose that under a special tax provision the tax on that income is deferred until Year 2. If the taxpayer can earn a 5 percent after-tax rate of return on the $100 of deferred tax, the value of deferral to the taxpayer is $4.76; by investing $95.24 at a 5 percent after-tax rate, the taxpayer will have $100 in Year 2 to pay the tax due in that year. The remaining $4.76 can be invested by the taxpayer (growing to $5 by Year 2) and retained as a permanent economic benefit. From the standpoint of the government, the situation is exactly the reverse. It has lost the use of the $100 for the year, resulting in a permanent revenue loss. Stated differently, the present value of the right to receive $100 of tax one year from now is $95.24. The concept of present value is an important one since it provides a mechanism by which a taxpayer can determine the present value of a future stream of deductions or exclusions and thus compare that value with that of alternative forms of investment. The time value of money concept and its effect on after-tax returns is considered in more detail in Chapter 8.

Because the value of accelerated deductions and deferred income may be quantified, the value can be compared with provisions such as the direct exclusion from income for state and local bond interest. The provisions that affect timing, although more subtle than outright exclusions from income, provide benefits that are just as real.

(b) Tax Expenditure Analysis

The concept of "tax expenditures" was developed by the U.S. Treasury Department beginning in the early 1960s and presented to Congress in 1969. Under this concept, special exclusions from gross income, special deductions and tax credits, and special accelerations of deductions or deferrals of income are viewed as the functional equivalents of federal spending programs. That is, a taxpayer who is granted a special exclusion from income is in the same economic position as if the tax had been paid on the full amount of economic income (without the exclusion) and the Treasury Department had returned a check to the taxpayer equal to the amount of the tax saving resulting from the income exclusion. Under this analytic technique, the special provisions are not viewed as "tax" provisions but instead represent a form of federal spending that is available to Congress as an alternative to direct spending programs. The term "tax expenditures" denotes the aspect of spending as well as the fact that the spending is conducted through the tax system. The tax expenditure concept thus posits that there are two components to the income tax system: the component consisting of the set of rules necessary to implement the normative elements of an income tax, as discussed in the preceding materials, and the tax expenditure component consisting of those special tax provisions that are the functional equivalents of direct spending programs.

The tax expenditure concept requires that the tax expenditure provisions be analyzed under criteria applied to spending programs rather than under criteria employed to test the operation of provisions that are part of the normative component of the income tax. Thus, with respect to each tax expenditure, the analysis should (i) inquire whether federal spending is needed or desirable; (ii) if so, how the program should be designed to distribute its benefits fairly, effectively, and efficiently; (iii) what controls, if any, should be placed on the program; and (iv) whether the program should be run through the direct expenditure budget or through the tax system. Tax expenditures have been grouped in the tax expenditure budget according to the functions utilized in the direct spending budget, and have been presented alongside the President's annual budget message since 1976. As of 2016, over 220 tax expenditure programs are categorized in the tax expenditure budget. Many of these tax expenditure items will be discussed throughout this book.

SECTION 2.   THE ROAD TO THE SIXTEENTH AMENDMENT AND THE MODERN FEDERAL INCOME TAX

A. INTRODUCTION

The history of federal taxation in the United States mirrors the history of the nation.[8] The demand for revenue by the federal government has arisen largely from the necessity of financing its expenditures. Crises of wars and economic recessions, the expansion of federal activities to meet complex social and economic problems, and the extent of the nation's role in world affairs have produced major effects on the level of federal expenditures and, in turn, on the federal tax system.

The annual volume of dollars collected by the government is merely one facet of the response of taxation to the pressures of the times. The total dollar figure, while itself revealing and easy to calculate, tells only part of the story. Figures reflecting total taxes collected from the citizenry tell us nothing about which citizens paid the taxes or what taxes the government imposed (the latter of which could actually provide some insight as to the former; that is, if the government imposed and collected property taxes, we could deduce that property-owners bore the burden of the tax).

The development of new methods of taxation, the decline or passing of older methods, and the degree to which the different revenue methods are relied upon can reveal the underlying social and economic history of the nation. For example, the change from customs receipts to excise taxes to income and social security taxes as the mainstay of our revenue system is one way of telling the story of a nation's economic growth, its developing administrative capacity, and its social policies and priorities. Moreover, the choice between a sales tax or other forms of tax on consumption and a progressive income tax determines which groups of our society will bear the burden of governmental expenditures, with sales and consumption taxes being born disproportionately by lower-income citizens and a progressive income tax being born disproportionately by higher-income citizens. These policy and design decisions depend on the resolution of all the pressures brought by representatives of those groups on the machinery of government as well as which groups can afford to be represented at the national level. Similarly, the choice between raising individual income tax rates and generating an equivalent amount of revenue by raising corporate income tax rates is rarely answered by legislators acting as tax technicians but rather by legislators acting as

---

[8]   For an overview of the relationship between the fiscal history of the United States and the general history of the country, see Brownlee, Federal Taxation in America: A History (3d ed. 2016) (examining all forms of taxation from 1789 to 2016, and identifying five prominent national crises—the formation of the republic, the Civil War, World War I, the Great Depression, and World War II—that provided the impetus for the five most significant stages of development in federal taxation).

politicians. Indeed, the tax system of the United States reflects the allocation of political strength among various constituencies at any particular time. In other words, tax is political.

B. THE EARLY YEARS

From 1789 to the Civil War, the federal government relied almost exclusively on customs receipts. This period produced a handful of notable, though short-lived, internal revenue developments. The last decade of the 18th century saw the imposition of excise taxes on distilled spirits, carriages,[9] sugar, snuff, property sold at auction, legal instruments, and bonds; a direct tax on dwelling houses, land, and slaves, apportioned among the states on the basis of population; and stamp taxes on legal instruments. These taxes were influenced by the provision in Article 1, Section 2 of the Constitution that allowed the federal government to impose direct taxation apportioned among the states by population.[10] By 1817, however, all of these internal taxes had been repealed. In fact, the federal government failed to enact any new internal taxes until the Civil War.

With the onset of hostilities between the North and South, the Lincoln administration was forced to locate new sources of revenue beyond tariffs and excises, increases to which, it was feared, would erode confidence in the Union government. In 1861, Northern Republican leaders passed the nation's first federal income tax. It was modest by today's standards, initially amounting to a flat rate of 3 percent on incomes above $800, a levy that affected only the top 1 percent of households. By war's end, Congress lowered the exemption to $600 and created a new rate schedule such that individuals with incomes over the exemption and up to $5,000 paid tax at 5 percent, while those with incomes above $5,000 paid 10 percent. The result was that tax liabilities for the richest Northerners doubled in less than five years.

At the conclusion of the Civil War, wealthy Americans demanded repeal of the income tax. It was meant to be a temporary measure, they argued, rather than a permanent part of the federal tax system. In 1872, Congress let the income tax expire. But it also reduced wartime excise taxes, a political move designed to induce non-wealthy Americans to accept the termination of the income tax, which was widely perceived to be a class-based tax. The federal government went back to relying on tariff revenues and excise taxes on liquor and tobacco. At the same time,

---

[9]   The carriage tax was held constitutional in Hylton v. United States, 3 U.S. 171 (1796), against the challenge that it was a direct tax and hence invalid because it was not properly apportioned among the states as required by the Constitution.

[10]   Art. 1, Sec. 2, Cl. 3 provides, "Taxes shall be apportioned among the several States which may be included within this Union, according to their respective Numbers, which shall be determined by adding to the whole number of free Persons, including those bound to Service for a Term of Years, and excluding Indians not taxed, three fifths of all other Persons."

the income tax had demonstrated its capacity to generate revenue during a time of crisis and to redistribute the tax burden.

C. THE 1894 INCOME TAX—LEGISLATIVE VICTORY AND JUDICIAL DEFEAT

Demand for an income tax was kept alive after 1872 by non-mainstream political groups, mostly in the West and South, and by farm and labor organizations. At the same time, business interests, principally prominent Eastern Republicans, opposed the tax. Rapidly deteriorating economic conditions in the 1890's resulted in a federal budget deficit and a dire need for new sources of revenue. A political battle ensued in Congress with Democrats from the West and South, allied with a strengthened Populist tide, arrayed against Republicans and Democrats from the East. The swelling Populist ranks called for a progressive tax on corporate profits and high incomes to reallocate the tax burden toward corporate monopolies and wealthy shareholders. In 1894, Congress enacted the nation's second federal income tax, which exempted the first $4,000 of personal income, taxed gifts and inheritances, and levied a 2 percent tax on individual and corporate incomes.

Even before the government could collect on the second federal income tax, the U.S. Supreme Court declared it unconstitutional. In Pollock v. Farmers' Loan and Trust Co., 158 U.S. 601 (1895), the Court held that a tax on income from land (for example, rents) or personal property was a direct tax that had to be apportioned among the states by population and the tax statute in question lacked such apportionment.

The Court's decision incited proponents of progressive taxation. According to one commentator, "the great majority of citizens" considered the Court's action "a radical reversal of long standing precedents and an unwarranted overthrow of the will of the people." Blakey, The New Income Tax, 4 Am. Econ. Rev. 25, 25 (1914). Neither Democrats nor Republicans could ignore the public outcry for progressive taxation. The Democratic Party included a progressive income tax in its 1896 presidential platform, while Republicans enacted a temporary progressive estate tax as well as an excise tax on the sugar and oil trusts to finance the Spanish-American War. In fact, by the early 1900s, prominent Republicans—from insurgent reformer Senator Bob La Follette of Wisconsin to party leaders Theodore Roosevelt and William Howard Taft—endorsed progressive income taxation. Previously confined to the West, Midwest, and South, the public clamor for a federal income tax crossed sectional boundaries and moved into northeastern urban centers. Progressive income taxation had risen to the top of the national policy agenda.

D. THE SIXTEENTH AMENDMENT AND THE RISE OF A MASS-BASED INCOME TAX

In 1909, Congress enacted a "corporation tax" and, at the same time, submitted to the states for ratification the Sixteenth Amendment, which read, "The Congress shall have the power to lay and collect taxes on incomes, from whatever source derived, without apportionment among the several States, and without regard to any census or enumeration." The ratification process got off to a rocky start, with New York, Massachusetts, and other powerful states rejecting it immediately. Nonetheless, in 1913, the amendment prevailed with three-quarters of the states ratifying the change to the Constitution.

In the same year, Congress enacted the Revenue Act of 1913, which instituted the nation's third federal income tax. The new levy assessed a "normal" tax of 1 percent on incomes above $3,000 for unmarried individuals and $4,000 for married couples in addition to a progressive "surtax" ranging from 1 percent to 6 percent on incomes above $20,000.[11] All taxpayers—single, married, with or without dependents—were subject to the same rate schedule.[12] As its Progressive Era advocates had envisioned, the tax fell disproportionately on the rich. Adjusted for inflation, the exemption levels created a tax-free threshold for singles and married couples, respectively, of $73,000 and $97,000 (in 2016 dollars). Meanwhile, only taxpayers with incomes exceeding $485,000 (in 2016 dollars) were subject to the higher surtax rates, with the top marginal rate only affecting incomes above $12 million (adjusted).[13] The class-based federal income tax with its generous zero-bracket levels exempted 98 percent of all households.

Despite its modest beginnings, the federal income tax quickly transformed into a potent source of revenue. Once more, crisis was the impetus, with the administration of President Woodrow Wilson relying heavily on the income tax to prosecute World War I. In the process, paying taxes became considerably more painful for wealthy Americans. The Revenue Act of 1916 more than doubled existing rates, raising the top marginal rate from 7 percent to 15 percent, while preserving the personal exemption levels. Revenue Act of 1916, ch. 463, 39 Stat. 756, 756–57, 761. The new tax statute also provided a graduated tax on estates exceeding $50,000 ($1.2 million in 2016 dollars) with a top rate of 10 percent on estates above $5,000,000 ($122 million in 2016 dollars).

---

[11]   Revenue Act of 1913, ch. 16, 38 Stat. 114, 166–68. The flat "normal" tax rate was assessed on taxable income above exemption levels and below an income ceiling of $20,000, while the graduated "surtax" rates were assessed on all taxable income above the ceiling.

[12]   By comparison, the current federal income tax contains four different rate schedules for individual taxpayers: married individuals filing joint returns and surviving spouses; heads of household; unmarried individuals; and married individuals filing separate returns. See I.R.C. § 1(a)–(d). For a discussion of the unit of taxation, see Chapter 38, Sections 1 & 2.

[13]   The top marginal rate of 7 percent began at $500,000, unadjusted for inflation.

High-income taxpayers charged the Wilson administration with pursuing a "soak-the-rich" campaign. They were right. In 1917, Congress gave the administration more of what it wanted, raising rates across the board, more than quadrupling the top marginal rate from 15 percent to 67 percent, while at the same time exposing lower levels of income to significantly higher taxes. Revenue Act of 1917, ch. 63, 40 Stat. 300, 300–01. The Act reduced personal exemption levels for individuals as well as married taxpayers, creating more than 100,000 new taxpayers. Despite lower exemptions, the federal income tax remained a class-based tax, affecting only 15 percent of all households. The richest 1 percent of Americans, moreover, accounted for 80 percent of the levy's receipts in 1918, and was subject to effective tax rates (including exemptions and deductions) exceeding 15 percent, up from 3 percent in 1916. The Revenue Act of 1918 raised rates again, such that by war's end, personal income tax rates ranged between 12 percent and 77 percent, while estate tax rates reached 25 percent. Revenue Act of 1918, ch. 18, 40 Stat. 1057, 1062–64.

In five years, the income tax had gone from a "rather tentative" revenue tool to "the foremost instrument of federal taxation."[14] Almost as quickly, opponents of progressive income taxation sought to roll back the power and reach of the federal income tax. In 1920, Republicans seized control of Congress, and newly elected President Warren Harding promised a "return to normalcy." The top marginal individual income tax rate fell from a wartime high of 77 percent to 58 percent in 1921, and to 25 percent by 1928. Congress also cut the estate tax rate to 20 percent, and increased the exemption to $100,000, excluding all but one-half of 1 percent of estates from tax. In addition to rate cutting, Republican Congresses undermined progressive taxation by punching loopholes in the Code. The 1920s witnessed the creation of the preferential treatment of capital gains, the oil and gas depletion allowances, and the exclusions for employer contributions to pensions and life insurance plans. In conjunction with reduced statutory rates, these new carve-outs lowered effective rates on high-income taxpayers, from 15.8 percent in 1920 to 7.4 percent by 1926.

The Republican retrenchment did not last long. Back-to-back national crises, this time the Great Depression and World War II, reversed the course of federal taxation once more. In 1932, in an effort to balance the budget, President Herbert Hoover endorsed higher taxes on the rich. That year's Revenue Act raised the top marginal income tax rate from 25 to 63 percent and the top estate tax rate from 20 to 45 percent.[15] The new law doubled the effective tax rate on the richest 1 percent of households, from 3.4 percent to 6.8 percent. It also pulled more middle-

---

[14]   W. Elliot Brownlee, "Historical Perspective on U.S. Tax Policy Toward the Rich," in *Does Atlas Shrug?: The Economic Consequences of Taxing the Rich*, 29, 41–42 (Slemrod ed., 2000).

[15]   Revenue Act of 1932, 47 Stat. 169, 174–77, 243–44 (1932).

income taxpayers into the federal income tax system by lowering personal exemptions for both unmarried and married taxpayers, while also raising tax rates throughout the middle-income range. But that was just the beginning. Congress upped taxes again in 1934 and 1935, and, as a result of wartime exigencies, almost every year between 1940 and 1944.

By the end of World War II, the federal income tax had transformed over a short thirty years from a class-based tax to a mass-based tax. As late as 1939, the federal government collected income taxes from just 4 million individuals. By 1945, sharply reduced personal exemptions increased the number of income taxpayers to 43 million. Moreover, the new, mass-based federal income tax contained steeply progressive rates, ranging from 22 percent to a staggering 94 percent (meaning that the very highest income earners kept just $0.06 of every additional dollar they earned). The tax also generated a near majority of all federal tax receipts. In 1939, the federal income tax yielded just $892 million, or 13.6 percent of federal tax revenues; by 1944, it produced $19.7 billion, or 45 percent of all federal tax dollars. World War II also ushered in significant developments in tax administration, most notably a vast new withholding system applied to wages and salaries that allowed tax officials to process (without the use of computers) tens of millions of new tax returns while at the same time relying on employers and third parties to collect tax in real time from tens of millions of new taxpayers.

In 1954 Congress re-drafted the Internal Revenue Code by configuring it into its current structure, and expanding the tax policy emphasis on tax incentives. The top marginal rate in the 1954 enactment was 91 percent and applied to very few returns, while the lowest bracket—20 percent—applied to 90 percent of taxpayers filing returns.[16] Tax revision in the following three decades reflected a pattern of declining marginal tax rates on the top income brackets and a shift of the burden of tax to lower- and middle-income tax brackets.[17] The 1964 act lowered rates by 20 percent across the board, which dropped the top rate to 70 percent. The Tax Reform Act of 1969 lowered the top rate on earned income still further to 50 percent, while the 1981 Act reduced the top rate on investment income to 50 percent.

The 1981 Act originated from President Reagan's proposals for a major tax reduction for individuals and a complete revision of the depreciation system for business. The Act included a number of new and expanded tax incentives for saving and investment, and instituted the principle of indexing individual tax brackets for inflation for the first time. The substantial reduction in revenues created by the 1981 Act,

---

[16]   Simmons, The Tax Reform Act of 1986: An Overview, 1987 BYU Law Rev. 151, 156–157.

[17]   See J. Pechman, Who Paid the Taxes 1966–1985 (Brookings Institute Studies of Government Finance (1985). Pechman attributes the increased tax burden on lower income taxpayers to increases in payroll taxes. (66–67).

coupled with continuing high levels of governmental expenditures and a weakened economy, led to large projected budget deficits. Subsequent tax bills passed in 1982, 1983, and 1984, reduced and eliminated some of the deficit-producing tax expenditures contained in the 1981 legislation, while also strengthening taxpayer compliance provisions, subjecting a portion of social security benefits to income taxation, and scaling back the generous depreciation rules that had been enacted in 1981.

The scope and complexity of the 1984 legislation fueled demands from tax practitioners and the general public for a simpler tax system.[18] Responding to these demands, the 1986 Act adopted a two-tier rate structure, with a top rate of 28 percent and a lower rate of 15 percent. The Act also included a 5-percent surtax on incomes above a certain threshold ($71,900 for married individuals filing jointly in 1986 dollars) that applied to a narrow range of income, effectively creating an anomalous 33 percent "bubble" rate on this band of income. In addition, the 1986 Act eliminated the preferential treatment for capital gains—previously taxed at 28 percent—by subjecting them to the same rates as ordinary income. The 1986 Act also reduced the impact of multiple tax incentives on individuals by imposing significant limitations on individual taxpayers' ability to take advantage of losses from passive activities to offset ordinary income. (discussed in Chapter 27, Section 2.B.). At the same time, the Act removed millions of low-income individuals and households from the tax rolls by increasing the standard deduction, raising the personal exemption, and expanding tax credits targeted to the working poor. Despite these innovations, decades of sharp tax cuts for upper incomes and a general flattening of the rate schedule shifted the relative tax burden from upper-income taxpayers to middle-income taxpayers.

Furthermore, the anticipated deficit reduction that was supposed to follow supply-side economic theories of cutting taxes on upper incomes did not materialize. As a result, Congress and the President in the 1990's were forced into a series of tax increases to address growing federal budget deficits. These actions included adding a top marginal rate in 1993 of 39.6 percent on ordinary income as well as continued taxation of capital gains at a maximum rate of 28 percent. By 1997, at the beginning of an economic expansion, Congress focused once more on tax reduction by, on the one hand, expanding and introducing tax expenditure items (including a new child tax credit that primarily benefited middle-income taxpayers) and, on the other hand, dramatically reducing tax rates on income from capital gains (an action that benefitted almost exclusively the highest income cohort). Finally, in the first decade of the current century rates fluctuated under provisions designed to sunset in 2010, with the top rate falling to 35 percent before being raised back to 39.6 percent in 2012.

---

[18]   See McDaniel, Federal Income Tax Simplification: The Political Process, 34 Tax L. Rev. 27 (1978); Gustafson (ed.), Federal Income Tax Simplification (1979).

In 2016, the federal income tax remains the lodestar of the federal revenue system. In fiscal year 2015, the federal government collected $3.2 trillion in federal revenues. Of that amount, individual federal income taxes reflected on more than 150 million tax returns (including returns of married couples treated as a single taxpaying unit) totaled 47 percent, or $1.5 trillion. Center on Budget and Policy Priorities, Where Do Federal Tax Revenues Come From? (2016). Another 11 percent came from the corporate income tax. Together, federal individual and corporate income taxes yielded close to two-thirds of all federal receipts. Those figures would have been even higher if Congress did not *spend* more than $1.2 trillion annually in foregone income tax revenues through "tax expenditures" (see Chapter 11 for the tax expenditure budget, and various other Chapters for specific tax expenditure items). On the whole, moreover, the federal income tax remains a progressive tax due to rising marginal rates, tax credits designed to help the working poor and middle class, and relatively generous zero-bracket amounts created by the standard deduction and personal exemptions. At the same time, the very highest-income households (those taxpayers with annual incomes above $5,000,000) enjoy declining rather than rising effective rates of tax due to lower rates on capital gain and dividend income, which accrue overwhelmingly to high-income households. Martin A. Sullivan, U.S. Income Tax Still Isn't Progressive at the High End, 152 Tax Notes 903 (2016).

Over the course of the next 38 Chapters, you will be exposed to the current strength and remaining untapped potential of the federal income tax, not just as a source of generating revenue but also as an instrument of influencing economic and social behavior.

SECTION 3.   THE FEDERAL INCOME TAX SYSTEM

A. THE LEGISLATIVE PROCESS

Tax legislation is a dynamic process. As the history of the income tax demonstrates, the income tax has been continually altered, often from year to year, to meet changing conditions. Since the fiscal policy of the Government must be responsive to current problems, and since the income tax is a vital part of our fiscal policy, this constant change is both inevitable and necessary.

Major tax legislation generally originates in response to Presidential recommendations. Occasionally, Congress takes the initiative, however. Because the Constitution requires that revenue legislation must originate in the House of Representatives,[19] historically the first Congressional step has involved a public hearing by the Committee on Ways and Means of the House of Representatives. In recent years,

---

[19]   Art. 1, Sec. 7, Cl. 1 provides: "All Bills for raising Revenue shall originate in the House of Representatives; but the Senate may propose or concur with Amendments as on other Bills."

hearings have been perfunctory, if they have been held at all. Usually a hearing is held against a background of general Presidential or Congressional proposals, but sometimes a particular bill (without such background) comes before the Committee. The first witness during these hearings is either a member of Congress who has proposed particular tax legislation, or the Secretary of the Treasury if a proposal originates with the Administration. The principal technical official of the Treasury Department who assists the Secretary in this regard and who is responsible for the direct supervision of tax legislation in the Executive branch is the Assistant Secretary for Tax Policy.[20]

Additional Administration witnesses may follow the Secretary of the Treasury, such as the Chair of the Council of Economic Advisors or the Director of the Office of Management and Budget, depending on the nature of the proposals. Representatives of various private interests concerned with the proposed legislation appear next. These persons include spokespersons for trade associations, business interests, labor unions, and farm organizations, as well as attorneys representing particular taxpayers and even taxpayers themselves. The testimony before the Committee is published under the title of Hearings on Tax Reform, or some similar title.

After the public hearings, the Committee on Ways and Means deliberates. All committee meetings are presumptively open to the public and a separate roll call vote is required to close any committee meeting. In these "mark up" deliberations, the Committee determines the main outlines of the bill that it reports to the full House. Its policy decisions are then translated into statutory form by members of the Office of the House Legislative Counsel, a group of expert legal drafters responsible for the drafting of nearly all the important legislation originating in the House. Generally, the same representatives of this Office work on tax legislation from year to year, thus facilitating continuity and building institutional knowledge. In addition, these drafting experts are assisted by technical representatives from the Treasury, the Internal Revenue Service, and the Staff of the Joint Committee on Taxation. This group also prepares a report to accompany the bill—a "Committee Report"— which contains material justifying its policies and explaining its provisions. The bill and Committee Report are then considered by the Committee and, when approved, reported to the full House. The bill is generally debated and voted on in the House under a "closed rule" procedure, which permits amendments to be offered only by the Committee (or perhaps a few amendments approved for consideration by

---

[20]   The Assistant Secretary is in charge of the Office of Tax Legislative Counsel, the Office of Benefits Counsel, the Office of International Tax Counsel, and the Office of Tax Analysis. The various Tax Legislative Counsels' Offices consist of staffs of lawyers who continuously consider the policy and technical aspects of proposals for legislative changes, originating within or without the Treasury Department. The Office of Tax Analysis is composed of economists who perform a similar function in regard to the economic aspects of tax issues and who are responsible for furnishing revenue estimates.

the House Rules Committee), which means that the bill as reported by the Committee is generally the bill as passed by the House.

A similar procedure occurs, often simultaneously, in the Senate.[21] The cast of characters, with Senators replacing Representatives, is much the same. The Senate Finance Committee makes its policy decisions, which may range from minor differences from the House bill to a completely different bill.[22] It then reports a bill with an accompanying Senate Finance Committee Report. The debate on the Senate floor is without restriction, and any Senator may propose an amendment dealing with any tax matter. Consequently, those interests desiring changes in the bill endeavor to secure the cooperation of a Senator or group of Senators in agreement with their objectives in order to change the bill on the floor of the Senate.

The House and Senate bills then go to a Committee of Conference of the House and Senate, composed of each party's ranking members, of the House Ways and Means Committee and the Senate Finance Committee. The House and Senate conferees adjust the differences between the two bodies, generally through compromises on the main issues. The two bills may have little resemblance, and the Conference Committee picks and chooses among the provisions of the different bills. In some instances, the Conference Committee adds provisions that were in neither the House nor the Senate bills. Often the Conference Report produced in Conference is the first time some provisions have seen the light of day and they are enacted without the benefit of critical examination in hearings and committee deliberations. The Conference action is set forth in a Conference Report that states the action on each Senate amendment and contains the language of Conference changes. The Report also contains a Joint Explanatory Statement of the Conference Committee by the Managers on the part of the House and the Senate that explains the actions taken, thus performing the function of a Committee Report.[23] The House and Senate act on the Conference Report, and almost always approve it. The final legislation is then sent to the President for action.

The legislative tools for the tax technician—the sources of legislative history—are created through this procedure: Presidential messages, Committee hearings, the successive stages of the bill and its amendments, Committee and Conference Reports, the Congressional debates, and a message accompanying the President's action on the bill. The Reports of Subcommittees, Treasury Department Statements,

---

[21]   The Constitutional requirement that revenue legislation originate in the House is satisfied by assigning the final bill the number of the original House bill, however different the two may be.

[22]   As in the House, committee meetings of the Senate are open to the public and a committee meeting may be closed only on a vote of the committee in order to discuss certain specified matters.

[23]   The Committee Reports through 1938 are contained in 1939–1 C.B., Part 2. Subsequent Committee reports are contained in the Cumulative Bulletin for the year of the legislation involved. All tax legislation is also reprinted in these Bulletins, issued by the Internal Revenue Service.

material prepared by the Staff of the Joint Committee on Taxation, and press conferences held by Committee Chairpersons provide additional interpretive material.

B. THE ADMINISTRATIVE PROCESS

(1) GENERAL ORGANIZATION OF THE INTERNAL REVENUE SERVICE

The Treasury tax staff is primarily concerned with the formulation of tax policy on behalf of the executive branch of the Government. The Commissioner of Internal Revenue and the officials and employees composing the IRS are responsible for the administration of federal taxes. Coordination between the Treasury and IRS is facilitated by the agency's location within the Treasury Department subject to the supervision of the Secretary.

The IRS is divided into a central supervisory and planning organization known as the National Office, located in Washington, D.C., and a much larger field organization located in the principal cities of the country.[24] The Commissioner, who is appointed by the President for a five-year term, is delegated direct responsibility for the assessment and collection of the federal taxes.

The Office of Chief Counsel of the Internal Revenue Service is headed by the Chief Counsel, the legal advisor to the Commissioner, who is also appointed by the President. Each of its principal operating divisions is supervised by an Associate Chief Counsel. The operating divisions are responsible for such matters as preparing regulations, analyzing legislative proposals, overseeing tax litigation, and preparing rulings on particular tax issues.

The day-to-day functions of the IRS are performed by several hierarchical divisions, which have been in a nearly constant state of reorganization in recent years. The actual collection of taxes is generally the responsibility of the Regional Service Centers. Most taxpayers are required to file their tax returns with one of the Service Centers, which process tax returns and related documents through the use of automatic and manual data processing systems.

Audit, and collection functions are performed primarily by four divisions (within which there are subgroups) based on the nature of the taxpayer involved; (1) Wage and Investment (W&I), which deals with most individual taxpayers; (2) Small Business and Self-Employed (SB&E), which deals with exactly what its title describes (including small corporate businesses); (3) Large Business and International (LB&I), which deals with the most significant corporations and partnerships; and (4) Tax-Exempt and Government Entities (TE/GE), which includes qualified pension plans. Each of these divisions has a centralized office,

---

[24]   An official description of the organization, functions and procedures of the Internal Revenue Service is contained in Part 601 of 26 Code of Federal Regulations.

but most taxpayer contacts are through IRS employees working in one of the many local offices. In addition, there is an independent Appeals Division, which provides an administrative review process for taxpayers who disagree with an initial IRS determination of a tax deficiency or a decision to place a lien on or to levy against a taxpayer's property to satisfy an unpaid tax liability.

(2) ADMINISTRATIVE INTERPRETATION OF THE TAX LAWS

The administrative interpretation of the tax laws is evidenced in a variety of forms, extending from general pronouncements to activity in the case of a particular taxpayer's return. The highest order of general pronouncement is a Treasury Regulation, which is prepared for each of the taxes administered by the IRS.[25] Treasury Regulations are first made public as Proposed Regulations so that interested parties may comment and urge changes.[26] A public hearing may be held. The final Regulations are then issued over the signature of the Commissioner and the Assistant Secretary for Tax Policy. Amendments of Regulations, which follow the same procedure, are known as Treasury Decisions. Under § 7805(b), only regulations issued within 18 months of the enactment of the statutory provision to which they relate may be completely retroactive.[27] Otherwise, a regulation may be retroactive only to the earliest of the following: (1) with respect to a temporary regulation, the date the regulation was filed with the Federal Register, (2) with respect to a final regulation, the date the proposed regulation was filed with the Federal Register, and (3) in any case, the date of a notice substantially describing to the public the expected content of the regulation. The Commissioner also may issue retroactive regulations to "prevent abuse," correct procedural defects in prior regulations, or that deal with internal policies, practices, and procedures.

The next level of interpretative pronouncement consists of the published Revenue Rulings of the IRS. These are rulings on a stated set of facts that usually involve a problem common to a number of taxpayers. Often they originate from requests for rulings by taxpayers. A reply to a request for technical advice on a substantive point by a field office may also be the subject of a published ruling. Published rulings issued by the IRS are designated by two numbers, with the first standing for the year of the ruling and the second reflecting the ruling number for that year (e.g., Rev. Rul. 2016–1 connotes the first Revenue Ruling issued in

---

[25] Regulations appear in Title 26, Code of Federal Regulations with the Income Tax Regulations designated as Part 1; the Estate Tax Regulations as Part 20; the Gift Tax Regulations as Part 25; and the Withholding Regulations as Part 31. Each particular Regulation has the same section number as the Code section to which it relates.

[26] In some cases, regulations are issued as both Proposed and Temporary Regulations. Taxpayers may rely on the latter while they are in effect with any subsequent changes to apply prospectively.

[27] For cases upholding the retroactivity of regulations see e.g., Pollack v. Commissioner, 392 F.2d 409 (5th Cir.1968); United States v. California Portland Cement Co., 413 F.2d 161 (9th Cir.1969); Danly Machine Corp. v. United States, 492 F.2d 30 (7th Cir.1974).

2016).[28] Revenue Procedures (e.g., Rev. Proc. 2016–1) historically have dealt with procedural aspects of taxpayer contact with the IRS. In recent years, however, the IRS has used Revenue Procedures to announce "safe-harbors," or circumstances under which the IRS will not challenge a taxpayer's position that a particular item is not reportable as income or is deductible. These administrative pronouncements are published on a current basis in the Internal Revenue Bulletin.

Generally, formally published interpretative pronouncements are binding on officials of the IRS. Of course, any given pronouncement may create an interpretative issue of its own. These pronouncements may be challenged by taxpayers in the courts, with success or failure depending upon the judicial doctrines pertaining to the weight given to administrative interpretations. Most regulations interpret specific statutory language under the general authority of § 7805 of the Code and are given a presumption of validity. Under time-honored standards announced by the Supreme Court in Commissioner v. South Texas Lumber Co., 333 U.S. 496 (1948), "Treasury regulations must be sustained unless unreasonable and plainly inconsistent with the words of the revenue statutes and * * * should not be overruled except for weighty reasons." In United States v. Correll, 389 U.S. 299 (1967), the Supreme Court added that in determining the validity of an interpretative regulation promulgated under authority of § 7805, "The role of the judiciary * * * begins and ends with assuring that the Commissioner's regulations fall within his authority to implement the congressional mandate in some reasonable manner."[29] More recently, the courts generally have applied the principles of Chevron USA, Inc. v. Natural Resources Defense Council, 467 U.S. 837 (1984). As applied to Treasury regulations, *Chevron* has been interpreted to mean that where "Congress has not directly spoken to the precise question at issue," and the regulations promulgated under authority of § 7805(a) "fill a gap left by the statutes, a court may not substitute its own construction for the reasonable interpretation of an agency." Peoples Federal Savings & Loan Association of Sidney v. Commissioner, 948 F.2d 289 (6th Cir.1991); see also Ohio Periodical Distributors, Inc. v. Commissioner, 105 F.3d 322 (6th Cir.1997) (under *Chevron*, "when Congress has not directly addressed the precise question, [the court] consider[s] whether the agency's interpretation is based on a permissible construction of the statute"; if the agency made a "reasonable policy choice," the regulation must be upheld).

---

[28]   Rev. Proc. 89–14, 1989–1 C.B. 814, sets forth the standards employed by the Internal Revenue Service for publication of Revenue Rulings and Revenue Procedures.

[29]   See also Lykes v. United States, 343 U.S. 118 (1952) (interpretative regulations are entitled to "substantial weight"); Commissioner v. Estate of Noel, 380 U.S. 678, 682 (1965) ("We have held in many cases that * * * a long-standing administrative interpretation, applying to a substantially re-enacted statute, is deemed to have received congressional approval and has the effect of law"). Compare Helvering v. Sabine Transportation Co., 318 U.S. 306 (1943) (regulations held invalid where they were contrary to "the unambiguous mandate of the statute * * * and amount to an attempt to legislate").

In Mayo Foundation v. United States, 562 U.S. 44 (2011), the Supreme Court clarified the level of deference that courts are required to give Treasury regulations. Before the decision in *Mayo*, it was unclear whether Treasury regulations were evaluated under administrative law's *Chevron* standard or under a different, tax-specific standard. It was also unclear prior to *Mayo* whether the appropriate level of deference depended on whether the regulation was issued pursuant to a specific directive in a particular Code section (a so-called "legislative regulation") or pursuant to § 7805(a)'s general authority to issue tax regulations wherever necessary (an "interpretive regulation"). In *Mayo*, the Court held that the *Chevron* standard applies to all Treasury regulations, regardless of whether they were issued pursuant to a specific directive or § 7805(a). Under step one of the *Chevron* standard, a reviewing court first determines whether Congress has directly addressed the precise question at issue or whether the statutory language is ambiguous on the point. If the statutory language is unambiguous, Congress's determination controls. If not, the reviewing court moves to step two, where it evaluates whether the regulation's interpretation of the statute is a reasonable one. If the interpretation is deemed reasonable, the regulation is upheld even though other reasonable interpretations might exist and even if the court would have chosen a different interpretation if it was interpreting the statute at issue without the benefit of a Treasury regulation on point.

Some Code provisions expressly authorize the issuance of regulations to govern the application of those provisions. These "legislative" regulations generally are given binding effect.[30]

The weight to be accorded Revenue Rulings is less clear. In Stubbs, Overbeck & Associates, Inc. v. United States, 445 F.2d 1142 (5th Cir.1971), the court stated: "A ruling is merely the opinion of a lawyer in the agency and must be accepted as such. It may be helpful in interpreting a statute, but it is not binding on * * * the courts. It does not have the effect of a regulation or a Treasury Decision." On the other hand, in Davis v. United States, 495 U.S. 472 (1990), the Supreme Court stated: "Although the IRS's interpretative rulings do not have the force and effect of regulations * * * we give an agency's interpretations and practices considerable weight where they involve a contemporaneous construction of a statute and where they have been in long use."[31] More recently, in United States v. Mead Corp., 533 U.S. 218 (2001), which involved a Customs Service ruling, the Supreme Court addressed the level of deference accorded to agency rulings that were issued without following the notice and comment process required for *Chevron*

---

[30]   See United States v. Vogel Fertilizer Co., 455 U.S. 16 (1982); Rowan Companies, Inc. v. United States, 452 U.S. 247 (1981). However, in Rite Aid Corp. v. United States, 255 F.3d 1357 (Fed.Cir.2001), the court invalidated a legislative regulation.

[31]   See also Johnson City Medical Center v. United States, 999 F.2d 973 (6th Cir.1993) (Revenue Rulings are entitled to "some deference" unless they conflict with the statute, legislative history or are "otherwise unreasonable").

deference. The Court concluded that the ruling in issue was not entitled to any judicial deference, but that the ruling was "eligible to claim respect according to its persuasiveness." Nevertheless, the opinion stated that "the fact that the [ruling] here was not a product of such formal process does not alone . . . bar the application of *Chevron,*" and "*Chevron* did not eliminate [the principle] that an agency's interpretation may merit some deference whatever its form." As a result of the ambiguous language, the courts have not interpreted *Mead* as completely eliminating deference to rulings promulgated without notice and comment. See American Express Co. v. United States, 262 F.3d 1376 (Fed.Cir.2001) ("The interpretation of a revenue procedure contained in a General Counsel Memorandum and an IRS decision under the revenue procedure is not reflected in a regulation adopted after notice and comment and probably would not be entitled to *Chevron* deference . . . [t]he Supreme Court has firmly established that agency interpretations of their own regulations are entitled to substantial deference.").

The Commissioner, by delegation from the Secretary of the Treasury, has the authority under § 7805(b) to make any interpretative pronouncement of the Treasury nonretroactive. Changes that are adverse to taxpayers are almost always made prospective in application to preserve reliance by taxpayers upon the previous interpretation.[32]

Taxpayers may request an administrative interpretation on prospective transactions or on completed transactions which are not involved in returns already filed. Generally, rulings are issued in response to these requests. In some cases, because the particular issue is deemed too uncertain, or because the matter is regarded as primarily one of fact (e.g., market value), no ruling may be issued. These "rulings," generally referred to as "private letter rulings," are issued by the National Office in Washington, D.C. "Determination letters" are issued in answer to taxpayer inquiries if the inquiry relates to situations governed by clearly established rules such as in the case of pension trusts and tax-exempt organizations.[33] The IRS charges a "user's fee" in varying amounts for different types of private letter rulings, ranging between $275 and $50,000 (adjusted periodically). A procedure known as a closing agreement (under § 7121) is available whereby the taxpayer and the Treasury may formally bind themselves to observe a particular interpretation, represented by the result agreed to with respect to a specified transaction.[34] In some cases, the IRS field office will ask

---

[32]   Rev. Proc. 89–14, 1989–1 C.B. 814, § 7.01(3) states: "When Revenue Rulings revoke or modify rulings previously published * * * the authority of section 7805(b) of the Code ordinarily is invoked to provide that the new rulings will not be applied retroactively to the extent that the new rulings have adverse tax consequences to taxpayers."

[33]   The procedures governing the issuance of private letter rulings and determination letters are described in a revenue procedure published as the first revenue procedure of each year. See e.g., Rev. Proc. 2016–1, 2016–1 I.R.B. 1. From time to time the Service publishes additional Revenue Procedures specifying issues on which it will not rule.

[34]   The procedures for entering into closing agreements on specific issues are described in annually issued revenue procedures.

Washington for "technical advice" in a particular case, in which event the taxpayer involved is afforded an opportunity to file a brief and obtain a hearing.[35]

As in the case of other administrative materials, private letter rulings and most documents reflecting advice to IRS field offices from the Chief Counsel's office (and related background documents) are available to the general public (after redactions of any information that could identify a particular taxpayer) and are published by various tax services. Section 6110 sets forth the procedures for obtaining and publishing such "written determinations." Section 6110(j)(3) provides that written determinations have no precedential status, except as otherwise provided by Regulations.[36] Section 6110 provides the exclusive method by which written determinations or background file documents may be disclosed.

Another source of administrative interpretation is the Internal Revenue Manual. This Manual is issued by the National Office to provide guidelines to IRS agents in their audits of various issues. The Manual is available to the public.

C. THE JUDICIAL PROCESS

(1) ORIGINAL JURISDICTION

The most important court of original jurisdiction in tax cases is the United States Tax Court (known as the Board of Tax Appeals or "B.T.A." until 1942). It has jurisdiction over taxpayers' appeals from tax deficiencies asserted by the Commissioner under the income, estate, and gift taxes. Proceedings before the Tax Court are suits by the taxpayer against the Commissioner, though the latter may assert additional deficiencies in the proceeding before the court. The hearing is *de novo*. The Tax Court has no jurisdiction in cases where the taxpayer is attempting to obtain a refund of a tax amount claimed to have been paid erroneously. A taxpayer may file an action in the Tax Court *only* within the 90-day period following issuance of a statutory notice of deficiency by the Commissioner. If jurisdiction is obtained on an asserted deficiency, however, the court may find that the proper result is a refund to the taxpayer.

The Tax Court is created under the legislative authority of Article I of the Constitution. It is not an Article III judicial court. The Tax Court is composed of 19 judges who are appointed by the President for a term of fifteen years. They are generally reappointed to office. The headquarters of the court is located in Washington, D.C. with individual

---

[35]   See Rev. Proc. 2016–2, 2016–1 I.R.B. 102. Changes to this revenue procedure are incorporated annually and published as the second revenue procedure of the year.

[36]   For a discussion of the use of private letter rulings for predictive or persuasive purposes, see Holden and Novey, Legitimate Uses of Letter Rulings Issued to Other Taxpayers—A Reply to Gerald Portney, 37 Tax Lawyer 337 (1984).

members holding trials in principal cities. The Commissioner is represented before the Tax Court by the IRS Office of the Chief Counsel.

Trials in the Tax Court are conducted by a single judge who prepares a decision consisting of findings of facts and an opinion. The Chief Judge determines whether the decision is to be reviewed by the entire court. Decisions reviewed by the entire court carry greater weight than unreviewed decisions. Memorandum decisions usually involve questions turning on factual issues or previously decided legal points and are less frequently cited as authorities by the Tax Court or other courts. The decisions, whether or not reviewed, are issued as published decisions, later bound in volumes cited 1 to 47 B.T.A. and 1 T.C. et seq., or in Memorandum Decisions which are not published in official reports but are published by the tax services.[37]

The other courts of original jurisdiction for tax matters are the District Courts of the United States and the United States Court of Federal Claims (formerly the Claims Court). The cases in these courts are known as refund suits, in that the taxpayer is seeking to obtain a refund of tax previously paid. The defendant in these courts is the United States. District Court suits generally must be brought in the district in which the taxpayer resides, or, in the case of a corporation, in the district in which it has its principal place of business.[38] The District Courts have jurisdiction in any tax case against the United States seeking a refund of tax regardless of the amount involved. A jury trial may be obtained in these suits. The Court of Federal Claims has jurisdiction over all tax suits against the United States regardless of amount. There is no jury trial. In all refund cases, the Government is represented by the Tax Division of the Department of Justice, which obtains the advice and assistance of the IRS Chief Counsel's office.

In order to sue for a refund in either the District Court or Court of Federal Claims, the taxpayer first must have sought the refund through administrative procedures. Generally speaking, a taxpayer has three years from the due date of a timely filed tax return to file a refund request with the IRS. If the administrative refund request is denied, the taxpayer has two years after the denial to file a refund suit. If the IRS fails to act on the refund request within six months, the taxpayer may file a refund suit without waiting for the IRS's denial of the refund claim.

Section 7421(a) provides that no suit shall be maintained in any court for the purpose of restraining the assessment or collection of any tax. While this section operates generally to prevent injunctive relief, injunctions are permitted under "exceptional circumstances." The federal declaratory judgment procedure is generally not available with respect to federal taxes, although the Tax Court has been given the power to

---

[37]   Citations in this book to Tax Court Memorandum decisions refer to the year and Tax Court number of the decision and do not correspond to the volume and page of any particular tax service. They are also easily located in any tax service.

[38]   28 U.S.C. § 1402(a)(1)–(2).

issue declaratory judgments in actions to determine the tax-exempt status of certain retirement plans and to determine whether interest on bonds issued by local governments is exempt from federal income taxation.[39]

(2) APPELLATE JURISDICTION

Appeals from the Tax Court are heard as a matter of right by the Courts of Appeals of the United States, with jurisdiction lying to the Circuit in which the taxpayer resided at the time the Tax Court petition was filed or, in the case of a corporation, in which it has its principal place of business. The parties may also agree to a particular court by stipulation. The appellate jurisdiction is exercised in the same manner as that over civil actions in District Courts tried without a jury.[40] Appeals from the District Courts in tax cases also go to the Courts of Appeals. Appeals from the Court of Federal Claims go to the Court of Appeals for the Federal Circuit. The Government in all appeals is represented by the Tax Division of the Department of Justice.

The Tax Court follows a Court of Appeals decision that is squarely on point where the appeal from the Tax Court decision would go to that Court of Appeals. Golsen v. Commissioner, 54 T.C. 742 (1970). The Tax Court does not, however, regard itself as bound by the decision of a particular Court of Appeals if the case in question would go to a different Circuit if appealed. In such cases, the Tax Court usually follows its own prior decision as precedent, even though it may have been reversed.

The decisions of the Courts of Appeals are reviewed by the Supreme Court under the certiorari procedure. Review is generally granted only when a conflict between Circuits exists or where the issue is of unusual importance to the administration of the tax laws. The Supreme Court reviews only a few tax cases each year. The Government is represented by the Office of the Solicitor General of the Department of Justice.

(3) IRS ACQUIESCENCE AND NON-ACQUIESCENCE

The IRS responds to some court decisions (other than Supreme Court decisions) with a notice of acquiescence or non-acquiescence in the decision. Acquiescence indicates acceptance of the legal interpretation, result, or both, while non-acquiescence means that the Tax Court's

---

[39] I.R.C. §§ 7476, 7478. In addition, § 7428 provides declaratory judgment jurisdiction in the Tax Court, the federal District Court for the District of Columbia, and the Court of Federal Claims with respect to the exempt status of certain non-profit organizations. See e.g., United Cancer Council, Inc. v. Commissioner, 100 T.C. 162 (1993).

[40] Section 7482(a) provides that Courts of Appeals review Tax Court decisions in the same manner as they review District Court decisions in civil actions without a jury. Rule 52(a) of the Federal Rules of Civil Procedure, applicable to review of a District Court's findings in a non-jury case, provides: "Findings of fact . . . shall not be set aside unless clearly erroneous, and due regard shall be given to the opportunity of the trial court to judge the credibility of the witnesses."

interpretation will not be followed. Acquiescences and non-acquiescences are published in the Internal Revenue Bulletin.[41]

D. INCOME TAX PROCEDURE[42]

(1) CURRENT PAYMENT

The individual income tax is collected during the year the income is earned. Current collection is effected through two principal devices—the withholding of tax on wages and salaries and the periodic payment by the taxpayer of an estimated tax on other forms of income. Under the withholding mechanism, an employer is required to withhold the specified tax from each payment of wages paid to an employee. The amount to be withheld is set forth in withholding tables based on graduated rates applied to the amount earned less the employee's prorated annual personal exemptions and an allowance for personal deductions. Assuming steady employment, the amount collected by withholding will closely approximate the correct tax on taxpayers whose total yearly income is in the form of wages. This withholding tax is merely a tentative tax collection; reconciliation with the current tax is by April 15 of the following year, as described below. The employer is responsible for the entire withholding process. Employers must make deposits of the amounts withheld to a designated Federal Reserve Bank at specified time intervals depending on the amount of withheld taxes involved. The employer must give the employee a statement showing the wages paid and tax withheld on the familiar Form W-2 by January 31 of the following year. Certain employment, such as farm labor, domestic service, and casual labor not in the employer's business, is not subject to withholding.[43]

By means of the withholding process, the great majority of wage and salary earners are kept current in their tax payments, so that lingering indebtedness for the income tax does not exist. At the same time, compliance with tax obligations is virtually assured on the part of these taxpayers, with their only real opportunity for evasion involving deliberate overstatement of deductions or exemptions claimed. Generally, the system results in over-withholding since many employees do not avail themselves of their full exemptions. As a result, most employees receive refunds each year.

---

[41]   In citations in this book, acquiescences are indicated as (Acq.) and non-acquiescences as (Nonacq.) after the court citation.

[42]   This survey is a very brief sketch of income tax procedure, designed to provide a background for the cases and materials to follow. Many of the rules are presented in general terms, with qualifications left unstated. A Statement of Procedural Rules, reflecting Internal Revenue Service practices and procedures, appears in 26 C.F.R. § 601.

[43]   Income tax withholding usually is combined with Social Security and Medicare tax withholding, and in such instances the employer may use one table, one return form, etc. Nonetheless, the statement provided to employees must state the taxes separately.

Current collection of individual income tax on other forms of income, such as interest and dividends, gains from the sale of property, or profits from operating an unincorporated business, is obtained through the payment of estimated taxes. Section 6654 requires individuals to remit payments of estimated taxes on April 15, June 15, September 15, and January 15. Generally speaking, each remittance must equal at least 90 percent of the tax liability with respect to income earned as of the due date for the payment. Estimated tax payments are computed by subtracting the amount of tax estimated to be collected through withholding. A penalty for the excess of actual tax over estimated tax paid is assessed if the total estimated tax paid is less than the amounts specified in § 6654. This estimated tax procedure helps persons with income from business and investments as well as those with income from wages or salaries large enough so that the graduated withholding tax does not approximate the correct tax keep current in their tax payments.

Corporations are required by § 6655 to make estimated tax payments.

(2) FILING OF RETURN AND FINAL PAYMENT

Every individual with a gross income above stated levels—generally the level of income that normally results in a positive income tax liability if the taxpayer has no dependents and before taking into account tax credits—is required to file a tax return by April 15 of the succeeding taxable year.[44] This filing is required even though no tax may be owed (which usually occurs due to claiming additional exemptions for dependents and qualifying for tax credits). The return is completed and signed by the taxpayer (or, alternatively, completed by the taxpayer's paid professional or tax preparation software and signed by the taxpayer). In this way, the income tax is regarded as a voluntary, self-assessed tax (even though § 7203 of the Code imposes a penalty of up to one-year in prison for "willful failure" to file a return). Consequently, the measure of compliance with the tax is dependent on the integrity and attitude of taxpayers as a group.

Form 1040 or one of its simplified variants is used by all individual taxpayers. Any individual whose taxable income is less than $50,000 and consists entirely of wages subject to withholding, interest or dividends, and certain other limited classes of income with respect to which the payor is required to file information returns may simply fill in a tax return form without computing the tax liability and send it to a Regional Service Center with copies of the withholding statement and other information returns. Under this procedure, the tax is computed by the Regional Service Center and the taxpayer receives a bill for income tax due or a refund check for any overpayment. Most taxpayers who compute their own tax liability do not have to work their way through the rate

---

[44]   The levels are set in § 6012(a)(1) as the sum of the taxpayer's personal exemptions plus the standard deduction.

schedules in § 1. Instead, they simply refer to tax tables prepared by the IRS, which incorporate the personal exemptions.

Tax returns are filed under penalty of perjury, and penalties are provided for late filing and for false or fraudulent returns.

Information disclosed on returns is confidential to the IRS. Under appropriate procedures it may be disclosed, however, to State tax officials, the House Ways and Means Committee, the Senate Finance Committee, and the Joint Committee on Taxation. In very limited circumstances, generally for statistical purposes, the information may be made available to other Congressional Committees and to Government agencies. Persons obtaining information from tax returns must keep that information confidential.[45]

(3) INVESTIGATION OF RETURNS AND SETTLEMENT PROCEDURE

The Regional Service Center makes a preliminary inspection of returns for mathematical errors. Any disclosed tax liability is billed at once and any excess payment is refunded immediately. The appropriate division of the IRS then examines the returns. Many of the audits are either "correspondence audits," carried on entirely by letter, or "office audits," in which the taxpayer must appear at a local IRS office with the records and information requested. The remaining audits are "field audits" in which the examining agent checks the taxpayer's books and records at his home or place of business. Returns subject to field audit are chosen primarily on the basis of a statistically-derived formula designed to identify returns with significantly understated tax liability. Correspondence audits are often based on discrepancies between the filed return and information returns from other persons.[46] Other factors that may result in audit include questions about returns of the taxpayer for prior years, Federal Reserve Bank notices of large cash withdrawals, information on significant real estate and insurance transactions, check-cashing activities, newspaper items, informant and anonymous tips, and similar leads.[47]

---

[45] See I.R.C. § 7216, which prohibits persons in the business of preparing returns from disclosing any information furnished in the course of the preparation of the returns.

[46] For example, persons paying salaries, annuities, interest, rent, etc. that exceed a threshold amount to any one person are required to file information returns; realtors are required to file information returns regarding real estate sales that they close on behalf of sellers; stock brokers are required to file information returns regarding sales of stocks and other securities by their customers; corporations are required to file information returns with respect to dividend and interest payments; any person engaged in business who pays another person more than $600 in compensation for services or the use of property must file an information return. The partnership and trust returns also operate as information returns.

[47] See General Accounting Office, Tax Administration: IRS' Return Selection Process, GAO/GGD–99–30 (Feb. 1999), for a discussion of some of the IRS methodologies.

The examining agent investigating a case (usually an accountant or an auditor) attempts to settle any dispute raised by the investigation.[48] An agreement reached at this stage concludes the matter.

If no agreement is reached at the agent level, the IRS field office will either drop the case or send a so-called "thirty-day letter" to the taxpayer. This letter contains the report of the examining agent and gives the taxpayer thirty days in which to choose one of three courses of action: (1) file a formal protest with the Appeals Office, which is a written statement of the taxpayer's case; (2) request (or receive through failure to respond) a statutory deficiency notice, a so-called "ninety-day letter," from which an appeal may be taken to the Tax Court; or (3) concede liability by executing the agreement form accompanying the thirty-day letter, thereby closing the case.

Conferences with the Appeals Office are informal in nature. No stenographic record is made. The taxpayer may bring witnesses to the hearing, but additional statements of fact to be added to the record must be submitted in affidavit form. Here also the effort is to settle the case, with the IRS rules pertaining to Appeals functions stating: "Appeals will ordinarily give serious consideration to an offer to settle a tax controversy on a basis which fairly reflects the relative merits of the opposing views in the light of the hazards which would exist if the case were litigated. However, no settlement will be made based upon nuisance value of the case to either party."[49] If the taxpayer elects not to have a conference, or if a settlement cannot be reached with the Appeals Office, a statutory deficiency notice is then issued. This letter constitutes a statement that there is a deficiency in tax (that is, additional tax is due) for the reasons stated in the notice. Assessment of tax cannot be made without the taxpayer's consent unless this statutory deficiency notice is issued, except in the case of a jeopardy assessment where the IRS believes any delay will jeopardize collection of the tax. On the issuance of this letter, the taxpayer has 90 days in which to petition the Tax Court for review. If this petition is not filed the tax must be paid and, if not paid, may be assessed and collected by appropriate procedures, including the use of liens and distraint (i.e., seizing the taxpayer's property). After payment, the taxpayer may still file a claim for refund and, if the claim is disallowed or not acted on within six months, bring suit in the District Court or Court of Federal Claims. The Tax Court procedure does, however, permit the taxpayer to obtain judicial consideration of the case without having to make prior payment of the deficiency claimed by the IRS.

The IRS has three years from the filing of the return to send a deficiency notice. I.R.C. § 6501(a). This period is extended to six years if

---

[48]   At the inception of the audit, the agent is required to provide the taxpayer with a pamphlet entitled "Your Rights as a Taxpayer," which sets forth in nontechnical language the rights of the taxpayer and the procedures to be followed.

[49]   26 C.F.R. § 601.106(f)(2).

the taxpayer omits from gross income an amount in excess of 25 percent of the gross income stated in the return, unless the taxpayer discloses the omission to the IRS. I.R.C. § 6501(e). The period is unlimited if no return is filed or if the return is false or fraudulent with intent to evade tax. I.R.C. § 6501(c)(1)–(3). These periods of limitation upon assessment may be extended by the taxpayer's written waiver, prescribing a longer period. Generally, the taxpayer acquiesces in a request for such a waiver, since the alternative is a deficiency notice that may be erroneous but is the only action the IRS can take if it has not had time to evaluate the case sufficiently.

(4) TAX COURT PROCEEDINGS

Proceedings in the Tax Court are initiated by a petition filed by the taxpayer in accordance with the rules of the Tax Court. This is a formal document in which the taxpayer assigns the errors claimed to exist with respect to the asserted deficiency and states supporting facts. The IRS may claim an additional deficiency in the answer to the petition and may raise affirmative issues, but as to these the burden is on the IRS. Once a petition has been filed, the IRS is barred from administratively assessing a further deficiency for the year. If the taxpayer pays the asserted deficiency, the Tax Court is deprived of jurisdiction.

After the petition has been filed, the taxpayer still may attempt to settle the case through conferences conducted by the Appeals Office. Settlement is effected by stipulation filed with the Tax Court.

If the case is not settled, the trial in the Tax Court is entirely *de novo* and is not restricted in any fashion by the data considered in the administrative stage. Review of the IRS's action is thus different from the review accorded to quasi-judicial administrative agencies. Briefs are filed after the trial.

The taxpayer generally has the burden of going forward with respect to disproving a deficiency. Prior to 1998, the taxpayer also bore the burden of proof in whatever forum the taxpayer chose to litigate the tax liability. Since 1998, however, § 7491 specifies that the burden of proof is on the government in any *court proceeding* pertaining to any factual issue with respect to which the taxpayer has introduced "credible evidence" if certain conditions set forth in § 7491(a)(2) have been satisfied. First, the taxpayer must have complied with any applicable substantiation or record keeping requirements imposed by the Code or regulations. Second, the taxpayer must have cooperated with reasonable requests by the IRS for witnesses, information, documents, meetings, and interviews, and must have exhausted administrative remedies. This requirement will result in the burden of proof remaining on the taxpayer in cases involving nonfilers and objective cheating as well as in more routine cases in which the taxpayer simply fails to cooperate through dilatory and evasive tactics. Furthermore, some taxpayers may conclude that the potential benefit of shifting the burden of proof is not worth the detriment of producing the required information before litigating the case. Finally, if the taxpayer is a corporation, partnership, or trust, the taxpayer's net worth may not exceed $7,000,000. Once the basic qualifying conditions have been met, shifting the burden of proof to the government requires that the taxpayer introduce credible evidence relevant to establishing the correct tax liability. If the taxpayer fails to introduce any such evidence, the burden of proof remains on the taxpayer, and the taxpayer very likely will have failed to carry that burden of proof. Section 7491 does not apply if another Code provision specifies who bears the burden of proof.

If the Tax Court finds a deficiency, the taxpayer either must pay or appeal and post a bond guaranteeing payment if the appeal is unsuccessful. Collection of a deficiency found by the Tax Court is not stayed simply by appeal; a bond is required. If the taxpayer does not appeal, the matter may not be relitigated by way of a claim for refund.

The Tax Court can hear cases involving small amounts on an informal basis. Where the deficiency does not exceed $50,000 for any single taxable year, the taxpayer may elect to have the case heard under a procedure following less formal rules and decided with a brief summary opinion rather than formal findings of facts by a trial judge. The small claims cases are not precedents for future cases and are not reviewable on appeal. The small claims procedures allow the taxpayer to present a claim to an impartial tribunal without the cost and delay of a full trial. In these proceedings, taxpayers generally appear without an attorney.

The administrative and court procedures thus provide the taxpayer—and hence the taxpayer's attorney—with numerous strategic choices. These choices include deciding how vigorously the taxpayer should argue the case with the examining agent who is not likely to consider finer points of law; technical legal discussions at this stage of the proceedings might not be very productive. In addition, the taxpayer has to decide whether to file a protest or instead pay the deficiency and continue the battle by way of refund claim. Many factors inform this decision, such as the taxpayer's ability to pay the deficiency, the fact that interest is payable on a deficiency if the taxpayer fails in Tax Court but is receivable on a refund if the taxpayer succeeds in District Court,[50] the perception of how quickly or slowly the IRS processes refunds, District Court precedents (if they favor the taxpayer, for instance, the taxpayer might also obtain favorable findings of fact on the theory that judges work hard to avoid reversal), and the opportunity for a jury trial in District Court. Most taxpayers resist the idea of paying the asserted tax due before commencing legal action and thus eschew seeking a refund of tax paid through a District Court. For those taxpayers who plan to resist without paying the tax asserted, yet another consideration involves whether to file a protest or to ask immediately for a deficiency letter. If the issue is one that is not likely to be settled, it may be advisable to

---

[50]   Sections 6601, 6611, 6621 and 6662 govern interest computations.

proceed to litigation rather than through conferences that might acquaint the IRS with the taxpayer's evidence. At the same time, most lawyers prefer to file the protest and go to the Appeals Office, because while this approach may educate the IRS it also educates the lawyer and offers insight into the IRS's position.

(5) REFUND PROCEDURE

A taxpayer who believes he has overpaid his tax may file a claim for refund.[51] An overpayment may have occurred with respect to the original tax paid when the return was filed or may have resulted from a later payment of a deficiency asserted by the IRS. The claim must state the grounds and facts relied upon, and it may be denied in whole or in part by the IRS. Refund claims are considered in a manner similar to that described above in deficiency cases. Any refund or over-assessment exceeding $2,000,000 is reviewed by the IRS Chief Counsel's office and the Congressional Joint Committee on Taxation.

The taxpayer has three years from the time the return was filed or two years from the time the tax was paid, whichever is later, to file a claim for refund. I.R.C. § 6511. Within that time, the IRS may make a refund payment without a claim, but it cannot do so after the period has run. If the period of limitation on assessment has been extended by waiver, generally the taxpayer may also file a refund claim within that extended period and six months thereafter.

If the claim for refund is denied, or not acted on within six months, the taxpayer may bring suit in the District Court or Court of Federal Claims, subject to the jurisdictional requirements. This suit must be brought within two years of the denial of the claim. I.R.C. § 6532(a).

(6) INTEREST, PENALTIES, AND ATTORNEYS' FEES

Delinquent payments of tax and payments of deficiencies in tax carry interest at the rate prescribed in § 6621 from the time the tax should have been paid, normally the return filing date for an individual. The running of interest is not suspended by litigation in the Tax Court. Interest is assessed and collected as part of the tax. Refunds of tax carry interest from the date the taxpayer pays the subsequently refunded remittance.

Section 6621 sets the interest on deficiencies and refunds at the "short-term federal rate" plus three percentage points. Generally speaking, the short-term federal rate is the rate at which the Treasury Department can borrow money for a term of three years or less. Interest rates are determined quarterly and announced by Revenue Ruling.

---

[51]   The taxpayer must pay the entire amount of any deficiency before contesting its correctness by a suit for refund. Flora v. United States, 357 U.S. 63 (1958), on rehearing, 362 U.S. 145 (1960).

Interest is compounded daily except in the case of interest on underpayment of estimated taxes. I.R.C. § 6622.

In addition to interest on deficiencies, the Internal Revenue Code provides a variety of penalties for failure to file a return or filing an incorrect return. Civil penalties are treated as additions to tax and collected as part of the tax through the deficiency procedure.

If any part of a deficiency is due to fraud with intent to evade the tax, the penalty equals 75 percent of the amount of the tax deficiency attributable to fraud. I.R.C. § 6663. While the normal burden of proof rules apply to show whether a deficiency exists, the Commissioner always has the burden of showing fraud once a deficiency is found. This civil penalty may be imposed even if a criminal penalty in the form of fine or imprisonment is also imposed.[52] Section 6663 applies only to fraudulent returns. The failure to file a return with fraudulent intent is governed by § 6651(f), which imposes a penalty of 15 percent of the tax due for each month after the due date that a return has not been filed, up to a maximum of 75 percent.

Section 6662 provides an array of penalties that will be assessed if a tax deficiency is attributable to culpable actions falling short of fraud. Under § 6662(a) and (b) the penalty is 20 percent of the amount of the "underpayment" attributable to: (1) "[n]egligence or disregard of rules or regulations," (2) "[a]ny substantial understatement of income tax," or (3) any substantial valuation misstatement, overstatement, or understatement (estate tax). An "underpayment" is the amount by which the tax finally determined to be due exceeds (1) the amount of tax due shown on the return plus any additional tax previously assessed, minus (2) prior abatements, refunds, and other repayments from the IRS. I.R.C. § 6664(a). Like the fraud penalty, the § 6662 penalties apply only when a return has been filed by the taxpayer. Only one of the § 6662 penalties may be assessed with respect to any item on a return, but different penalties may apply with respect to different portions of the deficiency.

"Negligence or disregard of rules or regulations" is defined in § 6662(c) as "any failure to make a reasonable attempt to comply with the provisions of this title," and "disregard" is defined to include "careless, reckless, or intentional disregard." For this purpose, "rules and regulations" include not just Treasury Regulations, but also revenue rulings, and notices (other than notices of proposed rulemaking).[53] Treas.

---

[52] A conviction for criminal fraud establishes the existence of civil fraud under § 6663 with the taxpayer thus collaterally estopped to introduce any evidence on the question of fraud in the civil proceedings. See Tomlinson v. Lefkowitz, 334 F.2d 262 (5th Cir.1964); Moore v. United States, 360 F.2d 353 (4th Cir.1965); Arctic Ice Cream Co. v. Commissioner, 43 T.C. 68 (1964) (Acq.). On the other hand, a failure to establish criminal fraud will not prevent a finding of civil fraud.

[53] Treas. Reg. § 1.6662–3(b)(2). A taxpayer who reports contrary to a revenue ruling has not "disregarded the rules and regulations" if the contrary position has a "realistic possibility" of success on the merits. This standard is met if the position has at least a one-in-three chance of being sustained on the merits if challenged. Treas. Regs. §§ 1.6662–3(a) and 1.6694–2(b).

Reg. § 1.6662–3(b) provides guidelines further defining negligence, and includes any failure to make a reasonable attempt to comply with the tax laws, to exercise ordinary and reasonable care in the preparation of a tax return, to keep adequate books and records, or to substantiate items properly. Failure to include an item reported on an information return or to attempt to verify a position that "would seem to a reasonable and prudent person to be too good to be true," is strong evidence of negligence.

The "substantial understatement of tax" penalty applies, without regard to negligence, if the excess of the tax required to be shown on the return over the actual tax shown on the return (minus any refunds or credits) exceeds the greater of $5,000 or ten percent of the tax required to be shown on the return. This penalty is not imposed if either (1) there is "substantial authority" supporting the taxpayer's position,[54] or (2) the relevant facts are adequately disclosed on the return and there is a "reasonable basis" for the taxpayer's position. The taxpayer is not required to prove that the authorities establish that the reporting position is "more likely than not" correct, but the standard for "substantial authority" is considerably more onerous than the "reasonable basis" standard. The regulations provide alternatively that there is substantial authority for a position only if the weight of authorities supporting the position relative to the weight of authorities for the contrary position is substantial (see Treas. Reg. § 1.6662–4(d)(3)(i)), and that a taxpayer may have substantial authority for a position that is supported only by a well-reasoned construction of a statute (see Treas. Reg. § 1.6662–4(d)(3)(ii)). Thus, the test for substantiality requires weighing existing authorities, considering well-reasoned arguments, and does not depend solely on a percentage-based estimate of the likelihood that the position is correct.

The substantial valuation misstatement penalty applies in a variety of circumstances where the taxpayer values property at 200 percent or more of its actual value, and thereby increases the amount of certain deductions, and the tax attributable to the misstatement exceeds $5,000. If the value is overstated by 400 percent or more, the penalty is increased to 40 percent of the understatement of tax.

Section 6662A imposes an additional penalty equal to 20 percent of any "reportable transaction understatement." A "reportable transaction understatement" involves an item with respect to either (1) a "listed transaction" or (2) a reportable transaction undertaken with a significant purpose of avoiding or evading federal income tax.[55] A listed transaction

---

[54] There is substantial authority for a position only if the weight of authorities supporting the position is substantial relative to the weight of authorities for the contrary position. Treas. Reg. § 1.6662–4(d)(3).

[55] Section 6707A imposes additional penalties for failure to disclose a reportable or listed transaction on a return. Section 6111 requires a material advisor in a tax shelter transaction to file a return describing the tax shelter and imposes penalties for failure to do so. Section 6112 requires each material advisor with respect to a reportable transaction to maintain a list of persons to whom the material advisor provided advice with respect to a reportable transaction, and further imposes penalties for failure to provide the list to the IRS when requested.

is one that is the same or substantially the same as a reportable transaction, but is specifically identified by the IRS as a tax avoidance transaction. See Treas. Reg. § 1.6011–4(b). Reportable transactions include transactions that incorporate a number of elements and transactions identified by the IRS as having the potential for tax avoidance or evasion. A reportable transaction understatement equals the sum of (1) the amount that results from applying the highest statutory tax rate to the increase in taxable income attributable to the difference between (a) the proper treatment of an item, and (b) the taxpayer's treatment of the item, and (2) the amount of the credits that would not have been taken if the reportable transaction had been reported correctly. The penalty is increased to 30 percent if the understatement is due to a listed transaction that is not disclosed as required by regulations under § 6011.

The §§ 6662 and 6662A penalties can be avoided if the taxpayer properly discloses to the IRS any nonfrivolous reporting positions. Such disclosure negates the negligence penalty for disregard of IRS rules and regulations if the taxpayer clearly states that the purpose of making the disclosure is to avoid the penalty and the taxpayer keeps adequate books and records. Treas. Reg. § 1.6662–3(c). At the same time, disclosure will not protect the taxpayer from penalties in the case of certain tax shelter transactions. Section 6664(d) requires that the taxpayer's position with respect to tax shelter transactions be based on substantial authority and that the taxpayer reasonably believed that the claimed tax treatment was more likely than not the proper tax treatment. See Treas. Reg. § 1.6664–4(d) and (f).

The Code also contains a "reasonable cause and good faith" defense to penalties in § 6664. The first step in determining whether the taxpayer deserves penalty abatement under § 6664 requires the taxpayer to prove reasonable cause for the underpayment of tax with respect to the underpayment and that the taxpayer acted in good faith in taking the position or undertaking the transaction. See § 6664(c)(1) and Treas. Reg. § 1.6664–4(a). The analysis evaluates the "extent of the taxpayer's effort to assess the taxpayer's proper tax liability," (Treas. Reg. § 1.6664–4(b)(1)), an inquiry that includes determining whether the taxpayer withheld relevant information from her tax advisor or provided false or misleading information, as well as whether she knew or should have known that her advisor "lacked knowledge in the relevant aspects of Federal tax law." Treas. Reg. § 1.6664–4(c)(1). In assessing whether the taxpayer's reliance on the advice of a tax professional was reasonable, the analysis accounts for the taxpayer's "education, sophistication, and business experience" (Treas. Reg. § 1.6664–4(c)(1)), with more sophisticated taxpayers being held to a higher standard in assessing their proper tax liability than less sophisticated taxpayers.[56]

---

[56]   See e.g., Crispin v. Commissioner, 708 F.3d 507, 518–20 (3d Cir.2013), cert. denied, 134 S.Ct. 784 (2013) (stating that taxpayer's " 'experience, knowledge, and education' as a

If the taxpayer meets these minimum thresholds of due care—that is, not actively concealing information, providing false information, or knowingly engaging an incompetent tax advisor—the reasonable cause/good faith inquiry shifts focus from the taxpayer to the taxpayer's tax advisor (if any) on which the taxpayer relied. See Treas. Reg. §§ 1.6664–4(c) and 1.6664–(d)(4)(B)(ii). Indeed, as courts have long recognized, "the concept of reliance on the advice of professionals is a hallmark of the exception for reasonable cause and good faith."[57] The tax practitioner's advice—which "does not have to be in any particular form" and can be oral or written (Treas. Reg. § 1.6664–4(c)(2))—must itself be reasonable, with the reasonableness inquiry turning on whether the practitioner met her professional standard of care in rendering the advice (see Treas. Reg. § 1.6664–4(b)(1)). In fact, section 6664 explicitly cross-references "rules applicable to advisors," and flags a handful of standards for special scrutiny, including Circular 230 (discussed in Section 3.E. of this Chapter) §§ 10.22 (pertaining to diligence as to accuracy) and 10.34 (pertaining to advising return positions and preparing or signing returns) as well as Treasury Regulations §§ 1.6694–1 through 1.6694–3 (pertaining to penalties for tax return preparers). See Treas. Reg. § 1.6664–4(c)(3). Section 6664 further reflects these standards in its own affirmative requirements, stating that advice must be based on "all pertinent facts and circumstances and the law as it relates to those facts and circumstances" (Treas. Reg. § 1.6664–4(c)(1)(i)), thereby invoking an advisor's due diligence obligations, and, furthermore, that the advice may not be based on "unreasonable factual or legal assumptions" or "unreasonably rely on the representations, statements, findings, or agreements of the taxpayer or any other person" (Treas. Reg. § 1.6664–4(c)(1)(ii)), which invokes duties of due diligence, communication, and avoiding conflicts of interest).

---

former CPA and chief financial officer also strongly suggest enough familiarity with tax matters that he should be expected to have understood the warnings" in his law firm's legal opinion); Fidelity Int'l Currency Advisor A Fund LLC v. United States, 747 F.Supp. 2d. 49, 213 (D.Mass. 2010) (finding taxpayers "highly sophisticated . . . with considerable business experience" and that they "knew or reasonably should have known that the legal advice they received . . . was not independent, and that the firms had an inherent conflict of interest"); Longino v. Commissioner, T.C. Memo 2013–80 *69 (2013) (finding taxpayer "is a licensed attorney who has been practicing law for decades, yet he failed to comply with established law governing the deduction and substantiation of business and other expenses"); Cheramie v. Commissioner, T.C. Summary Opinion 2013–92 *19 (2013) (granting reasonable cause/good faith defense to penalties and finding "[i]t is clear from the record that petitioner is very inexperienced in legal, financial, accounting, and tax matters"); Garcia v. Commissioner, T.C. Summary Opinion 2013–28 *19 (2013) (holding that taxpayer, "whose command of the English language is limited, made a good-faith effort to properly determine his 2008 Federal income tax liability and that the underpayment results from reliance on the advice of a return preparer, combined with an honest misunderstanding of fact or law that is reasonable in the light of his experience and knowledge").

[57]   Stobie Creek Invs., LLC v. United States, 82 Fed. Cl. 636, 717 (2008). See also United States v. Boyle, 469 U.S. 241, 251 (1985) ("When an accountant or attorney advises a taxpayer on a matter of tax law, such as whether a liability exists, it is reasonable for the taxpayer to rely on that advice.").

In the case of taxpayers filing "frivolous" returns, § 6702 authorizes an additional penalty of $5,000.[58] Meanwhile, for simple failure to file or failure to remit payment of taxes due with a filed tax return, § 6651 imposes a penalty of 5 percent of the amount of tax due for each month that the tax was not paid up to a maximum of 25 percent, unless the taxpayer can show that the failure to pay was due to "reasonable cause and not due to willful neglect."

The IRS always bears the burden of proof with respect to penalties and additions to tax. Section 7491(c), however, requires only that the IRS come forward with evidence that a particular penalty is appropriate. It does not require the IRS to prove that the taxpayer did not have "reasonable cause" or "substantial authority" for his position. The taxpayer must raise exculpatory circumstances that might negate application of penalty provisions. See Treas. Reg. § 1.6664–4(a).

Tax return preparers are subject to a variety of penalties for culpably preparing inaccurate returns. Section 6694(a) imposes a penalty in the amount of the greater of $1,000 or 50 percent of the income derived by the return preparer if a return or refund claim results in an understatement of liability with respect to an undisclosed position unless "there is or was substantial authority for the position." In the case of a properly disclosed position, the penalty applies if the position fails a "reasonable basis" standard. However, for positions with respect to tax shelters and reportable transactions as defined in § 6662A (pertaining to certain tax shelters designated by the IRS), the preparer penalty applies "unless it is reasonable to believe that the position would more likely than not be sustained on its merits." Section 6694(b) imposes a penalty in the amount of the greater of $5,000 or 50 percent of the income to be derived from preparing the return if the preparer willfully attempted to understate tax liability or recklessly or intentionally disregarded the rules or regulations. Although on its face § 6694 appears to apply narrowly, the definition of "tax return preparer" in § 7701(a)(36) and Treas. Reg. § 301.7701–15 expands its scope to include advisors who do not actually prepare tax returns. Thus attorneys advising taxpayers regarding reporting positions and transactions may be subject to the penalty. Section 6695 imposes a variety of other penalties on tax return preparers for more minor administrative transgressions. Section 6701 imposes a $1,000 penalty on any person who aids in the preparation of any document knowing or having reason to believe that it will be used in connection with a material matter arising under the tax laws and will result in an understatement of another person's tax liability.

In addition to civil penalties, criminal sanctions apply in certain circumstances. The principal criminal penalty is the felony penalty for willfully attempting in any manner to evade or defeat the tax, most commonly by fraudulent failure to file or by filing fraudulent returns.

---

[58]   The IRS routinely publishes a list of frivolous return positions. See e.g., Notice 2010–33; 2010–17 I.R.B. 609.

I.R.C. § 7201. Lawyers and other tax advisors need to be mindful that the criminal fraud provisions apply to anyone involved in the fraudulent scheme, including those who aid the taxpayer.[59] In addition, § 7206(2) provides criminal sanctions for anyone who willfully "aids or assists in or procures, counsels, or advises the preparation or presentation of a return, affidavit, claim, or other document, which is fraudulent or is false as to any material matter, whether or not such falsity or fraud is with the knowledge or consent of the person authorized or required to present such return, affidavit, claim, or document." Among the other criminal penalties, the most commonly encountered are the misdemeanor penalties for willful failure to file a return, pay a tax, keep required records, or supply required information.

Section 6673 provides that the Tax Court can assess up to a $25,000 penalty against a taxpayer if it is established that Tax Court proceedings were instituted or maintained primarily for delay, that the taxpayer's position in the proceedings was frivolous or groundless, or that the taxpayer unreasonably failed to pursue administrative remedies. Conversely, § 7430 provides that a taxpayer who prevails in a civil tax litigation may be awarded reasonable administrative and litigation costs, including attorneys' fees (at a maximum of $125 an hour, adjusted for inflation; in 2016, the award limitation was $200), if the taxpayer substantially prevails and the government does not establish that its position in the case was "substantially justified." Only costs incurred after the earlier of the receipt of notice of the decision of the IRS Appeals Office or a deficiency notice are taken into account. Attorneys' fee awards are not available to individuals whose net worth exceeds $2,000,000 or to other taxpayers, primarily corporations, whose net worth exceeds $7,000,000 or have more than 500 employees. As for counsel for both the taxpayer and the government, § 6673(a)(2) authorizes the Tax Court to require taxpayer counsel personally or the United States to pay any excess costs and attorneys' fees incurred by the other party if the attorney in question has "multiplied the proceedings in any case unreasonably and vexatiously." Finally, in the district courts and courts of appeals, attorneys are subject to the generally applicable sanctions (such as Federal Rule of Civil Procedure 11 sanctions) for improper behavior in prosecuting a case.

(7) CONCLUSION

There are more than 150 million individual income tax returns filed annually. See IRS, Statistics of Income, 2015 Filing Season Statistics (2016). These returns include self-assessments of tax owed made by taxpayers and their tax advisers. Proper administration of an income tax cannot rely solely on self-assessment, however. Instead, it must build

---

[59]   See United States v. Jerkins, 871 F.2d 598 (6th Cir.1989) (attorney convicted for conspiracy to commit tax fraud based on client's tax return); Tinkoff v. United States, 86 F.2d 868, 876 (7th Cir.1936) (accountant who prepared fraudulent returns for client).

upon the solid base provided by the self-assessment system. Underpayment of tax by one group of taxpayers can result in overpayment by other groups, at least to the extent the government addresses revenue shortfalls associated with noncompliance by raising taxes. The high level of taxpayer morale necessary to maintain the integrity of a self-assessment system can be accomplished only if taxpayers believe that government regulation and enforcement are working to ensure that all taxpayers pay their fair share.

In 2016, the IRS estimated the "voluntary compliance rate," defined as taxes paid voluntarily on time and in full, at 81.7 percent. IRS, Tax Gap Estimates for Tax Years 2008–2010 (2016). Meanwhile, the "net compliance rate," which includes IRS enforcement activities and receipt of late payments, was slightly higher at 83.7 percent. In either case, compliance rates for certain types and sources of income were considerably higher than for others. For income subject to withholding (such as wages and salaries) and substantial information reporting by third parties (such as interest and dividends), the compliance rate is a nearly perfect 99 percent. The compliance rate for income subject to substantial information reporting but not withholding is nearly as impressive at 93 percent. However, for income subject to little or no information reporting, such as nonfarm proprietor income (much of which is cash), the compliance rate plummets to 37 percent; in other words, nearly two-thirds of this income goes underreported or unreported every year.

Whatever the degree of withholding and information reporting implemented, adequate investigation of tax returns remains a necessary part of tax administration. Achieving "adequate" regulation and enforcement involves deploying carrots as well as sticks. The government cannot afford to investigate all taxpayers, either from the standpoint of budgetary cost and resources or projecting an image of top-down, coercive regulation. Indeed, investigating and enforcing tax compliance must be pursued in an efficient and selective manner in order to maintain high levels of compliance with the nation's tax laws.

The inevitable result of IRS audit activities involves a vast number of controversies arising between taxpayers and the agency administering our tax laws. Practically speaking, the overwhelming majority of these controversies must be settled at the administrative level to avoid the courts being inundated with tax controversies. The settlement procedure, which includes taxpayers and their representatives as well as IRS officials, must operate with this goal in mind. Moreover, the administrative mechanisms under which these procedures function must facilitate prompt resolution of disputes between taxpayers and the IRS, with courts only hearing and deciding controversies that cannot be resolved at the administrative level.

E. THE TAX ADVISER

Tax professionals—including most prominently attorneys, certified public accountants, and enrolled agents[60]—advise the majority of individual taxpayers in preparing and filing their annual federal income tax returns. See IRS, Statistics of Income, 2015 Filing Season Statistics (2016). In addition, nearly all non-individual taxpayers (primarily corporations, partnerships, and trusts) rely on tax advisers to plan and evaluate business transactions, and to determine the proper treatment of those transactions with respect to the federal income tax. In rendering tax advice and preparing tax returns, tax advisers must meet high ethical standards as reflected in the ethical rules promulgated by their professional organizations (such as the Rules of Professional Conduct governing lawyers promulgated by state bar associations and the American Bar Association). But as federal tax practitioners, they must also comport their conduct to the practice standards promulgated by the Treasury Department. These "Rules Governing Practice before the IRS" are commonly referred to as "Circular 230," and they provide detailed and disciplinary standards of conduct, violation of which can result in suspension or disbarment of one's ability to practice before the IRS in addition to significant monetary sanctions. The practice rules contained in Circular 230 also reinforce the standards of professional care required of tax advisers as reflected in the penalty provisions of the Internal Revenue Code and its underlying regulations.

The excerpted material below describes the affirmative and overlapping ethical obligations of tax advisers, with an emphasis on Circular 230 and the federal regulation of tax practice.

Ventry & Borden, Probability, Professionalism, and Protecting Taxpayers
68 Tax Law. 83, 96–105 (2014).

II. Regulating a Profession: Circular 230 as the (Gold) Standard of Care

Tax professionals are subject to more than one standard of care. For tax advisors who are also lawyers, the applicable standards include the ABA Model Rules of Professional Conduct (which every state except California has adopted in whole or in part),[62] ABA Formal Ethics

---

[60]   This grouping of tax professionals possesses unlimited practice rights with respect to representing taxpayers in federal tax matters before the Internal Revenue Service. Enrolled agent status is the highest credential awarded by the IRS. All enrolled agents must meet rigorous continuing education requirements, including 72 hours of coursework every three years.

[62]   Members of the California State Bar are regulated by the Rules of Professional Conduct, a compilation of ethical guidelines that for most of its existence resided in the state's Business and Professions Code. See Cal. Bus. & Prof. Code §§ 6000–6243 (West. 2014). * * *

Opinions interpreting the Model Rules as applied to tax lawyers,[63] and Circular 230, the Treasury regulations governing federal tax practice.[64] Tax professionals who are also certified public accountants are similarly subject to the strictures of Circular 230 in addition to the practice standards promulgated by the American Institute of Certified Public Accountants.[65] Finally, both tax lawyers and accountants must abide by the standards of care pertaining to tax return positions contained in the penalty provisions of the Code and the regulations promulgated thereunder, including most prominently sections 6662, 6664, and 6694.[66]

While each of the above standards possesses independent moral and legal authority, Circular 230 has emerged as *the* prevailing standard for tax professionals. No other standard provides such detailed rules of behavior for tax "practitioners" nationwide, not only for lawyers and accountants, but also for enrolled agents, enrolled actuaries, enrolled retirement plan agents, and registered tax return preparers.[67] No other

---

[63]   There are three such opinions: ABA Comm. on Ethics & Prof'l Responsibility, Formal Op. 85–352 (1985); ABA Comm. on Ethics & Prof'l Responsibility, Formal Op. 346 (rev.) (1982); ABA Comm. on Ethics & Prof'l Responsibility, Formal Op. 314 (1965).

[64]   See 31 C.F.R. § 10 (2014). Tax law is not the only practice area subject to federal regulation. Securities lawyers face particularized practice standards under the disciplinary rules governing the professional conduct of attorneys "appearing and practicing" before the Securities and Exchange Commission (SEC). See SEC, Standards of Professional Conduct for Attorneys Appearing and Practicing Before the Commission in the Representation of an Issuer, 17 C.F.R. § 205 (2012); SEC, Rules of Practice, 17 C.F.R. § 201.102(e) (2003).

[65]   For ethical standards governing CPAs, see American Institute of Certified Public Accountants, Code of Professional Conduct (2014); American Institute of Certified Public Accountants, Statements on Standards for Tax Services (2010).

[66]   While section 6694 applies most directly to practitioners by imposing penalties on return preparers for understatements of a taxpayer-client's tax liability, both section 6662 (pertaining to accuracy-related penalties imposed on taxpayers) and section 6664(c) (pertaining to the reasonable cause and good faith defense against penalties for taxpayers) implicate and inform practitioners' standard of care. See I.R.C. § 6694(a)(1); see also Reg. §§ 1.6694–1, 1.6694–2, 1.6694–3). For example, practitioners can avoid imposition of penalties by showing that a position on which they advised had "substantial authority," a level of certainty defined in Regulation section 1.6662–4(d) and explicitly cross-referenced in Regulation section 1.6694–1(a)(1), 1.6694(a)(1)(ii) and 1.6694–2(b)(1)–(3). In the same manner, Regulation section 1.6694–2(d)(2) adopts the definition of "reasonable basis" under Regulation section 1.6662–3(b)(3), while Regulation section 1.6694–2(d)(3) adopts the definition of "adequate disclosure" under Regulation section 1.6662–4(f). For its part, taxpayers can establish the section 6664 defense to penalties by showing reasonable reliance on professional tax advice, with the reasonableness inquiry turning on whether the taxpayer's advisor met her standard of care in rendering the advice. See Regulation section 1.6664–4(c). Throughout this Article, we discuss the overlap of the tax advisor's standard of care with that of the taxpayer's, with special focus on the "substantial authority" standard (see Part III.A.1) and the section 6664 defense to penalties (see Part III.E).

[67]   See 31 C.F.R. § 10.3(a)–(f) (2014). A recent U.S. Court of Appeals decision challenged the authority of the Treasury to regulate "tax return preparers" under Circular 230. See Loving v. IRS, 742 F.3d 1013 (D.C. Cir. 2014) (invalidating CLE and certification requirements—which the Service had imposed in an effort to tackle widespread fraud, on hundreds of thousands of unregulated tax return preparers—on grounds that the authorizing statute provides insufficient authority). The decision, at least as currently interpreted, has no bearing on the brand of tax practice and tax advising discussed in this Article. See also Lawrence B. Gibbs, "Loving v. IRS: Treasury's Authority to Regulate Tax Return Preparers," 141 Tax Notes 331, 337 (2013) (arguing that amendments in 2011 to Circular 230 covering tax return preparation by commercial preparers "are authoritative and should be upheld"); Brief for Former Commissioners of Internal Revenue as Amici Curiae Supporting Appellants, Loving v. IRS, 742 F.3d 1013 (D.C. Cir. 2014) (No. 13–061), 2013 WL 1386248, at *16–17 ("In 1884, Congress

standard, moreover, garners as much respect from tax professionals[68] or imposes such strictly enforced disciplinary rules rather than loosely enforced aspirational guidelines.[69] Furthermore, no other standard of conduct has influenced the development of the other standards as thoroughly as Circular 230,[70] or embedded its principles of accuracy and minimizing errors,[71] or been adopted as the standard of care in different jurisdictions and in both state and federal courts.[72]

For more than 125 years, the Treasury has enjoyed broad authority to regulate federal tax professionals. In 1884, Congress authorized the Secretary of the Treasury to promulgate rules and regulations "governing the recognition of agents ... representing claimants before his Department."[73] Under this statutory authority,[74] the Treasury issued relatively few rules of practice until 1921[75] when it first published Circular 230.[76] Subsequently, federal courts examining the Treasury's ability to regulate federal tax practice found that Treasury's "disciplinary

---

empowered the Treasury to regulate the conduct of claims agents pursuing financial benefits from the government; and in 2013 Treasury retains that authority to regulate the conduct of tax return preparers who similarly assist preparing and filing tax returns that present to the Treasury millions of claims worth billions of dollars each year."). But see Steve R. Johnson, "Loving and Legitimacy: IRS Regulation of Tax Return Preparation," 60 Vill. L. Rev. 515 (2014) (arguing that the statute authorizing Circular 230 does not confer authority to regulate tax return preparation).

[68]   As legal scholar Michael Lang writes, "When tax practitioners think of who addresses substandard behavior to their colleagues they think of the IRS Office of Professional Responsibility [which enforces Circular 230 rules] and they are right to do so." Michael B. Lang, "Thinking About Tax Malpractice," 32 ABA Section of Taxation News Quarterly 1 (Fall 2012). In addition, it is safe to say that tax lawyers are more likely to follow changes in the law pertaining to due diligence standards under Circular 230 (or the Code, for that matter) than under the ABA Model Rules. Moreover, they surely are more likely to know that section 10.22 of Circular 230 contains the Treasury's general due diligence requirements than that Model Rule 1.3 contains the ABA's (or their state bar's) diligence obligations.

[69]   See [notes 18–25 and accompanying text of original Ventry & Borden article] as well as infra notes 86–111 and accompanying text].

[70]   See [Part IV of original Ventry & Borden article].

[71]   See [Parts III and IV of original Ventry & Borden article].

[72]   See infra notes 74, 77–78 and accompanying text. See also Lang, supra note 68, at 28 (writing that "breaches of Circular 230 rules that either parallel state bar ethics rules or are designed to protect clients are likely to be treated like breaches of such state bar ethics rules," stating by way of example that breaches of sections 10.21 and 10.22 "are likely to be allowed to be offered in court as evidence of the breach of a duty to the client").

[73]   Act of July 7, 1884, § 3, 23 Stat. 258 (codified as 31 U.S.C. § 330, Practice before the Department).

[74]   See e.g., Falsone v. United States, 205 F.2d 734, 741 (5th Cir. 1953) (acknowledging Treasury's historical authority to promulgate rules and regulations "governing recognition of attorneys and agents representing persons before the Treasury Department"); Agran v. Shapiro, 127 Cal. App. 2d Supp. 807, 820–21 (Super. Ct. 1954) (recognizing the longstanding authority of the Treasury to promulgate and enforce regulations pertaining to the practice of persons appearing before it).

[75]   See Bryan T. Camp, " 'Loving' Return Preparer Regulation," 140 Tax Notes 457, 458 (2013) (quoting a 1927 article authored by the Chairman of the Treasury's Committee on Enrollment and Disbarment stating that, until 1921, "the rules governing practice were few, and applicants were enrolled without special investigation as to their character and qualifications"). Prior to 1921, the Treasury published at least three regulations governing federal tax practice: Circular 13 (Feb. 6, 1886) (pertaining to internal taxes), Circular 94, (Oct. 4, 1890) (same), and T.D. 32974 (Nov. 30, 1912) (pertaining to customs duties).

[76]   T.D. 38773, Circular No. 230 (Feb. 15, 1921).

authority clearly extends to all practitioners before the Treasury Department,"[77] and covers "in a general way, the activities of practitioners."[78] Moreover, Congress has repeatedly reauthorized this broad grant of authority,[79] which courts have found permits the Treasury "to judge the character, reputation, and competence of those who practice[ ] before it."[80]

Today, Circular 230 provides the prevailing standard of care for tax practitioners representing taxpayers "before the IRS."[81] It specifies sanctions for violating its rules.[82] And it prescribes disciplinary proceedings for adjudicating those violations.[83] The Treasury broadly defines "practice before the IRS" as "all matters connected with a presentation to the Internal Revenue Service or any of its officers or employees relating to a taxpayer's rights, privileges, or liabilities under laws or regulations administered by the Internal Revenue Service."[84] Moreover, "presentations" include "preparing and filing documents, corresponding and communicating with the Internal Revenue Service, rendering written advice with respect to any entity, transaction, plan or arrangement, or other plan or arrangement having a potential for tax avoidance or evasion, and representing a client at conferences, hearings and meetings."[85]

---

[77]   Poole v. United States, 84–2 U.S.T.C. ¶ 9612, 54 A.F.T.R.2d 5536 (D.D.C. 1984).

[78]   Id. at 9612, 54 A.F.T.R.2d. at 5537. For federal courts recognizing Circular 230 as the governing standard of care for federal tax practitioners, see Banister v. U.S. Dep't of the Treasury, 499 Fed. App'x 668 (9th Cir. 2012); Diaz v. Century Pac. Inv. Corp., 21 F.3d 1112 (9th Cir. 1994); Owrutsky v. Brady, 925 F.2d 1457 (4th Cir. 1991); Silverton v. U.S. Dept. of the Treasury, 644 F.2d 1341 (9th Cir. 1981); Pope v. United States, 599 F.2d 1383 (5th Cir. 1979); Harary v. Blumenthal, 555 F.2d 1113 (2d Cir. 1977); Falsone v. United States, 205 F.2d 734 (5th Cir. 1953); Ryan, LLC v. Lew, 934 F. Supp. 2d 159 (D.D.C. 2013) ("Simply stated, Circular 230 delineates who may practice before the Service, the standards and restrictions such persons must follow, and the sanctions imposed for violations of such standards and restrictions."); United States v. Tomlinson, 2013–2 U.S.T.C. ¶ 50,414, 111 A.F.T.R.2d 2431 (D.Kan. 2013); Loving v. IRS, 917 F. Supp. 2d 67, 71 (D.D.C. 2013); Legel v. U.S. Dept. of the Treasury, 2011 U.S. Dist. LEXIS 136257 (S.D. Fl. 2011); Banister v. U.S. Dep't of the Treasury, 2012–2 U.S.T.C. ¶ 50,680, 110 A.F.T.R.2d 6794 (N.D. Cal. 2011); Daniels v. United States, 2006–1 U.S.T.C. ¶ 50,310, 97 A.F.T.R.2d 2280 (N.D. Ga. 2006); Jordan v. United States, 2005 U.S. Dist. LEXIS 32076 (D.Conn. 2005); Sicignano v. United States, 127 F. Supp. 2d 325 (D.Conn. 2001); Inst. of Certified Practitioners v. Bentsen, 874 F.Supp. 1370 (N.D. Ga. 1994); Poole v. United States, 84–2 U.S.T.C. ¶ 9612, 54 A.F.T.R.2d 5536 (D.D.C. 1984). For state courts recognizing Circular 230 as the standard of care for tax practitioners, see N.Y. State Ass'n of Enrolled Agents, Inc. v. N.Y. State Dept. of Taxation and Fin., 29 Misc. 3d 332, 333–38 (N.Y. Sup. Ct. 2010); Estate of Heinz, 2006 N.Y. Misc. LEXIS 4230 *2 (Surrogate's Ct. of N.Y., New York Cnty. 2006); Carberry v. State Bd. of Accountancy, 28 Cal. App. 4th 770, 790 (Cal. Ct. App. 1994); N.Y. State Soc. of Enrolled Agents v. N.Y. State Div. of Tax Appeals, 161 A.D. 2d 1, 7 (N.Y. App. Div. 1990); Agran v. Shapiro, 127 Cal. App. 2d Supp. 807, 820–21 (Super. Ct. 1954).

[79]   See e.g., H.R. Rept. No. 82–2518, at 13 (1953); H.R. Rept. No. 89–1141, at 3 (1965) ("In imposing admission requirements on prospective practitioners, the Internal Revenue Service is acting under authority of the Act of July 7, 1884.").

[80]   *Poole*, 84–2 U.S.T.C. at 9612, 54 A.F.T.R.2d at 5537.

[81]   See 31 C.F.R. §§ 10.20–10.38 (2014).

[82]   See id. §§ 10.50–10.53 (2014).

[83]   See id. §§ 10.60–10.82 (2014).

[84]   Id. at § 10.2(a)(4) (2014).

[85]   Id.

Substantively, Circular 230 articulates affirmative obligations for practitioners, and proscribes behavior that violates those obligations[86] (or that otherwise demonstrates "incompetence and disreputable conduct"[87]) with the force of sanctions that include censure, monetary penalties, suspension, and disbarment.[88] The Treasury's Office of Professional Responsibility (OPR) handles "matters related to practitioner conduct and discipline"[89] with the OPR Director initiating disciplinary proceedings under section 10.60. The Director also has the authority to undertake "expedited proceedings" against practitioners under section 10.82 by suspending them from practice based on final prior adjudications in other judicial or administrative proceedings.[90]

Since 1998,[91] the Treasury has periodically published in the Internal Revenue Bulletin a list of disciplinary actions taken against practitioners.[92] The description of the action taken typically includes the disciplined practitioner's name, address, professional designation, a brief description of the disciplinary sanction, and effective dates of sanction.[93] As of February 24, 2014, the Treasury had published seventy-two such announcements describing disciplinary actions against more than 2,500 practitioners.[94] While the vast majority of disciplinary dispositions involve "expedited proceedings" under section 10.82,[95] the published descriptions of practitioner misconduct include a wide range of violations under Circular 230, including section 10.20 (information to be furnished to the Service),[96] section 10.22 (diligence as to accuracy),[97] section 10.29

---

[86]   See id. at § 10.52 (2014).

[87]   Id. at § 10.51 (2014).

[88]   See id. at § 10.50 (2014).

[89]   Id. at § 10.1(a)(1) (2014).

[90]   See id. at § 10.82(b) (2014). While the majority of these prior proceedings involves suspension or revocation of a professional license, they also include convictions of tax crimes, court sanctions relating to a taxpayer's liability or the practitioner's personal tax liability, and crimes "involving dishonesty or breach of trust, or any felony for which the conduct involved renders the practitioner unfit to practice before the Internal Revenue Service." Id.

[91]   See 1998–06 I.R.B. 1 (Feb. 2, 1998).

[92]   See 31 C.F.R. § 10.80 (2014).

[93]   Sanctions are published when (i) an Administrative Law Judge or the Secretary's delegate on appeal issues a final agency decision (discussed infra at notes 103–104 and accompanying text), (ii) OPR resolves a disciplinary matter with a signed "consent to sanction" by which the practitioner admits to violating one or more Circular 230 provisions, or (iii) OPR issues a decision in an expedited proceeding for suspension. See Circular 230 Disciplinary Proceedings, IRS, Aug. 20, 2014, at http://www.irs.gov/Tax-Professionals/Enrolled-Agents/Circular-230-Disciplinary-Proceedings.

[94]   For IRBs containing OPR "Announcements of Disciplinary Actions," see https://www.irs.gov/tax-professionals/enrolled-actuaries/disciplinary-sanctions-internal-revenue-bulletin.

[95]   See supra note 90 and accompanying text.

[96]   See e.g., Announcement 2012–08, 2012–07 I.R.B. 373–375); Announcement 2008–52, 2008–22 I.R.B. 1040–41.

[97]   See e.g., Announcement 2011–44, 2011–33 I.R.B. 166–67; Announcement 2011–41, 2011–28 I.R.B. 50–51; Announcement 2011–24, 2011–12 I.R.B. 571; Announcement 2010–53, 2010–36 I.R.B. 324; Announcement 2010–51, 2010–33 I.R.B. 264; Announcement 2009–75, 2009–42 I.R.B. 538; Announcement 2009–68, 2009–38 I.R.B. 390; Announcement 2009–65, 2009–36 I.R.B. 320; Announcement 2009–46, 2009–21 I.R.B. 1043; Announcement 2008–77, 2008–33 I.R.B. 396; Announcement 2008–52, 2008–22 I.R.B. 1041, 1046, 1050.

(conflicting interests),[98] section 10.30 (solicitation),[99] section 10.33 (tax shelter opinions, effective from 1984 and 2004, recodified as "Best practices" in 2004),[100] section 10.34 (standards for advising with respect to tax return positions and for preparing or signing returns),[101] and section 10.51 (disreputable conduct).[102]

In 2007, the OPR also began publishing Final Agency Decisions on disciplinary proceedings, which include un-appealed ALJ decisions, decisions of the designated Appellate Authority, and decisions of federal district courts and circuit courts.[103] As of February 24, 2014, the Treasury had published decisions in one hundred six proceedings involving seventy practitioners. These published decisions contain the usual trappings of judicial opinions, including statements of fact, fact to law analysis, discussion, and conclusion. Compared to the short, periodic summaries of disciplinary sanctions discussed above, these decisions allow for broader observations on the Treasury's disciplinary authority, on the public purposes of Circular 230, and, ultimately, on federal tax practitioners' professional responsibilities.[104]

The agency decisions recognize that federal agencies have long had the authority and power "to regulate those who practice before them," a power that the Treasury wields through Circular 230.[105] They further

---

[98]   See e.g., Announcement 2012–33, 2012–35 I.R.B. 327.

[99]   See e.g., Announcement 2008–52, 2008–22 I.R.B. 1046.

[100]   See e.g., Announcement 2010–43, 2010–27 I.R.B. 44.

[101]   See e.g., Announcement 2010–53, 2010–36 I.R.B. 324; Announcement 2008–52, 2008–22 I.R.B. 1050.

[102]   See e.g., Announcement 2010–53, 2010–36 I.R.B. 324; Announcement 2010–51, 2010–33 I.R.B. 263–64; Announcement 2010–43, 2010–27 I.R.B. 44; Announcement 2009–75, 2009–42 I.R.B. 538, 540–41; Announcement 2009–68, 2009–38 I.R.B. 390; Announcement 2008–52, 2008–22 I.R.B. 1041, 1046, 1050.

[103]   For final agency decisions, see Final Agency Decisions, available at https://www.irs.gov/tax-professionals/enrolled-actuaries/final-agency-decisions.

[104]   For additional analysis of these decisions and what they say about OPR's "thought process as it enforces Circular 230 professional standards," see Jeremiah Coder, "Circular 230 and Due Process," 135 Tax Notes 538 (2012); Jeremiah Coder, "OPR's Role in Guiding Practitioner Sanctions," 134 Tax Notes 1347 (2012); Jeremiah Coder, "Strong Headwinds for Those Facing Circular 230 Discipline," 131 Tax Notes 539 (2011).

[105]   Director, Office of Prof'l Responsibility v. Baldwin, No. 2010–08, slip-op at 5 (2010); see also Director, Office of Prof'l Responsibility v. Dwayne H. Coston, No. 2010–19, slip-op at 7 (2011); Director, Office of Prof'l Responsibility v. C. Wesley Craft, No. 2010–12, slip-op at 9 (2011); Director, Office of Prof'l Responsibility v. Donald A. Navatsyk, No. 2010–03, slip-op at 7 (2010); Director, Office of Prof'l Responsibility v. James E. Barr, No. 2009–09, slip-op at 5 (2010). Like the decisions from federal courts, see supra note 78 and accompanying text, the agency decisions adopt a broad interpretation of what it means to practice "before the Internal Revenue Service." See e.g., Director, Office of Prof'l Responsibility v. Philip G. Panitz, No. 2006–25, slip-op at 2 (2009) (finding jurisdiction over a practitioner, because he had practiced as a tax attorney for twenty years (including the years at issue), and thus "engaged in practice before the Service within the purview" of Circular 230 and "bound" by its rules and regulations); Director, Office of Prof'l Responsibility v. Leonard Fein, No. 2006–33, slip-op at 3–4 (2008) (subjecting a practitioner to the strictures of Circular 230, based on the fact that he was a CPA and that he had represented taxpayers before the Service earlier in his career); Director, Office of Prof'l Responsibility v. Joseph R. Banister, No. 2003–02, slip-op at 26–27 (2004) (finding that "with regard to oral and written representations made to either the Treasury or to a client in connection with any matter administered by the Internal Revenue Service, each attorney,

recognize that practicing before the Service "is a privilege," and "one cannot partake of that privilege without also taking on the responsibilities of complying with the regulations that govern such practice."[106] These duties include obligations to taxpayer-clients, to the general public, and to the tax system. Circular 230 provides "rules and regulations relating to a practitioner's activities as a taxpayer representative, as an adviser to taxpayers and relating to the practitioner's conduct of his or her own tax and other affairs."[107] As such, Treasury's practice rules "are designed to protect the Department and the public from persons unfit to practice before the IRS."[108] In meeting this "fitness to practice" standard, practitioners must conduct themselves as persons with " 'special skills' with regard to taxation" who "occup[y] a place of public trust"[109] and on whom "the IRS relies heavily . . . to perform their tasks diligently and responsibly."[110] "Breaches of professional responsibility by authorized practitioners," these decisions observe," jeopardize the achievement of the objectives of our tax laws and can inflict great damage on the public perception of fairness."[111]

The affirmative duties delineated in Circular 230 assist tax practitioners in fulfilling their professional responsibility to render accurate advice, which, in turn, informs accurate returns and facilitates compliance with the law. The standard of care contained in Circular 230 explicitly aims to reduce human error caused by carelessness, incompetence, lack of inquiry or communication, conflicting interests (including personal interests), lack of independent professional judgment, and otherwise flawed or biased practices or misaligned incentives. Consider a few examples of the most salient duties under Circular 230:

- The standards pertaining to *due diligence* require advisors to, among other things, investigate facts, to remain informed and abreast of the law, to evaluate all federal tax issues associated with a taxpayer-client's position or transaction, to track courts' use of anti-abuse regulations and doctrines as well as how the deployment of such doctrines varies across jurisdictions and venues, to know the government's litigating position and strategy with

---

certified public accountant, enrolled agent and enrolled actuary is required to exercise due diligence in determining the correctness of such statements").

[106] *Baldwin*, No. 2010–08 at 6; *Coston*, No. 2010–19 at 9; *Craft*, No. 2010–12 at 13; *Navatsyk*, No. 2010–03 at 9; *Barr*, No. 2009–09 at 7.

[107] *Banister*, No. 2003–02 at 14–15.

[108] *Baldwin*, No. 2003–02 at 5. For more on the "fitness to practice" standard, see Director, Office of Prof'l Responsibility v. Edgar H. Gee, Jr., No. 2009–31, slip-op at 38 (2011); *Coston*, No. 2010–19 at 9; *Craft*, No. 2010–12 at 13; Director, Office of Prof'l Responsibility v. Donald J. Petrillo, No. 2009–21, slip-p at 10 (2010); *Navatsyk*, No. 2010–03 at 9; *Barr*, No. 2009–09 at 6.

[109] *Gee*, No. 2009–31 at 39.

[110] Id.

[111] Id.

respect to material tax issues and tax avoidance transactions, and, at the end of the day, to articulate a conclusion as to the likelihood of success on the merits not just for each material tax issue comprising a transaction but also for the overall transaction.

- The standards for *communicating* with taxpayer-clients assist practitioners in reducing errors by helping them understand a client's purposes, goals, and motives in planning a transaction, taking a filing position, investing in litigation, or considering controverted issues. In so doing, the standards help practitioners become familiar with their clients' affairs, assist in meeting not just the above-noted due diligence standard but also in satisfying the informed consent requirement under the conflicting interests rules (see immediately below), and in reducing the likelihood of biased probability assessments associated with failing to learn or understand a client's risk profile or underlying motives in seeking tax reduction. The communication requirement also keeps taxpayer-clients informed of their options by, among other things, advising them of penalties that might apply to certain reporting positions and ways to avoid penalties through disclosure.

- For yet another example of Circular 230 helping practitioners and their clients reduce errors, consider the standard for avoiding *conflicts of interest*. This omnipresent standard forces practitioners to evaluate (and then reevaluate regularly) whether relationships, responsibilities, pecuniary incentives, fee structures, or other potential biases and misaligned incentives might adversely affect representation of a taxpayer-client or compromise the advisor's ability to render independent professional advice. The standard also requires practitioners to communicate any conflicts with taxpayer-clients, to discuss the potential implications of the conflicts, and to receive informed consent confirmed in writing to continue representation.

- Finally, Circular 230 rules further assist practitioners in rendering accurate advice by prohibiting *unconscionable fees* and by severely restricting *contingent fees*. Both kinds of fee arrangements can cloud professional judgment and result in biased, conflicted assessments of a reporting position or transaction's likelihood of success on the merits. Moreover, contingent fees exploit the "audit lottery" by encouraging taxpayer-clients to take overaggressive positions for which their tax advisor earns a fee only if the position avoids detection.

In emphasizing accurate advice and accurate returns, Circular 230's standard of care protects taxpayers, tax advisors, and the tax system. Taxpayer-clients can make more informed decisions about what to put on their returns, which protects them from having a return position challenged by the Service, litigated in court, invalidated on the merits, and subject to interest charges and penalties (with the latter levy often imposed by both federal and state tax authorities). For their part, tax advisors benefit by not subjecting taxpayer-clients to undue risk and liability, which, in addition to upholding the ethical axiom of "do no harm," protects the advisor from avoiding charges of professional misconduct (and in defending against such charges). Moreover, by fortifying its strictures of accurate advice with the palpable threat of disciplinary proceedings and sanctions, Circular 230 further protects tax professionals from losing clients to less ethical advisors. By the same token, accurate advice and accurate returns protect the tax system by raising compliance among taxpayers at all income levels and by bolstering fairness, both real and perceived, under the tax laws.

PART II

GROSS INCOME

CHAPTER 2

GENERAL PRINCIPLES OF GROSS INCOME

SECTION 1. INCOME

INTERNAL REVENUE CODE: Sections 61(a); 63(a).

REGULATIONS: Sections 1.61–1(a); –2(a)(1).

The tax imposed on individuals by § 1 of the Internal Revenue Code, or on corporations by § 11 of the Code, is imposed on "taxable income." Taxable income is derived in the first instance from "gross income" from which is subtracted the costs of producing that income as well as, in the case of individuals, multiple personal items that generally influence an individual's "ability to pay." The starting point for exploring the income tax is gross income.

The definition of gross income in § 61(a) begins with the catchall phrase "all income from whatever source derived" followed by a descriptive list of income items typically received by taxpayers. The sweeping definition of the catchall phrase remains largely unchanged from the original formulation in the Revenue Act of 1913, which referred to "gains or profits and income derived from any source whatever," and is similar to the language of the Sixteenth Amendment to the Constitution, which empowers Congress to collect taxes "on incomes, from whatever source derived." There is in fact little need for a precise statutory definition of "gross income," because the amount determined under § 61 is but the starting point in a long computation derived from the statutory language in other Code provisions. The resulting tax base can only very loosely be termed "net income." Section 61 might as easily define the "gross statutory amount" as including "all income from whatever source derived." However formulated, the starting point of the calculation is "income."

A. INCREASE IN NET WORTH

Commissioner v. Glenshaw Glass Co.

Supreme Court of the United States, 1955.
348 U.S. 426.

■ WARREN, CHIEF JUSTICE. This litigation involves two cases with independent factual backgrounds yet presenting the identical issue. The two cases were consolidated for argument before the Court of Appeals for the Third Circuit and were heard en banc. The common question is whether money received as exemplary damages for fraud or as the

61

*Issue
con't*

punitive two-thirds portion of a treble damage antitrust recovery must be reported by a taxpayer as gross income under § 22(a) of the Internal Revenue Code of 1939 [the predecessor of § 61(a)]. In a single opinion, 211 F.2d 928, the Court of Appeals affirmed the Tax Court's separate rulings in favor of the taxpayers. 18 T.C. 860, 19 T.C. 637. Because of the frequent recurrence of the question and differing interpretations by the lower courts of this Court's decisions bearing upon the problem, we granted the Commissioner of Internal Revenue's ensuing petition for certiorari. 348 U.S. 813.

The facts of the cases were largely stipulated and are not in dispute. So far as pertinent they are as follows:

FACTS — Glenshaw

*- Company rec.
money*
*- Some of the
money was for
punative damages
and antitrust
violations*
*- Company did not
report income*
*- Commissioner wants
them to report.*

Commissioner v. Glenshaw Glass Co.—The Glenshaw Glass Company * * * was engaged in protracted litigation with the Hartford-Empire Company, which manufactures machinery of a character used by Glenshaw. Among the claims advanced by Glenshaw were demands for exemplary damages for fraud and treble damages for injury to its business by reason of Hartford's violation of the federal antitrust laws. In December, 1947, the parties concluded a settlement of all pending litigation, by which Hartford paid Glenshaw approximately $800,000. Through a method of allocation which * * * is no longer in issue, it was ultimately determined that, of the total settlement, $324,529.94 represented payment of punitive damages for fraud and antitrust violations. Glenshaw did not report this portion of the settlement as income for the tax year involved. The Commissioner determined a deficiency claiming as taxable the entire sum less only deductible legal fees. As previously noted, the Tax Court and the Court of Appeals upheld the taxpayer.

*PH —
for this case*

Facts — Goldman

*Theater company
sues for violation
of anti-trust laws*
- Win $375,000
- Reported only $125,000
- Both courts uphold

Commissioner v. William Goldman Theatres, Inc.—William Goldman Theatres, Inc., a Delaware corporation operating motion picture houses in Pennsylvania, sued Loew's, Inc., alleging a violation of the federal antitrust laws and seeking treble damages. After a holding that a violation had occurred, William Goldman Theatres, Inc. v. Loew's, Inc., 150 F.2d 738, the case was remanded to the trial court for a determination of damages. It was found that Goldman had suffered a loss of profits equal to $125,000 and was entitled to treble damages in the sum of $375,000. William Goldman Theatres, Inc. v. Loew's, Inc., 69 F.Supp. 103, affirmed, 3 Cir., 164 F.2d 1021, certiorari denied, 334 U.S. 811, 68 S.Ct. 1016. Goldman reported only $125,000 of the recovery as gross income and claimed that the $250,000 balance constituted punitive damages and as such was not taxable. The Tax Court agreed, 19 T.C. 637, and the Court of Appeals, hearing this with the Glenshaw case, affirmed. 211 F.2d 928.

*Respondents
argument*

It is conceded by the respondents that there is no constitutional barrier to the imposition of a tax on punitive damages. Our question is one of statutory construction: are these payments comprehended by [§ 22 of the 1939 Code]?

Issue

The sweeping scope of the controverted statute is readily apparent:

"Sec. 22. Gross Income.

"(a) General Definition. 'Gross income' includes gains, profits, and income derived from salaries, wages, or compensation for personal service * * * of whatever kind and in whatever form paid, or from professions, vocations, trades, businesses, commerce, or sales, or dealings in property, whether real or personal, growing out of the ownership or use of or interest in such property; also from interest, rent, dividends, securities, or the transaction of any business carried on for gain or profit, *or gains or profits and income derived from any source whatever.* * * * " (Italics supplied.)

This Court has frequently stated that this language was used by Congress to exert in this field "the full measure of its taxing power." Helvering v. Clifford, 309 U.S. 331, 334; * * * . Respondents contend that punitive damages, characterized as "windfalls" flowing from the culpable conduct of third parties, are not within the scope of the section. But Congress applied no limitations as to the source of taxable receipts, nor restrictive labels as to their nature. And the Court has given a liberal construction to this broad phraseology in recognition of the intention of Congress to tax all gains except those specifically exempted. Commissioner v. Jacobson, 336 U.S. 28, 49 * * * . Thus, the fortuitous gain accruing to a lessor by reason of the forfeiture of a lessee's improvements on the rented property was taxed in Helvering v. Bruun, 309 U.S. 461. * * * Such decisions demonstrate that we cannot but ascribe content to the catchall provision of § 22(a), "gains or profits and income derived from any source whatever." The importance of that phrase has been too frequently recognized since its first appearance in the Revenue Act of 1913 to say now that it adds nothing to the meaning of "gross income."

Nor can we accept respondent's contention that a narrower reading of § 22(a) is required by the Court's characterization of income in Eisner v. Macomber, 252 U.S. 189, 207, as " 'the gain derived from capital, from labor, or from both combined.'" The Court was there endeavoring to determine whether the distribution of a corporate stock dividend constituted a realized gain to the shareholder, or changed "only the form, not the essence," of his capital investment. Id., 252 U.S. at page 210. It was held that the taxpayer had "received nothing out of the company's assets for his separate use and benefit." Id., 252 U.S. at page 211. The distribution, therefore, was held not a taxable event. In that context—distinguishing gain from capital—the definition served a useful purpose. But it was not meant to provide a touchstone to all future gross income questions. Helvering v. Bruun, supra, 309 U.S. at pages 468–469 * * * .

Here we have instances of undeniable accessions to wealth, clearly realized, and over which the taxpayers have complete dominion. The mere fact that the payments were extracted from the wrongdoers as punishment for unlawful conduct cannot detract from their character as taxable income to the recipients. Respondents concede, as they must, that the recoveries are taxable to the extent that they compensate for damages actually incurred. It would be an anomaly that could not be justified in the absence of clear congressional intent to say that a recovery for actual damages is taxable but not the additional amount extracted as punishment for the same conduct which caused the injury. And we find no such evidence of intent to exempt these payments.

[handwritten: Conclusion]

It is urged that reenactment of § 22(a) without change since the Board of Tax Appeals held punitive damages nontaxable in Highland Farms Corp., 42 B.T.A. 1314, indicates congressional satisfaction with that holding. Reenactment—particularly without the slightest affirmative indication that Congress ever had the Highland Farms decision before it—is an unreliable indicium at best. * * * Moreover, the Commissioner promptly published his nonacquiescence in this portion of the Highland Farms holding and has, before and since, consistently maintained the position that these receipts are taxable. It therefore cannot be said with certitude that Congress intended to carve an exception out of [§ 22(a)'s] pervasive coverage. Nor does the 1954 Code's legislative history, with its reiteration of the proposition that statutory gross income is "all-inclusive",[10] give support to respondent's position. The definition of gross income has been simplified, but no effect upon its present broad scope was intended.[11] Certainly punitive damages cannot reasonably be classified as gifts * * * , nor do they come under any other exemption provision in the Code. We would do violence to the plain meaning of the statute and restrict a clear legislative attempt to bring the taxing power to bear upon all receipts constitutionally taxable were we to say that the payments in question here are not gross income. * * *

[handwritten margin note: If money recieved for any reason other than a GIFT, it is taxable. Congress did not intend to exempt anything else. Conclusion →]

Reversed. *[handwritten: — Holding]*

DETAILED ANALYSIS

1. DEFINITION OF INCOME

Glenshaw Glass, with its focus on "undeniable accessions to wealth, clearly realized, and over which the taxpayers have complete dominion," makes it clear that the source of an increase in net worth is irrelevant for income definition purposes. Some earlier decisions had suggested that source distinctions might be relevant. See Eisner v. Macomber in Section 2 of this Chapter.

---

[10]   H.R.Rep. No. 1337, 83d Cong., 2d Sess. A18; S.Rep. No. 1622, 83d Cong., 2d Sess. 168.

[11]   In discussing § 61(a) of the 1954 Code the House Report states:

"This section corresponds to section 22(a) of the 1939 Code. While the language in existing section 22(a) has been simplified, the all-inclusive nature of statutory gross income has not been affected thereby. Section 61(a) is as broad in scope as section 22(a).

"Section 61(a) provides that gross income includes 'all income from whatever source derived.' This definition is based upon the 16th Amendment and the word 'income' is used in its constitutional sense." H.R.Rep. No. 1337, supra, note 11, at A18.

A virtually identical statement appears in S.Rep. No. 1622, supra, note 10 at 168.

In General American Investors Co., Inc. v. Commissioner, 348 U.S. 434 (1955), decided the same day as *Glenshaw Glass,* the Court held that a corporation that recovered from a director "insider profits" from prohibited trading in the corporation's stock derived gross income. "As in *Glenshaw*, the taxpayer realized the money in question free of any restrictions as to use. The payments in controversy were neither capital contributions nor gifts. * * * There is no indication that Congress intended to exempt them from coverage. In accordance with the legislative design to reach all gain constitutionally taxable unless specifically excluded, we conclude that the petitioner is liable for the tax and the judgment is affirmed."

2. WINDFALLS

Lottery winnings or other windfalls are clearly includable in gross income under *Glenshaw Glass*. Greisen v. United States, 831 F.2d 916 (9th Cir.1987), held that payments received by native-born Alaskan residents from the Alaska Permanent Fund, derived from mineral royalties collected by the state of Alaska, are includable in gross income.

In Haverly v. United States, 513 F.2d 224 (7th Cir.1975), an elementary school principal received unsolicited sample copies of textbooks from publishers, donated the books to his school library, and claimed a charitable contribution deduction. In holding that the taxpayer had gross income equal to the amount of the claimed deductions, the court stated:

> The receipt of textbooks is unquestionably an accession to wealth. Taxpayer recognized the value of the books when he donated them and took a $400 deduction therefor. Possession of the books increased the taxpayer's wealth. Taxpayer's receipt and possession of the books indicate the income was clearly realized. Taxpayer admitted that the books were given to him for his personal retention or whatever disposition he saw fit to make of them. Although the receipt of unsolicited samples may sometimes raise the question of whether the taxpayer manifested an intent to accept the property or exercised complete dominion over it, there is no question that this element is satisfied by the unequivocal act of taking a charitable deduction for donation of the property. * * *

> The Internal Revenue Service has apparently made an administrative decision to be concerned with the taxation of unsolicited samples only when failure to tax those samples would provide taxpayers with double tax benefits. It is not for the courts to quarrel with an agency's rational allocation of its administrative resources.

Haverly is consistent with Rev. Rul. 70–498, 1970–2 C.B. 6, which held that a newspaper's book reviewer must include in gross income the value of unsolicited books received from publishers, which are donated to a charitable organization and for which a charitable deduction is taken. This Ruling was issued to supersede an earlier ruling, Rev. Rul. 70–330, 1970–1 C.B. 14, that mere retention of unsolicited books was sufficient to cause them to be gross income.

3.   FOUND PROPERTY

Found money and other windfalls are income. Rev. Rul. 53–61, 1953–1 C.B. 17, following Treas. Reg. § 1.61–14(a), held: "The finder of treasure trove is in receipt of taxable income, for income tax purposes, to the extent of its value in United States currency, for the taxable year in which it is reduced to undisputed possession." Cesarini v. United States, 428 F.2d 812 (6th Cir.1970), held that $4,467 of cash found by the taxpayer in a piano purchased seven years earlier was taxable income in the year of discovery. However, no case has ever held that found property—for example, a watch picked up off the sidewalk—is required to be included in gross income.

B. INDIRECT RECEIPTS

Old Colony Trust Co. v. Commissioner
Supreme Court of the United States, 1929.
279 U.S. 716.

■ MR. CHIEF JUSTICE TAFT delivered the opinion of the Court.*

The facts certified to us are substantially as follows:

William M. Wood was president of the American Woolen Company during the years 1918, 1919 and 1920. In 1918 he received as salary and commissions from the company $978,725, which he included in his federal income tax return for 1918. In 1919 he received as salary and commissions from the company $548,132.27, which he included in his return for 1919.

August 3, 1916, the American Woolen Company had adopted the following resolution, which was in effect in 1919 and 1920:

"Voted: That this company pay any and all income taxes, State and Federal, that may hereafter become due and payable upon the salaries of all the officers of the company, including the president, William M. Wood * * * , to the end that said persons and officers shall receive their salaries or other compensation in full without deduction on account of income taxes, State or Federal, which taxes are to be paid out of the treasury of this corporation."

This resolution was amended on March 25, 1918, as follows:

"Voted: That, in referring to the vote passed by this board on August 3, 1916, in reference to income taxes, State and Federal, payable upon the salaries or compensation of the officers and certain employees of this company, the method of computing said taxes shall be as follows, viz.:

" 'The difference between what the total amount of his tax would be, including his income from all sources, and the amount of his tax when

---
*   [Ed.: The Old Colony Trust Company was the executor of the estate of William M. Wood.]

computed upon his income excluding such compensation or salaries paid by this company.'"

Pursuant to these resolutions, the American Woolen Company paid to the collector of internal revenue Mr. Wood's federal income and surtaxes due to salary and commissions paid him by the company * * * .

The decision of the Board of Tax Appeals here sought to be reviewed was that the income taxes of $681,169.88 and $351,179.27 paid by the American Woolen Company for Mr. Wood were additional income to him for the years 1919 and 1920.

The question certified by the Circuit Court of Appeals for answer by this Court is:

"Did the payment by the employer of the income taxes assessable *— Issue* against the employee constitute additional taxable income to such employee?"

* * *

Coming now to the merits of this case, we think the question *— Issue* presented is whether a taxpayer, having induced a third person to pay his income tax or having acquiesced in such payment as made in discharge of an obligation to him, may avoid the making of a return *— Courts answer* thereof and the payment of a corresponding tax. We think he may not do so. The payment of the tax by the employers was in consideration of the services rendered by the employee, and was a gain derived by the employee from his labor. The form of the payment is expressly declared to make no difference. [Former version of § 61(a).] It is therefore immaterial that the taxes were directly paid over to the government. The discharge by a third person of an obligation to him is equivalent to receipt *Application* by the person taxed. The certificate shows that the taxes were imposed upon the employee, that the taxes were actually paid by the employer, and that the employee entered upon his duties in the years in question under the express agreement that his income taxes would be paid by his employer. This is evidenced by the terms of the resolution passed August 3, 1916, more than one year prior to the year in which the taxes were imposed. The taxes were paid upon a valuable consideration, namely, the services rendered by the employee and as part of the compensation therefor. We think, therefore, that the payment constituted income to the *— Answer* employee.

* * *

It is next argued against the payment of this tax that if these payments by the employer constitute income to the employee, the employee will be called upon to pay the tax imposed upon this additional income, and that the payment of the additional tax will create further income which will in turn be subject to tax, with the result that there would be a tax upon a tax. This, it is urged, is the result of the government's theory, when carried to its logical conclusion, and results in an absurdity which Congress could not have contemplated.

In the first place, no attempt has been made by the Treasury to collect further taxes, upon the theory that the payment of the additional taxes creates further income, and the question of a tax upon a tax was not before the Circuit Court of Appeals, and has not been certified to this Court. We can settle questions of that sort when an attempt to impose a tax upon a tax is undertaken, but not now. * * * It is not, therefore, necessary to answer the argument based upon an algebraic formula to reach the amount of taxes due. The question in this case is, "Did the payment by the employer of the income taxes assessable against the employee constitute additional [gross] income to such employee?" The answer must be "Yes."

Conclusion —

DETAILED ANALYSIS

1.   THIRD-PARTY PAYMENTS

The *Old Colony* decision established the proposition that gross income under § 61(a) is not limited to situations in which cash is actually received by a taxpayer. Thus, in a companion case to *Old Colony*, payment by a lessee of the taxes of the lessor was held to be rental income to the lessor. United States v. Boston & Maine R.R., 279 U.S. 732 (1929). After *Glenshaw Glass* there is no question that the receipt of economic benefit from a third party is income. Similarly, corporate payment of tax fraud penalties imposed on the corporation's president-shareholder resulted in gross income to the president-shareholder (Sachs v. Commissioner, 277 F.2d 879 (8th Cir.1960), corporate payment of a civil fine imposed upon an employee in connection with a Ponzi scheme of the corporation in which the employee participated was included in the gross income of the employee (O'Malley v. Commissioner, 91 T.C. 352 (1988)), and payment of legal fees on behalf of an uncompensated trustee of a Teamster's Union pension trust, who was convicted of conspiracy to use trust funds to bribe a U.S. Senator was treated as gross income to the trustee (Huff v. Commissioner, 80 T.C. 804 (1983)). Inclusion in gross income of third party payments is necessary for the functioning of an income tax. Taxpayers must treat the economic benefit resulting from the payment of an obligation in the same way they would treat the receipt of cash that is used to discharge the obligation. Any other approach would make it too simple to avoid taxation by restructuring cash payments into payments to third parties that discharge the taxpayer's obligations.

Nevertheless, in Announcement 2015–22, 2015–35 I.R.B. 288, without articulating any rationale, the IRS announced it will not assert that an individual whose personal information may have been compromised in a data breach must include in gross income the value of the identity protection services provided by the organization that experienced the data breach, even if the organization that suffered the data breach and pays for the identity protection services is the person's employer. Perhaps the rationale is that the provision of such services is not disguised compensation and the person whose identity may have been compromised is not better off than before the data breach; rather, the person is merely being "made whole".

2.   THE TAX ON A TAX

In *Old Colony* the Government included in the taxpayer's gross income only the first "layer" of tax paid on behalf of the taxpayer. But the economic benefit to the taxpayer of having taxes paid can exceed this first layer, depending upon the arrangement between the employer and employee. Suppose, for example, that an employer agreed to pay an employee a stipulated salary of $100,000 plus any income tax on payments made by the employer. For the sake of illustration, assume the taxpayer has $20,000 of deductions unrelated to employment and personal exemptions, the taxpayer's taxable income is $80,000, and taxable income is taxed at 20%. The tax on the $100,000 cash salary minus the $20,000 of deductions would equal $16,000 ($80,000 × 20%). The taxpayer's gross income therefore would be $116,000 ($100,000 plus the $16,000 paid by the employer). After accounting for the $20,000 deduction, the tax on $96,000 would be $19,200 ($96,000 × 20%). This is the situation faced by the Court in *Old Colony*, with tax on a single layer of tax.

If the arrangement between the employer and employee is that the employer will pay the amount of tax required to ensure an after-tax salary, then the arrangement can result in pyramiding. For instance, to ensure that the taxpayer in this example had $100,000 of after-tax salary, the employer would have to pay the additional $3,200 ($19,200 − $16,000) of tax on tax. The employer's payment of that tax would increase the taxpayer's gross income to $119,200, and the employer would have to pay tax on the additional gross income. Such pyramiding would continue until the additional amount of tax became too small to matter. With pyramiding, the gross income would end up being $125,000. The tax liability, after accounting for the $20,000 of deductions would be $21,000. The difference between applying one "layer" of tax and "pyramiding" is thus significant. The amount of before-tax gross income to which the tax payment is equivalent may be computed by mathematical formula.[1]

Ironically, the computation in United States v. Boston & Maine Railroad, supra, the companion case to *Old Colony*, involved full pyramiding of each additional tax layer, although the Court seemed unaware of the issue. Prior to 1952, the IRS included in taxable income only the first layer of tax paid on behalf of a taxpayer. This policy was reversed by Mim. 6779, 1952–1 C.B. 8, and Mim. 51, 1952–2 C.B. 65, requiring that a taxpayer include in income *all* federal income taxes paid on a taxpayer's behalf. These rulings permit the taxpayer and the employer to agree on the mechanism for computing the tax, or on the amount of tax to be paid, thereby simplifying the calculation and avoiding some pyramiding of the tax. Many international organizations, such as the United Nations, World Bank, and International Monetary Fund, compensate their employees on the basis of a stipulated

---

[1]   The formula is the agreed upon net compensation divided by (1-Tax Rate). The calculation is complicated by the fact that the tax rate varies under the progressive rate tables so there may not be a single tax rate applicable to all of a taxpayer's taxable income.

salary plus any income tax resulting from that salary. These organizations in effect compute the total tax on a pyramided basis.

Whether pyramiding should apply will depend upon the agreement between an employer and employee and the timing of the tax payment. If the agreement provides that the employer will pay tax that results from the agreed upon compensation, pyramiding should not apply, and only the amount of the tax paid is included in gross income. If the agreement provides that the employer will pay an amount of tax necessary to ensure that the employee has a certain amount of after-tax compensation, then pyramiding could apply, but the timing of the tax payment could affect the application of pyramiding. For instance, if the taxing jurisdiction does not require payment of tax until after the close of a taxable year, then the payment arguably would not affect the gross income of the year during which the related compensation was paid. Instead, the payment of the tax arguably should be included in gross income for the year during which it was paid. If tax is paid on that gross income in a subsequent taxable year, then it would not result in pyramiding.

SECTION 2.   THE REALIZATION REQUIREMENT

REGULATIONS: Sections 1.1001–1(a), 1.1002–1.

Eisner v. Macomber

Supreme Court of the United States, 1920.
252 U.S. 189.

[The taxpayer was the owner of 2,200 shares of common stock in the Standard Oil Company of California. The corporation declared a 50 percent stock dividend and distributed one share of Standard Oil stock for each two shares held by the shareholders. The taxpayer received 1,100 additional shares of which 198.77 shares represented surplus of the corporation earned between March 1, 1913 and January 1, 1916, the latter date being the date of the stock dividend. The shares, representing the post March 1, 1913 surplus, had a par value of $19,877. The Commissioner treated the stock dividend as includable in gross income to the extent of the par value of such shares. Cash dividends in such an amount would have constituted income. The applicable statute expressly included stock dividends in income. The taxpayer asserted that the stock dividend was not income within the meaning of the Sixteenth Amendment. The District Court rendered judgment against the Government.]

■ MR. JUSTICE PITNEY delivered the opinion of the Court. * * *

In Towne v. Eisner, the question was whether a stock dividend made in 1914 against surplus earned prior to January 1, 1913, was taxable against the stockholder under the Act of October 3, 1913, * * * which provided * * * that net income should include "dividends," and also "gains or profits and income derived from any source whatever." * * * When the case came here, * * * we * * * disposed of it upon consideration of the essential nature of a stock dividend * * * saying (246 U.S. 426): "Notwithstanding the thoughtful discussion that the case received below we cannot doubt that the dividend was capital as well for the purposes of the Income Tax Law as for distribution between tenant for life and remainderman. What was said by this Court upon the latter question is equally true for the former. 'A stock dividend really takes nothing from the property of the corporation, and adds nothing to the interests of the shareholders. Its property is not diminished, and their interests are not increased. * * * The proportional interest of each shareholder remains the same. The only change is in the evidence which represents that interest, the new shares and the original shares together representing the same proportional interest that the original shares represented before the issue of the new ones.' Gibbons v. Mahon, 136 U.S. 549, 559, 560. In short, the corporation is no poorer and the stockholder is no richer than they were before. * * * If the plaintiff gained any small advantage by the change, it certainly was not an advantage of $417,450, the sum upon which he was taxed. * * * What has happened is that the plaintiff's old certificates have been split up in effect and have diminished in value to the extent of the value of the new."

This language aptly answered not only the reasoning of the District Court but the argument of the Solicitor General in this Court, which discussed the essential nature of a stock dividend. And if, for the reasons thus expressed, such a dividend is not to be regarded as "income" or "dividends" within the meaning of the Act of 1913, we are unable to see how it can be brought within the meaning of "incomes" in the Sixteenth Amendment; it being very clear that Congress intended in that act to exert its power to the extent permitted by the Amendment. * * *

The Sixteenth Amendment must be construed in connection with the taxing clauses of the original Constitution and the effect attributed to them before the Amendment was adopted. In Pollock v. Farmers' Loan & Trust Co., 158 U.S. 601, under the Act of August 27, 1894, * * * it was held that taxes upon rents and profits of real estate and upon returns from investments of personal property were in effect direct taxes upon the property from which such income arose, imposed by reason of ownership; and that Congress could not impose such taxes without apportioning them among the States according to population, as required by Art. I, § 2, cl. 3, and § 9, cl. 4, of the original Constitution.

Afterwards, and evidently in recognition of the limitation upon the taxing power of Congress thus determined, the Sixteenth Amendment was adopted, in words lucidly expressing the object to be accomplished: "The Congress shall have power to lay and collect taxes on incomes, from whatever source derived, without apportionment among the several States, and without regard to any census or enumeration." As repeatedly held, this did not extend the taxing power to new subjects, but merely removed the necessity which otherwise might exist for an apportionment among the States of taxes laid on income. Brushaber v. Union Pacific R.R. Co., 240 U.S. 1 * * * .

A proper regard for its genesis, as well as its very clear language, requires also that this Amendment shall not be extended by loose construction, so as to repeal or modify, except as applied to income, those provisions of the Constitution that require an apportionment according to population for direct taxes upon property, real and personal. This limitation still has an appropriate and important function, and is not to be overridden by Congress or disregarded by the Courts.

In order, therefore, that the clauses cited from Article I of the Constitution may have proper force and effect, save only as modified by the Amendment, and that the latter also may have proper effect, it becomes essential to distinguish between what is and what is not "income," as the term is there used; and to apply the distinction, as cases arise, according to truth and substance, without regard to form. Congress cannot by any definition it may adopt conclude the matter, since it cannot by legislation alter the Constitution, from which alone it derives its power to legislate, and within whose limitations alone that power can be lawfully exercised.

The fundamental relation of "capital" to "income" has been much discussed by economists, the former being likened to the tree or the land, the latter to the fruit or the crop; the former depicted as a reservoir supplied from springs, the latter as the outlet stream, to be measured by its flow during a period of time. For the present purpose we require only a clear definition of the term "income," as used in common speech, in order to determine its meaning in the Amendment; and, having formed also a correct judgment as to the nature of a stock dividend, we shall find it easy to decide the matter at issue.

After examining dictionaries in common use (Bouv.L.D.; Standard Dict.; Webster's Internat. Dict.; Century Dict.), we find little to add to the succinct definition adopted in two cases arising under the Corporation Tax Act of 1909 (Stratton's Independence v. Howbert, 231 U.S. 399, 415; Doyle v. Mitchell Bros. Co., 247 U.S. 179, 185)—"Income may be defined as the gain derived from capital, from labor, or from both combined," provided it be understood to include profit gained through a sale conversion of capital assets, to which it was applied in the Doyle Case * * * .

Brief as it is, it indicates the characteristic and distinguishing attribute of income essential for a correct solution of the present controversy. The Government, although basing its argument upon the definition as quoted, placed chief emphasis upon the word "gain," which was extended to include a variety of meanings; while the significance of the next three words was either overlooked or misconceived. "Derived-from-capital";—"the gain-derived-from-capital", etc. Here we have the essential matter: not a gain accruing to capital, not a growth or increment of value in the investment; but a gain, a profit, something of exchangeable value proceeding from the property, severed from the capital however invested or employed, and coming in, being "derived," that is, received or drawn by the recipient (the taxpayer) for his separate use, benefit and disposal;—that is income derived from property. Nothing else answers the description.]

The same fundamental conception is clearly set forth in the Sixteenth Amendment—"incomes, from whatever source derived"—the essential thought being expressed with a conciseness and lucidity entirely in harmony with the form and style of the Constitution.

Can a stock dividend, considering its essential character, be brought within the definition? To answer this, regard must be had to the nature of a corporation and the stockholder's relation to it. * * *

For bookkeeping purposes, the company acknowledges a liability in form to the stockholders equivalent to the aggregate par value of their stock, evidenced by a "capital stock account." If profits have been made and not divided they create additional bookkeeping liabilities under the head of "profit and loss," "undivided profits," "surplus account," or the like. None of these, however, gives to the stockholders as a body, much less to any one of them, either a claim against the going concern for any particular sum of money, or a right to any particular portion of the assets or any share in them unless or until the directors conclude that dividends shall be made and a part of the company's assets segregated from the common fund for the purpose. The dividend normally is payable in money, under exceptional circumstances in some other divisible property; and when so paid, then only (excluding, of course, a possible advantageous sale of his stock or winding-up of the company) does the stockholder realize a profit or gain which becomes his separate property, and thus derive income from the capital that he or his predecessor has invested.

A "stock dividend" shows that the company's accumulated profits have been capitalized, instead of distributed to the stockholders or retained as surplus available for distribution in money or in kind should opportunity offer. Far from being a realization of profits of the stockholder, it tends rather to postpone such realization, in that the fund represented by the new stock has been transferred from surplus to capital, and no longer is available for actual distribution.

The essential and controlling fact is that the stockholder has received nothing out of the company's assets for his separate use and benefit; on the contrary, every dollar of his original investment, together with whatever accretions and accumulations have resulted from employment of his money and that of the other stockholders in the business of the company, still remains the property of the company, and subject to business risks which may result in wiping out the entire investment. Having regard to the very truth of the matter, to substance and not to form, he has received nothing that answers the definition of income within the meaning of the Sixteenth Amendment.

* * *

We are clear that not only does a stock dividend really take nothing from the property of the corporation and add nothing to that of the shareholder, but that the antecedent accumulation of profits evidenced thereby, while indicating that the shareholder is the richer because of an increase of his capital, at the same time shows he has not realized or received any income in the transaction.

It is said that a stockholder may sell the new shares acquired in the stock dividend; and so he may, if he can find a buyer. It is equally true that if he does sell, and in doing so realizes a profit, such profit, like any other, is income, and so far as it may have arisen since the Sixteenth Amendment is taxable by Congress without apportionment. The same would be true were he to sell some of his original shares at a profit. But if a shareholder sells dividend stock he necessarily disposes of a part of his capital interest, just as if he should sell a part of his old stock, either before or after the dividend. What he retains no longer entitles him to the same proportion of future dividends as before the sale. His part in the control of the company likewise is diminished. * * *

Conceding that the mere issue of a stock dividend makes the recipient no richer than before, the Government nevertheless contends that the new certificates measure the extent to which the gains accumulated by the corporation have made him the richer. There are two insuperable difficulties with this: In the first place, it would depend upon how long he had held the stock whether the stock dividend indicated the extent to which he had been enriched by the operations of the company; unless he had held it throughout such operations the measure would not hold true. Secondly, and more important for present purposes, enrichment through increase in value of capital investment is not income in any proper meaning of the term.

It is said there is no difference in principle between a simple stock dividend and a case where stockholders use money received as cash dividends to purchase additional stock contemporaneously issued by the corporation. But an actual cash dividend, with a real option to the stockholder either to keep the money for his own or to reinvest it in new shares, would be as far removed as possible from a true stock dividend, such as the one we have under consideration, where nothing of value is taken from the company's assets and transferred to the individual ownership of the several stockholders and thereby subjected to their disposal.

* * *

Thus, from every point of view, we are brought irresistibly to the conclusion that neither under the Sixteenth Amendment nor otherwise has Congress power to tax without apportionment a true stock dividend made lawfully and in good faith, or the accumulated profits behind it, as income of the stockholder. The Revenue Act of 1916, in so far as it imposes a tax upon the stockholder because of such dividend, contravenes the provisions of Article I, § 2 cl. 3, and Article I, § 9, cl. 4, of the Constitution, and to this extent is invalid notwithstanding the Sixteenth Amendment.

Judgment affirmed. — *Holding*

■ MR. JUSTICE HOLMES, dissenting.

I think that Towne v. Eisner, 245 U.S. 418, was right in its reasoning and result and that on sound principles the stock dividend was not income. But it was clearly intimated in that case that the construction of the statute then before the Court might be different from that of the Constitution.* 245 U.S. 425. I think that the word "incomes" in the Sixteenth Amendment should be read in "a sense most obvious to the common understanding at the time of its adoption." Bishop v. State, 149 Indiana, 223, 230 * * *. For it was for public adoption that it was proposed. * * * The known purpose of this Amendment was to get rid of nice questions as to what might be direct taxes, and I cannot doubt that most people not lawyers would suppose when they voted for it that they put a question like the present to rest. I am of opinion that the Amendment justifies the tax. * * *

Helvering v. Bruun

Supreme Court of the United States, 1940.
309 U.S. 461.

■ MR. JUSTICE ROBERTS delivered the opinion of the Court.

The controversy had its origin in the petitioner's assertion that the respondent realized taxable gain from the forfeiture of a leasehold, the tenant having erected a new building upon the premises. The Court below held that no income had been realized. Inconsistency of the decisions on the subject led us to grant certiorari.

* * * [I]t appears that on July 1, 1915, the respondent, as owner, leased a lot of land and the building thereon for a term of ninety-nine years.

* * * The lessee was to surrender the land, upon termination of the lease, with all buildings and improvements thereon.

In 1929 the tenant demolished and removed the existing building and constructed a new one which had a useful life of not more than fifty years. July 1, 1933, the lease was canceled for default in payment of rent and taxes and the respondent regained possession of the land and building.

---

* 　[Ed.: Justice Holmes put it this way in Towne v. Eisner: "But it is not necessarily true that income means the same thing in the Constitution and the act. A word is not a crystal, transparent and unchanged, it is the skin of a living thought and may vary greatly in color and content according to the circumstances and the time in which it is used." 245 U.S. 418, 425 (1918).]

The parties stipulated "that as at said date, July 1, 1933, the building which had been erected upon said premises by the lessee had a fair market value of $64,245.68 and that the unamortized cost of the old building, which was removed from the premises in 1929 to make way for the new building, was $12,811.43, thus leaving a net fair market value as at July 1, 1933, of $51,434.25, for the aforesaid new building erected upon the premises by the lessee."

On the basis of these facts, the petitioner determined that in 1933 the respondent realized a net gain of $51,434.25. The Board overruled his determination and the Circuit Court of Appeals affirmed the Board's decision.

Procedural History →

* * *

The [taxpayer] insists that the realty,—a capital asset at the date of the execution of the lease,—remained such throughout the term and after its expiration; that improvements affixed to the soil became part of the realty indistinguishably blended in the capital asset; that such improvements cannot be separately valued or treated as received in exchange for the improvements which were on the land at the date of the execution of the lease; that they are, therefore, in the same category as improvements added by the respondent to his land, or accruals of value due to extraneous and adventitious circumstances. Such added value, it is argued, can be considered capital gain only upon the owner's disposition of the asset. The position is that the economic gain consequent upon the enhanced value of the recaptured asset is not gain derived from capital or realized within the meaning of the Sixteenth Amendment and may not, therefore, be taxed without apportionment.

Courts Answer/ Holding

We hold that the petitioner was right in assessing the gain as realized in 1933.

The respondent can not successfully contend that the definition of gross income in [§ 61 of the Code] is not broad enough to embrace the gain in question. That definition follows closely the Sixteenth Amendment. Essentially the respondent's position is that the Amendment does not permit the taxation of such gain without apportionment amongst the states. He relies upon * * * expressions found in the decisions of this Court dealing with the taxability of stock dividends to the effect that gain derived from capital must be something of exchangeable value proceeding from property, severed from the capital, however invested or employed, and received by the recipient for his separate use, benefit, and disposal.[8] He emphasizes the necessity that the gain be separate from the capital and separately disposable. These expressions, however, were used to clarify the distinction between an ordinary dividend and a stock dividend. They were meant to show that in the case of a stock dividend, the stockholder's interest in the corporate

---

[8]   See Eisner v. Macomber, 252 U.S. 189, 207; United States v. Phellis, 257 U.S. 156, 169.

assets after receipt of the dividend was the same as and inseverable from that which he owned before the dividend was declared. We think they are not controlling here.

While it is true that economic gain is not always taxable as income, it is settled that the realization of gain need not be in cash derived from the sale of an asset. Gain may occur as a result of exchange of property, payment of the taxpayer's indebtedness, relief from a liability, or other profit realized from the completion of a transaction. The fact that the gain is a portion of the value of property received by the taxpayer in the transaction does not negative its realization.

Here, as a result of a business transaction, the respondent received back his land with a new building on it, which added an ascertainable *— Conclusion* amount to its value. It is not necessary to recognition of taxable gain that he should be able to sever the improvement begetting the gain from his original capital. If that were necessary, no income could arise from the exchange of property; whereas such gain has always been recognized as realized taxable gain.

Judgment reversed. *— Holding*

DETAILED ANALYSIS

1. CONSTITUTIONAL STANDING OF THE REALIZATION REQUIREMENT

Eisner v. Macomber is the only decision holding that an income tax statute enacted by Congress is unconstitutional under the Sixteenth Amendment. The Court seemingly abandoned that stance in *Helvering v. Bruun* where it described the holding of Eisner v. Macomber as merely clarifying the distinction between ordinary dividends and stock dividends. In the term following its decision in Helvering v. Bruun, the Supreme Court described the realization requirement as "founded on administrative convenience" and as representing the "last step * * * taken by which he [the taxpayer] obtains the fruition of economic gain which has already accrued to him." Helvering v. Horst, 311 U.S. 112 (1940) (see Chapter 37, Section 2). In Commissioner v. Glenshaw Glass Co., 348 U.S. 426 (1955) (see Section 1 of this Chapter), the Court described Eisner v. Macomber as holding that the distribution of a stock dividend was not a "taxable event" adding that the definition of income adopted in that case was not intended to provide a "touchstone to all future gross income questions." Nonetheless, the Court in *Glenshaw Glass* maintained the realization requirement as part of its definition of income for purposes of § 61 as an accession to wealth clearly realized over which the taxpayer exercises dominion and control.

Following the Court's decisions in Helvering v. Bruun and Helvering v. Horst, a leading commentator described the decision in Eisner v. Macomber as an "historical relic." Surrey, The Supreme Court and the Federal Income Tax: Some Implications of the Recent Decisions, 35 Ill. L. Rev. 779, 792 (1941). Nonetheless, even without constitutional standing, the realization requirement remains one of the fundamental aspects of the determination of gross income under § 61. In recent years, Congress has enacted provisions that tax some gains on an accrual rather than a realization basis.[2] See I.R.C. §§ 475 and 1256, discussed at Chapter 6, Section 2.B.3.1.

2. THE PRACTICAL IMPACT OF EISNER v. MACOMBER

The income tax distinguishes between, on the one hand, the economic gains obtained by the taxpayers in *Old Colony* and *Glenshaw Glass* and, on the other hand, the gains obtained by Mrs. Macomber on the receipt of her stock dividend. As noted in Chapter 1, Section 1.B., Henry Simons defined "income" as the algebraic sum of amounts expended in consumption plus the net increment in the value of assets during the relevant period.[3] Eisner v. Macomber held that while "income" in any year may include capital growth that occurred over several years, clearly an economic gain, the annual increase in value of property is not treated as "income" under the Sixteenth Amendment until the date of an event on which the gain is "realized" by having been severed from the underlying investment. The holding in Eisner v. Macomber thus rejects the second prong of the Simons definition of income, formulating an entirely different measure of income. It is not at all clear that use of the word "income" in the Sixteenth Amendment necessarily requires the narrow definition adopted in Eisner v. Macomber, and a broader reading of the word "income," such as the Simons definition, very well might pass constitutional muster.

The deferral of tax on unrealized appreciation allowed by Eisner v. Macomber creates a tax advantage for investments in long-term growth assets relative to investments that return income in the form of current payments, such as interest and dividends. A simple example illustrates this tax advantage. Assume that a taxpayer in a 35 percent tax bracket invests $100 in each of two investments, one that grows at an annual rate of eight percent, which the taxpayer sells at the end of ten years, and one that pays eight percent taxable interest compounded annually, which the taxpayer accumulates for ten years. At the end of the ten-year period the former investment has returned $175.33, after tax, an annualized after-tax return of 5.76 percent, while the latter investment has returned $166.02, an annualized after-tax return of only 5.20 percent.

$100 INVESTMENT

	Growth Asset		Annual Income Asset		
Year	Interest	Year-End Value	Interest	After-Tax Return*	Year-End Value
1	$ 8.00	$108.00	$ 8.00	$5.20	$105.20
2	$ 8.64	$116.64	$ 8.42	$5.47	$110.67

---

[2]   See also Whitlock's Estate v. Commissioner, 494 F.2d 1297 (10th Cir.1974), upholding the constitutionality of § 951 of the Code, which includes certain undistributed income of a "controlled foreign corporation" in the shareholder's income.

[3]   H. Simons, Personal Income Taxation: The Definition of Income as a Problem of Fiscal Policy 49–50 (1938).

3	$ 9.33	$125.97	$ 8.85	$5.75	$116.43
4	$ 10.08	$136.05	$ 9.31	$6.05	$122.48
5	$ 10.88	$146.93	$ 9.80	$6.37	$128.85
6	$ 11.75	$158.69	$10.31	$6.70	$135.55
7	$ 12.69	$171.38	$10.84	$7.05	$142.60
8	$ 13.71	$185.09	$11.41	$7.42	$150.01
9	$ 14.81	$199.90	$12.00	$7.80	$157.81
10	$ 15.99	$215.89	$12.63	$8.21	$166.02

Gain on Sale	$115.89	
Less Tax@ 35%	$ 40.56	
Net Proceeds	$175.33	$166.02

*   After Tax Return = Interest × (1–.035)

3. BARGAIN PURCHASE AND COMPENSATORY DISCOUNTS

Where money is used as a medium of exchange, it is presumed that what is purchased has a value equal to the money paid. But the value *to the taxpayer* of the item purchased may be greater than the money paid. For example, an individual who purchases a shirt for $15 may have been willing to pay as much as $20. The tax system understandably makes no attempt to tax the economic benefit reflected in this "consumer surplus." Ascertaining the subjective value to the taxpayer would be an impossible administrative task. The price paid thus represents the minimum value to the taxpayer; if the taxpayer had valued the shirt for less than $15, the shirt would not have been purchased. What if the taxpayer pays $25 for an item in an antique shop and discovers that it is worth $10,000? Here the taxpayer now possesses an economic increment that was unknown at the time of the purchase, and could be said to have experienced a gain clearly realized over which the taxpayer has dominion and control.

In some instances, a particular taxpayer may obtain goods or services at a price below the generally prevailing market price, while other taxpayers pay the prevailing market price. The differential is not treated as gross income, even though valuation is not difficult. Pellar v. Commissioner, 25 T.C. 299 (1955) (Acq), held that taxpayers who were intentionally undercharged by a contractor for construction of their home because the contractor did business with corporations in which the father of one of the taxpayers had interests did not recognize any gross income. Rev. Rul. 91–36, 1991–2 C.B. 17, held that if a customer of an electric utility company participates in an energy conservation plan for which the customer receives a rate reduction or refundable credit on the customer's electric bill, the amount of the rate reduction or credit is not gross income to the customer.

The holdings in *Pellar* and Rev. Rul. 91–36 are arguably inconsistent with the definition of income in *Glenshaw Glass*. Generally, where a taxpayer is permitted to purchase property or services at a price below fair market because the seller intends to compensate the taxpayer for other goods or services provided to the seller, the taxpayer realizes gross income in the amount of the discount. I.R.C. § 83(a); Treas. Reg. § 1.61–2(d)(2). Employee discounts with respect to goods and services sold by the employer in the ordinary course of business, however, are subject to special rules under § 132 (see Chapter 3, Section 2.A.), and may be an excludable fringe benefit if certain conditions are met. Wentz v. Commissioner, 105 T.C. 1 (1995), held that an illegal premium kickback received from an insurance agent by the purchaser of a life insurance policy was income to the purchaser, not a price rebate. The amount could have been a price rebate only if it had been received from the insurance company, which was the seller of the policy.

Every major airline offers a "frequent flyer program" under which customers accumulate points or "miles" toward a "free" airline trip. The frequent flyer awards can be viewed as a "price rebate," reflecting a market bargain purchase price accorded by the airlines to frequent customers. This theory presents no problems if the purchased tickets that generated award trips involved personal travel. In practice, however, most frequent flyer points are generated by business travel that is not included in an employee's income or which is deducted by a self-employed business traveler. However, a large number of award trips accumulated by business travelers are used for personal purposes. In Announcement 2002–18, 2002–1 C.B. 621, the IRS announced that as a matter of administrative policy, "Consistent with prior practice, the IRS will not assert that any taxpayer has understated his federal tax liability by reason of the receipt or personal use of frequent flyer miles or other in-kind promotional benefits attributable to the taxpayer's business or official travel." The IRS cautioned, however, that this safe harbor is inapplicable to benefits that are converted to cash, to compensation paid in the form of benefits, or where these benefits "are used for tax avoidance purposes."

4.   STATUTORY TREATMENT OF STOCK DIVIDENDS

After the decision in Eisner v. Macomber, Congress provided that a stock dividend was not includable in gross income. At the same time, the Supreme Court made it clear that the receipt of a stock dividend that increased the shareholder's proportionate interest in the corporation represented income, which Congress could make subject to tax if it chose to do so. See Koshland v. Helvering, 298 U.S. 441 (1936); Helvering v. Gowran, 302 U.S. 238 (1937). Stock dividends that increased a shareholder's proportionate interest in the corporation were taxable under the 1936 Act.

In 1954, Congress provided a broad exclusion for stock dividends, requiring recognition of gross income on the receipt of a stock dividend only if any shareholder was given an election to take the dividend in stock or in cash, or the stock distribution was in lieu of dividend arrearages on preferred stock. The taxation of stock dividends was broadened in 1969 to include a distribution or a series of distributions that provide an increased proportionate interest in the distributing corporation to some shareholders and a taxable dividend in cash or other property to other shareholders (see I.R.C. § 305(b)(2)), and certain other distributions of or with respect to preferred stock (see I.R.C. § 305(b)(3)–(5)).

5.   STATUTORY TREATMENT OF LEASEHOLD IMPROVEMENTS

Like Eisner v. Macomber, Helvering v. Bruun also involved a question of income realization, but the situation was somewhat more complex. In *Bruun*, the Court considered several alternatives to when a taxpayer must realize gain attributable to tenant improvements of leased property: (a) the date on which the tenant completed construction of improvements to the lessor's land, (b) ratably over the remaining term of the lease as periodic rent, (c) the date on which the lessor obtained possession of the improvements, or (d) the date on which the lessor finally converts the land and improvements into cash or other property by disposition. In so doing, the Court evaluated whether the increment in value to the lessor's real estate attributable to the lessee's improvements were any different than the increment in value to Mrs. Macomber's stock added by corporate profits as reflected in the stock dividend.

Section 109, enacted in 1942, changed the result of the *Bruun* decision by providing that gross income does not include income derived by a lessor of real property on termination of a lease attributable to buildings or other improvements constructed by the lessee. Section 109 does not permanently exclude the value of improvements from income, however. Section 1019 prevents any adjustment to the lessor's basis (the recoverable cost on sale, see Chapter 6) as a result of improvements subject to exclusion from income under § 109, which means that gain attributable to lessee improvements is recovered by the lessor either on disposition of the property because a lower basis increases gain (or reduces loss), or as increased rental income from a future lease as the lessor's lower basis provides reduced depreciation deductions. Treas. Reg. § 1.109–1(a) provides that the exclusion under § 109 does not apply when the improvements are a bargained for consideration in lieu of cash rentals. In such a case, § 1019 is also inapplicable.

SECTION 3.   IMPUTED INCOME

The *Glenshaw Glass* definition of income includes all accessions to wealth clearly realized. As the court in *Old Colony Trust* makes clear, the economic benefit includable in gross income need not be in the form of cash receipts; indirect receipt of an economic benefit is also includable in gross income. The economic benefit derived from a person's use of the person's own capital, or the economic benefit derived from a person's own labor fit these definitions. For example, if a person utilizes capital to invest in a personal residence, that person realizes the economic benefit of the shelter, equivalent to the amount the person would be required to pay as rent for similar housing. Likewise, if a person washes his own automobile, that person derives the economic benefit of the personal services in an amount equivalent to what the person would pay someone else to perform the same service, an amount easily measured by the price charged at a local car wash. Yet none of these forms of "imputed income" are taken into account and included in gross income under the federal income tax. On the other hand, were this person to invest capital and pay rent to a property owner or pay someone else to wash his car, the tax system would treat those payments as gross income received by, respectively, the landlord and the owner of the car wash.

As one commentator noted many years ago:

Income in kind in the form of imputed income is in no way different so far as the individual is concerned. His power to consume and to accumulate is increased by its existence. A taxpayer who has acquired the sum of $20,000 (after payment of income tax) has the choice (among other, but similar, alternatives) of (1) investing the sum in, say, five per cent bonds, collecting $1,000 and spending the interest income left, after payment of income tax, on house rent; or (2) investing the $20,000 in a house, in which case he receives his rental services directly. If the tax is a flat 20 per cent with no exemptions, the first alternative leaves $800 for rent. The second alternative would yield rental services to the full value of $1,000 yearly, since the homeowner pays, under our statute, no tax upon his imputed income. Marsh, The Taxation of Imputed Income, 58 Pol.Sci.Q. 514 (1943).

The housekeeping services provided by a spouse represent one of the most significant forms of imputed income. As the same above commentator observed:

Another major source of imputed income is the tedious and unrequited labor of [housework]. Pigou has immortalized the innocent man who reduced the national income by marrying his housekeeper. Under our statute he would be able also to reduce his income tax liability, since he could maintain the same level of comfort with a smaller cash income than before. The imputed wages of his wife should be at least as great as the cash wages of his housekeeper. But the former do not appear in the taxpayer's accounts, and he receives tax free the excess of her imputed wages over the cost of her subsistence.

In the real world, decisions to marry or not to marry are unlikely to be much influenced by the possibilities of tax avoidance. But the alternatives may appear in another form. Thus, a [husband] and wife may have to consider whether [both] ought to continue [their] former occupation[s], using part of [their] earnings, after paying income taxes, to pay for household services; or whether [one should] keep house, earning imputed wages instead of cash and paying no income tax. Let us suppose that [one] is a competent school teacher, but an indifferent housekeeper. It may nevertheless be impossible * * * to earn sufficient money, after taxes, to pay for household service as good as [could be provided if that person] stayed at home. In this case, as in most other cases of imputed income from services, our tax laws tend to penalize specialization. Marsh, The Taxation of Imputed Income, supra.

Even if policy makers should want to tax the imputed income of persons who perform services for themselves out of a sense of fairness to those who earn taxable income and pay for the services with after-tax dollars, the administrative difficulty of doing so would be insurmountable. The IRS is not in a position to track every instance where the taxpayer washes the taxpayer's own car, mows the lawn or cleans the house in lieu of paying another to do so. In addition, maintaining complete equity in such a system would require capturing the foregone imputed income of the taxpayer who values and thus chooses leisure over maintaining the cleanliness of the automobile, the well-trimmed lawn, or the clean house. Nonetheless, as described in the Detailed Analysis, there have been instances when issues of imputed income have been considered.

DETAILED ANALYSIS

1.   RENTAL VALUE OF OWNER OCCUPIED HOUSING

Helvering v. Independent Life Ins. Co., 292 U.S. 371, 379 (1934), contains this dictum: "The rental value of the building used by the owner does not constitute income within the meaning of the Sixteenth Amendment." More than eighty years later, however, it is generally believed that no constitutional barrier exists to prevent the inclusion of this form of income. In addition, the Department of Commerce's Bureau of Economic Analysis (BEA) calculates imputed rent of owner-occupied housing and includes it in annual estimates of personal incomes. See BEA, Table 7.12, Imputations in the National Income and Product Accounts.

In some European countries, the imputed rental income from homes has been included in income for tax purposes. The treatment of imputed income from owner-occupied housing is considered in more detail at Chapter 21, Section 5.5.

2.   FARM PRODUCTS CONSUMED BY FARMER

In Morris v. Commissioner, 9 B.T.A. 1273 (1928) (Acq.), the court stated: "Products of a farm consumed by the operator thereof and his family do not appear to come within any of the categories of income enumerated in the taxing statutes and the administrative regulations of the Commissioner. * * * If products of a farm consumed thereon are income to the producer, it would seem to follow that the rental value of the farmer's home, the gratuitous services of his wife and children, and the value of the power derived from draft animals owned by the farmer and used without costs should also be so considered. It is obvious that such items are comparable to the rental value of a private residence, which has never been regarded as income."

Treas. Reg. § 1.61–4(c) provides: "If farm produce is exchanged for merchandise, groceries, or the like, the market value of the article received in exchange is to be included in gross income." Treas. Reg. § 1.61–4(a), states that "crop shares," i.e., the owner's share of the crops grown on his land under an arrangement with a third party, are to be included in the owner's gross income in the year in which the crop shares are reduced to money or the equivalent of money, whether or not they are considered as rent under state law.

3.   PAYMENTS TO ONE'S SELF

In Commissioner v. Minzer, 279 F.2d 338 (5th Cir.1960), the court held an insurance agent taxable on commissions received from the insurance company on insurance purchased on his own life. The Tax Court held similarly where a real estate salesman received commissions for purchases for his own account. Williams v. Commissioner, 64 T.C. 1085 (1975).

CHAPTER 3

COMPENSATION FOR SERVICES AND INDIRECT PAYMENTS

⌐As described in Chapter 2, the definition of gross income in § 61(a) includes all gains derived by the taxpayer from whatever source, which, as held in *Commissioner v. Glenshaw Glass*, includes any accession to wealth clearly realized.⌐ Section 61(a)(1) expressly enumerates "compensation for services, including fees, commissions, fringe benefits, and similar items" as income. Clearly cash payments for services are includable in the income of the recipient. In addition, *Old Colony Trust Company v. Commissioner* makes it clear that income includes a non-cash economic benefit, whether for services or otherwise. Nonetheless, methods for compensating a service provider raise difficult questions about identifying gross income. The materials in this chapter examine different forms of compensation in connection with services, some of which may or may not be included in gross income under statutory, judicial, or administrative interpretations.

SECTION 1. NONCASH ECONOMIC GAINS

INTERNAL REVENUE CODE: Sections 61(a)(1), 83(a).

REGULATIONS: Section 1.61–2(d)(1) and (2)(i).

Revenue Ruling 79–24
1979–1 C.B. 60.

FACTS

Situation 1. In return for personal legal services performed by a lawyer for a housepainter, the housepainter painted the lawyer's personal residence. Both the lawyer and the housepainter are members of a barter club, an organization that annually furnishes its members a directory of members and the services they provide. All the members of the club are professional or trades persons. Members contact other members directly and negotiate the value of the services to be performed.

Situation 2. An individual who owned an apartment building received a work of art created by a professional artist in return for the rent-free use of an apartment for six months by the artist.

LAW

The applicable sections of the Internal Revenue Code of 1954 and the Income Tax Regulations thereunder are 61(a) and 1.61–2, relating to compensation for services.

Section 1.61–2(d)(1) of the regulations provides that if services are paid for other than in money, the fair market value of the property or services taken in payment must be included in income. If the services were rendered at a stipulated price, such price will be presumed to be the fair market value of the compensation received in the absence of evidence to the contrary.

HOLDINGS

Situation 1. The fair market value of the services received by the lawyer and the housepainter are includable in their gross incomes under section 61 of the Code.

Situation 2. The fair market value of the work of art and the six months fair rental value of the apartment are includable in the gross incomes of the apartment-owner and the artist under section 61 of the Code.

DETAILED ANALYSIS

1.   RECEIPTS IN KIND GENERALLY

As illustrated in Rev. Rul. 79–24, goods or services received in exchange for services are income to the recipient. This principle follows the rationale of *Old Colony Trust Company v. Commissioner* that gain derived from labor is income regardless of the form of payment. Income in kind is not limited to compensation for services. Almost any form of income can be received in kind. Dean v. Commissioner, 187 F.2d 1019 (3d Cir.1951), held that a majority shareholder of a corporation who by virtue of her status as a shareholder resided in a home owned by the corporation realized dividend income as a result of the rent free use of the home. Strong v. Commissioner, 91 T.C. 627 (1988), held that the lessor of a cattle breeding herd realized rental income when the portion of the calves due as rent was added to the herd, which remained in the lessee's possession.

Armantrout v. Commissioner, 67 T.C. 996 (1977), involved distributions from an educational trust established by an employer to pay educational expenses of the children of its employees. The court held that distributions from the trust to schools in which the taxpayer-employee's children were enrolled were includable in the taxpayer's gross income as compensation for his services. As held in *Commissioner v. Glenshaw Glass*, income represents any accession to wealth, clearly realized, over which the taxpayer has dominion and control.

2.   FAIR MARKET VALUE

As noted by the IRS in Rev. Rul. 79–24, under Treas. Reg. § 1.61–2(d)(1) when economic benefits are received in the form of goods or services the fair market value of in-kind payments is included in income. Although "fair market value" is not defined in the Code or the Income Tax Regulations, the courts generally have adopted the definition in the Estate Tax Regulations: "The fair market value is the price at which the property would change hands between a willing buyer and a willing seller, neither being under any compulsion to buy or to sell and both having reasonable knowledge of relevant facts." Treas. Reg. § 20.2031–1(b).

In Rooney v. Commissioner, 88 T.C. 523 (1987), the Tax Court held that fair market value is measured by an objective standard; subjective valuation is not permitted. In *Rooney* the taxpayers, who were partners in a public accounting firm, agreed to accept goods and services from four clients who were delinquent on payments to the firm in lieu of amounts owed to the firm. However, the taxpayers believed that some of the provided goods and services were not satisfactory and attempted to discount the value of the goods and services below the retail price otherwise provided by the clients to customers. Upholding the IRS's position, the court stated "section 61 requires an objective measure of fair market value. * * * Under such standard the [taxpayers] may not adjust the acknowledged retail price of the goods and services received merely because they decide among themselves that such goods and services were overpriced." The court further opined:

> We are not persuaded by the petitioners' claims that they were compelled by circumstances to patronize these clients and that they were therefore "forced" to accept prices for the goods and services higher than they would have otherwise paid. We believe that their situation cannot be termed a forced purchase. The petitioners themselves made the decision to accept compensation in a form other than cash. Moreover, although the petitioners claim that they would not have willingly paid the retail prices for the goods and services received from the four clients, those prices were, so far as we know, accepted by other customers of those clients and thus represent the prices established in the marketplace. In our judgment, the petitioners must value their compensation by applying an objective measure of fair market value. For such reasons, we hold that the fair market value of the goods and services received by the petitioners is the prices charged by the partnership's clients to their retail customers. See sec. 20.2031–1(b), Estate Tax Regs.

In making a determination of fair market value, however, it is not always clear in which "market" a willing buyer and seller are deemed to operate. In McCoy v. Commissioner, 38 T.C. 841 (1962) (Acq.), the Commissioner asserted a tax based on the retail price of a car received as a prize. After receiving the car, a Lincoln which cost the taxpayer's employer $4,453, the taxpayer promptly traded it for a Ford station wagon with a retail price of $2,600 and $1,000 cash. The Tax Court held that the taxpayer was only taxable on the substantially lower amount that he realized on the disposition of the car, $3,600. In Turner v. Commissioner, T.C. Memo. 1954–38, the taxpayers won nontransferable, round-trip steamship tickets between the United States and South America. The court valued the tickets at approximately two-thirds of their retail value. The court's rationale was that the tickets did not provide the taxpayers with something that they would have purchased for themselves. The Tax Court's focus in *Turner* on the likelihood that a particular taxpayer would purchase an item does not appear to be consistent with the Tax Court's later position in *Rooney* on the retail price paid by others.

3.   ECONOMIC BENEFIT FOR THE CONVENIENCE OF THE PAYOR

3.1. *General*

In United States v. Gotcher, 401 F.2d 118 (5th Cir.1968), the taxpayer and his wife went on a twelve-day expense-paid trip to Germany to tour Volkswagen manufacturing facilities. Volkswagen paid seventy-five percent of the cost, while the remaining twenty-five percent was paid by Mr. Gotcher's employer, Economy Motors, in which Gotcher was considering purchasing an interest. Upon returning from the trip, Mr. Gotcher purchased twenty-five percent of the stock of Economy Motors. The court held that the payment for the cost of Mr. Gotcher's trip was not income because the trip primarily benefited Volkswagen, which was motivated to pay for the trip by its efforts to expand its share of the United States automobile market, and Mr. Gotcher "did nothing to earn that part of the trip paid by Economy Motors." The court summarized the principles as follows:

> [O]ne does not realize taxable income when he is serving a legitimate business purpose of the party paying the expenses. * * * The decisions also indicate that the tax consequences are to be determined by looking to the primary purpose of the expenses and that the first consideration is the intention of the payor.

Nevertheless, the cost attributable to Mrs. Gotcher accompanying Mr. Gotcher on the trip was gross income to him. The primary benefit of her expense-paid trip, according to the court, went not to Volkswagen, but to Mr. Gotcher, who was relieved of a nondeductible expense. Can the court's analysis in excluding the payment of Mr. Gotcher's expenses be squared with *Old Colony Trust*? What was the employer's purpose in paying Mr. Wood's income tax liability in *Old Colony Trust*?

Rev. Rul. 63–77, 1963–1 C.B. 177, concluded that the payment by a prospective employer of a prospective employee's travel expenses to attend an interview did not result in gross income to the prospective employee. This result is consistent with the quoted sentence from *Gotcher*.

Benaglia v. Commissioner, 36 B.T.A. 838 (1937) (Acq.), involved the manager of the Royal Hawaiian Hotel, who in addition to his salary received at no cost use of a suite of rooms for himself and his wife and all of their meals. Because the taxpayer was constantly on duty, the Board found that he received the meals and lodging "entirely for the convenience of his employer. * * * [N]either the [taxpayer] nor his employer ever regarded the meals and lodging as part of his compensation or accounted for them." Accordingly, the value of the meals and lodging was not gross income. The court explained its holding as follows:

> * * * The demands and requirements of guests are numerous, various, and unpredictable, and affect the meals, the rooms, the entertainment, and everything else about the hotel. The manager must be alert to all these things day and night. He would not consider undertaking the job and the owners of the hotel would not

consider employing a manager unless he lived there. This was implicit throughout his employment, and when his compensation was changed from time to time no mention was ever made of it. Both took it for granted. The corporation's books carried no accounting for petitioner's meals, rooms, or service.

Under such circumstances, the value of meals and lodging is not income to the employee, even though it may relieve him of an expense which he would otherwise bear. * * * The advantage to him was merely an incident of the performance of his duty, but its character for tax purposes was controlled by the dominant fact that the occupation of the premises was imposed upon him for the convenience of the employer.

The treatment of meals and lodging provided to an employee in the course of employment now is governed by § 119, discussed below. The "primary purpose" test of *Gotcher* and the "convenience of the employer" test of *Benaglia,* remain relevant in other contexts. For example, McDonell v. Commissioner, T.C. Memo. 1967–18, involved a salesman and his spouse who were selected by lottery to accompany a group of his employer's valued customers and their spouses on a ten-day trip to Hawaii paid for by the taxpayer's employer. The trip was a vacation for the customers, and the taxpayer's job responsibility on the trip was to accompany the customers at all times and "guide anticipated informal discussion relating to [the employer's] business." The court held that the value of the trip for both the employee and his spouse was not gross income:

> [T]he trip was not a vacation for the [taxpayers]. It was realistically a command performance to work. What was a social benefit to the contest winners was a work obligation to these [taxpayers]. More importantly, [the taxpayers] were expected to devote substantially all of their time on the trip to the performance of duties on behalf of [the employer] * * * . Nor do we consider it material that [taxpayers] enjoyed the trip. Pleasure and business, unlike oil and water, can sometimes be mixed. * * * It is noteworthy that neither of [taxpayers] went swimming or shopping during their entire stay, two activities for which Hawaii is famous.

In contrast, vacation travel expenses paid by an employer as a reward for job performance or intended to be additional compensation are gross income, even if nominally a business trip, such as a convention or seminar, if the primary purpose of the trip is pleasure. See e.g., Patterson v. Thomas, 289 F.2d 108 (5th Cir.1961); McCann v. United States, 696 F.2d 1386 (Fed.Cir.1983).

3.2. *Statutory Application of the Convenience of the Employer Doctrine to Meals and Lodging.*

Section 119 was enacted in 1954 to clarify the treatment of meals and lodging provided in connection with employment.[1] It excludes from gross

---

1　　Although the IRS initially acquiesced in *Benaglia,* it later retreated stating: "The 'convenience of the employer' rule is simply an administrative test to be applied only in cases in which the compensatory character of such benefits is not otherwise determinable." Mim. 6472,

income the value of meals and lodging provided for the convenience of the employer if the statutory tests are met. Section 119 applies to meals and lodging furnished for the convenience of the employer, even though they also were intended to be compensation and the exclusion applies even though the employee is also convenienced. Boykin v. Commissioner, 260 F.2d 249 (8th Cir.1958); Olkjer v. Commissioner, 32 T.C. 464 (1959) (Acq.).

The § 119 exclusion applies to meals and lodging furnished to the employee as well as the employee's spouse and dependents if the conditions of the section are satisfied. One justification for the extension of the exclusion to members of the employee's family is the obvious difficulty of valuing the portion of the food and lodging provided to individual family members.

3.2.1. *Convenience of the Employer*

Treas. Reg. § 1.119–1(a)(2) states that the "convenience of the employer" test is met with respect to meals if they are furnished for a "substantial noncompensatory business reason." Examples include a short lunch hour, insufficient eating facilities in the vicinity, and the need to be on call for emergencies. Treas. Reg. § 1.119–1(a)(2)(ii)(*a*), (*b*), (*c*).

Section 119(b)(4) provides that if more than one-half of the meals furnished to employees on an employer's business premises satisfy the "convenience of the employer test," then all meals furnished to all employees on those premises are deemed to have been provided for the convenience of the employer. Before § 119(b)(4) was enacted, the IRS held in Rev. Rul. 71–411, 1971–2 C.B. 103, that meals provided by the employer, whose business involved frequent telephone contacts with customers were provided for the employer's convenience to employees who were required to stay at their desks where they were served their lunch and to employees who had lunch in the dining room but were subject to call during the lunch hour. Meanwhile, meals provided to a third group of employees who were free to leave the building during the lunch period did not meet the convenience of the employer test. Under § 119(b)(4), because the first two groups of employees in Rev. Rul. 71–411 received more than one-half of the meals, the meals provided to the third group of employees also would be excluded. Furthermore, in Announcement 99–77, 1999–2 C.B. 243, the IRS stated that in applying § 119(a)(1) and the regulations it "will not attempt to substitute its judgment for the business decisions of an employer as to what specific business policies and practices are best suited to addressing the employer's business concerns." It does, however, caution taxpayers that "it would not [be] enough for [an employer] to waive a 'magic wand' and say it had a policy in order [for meals to qualify under § 119]." The IRS "will consider whether the employer's policies are reasonably related to the needs of the employer's business (apart from a desire to provide additional compensation to its

---

1950–1 C.B. 15. The Tax Court approved this position in several cases, including in gross income the fair market value of living quarters furnished when other factors indicated the lodging was provided as compensation. See e.g., Fisher v. Commissioner, 23 T.C. 218 (1954) (musician provided hotel quarters in lieu of higher cash salary), aff'd on other issues, 230 F.2d 79 (7th Cir.1956). Other cases allowed the exclusion on the basis of the "convenience of the employer" doctrine, without regard to consideration of the compensatory nature of the lodging. See e.g., Diamond v. Sturr, 221 F.2d 264 (2d Cir.1955).

employees) and whether these policies are in fact followed in the actual conduct of the business." If reasonable procedures are adopted and applied, and they preclude employees from obtaining a meal away from the employer's business premises during a reasonable meal period, § 119 will apply. It appears from this announcement that the IRS will not question an employer's judgment in prohibiting or restricting employees' ability to leave the business premises for meals, however unreasonable that judgment might be to outsiders, but it will demand that the employer actually prohibit or restrict employees from leaving the business premises for meals for § 119 to apply.

Section 119(b)(2) states that the fact employees are charged for employer-provided meals shall not to be taken into account in determining whether the meals are furnished for the convenience of the employer. Moreover, § 119(b)(3) excludes from the employee's gross income periodic fixed charges for employer-provided meals if such meals are provided for the convenience of the employer (under the usual tests), e.g., a firefighter's mess assessment. Section 119(b)(3) applies whether the employee pays the fixed charge out of stated compensation or out of her own funds, but only if the employee is required to make the payment whether she accepts or declines the meals.

Treas. Reg. § 1.119–1(a)(2)(i) provides that if employer-provided lodging meets the convenience of the employer test, any meals provided to the employee automatically meet the convenience of the employer test.

3.2.2. *Definition of Meals and Lodging*

Commissioner v. Kowalski, 434 U.S. 77 (1977), held that cash payments to New Jersey state troopers designated as meal allowances were not excludable under § 119: "By its terms, § 119 covers *meals* furnished by the employer and not *cash* reimbursements for meals. This is not a mere oversight. * * * [T]he form of § 119 which Congress enacted originated in the Senate and the Report accompanying the Senate bill is very clear: 'Section 119 applies only to meals or lodging furnished in kind.' S.Rep. No. 1622, 83d Cong., 2d Sess. 190 (1954)."

Tougher v. Commissioner, 51 T.C. 737 (1969), aff'd per curiam, 441 F.2d 1148 (9th Cir.1971), held that groceries supplied to the taxpayer by his employer did not constitute "meals" for purposes of § 119. But Jacob v. United States, 493 F.2d 1294 (3d Cir.1974), rejected the *Tougher* position and held that groceries cooked at the taxpayer's home on his employer's business premises qualified as "meals." The court could "see no logical reason why entitlement to the exclusion contained in § 119 should hinge upon who cooks the meal."

The IRS has ruled that "lodging" includes those utilities that are paid for by the employer, including utilities the cost of which is deducted from the employee's compensation. However, if the employee contracts directly with the utility company § 119 does not apply to the value of the utilities, which are not provided by the employer. Rev. Rul. 68–579, 1968–2 C.B. 61.

Section 119(b)(3) does not deal with the situation in which an employee is required to live on the employer's business premises and the employer deducts a charge for the rental value of the lodging from the employee's salary. Rev. Rul. 59–307, 1959–2 C.B. 48, held that the employee was not taxed on the portion of the salary retained by the employer. In light of *Kowalski,* however, this position appeared questionable, and Rev. Rul. 84–86, 1984–1 C.B. 26 (modified and superseded by Rev. Rul. 90–64, 1990–2 C.B. 35), reaffirmed the holding of Rev. Rul. 59–307 insofar as it applies to lodging furnished for the convenience of the employer; salary withheld to reimburse the employer for the employee's normal household expenses is taxable.[2]

3.2.3. *Condition of Employment*

For lodging to be excludable, acceptance of the lodging must be a condition of employment. This test is formally in addition to the "convenience of the employer" test, but the two are so closely connected that the distinction is often blurred in the cases. Treas. Reg. § 1.119–1(b) states that lodging is a condition of employment if its acceptance is required to enable the employee properly to perform his duties. Bob Jones University v. United States, 670 F.2d 167 (Ct.Cl.1982), held that this test was not met with respect to on-and off-campus housing provided to faculty members of a religious university. The lodging played only a "tangential role" in the employees' carrying out their responsibilities to the university. But Erdelt v. United States, 715 F.Supp. 278 (D.N.D.1989), aff'd by order, 909 F.2d 510 (8th Cir.1990), held that housing furnished to a rural school district superintendent near a school was excluded under § 119 because the superintendent's physical presence near the school was required for interaction with the school staff and community. The court stated that it "recognize[d] that its position is possibly reaching the extreme limits of the exclusion of section 119." Caratan v. Commissioner, 442 F.2d 606 (9th Cir.1971), applied § 119 to a farm manager whose duties required constant availability at the farm, even though other housing in which the farm manager could have lived was available nearby.

Section 119(d), added in 1986 partially in response to the *Bob Jones University* decision, provides a special rule for campus lodging provided to employees of educational institutions that fails to meet the conditions for exclusion under § 119(a). Only the amount by which the lesser of (1) 5 percent of the appraised value of the lodging premises, or (2) the average rental paid to the institution for comparable lodging by persons who are neither employees nor students over the rent paid by the employee is taxable.

3.2.4. *Business Premises*

Section 119(a) requires that the meals and lodging be provided on the employer's "business premises." This phrase has been the subject of substantial interpretation. In Commissioner v. Anderson, 371 F.2d 59 (6th Cir.1966), the taxpayer was a motel manager and was required to be on call at all times to oversee the management of the motel. His employer provided him with a house located "two short blocks" from the motel. The Tax Court held that the house satisfied the "business premises" test, 42 T.C. 410 (1964), but the Court of Appeals reversed. The adjacent house could not be considered part of the employer's business premises since the taxpayer did

---

[2]   Rev. Rul. 90–64 does not alter these conclusions.

not perform any significant portion of his duties there; simply being "on call" was not sufficient to make the house a part of the employer's "business premises." In Lindeman v. Commissioner, 60 T.C. 609 (1973) (Acq.), a hotel leased property directly across the street from the hotel to furnish its general manager with a residence. The court found the general manager performed "a significant portion of his duties" in the leased residence since he was on call 24 hours a day and had an office in the residence in which he occasionally performed some of his business activities. *Anderson* was distinguished on the ground that in that case the living quarters were not an "integral part" of the business property. See also Rev. Rul. 75–540, 1975–2 C.B. 53 (Governor's residence is business premises); Winchell v. United States, 564 F.Supp. 131 (D.Neb.1983), aff'd by order, 725 F.2d 689 (8th Cir.1983) (college president's house was not business premises because few job-related activities were performed there); Adams v. United States, 585 F.2d 1060 (Ct.Cl.1978) (residence provided to the American president of a Japanese subsidiary of a U.S. corporation qualified as business premises where the taxpayer used the residence for business-related entertainment between twelve and thirty-five times a year and received telephone calls on a regular basis; the special relation between business and social activities in Japan was considered a factor); McDonald v. Commissioner, 66 T.C. 223 (1976) (housing in Japan furnished to a corporate executive was not excluded because there was no evidence that proper performance of duties required such housing).

United States v. Morelan, 356 F.2d 199 (8th Cir.1966), held that meals furnished to a highway patrolman in restaurants near or adjacent to the highways were provided "on the business premises of the employer." Wilson v. United States, 412 F.2d 694 (1st Cir.1969), reached the opposite result finding that "[t]he state conducted no business in the public restaurant, [n]or was taxpayer performing, or going to perform, any business there. * * * [T]he restaurant was not 'a place where the employee performs a significant portion of his duties.' Rather, taxpayer was there because he was off duty."

Rev. Rul. 71–411, 1971–2 C.B. 103, dealt with the taxation of free meals furnished to employees who were served meals at branch offices other than those at which they "actually" worked. The ruling noted that although the "business premises" of the employer "generally means the place of employment of the employee * * * [i]n a case where the employee receives his meals at a place other than his place of employment, but at a place where the employer carries on a significant portion of his business," the business premises test is satisfied.

SECTION 2. EMPLOYEE FRINGE BENEFITS

Employers commonly provide compensatory benefits to employees in addition to their cash compensation. These fringe benefits range from free parking places or recreational facilities to employer-financed health care programs. The proper tax treatment of employee fringe benefits raises both theoretical and practical questions. While an employee can be said to benefit from a clean, well-lit, air-conditioned workplace, for example, the benefit is so intertwined with the employee's work that it may be considered as provided for the convenience of the employer and it may be presumed that no separate personal benefit is derived. Working conditions of this nature are thus appropriately not included in gross income. In other situations, it may be difficult to value compensatory benefits unrelated to the employee's general working conditions. Suppose, for example, the employer operates a health club and allows its employees to use the facility free of charge. A membership in the health club costs nonemployees $500. While the benefit of using the health club has value to the employee, the employee, unlike third parties using the facility, did not affirmatively choose to spend $500 on the benefit. Thus, it can be argued that the value to the employee is something less than $500 and it may not be appropriate to tax the employee for using the health club facility on the value that a third person must pay for that privilege. On the other hand, if the employer and the employee bargained with respect to the overall compensation package and the employee in effect received the benefit in lieu of $500 of cash income, then the fair market value approach clearly would be appropriate. Similarly, if the employee uses the facility extensively, even though the employee did not bargain for the benefit, the objective fair market value of the benefit may be the most appropriate measure of income.

Substantial fringe benefits provided by an employer are likely to be an inducement for prospective employees to accept employment and thus employees do provide valuable services for the benefits. A rule taxing the benefits at fair market value (taking into account any restrictions such as the standby nature of airline passes commonly granted to airline employees) would therefore be reasonable for many employees although it would overstate the value for some. On the other hand, it is difficult to develop meaningful distinctions between fringe benefits that are not taxed at fair market value because of restricted choice and benefits includable in gross income at fair market value.

Although the broad sweep of § 61(a) suggests that most fringe benefits are taxable, for most of the history of the income tax, in practice many fringe benefits have been excluded from gross income. Historically, fringe benefits were not that common and, when provided, were often small in amount. Even in cases in which theory indicates that it is appropriate to require inclusion of the fair market value of a fringe benefit, the valuation must actually be made by the payor or the recipient and monitored by the IRS. If the benefit is small in amount, the administrative burden to the government, the payor, and the recipient may justify exclusion from gross income on *de minimis* grounds.

A number of statutory provisions enacted over the years addressed various specific situations. Prior to 1984, the general taxation of fringe benefits was generally ignored, and most fringe benefits were controlled by § 61(a). As fringe benefits became increasingly popular among employers, Congress enacted § 132, dealing with fringe benefits not specifically addressed by other Code provisions. The 1984 legislation also added "fringe benefits" to the nonexclusive list in § 61 of specific items included in gross income, underscoring their taxation in the absence of a specific exclusion. I.R.C. § 61(a)(1). See also Treas. Reg. § 1.61–21(a)(1) and (2).

When taxable, fringe benefits must be included at fair market value. Treas. Reg. § 1.61–21(b)(2) specifies that for this purpose fair market value is "the amount that an individual would have to pay for the particular fringe benefit in an arm's length transaction." The special relationship between the employer and employee is ignored, as is the employee's subjective perception of the value of the fringe benefit. Taxable fringe benefits received by a member of the employee's family are includable in the gross income of the employee, not the income of the family member enjoying the benefit. Treas. Reg. § 1.61–21(a)(4)(i).

A. STATUTORY EXCLUSIONS BASED ON TAX POLICY AND ADMINISTRATIVE CONVENIENCE

INTERNAL REVENUE CODE: Sections 119(a)–(b); 132.

REGULATIONS: Sections 1.61–1(a); 1.61–21(a), (b)(1)–(4), (7), (d)(1), (g)(1), (4), (j), (k); 1.132–1(a)–(f); 1.132–2(a)–(c); 1.132–3(a)–(b)(iii), (c)(1), (2), (e); 1.132–4(a)(1); 1.132–5(a)–(b)(1), (3)(i), (k), (m)(i); 1.132–6; 1.132–7; 1.132–8(a)–(c)(1), (d)(1)–(2), (5), (f).

General Explanation of the Revenue Provisions of the Deficit Reduction Act of 1984

Staff of the Joint Committee on Taxation 840–61 (1984).

Reasons for Change

In providing statutory rules for exclusion of certain fringe benefits for income and payroll tax purposes, the Congress struck a balance between two competing objectives.

First, the Congress was aware that in many industries, employees may receive, either free or at a discount, goods and services which the employer sells to the general public. In many cases, these practices are long established, and generally have been treated by employers, employees, and the Internal Revenue Service as not giving rise to taxable income.

Although employees receive an economic benefit from the availability of these free or discounted goods or services, employers often have valid business reasons, other than simply providing compensation, for encouraging employees to avail themselves of the products which those employees sell to the public. For example, a retail clothing business will want its salespersons to wear, when they deal with customers, the clothing which it seeks to sell to the public, rather than clothing sold by its competitors. In addition, where an employer has only one line of business, the fact that the selection of goods and services offered in that line of business may be limited in scope makes it appropriate to provide a limited exclusion, when such discounts are generally made available to employees, for the income employees realize from obtaining free or reduced-cost goods or services. By contrast, allowing tax-free discounts for all lines of business of a conglomerate organization, where the employee might have unlimited choices among many products and services which individuals normally consume or use on a regular basis, would be indistinguishable in economic effect from allowing tax-free compensation in the form of cash or gift certificates. Also, the noncompensatory element involved in providing discounts on the particular products or services that the employee sells to the public may be marginal or absent where an employer offers discounts across all lines of business.

The Congress believed, therefore, that many present practices under which employers may provide to a broad group of employees, either free or at a discount, the products and services which the employer sells or provides to the public do not serve merely to replace cash compensation. These reasons support the decision to codify the ability of employers to continue many of these practices without imposition of income or payroll taxes.

The second objective of the new statutory rules is to set forth clear boundaries for the provision of tax-free benefits. * * *

Congress was concerned that without any well-defined limits on the ability of employers to compensate their employees tax-free by providing noncash benefits having economic value to the employee, new practices will emerge that could shrink the income tax base significantly. This erosion of the income tax base results because the preferential tax treatment of fringe benefits serves as a strong motivation to employers to substitute more and more types of benefits for cash compensation. * * * In addition, continuation of the dramatic growth in noncash forms of compensation in recent years—at a rate exceeding the growth in cash compensation—could further shift a disproportionate tax burden to those individuals whose compensation is in the form of cash.

Finally, an unrestrained expansion of noncash compensation would increase inequities among employees in different types of businesses, because not all employers can or will provide comparable compensation packages. For example, consumer-goods retail stores can offer their employees discounts on clothing, hardware, etc.; by contrast, a manufacturer of aircraft engines cannot give its workers compensation in the form of tax-free discounts on its products. Similarly, an unlimited exclusion for noncash benefits discriminates among employers. For example, if tax-free discounts were allowed across all lines of business of an employer, a large employer with many types of businesses (e.g., department store, hotel, airline, etc.) would be given a favorable edge by the tax system in competing for employees as compared with a small firm having one line of business (e.g., a specialty clothing store). Also, a failure to put any limits on the untaxed status of fringe benefits would encourage employers to provide further noncash forms of compensation and thus, in effect, restrict the employees' freedom of choice over how to spend or save their compensation.

Accordingly, the Congress determined that specific rules of exclusion should be set forth in the Code, with limitations on the availability, applicability, and scope of these statutory exclusions. These general limitations include a nondiscrimination rule, the line of business limitation, and the limitation on exclusions to benefits provided to the employee and the employee's spouse and dependent children. In addition, specific limitations apply to particular types of benefits.

The nondiscrimination rule is an important common thread among the types of fringe benefits which are excluded under [§ 132] from income and employment taxes. Under [§ 132], most fringe benefits may be made available tax-free to officers, owners, or highly compensated employees only if the benefits are also provided on substantially equal terms to other employees. The Congress believed that it would be fundamentally unfair to provide tax-free treatment for economic benefits that are furnished only to highly paid executives. Further, where benefits are limited to the highly paid, it is more likely that the benefit is being provided so that those who control the business can receive compensation in a nontaxable form; in that situation, the reasons stated above for allowing tax-free treatment would not be applicable. Also, if highly paid executives could receive free from taxation economic benefits that are denied to lower-paid employees, while the latter are compensated only in fully taxable cash, the Congress was concerned that this situation would exacerbate problems of noncompliance among taxpayers. In this regard, some commentators argued that the prior-law situation—in which the lack of clear rules for the tax treatment of nonstatutory fringe benefits encouraged the nonreporting of many types of compensatory benefits— led to nonreporting of types of cash income which are clearly taxable under present-law rules, such as interest and dividends.

In addition to enacting specific statutory exclusions covering many fringe benefit practices, the tax treatment of which had been uncertain under prior law, the Congress provided amendments in the Act to Code section 61, defining gross income, and to comparable employment tax provisions. These amendments made clear that any fringe benefit that does not qualify for exclusion under a specific Code provision is includable in the recipient's gross income, and in wages for withholding and other employment tax purposes, at the excess of the fair market value of the benefit over any amount paid by the recipient for the benefit.

The Congress recognized that the inclusion of taxable fringe benefits at fair market value raises valuation issues. However, the problem has been ameliorated because [§ 132] exempts from any taxation a significant portion of benefits made available under existing practices. In addition, the Congress has directed the Treasury to issue regulations, to the extent feasible, setting forth appropriate and helpful rules for the valuation of taxable fringe benefits, to assist both employers, employees, and the Internal Revenue Service.

Also, the Congress understood that valuation issues inherently arise whenever compensation is paid in the form of noncash benefits. For example, both under prior law and the Act, the personal use by an employee (including use by members of the employee's family) of an employer-provided car or plane is includable in income, thereby necessitating a determination of the fair market value of the personal use. While it is understood that as a matter of practice, some taxpayers have not been reporting the full fair market value of such benefits, and that the Internal Revenue Service may not have been actively pursuing the matter on audit, the Congress anticipated that with the enactment in the Act of statutory rules delineating exclusions for fringe benefits, the Internal Revenue Service will be more effective in assuring that all sources of income and wages are properly reported on employer and employee tax returns. The Congress believed that this will help achieve a greater fairness in the tax law, by treating alike employees having equivalent economic income.

* * *

Explanation of Provisions

a.   Overview

Under the Act, certain fringe benefits provided by an employer are excluded from the recipient employee's gross income for Federal income tax purposes, * * * if specified requirements are satisfied. Any fringe benefit that does not qualify for exclusion under the Act and that is not excluded under another specific statutory provision of the Code is includible in the recipient's gross income under Code sections 61 and 83, * * * at the excess of its fair market value over any amount paid by the recipient for the benefit.

* * * Some of the exclusions under the Act apply to benefits provided to the spouse and dependent children of a current employee, to former employees who separated from service because of retirement or disability (and their spouses and dependent children), and to the widow(er) of a deceased employee (and the dependent children of deceased employees).

In the case of a no-additional-cost service, a qualified employee discount, subsidized eating facilities, or a qualified tuition reduction, the exclusion applies with respect to benefits provided to officers, owners, or highly compensated employees only if the benefit is made available to employees on a basis which does not discriminate in favor of officers, owners, or highly compensated employees.

b.   No-additional-cost service

General rules

Under this category of excludable fringe benefits, the entire fair market value of any no-additional-cost service provided by an employer to an employee for the use of the employee * * * , or for use of the employee's spouse or dependent children, is excluded for income * * * tax purposes. The exclusion applies whether the no-additional-cost service is provided directly for no charge or at a reduced price, or whether the benefit is provided through a cash rebate of all or part of any amount paid for the service.

* * * [T]he exclusion applies only if the no-additional-cost service provided to the employee is of the type which the employer offers for sale to non-employee customers in the ordinary course of the line of business of the employer in which the employee is performing services. Also, the exclusion applies to officers, owners, or highly compensated employees only if the no-additional-cost service is available to employees on a nondiscriminatory basis. * * *

To qualify under this exclusion, the employer must incur no substantial additional cost in providing the service to the employee, as determined without regard to any amounts paid by the employee for the service. For this purpose, the term cost includes any revenue forgone because the service is furnished to the employee rather than to a nonemployee.

Generally, situations in which employers incur no additional cost in providing services to employees are those in which the employees receive, at no substantial additional cost to the employer, the benefit of excess capacity which otherwise would have remained unused because nonemployee customers would not have purchased it. Thus, employers that furnish airline, railroad, or subway seats or hotel rooms to employees working in those respective lines of business in such a way that nonemployee customers are not displaced, and telephone companies that provide telephone service to employees within existing capacity, incur no substantial additional cost in providing these services to employees, as this term is used in [§ 132(b)].

Line of business limitation

General rules

To be excluded under this category, a service must be the same type of service which is sold to the public (i.e., nonemployee customers) in the ordinary course of the line of business of the employer in which the employee is performing services. (Thus, types of services most of the employer's production of which are provided or sold to the employer's employees rather than to the public do not qualify for this exclusion.) The purpose of the line of business limitation is to avoid, to the extent possible, the competitive imbalances and inequities which would result from giving the employees of a conglomerate or other large employer with several lines of business a greater variety of tax-free benefits than could be given to the employees of a small employer with only one line of business. Thus, small businesses will not be disadvantaged in their ability to compete with large businesses that can provide discounts on an array of goods or services, and employees of small business will not be disadvantaged, in comparison to employees of multifaceted businesses, in terms of receiving tax-free economic benefits.

* * *

Reciprocal arrangements

Under [§ 132(i)], an exclusion is available to the employees of one employer for no-additional-cost services provided by an unrelated employer (i.e., another employer not under common control) only if the services provided to such employee (of the first employer) are the same type of services as provided to nonemployee customers by both the line of business (of the first employer) in which the employee works and the line of business (of the other employer) in which the services are provided to such employee. In addition, the exclusion is available to such employee only if both employers are parties to a written reciprocal agreement under which each employer's employees who work in such identical line of business may receive the service from the other employer, and only if neither employer incurs any substantial additional cost (including forgone revenue or payments to the other employer) in providing such service or pursuant to such agreement.

* * *

c.   Qualified employee discount

General rules

Under this category of excludable fringe benefits, the amount of employee discounts allowed by the employer from the selling price of qualified property or services of the employer is excluded, subject to certain limitations, for income and employment tax purposes. If an employee discount is excludable under this provision but the amount of the exclusion is subject to a specified limitation (described below) based on the employer's gross profit percentage in the case of qualified property or on the selling price of a qualified service, then any excess of the employee discount over the limitation amount is includible in the employee's gross income and wages.

The term employee discount is defined in [§ 132(c)(3)] as the amount by which the price at which the good or service is provided to the employee (for the use of the employee) by the employer is less than the price at which such good or service is being offered by the employer to customers who are not employees. The exclusion applies whether the qualified employee discount is provided through a direct reduction in price or through a cash rebate from the employer or a third party. By contrast to the exclusion for no-additional-cost services, the exclusion for qualified employee discounts is not available for any discounts on goods or services provided by an employer other than the employee's own employer, whether or not a reciprocal discount agreement exists between such employers and whether or not the line of business limitation would be satisfied had the discounted goods or services been provided by the employee's own employer.

Line of business limitation

General rules

To qualify under this exclusion, the qualified property or services on which the employee discount is available must be property or services which are offered for sale by the employer to nonemployee customers in the ordinary course of the employer's line of business in which the employee works. * * *

Amount of exclusion

General rule.—Under [§ 132(c)(1)], an employee discount is excluded only up to a specified limit. In the case of qualified property, the excludable amount of the discount is limited to the selling price of the property, multiplied by the employer's gross profit percentage. The discount exclusion for a qualified service may not exceed 20 percent of the selling price, regardless of the actual gross profit percentage.

* * *

d.   Working condition fringe

General rules

Under [§ 132(d)], the fair market value of any property or services provided to an employee of the employer is excludable for income * * * tax purposes as a working condition fringe only if and to the extent that payment for the property or services by the employee would have been deductible by the employee as an ordinary and necessary business expense (under Code secs. 162 or 167) had the employee, rather than the employer, paid for such property or services. * * *

The nondiscrimination rules applicable to certain other excludable fringe benefits under the Act do not apply as a condition for exclusion as a working condition fringe.

Examples

By way of illustration, the fair market value of use by an employee of a company car or corporate jet solely for section 162 business purposes is excludable as a working condition fringe (assuming any applicable substantiation requirements are satisfied). However, the fair market value of the use of a company car or plane by an employee (or members of the employee's family) for personal purposes is includible in the employee's income and wages. Merely incidental personal use of a company car, such as a small detour for a personal errand while on a business trip, might qualify for exclusion as a de minimis fringe, but regular personal use (e.g., after business hours or on weekends) or use on vacation trips cannot qualify for an exclusion.

* * *

Examples of other benefits excluded as working condition fringes are those provided by an employer primarily for the safety of its employees, if the costs of such safety precautions would be deductible by the employee as ordinary and necessary business expenses. For example, if strictly for security reasons the U.S. Government or a private business provides a bodyguard or car and driver to an employee, the fair market value of the bodyguard or use of the car and driver is treated as a working condition fringe, and hence is not includible in income or wages of the employee, to the extent the cost of such safety precautions would have been deductible under section 162 if paid by the employee. Other examples of excluded working condition fringes are employer expenditures for on-the-job training or travel by an employee if such expenditures, if paid by the employee, would meet the requirements (including any substantiation requirements) for deductibility under section 162.

* * *

e.   De minimis fringe

General rules

Under [§ 132(e)], if the fair market value of any property or service that otherwise would be includible in gross income of any person is so small that accounting for the property or service would be unreasonable or administratively impracticable, the value is excluded for income and employment tax purposes. [§ 132(e)(1)] provides that the frequency with which similar fringe benefits (otherwise excludable as de minimis fringes) are provided to such person is to be taken into account, among other relevant factors, in determining whether the fair market value of the property or service is so small as to make accounting for the property or service unreasonable or administratively impracticable.

The nondiscrimination rules applicable to certain other provisions of the Act do not apply as a condition for exclusion of property or a service as a de minimis fringe, except for subsidized eating facilities (as described below).

To illustrate, benefits that generally are excluded from income and employment taxes as de minimis fringes include the occasional typing of personal letters by a company secretary, occasional personal use of the company copying machine, * * * occasional company cocktail parties or picnics for employees, occasional supper money or taxi fare because of overtime work, traditional gifts on holidays of tangible personal property having a low fair market value (e.g., a turkey given for the year-end holidays), occasional theatre or sporting event tickets, and coffee and doughnuts furnished to employees. However, the frequency with which any such benefits are offered may make the exclusion unavailable for that benefit, regardless of difficulties in accounting for the benefits. By way of illustration, the exclusion is not available if traditional holiday gifts are provided to employees each month, or if sandwiches are provided free-of-charge to employees on a regular basis.

Subsidized eating facilities

If an employer provides and operates an eating facility for its employees on or near the employer's business premises and if revenue derived from the facility normally equals or exceeds the direct operating costs of the facility, the excess of the fair market value of a meal over the fee charged to the employee for such meal is excluded from income and wages under the Act as a de minimis fringe. * * *

h.   Nondiscrimination rules

Under [§§ 132(j)(1) and 117(d)(3)] relating to no-additional-cost services, qualified employee discounts, subsidized eating facilities, and qualified tuition reductions, the exclusion for such a benefit is available to an officer, owner, or highly compensated employee (the "highly compensated group") only if the benefit is available on substantially the same terms to each member of a group of employees which is defined under a reasonable classification set up by the employer that does not discriminate in favor of the highly compensated group.

If the availability of the fringe benefit does not satisfy these non-discrimination rules, the exclusion applies only to those employees (if any) receiving the benefit who are not members of the highly compensated group. For example, if an employer offers a 20-percent discount (which otherwise satisfies the requirements for a qualified employee discount) to rank-and-file employees and a 35-percent discount to the highly compensated group, the entire value of the 35-percent discount (not just the excess over 20 percent) is includible in gross income and wages of the members of the highly compensated group who make purchases at a discount.

* * *

DETAILED ANALYSIS

1.   NO-ADDITIONAL-COST SERVICES AND EMPLOYEE DISCOUNTS

1.1. *General*

The no-additional-cost service and employee discount exclusions are tied to the economic consequences of the employer providing the benefit. To qualify for exclusion, the no-additional-cost fringe benefit may not result in any substantial cost to the employer, including foregone revenue. I.R.C. § 132(b)(2). A qualified employee discount on property may not exceed the employer's gross profit percentage on all sales to customers of goods (not just the particular item purchased) sold in the line of business in which the employee works. If the discount exceeds the permissible percentage, the exclusion is not lost entirely. Rather, only the amount of the excess discount is includable. For example, if the employer's profit percentage was 30 percent and an employee is permitted to purchase for $55 an item that normally sold for $100, only $15 would be includable ($100 − 30 = $70; $70 − 55 = $15).

Discounts on real property and personal property of a type held for investment never qualify for exclusion under § 132(a)(2). I.R.C. § 132(c)(4). Thus, for example, if a home-building contractor sold a new home to an employee at a discount, the entire discount would be taxable to the employee without regard to its amount.

If a benefit is not intended to compensate employees, or if it can be provided at no additional cost to the employer, it may be difficult to infer that the employee has received a benefit equal to its fair market value. But these factors do not justify the total exclusion of such benefits from the tax base. In the employment context, where the benefits often are negotiated, it would appear reasonable to presume that substantial value (fair market value or a significant percentage of fair market value) has been received notwithstanding the absence of cost to the employer or the presence of a noncompensatory business reason.

Consider the following statement made by Congressman Holland regarding the taxation of standby airline passes for airline employees: "I don't personally believe that the airline pass should be taxed because I think that is a part of the inducement to get those employees to work for that company under what are not good conditions, admittedly, at all times." Hearings before the Subcommittee on Selected Revenue Measures, Ways and Means Committee, House of Representatives, 97th Cong., 1st Sess. 25 (1981). It is difficult to conceive of a stronger tax policy argument for, in fact, taxing these benefits!

1.2. *Nondiscrimination Requirement*

The nondiscrimination requirement in § 132(j)(1) applies to the no-additional-cost service and employee discount fringe benefits but not to the working conditions and *de minimis* fringe benefits. The nondiscrimination requirement highlights the fact that the exclusions for no-additional-cost services and employee discounts are not appropriate provisions for accurately determining net income; the exclusions are designed to achieve non-tax policy objectives.

Although the nondiscrimination requirement generally means that the benefit will be excludable by officers, owners, or highly compensated employees only if also offered generally to other employees, the exclusion still favors high-income employees. The economic value of the exclusion, even with the nondiscrimination requirement, is greater for higher-income employees. Suppose, for example, that a pilot in a 30 percent marginal tax bracket and a flight attendant in a 15 percent marginal bracket each take a free trip to Japan valued at $1,000. The effect of the exclusion is that the pilot has received the equivalent of $1,429 additional salary. Additional salary in that amount would be subject to tax of $429 leaving $1,000 to purchase the ticket. The flight attendant, however, has received the equivalent of only $1,176 additional salary, for it is that amount of pre-tax income that would be needed to produce sufficient after-tax funds to purchase the $1,000 ticket. Put differently, if the airline were to pay $1,000 in compensation to each employee, the benefit of excluding the payment from income would be $300 for the pilot but only $150 for the flight attendant.

1.3. *Reciprocal Agreements*

Section 132(i) allows an employee to exclude the value of a no-additional-cost fringe benefit provided by a company unrelated to the employee's employer if the benefit is provided pursuant to a reciprocal agreement. This rule permits the exclusion from taxation of free or discount airline passes used by airline employees even when they are granted by another airline. There is no provision for reciprocal agreements for qualified employee discounts under § 132(a)(2). See Treas. Reg. § 1.132–3(a)(3). In addition, while § 132(h) permits retired employees, employee's spouses, surviving spouses, and dependent children to receive tax-free qualified employee discounts, in the case only of free airline passes, § 132(h)(3) adds to this expansive list the employee's parents. It is difficult to discern any logical rationale for these differences, other than that Congress sought to confer a special benefit on airlines and their employees, who are the primary beneficiaries of the exclusion for no-additional-cost services fringe benefit.

2.   WORKING CONDITION AND DE MINIMIS FRINGE BENEFITS

While there are legitimate income tax policy and administrative reasons to exclude the value of working condition and *de minimis* fringe benefits from income, the precise scope of these exclusions is a matter of judgment.[3] With regard to working condition fringe benefits, § 132(d) provides that the exclusion extends to property and services which, if purchased by the employee, would be allowable as a deduction under § 162 or 167. This technique for defining the scope of working conditions has the virtue of providing consistent treatment for various property and services whether provided by the employer or purchased by the employee. In making this determination, limitations under § 274 on the deductibility of expenses for activities generally considered to be entertainment (see Chapter 19, Section 3) are taken into account, but the effect of the rules limiting employees to deducting business expenses as itemized deductions are not taken into account. See Treas. Reg. § 1.132–5(c). A disadvantage, however, is that the technique incorporates by reference existing flaws in the scope of §§ 162 and 167 as applied to employees. The § 132(d) definition needs to be considered in the context of the various deduction provisions discussed in Chapters 12, 19, and 20.

The *de minimis* fringe benefit exclusion applies to benefits which, considering the frequency with which the employer provides similar benefits, are unreasonable or administratively impractical to quantify. Under this standard, whether any given benefit qualifies for the exclusion depends upon the other benefits provided by that employer. Perhaps a more objective standard such as a total dollar amount should be provided, but such an objective standard could itself impose unreasonable administrative burdens.

---

[3]   Some special rules bring within the definition of working condition fringe benefits items that do not meet the general statutory definition. See § 132(j)(3).

Another approach would be to deny a deduction to the employer for the amount of the *de minimis* benefit, while still permitting employees to exclude the benefit, thus ensuring that it was not removed from the tax base altogether.

Exclusion on the ground that the amount involved is *de minimis* is limited to items received in-kind. American Airlines, Inc. v. United States, 204 F.3d 1103 (Fed.Cir.2000), held that $50 American Express vouchers charged to the employer's account that were provided to employees for their use at restaurants while traveling were not excludable as *de minimis* fringe benefits. As a practical matter the use of the vouchers was not restricted to employee travel. The court concluded that the vouchers were cash equivalents.

Section 132(e)(2) provides that subsidized meals at an eating facility on the employer's business premises are a *de minimis* fringe benefit if the revenues normally equal or exceed the direct operating costs. This rule does not apply, however, to "highly compensated employees" (as defined in § 414(q)), unless the facility is available on substantially equal terms to all employees or a reasonably classified group of employees that does not discriminate in favor of the highly compensated. Thus, a subsidized executive dining room does not qualify. It is hard to articulate a defensible policy reason for treating below market cost meals to employees as a tax-free fringe benefit when the aggregate value to certain employees could be substantial.

The nondiscrimination requirement of § 132(j)(1) generally does not apply to working condition or *de minimis* fringe benefits, a rule that effectively authorizes more benefits and better working conditions for highly compensated employees.

3. QUALIFIED TRANSPORTATION BENEFITS

Section 132(a)(5) excludes "qualified transportation fringe benefits" as defined in § 132(f). This exclusion applies to employer-provided parking, transit passes, and "commuter highway vehicle" use.[4] "Qualified parking" includes only parking at or near the employer's place of business or at or near a location from which the employee commutes to work in a car pool, on mass transit qualifying for the transit pass exclusion, or in a "commuter highway vehicle," as defined in § 132(f)(5)(B). Section 132(f)(2) limits the exclusion to $175 per month for qualified parking (adjusted for inflation; for 2016, the value is $255) and $100 per month in the aggregate for transit passes and qualified highway vehicle use (adjusted for inflation; for 2016, the value is $130). The anti-discrimination rules of § 132(j)(1) do not apply to qualified transportation benefits. Thus executives may be provided free parking while rank and file workers are not. Furthermore, § 132(f)(4) provides that if employees are offered a choice of free parking or cash and an employee accepts the free parking, no amount will be includable as a result of the employee having a choice between a cash or in-kind benefit. At the same

---

[4] Prior to the enactment of § 132(f), employer-provided parking at or near the employee's place of business was deemed to be an excludable working condition fringe benefit, even though commuting costs ordinarily are nondeductible.

time, this tax-free choice is not available for qualified transportation fringe benefits other than parking. See Treas. Reg. § 1.132–9 for detailed rules defining the scope of qualified transportation fringe benefits. The IRS has ruled that qualified transportation fringe benefits can be provided through smart cards, debit cards, or other electronic media issued to employees. To prevent abuse, electronically provided funds qualify for the exclusion only if the employer takes certain steps to ensure that all of the electronically provided funds are used solely for qualified transportation costs. Rev. Rul. 2006–57, 2006–47, 2 C.B. 911.

Thinking "green," Congress expanded the transportation fringe benefit to include any "qualified bicycle commuting reimbursement," which includes employer reimbursements "for the purchase of a bicycle and bicycle improvements, repair, and storage, if such bicycle is regularly used for travel between the employee's residence and place of employment." I.R.C. § 132(f)(5)(F)(i). The maximum amount of bicycle commuting reimbursements that may be excluded in any taxable year is $240. I.R.C. § 132(f)(5)(F)(ii).

4.   QUALIFIED RETIREMENT PLANNING SERVICES

Section 132(a)(7) excludes "qualified retirement planning services." Qualified retirement planning services are defined in § 132(m) as retirement planning advice or information provided to an employee and that employee's spouse by an employer maintaining a qualified pension plan. Qualifying advice is not limited to matters related to the qualified pension plan on which eligibility is based; it may extend to retirement income planning generally and how the employer's plan fits into the employee's overall retirement income planning. The exclusion under § 132(m) is subject to a nondiscrimination rule. The exclusion is available to highly compensated employees "only if such services are available on substantially the same terms to each member of the group of employees normally provided education and information regarding the employer's qualified employer plan." The legislative history indicates that this standard should permit employers to limit certain types of advice to individuals nearing retirement.

5.   QUALIFIED MOVING EXPENSE REIMBURSEMENT

Section 132(a)(6) excludes from income employer reimbursement for "qualified moving expenses." Section 132(g) defines qualified moving expense reimbursement as an amount paid on behalf of or to reimburse an employee for moving expenses that are deductible under § 217 (see Chapter 19, Section 2.4.), if paid by the employee. Only the reasonable expenses of moving household goods and personal effects and transportation and lodging to travel to an employee's new residence are excluded. Other moving expense reimbursements, including house-hunting expenses, are taxable.

6.   ATHLETIC FACILITIES

Section 132(j)(4) provides an additional, and otherwise unclassified tax-free fringe benefit, by excluding the value of the use of an athletic facility provided by the employer if the facility is operated by the employer on its business premises and substantially all the use of the facility is by employees, spouses, and dependents. It is not clear whether the exclusion is based on the difficulty of valuing the right to use an employer-provided athletic facility or to improve national physical fitness. Either way, not all employer-provided health club dues qualify as excludable fringe benefits.

7. EVALUATION OF SECTION 132

As originally enacted in 1984, § 132 might be viewed as a three-level response to the fringe benefits not otherwise governed by a special statutory provision. First, § 132 excludes working conditions and *de minimis* fringes for sound tax policy reasons (although the parameters of the exclusions may be questioned). Second, for reasons having little to do with tax policy, but to fulfill some other Congressional policies, § 132 exempts certain benefits, which typically have substantial value, while also trying to mitigate the negative impact of the exclusion on vertical equity by imposing a nondiscrimination requirement. Third, benefits not excluded by § 132 or another section are specifically includable in gross income under § 61(a)(1). However, the subsequent addition to § 132 of the qualified moving expense and qualified transportation expense fringe benefits (without subjecting either provision to nondiscrimination requirements) as well as the addition of qualified retirement planning services (which are subject to an anti-discrimination rule), indicates that Congress has deviated from the original justifications for § 132, and now simply considers the section a catchall for all tax-free fringe benefits.

8. SPECIAL VALUATION RULES

8.1. *General*

Although taxable fringe benefits generally are included at fair market value (Treas. Reg. § 1.61–21(b)(2)), the regulations provide special rules for valuing a variety of fringe benefits at other than fair market value. For example, Treas. Reg. § 1.61–21(d)–(f) provides rules governing valuation of the use of a company automobile for various purposes; Treas. Reg. § 1.61–21(g) provides rules for valuing noncommercial flights on company aircraft; Treas. Reg. § 1.61–21(h) provides rules for valuing flights on commercial aircraft; and Treas. Reg. § 1.61–21(j) provides rules for valuing meals at a company subsidized cafeteria.

8.2. *Below-Market Loans*

Section 7872 generally treats a compensation-related loan at a below-market interest rate as a payment of an amount equal to the foregone interest from the employer to the borrower (usually the employee) followed by a repayment to the employer. As a result, the employee realizes compensation income in the amount of the foregone interest. Whether the employee may claim an interest deduction under § 163 depends on the use to which the borrowed funds are put and whether the employee itemizes deductions (see Chapter 16, Section 2, Chapter 21, Section 5, and Chapter 22, Section 1.A.).

B. EMPLOYEE BENEFITS EXCLUDED FROM GROSS INCOME TO FURTHER SOCIAL POLICY GOALS

INTERNAL REVENUE CODE: Sections 79(a), (c), (d)(1)–(6); 105; 106(a); 117(d); 125(a), (b), (d); 127(a); 129(a); 137(a).

REGULATIONS: Section 1.61–1(a); 1.105–1, –2; 1.106–1.

Congress has enacted a number of provisions excluding specific fringe benefits of substantial value for the purpose of encouraging employers to offer the benefits to employees. These excluded fringe benefits include (1) health and accident insurance, (2) $50,000 face value of group term life insurance, (3) educational assistance, (4) dependent care assistance, and (5) adoption assistance. In each case Congress believed that worthy social goals would be advanced by providing a tax subsidy through the exclusion.

DETAILED ANALYSIS

1. HEALTH BENEFITS

In the absence of a specific statutory exclusion, payments by an employer that represent sickness, accident or similar benefits to the employee would constitute taxable compensation to the employee. See e.g., Waller v. United States, 180 F.2d 194 (D.C.Cir.1950) (taxing a pension for disabilities incurred in public health service); and Rev. Rul. 53–210, 1953–2 C.B. 114 (holding that the purchase by an employer of an individual accident insurance policy for an employee, with the employee having full rights thereunder, was income to the employee).

Sections 105 and 106 operate to provide an exclusion for health and accident benefits (including nursing home insurance[5]), but not for sick pay, provided by an employer, regardless of whether the provision of such benefits is through an insured plan or directly by the employer. Although the statutory explication of these rules is not straightforward, the results are reasonably clear. First, § 106 excludes any payments by an employer to a health or accident plan. Thus, medical or accident insurance premiums paid by an employer are excluded under § 106. Sections 104(a)(3) and 105 then govern the taxation of payments received from the accident or health plan, including in gross income payments received directly from the employer pursuant to an uninsured plan. While §§ 104(a)(3) and 105(a) appear to require inclusion of benefits, the effect of §§ 105(b) and (c) is to exclude benefits from employer-provided plans to the extent that the payments cover medical expenses (§ 105(b)) or are determined with reference to the type of injury suffered and do not relate to the period the employee is absent from work (I.R.C. § 105(c)).[6] The conditions for exclusion under §§ 105(b) and (c) are intended to prevent "sick pay" or similar disability insurance from

---

[5]   See I.R.C. § 7702B(a)(1), defining qualified long-term care insurance.

[6]   Compare the treatment of payments received under self-financed accident and health insurance, which are excluded from income by § 104(a)(3) except to the extent that they compensate the taxpayer for *past* medical expenses previously deducted under § 213. See Chapter 9, Section 3.A.

coming within the exclusion, thus leaving such receipts to be governed by § 105(a), rendering them taxable. See e.g., Beisler v. Commissioner, 814 F.2d 1304 (9th Cir.1987) (§ 105(c) excludes only amounts received from a "plan that varies the amount of payment according to the type and severity of the injury suffered by the employee"); Rosen v. United States, 829 F.2d 506 (4th Cir.1987) (§ 105 does not exclude payments received under a wage continuation plan following total disability); Berman v. Commissioner, 925 F.2d 936 (6th Cir.1991) (§ 105(c) does not exclude distributions received from a profit-sharing plan that treats retirement and permanent and total disability identically, i.e., the nature and amount of the payments are not determined with respect to the particular injury or illness). In Tuka v. Commissioner, 120 T.C. 1 (2003), the taxpayer argued that disability payments based on age, years of service, and salary, received from an employer sponsored plan were received under an insurance plan purchased by employees through wage concessions negotiated in a union contract, and therefore subject to exclusion under § 104(a)(3). The court rejected the taxpayer's argument, holding that the exclusion applied only if contributions to the accident and health plan were includable in the employee's gross income, while also noting that the contributions to the plan were directly made by the employer.

There are no anti-discrimination rules with respect to insured health and accident plans. Thus, for example, a closely held corporation may provide health insurance only for the shareholder-employees, and, unless the payments are recharacterized as a dividend rather than as an employee fringe benefit, §§ 105(b) and 106 will exclude both the insurance premiums and benefits. However, under § 105(h), the § 105(b) exclusion for medical cost reimbursements does not apply to benefits paid to highly compensated employees (as defined) if the plan is self-insured and discriminates in favor of that group as to coverage or benefits. Even if the plan discriminates, the exclusion remains in effect for other employees.

Section 106(b) excludes a limited amount of employer contributions to a qualified medical savings account (MSA) on behalf of an employee who is eligible to have an MSA. The exclusion applies only to employees whose employer-provided medical plans are "high deductible medical plans," as defined in § 220(c)(2). In addition, employees are not eligible if their employer had more than 50 employees in either of the two years preceding the first year in which a contribution to an MSA was made or employed an average of more than 200 employees on each day of any subsequent year in which a contribution is made. Unlike in the case of other health benefits excluded under § 106, a penalty tax is imposed on discriminatory MSA plans.

The exclusion of employer-provided medical benefits is one of the most significant tax expenditures in the Internal Revenue Code. For fiscal 2017, it is estimated to result in a revenue loss of $220 billion. Office of Management and Budget, Analytical Perspectives, Budget of the United States Government, Fiscal Year 2017 243 (2016). The tax treatment of expenditures for health care is an important national issue involving social and economic policy issues as well as revenue considerations. Although determining the proper theoretical treatment of employer paid medical benefits from a tax policy perspective is not difficult, assessing the proper tax treatment of medical expenses and benefits in practice must take into account these other policy issues as well.

2.   LIFE INSURANCE

Insurance premiums paid by the employer on policies on the life of an employee generally constitute taxable compensation where the employee's estate, spouse or children are the beneficiaries. See e.g., Genshaft v. Commissioner, 64 T.C. 282 (1975) (Acq.).

Section 79 provides an exception to this general rule by exempting the cost of up to $50,000 of group-term insurance coverage provided by the employer; coverage in excess of this amount is includable in gross income in an amount determined by tables appearing in the regulations. These tables are quite favorable to the taxpayer, reflecting a compromise between tax policy and non-tax policy considerations as described in Senate Finance Committee Report, S.Rep. No. 830, 88th Cong., 2d Sess. 46 (1964):

> [T]he tax-free status for employer-financed group term life insurance is inconsistent with the tax treatment of other types of life insurance protection furnished employees by their employers. * * * The employee in such case receives a substantial economic benefit from this insurance protection whether or not the policy for a specific year leads to a payment to his beneficiary." On the other hand, "from the standpoint of the economy as a whole, * * * it is desirable to encourage employers to provide life insurance protection for their employees. Provision of * * * a basic amount of insurance does much to keep together family units where the principal breadwinner dies prematurely.

For the technical definition of group-term life insurance for purposes of § 79, see Treas. Reg. § 1.79–1(a) and Rev. Rul. 71–360, 1971–2 C.B. 87.

Section 79(d) provides that if a group term life insurance plan is found to be discriminatory under the statutory tests, the premiums attributable to "key employees" are taxable, while the exclusion remains intact for other employees. This provision is designed to prevent group-term life insurance plans from discriminating in favor of key employees, either with respect to coverage or benefits available under the plan. At the same time, insurance benefits determined with respect to compensation, such as life insurance equal to twice annual compensation, are not considered discriminatory. I.R.C. § 79(d)(5).

3.   EDUCATIONAL BENEFITS

3.1. *Qualified Employer Educational Assistance Programs*

Section 127 excludes from an employee's income up to $5,250 per calendar year for amounts paid or incurred by the employer under a "qualified educational assistance program." Educational assistance that may be covered by employer payments includes tuition, fees, books, course supplies, and similar items, but does not include personal living expenses or any benefits for instruction involving recreational activities. Section 127 applies to graduate education as well as undergraduate education. A qualified educational assistance program must be established by a separate written plan of the employer, for the exclusive benefit of its employees, and must be nondiscriminatory both with respect to eligibility and to participation. No more than 5 percent of the employer's annual costs under the program may benefit officers, highly compensated individuals, or owners of more than 5 percent of the employer's stock, capital, or profits interests. A qualified plan may not permit employees to elect taxable compensation in lieu of educational assistance, nor may an employee claim any deduction or credit with respect to any amount excluded from income under § 127.

The avowed Congressional purposes in enacting § 127 were "to reduce the complexity * * * in this area" and to remove "the disincentive to upward mobility" occasioned by requiring "out-of-pocket tax payments for employer-provided educational assistance from those least able to pay, even though they receive only services, not an increased paycheck." S.Rep. No. 95–1263, 95th Cong., 2d Sess. 101 (1978).

3.2. *Tuition Remission Plans*

Section 117(d) excludes from gross income the amount of tuition reduction to an employee of an educational institution or certain family members for education below the graduate level at that institution or at another institution (generally one that has a reciprocal arrangement with the employee's institution). Officers, owners, and highly compensated employees may qualify for the exclusion only if the tuition reduction is available on a basis that does not discriminate in favor of those people.

4.   DEPENDENT CARE ASSISTANCE PROGRAMS

Section 129 excludes from an employee's gross income up to $5,000 paid by an employer for care—such as day care—of an employee's disabled dependents and dependent children under 13 years of age. See I.R.C. § 129(e)(1), incorporating by reference the disability requirement for dependents and age requirement for children in § 21(b)(2). Qualifying payments, which may be a reimbursement of the employee's out of pocket expenses, must be made pursuant to a written plan established by the employer. If the plan fails to meet statutory nondiscrimination requirements, benefits to certain highly compensated employees are taxable, but benefits to all other employees remain tax free as long as the plan meets the other statutory requirements.

5.   ADOPTION ASSISTANCE

Section 137 excludes from gross income qualified amounts paid pursuant to a qualified adoption assistance program maintained by an employer in connection with the employee's adoption of a child under 18 years of age or, if 18 years or older, a child physically or mentally incapable of caring for himself. Qualified adoption expenses include reasonable and necessary adoption fees, court costs, attorney's fees and other expenses to adopt an eligible child other than the taxpayer's spouse's child, which are not illegal or part of a surrogate parenting arrangement. The maximum amount excludable is $10,000 per child (adjusted for inflation; for 2016, the excludable amount is $13,460) regardless of the number of years over which the benefits are paid. For the adoption of "special needs" children, the full

$10,000 exclusion ($13,460 adjusted) is allowed regardless of the amount of qualified adoption expenses actually incurred. The exclusion is phased out ratably for employees whose adjusted gross income exceeds $150,000 (adjusted for inflation; for 2016, the figure is $201,920) and is completely phased out when the employee's adjusted gross income is $190,000 ($241,920 adjusted). The exclusion is not available to married taxpayers who file separate returns. To qualify, an adoption assistance program must be a separate written plan for the exclusive benefit of the employer's employees, eligible employees must receive reasonable notification of its existence and benefits, and the plan must not discriminate in favor of highly compensated employees or owner-employees.

6.   CAFETERIA PLANS

Despite their name, cafeteria plans do not necessarily involve food. The hallmark of cafeteria plans is that they allow an employee to choose among a buffet of cash and non-cash benefits. Section 125 provides that where employees may choose among benefits consisting of cash and certain statutory nontaxable benefits, the right to choose between taxable and non-taxable benefits will not cause a benefit otherwise excludable to be included in gross income. The statutory nontaxable benefits that may be offered include group-term life insurance, disability benefits, accident and health benefits (but not qualified long-term care insurance), dependent care, and qualified adoption assistance to the extent that such benefits are excluded from gross income. The exclusion granted by § 125 applies to highly compensated individuals only if the plan is nondiscriminatory as to coverage, eligibility, contributions, and benefits. An employee who chooses cash remains taxable on the cash payments.

7.   EVALUATION OF EXCLUSIONS OF FRINGE BENEFITS FOR SOCIAL POLICY PURPOSES

Many of the statutory exclusions from gross income for employer-provided benefits involve situations that do not raise the valuation issues discussed previously. Rather, they exclude benefits that have substantial value and substantial cost to the employer. Where the benefits are offered through a cafeteria plan, even the element of restricted choice is lacking. The nondiscrimination rules have no conceptual relationship to whether an item should be included in gross income.

Justification for most of these provisions must depend upon their success in achieving some nontax policy objective. Through these statutory exclusions Congress is in effect encouraging employers to provide (and employees to utilize) these benefits by making them more attractive than cash compensation. The employee is obviously better off receiving $100 of tax-free benefits than $100 of taxable compensation. From the employer's perspective, the cost of establishing a given level of after-tax compensation to the employee is reduced if a portion of that compensation can be paid through tax-free benefits. But such use of the tax system can have undesirable consequences. For instance, as previously discussed in connection with § 132, the value of the exclusion is greater for taxpayers in higher marginal brackets (even when the benefits are provided on a nondiscriminatory basis). Other problems are discussed in the following excerpt from U.S. Treasury Department, Tax Reform for Fairness, Simplicity, and Economic Growth, Vol. 1, 73–74 (1984), which proposed eliminating most of these statutory fringe benefits:

Many fringe benefits are not subject to tax under current law; among the most important fringe benefits presently excluded from tax are contributions to qualified retirement plans, and accident, health, and group term life insurance provided by employers. It is unfair that one taxpayer is excused from paying income tax on the value of a fringe benefit, while another who wants to enjoy the same good or service, but does not receive it as a fringe benefit, must purchase it with after-tax dollars. Nor is the solution to extend the exemption of fringe benefits even further, as some have suggested. Health care is made much more expensive for all because it is effectively subsidized through the tax system for some. The tax advantage now accorded some fringe benefits causes more of them to be consumed than if, like most goods and services, they could only be bought with after-tax income. This distortion of consumer choices would only be accentuated by widening the exemption of fringe benefits. Moreover, extending the scope of the exclusion of fringe benefits would exacerbate inequities in the treatment of employees receiving fringe benefits and those who receive income in other forms. Finally, the growing tendency to pay compensation in tax-exempt forms reduces the base for the social security taxes and thus weakens the social security system. These inequities and distortions can be reduced only if statutory fringe benefits are taxed more nearly like other income.

* * *

Presently the exclusion of fringe benefits from taxable income has gone so far that it has become necessary to offset the distorting effects of some tax provisions by allowing employers to offer a choice of tax-free benefits. On the one hand, current law encourages the use of tax-free forms of compensation, but on the other it attempts to counteract these incentives by allowing employers to offer employees the choice that is normally associated with payment of wages in cash. * * *

Taxing most statutory fringe benefits will greatly simplify the administration of the tax laws by relieving the pressure to pay compensation in non-taxable forms. Employers can continue, in effect, to offer certain goods and services for sale through salary deductions, but in the absence of tax inducements for paying wages as fringe benefits, most compensation will be in cash.

Employees will compare the full market prices of formerly subsidized consumption with other uses of their after-tax dollars. As a result, it is expected that employers will provide less life insurance and legal insurance, and that employees will purchase more directly. Purchases of insurance for marginal amounts of health coverage will also decline. These purchases are often quite inefficient because administrative costs, while small relative to large health bills, can be quite large relative to the cost of moderate or small amounts of health care. The rapidly rising cost of health care in the United States can be attributed in part to the large subsidy inherent in the current tax laws. The proposal to cap these health insurance benefits will help contain future increases in costs of health care.

Repeal of the current exemption of fringe benefits will require both employees and employers to reconsider the mix of fringe benefits offered and accepted. To allow time for adjustment, taxation of fringe benefits will be phased in gradually, as existing employment contracts expire.

CHAPTER 4

GIFTS, INHERITANCES, AND SIMILAR ITEMS

SECTION 1.   GIFTS AND INHERITANCES

A. EXCLUSION FOR GIFTS AND INHERITANCES

INTERNAL REVENUE CODE: Section 102.

REGULATIONS: Section 1.102–1(a), (b).

Section 102 excludes from the income of a donee the amount or value of any gift or inheritance (generally, "gratuitous transfers") received, but no provision allows the donor a deduction for gratuitous transfers. The appropriate treatment of gratuitous transfers in an income tax has been the subject of extensive discussion among tax theorists. There are three ways gratuitous transfers could be included in the base of an income tax: (1) inclusion by the donee with no deduction by the donor; (2) inclusion by the donee with a deduction for the donor; and (3) exclusion from gross income by the donee with no deduction by the donor.

Approach (1) was advocated by Henry Simons whose view was that inclusion of the gift in the income of the donee is required because the receipt of the gift produces an increase in net worth. The donor is not entitled to a deduction under this approach because the gift is a nondeductible consumption expenditure; the donor receives psychic satisfaction from the act of giving.

[handwritten margin note: when the donee rec the gift, it was an increase in their gain of wealth, the donor just gave something which made them feel good.]

Approach (2)—allowing a deduction to the donor and requiring the gift to be included in the income of the donee—avoids the creation of additional income that results from approach (1). This approach may be defended on the ground that the only consumption that occurs is when the donee spends or uses the gift. Because there is no consumption by the donor, the donor should be allowed a deduction. At the same time, this approach would facilitate avoidance of the progressive tax rates in § 1 by permitting high income family members to shift the incidence of taxation to lower income family members.

[handwritten margin note: Instead of rich paying taxes, they would just give their money to the poor.]

Approach (3), the current rule, is generally defended on the ground that an intrafamily gift does not generate additional economic income. This is in contrast to approach (1) where income inclusion for the donee without allowing a deduction for the donor assumes that the gift transaction increases total income. To illustrate: A earns $100 which A gives to B who spends it on food. The total amount of economic consumption in the economy is $100. Meanwhile, Approach (1) produces the result that the $100 gift has created $200 of consumption in the economy.

The current rule also is more easily administrable than the other two approaches. Including gratuitous transfers in income would present significant valuation problems where gifts of property were involved and would require distinguishing taxable gifts from tax-free support. Perhaps the major strength of the current rule lies in its avoiding these administrative difficulties.

This Section is concerned with identifying gifts and inheritances excluded by § 102 and distinguishing them from other receipts that are includable in gross income.

DETAILED ANALYSIS

1.   GIFTS AND INHERITANCES OF APPRECIATED PROPERTY

While the value of property transferred as a gift or at death is excluded from income under § 102, the income tax treatment of gifts and inheritances of property ultimately depends on the tax consequences to the transferee upon a subsequent sale. Generally speaking, the donee of a gift takes the same basis for computing gain or loss on a subsequent sale as the donor, and a person who inherits property takes a basis equal to the fair market value of the property on the date of the decedent's death. These issues are discussed in Chapter 7.

2.   GIFTS AND INHERITANCES OF INCOME

Income generated by the gift or inheritance is not itself excluded, Thus, while the value of cash or property received as a gift or inheritance is not included in gross income under § 102, interest, dividends, or other income received with respect to transferred property are included. This issue is discussed in greater detail in Chapter 7.

B.   THE MEANING OF "GIFT" OR "INHERITANCE"

INTERNAL REVENUE CODE: Sections 102(c); 274(b)(1); 1014(a), (b).

REGULATIONS: Section 1.274–3(a), (b)(1).

The treatment of intra familial gratuitous transfers as a gift or inheritance excluded by § 102 is fairly straightforward. More difficult issues arise, however, when a putative gift is received from a person with whom the taxpayer has some business or commercial relationship.

Commissioner v. Duberstein
Supreme Court of the United States, 1960.
363 U.S. 278.

■ MR. JUSTICE BRENNAN delivered the opinion of the Court.

These two cases concern the provision of the Internal Revenue Code which excludes from the gross income of an income taxpayer "the value

[handwritten margin note:] The "GIFT" you rec is not considered taxable income, BUT. If you make money from the gift or inheritance, then it is!

[handwritten margin note:] These two cases deal with property (value) rec. as a gift.

of property acquired by gift."[1] They pose the frequently recurrent question whether a specific transfer to a taxpayer in fact amounted to a "gift" to him within the meaning of the statute. The importance to decision of the facts of the cases requires that we state them in some detail.

No. 376, Commissioner v. Duberstein. The taxpayer, Duberstein, was president of the Duberstein Iron & Metal Company, a corporation with headquarters in Dayton, Ohio. For some years the taxpayer's company had done business with Mohawk Metal Corporation, whose headquarters were in New York City. The president of Mohawk was one Berman. The taxpayer and Berman had generally used the telephone to transact their companies' business with each other, which consisted of buying and selling metals. The taxpayer testified, without elaboration, that he knew Berman "personally" and had known him for about seven years. From time to time in their telephone conversations, Berman would ask Duberstein whether the latter knew of potential customers for some of Mohawk's products in which Duberstein's company itself was not interested. Duberstein provided the names of potential customers for these items.

One day in 1951 Berman telephoned Duberstein and said that the information Duberstein had given him had proved so helpful that he wanted to give the latter a present. Duberstein stated that Berman owed him nothing. Berman said that he had a Cadillac as a gift for Duberstein, and that the latter should send to New York for it; Berman insisted that Duberstein accept the car, and the latter finally did so, protesting however that he had not intended to be compensated for the information. At the time Duberstein already had a Cadillac and an Oldsmobile, and felt that he did not need another car. Duberstein testified that he did not think Berman would have sent him the Cadillac if he had not furnished him with information about the customers. It appeared that Mohawk later deducted the value of the Cadillac as a business expense on its corporate income tax return.

Duberstein did not include the value of the Cadillac in gross income for 1951, deeming it a gift. The Commissioner asserted a deficiency for the car's value against him, and in proceedings to review the deficiency, the Tax Court affirmed the Commissioner's determination. It said that "The record is significantly barren of evidence revealing any intention on the part of the payor to make a gift. * * * The only justifiable inference is that the automobile was intended by the payor to be remuneration for services rendered to it by Duberstein." The Court of Appeals for the Sixth Circuit reversed. 265 F.2d 28.

No. 546, Stanton v. United States. The taxpayer, Stanton, had been for approximately 10 years in the employ of Trinity Church in New York

---

[1]   The operative provision in the cases at bar is § 22(b)(3) of the 1939 Internal Revenue Code. The corresponding provision of the present Code is § 102(a).

City. He was comptroller of the Church corporation, and president of a corporation, Trinity Operating Company, the church set up as a fully owned subsidiary to manage its real estate holdings, which were more extensive than simply the church property. His salary by the end of his employment there in 1942 amounted to $22,500 a year. Effective November 30, 1942, he resigned from both positions to go into business for himself. The Operating Company's directors, who seem to have included the rector and vestrymen of the church, passed the following resolution upon his resignation: "BE IT RESOLVED that in appreciation of the services rendered by Mr. Stanton * * * a gratuity is hereby awarded to him of Twenty Thousand Dollars, payable to him in equal installments of Two Thousand Dollars at the end of each and every month commencing with the month of December, 1942; provided that, with the discontinuance of his services, the Corporation of Trinity Church is released from all rights and claims to pension and retirement benefits not already accrued up to November 30, 1942."

The Operating Company's action was later explained by one of its directors as based on the fact that, "Mr. Stanton was liked by all of the Vestry personally. He had a pleasing personality. He had come in when Trinity's affairs were in a difficult situation. He did a splendid piece of work * * *." And by another: "[W]e were all unanimous in wishing to make Mr. Stanton a gift. Mr. Stanton had loyally and faithfully served Trinity in a very difficult time. * * *"

On the other hand, there was a suggestion of some ill-feeling between Stanton and the directors, arising out of the recent termination of the services of one Watkins the Operating Company's treasurer, whose departure was evidently attended by some acrimony. At a special board meeting on October 28, 1942, Stanton had intervened on Watkins' side and asked reconsideration of the matter. * * * Stanton announced that in order to avoid any such embarrassment or question at any time as to his willingness to resign if the Board desired, he was tendering his resignation. It was tabled, though not without dissent. The next week, on November 5, at another special meeting, Stanton again tendered his resignation which this time was accepted.

The "gratuity" was duly paid. So was a smaller one to Stanton's (and the Operating Company's) secretary, under a similar resolution, upon her resignation at the same time. The two corporations shared the expense of the payments. There was undisputed testimony that there were in fact no enforceable rights or claims to pension and retirement benefits which had not accrued at the time of the taxpayer's resignation, and that the last proviso of the resolution was inserted simply out of an abundance of caution. The taxpayer received in cash a refund of his contributions to the retirement plans, and there is no suggestion that he was entitled to more. He was required to perform no further services for Trinity after his resignation.

The Commissioner asserted a deficiency against the taxpayer after the latter had failed to include the payments in question in gross income. After payment of the deficiency and administrative rejection of a refund claim, the taxpayer sued the United States for a refund in the District Court for the Eastern District of New York. The trial judge, sitting without a jury, made the simple finding that the payments were a "gift," and judgment was entered for the taxpayer. The Court of Appeals for the Second Circuit reversed. 268 F.2d 727.

The Government, urging that clarification of the problem typified by these two cases was necessary, and that the approaches taken by the Courts of Appeals for the Second and the Sixth Circuits were in conflict, petitioned for certiorari in No. 376, and acquiesced in the taxpayer's petition in No. 546. On this basis, and because of the importance of the question in the administration of the income tax laws, we granted certiorari in both cases. 361 U.S. 923.

The exclusion of property acquired by gift from gross income under the federal income tax laws was made in the first income tax statute passed under the authority of the Sixteenth Amendment, and has been a feature of the income tax statutes ever since. The meaning of the term "gift" as applied to particular transfers has always been a matter of contention. Specific and illuminating legislative history on the point does not appear to exist. Analogies and inferences drawn from other revenue provisions, such as the estate and gift taxes, are dubious. See Lockard v. Commissioner, 166 F.2d 409. The meaning of the statutory term has been shaped largely by the decisional law. With this, we turn to the contentions made by the Government in these cases.

First. The Government suggests that we promulgate a new "test" in this area to serve as a standard to be applied by the lower courts and by the Tax Court in dealing with the numerous cases that arise.[6] We reject this invitation. We are of opinion that the governing principles are necessarily general and have already been spelled out in the opinions of this Court, and that the problem is one which, under the present statutory framework, does not lend itself to any more definitive statement that would produce a talisman for the solution of concrete cases. The cases at bar are fair examples of the settings in which the problem usually arises. They present situations in which payments have been made in a context with business overtones—an employer making a payment to a retiring employee; a businessman giving something of value to another businessman who has been of advantage to him in his business. In this context, we review the law as established by the prior cases here.

The course of decision here makes it plain that the statute does not use the term "gift" in the common-law sense, but in a more colloquial

---

6   The Government's proposed test is stated: "Gifts should be defined as transfers of property made for personal as distinguished from business reasons."

sense. This Court has indicated that a voluntary executed transfer of his property by one to another, without any consideration or compensation therefor, though a common-law gift, is not necessarily a "gift" within the meaning of the statute. For the Court has shown that the mere absence of a legal or moral obligation to make such a payment does not establish that it is a gift. Old Colony Trust Co. v. Commissioner, 279 U.S. 716, 730. And, importantly, if the payment proceeds primarily from "the constraining force of any moral or legal duty," or from "the incentive of anticipated benefit" of an economic nature, Bogardus v. Commissioner, 302 U.S. 34, 41, it is not a gift. And, conversely, "[w]here the payment is in return for services rendered, it is irrelevant that the donor derives no economic benefit from it." Robertson v. United States, 343 U.S. 711, 714.[7] A gift in the statutory sense, on the other hand, proceeds from a "detached and disinterested generosity," Commissioner v. LoBue, 351 U.S. 243, 246; "out of affection, respect, admiration, charity or like impulses." Robertson v. United States, supra, at 714. And in this regard, the most critical consideration, as the Court was agreed in the leading case here, is the transferor's "intention." Bogardus v. Commissioner, 302 U.S. 34, 43. "What controls is the intention with which payment, however voluntary, has been made." Id., at 45 (dissenting opinion).[8]

The Government says that this "intention" of the transferor cannot mean what the cases on the common-law concept of gift call "donative intent." With that we are in agreement, for our decisions fully support this. Moreover, the Bogardus case itself makes it plain that the donor's characterization of his action is not determinative—that there must be an objective inquiry as to whether what is called a gift amounts to it in reality. 302 U.S., at 40. It scarcely needs adding that the parties' expectations or hopes as to the tax treatment of their conduct in themselves have nothing to do with the matter.

It is suggested that the Bogardus criterion would be more apt if rephrased in terms of "motive" rather than "intention." We must confess to some skepticism as to whether such a verbal mutation would be of any practical consequence. We take it that the proper criterion, established by decision here, is one that inquires what the basic reason for his conduct was in fact—the dominant reason that explains his action in making the transfer. Further than that we do not think it profitable to go.

---

[7]   The cases including "tips" in gross income are classic examples of this. See, e.g., Roberts v. Commissioner, 176 F.2d 221.

[8]   The parts of the Bogardus opinion which we touch on here are the ones we take to be basic to its holding, and the ones that we read as stating those governing principles which it establishes. As to them, we see little distinction between the views of the Court and those taken in dissent in Bogardus. The fear expressed by the dissent at 302 U.S., at 44, that the prevailing opinion "seems" to hold "that every payment which in any aspect is a gift is * * * relieved of any tax" strikes us now as going beyond what the opinion of the Court held in fact. In any event, the Court's opinion in Bogardus does not seem to have been so interpreted afterwards. The principal difference, as we see it, between the Court's opinion and the dissent lies in the weight to be given the findings of the trier of fact.

Second. The Government's proposed "test," while apparently simple and precise in its formulation, depends frankly on a set of "principles" or "presumptions" derived from the decided cases, and concededly subject to various exceptions; and it involves various corollaries, which add to its detail. Were we to promulgate this test as a matter of law, and accept with it its various presuppositions and stated consequences, we would be passing far beyond the requirements of the cases before us, and would be painting on a large canvas with indeed a broad brush. The Government derives its test from such propositions as the following: That payments by an employer to an employee, even though voluntary, ought, by and large, to be taxable; that the concept of a gift is inconsistent with a payment's being a deductible business expense; that a gift involves "personal" elements; that a business corporation cannot properly make a gift of its assets. The Government admits that there are exceptions and qualifications to these propositions. We think, to the extent they are correct, that these propositions are not principles of law but rather maxims of experience that the tribunals which have tried the facts of cases in this area have enunciated in explaining their factual determinations. Some of them simply represent truisms: it doubtless is, statistically speaking, the exceptional payment by an employer to an employee that amounts to a gift. Others are overstatements of possible evidentiary inferences relevant to a factual determination on the totality of circumstances in the case: it is doubtless relevant to the over-all inference that the transferor treats a payment as a business deduction, or that the transferor is a corporate entity. But these inferences cannot be stated in absolute terms. Neither factor is a shibboleth. The taxing statute does not make nondeductibility by the transferor a condition on the "gift" exclusion; nor does it draw any distinction, in terms, between transfers by corporations and individuals, as to the availability of the "gift" exclusion to the transferee. The conclusion whether a transfer amounts to a "gift" is one that must be reached on consideration of all the factors.

Specifically, the trier of fact must be careful not to allow trial of the issue whether the receipt of a specific payment is a gift to turn into a trial of the tax liability, or of the propriety, as a matter of fiduciary or corporate law, attaching to the conduct of someone else. The major corollary to the Government's suggested "test" is that, as an ordinary matter, a payment by a corporation cannot be a gift, and, more specifically, there can be no such thing as a "gift" made by a corporation which would allow it to take a deduction for an ordinary and necessary business expense. As we have said, we find no basis for such a conclusion in the statute; and if it were applied as a determinative rule of "law," it would force the tribunals trying tax cases involving the donee's liability into elaborate inquiries into the local law of corporations or into the peripheral deductibility of payments as business expenses. The former issue might make the tax tribunals the most frequent investigators of an important and difficult issue of the laws of the several States, and the latter inquiry would summon one difficult and delicate problem of federal tax law as an aid to the solution of another.[9] Or perhaps there would be required a trial of the vexed issue whether there was a "constructive" distribution of corporate property, for income tax purposes, to the corporate agents who had sponsored the transfer. These considerations, also reinforce us in our conclusion that while the principles urged by the Government may, in nonabsolute form as crystallizations of experience, prove persuasive to the trier of facts in a particular case, neither they, nor any more detailed statement than has been made, can be laid down as a matter of law.

Third. Decision of the issue presented in these cases must be based ultimately on the application of the fact-finding tribunal's experience with the mainsprings of human conduct to the totality of the facts of each case. The nontechnical nature of the statutory standard, the close relationship of it to the data of practical human experience, and the multiplicity of relevant factual elements, with their various combinations, creating the necessity of ascribing the proper force to each, confirm us in our conclusion that primary weight in this area must be given to the conclusions of the trier of fact. * * *

This conclusion may not satisfy an academic desire for tidiness, symmetry and precision in this area, any more than a system based on the determinations of various fact-finders ordinarily does. But we see it as implicit in the present statutory treatment of the exclusion for gifts, and in the variety of forums in which federal income tax cases can be tried. If there is fear of undue uncertainty or overmuch litigation, Congress may make more precise its treatment of the matter by singling out certain factors and making them determinative of the matter * * * . Doubtless diversity of result will tend to be lessened somewhat since federal income tax decisions, even those in tribunals of first instance turning on issues of fact, tend to be reported, and since there may be a natural tendency of professional triers of fact to follow one another's determinations, even as to factual matters. But the question here remains basically one of fact, for determination on a case-by-case basis.

One consequence of this is that appellate review of determinations in this field must be quite restricted. Where a jury has tried the matter upon correct instructions, the only inquiry is whether it cannot be said that reasonable men could reach differing conclusions on the issue. Baker v. Texas & Pacific R. Co., supra, at 228. Where the trial has been by a judge without a jury, the judge's findings must stand unless "clearly erroneous." Fed.Rules Civ.Proc., 52(a). "A finding is 'clearly erroneous' when although there is evidence to support it, the reviewing court on the entire evidence is left with the definite and firm conviction that a mistake

---

[9]   Justice Cardozo once described in memorable language the inquiry into whether an expense was an "ordinary and necessary" one of a business: "One struggles in vain for any verbal formula that will supply a ready touchstone. The standard set up by the statute is not a rule of law; it is rather a way of life. Life in all its fullness must supply the answer to the riddle." Welch v. Helvering, 290 U.S. 111, 115. The same comment well fits the issue in the cases at bar.

has been committed." United States v. United States Gypsum Co., 333 U.S. 364, 395. The rule itself applies also to factual inferences from undisputed basic facts, id., at 394, as will on many occasions be presented in this area. * * * And Congress has in the most explicit terms attached the identical weight to the findings of the Tax Court. I.R.C., § 7482(a).

Fourth. A majority of the Court is in accord with the principles just outlined. And, applying them to the *Duberstein* case, we are in agreement, on the evidence we have set forth, that it cannot be said that the conclusion of the Tax Court was "clearly erroneous." It seems to us plain that as trier of the facts it was warranted in concluding that despite the characterization of the transfer of the Cadillac by the parties and the absence of any obligation, even of a moral nature, to make it, it was at bottom a recompense for Duberstein's past services, or an inducement for him to be of further service in the future. We cannot say with the Court of Appeals that such a conclusion was "mere suspicion" on the Tax Court's part. To us it appears based in the sort of informed experience with human affairs that fact-finding tribunals should bring to this task.

As to *Stanton,* we are in disagreement. To four of us, it is critical here that the District Court as trier of fact made only the simple and unelaborated finding that the transfer in question was a "gift." To be sure, conciseness is to be strived for, and prolixity avoided, in findings; but, to the four of us, there comes a point where findings become so sparse and conclusory as to give no revelation of what the District Court's concept of the determining facts and legal standard may be. * * * While the standard of law in this area is not a complex one, we four think the unelaborated finding of ultimate fact here cannot stand as a fulfillment of these requirements. It affords the reviewing court not the semblance of an indication of the legal standard with which the trier of fact has approached his task. For all that appears, the District Court may have viewed the form of the resolution or the simple absence of legal consideration as conclusive. While the judgment of the Court of Appeals cannot stand, the four of us think there must be further proceedings in the District Court looking toward new and adequate findings of fact. In this, we are joined by MR. JUSTICE WHITTAKER, who agrees that the findings were inadequate, although he does not concur generally in this opinion.

Accordingly, in No. 376, the judgment of this Court is that the judgment of the Court of Appeals is reversed, and in No. 546, that the judgment of the Court of Appeals, is vacated, and the case is remanded to the District Court for further proceedings not inconsistent with this opinion.

It is so ordered.

* * *

■ MR. JUSTICE FRANKFURTER, concurring in the judgment in No. 376 and dissenting in No. 546.

As the Court's opinion indicates, we brought these two cases here partly because of a claimed difference in the approaches between two Courts of Appeals but primarily on the Government's urging that, in the interest of the better administration of the income tax laws, clarification was desirable for determining when a transfer of property constitutes a "gift" and is not to be included in income for purposes of ascertaining the "gross income" under the Internal Revenue Code. As soon as this problem emerged after the imposition of the first income tax authorized by the Sixteenth Amendment, it became evident that its inherent difficulties and subtleties would not easily yield to the formulation of a general rule or test sufficiently definite to confine within narrow limits the area of judgment in applying it. * * *

Despite acute arguments at the bar and a most thorough re-examination of the problem on a full canvass of our prior decisions and an attempted fresh analysis of the nature of the problem, the Court has rejected the invitation of the Government to fashion anything like a litmus paper test for determining what is excludable as a "gift" from gross income. Nor has the Court attempted a clarification of the particular aspects of the problem presented by these two cases, namely, payment by an employer to an employee upon the termination of the employment relation and non-obligatory payment for services rendered in the course of a business relationship. While I agree that experience has shown the futility of attempting to define, by language so circumscribing as to make it easily applicable, what constitutes a gift for every situation where the problem may arise, I do think that greater explicitness is possible in isolating and emphasizing factors which militate against a gift in particular situations.

Thus, regarding the two frequently recurring situations involved in these cases—things of value given to employees by their employers upon the termination of employment and payments entangled in a business relation and occasioned by the performance of some service—the strong implication is that the payment is of a business nature. The problem in these two cases is entirely different from the problem in a case where a payment is made from one member of a family to another, where the implications are directly otherwise. No single general formulation appropriately deals with both types of cases, although both involve the question whether the payment was a "gift." While we should normally suppose that a payment from father to son was a gift, unless the contrary is shown, in the two situations now before us the business implications are so forceful that I would apply a presumptive rule placing the burden upon the beneficiary to prove the payment wholly unrelated to his services to the enterprise. The Court, however, has declined so to analyze the problem * * * .

The Court has made only one authoritative addition to the previous course of our decisions. Recognizing Bogardus v. Commissioner, 302 U.S. 34, as "the leading case here" and finding essential accord between the

Court's opinion and the dissent in that case, the Court has drawn from the dissent in *Bogardus* for infusion into what will now be a controlling qualification, recognition that it is "for the triers of the facts to seek among competing aims or motives the ones that dominated conduct." 302 U.S. 34, 45 (dissenting opinion). * * *

* * * What the Court now does sets fact-finding bodies to sail on an illimitable ocean of individual beliefs and experiences. This can hardly fail to invite, if indeed not encourage, too individualized diversities in the administration of the income tax law. * * *

DETAILED ANALYSIS

1.   GIFTS TO EMPLOYEES

1.1. *"In Appreciation" Cases*

In *Stanton,* the companion case to *Duberstein,* the District Court on remand found the amount to be an exempt gift. This finding was upheld by the Court of Appeals, applying the *Duberstein* review standard, 287 F.2d 876 (2d Cir.1961), aff'g per curiam, 186 F.Supp. 393 (E.D.N.Y.1960). Schall v. Commissioner, 174 F.2d 893 (5th Cir.1949), and several other cases, held that payments to retired ministers were nontaxable gifts under § 102 in light of the close personal relationship between the recipient and the congregation, and in Rev. Rul. 55–422, 1955–1 C.B. 14, the IRS stated that it would follow those cases. Those clergy cases appear to be *sui generis*, however, and in Goodwin v. United States, 67 F.3d 149 (8th Cir.1995), cash payments to a minister from his congregation, which were called "special occasion gifts," were compensation, not gifts excludable under § 102, because they were regular, made by the congregation as a whole out of anonymous contributions, and were substantial in amount relative to the minister's annual salary.

The courts generally have found payments by employers to employees upon termination of employment to be taxable. See e.g., Miller v. United States, 362 F.Supp. 1242 (E.D.Tenn.1973) (monthly payments made by former employer until terminated corporate executive found substitute employment); Hubert v. Commissioner, 212 F.2d 516 (5th Cir.1954) ("honorarium" paid to law professor for services in connection with the state law institute). In a similar vein, employment-related payments at Christmas and other holidays have also generally been held to be taxable. See e.g., Teitelbaum v. Commissioner, 294 F.2d 541 (7th Cir.1961) (payments to an attorney by a client, denominated "Christmas Gift" but intended to cover additional expenses, held to be taxable as compensation and not a gift). Rev. Rul. 59–58, 1959–1 C.B. 17, held that the value of a turkey, ham, or other item of nominal value distributed to an employee by an employer at Christmas does not constitute income. But the theory of this ruling presumably is the *de minimis* nature of the item, not that it qualifies as a gift.

1.2. *Statutory Rule*

In 1986 Congress enacted § 102(c), foreclosing employees from claiming that payments from an employer are gifts. An exclusion for some "gifts" in kind may be allowed as a *de minimis* fringe benefit under § 132(a)(4), Chapter 3, Section 3.A.2. See Treas. Reg. § 1.132–6(e). Curiously, § 102(c) on its face applies only to a current employment relationship, and the legislative history does not clarify whether Congress intended the provision to bar gift treatment for an "in appreciation" payment to a former employee after retirement. Nor, apparently, does § 102(c) apply to independent contractors. Thus, cases such as *Teitelbaum* still may arise. Clearly, § 102(c) does not apply to a *Duberstein*-type situation.

Rev. Rul. 2003–12, 2003–1 C.B. 283, held that under § 102(c) amounts received by an individual from an employer to reimburse the individual for necessary medical, temporary housing, or transportation expenses incurred as a result of a flood are not excludable as a gift, but are excluded from gross income as qualified disaster relief under § 139 if the flood was a Presidentially declared disaster.

2.   EMPLOYEE DEATH BENEFITS CASES

The Supreme Court's refusal to give any guidance in the business gifts area and its decision to rely instead on the "fact-finding tribunal's experience with the mainsprings of human conduct" has led to widely disparate results. The treatment of payments made by corporations to surviving spouses of deceased corporate officers and executives has been a recurring problem. Section 102(c) does not expressly apply to these cases. As might be expected, the cases are not easy to classify. In general, the Tax Court has tended to find gross income while the District Courts by and large have found the payments to be gifts.

The Courts of Appeals, with their scope of review limited by *Duberstein,* generally have upheld the finding of the trier of fact. See e.g., Estate of Cronheim v. Commissioner, 323 F.2d 706 (8th Cir.1963) (Tax Court finding of taxable compensation affirmed since no "definite and firm conviction that a mistake has been committed"). Sometimes, however, the trial court has either been reversed or remanded for further findings. See e.g., Estate of Kuntz v. Commissioner, 300 F.2d 849 (6th Cir.1962) (reversal where the only indication of compensatory motivation was one statement in a corporate resolution).

In Estate of Carter v. Commissioner, 453 F.2d 61 (2d Cir.1971), the employer paid to the widow of a deceased employee an amount equal to the salary the employee would have earned under his contract if he had lived until the end of the fiscal year. The Tax Court found the payment to be income but the Court of Appeals reversed. After an exhaustive review of the precedents, the court observed that "the Tax Court and the district courts have been traveling different paths" and concluded: "We cannot believe the Supreme Court intended that, at least in an area where, in contrast to the entire field of controversy with respect to gifts versus compensation, similar fact patterns tend to recur so often, the result should depend on whether a widow could afford to pay the tax and sue for a refund rather than avail herself of the salutary remedy Congress intended to afford in establishing the Tax Court and permitting determination before payment. The 'mainsprings of human conduct' * * * do not differ so radically according to who tries the facts." In Bank of Palm Beach & Trust Co. v. United States, 476 F.2d 1343 (Ct.Cl.1973), the Court of Claims allowed a deduction to the employer for the same payments which were held nontaxable to the widow of the employee in *Estate of Carter*. Section 274(b), discussed below, limits the deduction for years after 1962.

3. LIMITATION ON DEDUCTIONS FOR "BUSINESS GIFTS"

Section 274(b)(1), as a general rule, disallows as a deduction all expenses for "gifts" to individuals in excess of $25 per person per year. The section by its terms applies to all payments excludable by the recipient under § 102.

In contrast to the intrafamilial gift situation, the amount of the "gift" in a business context typically constitutes a deductible business expense to the paying business. If the item is then excluded from the donee's income, it will never enter the income tax base. Thus, the arguments with respect to intrafamilial gifts are not applicable in the business context. In principle, the recipient should include the item in income. But it is often difficult as an administrative matter to include in the donee's income the value of business "gifts;" the individual item may be small in amount, there may be numerous recipients, and there may be problems of valuation. As a "second best" solution to these problems, the business "donor" may be denied a deduction. Such an action insures that the value of the gift is included in the income tax base, although tax is not imposed on the theoretically correct taxpayer, the donee. This second best approach was adopted by Congress with the enactment of § 247(b)(1) in 1962 to deal with the business gift situation.

The correct theoretical answer is that the cost of the "business gift" should be deductible, but that its value should be includable as income to the recipient. The solution in § 274(b) might inaccurately measure the tax base because the consumption value to the recipient will not necessarily be the same as the cost to the transferor. Nevertheless, it assures that consumption will not escape taxation altogether. Its effectiveness very well might be demonstrated by the substantial reduction of business-related gift cases arising after its enactment.

4. PAYMENTS BY OTHERS THAN EMPLOYERS

4.1. *Tips*

Tips are included in gross income. Treas. Reg. § 1.61–2; Roberts v. Commissioner, 176 F.2d 221 (9th Cir.1949) (upholding validity of Regulations). Olk v. United States, 388 F.Supp. 1108 (D.Nev.1975), found that "tokes" received from patrons by the taxpayer, a craps dealer in a Las Vegas casino, were gifts and not taxable income. The payments were not for any special services rendered by the dealer to a patron but were motivated by "sudden impulses of generosity" on the part of successful players to share their good fortune with others. Despite the *Duberstein* standard of review, the Court of Appeals reversed: "Tribute to the gods of fortune which it is hoped will be returned bounteously soon can only be described as an 'involved and intensely interested' act." Hence, the payments did not stem from the "detached or disinterested generosity" required by *Duberstein*. In holding that payments were not gifts, the court stated that "receipts by taxpayers engaged in rendering services contributed by those with whom the taxpayers have some personal or functional contact in the course of the performance of the services are taxable income when in conformity with the practices of the area and easily valued." 536 F.2d 876 (9th Cir.1976).

Determining the actual amount of tip income involves difficult factual questions. The IRS often has taken the position, as a rule of thumb, that 10 percent of gross receipts constitute tips. See e.g., *Roberts,* supra (taxi cab driver required to include 10 percent of his fares in income); Thomas v. Commissioner, T.C. Memo. 1973–261 (10 percent of a random sampling of a waitress' total weekly sales held to be average tip income). In some cases, the Commissioner has determined tipping rates by computing the average tips on credit card sales. See e.g., Applegate v. Commissioner, T.C. Memo. 1980–497. Compare Marvin v. Commissioner, T.C. Memo. 1980–509 (court reduced a tipping rate which had been established in such a manner; the method overstated the tipping rate since only 30 percent of the restaurant's sales were charged and tips on credit cards were considerably higher than cash tips).[1] In Schroeder v. Commissioner, 40 T.C. 30 (1963), a waitress reported only a little over 2 percent of her receipts as tips. The IRS asserted a deficiency based on tips at a rate of 12 percent. The court, in holding for the Government, stated: "We find it impossible to believe that the caliber of customers frequenting Frenchy's which serves gourmet food like Australian Kangaroo, Deep South Raccoon, and African Hippopotamus Steak, tip in the ridiculously low amounts claimed by petitioner."

The IRS has gone to great lengths to determine tip income of dealers and servers in casinos. In Ross v. Commissioner, T.C. Memo. 1989–682, aff'd by order, 967 F.2d 590 (9th Cir.1992), the tip income of a casino cocktail server was determined by multiplying the number of hours she worked by the average hourly tip rate for all casino cocktail servers as determined by the IRS through statistical analysis based on undercover surveillance of casinos.

Section 6053, dealing with the reporting of tip income by employers on the employee's form W-2, assumes an 8 percent tipping rate.

4.2. *Strike Benefits*

In Kaiser v. United States, 158 F.Supp. 865 (E.D.Wis.1958), a jury found that strike benefits were a gift. The lower court then held that as a matter of law the benefits were gross income and not gifts. The decision was reversed on appeal. Kaiser v. United States, 262 F.2d 367 (7th Cir.1958). The court stated that the benefits were not income, relying on cases and rulings involving wrongful death payments, social security and other public assistance payments, Red Cross disaster payments, and employer disaster

---

[1]   In U.S. v. Fior D'Italia, Inc., 536 U.S. 238 (2002), the Supreme Court validated the use of average tips on credit card sales for purposes of determining "wages" to employees for employment tax purposes, but this methodology cannot be applied to income tax cases because it determines only the aggregate tips received by all of the employer's employees and does not determine the amount of tips received by any particular employee.

payments. It then stated that in any event the payments were gifts because they were based upon need.

The Supreme Court, in United States v. Kaiser, 363 U.S. 299 (1960), affirmed on a different ground:

> We conclude, on the basis of our opinion in the *Duberstein* case, * * * that the jury in this case, as finder of the facts, acted within its competence in concluding that the assistance rendered here was a gift within section 102(a). * * * [The jury] had the power to conclude, on the record, taking into account such factors as the form and amount of the assistance and the conditions of personal need, of lack of other sources of income, compensation, or public assistance, and of dependency status, which surrounded the program under which it was rendered, that while the assistance was furnished only to strikers, it was not a recompense for striking.

Subsequent cases have resolved the factual issue against the taxpayer. Brown v. Commissioner, 398 F.2d 832 (6th Cir.1968) (strike benefits paid to airline pilots based on past salary and not conditioned on need held to be gross income despite the fact that there were no picketing duties required beyond not flying); Colwell v. Commissioner, 64 T.C. 584 (1975) (union strike benefits paid to a non-union member who supported the strike constituted gross income; the union made the payments to insure the economic feasibility of the strike rather than from detached and disinterested generosity); Osborne v. Commissioner, T.C. Memo. 1995–71 (fixed amount union-paid strike benefits that were not based on striker's individual financial needs were income; the payments were not gifts because the union's motivation was to promote the success of the strike, not detached and disinterested generosity).

4.3. *Testimonial Dinners, Public Appeals*

In Kralstein v. Commissioner, 38 T.C. 810 (1962) (Acq.), the taxpayer, vice president of a union, was honored at a testimonial dinner. The participants included the employers of the union members, other union officials, lawyers and doctors associated with the industry, and union employees. The taxpayer received $60,916.50, which was raised from dinner ticket sales and payments for insertions in a souvenir journal. The court found some of the participants made their contributions out of "disinterested generosity" but that others were primarily motivated by business reasons and held that $12,000 of the total amount raised qualified for the gift exclusion.

In Publishers New Press, Inc. v. Commissioner, 42 T.C. 396 (1964) (Acq.), the taxpayer published the newspaper "The Daily Worker." It made a public appeal for funds to continue operations and received some $300,000 over a three-year period. The Tax Court found the amounts taxable: "The mere absence of a legal consideration for the payment does not make the payment a gift under this statute. * * * The funds in question were contributions furnished by the contributors to obtain something the contributors desired. They were funds furnished in each instance by a person or organization in common with others for a common purpose, namely, the continued publication by petitioner of the newspaper. There is no indication that those who sent in money intended a gift."

4.4. *Friends and Acquaintances*

In Deisher v. Commissioner, T.C. Memo. 1990–347, a Rolex watch and Mercedes-Benz automobile given to the wife of a Fannie Mae official by a real estate developer were found to be income, not gifts, because the donor expected that as a result of the gifts transferred he would receive favorable treatment from Fannie Mae through the donee's husband.

United States v. Harris, 942 F.2d 1125 (7th Cir.1991), involved a criminal fraud prosecution against twin sisters who each received more than $500,000 over the course of several years from David Kritzik, "a wealthy widower partial to the company of young women." The evidence of the donor's intent was mixed. (He was deceased at the time of the trial.) Kritzik filed gift tax returns showing gifts to the sisters of only $90,000; one of the sisters applied for a bank loan listing Kritzik as her "employer;" and the sisters regularly picked up checks from the donor's secretary at his office. On the other hand, Kritzik had written love letters to one of the defendants stating that "so far as the things I give you are concerned—let me say that I get as great if not even greater pleasure in giving than you get in receiving." The Court of Appeals reversed the sisters' conviction of fraud for failure to report the receipts because the "current law on the tax treatment of payments to mistresses provided * * * no fair warning that her conduct was criminal."

> [A] person is entitled to treat cash and property received from a lover as gifts, as long as the relationship consists of something more than specific payments for specific sessions of sex. * * * The United States does not allege that Harris received specific payments for specific sessions of sex, so [the cases] support Harris' position.

> * * * The United States has not shown us, and we have not found, a single case finding tax liability for payments that a mistress received from her lover, absent proof of specific payments for specific sex acts. Even when such specific proof is present, the cases have not applied penalties for civil fraud, much less criminal sanctions. The broad principles contained in *Duberstein* do not fill this gap. Before she met Kritzik, Harris starred as a sorceress in an action/adventure film. She would have had to be a real life sorceress to predict her tax obligations under the current state of the law.

5.   DEFINITION OF INHERITANCE

Because § 1014 (discussed in Chapter 7, Section 2.) applies a special rule to determine the basis of property received by bequest or inheritance, § 1014(b) provides an extensive list of types of transfers that qualify. However, *Duberstein*-type questions arise in the context of bequests and devises as well. In Wolder v. Commissioner, 493 F.2d 608 (2d Cir.1974), the taxpayer was an attorney who received a bequest from a client in lieu of charging legal fees for work performed for the client before her death. The bequest was held to be includable in income even though under controlling state law the lawyer had received a bequest. See also Rev. Rul. 67–375, 1967–2 C.B. 60, holding that a bequest pursuant to written agreement to care for decedent was taxable; the term "bequest" as used in § 102(a) "generally implies bounty, gift, or gratuity."

Conversely, Lyeth v. Hoey, 305 U.S. 188 (1938), held that an amount received by a disinherited heir pursuant to a settlement of a will contest was excludable, even though the amount was not subject to state inheritance taxes because it was considered to have been received by contract. See also Getty v. Commissioner, 913 F.2d 1486 (9th Cir.1990) ($10 million received to settle a suit seeking to impose constructive trust as compensation for failure of J. Paul Getty to create an income interest in taxpayer's favor under J. Paul Getty's inter vivos trust was excludable under § 102).

SECTION 2.   LIFE INSURANCE DEATH BENEFITS

INTERNAL REVENUE CODE: Section 101(a), (d), (g), (j).

REGULATIONS: Sections 1.101–1(a)(1); –2(a)(1), (d); –4(a)(1).

Amounts paid under a life insurance contract by reason of the death of the insured are generally excluded from the beneficiary's income by § 101. In the case of term insurance, § 101 permanently excludes from tax any mortality gain from the contract—the proceeds less the premiums paid. In this respect § 101 closely resembles § 1014, which permanently excludes the unrealized appreciation of property transferred at death. Section 101 also permanently excludes the previously untaxed earnings from the investment portion of ordinary life insurance policies.

DETAILED ANALYSIS

1.   WHAT IS "LIFE INSURANCE?"

In Rev. Rul. 65–57, 1965–1 C.B. 56, the taxpayer purchased a life insurance contract under an arrangement with the insurance company whereby he was also required to purchase simultaneously a nonrefundable single premium annuity contract. The premium for the annuity contract was equal in amount to the face value of the life insurance policy. The IRS ruled that the proceeds of the life insurance policy would not be excluded under § 101 because there was no element of insurance risk (risk-shifting and risk distribution) in the transaction. See Helvering v. Le Gierse, 312 U.S. 531 (1941).

Section 7702, discussed Chapter 8, Section 5.B., provides a special definition of life insurance. If an insurance contract qualifies under the above rules and also meets the definitional standards of § 7702, the entire life insurance proceeds qualify under § 101. If a contract fails to meet the definition in § 7702, but is an insurance contract under the principles of *Le Gierse*, then only the amount of the death benefits in excess of the net surrender value of the contract is treated as received under a life insurance contract for purposes of § 101. I.R.C. § 7702(g)(2). Presumably, the net surrender value would be excludable from the income of the recipient of the proceeds under § 102, but the statute is not explicit on this point. The significance of § 7702 lies in the current income taxation of interest income earned on the savings portion of nonqualifying contracts. See Chapter 8, Section 5.B.

2. INSTALLMENT PAYMENTS MADE AFTER THE DEATH OF THE INSURED

If the only amount that the beneficiary of a life insurance policy can receive is the face amount of the policy, then the full amount of the proceeds is excludable under § 101(a) regardless of the method of payment of the proceeds. Thus, if the beneficiary of a $100,000 policy elects to receive the payment in ten equal installments, and no interest is paid on the installments, then each $10,000 payment will be excludable from income. Usually, however, if a beneficiary leaves the proceeds with the life insurance company under an option to pay the face amount in installments, the insurer will pay interest on each installment payment. Under § 101(d), amounts paid in excess of the policy's face amount, or the "interest" on the deferred payments, are includable in the income of the beneficiary. The death benefits withheld by the insurer are prorated over the period that payments are to be made and are excluded from each payment to determine the amount taken into gross income. If the policy provides for an option to receive a lump sum payment, the excludable amount is the amount of the lump sum payment. Otherwise, the excludable amount is the present value as of the date of the death of the insured of payments due to the beneficiary under the policy determined using the mortality tables and interest rate adopted by the insurance company to determine the payments. I.R.C. § 101(d)(2).

If payment of a lump sum insurance death benefit is deferred and upon receipt the beneficiary also receives interest on the deferred lump sum payment, the interest is includable in income by virtue of § 101(c).

3. RECEIPT OF PROCEEDS IN COMMERCIAL TRANSACTIONS

3.1. *General*

Life insurance policies are ordinarily acquired for the benefit of and are payable to the natural objects of the insured's bounty. But policies may also be used in commercial transactions, such as to secure a debt of the insured. In such situations, the issue is whether the recipient of the policy proceeds is entitled to the § 101(a) exclusion.

Creditors often insure the lives of debtors (at the debtors' expense) to secure repayment of the loan. If in order to collect the proceeds of the policy the creditor must prove not only the death of the insured, but the amount of the debt because the creditor may receive only that amount, the amount received by the creditor is received by reason of the debt, not "by reason of the death of the insured," and § 101(a) does not exclude the receipt. McCamant v. Commissioner, 32 T.C. 824 (1959). In Rev. Rul. 70–254, 1970–1 C.B. 31, a corporation sold home sites on an installment basis, taking out a life insurance policy on the purchaser for the unpaid balance of the purchase price. In the case of death, the corporation would receive the insurance proceeds and transfer title to the property to the heirs of the purchaser. The proceeds did not qualify as life insurance under § 101, but instead constituted a collection of the unpaid balance of the purchase price. The same result follows if the insured merely pledges policies with the creditor as security; the receipt of the proceeds is not covered by the insurance provisions but is governed by the rules ordinarily applicable to the payment of debts. Landfield Finance Co. v. United States, 418 F.2d 172 (7th Cir.1969). Where the amount to which the creditor is entitled under the insurance policy is not limited to the amount of the debt, some cases have excluded the policy proceeds received by the creditor, even though the debt had previously been deducted or charged off as a bad debt. Durr Drug Co. v. United States, 99 F.2d 757 (5th Cir.1938); L.C. Thomsen and Sons, Inc. v. United States, 484 F.2d 954 (7th Cir.1973).

In Tennessee Foundry and Machinery Co. v. Commissioner, 48 T.C. 419 (1967), aff'd per curiam, 399 F.2d 156 (6th Cir.1968), an employee of the taxpayer corporation committed suicide, leaving a note confessing to embezzlement of funds from the corporation. In settlement of an action brought by the corporation, the employee's widow assigned to the corporation life insurance policies of which her husband had been the owner and the insured, and she the beneficiary. The court held that the proceeds received by the corporation were taxable as a recovery of a previously deducted embezzlement loss and were not excluded as life insurance.

Section 101(j) limits the § 101 exclusion for life insurance death benefits received by an employer from an "employer-owned life insurance contract" on the life of an employee to the sum of the premiums and other amounts paid by the employer for the insurance contract. There are two exceptions to this limitation if certain qualifying conditions are met. First, a full exclusion under § 101(a) applies if the deceased insured (1) was an employee of the policyholder at any time during the twelve months preceding the employee's death, or (2) was a director, a "highly compensated employee," or a "highly compensated individual," as those terms are defined. Second, an exclusion is allowed for amounts received by the policyholder by reason of the death of the insured that are paid to a member of the insured's family, a designated beneficiary of the insured under the contract (other than the policyholder), a trust for the benefit of any such family member or designated beneficiary, or the insured's estate, including payments to purchase the deceased employee's equity interest in the policyholder-employer.

3.2. *Transfers for Valuable Consideration*

If the taxpayer receiving the proceeds had acquired the policy by the payment of consideration, then any gain resulting (excess of proceeds over such consideration plus later premiums and interest on loans to carry the policy that is not deductible by virtue of § 264(a)(4)) is generally taxable under § 101(a)(2) even though the entire proceeds would have been fully exempt if the policy had initially been taken out by the taxpayer. Section 101(a)(2)(B) provides some exceptions where the transfer is to a corporation or partnership in which the insured is involved or to a partner of the insured.

4. ACCELERATED DEATH BENEFITS

People with terminal illnesses, such as late-stage cancer, have sought to use the face amount of their life insurance policies to pay for medical expenses during their lifetimes. Insurance companies responded with plans that, in effect, prepaid death benefits under the policies. These arrangements raised the issue of whether such advance payments could be excluded under § 101. Congress reacted in 1996 by enacting § 101(g), which excludes from gross income amounts received under a life insurance policy during the lifetime of the insured if the insured individual is terminally ill, as well as certain amounts received under life insurance contracts on insureds who are chronically ill. An individual is "terminally ill" only if the person has been certified by a physician as having an illness or condition reasonably expected to result in death within 24 months. A complex definition of "chronically ill" is provided in § 7702B(c)(2). Amounts received with respect to a chronically ill insured, in contrast to a terminally ill insured, qualify for exclusion only if paid to cover otherwise unreimbursed costs of qualified long-term care services and the contract meets numerous statutory requirements. Section 101(g)(2) extends the exclusion to proceeds from the sale of a life insurance contract on a terminally or chronically ill insured to a viatical settlement provider (i.e., businesses that purchase life insurance policies from existing policy owners for more than its surrender value but less than its net death benefit). Only sales to viatical settlement providers regularly engaged in business qualify for the exclusion.

SECTION 3.   PRIZES

INTERNAL REVENUE CODE: Section 74.

Section 74, which expressly includes prizes and awards in gross income, was enacted in 1954 to overrule Washburn v. Commissioner, 5 T.C. 1333 (1945), and McDermott v. Commissioner, 150 F.2d 585 (D.C.Cir.1945). *Washburn* held that a $900 cash prize won from a radio show merely by answering the telephone when the radio show host called was excludable as a gift. *McDermott* held that a prize awarded for an essay submitted to the ABA Ross Essay competition was excludable from gross income. See S.Rep. No. 83–1622, 83d Cong., 2d Sess. 178–179 (1954).

As originally enacted, § 74(b) excluded prizes and awards in recognition of religious, charitable, scientific, educational, artistic, literary, or civic achievement if the recipient was selected without any action on the recipient's part to enter the contest and the recipient was not required to render any future services. Thus, for example, the recipient of a Nobel Prize or Pulitzer Prize incurred no tax liability. In effect, the failure to tax these prizes created a program of matching grants from the federal government in an amount equal to the taxes saved.

Since 1987 a prize or award is excludable only if it is transferred directly to a government or charity. This requirement was added because a prize or award for meritorious achievement "increases the recipient's net wealth and ability to pay taxes to the same extent as the receipt of * * * wages, dividends, or as a taxable award." S.Rep. No. 99–313, 99th

Cong., 2d Sess. 48 (1986). The continued exemption for prizes and awards for meritorious achievement that are transferred to a charity is an example of statutory complexity that may produce administrative simplification. But for the exclusion, a meritorious award recipient who transferred the award to a charity would be required to include the prize in income and would be allowed a charitable deduction under § 170, discussed in Chapter 21. There are, however, limitations on the ability to claim the charitable deduction, and to the extent any of these limitations reduces the allowable deduction below the amount of the award transferred to charity, the recipient would have some residual tax liability as a result of the award. Nevertheless, the rationale for this exclusion is elusive, because if a taxpayer performs personal services for a third party who agrees in advance to pay the charity rather than the taxpayer, the taxpayer nevertheless must include in income the amount paid to the charity and then claim a charitable contribution deduction under § 170, subject to the various limitations. See Treas. Reg. § 1.61–2(c).

In late 2016, infected with Olympic pride after the 2016 Rio Olympics, Congress added § 74(d) to exclude, "the value of any medal awarded in, or any prize money received from the United States Olympic Committee on account of, competition in the Olympic Games or Paralympic Games." The exclusion does not apply to an athlete who's adjusted gross income, including the prize money, exceeds $1,000,000.

Scholarships often are awarded as contest prizes. Section 74(a) expressly cedes jurisdiction over qualified (i.e., excludable) scholarships to § 117. See Section 4 below.

DETAILED ANALYSIS

1.   VALUATION OF TAXABLE PRIZES AND AWARDS

Noncash prizes and awards taxable under § 74 present significant valuation problems. Treas. Reg. § 1.74–1(a)(2) provides that prizes are to be included in income at their fair market value but the courts have not always followed this standard. In Turner v. Commissioner, T.C. Memo. 1954–38, the taxpayers received as a prize two round-trip first class steamship tickets for a cruise between New York City and Buenos Aires, Argentina. The tickets had a retail price of $2,200. The taxpayer, whose wife was born in Brazil, was able to negotiate with the steamship company to exchange the two first-class tickets to Argentina for four round-trip tourist tickets between New York City and Rio de Janeiro, Brazil, for the taxpayer, his wife, and two children. The taxpayer reported income of $520 but the Commissioner asserted a tax on the full retail price of the tickets. The Tax Court found the prize to be income in the amount of $1,400: "The winning of the tickets did not provide [the taxpayers] with something which they needed in the ordinary course of their lives and for which they would have made an expenditure in any event, but merely gave them an opportunity to enjoy a luxury otherwise beyond their means. Their value to the petitioners was not equal to their retail cost. They were not transferable and not salable and there were other restrictions on their use." See also McCoy v. Commissioner, 38 T.C. 841 (1962) (Acq.) (prize recipient, who immediately traded in the prize of a new car, was taxed on resale value, not on retail value). Compare this valuation approach with the objective standard applied in *Rooney*. See Chapter 3, Section 1.

2.   EMPLOYEE ACHIEVEMENT AWARDS

Section 74(c) excludes from income certain employee achievement awards. The technical rules for qualification are in § 274(j), which also limits the amount of the employer's deduction. To be excluded the award must (1) be tangible personal property, not cash, (2) be for length of service or a safety achievement, (3) be made as part of a "meaningful presentation," and (4) not create a significant likelihood of disguised compensation. Furthermore, unless the award is made pursuant to a "qualified plan," it must have cost the employer $400 or less. If the prize or award is made pursuant to a "qualified plan," the cost may not exceed $1,600. If the cost of the award exceeds the maximum allowable amount, the amount by which the greater of its cost or value exceeds the allowable cost will be taxable to the employee. Even if a prize or award is not excludable under § 74(c) it may be excludable as a de minimis fringe benefit under § 132(e) if it is of small value. See H.Rep. No. 99–426, 99th Cong., 1st Sess. 105 (1985).

Even though the employer's deduction is limited if the value of an employee achievement award exceeds the permitted ceilings, the value in excess of the deductible amount is includable by the employee. According to Congressional committee reports, the purpose of this two-pronged attack is to prevent employers from providing nontaxable disguised compensation, particularly to highly compensated employees, through nontaxable "awards" for regular job performance, such as productivity, rather than bonuses. See S.Rep. No. 99–313, 99th Cong., 2d Sess. 49 (1986).

SECTION 4.   SCHOLARSHIPS

INTERNAL REVENUE CODE: Section 117.

PROPOSED REGULATIONS: Section 1.117–6(b)–(d) [except (d)(4)].

General Explanation of the Tax Reform Act of 1986
Staff of the Joint Committee on Taxation 38–44 (1987).

* * *

Reasons for Change

By extending the exclusion for scholarship or fellowship grants to cover amounts used by degree candidates for regular living expenses (such as meals and lodging), [pre-1987] law provided a tax benefit not directly related to educational activities. By contrast, students who are not scholarship recipients must pay for such expenses out of after-tax dollars, just as individuals who are not students must pay for their food and housing costs out of wages or other earnings that are includible in income. The Congress concluded that the exclusion for scholarships should be targeted specifically for the purpose of educational benefits, and should not encompass other items that would otherwise constitute nondeductible personal expenses. The Congress also determined that, in the case of grants to nondegree candidates for travel, research, etc., that would be deductible as ordinary and necessary business expenses, an exclusion for such expenses is not needed, and that an exclusion is not appropriate if the expenses would not be deductible.

In addition, * * * the receipt of a nonexcludable scholarship amount by a student without other significant income will not result in tax liability so long as the individual's total income does not exceed the personal exemption (if available) and either the * * * standard deduction * * * or the taxpayer's itemized deductions. * * *

Under [pre-1987] law, controversies arose between taxpayers and the Internal Revenue Service over whether a particular stipend made in an educational setting constituted a scholarship or compensation for services. In particular, numerous court cases have involved resident physicians and graduate teaching fellows who have sought—often notwithstanding substantial case authority to the contrary—to exclude from income payments received for caring for hospitalized patients, for teaching undergraduate college students, or for doing research which inures to the benefit of the grantor. The limitation on the section 117 exclusion made by the Act, and the repeal of the special rule relating to degree candidates who must perform services as a condition of receiving a degree, should lessen these problems of complexity, uncertainty of tax treatment, and controversy.

The Congress concluded that the section 117 exclusion should not apply to amounts representing payment for teaching, research, or other services by a student, whether or not required as a condition for receiving a scholarship or tuition reduction, and that this result should apply whether the compensation takes the form of cash, which the student can use to pay tuition, or of a tuition reduction, pursuant to which there is no exchange of cash for payment of tuition. Thus, where cash stipends received by a student who performs services would not be excludable under the Act as a scholarship even if the stipend is used to pay tuition, the Congress believed that the exclusion should not become available merely because the compensation takes the form of a tuition reduction otherwise qualifying under section 117(d). The Congress concluded, consistently with the overall objectives of the Act, that principles of fairness require that all compensation should be given the same treatment; that is, some individuals (e.g., students who perform teaching services for universities) should not receive more favorable tax treatment of their compensation than all other individuals who earn wages.

* * *

Explanation of Provisions

In general

Degree candidates.—In the case of a scholarship or fellowship grant received by a degree candidate, an exclusion under section 117 is available only to the extent the individual establishes that, in accordance with the conditions of the grant, the grant was used for (1) tuition and fees required for enrollment or attendance of the student at an educational institution (within the meaning of sec. 170(b)(1)(A)(ii)), and (2) fees, books, supplies, and equipment required for courses of instruction at the educational institution ("course-related expenses"). This rule applies to all types of scholarship or fellowship grants, whether funded by a governmental agency, college or university, charitable organization, business, or other source, and whether designated as a scholarship or by some other name (e.g., "allowance").

The exclusion available under [section 117] for degree candidates is not limited to a scholarship or fellowship grant that by its express terms is required to be used for tuition or course-related expenses. Also, there is no requirement that the student be able to trace the dollars paid for tuition or course-related expenses to the same dollars that previously had been deposited in his or her checking account, for example, from a scholarship grant check. Instead, the amount of an otherwise qualified grant awarded to a degree candidate is excludable (after taking into account the amount of any other grant or grants awarded to the individual that also are eligible for exclusion) up to the aggregate amount incurred by the candidate for tuition and course-related expenses during the period to which the grant applies; any excess amount of the grant is includible in income. No amount of a grant is excludable if the terms of the grant earmark or designate its use for purposes other than tuition or course-related expenses (such as for room or board, or "meal allowances") or specify that the grant cannot be used for tuition or course-related expenses, even if the amount of such grant is less than the amount payable by the student for tuition or course-related expenses.

* * *

Performance of services

* * *

To prevent circumvention of the rule set forth in section 117(c), that rule is intended to apply not only to cash amounts received, but also to amounts (representing payment for services) by which the tuition of the person who performs services is reduced, whether or not pursuant to a tuition reduction plan described in Code section 117(d). The Act therefore explicitly provides that neither the section 117(a) exclusion nor the section 117(d) exclusion applies to any portion of the amount received that represents payment for teaching, research, or other services by the student required as a condition of receiving the scholarship or tuition reduction. If an amount representing reasonable compensation (whether paid in cash or as tuition reduction) for services performed by an employee is included in the employee's gross income and wages, then any additional amount of scholarship award or tuition reduction remains eligible for the section 117 exclusion as modified by the Act.

As noted, employees who perform required services for which they include in income reasonable compensation continue to be eligible to exclude amounts of tuition reduction. * * *

DETAILED ANALYSIS

1.   THE COMPENSATION LIMITATION

1.1. *General*

Section 117(c)(1) expressly limits the availability of the exclusion where a scholarship represents payment for teaching, research, or other services as a condition for receiving a qualified scholarship. Prop. Reg. § 1.117–6(d)(2) (1988) provides that a scholarship is payment for services when the grantor requires the recipient to perform services in return for the granting of the scholarship. A requirement that the recipient pursue studies, research, or other activities primarily for the benefit of the grantor is treated as a requirement to perform services. A scholarship grant is considered to be in return for services whether such services are required to be performed before, concurrent with, or after receipt of the scholarship. Section 117(c)(2), provides an exception for grants under the National Health Services Corps Scholarship Program and the Armed Forces Health Professions Scholarship and Financial Assistance Program, which are exempt from tax without regard to any service obligation imposed on the scholarship recipient.

1.2. *Professional Training and Graduate Students*

Under pre-1987 law most of the litigation involved professionals, usually physicians, who were paid while in training, e.g., interns or residents, and university graduate teaching assistants. See e.g., Adams v. Commissioner, 71 T.C. 477 (1978) (hospital intern's stipend was taxable); Rev. Rul. 82–57, 1982–1 C.B. 24 (amounts paid by Veterans Administration to psychology graduate students serving as staff assistants at VA hospitals were taxable). Because of § 117(c) and the limitation of the exclusion under § 117(a) to tuition, fees, books, supplies, and equipment, professional "in training" cases no longer should arise.

The treatment of graduate teaching and research assistants under § 117 is not as clear. Although § 117(d)(5) permits tax-free tuition remission to graduate teaching assistants, tax exemption under § 117(d), as under § 117(a), is expressly limited by § 117(c)(1). Prop. Reg. § 1.117–6(d)(1) (1988) provides that the portion of a scholarship grant that represents payment for services is included in gross income, regardless of whether such services are required of all candidates for the degree as a condition to receiving the degree. Prop. Reg. § 1.117–6(d)(3) (1988) requires that the grantor of the scholarship determine the portion of the scholarship that represents payment for services, and sets forth a number of factors to be considered in making that allocation. If the amount allocated by the grantor to payment for services represents reasonable compensation and the recipient includes that amount in gross income, the remainder of the scholarship received from the grantor is excludable.

Prop. Reg. § 1.117–6(d)(5) (1988) provides two examples of the application of these rules to graduate students:

> Example (5). On June 11, 1987, E receives a $6,000 scholarship for academic year 1987–1988 from University Y. As a condition to receiving the scholarship, E performs services as a researcher for Y. Other researchers who are not scholarship recipients receive $2,000 for similar services for the year. Therefore, Y allocates $2,000 of the scholarship amount to compensation for services performed by E. Thus, the portion of the scholarship that represents payment for services, $2,000, must be included in E's gross income as wages. However, if E establishes expenditures of $4,000 for qualified tuition and related expenses * * * , then $4,000 of E's scholarship is excludable from E's gross income as a qualified scholarship.

> Example (6). During 1987, F is employed as a research assistant to a faculty member at University Z. F receives a salary from Z that represents reasonable compensation for the position of research assistant. In addition to salary, F receives from Z a qualified tuition reduction (as defined in section 117(d)) to be used to enroll in an undergraduate course at Z. F includes the salary in gross income. Thus, the qualified tuition reduction does not represent payment for services and therefore, is not includable in F's gross income.

1.3. *Other Scholarships*

Rev. Rul. 68–20, 1968–1 C.B. 55, held that a Miss America beauty contest "scholarship" was taxable compensation where the winner was required to perform services for the contest organizer. See also, Miss Georgia Scholarship Fund, Inc. v. Commissioner, 72 T.C. 267 (1979) (same result where the scholarship could be forfeited if the contestant's contract obligations were not met). Contra, Wilson v. United States, 322 F.Supp. 830 (D.Kan.1971) (1971 Miss America scholarship was nontaxable). Athletic scholarships qualify for § 117 exclusion only if payment is not conditioned upon participation in the university's athletic program. Rev. Rul. 77–263, 1977–2 C.B. 47.

1.4. *Educational Loan Forgiveness*

Section 108(f) excludes from gross income forgiveness of student loans incurred to attend a qualified institution of higher learning if the discharge of the indebtedness is pursuant to a provision in the loan under which all or part of the debt would be discharged if the student works for a period of time in certain professions or for any broad class of employers. The exclusion applies only to loans made with funds provided by a governmental entity or to loans from a qualified educational organization under a program designed to encourage its students to serve in occupations with unmet needs or in areas with unmet needs and the services provided by the student are under the supervision of a governmental unit or tax-exempt charitable organization. Compare Porten v. Commissioner, T.C. Memo. 1993–73, holding that forgiveness of an Alaska student loan conditioned upon working in any capacity as a resident of Alaska was not an excludable scholarship.

Section 108(f)(4) excludes from gross income amounts received under the National Health Service Corps loan repayment program and under state loan repayment programs that receive Federal grants. Such programs require the recipient of the repayment to provide services in a geographic area identified as having a shortage of health-care professionals.

Under the Higher Education Act of 1965, the Department of Education pays makers of loans to qualified students for that portion of the interest that the lender agrees not to collect from the student-borrower. Rev. Rul. 75–537, 1975–2 C.B. 32, held that such interest payments qualify as a scholarship to the student under § 117.

2.   THE RELATIONSHIP OF SECTIONS 117, 102 AND 74

Treas. Reg. § 1.102–1(a) states that the § 102 gift exclusion does not apply to prizes and awards or scholarships and Treas. Reg. § 1.117–1(a) provides that if an amount is a scholarship or fellowship then § 117 controls, and §§ 74 and 102 are not applicable. See also Rev. Rul. 66–241, 1966–2 C.B. 40. Thus, the initial characterization of a payment is important to determine where it fits in the statutory scheme. For example, if the prize winner of the scholarship is not the student, § 74 will tax the scholarship. Zorc v. Commissioner, T.C. Memo. 1990–620 (tuition scholarship to private high school won by parents as a raffle prize was a taxable prize because they bore the responsibility for educating their child who attended the school and they were the persons who won the prize).

3.   EMPLOYER-PROVIDED EDUCATION BENEFITS

Where an employer pays, directly or indirectly, education costs of its employees, § 117(a) is not applicable, but in situations where the amounts are paid primarily for the benefit of the employer, or if the rules relating to qualified educational assistance fringe benefits are met, the payments nevertheless may be excludable as a tax-free fringe benefit.

4.   POLICY ISSUES

Many theorists argue that all scholarships or tuition remission benefits should be included in the recipient's income since they represent increases in net worth. (Whether deductions should be allowed with respect to the cost of education is considered in Chapter 23.) This result appears appropriate when the comparison is made between the working student who finances her education out of after-tax income and a scholarship recipient who, under § 117, finances his education in part out of untaxed income. But if the comparison is made to students who have their educational costs paid by gifts from family members, which are tax-free under § 102, scholarships, including room and board, arguably should be totally exempt, as they were before 1987. Unlike in the case of gifts, however, scholarships frequently are funded by charitable contributions and tax exempt income of the granting institutions. Hence, the failure to tax scholarships often results in the amount being omitted from the tax base altogether. From yet another perspective, scholarships provided by the educational institution itself that are limited to a net reduction in the price of room, board, tuition, fees, and books can be viewed simply as a bargain purchase that ought to be nontaxable. See Chapter 2, Section 2.

SECTION 5. GOVERNMENTAL SUBSIDIES AND RELATED ITEMS

The value of government goods and services provided to the public generally—public transportation, highways, public elementary and secondary education, below-cost postal service, flood control projects, etc.—are generally not seen to be within the reach of the income tax. The value of such benefits to any individual taxpayer would be nearly impossible to measure and attempts to include such items would not be administratively feasible. The line between nontaxable general public benefits and taxable subsidies cannot always be drawn with precision. Many government subsidies, however, are paid to specific persons based upon some particular status of the recipient: financial need, age, etc. From a tax policy perspective, where such benefits are in monetary form (or have a readily determinable market value), income inclusion generally would be appropriate unless administrative concerns militate otherwise.

A. BUSINESS SUBSIDIES

Governmental subsidies to business are generally includable in gross income. For example, Standley v. Commissioner, 99 T.C. 259 (1992), aff'd by order, 24 F.3d 249 (9th Cir.1994), held that payments from the Department of Agriculture under the Dairy Herd Termination Program to dairy farmers who sold cattle for slaughter at less than their fair market value for dairy purposes were taxable. Mortgage interest reduction payments made on behalf of the owner of low-income rental housing under § 236 of the National Housing Act were held to be taxable income to the property owner in Graff v. Commissioner, 74 T.C. 743 (1980), aff'd, 673 F.2d 784 (5th Cir.1982). There are, however, a few administrative and statutory exceptions to this general rule.

The taxpayer sometimes contends as to federal subsidies "that the intent cannot rationally be ascribed to Congress to bestow a benefit with one hand and to take it away with the other." Baboquivari Cattle Co. v. Commissioner, 135 F.2d 114, 116 (9th Cir.1943). But more is involved than merely taking back a portion of the subsidy's benefit. Under the progressive tax rate scale, the net effect of the benefit will depend on the taxpayer's marginal tax rate so that, if the income is taxable, taxpayers most in need of assistance in effect receive the greatest net benefit after taxes.

DETAILED ANALYSIS

1. OTHER EXAMPLES

The following are additional examples of the general rule that governmental subsidies are includable in the gross income of the recipient:

Acreage reduction payments under the Agricultural Adjustment Act, I.T. 2767, XIII–1 C.B. 35 (1934); payments to cotton exporters under the Agricultural Adjustment Act, Rev. Rul. 68–497, 1968–2 C.B. 312; subsidy to airlines that carry mail, paid in addition to the actual payment for mail carriage, Rev. Rul. 63–269, 1963–2 C.B. 293; subsidy to ship owners to enable them to meet foreign flag competition, Rev. Rul. 63–269, supra.

In contrast, Rev. Rul. 77–77, 1977–1 C.B. 11, held that grants made under the Indian Financing Act of 1974 to provide equity capital to expand Indian-owned profit-making enterprises located on or near reservations were not taxable because they were intended to promote social welfare. But Rev. Rul. 2005–46, 2005–2 C.B. 120, held that a grant received by a business under a state program to compensate businesses for damage or destruction of real and personal property on account of a disaster is not excludable from gross income under the general welfare exclusion, because "the payments are not based on individual or family needs." However, the taxpayer receiving the grant might be eligible to elect to defer gain under § 1033, discussed in Chapter 27.

Refundable state income and property tax credits in excess of the taxpayer's tax liability received under a New York program to subsidize business investment in targeted areas within the state were held to be an accession to wealth and thus income in Maines v. Commissioner, 144 T.C. 123 (2015). The court observed that there is no exclusion from gross income simply because a payment comes from a state and further held that the state law label of the credits as overpayments of prior taxes was not controlling for Federal tax purposes.

2. CONSERVATION COST-SHARING PAYMENTS

Section 126 provides an exclusion from gross income for certain payments received under a number of federal and state programs involving cost-sharing conservation arrangements. The exclusion applies to the extent the Secretary of Agriculture determines the payment is made "primarily for the purpose of conserving soil and water resources, protecting or restoring the environment, improving forests, or providing a habitat for wildlife" and is determined by the Secretary of the Treasury not substantially to increase the taxpayer's income. The subsidy must therefore not confer substantial gain to the recipient.

Section 126 provides that the excluded payments may not be included in the basis of property acquired with the payments. The effect of the basis reduction is to defer inclusion of the payment in income until the sale of the property. In addition, no deduction or credit may be taken with respect to any expenditure made using the excluded payments. The effect of these limitations, when applicable, is the same as including all or part of the payment in income. Additionally, if the property or improvements purchased with the excluded payments are disposed of within ten years, under § 1255 the gain is treated as ordinary income to the extent of the excluded payments. After the property has been held for ten years, the portion of the gain recaptured as ordinary income is reduced by 10 percent per year for each year the property is held in excess of ten years.

Sections 126 and 1255 provide that a taxpayer may elect that the exclusion-recapture rules of those sections not be applicable. The option is granted because the rules of §§ 126 and 1255 may be less favorable to some taxpayers than requiring income inclusion of cost-sharing payments, but allowing applicable tax deductions and credits in full for items for which the payments were expended. For example, Rev. Rul. 2006–46, 2006–2 C.B. 511, held that all or a portion of cost-share payments received under the Conservation Security Program (CSP)—a USDA program authorized under the provisions of §§ 1238–1238C of the Food Security Act of 1985 that supports ongoing conservation stewardship of agricultural lands by providing financial assistance to agricultural producers who maintain and enhance natural resources—are excludable under § 126, because the Secretary of Agriculture has determined that CSP is "substantially similar" to the types of programs described in § 126(a)(1) through (8), within the meaning of § 126(a)(9). See also Rev. Rul. 2004–8, 2004–1 C.B. 544 (all or a portion of cost-share payments received under the Forest Land Enhancement Program administered by the Department of Agriculture are eligible for exclusion from gross income under § 126).

B. SOCIAL WELFARE PAYMENTS

INTERNAL REVENUE CODE: Sections 85 and 86.

The federal and state governments provide a variety of welfare benefits to individuals. Subsidies may be made directly in cash (e.g., to provide a subsistence level of income for the poor or elderly), to third-party providers of particular types of services or goods (e.g., medical care, low-cost housing, job training, education), in the form of vouchers (e.g., food stamps), or in kind (e.g., public housing or health services for the poor, below-cost public transportation for the poor or elderly). Other governmental payments may be substitutes for taxable income, such as unemployment compensation, or for services that the government desires the individual to undertake. The tax policy issue is whether such subsidies should be included in the gross income of the recipient.

In general, the governing principles appear to require inclusion in gross income of those benefits that are substitutes for wages, but to exclude benefits based upon financial need. Although in theory all benefits generally should be included in the income of the recipients, where the benefits are based upon need, little if any tax is likely to be paid on these amounts and the exclusion is defensible on administrative grounds. But as Notice 99–3 indicates, exclusions also generate administrative problems.

Notice 99–3
1999–1 C.B. 271.

SECTION 1. PURPOSE

This notice addresses the federal income and employment tax consequences of payments received by individuals with respect to certain work activities performed in state programs under part A of title IV of the Social Security Act, as amended by the Personal Responsibility and Work Opportunity Reconciliation Act of 1996 (PRWORA), Pub. L. No. 104–193, 110 Stat. 2105 (August 22, 1996) (TANF payments). * * *

SECTION 3. BACKGROUND

Congress reformed the welfare system through the enactment of PRWORA, which replaced Aid to Families with Dependent Children (AFDC) with Temporary Assistance for Needy Families (TANF). AFDC required individuals to perform some work activities in order to continue to receive public assistance. TANF provides states with more flexibility than they had under AFDC to determine basic eligibility rules and benefit amounts. TANF also requires that specified percentages of individual recipients engage in work activities and imposes penalties on the states for non-compliance with that requirement.

For purposes of TANF, the term "work activities" is defined under § 407(d) of the Social Security Act, 42 U.S.C. § 607(d), as:

    (1)   unsubsidized employment;

    (2)   subsidized private sector employment;

    (3)   subsidized public sector employment;

    (4)   work experience (including work associated with the refurbishing of publicly assisted housing) if sufficient private sector employment is not available;

    (5)   on-the-job training;

    (6)   job search and job readiness assistance;

    (7)   community service programs;

    (8)   vocational educational training (not to exceed 12 months with respect to any individual);

    (9)   job skills training directly related to employment;

    (10) education directly related to employment, in the case of a recipient who has not received a high school diploma or a certificate of high school equivalency;

    (11) satisfactory attendance at secondary school or in a course of study leading to a certificate of general equivalence, in the case of a recipient who has not completed secondary school or received such a certificate; and

(12) the provision of child care services to an individual who is participating in a community service program.

SECTION 4. TREATMENT OF TANF PAYMENTS

.01 General Analysis.

The federal income and employment tax consequences of TANF payments generally are determined under the following analysis.

Payments by a governmental unit to an individual under a legislatively provided social benefit program for the promotion of the general welfare that are not basically for services rendered are not includible in the individual's gross income and are not wages for employment tax purposes, even if the individual is required to perform certain activities to remain eligible for the payments. See Rev. Rul. 71–425, 1971–2 C.B. 76; Rev. Rul. 75–246, 1975–1 C.B. 24. * * *

.02 Application of General Analysis to Certain TANF Payments.

Due to the flexibility TANF affords states to determine basic eligibility rules and benefit amounts, a TANF payment may be made both for the promotion of the general welfare and as compensation for services. In these cases, it is extremely difficult to characterize the basic purpose of the payments. It is also not practically feasible to determine the relative proportion of the payment each purpose represents.

In many of these cases, TANF payments are received in lieu of (and generally in amounts no greater than) payments the individual formerly received or would have received under AFDC based upon the individual's personal and family subsistence requirements. In these cases, the primary measure of the amount received is the personal or family need of the individual recipient rather than the value of any services performed.

These cases typically share, and can be identified by, common characteristics. In cases where the following three conditions are satisfied, TANF payments will be treated as made for the promotion of the general welfare and therefore will not be includible in an individual's gross income; will not be earned income for EIC purposes; and will not be wages for employment tax purposes:

(1) The only payments received by the individual with respect to the work activity are received directly from the state or local welfare agency (for this purpose, an entity with which a state or local welfare agency contracts to administer the state TANF program on behalf of the state will be treated as the state or local welfare agency);

(2) The determination of the individual's eligibility to receive any payment is based on need and the only payments received by the individual with respect to the work activity are funded entirely under a TANF program (including any payments with respect to qualified state expenditures (as defined in § 409(a)(7)(B)(i)(1) of the Social Security Act)) and the Food Stamp Act of 1977; and

(3) The size of the individual's payment is determined by the applicable welfare law, and the number of hours the individual may engage in the work activity is limited by the size of the individual's payment (as determined by applicable welfare law) divided by the higher of the federal or state minimum wage.

The federal income and employment tax treatment of TANF payments that do not satisfy each of these three conditions is determined under the general analysis described in section 4.01, above.

* * *

DETAILED ANALYSIS

1.   NEED-BASED PAYMENTS

The exclusion from income for payments made to achieve welfare objectives of the federal government is largely an administratively created exclusion. Prior to the adoption of specific statutory provisions, both Social Security Old-Age and Survivors Insurance payments (Rev. Rul. 70–217, 1970–1 C.B. 12, restating I.T. 3447, 1947–1 C.B. 191) and state unemployment benefits paid out of funds received from the Federal Unemployment Trust Fund (Rev. Rul. 70–280, 1970–1 C.B. 13) were excluded from gross income. Similarly, Rev. Rul. 70–341, 1970–2 C.B. 31, held that basic Medicare benefits are nontaxable since they are "in the nature of disbursements made in furtherance of the social welfare objective of the Federal government." See also Rev. Rul. 76–144, 1976–1 C.B. 17 (Disaster Relief Act of 1974 grants made to victims of natural disasters are not taxable); Rev. Rul. 74–205, 1974–1 C.B. 20 ("replacement housing payments" made to individuals who were displaced from their homes by federally-assisted urban renewal type programs are excludable as "payments made under legislatively provided social benefit programs for promotion of the general welfare"); Rev. Rul. 75–271, 1975–2 C.B. 23 (assistance payments made to mortgagee on behalf of low-income homeowners under § 235 of the National Housing Act are not includable in the gross income of the homeowner).

The same principles apply to social welfare benefits provided by the states. See Rev. Rul. 78–170, 1978–1 C.B. 24 (credits provided by a state to elderly or disabled utility customers are not includable); Rev. Rul. 73–87, 1973–1 C.B. 39 (payments made to certain families under an experimental welfare program were entitled to exclusion on a social welfare basis, despite the fact that the program was experimental and not part of a general welfare program); Rev. Rul. 74–74, 1974–1 C.B. 18 (payments made to victims of a crime under a state statute providing financial assistance to such victims were held to be excludable); Rev. Rul. 68–133, 1968–1 C.B. 36 (payments to school drop-outs and unemployed individuals under a state "job service corps" program are excludable).

On the other hand, Rev. Rul. 76–131, 1976–1 C.B. 16, held that special payments made by Alaska to persons 65 years or older who had resided in the state for at least 25 years were taxable. Rev. Rul. 85–39, 1985–1 C.B. 21, also held taxable "dividend payments" by Alaska residents of a certain percentage of the State's mineral income. In each of these Rulings, the payments were distinguished from those for the general welfare because no consideration was given to the recipient's financial status, health, education, or employment status. Rev. Proc. 2014–35, 2014–26 I.R.B. 1110, states that the IRS will not assert that non-compensatory benefits provided by Indian Tribal Governments pursuant to a governmental program of the tribe for the promotion of general welfare based on individual or family need are includable in gross income under the general welfare exclusion.

2. STATUTORY PROVISIONS

Various statutory provisions have reinforced or altered the administrative exclusions for social welfare payments. The two most significant provisions involve Social Security benefits and unemployment insurance, which are not restricted to low-income groups and thus can be said to fall outside the social welfare exception.

2.1. *Social Security*

2.1.1. *Generally*

Under § 86 up to eighty-five percent of the Social Security benefits received during the taxable year is includable in gross income. Determining the exact amount of Social Security benefits that must be included is inordinately complex. If the sum of the taxpayer's adjusted gross income, tax exempt interest, and one-half of Social Security benefits, exceeds a base amount of $25,000 for a single taxpayer or $32,000 for married taxpayers filing jointly, the lesser of (1) fifty percent of the amount of Social Security benefits, or (2) one-half of the amount by which the sum of the taxpayer's adjusted gross income, tax-exempt interest, and one-half of the Social Security benefits received exceeds the base amount, must be included. If the taxpayer's income, computed as above, exceeds $34,000 for a single taxpayer or $44,000 for married taxpayers filing jointly, the includable amount is the lesser of: (1) 85 percent of the taxpayer's total Social Security benefits for the year, or (2) the sum of (a) 85 percent of the amount by which the taxpayer's provisional income exceeds the applicable base amount, plus (b) the lesser of (i) the amount includable under the 50 percent inclusion rule or (ii) $4,500 for single taxpayers and $6,000 for married taxpayers filing a joint return.

2.1.2. *Policy Questions*

Social Security is a pay-as-you-go program under which currently employed workers and employers finance benefits for retired or disabled recipients. On the other hand, Social Security resembles (and is perceived as) a retirement program under which individuals make nondeductible contributions and later receive benefits. Under the former view, all benefits should be included in gross income. Under the latter view, the recipient should be allowed to offset contributions previously made against benefits received on return of capital principles. Yet another way to view the current rule of § 86 is that the income tax is being used to means-test social security payments by, in effect, reducing net social security benefits received by relatively higher income recipients.

2.2. *Qualified Disaster Relief Payments*

Section 139, enacted as part of The Victims of Terrorism Tax Relief Act of 2001 in response to the events of September 11, 2001, excludes "qualified disaster relief payments" from the gross income of an individual. The provision is very broad. Qualified disasters include not only disasters resulting from "terroristic or military action," but also all Presidentially declared disasters (such as hurricanes, floods, tornados, and earthquakes), disasters resulting from accidents involving common carriers, other events determined by the IRS to be of a catastrophic nature, and disasters determined by a governmental authority to warrant government assistance. I.R.C. § 139(c). Four types of qualified disaster relief payments qualify: (1) reimbursement or payment for personal, family, living or funeral expenses related to a qualified disaster; (2) reimbursement or payment for the expenses of repairing a personal residence (or repairing or replacing its contents) in response to a qualified disaster; (3) payments made by a common carrier by reason of death or personal injuries resulting from a qualified disaster; and (4) general welfare payments made by a federal, state or local government in connection with a qualified disaster. The exclusion applies only to the extent the taxpayer is not otherwise compensated (e.g., by insurance) for expenses reimbursed by relief payments. Further, although not expressly stated in the statute, the exclusion is not intended to apply to any payments in the nature of income replacement. See Joint Comm. on Taxation, Technical Explanation of the "Victims of Terrorism Tax Relief Act of 2001," JCX–93–01 (December 21, 2001). Moreover, as long as the amount of payments "can reasonably expected to be commensurate with the expenses incurred," payment recipients do not have to account for actual expenses in order to qualify for the exclusion. Id. at 16.

Some of the payments excludable under § 139 might arguably be excludable in any event under the nonstatutory general welfare exclusion (government disaster relief payments) or as a gift under § 102 (charitable disaster relief payments), but § 139 provides a statutory exclusion for some payments that otherwise would not be excludable. Compare Rev. Rul. 2003–12, 2003–1 C.B. 283 (amounts paid to an individual by an employer to reimburse the individual for necessary medical, temporary housing, or transportation expenses incurred as a result of a flood are not excludable as a gift under § 102, but are excluded from gross income as qualified disaster relief under § 139 if the flood was a Presidentially declared disaster) with Rev. Rul. 2005–46, 2005–2 C.B. 120 (a grant received by a business under a state program to compensate businesses for damage or destruction of real and personal property on account of a disaster is not excludable from gross income as a qualified disaster relief payment under § 139, which only applies to individuals).

2.3. *Other Special Rules*

Section 85 requires inclusion in income of the full amount of unemployment compensation.

Section 131 excludes certain payments made by states to foster parents to subsidize the care of foster children. See Cato v. Commissioner, 99 T.C.

633 (1992) (federal supplemental security income (SSI) benefits paid to foster parents through a state agency were excluded).

In other situations, the legislation creating the welfare program may exempt the payments from federal income tax. Thus, Title 38 U.S.C. § 5301(a) provides that benefits due under any law administered by the Veteran's Administration are exempt from tax. This exemption includes educational assistance allowances. Rev. Rul. 71–536, 1971–2 C.B. 78. The Uniform Relocation Assistance and Real Property Acquisition Policies Act of 1970, provides that payments to individuals and businesses displaced by federal or federally-assisted programs will not be considered as income for purposes of the income tax. 42 U.S.C. § 4636. But see Wolfers v. Commissioner, 69 T.C. 975 (1978) (basis reduction required). Grants paid to individuals to preserve historically significant structures under the National Historic Preservation Act are exempt from taxation under that Act. 16 U.S.C. § 470b.

CHAPTER 5

LOANS AND OTHER RECEIPTS BALANCED BY OFFSETTING OBLIGATIONS

SECTION 1.   LOANS

Money received in a loan transaction is not gross income. With the receipt there arises a duty to repay in accordance with the terms of the loan. The cash asset is offset by a corresponding liability and the borrower has no increase in net worth as a result of the loan transaction. Correspondingly, repayment of the principal amount of the loan has no income tax consequences to the borrower. (The lender has no income tax consequences because the repayment of the loan principal amount is a return of capital, discussed in Chapter 6.)

Milenbach, et al. v. Commissioner
United States Court of Appeals, Ninth Circuit, 2003.
318 F.3d 924.

■ TASHIMA, CIRCUIT JUDGE:

The Commissioner of Internal Revenue determined deficiencies in Petitioners-Appellants Sheldon and Phyllis Milenbach's federal income taxes for the years 1980 through 1982. The Commissioner also issued notices of Final Partnership Administrative Adjustments determining adjustments to the income of the Los Angeles Raiders, a California Limited Partnership, for the years 1983 through 1989. Petitioners (collectively the "Raiders") appeal from the Tax Court decisions affirming the contested determinations. *See Milenbach v. Comm'r*, 106 T.C. 184 (1996).

The Raiders own a professional football team and belong to the National Football League (the "NFL"). Prior to 1980, the Raiders played their home games at the Oakland-Alameda County Coliseum (the "Oakland Coliseum"). The Raiders' lease of the Oakland Coliseum expired at the end of the 1979 NFL season. During 1979, the Raiders negotiated with the Los Angeles Memorial Coliseum Commission (the "LAMCC") to allow the Raiders to begin playing their home games in the Los Angeles Memorial Coliseum (the "LA Coliseum"). In 1980, the Raiders announced that they intended to leave Oakland and play their home games at the LA Coliseum. This announcement set in motion a series of events that resulted in enormous controversy for the team, including several lawsuits, and a number of business transactions whose tax consequences are at issue here. * * *

I.   THE LAMCC PAYMENTS

A.   BACKGROUND

On March 1, 1980, the Raiders entered into a Memorandum of Agreement ("MOA") with the LAMCC providing for the relocation of the Raiders to Los Angeles beginning with the 1980 NFL season. The parties never implemented this MOA, however, because the City of Oakland ("Oakland") filed an action in eminent domain against the Raiders, seeking to condemn for public use the Raiders' NFL franchise, business, and physical assets. Both Oakland and the NFL obtained preliminary injunctions preventing the Raiders from relocating.

As a result, the Raiders played their 1980 and 1981 home games at the Oakland Coliseum. When the NFL injunction was lifted in 1982, the Raiders resumed negotiations with the LAMCC. On July 5, 1982, these negotiations produced a new Memorandum of Agreement (the "1982 MOA"). Pursuant to the 1982 MOA, in 1984, the parties executed a promissory note (the "Note") and a lease agreement for the LA Coliseum (the "Lease").

The 1982 MOA, the Note, and the Lease (collectively, the "LAMCC Agreement") provided that the LAMCC would loan the Raiders $6.7 million at 10 percent interest. The Raiders were to repay the loan from 12 percent of the net receipts from the operation of luxury suites to be constructed by the Raiders at the LA Coliseum. The repayment was to begin in the third year of suite rentals. The loan was secured by the to-be-constructed suites, with no recourse to the Raiders. The loan consisted of a $4 million cash payment to the Raiders in 1984 and credits totaling $2.7 million against rent due from the Raiders for the years 1982 through 1986.

As to the construction of the suites, the 1982 MOA provided that the Raiders "shall construct" approximately 150 private suites. The MOA went on to state that the construction "shall commence as soon as practicable as determined by [the Raiders] in [their] reasonable discretion, having in mind pending and potential litigation involving the parties hereto, or either of them, financial considerations, and other considerations reasonably deemed important or significant to the [Raiders]." The Lease further provided that the Raiders "shall use [their] best efforts to begin and complete Suite construction as soon as possible." The LAMCC Agreement was the result of arm's-length bargaining between the Raiders and the LAMCC.

The Raiders began playing their home games at the LA Coliseum starting with the 1982 season. Plans to construct the suites prior to the 1984 Summer Olympics were abandoned after the Los Angeles Olympic Committee voiced concerns over the timing of the construction. The

Raiders worked with architects and contractors on the planning of the suites throughout 1985 and 1986.

Actual construction began in early 1987, but was halted on February 18 of that year. On that date, the LAMCC demanded that suite construction stop because the Raiders had not obtained necessary performance bonds. The Raiders responded that they were willing and able to provide the required bonds, but stated that construction would cease because of the LAMCC's failure to make certain improvements to the LA Coliseum. Due to this dispute, construction never resumed and the suites were never completed.

The Raiders never made any payments on the LAMCC loan. In September 1987, the LAMCC filed a lawsuit claiming that the Raiders had breached the Lease by failing to construct the suites "as soon as practicable" and for failing to repay the $6.7 million loan. In January 1988, the Raiders answered the LAMCC's complaint, alleging that the LAMCC had breached a commitment to modernize and reconfigure the stadium. The lawsuit was settled on September 11, 1990.

* * * [T]he Commissioner * * * determined that the $4 million advance paid in 1984 was includable in the Raiders' 1984 gross income.

The Tax Court held that the "loan" payments from the LAMCC were includable in the Raiders' income in the years in which they were received. *Milenbach*, 106 T.C. at 198. It held that the obligation to construct the suites was illusory and, therefore, the LAMCC payments did not qualify as loans for tax purposes because the Raiders "controlled whether or not repayment of the $6.7 million would be triggered."

B. ANALYSIS

* * *

A loan is generally not taxable income because the receipt of the loan is offset by the obligation to repay the loan. *Comm'r v. Tufts*, 461 U.S. 300, 307 (1983). For this rule to apply, however, the loan must be an "existing, unconditional, and legally enforceable obligation for the payment of a principal sum." *Noguchi v. Comm'r*, 992 F.2d 226, 227 (9th Cir.1993); *see also Geftman v. Comm'r*, 154 F.3d 61, 68 (3d Cir.1998) (requiring "an unconditional obligation on the part of the transferee to repay the money, and an unconditional intention on the part of the transferor to secure repayment") (citation and internal quotation marks omitted).

Whether a transaction is a loan for federal income tax purposes is ultimately a question of federal law. *See Helvering v. Stuart*, 317 U.S. 154, 162 (1942) ("Once rights are obtained by local law, whatever they may be called, these rights are subject to the federal definition of taxability."). Initially, however, state law determines the rights and obligations of the parties to a transaction. *See id.* at 161–62. But once an obligation is created by local law, it is subject to the federal definition of taxability. *Id.* Here, the dispositive question is whether the LAMCC Agreement was sufficient, under California law, to subject the Raiders to a non-illusory and enforceable obligation to repay the LAMCC advances. If the Raiders were subject to an "existing, unconditional, and legally enforceable obligation" to repay the LAMCC advances, the advances are properly treated as loans for federal income tax purposes. *Noguchi*, 992 F.2d at 227.

Contrary to the Tax Court's conclusion, the Raiders' broad discretion in the timing of the construction of the suites did not make the contract illusory. Under California law, an obligation under a contract is not illusory if the obligated party's discretion must be exercised with reasonableness or good faith. *See Storek & Storek, Inc. v. Citicorp Real Estate, Inc.*, 122 Cal. Rptr. 2d 267, 281 (Ct. App. 2002) (holding that a promise to pay only if satisfied is not illusory if the ability to claim dissatisfaction is limited by the standard of reasonableness); *24 Hour Fitness, Inc. v. Superior Court*, 78 Cal. Rptr. 2d 533, 541 (Ct. App. 1998) ("[W]here the contract specifies performance the fact that one party reserves the power to vary it is not fatal if the exercise of the power is subject to prescribed or implied limitations such as the duty to exercise it in good faith and in accordance with fair dealings.") (citation and internal quotation marks omitted); *Frankel v. Bd. of Dental Exam'rs*, 54 Cal. Rptr. 2d 128, 136 (Ct. App. 1996) (holding that a contract is not illusory when the power to withdraw from the contract must be exercised in good faith).

Here, the Raiders were required to exercise their discretion reasonably and nothing in the LAMCC Agreement indicates that construction of the suites was optional. Both the 1982 MOA and the Lease state that the suites "shall be" constructed and both require the Raiders to use their "reasonable" discretion in deciding the exact timing in the construction of the suites. The Lease also required the Raiders to use their "best efforts" both to construct the suites as soon as possible and to operate them in such a way as to maximize the profits to be derived from them. At no point were the Raiders free to ignore their obligation to construct the suites. They could only delay the construction for a reasonable time and were required to use their best efforts to complete the suites and begin repayment of the loan. These limitations on the Raiders' discretion were sufficient to create a non-illusory obligation both to construct the suites and to repay the loan that would have been enforceable under California law. The fact that the obligations were later extinguished by the settlement of the 1987 lawsuit does not indicate that the obligation was illusory at the time the contract was made. Accordingly, we conclude that the Tax Court erred in holding that the LAMCC Agreement was illusory.

Because the Raiders had a non-illusory, unconditional obligation to repay the LAMCC loan, the payments were properly treated as loans and were excludable from income in the year in which they were received.[1]

DETAILED ANALYSIS

1. REQUIREMENT OF TRUE DEBT

As noted by the Court of Appeals in *Milenbach,* the Tax Court found that the obligation to construct skyboxes at the Los Angeles coliseum was completely within the Raiders' discretion and that any duties imposed on the Raiders were, therefore, illusory, thus requiring that the "loan" proceeds be included in gross income when received. Another issue in *Milenbach* was whether $10,000,000 received as the first disbursement on a $115 million nonrecourse loan to the Raiders by the City of Irwindale, which was made as part of a package to lure the Raiders to move from the Los Angeles Coliseum to a new coliseum to be built in Irwindale, was a true loan. The Irwindale loan agreement provided that the Raiders' obligation to repay the $10,000,000 advance would be canceled if the City of Irwindale failed to advance the remaining loan proceeds or failed to perform certain other acts relating to construction of a stadium that were required under the loan agreement. In contrast to its decision regarding the advance from the Los Angeles Memorial Coliseum Authority to the Raiders, the Tax Court held that at the time the funds were received from the City of Irwindale, they were not under the Raiders' complete dominion and control. Although the Raiders' obligation to repay could be canceled, the obligation was not conditional on the Raiders' own actions. Any cancellation would result from a condition subsequent that was within the *lender's* control.[1]

As indicated by the court in *Milenbach*, for a transaction to be characterized as a loan there "must have been, at the time the funds were transferred, an unconditional obligation on the part of the transferee to repay the money, and an unconditional intention on the part of the transferor to secure repayment." Geftman v. Commissioner, 154 F.3d 61, 68 (3d Cir.1998); Haag v. Commissioner, 88 T.C. 604, 616 (1987). For a purported loan to be recognized as such, repayment of a loan must be unconditional and not contingent upon some future event. See e.g., United States v. Henderson, 375 F.2d 36 (5th Cir.1967). If a purported indebtedness is not a true debt,

---

[1]   Our holding may or may not end the inquiry with respect to the taxability of the LAMCC loan. Although the Raiders were obligated to repay the loan at the time the payment was received and the rental offsets were made, at some point in time since then, that obligation was extinguished. Such a discharge of indebtedness must be treated as taxable income in the year in which the discharge occurred. 26 U.S.C. § 61(a)(12). The record does not disclose when, if ever, the Raiders recognized the LAMCC loan proceeds as income. Presumably, the Commissioner can further challenge that timing decision, but that issue is not before us.

[1]   The Tax Court also held that the Irwindale loan generated discharge of indebtedness income (see Chapter 10) in 1988 when the State of California enacted legislation that prevented Irwindale from issuing tax-exempt general obligation bonds to fund construction of a stadium for the Raiders. The Court of Appeals remanded this issue to the Tax Court to reconsider whether the discharge of the Raiders' obligation to repay the $10 million loan occurred in a later year.

the money received by the "borrower" will be currently taxable, and if and when the "loan" is repaid, that transaction then must be recharacterized.

In Karns Prime & Fancy Food, Ltd. v. Commissioner, 494 F.3d 404 (3d Cir. 2007), the taxpayer was a retailer that received a $1.5 million advance from a supplier that was evidenced by a promissory note with the proper indicia of debt. The parties concurrently entered into a supply agreement pursuant to which the debt would be forgiven if the taxpayer purchased the quantity of product required under the supply agreement over its term. The court held that the key question in determining whether a receipt of funds is a true loan is whether, at the time of receipt of the funds, the recipient was unconditionally obligated to make repayment. A receipt is not a loan if the taxpayer controls whether it will be entitled to retain the payment. The court found that in substance there was no unconditional obligation to repay the advance, because repayment under the note was due only if the taxpayer materially breached the supply agreement. Thus, since the taxpayer alone controlled whether it would meet the contractual requirements that would result in "forgiveness" of the "loan," the court concluded that receipt was not a true loan but was includable in gross income. Westpac Pacific Food v. Commissioner, 451 F.3d 970 (9th Cir. 2006), reached the opposite conclusion on substantially similar facts.[2]

In Frierdich v. Commissioner, 925 F.2d 180 (7th Cir.1991), the taxpayer was a lawyer in a firm representing the estate of a deceased client. The surviving spouse, executor of the deceased client's estate, "lent" the taxpayer $100,000, at a below-market rate of interest, with the loan due at the time the legal fees for representing the estate were due. Repayment of the note was expressly conditioned on the closing of the estate, and the note provided that the balance on the note could be set-off against the legal fees due from the estate. Because the trial court found as a matter of fact that the taxpayer had no intention of repaying the note, the court held that the $100,000 receipt was not a loan, but was prepaid legal fees includable in gross income.

2.   CANCELLATION OF INDEBTEDNESS INCOME

As indicated in footnote 1 of the opinion in *Milenbach*, the Court of Appeals observed that cancellation of the City of Los Angeles "loan" would result in cancellation of indebtedness income. If a debt is canceled and the borrower is relieved of the duty to repay the loan, that latter transaction must have tax consequences, either because the taxpayer's net worth has been increased or on the theory that the earlier benefit of receipt of cash without realization of income must be offset. Depending on which of these theories is applied, the consequences that would flow from the debt cancellation may differ. In United States v. Kirby Lumber Co., 284 U.S. 1 (1931), the Supreme Court held that when a debt is discharged for less than full repayment, the portion of the debt canceled without payment is income because the borrower's net worth has been increased. The rule that cancellation of indebtedness results in income realization has since been

---

[2]   In Rev. Proc. 2007–53, 2007–2 C.B. 233, the IRS announced that in similar situations it no longer will assert that the retailer realized gross income but will treat the amount as reduction in the price of inventory when purchased, i.e. a "trade discount."

codified in § 61(a)(12). Section 108, however, provides a number of exceptions to this rule, some of which reflect the "increase in net worth" origins of the rule in *Kirby Lumber*. The treatment of cancellation of indebtedness income is discussed in Chapter 10.

SECTION 2.   CLAIM OF RIGHT DOCTRINE

North American Oil Consolidated v. Burnet

Supreme Court of the United States, 1932.
286 U.S. 417.

■ MR. JUSTICE BRANDEIS delivered the opinion of the Court.

The question for decision is whether the sum of $171,979.22 received by the North American Oil Consolidated in 1917, was taxable to it as income of that year.

The money was paid to the company under the following circumstances. Among many properties operated by it in 1916 was a section of oil land, the legal title to which stood in the name of the United States. Prior to that year, the Government, claiming also the beneficial ownership, had instituted a suit to oust the company from possession; and on February 2, 1916, it secured the appointment of a receiver to operate the property, or supervise its operations, and to hold the net income thereof. The money paid to the company in 1917 represented the net profits which had been earned from that property in 1916 during the receivership. The money was paid to the receiver as earned. After entry by the District Court in 1917 of the final decree dismissing the bill, the money was paid, in that year, by the receiver to the company. United States v. North American Oil Consolidated, 242 Fed. 723. The Government took an appeal * * * to the Circuit Court of Appeals. In 1920, that Court affirmed the decree. 264 Fed. 336. In 1922, a further appeal to this Court was dismissed by stipulation. 258 U.S. 633.

The income earned from the property in 1916 had been entered on the books of the company as its income. It had not been included in its original return of income for 1916; but it was included in an amended return for that year which was filed in 1918. Upon auditing the company's income and profits tax returns for 1917, the Commissioner of Internal Revenue determined a deficiency based on other items. The company appealed to the Board of Tax Appeals. There, in 1927 the Commissioner prayed that the deficiency already claimed should be increased so as to include a tax on the amount paid by the receiver to the company in 1917. The Board held that the profits were taxable to the receiver as income of 1916; and hence made no finding whether the company's accounts were kept on the cash receipts and disbursements basis or on the accrual basis. 12 B.T.A. 68. The Circuit Court of Appeals held that the profits were taxable to the company as income of 1917, regardless of whether the company's returns were made on the cash or on the accrual basis. 50 F.(2d) 752. * * *

It is conceded that the net profits earned by the property during the receivership constituted income. The company contends that they should have been reported by the receiver for taxation in 1916; that if not returnable by him, they should have been returned by the company for 1916, because they constitute income of the company accrued in that year; and that if not taxable as income of the company for 1916, they were taxable to it as income for 1922, since the litigation was not finally terminated in its favor until 1922.

First. The income earned in 1916 and impounded by the receiver in that year was not taxable to him, because he was the receiver of only a part of the properties operated by the company.

Second. The net profits were not taxable to the company as income of 1916. For the company was not required in 1916 to report as income an amount which it might never receive. See Burnet v. Logan, 283 U.S. 404, 413. * * * There was no constructive receipt of the profits by the company in that year, because at no time during the year was there a right in the company to demand that the receiver pay over the money. Throughout 1916 it was uncertain who would be declared entitled to the profits. It was not until 1917, when the District Court entered a final decree vacating the receivership and dismissing the bill, that the company became entitled to receive the money. Nor is it material, for the purposes of this case, whether the company's return was filed on the cash receipts and disbursements basis, or on the accrual basis. In neither event was it taxable in 1916 on account of income which it had not yet received and which it might never receive.

Third. The net profits earned by the property in 1916 were not income of the year 1922—the year in which the litigation with the Government was finally terminated. They became income of the company in 1917, when it first became entitled to them and when it actually received them. If a taxpayer receives earnings under a claim of right and without restriction as to its disposition, he has received income which he is required to return, even though it may still be claimed that he is not entitled to retain the money, and even though he may still be adjudged liable to restore its equivalent. See Board v. Commissioner, 51 F.(2d) 73, 75, 76. * * * If in 1922 the Government had prevailed, and the company had been obliged to refund the profits received in 1917, it would have been entitled to a deduction from the profits of 1922, not from those of any earlier year. * * *

Affirmed.

DETAILED ANALYSIS

1. GENERAL

As *North American Oil* indicates, the general rule is that amounts received under a claim of right and without restriction as to their disposition constitute income in the year of receipt, even though the taxpayer might be required ultimately to restore an equivalent amount. The rule is based on the proposition that since the taxpayer has the free and unfettered use of funds from the time of receipt, the taxable year in which that receipt occurs is the appropriate time to fix tax liability. How is this situation different from the receipt of loan proceeds?

rule that comes from North American Oil.

Application of the claim of right doctrine does not depend upon the accounting method of the taxpayer. Items in the nature of gross income received by either cash or accrual method taxpayers are generally includable in gross income when received. Thus, in *North American Oil* the opinion does not consider whether the taxpayer is on the cash or accrual method of accounting.

The basic issue in *North American Oil* arises in a number of contexts. Some of them are considered in the following analysis material. Security deposits, which for many years prior to the Supreme Court directly addressing the issue were analyzed on the basis of *North American Oil,* are discussed in Section 4, and receipts by a taxpayer as a "conduit" are covered in Section 5.

2. EFFECT OF POSSIBILITY OF NON-RETENTION OF THE RECEIPT

The principles of *North American Oil* most commonly are applied in cases where a receipt clearly would be income if retained by the taxpayer, but there is a possibility that the receipt may be required to be returned. A string is in effect attached to the receipt. This string does not involve an obligation to repay, as in the case of a loan or a security deposit, so that it does not prevent the item from being in the nature of gross income. But, since a string that may result in a future repayment of the receipt does exist, the issue is whether the taxpayer should be required to include the receipt in gross income in the year when it is received despite the attached string. There are two basic situations in this area.

2.1. *Possibility of Return Present at Time of Receipt*

North American Oil is an illustration of this type of receipt. The amounts paid to the taxpayer in 1917 pursuant to the final decree of the District Court were subject to the cloud created by the Government's appeal. If the Government had prevailed in its appeal, the taxpayer would have been entitled to a deduction for the repayment in the year the repayment was made.

A number of cases have addressed the scope of the *North American Oil* rule. Where the taxpayer deposited in a bank account amounts received in satisfaction of a judgment and, although retaining absolute dominion, indicated in its account books its intention not to use the funds pending final resolution of the claim, the amounts received nevertheless were held includable in income. Commissioner v. Alamitos Land Co., 112 F.2d 648 (9th

Cir.1940). The filing of a bond as security for repayment also has been held to place no restriction of moneys received and thus does not remove the receipt from the claim of right doctrine. Commissioner v. Brooklyn Union Gas Co., 62 F.2d 505 (2d Cir.1933). The IRS has applied this rule to amounts received by a utility company pursuant to a rate increase and placed in a bank account under the joint control of the taxpayer and the surety company liable for repayment if so ordered by court. Rev. Rul. 55–137, 1955–1 C.B. 215.

Where the taxpayer is required to place contested amounts received out of its control, the claim of right doctrine does not require inclusion upon receipt. Thus, for example, in Rev. Rul. 69–642, 1969–2 C.B. 9, a corporation collected commissions from its customers in excess of the rate approved by a government agency. Under a court order, the taxpayer deposited the excess portion of the commissions with the court clerk pending final determination of the proper rates by the court. The taxpayer was held not to have income until ownership of the excess commissions was determined. In Mutual Telephone Co. v. United States, 204 F.2d 160 (9th Cir.1953), a telephone company was authorized in 1941 temporarily to increase installation charges, but was required to transfer the amounts into a special account until the regulatory commission agreed to the increase. The company intermingled the cash receipts, but kept marketable securities equal to the amount in the special account. In 1949 it was authorized to dispose of the special account. The court held that inclusion under the claim of right doctrine was not required in 1941 because the funds were not received without restriction at that time.

2.2. *Retention Appears Definite at Time of Receipt but Later Events Require Return of Item*

The cases in this category include situations where a salary payment must later be returned because an error in its computation is discovered. Since no issue of repayment existed when the receipt occurred, the item will have been included in income without question. When the unanticipated repayment occurs, a deduction is allowed for the year of repayment. See Chapter 29, Section 1.C.

SECTION 3.   ILLEGAL INCOME

REGULATIONS: Section 1.61–14(a).

James v. United States

Supreme Court of the United States, 1961.
366 U.S. 213.

■ MR. CHIEF JUSTICE WARREN announced the judgment of the Court and an opinion in which MR. JUSTICE BRENNAN and MR. JUSTICE STEWART concur.

The issue before us in this case is whether embezzled funds are to be included in the "gross income" of the embezzler in the year in which the funds are misappropriated under * * * § 61(a) of the Internal Revenue Code of 1954.

The facts are not in dispute. The petitioner is a union official who, with another person, embezzled in excess of $738,000 during the years 1951 through 1954 from his employer union and from an insurance company with which the union was doing business.[3] Petitioner failed to report these amounts in his gross income in those years and was convicted for willfully attempting to evade the federal income tax due for each of the years 1951 through 1954 in violation of [the predecessor of § 7201] and § 7201 of the Internal Revenue Code of 1954. He was sentenced to a total of three years' imprisonment. The Court of Appeals affirmed. 273 F.2d 5. Because of a conflict with this Court's decision in Commissioner of Internal Revenue v. Wilcox, 327 U.S. 404, a case whose relevant facts are concededly the same as those in the case now before us, we granted certiorari. 362 U.S. 974.

In Wilcox, the Court held that embezzled money does not constitute taxable income to the embezzler in the year of the embezzlement under [§ 61(a)]. Six years later, this Court held, in Rutkin v. United States, 343 U.S. 130, that extorted money does constitute taxable income to the extortionist in the year that the money is received under [§ 61(a)]. In Rutkin, the Court did not overrule Wilcox, but stated:

"We do not reach in this case the factual situation involved in Commissioner of Internal Revenue v. Wilcox, 327 U.S. 404. We limit that case to its facts. There embezzled funds were held not to constitute taxable income to the embezzler under [§ 61(a)]." Id., 343 U.S. at page 138.

However, examination of the reasoning used in Rutkin leads us inescapably to the conclusion that Wilcox was thoroughly devitalized.

The basis for the Wilcox decision was "that a taxable gain is conditioned upon (1) the presence of a claim of right to the alleged gain and (2) the absence of a definite, unconditional obligation to repay or return that which would otherwise constitute a gain. Without some bona fide legal or equitable claim, even though it be contingent or contested in nature, the taxpayer cannot be said to have received any gain or profit within the reach of [§ 61(a)]." Commissioner of Internal Revenue v. Wilcox, supra, 327 U.S. at page 408. Since Wilcox embezzled the money, held it "without any semblance of a bona fide claim of right," ibid., and therefore "was at all times under an unqualified duty and obligation to repay the money to his employer," ibid., the Court found that the money embezzled was not includible within "gross income." But Rutkin's legal claim was no greater than that of Wilcox. It was specifically found "that petitioner had no basis for his claim * * * and that he obtained it by extortion." Rutkin v. United States, supra, 343 U.S. at page 135. Both

---

[3] Petitioner has pleaded guilty to the offense of conspiracy to embezzle in the Court of Essex County, New Jersey.

Wilcox and Rutkin obtained the money by means of a criminal act; neither had a bona fide claim of right to the funds.[7] Nor was Rutkin's obligation to repay the extorted money to the victim any less than that of Wilcox. The victim of an extortion, like the victim of an embezzlement, has a right to restitution. Furthermore, it is inconsequential that an embezzler may lack title to the sums he appropriates while an extortionist may gain a voidable title. Questions of federal income taxation are not determined by such "attenuated subtleties." Lucas v. Earl, 281 U.S. 111 * * * . Thus, the fact that Rutkin secured the money with the consent of his victim * * * is irrelevant. Likewise unimportant is the fact that the sufferer of an extortion is less likely to seek restitution than one whose funds are embezzled. What is important is that the right to recoupment exists in both situations.

Examination of the relevant cases in the courts of appeals lends credence to our conclusion that the Wilcox rationale was effectively vitiated by this Court's decision in Rutkin. Although this case appears to be the first to arise that is "on all fours" with Wilcox, the lower federal courts, in deference to the undisturbed Wilcox holding, have earnestly endeavored to find distinguishing facts in the cases before them which would enable them to include sundry unlawful gains within "gross income."[9]

It had been a well-established principle, long before either Rutkin or Wilcox, that unlawful, as well as lawful, gains are comprehended within the term "gross income." Section II B of the Income Tax Act of 1913 provided that "the net income of a taxable person shall include gains, profits, and income * * * from * * * the transaction of any *lawful* business carried on for gain or profit, or gains or profits and income derived from any source whatever * * * ." (Emphasis supplied.) 38 Stat. 167. When the statute was amended in 1916, the one word "lawful" was omitted. This revealed, we think, the obvious intent of that Congress to tax income derived from both legal and illegal sources, to remove the incongruity of having the gains of the honest laborer taxed and the gains of the dishonest immune. Rutkin v. United States, supra, 343 U.S. at page 138; United States v. Sullivan, 274 U.S. 259, 263. Thereafter, the Court held that gains from illicit traffic in liquor are includible within "gross income." Ibid.

* * * And, the Court has pointed out, with approval, that there "has been a widespread and settled administrative and judicial recognition of

---

[7]   The Government contends that the adoption in Wilcox of a claim of right test as a touchstone of taxability had no support in the prior cases of this Court; that the claim of right test was a doctrine invoked by the Court in aid of the concept of annual accounting, to determine *when,* not *whether,* receipts constituted income.

[9]   For example, Kann v. Commissioner, 3 Cir., 210 F.2d 247, was differentiated on the following grounds: the taxpayer was never indicted or convicted of embezzlement; there was no adequate proof that the victim did not forgive the misappropriation; the taxpayer was financially able to both pay the income tax and make restitution; the taxpayer would have likely received most of the misappropriated money as dividends. In Marienfeld v. United States, supra, the court believed that the victim was not likely to repudiate. * * *

the taxability of unlawful gains of many kinds," Rutkin v. United States, supra, 343 U.S. at page 137. These include protection payments made to racketeers, ransom payments paid to kidnappers, bribes, money derived from the sale of unlawful insurance policies, graft, black market gains, funds obtained from the operation of lotteries, income from race track bookmaking and illegal prize fight pictures. Ibid.

The starting point in all cases dealing with the question of the scope of what is included in "gross income" begins with the basic premise that the purpose of Congress was "to use the full measure of its taxing power." Helvering v. Clifford, 309 U.S. 331, 334. And the Court has given a liberal construction to the broad phraseology of the "gross income" definition statutes in recognition of the intention of Congress to tax all gains except those specifically exempted. * * * The language of § 22(a) of the 1939 Code "gains or profits and income derived from any source whatever," and the more simplified language of § 61(a) of the 1954 Code, "all income from whatever source derived," have been held to encompass all "accessions to wealth, clearly realized, and over which the taxpayers have complete dominion." Commissioner of Internal Revenue v. Glenshaw Glass Co., 348 U.S. 426, 431. A gain "constitutes taxable income when its recipient has such control over it that, as a practical matter, he derives readily realizable economic value from it." Rutkin v. United States, supra, 343 U.S. at page 137. Under these broad principles, we believe that petitioner's contention, that all unlawful gains are taxable except those resulting from embezzlement, should fail.

When a taxpayer acquires earnings, lawfully or unlawfully, without the consensual recognition, express or implied, of an obligation to repay and without restriction as to their disposition, "he has received income which he is required to return, even though it may still be claimed that he is not entitled to retain the money, and even though he may still be adjudged liable to restore its equivalent." North American Oil Consolidated v. Burnet, supra, 286 U.S. at page 424. In such case, the taxpayer has "actual command over the property taxed—the actual benefit for which the tax is paid," Corliss v. Bowers, supra [281 U.S. 376]. This standard brings wrongful appropriations within the broad sweep of "gross income"; it excludes loans. When a law-abiding taxpayer mistakenly receives income in one year, which receipt is assailed and found to be invalid in a subsequent year, the taxpayer must nonetheless report the amount as "gross income" in the year received. United States v. Lewis, supra * * *. We do not believe that Congress intended to treat a law-breaking taxpayer differently. Just as the honest taxpayer may deduct any amount repaid in the year in which the repayment is made, the Government points out that, "If, when, and to the extent that the victim recovers back the misappropriated funds, there is of course a reduction in the embezzler's income." Brief for the United States, p. 24.

Petitioner contends that the Wilcox rule has been in existence since 1946; that if Congress had intended to change the rule, it would have done so; that there was a general revision of the income tax laws in 1954 without mention of the rule; that a bill to change it[11] was introduced in the Eighty-sixth Congress but was not acted upon; that, therefore, we may not change the rule now. But the fact that Congress has remained silent or has re-enacted a statute which we have construed, or that congressional attempts to amend a rule announced by this Court have failed, does not necessarily debar us from re-examining and correcting the Court's own errors. * * * There may have been any number of reasons why Congress acted as it did. Helvering v. Hallock, supra. * * * One of the reasons could well be our subsequent decision in Rutkin which has been thought by many to have repudiated Wilcox. Particularly might this be true in light of the decisions of the Courts of Appeals which have been riding a narrow rail between the two cases and further distinguishing them to the disparagement of Wilcox. * * *

We believe that Wilcox was wrongly decided and we find nothing in congressional history since then to persuade us that Congress intended to legislate the rule. Thus, we believe that we should now correct the error and the confusion resulting from it, certainly if we do so in a manner that will not prejudice those who might have relied on it. * * * We should not continue to confound confusion, particularly when the result would be to perpetuate the injustice of relieving embezzlers of the duty of paying income taxes on the money they enrich themselves with through theft while honest people pay their taxes on every conceivable type of income.

But, we are dealing here with a felony conviction under statutes which apply to any person who "willfully" fails to account for his tax or who "willfully" attempts to evade his obligation. In Spies v. United States, 317 U.S. 492, 499, the Court said that [§ 7201] embodied "the gravest of offenses against the revenues," and stated that willfulness must therefore include an evil motive and want of justification in view of all the circumstances. Id., 317 U.S. at page 498. Willfulness "involves a specific intent which must be proven by independent evidence and which cannot be inferred from the mere understatement of income." Holland v. United States, 348 U.S. 121, 139.

We believe that the element of willfulness could not be proven in a criminal prosecution for failing to include embezzled funds in gross income in the year of misappropriation so long as the statute contained the gloss placed upon it by Wilcox at the time the alleged crime was committed. Therefore, we feel that petitioner's conviction may not stand and that the indictment against him must be dismissed.

■ Since MR. JUSTICE HARLAN, MR. JUSTICE FRANKFURTER, and MR. JUSTICE CLARK agree with us concerning Wilcox, that case is overruled. MR. JUSTICE BLACK, MR. JUSTICE DOUGLAS, and MR. JUSTICE WHITTAKER believe that petitioner's conviction must be reversed and the case dismissed for the reasons stated in their opinions.

---

[11]   H.R. 8854, 86th Cong., 1st Sess.

Accordingly, the judgment of the Court of Appeals is reversed and the case is remanded to the District Court with directions to dismiss the indictment.

It is so ordered.

■ MR. JUSTICE BLACK, whom MR. JUSTICE DOUGLAS joins, concurring in part and dissenting in part. * * *

[T]he arguments * * * against taxability of [embezzled] funds * * * can best be obtained from the court's opinion in McKnight v. Commissioner, written by Judge Sibley * * * . He recognized that the taxpayer could not rely upon the unlawfulness of his business to defeat taxation if he had made a "gain" in that business. He pointed out, however, that the ordinary embezzler "got no title, void or voidable, to what he took. He was still in possession as he was before, but with a changed purpose. He still had no right nor color of right. He claimed none." Judge Sibley's opinion went on to point out that the "first takings [of an embezzler] are, indeed, nearly always with the intention of repaying, a sort of unauthorized borrowing. It must be conceded that no gain is realized by borrowing, because of the offsetting obligation." Approaching the matter from a practical standpoint, Judge Sibley also explained that subjecting the embezzled funds to a tax would amount to allowing the United States "a preferential claim for part of the dishonest gain, to the direct loss and detriment of those to whom it ought to be restored." He was not willing to put the owner of funds that had been stolen in competition with the United States Treasury Department as to which one should have a preference to get those funds.

* * *

It contributes nothing new to the analysis of this problem to say repeatedly that the dishonest man must be subject to taxation just as the honest. As already said, Chief Justice Stone and the others sitting with him on the Wilcox Court fully accepted that general principle and we do still. Applying it here, we would say the embezzler should be treated just like the law-abiding, honest borrower who has obtained the owner's consent to his use of the money. It would be unthinkable to tax the borrower on his "gain" of the borrowed funds and thereby substantially impair the lender's chance of ever recovering the debt. The injury that the Government would inflict on the lender by making the borrower less able to repay the loan surely would not be adequately compensated by telling the lender that he can take a tax deduction for the loss, and it is equally small comfort to the embezzlement victim for the Government, after taking part of his property as a tax on the embezzler, to tell the victim that he can take a deduction for his loss if he has any income against which to offset the deduction. There is, of course, one outstanding distinction between a borrower and an embezzler, and that is that the embezzler uses the funds without the owner's consent. This distinction can be of no importance for purposes of taxability of the funds, however, because as a matter of common sense it suggests that there is, if anything, less reason to tax the embezzler than the borrower. But if this distinction is to be the reason why the embezzlement must be taxed just as "the gains of the honest laborer," then the use of this slogan in this case is laid bare as no more than a means of imposing a second punishment for the crime of embezzlement without regard to revenue considerations, the effect on the rightful owner, or the proper role of this Court when asked to overrule a criminal statutory precedent. The double jeopardy implications would seem obvious, and discussion of the serious inadvisability for other reasons of thus injecting the Federal Government into local law enforcement can be found in the dissenting opinion in Rutkin.

* * *

■ MR. JUSTICE WHITTAKER, whom MR. JUSTICE BLACK and MR. JUSTICE DOUGLAS join, concurring in part and dissenting in part. * * *

An embezzler, like a common thief, acquires not a semblance of right, title, or interest in his plunder, and whether he spends it or not, he is indebted to his victim in the full amount taken as surely as if he had left a signed promissory note at the scene of the crime. Of no consequence from any standpoint is the absence of such formalities as (in the words of the prevailing opinion) "the consensual recognition, express or implied, of an obligation to repay." The law readily implies whatever "consensual recognition" is needed for the rightful owner to assert an immediately ripe and enforceable obligation of repayment against the wrongful taker. These principles are not "attenuated subtleties" but are among the clearest and most easily applied rules of our law. They exist to protect the rights of the innocent victim, and we should accord them full recognition and respect.

The fact that an embezzler's victim may have less chance of success than other creditors in seeking repayment from his debtor is not a valid reason for us further to diminish his prospects by adopting a rule that would allow the Commissioner of Internal Revenue to assert and enforce a prior federal tax lien against that which "rightfully and completely belongs" to the victim. Commissioner of Internal Revenue v. Wilcox, supra, 327 U.S. at page 410. The Chief Justice's opinion quite understandably expresses much concern for "honest taxpayers," but it attempts neither to deny nor justify the manifest injury that its holding will inflict on those honest taxpayers, victimized by embezzlers, who will find their claims for recovery subordinated to federal tax liens. Statutory provisions, by which we are bound, clearly and unequivocally accord priority to federal tax liens over the claims of others, including "judgment creditors."

However, if it later happens that the debtor-creditor relationship between the embezzler and his victim is discharged by something other than full repayment, such as by the running of a Statute of Limitations against the victim's claim, or by a release given for less than the full amount owed, the embezzler at that time, but not before, will have made a clear taxable gain and realized "an accession to income" which he will be required under full penalty of the law to report in his federal income tax return for that year. No honest taxpayer could be harmed by this rule.

* * *

DETAILED ANALYSIS

1. EFFECT OF REPAYMENT

In line with the suggestion in the *James* opinion, it has been held that subsequent repayments of embezzled funds qualify for a loss deduction under § 165(c)(2). Rev. Rul. 65–254, 1965–2 C.B. 50. Stephens v. Commissioner, 905 F.2d 667 (2d Cir.1990), allowed a deduction under § 162(c) for the judicially ordered repayment of profits derived from a criminally fraudulent scheme. But see Waldman v. Commissioner, 88 T.C. 1384 (1987), aff'd by order, 850 F.2d 611 (9th Cir.1988) (disallowing by analogy to § 162(f), discussed in Chapter 12, Section 5.A., a deduction for restitution to fraud victim that was a condition of probation).

2. EFFECT OF FORFEITURE STATUTES

Gambina v. Commissioner, 91 T.C. 826 (1988), held that profits derived from illegal activities and forfeited to the government under the Racketeer Influenced and Corrupt Organizations Act (RICO) must be included in gross income even though RICO provides that title to the money vests in the government at the time the illegal act is committed. Vasta v. Commissioner, T.C. Memo. 1989–531, likewise held that a convicted cocaine dealer was required to include in gross income $6.8 million attributable to cash and cocaine in his possession and seized at time of arrest, even though the cash and cocaine were forfeited to the United States government and, under § 280E, no § 165 loss deduction was available with respect to the seizure. The taxpayer's argument that he had owned the cash and cocaine for only eight days before they were seized and therefore did not possess the requisite dominion and control under *James* was rejected. See also Ianniello v. Commissioner, 98 T.C. 165 (1992), holding that a forfeiture under RICO of illegal profits is deductible in the year of actual repayment; the RICO provision that title to illegal profits vests in the government *ab initio* does not apply to permit exclusion from gross income.

3. THE CONSENSUAL RECOGNITION TEST

The "consensual recognition, expressed or implied, of an obligation to repay," which the "majority" opinion in *James* saw as the test of nonincludability, has given rise to some interesting litigation. In Norman v. Commissioner, T.C. Memo. 1968–40, aff'd per curiam, 407 F.2d 1337 (3d Cir.1969), the taxpayer had been embezzling from his employer and, when discovered, agreed to make repayment of the funds taken. The court held that the subsequent "consensual recognition" did not relate back to the time of the taking and thus did not retroactively convert the transaction into a loan. See also Moore v. United States, 412 F.2d 974 (5th Cir.1969) (attempt by taxpayer to characterize embezzlement scheme as a loan failed because, though there may have been an intention to repay, there was no actual agreement between the party providing the money and the party receiving it and hence no "consensual recognition" as required by *James*). In Buff v. Commissioner, 58 T.C. 224 (1972), the taxpayer embezzled $22,000 in 1965. In the same year, he executed a confession of judgment to his employer agreeing to repay the embezzled funds and make some payments in that year. The IRS treated the embezzled funds as income in 1965 but the Tax Court held that no income was realized because of the offsetting obligation to repay: "Where there is a 'consensual recognition' of indebtedness within the same taxable year, formalized by a confession of judgment, such a transaction does not result in the realization of taxable gain." The Court of Appeals reversed on the ground that the confession of judgment was of "no value" at the time it was given and the funds were not in fact subsequently repaid. 496 F.2d 847 (2d Cir.1974). A different result was reached in Collins v. Commissioner, 3 F.3d 625 (2d Cir.1993), where an off-track betting clerk embezzled tickets but turned himself in at the end of the day and made immediate restitution of the proceeds from the winning tickets. The court held that the clerk realized income equal to the retail price of all of the embezzled tickets minus the face value of the returned winning tickets.

A subsequently arising consensual obligation to repay in the year of receipt seems irrelevant to the question of income inclusion unless the transaction can be viewed as a loan, which *James* ruled out with regard to embezzled funds. The real significance of the obligation to repay is whether it can justify a current deduction for the taxpayer (prior to actual repayment) unavailable for taxpayers on the cash method of accounting. See Chapter 28, Section 2.B. Quinn v. Commissioner, 524 F.2d 617 (7th Cir.1975), followed this approach, focusing on the deduction issue.

In Gilbert v. Commissioner, 552 F.2d 478 (2d Cir.1977), the president and principal shareholder of a corporation acquired shares of another corporation on margin intending ultimately to merge the two companies. Because of a drop in the stock market, the taxpayer was required to put up almost $2 million additional margin. Funds from his corporation were used for that purpose. The taxpayer intended from the outset to repay the funds to the corporation and thought he was acting in the corporation's best interest in protecting his position with respect to the stock purchase. He informed some of the directors of the action and, within a few days after the deposit of the funds, the taxpayer executed a demand note to the corporation and assigned all his assets as security for the note. The board of directors accepted the note but refused to ratify the withdrawal of the funds. The court concluded that this was not a "typical embezzlement case" and did not interpret *James* to require "income realization in every case of unlawful withdrawals by a taxpayer" as urged by the Government. By virtue of the assignment, there was no net accretion to the taxpayer's wealth since the value of the assigned assets exceeded the amount withdrawn from the corporation: "We conclude that where a taxpayer withdraws funds from a corporation which he fully intends to repay and which he expects with reasonable certainty he will be able to repay, where he believes that his withdrawals will be approved by the corporation, and where he makes a prompt assignment of assets sufficient to secure the amount owed, he does not realize income under the *James* test."

4.   PRIORITY OF CLAIMS TO STOLEN FUNDS

The Government's claim against the embezzler for the tax due on stolen funds is often in competition with the owner's claim for repayment. Where the defrauder's assets are few, the Government's lien established under the tax lien provisions (§§ 6321–6323) often competes for priority with the lien of the defrauded creditor. Normally, the rule "first in line is first in time" governs the priority of liens. However, the defrauded party who under state law would have priority may be subordinated to a subsequently-filed tax lien where his lien is "inchoate" or unperfected prior to the filing of the tax lien. United States v. Security Trust & Savings Bank, 340 U.S. 47 (1950). But where under state law the thief did not acquire any title to the stolen money, no federal tax lien attaches, Aquilino v. United States, 363 U.S. 509 (1960), and the rightful owner may recover from the government taxes paid by a thief out of stolen funds. Dennis v. United States, 372 F.Supp. 563 (E.D.Va.1974); Carter v. United States, 49 A.F.T.R.2d 1016 (N.D.Cal.1982).

In instances where the defrauder has been adjudicated a bankrupt under the Bankruptcy Act, these priority problems may become more complicated because tax liens have a special priority. See § 507 of the Bankruptcy Act. In United States v. Rochelle, 384 F.2d 748 (5th Cir.1967), the court, after finding that amounts obtained under false pretenses were not "loans" and hence were subject to tax in the hands of the "borrower," made the following observation: "The Referee in Bankruptcy and the district court below apparently considered it significant that the dispute here involves a contest between the United States and the defrauded lenders, who are the claimants in the Bankruptcy proceeding. While we are not without sympathy for these victims of [the defrauder's] schemes, we do not perceive the relevance of the procedural posture of the case in this respect. It is for Congress, and not the Courts, to determine priorities in both taxation and Bankruptcy. Since Congress has decided that income shall be taxable, and that a properly obtained lien for taxes shall have * * * priority in Bankruptcy, it is their decision and not ours that the United States shall take all and the other claimants nothing."

SECTION 4.   DEPOSITS

REGULATIONS: Section 1.61–8(b).

Commissioner v. Indianapolis Power & Light Co.

Supreme Court of the United States, 1990.
493 U.S. 203.

■ JUSTICE BLACKMUN delivered the opinion of the Court.

Respondent Indianapolis Power & Light Company (IPL) requires certain customers to make deposits with it to assure payment of future bills for electric service. Petitioner Commissioner of Internal Revenue contends that these deposits are advance payments for electricity and therefore constitute taxable income to IPL upon receipt. IPL contends otherwise.

I

IPL is a regulated Indiana corporation that generates and sells electricity in Indianapolis and its environs. It keeps its books on the accrual and calendar year basis. During the years 1974 through 1977, approximately 5% of IPL's residential and commercial customers were required to make deposits "to insure prompt payment," as the customers' receipts stated, of future utility bills. These customers were selected because their credit was suspect. * * *

In March 1976, IPL amended its rules governing the deposit program. * * * Under the amended rules, the * * * interest rate was raised to 6% but was payable only on deposits held for 12 months or more. A deposit was refunded when the customer made timely payments for either 9 consecutive months, or for 10 out of 12 consecutive months so long as the 2 delinquent months were not themselves consecutive. A customer could obtain a refund prior to that time by satisfying the credit test. As under the previous rules, the refund would be made in cash or by check, or, at the customer's option, applied against future bills. Any deposit unclaimed after seven years was to escheat to the State. See Ind.Code § 32–9–1–6(a) (1988).

IPL did not treat these deposits as income at the time of receipt. Rather, as required by state administrative regulations, the deposits were carried on its books as current liabilities. Under its accounting system, IPL recognized income when it mailed a monthly bill. If the deposit was used to offset a customer's bill, the utility made the necessary accounting adjustments. Customer deposits were not physically segregated in any way from the company's general funds. They were commingled with other receipts and at all times were subject to IPL's unfettered use and control. It is undisputed that IPL's treatment of the deposits was consistent with accepted accounting practice and applicable state regulations.

Upon audit of respondent's returns for the calendar years 1974 through 1977, the Commissioner asserted deficiencies. * * * The Commissioner took the position that the deposits were advance payments for electricity and therefore were taxable to IPL in the year of receipt. He contended that the increase or decrease in customer deposits outstanding at the end of each year represented an increase or decrease in IPL's income for the year. IPL disagreed and filed a petition in the United States Tax Court for redetermination of the asserted deficiencies.

In a reviewed decision, with one judge not participating, a unanimous Tax Court ruled in favor of IPL. 88 T.C. 964 (1987). The court * * * relied on several factors in concluding that the deposits in question were properly excluded from gross income. It noted, among other things, that only 5% of IPL's customers were required to make deposits; that the customer rather than the utility controlled the ultimate disposition of a deposit; and that IPL consistently treated the deposits as belonging to the customers, both by listing them as current liabilities for accounting purposes and by paying interest. * * *

The United States Court of Appeals for the Seventh Circuit affirmed the Tax Court's decision. 857 F.2d 1162 (1988). The court stated that "the proper approach to determining the appropriate tax treatment of a customer deposit is to look at the primary purpose of the deposit based on all the facts and circumstances. . . ." * * * The court appeared to place primary reliance, however, on IPL's obligation to pay interest on the deposits. It asserted that "as the interest rate paid on a deposit to secure income begins to approximate the return that the recipient would be expected to make from 'the use' of the deposit amount, the deposit begins to serve purposes that comport more squarely with a security deposit." * * * Noting that IPL had paid interest on the customer deposits throughout the period in question, the court upheld, as not clearly erroneous, the Tax Court's determination that the principal purpose of these deposits was to serve as security rather than as prepayment of income. * * *

Because the Seventh Circuit was in specific disagreement with the Eleventh Circuit's ruling in City Gas Co. of Florida, supra, we granted certiorari to resolve the conflict. 490 U.S. 1033 (1989).

II

We begin with the common ground. IPL acknowledges that these customer deposits are taxable as income upon receipt if they constitute advance payments for electricity to be supplied. The Commissioner, on his part, concedes that customer deposits that secure the performance of non-income-producing covenants—such as a utility customer's obligation to ensure that meters will not be damaged—are not taxable income. And it is settled that receipt of a loan is not income to the borrower. * * * IPL, stressing its obligation to refund the deposits with interest, asserts that the payments are similar to loans. The Commissioner, however, contends that a deposit which serves to secure the payment of future income is properly analogized to an advance payment for goods or services. See Rev. Rul. 72–519, 1972–2 C.B. 32, 33 ("When the purpose of the deposit is to guarantee the customer's payment of amounts owed to the creditor, such a deposit is treated as an advance payment, but when the purpose of the deposit is to secure a property interest of the taxpayer the deposit is regarded as a true security deposit").

In economic terms, to be sure, the distinction between a loan and an advance payment is one of degree rather than of kind. A commercial loan, like an advance payment, confers an economic benefit on the recipient: a business presumably does not borrow money unless it believes that the income it can earn from its use of the borrowed funds will be greater than its interest obligation. * * * Even though receipt of the money is subject to a duty to repay, the borrower must regard itself as better off after the loan than it was before. The economic benefit of a loan, however, consists entirely of the opportunity to earn income on the use of the money prior to the time the loan must be repaid. And in that context our system is content to tax these earnings as they are realized. The recipient of an advance payment, in contrast, gains both immediate use of the money (with the chance to realize earnings thereon) and the opportunity to make a profit by providing goods or services at a cost lower than the amount of the payment.

The question, therefore, cannot be resolved simply by noting that respondent derives some economic benefit from receipt of these deposits. Rather, the issue turns upon the nature of the rights and obligations that IPL assumed when the deposits were made. In determining what sort of economic benefits qualify as income, this Court has invoked various formulations. It has referred, for example, to "undeniable accessions to wealth, clearly realized, and over which the taxpayers have complete dominion." Commissioner v. Glenshaw Glass Co., 348 U.S. 426, 431 (1955). It also has stated: "When a taxpayer acquires earnings, lawfully or unlawfully, without the consensual recognition, express or implied, of an obligation to repay and without restriction as to their disposition, 'he has received income.'" James v. United States, 366 U.S., at 219, quoting North American Oil Consolidated v. Burnet, 286 U.S. 417, 424 (1932). IPL hardly enjoyed "complete dominion" over the customer deposits entrusted to it. Rather, these deposits were acquired subject to an express "obligation to repay," either at the time service was terminated or at the time a customer established good credit. So long as the customer fulfills his legal obligation to make timely payments, his deposit ultimately is to be refunded, and both the timing and method of that refund are largely within the control of the customer.

The Commissioner stresses the fact that these deposits were not placed in escrow or segregated from IPL's other funds, and that IPL therefore enjoyed unrestricted use of the money. That circumstance, however, cannot be dispositive. After all, the same might be said of a commercial loan; yet the Commissioner does not suggest that a loan is taxable upon receipt simply because the borrower is free to use the funds in whatever fashion he chooses until the time of repayment. In determining whether a taxpayer enjoys "complete dominion" over a given sum, the crucial point is not whether his use of the funds is unconstrained during some interim period. The key is whether the taxpayer has some guarantee that he will be allowed to keep the money. IPL's receipt of these deposits was accompanied by no such guarantee.

Nor is it especially significant that these deposits could be expected to generate income greater than the modest interest IPL was required to pay. Again, the same could be said of a commercial loan, since, as has been noted, a business is unlikely to borrow unless it believes that it can realize benefits that exceed the cost of servicing the debt. A bank could hardly operate profitably if its earnings on deposits did not surpass its interest obligations; but the deposits themselves are not treated as income.[5] Any income that the utility may earn through use of the deposit money of course is taxable, but the prospect that income will be generated provides no ground for taxing the principal.

The Commissioner's advance-payment analogy seems to us to rest upon a misconception of the value of an advance payment to its recipient. An advance payment, like the deposits at issue here, concededly protects the seller against the risk that it would be unable to collect money owed it after it has furnished goods or services. But an advance payment does much more: it protects against the risk that the purchaser will back out of the deal before the seller performs. From the moment an advance payment is made, the seller is assured that, so long as it fulfills its contractual obligation, the money is its to keep. Here, in contrast, a customer submitting a deposit made no commitment to purchase a specified quantity of electricity, or indeed to purchase any electricity at all.[6] IPL's right to keep the money depends upon the customer's purchase of electricity, and upon his later decision to have the deposit applied to future bills, not merely upon the utility's adherence to its contractual duties. Under these circumstances, IPL's dominion over the fund is far less complete than is ordinarily the case in an advance-payment situation.

The Commissioner emphasizes that these deposits frequently will be used to pay for electricity, either because the customer defaults on his obligation or because the customer, having established credit, chooses to apply the deposit to future bills rather than to accept a refund. When this occurs, the Commissioner argues, the transaction, from a cash-flow standpoint, is equivalent to an advance payment. In his view this economic equivalence mandates identical tax treatment.[7]

Whether these payments constitute income when received, however, depends upon the parties' rights and obligations at the time the payments are made. The problem with petitioner's argument perhaps can best be understood if we imagine a loan between parties involved in

---

[5]   Cf. Rev. Rul. 71–189, 1971–1 Cum.Bull. 32 (inactive deposits are not income until bank asserts dominion over the accounts). * * *

[6]   A customer, for example, might terminate service the day after making the deposit. Also, IPL's dominion over a deposit remains incomplete even after the customer begins buying electricity. As has been noted, the deposit typically is set at twice the customer's estimated monthly bill. So long as the customer pays his bills in a timely fashion, the money he owes the utility (for electricity used but not yet paid for) almost always will be less than the amount of the deposit. If this were not the case, the deposit would provide inadequate protection. Thus, throughout the period the deposit is held, at least a portion is likely to be money that IPL has no real assurance of ever retaining.

[7]   The Commissioner is unwilling, however, to pursue this line of reasoning to the limit of its logic. He concedes that these deposits would not be taxable if they were placed in escrow, Tr. of Oral Arg. 4; but from a cashflow standpoint it does not make much difference whether the money is placed in escrow or commingled with the utility's other funds. In either case, the utility receives the money and allocates it to subsequent purchases of electricity if the customer defaults or chooses to apply his refund to a future bill.

an ongoing commercial relationship. At the time the loan falls due, the lender may decide to apply the money owed him to the purchase of goods or services rather than to accept repayment in cash. But this decision does not mean that the loan, when made, was an advance payment after all. The lender in effect has taken repayment of his money (as was his contractual right) and has chosen to use the proceeds for the purchase of goods or services from the borrower. Although, for the sake of convenience, the parties may combine the two steps, that decision does not blind us to the fact that in substance two transactions are involved.[8] It is this element of choice that distinguishes an advance payment from a loan. Whether these customer deposits are the economic equivalents of advance payments, and therefore taxable upon receipt, must be determined by examining the relationship between the parties at the time of the deposit. The individual who makes an advance payment retains no right to insist upon the return of the funds; so long as the recipient fulfills the terms of the bargain, the money is its to keep. The customer who submits a deposit to the utility, like the lender in the previous hypothetical, retains the right to insist upon repayment in cash; he may choose to apply the money to the purchase of electricity, but he assumes no obligation to do so, and the utility therefore acquires no unfettered "dominion" over the money at the time of receipt.

When the Commissioner examines privately structured transactions, the true understanding of the parties, of course, may not be apparent. It may be that a transfer of funds, though nominally a loan, may conceal an unstated agreement that the money is to be applied to the purchase of goods or services. We need not, and do not, attempt to devise a test for addressing those situations where the nature of the parties' bargain is legitimately in dispute. This particular respondent, however, conducts its business in a heavily regulated environment; its rights and obligations vis-a-vis its customers are largely determined by law and regulation rather than by private negotiation. That the utility's customers, when they qualify for refunds of deposits, frequently choose to apply those refunds to future bills rather than taking repayment in cash does not mean that any customer has made an unspoken commitment to do so.

Our decision is also consistent with the Tax Court's long-standing treatment of lease deposits—perhaps the closest analogy to the present situation. The Tax Court traditionally has distinguished between a sum designated as a prepayment of rent—which is taxable upon receipt—and a sum deposited to secure the tenant's performance of a lease agreement. See, e.g., J. & E. Enterprises, Inc. v. Commissioner, 26 T.C. M. (CCH) 944 (1967). In fact, the customer deposits at issue here are less plausibly

---

[8]   The Commissioner contends that a customer's decision to take his refund while making a separate payment for services, rather than applying the deposit to his bill, would amount to nothing more than an economically meaningless "exchange of checks." But in our view the "exchange of checks," while less convenient, more accurately reflects the economic substance of the transactions.

regarded as income than lease deposits would be. The typical lease deposit secures the tenant's fulfillment of a contractual obligation to pay a specified rent throughout the term of the lease. The utility customer, however, makes no commitment to purchase any services at all at the time he tenders the deposit.

We recognize that IPL derives an economic benefit from these deposits. But a taxpayer does not realize taxable income from every event that improves his economic condition. A customer who makes this deposit reflects no commitment to purchase services, and IPL's right to retain the money is contingent upon events outside its control. We hold that such dominion as IPL has over these customer deposits is insufficient for the deposits to qualify as taxable income at the time they are made.

The judgment of the Court of Appeals is affirmed.

DETAILED ANALYSIS

1. SECURITY DEPOSIT VERSUS PREPAYMENT FOR GOODS OR SERVICES

Section 451 generally has been interpreted to require inclusion in the year of receipt of advance payments for goods or services. See Chapter 28, Section 3.A.(2). There is some tension between the decision in *Indianapolis Power & Light* and the earlier Supreme Court cases requiring current inclusion of advance receipts. This tension is evidenced by the divergent results in cases applying *Indianapolis Power & Light*. In a number of cases, the Tax Court has applied expansively the principles articulated by the Supreme Court in *Indianapolis Power & Light*.

In Oak Industries, Inc. v. Commissioner, 96 T.C. 559 (1991), the Tax Court excluded from income deposits received by a cable television service because the deposits, although non-interest-bearing and required of all customers, were conditionally refundable to the customers. Originally, the Tax Court had required Oak Industries to include the deposits in income because it had unrestricted use of the funds between the time they were received and the time a refund was due. T.C. Memo. 1987–65.

In Kansas City Southern Industries, Inc. v. Commissioner, 98 T.C. 242 (1992), a railroad company collected "sidetrack deposits" from customers who wanted a railroad siding to their manufacturing facility installed. The deposits were refundable only as a rebate against future freight charges, while unrebated deposits were forfeited to the railroad after five years. The Tax Court held that under *Indianapolis Power & Light* the deposits were not currently includable. See also Buchner v. Commissioner, T.C. Memo. 1990–417 (applying *Indianapolis Power & Light* to exclude refundable deposits received by direct mail advertising firm from customers to assure repayment of postage expenses).

In Highland Farms, Inc. v. Commissioner, 106 T.C. 237 (1996), the Tax Court again broadly construed *Indianapolis Power & Light* to permit exclusion of deposits that were conditionally refundable. The taxpayer operated a residential retirement community and received "entry fees" from residents who rented its rental units. The entry fees were partially refundable, on a sliding scale, if the resident vacated a rental unit within a specified period of time, either five years or twenty years, depending on the nature of the rental unit. The Commissioner asserted that the "entry fees" were includable as prepaid rent in the year received, but the court permitted the taxpayer to include the deposits as income only as they became nonrefundable.

In contrast, in Herbel v. Commissioner, 106 T.C. 392 (1996), the Tax Court declined to apply *Indianapolis Power & Light* where there was merely "some likelihood" that the recipient of an advance payment might have to refund the amount received. The taxpayer owned gas wells and entered into a contract with a public utility to supply gas as required by the utility. The public utility was required to pay for a minimum amount of gas whether or not it took delivery of the gas. Payments in excess of the value of the gas taken could be recouped by the public utility company in future years. In the year in question, the taxpayer received $1,850,000, which the public utility could recoup from future gas purchases. The payment was refundable only if the taxpayer canceled the contract or the gas wells were depleted before the payment was recouped by the public utility through future gas deliveries. Although there was "some likelihood" that the taxpayer might have to refund the amount received, because the event that might trigger a refund was not within the taxpayer's control, the payment was not an excludable deposit, but was currently includable. This decision is difficult to reconcile with *Kansas City Southern Industries, Inc.*, supra.

In Johnson v. Commissioner, 108 T.C. 448 (1997), the Tax Court attempted to explain the difference between a refundable deposit that is excludable under *Indianapolis Power & Light* and an includable refundable payment for contingent services. The taxpayers in *Johnson* were motor vehicle dealers who had entered into multi-year vehicle service contracts, receiving a flat fee in advance for work to be performed under the contracts. The contracts could be canceled by the customers, and in the event of cancellation the customer would receive a refund determined related to the period of time the contract had been in force and the number of miles the vehicle had been driven. The amount of repairs performed on the vehicle generally was not a factor in determining the refund. If the amount of repair work actually performed determined the extent of the taxpayer's right to retain the fees, they would have been deposits that were not includable. Because the taxpayer's right to keep the advance payment was not dependent on the customer's actual demand for repair services, but rather on other factors, the payments were includable as prepayments for services and were not excludable deposits.

Alexander Shokai, Inc. v. Commissioner, 34 F.3d 1480 (9th Cir.1994), also presented facts to which *Indianapolis Power & Light* did not apply. The taxpayer entered into a contract under which it was to earn commissions on U.S. sales of products made in Japan. An oral agreement between the seller and the sole shareholder of the taxpayer required the shareholder to return part of the commissions if the Japanese tax administration disallowed deductions to the seller for the commissions it paid. All commissions were deposited in the sole shareholder's bank account. The court held that the shareholder was taxable on the funds under the claim of right doctrine. The shareholder's argument that the "complete dominion" test in *Indianapolis Power & Light* should have been applied was rejected. The court distinguished *Indianapolis Power & Light* on the basis that the taxpayer in that case had an "absolute obligation" to repay the deposits upon request. The shareholder of the taxpayer in *Alexander Shokai, Inc.*, however, had an obligation to repay only if the seller's tax deduction was disallowed.

SECTION 5.   CONDUIT SITUATIONS

Revenue Ruling 68–512
1968–2 C.B. 41.

Advice has been requested whether, under the circumstances described below, campaign contributions received by a committee formed to aid a candidate campaigning for an elective office of a labor union are includible in the candidate's income for Federal income tax purposes.

The amounts received by the committee are contributions from donors conditioned upon their use only for the campaign expenses of the candidate. The treasurer of the committee handled the funds and made the distributions, all of which were for payment of the expenses of the candidate's campaign. The candidate did not know how much was collected, nor how the funds were disbursed. No part of the contributions received were used for any personal purposes by or on behalf of the candidate.

Political contributions are not taxable to a political candidate by or for whom they are collected if they are used for expenses of a political campaign or some similar purpose. However, any amount diverted from the channel of campaign activity and used by the political candidate for any personal purpose is income taxable to such candidate for the year in which funds are so diverted. See I.T. 3276, C.B. 1939–1 (Part 1), 108, Rev. Rul. 54–80, C.B. 1954–1, 11, and Rev. Proc. 68–19, C.B. 1968–1, 810.

Accordingly, since the amounts received by the committee in the instant case were campaign contributions used only for the campaign expenses of the candidate and were not diverted to the personal use of the candidate, no portion of the funds are includible in the candidate's gross income.

DETAILED ANALYSIS

1.   RECEIPTS SUBJECT TO RESTRICTION ON USE

Receipts that never have to be repaid but which are subject to restrictions on their use often are excluded from gross income because the taxpayer is required to devote the funds to a particular beneficial use. In Ford Dealers Advertising Fund v. Commissioner, 55 T.C. 761 (1971), aff'd per curiam, 456 F.2d 255 (5th Cir.1972), a non-profit corporation received funds from its member Ford dealers under a contract that required the corporation to expend the funds for its not-for-profit purpose of advertising the products and services of its members. The court held that the funds received did not constitute income to the corporation on the basis that where the "taxpayer receives trust funds, which he is obligated to spend in entirety for a specified purpose and no profit, gain, or other benefit is to be received by him in so doing," the funds received are not includable in income. 55 T.C. at 771. Under such circumstances the recipient is treated as a mere conduit for the funds. In Rev. Rul. 74–318, 1974–2 C.B. 14, the IRS indicated that it would not follow this decision. But Rev. Rul. 87–2, 1987–1 C.B. 18, held that interest on attorneys' client trust accounts that were controlled by the state supreme court was not taxable to either the lawyers or clients because neither had any right to, or control over, the interest.

Brown v. Commissioner, T.C. Memo. 1996–310, held that the portion of tips received by a waitress that was passed on to busboys, cooks, bartenders, and similar employees was not includable in the waitress' gross income; the sharing of tips carried out the "pass-through intent of the customer." In Dri-Powr Distributors Association Trust v. Commissioner, 54 T.C. 460 (1970) (Nonacq.), no income was derived by a trust from payments by member distributors where the trust was required to expend receipts to pay freight, advertising, and unified product promotion expenses of the distributors. In Angelus Funeral Home v. Commissioner, 47 T.C. 391 (1967), aff'd, 407 F.2d 210 (9th Cir.1969), amounts received by a funeral home pursuant to prepaid funeral contracts requiring the funds to be segregated and withdrawn to pay funeral expenses only upon proof of death of the payor were not currently includable, but receipts under other prepaid funeral contracts, which permitted the taxpayer to withdraw the funds prior to proof of death of the payor, were gross income when originally received.

The opinions in the "conduit" cases are not entirely satisfactory in articulating the ground for the decisions. On the one hand, there is some indication that the claim of right doctrine is applicable in these cases. Under this rationale, the issue is whether the restrictions on use are so substantial that the basic test of the doctrine is not satisfied. On the other hand, in *Dri-Powr* the court indicated that the claim of right doctrine should be confined to cases involving the question *when* income is taxable and not to the question *whether* a receipt constitutes income and, if so, *who* is taxable. But it then proceeded to analyze the case itself in terms of claim of right principles.

2.   POLITICAL CONTRIBUTIONS

2.1. *Campaign Contributions*

Rev. Rul. 68–512 cites no authority other than prior IRS pronouncements for excluding political contributions from gross income of the candidate, although I.T. 3276, cited in Rev. Rul. 68–512, referred to "political gifts." Are political contributions excludable under § 102 because they are gifts? Do donors to political campaigns typically make their contributions out of "detached and disinterested generosity," which *Duberstein,* Chapter 4, Section 1.B., suggests is the standard for determining whether a transfer is a gift in a nonfamilial context? What is the relevance of the use to which the candidate puts the contributed funds in determining whether the receipt of the contribution is gross income? Does the apparent relevance of the use to which the funds are put suggest that the rationale for exclusion is that the candidate is a mere custodian expending the funds for the benefit of the donor? Is this a realistic assumption?

Section 527 provides for the taxation of political organizations. A political organization, as defined in § 527(e)(1), is a committee, association or fund maintained to accept contributions or make expenditures, or both, for an exempt function. Section 527(e)(2) provides that an exempt function includes all activities directly related to the process of selection, nomination, or election of an individual. Basically, contributions to such organizations constitute "exempt function income" and are not subject to tax. Investment income, however, including capital gains, is taxable, the organization being taxed as a corporation. The fact that contributions are characterized as "income," although exempt from tax, may indicate that, in the Congressional view, they generally would not fall within an exclusion to gross income.

With regard to the individual candidate, Treas. Reg. § 1.527–5(a) provides that amounts expended by the organization directly or indirectly for the personal benefit of the candidate constitute income to the candidate. The Regulations reflect the position earlier reached by the IRS through a series of administrative pronouncements. See e.g., Rev. Rul. 71–449, 1971–2 C.B. 77 (where a candidate for political office received contributions of $1,000 and used $600 for campaign purposes and the balance to reduce the mortgage on his personal residence, the $400 diverted from political purposes was taxable to the candidate). Not all indirect benefits to candidates and office holders provided by a § 527 organization are includable in income. The legislative history of § 527 indicates that incidental expenses, such as self-improvement courses "for the primary purpose of benefiting the candidate directly in connection with his campaign are not to be treated as amounts diverted for the personal benefit of the candidate." S.Rep. No. 93–1357, 93rd Cong. 2d Sess. 25, 31 (1974). The legislative history also indicates that payment of the candidate's "transition" expenses is not gross income to the candidate. Treas. Reg. § 1.527–2(c)(5), Exs. (2), (3), (4) and (5), allow a tax-exempt campaign organization to provide candidates with such things as speech lessons, travel expenses for the candidate's spouse, tickets to testimonial dinners, and subscriptions to periodicals, as long as the items are related to the campaign. In addition, § 527(g) treats a newsletter fund maintained by an office holder or candidate as a political organization.[3] This provision permits the office holder or candidate to maintain a separate vehicle for raising tax-exempt contributions to communicate to voters and constituents. See generally, Simmons, An Essay on Federal Income Taxation and Campaign Finance Reform, 54 Fla. L.Rev. 1, 37 (2002). Section 527(e)(2) permits a section 527 political organization to pay an office holder's ordinary and necessary

---

[3]   Excluding the payments from income avoids "distortions" that would occur in the officer holder's income due to increases in adjusted gross income that affect the taxpayer's deduction of medical expenses and casualty losses, as well as the impact of various phase-out provisions that are based on adjusted gross income. See S. Rep. No. 93–1357 at 31–32.

expenses incurred in the course of the office holder's political employment, which is not includable in the office holder's gross income.[4]

Rev. Rul. 75–103, 1975–1 C.B. 17, held that contributions to a political campaign in exchange for a promise by a candidate that he would vote according to the contributor's direction on certain legislation were income to the candidate under § 61 and James v. United States (see Chapter 5, Section 3). Under the circumstances, "the payments were not made as a result of or in exchange for promises of a traditional and legitimate political nature."

2.2. *Other Contributions*

Rev. Rul. 75–146, 1975–1 C.B. 23, involved an intern program run by a U.S. Congressman to provide education and training in governmental functions and the legislative process. The program was funded by amounts that the Congressman had received from his constituency. The ruling held that the contributions did not qualify as gifts since the contributors donated the money with the intention of obtaining a more efficient public servant through supporting the intern program. The amounts were includable in the Congressman's income, but he was entitled to deduct amounts paid to the interns as ordinary and necessary business expenses.

Similarly, payments made to a trust set up to defray traveling expenses of a Congressman were held to be gross income. The payments did not qualify for the gift exclusion under § 102 because they were made by the constituents in the hope of obtaining more effective representation in Congress. Rev. Rul. 76–276, 1976–2 C.B. 14.

3.   CONDUITS FOR POLITICAL CONTRIBUTIONS

The taxpayer in Reichert v. Commissioner, 19 T.C. 1027 (1953), aff'd on other issues, 214 F.2d 19 (7th Cir.1954), was the mayor of Evansville, Indiana, and chairman of the Vanderburgh County Republican Party. The Commissioner asserted that Reichert had received approximately $20,000 from tavern-keepers, bookies, and others as a " 'pay off' for political favor rendered or the 'sale of political influence.' " A portion of the funds was not included in the taxpayer's income because the court found that the funds were "received by him as campaign contributions for use in Evansville and that they were used, as indicated by the testimony of witnesses, as 'pay offs' to precinct committeemen and precinct workers, * * * the major portion being distributed on the eves of elections." The balance, however, which was received from tavern-keepers whose licenses were up for renewal and was not reported to the local Republican Party, constituted gross income to the taxpayer.

Liddy v. Commissioner, 808 F.2d 312 (4th Cir.1986), involved the tax treatment of $386,000 raised by the Committee to Reelect the President (CREEP) and controlled by G. Gordon Liddy in connection with the infamous Watergate break-in and other activities directed toward the reelection of Richard Nixon. The court held that Liddy was not taxable on the $340,000 that he proved was used to further CREEP activities, but that Liddy was

---

[4]   This provision conforms the treatment of political office holders with respect to reimbursements from a political organization to provisions that allow an employee to disregard business expenses reimbursed by an employer, discussed at Chapter 3, Section 3.A.2.

taxable on the portion of the funds for which he could not prove that he was a mere conduit. The dissent would have taxed Liddy only on the $11,000 found in his possession after he was arrested for the Watergate break-in.

CHAPTER 6

INCOME FROM THE DISPOSITION OF PROPERTY

SECTION 1. INTRODUCTION

INTERNAL REVENUE CODE: Sections 61(a)(3); 1001(a)–(c); 1011(a); 1012.

If A purchases land for $200,000 and sells it several years later for $300,000 there are at least three possibilities for determining the amount of A's income: (1) A has no gross income because the $300,000 sales proceeds merely represents a change in the form of A's wealth, but not an increase in wealth, (2) A has $300,000 of gross income because that is the amount that A has available for consumption after the sale, or (3) A has $100,000 of gross income because A has $100,000 more than A paid for the property. These questions were addressed by the Supreme Court in Doyle v. Mitchell Brothers Company, 247 U.S. 179 (1918), interpreting the Corporation Excise Tax of 1909. The Court in *Doyle* rejected the first two options and held that an income tax system requires use of the third option.[1]

With respect to the argument that a sale of property cannot give rise to income because it is merely a change in the form of capital, the Court made the following observation:

> The suggestion that the entire proceeds of the conversion should be still treated as the same capital, changed only in form and containing no element of income although including an increment of value, we reject at once as inconsistent with the general purpose of the act. Selling for profit is too familiar a business transaction to permit us to suppose that it was intended to be omitted from consideration in an act for taxing the doing of business in corporate form upon the basis of the income received "from all sources."

The 1909 Act allowed deductions for items such as expenses of maintenance and operation of the business and property, rentals, uncompensated losses, depreciation, interest, and taxes, but there was no express provision for a deduction of the cost of the goods sold. The Court remedied the omission with the following analysis:

---

[1]   The taxpayer was a lumber manufacturing corporation that claimed in computing its net income it should be permitted to deduct from its gross receipts from timber sales the amount of its capital investment in timber as of the effective date of the income tax, rather than its lower cost for the timber incurred before the effective date of the act. The Court allowed recovery of the full value of the taxpayer's capital investment as of the effective date of the 1909 Act before the taxpayer realized gain.

Yet it is plain, we think, that by the true intent and meaning of the act the entire proceeds of a mere conversion of capital assets were not to be treated as income. Whatever difficulty there may be about a precise and scientific definition of "income," it imports, as used here, something entirely distinct from principal or capital either as a subject of taxation or as a measure of the tax; conveying rather the idea of gain or increase arising from corporate activities. * * *

Understanding the term in this natural and obvious sense, it cannot be said that a conversion of capital assets invariably produces income. If sold at less than cost, it produces rather loss or outgo. Nevertheless, in many if not in most cases there results a gain that properly may be accounted as a part of the "gross income" received "from all sources"; and by applying to this the authorized deductions we arrive at "net income." In order to determine whether there has been gain or loss, and the amount of the gain, if any, we must withdraw from the gross proceeds an amount sufficient to restore the capital value that existed at the commencement of the period under consideration. * * *

The final sentence of the opinion in Doyle v. Mitchell Brothers Co. quoted here states a principle that is fundamental to the present income tax. Income for purposes of § 61 contemplates the realization of gain only after recovery of the taxpayer's original capital investment. This rule is now embedded in the statutory scheme.

Section 61(a)(3) specifically includes in gross income, "gains derived from dealings in property." Section 1001(a) defines gains and losses from dispositions of property as the difference between the amount realized on disposition, defined in § 1001(b) as the amount of money and fair market value of property received, and the "adjusted basis" of the property transferred. In general, under § 1012, "adjusted basis" reflects the taxpayer's "cost" (or invested capital) adjusted, as required by § 1016, for additions to and recoveries of cost subsequent to the taxpayer's acquisition of the property. Amount realized and basis are considered in Section 3. Special basis rules apply to property acquired by gift or inheritance. See Chapter 7.

In the example above, A's purchase of the land for $200,000 and subsequent sale for $300,000 results in $100,000 of gross income. Now suppose that instead of selling the property for cash, A incurs additional expenses of $50,000 to improve the property. A's adjusted basis in the property is now $250,000. After holding the property for several years, A exchanges the property for stock worth $400,000. A's amount realized under § 1001 is the fair market value of the stock. A's realized gain on disposition of the property is $150,000 ($400,000—$250,000). Gain realized on the sale or exchange of property must be recognized—included in gross income under § 61—unless there is a specific provision of the Code providing otherwise. I.R.C. § 1001(c). A's basis in the stock

determining that as the bonus was paid in property, "the basis of calculation of the amount thereof is the cost of such property and not its market value as claimed on the return." * * * Taxpayer filed a petition with the Tax Court for a redetermination of the deficiency thus determined. By an amended answer, the Commissioner, in the alternative, alleged that if it were held that the taxpayer was entitled to a deduction in the amount of $24,858.75 on account of the payment of bonus in stock, then the taxpayer realized a taxable profit of $8,705.39 on the disposition of the shares, and taxpayer's net taxable income otherwise determined should be increased accordingly.

The Tax Court held that taxpayer was entitled to a deduction for compensation paid in the year 1936 in the amount of $24,858.75. The Tax Court decided for the Commissioner, however, on the defense set forth in the Commissioner's amended answer, holding that taxpayer realized a gain of $8,705.39 in 1936 by paying the class B bonus in stock which had cost taxpayer $8,705.39 less than its market value when taxpayer transferred the stock to its employees. * * * From that decision the taxpayer seeks review.

■ FRANK, CIRCUIT JUDGE.

1.   [Ed.: The Court of Appeals upheld the Tax Court ruling that the taxpayer was entitled to deduct as compensation to employees the full value of the duPont stock transferred to its employees.]

2.   We turn to the question whether the transaction resulted in taxable gain to taxpayer. We think that the Tax Court correctly held that it did. * * *

[A]s the delivery of the shares here constituted a disposition for a valid consideration, it resulted in a closed transaction with a consequent realized gain. It is of no relevance that here the taxpayer had not been legally obligated to award any shares or pay any additional compensation to the employees; bonus payments by corporations are recognized as proper even if there was no previous obligation to make them; although then not obligatory, they are regarded as made for a sufficient consideration. Since the bonuses would be invalid to the extent that what was delivered to the employees exceeded what the services of the employees were worth, it follows that the consideration received by the taxpayer from the employees must be deemed to be equal at least to the value of the shares in 1936. Here then, as there was no gift but a disposition of shares for a valid consideration equal at least to the market value of the shares when delivered, there was a taxable gain equal to the difference between the cost of the shares and that market value.

For § [1001(a) of the Code] provides that the gain from "the sale or other disposition of property" shall be the excess of "the amount realized therefrom" over "the adjusted basis" provided in § [1011]—in the light of § [1012]—makes the "basis" the cost of such property. True, § [1001(b)] provides that "the amount realized" is the sum of "any money received plus the fair market value of the property (other than money) received." Literally, where there is a disposition of stock for services, no "property" or "money" is received by the person who thus disposes of the stock. But, in similar circumstances, it has been held that "money's worth" is received and that such a receipt comes within § [1001(b)]. See Commissioner v. Mesta, 3 Cir., 123 F.2d 986, 988 * * * .[5]

The taxpayer properly asks us to treat this case "as if there had been no formal bonus plan" and as if taxpayer "had simply paid outright 150 shares of duPont stock to selected employees as additional compensation." On that basis, surely there was a taxable gain. For to shift the equation once more, the case supposed is the equivalent of one in which the taxpayer in the year 1936, without entering into a previous contract fixing the amount of compensation, had employed a transposition expert for one day and, when he completed his work, had paid him 5 shares of duPont stock having market value at that time of $500 but which it had bought in a previous year for $100. There can be no doubt that, from such a transaction, taxpayer would have a taxable gain. And so here.

The order of the Tax Court is affirmed.

DETAILED ANALYSIS

1. AMOUNT REALIZED ON THE TRANSFER OF PROPERTY IN SATISFACTION OF A CLAIM

International Freighting holds that the transfer of property as compensation for services rendered is a disposition subject to § 1001[2] Amount realized, the fair market value of the property received, includes the value of the employees' claim for compensation that is released in exchange for the property. See also Montana Power Co. v. United States, 171 F.Supp. 943 (Ct.Cl.1959) (taxpayer allowed a loss, determined by reference to fair market value, on stock transferred to obtain a release of the taxpayer from a 10-year contract to supply oil to the transferee and to obtain the transferee's approval to a dissolution of the taxpayer). The holding that amount realized includes the value of claims against the taxpayer released in exchange for property has been significant in a variety of situations.

In United States v. Davis, 370 U.S. 65 (1962), the taxpayer transferred appreciated stock to his wife in exchange for a release of the wife's marital rights in the context of a divorce. The taxpayer argued that the stock transfer was part of a nontaxable division of jointly owned property. The Court held that under Delaware law the wife's interest in her husband's property was

---

[5]   In these cases the taxpayer paid a money claim by delivering stock. What the taxpayer received was literally neither property nor money, yet it was held that there was a taxable transaction under § [1001(b)].

[2]   Note that on the specific facts of *International Freighting*—the use by a subsidiary corporation of its parent corporation's stock to pay an expense or acquire property—Treas. Reg. § 1.1032–3 provides for nonrecognition of the gain under limited circumstances. If the specific facts of *International Freighting* were to arise today, however, Treas. Reg. § 1.1032–3 would not apply. Treas. Reg. § 1.1032–3(c)(2).

more in the nature of a personal liability of the husband than a co-ownership interest in property. Thus the Court concluded that the stock was transferred to the wife in satisfaction of her claim against the husband, a taxable event. The amount realized on the taxpayer's disposition of the stock was the fair market value of the wife's marital rights released in exchange for the stock. The Court of Claims had held that there was no way to determine the fair market value of the wife's marital rights and thus that it was impossible to determine the amount realized under § 1001(a). The Supreme Court held, however, that since the parties in the transaction were acting at arm's length, it could be assumed that the marital rights were equal in value to the property for which they were exchanged. Thus the fair market value of the marital rights was treated as equivalent to the value of the stock transferred by the husband in exchange for the release. The same result was reached in *International Freighting* where the employee's services were presumed to be equal in value to the value of the transferred stock. Section 1041, discussed in Chapter 38, Section 3, enacted in 1984, reverses the result on the facts of *Davis* by providing that gain or loss will not be recognized on transfers between spouses and transfers incident to divorce. Nonetheless, *Davis* remains an important precedent with regard to the transfer of appreciated property in satisfaction of a claim.

In Kenan v. Commissioner, 114 F.2d 217 (2d Cir.1940), the taxpayer, a trust, transferred appreciated stock in partial satisfaction of a $5,000,000 pecuniary bequest to a trust beneficiary. The court held that the trust realized gain on a taxable disposition of the stock for the amount of the bequest that was satisfied by the stock transfer. The court rejected the trust's argument that the transferred stock itself represented the bequest to the beneficiary, pointing out that the beneficiary had a fixed dollar claim against the trust that was satisfied by the disposition of appreciated property. See also Rev. Rul. 74–178, 1974–1 C.B. 196, and Rev. Rul. 66–207, 1966–2 C.B. 243, holding that the transfer of appreciated stock to a creditor of an estate results in a disposition under § 1001 of the stock for the amount of the claim.

The same principle is applied to the transfer of property to a person who satisfies a third party's claim against the transferor. In Diedrich v. Commissioner, 457 U.S. 191 (1982), the taxpayer transferred appreciated stock to his children on the condition that the donees pay the taxpayer's gift tax liability on the transfer. The gift taxes paid by the donees were in excess of the taxpayer's basis for the transferred stock. The court treated the transfer as a disposition of the stock for the amount of the gift tax liability paid by the donees. The court rejected the taxpayer's argument that the transfer represented a net gift of the property less the amount of the gift tax. The taxpayer realized gain in the amount of the difference between the gift taxes, treated as amount realized, and the taxpayer's basis for the transferred stock. Part gift, part sale issues raised by *Diedrich* are discussed in Chapter 7, Section 1.3.

2. BASIS

2.1. *Adjustments to Basis*

Section 1016 provides for adjustments to the taxpayer's original cost basis to reflect additional capital expenditures attributable to the property and withdrawals of invested capital through such items as depreciation and other deductions that reflect a recovery of basis over time. Thus basis is increased for the cost of improvements to property. I.R.C. § 1016(a)(1). Adjustments to basis for depreciation and other deductions are discussed Chapter 14, Section 1.3.

2.2. *Special Basis Rules—Gifts and Inheritances*

Although a taxpayer's gain or loss on disposition of property is normally determined from the taxpayer's investment in the property, the Code contains special rules for determining the basis of property acquired by gift or inheritance. See Chapter 7.

2.3. *Cost of Goods Sold*

As noted by the Court in Doyle v. Mitchell Brothers Company, *supra* Section 1, the Code does not provide a specific deduction for the cost of goods sold by a manufacturer or merchant. However, the rule of Doyle v. Mitchell Brothers Co. is reflected in Treas. Reg. § 1.61–3(a), which provides that gross income derived from business means sales less the cost of goods sold. "Cost of goods sold" is essentially the manufacturer's or merchant's basis in its inventory of goods. Furthermore, § 471 authorizes Treasury regulations prescribing the maintenance of inventories as a method of determining the cost of goods sold whenever necessary in order to clearly reflect a taxpayer's income. Section 1013 adds that the basis of property required to be included in a taxpayer's closing inventory will be the inventory value of the property. Inventory accounting is discussed in Chapter 28, Section 4.

3. ALLOCATION OF BASIS BETWEEN TRANSFERRED AND RETAINED PROPERTY

3.1. *General*

Treas. Reg. § 1.61–6(a) provides that when part of a larger property is sold, the cost or other basis of the property must be "equitably apportioned" among the parts. However, in Inaja Land Co. v. Commissioner, 9 T.C. 727 (1947), the taxpayer was permitted to defer realization of gain on the receipt of a cash payment of approximately $50,000 from the City of Los Angeles in exchange for a grant of an easement over the taxpayer's land. The easement was granted to permit overflows of water from the Mono Craters Tunnel constructed up river from the taxpayer's property as part of the Los Angeles Owens River water project. The taxpayer's basis in the whole property was $61,000. The taxpayer claimed that no part of the $50,000 payment was realized gain because it would be impossible to apportion a definite basis to the easement transferred to the City of Los Angeles. Quoting from Strother v. Commissioner, 55 F.2d 626 (4th Cir.1932), the Tax Court agreed:

> " * * * A taxpayer * * * should not be charged with gain on pure conjecture unsupported by any foundation of ascertainable fact."
> See Burnet v. Logan, 283 U.S. 404 * * * .

This rule is approved in the recent case of Raytheon Production Corporation v. Commissioner, [1 T.C. 952, aff'd 144 F.2d 110 (1st Cir.1944)]. Apportionment with reasonable accuracy of the amount received not being possible, and this amount being less than petitioner's cost basis for the property, it can not be determined that petitioner has, in fact, realized gain in any amount. Applying the rule as above set out, no portion of the payment in question should be considered as income, but the full amount must be treated as a return of capital and applied in reduction of petitioner's cost basis. Burnet v. Logan, 283 U.S. 404.

The $50,000 received by the Inaja Land Company is not completely without tax effect as the $50,000 reduced that taxpayer's unrecovered capital invested in the property, adjusted basis, to $11,000. Thus, a subsequent sale of the property for $61,000 would have resulted in $50,000 of realized gain ($61,000—$11,000). If the Inaja Land Company had received $70,000, net of expenses, in exchange for the easement it would have realized $9,000 of gain ($70,000—$61,000) as its amount realized exceeded its total investment.

What if the Inaja Land Company had purchased 6.1 acres of indistinguishable land for $61,000 and had transferred one of those acres to the city of Los Angeles for $50,000? In Fasken v. Commissioner, 71 T.C. 650 (1979), the taxpayers sold easements for pipelines, powerlines, and other facilities. The taxpayers attempted to treat the consideration received as a return of capital reducing their basis in the overall property, as did the taxpayer in *Inaja Land Company*. The court required the taxpayers to recognize gain in an amount equal to the consideration received less the portion of adjusted basis proportionately allocated to the area covered by the grant of easements. The court held that whether to apportion basis to a transferred easement is a question of fact and the taxpayer failed to establish that an apportionment of basis to the easements was impossible or impracticable. See also Rev. Rul. 68–291, 1968–1 C.B. 351 (taxpayer was allowed to allocate only a portion of basis of farmland to the specific portion of the entire tract over which the taxpayer granted an easement for power lines; the taxpayer recognized gain to the extent that the consideration received for the easement exceeded the portion of basis allocated to the tract over which the easement was granted). In Rev. Rul. 70–510, 1970–2 C.B. 159, however, the IRS followed *Inaja Land Company* to allow the taxpayer to treat as a return of capital an amount paid by the Government for an easement to allow flood waters to flow over the taxpayer's property. The payment was based on 20 percent of the value of the fee interest in the property. The ruling notes that the taxpayer did not sell the land or improvements and that the payment was not a payment in advance for anticipated future damage to the taxpayer's trade or business. The ruling concluded that the payment should be applied against the basis of the property to which the easement appertains in determining gain or loss from subsequent sale or other disposition of the property.

In Gladden v. Commissioner, 262 F.3d 851 (9th Cir.2001), the taxpayer, who was engaged in a farming business, received from the Department of the Interior payments in exchange for surrender of the taxpayer's rights to a water allotment, which were appurtenant to the land, from the Colorado River. The Tax Court held the taxpayer, who acquired the land in 1976 and acquired the appurtenant water rights in 1983, could not allocate any portion of the basis of the land to the water rights under Treas. Reg. § 1.61–6(a) because the water rights were not vested at the time the land was purchased. The Court of Appeals reversed. The Court of Appeals rejected the taxpayer's argument that it should follow *Inaja Land Co.* to permit the taxpayer simply to apply the amount received against his basis in the land. The court reasoned that if there had been no expectation of a subsequent allocation of water rights to the land at the time of its purchase, none of the cost of the land would have been apportionable to the water rights. But because there had been an expectation of a subsequent allocation of water rights to the land at the time of its purchase, the land could have commanded a premium that properly should have been allocated to the basis of the water rights. Thus, the Court of Appeals remanded the case for a factual determination of what portion of the cost of the land was a premium paid for the water rights later acquired, or whether it was "impracticable or impossible" to determine what that premium may have been.

In Beaver Dam Coal Company v. United States, 370 F.2d 414, 417 (6th Cir.1966), the taxpayer purchased farm land in order to strip mine coal. In order to get access to lands useful in its mining operations, the taxpayer was required to pay a premium price for portions of acquired properties with no access to coal. The court rejected the Commissioner's assertion that the taxpayer was required to allocate its cost equally among all of the acquired acres and allowed the taxpayer to allocate a larger portion of its acquisition cost to the coal bearing lands. The Court held that the equitable apportionment required by Treas. Reg. § 1.61–6(a) means that the relative values of the various parts must be taken into account. Thus, basis is not necessarily allocated based on the relative size of parcels of land, but on the relative values of different plots. See also Fairfield Plaza, Inc. v. Commissioner, 39 T.C. 706 (1963) (larger portion of basis allocated to portions of shopping center land fronting major streets).

3.2. *Blocks of Stock*

Treas. Reg. § 1.1012–1(c) provides a specific rule for determining the basis on disposition of shares of stock that were acquired on different dates or at different prices. If the transferred block of stock can be identified, the cost basis of the particular block is used in calculating gain or loss. A block of stock is adequately identified either by delivery of a certificate or, if the stock is left in the custody of the taxpayer's stock broker or an agent, through identification to the stock broker or agent of the block that is to be sold followed by a written confirmation to the taxpayer from the broker or agent. If the transferred certificates are not so identified, the regulations adopt a first-in first-out rule so that the cost of the earliest acquired stock is used to calculate gain or loss on the disposition.

B. BASIS OF PROPERTY RECEIVED IN AN EXCHANGE

Philadelphia Park Amusement Co. v. United States

United States Court of Claims, 1954.
126 F.Supp. 184.

■ LARAMORE, JUDGE.

The taxpayer corporation sues to recover $42,864.50, with interest thereon, representing alleged overpayment of income taxes for the calendar years 1944 and 1945. * * * The issue presented in this case is whether or not the taxpayer is entitled to include as a part of the cost of its franchise, for purposes of determining depreciation and loss due to abandonment, the undepreciated cost of a bridge exchanged for a 10-year extension of the franchise. The facts which have been stipulated by the parties may be summarized as follows: The taxpayer's predecessor was granted on July 6, 1889, by the City of Philadelphia, a franchise to construct, operate, and maintain for 50 years a passenger railway in Fairmount Park at its own cost and expense. * * *

Pursuant to the franchise the taxpayer's predecessor constructed the bridge in question, commonly known as Strawberry Bridge, over the Schuylkill River at a cost of $381,000. The bridge * * * carried pedestrian and vehicular traffic in addition to taxpayer's streetcars. The taxpayer's principal business was the operation of an amusement park and the street railway was employed in the transportation of customers to the park. With the increase in automobile transportation the proportion of customers carried to the amusement park by the taxpayer's streetcars decreased over the years and during the latter years of its operation losses were sustained. Early in 1934 the City, in writing the taxpayer, pointed out that Strawberry Bridge was in need of extensive repairs, that it was taxpayer's obligation to make the repairs at taxpayer's expense, and threatened to close the bridge unless the repairs were made promptly. The taxpayer wrote the City explaining that its financial condition prevented the making of extensive repairs to the bridge and offered to transfer the ownership of the bridge to the City in exchange for a 10-year extension of the railway franchise. The City accepted the offer and on August 3, 1934, Strawberry Bridge was transferred to the City. The taxpayer reserved its right-of-way over the bridge for the duration of its franchise and agreed to maintain its facilities thereon. On November 14, 1934, the City amended the franchise and extended it from July 24, 1939, to July 24, 1949. The adjusted basis, i.e., the undepreciated or unrecovered cost of Strawberry Bridge at the time of the exchange was $228,852.74. The taxpayer's bookkeeper took depreciation on the bridge for the part of 1934 that taxpayer owned it and promptly wrote the asset off the books by a direct debit to surplus of $228,852.74, without reporting any gain or loss on the exchange or adding the undepreciated cost or fair market value of the bridge to the cost of the franchise. From that time until 1946 the taxpayer's bookkeeper did not record on the taxpayer's books or claim a deduction on its returns for the amortization of this cost. He also failed to take the undisputed deduction for the amortization of the undepreciated portion, $50,000, of the original cost of the franchise. In 1946 the taxpayer arranged with a bus company to give passenger service to its amusement park, ceased operation of the railway, and abandoned its franchise. In its 1946 tax return the taxpayer claimed a loss due to abandonment of the railroad of $336,380.04, $74,445.89 of which was claimed to represent the undepreciated cost of the franchise. This produced a $128,897.97 net loss for the year 1946, and taxpayer claimed a net operating loss carry-back to 1944 and 1945 under section 122(b) of the Code.

* * *

[Ed.: The taxpayer filed claims for refund of its 1944 and 1945 taxes claiming a net operating loss carryback of its 1946 abandonment loss and additional deductions in 1944 and 1945 for depreciation of the basis of the 10 year extension of the franchise. The Court agreed that the taxpayer was entitled to amortize the basis of the franchise over its term and to claim a loss deduction for the unrecovered basis of the franchise.]

This brings us to the question of what is the cost basis of the 10-year extension of taxpayer's franchise. Although defendant contends that Strawberry Bridge was either worthless or not "exchanged" for the 10-year extension of the franchise, we believe that the bridge had some value, and that the contract under which the bridge was transferred to the City clearly indicates that the one was given in consideration of the other. * * * [I]t was a taxable exchange under section [1001] of the Code.

The gain or loss, whichever the case may have been, should have been recognized, and the cost basis under section [1012] of the Code, of the 10-year extension of the franchise was the cost to the taxpayer. The succinct statement in section [1012] that "the basis of property shall be the cost of such property" although clear in principle, is frequently difficult in application. One view is that the cost basis of property received in a taxable exchange is the fair market value of the property given in the exchange. The other view is that the cost basis of property received in a taxable exchange is the fair market value of the property received in the exchange. As will be seen from the cases and some of the Commissioner's rulings the Commissioner's position has not been altogether consistent on this question. The view that "cost" is the fair market value of the property given is predicated on the theory that the cost to the taxpayer is the economic value relinquished. The view that "cost" is the fair market value of the property received is based upon the theory that the term "cost" is a tax concept and must be considered in the light of the designed interrelationship of sections [1001] * * * and [1012], and the prime role that the basis of property plays in determining tax liability. We believe that when the question is considered in the latter context that the cost basis of the property received in a taxable exchange is the fair market value of the property received in the exchange. When property is exchanged for property in a taxable exchange the taxpayer is taxed on the difference between the adjusted basis of the property given in exchange and the fair market value of the property received in exchange. For purposes of determining gain or loss the fair market value of the property received is treated as cash and taxed accordingly. To maintain harmony with the fundamental purpose of these sections, it is necessary to consider the fair market value of the property received as the cost basis to the taxpayer. The failure to do so would result in allowing the taxpayer a stepped-up basis, without paying a tax therefor, if the fair market value of the property received is less than the fair market value of the property given, and the taxpayer would be subjected to a double tax if the fair market value of the property received is more than the fair market value of the property given. By holding that the fair market value of the property received in a taxable exchange is the cost basis, the above discrepancy is avoided and the basis of the property received will equal the adjusted basis of the property given plus any gain recognized, or that should have been recognized, or minus any loss recognized, or that should have been recognized.

Therefore, the cost basis of the 10-year extension of the franchise was its fair market value on August 3, 1934, the date of the exchange. The determination of whether the cost basis of the property received is its fair market value or the fair market value of the property given in exchange therefor, although necessary to the decision of the case, is generally not of great practical significance because the value of the two properties exchanged in an arms-length transaction are either equal in fact, or are presumed to be equal. The record in this case indicates that the 1934 exchange was an arms-length transaction and, therefore, if the value of the extended franchise cannot be determined with reasonable accuracy, it would be reasonable and fair to assume that the value of Strawberry Bridge was equal to the 10-year extension of the franchise. The fair market value of the 10-year extension of the franchise should be established but, if that value cannot be determined with reasonable certainty, the fair market value of Strawberry Bridge should be established and that will be presumed to be the value of the extended franchise. This value cannot be determined from the facts now before us since the case was prosecuted on a different theory.

* * * If the value of the extended franchise or bridge cannot be ascertained with a reasonable degree of accuracy, the taxpayer is entitled to carry over the undepreciated cost of the bridge as the cost basis of the extended franchise. Helvering v. Tex-Penn Oil Co., 300 U.S. 481 * * * . However, it is only in rare and extraordinary cases that the value of the property exchanged cannot be ascertained with reasonable accuracy. We are presently of the opinion that either the value of the extended franchise or the bridge can be determined with a reasonable degree of accuracy. * * *

We, therefore, conclude that the 1934 exchange was a taxable exchange and that the taxpayer is entitled to use as the cost basis of the 10-year extension of its franchise its fair market value on August 3, 1934, for purposes of determining depreciation and loss due to abandonment, as indicated in this opinion.

DETAILED ANALYSIS

1. BASIS OF ACQUIRED PROPERTY INCLUDED IN INCOME

Where the property is acquired under circumstances making the property itself an item of gross income, such as a dividend or compensation for services, the basis of property is the amount includable in gross income, which is the fair market value of the property received. See Treas. Reg. § 1.61–2(d)(2) (last sentence). Thus, for example, if an employee receives stock for services the fair market value of the stock is includable in gross income and becomes the employee's basis of the stock. The basis is thus the basis of property given up, zero in this case, increased by the gain recognized, the amount included in the recipient's gross income. Alternatively, the transaction may be viewed as if the employer had paid cash to the employee in an amount equal to the fair market value of the stock and the stock was then purchased for this amount. Whatever the interpretation, the result is an accepted and necessary application of the term "cost" as used in § 1012.

2. PROPERTY ACQUIRED IN EXCHANGE FOR PROPERTY

In *Philadelphia Park* the court described the basis of property (other than cash) received in a taxable exchange for other property as the fair market value of the property received. The Court noted that under this formulation the basis of property received is equivalent to the adjusted basis of the property given up, plus any gain recognized (or that should have been recognized) on the exchange, or minus any loss recognized (or that should have been recognized).[3] Describing basis in these terms accounts for the taxpayer's tax cost of property. If, for example, the taxpayer were to purchase property for $10 and exchange that property for property with a fair market value of $30, the taxpayer would realize and recognize $20 of gain (assuming the exchange is not subject to a nonrecognition provision discussed in Chapter 26). In terms of the dollars on which the taxpayer has paid tax, the basis of the new property must include the $10 original investment (the adjusted basis of the property given up), plus the $20 of gain that the taxpayer must include in income in the taxable year of the exchange (the gain recognized). Thus the taxpayer has a basis of $30 reflecting the $30 of investment upon which tax has been paid.

The formulation of basis in *Philadelphia Park* as equivalent to the fair market value of property received is derived algebraically from the definitions of gain and amount realized in § 1001. If, as described above—

---

[3]   This description of basis is codified in §§ 358 and 1031(d) with respect to nonrecognition transactions.

Basis of Property Received =

(Basis of Property Given Up) + (Gain (Loss) Recognized)

And under § 1001(a) and (b)—

Gain (Loss) Recognized =

(Fair Market Value of Property Received) – (Basis of Property Given)

Then—

Fair Market Value of Property Received =

(Basis of Property Given) + (Gain (Loss) Recognized)

Therefore, Basis of Property Received = Fair Market Value of Property Received.[4]

Defining the basis of property as the basis of property given up plus any gain recognized on the exchange, or minus any loss recognized on the exchange, will always produce the correct result, a measurement of the after-tax capital invested in the property. That is also true where the exchange involves payment of money for property because the basis of the money given up is always its face amount. However, describing the basis of property received as the fair market value of property received is not always accurate. See e.g., the discussion of options in part 4, below.

Where property is acquired in a taxable exchange for other property, as in the *Philadelphia Park* case, the fair market value of the properties normally will be the same. Therefore, whether the value of the acquired property or the property transferred is used in basis determination will ordinarily have no practical consequence. However, if the market values do differ, adopting the fair market value of the property received as the basis of that property, as derived from the basis of property given up plus gain (or minus loss) recognized, accurately will reflect the economic consequences to the taxpayer. Suppose, for example, that a taxpayer owns property A with a cost basis of $4,500 and a fair market value of $6,000 that is exchanged for property B with a fair market value of $5,000. The discrepancy in values arises from the taxpayer's desire to dispose of property A quickly. The taxpayer's gain on the exchange is $500, the difference between the fair market value of the property received ($5,000) and the taxpayer's basis in the property transferred ($4,500); the taxpayer's basis in property B would then be $5,000 consisting of the $4,500 basis of the property given up plus $500 gain recognized. A subsequent sale of property B for $6,000 would result in a further recognized gain of $1,000. The recognized gain on both transactions is equivalent to the taxpayer's economic gain of $1,500.

On the other hand, if the basis of the property acquired were determined by reference to the value of the property transferred, there could be a discrepancy in the amount of gain or loss recognized when the property subsequently was sold or exchanged. Thus, if the taxpayer's basis in property

---

[4]　This is the algebraic transitive property of equality which provides that if a = b and b = c, then a = c. A simplified version of the equations shows the transitive property clearly. If Basis of Property Received is Br, Basis of Property Given is Bg, Gain (Loss) Recognized is G, and the Fair Market Value of Property Received is $FMVr$, the transitive can be written simply as $Br = Bg + G$, $Bg + G = FMVr$, so $Br = FMVr$.

B were $6,000, a subsequent sale of property B for $6,000 would result in no further gain or loss. The taxpayer would have been taxed on only $500 of recognized gain despite the fact that an economic gain of $1,500 was realized as a result of both transactions. The *Philadelphia Park* interpretation of cost as the value of the property received prevents this result by coordinating the basis provisions with the amount realized.[5]

If the fair market value of the property received cannot be ascertained, then the fair market value of the property transferred will be presumed to be equal and will thereby be used to determine amount realized. United States v. Davis, 370 U.S. 65, 73 (1962). As a result, the basis of the property received will be the fair market value of the property given up, but only because that value will be equivalent to the basis of the property given plus gain recognized.

3.   BASIS OF PROPERTY RECEIVED IN AN EXCHANGE WHERE GAIN OR LOSS IS NOT RECOGNIZED

Where neither asset has a determinable fair market value, the basis of the transferred property should be taken as the basis for the property received, as *Philadelphia Park* intimates. This result is appropriate because when neither the value of the property received nor the value of the property given up can be ascertained, it is not possible to determine the amount realized and hence the amount of realized gain or loss. Thus no gain or loss is recognized, although, as discussed in Chapter 31, Section 1, this nonrecognition will occur only in extraordinary circumstances. See Burnet v. Logan, 283 U.S. 404 (1931); Treas. Reg. § 15a.453–1(d)(2)(iii). The basis of property received in this nonrecognition transaction is equivalent to the basis of property given plus or minus the zero gain or loss recognized.

In an exchange of properties in which gain or loss, even if realized, is not recognized, adoption of the basis of the property transferred as the basis of the property received will defer recognition of gain or loss until final disposition of the property received. The taxpayer does not completely escape paying tax on gain or lose the deduction for loss. For example, if appreciated property A purchased for $4,000 is exchanged for property B in a transaction in which gain or loss is properly not recognized, the basis of property B will be $4,000. Disposition of property B for $6,000 of cash will require the taxpayer to recognize $2,000 of gain. This gain will include any appreciation or depreciation in the value of property A at the time of the exchange for property B. Statutory provisions permitting nonrecognition of gain or loss in certain transactions adopt this deferral approach by providing in general that the basis of property given up will be transferred to the basis of the property received. See, e.g., § 1031(d), in Chapter 26, Section 1.

4.   PROPERTY ACQUIRED ON THE EXERCISE OF AN OPTION

Where property is acquired by the exercise of an option, the basis of the acquired property is the amount paid on the exercise plus any amount paid for the option itself. Thus, if a taxpayer paid $1,000 for an option to purchase property for $10,000, and then exercised the option and purchased the

---

[5]   There is dictum in United States v. Davis, 370 U.S. 65, 73 (1962), that is inconsistent with the approach of *Philadelphia Park,* but *Davis* has not been followed on this point.

property when it had a value of $15,000, the basis for the property is $11,000. See e.g., Moore v. Commissioner, 425 F.2d 713 (9th Cir.1970). Gain is not recognized as to the option itself, so that the $4,000 appreciation in value of the option does not result in a gain on its exercise, and thus does not enter into the basis of the acquired property. Helvering v. San Joaquin Fruit & Investment Co., 297 U.S. 496 (1936). Adopting the fair market value of the acquired property as its basis would require treating the exercise of the option as a realization event to prevent overstating of basis. The basis of the acquired property in this example reflects the "cost" to the taxpayer in after-tax dollars given up, $1,000 plus $10,000. The basis of property acquired on the exercise of an option accurately can be expressed as the basis of the property given up, the $11,000 cash paid, increased by the gain recognized, zero.

C. THE ROLE OF DEBT IN AMOUNT REALIZED AND BASIS

REGULATIONS: Section 1.1001–2.

Few major property acquisitions and dispositions involve only cash, especially transactions in real estate. Frequently the purchaser of property will borrow the purchase price from a third party lender, such as a bank, or acquire the property under an installment payment arrangement pursuant to which the seller finances the acquisition by taking deferred payments. A debt-financed acquisition of property often is secured by a mortgage or other security interest in the acquired property in favor of the lender. On disposition of property secured by a debt, the purchaser will often assume the seller's liability (i.e., promise the seller, and sometimes the lender, to pay the debt as it falls due), or, in the case of nonrecourse debt, take the property subject to the debt (without expressly promising the seller to pay the debt as it falls due). In general, basis under § 1012 includes borrowed funds used to acquire property. Conversely, on the transfer of property the amount of debt assumed by the buyer, or subject to which the buyer takes the property, is included in amount realized. See Treas. Reg. § 1.1001–2. Special issues that are raised with respect to borrowed funds for which the borrower is not personally liable (i.e., nonrecourse debt) are considered in Chapter 34.

DETAILED ANALYSIS

1. DEBT IN BASIS

Assume that A purchases property for $100 cash. The $100 is included in basis, as cost, for purposes of determining gain or loss on disposition and for purposes of calculating capital recovery deductions (depreciation and the like), discussed in Chapter 14. On disposition of the property, A is entitled to recover the $100 invested capital before any gain is realized. Now suppose A borrows the $100 purchase price from a bank. The receipt of the borrowed funds is not included in income because of A's obligation to return the capital to the bank. See Milenbach v. Commissioner, 318 F.3d 924 (9th Cir.2003),

Chapter 5, Section 1. If A uses the $100 to purchase property, again A has made a $100 investment in the property, but with borrowed funds. A cannot derive an economic gain from the property unless A sells the property for an amount in excess of the $100 due to the lender. Therefore, the $100 of borrowed capital must be included in A's basis in order to properly determine A's gain. If A sells the property for $110 of cash, A realizes $10 of gain that is subject to recognition as gross income. If $100 of the proceeds remains impressed with A's obligation to repay the lender, the borrowed $100 does not represent income to A.

The situation does not change when A acquires property from the seller in exchange for A's promise to pay $100 in the future evidenced by a note to the seller secured by the property, rather than borrowing cash that is used to acquire property. Again, before A can realize an economic gain, A must dispose of the property for an amount in excess of $100. Thus, the full $100 must be accounted for in basis as capital recoverable tax-free to compute taxable gain. The transaction differs from the first example, the borrowing of cash that is invested in property, only by the fact that no money has changed hands between borrower and seller. As a consequence, this transaction might be treated as if A's basis in the property were zero and the $100 will be included in basis only as payments of principal are made on the note. Nevertheless, from A's point of view, the transaction is economically equivalent to the first. In both cases A has a property purchased for $100 and a $100 liability. There is, therefore, no reason to treat the two transactions differently. In addition, limiting A's basis to A's equity investment in the property would limit capital recovery deductions to A's equity investment plus the amount paid on the debt principal, see Chapter 14. If that were the case, the purchase money borrower would be at a tax disadvantage relative to the borrower who receives cash that is subsequently invested in property. Thus, in general, the purchase money situation is treated in the same fashion from the borrower's point of view as a loan from a third party. This is a case of the economic substance of the transaction controlling over its form.

Note that the payment of the debt does not change A's basis in the property. By repaying the debt, A replaces a portion of the cash received tax free subject to an obligation to repay, with cash accounted for as gross income. A's investment in the property recoverable free of tax remains $100.

2.   DEBT AND AMOUNT REALIZED

Typically, when property encumbered by a debt is sold, a portion of the sales proceeds is paid directly to the lender to discharge the debt. Even though the seller has not personally received the portion of the proceeds paid to discharge the debt, that amount is included in the seller's amount realized under the principles of *Old Colony Trust*, Chapter 2, Section 1.B. Other times the buyer assumes the seller's liability (or in the case of nonrecourse debt takes the property subject to the debt). When a buyer assumes a liability of the seller upon the disposition of property, the seller has received a valuable contract right from the buyer in exchange for the property. That contract right should be included in the seller's amount realized on the sale of the property, along with any cash or other property received in the transaction.

See Brons Hotels, Inc. v. Commissioner, 34 B.T.A. 376, 379–80 (1936). For example, the transfer of property worth $100, but encumbered by a debt of $40 that the buyer assumes, for $60 of cash results in an amount realized of $100, the sum of the $60 of cash and the $40 value of the buyer's contractual promise to pay the debt that the buyer has received. The fact that this treatment is necessary to reach the proper result is most obvious in the case of purchase money debt. The symmetry between basis and amount realized that formed the decision in *Philadelphia Park* requires that since debt incurred to acquire property is included in basis, a release of debt that occurs on disposition of property must be included in the amount realized on the sale or exchange. In Brons Hotel, Inc. v. Commissioner, supra, the Board of Tax Appeals (the Tax Court's predecessor) described this symmetry as follows:

> Petitioner, as the owner of the Walton Hotel, was entitled to take— and required to take—as a basis for determining gain or loss upon the sale or other disposition of such property the *cost* thereof (sec. [1012]). When it acquired the property, it received, as part of its cost, the benefit of the mortgage which it assumed, although it actually acquired only an equity in the property. During the time it owned the property it was allowed depreciation on the improvements located thereon and not merely upon its equity in such improvements. * * * It has been said that it is only equitable that, when relieved of the debt burden which it has been allowed to use as part of the cost, it should be deemed to have received cash equivalent in the passing on of that debt to its vendee. Of course, neither the administrative officers of the department nor this Board have equity powers; but as a mere abstraction the above statement undoubtedly is correct.

The "equitable" argument for inclusion of debt in both basis and amount realized articulated in *Brons Hotel, Inc.* is supported by economic analysis and proper accounting for realized gains and losses. Assume, for example, that A purchases property worth $100 for $20 of cash plus a debt to the seller, secured by the property, of $80. A's basis in the property includes the $20 invested by A, plus the additional $80 that A promised to invest by paying the debt. A's receipt of $100 of property for a contemporaneous payment of only $20 currently is not income because of A's offsetting obligation to pay an additional $80 to the seller. When the property has appreciated in value to $130, A transfers the property to a purchaser who pays A $50 of cash and assumes A's original $80 debt. A's amount realized is $130, including both the $50 cash and the contract right worth $80. (That the contract right received by A is worth $80 is even clearer when, as a result of a novation—a three party contract between A, the purchaser, and the lender—the lender releases A from liability in connection with the purchaser's assumption of the debt). A thereby realizes $30 of gain on the disposition of the property ($130 − $100). That is obviously the correct result. A initially received $100 of property for payment of $20 plus the receipt of $80 of value offset by A's obligation to repay the debt. Including the full $100 in basis reflects the full capital investment in the property in terms of both A's actual current payment and future payments of the loan principal. Additionally, before A realizes economic gain on disposition of the property, A must realize $100 to recover A's initial capital investment and repay the loan. On disposition of the property to a purchaser who assumes A's obligation to repay the debt, including in A's amount realized the amount of the debt the purchaser has promised to pay (in effect, relief from the liability) accounts for A's initial tax-free receipt of $80 of value that had been offset by A's obligation to repay the debt. In other words, A's tax-free basis credit for $80 of borrowed capital is repaid within the tax accounting system by A's inclusion of the amount of the unpaid liability in amount realized on disposition of the property. The $50 of cash returns A's initial $20 of cash investment, leaving A with a $30 gain. Although this transaction could be accounted for by excluding the debt from both sides of the equation, doing so would cause distortions in accounting for the full capital cost of the property in the context of the capital recovery provisions.

Treas. Reg. § 1.1001–2 does not generally distinguish debt for which the seller is personally liable from debt for which the lender's only recourse is against the property ("nonrecourse debt"). The rationale for treating nonrecourse debt in the same manner as recourse debt is explored further in Chapter 34. The only instance in which the two types of debt are treated differently is when the encumbered property is transferred to the lender in full satisfaction of the debt. If the property is transferred to the lender in exchange for a release of personal liability, the debt is included in amount realized only to the extent of the fair market value of the property. Any debt in excess of the value of transferred property is treated as cancellation of indebtedness income, discussed in Chapter 10. In the case of nonrecourse debt for which there is no personal liability, the full amount of the debt is included in amount realized regardless of the fair market value of the encumbered property. Treas. Reg. § 1.1001–2(b); *Commissioner v. Tufts*, 461 U.S. 300 (1983), Chapter 34, Section 1. The different treatment of recourse and nonrecourse debt is important when determining the portion of the gain that is treated as gain from the disposition of the property (the excess of the amount realized over basis), which might be capital gain, and the portion of the gain that results from cancellation of the debt, which will be ordinary income and possibly excludable in certain circumstances. The distinction is discussed further in Chapter 34, Section 1.3.

3.   POST-ACQUISITION INDEBTEDNESS

Assume, as in the previous example, that A purchases property for $20 cash plus a note for $80. When the property has appreciated in value to $130, A borrows an additional $50, pledging the appreciated property as security for the second loan as well as the first. As indicated by *Woodsam Associates,* in Section 3.A., A does not realize gain on the subsequent borrowing even though A benefits from the $50 of appreciation at the time of the borrowing. Just as with the initial $80 purchase-money note, A's receipt of the $50 cash is offset by A's obligation to repay the $50 to the lender, and is, therefore, not includable in income. However, unless A invests the borrowed $50 in improvements to the property, the subsequent $50 of debt *does not* increase A's basis in the property that secures the additional borrowing. Rather, the subsequent borrowing produced $50 of additional cash which A could use for other purposes.[6] If A were to transfer the property to a buyer who assumes the liabilities, without more, A's amount realized is $130, representing the value of the assumption of both the original $80 debt and the subsequent $50 debt. A's realized gain is $30, the amount realized of $130 less A's basis of $100. A's overall taxable gain on the transaction reflects A's initial cost for the property of $20 of cash, plus A's obligation to repay $80 of purchase money debt, and A's receipt of $50 without tax at the time of the second loan, which A will not be required to repay. Overall, A has received $30 in excess of A's total investment. A's net gain of $30 is includable as gross income. The same results would occur if the second loan were nonrecourse and the buyer took the property subject to the loan, but the theoretical reasons for the result would be slightly different.

SECTION 3.   COMPLEX ASPECTS OF REALIZATION

REGULATIONS: Sections 1.1001–1(a); 1.1002–1(a).

Eisner v. Macomber, 252 U.S. 189 (1920), Chapter 2, Section 2, held that the term "derived" as used both in the Sixteenth Amendment and § 61, requires that gain inherent in property is not includable in gross income until a disposition of the property or other event in which the gain is "realized" for tax purposes. This requirement is applicable both for purposes of recognizing gain includable in income and for purposes of identifying recognized losses that may be deductible in reducing taxable income. The deduction of losses is considered in Chapter 15. Identifying the taxable event that represents a realization of gain or loss presents its own definitional difficulties.

A. MORTGAGING PROPERTY AS A DISPOSITION

Woodsam Associates, Inc. v. Commissioner
United States Court of Appeals, Second Circuit, 1952.
198 F.2d 357.

■ CHASE, CIRCUIT JUDGE

On December 29, 1934, Samuel J. Wood and his wife organized the petitioner and each transferred to it certain property in return for one-half of its capital stock. One piece of property so transferred by Mrs. Wood was [a] parcel of improved real estate consisting of land in the City of New York and a brick building thereon divided into units suitable for use, and used, in retail business. The property was subject to a $400,000

---

[6]   It might be said that A has a basis of $50 in the cash, which in effect includes the full amount of the debt in the property acquired for A's note. If A uses the $50 to acquire other property, A will have a $50 basis in that other property. Similarly, if A had used the $50 to improve the mortgaged property, its basis then would be $130 and the transfer solely for assumption of the $130 indebtedness would have resulted in no gain.

mortgage on which Mrs. Wood was not personally liable and on which the petitioner never became personally liable. Having, thus, acquired the property in a tax free exchange, I.R.C. [§ 351], the petitioner took the basis of Mrs. Wood for tax purposes. [I.R.C. § 362.] Upon the final disposition of the property at the foreclosure sale there was still due upon the mortgage the principal amount of $381,000 and, as the petitioner concedes, the extent to which the amount of the mortgage exceeds its adjusted basis was income taxable to it even though it was not personally liable upon the mortgage. Crane v. C.I.R., 331 U.S. 1 * * * .

Turning now to the one item whose effect upon the calculation of the petitioner's adjusted basis is disputed, the following admitted facts need to be stated. Mrs. Wood bought the property on January 20, 1922 at a total cost of $296,400. She paid $101,400 in cash, took the title subject to an existing mortgage for $120,000 and gave a purchase money bond and second mortgage for $75,000. She had made payments on the first mortgage reducing it to $112,500, when, on December 30, 1925, both of the mortgages were assigned to the Title Guarantee and Trust Company. On January 4, 1926 Mrs. Wood borrowed $137,500 from the Title Guarantee & Trust company and gave it a bond and mortgage for $325,000 on which she was personally liable, that being the amount of the two existing mortgages, which were consolidated into the new one, plus the amount of the cash borrowed. On June 9, 1931 this consolidated mortgage was assigned to the East River Savings Bank and, shortly thereafter, Mrs. Wood borrowed an additional $75,000 from that bank which she received upon the execution of a second consolidated mortgage for $400,000 comprising the principal amount due on the first consolidated mortgage plus the additional loan. However, this transaction was carried out through the use of a "dummy" so that, under New York law, Mrs. Wood was not personally liable on this bond and mortgage. See In re Childs Co., 2 Cir., 163 F.2d 379. This was the mortgage, reduced as above stated, which was foreclosed.

The contention of the petitioner may now be stated quite simply. It is that, when the borrowings of Mrs. Wood subsequent to her acquisition of the property became charges solely upon the property itself, the cash she received for the repayment of which she was not personally liable was a gain then taxable to her as income to the extent that the mortgage indebtedness exceeded her adjusted basis in the property. That being so, it is argued that her tax basis was, under familiar principles of tax law, increased by the amount of such taxable gain and that this stepped up basis carried over to the petitioner in the tax free exchange by which it acquired the property.

While [this conclusion] would be sound if the premise on which it is based were correct, we cannot accept the premise. It is that the petitioner's transferor made a taxable disposition of the property, within the meaning of I.R.C. [§ 1001] when the second consolidated mortgage was executed, because she had, by then, dealt with it in such a way that she had received cash, in excess of her basis, which, at that time, she was freed from any personal obligation to repay. Nevertheless, whether or not personally liable on the mortgage, "The mortgagee is a creditor, and in effect nothing more than a preferred creditor, even though the mortgagor is not liable for the debt. He is not the less a creditor because he has recourse only to the land, unless we are to deny the term to one who may levy upon only a part of his debtor's assets." C.I.R. v. Crane, 2 Cir., 153 F.2d 504, 506. Mrs. Wood merely augmented the existing mortgage indebtedness when she borrowed each time and, far from closing the venture, remained in a position to borrow more if and when circumstances permitted and she so desired. And so, she never "disposed" of the property to create a taxable event which [§ 1001] makes a condition precedent to the taxation of gain. "Disposition," within the meaning of [§ 1001] is the " 'getting rid, or making over, of anything; relinquishment.' " * * * Nothing of that nature was done here by the mere execution of the second consolidated mortgage; Mrs. Wood was the owner of this property in the same sense after the execution of this mortgage that she was before. As was pointed out in our decision in the Crane case, supra, 153 F.2d at 505–506, " * * * the lien of a mortgage does not make the mortgagee a cotenant; the mortgagor is the owner for all purposes; indeed that is why the 'gage' is 'mort,' as distinguished from a *vivum vadium*.' Kortright v. Cady, 21 N.Y. 343 * * * . He has all the income from the property; he manages it; he may sell it; any increase in its value goes to him; any decrease falls on him, until the value goes below the amount of the lien." Realization of gain was, therefore, postponed for taxation until there was a final disposition of the property at the time of the foreclosure sale. * * * Therefore, Mrs. Wood's borrowings did not change the basis for the computation of gain or loss.

DETAILED ANALYSIS

1. RECEIPT OF LOAN PROCEEDS AS A REALIZATION EVENT

The receipt of the proceeds of a loan normally does not constitute income since the loan creates an offsetting obligation for the borrower. There is thus no increase in the taxpayer's net worth. The issue raised by *Woodsam* is whether this result should be any different where the borrower is not personally liable for repayment of the debt and repayment of the loan is secured only by appreciated property of the taxpayer—a nonrecourse liability.

Suppose, for example, that the taxpayer has land with a fair market value of $100,000 and an adjusted basis of $10,000. The taxpayer needs cash but does not want to sell the property because the taxpayer believes there will be further substantial appreciation. A bank agrees to lend the taxpayer $50,000 on a nonrecourse basis. Thus, in the event of default, the bank's only remedy is to foreclose upon the property; the taxpayer is not personally liable for repayment. In this situation, the taxpayer and the bank have in effect agreed that the taxpayer can always satisfy the loan obligation by transferring to the bank the property securing the loan. Thus, the risk that the property might decline in value below the loan amount is borne by the bank. The taxpayer has "locked in" a portion of the gain with respect to the property since the taxpayer no longer bears the risk of loss of a decline in value of the property below $50,000.

Under these circumstances, it would be plausible to treat the "loan" as a partial disposition of the underlying property, with the proceeds constituting an amount realized. This approach would require deciding how the basis should be allocated in connection with this partial disposition. The taxpayer in *Woodsam* apparently contended that only the excess of the "borrowing" over the entire basis was the gain realized. This approach has the virtue of not requiring a valuation of the property that an allocation of basis approach would entail. Thus, in the preceding example, the realized gain would be $40,000 ($50,000–$10,000 basis) under this approach and $45,000 [$50,000–(($50,000 cash/$100,000 value) $10,000 basis)] under an allocation of basis approach.

The *Woodsam* court, however, rejected the sale characterization entirely. Thus no gain is recognized on a nonrecourse borrowing. Accounting for the liability for tax purposes must await the ultimate disposition of property.

B. REALIZATION AS MATERIAL CHANGE

Cottage Savings Association v. Commissioner*

Supreme Court of the United States, 1991.
499 U.S. 554.

■ JUSTICE MARSHALL delivered the opinion of the Court. The issue in this case is whether a financial institution realizes tax-deductible losses when it exchanges its interests in one group of residential mortgage loans for another lender's interests in a different group of residential mortgage loans. We hold that such a transaction does give rise to realized losses.

I

Petitioner Cottage Savings Association (Cottage Savings) is a savings and loan association (S & L) formerly regulated by the Federal Home Loan Bank Board (FHLBB). Like many S & L's, Cottage Savings held numerous long-term, low-interest mortgages that declined in value when interest rates surged in the late 1970's. These institutions would have benefited from selling their devalued mortgages in order to realize tax-deductible losses. However, they were deterred from doing so by FHLBB accounting regulations, which required them to record the losses on their books. Reporting these losses consistent with the then-effective FHLBB accounting regulations would have placed many S & L's at risk of closure by the FHLBB.

---

*   [Ed. A companion case, U.S. v. Centennial Savings Bank FSB was decided at the same time.]

The FHLBB responded to this situation by relaxing its requirements for the reporting of losses. In a regulatory directive known as "Memorandum R–49," dated June 27, 1980, the FHLBB determined that S & L's need not report losses associated with mortgages that are exchanged for "substantially identical" mortgages held by other lenders.[2] The FHLBB's acknowledged purpose for Memorandum R–49 was to facilitate transactions that would generate tax losses but that would not substantially affect the economic position of the transacting S & L's.

This case involves a typical Memorandum R–49 transaction. On December 31, 1980, Cottage Savings sold "90% participation interests" in 252 mortgages to four S & L's. It simultaneously purchased "90% participation interests" in 305 mortgages held by these S & L's.[3] All of the loans involved in the transaction were secured by single-family homes, most in the Cincinnati area. The fair market value of the package of participation interests exchanged by each side was approximately $4.5 million. The face value of the participation interests Cottage Savings relinquished in the transaction was approximately $6.9 million. * * *

On its 1980 federal income tax return, Cottage Savings claimed a deduction for $2,447,091, which represented the adjusted difference between the face value of the participation interests that it traded and the fair market value of the participation interests that it received. As permitted by Memorandum R–49, Cottage Savings did not report these losses to the FHLBB. After the Commissioner of Internal Revenue disallowed Cottage Savings' claimed deduction, Cottage Savings sought a redetermination in the Tax Court. The Tax Court held that the deduction was permissible. * * *

On appeal by the Commissioner, the Court of Appeals reversed. 890 F.2d 848 (C.A.6 1989). * * *

Because of the importance of this issue to the S & L industry and the conflict among the Circuits over whether Memorandum R–49 exchanges produce deductible tax losses, we granted certiorari. * * * We now reverse.

II

Rather than assessing tax liability on the basis of annual fluctuations in the value of a taxpayer's property, the Internal Revenue Code defers the tax consequences of a gain or loss in property value until the taxpayer "realizes" the gain or loss. The realization requirement is implicit in § 1001(a) of the Code, * * * which defines "the gain [or loss] from the sale or other disposition of property" as the difference between "the amount realized" from the sale or disposition of the property and its

---

[2] Memorandum R–49 listed 10 criteria for classifying mortgages as substantially identical. * * *

[3] By exchanging merely participation interests rather than the loans themselves, each party retained its relationship with the individual obligors. Consequently, each S & L continued to service the loans on which it had transferred the participation interests and made monthly payments to the participation-interest holders. * * *

"adjusted basis." As this Court has recognized, the concept of realization is "founded on administrative convenience." Helvering v. Horst, 311 U.S. 112, 116 (1940). Under an appreciation-based system of taxation, taxpayers and the Commissioner would have to undertake the "cumbersome, abrasive, and unpredictable administrative task" of valuing assets on an annual basis to determine whether the assets had appreciated or depreciated in value. * * * In contrast, "[a] change in the form or extent of an investment is easily detected by a taxpayer or an administrative officer." * * *

Section 1001(a)'s language provides a straightforward test for realization: to realize a gain or loss in the value of property, the taxpayer must engage in a "sale or other disposition of [the] property." The parties agree that the exchange of participation interests in this case cannot be characterized as a "sale" under § 1001(a); the issue before us is whether the transaction constitutes a "disposition of property." The Commissioner argues that an exchange of property can be treated as a "disposition" under § 1001(a) only if the properties exchanged are materially different. The Commissioner further submits that, because the underlying mortgages were essentially economic substitutes, the participation interests exchanged by Cottage Savings were not materially different from those received from the other S & L's. Cottage Savings, on the other hand, maintains that any exchange of property is a "disposition of property" under § 1001(a), regardless of whether the property exchanged is materially different. Alternatively, Cottage Savings contends that the participation interests exchanged were materially different because the underlying loans were secured by different properties.

We must therefore determine whether the realization principle in § 1001(a) incorporates a "material difference" requirement. If it does, we must further decide what that requirement amounts to and how it applies in this case. We consider these questions in turn.

A

Neither the language nor the history of the Code indicates whether and to what extent property exchanged must differ to count as a "disposition of property" under § 1001(a). Nonetheless, we readily agree with the Commissioner that an exchange of property gives rise to a realization event under § 1001(a) only if the properties exchanged are "materially different." The Commissioner himself has by regulation construed § 1001(a) to embody a material difference requirement:

> "Except as otherwise provided . . . the gain or loss realized from the conversion of property into cash, *or from the exchange of property for other property differing materially either in kind or in extent,* is treated as income or as loss sustained." Treas. Reg. § 1.1001–1, * * * (1990) (emphasis added).

Because Congress has delegated to the Commissioner the power to promulgate "all needful rules and regulations for the enforcement of [the

Internal Revenue Code]," 26 U.S.C. § 7805(a), we must defer to his regulatory interpretations of the Code so long as they are reasonable, see National Muffler Dealers Assn., Inc. v. United States, 440 U.S. 472, 476–477 (1979).

We conclude that Treasury Regulation § 1.1001–1 is a reasonable interpretation of § 1001(a). Congress first employed the language that now comprises § 1001(a) of the Code in § 202(a) of the Revenue Act of 1924, * * * ; that language has remained essentially unchanged through various reenactments. And since 1934, the Commissioner has construed the statutory term "disposition of property" to include a "material difference" requirement. As we have recognized, " 'Treasury regulations and interpretations long continued without substantial change, applying to unamended or substantially reenacted statutes, are deemed to have received congressional approval and have the effect of law.' " United States v. Correll, 389 U.S. 299, 305–306 (1967), quoting Helvering v. Winmill, 305 U.S. 79, 83 (1938).

Treasury Regulation § 1.1001–1 is also consistent with our landmark precedents on realization. In a series of early decisions involving the tax effects of property exchanges, this Court made clear that a taxpayer realizes taxable income only if the properties exchanged are "materially" or "essentially" different. See United States v. Phellis, 257 U.S. 156, 173 (1921); Weiss v. Stearn, 265 U.S. 242, 253–254 (1924); Marr v. United States, 268 U.S. 536, 540–542 (1925); see also Eisner v. Macomber, 252 U.S. 189, 207–212 (1920) (recognizing realization requirement). Because these decisions were part of the "contemporary legal context" in which Congress enacted § 202(a) of the 1924 Act, see Cannon v. University of Chicago, 441 U.S. 677, 698–699 (1979), and because Congress has left undisturbed through subsequent reenactments of the Code the principles of realization established in these cases, we may presume that Congress intended to codify these principles in § 1001(a) * * * . The Commissioner's construction of the statutory language to incorporate these principles certainly was reasonable.

B

Precisely what constitutes a "material difference" for purposes of § 1001(a) of the Code is a more complicated question. The Commissioner argues that properties are "materially different" only if they differ in economic substance. To determine whether the participation interests exchanged in this case were "materially different" in this sense, the Commissioner argues, we should look to the attitudes of the parties, the evaluation of the interests by the secondary mortgage market, and the views of the FHLBB. We conclude that § 1001(a) embodies a much less demanding and less complex test.

Unlike the question whether § 1001(a) contains a material difference requirement, the question of what constitutes a material difference is not one on which we can defer to the Commissioner. For the Commissioner has not issued an authoritative, prelitigation interpretation of what property exchanges satisfy this requirement. Thus, to give meaning to the material difference test, we must look to the case law from which the test derives and which we believe Congress intended to codify in enacting and reenacting the language that now comprises § 1001(a). * * *

We start with the classic treatment of realization in *Eisner v. Macomber,* supra. In *Macomber,* a taxpayer who owned 2,200 shares of stock in a company received another 1,100 shares from the company as part of a *pro rata* stock dividend meant to reflect the company's growth in value. At issue was whether the stock dividend constituted taxable income. We held that it did not, because no gain was realized. * * * We reasoned that the stock dividend merely reflected the increased worth of the taxpayer's stock, * * * and that a taxpayer realizes increased worth of property only by receiving "something of exchangeable value proceeding from the property," * * * .

In three subsequent decisions—*United States v. Phellis,* supra; *Weiss v. Stearn,* supra; and *Marr v. United States,* supra—we refined *Macomber's* conception of realization in the context of property exchanges. In each case, the taxpayer owned stock that had appreciated in value since its acquisition. And in each case, the corporation in which the taxpayer held stock had reorganized into a new corporation, with the new corporation assuming the business of the old corporation. While the corporations in *Phellis* and *Marr* both changed from New Jersey to Delaware corporations, the original and successor corporations in *Weiss* both were incorporated in Ohio. In each case, following the reorganization, the stockholders of the old corporation received shares in the new corporation equal to their proportional interest in the old corporation.

The question in these cases was whether the taxpayers realized the accumulated gain in their shares in the old corporation when they received in return for those shares stock representing an equivalent proportional interest in the new corporations. In *Phellis* and *Marr,* we held that the transactions were realization events. We reasoned that because a company incorporated in one State has "different rights and powers" from one incorporated in a different State, the taxpayers in *Phellis* and *Marr* acquired through the transactions property that was "materially different" from what they previously had. *United States v. Phellis*; 257 U.S., at 169–173; see *Marr v. United States*, supra, at 540–542 (using phrase "essentially different"). In contrast, we held that no realization occurred in *Weiss.* By exchanging stock in the predecessor corporation for stock in the newly reorganized corporation, the taxpayer did not receive "a thing really different from what he theretofore had." Weiss v. Stearn, supra, at 254. As we explained in *Marr,* our determination that the reorganized company in *Weiss* was not "really different" from its predecessor turned on the fact that both companies were incorporated in the same State. See *Marr v. United States*, supra, at 540–542 (outlining distinction between these cases).

Obviously, the distinction in *Phellis* and *Marr* that made the stock in the successor corporations materially different from the stock in the predecessors was minimal. Taken together, *Phellis, Marr,* and *Weiss* stand for the principle that properties are "different" in the sense that is "material" to the Internal Revenue Code so long as their respective possessors enjoy legal entitlements that are different in kind or extent. Thus, separate groups of stock are not materially different if they confer "the same proportional interest of the same character in the same corporation." Marr v. United States, 268 U.S., at 540. However, they are materially different if they are issued by different corporations, Id., at 541; United States v. Phellis, supra, at 173, or if they confer "different rights and powers" in the same corporation, Marr v. United States, supra, at 541. No more demanding a standard than this is necessary in order to satisfy the administrative purposes underlying the realization requirement in § 1001(a). * * * For, as long as the property entitlements are not identical, their exchange will allow both the Commissioner and the transacting taxpayer easily to fix the appreciated or depreciated values of the property relative to their tax bases.

In contrast, we find no support for the Commissioner's "economic substitute" conception of material difference. According to the Commissioner, differences between properties are material for purposes of the Code only when it can be said that the parties, the relevant market (in this case the secondary mortgage market), and the relevant regulatory body (in this case the FHLBB) would consider them material. Nothing in *Phellis, Weiss,* and *Marr* suggests that exchanges of properties must satisfy such a subjective test to trigger realization of a gain or loss.

Moreover, the complexity of the Commissioner's approach ill serves the goal of administrative convenience that underlies the realization requirement. In order to apply the Commissioner's test in a principled fashion, the Commissioner and the taxpayer must identify the relevant market, establish whether there is a regulatory agency whose views should be taken into account, and then assess how the relevant market participants and the agency would view the transaction. The Commissioner's failure to explain how these inquiries should be conducted further calls into question the workability of his test.

Finally, the Commissioner's test is incompatible with the structure of the Code. Section 1001(c) of Title 26 provides that a gain or loss realized under § 1001(a) "shall be recognized" unless one of the Code's nonrecognition provisions applies. One such nonrecognition provision withholds recognition of a gain or loss realized from an exchange of properties that would appear to be economic substitutes under the Commissioner's material difference test. This provision, commonly known as the "like kind" exception, withholds recognition of a gain or loss realized "on the exchange of property held for productive use in a trade or business or for investment . . . for property of like kind which is to be held either for productive use in a trade or business or for investment." 26 U.S.C. § 1031(a)(1). If Congress had expected that exchanges of similar properties would not count as realization events under § 1001(a), it would have had no reason to bar recognition of a gain or loss realized from these transactions.

C

Under our interpretation of § 1001(a), an exchange of property gives rise to a realization event so long as the exchanged properties are "materially different"—that is, so long as they embody legally distinct entitlements. Cottage Savings' transactions at issue here easily satisfy this test. Because the participation interests exchanged by Cottage Savings and the other S & L's derived from loans that were made to different obligors and secured by different homes, the exchanged interests did embody legally distinct entitlements. Consequently, we conclude that Cottage Savings realized its losses at the point of the exchange.

The Commissioner contends that it is anomalous to treat mortgages deemed to be "substantially identical" by the FHLBB as "materially different." The anomaly, however, is merely semantic; mortgages can be substantially identical for Memorandum R–49 purposes and still exhibit "differences" that are "material" for purposes of the Internal Revenue Code. Because Cottage Savings received entitlements different from those it gave up, the exchange put both Cottage Savings and the Commissioner in a position to determine the change in the value of Cottage Savings' mortgages relative to their tax bases. Thus, there is no reason not to treat the exchange of these interests as a realization event, regardless of the status of the mortgages under the criteria of Memorandum R–49.

IV

For the reasons set forth above, the judgment of the Court of Appeals is reversed, and the case is remanded for further proceedings consistent with this opinion.

So ordered.

■ JUSTICE BLACKMUN, with whom JUSTICE WHITE joins, concurring in part and dissenting in part * * * .

I dissent * * * from the Court's conclusions in these two cases that Centennial and Cottage Savings Association realized deductible losses for income tax purposes when each exchanged partial interests in one group of residential mortgage loans for partial interests in another like group of residential mortgage loans. I regard these losses as not recognizable for income tax purposes because the mortgage packages so exchanged were substantially identical and were not materially different.

The exchanges, as the Court acknowledges, were occasioned by the Federal Home Loan Bank Board's (FHLBB) Memorandum R–49 of June 27, 1980, and by that Memorandum's relaxation of theretofore-existing accounting regulations and requirements, a relaxation effected to avoid placement of "many S & L's at risk of closure by the FHLBB" without substantially affecting the "economic position of the transacting S & L's." * * * But the Memorandum, the Court notes, also had as a purpose "the facilitation of transactions that would generate tax losses." * * * I find it somewhat surprising that an agency not responsible for tax matters would presume to dictate what is or is not a deductible loss for federal income tax purposes. I had thought that was something within the exclusive province of the Internal Revenue Service, subject to administrative and judicial review. Certainly, the Bank Board's opinion in this respect is entitled to no deference whatsoever. * * * The Commissioner, of course, took the opposing position. See Rev. Rul. 85–125, 1985–2 Cum.Bull. 180; Rev. Rul. 81–204, 1981–2 Cum.Bull. 175.

* * *

In applying the realization requirement to an exchange, the properties involved must be materially different in kind or in extent. Treas. Reg. § 1.1001–1(a) * * * . This has been the rule recognized administratively at least since 1935, * * * . This makes economic as well as tax sense, for the parties obviously regard the exchanged properties as having equivalent values. In tax law, we should remember, substance rather than form determines tax consequences. Commissioner v. Court Holding Co., 324 U.S. 331, 334 (1945) * * * . Thus, the resolution of the exchange issue in these cases turns on the "materially different" concept. The Court recognizes as much. * * *

That the mortgage participation partial interests exchanged in these cases were "different" is not in dispute. The materiality prong is the focus. A material difference is one that has the capacity to influence a decision. * * *

The application of this standard leads, it seems to me, to only one answer—that the mortgage participation partial interests released were not materially different from the mortgage participation partial interests received. Memorandum R–49, as the Court notes, * * * , lists 10 factors that, when satisfied, as they were here, serve to classify the interests as "substantially identical." These factors assure practical identity; surely, they then also assure that any difference cannot be of consequence. Indeed, nonmateriality is the full purpose of the Memorandum's criteria. The "proof of the pudding" is in the fact of its complete accounting acceptability to the FHLBB. Indeed, as has been noted, it is difficult to reconcile substantial identity for financial accounting purposes with a material difference for tax accounting purposes. * * * Common sense so dictates.

This should suffice and be the end of the analysis. Other facts, however, solidify the conclusion: The retention by the transferor of 10% interests, enabling it to keep on servicing its loans; the transferor's continuing to collect the payments due from the borrowers so that, so far as the latter were concerned, it was business as usual, exactly as it had been; the obvious lack of concern or dependence of the transferor with the "differences" upon which the Court relies (as transferees, the taxpayers made no credit checks and no appraisals of collateral, see 890 F.2d 848, 849 (C.A.6 1989)) * * *; the selection of the loans by computer programmed to match mortgages in accordance with the Memorandum R–49 criteria; the absence of even the names of the borrowers in the closing schedules attached to the agreements; Centennial's receipt of loan files only six years after its exchange, 682 F.Supp., at 1392, n. 5; the restriction of the interests exchanged to the same State; the identity of the respective face and fair market values; and the application by the parties of common discount factors to each side of the transaction—all reveal that any differences that might exist made no difference whatsoever and were not material. This demonstrates the real nature of the transactions, including nonmateriality of the claimed differences.

We should be dealing here with realities and not with superficial distinctions. As has been said many times, and as noted above, in income tax law we are to be concerned with substance and not with mere form. When we stray from that principle, the new precedent is likely to be a precarious beacon for the future.

DETAILED ANALYSIS

1. IMMEDIATE RECOGNITION VERSUS DEFERRAL OF GAIN OR LOSS

Treas. Reg. § 1.1001–1(a), at issue in *Cottage Savings,* applies to both gains and losses. Would the taxpayer in *Cottage Savings* have taken the same position if the value of its mortgage portfolio had appreciated? Conversely, a victory for the Commissioner in *Cottage Savings* might have come back to haunt the fisc in terms of lost revenue as taxpayers who have derived gains on exchanges of closely related property would have claimed income deferral under a narrow definition of material change.

Has the investor who moves her capital from one publicly traded security to another actually materially changed her position so that gain or loss should be recognized by the tax system, or should the system allow further deferral of gain or loss until the investment is completely removed from the market? In some circumstances the Code allows deferral of realized gains when the taxpayer changes the form of an investment into similar property. For example, under § 1031, discussed in Chapter 26, gain is not recognized on the exchange of investment or business property for property of "like-kind." This provision allows real estate investors to exchange one property for another without recognizing gain, but does not permit the tax-free receipt of cash, even if it is promptly reinvested. Similarly, taxpayers are permitted to contribute property to a controlled corporation in exchange for stock (§ 351), or to a partnership in exchange for a partnership interest (§ 721), without recognition of gain or loss. An extensive set of rules permits nonrecognition of gain or loss on the exchange of the stock of one corporation for the stock of another in corporate reorganizations, including statutory mergers and the acquisition of the assets of one corporation by another in exchange for the stock of the acquiring corporation. The corporate reorganization provisions also allow reincorporation in a different state without recognition of gain, thus reversing the holdings in United States v. Phellis, 257 U.S. 156 (1921), and Marr v. United States, 268 U.S. 536 (1925), discussed in *Cottage Savings*. These nonrecognition provisions are based, to some extent, on the view that the taxpayer's continued investment in related property justifies deferral of income tax to the time of a more complete termination of the taxpayer's investment. As in the case of § 1031, if any cash is received in a transaction otherwise subject to these provisions, the cash generally either will be taxable or result in disqualifying the transaction for nonrecognition status.

2. THE *COTTAGE SAVINGS* REGULATIONS

The *Cottage Savings* decision generated a concern that a significant modification of a debt instrument, for example, a refinancing that altered the interest rate, due date, or even the principal amount, would constitute a realization event for both the creditor and the debtor, i.e., the creditor constructively exchanging the original promissory note to the debtor for a new promissory note. The creditor may recognize gain or loss because, while the fair market values of the obligations presumably will be identical at the time of the exchange, the creditor's basis for the obligation may differ, in most cases being higher than the fair market value at the time of the refinancing. As for the debtor, if the principal amount of the new debt instrument is less than the principal amount of the original debt instrument, discharge of indebtedness income may result. See Chapter 10. The IRS responded to these concerns regarding the implications of *Cottage Savings* by promulgating Treas. Reg. § 1.1001–3, dealing with the circumstances under which modification of a debt instrument is deemed to be an exchange of the original debt instrument for a new debt instrument.

An exchange, and thus a realization event, occurs whenever there is a "modification" that is "significant," whether through an agreement of the debtor and creditor or a unilateral waiver of rights. Changes of legal rights or responsibilities pursuant to the original terms of the debt instrument generally are not modifications. For example, the conversion of a variable rate mortgage to a fixed rate mortgage at the borrower's option as provided in the original investment is not a significant modification. Treas. Reg. § 1.1001–3(d), Ex.(8). Certain alterations pursuant to the original instrument, however, are designated as modifications by Treas. Reg. § 1.1001–3(c)(2). Modifications that are deemed to be significant under Treas. Reg. § 1.1001–3(e) include: (1) changing the annual yield by an amount in excess of 1/4 of one percent or by more than 5 percent of the yield of the unmodified instrument (unless attributable to a formula in the original instrument) through either an adjustment to the interest rate or a reduction of the principal, (2) changing the timing or amount of payments to materially defer payment (an extension exceeding the lesser of five years or 50 percent of the original term of the instrument), (3) substituting a new obligor on a recourse instrument, (4) altering collateral or guarantees securing a nonrecourse note (unless the collateral is fungible), (5) altering collateral or guarantees securing a recourse debt if the alteration changes payment expectations, and (6) changing an instrument from recourse to nonrecourse or vice versa (other than changing a secured debt from recourse to nonrecourse without a change in repayment expectations). In addition, any modification that, based on all of the facts and circumstances, alters the legal rights or obligations of the parties to the extent the alterations are "economically significant" would trigger realization.

3.   MARK-TO-MARKET RULES

3.1. *Inventory Held by Securities Dealers*

Section 475 requires securities dealers annually to mark their securities to market and report the accrued gains and losses as taxable income even though no realization event has occurred. The term "security" is defined in § 475(c)(2) to include not only corporate stocks and bonds, but also interests in publicly traded partnerships and trusts and a variety of financial instruments and currency exchange contracts. This provision applies both to inventory and other securities owned by the dealer except those specially excepted by statute. Securities held for investment, which have been so identified on the dealer's books before the close of the day they were acquired, are not subject to § 475. The general rule of § 475 is a clear-cut abrogation of the realization requirement, but it conforms to industry accounting practices.

3.2. *Commodity Futures and Options*

Section 1256 accounts on an annual basis for gains and losses from various futures and options contracts traded on specified exchanges. Because of the mark-to-market rules of these exchanges, under which cash withdrawals of profits are generally permitted and cash contributions required in case of loss, this section may be viewed as an application of the doctrine of constructive receipt, discussed in Chapter 28, Section 2.A. See Murphy v. United States, 992 F.2d 929 (9th Cir.1993) (mark-to-market rules in § 1256 are an application of constructive receipt based on the unique financial structure of futures contracts). Nevertheless, the annual accounting of § 1256 generally is the same as would apply to annual taxation of accrued gains from other property.

In addition, § 475(e) allows commodities dealers to elect to apply the mark-to-market regime to their positions in actively traded commodities (and derivative instruments based on commodity prices) that are not subject to § 1256. Only commodities clearly identified on the taxpayer's records by the close of the day the commodity was acquired as held in dealer status are subject to the elective mark-to-market rules.

3.3. *Elective Mark to Market Regime for "Traders"*

Section 475(f) extends the mark-to-market regime to "traders" in securities and commodities on an elective basis. A mark-to-market election applies to all securities or commodities held by the trader except any securities or commodities that the taxpayer can establish to the Commissioner's satisfaction are not related to the taxpayer's trading activities and which are clearly identified in the taxpayer's records by the close of the acquisition date as not being related to the taxpayer's trading activities. Any gain or loss recognized under the elective mark-to-market regime is ordinary gain or loss, not capital gain or loss. An election under § 475(f) may not be revoked without the Commissioner's consent. See generally H. Rep. No. 148, 105th Cong., 1st Sess. 445 (1997). As to when a taxpayer's activities result in classification as a trader, see Chapter 24, Section 2.A.6.

4.　CONSTRUCTIVE SALES OF FINANCIAL INSTRUMENTS

Section 1259 requires constructive realization of gains, but not losses, with respect to certain appreciated financial instruments that are not subject to § 475. A typical transaction to which this provision applies is the so-called "short sale against the box," in which a taxpayer who owns appreciated stock borrows and sells stock identical to the stock he holds to lock-in the unrealized appreciation on the stock he holds. For example, assume that B holds 100 shares of Intel stock that B purchased for $15 per share. When Intel is trading at $20 per share, B enters into short sale of 100 shares of Intel by borrowing 100 shares from B's broker and selling the shares for $2,000. B does not realize gain on this sale because B's basis in the borrowed shares is $2,000. B continues to hold B's original 100 shares. By maintaining precisely offsetting positions, B is insulated from fluctuations in value. When B is required to repay the loan of 100 shares, B can either purchase 100 additional shares and maintain his position in Intel stock or use the original 100 shares and close is position. While the short sale against the box is in place, the taxpayer effectively converts the investment to cash without actually selling it.[7] Investment bankers have devised many other transactions having similar effect, all of which can shift the risk of loss and opportunity for gain with respect to the stock to another party.

Section 1259 applies to appreciated "positions" with respect to stock, partnership interests, and certain debt instruments. A "position" includes not only ownership of a stock, debt, or partnership interest, but also futures or forward contracts, options, or short sales with respect to such interests. In general, § 1259 treats a taxpayer as constructively selling a position in an appreciated financial instrument when the taxpayer enters into (1) a short sale of the same or substantially identical property, (2) an offsetting notional principal contract with respect to the same or substantially identical property, or (3) a futures or forward contract to deliver the same or substantially identical property. If a taxpayer without an existing position in an appreciated financial instrument engages in a short sale, a notional principal contract, or a futures or forward contract with respect to a financial

---

[7]　Section § 1233(h) provides that if a taxpayer engages in a short sale of property that subsequently becomes worthless, the taxpayer recognizes gain on the short sale as if it were closed with identical worthless property at the time it became worthless. Section 1233(h)(2) provides an extended statute of limitations for assessing a deficiency based on worthlessness of the property subject to the short sale.

instrument, the taxpayer is treated as making a constructive sale when the taxpayer acquires the same property as the underlying property for the position. Section 1259(b)(2) excepts from constructive sale treatment appreciated financial instruments that are not marketable securities (within the meaning of § 453(f)) if an offsetting position is settled within one year after the date it is entered into.

5. RESCISSION

Even though a sale has been closed and gain thus realized, if the transaction is rescinded prior to the close of the taxable year in which it occurred, the original sale might be ignored and the status quo ante restored for tax purposes. This doctrine applies only to a rescission directly between the seller and the buyer. See Rev. Rul. 80–58, 1980–1 C.B. 181. Thus, for example, if an agent sells property on behalf of a principal without authorization and the agent subsequently assists the principal in acquiring fungible replacement property, the gain on the original sale is realized and must be recognized. See Hutcheson v. Commissioner, T.C. Memo. 1996–127 (when taxpayer instructed broker to sell $100,000 worth of Wal-Mart stock but broker sold 100,000 shares of stock from taxpayer's account, the repurchase of Wal-Mart stock through the broker was a separate transaction).

SECTION 4.   EXCLUSION OF GAINS FROM THE SALE OF A PRINCIPAL RESIDENCE

INTERNAL REVENUE CODE: Section 121(a)–(c), (d)(1), (6), (f).

Not all realized gains are currently taxed—"recognized" in tax parlance—and some gains that are currently recognized are taxed at preferential rates. Later chapters will deal with deferred recognition of gains from "like-kind" exchanges[8] and "involuntary conversions,"[9] as well as preferential tax rates accorded to gains from the sale of "capital assets."[10] This section introduces the concept of preferential treatment of certain types of recognized gains by focusing on gains recognized on the sale of the taxpayer's principal residence.

The return on investment in home ownership is highly tax favored. Not only does the income tax exclude the imputed income derived from the use of a personal residence owned by the taxpayer (see the discussion in Chapter 2, Section 3), § 121 provides that a taxpayer may exclude up to $250,000 of gain on the sale of a principal residence.[11] To qualify for the exclusion the taxpayer must have both owned and occupied the property as a principal residence for two out of the five taxable years preceding a sale or exchange. Married taxpayers, whether or not they file jointly, each may exclude up to $250,000 of gain on the sale of jointly-

---

[8]   See Chapter 26.

[9]   See Chapter 27.

[10]   See Chapters 24 and 25.

[11]   In addition to these benefits, interest on home mortgages and property taxes are deductible. See Chapter 21, Sections 4 and 5.

owned or community property, as long as they each meet the statutory two-out-of-five-years occupancy test. If only one spouse owned the property but both spouses satisfy the occupancy test, § 121(b)(2) permits an exclusion of up to $500,000 on a joint return. In addition, under § 121(b)(3), the exclusion only is available if the taxpayer had not claimed the exclusion on the sale of a principal residence within the immediately preceding two-year period.

Detailed Analysis

1. TWO-OUT-OF-FIVE-YEARS OWNERSHIP AND USE TEST

1.1. *In General*

To qualify for exclusion under § 121, the taxpayer must have owned and used the property as her principal residence for two of the five years preceding the date of the sale. Section 121(d)(7) relaxes the use requirement for taxpayers who were physically or mentally incapable of self-care during the five years preceding the sale of their principal residence and resided in a licensed health care facility or nursing home. In such a case, if the taxpayer actually used the residence for one year in the five-year test period, then the time the taxpayer resided in the health care facility also counts toward the two-out-of-five-years test. In addition, the two-out-of-five-years rule permits the sale of a principal residence that was abandoned and converted to rental use not more than three years previously to qualify for the exclusion, as long as it was continuously owned and used as a principal residence for at least two years prior to its conversion to rental property.

To qualify for the exclusion the property must be sold by the individual taxpayer who owned and occupied the property as a principal residence. Thus, property sold by estates and trusts generally does not qualify for the exclusion. However, if the taxpayer's principal residence is held by a trust, the taxpayer is treated as the owner and the seller of the residence during the period that the taxpayer is treated as the owner of the trust or the portion of the trust that includes the residence under §§ 671 through 679 (the grantor trust rules in Chapter 38, Section 4.A.). Treas. Reg. § 1.121–1(c)(3)(i). Sales by an individual's bankruptcy trustee qualify for the § 121 exclusion. Treas. Reg. § 1.1398–3.

Section 121(b)(2) permits an exclusion of up to $500,000 of gain on a joint return if either spouse owned the property, both spouses satisfy the two-out-of-five-years occupancy test, and neither spouse had claimed the benefit of a § 121 exclusion for another sale within the 24 months preceding the sale in question. If one spouse is not eligible for the exclusion, for example, because he or she did not meet the two-out-of-five-years use test or because of the one-sale-every-two-years limitation of § 121(b)(3), then under § 121(b)(2)(B), the ceiling on the exclusion on a joint return is computed as if the husband and wife were single, except that the ownership of one continues to be attributed to the other. Thus, for example, if either spouse fails the use test, the ceiling is only $250,000. Similarly, if § 121(b)(2) does not apply because one spouse (but not the other) had sold another house within the prior two years and claimed an exclusion under § 121 (and that spouse was not eligible for exclusion with a reduced ceiling under § 121(c)), then the exclusion ceiling on the joint return would be only the $250,000 attributable to the fully eligible spouse. Section 121(b)(2)(B) is also applicable when taxpayers marry and then sell one or both of the principal residences they previously occupied when they were single, capping the exclusion of gain on the sale of each such residence at $250,000. See generally Treas. Reg. § 1.121–2. The $500,000 exclusion also is available if a surviving spouse sells a principal residence within two years of the death of the other spouse. I.R.C. § 121(b)(4).

1.2. *Divorce Situations*

Section 121(d)(3)(B) provides a special rule dealing with divorce situations in which one spouse is granted exclusive use of the family residence pursuant to a divorce decree, but the residence continues to be jointly owned or owned by the other spouse. Section 121(d)(3)(B) treats the use of a residence by a former spouse pursuant to a divorce or separation instrument as use by the other former spouse during any period in which that spouse retains an ownership interest. Thus, for example, if A and B were divorced in 2004 and B was awarded use of their jointly-owned home for seven years, upon the sale of the home in 2008 A and B each could claim an exclusion for their individual share of the gain of up to $250,000.

Section 121(d)(3)(A) provides another special rule dealing with divorce situations. If property is acquired in a transfer to which § 1041 applies—as in the case of transfers incident to a divorce, discussed in Chapter 38, Section 3—the transferee spouse may tack the transferor spouse's ownership period. Thus for example, if A purchased a family residence into which A and B moved on July 1, 2014, and on December 31, 2015, A and B were divorced and the family residence transferred to B, B would satisfy the ownership requirement as of July 2, 2016. (Under the normal two-out-of-five-years ownership and use test, if spouse A owned the family residence, but it was awarded to spouse B in a divorce proceeding, spouse B would not meet the ownership test and not be eligible for nonrecognition for two years following the transfer.) Because § 121(d)(3)(A) applies to all transfers between spouses, § 121(d)(3)(A) also assures that the ownership test is met whenever for any purpose there is a transfer of interests in the family's principal residence between spouses within two years preceding the sale of the residence, provided, however, that one or the other of the spouses owned the residence for at least two years prior to sale.[12]

1.3. *Denial of Exclusion for Certain Residences Acquired in a Like-Kind Exchange*

Section 121(d)(10) denies the exclusion if the residence was acquired in a tax-deferred § 1031 like-kind exchange within the 5-year period preceding the date of sale. Congress was apparently concerned that taxpayers would exchange investment property, such as residential rental property, for property that they then converted into a principal residence with the result that gain intended to be deferred only under § 1031 (discussed in Chapter

---

[12]   Section 121(d)(2) provides a similar tacking rule when one spouse acquires an interest in a principal residence by reason of the other spouse's death.

26) would be permanently excluded under § 121. By in effect increasing the minimum holding period in the case of property acquired in a § 1031 exchange, Congress reduced the shelter potential of combining the two provisions while retaining the benefit provided by § 121.

1.4. *Limitation on Excluded Gains from Converted Property*

Section 121(b)(4) provides that gain on the sale of a personal residence is not excluded from gross income to the extent that the gain is allocable to periods of "nonqualified use" of the residence. In general, periods of nonqualified use include periods in which the property is not used as a principal residence of the taxpayer (or of the taxpayer's current or former spouse). However, (1) use prior to January 1, 2009 is not treated as nonqualified use, (2) use after the last date that the taxpayer used the property as a principal residence is not treated as a nonqualified use, (3) use while the taxpayer is on certain official governmental extended duty (e.g., military) is not nonqualified use, and (4) use during any other period of temporary absence (for up to an aggregate period of two years) is not nonqualified use if the absence is due to specified unforeseen circumstances. The amount of gain not excluded by reason of § 121(b)(4) is determined by allocating the total gain to periods of nonqualified use based on the ratio that the aggregate period of nonqualified use bears to the total time the taxpayer owned the property. For example, assume that a taxpayer bought a property on January 1, 2009, for $500,000, and uses it exclusively as a vacation home for four years. On January 1, 2013, the taxpayer converts the property to his principal residence. On January 1, 2015, the taxpayer sells the property for $800,000. The four years of vacation use is a period of nonqualified use that is two-thirds of the taxpayer's six-year period of ownership; accordingly, two-thirds ($200,000) of the $300,000 total gain is allocated to the period of nonqualified use and is therefore not eligible for exclusion under § 121. The remaining $100,000 of gain is excluded from gross income.

2. ONE SALE EVERY TWO YEARS LIMITATION

Section 121(b)(3) limits taxpayers to one exclusion under § 121 every two years. The measuring period is the actual period between sales, not taxable years. Thus, for example, if a taxpayer sold a principal residence on November 1, 2013 and excluded all or part of the gain, the taxpayer would not be eligible to claim nonrecognition on any sale of a subsequent primary residence until November 2, 2015.

The one-sale-every-two-years rule can affect the amount of the exclusion allowed on a joint return if one spouse owns and sells a principal residence that otherwise qualifies for the $500,000 exclusion rather than the $250,000 exclusion, but the other spouse had sold a principal residence within the preceding two years. Assume, for example, that on December 1, 2013, A married B and moved into B's principal residence (which B had owned for several years). On December 31, 2013, A sold A's recently abandoned principal residence and validly excluded the gain under § 121. A and B continued to live in B's house until December 15, 2014, when B sold the house and A and B moved. Although B is eligible to exclude $250,000, the $500,000 exclusion under § 121(b)(2) is not available because A is ineligible to claim the exclusion on any sale before January 1, 2015. To claim the $500,000 exclusion, neither spouse may have claimed the exclusion, even on a separate return, for a sale within the two years preceding the sale in question. I.R.C. § 121(b)(2)(A)(iii). See H. Rep. No. 148, 105th Cong., 1st Sess. 348 (1997).

3. PARTIAL NONRECOGNITION

If a taxpayer realizes gain on more than one sale within a two-year period in circumstances where the decision to move was not entirely within the taxpayer's control, the one-sale-every-two-years rule could have a harsh effect if not mitigated. Section 121(c) provides some relief in the form of partial nonrecognition if a taxpayer fails to meet either the two-year use and ownership requirements of § 121(a) or the one-sale-every-two-years limitation of § 121(b)(3) and the sale is due to a change in the taxpayer's place of employment or health. Qualifying conditions are detailed in Treas. Reg. § 1.121–3. The regulations extend the partial nonrecognition rule to unforeseen circumstances such as unemployment, a change in employment status that makes the taxpayer's living situation unaffordable, divorce or separation, or multiple births. See Treas. Reg. § 1.121–3(e). Since both the use and ownership test and the one-sale-every-two-years limitation employ the same base, § 121(c) reduces the ceiling on the amount of excludable gain. When § 121(c) applies, the $250,000 or $500,000 ceiling in § 121(a) or (b) is reduced by multiplying it by a fraction, the numerator of which is the number of months the taxpayer owned and used as a principal residence the house that was sold and the denominator of which is 24. Assume, for example, that in March 2013, the taxpayer was transferred by her employer to Indianapolis and purchased a home for $100,000. Two years later, in April 2015, the taxpayer was transferred by her employer to Boston and purchased a home in Boston for $210,000. In June 2015, the taxpayer sold the Indianapolis home for $110,000 and excluded the $10,000 gain under § 121. In October 2016, the taxpayer was transferred to San Francisco, and sold her Boston home for $420,000, realizing a $210,000 gain. The gain on the sale of the Boston home cannot be completely excluded under § 121(a) because the taxpayer resided in the Boston home for less than two years, and because she sold her Indianapolis home within two years of the sale of her Boston home. Under § 121(c) the ceiling on excludable gain is reduced to $187,500 ($250,000 × 18/24). Thus, the taxpayer may exclude $187,500 of her gain and must recognize the remaining $22,500 of the gain.

4. "PRINCIPAL RESIDENCE"

The exclusion is available only with respect to a sale of the taxpayer's "principal residence." Thus, gain realized on the sale of a vacation home or other secondary residence must be recognized. This is true even if the taxpayer rents the taxpayer's principal residence, for example, an apartment in Chicago, and the taxpayer sells the taxpayer's owner-occupied secondary residence, for example, a fishing camp in Minnesota. Whether a particular dwelling unit was the taxpayer's principal residence for two of the five years is a factual issue. Treas. Reg. § 1.121–1(b)(2) provides a nonexclusive list of factors relevant to identifying the taxpayer's principal residence, which include the taxpayer's place of employment, the principal abode of the taxpayer's family, the address used for filing tax returns, the address for the taxpayer's driver's license, automobile registration and voter's registration, the taxpayer's mailing address for bills and correspondence, the location of the taxpayer's banks, and the location of the taxpayer's social clubs and place of worship. These factors cannot be conclusive because they can produce inconsistent evidence. For example, a taxpayer may receive bills and subscriptions and join social clubs and places of worship at two distant residences, and might hold a driver's license with an address different than the one used for filing tax returns. The regulation also provides that if a taxpayer alternates between two residences during the year, the one that is used for the majority of the time will be the taxpayer's principal residence.

In Gates v. Commissioner, 135 T.C. 1 (2010), the Tax Court addressed the question of whether the taxpayer was required to have physically resided in the particular dwelling unit that was sold to be eligible to claim the § 121 exclusion. In that case, the married taxpayers had owned and occupied a house as a principal residence for at least two years. They wanted to enlarge and remodel the house but were advised by an architect that more stringent building and permit restrictions had been enacted since the house was built. In 1999, rather than remodel the house, they demolished it and constructed a new house on the property. The taxpayers never occupied the new house, and subsequently sold it, realizing a gain of over $500,000. They claimed that $500,000 of the gain was excludable under § 121, but the IRS denied the exclusion because they had never occupied the new structure and it thus never was their "principal residence," even though it occupied land on which had been located their former principal residence. The IRS's argument interpreted "the term 'property' [in § 121(a)] to mean, or at least include, a dwelling that was owned and occupied by the taxpayer as his 'principal residence' for at least 2 of the 5 years immediately preceding the sale." The taxpayers argued that the term "property" in § 121(a) includes not only the dwelling but also the land on which the dwelling is situated, and that the requirements of § 121(a) are satisfied if the taxpayer lived in any dwelling on the property for the required 2-year period, even if that dwelling is not the dwelling that was sold. Under the taxpayer's theory, because they used the original house and the land on which it was situated as their principal residence for the required term, the land and building that were sold qualified as their principal residence. Finding that the statute did not define the terms "property" and "principal residence," the majority of the Tax Court examined the background of § 121, including its statutory predecessors, former § 1034 and its predecessor in the 1939 Code, and held that:

> Congress intended the term "principal residence" to mean the primary dwelling or house that a taxpayer occupied as his principal residence. . . . Although a principal residence may include land surrounding the dwelling, the legislative history supports a conclusion that Congress intended the section 121 exclusion to apply only if the dwelling the taxpayer sells was actually used as his principal residence for the period required by section 121(a).

The court noted in a footnote that Treas. Reg. § 1.121–1(b)(3), as currently in effect, allows gain from the sale of land alone to qualify under

§ 121 if the taxpayer also sells "a 'dwelling unit' that meets the requirements under § 121 within 2 years before or after the sale of the land." The dissenting opinion would have allowed the exclusion, treating the demolition and reconstruction no differently from a renovation. It expressed concern that drawing the line between a "remodeling," which presumably would not start the 2-year clock running anew and a "rebuilding," which under the majority opinion does start the 2-year clock running anew is a difficult line to draw, asking rhetorically "is there some level of remodeling that does (1) terminate the use of the home as the taxpayer's principal residence and (2) set the temporal clock to zero?"

A taxpayer's principal residence need not be a traditional house. In addition to mobile homes, which long have been recognized as residences, a taxpayer's principal residence may be a boat or recreational vehicle with appropriate accommodations and facilities. Thus, for example, gain on a houseboat or yacht could be excluded under § 121 if it was the taxpayer's principal residence. See Treas. Reg. § 1.121–1(b)(1). In addition, Treas. Reg. § 1.121–1(b)(3) extends the exclusion to gain on the sale of vacant land that is adjacent to the taxpayer's principal residence, and which is owned and used by the taxpayer as part of the principal residence. The gain on the taxpayer's dwelling unit and the vacant land are combined so that only a single exclusion is allowed.

If a taxpayer owns and lives in a multi-unit dwelling, only the portion of the gain attributable to the owner-occupied unit is excludable. Treas. Reg. § 1.121–1(e)(1). For example, if the taxpayer owns an apartment building with four units and occupies one as a residence, only one-fourth of gain on the sale of the apartment building would qualify as gain on disposition of the principal residence. See Treas. Reg. § 1.121–1(e)(4), Ex. (2) and Ex. (3). With respect to the sale of land and buildings attached to a dwelling unit that are used in a business, such as the sale of a farm, only the gain allocable to the dwelling unit is excludable under § 121. Treas. Reg. § 1.121–1(e)(1) and (4), Ex. (1).

5.   EFFECT OF PARTIAL BUSINESS USE

Special problems arise with respect to the treatment of gains realized on the sale of a principal residence that has been used partially for business purposes, for example, a home office or a home that has been rented by the taxpayer at some time during the period of ownership. Property held for rental can qualify for § 121 treatment as long as the two-out-of-five-years test has been met. However, § 121(d)(6) provides that § 121 nonrecognition is not available to the extent that the gain does not exceed prior depreciation allowable with respect to the property for periods after May 7, 1997, e.g. the exclusion applies only to gain in excess of post 1997 depreciation deductions. Assume for example, that in 2006 the taxpayer purchased a principal residence for $150,000. For the years 2006 through 2015, the taxpayer is allowed depreciation deductions totaling $5,000 with respect to a home office in the principal residence. If the taxpayer sells the principal residence in 2015 for $260,000, realizing a $115,000 gain ($260,000–[$150,000–$5,000]) only $110,000 would be excluded under § 121; the other $5,000 of gain—an amount equal to the prior depreciation deductions—would be recognized. See

Treas. Reg. § 1.121–1(e)(4), Ex. (5). The regulations provide that in the case of a home office within the dwelling unit of the principal residence the gain need not be apportioned between the portion of the dwelling unit that is used for business and the portion of the dwelling unit that is used as a principal residence.

6.   POLICY ANALYSIS

The normative structure of an income tax requires the recognition of gain on the sale of a personal residence. The exclusion provided under § 121, in addition to relieving perceived hardships and facilitating replacement of a principal residence, provides taxpayers with a tax-free source of consumption. According to an estimate by the Staff of the Joint Committee on Taxation, § 121 will cost nearly $150 billion in lost revenue for the years 2015 through 2019. JCT, Estimates of Federal Tax Expenditures for Fiscal Years 2015–2019 32 JCX–141R–15 (Dec. 7, 2015).

If § 121 were analyzed as a spending provision (see the discussion of tax expenditures in Chapter 11), an initial question is whether there is a need for this subsidy to homeownership. From an economic perspective a subsidy might be justified if either it corrects a market failure or there are beneficial "externalities" generated by the subsidy. Evidence of market failure might include showing that individuals are deterred from moving from smaller to larger houses because they cannot generate enough after-tax cash for a down payment or that the residential housing lending market was insufficient to meet borrowing needs of homeowners who wish to move to a different residence. Externalities that might justify a home ownership subsidy could include data that home ownership promotes more stable communities, greater involvement in the community, and the like. If it were thought that either of these justifications were present in the case of homeowners, none was offered by Congress. If either were present, then the question would turn to whether the cost/benefit ratio was appropriate.

Analysis of the provision as a tax subsidy also requires an examination of the program design to see if it effectively meets the goals that justify the subsidy. In the case of § 121, the subsidy is delivered at the point of sale for a personal residence. The exemption is available whether the selling homeowner reinvests in another personal residence or not. Thus, this feature of the subsidy would appear to undercut the case that it generates valuable externalities. A subsidy to first-time purchasers of residences would seem more suitably targeted to encourage homeownership and thus create potential beneficial externalities. Moreover, since a sale is required to generate the federal subsidy, it is unlikely that the subsidy is an efficient mechanism to offset any market failure generated because of inadequacies in the market for financing home acquisition.

Finally, because the exclusion technique was adopted, the amount of the subsidy increases both with income and with the value of the residence sold, which undercuts the above-asserted justifications for the subsidy.

It is true that § 121 reduces record-keeping requirements for most homeowners relative to the rollover relief of former § 1034, and thus could be viewed as a beneficial simplification over prior law. But few, if any, direct subsidies are granted on the basis of relieving individuals or businesses from the burden of keeping and substantiating records. Furthermore, § 121 raises its own set of technical and record-keeping issues as discussed above.

CHAPTER 7

THE RELATIONSHIP OF BASIS TO INCOME RECOGNITION

SECTION 1. GIFTS OF PROPERTY: TRANSFERRED BASIS

INTERNAL REVENUE CODE: Sections 61(a)(3); 102; 1001(a)–(c); 1015.

REGULATIONS: Sections 1.1015–1(a); –4.

Taft v. Bowers
Supreme Court of the United States, 1929.
278 U.S. 470.

■ MR. JUSTICE MCREYNOLDS delivered the opinion of the Court.

Petitioners, who are donees of stocks, seek to recover income taxes exacted because of advancement in the market value of those stocks while owned by the donors. The facts are not in dispute. Both causes must turn upon the effect of [the provision of the] Revenue Act, 1921 [similar to present § 1015(a) with regard to the computation of the donee's gain], which prescribes the basis for estimating taxable gain when one disposes of property which came to him by gift. The records do not differ essentially and a statement of the material circumstances disclosed by No. 16 will suffice.

During the calendar years 1921 and 1922 the father of petitioner, Elizabeth C. Taft, gave her certain shares of Nash Motors Company stock, then more valuable than when acquired by him. She sold them during 1923 for more than their market value when the gift was made.

The United States demanded an income tax reckoned upon the difference between cost to the donor and price received by the donee. She paid accordingly and sued to recover the portion imposed because of the advance in value while the donor owned the stock. The right to tax the increase in value after the gift is not denied.

Abstractly stated, this is the problem:

In 1916 A purchased 100 shares of stock for $1,000, which he held until 1923 when their fair market value had become $2,000. He then gave them to B who sold them during the year 1923 for $5,000. The United States claim that under the Revenue Act of 1921 B must pay income tax upon $4,000, as realized profits. B maintains that only $3,000—the appreciation during her ownership—can be regarded as income; that the increase during the donor's ownership is not income assessable against her with intendment of the Sixteenth Amendment. * * *

We think the manifest purpose of Congress * * * was to require the petitioner to pay the enacted tax.

The only question subject to serious controversy is whether Congress had power to authorize the exaction.

It is said that the gift became a capital asset of the donee to the extent of its value when received and, therefore, when disposed of by her no part of that value could be treated as taxable income in her hands.

The Sixteenth Amendment provides:

"The Congress shall have power to lay and collect taxes on incomes, from whatever source derived, without apportionment among the several states, and without regard to any census or enumeration."

Income is the thing which may be taxed-income from any source. The amendment does not attempt to define income or to designate how taxes may be laid thereon, or how they may be enforced.

Under former decisions here the settled doctrine is that the Sixteenth Amendment confers no power upon Congress to define and tax as income without apportionment something which theretofore could not have been properly regarded as income.

Also, this court has declared: " 'Income may be defined as the gain derived from capital, from labor, or from both combined,' provided it be understood to include profit gained through a sale or conversion of capital assets." Eisner v. Macomber, 252 U.S. 189, 207, 40 S.Ct. 189, 193 * * * . The "gain derived from capital," within the definition, is "not a gain accruing to capital, nor a growth or increment of value in the investment, but a gain, a profit, something of exchangeable value proceeding from the property, severed from the capital however invested, and coming in, that is, received or drawn by the claimant for his separate use, benefit and disposal." United States v. Phellis, 257 U.S. 156, 169, 42 S.Ct. 63, 65 * * * .

If, instead of giving the stock to petitioner, the donor had sold it at market value, the excess over the capital he invested (cost) would have been income therefrom and subject to taxation under the Sixteenth Amendment. He would have been obliged to share the realized gain with the United States. He held the stock—the investment—subject to the right of the sovereign to take part of any increase in its value when separated through sale or conversion and reduced to his possession. Could he, contrary to the express will of Congress, by mere gift enable another to hold this stock free from such right, deprive the sovereign of the possibility of taxing the appreciation when actually severed, and convert the entire property into a capital asset of the donee, who invested nothing, as though the latter had purchased at the market price? And after a still further enhancement of the property, could the donee make a second gift with like effect, etc.? We think not.

In truth the stock represented only a single investment of capital— that made by the donor. And when through sale or conversion the increase was separated therefrom, it became income from that investment in the hands of the recipient subject to taxation according to the very words of the Sixteenth Amendment. By requiring the recipient of the entire increase to pay a part into the public treasury, Congress deprived her of no right and subjected her to no hardship. She accepted the gift with knowledge of the statute and, as to the property received, voluntarily assumed the position of her donor. When she sold the stock she actually got the original sum invested, plus the entire appreciation and out of the latter only was she called on to pay the tax demanded.

[handwritten margin note: When the daughter recieved the stock (however) it became income to her which is subjected to be taxed by 16th Amend.]

[handwritten margin note: When she got the stock + then sold it, she made money from the original + whatever else.]

The provision of the statute under consideration seems entirely appropriate for enforcing a general scheme of lawful taxation. To accept the view urged in behalf of petitioner undoubtedly would defeat, to some extent, the purpose of Congress to take part of all gain derived from capital investments. To prevent that result and insure enforcement of its proper policy, Congress had power to require that for purposes of taxation the donee should accept the position of the donor in respect of the thing received. And in so doing, it acted neither unreasonably nor arbitrarily.

[handwritten margin note: courts reasing]

There is nothing in the Constitution which lends support to the theory that gain actually resulting from the increased value of capital can be treated as taxable income in the hands of the recipient only so far as the increase occurred while he owned the property. * * *

[handwritten margin note: — conclusion/ (Holding]

The judgment below is affirmed.

DETAILED ANALYSIS

1. GENERAL

The basis of property received as a gift is generally determined by reference to the donor's basis in the property. The donor's basis transfers to the donee, thus assuring that any appreciation in value of the property at the time of the gift will be taxed to the donee when the gain is ultimately recognized. Thus, for example, if A purchased Blackacre for $20,000 in 2014, and in 2016, when Blackacre was worth $35,000, A gave Blackacre to B, § 102 would exclude the $35,000 value of Blackacre from B's income. But if in 2016 B sold Blackacre for $45,000, B would recognize a gain of $25,000 ($45,000—$20,000) in that year. The transferred basis rules contained in § 1015 are required by the policy decision not to tax accrued gains upon the disposition of property by gift. Consistent with Taft v. Bowers, the accrued gain retains its potential for taxation in the hands of the donee, awaiting a subsequent realization event to trigger the tax. In some gift situations, Congress has not been content to let the accrued gains continue to go untaxed in the donee's hands. Here, Congress has treated the gift as a realization event. These situations are discussed in Part 4 of the Detailed Analysis.

A special rule applies where the value of the property at the time of the gift is less than the donor's basis. In these circumstances, the donee's basis for purposes of determining the amount of *loss* realized upon a subsequent disposition of the property is the fair market value of the property at the time of the gift. This rule prevents the donor from shifting an unrealized loss to the donee. If the value of the property at the time of the gift is less than the donor's basis but subsequently increases above the donor's basis, and is then sold, the normal transferred basis rule applies. See Treas. Reg. § 1.1015–1(a)(2).

2.   EFFECT ON BASIS OF GIFT TAX PAID

Section 1015(d) provides that the basis of property acquired by gift shall be increased by the amount of the gift tax paid that is allocable to any appreciation in the property at the time of the gift. The gift tax attributable to the appreciation is determined by allocating the total gift tax paid between the appreciation and the basis in the property to the donor. Prior to 1976, a basis increase was allowed for the full amount of the gift tax paid. The House Ways and Means Committee Report, H.Rep. No. 94–1380, 94th Cong., 2d Sess. 44 (1976), explained the reason for the change as follows:

> The purpose of the increase in basis for gift taxes paid on the gift is to prevent a portion of the appreciation in the gift (equal to the gift tax imposed on the appreciation) from also being subject to income tax, that is, to prevent the imposition of a tax on a tax. However, [pre-1976] law was too generous in that it permitted the basis of the gift to be increased by the full amount of the gift tax paid on the gift and not just the gift tax attributable to the appreciation at the time of the gift.

As a result of the limitation in § 1015(d)(6), the overall tax consequence (except for deferral) of a donative transfer of appreciated property is the same whether the donor sells the property and transfers the proceeds or transfers the property to the donee who sells the property and pays the tax on the gain.[1] If, however, the gift tax is viewed as an excise tax imposed on the transfer, the entire gift tax paid could be viewed as a cost to the donor that should be included in the basis of the property (the result under pre-1976 law). On the other hand, transfer taxes may be viewed as taxes that are in addition to the income tax and thus should not increase the basis of the property at all.

3.   PART GIFT AND PART SALE

Suppose that a parent transfers property with a basis of $30 and a fair market value of $100 to a child for $40, intending a gift of the $60 difference. The transfer is thus part gift and part sale and requires a determination of how the basis in the property should be allocated between these two aspects of the transaction. Treas. Reg. §§ 1.1001–1(e) and 1.1015–4, in effect, allocate

---

[1]   Suppose, for example, that the donor contemplates transferring property worth $25,000 with a basis of $5,000. The donor and the donee are both in the 35% bracket, subject to a 15% maximum tax on capital gains, and the gift tax rate is 50%. If the donor sells the property and transfers the net proceeds, the donor will pay income tax of $3,000 on the $20,000 gain and a gift tax of $11,000 ([$25,000 − $3,000] × 50%) on the gift. The combined gift and income tax is $14,000. If, on the other hand, the donor transfers the $25,000 property as a gift, paying a gift tax of $12,500 ($25,000 × 50%), the donee's basis in the property will be $15,000, consisting of the donor's basis of $5,000, plus a gift tax adjustment of $10,000 ($20,000 × 50%). Upon sale of the property for $25,000, the donee will recognize gain of $10,000 and pay tax of $1,500 on the gain. Again the total tax liability of the donor and donee is $14,000 ($12,500 + $1,500).

the entire basis in the property to the sale. Thus, in the example above, the parent would realize only $10 of gain ($40–$30).

In Diedrich v. Commissioner, 457 U.S. 191 (1982), the taxpayer transferred stock to his children on the condition that they pay the taxpayer's gift tax liability arising from the transfer, which was in excess of the taxpayer's basis in the transferred stock. For income tax purposes, the court treated the transfer as a sale of the stock for the amount of the gift taxes paid by the children. The taxpayer's gain was determined by treating the gift tax relief as amount realized and subtracting the full amount of the taxpayer's basis from the amount realized.

Where, however, the bargain sale is to a charity, § 1011(b) requires that the basis be allocated between the sale and gift aspects in proportion to the amounts of the sale and contribution respectively. Thus, in the example above, $12 of the $30 basis ($30 × $40/$100) would be allocated to the $40 received on the sale portion of the transaction and the remaining $18 of basis would be allocated to the gift portion; the transferor would have a gain of $28 ($40 less $12) and the transferee would have a basis of $58 ($18 donor's basis plus $40 cost). This allocation of basis rule achieves an accurate apportionment and should be extended to noncharitable transactions.

4. SPECIAL RECOGNITION RULES

Section 84 provides that a transfer of appreciated property to a political organization (as defined in § 527(e)(1)) is a recognition event to the transferor. The gain is thus taxable to the transferor and the political organization acquires a basis equal to the fair market value of the property on the date of the transfer. Any subsequent change in the value would be reflected in the tax account of the political organization which, under § 527, is for limited purposes made a taxable entity at the corporate tax rate.

In addition, gain recognition is required by § 453B, discussed in Chapter 31, Section 2.5., in the case of disposition of an installment note by gift.

SECTION 2.   TRANSFERS AT DEATH: FAIR MARKET VALUE BASIS

INTERNAL REVENUE CODE: Section 1014(a), (b)(1)–(4), (9), (c), (f).

REGULATIONS: Sections 1.1014–1(a); –3(a), (c), (e).

Unlike the case of gifts of appreciated property, under current law the exclusion under § 102 for inherited appreciated property is complete and permanent. Section 1014 provides the transferee with a basis equal to the fair market value of the property at the decedent's death. Thus for example, if C purchased Whiteacre for $2,000 in 2008, and in 2016, when Whiteacre was worth $10,000, C died and devised Whiteacre to D, § 102 would exclude the $10,000 value of Whiteacre from D's income. If in 2016 D sold Whiteacre for $11,000, D would recognize a gain of only $1,000. Congress has made a policy decision that death is not an appropriate time to impose a tax on gains that have accrued in property transferred by the decedent. By granting a "step-up" in basis equal to the fair market value of the property at the date of death, however, § 1014 adds a much more important policy decision. The effect of stepping up the basis of appreciated assets held at death is to exempt forever the appreciation in the property that accrued in the hands of the decedent. Thus, unlike the donee in the gift situation, an individual who inherits appreciated property will never be subject to tax on the appreciation that occurred while the asset was owned by the transferor. Conversely, if inherited property has declined in value, the loss accrued prior to the decedent's death will never be recognized. Thus, well-advised taxpayers will sell depreciated property before death while continuing to hold appreciated property subject to the step-up in basis.

The decision to grant a step-up in basis in the case of appreciated assets transferred at death itself requires a set of technical rules to implement that decision.

DETAILED ANALYSIS

1. STATUTORY STRUCTURE

Under current law, property acquired from a decedent generally receives a basis under § 1014(a) equal to the fair market value of the property at the date of the decedent's death. Where the asset transferred by the decedent is a stream of income, such as a deferred compensation payment, Congress has been unwilling to grant a step-up in basis and has provided for a transferred basis. Section 1014(c) excludes property which is income in respect of a decedent under § 691. This limitation is discussed in Section 4 of this Chapter. The definition of property that is "acquired from the decedent" is provided in § 1014(b). Section 1014(b)(1)–(8) enumerate specific types of situations that qualify under § 1014(a). Section 1014(b)(9) extends the application of § 1014 to all property acquired by reason of death, regardless of form of ownership or other condition, if included in the decedent's gross estate. The most important application of § 1014(b)(9) is to provide a fair market value at death basis in one-half of the property owned by the surviving joint tenant upon the death of the other joint tenant. Section 1014(b)(10) further extends this concept by in effect applying § 1014(b)(9) to property included in the gross estate under § 2044.

There are some unusual aspects to § 1014(b). For example, § 1014(b)(6) defines property "acquired from the decedent" to include the surviving spouse's share of community property even though that share was not obtained from the decedent. Thus, if husband and wife own community property and the wife dies leaving her one-half share to the children, the basis of the husband's one-half share changes automatically to the fair market value at the wife's death. See Rev. Rul. 92–37, 1992–1 C.B. 195, for an application of this rule. In contrast, the basis of a surviving spouse's interest in similar jointly held property is increased only to the extent the property is includable in the decedent's gross estate.

In the case of a qualified joint interest between spouses created after 1976 (and thus governed by current § 2040(b)(2) for estate tax purposes), the amount included in the deceased spouse's estate is one-half of the joint property. In all other cases, the portion of the property to which the § 1014 basis rule applies depends on the portion of the consideration provided by the deceased joint tenant. See e.g. Gallenstein v. United States, 975 F.2d 286 (6th Cir.1992) (surviving joint tenant-spouse took a date-of-death fair market value basis in entire property because the joint tenancy was created before the effective date of current § 2040(b) and the deceased spouse provided all the consideration.)

2.   SOME EXAMPLES OF THE APPLICATION OF SECTION 1014

In Diebold v. Commissioner, 194 F.2d 266 (3d Cir.1952), on his death a shareholder of a closely held corporation bequeathed his stock and other property to the corporation. The court allocated the value of the stock among the remaining shareholders and added it to the basis of their stock, on the theory that the enlargement of the proportional interest represented by the decedent's stock had been acquired by bequest. But the court did not increase the remaining stock basis because of the bequest of the other property to the corporation, saying that this bequest merely increased the value of the stock. Where a bequest of property is intended to benefit the surviving shareholders rather than the corporation itself, the bequest may be treated as if it had been made directly to the shareholders in proportion to their respective interests followed by a contribution to the capital of the corporation, thus allowing the shareholders to increase their basis in the shares of the corporation by the fair market value of the property which the corporation received from the decedent. Rev. Rul. 74–329, 1974–2 C.B. 269.

In Rev. Rul. 67–96, 1967–1 C.B. 195, the testator's will granted to his son an option to purchase stock from the testator's estate at a price below fair market value. The IRS ruled that the option itself acquired a basis under § 1014(a), presumably equal to the difference between the fair market value of the stock subject to the option and the option price, and that the basis of the option was to be added to the option price to determine the basis of the property received upon exercise of the option by the son. Thus, if the will granted the testator's son the option to purchase for $60 stock which had a fair market value at death of $100, the son would have $100 basis in the stock consisting of the $40 basis derived from the option under § 1014(a) plus a $60 cost basis. See also Kalbac v. Commissioner, 298 F.2d 251 (8th Cir.1962).

In Connecticut Nat'l Bank v. United States, 937 F.2d 90 (2d Cir.1991), an estate sold property after the death of the decedent's widow, who was the beneficiary of the estate but who had died without receiving full distribution of the assets. The question was whether the estate's basis for the property was its fair market value on the date of the husband's death or its value on the later date of death of the wife. Because the wife was the beneficial owner of the estate assets, the court held that the basis of the property was determined with reference to the wife's date of death.

3.   RELATIONSHIP TO ESTATE TAX VALUE

Section 1014(f) provides that the basis of any property taking a § 1014 date-of-death-value shall not exceed the final value as determined for estate tax purposes, or, if the value of the property has not been finally determined for estate tax purposes, the value stated in a statement (required by § 6035(a) to be provided by the executor of any estate required to file an estate tax return) identifying the value of the property. Section 1014(f)(2), somewhat inartfully, provides that this mandatory consistency rule does not apply with respect to any property passing from a decedent for whom no estate tax return is required to be filed. The basis has been finally determined for estate tax purposes only if (1) the value of the property as shown on the estate tax return was not contested by the IRS before the statute of limitations expired, (2) the value is specified by the IRS on audit and was not timely contested by the executor of the estate, or (3) the value is determined by a court or pursuant to a settlement with the IRS.

Section 6035 requires the executor of any estate required to file an estate tax return to report to the IRS and each beneficiary acquiring any interest in property included in the decedent's gross estate a statement identifying the value of each interest in such property as reported on such return and any other information as the Treasury and IRS may prescribe. Section 6035(b) directs the Treasury Department to promulgate regulations as necessary to carry out the new provision, including regulations relating to (1) the application of § 6035 to property with regard to which no estate tax return is required to be filed, and (2) situations in which the surviving joint tenant or other recipient may have better information than the executor regarding the basis or fair market value of the property.

Section 6662(b)(8) extends the 20 percent accuracy related penalty to "any inconsistent estate basis," which is defined in § 6662(k) as a basis claimed on an income tax return that exceeds the basis determined under § 1014(f).

SECTION 3.   GIFTS AND INHERITANCES OF SPLIT INTERESTS

INTERNAL REVENUE CODE: Section 102(b).

REGULATIONS: Sections 1.1014–5(a)–(b); 1.1015–1(b); –2.

Irwin v. Gavit

Supreme Court of the United States, 1925.
268 U.S. 161.

■ MR. JUSTICE HOLMES delivered the opinion of the Court.

This is a suit to recover taxes and penalties exacted by the Collector under the Income Tax Act of October 3, 1913. * * *

Issue — [The question is whether the sums received by the plaintiff under the will of Anthony N. Brady in 1913, 1914 and 1915, were income and taxed.] The will, admitted to probate August 12, 1913, left the residue of the estate in trust to be divided into six equal parts, the income of one part to be applied so far as deemed proper by the trustees to the education and support of the testator's granddaughter, Marcia Ann Gavit, the balance [of the income of such part] to be divided into two equal parts and one of them to be paid to the testator's son-in-law, the plaintiff, in equal quarter-yearly payments during his life. But on the granddaughter's reaching the age of twenty-one or dying the fund went over, so that, the granddaughter then being six years old, it is said, the plaintiff's interest could not exceed fifteen years. The Courts below held that the payments received were properly acquired by bequest, were not income and were not subject to tax.

The statute provides that there shall be levied a tax "upon the entire net income arising or accruing from all sources in the preceding calendar year to every citizen of the United States." If these payments properly may be called income by the common understanding of that word and the statute has failed to hit them it has missed so much of the general purpose that it expresses at the start. Congress intended to use its power to the full extent. Eisner v. Macomber, 252 U.S. 189 * * * . [The statute provides that] the net income is to include "gains or profits and income derived from any source whatever, including the income from but not the value of property acquired by gift, bequest, devise or descent." [It further states that] trustees are to make "return of the net income of the person for whom they act, subject to this tax," and trustees and others, having the control or payment of fixed or determinable gains, etc., of another person who are required to render a return on behalf of another are "authorized to withhold enough to pay the normal tax." The language quoted leaves no doubt in our minds that if a fund were given to trustees for A for life with remainder over, the income received by the trustees and paid over to A would be income of A under the statute. It seems to us hardly less clear that even if there were a specific provision that A should have no interest in the corpus, the payments would be income none the less, within the meaning of the statute and the Constitution, and by popular speech. In the first case it is true that the bequest might be said to be of the corpus for life, in the second it might be said to be of the income. But we think that the provision of the act that exempts bequests assumes the gift of a corpus and contrasts it with the income arising from it, but was not intended to exempt income property so-called simply because of a severance between it and the principal fund. No such conclusion can be drawn from Eisner v. Macomber, 252 U.S. 189 * * * . The money was income in the hands of the trustees and we know of nothing in the law that prevented its being paid and received as income by the donee.

The courts below went on the ground that the gift to the plaintiff was a bequest and carried no interest in the corpus of the fund. We do not regard those considerations as conclusive, as we have said, but if it were material a gift of the income of a fund ordinarily is treated by equity as creating an interest in the fund. Apart from technicalities we can perceive no distinction relevant to the question before us between a gift of the fund for life and a gift of the income from it. The fund is appropriated to the production of the same result whichever form the gift takes. Neither are we troubled by the question where to draw the line. That is the question in pretty much everything worth arguing in the law. * * * But the distinction between * * * a gift from the corpus of the estate payable in installments and the present seems to us not hard to draw, assuming that the gift supposed would not be income. This is a gift from the income of a very large fund, as income. It seems to us immaterial that the same amounts might receive a different color from their source. We are of opinion that quarterly payments, which it was hoped would last for fifteen years, from the income of an estate intended for the plaintiff's child, must be regarded as income within the meaning of the Constitution and the law. It is said that the tax laws should be construed favorably for the taxpayers. But that is not a reason for creating a doubt or for exaggerating one when it is no greater than we can bring ourselves to feel in this case.

Judgment reversed.

DETAILED ANALYSIS

1.   ANALYSIS OF IRWIN v. GAVIT

Section 102(b) incorporates the rule of Irwin v. Gavit that allocates the full basis to the corpus of a split interest and none to the income interest. Irwin v. Gavit and § 102(b) provide an easily administrable rule for allocating the § 102 exclusion. Yet the rule does not comport with the economic realities of the transaction. The right to receive the trust income for a specified period is no less an economic right than the right to receive the principal. The recipient obtains as a bequest the present value of the specified income stream. Suppose that $100,000 is left in trust with the income interest to be paid to A for five years and the principal then to be distributed to B. The rule of Irwin v. Gavit assumes that the entire amount of the $100,000 exclusion should be allocated to B, the remainder interest holder, with the entire income interest received by A thus being fully taxable. The income interest has a present value of approximately $30,000 (assuming an 8 percent discount rate) and the remainder interest correspondingly has a value of $70,000. It would be possible to "divide up" the § 102 exclusion based on the relative values of the transferred interests and allow the income beneficiary to exclude a portion of the income payments received in such a manner that, by the time the income interest ended, $30,000 would have been excluded from income. Compare the treatment of annuities, discussed in Chapter 8, Section 5.A. Similarly, only $70,000, rather than the full $100,000, would be excluded by the remainder interest holder. Such an approach, though more complex than the approach in § 102(b), better reflects the economics of the situation.

The Irwin v. Gavit situation has had a counterpart in the assignment of income area where the right to interest payments on a bond is "stripped" from the bond, thus severing the "income" from the "principal." In this case, however, the economically accurate allocation described above often is required. See Chapter 37, Section 2.6.

2. BASIS ISSUES INVOLVING SPLIT INTERESTS—THE UNIFORM BASIS RULE

Where there is a gift in the form of a transfer in trust, the basis to the trust is governed by § 1015(b). The beneficiaries have a basis for their respective interests determined under Treas. Reg. § 1.1015–1(b), which apportions the total basis among them. Treas. Reg. § 1.1015–1(b) also apportions the § 1015 transferred basis between a life tenant and a remainder interest-holder in the case of a gift of a split interest by the creation of legal estates rather than through a trust.

Treas. Reg. § 1.1014–5 deals with the basis of property where a life estate (or term for years) and a remainder interest are created at death. The regulations provide that the aggregate basis of the separate life and remainder interests remains uniform. The basis of each component, however, constantly changes, with the basis of the life interest decreasing with the passage of time and the basis of the remainder interest correspondingly increasing.

The application of these rules to life interests is of limited significance. Under Irwin v. Gavit and § 102(b), the annual distributions to the owner of the life interest are not eligible for exclusion under § 102 or otherwise treated as a return of capital, and § 273 provides that the basis of a life estate cannot be amortized over its expected life. Thus payments received by the beneficiary of an inter-vivos income interest generally are includable in gross income in their entirety. The life tenant's allocable share of the basis is also generally disregarded under § 1001(e) if the interest is sold unless the limited exceptions in § 1001(e)(3) apply. The rules do have some significance for dispositions of remainder interests.

The basis of a remainder interest increases to reflect the increasing value of the interest as the date of its receipt approaches, thus reducing the amount of gain recognized on a sale of the remainder interest. In this case, basis is acquired without a corresponding income inclusion. For an example of the application of these rules, see Rev. Rul. 69–239, 1969–1 C.B. 198.

SECTION 4.   INCOME IN RESPECT OF A DECEDENT

INTERNAL REVENUE CODE: Sections 61(a)(14); 691(a)(1)–(3), (c)(1)(A); 443(a)(2).

REGULATIONS: Sections 1.691(a)–1; –2; –3.

Prior to the adoption of the predecessor to § 691, income that was "earned" by the decedent but was not includable in the decedent's final income tax return, because of the decedent's accounting method or otherwise, was entitled to a step-up in basis and thus escaped tax. For example, in Hatch v. Commissioner, 190 F.2d 254 (2d Cir.1951), arising prior to the adoption of the income in respect of a decedent exception, the court held that where annual salary payments were to be paid to an employee's estate for ten years after his death, the value of the right to receive the payments was entitled to a basis that could be amortized over the ten-year period. Thus, only the excess of the payments over that value was income.

Section 691 was designed to reverse this result. The § 1014(a) rule of fair market value basis does not apply to income in respect of a decedent as defined in § 691. I.R.C. § 1014(c). Income in respect of a decedent has presented significant definitional problems as illustrated in the following materials.

Edward D. Rollert Residuary Trust v. Commissioner*

United States Tax Court, 1983.
80 T.C. 619.

■ WHITAKER, JUDGE: * * *

For several years prior to his death on November 27, 1969, Edward D. Rollert had been employed as an executive vice president of General Motors Corp. and had participated in the corporation's stock option plan and its bonus plan. These plans were designed to compensate corporate executives and other employees by providing cash and stock bonuses payable in installments in subsequent years. * * *

During the period between the award of bonus rights under either of these plans and the employee's receipt of the final installment payment attributable to such rights, the employee had to "earn out" his or her right to the award by continuing to be employed by the corporation and not committing acts inimical to the best interests of the corporation. Death relieved an employee from the duty of earning out a bonus; thus, upon an employee's death, his or her estate, or the party entitled to the right, possessed a nonforfeitable right to subsequent installments of the bonus award.

General Motors made awards to Mr. Rollert under both the bonus plan and the stock option plan for each of the years 1964 through 1968. These awards, which exceeded $300,000 for each of these years, are referred to collectively as the "lifetime" bonus awards. * * *

On March 2, 1970, decedent was awarded a bonus under the bonus plan of 1,786 shares of General Motors common stock and $285,763 cash with respect to his almost 11-months employment with the corporation in 1969. This is referred to hereafter as the "postmortem bonus award." The parties have stipulated that decedent "had no rights to the post-mortem bonus award during his lifetime." This bonus was to be paid in five annual installments, with the first installment in March 1970, and the subsequent installments on January 10 of the next 4 years. * * *

We are, * * * squarely faced with the issue whether payments of the postmortem bonus award were income in respect of a decedent. Petitioner argues that Mr. Rollert had no right or entitlement to a bonus award with respect to his employment in 1969 since the bonus was not formally

---

*   [Ed.: The decision of the Tax Court was affirmed, 752 F.2d 1128 (6th Cir.1985).]

awarded by General Motors until March 2, 1970—over 3 months after his death. We disagree. For purposes of section 691, we believe that as of the date of his death, Mr. Rollert had a right to a bonus award for 1969, in view of General Motors' established practices in awarding bonuses and its tentative decisions to assign substantial funds to the bonus pool for 1969 and to award bonuses to all executive vice presidents.

* * *

In determining whether particular receipts should be treated as income in respect of a decedent, courts have focused on whether the decedent had a *right* or *entitlement* to receive income as of the date of his death. Estate of Peterson v. Commissioner, 667 F.2d [675, 679 (8th Cir.1981), aff'g 74 T.C. 630 (1980)], and cases cited therein. The parties have stipulated in this case that Mr. Rollert "had no rights to the post-mortem bonus award during his lifetime." Respondent takes the position that for purposes of the stipulation, the term "rights" should be read as referring to contract rights or other legally enforceable rights, and that the stipulation establishes only that the decedent had during his lifetime no legally enforceable right to an award not yet made. Petitioner contends, however, that the stipulation establishes that decedent had no right or entitlement to the postmortem bonus and that the installment payments of this bonus were therefore not income in respect of a decedent. * * *

In [Halliday v. United States, 655 F.2d 68 (5th Cir.1981)], the Fifth Circuit rejected the view that a legally enforceable right was necessary in order for income to be taxed under section 691. The court characterized the right-to-income test as simply a "more precise" definition of income in respect of a decedent, rather than as a repudiation of the line of cases that had found the existence of income in respect of a decedent in the absence of a legally enforceable right. It elaborated on the right-to-income test as follows:

> We find that for purposes of Section 691, a right to income arises where the evidence shows a substantial certainty that benefits directly related to the decedent's past economic activities will be paid to his heirs or estate upon his death, notwithstanding the absence of a legally enforceable obligation. * * * [655 F.2d at 721]

The fact situation in *Halliday* was quite similar to that now presented to us. The *Halliday* court was asked to decide whether section 691 applied to life insurance renewal commissions received by the estate of an insurance agent after his death. The agent had no contractual right to the payment of these renewal commissions. Nevertheless, the insurance company had a longstanding policy of paying benefits at a set rate to the beneficiaries of a deceased agent, and this policy had been embodied in corporate resolutions. On the basis of these facts, the court found that the decedent had a right, albeit not necessarily a legally enforceable one, to post-death renewal commissions, and therefore that the benefits paid to his estate by the insurance company constituted income in respect of a decedent.

The "substantial certainty" approach adopted in the *Halliday* opinion is consistent with the approach we took in Estate of Peterson v. Commissioner, supra. That case involved the tax treatment of sales proceeds under a contract for the sale of calves, which had been entered into by the decedent prior to his death. Based on our review of the case law and regulations, we found in *Estate of Peterson* that the following four requirements have been applied to test whether a decedent possessed the requisite right to sales proceeds at the time of death: (1) Whether the decedent entered into a legally significant arrangement regarding the subject matter of the sale; (2) whether the decedent performed the substantive acts required as preconditions to the sale; (3) whether there existed at the time of decedent's death any economically material contingencies which might have disrupted the sale; and (4) whether the decedent would have eventually received the sales proceeds if he or she had lived.[6] We found that the proceeds from the contract for the sale of the calves satisfied three of these four requirements but did not satisfy the second requirement. Substantial and essential acts that the decedent had been required to perform under the contract had not been completed as of the date of his death since one-third of the calves were too young to be deliverable as of that date and had to be raised by the estate for more than 1 month thereafter. We therefore held that the sales proceeds were not income in respect of a decedent.

We now apply to the facts of this case the right-to-income test as elaborated in Halliday v. United States, supra, and Estate of Peterson v. Commissioner, supra.

General Motors had no contractual obligation as of the date of decedent's death to pay him a bonus with respect to 1969. However, the decedent had a longstanding contractual employment relationship with General Motors, and under the terms of his employment, he was eligible to participate in the bonus plan, which was a formalized deferred compensation arrangement and under which bonuses had been paid consistently in preceding years. In this factual context, it is apparent that the bonus payments were made in relation to "a legally significant arrangement" between the decedent and General Motors. See Estate of Peterson v. Commissioner, 74 T.C. at 639. It is also clear that decedent's 11-months employment with General Motors in 1969 and his refraining from taking any actions that would have disqualified him from bonus eligibility for that year constituted his performance of all the substantive

---

6   In Estate of Peterson v. Commissioner, 74 T.C. 630, 639 n.9 (1980), affd. 667 F.2d 675 (8th Cir.1981), we cautioned that the four factors were not meant to be an ironclad formula but might change based on the type of transaction to be analyzed.

acts required as a precondition of his being awarded a bonus for 1969. * * *

* * *

It is also clear that Mr. Rollert was assured prior to his death of being one of the individuals to whom awards would be made for 1969. The committee had never denied an award to an executive vice president, and Mr. Rollert had received bonuses in excess of $300,000 for each of the 5 years preceding 1969. More importantly, over 3 weeks before Mr. Rollert's death, the committee had made a determination (albeit a tentative one) to grant bonus awards for 1969 to all executive vice presidents. * * *

The bonus plan provided the committee with discretion in determining the eligibility of employees for consideration for bonuses in the year their employment terminated, but the existence of this discretion did not significantly affect Mr. Rollert's chances of receiving a bonus for 1969. The committee had no written rules or guidelines circumscribing their discretion with respect to terminated employees. However, the committee's established practice had been to make awards to terminated employees who were otherwise qualified so long as they had at least 2-months active service in the year for which the award was being granted. Halliday v. United States, * * * paid particular attention to the fact that the corporation had consistently followed its established policy of paying post-death benefits even absent a contractual obligation. Here, it is equally clear that under established practices, the bonus award with respect to Mr. Rollert's service in 1969 would not have been denied on the basis of his cessation of employment in that year. Thus, as of the date of Mr. Rollert's death, there was no material contingency comparable to that in Keck v. Commissioner, supra, that might have resulted in denial of a bonus award for 1969. On these facts, it is established that Mr. Rollert had a substantial certainty as of the date of his death of receiving a bonus award for 1969.

Thus, the analyses in the *Halliday* and *Estate of Peterson* opinions lead us to the conclusion that as of the date of his death, Mr. Rollert had a right or entitlement to a bonus for 1969. Accordingly, the payments under the postmortem bonus award were income in respect of a decedent when received by the estate or petitioner.

DETAILED ANALYSIS

1. OTHER EXAMPLES OF INCOME IN RESPECT OF A DECEDENT

1.1. *Income from the Disposition of Property*

Proceeds received after the decedent's death from sales completed prior to death are income in respect of a decedent. Section 691(a)(4) specifically treats payments under installment obligations acquired from the decedent as income in respect of a decedent.

Where there is a contract of sale at the time of death, the cases generally look to whether there are significant contingencies to the completion of the sale. One such case, Trust Company of Georgia v. Ross, 392 F.2d 694 (5th Cir.1967), cited in *Rollert Trust,* involved the owner of a hotel chain who entered into a contract for the sale of his stock. The stock was placed in escrow to await payment of the purchase price. The sale was not closed until after the death of the decedent. The matters that remained to be completed prior to the closing were not of a substantive nature. The District Court had held that the sales proceeds were income in respect of a decedent. The Court of Appeals affirmed, indicating that the appropriate test was one of "entitlement" to income:

> Although it is pertinent to inquire whether the income received after death was attributable to activities and economic efforts of the decedent in his lifetime, these activities and efforts must give rise to a right to that income. And the right is to be distinguished from the activity which creates the right. Absent such a right, no matter how great the activities or efforts, there would be no taxable income under § 691. * * *

> It is implicit in the statute and in the definition that this condition or limitation has reference to the date of death of the decedent. That is, income is to be included if decedent was entitled to the income at the date of his death.

The cases discussed in *Rollert Trust* indicate the subsequent development of the "entitlement" approach to the definitional problem.

1.2. *Interest*

Rev. Rul. 58–435, 1958–2 C.B. 370, held that interest paid on debt obligations owed to the decedent constitutes income in respect of a decedent to the extent attributable to the period of time that the debt instrument was held by the decedent. Interest earned after the date of death constitutes income to the recipient under § 61. (The debt instrument itself obtains a step-up in basis under § 1014).

Deferred interest on United States Savings Bonds constitutes income in respect of a decedent. Rev. Rul. 64–104, 1964–1 C.B. 223.

1.3. *Royalties*

Considerable difficulties arise in determining whether post-death payments received under royalty arrangements constitute income in respect of a decedent. The issue in these cases turns on whether the transaction entered into prior to death by the author or inventor constituted a "sale" or a "license."

In Rev. Rul. 57–544, 1957–2 C.B. 361, royalties under a deceased author's contract arising after his death were income in respect of a decedent where the contract constituted a "sale" of the author's rights. The recipient of the royalties thus did not receive a step-up in basis for the contract rights. On the other hand, in Rev. Rul. 60–227, 1960–1 C.B. 262, royalties received under a license were held to constitute income in respect of a decedent only to the extent of payments due and accrued prior to the date of death. The contract rights received a step-up in basis under § 1014 and the recipients were entitled to amortization deductions based on that value to offset the post-death royalty income. This distinction was accepted in Grill v. United States, 303 F.2d 922 (Ct.Cl.1962).

In Dorsey v. Commissioner, 49 T.C. 606 (1968), the stockholders of a corporation owning the patents on the first workable automatic pin setting machine for bowling assigned all interests in the invention to another corporation for cash, stock and one percent of the receipts by the acquiring corporation from the sale or license of the machine for 20 years. The transferor corporation was then liquidated. The court held that the subsequent amounts received under the contract by the estate of one of the deceased stockholders of the transferor corporation constituted income in respect of a decedent under § 691. The transaction assigning the invention constituted a "sale" and the court held that the principles of Rev. Rul. 57–544, rather than Rev. Rul. 60–227, were applicable.

2.   INCOME TAX DEDUCTION FOR ESTATE TAXES PAID: SECTION 691(c)

Section 691(c) provides an income tax deduction to the recipient of income in respect of a decedent for the federal estate taxes paid with respect to the item. The allowable § 691(c) deduction is the excess of the estate tax actually paid over the estate tax that would have been payable had the income in respect of a decedent not been included in the gross estate. In effect, this rule grants a deduction for the estate taxes paid at the highest marginal rate achieved by the estate and insures that in general the aggregate income and estate taxes will be substantially the same whether the income is realized before or after death.

SECTION 5.   TAX POLICY ASPECTS OF GRATUITOUS TRANSFERS OF APPRECIATED PROPERTY

In 1942 the Treasury recommended that the recipient of property transferred at death take the same basis as the decedent, thus conforming the basis rules for lifetime gifts and transfers at death. The Treasury recommendation was not adopted. See Statement of Randolph Paul, Tax Advisor to the Secretary of the Treasury, House Ways and Means Committee, Revenue Revision of 1942, 77th Cong., 2d Sess., vol. 1, 89 (1942). In 1976, Congress adopted a provision applying a transferred basis rule to transfers at death. The provision was strongly attacked by the Tax Section of the American Bar Association and the American Bankers Association. The effective date of the provision was repeatedly postponed until finally, in 1980, the provision was retroactively repealed. See Committee on Ways and Means, Hearings on Carryover Basis, 96th Cong., 1st Sess. (1979). One of the major complaints involved the difficulty of ascertaining the decedent's basis in property held for long periods.

In 1963, the President's Tax Message went further than the transferred basis proposals by recommending recognition of gain, and thus imposition of a tax, on accrued gains at death. The President's proposal was not adopted. See Hearings on President's 1963 Tax Message, House Ways and Means Committee, 88th Cong., 1st Sess. 20, 49, 122 (1963). In 1968, the Treasury again proposed taxation of such gains at death, but again Congress did not adopt the proposal.

Congress's view of appropriate tax policy is never set in stone. As part of the prospective repeal of the estate tax in the 2001 Act, Congress eliminated the step-up in basis at death in favor of a transferred basis regime. However, § 1022, which imposed a transferred basis regime similar to the structure of § 1015 but with a step-up in basis for $1.3 million of value ($3 million in the case of transfers to a spouse), was not effective until January 1, 2010, and like all provisions of the 2001 Act, § 1022 expired on December 31, 2010, and was thus in effect for only a single year.

SECTION 6.   NONSHAREHOLDER CONTRIBUTIONS TO CAPITAL

INTERNAL REVENUE CODE: Sections 118; 362(a), (c).

REGULATIONS: Sections 1.118–1 (fourth sentence to end); 1.362–2(a).

When a corporation receives money or property in consideration of issuing stock, it does not recognize income. I.R.C. § 1032. Similarly, a corporation does not recognize income when a shareholder makes an additional capital contribution without receiving stock. This treatment might be justified on the grounds that the transfer is a mere change in the form of ownership of the money or property contributed for the stock. Consistent with this theory, § 362(a) provides the corporation with a transferred basis from the shareholder in any contributed property (but with a limitation in § 362(e) if the aggregate basis of the transferred properties exceeds their aggregate fair market value). Nonshareholder contribution of capital to a corporation, such as a contribution of land by state or local government to induce the corporation to build a factory in a particular location, are excluded from income under § 118, but § 362(c) provides that the basis of property received as a nonshareholder contribution to capital will be zero. See also Edwards v. Cuba Railroad Co., 268 U.S. 628 (1925), which held that nonshareholder contributions to the capital of a corporation by a government were not income.

DETAILED ANALYSIS

1.   STATUTORY STRUCTURE

Section 118 excludes contributions to the capital of a corporation from the corporation's current gross income. Although § 118 principally applies to contributions to a corporation by its shareholders, Treas. Reg. § 1.118–1 provides that "[s]ection 118 also applies to contributions to capital made by persons other than shareholders. For example, the exclusion applies to the value of land or other property contributed to a corporation by a governmental unit or by a civic group for the purpose of inducing the corporation to locate its business in a particular community, or for the purpose of enabling the corporation to expand its operating facilities. However, the exclusion does not apply to any money or property transferred to the corporation in consideration for goods or services rendered, or to subsidies paid for the purpose of inducing the taxpayer to limit production."

Although a nonshareholder contribution to capital qualifying under § 118 initially is excluded from income, § 362(c) provides that the property contributed, or the property purchased with contributed funds, has a tax basis of zero. As a result, the issue in the case of nonshareholder contributions to capital is not whether the receipt will be included in income, but *when* the item will be included in income. Assume that a nonshareholder contributes $100 in cash to a corporation, money that the corporation uses to purchase vacant real estate. While § 118 excludes the $100 from the corporation's income, under § 362(c) the corporation would have a zero basis in the real estate. Upon a sale of the real estate after it had doubled in value, the corporation would include $200 in income, consisting of the $100 in appreciation in value and the original $100 attributable to the contribution to capital. In contrast, if the original $100 contribution had not qualified as a contribution to capital under § 118, and therefore was includable in gross income in the year of receipt, § 362(c) would not apply; the corporation would have a $100 basis in the real estate. Upon a sale for $200, the corporation would realize only $100 in gain. The taxpayer in both situations includes the same aggregate amount in gross income. But in the case of a contribution to capital qualifying under § 118, the income is accounted for later by virtue of the exclusion at the time of contribution and reduced basis.

2.   THE DEFINITION OF CONTRIBUTION TO CAPITAL

The Supreme Court addressed the treatment of nonshareholder contributions to capital in United States v. Chicago, Burlington & Quincy Railroad Co., 412 U.S. 401 (1973). The railroad entered into contracts with a number of states under which the states would fund the cost of construction of items including highway undercrossings and overcrossings, crossing signals, signs, and floodlights. The railroad agreed to maintain the improvements once installed. The Court articulated the test for determining whether a receipt is a contribution to capital as follows:

> We can distill from [Detroit Edison Co. v. Commissioner, 319 U.S. 98 (1943), and Brown Shoe Co. v. Commissioner, 339 U.S. 583 (1950)] some of the characteristics of a nonshareholder contribution to capital under the Internal Revenue Codes. It certainly must become a permanent part of the transferee's working capital structure. It may not be compensation, such as a direct payment for a specific, quantifiable service provided for the transferor by the transferee. It must be bargained for. The asset transferred foreseeably must result in benefit to the transferee in an amount commensurate with its value. And the asset ordinarily, if not always, will be employed in or contribute to the production of additional income and its value assured in that respect.

The Court went on to conclude that the facilities were not a contribution to capital. The transaction was unilateral; C.B. & Q. only agreed to accept the facilities paid for by the state. The railroad did not bargain to receive the facilities, they were peripheral to its business, did not contribute further to the production of income, and the economic benefit it realized from them was only marginal. Thus the test was not satisfied.

United States v. Coastal Utilities, Inc., 483 F.Supp.2d 1232 (S.D. Ga. 2007), aff'd per curiam, 514 F.3d 1184 (11th Cir. 2008), held that payments received by a telephone company from the Universal Service Administration Company and the State of Georgia Access Funds were not contributions to capital excluded from gross income under § 118. The payments were part of state and federally mandated programs, funded by fees collected from telecommunications carriers based on revenues, and were made to carriers with high cost obligations to provide universal access to telephone services. The purpose of the payments was to supplement revenue, and thus they were not non-shareholder contributions to capital. Although the formula used to determine the amount of the payments largely related to investment expenditures, it took into account operation, maintenance, administrative, and other expenses that were unrelated to capital investment.

3.   PAYMENTS FROM NONGOVERNMENTAL SOURCES

The contribution to capital exclusion was applied both before and after the enactment of § 118 to contributions by future customers to the cost of constructing facilities needed to extend service to them, such as railroads, spur tracks, and electrical power lines. See e.g., Appeal of Liberty Light & Power Co., 4 B.T.A. 155 (1926) (Acq.). But in Teleservice Company of Wyoming Valley v. Commissioner, 254 F.2d 105 (3d Cir.1958), the taxpayer constructed a community antenna television system to facilitate reception in hilly terrain. The construction of the basic system and extension of service were financed by prospective customers; any person who moved into the house of an old contributor was required to contribute to use the system. The court held *Cuba Railroad* inapplicable and instead considered the contributions as payments for services to be rendered. Though the case questioned the validity of the railroad and public utility cases, the Service issued Rev. Rul. 58–555, 1958–2 C.B. 25, indicating that it would continue to follow them in cases involving regulated public utilities.

After the *Chicago, Burlington & Quincy* decision, the IRS issued Rev. Rul. 75–557, 1975–2 C.B. 33, withdrawing its acquiescence in *Liberty Light & Power Co.*, supra, and revoking Rev. Rul. 58–555, supra. The ruling stated that the distinction drawn between regulated and nonregulated businesses would no longer be followed. In the ruling, connection fees paid by customers to connect their houses to water lines constituted taxable income to a regulated public utility.

Section 118 was amended between 1976 and 1986 to provide that contributions in aid of construction made to a regulated public utility that provides water or sewage disposal service constitute nontaxable contributions to capital under § 118(a) in certain circumstances. In 1986, § 118 was amended again, with the addition of § 118(b) in its current form, to exclude from the term "contribution in aid of construction" any amounts paid by customers or potential customers.

These amendments to § 118 do not restrict its application to contributions from governmental sources. In Board of Trade of City of Chicago v. Commissioner, 106 T.C. 369 (1996), the taxpayer corporation, which operated a futures exchange, received "transfer fees" when a membership on the exchange was transferred. Under the Board of Trade's bylaws, the receipts were required to be used to retire the outstanding indebtedness that encumbered the Board of Trade Building, which housed its trading floor. The transfer fees were held to be nontaxable contributions to capital, rather than taxable payments for services, because the transferees of memberships had an "investment motive" in paying the fees. The earmarking of the fees to reduce the Board of Trade's indebtedness resulted in an increase in the members' equity in the Board of Trade.

4.   ANALYSIS

The appropriate treatment of nonshareholder contributions to capital and the scope of this special category depend upon the extent to which the contributions represent a gain to the corporation. This becomes an important issue in the context of state and local governmental competitions to attract corporate development with promises of substantial benefits.

Where no restrictions are imposed, the money or property is includable in gross income, because no contribution to capital has occurred. Thus, governmental subsidies that are not restricted as to use are includable in gross income. Similarly, payments received for future services are generally includable in gross income when received under the claim of right doctrine if the taxpayer is not restricted as to the use of the money. Both Edwards v. Cuba Railroad and United States v. Chicago, Burlington & Quincy Railroad Co., state that payments for services do not qualify as contributions to capital.

But where restrictions are imposed and the payments are not in consideration for services to be rendered, theoretical valuation problems arise. The *Chicago, Burlington & Quincy* case illustrates how the value to the taxpayer of what was received may have been substantially less than the amount of the state grants. The improvements in that case were only indirectly related to the production of income by the railroad.

The reasoning used in the *Chicago, Burlington & Quincy* opinion to reach the conclusion that the items were not contributions to capital suggests that they did not constitute income to C.B. & Q. because although the construction cost to the state was significant, the value to C.B. & Q. was negligible. If this is correct, the situations in this area can be characterized as follows: (1) governmental subsidies includable in income and which generate basis, (2) contributions to capital governed by §§ 118 and 362(c), or (3) neither taxable subsidies nor contributions to capital, because of the absence of significant value to the taxpayer, and which do not generate basis.

5.   QUALIFIED LESSEE CONSTRUCTION ALLOWANCES

Section 110, which is applicable to both individuals and corporations, operates in a manner analogous to § 118 with respect to the relationship of income exclusion and basis, although its triggering conditions differ from those of § 118. In general, § 110 excludes amounts received by lessees from lessors, whether received in cash or as a rent reduction, that are applied by the lessee to the construction of leasehold improvements that will be used in the lessee's trade or business. The provision applies only if the lease is for the use of retail space for 15 years or less, and the leasehold improvements must revert to the lessor at the end of the lease. Any leasehold improvements constructed with an excludable qualified leasehold construction allowance are treated as the lessor's property rather than as the lessee's property.

CHAPTER 8

TAXATION OF PERIODIC INCOME FROM CAPITAL

SECTION 1. INTRODUCTION

INTERNAL REVENUE CODE: Sections 61(a)(4)–(7); 103(a).

Determining the appropriate level of tax on investment income is a central issue in policy debates about the income tax. Fixed or periodic returns on invested capital such as interest, rents, dividends, and royalties are expressly included in gross income by § 61(a). Periodic returns on capital are generally subject to tax at normal rates as ordinary income. However, certain dividends are treated as adjusted net capital gain and subject to preferential rates ranging between 0 and 23.8 percent. See Section 3 of this Chapter.

Under the Haig-Simons definition of income, fixed and periodic returns on invested capital are clearly income when received and are, therefore, properly includable in gross income on an annual basis, even when interest or dividends are reinvested into a savings account or additional stock. However, from an investor's perspective, current taxation of re-invested periodic earnings imposes a cost that must be taken into account in comparing investment opportunities. Conversely, various forms of tax deferral or exemption reduce the cost of tax favored investments. Assessing relative rates of return on investment alternatives requires a determination of "after-tax" rates of return. For example, an investment in a corporate bond bearing a five percent interest rate before tax will return 5 percent (1 – Tax Rate) after tax. Thus, for an investor in a 35 percent marginal tax bracket, the after-tax rate of return on a bond with a 5 percent interest rate is 5 percent (1 – .35), or 3.25 percent. Under some forms of comparative analysis, the actual tax burden on returns from investment might be higher than the investor's marginal tax rate. This phenomenon has led to assertions that investment income is subject to "double tax." However, critics of the "double tax" argument maintain that it significantly overstates the number of real-world examples in which income actually gets taxed twice.

For taxable years beginning after December 31, 2012, a new surtax is imposed on the net investment income earned by higher-income individuals. While the tax imposed by new § 1411 is part of the Code's employment tax provisions and matches the 3.8 percent Medicare tax imposed on wages and self-employment income of higher-income individuals, it operates as a surtax on investment income, and revenue from the tax does not go into the Medicare Trust Fund. The provision was enacted as part of the Patient Protection and Affordable Care Act of 2010 to help fund the subsidies provided to lower-income individuals to purchase health insurance. The § 1411 surtax applies to the lesser of (1) net investment income or (2) the excess of adjusted gross income over a threshold amount. The threshold amount is $250,000 for spouses filing a joint return and $200,000 for single taxpayers. Net investment income generally includes interest, dividends, royalties, rents, and capital gains, except to the extent these items are derived in a trade or business.

DETAILED ANALYSIS

1. AFTER-TAX RETURNS ON INVESTMENT INCOME

Interest and dividends are included in gross income in the year that the item becomes due to the investor, even though the income may be reinvested or retained with the principal. For example, interest received on a savings account may be left in the account and accrue additional interest on the reinvested interest. In this case, the return on the investment is compounded as interest is paid on the reinvested interest. The impact of the annual tax on investment return also is compounded as each year's tax liability reduces the benefit of the compounded interest. To illustrate, assume the taxpayer invests $1,000 in a bond mutual fund that earns 5 percent interest, compounded semi-annually, for ten years. The semi-annual interest is reinvested in the fund, which enhances principal. The interest rate is 2.5 percent each six-month period, representing an effective annual interest rate of 5.063 percent. The future value of a $1,000 investment at 5 percent interest compounded semi-annually at the end of ten years is $1,638.62.[1] The return on the bond mutual fund before taking taxes into account is shown in Table 1.

Table 1

Year	Period	Principal	Interest
1	1	$1,000.00	$25.00
	2	$1,025.00	$25.63
2	3	$1,050.63	$26.27
	4	$1,076.89	$26.92
3	5	$1,103.81	$27.60
	6	$1,131.41	$28.29
4	7	$1,159.69	$28.99
	8	$1,188.69	$29.72
5	9	$1,218.40	$30.46
	10	$1,248.86	$31.22

---

[1]   The future value (FV) can be calculated from the formula $FV = PV(1+r)^n$ where PV is the present value of the starting amount, r is the interest rate, and n is the number of periods that the interest rate r will be paid. Thus $1,000 $(1 + .025)^{20} = $1,638.62.

6	11	$1,280.08	$32.00
	12	$1,312.09	$32.80
7	13	$1,344.89	$33.62
	14	$1,378.51	$34.46
8	15	$1,412.97	$35.32
	16	$1,448.30	$36.21
9	17	$1,484.51	$37.11
	18	$1,521.62	$38.04
10	19	$1,559.66	$38.99
	20	$1,598.65	$39.97
Ending Principal		$1,638.62	
Total Interest			$638.62

Compare the return on the investment if each year's interest payment is subject to tax at a 35 percent tax rate and only interest net of taxes is reinvested.[2] Each year the interest payment that is added to principal is reduced by 35 percent. The compounded interest paid on the after-tax interest added to principal is again subject to tax at the full 35 percent rate. In effect, the impact of the income tax is compounded as it affects the overall after-tax return on the investment.

Table 2

Year	Period	Principal	Interest	Tax	Net Return
1	1	$1,000.00	$25.00	$8.75	$16.25
	2	$1,016.25	$25.41	$8.89	$16.51
2	3	$1,032.76	$25.82	$9.04	$16.78
	4	$1,049.55	$26.24	$9.18	$17.06
3	5	$1,066.60	$26.67	$9.33	$17.33
	6	$1,083.93	$27.10	$9.48	$17.61
4	7	$1,101.55	$27.54	$9.64	$17.90
	8	$1,119.45	$27.99	$9.80	$18.19
5	9	$1,137.64	$28.44	$9.95	$18.49
	10	$1,156.13	$28.90	$10.12	$18.79
6	11	$1,174.91	$29.37	$10.28	$19.09
	12	$1,194.00	$29.85	$10.45	$19.40

---

[2]   The financial analysis is identical regardless of the source of payment of the tax due, but the assumption that the taxes paid reduce the reinvested annual interest renders the analysis more transparent.

7	13	$1,213.41	$30.34	$10.62	$19.72
	14	$1,233.13	$30.83	$10.79	$20.04
8	15	$1,253.16	$31.33	$10.97	$20.36
	16	$1,273.53	$31.84	$11.14	$20.69
9	17	$1,294.22	$32.36	$11.32	$21.03
	18	$1,315.25	$32.88	$11.51	$21.37
10	19	$1,336.63	$33.42	$11.70	$21.72
	20	$1,358.35	$33.96	$11.89	$22.07

Ending Principal	$1,380.42		
Total Interest		$585.26	$380.42

Comparing the after-tax net return on the investment with the before-tax return on the same investment reveals that the after-tax return is 59.57 percent of the before-tax return ($380.42/$638.62). One might assert, therefore, that the actual tax burden on the income derived from the taxed investment is 40.43 percent, notwithstanding the fact that the nominal rate of tax is 35 percent.[3] The appearance of a higher overall tax burden on the investment income is due to the fact that each year the addition to principal that results from the reinvested compounded interest is reduced by the tax on the annual interest increment. As a consequence, the cumulative annual additions to principal on which each year's interest is earned are an increasingly lesser amount than would have been added to principal had the interest not been taxed. Is this actually a double tax on the interest income?

The effective tax rate on the annual percentage yield from the investment is still the same as the 35 percent nominal tax rate. We can demonstrate this result by comparing the annual interest rate on the before-tax and after-tax results. The interest rate on a $1,000 investment that produces a future value of $1,638.62 at the end of a 10-year term is 5.0 percent compounded semi-annually.[4] Table 2 illustrates that if the same investment were subject to annual tax on the interest income of 35 percent, the future value of the investment is $1,380.42 at the end of ten years. The interest rate on a $1,000 investment that produces a future value of $1,380.42 at the end of ten years is 3.25 percent compounded semi-annually.[5] Comparing the investment yields before and after tax produces an effective tax rate of 35 percent (1 − [3.25%/5.00%]). Since all of the income from the investment is taxed at the same 35 percent rate, the after-tax yield from the investment will be 35 percent less than the before tax yield.

Deferring tax on income from capital until the date on which the gain is derived from the investment, as is the case under the realization model of

---

[3]   The term "tax burden" is used to reflect the percentage of income that is paid in taxes over the course of the investment. The tax burden can be expressed as 1 − (after-tax income/before-tax income) = the tax burden. On our ten year bond fund, 1 − ($380.42/$638.63) equals a tax burden of 40.43 percent.

[4] $r = (FV/PV)1/n − 1$. Thus, ($1,638.62/$1,000)1/20 − 1 = 0.025, or 5 percent compounded semi-annually.

[5]   ($1,380.42/$1,000)1/20 − 1 = 0.01625, or 3.25 percent compounded semi-annually.

Eisner v. Macomber (see Chapter 2, Section 2) also produces an effective tax burden on the income that is the same as the nominal tax rate. For example, if the income of the mutual bond fund in Table 1 were taxed at the 35 percent rate only on termination of the investment in year ten, the $638.62 of income would be subject to tax of $223.52, reducing the net after-tax income to $415.10. The effective tax burden on the gain from the investment is 35% (1 − ($415.10/$638.62)), the same as the nominal rate. This deferral is the basis of favorable taxation of deferred annuities, discussed in Section 4 of this Chapter.

The different conclusions about tax burdens in these approaches demonstrate the need to exercise caution in assessing claims of over-taxation of investment income. To an individual in the same marginal tax bracket, each year's investment income is taxed at the same rate as compensation for services. The annual tax on investment income achieves horizontal equity by taxing annual income at the same rate regardless of the source of that income. However, the comparison of Tables 1 and 2 suggests that the taxpayer who reinvests after-tax income pays a higher overall rate of tax on accumulated periodic returns, and is at an economic disadvantage, relative to the taxpayer who spends annual income on consumption.

The claimed tax disadvantage to investment relative to current consumption can be further illustrated by comparing the current value of consumption to the net after-tax value of deferred consumption. Assume that individuals A and B, who are in a 35 percent marginal tax bracket, each have $2,000 of discretionary pre-tax earned income that they can invest for ten years in an asset that will grow in value (unrealized gain) at a 5 percent annual return, compounded semi-annually, or they can spend it on immediate consumption such as travel, recreation, or entertainment. Each must pay tax of $700 on their earned income, leaving $1,300 for investment or consumption. Taxpayer A spends the $1,300 on a ski vacation, thereby obtaining $1,300 of present value in the form of immediate satisfaction. Taxpayer B invests the $1,300 for ten years. At the end of the ten year period B's investment has grown to $2,130.20.[6] At B's 35 percent tax bracket, sale of the asset requires payment of $290.57[7] of tax, leaving a net after-tax return of $1,839.63, which B now has available for consumption.[8] At the same 5 percent discount rate, the discounted present value in year 1 of the $1,839.63 available for B's consumption in year 10 is only $1,122.67.[9] In other words, measured by the discounted present value in year 1, A has achieved a higher level of consumption, $1,300, than B who deferred consumption and invested.[10]

---

[6]　$FV = PV(1+r)^n$ so $\$1,300\,(1+.025)^{20} = \$2,130.20$.

[7]　$35\% \times (\$2130.20 - \$1,300)$.

[8]　Note that the effective rate of tax on the income from this investment is 35 percent, 1 − ($539.63/$830.20).

[9]　$PV = FV/(1+r)^n$ so $\$1,839.63/(1 + .025)^{20} = \$1,122.67$.

[10]　The lower 15 percent tax rate on long term capital gain does not change the analysis. If B's realized gain in year 10 were taxed at 15 percent, B would have $2,005.67 available for consumption at that time. The present value in year one of B's $2,005.67 is $1,224.00, which is still less than the present value of A's $1,300 of immediate consumption.

Table 3

	A	B
Discretionary Income	$2,000.00	$2,000.00
Tax	$ 700.00	$ 700.00
Consumption/Investment	$1,300.00	$1,300.00
Ten Year Return		$2,130.20
Tax (35%)		$ 290.57
Net Return		$1,839.63
Year One Present Value	$1,300.00	$1,122.67

Whether the tax is imposed on fixed and periodic returns on investment, or is deferred and imposed on gains realized at the termination of an investment, in terms of discounted present values, the income tax system appears to favor immediate consumption over savings and investment.[11] These computations and the consequent conclusions, however, contain two major controversial assumptions for purposes of the comparison: (1) that the utility of immediate consumption to A is the same as that of B's deferred consumption, making economic present value the only factor at issue, and (2) that the anticipated discount rate is constant over the period of the investment.

2.   THE CONSUMPTION TAX ALTERNATIVE

The purported disincentive to savings and investment inherent in the income tax has led to proposals to replace the income tax with a system that taxes only consumption rather than both consumption and savings as does an income tax. See the discussion at Chapter 1, Section 1.B. Whether a consumption tax is structured as a value-added tax (VAT), a retail sales tax, or as a cash flow income tax, all of the models share the same fundamental feature: The measure of the tax is the amount expended on consumption. Consumption can be determined by computing income and adding borrowing, then subtracting savings and investment.[12] See Andrews, A Consumption-Type or Cash Flow Personal Income Tax, 87 Harv. L. Rev. 1113 (1974). Under a consumption tax regime, the tax system is neutral with respect to the decision to consume discretionary income or to save and invest. In the example in Table 3, assuming the same tax rates for purposes of comparison, individual A would pay tax on $2,000 of earnings and retain $1,300 for consumption. A can thus purchase the $1,300 ski trip, just as under an income tax. B on the other hand, would receive a current deduction

---

[11]   Comparing the effective rate of tax burden on A and B also illustrates that the percentage tax cost to B of saving rather than consuming the $2,000 is higher than the tax cost borne by A's immediate consumption. A's effective tax burden is 35 percent (1 − $1,300/$2,000). If B's income were not subject to tax, B's ten-year investment would grow to $3,277.23. Comparing B's after-tax return to the return of an un-taxed investment produces an effective tax burden of 43.87 percent. Thus, B's saving and deferred consumption is subject a higher overall tax burden.

[12]   This can be seen by the application of a little algebra to the Haig-Simons definition of income, discussed in Chapter 1, Section 1.B. If Personal Income = a Change in Net Worth + Consumption, then Consumption = Personal Income − a Change in Net Worth.

(or reduction in the total tax base) for the full $2,000 of earned income that is saved.[13] After ten years, at a 5 percent interest rate compounded semi-annually, B's $2,000 investment grows to $3,277.23. On disposition of the investment and use of the proceeds for consumption, at a 35 percent tax rate, B will be liable for tax of $1,147.03, leaving $2,130.20 for consumption.[14] The present value in year one, again using a 5 percent discount rate compounded semi-annually, of B's deferred consumption in year ten of $2,130.20 is $1,300, as shown in Table 4.

Table 4

	A	B
Discretionary Income	$2,000.00	$2,000.00
Tax	$ 700.00	$ 0
Consumption/Investment	$1,300.00	$2,000.00
Ten Year Return		$3,277.23
Tax (35%)		$1,147.03
Net Return		$2,130.20
Year One Present Value	$1,300.00	$1,300.00

Thus, in discounted present value terms, the tax impact on A's decision to consume and B's decision to invest is the same. In addition, both A and B are subject to the same 35 percent effective tax burden whether the $2,000 earned income is consumed immediately (A's effective tax burden is 1 − ($1,300/$2000) = 35%) or invested and consumed later (B's effective burden is 1 − ($2130/$3277) = 35%).

A similar result occurs with respect to the government's revenue. The government collects $700 of tax from A in year one. The government collects $1,147.03 of tax from B after ten years. The discounted present value of B's tax liability as of year one at 5 percent interest compounded semi-annually is $700.[15] Thus the government also is neutral as to B's decision to consume or save.

Although ostensibly neutral between current consumption versus savings and investment—which consumption tax advocates claim makes it preferable to income taxation given the latter's less favorable treatment of investment—a consumption tax ultimately benefits taxpayers who can save more over many years; i.e., the wealthy. Indeed, while the tax burdens of consumers and savers are equivalent in present value terms (as demonstrated in the preceding example), a consumption tax affords the population of savers greater real consumption over their lifetimes than those

---

[13]   This example is a tax on income with a deduction for savings, a feature of most "flat-tax" proposals. Under a value-added tax or a retail sales tax model, A's immediate consumption would be taxable. B is subject to tax only on B's deferred consumption. The economic result is the same. Tax is imposed to the degree that earnings are expended in consumption. Earnings that are saved or invested are not included in the tax base.

[14]   Under a consumption tax, the tax to B on disposition of the investment will be the same whether the investment produces a periodic return such as interest or dividends, or whether gains represent capital appreciation of an asset.

[15] $1,147.03/(1 + .025)^{20} = $700.

who choose to (or must) consume immediately all of their income. Note that in the example to which Tables 3 and 4 relate, absent an inflationary increase in the price of the ski trip raising its cost to $2,130.20, B has enjoyed more real consumption than A has enjoyed. If the price of the ski trip remains $1,300, in addition to the ski trip in year 10, B obtains $830.20 of consumption—a separate fishing trip, perhaps—that A never realizes. From this perspective, the "neutrality" of the consumption tax is illusory.

The foregoing example compared two individual taxpayers who, apart from the decision to save versus consume in the first year were otherwise identical. But the choice of a tax base involves additional considerations. Review Chapter 1, Section 1.B.1. The policy choices that underlie taxation involve decisions as to which groups of citizens and which sectors of the economy should bear the burden of funding governmental activities. Relative to the distribution of tax burdens under an income tax, a consumption tax removes from the tax base income that is saved, including any reinvested returns on earlier savings. Thus, a portion of the income of individuals who have sufficient discretionary income for savings and investment is freed from tax, perhaps permanently. Moving from an income tax base to a consumption tax base thereby shifts the burden of taxation from individuals who can afford to save and invest (and have the option to consume as an alternative) to individuals who must consume their income for subsistence. In other words, the consumption tax benefits higher income individuals by reducing their tax burden on savings and investment. In fact, under certain assumptions, the favorable treatment of savings is equivalent to exempting investment income from tax altogether such that the resultant system taxes only wages. In addition, the consumption tax base shifts the burden of tax both to younger families who are in the process of acquiring basic necessities and modest luxuries as well as to retired individuals who are consuming life-long savings and away from individuals in their highest earnings years.

Oddly, proponents of moving from an income tax to a consumption tax maintain that permitting taxpayers to deduct savings from earnings offers a fairer alternative to our current system. They bolster such claims with talk of "tax simplification" through eliminating most deductions, exclusions, exemptions, and credits. They often integrate such proposals with plans to replace the income tax with a flat tax, a form of consumption taxation that imposes a single, low rate on all taxpayers.

Claims for fairness, simplification, and low rates under a consumption tax are misleading. First, all of the proposals preserve the most popular and expensive tax expenditures, such as the deductions for charitable contributions and mortgage interest, which overwhelmingly benefit high-income taxpayers (less than one-third of all taxpayers itemize deductions and thus are the beneficiaries of these tax dispensations, while more than two-thirds of taxpayers must take the standard deduction and realize no tax savings associated with these expenditures). At the same time, the proposals eliminate assistance for child-care and medical expenses as well as provisions aimed at low-income taxpayers such as the earned income credit.

Second, even if consumption tax plans eliminated all existing tax "loopholes" in the income tax (the majority of which benefit wealthy taxpayers, both in number and cost) a consumption tax replacement would still overwhelmingly benefit wealthy taxpayers. Under current law, the top marginal income tax rate reaches 39.6 percent, while consumption tax proposals promise maximum rates of only 15 to 20 percent (although without promising revenue neutrality, which would force the rates up); in other words, these plans would bestow an immediate tax cut of at least 50 percent or higher for top earners. It is no wonder that two early and famous proponents of the flat tax conceded that their plan would be "a tremendous boon to the economic elite," and raise taxes on the lowest income families by 78 percent while cutting taxes on the wealthiest families by 41 percent. Hall & Rabushka, Low Tax, Simple Tax, Flat Tax, Appendix (1983).

If consumption tax advocates truly cared about removing inequitable and inefficient tax expenditure items, they could accomplish the goal of broadening the tax base—while trading tax reform for tax cuts—within the current income tax system. In this way, they could also improve and rationalize the current treatment of savings and investment by expanding existing consumption tax elements such as Individual Retirement Accounts (IRAs), discussed in the next section.

Finally, it is worth pointing out that moving from an income tax to a consumption tax would create serious transition problems. In effect, the change imposes a one-time tax on all existing capital, an unappealing result, particularly to retired persons who do not have adequate time to bring their savings back up to existing levels.

SECTION 2.   TAX DEFERRED AND TAX-EXEMPT INVESTMENT ACCOUNTS

INTERNAL REVENUE CODE: Sections 219(a)–(c); 408(a), (d)(1), (e)(1), (g); 408A(a)–(c), (d)(1) and (2).

The consumption tax proposals analyzed in the preceding section are based on a tax base that allows a reduction for income that is saved or invested. The current income tax system adopts this model to encourage savings for retirement through Individual Retirement Accounts (IRAs), which provide for a deduction of the annual contributions to a qualified trust. I.R.C. § 219(a). Income earned by the qualified trust is not subject to taxation until the funds are withdrawn, at which time the full amount of withdrawals is included in gross income. Qualified defined contribution plans providing deferred compensation to employees provide the same tax benefit. Compensation income is exempted from inclusion in gross income when it is deposited in a qualified trust for the benefit of the employee. The trust income and principal are included in the employee's gross income when received as deferred compensation, generally upon retirement. The presence of these savings vehicles in the Internal Revenue Code may be seen to transform the income tax into a hybrid system that has elements of both an income tax and a consumption tax to the extent that income saved in an IRA or qualified employee pension plan is not included in the tax base until consumed.

The deferred taxation constitutes a very large tax expenditure in an income tax system. See Office of Management and Budget, Analytical Perspectives: Budget of the U.S. Government, Fiscal Year 2017, 231 (2016) (estimating the tax expenditure for IRAs at nearly $220 billion between 2016–25 and for employee pension plans at $620 billion).

The Roth IRA provided by § 408A, on the other hand, is funded with after-tax contributions, but the income earned by the account is exempt from tax. The Roth IRA thereby represents a tax on wages, with an exclusion for investment income. Assuming identical positive yields and that tax rates are the same, the impact of the deduction for contributions to a regular IRA and exemption from income for the earnings of the Roth IRA is the same. Each of these approaches basically exempts income earned on the investment from taxation.[16]

To illustrate the economic benefit of these various approaches to tax favored investment accounts, consider taxpayers A, B and C, each of whom earn $5,000 that is available for savings or investment. Assume that A, B, and C will each pay a marginal tax rate of 35 percent on all income. A pays tax on the income and deposits the after-tax remainder in an interest-bearing savings account that pays 5 percent interest compounded semi-annually. The interest from the savings account is subject to tax each year, and only the net proceeds after tax are retained in the account. B deposits $5,000 in a qualified IRA, which allows for a deduction of the amount contributed to the IRA and inclusion in gross income of the proceeds on withdrawal. C pays tax on the income and deposits the after-tax proceeds in a Roth IRA, which exempts from tax all of the earnings on the account. Each taxpayer withdraws the proceeds at the end of 10 years. The results to the three taxpayers and the result in a no-tax world are shown in Table 5.

---

[16]   The same can be said about a consumption tax, which would, in the context of an income tax, exempt income from saving and investment from the tax.

Table 5

	Zero Tax	A Savings Account	B IRA	C Roth IRA
Earned Income	$5,000.00	$5,000.00	$5,000.00	$5,000.00
Immediate Tax		$1,750.00	$ 0.00	$1,750.00
Deposit	$5,000.00	$3,250.00	$5,000.00	$3,250.00
Grows To	$8,193.08	$4,486.36	$8,193.08	$5,325.50
Tax at Withdrawal		$ 0	$2,867.58	$ 0
Net Return	$8,193.08	$4,486.36	$5,325.50	$5,325.50
Overall Tax Burden[17]	0.00%	45.24%	35.00%	35.00%
Tax Burden on Investment Income	0.00%	40.43%	0.00%	0.00%

The overall effective burden for each taxpayer combines the taxes on both the earned income and the income from invested capital. The example illustrates that under both the regular IRA and the Roth IRA, only the taxpayer's wage income was subject to taxation. In contrast, the effective tax burden to A on the savings account reflects the compound influence of both the reduction in income remaining for deposit because of the tax on earned income and the reduction in annual return attributable to the annual tax on income. However, the effective tax rate on the investment income alone is 40.43 percent,[18] which is the same as the effective tax rate in Table 1, Section 1 of this Chapter.

DETAILED ANALYSIS

1. INDIVIDUAL RETIREMENT ACCOUNTS

1.1. Contributions and Distributions

Individuals who are not covered by an employer maintained qualified retirement plan (discussed at Chapter 30) may deduct contributions to an Individual Retirement Account (IRA) up to the lesser of $5,000, adjusted for inflation, or the individual's gross income from compensation. I.R.C. § 219. For 2016, the inflation-adjusted contribution limit was $5,500. If spouses file a joint return and one spouse has no compensation income during the year,

---

[17] The effective tax burden is 1 − (after tax return/no-tax return). One can come to the same conclusions regarding effective tax rates by comparing the net present value of the return from each investment.

[18] $(1 - ([4,486.36 - 3,250]/[5,325.50 - 3,250]))$.

an additional $5,500 may be contributed to an IRA for that spouse. In addition, taxpayers age 50 and older may deduct an additional "catch-up" contribution of $1,000. The IRA must be a trust or custodial account with a bank or other qualified trustee.

Meanwhile, income earned in the IRA is not currently taxed. I.R.C. § 408(e)(1). Distributions are taxed as an annuity under the rules of § 72, discussed in Section 4 of this Chapter. If a taxpayer made only deductible contributions to an IRA, the taxpayer has no "after-tax investment" in the IRA and distributions are fully taxable.

Distributions from an IRA before the taxpayer reaches age 59½ (unless the taxpayer becomes disabled) are subject to a penalty tax equal to 10 percent of the taxable distribution in addition to normal income taxes. I.R.C. § 72(t). The penalty tax does not apply if distributions are made to purchase medical insurance or pay certain other medical expenses while the taxpayer is unemployed, to purchase an owner-occupied principal residence by a taxpayer who has not owned his or her principal residence at any time within the prior two years, or to pay qualified higher education expenses of the taxpayer or the taxpayer's dependents.

Conversely, to prevent excessive tax-deferred accumulations that are more likely to end up as a bequest rather than to secure retirement income, contributions may not be made and distributions must commence after the taxpayer reaches age 70½. I.R.C. §§ 219(d)(1) and 408(a)(6). Section 4974 imposes an excise tax if the minimum distribution requirement has not been met.

If an individual has more than one IRA, contributions to one or more of which were not entirely deductible, all of the taxpayer's IRAs are treated as a single IRA and all distributions are aggregated. I.R.C. § 408(d)(2). Suppose an individual made $16,000 of deductible contributions to IRA #1 and $4,000 of non-deductible contributions to IRA #2. The taxpayer receives distributions of $200 from IRA #1 and $1,800 from IRA #2. The $2,000 in total distributions would be treated as a $400 return of capital as a proportion of the total nondeductible contributions [($200 + $1,800) $4,000/($16,000 + $4,000) = ($2,000) 1/5], and $1,600 of gross income (($2,000) 4/5).

1.2. *Participation in a Qualified Plan*

If either the taxpayer or the taxpayer's spouse participates in an employer sponsored qualified plan during the year, the allowable deduction is reduced under § 219(g) by an amount equal to the otherwise allowable deduction multiplied by a fraction. In 2016, the numerator is the amount by which the taxpayer's adjusted gross income (with certain modifications) exceeds $98,000 for taxpayers filing a joint return or $61,000 for single taxpayers (adjusted periodically for inflation). The denominator is $20,000 for taxpayers filing a joint return or $10,000 for single taxpayers. Thus, the deduction is completely phased out for married taxpayers filing a joint return with $118,000 of modified AGI ($118,000 less $98,000 = $20,000, and $20,000/$20,000 = 1) and for single taxpayers with $71,000 of modified AGI ($71,000 less $61,000 = $10,000, and $10,000/$10,000 = 1). An individual who does not participate in a qualified plan at any time during the year but has a spouse who does participate in a qualified plan is subject to a different phase-out rule. The "applicable dollar amount" for the nonparticipating spouse is $184,000 (adjusted for inflation), and the deduction is phased out over a $10,000 range. Even if § 219(g) applies, the taxpayer may make a nondeductible contribution to an IRA up to the generally allowable amount. I.R.C. § 408(o).

Wade v. Commissioner, T.C. Memo. 2001–114, suggests that participation in a qualified pension plan for purposes of determining whether the phase-out rules apply is strictly interpreted. Mrs. Wade was a part-time community college teacher who was an active participant in a qualified plan by virtue of an $84.89 mandatory contribution to a defined benefit plan in a year in which she accrued approximately 1/120th of the service required for benefits to vest. As a result, both Mrs. and Mr. Wade, whose combined AGI exceeded the then applicable phase out threshold, were denied deductions for their IRA contributions under the § 219(g) phase-out rule.

2. NONDEDUCTIBLE "ROTH" IRAs

2.1. *General*

Section 408A provides for "Roth IRAs," which are significantly different than regular IRAs. Unlike the conventional IRA, there is no deduction for contributions to a Roth IRA, which, therefore, is funded with after-tax investment. The Roth IRA trust is tax exempt and distributions from the Roth IRA are not includable in gross income. As a result the earnings never are taxed. In this respect a Roth IRA resembles tax-exempt interest on a municipal bond, see § 103 discussed in Section 3 of this Chapter. But unlike a municipal bond, on which any capital appreciation (due to a decrease in market interest rates) is taxable if the bond is sold, capital appreciation in a Roth IRA permanently escapes taxation. As shown in Table 5, given a constant rate of return on equivalent investments, and the same tax rates, the economic benefit of a Roth IRA is the same as a regular IRA. Nonetheless, there are some distinct advantages to the Roth IRA. Even with the same contribution limits, more pre-tax earnings can be set aside in the Roth IRA. See Table 5, infra. An IRA is normally a conventional IRA unless it is designated as a Roth IRA at the time it is established. I.R.C. § 408A(b).

2.2. *Contribution Limits*

In general, the maximum amount that a taxpayer may contribute to a Roth IRA is an amount equal to that which the taxpayer could have deducted as a contribution to a deductible IRA (disregarding the limitations on deductions based on the taxpayer's participation in a qualified plan and the prohibition on contributions to a deductible IRA after age 70½) minus the amount that the taxpayer actually contributed to a deductible IRA. For example, if in 2016 a single person with a modified adjusted gross income of $50,000, who did not participate in a qualified plan, contributed $3,500 to a deductible IRA, the taxpayer could contribute an additional $2,000 to a Roth IRA (contribution limits are adjusted periodically for inflation).

The ceiling on allowable contributions to a Roth IRA is phased out ratably over a $10,000 range for married taxpayers filing joint returns with a modified adjusted gross income equal to or exceeding $183,000 (thus being unavailable for taxpayers with at least $193,000 of modified adjusted gross income). For all other taxpayers with a modified adjusted gross income equal to or greater than $116,000, the ceiling is phased out over a $15,000 range (thus being unavailable for modified adjusted gross income exceeding $131,000). I.R.C. § 408A(c)(3)(A), (c)(3)(C), with the phase-out ranges adjusted for inflation. The phase-out rules apply whether or not the taxpayer is a participant in an employer provided qualified plan. A penalty tax under § 4973(f) applies to excess contributions to a Roth IRA.

Because there is no deduction for contributions to a Roth IRA, the contribution limit applies to contributions made from after-tax income. Thus, where a taxpayer in a 28 percent tax bracket only may contribute $5,500 of earned income to a conventional IRA, the same taxpayer requires $7,638.89 of earned income to fund a Roth IRA with a $5,500 after-tax contribution.[19] In effect, a taxpayer is permitted to set aside a larger proportion of earnings in the Roth IRA. Thus, for a taxpayer in a 28 percent tax bracket who maximizes IRA contributions, and who receives a 5 percent return on the investment compounded semi-annually, the appropriate comparison over a ten year investment horizon is as shown in Table 6.

Table 6

	IRA	Roth IRA
Earned Income	$5,500.00	$7,638.89
Immediate Tax	$ 0	$2,138.80
Deposit	$5,500.00	$5,500.00
Grows To	$9,012.39	$9,012.39
Tax at Withdrawal	$2,523.47	$ 0
Net Return	$6,488.92	$9,012.39
Overall Tax Burden	28.00%	28.00%

While the overall tax burden is the same on the combined earned income and investment income with respect to both forms of individual retirement accounts, the Roth IRA provides its benefits to a larger accumulation of income. However, the conventional IRA offers an offsetting benefit to the taxpayer who anticipates being subject to higher tax rates at the time of the contribution and lower tax rates at the time of withdrawal, while the Roth IRA is beneficial to a taxpayer who is subject to lower rates at the time of contribution and higher rates at the time of withdrawal.

2.3. *Distributions*

Distributions from a Roth IRA prior to the taxpayer attaining age 59½ generally are not qualified for full exclusion treatment, unless attributable to the taxpayer's death or disability. I.R.C. § 408A(d)(2)(A)(ii) and (iii).

---

[19]   Total earned income necessary = $5,500/(1 – the tax rate). Thus, $5,500/(1 – 28%) = $7,638.89.

An individual may roll-over or convert a regular IRA into a Roth IRA at any time.[20] The conversion is treated as a distribution from the regular IRA and the converted amounts are thus included in the beneficiary's gross income for the year of the conversion. However, the distribution is not subject to the ten percent penalty tax of § 72(t). I.R.C. §§ 402A(c)(3), 408(d)(3)(A).

3. ANALYSIS

The comparison of the regular IRA and the Roth IRA in Table 6 is based on a constant investment yield. Not all investors will be equally successful under the two savings alternatives, however. The regular IRA is based on a consumption tax model. The taxpayer is allowed a deduction for earned income that is saved in the IRA, then subject to taxation at regular rates on the full amount withdrawn from the IRA, including both the original contribution plus the full amount of earnings derived on the contribution. Thus, all investors in regular IRAs are taxed the same—that is, at their marginal rates—regardless of the success or failure of the investment within the retirement account. The Roth IRA, on the other hand, represents a tax only on earned income (or wages), with a complete exemption from tax for investment income. As a consequence, the highly successful investor, who derives higher income from the Roth IRA investment, pays the same tax on earned income (and no tax on investment income) as the unsuccessful investor.

Consider, for example, two young taxpayers in the same tax bracket, Investor A and Investor B, each of whom invests $5,000 in a Roth IRA for five years, for a total of $25,000. Assume that neither investment generates a return during the first five years. However, over the subsequent fifty years, the returns diverge sharply such that Investor A's initial investment generates no increase in value over and above the original $25,000, while Investor B's initial investment generates an annual 12-percent rate of return, growing from $25,000 to nearly $10 million. Despite the wildly different rates of return (0 vs. 12 percent) and appreciation ($0 vs. $10 million), Investors A and B pay the same amount of tax on their investment returns; that is, $0.00.

---

[20] Section 408A(e) permits taxpayers to roll-over distributions from certain qualified retirement plans to Roth IRAs, subject to the rules applicable to roll-overs from regular IRAs to Roth IRAs.

SECTION 3.   SPECIAL TREATMENT OF CORPORATE DIVIDENDS

INTERNAL REVENUE CODE: Section 1(h)(11)(A), (B)(i), (C)(i), (ii).

Jobs and Growth Tax Relief Reconciliation Act of 2003, Report of the Committee on Ways and Means, House of Representatives

H. Rep. No. 108–094, 108th Cong., 1st Sess. (2003).

Reasons for Change

The Committee believes it is important that tax policy be conducive to economic growth. The Committee believes that reducing the individual tax on dividends lowers the cost of capital and will lead to economic growth and the creation of jobs. Economic growth is impeded by tax-induced distortions in the capital markets. Mitigating these distortions will improve the efficiency of the capital markets. In addition, reducing the aggregate tax burden on investments made by corporations will lower the cost of capital needed to finance new investments and lead to increases in aggregate national investment and increases in private sector employment. It is through such investment that the United States' economy can increase output, employment, and productivity. It is through increases in productivity that workers earn higher real wages and all Americans benefit from a higher standard of living.

The Committee observes that present law imposes different total tax burdens on income from different investments. The Committee believes that, by placing different tax burdens on different investments, the present system results in economic distortions. The Committee observes that present law distorts individual and corporate financial decisions. The Committee observes that because interest payments on the debt are deductible, present law encourages corporations to finance using debt rather than equity. The Committee believes that the increase in corporate leverage, while beneficial to each corporation from a tax perspective, may place the economy at risk of more bankruptcies during an economic downturn. In addition, the Committee finds that present law, by taxing dividend income at a higher rate than income from capital gains, encourages corporations to retain earnings rather than to distribute them as taxable dividends. If dividends are discouraged, shareholders may prefer that corporate management retain and reinvest earnings rather than pay out dividends, even if the shareholder might have an alternative use for the funds that could offer a higher rate of return than that earned on the retained earnings.

This is another source of inefficiency as the opportunity to earn higher pre-tax returns is bypassed in favor of lower pre-tax returns.

Explanation of Provision

Under the provision, dividends received by an individual shareholder from domestic corporations are taxed at the same rates that apply to net capital gain. This treatment applies for purposes of both the regular tax and the alternative minimum tax. Thus, under the provision, dividends will be taxed at rates of five and 15 percent.

If a shareholder does not hold a share of stock for more than [60] days during the [121]-day period beginning [60] days before the ex-dividend date (as measured under section 246(c)) [and as explained below], dividends received on the stock are not eligible for the reduced rates. . . .

If an individual receives an extraordinary dividend (within the meaning of section 1059(c)) eligible for the reduced rates with respect to any share of stock, any loss on the sale of the stock is treated as a long-term capital loss to the extent of the dividend.

DETAILED ANALYSIS

1.   PREFERENTIAL RATES

Under § 1(h)(11) certain dividends—known as "qualified" dividends—received by taxpayers other than corporations generally are taxed at the same rate as long-term capital gains (discussed in Chapter 24): 20 percent for income otherwise in the 39.6 percent bracket, 15 percent for income otherwise in the 25 percent or higher bracket (but below the 39.6 percent bracket), and zero for income otherwise in the 10 or 15 percent bracket. I.R.C. § 1(h)(11). An additional tax of 3.8 percent may also be assessed on these dividends under § 1411 for upper-income taxpayers with sufficiently large amounts of net investment income. See Section 1 of this Chapter.

2.   ANTI-ABUSE RULES RELATING TO PREFERENTIAL RATES FOR QUALIFIED DIVIDENDS

Section 1(h)(11)(B)(iii) is aimed at preventing taxpayers from obtaining unwarranted tax benefits in some situations. The 15 percent preferential rate for qualified dividends, coupled with capital loss resulting from the short-term holding of stock purchased in anticipation of receiving a dividend, creates inappropriate tax arbitrage benefits. Section 1(h)(11)(B)(iii) provides that the preferential rate for qualified dividends does not apply to any dividends on any share of stock that is held for less than 60 days during the 121 day period beginning on the date that is 60 days before the date on which the stock becomes ex-dividend. (Under stock exchange rules, stock generally becomes ex-dividend three business days before the "record date" for paying dividends.) For preferred stock, if the dividends received are attributable to a period in excess of 366 days, the holding period is extended to 120 days during the 180-day period beginning on the date that is 120 days before the date on which the stock becomes ex-dividend.

Congress considered § 1(h)(11)(B)(iii) to be adequate to deal with only some of the tax avoidance possibilities created by the availability of the preferential rate for dividends as applied to extraordinarily large dividends.

If an extraordinarily large dividend was expected to be paid on stock of a corporation, the investor owning the stock would be willing to hold the stock for the period required to avoid the limitation in § 1(h)(11)(B)(iii). Section 1(h)(11)(D)(ii) provides that if an individual receives an "extraordinary dividend," as defined in § 1059(c), taxed at the preferential rate, any loss on the sale of the stock on which the dividend was paid is treated as a long-term capital loss to the extent of the dividend, even if the actual holding period of the stock was short-term. Thus, to the extent an extraordinary dividend is taxed at the preferential rate, any loss recognized on the sale of the stock that is attributable to a decline in value caused by the dividend first offsets long-term capital gain that would have been taxed at preferential rates before offsetting short-term capital gain that would be taxed at normal rates. See I.R.C. § 1211, Chapter 24, Section 1.3.

3.   ANALYSIS

Reducing the tax rate on dividend income for qualified dividends from as high as 39.6 percent to 20 percent (and even 15 percent or 0 percent) while wages, interest, and other ordinary income items remain taxable at normal rates, provides an extraordinary tax preference to a very small number of taxpayers. For tax year 2013, only 17 percent of all taxpayers received qualified dividend income with the majority of the tax savings accruing to wealthy taxpayers. Just 9 percent of all taxpayers with adjusted gross income under $50,000 (an AGI category representing nearly 65 percent of all tax returns) received dividend income. By comparison, two-thirds of taxpayers with AGI exceeding $200,000 (representing 3.75 percent of all returns) reported dividend income, as did 86 percent of taxpayers with AGI of over $1 million (0.24 percent of all returns) and 94 percent of taxpayers with AGI exceeding $10 million (0.01 percent of all returns). Not only do upper-income taxpayers receive qualified dividend income at higher rates than other taxpayers; they also capture a disproportionate percentage of the tax-favored income. Households with AGI under $50,000 reporting qualified dividends received less than 10 percent of all income from that source with each household averaging roughly $1,790. Meanwhile, taxpayers with more than $200,000 in AGI received more than 60 percent of all qualified dividend income with each household averaging $17,445, while returns with more than $1 million in AGI garnered 35 percent of all such income for an average benefit of $157,000. The numbers are even more staggering for the super wealthy with AGI over $10 million. This select group of 12,839 returns reported nearly 16 percent of all qualified dividend income (or $25 billion) for an average benefit of nearly $2 million per household. Calculated from Internal Revenue Service, Individual Income Tax Returns, Table 1.4, All Returns: Sources of Income, Adjustments, and Tax Items by Size of Adjusted Gross Income, Tax Year 2013 (2015).

SECTION 4.   TAX-EXEMPT INTEREST ON STATE AND LOCAL BONDS

INTERNAL REVENUE CODE: Sections 61(a)(4); 103; 141(a), (e).

REGULATIONS: Section 1.103–1.

Interest income derived from investments in state and local bonds is tax favored by virtue of § 103(a), which excludes such interest from gross income. The exclusion permits an issuer to offer bonds at a lower interest rate, thereby subsidizing the cost of capital to state and local governments. There are two general categories of bonds issued in the name of state and local governments. The first category consists of bonds issued to finance public activities such as schools, roads and governmentally-operated utilities including water and electricity. The second category consists of bonds issued to finance private activities, including activities of both non-profit charitable organizations (including schools) and various private businesses and individuals. The major categories of private noncharitable bonds include industrial development bonds (IDBs) used to finance private business enterprises (such as the construction of a factory), student loan bonds issued in connection with certain programs of the U.S. Department of Education, and mortgage subsidy bonds (MSBs), which generally are used to provide below market mortgage loans to first-time homebuyers or veterans. Private charitable bonds include bonds issued for the benefit of private universities and private hospitals.

Under a pure income tax, the interest on state and local government obligations should be included in gross income. The interest income from a state or local governmental bond is no less an economic benefit clearly realized than interest on a corporate bond. The exclusion, although at one time thought to be required as a matter of constitutional law, today is justified solely as a subsidy to state and local government.[21] As such, it is a form of federal financial aid and must be evaluated as would any direct federal program designed to reduce borrowing costs to state and local governments. The "tax expenditure" aspect of such subsidies is considered in Chapter 11.

The subsidy to the state and local governments (and the private parties on whose behalf private purpose bonds are issued) is provided by excluding the bond interest from the gross income of the bondholders.

---

[21]   In South Carolina v. Baker, 485 U.S. 505 (1988), the Court stated:

"We thus confirm that subsequent case law has overruled the holding in *Pollock* [see Chapter 1, Section 2.C].that state bond interest is immune from a nondiscriminatory federal tax. We see no constitutional reason for treating persons who receive interest on government bonds differently than persons who receive income from other types of contracts with the government, and no tenable rationale for distinguishing the costs imposed on States by a tax on state bond interest from the costs imposed by a tax on the income from any other state contract. * * * [T]he owners of state bonds have no constitutional entitlement not to pay taxes on income they earn from state bonds, and States have no constitutional entitlement to issue bonds paying lower interest rates than other issuers. * * * "

The subsidy thus takes the form of an incentive (1) that is provided to parties other than the intended beneficiaries and (2) that varies with their marginal tax bracket. The characteristics interact to provide a subsidy that is both inefficient and unfair.

Suppose that the rate of interest on taxable bonds is 10 percent. An investor in a 35 percent marginal tax bracket should be neutral between purchasing a 10 percent taxable bond, which would return 6.5 percent after-tax, and a tax-exempt bond that returns 6.5 percent, assuming all risks are equal. A tax-exempt interest rate of about 6.5 percent would, therefore, be sufficient to attract a 35 percent bracket investor to the tax-exempt investment. If there were sufficient investors in the 35 percent marginal bracket bidding for these bonds, the tax-exempt interest rate could be expected to be about 6.5 percent, or 65 percent of the taxable interest rate (1 − tax rate). But in fact there are not enough 35 percent bracket investors to purchase all of the bonds that state and local governments desire to issue. Accordingly, the rate must be high enough to make the bonds attractive to lower-bracket taxpayers. The exempt rate must be at least 6.7 percent to attract 33 percent bracket taxpayers, 7.2 percent to attract 28 percent bracket taxpayers, and so forth. As the tax-exempt interest rate rises to attract lower-bracket investors, the 35 percent bracket taxpayers receive a windfall; after all, a 6.5 percent rate was all that was necessary to attract this investment. Thus, if the tax-exempt rate were 7.2 percent, anyone investing who is in a marginal rate bracket above 28 percent (the break-even point) also would receive a windfall. The windfall increases in proportion to the marginal rate bracket; the higher the bracket, the greater the windfall.

The windfall effect described above means that the full amount of the federal subsidy does not reach the state and local governments. Thus, if, in the preceding example, the tax-exempt rate is 7.2 percent, the 35 percent marginal tax rate investor would receive a windfall of 0.7 percent. This is the after-tax rate of return on the bond (7.2 percent) less the after-tax rate on a comparable taxable investment (6.5 percent). The federal revenue loses 3.5 percent of the interest that would otherwise be payable as federal income tax. The state or local government receives 2.8 percent in the form of reduced interest expense. This is the difference between what the governmental unit would have had to pay in interest if the bonds were taxable, less the actual interest expense. As a result, the tax exemption mechanism under the assumed conditions is an inefficient technique for providing federal aid to state and local governments since a significant portion of the subsidy is retained by some investors.

The lower rate of return on tax-exempt bonds represents an implicit tax to the investor that exists unless the tax-exempt rate equals the taxable rate. As in the above example, when the tax-exempt interest rate is 6.5 percent and the interest rate on taxable obligations is 10 percent, the investor incurs an implicit tax equal to 35 percent. An investment in tax-exempt bonds will be preferable to an investment in taxable bonds anytime this implicit tax is less than the explicit tax on taxable income. The after-tax return on a taxable and comparable tax-exempt bond is the same.[22] When the tax-exempt rate rises to 7.2 percent, the 35 percent bracket investor incurs a 28 percent implicit tax rate on the bonds issued by state and local governments, which is less than the explicit 35 percent rate on taxable bond interest. The implicit tax borne by investors in tax-exempt bonds is always the difference between the yield on taxable bonds and the yield on tax-exempt bonds expressed as a percentage of the yield on taxable bonds.

At any given time, the implicit rate of tax incurred by an investor in tax-exempt bonds can be calculated by determining the ratio between the long-term tax-exempt yield and the long-term taxable bond yield and subtracting the resulting percentage from 100 percent. The implicit tax is thus equal to 1—(the tax-exempt yield/taxable yield). For example, if the average long-term tax-exempt rate is 6 percent and the average long-term taxable bond rate is 7.5 percent, the ratio between them is .80 and the implicit tax rate is 20 percent (1 − [6.0/7.5]). If the top marginal income tax rate is 35 percent, there is a difference of 15 percentage points between the two rates and the investment in the tax-exempt instrument is highly favored. This difference is an indicator of the inefficiency of the subsidy mechanism under the assumed conditions. If the top marginal rate were increased to 50 percent and bond yields remained the same, the subsidy would become even more inefficient as the gap between the implicit and marginal rates widened. The benefit to the taxpayer from the subsidy and the cost to the Treasury rise and fall with changes in tax rates.

There are two other significant aspects of the subsidy provided to state and local governments by § 103. First, the federal subsidy is available for any public activity the state and local government officials choose; unlike most direct subsidies, the federal government exercises no control over the type of projects that will qualify for the subsidy. Second, the amount of the subsidy for public activities is open ended, depending solely upon the volume of tax-exempt bonds issued and the interest differential between the tax-exempt rate and the taxable rate. In this regard, the subsidy more closely resembles an entitlement program than a direct appropriation of federal funds that typically is subject to a maximum total amount. These two characteristics have been the

---

[22]   If the exemption were recast as a direct federal spending program, the 35 percent bracket taxpayer could be seen as making an imputed tax payment equal to the difference between the tax-exempt rate (assume 6.5 percent) and the 10 percent taxable rate. The federal government in turn remits this 3.5 percent imputed payment back to the investor who in turn remits it to the local government issuing the bond. If the tax-exempt rate is 7.2 percent, the investor remits a 2.8 percent imputed payment to the local government and retains 0.7 percent in addition to the 6.5 percent after-tax bond rate. Thus, if the federal government were to collect the full tax on $10 of interest on a 10 percent bond and pass on the payment to a municipal government, the direct expenditure would be $3.50. However, if the tax-exempt bond rate is 7.2 percent, $3.50 in tax savings is provided to the investor, while only $2.80 is transferred to the municipal government.

principal reasons why governors, mayors, and other local government officials have vigorously opposed any effort to modify or replace the existing tax expenditure for general purpose state and local government bonds.

The exclusion for interest on state and local government bonds, which has been in the Internal Revenue Code since its inception in 1913, was intended for bonds issued for governmental purposes. Subsequently, some state and local governments, bolstered by favorable IRS rulings, began issuing bonds for the purpose of financing various nongovernmental activities. The most common situation involved "industrial development bonds" that nominally were issued by the governmental unit but which financed construction of a facility to be used by a private business. The bonds typically were issued either to attract or keep the business at that particular location. The corporation agreed to "rent" the facility for exactly the amount needed to pay the interest and amortize the principal of the bonds. The municipality was not liable for either the principal or interest on the bonds. In effect, the municipality was a mere conduit passing on the benefit of its tax-exempt status, the reduced interest rate, to the private business in the form of reduced "rent."

Beginning in 1968, Congress began to limit the growth and use of exempt bonds for the benefit of private businesses. Congress added further restrictions in the 1986 Act, the reasons for which are set forth in the following excerpt from a document prepared by the staff of the Joint Committee on Taxation.

General Explanation of the Tax Reform Act of 1986
Staff of the Joint Committee on Taxation, 1151–52 (1987).

Reasons for Change
General considerations

Congress was concerned with the large and increasing volume of tax-exempt bonds being issued under prior law. The effects of this increasing volume included an inefficient allocation of capital; an increase in the cost of financing traditional governmental activities; the ability of higher-income persons to avoid taxes by means of tax-exempt investments; and mounting revenue losses.

At the same time, Congress recognized the important cost savings that tax-exempt financing could provide for State and local governments, in a period marked by reductions in direct Federal expenditures for such purposes. To the extent possible, Congress desired to restrict tax-exempt financing for private activities without affecting the ability of State and local governments to issue bonds for traditional governmental purposes.

Between 1975 and 1985, the volume of long-term tax-exempt obligations for private activities (including tax-exempt IDBs [Industrial

Development Bonds], student loan bonds, mortgage revenue bonds, and bonds for use by certain nonprofit charitable organizations) increased from $8.9 billion to $116.4 billion. As a share of total State and local government borrowing, financing for these activities increased from 29 percent to 53 percent. Essentially, these bonds provided an indirect Federal subsidy to private activities. This affected the efficiency and equity of the tax system in several ways.

First, the large volume of nongovernmental tax-exempt bonds increased the interest rates that State and local governments were required to pay to finance their activities. As the total volume of tax-exempt bonds increases, the interest rate on the bonds must increase to attract investment from competing sources. The additional bond volume caused by nongovernmental use thus increases the cost of financing essential government services.

Second, tax-exempt financing for certain activities of nongovernmental persons resulted in a misallocation of capital. Efficient allocation of capital requires that the return from a marginal unit of investment be equal across activities. This can result, in turn, only if there is no preferential treatment for investment in certain activities. By restricting the ability of nongovernmental activities to qualify for tax-exempt financing, the Act reduces preferential treatment for certain activities and allows capital to be allocated more efficiently.

Third, the equity of the tax system was harmed as high-income taxpayers and corporations limited their tax liability by investing in tax-exempt securities. Because of the large volume of nongovernmental tax-exempt obligations, tax-exempt yields were often close to taxable yields. Taxpayers with high marginal tax rates accordingly received an after-tax yield on tax-exempt bonds significantly higher than the yield they would have received from taxable investments. A perception of inequity arises when such investors are able to reduce their tax liability and still receive a rate of return nearly as high as that on taxable investments.

Finally, rapid growth in the issuance of nongovernmental tax-exempt bonds resulted in mounting revenue losses.

Bonds for governmental activities

The Act retains the ability of qualified governmental units to issue tax-exempt debt for the financing of traditional governmental activities. These include general government operations and the construction and operation of such governmental facilities as schools, roads, government buildings, and governmentally owned and operated sewage, solid waste, water, and electric facilities.

While retaining the ability to issue bonds for governmental purposes, Congress was concerned that, under prior law, a significant amount of bond proceeds from governmental issues was being used to finance private activities not specifically authorized to receive tax-exempt financing. Abuses were noted whereby governmental bond issues were structured intentionally to maximize private use without violating the 25-percent private use limit of prior law. Other bond issues were intentionally structured to "fail" the prior-law IDB security interest test, when the bonds otherwise would be considered IDBs or would not qualify for tax-exemption. Congress believed that this diversion of governmental bond proceeds to nongovernmental users should be limited, but without setting the threshold amount so low that *de minimis* or incidental usage of government facilities and services by private users might cause interest on an issue to be taxable.

To accomplish this, the Act generally defines as a private activity (*i.e.,* nongovernmental) bond any bond of which more than 10 percent of the proceeds is to be used in a trade or business of any person or persons other than a governmental unit, and which is to be directly or indirectly repaid from, or secured by, revenues from a private trade or business. (This is similar to the IDB definition of prior law.) Additionally, a bond is a private activity bond if an amount exceeding the lesser of 5 percent or $5 million of the proceeds is to be used for loans to any person or persons other than a governmental unit. Congress believed that these rules provide an appropriate limit for preventing the diversion of governmental bond proceeds for conduit financing for nongovernmental users, without affecting the availability of tax-exempt financing for traditional governmental activities. * * *

DETAILED ANALYSIS

1.   PROPOSALS TO RESHAPE THE SUBSIDY

Several proposals have sought to reduce the inefficiency and vertical inequities of the current system for dealing with interest on state and local bonds without limiting either the freedom of the state and local governmental units to choose the projects to be financed or the total amount to be provided. For example, consideration has been given to creating a taxable bond option which would provide a federal subsidy payable to a state or local government which elected to issue taxable rather than tax exempt bonds. The subsidy would be equal to some specified percentage of the interest due on the bonds. The percentage would be set so that the net interest rates paid by state and local governments on taxable bonds would be less than would be required if they issued tax exempt bonds.

While several presidential administrations have proposed the taxable bond option (or variants thereof), Congress has never enacted the proposals. In its version of the Tax Reform Act of 1969, the House Ways and Means Committee developed a taxable bond option alternative to tax exemption. Its bill provided that if a state or local government elected to issue a taxable bond, the Treasury Department would be required to pay periodically to the issuing local government, as bond interest payments fell due, from 30 to 40 percent of the interest payment.[23] The provision was not included in the final legislation.

The Senate Finance Committee version of the Revenue Act of 1978 contained an optional tax credit to bondholders who elected to include the interest in taxable income;[24] the provision was deleted on the Senate floor.

2. ARBITRAGE BONDS

During the 1960's, state and local governments utilized their tax-exempt status to engage in "arbitrage" transactions. The governmental unit would issue tax-exempt bonds to private investors and then invest the proceeds in higher yield U.S. securities, which in effect secured the payment of interest and principal of the exempt bonds. The difference between the interest paid by the local government on its bonds and the higher nontaxable interest it received on the U.S. securities constituted profit to be used by the local government for its own purposes. The private higher bracket investors in effect would obtain a federally guaranteed tax-exempt bond. Unchecked, this practice would have no legal limit except the total amount of U.S. obligations outstanding.

In 1969, Congress added a provision to limit the amount of arbitrage that could be earned without the loss of the tax exemption. Under the structure established by the 1986 Act, § 103(b)(2) provides that interest on arbitrage bonds does not qualify for the exemption under § 103(a). Section 148(a) defines an arbitrage bond as an issue in which any portion of the proceeds is used to acquire a higher yield investment or to replace funds that have been so used. While this rule generally results in the inclusion in gross income of the interest on arbitrage bonds, § 148 includes various special rules and exemptions that have the effect of restoring the § 103(a) exemption in certain cases, for example, with issues of general purpose governmental bonds of less than $5 million. Subsequent Acts have refined § 148, a process that can be expected to continue.

3. PRIVATE ACTIVITY BONDS

Even after the 1986 Act, described in the General Explanation above, tax-exempt private activity bonds may still be issued to finance facilities that benefit private sector profit-seeking activities. As noted in the excerpt, an issue qualifies as a private activity bond if more than 10 percent of the proceeds are directed to "private business use," which is defined as use in a trade or business carried on by any person other than a government. I.R.C. § 141(b)(1), (b)(6)(A). There are numerous exceptions, however, that permit the issue of qualified bonds for private activities. Section 144(a) provides an exception for a qualified small issue bond, which is a bond issue of $1 million or less face amount, 95 percent of the proceeds of which are used for the acquisition, construction, or improvement of land or depreciable property. In some circumstances the allowable figure is increased to $10 million, but taking into account capital expenditures under previous bond issues within

---

[23] House Ways and Means Comm., Tax Reform Act of 1969, H.Rep. No. 91–413, 91st Cong. 1st Sess. 172–173 (1969).

[24] Senate Finance Comm., Revenue Act of 1978, S.Rep. No. 95–1263, 95th Cong., 2d Sess. 143–150 (1978).

a 6-year period beginning 3 years before the date of the issue and ending 3 years after the date of the issue. In any event, the qualified small issue bond remains a significant opportunity to direct the benefit of tax-exempt funding to private activity.

Section 142(a) permits the issue of bonds for exempt facilities including, among others, qualified residential rental projects, airports, docks, wharves, mass commuting facilities, sewage facilities, solid waste disposal facilities, facilities for the local furnishing of electric energy, gas, or water, qualified hazardous waste disposal facilities, high speed intercity rail facilities, and environmental enhancements for certain hydroelectric generation facilities. Section 142(a) also provides for issue of bonds for investment in certain empowerment and enterprise zone facilities, as well as to fund "qualified public educational facilities," which are public elementary or secondary school facilities owned by a private corporation pursuant to a partnership agreement with a state or local government, see I.R.C. § 142(k). Section 141(e)(1)(F) allows "qualified redevelopment bonds" to fund acquisition and rehabilitation of property in designated blighted redevelopment areas, see I.R.C. § 144(c).

Tax-exempt bonds may be issued by state and local governments that benefit specific individuals in the form of qualified mortgage bonds (generally restricted to lower-income first-time homebuyers) and qualified mortgage bonds for veterans (I.R.C. § 143), and bonds to finance a student loan program (I.R.C. § 144(b)(1)).

Allowable private activity bonds are subject to overall limitations applicable at the local and state-wide levels. I.R.C. § 146. The aggregate maximum amount of outstanding private activity bonds issued within any state is limited to the greater of $100 multiplied by the state population or $300 million (adjusted annually for inflation). Governmental agencies within a state are limited to 50 percent of the state limitation, allocated among agencies in proportion to the population within each bond-issuing jurisdiction. A state may provide for a different method of allocation. I.R.C. § 146(e). Section 147 provides additional restrictions, including: (i) limiting the maturity of private activity bonds to 120 percent of the economic life of facilities acquired with the bond proceeds; (ii) requiring that the issue be approved by a public governmental body; (iii) limiting the use of proceeds for the acquisition of land to 25 percent (50 percent in the case of an industrial development park); (iv) prohibiting the acquisition of land for farming; (v) requiring that the first use of property acquired with bond proceeds is in connection with the acquisition; and (vi) denying exempt treatment if the bonds are held by a substantial user of property acquired with the bond proceeds. Also, under § 147(e) a private activity bond will not qualify for tax exemption if proceeds are used to provide certain luxuries such as an airplane, skybox, health club, facilities used for gambling, or a liquor store.

4.   INTEREST EXPENSE RELATED TO TAX-EXEMPT INCOME

For a discussion of limitations on the deductibility of interest on indebtedness incurred or continued to purchase or carry tax-exempt bonds, see Chapter 16, Section 3.C.

SECTION 5.   TREATMENT OF THE OWNER OF ANNUITY AND LIFE INSURANCE CONTRACTS

The purchaser of an annuity or a whole life insurance contract makes an initial capital investment in the form of the payment of premiums. The issuer of the contract, usually an insurance company, retains the capital investment represented by the premium payments and returns an interest element that reflects an annual growth in the value of the annuity or insurance policy plus the original investment. An annuity contract provides for periodic payments to the annuitant for a term of years, or for the life of the annuitant. Each payment represents a return of the capital originally invested as payments of premiums, plus an interest element. In the case of whole life insurance policies, the return on the contract includes a return of the invested premiums, the interest element, plus a death benefit. Taxation of annuity and life insurance contracts must account for a return of the capital investment in the contract. In addition, an income tax must address whether and when to include in gross income the growth element of these contracts.

A. ANNUITIES

INTERNAL REVENUE CODE: Sections 61(a)(9); 72(a)–(c), (e)(1)–(4), (q), (u).

REGULATIONS: Sections 1.72–4(a); –5(a)(1)–(3); –9 (Table V).

An annuity represents a current payment of premium in exchange for a promise to make periodic fixed payments to the annuitant in the future, often for the life of the annuitant. Assume, for example, that a taxpayer, age 50, desires to provide for a steady source of income for the taxpayer's his life. The taxpayer purchases an annuity from a life insurance company by paying a single premium in the amount of $100,000. The company agrees to make monthly payments of $1,000 to the taxpayer for the rest of the taxpayer's life. The total number of payments expected to be received is determined by the taxpayer's life expectancy. If the taxpayer is expected to live 33 years, the total amount expected to be received under the contract will be nearly $396,000. The amount of the monthly payment that the insurance company is willing to provide for a given premium depends upon the insurance company's actuarial assumptions about the taxpayer's life expectancy and the rate of interest the company will pay on the taxpayer's initial investment.[25] Thus, payments under the annuity contract reflect not only a return of the taxpayer's initial $100,000 investment, but also an income element since the total anticipated payments based on the taxpayer's life expectancy will exceed the capital invested.

The application of the return of capital concept to annuities raises several questions because the taxpayer recovers the investment over a

---

[25]   If the taxpayer's expected life is 33 years, this annuity represents an annual return of approximately 9.8 percent.

series of payments instead of receiving a single payment. Should all payments received by the taxpayer be treated as a replacement of capital until the total amount of the premium payment has been recovered, with the interest element taxed only after the amount of the premium has been restored? Or should each payment be divided into a capital and income element? In enacting § 72, Congress chose to treat each payment as part capital recovery and part taxable income. The Code and regulations provide detailed rules to determine the method of allocating each annuity payment between taxable interest income and tax-free return of capital. In general, § 72 enables a taxpayer to recover tax free the taxpayer's total investment in the annuity contract ratably over the taxpayer's projected life expectancy. This treatment defers taxation on the growth element in the annuity until payments are received.

Isn't the investment already taxed money?

The amount of each annuity payment excluded from income is determined by the "exclusion ratio" as defined in § 72(b). Treas. Reg. § 1.72–4. The numerator of the ratio is the "investment in the contract" (Treas. Reg. § 1.72–6) and the denominator is the "expected return under the contract" (Treas. Reg. § 1.72–5). The expected return under the contract is determined from actuarial tables set forth in Treas. Reg. § 1.72–9.

In the case of the 50-year-old taxpayer described above, Treas. Reg. § 1.72–9 (Table V) indicates that the taxpayer's life expectancy (at least for tax purposes) is 33.1 years. The expected return is therefore $397,200 ($1,000 × 12 months × 33.1 years). The exclusion ratio is 25.2 percent ($100,000/$397,200), so $252 of each monthly payment is a return of capital, while the remaining $748 is included in gross income.

Most annuity contracts provide for a refund of a portion of the premium if the annuitant does not survive for a specified minimum number of years. (Often this feature is required by state law.) Section 72(c)(2) requires that the actuarial value of the refund feature be subtracted from the taxpayer's investment in the contract in computing the exclusion ratio (which, in the above example, would reduce the exclusion ratio and thereby increase the amount allocated to taxable income in each payment). The value of the refund feature is determined under Treas. Regs. §§ 1.72–7 and –9 (Table VII).

Naturally, an annuitant may die before or after the date assumed by his projected life expectancy. If the individual lives longer than the individual's projected life expectancy, the individual realizes what is called a "mortality gain." That is to say, the individual realizes more on the annuity contract than was originally anticipated. Conversely, if the taxpayer dies before the taxpayer's projected life expectancy, a mortality loss occurs when the taxpayer does not receive payment sufficient to recover the investment in the contract. Section 72(b)(2) limits the exclusion under § 72(b)(1) to the taxpayer's unrecovered investment in the contract. As a result, mortality gains are taxed in full as payments are received. Section 72(b)(3) permits a deduction for mortality losses if payments cease by reason of the death of the taxpayer and the taxpayer has not recovered the investment in the contract. The deduction is only available if the annuitant's date of death is after the annuity starting date. Thus, no deduction is allowed if the annuitant dies before payments under the annuity have begun. See I.R.C. § 72(b)(3)(A)(i).

If amounts that are not annuity payments are received after the annuity starting date, § 72(e) applies rather than § 72(b). Thus, for example, policy dividends received after the annuity starting date are included in income in full and are not subject to the exclusion ratio of § 72(b). See I.R.C. § 72(e)(2)(A). Loans from an annuity contract are treated as distributions includable in income to the extent that cash surrender value exceeds the investment in the contract. I.R.C. § 72(e)(4)(A). If, however, the payments are received on the surrender, redemption, or maturity of the contract, the amount taxable is the excess of the amount received over the investment in the contract. I.R.C. § 72(e)(5)(A), (E) and (6). If, on the surrender of the contract, the taxpayer receives less than the original investment in the contract, reduced by previous exclusions, the resulting loss is deductible. Rev. Rul. 61–201, 1961–2 C.B. 46.

DETAILED ANALYSIS

1. DEFERRED ANNUITIES

Suppose that the 50-year-old taxpayer described above, rather than purchasing an annuity providing for payments commencing immediately, purchases an annuity under which payments do not commence until the taxpayer reaches age 65. During the period between payment of the premium and commencement of the annuity payments (15 years in this example), interest is earned on the annuity policy and, for purposes of computing the amount of the monthly payments commencing when the taxpayer reaches age 65, the insurance company treats the interest accruals as additional purchase price. Inclusion of the interest in income is deferred for tax purposes until the taxpayer receives payments under the annuity. The interest will not be treated under § 72 as investment in the contract and normally will be taxed to the annuitant under the rules of § 72(b) when the payments are received. Thus, the interest accrues free of tax until withdrawn as part of the annuity payment.

Deferred annuity policies typically permit amounts to be withdrawn prior to the annuity starting date. Prior to 1982, early withdrawals were treated as representing a return of capital and were tax free until the full amount of the taxpayer's investment in the contract had been received. Only withdrawals in excess of the amount invested were taxable. In the late 1970's insurance companies began to market deferred annuities, emphasizing how the benefits of tax deferral and the favorable treatment given to withdrawals prior to the annuity starting date allowed the interest income to be distributed without producing gross income. In 1982, Congress revised the treatment in § 72(e) for payments received before the annuity starting date because, while it believed that existing rules were appropriate for annuity contracts intended "to meet long-term investment goals, such as income security * * * their use for short-term investment and income tax deferral should be discouraged." Senate Finance Committee Report, S.Rep. No. 97–494, vol. 1, 97th Cong., 2d Sess. 350 (1982).

Under § 72(e)(2)(B) and (3), cash withdrawals (including policy loans) are includable in income to the extent the cash value of the contract exceeds the annuity owner's investment in the contract at the time of withdrawal. These provisions reverse the ordering rule of prior law (cash withdrawals first applied to a return of capital) and cause the previously-deferred interest to be taxed first; only after the interest has been fully included in income do the amounts received constitute tax-free returns of capital. Section 72(e)(5)(C) and (D) continue the ordering rule of prior law for amounts withdrawn under life insurance and endowment contracts and qualified employee retirement plans.

Section 72(e)(4)(C) provides that an owner of an annuity who transfers the contract for less than adequate consideration realizes income under § 72(e)(2)(B) equal to the excess of the cash surrender value of the contract at the time of the transfer over the owner's investment in the contract. Thus, the owner of an annuity contract cannot shift the tax-deferred inside build-up by, for example, making a gift of the contract to a child or a trust for the child. The transferee has an investment in the annuity contract equal to the original owner's investment plus the income recognized under § 72(e)(4)(C). In addition, § 72(u) eliminates the deferral of tax on the inside build-up of annuity contracts where the holder of the contract is not a "natural person," e.g., a corporation.

If the owner-annuitant of a deferred annuity contract dies before the annuity starting date, any amounts received by a beneficiary in excess of the owner-annuitant's investment in the contract are includable in gross income as income in respect of a decedent under § 691 (discussed at Chapter 7, Section 4), subject to the rules of § 72 if the beneficiary receives an annuity rather than a lump-sum. Rev. Rul. 2005–30, 2005–1 C.B. 1015.

Section 72(q) imposes a penalty on amounts withdrawn prior to the annuity starting date. This provision is designed to deter taxpayers from purchasing deferred annuities for the benefits of tax deferral and then cashing the policy before any annuity payments are made. The penalty is equal to 10 percent of the amount which is includable in the income of the taxpayer under the rules discussed above. Section 72(q)(2) sets forth exceptions to the penalty provision including distributions by reason of the death or disability of the annuitant and distributions made after the annuitant has reached age 59½.

2. TAX INCENTIVES

The benefit of deferred annuities can be illustrated by comparison with the illustration at the beginning of this section. If a 50 year old taxpayer purchases a deferred annuity for $100,000 that is calculated on a rate of return of 5 percent compounded semi-annually, and which begins semi-annual payments at age 65 for the remainder of the taxpayer's life expectancy, say 18 years, the annuity payments will be $8,905 at the end of each six-month period.[26] The expected payment over the remaining 18 years of the taxpayer's life expectancy is $320,562, an overall gain of $220,562. Thus, the exclusion ratio for each payment is $100,000/$320,562. Each payment represents $2,778 return of capital and $6,127 of gain. At the 35 percent tax bracket, the taxpayer's net return on each payment is $6,761 after tax and thus the taxpayer's total after-tax return on the annuity (assuming the annuity ceases at age 83) is $243,365 consisting of $100,000 return of initial capital and $143,365 of net after-tax gain.[27] The tax burden on this gain is 35 percent, the same as the taxpayer's nominal tax rate (1 − $143,365/$220,562).

If instead of purchasing an annuity contract, the taxpayer had at age 50 deposited $100,000 in a savings account paying 5 percent interest, compounded semi-annually, which is subject to tax each year, at age 65 the taxpayer would have accumulated $162,187. If that amount were converted into an annuity payable over the remaining 18 years of the taxpayer's life expectancy, the taxpayer would receive $6,885 every six-months. The investment in the contract is $162,187 and the taxpayer's expected payments are $247,864. Each payment consists of $4,505 return of capital ($6,885 $162,187/$247,864), $2,380 of income, and the tax liability is $833, leaving the taxpayer with $6,052 after tax. Here the taxpayer ends up with a total return of $217,877 consisting of $100,000 return of initial capital and $117,877 of net after-tax gain. Comparing this gain with the gain on the investment before-tax produces a total tax burden of 46.56 percent, which is 11.56 percent higher than the total tax burden imposed on the purchased annuity. The difference in these tax burdens will vary with the length of deferral and the yield in the annuity contract, the longer the period of deferral and the higher the yield, the more valuable the tax benefit.

---

[26]   The cash value of the $100,000 initial investment grows to $209,757 by the time the taxpayer reaches age 65. The taxpayer's remaining life expectancy is 18 years. At 5 percent compounded semi-annually, the annuity would provide for semi-annual payments of $8,905. These numbers are rounded off which creates some discrepancies in the totals.

[27]   The net return consists of $109,757 of tax-deferred inside build-up for the first 15 years of the contract, plus an additional $110,805 of interest accrued during the annuity pay-out period.

Table 7

	Deferred Annuity	Savings Account
Initial Deposit	$100,000	$100,000
After-tax Value, Age 65	$209,757	$162,187
Annuity Payments	$ 8,905	$ 6,885
Return of Capital	$ 2,778	$ 4,505
Gross Income	$ 6,127	$ 2,380
Tax	$ 2,145	$ 833
Net Annuity Payment	$ 6,761	$ 6,052
Overall Tax Burden	35.00%	46.56%

The difference between the net after-tax return on the taxpayer's investment in a deferred annuity and the amount that would be paid if the taxpayer had utilized a taxable savings vehicle during the deferral period, $25,488, would likely be captured in part by the insurance company selling the annuity. A deferred annuity will typically pay a lower rate of interest than taxable investment vehicles, or sell for a higher price (which is effectively the same thing). The reduction in explicit tax achieved from the favorable tax treatment is converted into an implicit tax in the form of a lower before-tax rate of return.

3. VARIABLE ANNUITIES

In the 1970's, insurance companies began marketing contracts that not only promised tax deferral for high-yield investments, but also permitted the policy holder to designate the investments into which the premium payments were to be made by the insurance company, so-called "wrap-around" or "investment annuities." Rev. Rul. 77–85, 1977–1 C.B. 12, held that income earned under such "investment annuities" did not qualify for the tax deferral privilege accorded ordinary annuity contracts and treated the policyholder as the owner of the underlying investments. As a result, the income from the investments was currently taxed directly to the policyholder. Insurance companies also offered deferred annuity policies in which, though the policyholder did not have the right to direct the investment, the insurance company agreed to invest the premiums in specified assets, such as certificates of deposit or a mutual fund. In Rev. Rul. 80–274, 1980–2 C.B. 27, and Rev. Rul. 81–225, 1981–2 C.B. 12, the IRS ruled that in those situations the insurance company was simply a conduit between the policyholders and the underlying assets; as a result, the assets were treated as owned for tax purposes directly by the policyholders.

In 1984, Congress enacted § 817(h) to discourage the use of annuities and life insurance contracts as investment vehicles. It requires that premiums be aggregated into a segregated asset account, which is an account separate from the general asset accounts of the company issuing an annuity or life insurance contract. Section 817(h) provides that the arrangement will not be treated as an annuity or life insurance contract unless the segregated asset account is adequately diversified in accordance with regulations. Treas. Reg. § 1.817–5(b)(1) requires that no more than 55 percent of the assets of a segregated fund may be invested in a single asset, that no more than 70 percent of the assets may be invested in any two assets, that no more than 80 percent of the fund may be invested in any three assets, and that no more than 90 percent of the fund may be invested in any four assets. Treas. Reg. § 1.817–5(f) provides a "look-thru" rule in the case of an investment in certain partnerships or other entities that applies the diversification test to the assets of the entity, rather than treating the entity as a single asset.

In Rev. Rul. 2003–91, 2003–2 C.B. 347, the IRS ruled that an annuity or life insurance contract that permitted the policy holder to allocate the policy premium among as many as 20 sub-accounts reflecting different investment strategies (each of which met the asset diversification requirements of Treas. Reg. § 1.817–5) is a valid annuity or life insurance arrangement. The ruling concluded that, "The investment strategies of the Sub-accounts currently available are sufficiently broad to prevent [the taxpayer] from making particular investment decisions through investment in a Sub-account." In Rev. Rul. 2003–92, 2003–2 C.B. 350, however, the IRS held that an arrangement failed to qualify as an annuity or life insurance contract where policy holders were permitted to allocate premiums among sub-accounts that invested in partnership interests that were available to the public in private placements (i.e., non-publicly traded partnership interests exempt from securities registration). The policy holders were required to include earnings from the investments in gross income as the owners of the underlying assets.[28]

4. POLICY ASPECTS OF DEFERRED ANNUITIES

The discussion of deferred annuities and wrap-around annuities underscores the problems that arise from providing different tax consequences for similar types of investment. Even when the policyholder has no right to choose directly or indirectly the investment portfolio of the insurance company, the question is whether the deferral of tax provided by the traditional annuity rules is appropriate during the period prior to the beginning of the payout under the annuity policy. The 1982 amendments discussed above continued the basic policy of deferral, but provided that to the extent of the interest build-up certain withdrawals are income and not a return of capital. Legislation proposed in 1978, but not enacted, would have taxed the policyholder currently on income earned during the accumulation period. U.S. Treas. Dept., The President's 1978 Tax Program, 180–192 (1978). A similar proposal (also not enacted) was made by the Treasury Department in 1984 and incorporated into the President's 1985 tax reform proposals:

> Investment income earned on deferred annuities is similar to investment income earned on other savings instruments with other financial institutions. Interest on savings accounts and certificates

---

[28] Treas. Reg. § 1.817–5(f)(2) provides that investments in partnership interests that are available for purchase by persons other than insurance companies are not subject to the look-through rules of Treas. Reg. § 1.817–5(f).

of deposits is taxed currently, however, while investment income earned on annuities is not taxed until withdrawal. * * *

Since tax-favored annuities can be purchased only from life insurance companies, this tax deferral directs the flow of savings toward life insurance companies and away from other financial institutions. There is no reason to favor savings through insurance companies over savings through competing financial institutions.

The deferral of tax on investment income credited to deferred annuities is available only to persons with disposable income available for savings and is of greatest benefit to persons in the highest tax brackets. The tax deferral thus favors wealthier individuals.

U.S. Treasury Department, Tax Reform for Fairness, Simplicity, and Economic Growth, Vol. 2, 266 (1984); President Reagan's "Tax Proposals to the Congress for Fairness, Growth and Simplicity," Chapter 10.07 (1985).

5.   PRIVATE ANNUITIES

In some situations, an individual owning property may desire to exchange property for an annuity, but to keep the property within the family unit. For example, a parent owning stock of a closely held corporation or a family farm may transfer the property to a child in return for the promise of the child to pay the parent an annuity for life. The return of capital and ordinary income elements of each payment are generally determined as in the case of commercial annuities, although different actuarial assumptions may be required.

If the property transferred in exchange for a private annuity has appreciated in value, a capital gain may result. Rev. Rul. 69–74, 1969–1 C.B. 43, provides that gain realized on the exchange is recognized as payments are received by the annuitant.[29] Since realized gain is not recognized on the transfer of appreciated property for an annuity, the annuitant's investment in the contract is the adjusted basis of the transferred property, not its fair market value.

Proposed regulations, first published in 2006 and still pending, would significantly change the treatment of private annuities to align their taxation with the treatment of commercial annuities. Prop. Reg. § 1.1001–1(j) (2006) would provide that if property is exchanged for an annuity, the amount realized attributable to the annuity contract is its fair market value (determined under § 7520) at the time of the exchange. The entire amount of the gain or loss realized on the exchange must be recognized in the year of the exchange. At the same time, the initial investment in the annuity contract under § 72(c)(1) equals the amount realized with respect to the annuity contract (i.e., the fair market value of the annuity contract). Prop. Reg. § 1.72–6(e)(1) (2006). Thus, under the proposal, if the fair market value of the exchanged property equals the fair market value of the received

---

[29]   Under Rev. Rul. 69–74, gain is determined by treating the present value of the annuity as the amount realized for the property. The excess of the fair market value of the property, if any, over the present value of the annuity is treated as a gift from the annuitant to the other party.

annuity contract, the investment in the annuity contract would equal the fair market value of the exchanged property.

6.   EMPLOYEE ANNUITIES

A retired employee may receive a pension in the form of an annuity. Section 72(d) provides special rules for the treatment of such payments when made under qualified employee retirement benefit plans.

B. LIFE INSURANCE

INTERNAL REVENUE CODE: Sections 61(a)(10); 72(e)(1), (2), (5)(A)–(C), (6); (h); 101(a), (c), (d); see also 7702; 7702A.

REGULATIONS: Sections 1.101–1(a)(1); –2(a), (d); –4(a)(1).

Section 101(a)(1) excludes from gross income the payment of benefits under a life insurance policy on the death of the insured.

The owner of a life insurance policy makes an investment in the life insurance contract with the payment of premiums. (The owner of the policy is often the insured, but may also be a family member, trust, or someone with a business relationship to the insured.) The nature of that investment depends on the type of life insurance. In the case of term life insurance, the owner is purchasing life insurance protection only. In purchasing term insurance the owner is in effect making an annual bet with the life insurance company as to whether the insured will survive the period of insurance protection. If the owner of the policy "wins" the wager, the beneficiaries will receive a tax-free payment at the death of the insured that is far in excess of the cost of the policy. If the owner "loses" the wager, the insured will have lost the premium for the insurance protection in the period concerned. The owner may not feel the owner has truly lost, however, because the owner has had the security provided by the presence of the insurance during the year. As to the insurance company, the risk of losing this wager is spread over a large number of policies so that, in the aggregate, the amount received as premiums will be sufficient to provide death benefits to insureds who die during the year. To determine the cost of term insurance, the insurance company thus will collect premiums from each member of the group of insureds within an age bracket sufficient to pay benefits to members of the group who die during the year. Each year as the group of insureds within an age bracket gets smaller, and the risk of death increases because of age, the premium charged by the insurance company increases.

The pure life insurance protection provided by term insurance is to be contrasted with the more complex investment made by the taxpayer who purchases a so-called *ordinary* (or whole) life insurance contract. Rather than having the premiums increase as the actuarial risk increases, ordinary life insurance contracts provide for a level premium payment throughout the period of the policy. These payments exceed the cost of pure life insurance protection during the early years of the policy and the excess payments plus the earnings on those payments (the policy's "terminal reserve") in effect fund an increasing portion of the cost of pure life insurance protection in the later years of the policy. Thus, the ordinary life insurance policy represents both the acquisition of insurance protection and a savings element. The savings element—the excess of the premium paid over the cost of the pure insurance protection—is invested by the company and earns interest. As the pool of money representing the savings element increases, the amount of term insurance necessary to pay the death benefit is reduced. As a consequence, the accumulation of interest income under the policy reduces the amount of continued term insurance, and thereby reduces the premium. The accrued interest also avoids increased premiums as the pool of insureds in any given age group gets smaller. Under current law, the interest element accruing on the portion of the taxpayer's premium which represents savings is not currently taxed. Section 101 permits the tax-free receipt of both the savings element and the insurance proceeds on the death of the insured.

An insured who surrenders an ordinary life policy during life will receive a payment that includes the savings portion of the policy premiums and the earnings on that portion (less a charge for expenses and a profit factor, the so-called "load factor"). Under § 72(e)(5) and (6), the taxpayer will be taxed only on the excess of the amount received over the investment in the contract, which is defined to include the total amount of the premiums paid, including the portions representing the purchase of pure insurance protection and the load factor. The taxpayer is, in effect, allowed to deduct the personal costs of maintaining life insurance for the period the policy was in effect from the gross income upon surrender of the policy. The taxpayer who surrenders the policy during life receives a double benefit: the tax on the earnings element in the policy is deferred to the date of surrender and, in addition, the taxpayer is allowed to offset a portion of the taxpayer's personal costs for insurance, which was funded by untaxed earnings, against the amounts received. The advantage becomes clearer if one compares the purchase of an ordinary life policy with someone who purchases term insurance and invests the difference between the ordinary premium and the term premium in a bank account. The interest accruing on the bank account will be taxable currently and the amount spent for insurance protection including any sales commission will be a nondeductible personal cost that cannot be used to offset the interest for purposes of computing income.

Various types of life insurance policies have savings elements that are significantly greater, in relation to the amount of pure insurance protection, than the savings element present in ordinary life insurance. The enhanced savings feature is achieved by charging even larger premium payments during the earlier years of the policy than under ordinary life insurance.

DETAILED ANALYSIS

1.   DEFINITION OF INSURANCE

Various policies, often referred to as "flexible premium" or "universal life" policies, historically allowed the owner to determine the mix of the savings and the protection elements of a life insurance policy. These policies often provided high guaranteed interest rates (at least for short time periods) and were marketed to compete with noninsurance investments. Flexible premium policies often were comprised almost entirely of savings; a nominal amount of life insurance protection was provided to attempt to make the earnings exempt from taxation.

Section 7702 defines life insurance in a way that limits the extent to which policies may emphasize the savings feature. Congress enacted this provision because policies were becoming "overly investment oriented by allowing large cash value build-ups without requiring a continued reasonable amount of pure insurance protection." S.Rep. No. 97–494, 97th Cong., 2d Sess. 352 (1982). Extremely complicated and detailed, § 7702 provides that a policy, to qualify as life insurance for tax purposes, must meet one of two alternative tests. One of these tests, the "cash value accumulation test" was "intended to allow traditional whole life policies, with cash values that accumulate based on reasonable interest rates, to continue to qualify as life insurance contracts. Certain contracts that have been traditionally sold by life insurance companies, such as endowment contracts [which provide a fixed return on the earlier of the death of the insured or the end of a fixed period] will not continue to be classified as life insurance contracts because of their innate investment orientation." Staff of the Joint Committee on Taxation, General Explanation of the Revenue Provisions of the Deficit Reduction Act of 1984, 647 (Dec. 31, 1984).

If a life insurance contract fails to meet the standards of § 7702, the interest income element of the contract is taxable to the policyholder as ordinary income in the year in which the income is paid or accrued, thereby eliminating the benefit of deferral. I.R.C. § 7702(g)(1). Payments on the death of the insured in excess of the cash surrender value are treated as paid under a life insurance contract for purposes of § 101. I.R.C. § 7702(g)(2). Presumably, the net surrender value would be excludable from the income of the recipient of the proceeds under § 101 but the statute is not explicit on this point.

In 1988, Congress further tightened the definition of life insurance by enacting § 7702A. Section 7702A was intended to increase the level of insurance protection provided by a contract during the first seven years of the contract. H.Rep. No. 100–795, 100th Cong., 2d Sess. 479 (1988). An insurance contract that fails the so-called "7-pay test"[30] of § 7702A is treated as a "modified endowment contract." Although the inside build-up in value of a modified endowment contract is not taxed currently, any payments

---

[30]   The 7-pay test is met if the cumulative amount paid under the contract at any time during the first 7 years of the contract exceeds the sum of the net level premiums that would have been paid on or before such time had the contract provided for paid-up future benefits after the payment of 7 level annual premiums. I.R.C. § 7702A(b).

received under the contract (including loans) during the owner's lifetime must be included in income first (before there is any recovery of capital) to the extent that cash surrender value exceeds the investment in the contract. I.R.C. § 72(e)(10). In addition, the 10 percent penalty tax under § 72(q) is imposed on payments received under a modified endowment contract that must be included in gross income.

2.   TAX POLICY ASPECTS

The annual increase in the cash value of a life insurance policy during the insured's life represents an increase in the policyholder's net worth that is readily accessible and, from a tax policy perspective, should be taxed currently. Modern electronic data processing methods render current taxation of the accruing income administratively feasible. The preferential treatment currently given to the savings element in life insurance policies is sometimes justified on the ground that the purchase of life insurance protection should be encouraged by the government to help ensure that those dependent on family breadwinners have sufficient funds when that source of financial support is gone. This nontax policy objective could be implemented through the tax system by exempting from taxation only the mortality gain with respect to the pure insurance element of policies with an investment feature. But the current rules continue to provide disproportionate incentive for the investment feature of ordinary life insurance relative to other savings and investment alternatives.

If the increase in cash value is not taxed currently, this income element should at least be taxed when withdrawn as in the case of annuities and modified endowment contracts. In calculating the amount includable in income, an appropriate adjustment in the taxpayer's investment in the policy would be made to reflect the portion of the premiums paid attributable to the protection element of the policy. This approach would still allow the advantage of tax deferral but would eliminate the current failure to tax the interest element that is offset against the premium charge attributable to life insurance protection.

The 1984 Treasury Proposals and President's Reagan's 1985 Proposals recommended current taxation of the annual increase in the cash value of life insurance policies (for many of the same reasons that it recommended currently taxing income of deferred annuities during the accumulation period). The following excerpt from U.S. Treasury Department, Tax Reform for Fairness, Simplicity, and Economic Growth, Vol. 2, 259–262 (1984) lists some of these reasons, all of which remain relevant today as policymakers consider the equity and efficiency effects of how we tax life insurance policies and annuities:

> The benefit of deferring or avoiding tax on the inside interest build-up on life insurance policies goes only to individuals with excess disposable income that enables them to save, and particularly to individuals in high tax brackets. This benefit is not available to lower income taxpayers and other individuals buying term insurance since it derives solely from the investment

component of a policy (which is not present in a term insurance policy).

The tax-favored treatment of inside interest build-up encourages individuals to save through life insurance companies rather than other financial institutions and perhaps to purchase life insurance that they would not buy except to gain access to the favorable tax treatment of the investment income. This distorts the flow of savings and investment in the economy.

The Treasury Department further detailed the inequitable distribution of cash value life insurance policies by household income. High-income families were not only more likely to invest in cash value policies; they also derived significantly greater amounts of annual, tax-deferred interest income from both insurance and annuity policies. The Treasury estimated that in 1983, the average tax-deferred inside build-up under these policies for families with income over $200,000 (about $480,000 in 2016 dollars) exceeded $3,000 annually ($7,200 adjusted) compared to less than $200 ($480 adjusted) for families with income under $30,000 ($72,000 adjusted). In concluding its discussion of the inequitable distribution of tax benefits, the Treasury correctly predicted that "the difference between the amount of inside interest build-up earned by wealthier individuals and that earned by less wealthy individuals is expected to grow in the future."

CHAPTER 9

DAMAGE AWARDS AND SETTLEMENTS AND INSURANCE RECOVERIES

Determining the treatment of damage awards can be complex. No single unifying theory explains the varying answers in all cases. The complexity is attributable, in part, to the special statutory treatment accorded certain damage awards and similar receipts under § 104. Complexity also results from judicial decisions interpreting the statutory predecessors of § 61, which focus on identifying the loss for which the damages were received. If the damages are received in lieu of receipts that would have been taxable, such as lost business profits or lost wages, then the damage award is taxable, but if the damage award was received in lieu of nontaxable receipts or to compensate for a loss of capital, then the damage award is not taxable. When damages are received with respect to stolen or damaged property, the award may compensate the owner for the cost of the property, unrealized appreciation, and lost income, thus requiring a complex allocation of the damages, which might not have occurred in the damage suit itself, in order to characterize the receipts for tax purposes.

As early as 1918, the statutory predecessor of § 104(a)(2) provided a broad exclusion for damages received on account of "personal injury." Early cases and rulings extended the "recovery of capital" principle to damage awards for loss of and injuries to personal rights, often without express reliance on the statutory exclusion. See e.g., Rev. Rul. 54–19, 1954–1 C.B. 179 (damages for wrongful-death), obsoleted by Rev. Rul. 2007–14, 2007–1 C.B. 747; Rev. Rul. 55–132, 1955–1 C.B. 213 (payments to prisoners of war because of enemy violations of the Geneva Convention regarding obligations respecting the treatment of prisoners); Rev. Rul. 69–212, 1969–1 C.B. 34 (pension payments by the Austrian government to victims of Nazi persecution), obsoleted by Rev. Rul. 2007–14, 2007–1 C.B. 747; Hawkins v. Commissioner, 6 B.T.A. 1023 (1927) (Acq.) (damages for libel and slander).

SECTION 1.   DAMAGES RECEIVED ON ACCOUNT OF PROPERTY AND LOST PROFITS

Clark v. Commissioner

United States Board of Tax Appeals, 1939.
40 B.T.A. 333.

■ LEECH: This is a proceeding to redetermine a deficiency in income tax for the calendar year 1934 in the amount of $10,618.87. The question presented is whether petitioner derived income by the payment to him of an amount of $19,941.10, by his tax counsel, to compensate him for a loss suffered on account of erroneous advice given him by the latter. [Tax counsel had advised the filing of a joint return by petitioner and his wife whereas the filing of separate returns would have saved $19,941.10 in taxes.] * * *

The theory on which the respondent included the above sum of $19,941.10 in petitioner's gross income for 1934, is that this amount constituted taxes paid for petitioner by a third party and that, consequently, petitioner was in receipt of income to that extent. The cases of Old Colony Trust Co. v. Commissioner, 279 U.S. 716; United States v. Boston & Maine Railroad, 279 U.S. 732, are cited as authority for his position. Petitioner, on the contrary, contends that this payment constituted compensation for damages or loss caused by the error of tax counsel, and that he therefore realized no income from its receipt in 1934.

We agree with petitioner. The cases cited by the respondent are not applicable here. Petitioner's taxes were not paid for him by any person— as rental, compensation for services rendered, or otherwise. He paid his own taxes.

When the joint return was filed, petitioner became obligated to and did pay the taxes computed on that basis. * * * In paying that obligation, he sustained a loss which was caused by the negligence of his tax counsel. The $19,941.10 was paid to petitioner, not qua taxes * * *, but as compensation to petitioner for his loss. The measure of that loss, and the compensation therefor, was the sum of money which petitioner became legally obligated to and did pay because of that negligence. The fact that such obligation was for taxes is of no moment here.

* * *

[T]he fact that the payment of the compensation for such loss was voluntary, as here, does not change its exempt status. Rice, Barton & Fales Inc. v. Commissioner, 41 F.2d 339. It was, in fact, compensation for a loss which impaired petitioner's capital.

Moreover, so long as petitioner neither could nor did take a deduction in a prior year of this loss in such a way as to offset income for the prior year, the amount received by him in the taxable year, by way of

recompense, is not then includable in his gross income. Central Loan &
Investment Co., 39 B.T.A. 981.

Decision will be entered for the petitioner.   *— Holding*

Raytheon Production Corp. v. Commissioner

United States Court of Appeals, First Circuit, 1944.
144 F.2d 110.

■ MAHONEY, CIRCUIT JUDGE.

This case presents the question whether an amount received by the *— Issue*
taxpayer in compromise settlement of a suit for damages under the
Federal Anti-Trust Laws, 15 U.S.C.A. § 1 et seq., is a non-taxable return
of capital or income. * * * The original Raytheon Company was a pioneer
manufacturer of a rectifying tube which made possible the operation of a
radio receiving set on alternating current instead of on batteries. In 1926
its profits were about $450,000; in 1927 about $150,000; and in 1928,
$10,000. The Radio Corporation of America had many patents covering
radio circuits and claimed control over almost all of the practical circuits.
Cross-licensing agreements had been made among several companies
including R.C.A., General Electric Company, Westinghouse, and
American Telephone & Telegraph Company. R.C.A. had developed a
competitive tube which produced the same type of rectification as the *FACTS*
Raytheon tube. Early in 1927, R.C.A. began to license manufacturers of
radio sets and in the license agreement it incorporated "Clause 9", which
provided that the licensee was required to buy its tubes from R.C.A. In
1928 practically all manufacturers were operating under R.C.A. licenses.
As a consequence of this restriction, Raytheon was left with only
replacement sales, which soon disappeared. When Raytheon found it
impossible to market its tubes in the early part of 1929, it obtained a
license from R.C.A. to manufacture tubes under the letters patent on a
royalty basis. The license agreement contained a release of all claims of
Raytheon against R.C.A. by reason of the illegal acts of the latter under
Clause 9 but by a side agreement such claims could be asserted if R.C.A.
should pay similar claims to others. The petitioner was informed of
instances in which R.C.A. had settled claims against it based on Clause
9. On that ground it considered itself released from the agreement not to
enforce its claim against R.C.A. and consequently, on December 14, 1931,
the petitioner caused its predecessor, Raytheon, to bring suit against
R.C.A. in the District Court of Massachusetts alleging that the plaintiff
had by 1926 created and then possessed a large and valuable good will in
interstate commerce in rectifying tubes for radios and had a large and
profitable established business therein so that the net profit for the year
1926 was $454,935; that the business had an established prospect of
large increases and that the business and good will thereof was of a value
of exceeding $3,000,000; that by the beginning of 1927 the plaintiff was
doing approximately 80% of the business of rectifying tubes of the entire
United States; that the defendant conspired to destroy the business of

the plaintiff and others by a monopoly of such business and did suppress and destroy the existing companies; that the manufacturers of radio sets and others ceased to purchase tubes from the plaintiffs; that by the end of 1927 the conspiracy had completely destroyed the profitable business and that by the early part of 1928 the tube business of the plaintiff and its property and good will had been totally destroyed at a time when it had a present value in excess of $3,000,000, and thereby the plaintiff was injured in its business and property in a sum in excess of $3,000,000. The action against R.C.A. was referred to an auditor who found that Clause 9 was not the cause of damage to the plaintiff but that the decline in plaintiff's business was due to advancement in the radio art and competition. The auditor, however, also found that if it should be decided that Clause 9 had turned the development of the radio art away from plaintiff's type of tube, then the damages would be $1,000,000.

In the spring of 1938, after the auditor's report and just prior to the time for the commencement of the trial before a jury, the Raytheon affiliated companies began negotiations for the settlement of the litigation with R.C.A. In the meantime a suit brought by R.C.A. against the petitioner for the non-payment of royalties resulted in a judgment of $410,000 in favor of R.C.A. R.C.A. and the petitioner finally agreed on the payment by R.C.A. of $410,000 in settlement of the anti trust action. R.C.A. required the inclusion in the settlement of patent license rights and sublicensing rights to some thirty patents but declined to allocate the amount paid as between the patent license rights and the amount for the settlement of the suit. The agreement of settlement contained a general release of any and all possible claims between the parties.

The officers of the Raytheon companies testified that $60,000 of the $410,000 received from R.C.A. was the maximum worth of the patents, basing their appraisal on the cost of development of the patents and the fact that few of them were then being used and that no royalties were being derived from them. In its income tax return the petitioner returned $60,000 of the $410,000 as income from patent licenses and treated the remaining $350,000 as a realization from a chose in action and not as taxable income. The Commissioner determined that the $350,000 constituted income on the following ground contained in the statement attached to his notice of deficiency: "It is the opinion of this office that the amount of $350,000 constitutes income under [§ 61]. There exists no clear evidence of what the amount was paid for so that an accurate apportionment can be made as to a specific consideration for patent rights transferred to Radio Corporation of America and a consideration for damages. The amount of $350,000 has therefore been included in your taxable income." * * *

Damages recovered in an antitrust action are not necessarily nontaxable as a return of capital. As in other types of tort damage suits, recoveries which represent a reimbursement for lost profits are income. Swastika Oil & Gas Co. v. Commissioner, 6 Cir., 1941, 123 F.2d 382, certiorari denied 1943, 317 U.S. 639; H. Liebes & Co. v. Commissioner, 9 Cir., 1937, 90 F.2d 932; * * * . The reasoning is that since the profits would be taxable income, the proceeds of litigation which are their substitute are taxable in like manner.

Damages for violation of the anti-trust acts are treated as ordinary income where they represent compensation for loss of profits. Commercial Electrical Supply Co. v. Commissioner, 1927, 8 B.T.A. 986 * * * .

The test is not whether the action was one in tort or contract but rather the question to be asked is "In lieu of what were the damages awarded?" Farmers' & Merchants' Bank v. Commissioner, 6 Cir., 1932, 59 F.2d 912; Swastika Oil & Gas Co. v. Commissioner, supra * * * . Where the suit is not to recover lost profits but is for injury to good will, the recovery represents a return of capital and, with certain limitations to be set forth below, is not taxable. Farmers' & Merchants' Bank v. Commissioner, supra. * * *

Upon examination of Raytheon's declaration in its anti-trust suit we find nothing to indicate that the suit was for the recovery of lost profits. The allegations were that the illegal conduct of R.C.A. "completely destroyed the profitable interstate and foreign commerce of the plaintiff and thereby, by the early part of 1928, the said tube business of the plaintiff and the property good will of the plaintiff therein had been totally destroyed at a time when it then had a present value in excess of three million dollars and thereby the plaintiff was then injured in its business and property in a sum in excess of three million dollars." This was not the sort of antitrust suit where the plaintiff's business still exists and where the injury was merely for loss of profits. The allegations and evidence as to the amount of profits were necessary in order to establish the value of the good will and business since that is derived by a capitalization of profits. A somewhat similar idea was expressed in Farmers' & Merchants' Bank v. Commissioner, supra, 59 F.2d at page 913. "Profits were one of the chief indications of the worth of the business; but the usual earnings before the injury, as compared with those afterward, were only an evidential factor in determining actual loss and not an independent basis for recovery." Since the suit was to recover damages for the destruction of the business and good will, the recovery represents a return of capital. Nor does the fact that the suit ended in a compromise settlement change the nature of the recovery; "the determining factor is the nature of the basic claim from which the compromised amount was realized." * * *

But, to say that the recovery represents a return of capital in that it takes the place of the business good will is not to conclude that it may not contain a taxable benefit. Although the injured party may not be deriving a profit as a result of the damage suit itself, the conversion thereby of his property into cash is a realization of any gain made over the cost or other basis of the good will prior to the illegal interference. Thus A buys

Blackacre for $5,000. It appreciates in value to $50,000. B tortiously destroys it by fire. A sues and recovers $50,000 tort damages from B. Although no gain was derived by A from the suit, his prior gain due to the appreciation in value of Blackacre is realized when it is turned into cash by the money damages.

Compensation for the loss of Raytheon's good will in excess of its cost is gross income. * * *

* * * As the Tax Court pointed out, the record is devoid of evidence as to the amount of that basis and "in the absence of evidence of the basis of the business and good will of Raytheon, the amount of any nontaxable capital recovery cannot be ascertained." 1 T.C. 952. * * *

Where the cost basis that may be assigned to property has been wholly speculative, the gain has been held to be entirely conjectural and not taxable. In Strother v. Commissioner, 4 Cir., 1932, 55 F.2d 626, affirmed on other grounds, 1932, 287 U.S. 308, * * * a trespasser had taken coal and then destroyed the entries so that the amount of coal taken could not be determined. Since there was no way of knowing whether the recovery was greater than the basis for the coal taken, the gain was purely conjectural and not taxed. Magill explains the result as follows: "as the amount of coal removed could not be determined until a final disposition of the property, the computation of gain or loss on the damages must await that disposition." Taxable Income, pp. 339–340. The same explanation may be applied to Farmers' & Merchants' Bank v. Commissioner, supra, which relied on the Strother case in finding no gain. The recovery in that case had been to compensate for the injury to good will and business reputation of the plaintiff bank inflicted by defendant reserve banks' wrongful conduct in collecting checks drawn on the plaintiff bank by employing "agents who would appear daily at the bank with checks and demand payment thereof in cash in such a manner as to attract unfavorable public comment". Since the plaintiff bank's business was not destroyed but only injured and since it continued in business, it would have been difficult to require the taxpayer to prove what part of the basis of its good will should be attributed to the recovery. In the case at bar, on the contrary, the entire business and good will were destroyed so that to require the taxpayer to prove the cost of the good will is no more impractical than if the business had been sold.[2]

DETAILED ANALYSIS

1.   EXCLUSION OF DAMAGES AS A RECOVERY OF CAPITAL

The situation in *Clark* can be analogized to the recovery of capital in computing gain from the disposition of property, discussed at Chapter 6, Section 1. Under this analogy, Clark realized no gain on the recovery of an

---

[2]   Since the plant and other physical assets of the taxpayer were not destroyed but were used by it in the new tube business under licenses from R.C.A., the recovery was only for the destruction of business good will and not the physical assets.

amount previously lost. This result differs if in an earlier year Clark had been able to deduct the loss for which the damages ultimately were received, because Clark would have derived a tax benefit from the deduction. The tax benefit rule, which governs related situations, is discussed at Chapter 29, Section 2.B.

The capital recovery analogy of *Clark* was followed in Cosentino v. Commissioner, T.C. Memo. 2014–186, to exclude from gross income a portion of damages recovered in a settlement from tax advisors in an abusive tax shelter scheme who were alleged to have been negligent and in breach of their fiduciary duties to the taxpayer by advising them to pursue what was ultimately determined to be a fraudulent tax shelter. The recovery was not includable in gross income except to the extent that damages were received as compensation for amounts claimed as deductions that had been allowed, and certain damages recovered for amounts that the taxpayer did not incur or incurred in amounts that were less than the amounts of damages alleged in the complaint.

2. COMPENSATION FOR LOST PROFITS VERSUS COMPENSATION FOR PROPERTY LOSS

Damage awards compensating the taxpayer for lost business profits or wages arising from a breach of contract or business related tort obviously are gross income under § 61. See Kurowski v. Commissioner, 917 F.2d 1033 (7th Cir.1990) (payment to tenured teacher in exchange for resignation to settle contested removal hearing was taxable). "Liquidated damages" provided in a contract for nonperformance are treated as ordinary income, not a recovery of capital. Mittleman v. Commissioner, 56 T.C. 171 (1971).

Determining whether a payment is for lost profits or for damage to property, however, may be difficult where a suit seeks damages on account of both lost profits and injury to property or property rights or where a suit is settled without a verdict. Compare State Fish Corporation v. Commissioner, 48 T.C. 465 (1967) (Acq.) (breach of covenant not to compete was treated as an injury to goodwill; evidence with respect to lost profits was only indicative of the measure of damage), and Sager Glove Corporation v. Commissioner, 311 F.2d 210 (7th Cir.1962) (payments in settlement of an antitrust action were taxable as ordinary income, not excludable as a return of capital, because the amount of the settlement was nearly the same amount that the taxpayer had claimed in the antitrust suit to have been lost profits). In Gail v. United States, 58 F.3d 580 (10th Cir.1995), a damage award was received by the owner of mineral rights for conversion of oil and gas through unlawful extraction. The amount of the award was bifurcated into an amount received in lieu of lost royalties, which was taxable as ordinary income, and an amount received as compensation for diminution in value of the land and mineral estate, which was taxable as capital gain to extent that the allocable damages exceeded the allocable portion of basis.

The taxpayer bears the burden of proof that damages were received for impairment of goodwill rather than for lost profits. The taxpayer in Milenbach v. Commissioner, 106 T.C. 184 (1996), aff'd on this issue, rev'd on other issues, 318 F.3d 924 (9th Cir.2003), was a partner in the Oakland

Raiders football team. The partnership received a settlement in a suit against the City of Oakland for inverse condemnation of the Oakland Raiders football team arising from the City's efforts to prevent the Raiders from moving to Los Angeles. The settlement proceeds were taxed as ordinary income, received in lieu of lost profits, rather than as a recovery of capital. Although the settlement agreement stated that it resolved a claim for "restoration of lost franchise value," the taxpayer's damages study prepared by an expert in connection with the underlying suit indicated that the Raiders' claim against the City was based entirely on lost profits.

3.   DAMAGES FOR INJURY TO PROPERTY

Assuming the taxpayer can establish that a damage award is related to injury to property (whether used for business or personal purposes), the next inquiry is the second issue in the *Raytheon* case, the question of the portion of the taxpayer's basis in the property that may be allocated to the recovery. As the Blackacre example in the *Raytheon* opinion indicates, the fact that the taxpayer has been compensated for an economic loss does not mean that income has not been realized for tax purposes. A taxpayer is entitled to a tax-free return only of the investment, the taxpayer's basis, in the property. Basis for this purpose is determined in the same manner as it is determined in computing gain (or loss) on the sale of property. The taxpayer in the Blackacre example had a basis of only $5,000 because the unrealized appreciation in the property was not taken into income for tax purposes prior to the loss. Accordingly, the conversion of the appreciation into cash represents a realization of income, not a return of capital.

Suppose the property in the Blackacre example had been damaged, but not completely destroyed, and the taxpayer received $5,000 instead of $50,000. Should the $5,000 be treated as representing recovery of (a) appreciation in the property and thus taxable in full; (b) basis in the property and hence tax free as a return of capital; or (c) part return of capital and part income in the proportion that the basis bears to fair market value. Inaja Land Co. v. Commissioner, 9 T.C. 727 (1947) (Acq.) (see Chapter 6, Section 3.A.3.) indicates that at least where the damaged portion of the property is not divisible from the undamaged portion, the recovery is entirely a return of capital up to the amount of basis. Suppose alternatively that Blackacre consisted of land and two buildings, and at the time it was purchased for $5,000 the fair market values of the components were: Land, $1,000; Building #1, $1,000; and Building #2, $3,000. If Building #1 was destroyed, leading to recovery of a $5,000 damage award, only $1,000 would be excludable as a recovery of capital and the remaining $4,000 would be taxable gain.

Where the taxpayer's property is tortiously destroyed and the taxpayer recovers damages (or insurance proceeds), current recognition of gain can be avoided if the taxpayer purchases property "similar or related in service or use" before the end of the second taxable year after the year the damage occurred. See Chapter 27.

4.   PUNITIVE DAMAGES

Commissioner v. Glenshaw Glass Co., 348 U.S. 426 (1955) (see Chapter 2, Section 1.A.) established that punitive damages are gross income under § 61(a). General American Investors Co., Inc. v. Commissioner, 348 U.S. 434 (1955), reached the same result with respect to an award of "insider profits" recovered by a corporation from a director pursuant to § 16(b) of the Securities Exchange Act. Unlike compensatory damages, there is no possibility that punitive damage payments constitute a return of capital.

5.   INTEREST

In most actions for damages, a prevailing plaintiff is entitled to interest on the damage award. Such interest is taxed as such, and is not a recovery of capital or gain resulting from a property transaction. See Leonard v. Commissioner, 94 F.3d 523 (9th Cir.1996) (interest on a judgment for destruction or conversion of the taxpayer's property is taxed as interest income, not as gain from a property transaction).

SECTION 2.   DAMAGE AWARDS FOR PERSONAL INJURY

INTERNAL REVENUE CODE: Section 104(a)(2) and flush material, second and third sentences.[1]

REGULATIONS: Section 1.104–1(c).

A typical action for personal injuries includes claims for (1) lost wages, (2) loss in future earning power, (3) reimbursement for medical expenses incurred or to be incurred in the future, (4) pain and suffering, and (5) punitive damages. If the principles of Raytheon Production Co. v. Commissioner (see Section 1 of this Chapter) were applied to damages for personal injury, each component of a personal injury damage award would be separately examined to determine the extent to which the damage award was includable in gross income. Under the principles developed in *Raytheon,* damages as a substitute for lost income would constitute ordinary income; damages for reduced earning power, in effect goodwill, would be nontaxable but only to the extent that the taxpayer was able to establish a cost basis in the item.

To a large extent, however, such an inquiry has been obviated by statute. Prior to 1996, § 104(a)(2) excluded from gross income damages "received on account of personal injury or sickness." Historically, § 104(a)(2) was liberally construed, and the results were not always consistent with the principles considered previously. Rev. Rul. 85–97, 1985–2 C.B. 50, held that the portion of a settlement of a suit for personal injuries incurred in a bus accident and attributable to lost wages was excludable under § 104(a)(2). In practice this ruling has been applied to compensation for lost future earning power as well.

Section 104(a)(2) reaches the correct result to the extent that the payments are reimbursement for medical costs. In the situation where

---

[1]   Flush material (also often referred to as "flush language") is the unnumbered language at the end of a statutory provision.

the payment is made by the tortfeasor (or the tortfeasor's insurance company), the taxpayer should be entitled to receive the payment free of tax as a return of capital because, like the taxpayer in *Clark,* the taxpayer in effect has a cost basis in a claim against the tortfeasor in an amount equal to the medical costs incurred for which a deduction under § 213 (see Chapter 21, Section 2) has not been claimed.

With respect to damages for pain and suffering, it may be argued that § 104(a)(2) properly excludes the recovery as compensation for injuries to good health. Even though the taxpayer has no basis in "good health," good health is not something that could have been sold in a market-place transaction, and thus it might be conceptualized as taking a "deemed basis" equal to fair market value, which is, in turn, determined with reference to the damages received. Another variation of this argument is that damages received as a measure of suffering simply do not represent an accession to wealth.

Because of the high stakes involved, the scope of § 104(a)(2) has been a matter of considerable controversy. The broad statutory exclusion could result in complete exclusion of personal injury damage awards in many cases. Thus, the meaning of the phrases "on account of" and "personal injury" has engendered much litigation. Prior to enactment of the 1996 amendments to § 104(a)(2), explained in the excerpt from the General Explanation of the Small Business Job Protection Act of 1996, which follows this discussion, the IRS and the courts often excluded damages received on account of nonphysical personal injuries, such as defamation. Many courts also extended the exclusion of § 104(a)(2) to damages received in suits primarily seeking economic damages if the action sounded in tort and loosely could be characterized as a personal injury. For example, damages received for deprivation of constitutional rights were held to be excludable under § 104(a)(2) because actions to enforce such rights are analogous to tort suits. Bent v. Commissioner, 835 F.2d 67 (3d Cir.1987), excluded damages received under 42 U.S.C. § 1983 for deprivation of a public school teacher's right to freedom of speech, even though most of the damages represented lost wages as a result of his unlawful dismissal. In Roemer v. Commissioner, 716 F.2d 693 (9th Cir.1983), rev'g 79 T.C. 398 (1982), the Court of Appeals for the Ninth Circuit held that defamation was inherently a personal injury even in a case in which the defamation related solely to the taxpayer's business practices and was communicated only to the taxpayer's business associates, and the damages received were limited to lost profits.

After *Roemer,* the courts were deluged with cases involving the application of § 104(a)(2) to exclude damages received on account of violations of employment-related civil rights statutes. In general, the lower courts broadly interpreted § 104(a)(2) and excluded almost all damages received under such statutes. See e.g., Byrne v. Commissioner, 883 F.2d 211 (3d Cir.1989) (damages under Fair Labor Standards Act and Equal Opportunity in Employment Act were excluded); Pistillo v.

Commissioner, 912 F.2d 145 (6th Cir.1990) (damages under Age Discrimination in Employment Act were excluded). In United States v. Burke, 504 U.S. 229 (1992), however, the Supreme Court held that § 104(a)(2) did not exclude back pay awards under Title VII of the Civil Rights Act (as in effect before its amendment in 1991). Because the sole monetary remedy available to the taxpayer in *Burke* under pre-1991 Title VII was a back-pay award, the Court concluded that the Title VII statute provided a remedy for an economic injury, not a "tort-like personal" injury.

Three years later, in Commissioner v. Schleier, 515 U.S. 323 (1995), the Supreme Court held that both back pay and liquidated damages received under the ADEA were fully includable in gross income. Although the wrongful discharge from employment might have caused a personal injury, the discharge from employment itself was not a personal injury, and the back pay award was received as compensation for the economic losses arising from the wrongful discharge, not on account of any tortious personal injury occasioned by the wrongful discharge. The court noted that in contrast, in a case in which damages for lost wages are received on account of a physical injury, the loss of wages is caused by the physical injury that rendered the injured taxpayer unable to work.

In an effort to curtail controversy regarding the scope of the exclusion under § 104(a)(2), in 1996 Congress amended § 104(a)(2) in two important respects, as explained in the following excerpt from the General Explanation of the Small Business Job Protection Act of 1996.

General Explanation of Tax Legislation Enacted in the 105th Congress

Staff of the Joint Committee on Taxation, 222–224 (1996).

Taxation of punitive damages received on account of personal injury or sickness * * * .

[Pre-1996] Law

Under [pre-1996] law, gross income generally does not include any damages received (whether by suit or agreement and whether as lump sums or as periodic payments) on account of personal injury or sickness (sec. 104(a)(2)). Under [pre-1996] law, the statute specifically provides that this exclusion does not apply to punitive damages received in connection with a case not involving physical injury or sickness. Under [pre-1996] law, courts differed as to whether the exclusion applied to punitive damages received in connection with a case involving a physical injury or physical sickness.[168] Certain States provide that, in the case of

---

[168]   However, the Supreme Court has held that punitive damages received by the husband and children of a woman who died of toxic shock syndrome were not received "on account of" personal injuries and, therefore, the exclusion did not apply. O'Gilvie v. U.S., [519 U.S. 79 (1996)]. Also, the Tax Court recently held that if punitive damages are not of a compensatory nature, they are not excludable from income, regardless of whether the underlying claim

claims under a wrongful death statute, only punitive damages may be awarded.

Under [pre-1996] law, courts interpreted the exclusion from gross income of damages received on account of personal injury or sickness broadly in some cases to cover awards for personal injury that do not relate to a physical injury or sickness. * * *

Reasons for Change

Punitive damages are intended to punish the wrongdoer and are not intended to compensate the claimant (e.g., for lost wages or pain and suffering). Thus, they are a windfall to the taxpayer and appropriately should be included in taxable income. Further, including all punitive damages in taxable income provides a brightline standard which avoids prospective litigation on the tax treatment of punitive damages received in connection with a case involving a physical injury or physical sickness.

Damages received on a claim not involving a physical injury or physical sickness (e.g., employment discrimination or injury to reputation) are generally to compensate the claimant for lost profits or lost wages that would otherwise be included in taxable income. The confusion as to the tax treatment of damages received in cases not involving physical injury or physical sickness has led to substantial litigation, including two Supreme Court cases within the last four years. The Congress believed that the taxation of damages received in cases not involving a physical injury or physical sickness should not depend on the type of claim made.

Explanation of Provision

Include in income all punitive damages

[As amended in 1996, § 104(a)(2)] provides that the exclusion from gross income does not apply to any punitive damages received on account of personal injury or sickness whether or not related to a physical injury or physical sickness. * * * [P]rior law continues to apply to [exclude] punitive damages received in a wrongful death action if the applicable State law (as in effect on September 13, 1995 without regard to subsequent modification) provides, or has been construed to provide by a court decision issued on or before such date, that only punitive damages may be awarded in a wrongful death action.* * * *

Include in income damage recoveries for nonphysical injuries.

The Small Business Act provides that the exclusion from gross income only applies to damages received on account of a personal physical injury or physical sickness. If an action has its origin in a physical injury or physical sickness, then all damages (other than punitive damages) that flow therefrom are treated as payments received on account of physical injury or physical sickness whether or not the

---

involved a physical injury or physical sickness. Bagley v. Commissioner, 105 T.C. 396 (1995) [aff'd 121 F.3d 393 (8th Cir.1997)].

recipient of the damages is the injured party. For example, damages (other than punitive damages) received by an individual on account of a claim for loss of consortium due to the physical injury or physical sickness of such individual's spouse are excludable from gross income. In addition, damages (other than punitive damages) received on account of a claim of wrongful death continue to be excludable from gross income as under prior law.

* * *

[E]motional distress is not considered a physical injury or physical sickness.[171] Thus, for example, the exclusion from gross income does not apply to any damages received (other than for medical expenses as discussed below) based on a claim of employment discrimination or injury to reputation accompanied by a claim of emotional distress. However, because all damages received on account of physical injury or physical sickness are excludable from gross income, the exclusion from gross income applies to any damages received based on a claim of emotional distress that is attributable to a physical injury or physical sickness. In addition, the exclusion from gross income specifically applies to the amount of damages received that is not in excess of the amount paid for medical care attributable to emotional distress (regardless of whether the emotional distress is due to a physical injury or physical sickness). * * *

DETAILED ANALYSIS

1. THE RELEVANCE OF A "TORT" CLAIM

As amended in 2012, Treas. Reg. § 1.104–1(c) eliminates a requirement in the former regulations that to be excludable under § 104(a)(2) damages must have been "based upon tort or tort type rights." This change allows damages for physical injuries to qualify for exclusion under § 104(a)(2) even though the injury giving rise to the damages is not defined as a tort under state or common law. The Treasury Department promulgated the change because of its concern that the Supreme Court's interpretation of the tort type rights test in United States v. Burke, 504 U.S. 229 (1992), limiting the § 104(a)(2) exclusion to damages for personal injuries for which the full range of tort-type remedies is available, could preclude an exclusion under § 104(a)(2) for redress of physical personal injuries under a "no-fault" statute that does not provide traditional tort remedies.

In Perez v. Commissioner, 144 T.C. 51 (2015), the Tax Court held that the 2012 amendments to Treas. Reg. § 1.104–1(c) were not intended to extend the exclusion to instances where there was no lawsuit or threat of a lawsuit. The taxpayer, a human egg donor, was required to include in income as compensation for services a $10,000 payment for "[d]onor's time, effort, inconvenience, pain, and suffering in donating her eggs."

---

[171] As discussed above, * * * punitive damages received in certain wrongful death actions may be still excludable from gross income to the extent they were excludable under prior law. However, see O'Gilvie v. U.S., supra.

2.   NONPHYSICAL PERSONAL INJURIES AFTER THE 1996 ACT

As discussed in the excerpt from the General Explanation of the Small Business Job Protection Act of 1996, § 104(a)(2) no longer applies to exclude damages received on account of nonphysical personal injuries, even though the action sounds in tort. Congress' primary reason for so amending § 104(a)(2) appears to have been to require inclusion of damages received in employment-related statutory civil rights actions, such as Title VII of the Civil Rights Act, the ADEA, and the ADA, as well as state law wrongful discharge from employment and unfair competition suits. See Rev. Rul. 96–65, 1996–2 C.B. 6 (under 1996 amendments to § 104(a)(2), neither back pay nor damages for emotional distress received on account of disparate treatment employment discrimination under Title VII of the Civil Rights Act are excludable). As amended, however, § 104(a)(2) also no longer excludes damages received in tort suits for defamation, malicious prosecution, invasion of privacy, and possibly assault and false imprisonment (without an attendant battery), whether or not the tort was business related. Stadnyk v. Commissioner, T.C. Memo. 2008–289 (2008), aff'd, 367 Fed.Appx. 586 (6th Cir. 2010), held that damages received on account of false imprisonment were not excludable under § 104(a)(2), even though the taxpayer was detained, handcuffed, and searched, because she suffered no physical harm. Instead, the court determined that the taxpayer received the damages on account of her emotional distress, mortification, humiliation, mental anguish, and reputational harm.

Treas. Reg. § 1.104–1(c) provides, consistent with its legislative history, that emotional distress is not considered a physical injury or physical sickness. However, the regulation also provides that damages for emotional distress that are attributable to a physical injury or physical sickness are excludable under § 104(a)(2). Cases that predated the regulation were consistent with this approach. Lindsey v. Commissioner, 422 F.3d 684 (8th Cir. 2005), held that physical symptoms that are merely manifestations of the underlying emotional distress for which damages are received do not result in the damages being treated as received on account of personal injury if there is no "direct causal link between any physical sickness suffered by [the taxpayer] and any damages paid out to him". In that case, the taxpayer's physician testified that the taxpayer "suffered from hypertension and stress-related symptoms, including periodic impotency, insomnia, fatigue, occasional indigestion, and urinary incontinence" as a result of the emotional distress inflicted by the defendant, but the settlement agreement identified taxpayer's claims solely as tort claims for damage to his "emotions, reputation and character." Thus, § 104(a)(2) did not exclude the damages received pursuant to the settlement.

Murphy v. IRS, 493 F.3d 170 (D.C. Cir. 2007), similarly held that damages received by the taxpayer from her former employer under whistle-blower environmental statutes for mental pain and injury to her reputation were not received on account of personal physical injury as required by § 104(a)(2), even though the taxpayer suffered from "bruxism" (teeth grinding often associated with stress), which may cause permanent tooth damage, and other physical manifestations of stress, including anxiety attacks, shortness of breath, and dizziness caused by the emotional distress. The court emphasized that the administrative law judge that made the award and the Department of Labor Administrative Review Board that upheld the award specifically awarded the damages "on account of" her mental distress and reputational loss, not her bruxism or other physical symptoms.

As the General Explanation of the 1996 Act noted, damages for loss of consortium or emotional distress arising from a physical injury are intended to be excludable, even if the emotional distress is suffered by a taxpayer other than the taxpayer who suffered the physical injury, for example, damages received by a family member for the emotional distress of seeing a relative physically injured. Conversely, the legislative history indicates that physical manifestations of emotional distress, such as insomnia, headaches, and stomach disorders, are not to be treated as physical injury. See H. Rep. No. 104–737, 104th Cong., 2d Sess. 301, n.56 (1996). In some cases of nonphysical injury, particularly defamation, the damages received may correlate very closely to lost profits, and the bright line of the 1996 legislation standard may reach the correct result—assuming that any exclusion for personal injury damages is sensible. But other cases involving nonphysical personal injuries—for example, false imprisonment—are difficult to distinguish theoretically from a tortious physical personal injury. A more rational distinction would have been to draw a line between claims originating in business activities and claims originating in personal activities, although, admittedly, this line itself sometimes may be difficult to discern. The current rule might be an adequate proxy in many cases but not others.

3. APPORTIONMENT OF DAMAGES FOR MULTIPLE CLAIMS

Where the taxpayer has received a lump sum unapportioned award or settlement with respect to multiple claims, some of which are for physical personal injury or sickness and some of which are for breach of contract or other nonexcludable damages, the total amount must be apportioned into taxable and nontaxable components. When cases are settled, it is sometimes difficult to determine the nature of the claim with respect to which the settlement amount was received. The terms of the settlement agreement itself are important. Rivera v. Baker West, Inc., 430 F.3d 1253 (9th Cir. 2005), held that no portion of the settlement of a claim for unlawful workplace discrimination and unlawful termination was compensation for physical personal injuries where the settlement agreement was silent regarding the nature of the injuries addressed and the only evidence of the payor's intent regarding the claims settled was a statement that the defendant would pay taxpayer a sum of money "less all lawfully required withholdings;" the inference of the withholding clause was that the defendant considered some or all of the payment to represent back pay.

Rev. Rul. 85–98, 1985–2 C.B. 51, held that where an unapportioned award is received pursuant to a jury verdict, the award should be prorated among the various claims in proportion to the damages requested in the complaint. In Stocks v. Commissioner, 98 T.C. 1 (1992), the Tax Court dealt with apportioning the proceeds from a pre-trial settlement of a claim for both breach of contract and racial discrimination (at a time when damages for racial discrimination were excludable under § 104(a)(2)) where there was no documentation of the amount paid with respect to the different claims. The court held that absent any formal basis for determining the nature of the claim settled, the payor's intent was the most important factor. Based on testimony of the person who conducted the settlement negotiations for the taxpayer's employer that his primary intent was to settle the breach of contract claim, but that he would not have settled without an agreement covering a racial discrimination claim, the court concluded that the settlement proceeds were partly for the breach of contract claim and taxable and partly for the racial discrimination claim and not taxable. As is often true in apportionment cases, the amounts allocated to each claim appeared to be arbitrary. Compare McKay v. Commissioner, 102 T.C. 465 (1994), rev'd by order on other grounds, 84 F.3d 433 (5th Cir.1996), in which the Tax Court deferred completely to a post-judgment settlement agreement because the parties were genuinely adverse, with Robinson v. Commissioner, 102 T.C. 116 (1994), aff'd on this issue, rev'd on other issues, 70 F.3d 34 (5th Cir.1995), in which a post-judgment allocation was not respected because it was not the result of an arm's length agreement between the parties and the court instead adopted the same allocation as had been made in the prior jury verdict.

In Bagley v. Commissioner, 121 F.3d 393 (8th Cir.1997), a jury had awarded the taxpayer $1,500,000 of compensatory damages and $7,500,000 of punitive damages on a personal injury suit. After certain portions of the award were vacated on appeal, pending a new trial the taxpayer settled for $1,500,000. The settlement agreement provided that the payment was for "personal injuries," without any mention of punitive damages. The court of appeals held that the Tax Court properly allocated $500,000 of the settlement to punitive damages. The reality of the settlement negotiations was that even if the defendant won all of the issues to be retried, it still would have had to pay $250,000 of punitive damages, and it faced a significant risk of having to pay another $1,500,000 of punitive damages. The court determined that even if a settlement agreement allocates nothing to a particular class of damages, if the defendant almost certainly would have been liable for an amount of a particular type of damages absent the settlement, apportionment of some portion of the settlement to that class of damages may be proper. This is particularly true with respect to punitive damages, because it is almost always to the defendant's advantage for nontax purposes to avoid characterizing any portion of the settlement as attributable to punitive damages (which might not be covered by insurance and could lead to greater adverse publicity) and to the plaintiff's advantage to avoid such a characterization because of tax consequences. Thus the parties to the agreement lacked adverse interests in bargaining over the characterization of the settlement.

In Amos v. Commissioner, T.C. Memo 2003–329 (2003), the taxpayer was a television cameraman who was kicked and injured by NBA basketball player Dennis Rodman after Rodman ran out of bounds and tripped, landing on the taxpayer—i.e., the kick took extra effort by Rodman. The taxpayer settled any claims he had against Rodman for $200,000, and the settlement agreement expressly provided that Rodman paid the taxpayer a portion of the settlement amount at issue in return for the taxpayer's agreement not to: (1) defame Rodman, (2) disclose the existence or the terms of the settlement agreement, (3) publicize facts relating to the incident, or (4) assist in any criminal prosecution against Rodman with respect to the incident. The Tax Court characterized these four provisions collectively as "the nonphysical injury provisions," and found, as a fact-finding matter, that $80,000 of the settlement was attributable to these provisions and that only $120,000 of the settlement was "on account of" personal physical injury and therefore excludable.

In Domeny v. Commissioner, T.C. Memo. 2010–9, the taxpayer received approximately $33,000 from her former employer to settle a claim for wrongful termination of employment and violations of various civil rights statutes (of which $8,000 was paid to her lawyer). The employer issued her a Form W-2 that reflected approximately $8,000 as employee compensation, and $17,000 to the taxpayer that was shown on a Form 1099-MISC as "nonemployee compensation." The $8,000 paid directly to the taxpayer was includable wage compensation, and the remaining amount was excludable under § 104(a)(2) as damages for physical injuries attributable to exacerbation of the employee's multiple sclerosis caused by a hostile work environment. The employer's intent in settling the claim was evidenced by the issuance of separate checks and different information returns, facts indicating that the employer intended the amount in excess of wages due to be in settlement of tort claims for physical injuries. Likewise, in Parkinson v. Commissioner, T.C. Memo. 2010–142, the Tax Court determined that one-half of the amount received by the taxpayer in settlement of a claim for intentional infliction of emotional distress was excludable under § 104(a)(2), because the payor intended that portion to be compensation for a heart attack suffered as a result of the emotional distress. The court reasoned that "a heart attack and its physical aftereffects constitute physical injury or sickness rather than mere subjective sensations or symptoms of emotional distress." The other one-half of the settlement was not excludable, because it represented compensation for emotional distress.

4. ATTORNEYS' FEES AWARDS AND INTEREST ON JUDGMENTS

When a plaintiff in a tort suit receives a judgment or settles the case, the defendant typically pays the damage award or settlement to the plaintiff's lawyer, who retains the agreed-upon contingent fee and remits the net amount to the plaintiff-taxpayer. Fite v. Commissioner, T.C. Memo. 1993–594, rev'd by order on other grounds, 79 F.3d 1148 (6th Cir.1995), held that attorney's fees and court costs awarded to a prevailing plaintiff in a personal injury action are excluded under § 104(a)(2). Since the 1996 amendments to § 104(a)(2), this principle generally applies only to attorney's fees received in a suit for a physical personal injury. See Sinyard v. Commissioner, 268 F.3d 756 (9th Cir.2001) (including in plaintiff's gross income an award of attorney's fees payable directly from the defendant to the plaintiff's attorney under the Age Discrimination in Employment Act). In Commissioner v. Banks, 543 U.S. 426 (2005), the Supreme Court held that in cases in which the damages are not excludable under § 104(a)(2), the plaintiff must include the full amount of the damage award in gross income and then claim any allowable deduction for the attorney's fees.

Kovacs v. Commissioner, 100 T.C. 124 (1993), aff'd by order, 25 F.3d 1048 (6th Cir.1994), Aames v. Commissioner, 94 T.C. 189 (1990), Brabson v. United States, 73 F.3d 1040 (10th Cir. 1996), and Chamberlain v. United States, 401 F.3d 335 (5th Cir.2005), all held that statutory prejudgment interest awarded in a personal injury suit is not excludable under § 104(a)(2) because it is compensation for the lost time value of money, not compensation for the personal injury. Where a suit is settled after the trial verdict but pending appeal, however, it may be possible to avoid characterizing any part of the settlement as interest. In McShane v. Commissioner, T.C. Memo. 1987–151, none of a settlement for an amount in excess of the verdict was treated as interest because pending appeal there was no final judgment and thus no fixed obligation; the settlement amount was based on the hazards of litigation. On the other hand, Forest v. Commissioner, T.C. Memo. 1995–377, aff'd by order, 104 F.3d 348 (1st Cir.1996), appears to have held that an allocation of a portion of any post-judgment settlement to statutory prejudgment interest is required, even if the settlement is for less than the jury verdict. In Delaney v. Commissioner, 99 F.3d 20 (1st Cir.1996), a portion of a post-judgment settlement was allocated to prejudgment interest, even though the settlement agreement specifically provided that no portion of the settlement was attributable to interest, because the settlement agreement was not an arms' length bargain. The amount of interest was the same percentage of the settlement as the interest component of the jury verdict was of the total jury verdict.

5. DEFERRED PAYMENTS

Although express interest on a damage award excluded by § 104(a)(2) is taxable, the exclusion provided by § 104(a)(2) applies to amounts received as stated-sum periodic payments as well as to amounts received in a lump sum. Thus, for example, if instead of receiving a lump sum payment of $100,000, a taxpayer instead receives $20,000 a year for seven years, the entire $140,000 (assumed to be the actuarial equivalent) is excluded from gross income. The extra $40,000 received is actually interest on the $100,000 and would have been taxable if the taxpayer had received the $100,000 and invested it in assets yielding taxable income. See Rev. Rul. 79–220, 1979–2 C.B. 74 (payee of annuity to satisfy claim for personal injury is allowed to exclude the full amount of payments, not merely the discounted present value); Rev. Rul. 79–313, 1979–2 C.B. 75 (taxpayer receiving 50 annual payments, each of which is increased by 5% over the amount of the preceding payment, is allowed to exclude full amount of each payment). When periodic payments result from a settlement, the extent to which the taxpayer benefits from the added exclusion depends on whether the party holding the $100,000 pays tax on the investment income and the timing of the payor's deduction, if any, for payments made, which will affect the implicit rate of interest. Section 461(h) (see Chapter 28, Section 3.B.2.) defers a payor's deduction until actual payment is made, and § 468B provides that "settlement funds" are taxable entities. Thus, in many cases the exemption for the implicit interest may be shared with or shifted to the payor.

6. JURY INSTRUCTIONS

It is not clear whether taxpayers who receive damages excludable under § 104(a)(2) actually receive the benefit of the exclusion at all. The Supreme Court held that in assessing damages for personal injuries under the Federal Employer's Liability Act the tax consequences may be taken into account, Norfolk & Western Railway Co. v. Liepelt, 444 U.S. 490 (1980), and jury instructions on the tax exemption for damages in personal injury cases are commonplace. The award therefore may be less (in before tax dollars) than it otherwise would have been.

SECTION 3.   INSURANCE RECOVERIES

The treatment of the receipt of insurance proceeds depends on the type of insurance and the circumstances under which the proceeds have been received. Damage awards in tort suits, discussed in the preceding material in this chapter, often are paid by insurance companies on behalf of an insured defendant. The treatment of the plaintiff-taxpayer in those cases is not dependent on whether the damages have been paid by the defendant or the defendant's insurance company. Interestingly, without any statutory, regulatory, or judicial authority dealing with the issue, the practice, long accepted by the IRS, has been *not to apply* the principles of Old Colony Trust Co. v. Commissioner, 279 U.S. 716 (1929) (see Chapter 2, Section 1.B.) to require that the insured defendant include in gross income as an indirect receipt the amount that the insurance company has paid to the plaintiff on the insured defendant's behalf.

When a taxpayer-insured receives a payment from a casualty insurance company with respect to a loss to property, the taxpayer will recognize a gain if the insurance proceeds exceed the basis of the damaged property or realize a lesser casualty loss if the insurance proceeds do not exceed the basis of the damaged property. These issues, which are determined under sections relating to gain and loss generally, are discussed at Chapter 6, Section 1 and Chapter 27, Section 1.

The tax treatment of a few categories of insurance proceeds is addressed by specific Code sections. The most important of such sections are discussed in the following material.

A.   COMPENSATION FOR PERSONAL INJURIES OR SICKNESS

(1)   WORKER'S COMPENSATION

INTERNAL REVENUE CODE: Section 104(a)(1).

REGULATIONS: Section 1.104–1(b).

Section 104(a) excludes a number of insurance and similar recoveries that are analogous to damages excluded under § 104(a)(2). Section 104(a)(1) excludes "amounts received under workmen's compensation acts as compensation for personal injuries or sickness." Treas. Reg. § 1.104–1(b) "extends the ambit of this provision to include any statute in the nature of a workmen's compensation act which provides compensation to employees for personal injuries or sickness incurred in the course of employment." See Givens v. Commissioner, 90 T.C. 1145 (1988) (Nonacq.) (payments to county deputy sheriff injured in the line of duty that were made pursuant to county employee general sick leave regulations were excludable because they were in the nature of workers compensation). Section 104(a)(1) does not apply, however, to employer-provided sick-pay or to compensation for injuries not related to employment. Amounts may not be excluded under § 104(a)(1) to the extent the recovered amounts reimburse the taxpayer for previously deducted medical expenses.

(2) ACCIDENT AND HEALTH INSURANCE

INTERNAL REVENUE CODE: Section 104(a)(3)–(5).

REGULATIONS: Section 1.104–1(d).

Section 104(a)(3) excludes amounts received through accident or health insurance for personal injuries or sickness that are attributable to insurance premiums paid by the taxpayer or included in the taxpayer's gross income. Accident and health insurance proceeds attributable to employer-financed fringe benefit plans are governed by § 105 (see Chapter 3, Section 3.B.), which unlike § 104(a)(3), excludes insurance proceeds only up to the amount necessary to cover actual medical expenses. For the determination of the amount excludable under § 104(a)(3) when the taxpayer receives insurance proceeds attributable to both employer-financed insurance and self-financed insurance, see Rev. Rul. 69–154, 1969–1 C.B. 46.

Amounts may not be excluded under § 104(a)(3) to the extent the recovered amounts reimburse the taxpayer for previously deducted medical expenses. Exclusion of such amounts would produce a double tax benefit, effectively shielding from taxation some of the taxpayer's other income, which was not used to pay medical expenses. On the other hand, § 104(a)(3) excludes insurance proceeds in excess of medical expenses incurred. Thus, amounts replacing lost wages or even pure windfalls can be received tax-free. The theory for exclusion of such receipts appears to be akin to the theory for exclusion of recoveries under § 104(a)(2). The compassionate theory of § 104(a)(3) apparently does not apply, however, to taxpayers who assiduously plan to avail themselves of its benefit. Dodge v. Commissioner, 96 T.C. 172 (1991), aff'd in part, rev'd in part, 981 F.2d 350 (8th Cir.1992), denied an exclusion for $257,000 received pursuant to illegal multi-policy insurance speculation scheme with respect to hospitalization costing $29,445.

B. INSURANCE PAYMENTS FOR LIVING EXPENSES

INTERNAL REVENUE CODE: Section 123.

REGULATIONS: Section 1.123–1(a)(1)–(3).

Section 123 provides that insurance payments to compensate an individual for additional living expenses incurred by the individual and family members because of the loss of the use of the individual's principal residence are not includable in gross income to the extent that the additional living expenses exceed the taxpayer's normal living expenses. Prior to the enactment of § 123, the cases had generally found such payments includable in income and the additional living expenses nondeductible personal expenses. See, e.g., Millsap v. Commissioner, 387 F.2d 420 (8th Cir.1968) (citing the broad definition of income in *Glenshaw Glass*, see Chapter 2, Section 1.A., and § 262, which denies deductions for "personal, living, or family expenses" except for specific statutory exceptions).

The discussion with respect to § 104 (see Section 2 of this Chapter) is equally applicable to § 123. McCabe v. Commissioner, 54 T.C. 1745 (1970), involving taxable years prior to the enactment of § 123, rejected the argument that the insurance proceeds are excludable because the use and occupancy of the house (imputed rent) is not taxed and the insurance is a substitute for a nontaxable type of income. The court stressed instead that inclusion was required because of the lack of a "cost basis" for the insurance proceeds.

CHAPTER 10

INCOME FROM THE CANCELLATION OF INDEBTEDNESS

INTERNAL REVENUE CODE: Section 61(a)(12).

REGULATIONS: Section 1.61–12(a).

Viewing a loan transaction as a whole, when a borrower receives money with a promise to repay and is later discharged from the liability without repaying the debt the borrower has had an accession to wealth. Recognizing the existence of income in this situation generally is not a problem for the income tax system. The initial receipt of $10 of borrowed cash is not income because the receipt is offset by an obligation to repay $10, but elimination of the obligation produces an accession to wealth which should be included in gross income. However, the existence of an accession to wealth is not as clear when the initial consideration for the borrower's indebtedness is something other than the receipt of cash in an amount equal to the face amount of the borrower's note.

Although inclusion of "discharge of indebtedness" or "cancellation of debt" in gross income originated in judicial decisions, § 61(a)(12) now specifically includes income from the "discharge of indebtedness" in gross income. While the Code refers to " 'discharge of indebtedness' income," tax lawyers most often refer to the concept as "cancellation of indebtedness income," and we will do so in this text. This slight change in terminology reflects the fact that § 61(a)(12) applies when a debt is "discharged" for less than full payment received by the creditor, or is "cancelled" in whole or in part, but § 61(a)(12) has no relevance when a debt is "discharged" either by payment or by a novation agreement under which a third party assumes the taxpayer's liability for the debt.

As the following materials demonstrate, the courts have struggled with the theory under which cancellation of debt produces gross income.

SECTION 1.   GENERAL PRINCIPLES

United States v. Kirby Lumber Company

Supreme Court of the United States, 1931.
284 U.S. 1.

■ MR. JUSTICE HOLMES delivered the opinion of the Court.

In July, 1923, the plaintiff, the Kirby Lumber Company, issued its own bonds for $12,126,800 for which it received their par value. Later in the same year it purchased in the open market some of the same bonds at less than par, the difference of price being $137,521.30. The question is whether this difference is a taxable gain or income of the plaintiff for the year 1923. By the Revenue Act of (November 23,) 1921, c. 136, § 213(a) gross income includes "gains or profits and income derived from any source whatever," and by the Treasury Regulations authorized by § 1303, that have been in force through repeated reenactments, "If the corporation purchases and retires any of such bonds at a price less than the issuing price or face value, the excess of the issuing price or face value over the purchase price is gain or income for the taxable year." Article 545(1)(c) of Regulations 62, under Revenue Act of 1921. * * * We see no reason why the Regulations should not be accepted as a correct statement of the law.

In Bowers v. Kerbaugh-Empire Co., 271 U.S. 170, the defendant in error owned the stock of another company that had borrowed money repayable in marks or their equivalent for an enterprise that failed. At the time of payment the marks had fallen in value, which so far as it went was a gain for the defendant in error, and it was contended by the plaintiff in error that the gain was taxable income. But the transaction as a whole was a loss, and the contention was denied. Here there was no shrinkage of assets and the taxpayer made a clear gain. As a result of its dealings it made available $137,521.30 assets previously offset by the obligation of bonds now extinct. We see nothing to be gained by the discussion of judicial definitions. The defendant in error has realized within the year an accession to income, if we take words in their plain popular meaning, as they should be taken here. Burnet v. Sanford & Brooks Co., 282 U.S. 359, 364.

Judgment reversed.

DETAILED ANALYSIS

1.   COMPETING THEORIES DERIVED FROM *KIRBY LUMBER*

1.1. *In General*

The Court's reference in *Kirby Lumber* to the freeing of the taxpayer's assets from the obligation of its cancelled indebtedness raises a question whether it is simply the balance sheet improvement resulting from eliminating the offsetting obligation that creates gross income on cancellation of indebtedness, or whether the existence of cancellation of indebtedness income depends on the presence of some other factor. If a taxpayer signs a note for $10,000, but receives only $9,000 of cash, and is subsequently relieved of the $10,000 debt by the payment of $9,000, is there $1,000 of cancellation of indebtedness income?[1] The taxpayer's assets have been freed from a balance sheet liability of $10,000 resulting in a $1,000 balance sheet gain. On the other hand, viewing the transaction as a whole,

---

[1]   As discussed in Chapter 32, the $1,000 difference is properly viewed as interest and may be so treated under the original issue discount rules of § 1271, et seq.

the taxpayer has received cash assets of $9,000 and returned cash in the amount of $9,000, resulting in a net accession to wealth of zero.[2]

In at least one application of *Kirby Lumber,* the Court has repeated both formulations. Commissioner v. Jacobson, 336 U.S. 28 (1949), held that an individual taxpayer recognized cancellation of indebtedness income on the repurchase of his personal bonds for an amount less than their issue price. The Court pointed out that the taxpayer's acquisition of his bonds improved his "net worth" by the difference between the face amount of the bonds and the acquisition price. The Court also noted that, "In the first instance [Jacobson] had received the full face amount in cash for these bonds so that his repurchase of them for 50 percent, or less, of that amount reflected a substantial benefit which he had derived from the use of that borrowed money."

Other courts have analyzed *Kirby Lumber* by comparing the consideration received in exchange for the taxpayer's note with the payment made to discharge the obligation. In Commissioner v. Rail Joint Co., 61 F.2d 751 (2d Cir.1932), the taxpayer issued bonds as a dividend to shareholders and accounted for the bonds on the corporate books at their face value. When the corporation repurchased the bonds for less than their face amount the Commissioner asserted that the corporation realized cancellation of indebtedness income because its balance sheet was improved by removing the face amount of the bonds as a corporate indebtedness. The court disagreed and held that in applying *Kirby Lumber,* "the consideration received for the obligation evidenced by the bond as well as the consideration paid to satisfy that obligation must be looked to in order to determine whether gain or loss is realized when the transaction is closed; i.e., when the bond is retired." 61 F.2d at 751–752. The Rail Joint Company did not have cancellation of indebtedness income on retirement of its bonds because the corporation did not receive an increment to its assets at the time the bonds were issued. Viewing the transaction as a whole, the corporation received no asset that it did not possess prior to the opening and closing of the bond transaction. There was no gain to be treated as income. The Tax Court reached the same conclusion in Fashion Park, Inc. v. Commissioner, 21 T.C. 600 (1954) (corporation retired dividend bonds for less than face value).

Hahn v. Commissioner, T.C. Memo. 2007–75, held that cancellation of indebtedness income can be realized under the *Kirby Lumber Co.* "freeing of assets" rationale even though the debtor did not receive any cash or other property when he incurred the liability. In *Hahn* the taxpayer was discharged from an obligation to pay accrued but unpaid interest. The court held that when a creditor writes off accrued but unpaid interest owed by a cash method debtor, discharge of indebtedness income is realized, unless the

---

[2]   It is not clear whether the taxpayer in *Kirby Lumber* actually received full value for the issue of its bonds. See Bittker, *Income from the Cancellation of Indebtedness: A Historical Footnote to the* Kirby Lumber Co. *Case,* 4 J. Corp.Tax 124 (1977). The case was tried before the Court of Claims on a stipulation that the bonds had been issued for their par value. Both the Court of Claims, 44 F.2d 885, 886 (Ct.Cl.1930), and the Supreme Court stated that the company had received par value when the bonds were issued. These express statements plus the tenor of the Supreme Court's opinion lead to the conclusion that the Court's analysis is based upon the assumption that the Kirby Lumber Company received full value on issue of the bonds.

interest would have been deductible if it had been paid and § 108(e)(2), infra, thus would have excluded the amount. The court reasoned that "[t]he right to use money represents a valuable property interest." *Rail Joint Company* and *Fashion Park, Inc.*, *supra*, both of which appear to be analytically inconsistent, were distinguished as limited to their particular facts. Accordingly, the taxpayer's motion for summary judgment was denied because whether the interest expense incurred in a horse breeding activity was deductible as a trade or business expense was a question of fact on which a trial was necessary. A similar result was reached in Payne v. Commissioner, T.C. Memo. 2008–66, *aff'd,* 357 Fed. Appx. 734 (8th Cir. 2009), where the taxpayer compromised a credit card debt, including interest, incurred for personal living expenses. The court held that the taxpayer realized cancellation of debt income, holding that § 108(e)(5) is inapplicable where the only relationship between the debtor and creditor is the debtor-creditor relationship and there was no property sale and purchase that could be said to give rise to the debt.

In Bradford v. Commissioner, 233 F.2d 935 (6th Cir.1956), the taxpayer substituted her personal note in the amount of $100,000 for her husband's note to a bank in the same amount. Later, the creditor bank accepted a $50,000 payment from the taxpayer in full satisfaction of her debt. The court rejected the Commissioner's assertion that the taxpayer realized cancellation of indebtedness income from the retirement of her debt for $50,000 less than its face amount. The court noted that the taxpayer did not realize any economic gain from what was a loss transaction and cited Bowers v. Kerbaugh-Empire Co., 271 U.S. 170 (1926), discussed in *Kirby Lumber*, for the proposition that a court need not find income from cancellation of indebtedness if the net effect of an entire transaction is a loss.

The result in *Kerbaugh-Empire Co.*, discussed in *Kirby Lumber Company*, is questionable because the court tied the taxpayer's borrowing of German marks to the taxpayer's subsequent investment of the borrowed proceeds in a subsidiary corporation. The Court failed to recognize the presence of two distinct transactions, the borrowing and repayment of marks, and the investment in stock of a subsidiary. (Section 988 now expressly requires assigning independent tax consequences to the two transactions.) For the most part, *Kerbaugh-Empire Co.* is now treated as an anomaly, and the courts rarely, if ever, apply the case to find that there has been no cancellation of indebtedness. See Vukasovich, Inc. v. Commissioner, 790 F.2d 1409 (9th Cir.1986) (declining to follow *Kerbaugh-Empire Co.*); Zarin v. Commissioner, 92 T.C. 1084 (1989) (settlement for $500,000 of $3.4 million gambling debt owed to casino resulted in $2.9 million cancellation of indebtedness income even though transaction as a whole was a loss; declining to follow *Kerbaugh-Empire Co.*), rev'd on other grounds, 916 F.2d 110 (3d Cir.1990) (debtor realized no income because debt was not enforceable under state law); Rev. Rul. 92–99, 1992–2 C.B. 35 (*Kerbaugh-Empire* has been discredited by subsequent Supreme Court cases).

1.2. *Compromise of Loan Guarantees*

Notwithstanding that *Kerbaugh-Empire Co.* generally is considered to have been discredited as precedent, the nature of the origin of the debt sometimes may be important in determining whether cancellation of debt income has been realized. In Payne v. Commissioner, T.C. Memo. 1998–227, rev'd on other grounds, 224 F.3d 415 (5th Cir.2000), the taxpayer had guaranteed a debt of $705,000 owed by a corporation (Payne & Potter) of which he was a shareholder. After the corporation defaulted on the loan, the taxpayer made a partial payment and the debt was restructured to reduce his obligation on the guarantee by $349,500, which the IRS treated as cancellation of debt income. The Tax Court rejected the Commissioner's argument and found for the taxpayer, holding that the guarantor of a promissory note does not recognize any cancellation of debt income when the amount of the debt is compromised:

> In Landreth v. Commissioner, 50 T.C. 803, 812–813 (1968), we distinguished the situation involving a guarantor of a debt from that of a primary obligor on a debt, and we concluded that a guarantor of a debt, upon the payment of the debt by the primary obligor, does not realize cancellation of indebtedness income when relieved of an obligation under a guaranty. We stated as follows:

>> The situation of a guarantor is not like that of a debtor who as a result of the original loan obtains a nontaxable increase in assets. * * * Where a debtor is relieved of his obligation to repay the loan, his net worth is increased over what it would have been if the original transaction had never occurred. This real increase in wealth may be properly taxable. However, where the guarantor is relieved of his contingent liability, either because of payment by the debtor to the creditor or because of a release given him by the creditor, no previously untaxed accretion in assets thereby results in an increase in net worth. * * *

> On the evidence before us, we conclude that the discharge of the balance due on Payne & Potter's $705,000 debt obligation to TexCommBk may have resulted in discharge of indebtedness income to Payne & Potter but not to petitioner. When petitioner's contested liability as guarantor of the debt obligation was settled, petitioner did not realize an increase in net worth, and petitioner is not to be charged with discharge of indebtedness income with regard thereto.

A similar result was reached in Mylander v. Commissioner, T.C. Memo. 2014–191, in which the court also held that the taxpayer did not recognize COD income when he was released from a guarantee on which the principal obligor had defaulted, reasoning that "at no point did [the taxpayer] receive an untaxed accretion of assets with respect to the guaranty." In Friedland v. Commissioner, T.C. Memo. 2001–236, the taxpayer pledged appreciated stock in a closely held corporation to a bank to secure a debt his adult son owed to the bank. When the son defaulted on the loan, the taxpayer's stock was transferred to the bank in satisfaction of the son's debt. The court held that the taxpayer did not recognize any gain because no amount was realized on the transfer. Citing Landreth v. Commissioner, 50 T.C. 803 (1968), supra, the court held that Treas. Reg. § 1.1001–2(a)(1) treats as an amount realized only the amount of the taxpayer's own indebtedness that is discharged by the transfer of property—not the amount of indebtedness of a third party. In a guarantee situation, satisfaction of the debt obligation by a guarantor creates a debt from the original debtor to the guarantor. Thus, in *Friedland*, failure by the son to pay this debt to the father would produce either cancellation of debt income or a nontaxable gift to the son.

2.   WHEN HAS A DEBT BEEN CANCELLED

Any reduction in the amount due triggers realization of cancellation of debt income regardless of whether a new obligation has been substituted or the creditor simply agrees to accept a lesser amount in satisfaction of the debt. See Michaels v. Commissioner, 87 T.C. 1412 (1986) (discount of principal balance due granted by lender on prepayment of home mortgage). This is true even if the debtor's obligation that was cancelled is subject to revival upon the occurrence of some highly contingent future event. In Jelle v. Commissioner, 116 T.C. 63 (2001), the taxpayer owed $269,828 to the Farmers Home Administration (FmHA) on a mortgage loan secured by the taxpayer's farm, which was appraised at a value of $92,057. The taxpayer paid the FmHA the $92,057 "net recovery value" of the loan in exchange for cancellation of the remaining $177,772 of debt, but the cancellation was subject to a "net recovery buyout recapture agreement" under which the taxpayer agreed to repay *pro tanto* the amounts written off by the FmHA in the event he disposed of the farm within a 10-year period for a price that exceeded the $92,057 net recovery value. The taxpayer argued that the debt had not been cancelled before the end of the 10-year period because the "net recovery buyout recapture agreement" was a continuing obligation. The Tax Court disagreed and held that the overall agreement resulted in immediate cancellation of indebtedness income of $177,772 because there was only "the mere chance of some future repayment." The recapture agreement was not a substitute for the taxpayer's former obligation.

In Johnston v. Commissioner, T.C. Memo. 2015–91 (2015), the court held that the mere fact that a creditor fails to take collection action before the period of limitations for collection of a debt has expired does not conclusively give rise to cancellation of debt income for the debtor; "[t]his is because the expiration of the period of limitations generally does not cancel an underlying debt obligation but simply provides an affirmative defense for the debtor in an action by the creditor." In that case the record supported findings that the creditor corporation considered the debt outstanding and expected that the taxpayer would repay the debt, and that the taxpayer was continuing to pay the debt in installments. Furthermore, the creditor had not issued an information return reporting cancellation of debt income and had not claimed a bad debt deduction.

In many cases, a debtor's obligation may be modified with respect to terms other than the principal amount, for example, to extend the time for payment, reduce the interest rate, release collateral, or eliminate restrictions imposed by a loan agreement, without reducing the principal amount due. Historically, changes of this type did not result in the realization of cancellation of indebtedness income even if the fair market value of the new debt obligation was less than the face amount of the old debt that was cancelled. See Rev. Rul. 58–546, 1958–2 C.B. 143. Since 1990, however, § 108(e)(10) has provided that cancellation of indebtedness income is realized whenever a new debt instrument is issued in satisfaction of an existing debt instrument if the "issue price" of the new instrument, determined under the original issue discount (OID) rules, discussed in Chapter 32, is less than the principal amount of the old debt obligation. Whether a new debt instrument has been issued is determined with reference to the principles applied to determine whether a modification is sufficient to treat the creditor as realizing gain or loss on an exchange under § 1001. See Treas. Reg. § 1.1001–3, discussed in Chapter 6, Section 2.B.2. Generally speaking, the result under the regulations is that the debtor realizes cancellation of debt income whenever the creditor realizes a bad debt deduction or loss on the exchange.

3.   EFFECT OF TRANSACTION COSTS ON AMOUNT OF CANCELLATION OF DEBT INCOME

Unless the taxpayer is in a trade or business or the debt relates to a transaction entered into for profit, transaction costs incurred to secure the cancellation of the debt are neither deductible nor an offset against the amount of the debt cancellation that must be included under § 61(a)(12). In Melvin v. Commissioner, T.C. Memo. 2009–199, the taxpayers owed a bank $13,084 on a consumer credit card. The bank agreed to accept $4,579 to settle the debt, and the taxpayers paid a third-party 25 percent of the $8,505 savings, or $2,126 to negotiate the compromise. The court rejected the taxpayer's argument that under § 61(a)(12) only the net benefit of the debt cancellation, i.e., $6,379, was includable in gross income.

SECTION 2.   STATUTORY CODIFICATION OF CANCELLATION OF INDEBTEDNESS RULES

INTERNAL REVENUE CODE: Sections 61(a)(12); 108(a), (b)(1)–(2), (c), (d)(1)–(5), (e)(1), (2), (4), (5); 1017(a), (b)(1)–(3)(B).

REGULATIONS: Sections 1.61–12(a); 1.1017–1(a), (b)(1), (3).

Although § 61(a)(12) specifically includes income from the "discharge of indebtedness" in gross income, § 108 is the principal section interpreted in most litigated cases involving cancellation of indebtedness income. Section 108 provides a number of exceptions to § 61(a)(12) under which a taxpayer may be excused from recognizing cancellation of indebtedness income. In addition, § 108 provides a number of operating rules for calculating the precise amount of cancellation indebtedness income where the amount is not necessarily clear on the face of the transactions.

DETAILED ANALYSIS

1. EXCEPTIONS TO RECOGNITION OF CANCELLATION OF INDEBTEDNESS INCOME—GENERAL

Cancellation of indebtedness income realized in a bankruptcy case or by a taxpayer who is insolvent is excluded by § 108(a)(1)(A) and (B). Section 108(a)(1)(C) excludes from income the cancellation of certain indebtedness incurred in the trade or business of farming.

When cancellation of indebtedness income is excluded under § 108(a)(1), the taxpayer is required to reduce certain tax attributes by the amount of income excluded under § 108. Thus § 108, in large part, operates to defer tax liability rather than to absolutely exclude cancelled debt as income. Section 108(b)(2) requires the taxpayer first to reduce any net operating loss carryovers,[3] then general business credits, capital loss carryovers, and, finally, the basis of property owned by the taxpayer.[4] These attribute reductions will increase the taxpayer's taxable income, or gain on disposition of its property, in future years. In lieu of the reductions mandated by § 108(b)(2), the taxpayer may elect under § 108(b)(5) to reduce the basis of depreciable property. See I.R.C. § 1017. The result will be lower depreciation deductions in future years thereby increasing future taxable income by the amount of the deferred cancellation of indebtedness income. See I.R.C. § 1017(b)(3).

The taxpayer's tax liability for the year of cancellation is determined without any reduction in attributes under § 108(b) to ascertain the amount, if any, of the tax attributes that will be reduced. Treas. Reg. § 1.108–7. "This ordering rule affords the taxpayer the use of certain of its tax attributes described in § 108(b)(2), including any losses carried forward to the taxable year of cancellation, for purposes of determining its tax for the taxable year of discharge, before subjecting those attributes to reduction." T.D. 9080, Reduction of Tax Attributes Due to Discharge of Indebtedness, 68 F.R. 42590 (July 21, 2003) (preamble). Basis reductions under § 1017 occur at the beginning of the taxable year following the year in which the cancellation occurred. See Treas. Reg. § 1.1017–1(b)(4).

Section 108(e)(5) excludes cancellation of indebtedness income that qualifies as a purchase price reduction. Note that § 108(e)(5) acts as a deferral provision since the exclusion requires a reduction in basis that results in decreased future depreciation deductions or loss on disposition, or increased gain on future disposition.

2. INSOLVENCY AND BANKRUPTCY EXCEPTIONS

Relying in part on the freeing of assets theory of *Kirby Lumber,* the Board of Tax Appeals held in Lakeland Grocery Company v. Commissioner, 36 B.T.A. 289 (1937), that an insolvent taxpayer did not recognize income on the cancellation of its indebtedness. However, because the exclusion was

---

[3]   For net operating loss deductions, see Chapter 29, Section 2.

[4]   Section 1017(d) provides that basis reductions under this provision be treated as adjustments to basis requiring recapture as ordinary income under §§ 1245 and 1250, discussed in Chapter 25, Section 1.

grounded in the absence of a balance sheet improvement for the insolvent taxpayer, the exclusion was available only to the extent of the taxpayer's insolvency. Cancellation of indebtedness income was realized to the extent the taxpayer's assets exceeded liabilities after the cancellation.

This judicial insolvency exception has been incorporated into §§ 108(a)(1)(B), (a)(3) and (d)(3), which exclude cancellation of indebtedness income of a taxpayer if the taxpayer is insolvent immediately before the cancellation. In Gitlitz v. Commissioner, 531 U.S. 206 (2001), the Supreme Court held that the enactment of § 108(e) pre-empted the field: the statutory insolvency exception is exclusive, and prior judicial principles cannot be applied to expand or narrow the statutory rules.

Exclusion of cancellation of indebtedness income under the insolvency exception is limited to the amount by which the taxpayer is insolvent, thus requiring inclusion to the extent that the cancellation of indebtedness renders the taxpayer solvent. Insolvency is defined in § 108(d)(3) as the excess of the taxpayer's liabilities over the fair market value of assets. In Carlson v. Commissioner, 116 T.C. 87 (2001), the Tax Court held that the definition of "insolvent" in § 108(d)(3) requires that all of the taxpayer's assets, including assets exempt from the claims of creditors under state law, be included in determining whether the taxpayer's liabilities exceed his assets. The taxpayer had argued that assets exempt from creditors' claims under state law should be excluded from the calculation, thus making it easier for a taxpayer to demonstrate insolvency. The court rejected this argument. It compared the definition of "insolvent" under the Bankruptcy Code, 11 U.S.C. § 101(26), which expressly excludes exempt property from the calculation, with the definition under § 108(d)(3), which does not do so, and concluded that the difference was intentional. By using the different definition Congress intended exempt assets not to be excluded from the calculation in determining whether the taxpayer is insolvent for purposes of § 108.

Section 108(a)(1)(A) excludes cancellation of indebtedness income that occurs in a Title 11 bankruptcy case. A Title 11 case is any case in which the taxpayer is subject to the jurisdiction of the court under Title 11 of the United States Code (relating to bankruptcy). I.R.C. § 108(d)(2).

There is little theoretical justification in tax policy for the relief from cancellation of indebtedness income provided to insolvent or bankrupt taxpayers. This form of income is excluded, while income derived from other sources by an insolvent taxpayer remains subject to tax. See e.g., Parkford v. Commissioner, 133 F.2d 249 (9th Cir.1943) (insolvent individual has income from compensation); Estate of Delman v. Commissioner, 73 T.C. 15, 31–33 (1979) (insolvent individual required to recognize gain on disposition of property).

3.   PURCHASE PRICE REDUCTION

In Hirsch v. Commissioner, 115 F.2d 656 (7th Cir.1940), the taxpayer acquired property for cash plus the assumption of a mortgage held by a third party. The value of the property declined below the face amount of the mortgage and the taxpayer offered to convey the property to the creditor in exchange for cancellation of the debt. The creditor refused the offer but agreed to reduce the amount of the mortgage by $7,000. The Commissioner asserted that the taxpayer realized cancellation of indebtedness income as a result of a $7,000 balance sheet improvement resulting from reduction of the mortgage. The court held there was no cancellation of indebtedness income, concluding instead that the taxpayer had merely obtained a reduction in the cost of the property. With a reference to the whole transaction approach of *Bowers v. Kerbaugh-Empire Co.,* supra, the *Hirsch* court stated: "[The taxpayer's] ultimate gain or loss cannot be determined until liquidation of his capital investment. When costs go into property, whether one is to gain or lose must of necessity remain undecided until the property is sold. Credits upon the cost of the investment do not become gain until we find that what is realized upon sale exceeds the total cost, after deducting such voluntary reductions." 115 F.2d at 658. In Fifth Avenue-Fourteenth Street Corp. v. Commissioner, 147 F.2d 453 (2d Cir.1944), the court described the purchase price reduction exception as irrational and held that where the doctrine is to be applied, it is limited to direct negotiations between the seller and purchaser of encumbered property.

The purchase price reduction exception is now codified in § 108(e)(5), which provides that cancellation of indebtedness income does not include a reduction of an obligation from the purchaser of property to the seller of the property when the obligation arose out of the sale of the property. The reduction or cancellation of purchase money debt is treated as a reduction of the purchase price, resulting in a reduction of the basis of the property. The purchase price reduction exception does not apply, however, if the reduction occurred in a Title 11 case or if the purchaser was insolvent. The result of this ordering rule is not to require inclusion in gross income of the cancelled indebtedness, but to invoke the reduction of tax attributes rules of § 108(b).

Section 108(e)(5) was enacted to end disputes between the IRS and taxpayers over whether cancellation of indebtedness attributable to the purchase of property should be treated as income or as a true reduction in the purchase price of property. S.Rep. No. 96–1035, 96th Cong., 2d Sess. 16 (1980). Legislative history indicates that the provision applies only to a reduction of debt resulting from direct negotiations between buyer and seller. The purchase price reduction is not available if there has been a transfer of either the debt or the purchased property to a third party. S.Rep. No. 96–1035 at 16–17. In Michaels v. Commissioner, 87 T.C. 1412 (1986), the taxpayer was required to recognize cancellation of indebtedness income on prepayment at a discount of a purchase money home mortgage debt to a third-party lender. The court rejected the taxpayer's argument that the cancellation of indebtedness income was excludable under § 108(e)(5).

The purchase price reduction provision is limited to debt relief negotiated between the buyer and seller of property. However, a purchaser of property financed by a loan from a third-party lender, as in *Hirsch,* who subsequently negotiates a reduction in the amount of the debt, appears to be in the same position as the purchaser who negotiates a reduction in purchase money debt held by the seller.[5] In either case the ultimate cost of the property to the taxpayer is reduced by the amount of debt reduction. However, the purchaser who borrows from a third party may be in control of cash for a period of time. In addition, the seller who is financing the acquisition may be tempted to inflate the purchase price of the property while a third-party lender will be more concerned that the financed purchase price reflects the value of the property.

The argument that *Hirsch* and its progeny created a judicial purchase price exception that survives enactment of § 108(e)(5) was rejected in Preslar v. Commissioner, 167 F.3d 1323 (10th Cir. 1999), which held that the enactment of § 108(e)(5) preempted any preexisting "common law" purchase price adjustment exception. The exception applies only to indebtedness owed by the purchaser to the seller of property. As in *Preslar*, the courts have consistently held that relief from recognition of the cancellation of debt income is limited to negotiations between the buyer and the seller who holds the buyer's debt instrument. Section 108(e)(5) does not apply to cancellation of purchase money debt owed to a third-party lender. In Rev. Rul. 92–99, 1992–2 C.B. 35, the IRS expressly rejected the application of *Hirsch* to a reduction by a third-party lender of nonrecourse debt that was incurred to purchase property that had declined in value. Nevertheless, in the same ruling the IRS indicated that it would treat debt reduction by a third-party lender as a purchase price reduction to the extent that the debt reduction is based on an infirmity that clearly relates back to the original sale, such as a misrepresentation of a material fact or fraud.

4.   LOST DEDUCTIONS

Section 108(e)(2) provides that no cancellation of indebtedness income is realized from the cancellation of a debt that would have given rise to a deduction if it had been paid. This provision applies primarily to the accounts payable of a cash method trade or business, but it may apply to other items, such as home mortgage interest deductible under § 163(h). It does not apply to accounts payable of accrual method taxpayers because a deduction is allowed when the debt is incurred. See Rev. Rul. 67–200, 1967–1 C.B. 15, clarified by Rev. Rul. 70–406, 1970–2 C.B. 16. No real exclusion is provided by this provision, however, since the deduction is lost by virtue of the debt not having been paid. Section 108(e)(2) simply eliminates the requirement that the cancelled amount be included in income and then subsequently be treated as constructively paid, thus giving rise to an offsetting deduction.

5.   REAL PROPERTY BUSINESS DEBT

Section 108(a)(1)(D) and (c) allow noncorporate taxpayers to elect to exclude income arising from cancellation of "qualified real property business indebtedness." Qualified real property business indebtedness is indebtedness incurred in connection with, and secured by, real property used in a trade or business. If the taxpayer elects the exclusion, the taxpayer must reduce the basis of depreciable real property by the amount excluded. I.R.C.

---

[5]   *Hirsch* was decided on the basis that gain is not realized until disposition of the underlying property. An answer to *Hirsch* may be that this exclusion of cancellation of indebtedness income is wrong because the realization requirement itself distorts income.

§ 108(c)(1)(A). Treas. Reg. § 1.1017–1(c) provides ordering rules under which the basis of the qualifying real property is reduced first, and any remaining excluded cancellation of debt income is applied to reduce the basis of other real property held by the taxpayer for use in a trade or business or as an investment. The purpose of this provision is to facilitate refinancing of failing real estate projects. Thus § 108(c)(2)(A) limits the exclusion to the amount by which the outstanding principal amount of the debt before the cancellation exceeds the fair market value of the property (minus the principal amount of any other qualified real property business indebtedness secured by the property). To assure that the exclusion results only in deferral and not permanent exclusion, § 108(c)(2)(B) further limits the amount of the exclusion to the aggregate adjusted basis of depreciable real property held by the taxpayer immediately before the cancellation. If a debtor is insolvent at the time of the cancellation, the insolvency exception rules take precedence. I.R.C. § 108(a)(2)(B).

6.   DISCHARGE OF STUDENT LOANS

Section 108(f) provides an exclusion for gross income resulting from the discharge (in whole or in part) of any student loan (or any loan made to refinance a student loan) if the discharge was pursuant to a loan provision that provided for the discharge if the borrower worked for a certain period of time in certain professions for any of a broad class of employers. Loan repayment assistance programs (LRAP) now provided by law schools are often designed to qualify for exclusion under this provision. These programs make loans to students to allow them to remit scheduled payments on their student loans; the LRAP loans are subsequently forgiven by law schools if the student works for specified periods of time for the government or for public interest organizations. See Rev. Rul. 2008–34, 2008–2 C.B. 76 (analyzing a typical LRAP loan and concluding that its forgiveness would qualify under § 108(f)).

SECTION 3.   THE DISPUTED DEBT, OR CONTESTED LIABILITY, DOCTRINE

INTERNAL REVENUE CODE: Section 108(e)(5).

Preslar v. Commissioner

United States Court of Appeals, Tenth Circuit, 1999.
167 F.3d 1323.

■ BRISCOE, CIRCUIT JUDGE.

The Commissioner of Internal Revenue appeals the United States Tax Court's decision to redetermine the tax deficiency assessed against Layne and Sue Preslar for underpayment of 1989 federal income taxes. The Tax Court held the Preslars' settlement of a loan obligation for less than the face amount of the loan did not create taxable income because the contested liability/disputed debt exception to the general discharge-of-indebtedness income rule rendered the write-off nontaxable. We * * * reverse and remand.

I.

Layne Preslar, a real estate agent of twenty-five years, commenced negotiations in 1983 to purchase a 2500-acre ranch near Cloudcroft, New Mexico. High Nogal Ranch, Inc., owned the ranch and was a debtor-in-possession in a Chapter 11 bankruptcy proceeding. Citizens State Bank of Carrizozo, Security Bank and Trust of Alamogordo, and Moncor Bank held mortgages in the ranch. Moncor Bank, which had been experiencing serious financial difficulties and whose interest was subordinate to the other banks, took the lead in assisting in negotiations between High Nogal and Preslar. * * *

On July 12, 1983, after six months of talks, Layne and Sue Preslar agreed to purchase the ranch for $1 million, with the sale to be financed by Moncor Bank. The agreement expressly referred to the fact that Moncor Bank was financing the purchase, but only the Preslars and the president of High Nogal signed the contract on September 1, 1983. The Preslars executed a $1 million promissory note in favor of Moncor Bank, secured by a mortgage on the ranch. The Preslars were to pay fourteen annual installments of $66,667, with interest at twelve percent per annum, with final payment due September 1, 1998. * * *

The Preslars intended to develop the ranch as a sportsman's resort. * * *

Moncor Bank permitted the Preslars to repay their loan by assigning the installment sales contracts of purchasers of cabin lots to Moncor Bank at a discount. There is no reference to this unique repayment arrangement in the loan documents. * * * When each cabin lot was sold, the Preslars assigned and physically transferred the written sales contract to Moncor Bank. In return, Moncor Bank credited the Preslars' debt obligation in an amount equal to 95 percent of the stated principal contract price, regardless of actual payments received from the purchaser. Moncor Bank received a security interest in each lot sold to protect its interests in the event a purchaser defaulted. Between September 1983 and August 1985, the Preslars sold nineteen cabin lots and had assigned most of the contracts to Moncor Bank prior to its declared insolvency. Moncor Bank had credited the Preslars' principal loan balance with approximately $200,000. Funds applied to interest are not included in this amount; thus, the aggregate amount of discounted installment contracts assigned to Moncor Bank exceeded $200,000.

In August 1985, Moncor Bank was declared insolvent and the Federal Deposit Insurance Corporation (FDIC) was appointed as receiver. The FDIC notified the Preslars of the insolvency and advised them to make all future payments on their loan to the FDIC. The FDIC refused to accept further assignments of sale contracts as repayment and ordered the Preslars to suspend sales of cabin lots. The Preslars complied with the suspension directive, but made no further payments on the loan.

The Preslars filed an action against the FDIC for breach of contract in September 1985, seeking an order requiring the FDIC to accept assignment of sales contracts as loan repayment. The parties settled the action in December 1988 after the FDIC agreed to accept $350,000 in full satisfaction of the Preslars' indebtedness. The Preslars borrowed the $350,000 from another bank and, after the funds were remitted to the FDIC, the original $1 million promissory note was marked "paid."

At the time of the settlement, the unpaid balance on the Preslars' loan was $799,463. The Preslars paid a total of $550,537 on the loan ($350,000 settlement plus $200,537 credited for assignment of sales contracts). Therefore, as a result of the settlement, the Preslars' outstanding debt obligation was reduced by $449,463 ($1 million less $550,537).

The Preslars did not include the $449,463 debt write-off as discharge-of-indebtedness income on their 1989 joint tax return. Rather, they opted to reduce their basis in the ranch by $430,000 pursuant to Internal Revenue Code § 108(e)(5), 26 U.S.C. § 108(e)(5). The Preslars' 1989 tax return was audited and they were assessed a deficiency because (1) they had realized $449,463 in discharge-of-indebtedness income, and (2) they were not eligible to treat such income as a purchase price adjustment under § 108(e)(5). * * *

The Preslars sought a redetermination of the deficiency in United States Tax Court, insisting they were free to treat their settlement with the FDIC as a purchase price adjustment pursuant to § 108(e)(5) and/or common law. They supported this theory in part by claiming the FDIC's refusal to honor their repayment agreement with Moncor Bank amounted to an infirmity relating back to the original sale, thereby negating the general prohibition against treating debt reductions as purchase price adjustments. * * * At no time, however, did the Preslars dispute their underlying liability on the $1 million note.

* * *

The Tax Court ruled in favor of the Preslars without addressing the purchase price adjustment issue. Instead, the court *sua sponte* invoked the contested liability doctrine and held the Preslars' unusual payment arrangement with Moncor Bank caused their liability for the full $1 million loan to be brought into question. The court determined the true amount of the Preslars' indebtedness was not firmly established until they settled with the FDIC; thus, no discharge-of-indebtedness income could have accrued to the Preslars as a result of the settlement. * * *

II.

* * *

Discharge-of-Indebtedness Income

* * *

This case centers around the Commissioner's determination of the Preslars' discharge-of-indebtedness income after they settled their loan obligation with the FDIC in December 1988. The concept of discharge-of-indebtedness income, first articulated in United States v. Kirby Lumber Co., 284 U.S. 1(1931), and later codified in 26 U.S.C. § 61(a)(12), requires taxpayers who have incurred a financial obligation that is later discharged in whole or in part, to recognize as taxable income the extent of the reduction in the obligation. Two rationales have been identified for this rule:

> This rule is based on the premise that the taxpayer has an increase in wealth due to the reduction in valid claims against the taxpayer's assets. In the alternative it has been suggested that taxation is appropriate because the consideration received by a taxpayer in exchange for [his] indebtedness is not included in income when received because of the obligation to repay and the cancellation of that obligation removes the reason for the original exclusion.

2 Jacob Mertens, Jr., Mertens Law of Federal Income Taxation § 11.01 (1996). [Loans ordinarily are not taxable because the borrower has assumed an obligation to repay the debt in full at some future date.]* * * Discharge-of-indebtedness principles come into play, however, if that assumption of repayment proves erroneous. Otherwise, taxpayers could secure income with no resulting tax liability.

It is undisputed that the Preslars financed their purchase of the ranch in 1983 by executing a $1 million promissory note in favor of Moncor Bank. It is similarly uncontested that when the Preslars settled their lawsuit with the FDIC in 1988, thereby extinguishing all obligations arising from the 1983 loan, only $550,537 had been paid on the loan principal. Nevertheless, the Tax Court ruled the Preslars' underlying debt was disputed and fell within the judicially-created "contested liability" exception to discharge-of-indebtedness income.

Contested Liability/Disputed Debt Exception

The "contested liability" or, as it is occasionally known, "disputed debt" doctrine rests on the premise that if a taxpayer disputes the *original amount* of a debt in good faith, a subsequent settlement of that dispute is "treated as the amount of debt cognizable for tax purposes." Zarin v. Commissioner, 916 F.2d 110, 115 (3d Cir.1990). In other words, the "excess of the original debt over the amount determined to have been due" may be disregarded in calculating gross income. Id. The few decisions that have interpreted this doctrine have generated considerable controversy.

The origins of the contested liability doctrine can be traced to N. Sobel, Inc. v. Commissioner, 40 B.T.A. 1263 (1939) * * * . In that case, a New York corporation purchased 100 shares of a bank's stock and signed a $21,700 note as payment. When the note matured, the stock was worthless. The corporation sued the bank for rescission, insisting the loan contravened state law and the bank had failed to fulfill its promise to guarantee the corporation against loss. Shortly thereafter, the state superintendent of banks closed the bank because of insolvency and initiated a countersuit against the corporation for the amount of the note. The parties ultimately settled the consolidated proceedings with the corporation paying the superintendent $10,850 in return for discharge of the debt. The corporation then took a $10,850 deduction in the year of settlement. The Commissioner disallowed the deduction and assessed a $10,850 deficiency, representing the amount of the original loan over the settlement figure. The Board of Tax Appeals reversed the ruling and upheld the deduction, concluding the corporation's ownership of the shares and the degree of liability on the note were highly unclear. * * * The Board found the corporation's financial obligations could not be assessed definitively prior to resolution of its dispute with the superintendent and, since settlement compromised the parties' claims and precluded recognition of their legal rights, the existence and amount of the corporation liability were not fixed until the date of settlement. Thus, release of the note did not amount to a gain for the corporation.

In *Zarin*, the court embraced the reasoning of *N. Sobel* while reversing the Commissioner's recognition of discharge-of-indebtedness income. The state gaming commission identified Zarin as a compulsive gambler and ordered an Atlantic City casino to refrain from issuing him additional credit, but the casino ignored the commission. When Zarin's debt surpassed $3.4 million, the casino filed a state action to collect the funds. Zarin initially denied liability on the grounds the casino's claim was unenforceable under New Jersey law. The parties later settled the dispute for $500,000. After Zarin failed to account for the debt write-off on his tax return, the Commissioner assessed a deficiency for approximately $2.9 million, the amount by which Zarin's underlying debt exceeded his settlement with the casino. The Tax Court affirmed. However, a divided Third Circuit held Zarin had no discharge-of-indebtedness income because, inter alia, his transaction with the casino arose from a contested liability. * * * Citing no authority, the majority reasoned that "[w]hen a debt is unenforceable, it follows that the amount of the debt, and not just the liability thereon, is in dispute." * * * Therefore, the $500,000 settlement "fixed the amount of loss and the amount of debt cognizable for tax purposes." * * *

The problem with the Third Circuit's holding is it treats liquidated and unliquidated debts alike. The whole theory behind requiring that the *amount* of a debt be disputed before the contested liability exception can be triggered is that only in the context of disputed debts is the Internal Revenue Service (IRS) unaware of the exact consideration initially exchanged in a transaction. * * * The mere fact that a taxpayer challenges the enforceability of a debt in good faith does not necessarily mean he or she is shielded from discharge-of-indebtedness income upon resolution of the dispute. To implicate the contested liability doctrine, the original amount of the debt must be unliquidated. A total denial of liability is not a dispute touching upon the amount of the underlying debt. One commentator has observed:

> Enforceability of the debt * * * should not affect the tax treatment of the transaction. If the parties initially treated the transaction as a loan when the loan proceeds were received, thereby not declaring the receipt as income, then the transaction should be treated consistently when the loan is discharged and income should be declared in the amount of the discharge.

Gregory M. Giangiordano, Taxation—Discharge of Indebtedness Income—Zarin v. Commissioner, 64 Temp. L.Rev. 1189, 1202 n.88 (1991). A holding to the contrary would strain IRS treatment of unenforceable debts and, in large part, disavow the Supreme Court's mandate that the phrase "gross income" be interpreted as broadly as the Constitution permits. See Glenshaw Glass, 348 U.S. at 432 & n. 11.

This conclusion is underscored by the Supreme Court's holding in *Tufts* that a nonrecourse mortgage (i.e., taxpayer has no personal liability upon default) must be treated as an enforceable loan both when it is made and when it is discharged. 461 U.S. at 311–13. The Court reasoned that because the indebtedness is treated as a true debt when it is incurred, it must be treated as a true debt when it is discharged, with all the attendant tax consequences. Id. at 309–10. It seems evident from this ruling that if the distinction between the recourse and nonrecourse nature of a loan has no bearing on calculation of gross income, the enforceability of a debt should be of equally minimal importance. Of course, if the debt is unenforceable as a result of an infirmity at the time of its creation (e.g., fraud or misrepresentation), tax liability may be avoided through a purchase price reduction under 26 U.S.C. § 108(e)(5) or an "infirmity exception."

* * *

In this case, the Tax Court observed that "the unusual payment arrangement between [the Preslars] and Moncor Bank relating to the Bank loan casts significant doubt on [the Preslars'] liability for the total $1 million stated principal amount of the Bank loan." Tax Ct. Op. at 8. Accepting the Preslars' contention that their $1 million purchase price had been inflated and did not reflect the fair market value of the ranch, the Tax Court suggested the Preslars had agreed to the terms of the financing arrangement only after Moncor Bank assented to a favorable repayment scheme involving assignment of installment sales contracts. The court held when the FDIC refused to honor this payment arrangement, "a legitimate dispute arose regarding the nature and amount of [the Preslars'] liability on the Bank loan." Id. Only after the Preslars and the FDIC settled their subsequent lawsuit, the court reasoned, was the amount of liability on the loan finally established.

It is conceivable that two parties could negotiate a loan transaction in which the underlying amount of a debt is tied to the existence or nonexistence of some post-execution event. Indeed, the IRS has defined "indebtedness" as "an obligation, absolute and not contingent, to pay on demand or within a given time, in cash or another medium, a fixed amount." Treas. Reg. § 1.108(b)–1(c), 26 C.F.R. § 1.108(b)–1(c) (1998). Contrary to the Tax Court's representations, however, there is no evidence of such an agreement here.

The Preslars advanced no competent evidence to support their theory that their loan obligation was linked to the repayment scheme. * * * Neither the May 1984 letter from Moncor Bank to Layne Preslar nor the unsigned 1985 Dealer Agreement * * * contains any statement evincing an intent to link the underlying liability with the repayment scheme. * * * Preslar's own self-serving testimony regarding the intentions of the parties to the original loan agreement is not sufficient to support the Preslars' integrated transaction theory. * * *

* * *

Although ultimately irrelevant, the Preslars offered no evidence, other than Layne Preslar's self-serving testimony, that the fair market value of the ranch differed from their $1 million purchase price. * * * Moreover, even if the Preslars could demonstrate the property was worth less than the purchase price, they still could not invoke the contested liability doctrine in the absence of proof the loan they executed was tainted by fraud or material misrepresentations, because the underlying amount of their debt obligation remained liquidated. * * * There are no allegations of fraud or misrepresentation in this case.

* * *

Purchase Price Adjustment

Another method by which taxpayers can avoid discharge-of-indebtedness income is to classify their debt reductions as purchase price adjustments. This rule permits taxpayers to reflect their debt reduction by adjusting the basis of their property rather than recognizing an immediate gain as cancellation of indebtedness. Although this principle had been part of the common law for decades, Congress codified the rule as part of the Bankruptcy Tax Act of 1980, Pub.L. No. 96–589, § 2(a), 94 Stat. 3389, 3389–90 (1980) (codified at 26 U.S.C. § 108(e)(5)).

* * *

The Preslars cannot treat their settlement with the FDIC as a purchase price reduction. Section 108(e)(5) applies only to direct agreements between a purchaser and seller. S.Rep. No. 96–1035 at 16 (1980) * * * . "If the debt has been transferred by the seller to a third party (whether or not related to the seller), or if the property has been transferred by the buyer to a third party (whether or not related to the buyer)," the purchase price reduction exception is not available and normal discharge-of-indebtedness rules control. * * * Although Moncor Bank helped negotiate the terms of the sale, it did so only in its capacity as a mortgage holder. * * *

Common Law Purchase Price Reduction Doctrine

The Preslars insist the common law purchase price reduction doctrine may be invoked in cases where 26 U.S.C. § 108(e)(5) is inapplicable. The Commissioner responds that § 108(e)(5) has displaced the common law on this issue and, in any event, a debt reduction by a third-party lender was not considered a purchase price adjustment under common law. See Fifth Ave-Fourteenth St. Corp. v. Commissioner, 147 F.2d 453, 456–57 (2d Cir.1944) (doctrine does not apply where reduction results from arms-length transaction relating solely to debt itself).

It is clear the case law developed prior to enactment of § 108(e)(5) did not extend the purchase price reduction exception to debt settlements outside the purchase money mortgage context. * * * The case law was not consistent, however, with respect to purchase money mortgages involving third parties. Compare Fifth Ave., 147 F.2d at 456–57 (doctrine does not apply to third-party transactions), with Hirsch v. Commissioner, 115 F.2d 656, 657–59 (7th Cir.1940) (doctrine does apply to third-party transactions).

The Hirsch case relied on Bowers v. Kerbaugh-Empire Co., 271 U.S. 170 (1926), a decision implicitly repudiated in subsequent years. See Glenshaw Glass, 348 U.S. at 429–32 & n. 11; Kirby Lumber, 284 U.S. at 2. Further, § 108(e)(5) was intended, at least in part, to create uniformity in this jurisprudence. See S.Rep. No. 96–1035 at 16–17 (1980) ("This provision is intended to eliminate disagreements between the Internal Revenue Service and the debtor as to whether, in a particular case to which the provision applies, the debt reduction should be treated as discharge income or a true price adjustment."). If, as the Preslars argue, the common law rule remains viable and permits taxpayers involved in third-party transactions to treat their debt reductions as purchase price adjustments rather than additions to their gross income, § 108(e)(5) would be rendered meaningless. We agree with the Commissioner's rationale for imposing the direct seller-purchaser negotiation requirement, as articulated in a 1992 revenue ruling:

> An agreement to reduce a debt between a purchaser and a third-party lender is not a true adjustment of the purchase price paid for the property because the seller has received the entire purchase price from the purchaser and is not a party to the debt

reduction agreement. The debt reduction relates solely to the debt and results in discharge of indebtedness income to the debtor.

Rev. Rul. 92–99, 1992–2 C.B. 35. Accordingly, the Preslars may not treat their settlement with the FDIC as a common law purchase price reduction.

III.

Conclusion + Holding

We REVERSE the Tax Court's vacatur of the Commissioner's determination of tax deficiency and * * * REMAND the case with instructions to enter judgment in favor of the Commissioner.

DETAILED ANALYSIS

1. CANCELLATION OF INDEBTEDNESS AND THE NATURE OF THE TRANSACTION

The *Zarin* case, which was discussed and criticized by the Tenth Circuit in *Preslar*, has generated much debate. Mr. Zarin, a compulsive gambler, had borrowed from an Atlantic City casino over $3.4 million, which he contemporaneously lost back to the casino. Zarin's liability to repay the debt was unenforceable under New Jersey law. Ultimately, Zarin settled the debt for $500,000. Between the Tax Court and the Court of Appeals, six different judges wrote extensive opinions with differing analyses of whether and why Zarin should or should not have recognized income. In the various opinions Zarin's recognition of gross income depended upon whether he was deemed to have received for his markers (a) cash or cash equivalents in which case repayment of the debt for less should have produced income (Zarin v. Commissioner, 92 T.C. 1084 (1989) majority opinion), (b) casino chips that were property of contested value in which case cancellation of indebtedness income was excludable under § 108(e)(5) (92 T.C. at 1107, Ruwe J. dissenting), or (c) an opportunity to partake of the gambling services provided by the casino, which was either something of value (Tax Court majority, supra) or a service for which liability for payment was disputed or unenforceable. In each of the different opinions Zarin's receipt of gross income is characterized by reference to the nature of the initial part of the transaction.

In United States v. Hall, 307 F.2d 238 (10th Cir.1962), the court held that the taxpayer's settlement of a disputed gambling debt by a transfer of cattle to the creditor did not result in cancellation of indebtedness income even though the value of the transferred cattle was less than the debt.[6] In contrast to the Third Circuit's analysis in *Zarin*, the court in *Hall* expressly stated that the result in the case was not based on the contested amount of the taxpayer's gambling debt. 307 F.2d at 241. Rather, citing *Kerbaugh-Empire Co.*, discussed in *Kirby Lumber, supra*, and quoting extensively from Bradford v. Commissioner, 233 F.2d 935 (6th Cir. 1956), *supra*, the court in

---

[6] The court also held that the taxpayer should recognize gain on the disposition of the cattle in an amount equal to the value of cattle accepted in cancellation of the debt less the taxpayer's basis in the cattle.

Hall concluded that the overall transaction did not result in income: "The cold fact is that taxpayer suffered a substantial loss from gambling, the amount of which was determined by the transfer [of cattle]." Thus, in *Hall*, the characterization of the cancellation of the debt was not determined with reference to the initial part of the transaction but with reference to the whole transaction.

In line with the result in *Hall*, the taxpayer in *Zarin* argued that he did not realize income because his overall gambling transaction resulted in a loss. The Tax Court majority, however, rejected the taxpayer's argument and concluded that Zarin was required to recognize cancellation of indebtedness income. The Tax Court majority refused to follow the doctrine of *Kerbaugh-Empire Co.* and rejected the application of *Hall* to Zarin's gambling debt. Instead the Tax Court relied on Vukasovich, Inc. v. Commissioner, 790 F.2d 1409 (9th Cir.1986). In *Vukasovich* the taxpayer borrowed money to invest in a cattle-feeding venture. The taxpayer sold his interest for less than the borrowed amount. The taxpayer was then able to settle his debt with the creditor for less than the amount originally borrowed. The *Vukasovich* court refused to treat the taxpayer's borrowing and investment of borrowed proceeds in a cattle-feeding operation as a single transaction resulting in an overall loss and required the taxpayer to recognize cancellation of indebtedness income in the year the taxpayer's indebtedness was settled for less than the amount of the borrowed proceeds. The court in *Vukasovich* concluded that the unitary transactional approach of *Kerbaugh-Empire Co.* had been repudiated by subsequent Supreme Court decisions, including *Kirby Lumber*. The court noted, however, that "requiring some benefit to the taxpayer from the transaction creating the indebtedness explains such cases as *Commissioner v. Rail Joint*," *supra*, and added: "We have no doubt that an increase in wealth from the cancellation of indebtedness is taxable where the taxpayer received something of value in exchange for the indebtedness." 790 F.2d at 1415. Accepting this logic, the Tax Court majority in *Zarin* stated:

> We conclude here that the taxpayer did receive value at the time he incurred the debt and that only his promise to repay the value received prevented taxation of the value received at the time of the credit transaction. When, in the subsequent year, a portion of the obligation to repay was forgiven, the general rule that income results from forgiveness of indebtedness, section 61(a)(12), should apply.

By comparison, the result in *Hall* was wholly dependent on the now largely discredited "entire-transaction" approach of *Kerbaugh-Empire Co.*, which failed to recognize that the taxpayer actually had engaged in two separate and distinct transactions.

2. ENFORCEABILITY OF THE OBLIGATION AND CONTESTED LIABILITIES

In *Preslar*, the Tenth Circuit did not attempt to distinguish the Third Circuit's *Zarin* opinion, but rather confronted it head on and dismissed *Zarin* as an erroneous application of the contested debt doctrine. The Third Circuit reversed the Tax Court in *Zarin* based on its conclusion that because Zarin's obligation was not enforceable under state law, there was no debt to be cancelled. Alternatively, the Third Circuit concluded that Zarin's liability was contested, so that subsequent settlement of the liability did not result in an accession to wealth.

The Third Circuit suggested in *Zarin* that it would have reached the same result if Zarin had received $3 million cash in exchange for his notes and used the cash to purchase the chips. The court stated:

> [I]f a taxpayer took out a loan for $10,000, refused in good faith to pay the full $10,000 back, and then reached an agreement with the lendor (sic) that he would pay back only $7000 in full satisfaction of the debt, the transaction would be treated as if the initial loan was $7000. When the taxpayer tenders the $7000 payment, he will have been deemed to have paid the full amount of the initially disputed debt. Accordingly, there is no tax consequence to the taxpayer upon payment.

The fact that the obligation is not enforceable should not disguise a $3 million accession to wealth in such a case. Similarly, if the taxpayer initially borrowed $10,000 of *cash,* the presence of a dispute over the enforceability of the debt does not change the fact that the taxpayer has received a $3,000 accession to wealth on this transaction.

In *Preslar*, the Tenth Circuit had no difficulty in finding gross income in this situation. A dispute over enforceability or the amount of a debt should affect the recognition of gain on cancellation only if the debt is incurred in exchange for the receipt of something other than cash, such as goods or services which the taxpayer later claims were not worth the original purchase price. In the case of a cash receipt there is no room for a dispute regarding the presence of an accession to wealth on cancellation of the debt for less than the amount of cash received.

The same issue arises when collection of a debt is barred by a statute of limitations. In Estate of Bankhead v. Commissioner, 60 T.C. 535 (1973), the taxpayer was required to recognize cancellation of indebtedness income on loans that became unenforceable because the creditor failed to file necessary claims in the probate of the deceased taxpayer's estate. The court pointed out that the debtor was "enriched by the abolition of a duty to repay money he has previously received and had the unlimited use of. It is this undeniable economic benefit that creates income * * * ." 60 T.C. at 540. See also Carl T. Miller Trust v. Commissioner, 76 T.C. 191 (1981) (same result).

In Johnston v. Commissioner, T.C. Memo. 2015–9, the Tax Court held that the mere fact that a creditor fails to take collection action before the period of limitations for collection of a debt has expired does not conclusively give rise to cancellation of debt income for the debtor. In *Johnston*, the taxpayer's employer lent him $450,000, repayment of which would become due upon the termination of his employment. When the taxpayer left his position with the employer, the employer did not demand repayment. Subsequently, the taxpayer returned to his position with his original employer. Two years later the statute of limitations on collection of the loan expired. The IRS asserted that the taxpayer realized COD income upon the expiration of the statute of limitations on collection. The Tax Court based its holding on the reasoning that "the expiration of the period of limitations generally does not cancel an underlying debt obligation but simply provides an affirmative defense for the debtor in an action by the creditor." An officer of the creditor corporation testified that the corporation considered the debt outstanding and expected that the taxpayer would repay the debt. The taxpayer was repaying the debt via payroll deductions of $1,000 per month from his paycheck. Furthermore, the creditor had not issued a Form 1099-C and had not claimed a bad debt deduction.

As an alternative analysis, even if the transaction in *Zarin* is not viewed in accession-to-wealth terms, one might argue that Zarin received personal consumption value from the gambling experience that approached the full $3.4 million in chips that he lost. In that case, Zarin should be taxed on the difference between what he paid for the gambling experience ($500,000) and the value that he received from the experience ($3.4 million), or $2.9 million.

SECTION 4. CANCELLATION OF INDEBTEDNESS AS A MEDIUM OF PAYMENT

As noted earlier in this chapter, not every discharge of indebtedness results in the realization of cancellation of indebtedness income under § 61(a)(12). If the creditor receives full satisfaction of the debt in some form other than cash, the debtor does not realize any cancellation of indebtedness income even though the debt is discharged. It is true that the debt has been "discharged" but in these cases it has been discharged by payment or some other satisfaction.

DETAILED ANALYSIS

1. SATISFACTION OF INDEBTEDNESS BY TRANSFER OF PROPERTY

As was discussed in Chapter 6, Section 2.1., if a debtor transfers property to satisfy a debt to the transferee, the transfer is treated as a sale or exchange of the property. The debt is included in the amount realized, and under § 1001 the debtor-transferor realizes either a gain includable under § 61(a)(3) or a loss, which might be deductible under § 165. This conclusion assumes that the fair market value of the property transferred is at least equal to the amount of the debt satisfied. Suppose that A, who is indebted to B for $10,000, offers to transfer to B property with a basis of $5,000 and a fair market value of $8,000, in full satisfaction of the debt. Treas. Reg. § 1.1001–2(a) provides that the debt is included in the amount realized only to the extent of the fair market value of the property, so that A realizes a gain of $3,000 on the sale or exchange of the property and $2,000 of cancellation of indebtedness income under § 61(a)(12). See Gehl v. Commissioner, 102 T.C. 784 (1994), aff'd, 50 F.3d 12 (8th Cir.1995) (reaching this result); Treas. Reg. § 1.1001–2(c), Ex. (8). This distinction is important, because only the $2,000 of cancellation of indebtedness income is eligible for exclusion under § 108. Thus, for example, if A were insolvent both before and after the transfer, A would recognize the $3,000 gain from the property, but A would not recognize the $2,000 cancellation of indebtedness income.

Bifurcation of the transaction, as required by the regulations, may be justified by the fact that the debt is satisfied by the transfer of property only to the extent of the fair market value of the property. Thus, although the debt in the preceding example was not paid in full, $8,000 of the debt was paid by the transfer of the property; only $2,000 of the debt was canceled, i.e., extinguished without payment to the creditor.

If the debt is a secured debt on which the debtor is not personally liable (i.e., a nonrecourse debt), then the full amount of the debt is treated as the amount realized on the transfer of the property, and no cancellation of indebtedness income is realized. Treas. Reg. § 1.1001–2(a)(4), (b), (c), Ex. (7). The reason for this differing treatment is discussed in Chapter 34, Section 1.

2. CANCELLATION OF INDEBTEDNESS AS A MEDIUM OF PAYMENT

In some cases cancellation of indebtedness is the medium through which payment is made in a form other than cash or property. For example, the taxpayer in Spartan Petroleum Company v. United States, 437 F.Supp. 733 (D.S.C.1977), was a distributor for the Atlantic Richfield Company (ARCO). The taxpayer was indebted to ARCO in the approximate amount of $233,000 for the proceeds of direct borrowings from ARCO and for an indebtedness from a third party assumed by the taxpayer on acquisition of assets from that party. ARCO canceled the taxpayer's distribution agreement and agreed to pay the taxpayer approximately $1.6 million in exchange for the taxpayer's rights under the distribution agreement. Rather than accept ARCO's check for $1.6 million and repay its debt with an offsetting check for $233,000, the taxpayer requested that ARCO give it a check for the net amount. The taxpayer claimed that the cancellation of its debt was cancellation of indebtedness income excludable under § 108.[7] The court rejected the taxpayer's characterization and treated ARCO's cancellation of the taxpayer's obligation as a part of the payment in exchange for the distributorship contract. Thus, the taxpayer realized no cancellation of indebtedness income and § 108 was not applicable. See also OKC Corp. v. Commissioner, 82 T.C. 638 (1984) (property seller's agreement to satisfy taxpayer's purchase money obligation to bank as part of the settlement of a dispute involving an oil contract not treated as cancellation of indebtedness).

In United States v. Centennial Savings Bank FSB, 499 U.S. 573 (1991), the taxpayer, a savings and loan association, was relieved of certain interest obligations to depositors as the result of penalties imposed on the depositors for early withdrawal of savings accounts. The IRS asserted that the amount of the early withdrawal penalties was includable in gross income. The Court rejected the taxpayer's argument that the interest penalties forfeited to it

---

[7]   At the time of the transaction § 108 excluded from income cancellation of an indebtedness that was incurred in connection with property used in the taxpayer's trade or business provided that the taxpayer consented to a reduction in the basis of business assets. Thus, it was to the taxpayer's advantage to treat income as cancellation of indebtedness income and defer recognition with a basis reduction.

represented cancellation of indebtedness income excludable under former § 108(d)(4). The Court held that the agreement between the savings and loan association and its depositors provided that the depositor was entitled to a return of principal and accrued interest less the penalty applicable to early withdrawal. The depositor does not "discharge" the bank from an "obligation" when the depositor accepts principal and accrued interest less the penalty on early withdrawal. The Court noted that "to determine whether the debtor has realized 'income by reason of the discharge . . . of indebtedness,' it is necessary to look at *both* the end result of the transaction *and* the repayment terms agreed to by the parties at the outset of the debtor-creditor relationship."

Rev. Rul. 2004–37, 2004–1 C.B. 583, involved a transaction that superficially appeared to be a purchase price adjustment subject to the § 108(e)(5) exception to the inclusion under § 61(a)(12) of cancellation of debt income, discussed above, but which on closer examination gave rise to compensation. In that ruling, an employee purchased stock from his employer by giving the employer a promissory note and the employer and employee subsequently agreed to reduce the principal amount of the note. The ruling held that the employee recognized compensation income, rather than excluded cancellation of debt income, when the amount of the debt was reduced.

3.   CANCELLATION OF INDEBTEDNESS AS A GIFT

In Helvering v. American Dental Company, 318 U.S. 322 (1943), the Court held that the gratuitous receipt of financial advantage from the cancellation of a debt was a gift excludable from income under the predecessor to § 102. However, in Commissioner v. Jacobson, 336 U.S. 28 (1949), the Court rejected the taxpayer's argument that cancellation of indebtedness income on the taxpayer's acquisition of personal bonds from bond holders for less than their face amount was excludable from income as a gift. The Court in *Jacobson* determined that the taxpayer's acquisition of his bonds from the holders was an arm's-length transaction in which the bondholders were acting solely in their own interest. The Court was not willing to find that the bond sellers intended to make a gift to the taxpayer. It remains possible, however, for the taxpayer to argue that debt is canceled as a gift under the standards of Commissioner v. Duberstein, Chapter 4, Section 1. Compare Bosse v. Commissioner, T.C. Memo. 1970–355 (cancellation of debt treated as a gift) with Dosek v. Commissioner, T.C. Memo. 1971–160 (gift status rejected).

CHAPTER 11

TAX EXPENDITURES

SECTION 1. THE CONCEPT OF TAX EXPENDITURES

A. INTRODUCTION

The preceding material indicates that certain items, such as recoveries of capital, are excluded from the tax base as necessary parts of a tax structure intended to tax only realized "income." Other items, although clearly covered by the concept of "income," are nonetheless excluded from the tax base to achieve some specific economic or social objective. Some of these provisions, frequently referred to as "tax incentives," are intended to encourage certain types of activity. Others are designed to achieve other social objectives such as relieving personal hardship. These special tax provisions are termed "tax expenditures" because they represent government expenditures provided through the tax system.

The federal income tax system consists of two parts: one part comprises the structural provisions necessary to implement the income tax; the second part comprises a system of tax expenditures under which governmental financial assistance programs are carried out through tax provisions rather than through direct government expenditures. This second system is not necessary to the operation of the structure of the income tax. Rather, it is a vast subsidy apparatus that uses the mechanics of the income tax to deliver government financial assistance.

The tax expenditure concept was developed by the late Professor Stanley S. Surrey. His classic discussion of the concept is contained in Surrey, Pathways to Tax Reform (1973). A sequel to that volume is Surrey and McDaniel, Tax Expenditures (1985).

Tax expenditure analysis treats tax expenditure provisions as involving two payments: the imputed tax payment that would have been made in the absence of the special provision (all else remaining the same) and the simultaneous expenditure by the Government as a direct grant or loan to the beneficiary of the special provision. Since the hypothetical direct grant itself may constitute income, the tax on this income could also be viewed as part of the tax expenditure.

Tax expenditures take a variety of forms, including exclusions from income, deductions, credits against tax, preferential rates of tax, negative rates of tax, and deferral of tax. The exclusion technique, for example, is employed for interest on state and local bonds, while the deduction method is used for qualifying charitable contributions and mortgage interest, among other expense items. Tax expenditures taking the form of a tax credit include the credit for certain research expenses.

Meanwhile, tax expenditures that provide negative rates of tax include the portion of the Earned Income Credit paid out as cash over and above its offset to tax liability. Other tax expenditures, such as the preferential treatment of capital gains and dividends, provide a special rate of tax. Still other tax expenditures accelerate the timing of deductions or defer the inclusion of income. Items such as accelerated depreciation and the deduction for intangible drilling and development costs are examples of accelerated deductions while the treatment of qualified employee retirement plans illustrates the deferral of income.

Tax expenditure analysis is included at this point to facilitate consideration of items excluded from gross income. Consider which of the exclusions from gross income discussed so far are integral parts of a tax structure designed to tax income and which are tax expenditures. The tax expenditure analysis also should be utilized as an additional analytical tool in the evaluation of the materials in succeeding chapters.

B. IDENTIFYING TAX EXPENDITURES

Classification of a provision as a tax expenditure depends upon whether it is considered as part of the structure of an income tax or is viewed as a mechanism to promote some desired activity or conduct or to relieve personal hardship. In the vast majority of cases this determination is straightforward. In some cases, however, the determination depends upon one's definition of income.

In one of the government's first published examinations of the tax expenditure concept, the Report of the Secretary of the Treasury for fiscal year 1968 embraced "widely accepted definitions of income." It leaned heavily towards the Haig-Simons articulation of income defined as the increase in net worth between two points in time plus consumption during the period. The description and analysis of tax expenditures contained in the Treasury's report used the following guidelines:

[The analysis] lists the major respects in which the current income tax bases deviate from widely accepted definitions of income and standards of business accounting and from the generally accepted structure of an income tax. * * *

The study does not attempt a complete listing of all the tax provisions which vary from a strict definition of net income. Various items that could have been added have been excluded for one or more of several reasons:

(a) Some items were excluded where there is no available indication of the precise magnitude of the implicit subsidy. This is the case, for example, with depreciation on machinery and equipment where the accelerated tax methods may provide an allowance beyond that appropriate to the measurement of net income but where it is difficult to measure that difference because the true economic deterioration or obsolescence factor cannot be readily determined. [Ed.: Subsequently, measurement techniques were developed and accelerated depreciation is included in tax expenditure accounts.]

(b) Some items were excluded where the case for their inclusion in the income base stands on relatively technical or theoretical tax arguments. This is the case, for example, with the imputed rent on owner-occupied homes, which involves not only a conceptual problem but difficult practical problems such as those of measurement. [Ed.: Subsequently, the Treasury Department began including net imputed rental income in its tax expenditure estimates.]

(c) Some items were omitted because of their relatively small quantitative importance.

Other features of our income tax system are considered not as variations from the generally accepted measure of net income or as tax preferences but as part of the structure of an income tax system based on ability to pay. Such features include personal exemptions and the rate schedules under the individual income tax, including the income splitting allowed for married couples filing joint returns or for heads of households. A discussion of income splitting and the dependent's personal exemption is thus considered outside the scope of this study on tax expenditures.

It must be recognized that these exclusions are to some extent arbitrary * * * . The immediate objective, however, of this study is to provide a list of items that would be generally recognized as more or less intended use of the tax system to achieve results commonly obtained by government expenditures. The design of the list seems best served by constructing what seemed a minimum list rather than including highly complicated or controversial items that would becloud the utility of this special analysis.

* * *

* * * The assumption inherent in current law, that corporations are separate entities and subject to income taxation independently from their shareholders, is adhered to in this analysis.

The Congressional Budget Act of 1974, which required the Treasury to publish an annual, current-year tax expenditure budget to be considered alongside the annual direct expenditure budget, embodied the Treasury's earlier approach in 1968 to identify tax expenditures as: "[T]hose revenue losses attributable to provisions of the Federal tax laws which allow a special exclusion, exemption or deduction from gross income or which provide a special credit, a preferential rate of tax or a deferral of tax liability * * * ."

The legislative history of the 1974 Budget Act makes clear that the classification of an item as "special" was to be made by employing the techniques that had been used by Treasury and congressional staff technicians to develop the previously published tax expenditure lists.[1]

Pursuant to the 1974 Budget Act, all budgets submitted to Congress have contained a special analysis titled "Tax Expenditures" providing a detailed tabulation of income tax expenditures. In addition, the Staff of the Joint Committee on Taxation (JCT Staff) has published annual reports on tax expenditures.

For a number of years after the 1974 Act, there was little controversy over the classification as tax expenditures of most of the items that have been included in the tax expenditure lists.[2] This is not to say that controversy was not engendered by the introduction of the tax expenditure concept. Some tax policy analysts accept the general framework of tax expenditure analysis, but have argued that certain items included in the tax expenditure budget should not be classified as tax expenditures. Generally, these arguments have centered on the classification of items such as the medical expense[3] and casualty loss deductions. Others have also accepted the analytical framework of the tax expenditure concept, but have argued that the basic definition of income adopted (generally, the Haig-Simons definition) is not the proper definition. Finally, there are some who would argue that there is no generally accepted definition of income at all which can stand as the benchmark against which provisions can be assessed to determine if they constitute tax expenditures. Under this view, each exclusion from income or deduction is simply a tax provision which Congress has decided to enact and no further analysis of the provisions as spending programs can be undertaken.[4]

C. THE TAX EXPENDITURE BUDGET

The following tax expenditure budget prepared by the Staff of the Joint Committee on Taxation shows the amount of tax expenditures by budget function for fiscal years 2015–2019 and the assumptions used in its preparation:

---

[1]   For discussions of the legislative history of the inclusion of tax expenditures in the Congressional Budget Act of 1974, see Surrey and McDaniel, The Tax Expenditure Concept and the Budget Reform Act of 1974, 17 B.C. Ind. & Comm. L. Rev. 679 (1976); Surrey and McDaniel, Tax Expenditures; How to Identify Them: How to Control Them, 15 Tax Notes 595 (1982).

[2]   The history of developments in the use of tax expenditure analysis is set forth in Surrey and McDaniel, Tax Expenditures (1985).

[3]   See Andrews, Personal Deductions in an Ideal Income Tax, 86 Harv. L. Rev. 309 (1972). Professor Andrews also maintains in this article that charitable contributions should be deductible under an income tax and thus the deduction is not properly categorized as a tax expenditure.

[4]   This appears to be the view set forth in Bittker, Accounting For Federal "Tax Subsidies" in the National Budget, 22 Nat'l Tax J. 244 (1969).

Estimates of Federal Tax Expenditures
for Fiscal Years 2015–2019

Joint Committee on Taxation, (JCX–141R–15).
December 7, 2015.

I. THE CONCEPT OF TAX EXPENDITURES

Overview

"Tax expenditures" are defined under the Congressional Budget and Impoundment Control Act of 1974 ("the Budget Act") as "revenue losses attributable to provisions of the Federal tax laws which allow a special exclusion, exemption, or deduction from gross income or which provide a special credit, a preferential rate of tax, or deferral of tax liability."[4] Thus, tax expenditures include any reductions in income tax liabilities that result from special tax provisions or regulations that provide tax benefits to particular taxpayers.

Special income tax provisions are referred to as tax expenditures because they may be analogous to direct outlay programs and may be considered as alternative means of accomplishing similar budget policy objectives. Tax expenditures are similar to direct spending programs that function as entitlements to those who meet the established statutory criteria.

Estimates of tax expenditures are prepared for use in budget analysis. They are a measure of the economic benefits that are provided through the tax laws to various groups of taxpayers and sectors of the economy. The estimates also may be useful in determining the relative merits of achieving specific public goals through tax benefits or direct outlays. It is appropriate to evaluate tax expenditures with respect to cost, distributional consequences, alternative means of provision, and economic effects and to allow policymakers to evaluate the tradeoffs among these and other potentially competing policy goals.

The legislative history of the Budget Act indicates that tax expenditures are to be defined with reference to a normal income tax structure (referred to here as "normal income tax law"). The determination of whether a provision is a tax expenditure is made on the basis of a broad concept of income that is larger in scope than "income" as defined under general U.S. income tax principles. The Joint Committee staff uses its judgment in distinguishing between those income tax provisions (and regulations) that can be viewed as a part of normal income tax law and those special provisions that result in tax expenditures. A provision traditionally has been listed as a tax expenditure by the Joint Committee staff if there is a reasonable basis for such classification and the provision results in more than a *de minimis* revenue loss, which solely for this purpose means a total revenue

---

4   Congressional Budget and Impoundment Control Act of 1974, Pub. L. No. 93–344, sec. 3(3).

loss of less than $50 million over the five fiscal years 2015–2019. The Joint Committee staff emphasizes, however, that in the process of listing tax expenditures, no judgment is made, nor any implication intended, about the desirability of any special tax provision as a matter of public policy.

* * *

Individual Income Tax

Under the Joint Committee staff methodology, the normal structure of the individual income tax includes the following major components: one personal exemption for each taxpayer and one for each dependent, the standard deduction, the existing tax rate schedule, and deductions for investment and employee business expenses. Most other tax benefits for individual taxpayers are classified as exceptions to normal income tax law.

The Joint Committee staff views the personal exemptions and the standard deduction as defining the zero-rate bracket that is a part of normal tax law. An itemized deduction that is not necessary for the generation of income is classified as a tax expenditure, but only to the extent that it, when added to a taxpayer's other itemized deductions, exceeds the standard deduction.

All employee compensation is subject to tax unless the Code contains a specific exclusion for the income. Specific exclusions for employer-provided benefits include: coverage under accident and health plans,[8] accident and disability insurance, group term life insurance, educational assistance, tuition reduction benefits, transportation benefits (parking, van pools, and transit passes), dependent care assistance, adoption assistance, meals and lodging furnished for the convenience of the employer, employee awards, and other miscellaneous fringe benefits (e.g., employee discounts, services provided to employees at no additional cost to employers, and *de minimis* fringe benefits). Each of these exclusions is classified as a tax expenditure in this report.

* * *

The individual income tax does not include in gross income the imputed income that individuals receive from the services provided by owner-occupied homes and durable goods.[10] However, the Joint

---

[8]   Present law contains an exclusion for employer-provided coverage under accident and health plans (sec. 106) and an exclusion for benefits received by employees under employer-provided accident and health plans (sec. 105(b)). These two exclusions are viewed as a single tax expenditure. Under normal income tax law, the value of employer-provided accident and health coverage would be includible in the income of employees, but employees would not be subject to tax on the accident and health insurance benefits (reimbursements) that they might receive.

[10]   The National Income and Product Accounts include estimates of this imputed income. The accounts appear in *Survey of Current Business,* published monthly by the U.S. Department of Commerce, Bureau of Economic Analysis. However, a taxpayer-by-taxpayer accounting of imputed income would be necessary for a tax expenditure estimate.

Committee staff does not classify this exclusion as a tax expenditure.[11] The measurement of imputed income for tax purposes presents administrative problems and its exclusion from taxable income may be regarded as an administrative necessity.[12]

* * *

Business Income Taxation

* * *

One of the most difficult issues in defining tax expenditures for business income relates to the tax treatment of capital costs. Under present law, capital costs may be recovered under a variety of alternative methods, depending upon the nature of the costs and the status of the taxpayer. For example, investments in equipment and structures may qualify for tax credits, expensing, accelerated depreciation, or straight-line depreciation. The Joint Committee staff generally classifies as tax expenditures cost recovery allowances that are more favorable than those provided under the alternative depreciation system (sec. 168(g)), which provides for straight-line recovery over tax lives that are longer than those permitted under the accelerated system.

* * *

III. Tax Expenditure Estimates

Tax expenditures are grouped in Table 1 in the same functional categories as outlays in the Federal budget. Estimates are shown separately for individuals and corporations. Those tax expenditures that do not fit clearly into any single budget category have been placed in the most appropriate category. Totals for each tax expenditure are presented for the five-year period covering fiscal years 2015–2019, respectively.

Several of the tax expenditure items involve small amounts of revenue, and those estimates are indicated in Table 1 by footnote 4. For each of these items, the footnote means that the tax expenditure is less than $50 million in the fiscal year.

* * *

---

[11]   The Treasury Department provides a tax expenditure calculation for the exclusion of net rental income of homeowners that combines the positive tax expenditure for the failure to impute rental income with the negative tax expenditure for the failure to allow a deduction for depreciation and other costs.

[12]   If the imputed income from owner-occupied homes were included in adjusted gross income, it would be proper to include all mortgage interest deductions and related property tax deductions as part of the normal income tax structure, since interest and property tax deductions would be allowable as a cost of producing imputed income. It also would be appropriate to allow deductions for depreciation and maintenance expenses for owner-occupied homes.

Table 1.—Tax Expenditure Estimates By Budget Function, Fiscal Years 2015 - 2019 [1]

[Billions of Dollars]

Function	Corporations					Individuals					Total
	2015	2016	2017	2018	2019	2015	2016	2017	2018	2019	2015-19
National Defense											
Exclusion of benefits and allowances to armed forces personnel	--	--	--	--	--	5.8	6.0	6.4	6.8	7.0	31.9
Exclusion of military disability benefits	--	--	--	--	--	0.3	0.3	0.3	0.3	0.3	1.4
Deduction for overnight-travel expenses of national guard and reserve members	--	--	--	--	--	0.1	0.1	0.1	0.1	0.1	0.5
Exclusion of combat pay	--	--	--	--	--	1.4	1.4	1.5	1.6	1.6	7.5
International Affairs											
Exclusion of certain allowances for Federal employees abroad	--	--	--	--	--	2.1	2.2	2.3	2.3	2.4	11.2
Exclusion of foreign earned income:											
Housing	--	--	--	--	--	1.3	1.3	1.4	1.5	1.6	7.1
Salary	--	--	--	--	--	6.4	6.7	7.2	7.6	8.0	35.7
Inventory property sales source rule exception	1.7	1.7	1.8	1.8	1.8	--	--	--	--	--	8.8
Deduction for foreign taxes instead of a credit	0.3	0.3	0.3	0.3	0.3	--	--	--	--	--	1.3
Interest expense allocation:											
Unavailability of symmetric worldwide method*	-1.2	-1.2	-1.2	-1.3	-1.3	--	--	--	--	--	-6.2
Separate grouping of affiliated financial companies	0.5	0.5	0.5	0.5	0.5	--	--	--	--	--	2.5
Apportionment of research and development expenses for determination of foreign tax credits	0.2	0.2	0.2	0.2	0.2	--	--	--	--	--	1.1
Special rules for interest-charge domestic international sales corporations	0.6	0.6	0.6	0.7	0.7	--	--	--	--	--	3.2
Tonnage tax	0.1	0.1	0.1	0.1	0.1	--	--	--	--	--	0.5

Table 1.—Tax Expenditure Estimates By Budget Function, Fiscal Years 2015 - 2019 [1]

[Billions of Dollars]

Function	Corporations					Individuals					Total
	2015	2016	2017	2018	2019	2015	2016	2017	2018	2019	2015-19
National Defense											
Exclusion of benefits and allowances to armed forces personnel	---	---	---	---	---	5.8	6.0	6.4	6.8	7.0	31.9
Exclusion of military disability benefits	---	---	---	---	---	0.3	0.3	0.3	0.3	0.3	1.4
Deduction for overnight-travel expenses of national guard and reserve members	---	---	---	---	---	0.1	0.1	0.1	0.1	0.1	0.5
Exclusion of combat pay	---	---	---	---	---	1.4	1.4	1.5	1.6	1.6	7.5
International Affairs											
Exclusion of certain allowances for Federal employees abroad	---	---	---	---	---	2.1	2.2	2.3	2.3	2.4	11.2
Exclusion of foreign earned income:											
Housing	---	---	---	---	---	1.3	1.3	1.4	1.5	1.6	7.1
Salary	---	---	---	---	---	6.4	6.7	7.2	7.6	8.0	35.7
Inventory property sales source rule exception	1.7	1.7	1.8	1.8	1.8	---	---	---	---	---	8.8
Deduction for foreign taxes instead of a credit	0.3	0.3	0.3	0.3	0.3	---	---	---	---	---	1.3
Interest expense allocation:											
Unavailability of symmetric worldwide method*	-1.2	-1.2	-1.2	-1.3	-1.3	---	---	---	---	---	-6.2
Separate grouping of affiliated financial companies	0.5	0.5	0.5	0.5	0.5	---	---	---	---	---	2.5
Apportionment of research and development expenses for determination of foreign tax credits	0.2	0.2	0.2	0.2	0.2	---	---	---	---	---	1.1
Special rules for interest-charge domestic international sales corporations	0.6	0.6	0.6	0.7	0.7	---	---	---	---	---	3.2
Tonnage tax	0.1	0.1	0.1	0.1	0.1	---	---	---	---	---	0.5

Function	Corporations					Individuals					Total
	2015	2016	2017	2018	2019	2015	2016	2017	2018	2019	2015-19
Special rule to implement electric transmission restructuring	-0.2	-0.2	-0.2	-0.2	-0.2	---	---	---	---	---	-1.0
Credits for investments in clean coal facilities	0.2	0.2	0.2	0.2	0.2	---	---	---	---	---	1.0
Coal production credits:											
Refined coal	[4]	[4]	[4]	[4]	[4]	---	---	---	---	---	0.1
Indian coal	[4]	[4]	[4]	[4]	[4]	---	---	---	---	---	0.1
Credits for alternative technology vehicles:											
Other alternative fuel vehicles	[4]	[4]	[4]	[4]	[4]	---	---	---	---	---	0.1
Residential energy-efficient property credit	---	---	---	---	---	1.1	1.2	0.7	---	---	3.0
Credit for plug-in electric vehicles	[4]	[4]	[4]	[4]	[4]	0.2	0.2	0.2	0.2	0.2	1.2
Credit for investment in advanced energy property	0.2	0.2	0.2	0.1	0.1	0.1	0.1	0.1	0.1	0.1	1.2
Exclusion of interest on State and local government qualified private activity bonds for energy production facilities	[4]	[4]	[4]	[4]	[4]	[4]	[4]	[4]	[4]	[4]	0.2
Expensing of exploration and development costs, fuels:											
Oil and gas	1.0	1.1	1.1	1.1	1.0	0.3	0.4	0.3	0.3	0.3	7.0
Other fuels	[4]	[4]	[4]	[4]	[4]	[4]	[4]	[4]	[4]	[4]	0.5
Excess of percentage over cost depletion, fuels:											
Oil and gas	1.4	1.3	1.4	1.6	1.6	[4]	[4]	[4]	[4]	[4]	7.4
Other fuels	0.2	0.2	0.3	0.3	0.3	[4]	[4]	[4]	[4]	[4]	1.4
Amortization of geological and geophysical expenditures associated with oil and gas exploration	0.1	0.1	0.1	0.1	0.1	[4]	[4]	[4]	[4]	[4]	0.7
Amortization of air pollution control facilities	0.4	0.4	0.3	0.3	0.3	---	---	---	---	---	1.7
Depreciation recovery periods for energy-specific items:											
Five-year MACRS for certain energy property (solar, wind, etc.)	0.3	0.3	0.3	0.2	0.2	[4]	[4]	[4]	[4]	[4]	1.3
10-year MACRS for smart electric distribution property	0.2	0.2	0.2	0.2	0.2	---	---	---	---	---	1.0
15-year MACRS for certain electric transmission property	0.2	0.2	0.2	0.2	0.2	---	---	---	---	---	1.0
15-year MACRS for natural gas distribution line	0.2	0.2	0.1	0.1	0.1	---	---	---	---	---	0.8

Function	Corporations					Individuals					Total
	2015	2016	2017	2018	2019	2015	2016	2017	2018	2019	2015-19
Exceptions for publicly traded partnership with qualified income derived from certain energy-related activities.	---	---	---	---	---	1.1	1.2	1.2	1.2	1.2	5.9
Natural Resources and Environment											
Special depreciation allowance for certain reuse and recycling property.	[4]	[4]	[4]	[4]	[4]	[4]	[4]	[4]	[4]	[4]	0.1
Expensing of exploration and development costs, nonfuel minerals.	0.1	0.1	0.1	0.1	0.1	[4]	[4]	[4]	[4]	[4]	0.5
Excess of percentage over cost depletion, nonfuel minerals.	0.1	0.1	0.1	0.1	0.1	[4]	[4]	[4]	[4]	[4]	0.5
Expensing of timber-growing costs.	0.3	0.3	0.3	0.3	0.3	[4]	[4]	[4]	[4]	[4]	1.5
Special rules for mining reclamation reserves.	[4]	[4]	[4]	[4]	[4]	[4]	[4]	[4]	[4]	[4]	0.2
Special tax rate for nuclear decommissioning reserve funds.	0.2	0.2	0.3	0.3	0.3	---	---	---	---	---	1.3
Exclusion of contributions in aid of construction for water and sewer utilities.	[4]	[4]	[4]	[4]	[4]	---	---	---	---	---	0.2
Exclusion of earnings of certain environmental settlement funds.	[4]	[4]	[4]	[4]	[4]	---	---	---	---	---	0.1
Amortization and expensing of reforestation expenditures.	0.1	0.1	0.1	0.2	0.2	0.1	0.1	0.1	0.1	0.1	1.3
Special tax rate for qualified timber gain (including coal and iron ore).	---	---	---	---	---	0.3	0.3	0.4	0.4	0.4	1.8
Treatment of income from exploration and mining of natural resources as qualifying income under the publicly-traded partnership rules.	---	---	---	---	---	0.1	0.1	0.1	0.1	0.1	0.5
Agriculture											
Expensing of soil and water conservation expenditures.	[4]	[4]	[4]	[4]	[4]	0.1	0.1	0.1	0.1	0.1	0.6
Expensing of the costs of raising dairy and breeding cattle.	[4]	[4]	[4]	[4]	[4]	0.2	0.2	0.2	0.2	0.1	0.9
Exclusion of cost-sharing payments.	[4]	[4]	[4]	[4]	[4]	[4]	[4]	[4]	[4]	[4]	0.1
Exclusion of cancellation of indebtedness income of farmers.	---	---	---	---	---	0.1	0.1	0.1	0.1	0.1	0.5

Function	Corporations 2015	2016	2017	2018	2019	Individuals 2015	2016	2017	2018	2019	Total 2015-19
Income averaging for farmers and fishermen	---	---	---	---	---	0.1	0.2	0.2	0.2	0.2	0.9
Five-year carryback period for net operating losses attributable to farming	[4]	[4]	[4]	[4]	[4]	0.1	0.1	0.1	0.1	0.1	0.4
Expensing by farmers for fertilizer and soil conditioner costs	[4]	[4]	[4]	[4]	[4]	0.1	0.2	0.2	0.2	0.2	0.9
Cash accounting for agriculture	[4]	[4]	[4]	[4]	[4]	[4]	[4]	[4]	[4]	[4]	0.1
Commerce and Housing											
Housing:											
Deduction for mortgage interest on owner-occupied residences	---	---	---	---	---	71.0	77.0	84.3	91.1	96.4	419.8
Deduction for property taxes on real property	---	---	---	---	---	32.4	34.7	36.9	39.2	41.3	184.5
Exclusion of capital gains on sales of principal residences	---	---	---	---	---	24.1	29.0	30.6	32.2	34.0	149.9
Exclusion of interest on State and local government qualified private activity bonds for owner-occupied housing [5]	0.3	0.4	0.4	0.4	0.4	0.9	0.9	1.0	1.1	1.1	6.9
Credit for low-income housing	7.3	7.8	8.3	8.6	9.2	0.3	0.3	0.4	0.4	0.4	43.0
Credit for rehabilitation of historic structures	0.7	0.7	0.7	0.8	0.8	0.2	0.2	0.2	0.2	0.2	4.6
Credit for rehabilitation of structures, other than historic structures	[4]	[4]	[4]	[4]	[4]	[4]	[4]	[4]	0.1	0.1	0.3
Exclusion of interest on State and local government qualified private activity bonds for rental housing	0.3	0.3	0.3	0.3	0.3	0.7	0.7	0.8	0.8	0.9	5.4
Depreciation of rental housing in excess of alternative depreciation system	0.5	0.4	0.4	0.4	0.4	4.2	4.0	3.9	3.9	3.8	22.0
Other business and commerce:											
Exclusion of interest on State and local government small-issue qualified private activity bonds	0.1	0.1	0.1	0.1	0.1	0.3	0.3	0.3	0.3	0.3	2.1
Carryover basis of capital gains on gifts	---	---	---	---	---	-4.6	11.3	10.5	8.9	9.3	35.4
Deferral of gain on non-dealer installment sales	6.9	6.8	6.7	6.7	6.7	2.1	1.7	1.4	1.2	1.2	41.3
Deferral of gain on like-kind exchanges	11.0	11.1	11.4	11.7	12.2	5.8	5.9	6.0	6.2	6.4	87.7

Function	Corporations					Individuals					Total
	2015	2016	2017	2018	2019	2015	2016	2017	2018	2019	2015-19
Expensing under section 179 of depreciable business property	4.8	1.8	0.8	0.8	0.6	7.8	2.9	1.3	1.2	1.0	22.9
Amortization of business startup costs	[4]	[4]	[4]	[4]	0.1	[4]	[4]	[4]	0.1	0.1	0.2
Reduced rates on first $10,000,000 of corporate taxable income	4.0	4.2	4.2	4.2	4.2	---	---	---	---	---	20.8
Exemptions from imputed interest rules	[4]	[4]	[4]	[4]	[4]	0.6	0.6	0.7	0.7	0.7	3.4
Expensing of magazine circulation expenditures	0.1	0.1	[4]	[4]	[4]	[4]	[4]	[4]	[4]	[4]	0.1
Special rules for magazine, paperback book, and record returns	[4]	[4]	[4]	[4]	[4]	[4]	[4]	[4]	[4]	[4]	0.2
Completed contract rules	0.9	0.9	0.9	1.0	1.0	0.1	0.1	0.1	0.1	0.1	5.2
Cash accounting, other than agriculture	0.3	0.3	0.3	0.3	0.3	1.8	1.9	1.9	2.0	2.0	11.1
Credit for employer-paid FICA taxes on tips	0.6	0.6	0.6	0.7	0.7	0.7	0.7	0.7	0.8	0.8	6.9
Deduction for income attributable to domestic production activities	11.7	12.1	12.3	12.6	12.8	4.5	4.6	4.7	4.8	4.8	84.8
Credit for the cost of carrying tax-paid distilled spirits in wholesale inventories	[4]	[4]	[4]	[4]	[4]	---	---	---	---	---	[4]
Reduced rates of tax on dividends and long-term capital gains	---	---	---	---	---	131.7	134.6	137.1	140.9	145.4	689.6
Surtax on net investment income*	---	---	---	---	---	-34.8	-35.9	-36.9	-38.3	-40.0	-186.0
Exclusion of capital gains at death	---	---	---	---	---	32.4	32.9	33.8	35.2	36.8	171.3
Expensing of costs to remove architectural and transportation barriers to the handicapped and elderly	[4]	[4]	[4]	[4]	[4]	[4]	[4]	[4]	[4]	[4]	0.1
Exclusion for gain from certain small business stock	---	---	---	---	---	0.9	1.0	1.0	1.1	1.1	5.1
Distributions in redemption of stock to pay various taxes imposed at death	---	---	---	---	---	[4]	[4]	[4]	[4]	[4]	0.2
Inventory methods and valuation:											
Last in first out	1.5	1.6	1.6	1.6	1.7	0.3	0.3	0.3	0.3	0.3	9.4
Lower of cost or market	0.1	0.1	0.1	0.1	0.1	[4]	[4]	[4]	[4]	[4]	0.4
Specific identification for homogeneous products	[4]	[4]	[4]	[4]	[4]	[4]	[4]	[4]	[4]	[4]	0.1

Function	Corporations					Individuals					Total
	2015	2016	2017	2018	2019	2015	2016	2017	2018	2019	2015-19
Exclusion of gain or loss on sale or exchange of brownfield property	[4]	[4]	[4]	[4]	[4]	---	---	---	---	---	0.1
Income recognition rule for gain or loss from section 1256 contracts	0.1	0.1	0.1	0.1	0.1	1.0	1.0	1.0	1.0	1.0	5.3
Net alternative minimum tax attributable to net operating loss limitation*	-0.5	-0.5	-0.5	-0.5	-0.5	-0.1	-0.1	-0.1	-0.1	-0.1	-3.0
Exclusion of interest on State and local qualified private activity bonds for green buildings and sustainable design projects	[4]	[4]	[4]	[4]	[4]	[4]	[4]	[4]	[4]	[4]	0.1
Depreciation of buildings other than rental housing in excess of alternative depreciation system	0.2	0.2	0.2	0.2	0.2	0.2	0.2	0.2	0.2	0.2	2.2
Depreciation of equipment in excess of the alternative depreciation system [6]	-20.0	-18.0	-3.1	6.4	13.8	-8.2	-7.4	-1.3	2.6	5.7	-29.6
Financial institutions Exemption of credit union income	2.2	2.4	2.5	2.7	2.9	---	---	---	---	---	12.7
Insurance companies:											
Small life insurance company taxable income adjustment	[4]	[4]	[4]	[4]	[4]	---	---	---	---	---	0.2
Special treatment of life insurance company reserves	2.9	3.2	3.3	3.3	3.3	---	---	---	---	---	16.0
Special deduction for Blue Cross and Blue Shield companies	0.4	0.4	0.4	0.4	0.5	---	---	---	---	---	2.2
Tax-exempt status and election to be taxed only on investment income for certain small property and casualty insurance companies	0.1	0.1	0.1	0.1	0.1	---	---	---	---	---	0.5
Interest rate and discounting period assumptions for reserves of property and casualty insurance companies	2.3	2.6	2.6	2.6	2.6	---	---	---	---	---	12.7
Proration for property and casualty insurance companies	0.4	0.4	0.4	0.4	0.5	---	---	---	---	---	2.1

Function	Corporations					Individuals					Total
	2015	2016	2017	2018	2019	2015	2016	2017	2018	2019	2015-19
Transportation											
Exclusion of employer-paid transportation benefits (parking, van pools, and transit passes)	---	---	---	---	---	5.0	5.2	5.5	5.7	5.9	27.2
Deferral of tax on capital construction funds of shipping companies	0.1	0.1	0.1	0.1	0.1	---	---	---	---	---	0.5
Exclusion of interest on State and local government qualified private activity bonds for highway projects and rail-truck transfer facilities	[4]	[4]	[4]	0.1	0.1	0.1	0.1	0.1	0.1	0.1	0.6
Exclusion of interest on State and local government qualified private activity bonds for high-speed intercity rail facilities	[4]	[4]	[4]	[4]	[4]	[4]	[4]	[4]	[4]	[4]	0.1
Exclusion of interest on State and local government qualified private activity bonds for private airports, docks, and mass-commuting facilities	0.2	0.3	0.3	0.3	0.3	0.7	0.7	0.7	0.7	0.8	4.9
Community and Regional Development											
Empowerment zone tax incentives	0.2	[4]	[4]	[4]	[4]	0.2	[4]	[4]	[4]	[4]	0.2
New markets tax credit	1.1	1.1	1.2	1.1	1.0	[4]	[4]	[4]	[4]	[4]	5.5
District of Columbia tax incentives	[4]	[4]	[4]	[4]	[4]	[4]	[4]	[4]	[4]	[4]	0.1
Credit for Indian reservation employment	[4]	[4]	[4]	[4]	[4]	[4]	[4]	[4]	[4]	[4]	[4]
Exclusion of interest on State and local government qualified private activity bonds for sewage, water, and hazardous waste facilities	0.1	0.1	0.1	0.1	0.1	0.3	0.3	0.3	0.4	0.4	2.3
Recovery zone economic development bonds [2] [3]	[4]	[4]	[4]	[4]	[4]	0.2	0.2	0.2	0.2	0.2	0.9
Eliminate requirement that financial institutions allocate interest expense attributable to tax-exempt interest	0.5	0.5	0.5	0.5	0.5	---	---	---	---	---	2.6
Disaster Relief:											
National disaster relief	- Estimate Contained in Other Provisions - - - - - - - - - - - - - - -										

Education, Training, Employment, and Social Services

Education and training:

Function	Corporations					Individuals					Total
	2015	2016	2017	2018	2019	2015	2016	2017	2018	2019	2015-19
Deduction for interest on student loans	---	---	---	---	---	2.0	2.1	2.2	2.3	2.4	11.1
Exclusion of earnings of Coverdell education savings accounts	---	---	---	---	---	0.1	0.1	0.1	0.1	0.1	0.5
Exclusion of scholarship and fellowship income	---	---	---	---	---	2.7	2.9	3.0	3.2	3.4	15.2
Exclusion of income attributable to the discharge of certain student loan debt and NHSC and certain state educational loan repayments	---	---	---	---	---	0.2	0.2	0.2	0.2	0.2	0.8
Exclusion of employer-provided education assistance benefits	---	---	---	---	---	1.2	1.2	1.2	1.3	1.3	6.2
Exclusion of employer-provided tuition reduction benefits	---	---	---	---	---	0.3	0.3	0.3	0.3	0.3	1.6
Parental personal exemption for students aged 19 to 23	---	---	---	---	---	4.5	4.7	4.9	5.2	5.5	24.7
Exclusion of interest on State and local government qualified private activity bonds for student loans	0.2	0.2	0.2	0.2	0.2	0.4	0.4	0.4	0.5	0.5	3.0
Exclusion of interest on State and local government qualified private activity bonds for private nonprofit and qualified public educational facilities	1.0	1.0	1.0	1.1	1.1	2.6	2.6	2.8	2.9	3.1	19.1
Credit for holders of qualified zone academy bonds [2] [3]	0.2	0.2	0.2	0.2	0.2	0.1	0.1	0.1	0.1	0.1	1.4
Deduction for charitable contributions to educational institutions	0.3	0.4	0.4	0.4	0.4	6.2	6.4	6.6	6.8	7.1	35.0
Credits for tuition for post-secondary education [3]	---	---	---	---	---	19.7	21.0	21.2	12.5	9.6	84.0
Exclusion of tax on earnings of qualified tuition programs:											
Prepaid tuition programs	---	---	---	---	---	---	---	0.1	0.1	0.1	0.3
Savings account programs	---	---	---	---	---	0.7	0.9	1.1	1.3	1.4	5.5
Qualified school construction bonds [2] [3]	[4]	[4]	[4]	[4]	[4]	1.0	1.1	1.2	1.3	1.4	6.0

Function	Corporations 2015	2016	2017	2018	2019	Individuals 2015	2016	2017	2018	2019	Total 2015-19
Employment:											
Exclusion of employee meals and lodging (other than military)	---	---	---	---	---	2.1	2.1	2.2	2.3	2.4	11.1
Exclusion of benefits provided under cafeteria plans [7]	---	---	---	---	---	35.2	36.1	37.6	39.4	40.2	188.5
Exclusion of housing allowances for ministers	---	---	---	---	---	0.8	0.8	0.8	0.8	0.8	4.0
Exclusion of miscellaneous fringe benefits	---	---	---	---	---	7.5	7.7	7.8	8.0	8.2	39.2
Exclusion of employee awards	---	---	---	---	---	0.3	0.3	0.3	0.3	0.4	1.7
Exclusion of income earned by voluntary employees' beneficiary associations	---	---	---	---	---	3.2	3.2	3.3	3.3	3.4	16.4
Special tax provisions for employee stock ownership plans (ESOPs)	1.4	1.5	1.6	1.6	1.7	0.1	0.1	0.1	0.1	0.1	8.3
Deferral of taxation on spread on acquisition of stock under incentive stock option plans*	-1.1	-1.2	-1.2	-1.1	-1.1	0.4	0.4	0.3	0.3	0.3	-4.1
Deferral of taxation on spread on employee stock purchase plans*	-0.1	-0.2	-0.2	-0.2	-0.2	[4]	[4]	0.1	0.1	0.1	-0.6
Disallowance of deduction for excess parachute payments (applicable if payments to a disqualified individual are contingent on a change of control of a corporation and are equal to or greater than three times the individual's annualized includible compensation) [8]*	-0.2	-0.2	-0.2	-0.2	-0.2						-1.2
Limits on deductible compensation [8]*	-0.8	-0.8	-0.9	-0.9	-0.9	---	---	---	---	---	-4.3
Work opportunity tax credit	0.4	0.1	---	---	---	0.1	[4]	[4]	[4]	[4]	0.6
Social services:											
Credit for children under age 17 [3]	---	---	---	---	---	57.1	56.0	55.8	55.6	42.5	267.0
Credit for child and dependent care and exclusion of employer-provided child care [3] [9]	---	---	---	---	---	4.7	4.8	4.8	4.8	4.9	24.0
Credit for employer-provided dependent care	[4]	[4]	[4]	[4]	[4]	[4]	[4]	[4]	[4]	[4]	0.1
Exclusion of certain foster care payments	---	---	---	---	---	0.4	0.4	0.4	0.4	0.4	2.1

Function	Corporations					Individuals					Total
	2015	2016	2017	2018	2019	2015	2016	2017	2018	2019	2015-19
Adoption credit and employee adoption benefits exclusion	---	---	---	---	---	0.4	0.4	0.4	0.5	0.5	2.2
Deduction for charitable contributions, other than for education and health [10]	1.0	1.1	1.1	1.1	1.1	36.2	37.3	38.5	39.8	41.1	198.4
Credit for disabled access expenditures	[4]	[4]	[4]	[4]	[4]	[4]	[4]	[4]	[4]	[4]	0.3
Health											
Exclusion of employer contributions for health care, health insurance premiums, and long-term care insurance premiums [11]	---	---	---	---	---	145.5	143.8	151.4	159.6	169.4	769.8
Exclusion of medical care and TRICARE medical insurance for military dependents, retirees, and retiree dependents not enrolled in Medicare	---	---	---	---	---	2.6	2.7	2.8	2.9	2.9	13.9
Exclusion of health insurance benefits for military retirees and retiree dependents enrolled in Medicare	---	---	---	---	---	0.9	0.9	1.0	1.0	1.1	4.9
Deduction for health insurance premiums and long-term care insurance premiums by the self-employed	---	---	---	---	---	5.2	5.1	5.4	4.8	4.8	25.3
Deduction for medical expenses and long-term care expenses	---	---	---	---	---	10.1	11.1	11.4	12.2	13.7	58.5
Exclusion of workers' compensation benefits (medical benefits)	---	---	---	---	---	4.9	5.0	5.1	5.2	5.3	25.6
Health savings accounts	---	---	---	---	---	1.8	2.1	2.4	2.8	3.3	12.4
Exclusion of interest on State and local government qualified private activity bonds for private nonprofit hospital facilities	0.7	0.7	0.7	0.7	0.7	1.8	1.8	2.0	2.0	2.1	13.1
Deduction for charitable contributions to health organizations	1.9	1.9	2.0	2.0	2.1	3.2	3.3	3.4	3.5	3.6	26.7
Credit for purchase of health insurance by certain displaced persons [3]	---	---	---	---	---	---	[4]	[4]	[4]	[4]	0.2
Credit for orphan drug research	0.8	1.0	1.1	1.2	1.3	[4]	[4]	[4]	[4]	[4]	5.3

Function	Corporations					Individuals					Total
	2015	2016	2017	2018	2019	2015	2016	2017	2018	2019	2015-19
Tax credit for small businesses purchasing employer insurance	0.2	0.2	0.1	0.1	0.2	1.2	0.9	0.6	0.8	0.9	5.2
Subsidies for insurance purchased through health benefit exchanges [3]	---	---	---	---	---	29.6	53.5	72.5	82.1	84.8	322.5
Income Security											
Exclusion of workers' compensation benefits (disability and survivors payments)	---	---	---	---	---	2.7	2.9	3.0	3.2	3.3	15.1
Exclusion of damages on account of personal physical injuries or physical sickness	---	---	---	---	---	1.7	1.7	1.7	1.7	1.8	8.5
Exclusion of special benefits for disabled coal miners	---	---	---	---	---	[4]	[4]	[4]	[4]	[4]	0.1
Net exclusion of pension contributions and earnings:											
Plans covering partners and sole proprietors (sometimes referred to as "Keogh plans")	---	---	---	---	---	8.0	9.3	10.7	15.5	17.7	61.1
Defined benefit plans	---	---	---	---	---	48.6	57.4	62.9	69.6	77.0	315.6
Defined contribution plans	---	---	---	---	---	72.8	82.7	98.9	117.6	132.9	504.8
Individual retirement arrangements:											
Traditional IRAs	---	---	---	---	---	20.9	12.9	13.6	14.5	15.3	77.2
Roth IRAs	---	---	---	---	---	7.1	7.0	7.7	8.5	9.2	39.5
Credit for certain individuals for elective deferrals and IRA contributions	---	---	---	---	---	1.2	1.2	1.2	1.2	1.2	6.0
Exclusion of other employee benefits:											
Premiums on group term life insurance	---	---	---	---	---	3.2	3.2	3.3	3.3	3.4	16.4
Premiums on accident and disability insurance	---	---	---	---	---	4.1	4.2	4.4	4.6	4.8	22.2
Additional standard deduction for the blind and the elderly	---	---	---	---	---	2.7	2.8	3.0	3.3	3.5	15.3
Deduction for casualty and theft losses	---	---	---	---	---	0.4	0.5	0.5	0.5	0.6	2.5
Earned income credit [3]	---	---	---	---	---	72.7	73.3	76.0	73.8	75.6	371.4

Function	Corporations					Individuals					Total
	2015	2016	2017	2018	2019	2015	2016	2017	2018	2019	2015-19
Phase out of the personal exemption for the regular income tax, and disallowance of the personal exemption and the standard deduction against the alternative minimum tax*	---	---	---	---	---	-15.0	-15.9	-16.9	-17.9	-19.0	-84.6
Exclusion of survivor annuities paid to families of public safety officers killed in the line of duty	[4]	---	---	---	---	[4]	[4]	[4]	[4]	[4]	0.1
Exclusion of disaster mitigation payments	[4]	[4]	[4]	[4]	[4]	[4]	[4]	[4]	[4]	[4]	0.2
ABLE accounts [12]	---	---	---	---	---	[4]	[4]	[4]	[4]	0.1	0.1
Social Security and Railroad Retirement											
Exclusion of untaxed Social Security and railroad retirement benefits	---	---	---	---	---	37.6	39.6	41.9	44.2	46.8	210.1
Veterans' Benefits and Services											
Exclusion of veterans' disability compensation	---	---	---	---	---	6.8	7.6	7.4	7.1	7.9	36.8
Exclusion of veterans' pensions	---	---	---	---	---	0.2	0.2	0.2	0.2	0.2	0.9
Exclusion of veterans' readjustment benefits	---	---	---	---	---	1.6	1.8	1.8	1.9	2.0	9.1
Exclusion of interest on State and local government qualified private activity bonds for veterans' housing	[4]	[4]	[4]	[4]	[4]	[4]	[4]	[4]	[4]	[4]	0.3
General Purpose Fiscal Assistance											
Exclusion of interest on public purpose State and local government bonds	9.7	9.8	10.1	10.3	10.6	25.6	26.0	26.7	29.1	29.9	187.7
Deduction of nonbusiness State and local government income taxes, sales taxes, and personal property taxes	---	---	---	---	---	62.2	65.1	68.4	71.7	74.9	342.3
Build America bonds [2] [3]	---	---	---	---	---	3.2	3.2	3.2	3.2	3.2	16.0

Function	Corporations					Individuals					Total
	2015	2016	2017	2018	2019	2015	2016	2017	2018	2019	2015-19
Interest											
Deferral of interest on savings bonds	---	---	---	---	---	1.2	1.3	1.3	1.3	1.3	6.4

Joint Committee on Taxation

NOTE: Details may not add to totals due to rounding. An "*" indicates a negative tax expenditure for the 2015-2019 period.

[1] Reflects legislation enacted by September 30, 2015.
[2] Estimate includes an outlay to State and local governments. For the purposes of this table outlays are attributed to individuals.
[3] Estimate includes refundability associated with the following outlay effects:

	Corporations					Individuals					Total
	2015	2016	2017	2018	2019	2015	2016	2017	2018	2019	2015-19
Credit for holders of clean renewable energy bonds	---	---	---	---	---	[4]	[4]	[4]	[4]	[4]	0.2
Credit for holders of qualified energy conservation bonds	---	---	---	---	---	[4]	[4]	[4]	[4]	[4]	0.3
Recovery zone economic development bonds	---	---	---	---	---	0.2	0.2	0.2	0.2	0.2	0.8
Credit for holders of qualified zone academy bonds	---	---	---	---	---	0.1	0.1	0.1	0.1	0.1	0.3
Credits for tuition for post-secondary education	---	---	---	---	---	6.4	7.4	7.8	8.0	---	29.6
Qualified school construction bonds	---	---	---	---	---	1.0	1.1	1.2	1.3	1.4	5.9
Credit for children under age 17	---	---	---	---	---	33.7	33.9	34.5	35.0	22.1	159.2
Credit for child and dependent care and exclusion of employer-provided child care	---	---	---	---	---	0.9	1.0	1.0	0.9	0.9	4.7
Credit for purchase of health insurance by certain displaced persons	---	---	---	---	---	---	[4]	[4]	[4]	[4]	0.1
Subsidies for insurance purchased through health benefit exchanges	---	---	---	---	---	25.8	46.3	63.0	71.3	73.7	280.1
Earned income credit	---	---	---	---	---	63.3	63.7	66.1	63.8	65.3	322.1
Build America bonds	---	---	---	---	---	3.2	3.2	3.2	3.2	3.2	16.0

[Footnotes for the Table continue on the following page]

Footnotes for the Table continued:

[4] Positive tax expenditure of less than $50 million.

[5] Estimate includes effect of credit for interest on certain home mortgages (Section 25).

[6] Includes bonus depreciation and general acceleration under MACRS.

[7] Estimate includes amounts of employer-provided health insurance purchased through cafeteria plans and employer-provided child care purchased through dependent care flexible spending accounts. These amounts are also included in other line items in this table.

[8] Estimate does not include effects of changes made by the Emergency Economic Stabilization Act of 2008.

[9] Estimate includes employer-provided child care purchased through dependent care flexible spending accounts.

[10] In addition to the general charitable deduction, the tax expenditure accounts for the higher percentage limitation for public charities, the fair market value deduction for related-use tangible personal property, the enhanced deduction for inventory, the fair market value deduction for publicly traded stock and exceptions to the partial interest rules.

[11] Estimate includes employer-provided health insurance purchased through cafeteria plans and TRICARE medical insurance, which are also included in other line items on this table.

[12] Estimate does not include outlays due to Medicaid.

DETAILED ANALYSIS

1. PREPARATION OF TAX EXPENDITURE LISTS

Governmental tax expenditure lists are published annually by two bodies. The Executive Branch tax expenditure list appears in Analytical

Perspectives, "Tax Expenditures," which accompanies the annual Budget submitted by the President, and provides estimates over an eleven-year window (prior year, current year, and nine succeeding years). For its part, the Staff of the Joint Committee on Taxation publishes its list in "Estimates of Federal Tax Expenditures," and provides estimates over a five-year window (current year and four succeeding years).[5] We use the JCT list in this chapter and throughout the casebook because Congress requires that the Congressional Budget Office rely exclusively on JCT estimates when analyzing the revenue effects of proposed legislation.[6]

2. REVENUE ESTIMATING CONVENTIONS

The following excerpt from Staff of the Joint Committee on Taxation, Estimates of Federal Tax Expenditures for Fiscal Years 2015–2019, explains the methodology employed to estimate the revenue costs of tax expenditures:

> A tax expenditure is measured by the difference between tax liability under present law and the tax liability that would result from a recomputation of tax without benefit of the tax expenditure provision. Taxpayer behavior is assumed to remain unchanged for tax expenditure estimate purposes. * * *
>
> The tax expenditure calculations in this report are based on the January 2014 CBO revenue baseline and Joint Committee staff projections of the gross income, deductions, and expenditures of individuals and corporations for calendar years 2013–2018. These projections are used to compute tax liabilities for the present-law revenue baseline and tax liabilities for the alternative baseline that assumes that the tax expenditure provision does not exist.
>
> Internal Revenue Service ("IRS") statistics from recent tax returns are used to develop projections of the tax credits, deductions, and exclusions that will be claimed (or that will be denied in the case of negative tax expenditures) under the present-law baseline. These IRS statistics show the actual usage of the various tax expenditure provisions. * * *

---

[5]   The two official lists of tax expenditures differ in other respects. First, the JCT and Treasury staffs use different methodologies for measuring the cost of individual tax expenditures: the JCT measures the difference between tax liability under present law and tax liability if the exclusion were repealed with taxpayers also being allowed to claim the next best tax treatment for the particular income or expense, while the Treasury measures the difference in tax liability before and after repeal without permitting taxpayers to take advantage of second-best tax expenditure provisions. Second, the JCT methodology uses a broader definition of the normal income tax base, which results in JCT's list including more items than Treasury's. Third, the JCT calculations rely on economic forecasts prepared by the Congressional Budget Office (CBO), while the Treasury uses forecasts created by the Office of Management and Budget (OMB). Fourth, the JCT list excludes tax expenditure provisions costing less than $50 million over a five-year horizon, while the Treasury excludes provisions costing less than $5 million every year over an 11-year horizon. And finally, the JCT estimates integrate "negative tax expenditures" (i.e., tax provisions that provide *less* favorable treatment than normal tax law, and that are not related to progressivity) into its standard presentation, while the Treasury calculations ignore such scenarios (an example of a negative tax expenditure is the current law's failure to allow homeowners a deduction for depreciation and other costs).

[6]   See Pub. L. No. 99–177, sec. 173, codified at 2 U.S.C. 601(f).

Some tax expenditure calculations are based partly on statistics for income, deductions, and expenses for prior years. Accelerated depreciation is an example. Estimates for this tax expenditure are based on the difference between tax depreciation deductions under present law and the deductions that would have been claimed in the current year if investments in the current year and all prior years had been depreciated using the alternative (normal income tax law) depreciation system.

Each tax expenditure is calculated separately, under the assumption that all other tax expenditures remain in the Code. If two or more tax expenditures were estimated simultaneously, the total change in tax liability could be smaller or larger than the sum of the amounts shown for each item separately, as a result of interactions among the tax expenditure provisions.

3.   GROWTH IN TAX EXPENDITURE PROGRAMS

There has been rapid growth in the use of tax expenditure programs to fund various federal initiatives. The Joint Committee staff report for FY 2015–2019 lists more than 200 different tax expenditure programs costing over $1 trillion in foregone tax revenue. In past years, the total number of tax expenditure programs approached 250, but the Joint Committee stopped listing tax expenditures costing less than $50 million over the JCT's five-year reporting window. By contrast, and reflective of the recent explosion in tax expenditure programs, FY 1994–1998 estimates from the JCT contained a "mere" 126 tax expenditure items. The FY 2006–2010 report listed 70 new or extended tax expenditures enacted in 2005 alone. Part of the increase is attributable to Congress' penchant for using the tax expenditure budget to fund temporary and emergency priorities with tax provisions that "sunset" or expire after a period of years. The JCT report for FY 2015–19 listed 44 provisions that expired in 2014 or were expected to expire at the end of 2015.

4.   USES OF THE TAX EXPENDITURE CONCEPT

The Tax Expenditure Budget is a useful tool for analyzing the public policy purpose of numerous tax provisions.

4.1. *"Tax" Policy Questions*

Overall Consideration of Income Tax Revision and "Tax" Reform. An understanding that the income tax system consists of two elements serving different functions makes a difference in the approach to tax revision or tax reform. Tax reform is one thing if it means looking at a part of the inherent income tax structure that is not working well and asking just where did the tax experts go wrong in shaping that part. The issues posed and the answers to be explored are considered within the premises of an income tax and can be judged accordingly. But tax reform is quite another matter if it means examining a program of financial assistance to a particular group to decide whether that assistance should be given, in what amount, and on what terms. The latter process is not tax reform at all but rather "expenditure reform," and the issues and answers to be explored involve different premises and require different experts.

Effective "Tax" Rate Analysis. A traditional method of making interpersonal comparisons of the tax burden is "effective tax rate analysis." Under this method of analysis, the actual tax check remitted to the government is divided by the taxpayer's economic income and the resulting percentage figure is treated as the effective tax rate. Where two taxpayers with the same economic incomes are shown to have different effective tax rates under this analysis, it is asserted that horizontal equity has been violated and that the provisions causing the differences in effective tax rates are therefore objects of tax reform.

Tax expenditure analysis conflicts with and questions this traditional method of using effective rate analysis. Under the tax expenditure analytic technique, the taxpayer is deemed to have paid the tax on the total economic income (the taxpayer's "economic tax check"). The taxpayer in turn receives a check from the Treasury equal to the total of the tax expenditures for which the taxpayer has qualified (the taxpayer's "tax subsidy check"). Of course, these two checks are not actually exchanged. Instead, in the computation of tax liability on the tax return, the taxpayer in effect nets the economic tax check with the tax subsidy check and remits the balance to the Treasury. Although this check has traditionally been referred to as the taxpayer's "tax liability," and is so used in effective rate analysis, the number is simply the mathematical netting of the two checks. Under this analysis, the effective tax rate ratio is defective because the fraction involves two quite different numbers. The denominator of the fraction includes total economic income; but the numerator is not the taxpayer's total economic "tax." As a result, effective tax rates can give misleading information about the impact of the normal tax structure on taxpayers. To illustrate this point most dramatically, if all tax expenditures were repealed and were replaced by identical direct expenditure programs, every taxpayer's effective tax rate would immediately rise. Yet, the taxpayer's economic position would be unchanged. In short, traditional effective rate analysis actually tells policymakers very little. A low effective rate is usually an indication that the taxpayer is in the receipt of a significant amount of tax expenditures.

This is not to say that there is no role for effective rate analysis. The correct determination of taxpayers' effective tax rates can be obtained by comparing the economic tax to economic income. If differing effective rates occur at the same income level, that difference will result from defects within the normal structure of the tax itself and can be addressed.

For a discussion of these issues, see McDaniel, Identification of the "Tax" in "Effective Tax Rates," "Tax Reform" and "Tax Equity," 38 Nat'l Tax J. 273 (1985); Bittker, Effective Tax Rates: Fact or Fancy?, 122 U. Pa. L. Rev. 780 (1974).

"Tax" Simplification and "Tax" Complexity. In much the same way, tax expenditure analysis permits one to consider the matter of tax simplification—or tax complexity—in a different way from that usually followed. The perennial desire for tax simplification always makes it a primary objective of tax revision and tax reform efforts. Yet the income tax system becomes increasingly complex as each revision or reform passes into history. The efforts at tax simplification are rarely preceded by a

consideration of what factors are inherent in an income tax or instead are the result of faulty policies or faulty techniques. But tax expenditure analysis indicates that one significant source of complexity is the presence of the tax expenditure apparatus within the income tax system. One is thus led to inquire how much of the complexity of the present tax system stems from that apparatus and how much follows just from having an income tax itself. An income tax is an inherently complex tax, but it is made much more complicated when it is tasked with carrying out a host of expenditure programs.

Tax Administration. Problems of tax administration also are complicated by the presence of tax expenditures. In effect, the Commissioner of Internal Revenue is required to administer programs that otherwise would fall within the purview of some other executive branch department or agency. For each tax expenditure program, regulations must be prepared, rulings issued, agents trained, audits conducted, and litigation pursued. In turn, the Commissioner inevitably becomes involved in issues that have nothing to do with the collection of revenue, but rather with the administration of spending programs.

4.2. *Spending Program Questions*

Evaluation Techniques. Tax expenditure analysis suggests that preferential tax provisions should be analyzed and evaluated under the same criteria as are applied to direct spending programs. Moreover, because tax expenditures cover areas that are also affected by direct spending or regulatory programs, comparisons between the tax and direct spending programs are required to insure that consistent government policies are being followed by the two approaches.

Budget Issues. The Budget Act of 1974 reflected Congressional understanding that basically the same procedures should be applied to tax expenditures as to direct expenditures if Congress is to exercise any meaningful control over the budget process. In theory, almost any proposed or existing direct spending program can be drafted as a tax expenditure. Congress understood, therefore, that exclusion of tax expenditures from the budget process would permit certain spending provisions to operate free of the budgetary constraints envisioned by the Act.

Legislative Process. Tax expenditure analysis also has illuminated some issues in the legislative process. It has made clear, for example, that the tax-writing committees, when they enact or expand tax expenditures, serve both as authorizing and as appropriations committees. Whether this procedure is desirable or not needs to be evaluated by policymakers.

Some steps have been taken by Congress to provide greater coordination between consideration of tax and direct spending programs. The budget process obviously has a role to play. But the issue is not simply a budget matter, and the preliminary steps that have been taken need to be improved to insure more effective Congressional oversight of all federal expenditure programs. The coordination task is not easy, because it involves sensitive issues of committee jurisdiction.

Judicial Process. There have been surprisingly few constitutional challenges to tax expenditure provisions. Nevertheless, in some situations, the courts have been required to examine the effects of using the tax expenditure versus the direct expenditure technique. Most notably, challenges have been raised to federal expenditures effected through the charitable contribution deduction which allegedly would not have survived constitutional scrutiny as a direct expenditure program. In cases involving segregated tax-exempt organizations and aid to religion the courts have sustained constitutional or statutory challenges to the tax expenditure provision. See Chapter 21, Section 3.8. Indeed, now that (a) Congress has defined special tax provisions as spending programs, (b) both Congress and the executive branch publish lists of tax expenditures, and (c) tax committees are required to identify new tax expenditures, it is difficult to see how the courts could refuse to apply direct spending tests to tax expenditure provisions if such a challenge is raised. The Supreme Court's narrowing of standing, however, generally has precluded such challenges. More specifically, the Court has ruled that individual taxpayers lack standing to file lawsuits against the federal government merely because they disapprove of how the federal government spends taxpayer dollars (either directly or through tax provisions).

International Aspects. Other countries publish tax expenditure accounts for the tax systems they employ, including Canada, Finland, France, Austria, Spain, Sweden, the United Kingdom, and West Germany. Comparative studies have examined the use of tax expenditures by selected industrialized countries, and the possible utility of the concept in working out international tax relationships.[7]

Tax expenditures have also been the subject of proceedings under the World Trade Organization (WTO) agreements. For example, three successive tax expenditures intended to increase U.S. exports were held to violate U.S. obligations under the WTO agreements, with the WTO hearing panels undertaking tax expenditure analysis to reach their conclusions.[8]

5.   EVALUATION OF TAX EXPENDITURE PROGRAMS

The Tax Expenditure Budget enables an examination of income tax provisions as expenditure programs rather than technical tax provisions. When these tax provisions are understood to be carrying out programs of financial assistance for particular groups and activities, rather than as inherent parts of an income tax structure, the analysis requires a number of expenditure oriented questions.

Is There a Need for Federal Financial Aid? Tax expenditures involve spending federal money. If a tax expenditure is adopted or continued, fewer tax dollars will be available for reductions in tax rates or for direct spending programs, which has the same effect as continuing or adopting new direct spending programs. Therefore, the same proof of need for federal financial

---

[7]   See McDaniel and Surrey (eds.), International Aspects of Tax Expenditures: A Comparative Study (Kluwer: 1985); OECD, Tax Expenditures: Recent Experiences (1996).

[8]   The WTO proceedings are analyzed in McDaniel, Trade Agreements and Income Taxation: Interactions, Conflicts, and Resolutions, 57 Tax L. Rev. 275 (2004).

aid must be imposed on the proponents of a tax expenditure program as is imposed on proponents of a direct spending program. Advocates of a particular tax expenditure should be required to identify the specific problems that need resolution, and the reasons why the market mechanism cannot solve the identified problems; in other words, they should be required to articulate the need for governmental intervention in the first instance. Detailed analysis of the specific causes of the problem should also be required, and would include examining the industries and groups of individuals that might be affected, whether all businesses and individuals within the group are affected in the same way, and whether all affected parties need the same type and amount of aid.

What Is the Optimal Form of Federal Assistance? If a need for federal aid is established, the appropriate form of federal assistance must be determined. In general, Congress can choose among such techniques as direct grants, loans, interest subsidies, and loan guarantees.[9] Therefore, the next requirement in delivering benefits is to recommend the form of program that is best suited to address the problems that have been identified, and to provide the assistance that is needed.

The task is to produce the proper program *without* considering at this stage whether that program is to be implemented through a tax expenditure or direct expenditure mechanism. In this effort, the expertise of those involved in the particular program area must be drawn upon. This means that those in the executive branch department with responsibility for the program area should be consulted, as should members and the staffs of the non-tax congressional committees that have legislative responsibility for the general program area. Non-tax experts outside of government also should be involved. Comparable existing direct programs should be reviewed, not only to obtain information on appropriate program design, but also to insure proper coordination of the program under review with those already in existence.

In evaluating an existing or proposed tax expenditure, Treasury officials and the Congressional tax-writing committees should require their staffs:

— First, to determine the optimal form of a federal expenditure program to meet the identified need.

— Second, to reconstruct the tax expenditure under review as a direct expenditure program.

— Third, to compare the restructured tax expenditure to the optimal direct program to existing direct programs.

— Fourth, to identify the points at which differences exist in the tax and direct expenditure programs, and to ask whether these differences produce results that are rational and desirable.

The translation and consequent restatement of a tax expenditure program in direct expenditure terms generally show an "upside-down" result at variance with usual expenditure policies. This upside-down effect, with greater tax savings accruing to higher-income households, occurs because

---

9   See Salamon (ed.) Beyond Privatization: The Tools of Government Action (1989).

the value of a tax expenditure is a function of the marginal tax bracket of the taxpayer who utilizes the special provision. Thus, for individuals with incomes below the poverty level and no positive income tax liability due to a marginal tax bracket of zero, tax expenditures typically provide no benefit at all (this generalization does not apply to tax credits, see Chapter 22, Section 2). As income and rates rise, the benefit of a tax expenditure also rises. For example, consider the exclusion from income for employer contributions for medical insurance, discussed at Chapter 3, Section 3.B. Under a normative income tax system, the amount of the employer's contribution would be included in an employee's income. The exclusion in effect means that the government is paying a portion of the health care premium cost for the employee. If the tax expenditure program were translated into a direct expenditure program, the program would look as follows (using tax rates and brackets from tax year 2015, payable in April 2016):

— For a married couple filing a joint return with $500,000 in taxable income, the Department of Health and Human Services (HHS) would pay the insurance company $39.60 for each $100 of premium payments (reflecting the couple's 39.6 percent marginal tax rate), leaving the couple responsible for paying $60.40 from their own funds.

— For a married couple filing jointly with $200,000 in taxable income, HHS would pay the insurance company $28.00 for each $100 of premium payments, leaving the couple responsible for paying $72.00 from their own funds.

— For a married couple filing jointly with taxable income of $50,000, HHS would pay the insurance company $15 for each $100 of insurance premium, with the couple paying the remaining $85.

— For a married couple filing jointly with taxable income of $15,000, HHS would pay the insurance company $10 for each $100 of insurance premium, leaving the couple responsible for paying $90.

— And for a married couple too poor to be subject to the federal income tax, HHS would pay nothing to the insurance company, leaving the couple responsible for paying the entire $100 premium.

No HHS Secretary (indeed, no agency executive, no president, and no legislator) would ever recommend such an upside-down direct expenditure program to Congress with benefits accruing disproportionately to taxpayers least in need of assistance and nothing to those most in need of assistance.[10]

Techniques have been developed to design tax expenditures that eliminate the upside-down effect of most existing tax expenditures as well as the lack of benefit to non-taxpayers. The upside-down effect can be eliminated by using a tax credit, the amount of which is included in gross income (see e.g., the alcohol fuels tax credit, Chapter 17, Section 3.1.), or that

---

[10]   In some tax expenditures, the upside-down effect may be reduced or even eliminated because all or part of the nominal benefit may be shifted to others in the form of higher prices. The exemption for interest on certain state and local government bonds illustrates how this may occur. See Chapter 8, Section 4.

is phased out as income rises (see e.g., the child tax credit, Chapter 22, Section 2.A.(2).). Also, the benefit of a tax expenditure can be provided to low-income individuals by employing a tax credit which is "refundable" by delivering cash payments to individuals either with no positive tax liability or insufficient tax liability to take full advantage of the credit amount (see e.g., the earned income credit, Chapter 22, Section 2.A.1.).

Where a tax expenditure is included in income, there is no tax policy objection to using the tax expenditure mechanism; for income measurement purposes, the tax expenditure is treated the same as a taxable direct government outlay. Similarly, where a tax expenditure program is the equivalent of a loan program, tax policy concerns are satisfied if an appropriate interest charge is imposed on the loan.

6.   CRITERIA FOR CHOOSING BETWEEN TAX AND DIRECT EXPENDITURES

Tax expenditure analysis makes clear that when the government wishes to implement a spending program, it has the choice between two techniques: direct expenditure programs or tax expenditure programs. Whereupon the issue becomes identifying the criteria to determine which alternative to implement. At this juncture, some observers perceive inherent differences in the two approaches, particularly those involving control of costs, government red tape and bureaucracy, and administrative ease or complexity. However, experience reveals that these differences amount to debates over program design rather than innate differences between the tax and direct spending mechanism. Furthermore, these debates over program design and administration can be resolved by accounting for the following considerations:

Program Design: Type of program, costs and benefits, effectiveness, distribution of benefits, methods of review and evaluation, and income tax treatment of the benefits.[11]

Degree of Government Control: The "red tape" issue presents itself because a government bureaucracy must administer the program, which necessarily involves government procedures and protocol. The tax expenditure approach shifts governmental administration to the IRS, often without a budget adjustment to reflect alternative costs of administration.

Budget Effects: The impact on the budget, the need for a cap on the revenue loss, and resolution of budget priorities.

Constitutional Questions: Whether federal aid can be given at all to certain potential program beneficiaries.

Effects on inflation: Whether the program reduces or increases inflationary pressures in the economic activity affected.

Effects on Competitive Behavior: Whether the subsidy enhances competition or facilitates corporate concentration.

---

[11]   See Zelinsky, Efficiency and Income Taxes: The Rehabilitation of Tax Incentives, 64 Tex. L. Rev. 973 (1986) (demonstrating that there is no inherent reason why a tax expenditure should be more or less efficient, in the various ways that term is used, than an identical direct outlay program).

Committee Jurisdiction: If a direct expenditure program is utilized, the respective legislative and appropriations committees obtain jurisdiction. If the tax expenditure approach is used, the tax-writing committees obtain jurisdiction over both the authorizing and appropriations functions.

Closely related to the jurisdictional issues is the question of staff resources and expertise. If the tax expenditure route is followed, problems of housing, pollution control, energy, and constitutionality become the responsibilities of tax lawyers and economists, many of whom may be required to become experts in subjects far outside their usual areas of expertise. Again, the difference is not inevitable as the tax-writing committees could employ non-tax staff members in the various areas covered by tax expenditures.

Whether these differences in committee jurisdiction and staff expertise (and more fundamentally, in the legislative process followed) are desirable or undesirable is beyond the scope of tax expenditure analysis.[12] But under present procedures the differences may be important in deciding whether to implement a program either through the tax expenditure or direct expenditure legislative process.

Executive Branch Administration: Generally, different executive branch agencies will administer a program, depending on whether it is a tax expenditure or a direct expenditure. Thus, for example, the major program to provide financial assistance to homeowners (through deductions for mortgage interest and property taxes and exclusion of gain on sale) is in the Internal Revenue Code and is administered by the Treasury and Internal Revenue Service. An identical direct homeowner's subsidy would be administered by the Department of Housing and Urban Development. Present procedures thus produce a real difference between the tax expenditure and direct expenditure approaches, because the Treasury and Internal Revenue Service will have exclusive or joint control of the former approach and would typically not be involved in the latter approach.

Level of Program Benefits: If the tax expenditure approach is adopted, program benefits and costs can rise and fall as a result of unrelated tax changes. Every tax rate increase or decrease can produce a corresponding increase or decrease in the amount of assistance provided through tax expenditures.

Similarly, increases in the standard deduction or in the personal exemptions may reduce the scope and cost of tax expenditures implemented by itemized personal deductions and most tax credits. This corresponding change in the level of federal funding does not occur where direct programs are concerned. Of course, tax increases or tax reductions have an impact on the overall amounts of federal funds available for direct programs, but a change in tax rates does not automatically change the federal revenue cost of each direct spending program.

Whether the automatic effect on the cost of tax expenditure programs resulting from unrelated tax changes is desirable or undesirable raises

---

[12]   See McDaniel, Federal Income Tax Simplification: The Political Process, 34 Tax L. Rev. 27 (1978).

questions both of a programmatic and political nature. But the effect is peculiar to the tax expenditure approach. Although one could conceive of Congress adjusting each tax expenditure program when it makes a tax rate change so as to eliminate this difference, such an approach is not a practical possibility in the existing legislative process.

Psychological Aspects: Some observers believe that program beneficiaries may exhibit a different psychological response to tax and direct expenditure programs. In part, the expressed psychological preference of some persons for the tax expenditure approach may reflect a desire to obscure the appearance that they are receiving a federal subsidy. In other cases, the psychological response may be conditioned by the program design differences that have characterized the tax and direct spending approaches, with the beneficiaries preferring to receive tax benefits as opposed to direct spending handouts. But, as discussed above, program design differences are neither inevitable nor desirable.

While psychological factors may be present in the public perception of tax versus direct expenditures, it is difficult to assess how much weight a government seeking to retain control of its tax and budget policy should give them. Little weight should be accorded to psychological responses based on misconceptions or historical accident, because such responses can be altered though education and exposure to different approaches or techniques. Further analysis is warranted to see if there are additional and deeper concerns involved.

In summary, there are some significant and important differences between using the tax and direct expenditure techniques. These differences are not the ones usually identified in popular or political debate. Frequently, as we have seen, those "differences" turn out to be neither inevitable nor desirable. In situations where differences depend on which approach is selected, tax expenditure analysis does not dictate that one approach is preferable to another. It simply requires policymakers to ensure that unnecessary and undesirable differences in the two techniques are minimized as much as possible, and that the criteria that differentiate the two approaches are clearly identified and rationally applied in a transparent manner.

SECTION 2.   APPLICATION OF TAX EXPENDITURE ANALYSIS

DETAILED ANALYSIS

1.   TAX EXPENDITURES RECONSIDERED

This chapter's discussion of tax expenditure analysis assists in better understanding the material in preceding chapters. In particular, it can help evaluate why certain Internal Revenue Code sections—and the revenues lost to those sections—might be classified as structural expenditures versus tax expenditures.

Below, you will find a list of expenditure items discussed in previous chapters. As you revisit each item, consider how tax expenditure analysis may alter your previous understanding of the individual provisions' purposes and effectiveness. Ask whether the program should exist in the first place; whether it should be administered by the Internal Revenue Service or some other federal agency; if the former, ask whether it should take the form of an individual tax expenditure or become part of the "normal" tax system; and if a tax expenditure seems appropriate, ask whether the tax benefits should be delivered through an exclusion, deduction, exemption, or credit based on a variety of factors, including targeted beneficiaries, distributional consequences, treatment of similarly situated taxpayers, cost, potential behavioral responses, and other competing policy goals.

Later chapters, particularly Chapters 17 and 23, will provide additional opportunities to undertake a closer look at specific tax expenditure provisions contained in the Code.

Budget Function	Revenue Cost, 2015–2019 (in $billions)
Energy	
• Exclusion of interest on private activity bonds (PABs) for energy production facilities	0.2
Agriculture	
• Exclusion of conservation cost-sharing payments	0.1
Commerce and Housing	
• Exclusion of capital gains on sales of principal residences	149.9
• Exclusion of interest on PABs for owner-occupied housing	6.9
• Exclusion of interest on PABs for rental housing	5.4
• Exclusion of accrued gains at death	171.3
• Carryover basis for gifts	35.4
Transportation	
• Exclusion of employer-paid transportation benefits	27.2

- Exclusion of interest on PABs for highway projects   0.6

Education (see also Chapter 23), **Training, and Social Services**

- Exclusion of employee meals and lodging   11.1

- Exclusion of benefits under cafeteria plans   188.5

- Miscellaneous excluded fringe benefits   39.2

- Exclusion of employee awards   1.7

Health

- Exclusion of employer contributions for health insurance and health-care   769.8

- Exclusion of worker's compensation benefits (medical benefits)   25.6

Income Security

- Exclusion of worker's compensation benefits   15.1

- Exclusion of damages for personal physical injuries or sickness   8.5

- Individual retirement accounts   116.7

- Exclusion of premiums on group life insurance   16.4

- Exclusion of premiums on accident and disability insurance   22.2

Social Security

- Untaxed benefits   210.1

General Purpose Fiscal Assistance

- Exclusion of interest on public purpose state and local bonds   187.7

2. EXCLUSIONS CLASSIFIED AS STRUCTURAL

- Realization requirement
- Imputed income
- Certain fringe benefits
- Gifts and inheritances
- Life insurance death benefits
- Social welfare subsidies
- Loans
- Deposits

PART III

BUSINESS DEDUCTIONS AND CREDITS

CHAPTER 12

ORDINARY AND NECESSARY BUSINESS AND PROFIT-SEEKING EXPENSES

There is no one central Code section for deductions that functions in the same manner as § 61(a) does for gross income. Rather, deductions are available only if expressly authorized. Thus, the deduction sections are an enumeration of specific items. The closest that the Code comes to having provisions of general application with respect to deductions are §§ 162 and 212, which in general grant deductions for the expenses of producing income. These sections are supplemented by other provisions establishing the deductibility of specific types of expenses. The basic function of these sections is to reduce gross income to net income, thus establishing the gain or profit central to the concept of income.

Two principal limitations generally apply to these sections. First, in most situations only profit-seeking expenses are deductible. The costs of producing income must be distinguished from costs of personal consumption. The difficulties of distinguishing deductible profit-seeking expenses from nondeductible personal expenses are discussed in Chapter 19, which deals with deductions for items such as meals, entertainment, and travel.

Second, even if the expense relates to a profit-seeking activity, it must be an expense that reduces the taxpayer's net worth. Some costs, such as the cost of purchasing a machine, merely convert one form of capital, cash, into another form of capital, the machine. Therefore, these costs are not currently deductible. Such costs create basis in the acquired item (see Chapter 13) and that basis will be recovered in later years either through some cost recovery technique (see Chapter 14) or by offsetting the amount realized if the item is sold or otherwise disposed of. The issue in these situations is one of *timing*—determining when the cost will be recovered. The materials in Chapter 13 discuss the rules used to differentiate currently deductible costs from costs that are not currently deductible.

In addition to these two major limitations, a number of other interpretive issues arise, which are discussed in this Chapter. Although both §§ 162 and 212 cover the costs of generating income, they use different terminology and have been found to cover different types of activities. Section 162 applies to trade or business expenses, while § 212 applies to other profit-seeking expenses. Section 1 of this Chapter discusses the differences between "business" expenses deductible under § 162 and non-business profit-seeking expenses deductible under § 212.

Both §§ 162 and 212 allow a deduction only for "ordinary and necessary" expenses. Section 2 of this Chapter considers whether these words further limit the deductibility of personal and capital costs and, if so, the nature of that limitation. Section 162(a) and Treas. Reg. § 1.212–1(d) apply the qualifying term "reasonable" to some costs of producing income. Section 3 of this Chapter discusses a specific application of this limitation. Additional issues arise if the income to which the profit-seeking expense relates is tax-exempt or given preferential tax treatment. Section 4 deals with these issues. Section 5 considers tax penalties—provisions designed to achieve non-tax policy objectives by limiting the deductibility of some costs of producing income.

Finally, a note on the relative value of deductions: Not all deductions are created equal. As explained in Chapter 22, some deductions are always available to taxpayers and will therefore always reduce the amount of income subject to tax. These are therefore the most attractive deductions. Other deductions, including deductions allowed by § 212, are available only to taxpayers who elect to take them in lieu of taking a more "standard" deduction. These deductions can be less valuable because their availability comes at a price. Moreover, some of these deductions are subject to additional limitations which further reduce their attractiveness. Although we will explore the differences in deductions later, for now it suffices to observe that not all deduction dollars reduce a taxpayer's income by the same final amount.

SECTION 1.   THE RELEVANCE OF "TRADE OR BUSINESS" VERSUS "PROFIT-SEEKING" EXPENSES

INTERNAL REVENUE CODE: Sections 162(a); 212; 7701(a)(26).

REGULATIONS: Section 1.212–1(a), (b), (g)–(i), (m).

Section 162(a) allows a deduction for the "ordinary and necessary expenses" of "carrying on any trade or business." Although the phrase "ordinary and necessary" presents a number of significant issues, the threshold question is whether expenses were incurred in a trade or business. Limiting the deduction to expenses paid or incurred in carrying on a trade or business precludes any deduction under § 162 for personal living expenses. This limitation is reinforced by the express proscription of any such deduction in § 262. The fact that an expense is not a personal living expense does not necessarily mean that it is deductible under § 162. Expenses incurred by an investor—for example, investment advisory expenses and the cost of subscribing to financial news publications incurred by an individual who purchases and holds publicly traded stocks for speculative appreciation, as well as dividend income— are not expenses incurred in a trade or business.

In Higgins v. Commissioner, 312 U.S. 212 (1941), the Supreme Court held that the managing of portfolio investments was not a trade or business and that expenses incurred to manage such investments were not deductible under the predecessor of § 162, even though the expenses clearly were not personal but were the cost of earning income. Congress responded with the enactment of the statutory predecessor of § 212(1) and (2). Generally speaking the purpose of § 212 is to provide a deduction for "ordinary and necessary" profit-seeking expenses incurred in holding investment property, such as stocks and bonds and speculative real estate. Thus, ordinary and necessary expenses of managing investments, such as the cost of investment advice and subscriptions to financial publications, are governed by § 212. Its scope goes beyond the type of activities involved in *Higgins* however, and it extends to the cost of acquiring any items includable in income that are received outside of a trade or business. See e.g., Kanelos v. Commissioner, T.C. Memo. 1943–429 (cost of traveling to Dublin to collect on a winning ticket in Irish Sweepstakes was deductible). Although § 212 literally covers both business and investment expenses, the presence of § 162(a) and the circumstances surrounding the enactment of § 212 serve to confine § 212 to the expenses of profit-seeking activities that do not constitute a trade or business.

The distinction between §§ 162 and 212 would be of little practical relevance if the two provisions allowed deductions under similar circumstances and to the same extent. However, that is not the case. Although most § 162 trade or business expenses are deductible by all taxpayers regardless of what other deductions are available to them, and are not limited by other provisions, § 212 profit-seeking expenses are deductible only as itemized deductions.[1] This means that many taxpayers who incur such expenses will not in fact be able to deduct them because they do not and should not itemize deductions. (Chapter 22 explains why many taxpayers do not itemize deductions.) Furthermore, even for individuals who itemize deductions, § 212 deductions are subject to a number of complex limitations, which are discussed in Chapter 21. In sum, § 162 deductions are significantly more attractive than § 212 deductions. There is no policy justification for this differing treatment of business and other profit-seeking expenses, and the reason for it is probably historical.

Section 199 provides a deduction for "domestic production activities," which is in effect available only if the activity is part of a trade or business. In computing the amount of the deduction, only items attributable to the actual conduct of a trade or business can be taken into account. I.R.C. § 199(d)(5). As a result, the consequences that attend the determination that a taxpayer is engaged in the conduct of a trade or business rather than engaging in an activity for the production of income now go beyond the availability of deductions under §§ 162 or 212.

---

[1] In addition, § 212 deductions are not allowable for purposes of the alternative minimum tax, but almost all § 162 deductions are.

DETAILED ANALYSIS

1.   TRADE OR BUSINESS DEFINED: THE SCOPE OF SECTION 162

In Deputy v. du Pont, 308 U.S. 488, 499 (1940), Justice Frankfurter, in a concurring opinion, stated that for purposes of § 162 carrying on any trade or business "involves holding one's self out to others as engaged in the selling of goods or services." Nevertheless, in Commissioner v. Groetzinger, 480 U.S. 23 (1987), the Supreme Court rejected this formulation. In *Groetzinger* the Court concluded that holding oneself out to others as being engaged in the selling of goods or services is not a prerequisite for being engaged in a trade or business. It thus held that a full-time gambler who spent between sixty and eighty hours a week wagering on dog races for his own account was engaged in a trade or business. The Court announced that "to be engaged in a trade or business, the taxpayer must be involved in the activity with continuity and regularity and . . . the taxpayer's primary purpose for engaging in the activity must be for income or profit."

Under this standard, individuals may be in the trade or business of buying and selling stock and other investment securities on an exchange for their own account, so-called "traders," if the primary source of profits is short-term price fluctuations and arbitrage. To have such activity treated as a business rather than an investment, taxpayers must personally manage the activity and make the investment decisions; hiring professional financial managers results in the activity being considered a profit-seeking investment activity, subject to § 212 rather than § 162. Mayer v. United States, 32 Fed. Cl. 149 (1994).

Holding real estate for rental purposes generally is considered to be a trade or business, even though the activity may require very little time and energy of the owner. See e.g., Hazard v. Commissioner, 7 T.C. 372 (1946) (Acq.). Two cases illustrate the limits of this rule. First, where a single property is leased for a long period of time to a single tenant and the lessor's actual effort is minimal and requires no employees, the activity may be found to be a nonbusiness profit seeking activity. Grier v. United States, 218 F.2d 603 (2d Cir.1955). Second, holding real estate for speculative appreciation is not a trade or business, but it is a profit seeking activity, and the expenses of the activity generally are deductible under § 212, rather than § 162. Harris v. Commissioner, T.C. Memo. 1978–332.

If an activity purporting to be a trade or business does not have a profit motive, it cannot be a trade or business, and § 162 thus is inapplicable.[2] In Sloan v. Commissioner, T.C. Memo. 1988–294, aff'd by order, 896 F.2d 547 (4th Cir.1990), a government computer analyst who was a licensed attorney was denied any deduction for expenses of a law practice conducted only on weekends. The activity was not continuous and regular and the taxpayer rarely charged clients. Because the primary purpose of the weekend law practice was to gain experience, it did not constitute the conduct of a trade or business.

---

[2]   Section 183, discussed in Chapter 18, allows deductions with respect to an activity conducted without a profit motive, but only to the extent of gross income realized from the particular activity.

2.   SCOPE OF SECTION 212

Section 212 allows a deduction for expenses of managing and conserving income producing property, as well as expenses for the production of income. Thus, as long as an expense bears one of the requisite statutory relationships to income producing property, it may be eligible for deduction under § 212. For example, Bingham's Trust v. Commissioner, 325 U.S. 365 (1945), allowed a deduction under the predecessor of § 212 to a trust for expenses incurred in connection with the payment of certain legacies. Even though the expenses themselves were not directed to producing income, the expenses were incurred in the management of income producing property. There are limits, however. To be deductible under § 212 the expense must bear some relationship to a profit-seeking purpose with respect to income producing property. Personally motivated expenses incurred with respect to income producing property, such as the cost of a will to bequeath income producing property to a relative, are not deductible.

Furthermore, not all profit-seeking expenses incurred with respect to investment property are deductible under § 212. Some expenses incurred to prevent the loss of income producing property may not be deducted. For example, Accardo v. Commissioner, 942 F.2d 444 (7th Cir.1991), held that legal fees incurred in the successful defense of criminal RICO charges were not deductible merely because a conviction would have resulted in the forfeiture of $1.5 million of income producing assets. But expenses to conserve income producing property are deductible under § 212. Cruttenden v. Commissioner, 644 F.2d 1368 (9th Cir.1981), held that expenses incurred to recover a stock certificate loaned to another person to use as security for a third-party loan were deductible because there was no dispute as to title.

SECTION 2.   THE "ORDINARY AND NECESSARY" LIMITATION

A.   THE SUPREME COURT DECISIONS

INTERNAL REVENUE CODE: Sections 63(a); 161; 162(a); 212.

REGULATIONS: Section 1.162–1(a)–6.

Welch v. Helvering

Supreme Court of the United States, 1933.
290 U.S. 111.

[A former officer of a bankrupt corporation, the stock of which had been owned by the officer and his father, went into a similar business for himself. In an effort to reestablish relations with his customers and to solidify his credit and standing, he paid the debts of the bankrupt corporation. The Board of Tax Appeals disallowed the deduction, and the Court of Appeals for the Eighth Circuit affirmed.]

■ MR. JUSTICE CARDOZO delivered the opinion of the Court:

* * *

We may assume that the payments to creditors of the Welch Company were necessary for the development of the petitioner's business, at least in the sense that they were appropriate and helpful. * * *. He certainly thought they were, and we should be slow to override his judgment. But the problem is not solved when the payments are characterized as necessary. Many necessary payments are charges upon capital. There is need to determine whether they are both necessary and ordinary. Now, what is ordinary, though there must always be a strain of constancy within it, is none the less a variable affected by time and place and circumstance. Ordinary in this context does not mean that the payments must be habitual or normal in the sense that the same taxpayer will have to make them often. A lawsuit affecting the safety of a business may happen once in a lifetime. The counsel fees may be so heavy that repetition is unlikely. None the less, the expense is an ordinary one because we know from experience that payments for such a purpose, whether the amount is large or small, are the common and accepted means of defense against attack. * * *. The situation is unique in the life of the individual affected, but not in the life of the group, the community, of which he is a part. At such times there are norms of conduct that help to stabilize our judgment, and make it certain and objective. The instance is not erratic, but is brought within a known type.

The line of demarcation is now visible between the case that is here and the one supposed for illustration. We try to classify this act as ordinary or the opposite, and the norms of conduct fail us. No longer can we have recourse to any fund of business experience, to any known business practice. Men do at times pay the debts of others without legal obligation or the lighter obligation imposed by the usages of trade or by neighborly amenities, but they do not do so ordinarily, not even though the result might be to heighten their reputation for generosity and opulence. Indeed, if language is to be read in its natural and common meaning, * * *, we should have to say that payment in such circumstances, instead of being ordinary is in a high degree extraordinary. There is nothing ordinary in the stimulus evoking it, and none in the response. Here, indeed, as so often in other branches of the law, the decisive distinctions are those of degree and not of kind. One struggles in vain for any verbal formula that will supply a ready touchstone. The standard set up by the statute is not a rule of law; it is rather a way of life. Life in all its fullness must supply the answer to the riddle.

The Commissioner of Internal Revenue resorted to that standard in assessing the petitioner's income, and found that the payments in controversy came closer to capital outlays than to ordinary and necessary expenses in the operation of a business. * * * Unless we can say from facts within our knowledge that these are ordinary and necessary expenses according to the ways of conduct and the forms of speech prevailing in the business world, the tax must be confirmed. But nothing told us by this record or within the sphere of our judicial notice permits us to give that extension to what is ordinary and necessary. Indeed, to do so would open the door to many bizarre analogies. One man has a family name that is clouded by thefts committed by an ancestor. To add to his own standing he repays the stolen money, wiping off, it may be, his income for the year. The payments figure in his tax return as ordinary expenses. Another man conceives the notion that he will be able to practice his vocation with greater ease and profit if he has an opportunity to enrich his culture. Forthwith the price of his education becomes an expense of the business, reducing the income subject to taxation. There is little difference between these expenses and those in controversy here. * * *

Many cases in the federal courts deal with phases of the problem presented in the case at bar. To attempt to harmonize them would be a futile task. They involve the appreciation of particular situations, at times with borderline conclusions. * * *

The decree should be affirmed. —> Holding / conclusion

DETAILED ANALYSIS

1. THE "ORDINARY AND NECESSARY" LIMITATION: REDUNDANT OR ADDITIONAL?

In Deputy v. du Pont, 308 U.S. 488 (1940), the Supreme Court again considered the "ordinary" requirement. The taxpayer, owner of about 16 percent of stock in E.I. du Pont de Nemours & Co., sold stock to executives of the company. The company wanted the executives to have a financial interest in it but for legal reasons could not sell the stock to them directly. The taxpayer-shareholder had to borrow the shares and, as a result of the borrowing, had to pay various amounts to the lender. The Court held that even assuming taxpayer's activities amounted to a trade or business, his payments were not ordinary: "There is no evidence that stockholders or investors, in furtherance of enhancing and conserving their estates, ordinarily or frequently lend such assistance to employee stock purchase plans of their corporations."

Over 20 years later, in Commissioner v. Tellier, 383 U.S. 687 (1966), the Supreme Court formulated the ordinary and necessary limitation as follows:

> Our decisions have consistently construed the term "necessary" as imposing only the minimal requirement that the expense be "appropriate and helpful" for the "development of the [taxpayer's] business." Welch v. Helvering, 290 U.S. 111, 113 * * * . The principal function of the term "ordinary" in § 162(a) is to clarify the distinction, often difficult, between those expenses that are currently deductible and those that are in the nature of capital expenditures, which, if deductible at all, must be amortized over the useful life of the asset.

Under the approach suggested by the quoted language from *Tellier,* the requirement that the expenditure be "necessary" emphasizes the business connection of the expenditure and distinguishes it from a nondeductible personal expense. Similarly, "ordinary" is not to be understood as contrasting with unusual or extraordinary but only as underlining the distinction between currently deductible expenses and non-deductible capital expenditures discussed in Chapter 13. If this view is correct, the "ordinary and necessary" limitation adds nothing to the basic statutory pattern of the rules governing deductibility of expenditures because § 262 prohibits the deduction of expenses which are personal in nature and § 263 disallows current deductions for capital expenditures.

The lack of clarity in the Supreme Court opinions has led to considerable confusion among the lower courts. Thus, a number of cases, both before and after *Tellier,* have applied the ordinary and necessary language literally as independent limitations, disallowing deductions where the expenditure was unusual or voluntary. Many of these cases appear to reach the correct result for the wrong reason: often the "unusual" character of an expenditure is a sign of its capital nature and, similarly, the voluntariness of a payment may evidence a personal rather than business relationship. The latter point may help explain the decision in Friedman v. Delaney, below.

B. THE "ORDINARY AND NECESSARY" LIMITATION IN THE LOWER COURTS

Friedman v. Delaney

United States Court of Appeals, First Circuit, 1948.
171 F.2d 269.

■ PETERS, DISTRICT JUDGE. * * * It appears that the plaintiff, Mr. Friedman, a Boston lawyer of long experience, had a valued client in whom he had confidence, one Louis H. Wax, whose proposed composition in bankruptcy required the deposit in court of the sum of $7000. The record shows that Mr. Friedman made this deposit in February, 1938, accompanying it with a caveat to the effect that no part of the money came from Wax or his estate. In November, 1939, Mr. Friedman entered a petition in bankruptcy court alleging "that the money deposited for the proposed composition, which has been abandoned," was deposited by him and was not the property of the bankrupt, and asking that it be ordered returned. The petition was denied in November, 1941, and thereupon Mr. Friedman filed an undertaking that he would not further oppose transfer of the money to the trustee in bankruptcy, at the same time alleging that slightly over $5000 of the amount deposited was his own money.

It seems that the reason Mr. Friedman furnished this money from his own funds in the bankruptcy proceeding was because, in conversations with attorneys for creditors, when he was urging the acceptance of the proposed composition, he had personally assured them that the money to carry it out would be forthcoming. He did this without informing Mr. Wax and without intending to subject him to any legal liability, presumably feeling certain that the money would be obtained from a certain life insurance policy, which he had in his possession. This policy on the life of Wax, payable to his wife, could be pledged for $5000, but when it came to that point Mr. and Mrs. Wax refused to have it so used, which left Mr. Friedman in the breach. Commendably recognizing his moral obligation, in view of the assurances he had given, he paid the money to the clerk of the bankruptcy court.

The question presented is whether the $5000, which the plaintiff in his complaint alleged was "lost by him in connection with the bankruptcy proceedings of one Louis H. Wax", and which he claimed as a deduction from income in his return for 1941, was wrongfully disallowed by the Commissioner, the plaintiff now claiming that it should have been allowed as an ordinary and necessary expense in carrying on business under [the predecessor of section 162(a)] * * * .

The parties are in agreement that the plaintiff, to recover, must show the applicability of [that] Section. We agree with the District Court that he has failed to do so.

The plaintiff contends that the loss of the amount in question was due to his keeping his word, which the ethics of his profession, as well as his own conscientiousness compelled him to do and argues that consequently the payment was made and the loss incurred in his law business, and should have been allowed as a deduction from income under one or the other of the sections referred to. His position is illustrated by his rhetorical question: Is it not part of a lawyer's business to keep his word? It might be answered that it is everybody's business to do so, but that is wide of the mark. We are obliged to inquire whether the circumstances of this loss—no matter how creditably incurred—are clearly within the coverage of either Section referred to. Nor can equitable considerations be allowed to control. The matter of deductions from income " * * * 'depends upon legislative grace; and only as there is clear provision therefor can any particular deduction be allowed.' " Deputy v. du Pont, 308 U.S. 488 * * * .

It is necessary to consider the origin of the obligation under which the taxpayer considered himself to be under when he made the payment in question, in determining whether it is a permissible deduction under either Section of the statute. It arose from the gratuitous assurance given attorneys for creditors of Wax by Mr. Friedman that the money for the composition would be forthcoming if they would approve it. In effect, it was the voluntary underwriting of the obligation of another. It was of course, the duty of the client to furnish the money, not of his attorney. Payment of the $5000 by the attorney was made as a consequence of his undertaking and in pursuance of it and was no less voluntary than the assurance which occasioned it. From any point of view his loss was caused by his voluntary action.

As was said by this Court in the very similar case of W.F. Young, Inc. v. Commissioner, 120 F.2d 159, 166, "Even if the credit and reputation of the taxpayer would have been improved by these payments and even though they would in any way benefit the taxpayer, voluntary payments are not deductible as ordinary and necessary business expenses or losses." * * *

The emphasis placed by the plaintiff upon his moral obligation to keep his professional word should not obscure the fact that the transaction on his part was voluntary from the beginning.

That the circumstances of the taxpayer's payment preclude its being considered either an "ordinary and necessary expense" of his business or a loss incurred in business is clear both from the Regulations promulgated under the Internal Revenue Code and the construction [sections 162(a) and 165(a) and (c)(1)] have received by the Courts.

The business expenses covered by the former Section are limited to those described as being "ordinary and necessary"; such as are directly connected with and proximately resulting from carrying it on; those normally originating in a liability created in the course of its operation. Deputy v. du Pont, supra. Welch v. Helvering, 290 U.S. 111 * * * .

The moral obligation which the taxpayer recognized here, to his financial detriment, was an extra-professional liability which resulted in a loss which is certainly not clearly covered by [section 162(a)] according to the accepted construction of that Section.

* * *

■ MAGRUDER, CHIEF JUDGE. I concur in the result. But I would stress certain additional facts which apparently have not been regarded as significant either by the district court or by my brethren. [Chief Judge Magruder then recited the facts, in somewhat greater detail than the majority].

If these were all the relevant facts, I should hate to have to hold that the payment of $5000 by Friedman under the circumstances stated was not an "ordinary and necessary" expense paid in carrying on his professional business. The statutory language is pretty flexible. Cf. Welch v. Helvering, 1933, 290 U.S. 111 * * *: "One struggles in vain for any verbal formula that will supply a ready touchstone. The standard set up by the statute is not a rule of law; it is rather a way of life. Life in all its fullness must supply the answer to the riddle." I do not think that the fact that the making of the deposit was "voluntary", in the sense that it was not in pursuance of an enforceable legal obligation, is conclusive against deductibility. Dunn & McCarthy, Inc. v. Commissioner, 2 Cir., 1943, 139 F.2d 242. * * * "Whether an expenditure is directly related to a business and whether it is ordinary and necessary are doubtless pure questions of fact in most instances." Commissioner v. Heininger, 1943, 320 U.S. 467 * * * . Hence the finding of the district court in the present case that the payment was not an ordinary and necessary expense incident to Friedman's practice of law would have to be accepted by the appellate courts unless "clearly erroneous." In view of the further facts to which I shall now advert, I think that on the record as a whole it would have been improper to find that the $5000 item was an ordinary and necessary business expense. * * *

As already stated, Friedman made the deposit to make good on his assurance that funds would be available to satisfy a composition of ten cents on the dollar if Wax's creditors should accept the offer of settlement. That was the only purpose of the deposit; and that was the full extent of the professional obligation of honor which Friedman scrupulously recognized. Friedman certainly had no obligation, moral or legal, to make a general and unrestricted contribution to the bankrupt estate out of his own pocket. * * *

Now it appears from the record that the proposed composition was never effectuated and that Friedman's $5000 was never applied to the limited purpose for which the deposit had been made. Upon the failure of the composition proposal, Wax was adjudicated a bankrupt. * * * After some negotiations in which the trustee, the Malden Trust Company, Friedman, and others participated, a compromise agreement was worked out under which the trustee agreed to accept from the Malden Trust Company the sum of $4000 in full settlement of the equity suit; and as part of the compromise Friedman agreed not to press his petition for the return to him of the $5000 deposit and not to oppose the entry of an order by the referee extinguishing Friedman's claim to the deposit and transferring it to the trustee in bankruptcy for the general purposes of the bankruptcy administration. * * * Then and there Friedman lost his $5000.

The record is silent as to the reasons which led Friedman to agree in 1941 that the $5000 deposit (to the return of which he was clearly entitled upon the failure of its purpose) should be turned over to the trustee in bankruptcy to be dealt with without restriction as part of the bankrupt's estate. This agreement does not appear to have been related in any way to the assurances which Friedman had given to the referee and to attorneys for Wax's creditors back in 1937 as a result of which Friedman had felt morally bound to make the deposit so that funds would be available to satisfy the proposed agreement of composition then pending. As above stated, the composition was never consummated and Wax was adjudicated a bankrupt. Friedman's relinquishment in 1941 of his claim for refund of the $5000 deposit can therefore not be deemed to have been an ordinary and necessary expense by way of fulfilling a professional commitment made in the course of his practice of the law— which is the main ground urged by Friedman in support of his claim that the $5000 item was properly deductible. * * *

DETAILED ANALYSIS

1. UNUSUAL EXPENDITURES: UNCLEAR LANGUAGE AND MUDDLED REASONING

The courts have not been paragons of clarity or consistency in interpreting the statutory terms. *Friedman* illustrates the confusion, with Judge Magruder requiring additional facts to reach the conclusion that his colleagues reached without those facts. Although sometimes deductions are disallowed because they reflect peculiar judgment, more often the unusual nature of outlays that do not qualify as "ordinary" suggests that the item is a personal expense or capital expenditure. For example, if an expense is commonly incurred by people in a given business, then it is likely that the amount is neither personal nor a capital expenditure. Consider the extent to which courts are applying the personal or capital analysis in the cases described below.

In Henry v. Commissioner, 36 T.C. 879 (1961), a tax lawyer claimed deductions for depreciation, maintenance, and insurance on a yacht named "Bar Bill 2nd." It was his practice to anchor the yacht and fly a flag which had the numeral "1040" on it. When passers-by stopped to investigate the significance of the flag, not a usual naval pennant, the taxpayer indicated that it was the number of the federal tax form for individuals and that he was a tax expert who could assist them in their tax planning problems. The taxpayer claimed that these promotional activities had generated additional income. The Tax Court found that the taxpayer failed to show that the expenses were necessary since they "may well have been made to further ends which are primarily personal." In addition, the expenses were not ordinary since promotional and advertising expenses of this kind were, in the court's view, not ordinarily incurred by lawyers or accountants. In contrast Bower v. Commissioner, T.C. Memo. 1990–16, allowed a commodities broker to deduct the expenses of sponsoring an Amateur Athletic Union basketball team whose jerseys bore the name of his business.

In Trebilcock v. Commissioner, 64 T.C. 852 (1975), aff'd by order, 557 F.2d 1226 (6th Cir.1977), the taxpayer was the sole proprietor of a business engaged in the brokerage of wood products. He employed an ordained minister, to whom he paid $7,020 per year, primarily to minister spiritually to petitioner and his employees. The minister conducted prayer meetings to "raise the level of spiritual awareness of the participants" and counseled the taxpayer and his other employees regarding their business and personal problems. "When he offered advice about business problems it was not based upon his knowledge of the brokerage business for he had no such knowledge. Rather, he would receive a problem, turn to God in prayer, and then propose an answer resulting from that prayer." He also visited sawmills, ran errands, and mailed materials for the business.

The Tax Court allowed a deduction only for the portion of the minister's salary attributable to visiting the sawmills, running errands, and the like. It specifically disallowed any deduction for the portion of the advice rendered to the taxpayer:

> When [the minister] counseled [the taxpayer] and his
> employees about business problems * * * [t]he solutions * * *
> offered were not based upon his expertise in the brokerage of wood
> products; he admits he had no such expertise. Rather, his solutions
> came through prayer from God. A deduction under section 162(a) is
> allowed for all ordinary and necessary expenses paid or incurred
> during the taxable year in carrying on a trade or business.
> "Ordinary," as used in section 162(a), refers to items which arise
> from "transactions * * * of common or frequent occurrence in the
> type of business involved." Lilly v. Commissioner, 343 U.S. 90, 93
> (1952). * * * Petitioner has offered no proof that his payments to
> [the minister] for solutions to business problems, considering the
> method [the minister] used, were "ordinary" in his type of business.

In Raymond Bertolini Trucking Co. v. Commissioner, 736 F.2d 1120 (6th
Cir.1984), the taxpayer made certain kickback payments in order to obtain
work on a construction project. The payments were legal under state law.
Before allowing a deduction for the expense, the court discussed the
"ordinary" requirement as follows:

> Petitioner and the Commissioner advocate two distinct views
> of the meaning of "ordinary" in the statute. The Commissioner
> promotes the view that "ordinary" means "normal" or "habitual."
> Petitioner advances the view that the word "ordinary" is in the
> statute simply to distinguish between expenditures which are
> ordinary, i.e., currently deductible, and those which must be
> capitalized and deducted over the life of the asset or benefit
> acquired. There is apparently no meaningful legislative history on
> this point, though the phrase "ordinary and necessary" has been
> with us to delimit allowable business expenses deductions since
> 1909. * * *

> We believe that the confusion regarding the meaning of
> "ordinary" stems from the fact that the two views advanced here
> are both to a certain extent correct, and are not mutually exclusive.
> * * * Whether an expenditure is "normal" or "habitual" is a criterion
> to be used in determining whether it is currently deductible, or
> whether it must be capitalized. An expenditure may be
> extraordinary and unusual because it is a purchase of an asset
> requiring an unusually large cash outlay, or because the
> expenditure was occasioned by an extraordinary disaster. These
> will generally be capital, or non-ordinary expenditures.

However, in Car-Ron Asphalt Paving Co., Inc. v. Commissioner, 758
F.2d 1132 (6th Cir.1985), a different panel of the same Circuit disallowed a
deduction for kickback payments made by another subcontractor working on
the same project on the ground that the payments, while "ordinary," were
not "necessary." The "necessary" issue was not considered in Bertolini.

2.   FAILURE TO SEEK AVAILABLE REIMBURSEMENT

Concern that an expense properly belongs to a person other than the
taxpayer claiming it, first expressed in Deputy v. du Pont, supra, has led to

a series of cases denying deductions for business expenses for which the taxpayer voluntarily refrained from seeking reimbursement that might have been available from another person.

Employees are considered to be engaged in the trade or business of being employees in the line of business in which their employer is engaged. See Noland v. Commissioner, 269 F.2d 108 (4th Cir.1959) ("every person who works for a living is engaged in the business of earning his pay"). Thus, subject to certain limitations (see §§ 62, 63, and 67), employees generally are permitted to deduct unreimbursed expenses incurred in the course of their employment. An employee entitled to reimbursement, however, may fail to seek reimbursement from the employer for a variety of business related reasons, ranging from an effort to appear efficient to mere oversight. A number of cases have denied employees any deduction for unreimbursed business expenses where reimbursement was available but they declined to request it. Heidt v. Commissioner, 274 F.2d 25 (7th Cir.1959), involved a corporate executive who was responsible for approving expense account applications. He declined to seek reimbursement for his own automobile expenses because he wanted "to avoid possible criticism." Citing Deputy v. du Pont, the court disallowed the deduction because the taxpayer was "attempting to convert the employer's right to a deduction into his own." *Heidt* has been applied in a number of subsequent cases. Cavitt v. Commissioner, T.C. Memo. 1990–366, read these cases to establish a general principle of law: "A trade or business expense deduction is not allowable to an employee to the extent that the employee is entitled to reimbursement from his or her employer for an expenditure related to his status as an employee." This rule is strictly applied; an employee may be denied a deduction if the employer's policy is to reimburse expenses, even though the employee was unaware of that policy. Orvis v. Commissioner, 788 F.2d 1406 (9th Cir. 1986).

Application of the principle that it is not "ordinary" to decline to seek reimbursement applies to self-employed individuals as well as to employees. Rev. Rul. 78–141, 1978–1 C.B. 58, held that an attorney who reimbursed a client for a loss caused by the attorney's erroneous advice cannot deduct a payment to the client if the attorney refrains from filing a malpractice insurance claim because of fear that premiums will be increased or the policy cancelled. The court in Campbell v. Commissioner, T.C. Memo. 1987–480, denied a deduction to an actuarial firm for a payment made to a client to compensate the client for a loss occasioned by the negligence of a firm employee; the expense was not "necessary" because the firm had an errors and omissions insurance policy but declined to file a claim. Note that this construction of the word "necessary" in § 162 is completely at odds with the meaning ascribed to the word by the Supreme Court in *Tellier, supra* Section 2.A.

SECTION 3.   THE LIMITATION OF "UNREASONABLE" COMPENSATION

INTERNAL REVENUE CODE: Section 162(a)(1).

REGULATIONS: Sections 1.162–7; –8; 1.212–1(d).

Exacto Spring Corporation v. Commissioner
United States Court of Appeals, Seventh Circuit, 1999.
196 F.3d 833.

■ POSNER, CHIEF JUDGE. This appeal from a judgment by the Tax Court, T.C. Memo 1998–220, 75 T.C.M. (CCH) 2522 (1998), requires us to interpret and apply 26 U.S.C. § 162(a)(1), which allows a business to deduct from its income its "ordinary and necessary" business expenses, including a "reasonable allowance for salaries or other compensation for personal services actually rendered." In 1993 and 1994, Exacto Spring Corporation, a closely held corporation engaged in the manufacture of precision springs, paid its cofounder, chief executive, and principal owner, William Heitz, $1.3 and $1.0 million, respectively, in salary. The Internal Revenue Service thought this amount excessive, that Heitz should not have been paid more than $381,000 in 1993 or $400,000 in 1994, with the difference added to the corporation's income, and it assessed a deficiency accordingly, which Exacto challenged in the Tax Court. That court found that the maximum reasonable compensation for Heitz would have been $900,000 in the earlier year and $700,000 in the later one—figures roughly midway between his actual compensation and the IRS's determination—and Heitz has appealed.

In reaching its conclusion, the Tax Court applied a test that requires the consideration of seven factors, none entitled to any specified weight relative to another. The factors are, in the court's words, "(1) the type and extent of the services rendered; (2) the scarcity of qualified employees; (3) the qualifications and prior earning capacity of the employee; (4) the contributions of the employee to the business venture; (5) the net earnings of the employer; (6) the prevailing compensation paid to employees with comparable jobs; and (7) the peculiar characteristics of the employer's business." 75 T.C.M. at 2525. It is apparent that this test, though it or variants of it (one of which has the astonishing total of 21 factors, Foos v. Commissioner, 1981 T.C. Memo 61, 41 T.C.M. (CCH) 863, 878–79 (1981)), are encountered in many cases, * * * leaves much to be desired—being, like many other multi-factor tests, "redundant, incomplete, and unclear." Palmer v. City of Chicago, 806 F.2d 1316, 1318 (7th Cir.1986).

To begin with, it is nondirective. No indication is given of how the factors are to be weighed in the event they don't all line up on one side. And many of the factors, such as the type and extent of services rendered, the scarcity of qualified employees, and the peculiar characteristics of the employer's business, are vague.

Second, the factors do not bear a clear relation either to each other or to the primary purpose of section 162(a)(1), which is to prevent dividends (or in some cases gifts), which are not deductible from corporate income, from being disguised as salary, which is. * * * Suppose that an employee who let us say was, like Heitz, a founder and the chief executive officer and principal owner of the taxpayer rendered no services at all but received a huge salary. It would be absurd to allow the whole or for that matter any part of his salary to be deducted as an ordinary and necessary business expense even if he were well qualified to be CEO of the company, the company had substantial net earnings, CEOs of similar companies were paid a lot, and it was a business in which high salaries are common. The multifactor test would not prevent the Tax Court from allowing a deduction in such a case even though the corporation obviously was seeking to reduce its taxable income by disguising earnings as salary. The court would not allow the deduction, but not because of anything in the multi-factor test; rather because it would be apparent that the payment to the employee was not in fact for his services to the company. * * *

Third, the seven-factor test invites the Tax Court to set itself up as a superpersonnel department for closely held corporations, a role unsuitable for courts, as we have repeatedly noted in the Title VII context, e.g., Jackson v. E.J. Brach Corp., 176 F.3d 971, 984 (7th Cir.1999), and as the Delaware Chancery Court has noted in the more germane context of derivative suits alleging excessive compensation of corporate employees. Gagliardi v. TriFoods Int'l, Inc., 683 A.2d 1049, 1051 (Del. Ch. 1996). The test * * * invites the court to decide what the taxpayer's employees *should* be paid on the basis of the judges' own ideas of what jobs are comparable, what relation an employee's salary should bear to the corporation's net earnings, what types of business should pay abnormally high (or low) salaries, and so forth. The judges of the Tax Court are not equipped by training or experience to determine the salaries of corporate officers; no judges are.

Fourth, since the test cannot itself determine the outcome of a dispute because of its nondirective character, it invites the making of arbitrary decisions based on uncanalized discretion or unprincipled rules of thumb. The Tax Court in this case essentially added the IRS's determination of the maximum that Mr. Heitz should have been paid in 1993 and 1994 to what he was in fact paid, and divided the sum by two. It cut the baby in half. One would have to be awfully naive to believe that the seven-factor test generated this pleasing symmetry.

Fifth, because the reaction of the Tax Court to a challenge to the deduction of executive compensation is unpredictable, corporations run unavoidable legal risks in determining a level of compensation that may be indispensable to the success of their business.

The drawbacks of the multi-factor test are well illustrated by its purported application by the Tax Court in this case.

* * * [The court then examined the Tax Court's application of each factor.]

Having run through the seven factors, all of which either favored the taxpayer or were neutral, the [tax] court reached a stunning conclusion: "We have considered the factors relevant in deciding reasonable compensation for Mr. Heitz. On the basis of all the evidence, we hold that reasonable compensation for Mr. Heitz" was much less than Exacto paid him. * * * The court's only effort at explaining this result when Heitz had passed the seven-factor test with flying colors was that "we have balanced Mr. Heitz' unique selling and technical ability, his years of experience, and the difficulty of replacing Mr. Heitz with the fact that the corporate entity would have shown a reasonable return for the equity holders, after considering petitioners' concessions." * * * But "the fact that the corporate entity would have shown a reasonable return for the equity holders" after the concessions is on the same side of the balance as the other factors; it does not favor the Internal Revenue Service's position. The government's lawyer was forced to concede at the argument of the appeal that she could not deny the possibility that the Tax Court had pulled its figures for Heitz's allowable compensation out of a hat.

The failure of the Tax Court's reasoning to support its result would alone require a remand. But the problem with the court's opinion goes deeper. The test it applied does not provide adequate guidance to a rational decision. We owe no deference to the Tax Court's statutory interpretations, its relation to us being that of a district court to a court of appeals, not that of an administrative agency to a court of appeals. * * * The federal courts of appeals, whose decisions do of course have weight as authority with us even when they are not our own decisions, have been moving toward a much simpler and more purposive test, the "independent investor" test. Dexsil Corp. v. Commissioner, [147 F.3d 96 (2d Cir.1998)]; Elliotts, Inc. v. Commissioner, [716 F.2d 1241 (9th Cir.1983)]; Rapco, Inc. v. Commissioner, [85 F.3d 950 (2d Cir.1996)]. We applaud the trend and join it.

Because judges tend to downplay the element of judicial creativity in adapting law to fresh insights and changed circumstances, the cases we have just cited prefer to say (as in Dexsil and Rapco) that the "independent investor" test is the "lens" through which they view the seven (or however many) factors of the orthodox test. But that is a formality. The new test dissolves the old and returns the inquiry to basics. The Internal Revenue Code limits the amount of salary that a corporation can deduct from its income primarily in order to prevent the corporation from eluding the corporate income tax by paying dividends but calling them salary because salary is deductible and dividends are not. (Perhaps they should be, to avoid double taxation of corporate earnings, but that is not the law.) In the case of a publicly held company, where the salaries of the highest executives are fixed by a board of directors that those executives do not control, the danger of siphoning corporate earnings to executives in the form of salary is not acute. The danger is much greater in the case of a closely held corporation, in which ownership and management tend to coincide; unfortunately, as the opinion of the Tax Court in this case illustrates, judges are not competent to decide what business executives are worth.

There is, fortunately, an indirect market test, as recognized by the Internal Revenue Service's expert witness. A corporation can be conceptualized as a contract in which the owner of assets hires a person to manage them. The owner pays the manager a salary and in exchange the manager works to increase the value of the assets that have been entrusted to his management; that increase can be expressed as a rate of return to the owner's investment. The higher the rate of return (adjusted for risk) that a manager can generate, the greater the salary he can command. If the rate of return is extremely high, it will be difficult to prove that the manager is being overpaid, for it will be implausible that if he quit if his salary was cut, and he was replaced by a lower-paid manager, the owner would be better off; it would be killing the goose that lays the golden egg. The Service's expert believed that investors in a firm like Exacto would expect a 13 percent return on their investment. Presumably they would be delighted with more. They would be *overjoyed* to receive a return more than 50 percent greater than they expected— and 20 percent, the return that the Tax Court found that investors in Exacto had obtained, is more than 50 percent greater than the benchmark return of 13 percent.

When, notwithstanding the CEO's "exorbitant" salary (as it might appear to a judge or other modestly paid official), the investors in his company are obtaining a far higher return than they had any reason to expect, his salary is presumptively reasonable. We say "presumptively" because we can imagine cases in which the return, though very high, is not due to the CEO's exertions. Suppose Exacto had been an unprofitable company that suddenly learned that its factory was sitting on an oil field, and when oil revenues started to pour in its owner raised his salary from $50,000 a year to $1.3 million. The presumption of reasonableness would be rebutted. There is no suggestion of anything of that sort here and likewise no suggestion that Mr. Heitz was merely the titular chief executive and the company was actually run by someone else, which would be another basis for rebuttal.

The government could still have prevailed by showing that while Heitz's salary may have been no greater than would be reasonable in the circumstances, the company did not in fact intend to pay him that amount as salary, that his salary really did include a concealed dividend though it need not have. This is material (and the "independent investor" test, like the multifactor test that it replaces, thus incomplete, though invaluable) because any business expense to be deductible must be, as we noted earlier, a bona fide expense as well as reasonable in amount. The fact that Heitz's salary was approved by the other owners of the corporation, who had no incentive to disguise a dividend as salary, goes far to rebut any inference of bad faith here, which in any event the Tax Court did not draw and the government does not ask us to draw.

The judgment is reversed with directions to enter judgment for the taxpayer.

DETAILED ANALYSIS

1. REASONABLE COMPENSATION

1.1. *General*

The regulations explicitly state that the test for deductibility is that the payments are "reasonable and are in fact payments purely for services." Treas. Reg. § 1.162–7(a). In Pediatric Surgical Associates, P.C. v. Commissioner, T.C. Memo. 2001–81, the Tax Court distinguished the two prongs of that test. Although it saw no question regarding the reasonableness of the compensation, it found a significant question regarding whether the amounts paid to shareholder-physicians represented solely compensation for services. After carefully analyzing the medical corporation's finances, the court concluded that the shareholder-physicians received a portion of the profits attributable to the work of the physicians who were not shareholders. That portion of the payments was not considered compensation for services and was therefore not deductible.

Most cases are not so analytically clear. In the vast majority of cases, courts conclude that the compensation is "unreasonable" when they feel that the payment in question is not appropriately characterized as compensation. For example, the payment may be a disguised dividend, a gift, or a payment for property. See e.g., Paul E. Kummer Realty Co. v. Commissioner, 511 F.2d 313 (8th Cir.1975) (compensation unreasonable where purported bonuses were closely related to the percentage of stock owned by the employee); Petro-Chem Marketing Co., Inc. v. United States, 602 F.2d 959 (Ct.Cl.1979) (bonuses paid to officer-shareholders were unreasonable where the bonuses exceeded the annual salaries and were computed on no apparent predetermined basis except the availability of funds); Charles Schneider and Co., Inc. v. Commissioner, 500 F.2d 148 (8th Cir.1974) (purported compensation paid to officer-shareholders calculated by dividing up the profits of the corporation after setting aside 2 percent of net sales for retained earnings constituted a disguised distribution of profits).

1.2. *Factors Considered in Determining Reasonableness of Compensation*

The reasonableness of compensation is a question of fact. As Judge Posner explained in *Exacto Spring*, courts have considered various factors in making the determination. Despite Judge Posner's exhortation, other courts of appeal have declined to jettison the multifactor test. In Eberl's Claim Service, Inc. v. Commissioner, 249 F.3d 994 (10th Cir.2001), the court appeared moved by Judge Posner's arguments but nevertheless concluded that "[w]hatever the relative wisdom of the two approaches, absent *en banc* rehearing we are bound to the use of a multi-factor approach by our prior decision in Pepsi-Cola Bottling [578 F.2d 176 (10th Cir.1976)]." After noting that "[t]he factors to be considered have been 'stated innumerable times' but never reduced to a definitive list," the Court of Appeals in *Eberl's Claim Service* listed twelve factors applied by the Tax Court in that case:

> (1) the employee's qualifications; (2) the nature and scope of the employee's work; (3) the size and complexity of the business; (4) general economic conditions; (5) the employer's financial condition; (6) a comparison of salaries paid with sales and net income; (7) distributions to shareholders and retained earnings; (8) whether the employee and the employer dealt at arm's length, and, if not, whether an independent investor would have approved the compensation; (9) the employer's compensation policy for all employees; (10) the prevailing rate of compensation for comparable positions in comparable companies; (11) compensation paid in prior years; and (12) whether the employee guaranteed the employer's debt.

Although the Court of Appeals did not review the Tax Court's finding on every factor, it concluded that the Tax Court's holding was not clearly erroneous.

The Tax Court, constrained by its need to follow the Courts of Appeal, has explained its position as follows:

> Recently, the Court of Appeals for the Seventh Circuit has expressed its disagreement with a multifactor test, opting instead to rest its analysis of the reasonableness of compensation primarily on whether an independent investor would have approved of the amount of compensation paid to the employee. Exacto Spring Corp. v. Commissioner, 196 F.3d at 838–839. The court observed that the Courts of Appeals for the Second and Ninth Circuits have concluded somewhat differently by requiring that the various factors of the traditional test be analyzed from the perspective of an independent investor * * * . Our jurisprudence has also applied a multifactor test through the lens of an independent investor, in the setting of a case that was not appealable to a circuit that had already recognized such an application. Wagner Constr., Inc. v. Commissioner, T.C. Memo. 2001–160 (venue was the Eighth Circuit). We follow that jurisprudence here and apply the multifactor test through the lens of an independent investor.

Haffner's Service Stations v. Commissioner, T.C. Memo 2002–38. On appeal, affirming the Tax Court, the First Circuit applied a multifactor test. Regarding application of *Exacto Spring*, the First Circuit Court of Appeals stated:

> There is always a balance to be struck between simplifying doctrine and accuracy of result, and for the present we think that multiple factors often may be relevant. *Exacto* remains a useful reminder that reasonableness under section 162(a)(1) is not a moral concern

or a matter of fairness; the inquiry aims at what an arm's length owner would pay an employee for his work. The problem is that the actual payment—ordinarily a good expression of market value in a competitive economy—does not decisively answer this question where the employee controls the company and can benefit by re-labeling as compensation what would otherwise accrue to him as dividends.

Haffner's Service Stations v. Commissioner, 326 F.3d 1 (1st Cir.2003). Nevertheless, the Tax Court's recent decisions tend to discuss the question of investment returns, and in some cases that factor seems to be pivotal. See e.g., Damron Auto Parts, Inc. v. Commissioner, T.C. Memo 2001–197. The Tax Court's opinion in B & D Foundations, Inc. v. Commissioner, T.C. Memo 2001–262, includes an extensive discussion of the return to a hypothetical independent investor as a factor, even though the circuit to which the case was appealable (the Tenth) has declined to adopt the independent investor test. In Brewer Quality Homes, Inc. v. Commissioner, T.C. Memo 2003–200, aff'd, 122 Fed. Appx. 88 (5th Cir. 2004), the Tax Court employed the traditional multifactor analysis but observed that courts have described the independent investor test as a "lens through which the entire analysis should be viewed."

1.3. *Contingent Compensation*

A number of unreasonable compensation cases deal with contingent compensation situations. In Harolds Club v. Commissioner, 340 F.2d 861 (9th Cir.1965), the taxpayer corporation employed the father of its principal shareholders. The father's salary was composed of a fixed amount of compensation plus a certain percentage of corporate profits. Both the Tax Court and the Court of Appeals upheld the disallowance of part of the compensation on the ground that the amount of the compensation was unreasonable and the agreement to pay the contingent compensation was not the result of a "free bargain" between the corporation and the employee because of the family relationships involved. In Kennedy v. Commissioner, 671 F.2d 167 (6th Cir.1982), the taxpayer entered into a compensation agreement with a corporation under the terms of which he was to receive a fixed monthly salary plus a percentage of the profits. In the nine years during which the agreement was in effect, the taxpayer's salary rose from $6,000 to $330,000. The Tax Court found the salary unreasonable but the Court of Appeals reversed, holding that the contract was an arm's length agreement which was reasonable when entered into, the taxpayer had been highly instrumental in contributing to the growth of the corporation, and the high level of compensation was thus justified. See Treas. Reg. § 1.162–7(b)(2), indicating that in situations involving contingent compensation the amounts paid may be greater than those which might ordinarily be expected.

2. TAX TREATMENT OF THE RECIPIENT OF DISBURSEMENTS DISALLOWED AS DEDUCTIONS

In Smith v. Manning, 189 F.2d 345 (3d Cir.1951), the IRS disallowed in part a deduction for salaries paid by a sole proprietor to his daughters who worked in the business. Thereupon the daughters, who had paid income tax on the amounts they received as salaries, filed claims for refunds on the theory that the payments represented gifts from the father. The Court of Appeals rejected the refund claim on the ground that the IRS did not disallow the salary deductions because they were gifts but simply because they constituted unreasonable compensation. The court went on to find additionally that, because the parties had originally treated the payments as salary, there could be no donative intent and hence no gift for income tax purposes.

In Sterno Sales Corp. v. United States, 345 F.2d 552 (Ct.Cl.1965), a corporation received compensation for services from a related corporation. The Tax Court in a separate case had disallowed a deduction to the payor corporation for a portion of the payment on the ground that it constituted unreasonable compensation. The corporation receiving the compensation attempted to argue that the payment had been in effect a dividend which qualified for the intercorporate dividends received deduction under § 243. The Court of Claims rejected the argument: "Compensation remains compensation even if it is held unreasonable in amount and, accordingly, not deductible as a business expense. The payment does not change character solely because it is characterized as excessive or undue * * * . [However, if] a payment originally labeled compensation is determined to be a dividend, the taxpayer (or other affected taxpayer) may well be able to get whatever benefits may lie in that re-evaluation. They can take the Government or the court at its word." Since in this case the reason for the Tax Court's denial of the deduction was simply that the compensation was excessive, the attempted recharacterization as a dividend failed.

These cases indicate some of the difficulties that follow from treating the reasonable compensation requirement as an independent limitation rather than as an indication that purported compensation should be more accurately characterized as something else, such as a dividend or a gift.

SECTION 4.   EXPENSES RELATED TO TAX-EXEMPT INCOME

INTERNAL REVENUE CODE: Sections 265(a)(1); 264.

REGULATIONS: Section 1.265–1(c).

Revenue Ruling 83–3
1983–1 C.B. 72.

FACTS

Situation 1. During a taxable year, an unmarried veteran with no dependents, who is an attorney employed by a law firm, received five monthly payments totaling $780 from the Veterans' Administration pursuant to 38 U.S.C. section 1651 et seq., which provides for educational assistance allowances. The purpose of the allowance is to meet, in part, the expenses of a veteran's subsistence, tuition, fees, supplies, books, equipment, and other educational costs. 38 U.S.C. section 1681(a) (1979).

Based upon the legislative history behind 38 U.S.C. section 1681 (1979), it is determined that Congress intended one-half of the allowance to be attributable to subsistence and one-half to be attributable to educational costs. See S.Rep. No. 269, 89th Cong., 1st Sess. 17 (1965). These payments are exempt from taxation under 38 U.S.C. section 3101(a) (1979). The taxpayer incurred expenses for tuition, fees, books, and other expenses in connection with three courses of advanced law education taken at a local university. The employer required the attorney to take the three courses as a condition of continued employment.

During the year, the veteran incurred and paid expenses of $1,054 for the education.

Educational expenses for courses required by the employer as a condition of continued employment generally are deductible as ordinary and necessary business expenses under the provisions of section 162 of the Code, provided the taxpayer elects to itemize deductions.

* * *

Situation 3. Same as in *Situation 1,* except the taxpayer is not a veteran and the $780 qualified as an amount received as a scholarship solely attributable to tuition that is excludable from gross income under section 117 of the Code.

LAW AND ANALYSIS

* * *

Section [265(a)(1)] of the Code provides that no deduction shall be allowed for any amount otherwise allowable as a deduction that is allocable to one or more classes of income other than interest (whether or not any amount of income of that class or classes is received or accrued) wholly exempt from the taxes imposed by subtitle A of the Internal Revenue Code, or any amount otherwise allowable under section 212 that is allocable to interest (whether or not any amount of such interest is received or accrued) wholly exempt from the taxes imposed by subtitle A.

Section 1.265–1(c) of the Income Tax Regulations provides that expenses and amounts otherwise allowable that are directly allocable to any class or classes of exempt income shall be allocated thereto, and expenses and amounts directly allocable to any class or classes of nonexempt income shall be allocated thereto. If an expense or amount otherwise allowable is indirectly allocable to both a class of nonexempt income and a class of exempt income, a reasonable proportion thereof determined in the light of all the facts and circumstances in each case shall be allocated to each.

The purpose of section 265 of the Code is to prevent a double tax benefit. In United States v. Skelly Oil Co., 394 U.S. 678 (1969), 1969–1 C.B. 204, the Supreme Court of the United States said that the Internal Revenue Code should not be interpreted to allow the practical equivalence of double deductions absent clear declaration of intent by

Congress. Section [265(a)(1)] applies to otherwise deductible expenses incurred for the purpose of earning or otherwise producing tax-exempt income. It also applies where tax exempt income is earmarked for a specific purpose and deductions are incurred in carrying out that purpose. In such event, it is proper to conclude that some or all of the deductions are allocable to the tax exempt income. See Heffelfinger v. Commissioner, 5 T.C. 985 (1945), which held that Canadian income taxes on income exempt from U.S. tax are not deductible in computing U.S. taxable income; Banks v. Commissioner, 17 T.C. 1386 (1952), which held that certain educational expenses paid by the Veterans' Administration that were exempt from income tax, were not deductible; Christian v. United States, 201 F. Supp. 155 (E.D. La.1962), where a school teacher was denied deductions for expenses incurred for a literary research trip to England because the expenses were allocable to a tax-exempt gift and fellowship grant * * * .

In Manocchio v. Commissioner, 78 T.C. 989 (1982), a taxpayer attended a flight-training course that maintained and improved skills required in the taxpayer's trade or business. As a veteran, the taxpayer was entitled to an educational assistance allowance from the Veterans' Administration pursuant to 38 U.S.C. section 1677 (1976) equal to 90 percent of the costs incurred. Because the payments received were exempt from taxation under 38 U.S.C. section 310(a) (1976), the taxpayer did not report them as income. The taxpayer did, however, deduct the entire cost of the flight training course, including the portion that had been reimbursed by the Veterans' Administration. In a reviewed opinion, the court held that the reimbursed flight-training expenses were nondeductible under section [265(a)(1)] of the Code.[*]

* * *

In [both] situations, the taxpayer has incurred expenses for the purposes for which the tax-exempt income was received. Permitting a full deduction in each situation would lead to a double benefit not allowed under section 265 of the Code.

HOLDINGS

In *Situation 1* and *Situation 3,* the amount of the itemized deductions for tuition, books and other expenses connected with further education must be decreased to the extent the expense is allocable to the amounts received for such expenses from the Veterans' Administration or as a scholarship, as the case may be.

* * *

The following demonstrates one reasonable method of allocation under section 1.265–1(c) of the regulations that will be accepted by the Internal Revenue Service.

---

*   [Ed.: The Court of Appeals affirmed the Tax Court decision on other grounds without reaching the section 265(a)(1) issue, 710 F.2d 1400 (9th Cir.1983).]

In *Situation 1,* the $1,054 of educational expenses that otherwise qualify for deduction is decreased by one-half of $780 (or $390), computed by multiplying $1,054 (the amount of the expense that is otherwise deductible) by a fraction, the numerator of which is $390 (the amount of the reimbursement allocable to deductible educational costs) and the denominator of which is $1,054 (the total of all expenditures to which the reimbursement is applicable): $1,054 × $390 ÷ $1,054 = $390. Therefore, the itemized deduction for educational expenses under section 162 is $664 ($1,054 – $390).

* * *

In *Situation 3,* the $1,054 of educational expenses that otherwise qualify for deduction is decreased by $780; computed by multiplying $1,054 (the amount of the expense otherwise deductible) by a fraction, the numerator of which is $780 (the amount of the scholarship) and the denominator of which is $1,054 (the total of all expenditures to which the reimbursement is applicable): $1,054 × $780 ÷ $1054 = $780. Therefore, the itemized deduction for educational expenses allowable under section 162 is $274 ($1,054 – $780).

* * *

DETAILED ANALYSIS

1.   GENERAL PRINCIPLES: SECTION 265(a)(1)

A corollary to the principle that expenses incurred in generating taxable income should be deductible is that expenses related to earning tax-exempt income should not be taken into account in computing taxable income. The statutory embodiment of this principle takes a variety of forms and the principle is not always applied consistently. In general, § 265(a)(1) provides that with respect to tax-exempt income other than interest, no deduction is allowed for any expense which is "allocable" to any class of income that is wholly exempt from tax. The regulations indicate that "class of exempt income" means income exempt under a specific statutory provision and thus does not include, for example, imputed income. Treas. Reg. § 1.265–1(b).

Rev. Rul. 87–102, 1987–2 C.B. 78, is a rather straightforward application of § 265(a)(1). That ruling involved a taxpayer who paid legal fees of $1,500 in connection with a claim for social security disability benefits. The taxpayer received benefits of $7,000, and because the taxpayer's income exceeded $31,000, under § 86, discussed in Chapter 4, Section 5.B., one-half of the social security benefits were taxable; the other one-half was tax exempt. The ruling held that § 265(a)(1) limited the deduction for legal fees under § 212 to only $750, one-half of the legal fees paid. See also Rugby Productions Ltd. v. Commissioner, 100 T.C. 531 (1993) (§ 265(a)(1) applied to disallow an employer's deduction of disability insurance policy premiums paid with respect to an employee because the employer was the beneficiary and the policy proceeds would be excluded by § 104(a)(3)). In contrast to Rev. Rul. 87–102, which deals with disallowing deductions for payments to *obtain* tax exempt income, Rev. Rul. 83–3 deals with disallowing deductions for payments *made with* tax exempt income.

If the expense involved is directly related to an item of tax-exempt income, the deduction is disallowed in its entirety. See e.g., Bent v. Commissioner, 87 T.C. 236 (1986), aff'd on other issues, 835 F.2d 67 (3d Cir.1987) (disallowing deduction for legal fees incurred to recover damages that were tax exempt under § 104(a)(2)). In the case of indirect expenses, some reasonable apportionment method must be used. Treas. Reg. § 1.265–1(c).

With respect to tax-exempt interest income, § 265(a)(1) is more limited and disallows only those deductions that would otherwise be allowable under § 212. Thus, for example, an allocable portion of investment expenses involved in the production of income that is composed in part of tax-exempt interest cannot be deducted. See e.g., Alt v. Commissioner, T.C. Memo. 1969–292 (allocation of investment management advice on basis of relative value of taxable and tax-exempt securities).

In Manufacturers Hanover Trust Co. v. Commissioner, 431 F.2d 664 (2d Cir.1970), the taxpayer claimed deductions for amortization of the cost of a purchased life estate by prorating the cost of the life estate over its expected duration. The taxpayer was receiving income from the life estate that was composed in part of tax-exempt interest. The Commissioner disallowed the portion of the deduction for amortization that related to the tax-exempt interest. The Court of Appeals allowed the deduction on the ground that § 265(a)(1) was specifically limited in the case of tax-exempt interest to deductions allowable under § 212 and the amortization deduction was not under § 212 but was based on § 167, relating to depreciation. The court refused to accept the Government's argument that Congress could not have intended to prohibit only § 212 deductions, in the light of the explicit statutory language: "If the facts of this case demonstrate a tax loophole Congress, not the courts, should plug it."

2. COSTS INCURRED IN CONNECTION WITH INSURANCE CONTRACTS: SECTION 264

Section 264 also is directed to the problem of expenses related to tax-exempt income. A business often takes out so-called "key person" life insurance on an important employee or life insurance on a debtor of the business. Section 264(a)(1) denies any deduction for premiums paid on any life insurance policy, annuity, or endowment contract covering any individual if the taxpayer is directly or indirectly a beneficiary of the policy or contract. (This deduction disallowance rule does not apply to premiums paid with respect to certain qualified pension plans and retirement annuities or to premiums with respect to an annuity the current income of which is taxed to the owner under § 72(u). See I.R.C. § 264(b).) The proceeds of the life insurance policy are excluded from the beneficiary's income under § 101(a)(1), and hence disallowance of the deduction for the premium carries out the same policy as § 265.

Section 264(a)(2) and (3), disallowing a deduction for interest on indebtedness incurred or continued to purchase or carry a life insurance, endowment or annuity contract in certain defined circumstances, are discussed in Chapter 16, Section 3.D.

SECTION 5. "PUBLIC POLICY" LIMITATIONS: TAX PENALTIES

Just as it is possible for a special provision in the income tax to create the functional equivalent of a direct spending program—a tax expenditure—so too a special provision may operate as the equivalent of a government regulatory program. The latter type of provision causes the government to collect more revenue than it would under a normative income tax and is appropriately analyzed as the equivalent of a directly imposed governmental fine or penalty. Such provisions are referred to as "tax penalties." It is important to identify and analyze tax penalties since they constitute government interventions in social or economic activities in the same manner as directly-imposed fines and penalties.

In an income tax, a tax penalty generally is created by the denial of a deduction for an expenditure that constitutes a cost of producing income. For example, § 162(c)(1) denies a deduction for certain payments to a foreign government official to obtain a business contract in the foreign country when those payments are unlawful under the Foreign Corrupt Practices Act. Nevertheless, the expenditures are costs of producing income and in principle should be deductible. Denial of the deduction is the functional equivalent of the imposition of a direct governmental fine, varying with the taxpayer's marginal rate, for engaging in the proscribed activity.

All of the "public policy limitations" discussed in this section can be viewed as tax penalties. In each case, it would be possible to impose (or increase) a direct financial penalty or a regulatory restraint to penalize or restrict the activity involved. That is, instead of denying a deduction for the taxable damages portion of an antitrust payment, as provided in § 162(g), the antitrust law itself could be amended to increase the penalty to six, eight or ten times actual damages (the appropriate figure being determined by the after-tax cost Congress desired the violator to bear).

As in the case of tax expenditures, the various tax penalty provisions have no effect on the behavior of tax-exempt organizations or individuals or businesses that have no positive tax liability. In addition, varying the degree of the penalty with reference to the taxpayer's marginal tax bracket rather than the seriousness of the targeted offense appears to be questionable policy.

Denial of a deduction for a cost of producing income does not always result in a tax penalty. For example, denying a deduction on grounds of tax administration does not constitute a tax penalty but rather imposes a surrogate tax on the payor. Provisions denying deductions for costs for which a tax credit is given do not constitute tax penalties. Instead, such provisions in effect insure that the amount of the credit is itself included in taxable income. Provisions that directly impose limits on the use of a tax expenditure likewise do not constitute tax penalties; their function is to limit the federal tax subsidy. See for example, § 41(d)(4)(F) (denying the research credit for foreign research) and § 41(d)(4)(G) (denying the research credit for research in the social sciences, arts, or humanities).

As in the case of tax expenditures, the critical policy questions with respect to tax penalties include (1) whether and why the tax penalty technique is preferable to a nontax penalty or regulation approach; and (2) to what extent are existing tax penalties consistent with or different from programs involving directly imposed penalties in the same area.

A. BRIBES, FINES, AND PENALTIES

INTERNAL REVENUE CODE: Section 162(c), (f), (g).

REGULATIONS: Sections 1.162–1(a); –15; –18; –21; 1.212–1(p).

Tank Truck Rentals, Inc. v. Commissioner

Supreme Court of the United States, 1958.
356 U.S. 30.

■ MR. JUSTICE CLARK delivered the opinion of the Court.

In 1951 petitioner Tank Truck Rentals paid several hundred fines imposed on it and its drivers for violations of state maximum weight laws. This case involves the deductibility of those payments as "ordinary and necessary" business expenses under [the predecessor of § 162(a)]. Prior to 1950 the Commissioner had permitted such deductions, but a change of policy that year caused petitioner's expenditures to be disallowed. The Tax Court, reasoning that allowance of the deduction would frustrate sharply defined state policy expressed in the maximum weight laws, upheld the Commissioner. 26 T.C. 427. The Court of Appeals affirmed on the same ground, 242 F.2d 14, and we granted certiorari. 354 U.S. 920 (1957). In our view, the deductions properly were disallowed.

Petitioner, a Pennsylvania corporation, owns a fleet of tank trucks which it leases, with drivers, to motor carriers for transportation of bulk liquids. The lessees operate the trucks throughout Pennsylvania and the surrounding States of New Jersey, Ohio, Delaware, West Virginia, and Maryland, with nearly all the shipments originating or terminating in Pennsylvania. In 1951, the tax year in question, each of these States imposed maximum weight limits for motor vehicles operating on its highways. Pennsylvania restricted truckers to 45,000 pounds, however, while the other States through which petitioner operated allowed maximum weights approximating 60,000 pounds. It is uncontested that trucking operations were so hindered by this situation that neither petitioner nor other bulk liquid truckers could operate profitably and also observe the Pennsylvania law. * * *

Confronted by this dilemma, the industry deliberately operated its trucks overweight in Pennsylvania in the hope, and at the calculated risk, of escaping the notice of the state and local police. This conduct also constituted willful violations in New Jersey, for reciprocity provisions of the New Jersey statute subjected trucks registered in Pennsylvania to Pennsylvania weight restrictions while traveling in New Jersey. In the remainder of the States in which petitioner operated, it suffered overweight fines for several unintentional violations, such as those caused by temperature changes in transit. During the tax year 1951, petitioner paid a total of $41,060.84 in fines and costs for 718 willful and 28 innocent violations. Deduction of that amount in petitioner's 1951 tax return was disallowed by the Commissioner.

It is clear that the Congress intended the income tax laws "to tax earnings and profits less expenses and losses," Higgins v. Smith, 308 U.S. 473, 477 (1940), carrying out a broad basic policy of taxing "net, not . . . gross, income. . . ." McDonald v. Commissioner, 323 U.S. 57, 66–67 (1944). Equally well established is the rule that deductibility under [the predecessor of § 162(a)] is limited to expenses that are both ordinary and necessary to carrying on the taxpayer's business. Deputy v. du Pont, 308 U.S. 488, 497 (1940). A finding of "necessity" cannot be made, however, if allowance of the deduction would frustrate sharply defined national or state policies proscribing particular types of conduct, evidenced by some governmental declaration thereof. Commissioner v. Heininger, 320 U.S. 467, 473 (1943) * * * .

Here we are concerned with the policy of several States "evidenced" by penal statutes enacted to protect their highways from damage and to insure the safety of all persons using them. Petitioner and its drivers have violated these laws and have been sentenced to pay the fines here claimed as income tax deductions. It is clear that assessment of the fines was punitive action and not a mere toll for use of the highways: the fines occurred only in the exceptional instance when the overweight run was detected by the police. Petitioner's failure to comply with the state laws obviously was based on a balancing of the cost of compliance against the chance of detection. Such a course cannot be sanctioned, for judicial deference to state action requires, whenever possible, that a State not be thwarted in its policy. We will not presume that the Congress, in allowing deductions for income tax purposes, intended to encourage a business enterprise to violate the declared policy of a State. To allow the deduction sought here would but encourage continued violations of state law by increasing the odds in favor of noncompliance. This could only tend to destroy the effectiveness of the State's maximum weight laws.

This is not to say that the rule as to frustration of sharply defined national or state policies is to be viewed or applied in any absolute sense. "It has never been thought . . . that the mere fact that an expenditure bears a remote relation to an illegal act makes it nondeductible." Commissioner v. Heininger, supra, at 474. Although each case must turn on its own facts, * * * the test of nondeductibility always is the severity and immediacy of the frustration resulting from allowance of the deduction. The flexibility of such a standard is necessary if we are to accommodate both the congressional intent to tax only net income, and the presumption against congressional intent to encourage violation of declared public policy.

Analysis →

Certainly the frustration of state policy is most complete and direct when the expenditure for which deduction is sought is itself prohibited by statute. See Boyle, Flagg & Seaman, Inc. v. Commissioner, 25 T. C. 43. If the expenditure is not itself an illegal act, but rather the payment of a penalty imposed by the State because of such an act, as in the present case, the frustration attendant upon deduction would be only slightly less remote, and would clearly fall within the line of disallowance. Deduction of fines and penalties uniformly has been held to frustrate state policy in severe and direct fashion by reducing the "sting" of the penalty prescribed by the state legislature.

There is no merit to petitioner's argument that the fines imposed here were not penalties at all, but merely a revenue toll. * * *

Petitioners argument →

Finally, petitioner contends that deduction of the fines at least for the innocent violations will not frustrate state policy. But since the maximum weight statutes make no distinction between innocent and willful violators, state policy is as much thwarted in the one instance as in the other. * * *

Holding + conclusion →

Affirmed.

DETAILED ANALYSIS

1.   FINES AND PENALTIES VERSUS COMPENSATORY DAMAGES

In 1969 Congress enacted § 162(f), which denies a deduction for any "fine or similar penalty." As the court explained in True v. United States, 894 F.2d 1197 (10th Cir.1990), where the question was the deductibility of a civil penalty:

> Whether the statute is determined to be "criminal" or "civil" is not conclusive. Rather, the nondeductibility exception for "fines and similar penalties" includes criminal fines and any similar retributive civil penalty intended to sanction conduct the state specifically seeks to prohibit. It follows implicitly that compensatory or remedial payments are beyond the scope of section 162(f). In addition, civil penalties for the violation of reporting requirements, filing deadlines, and other procedural failings which do not frustrate the primary purpose of the statutory scheme also remain deductible.

The court then went on to hold that Treas. Reg. § 1.162–21, which restates that civil penalties are not deductible but provides that "[c]ompensatory damages * * * paid to a government do not constitute a fine or penalty," is valid and precludes the deduction of a civil penalty assessed for the discharge of oil in violation of a federal statute. The court reasoned that since the amount of the penalty bore no relation to the cost of the cleanup or the damage inflicted, and a different statutory provision allowed the government to recoup those costs, the penalty was not compensatory.

Other cases have reached results similar to *True* with respect to similar penalties. Southern Pacific Transportation Co. v. Commissioner, 75 T.C. 497 (1980), disallowed a deduction for civil penalties levied against a railroad for violation of various health and safety regulations. The civil penalty was imposed to enforce the regulations and as punishment for violation. Its purpose was the same as a fine exacted under a criminal statute and the penalty was "similar" to a fine. Colt Industries, Inc. v. United States, 880 F.2d 1311 (Fed.Cir.1989), held that it is not necessary to determine affirmatively that a penalty serves the same purpose as a fine in order for it to be nondeductible; *only* compensatory penalties are deductible. On the other hand, in Mason & Dixon Lines, Inc. v. United States, 708 F.2d 1043 (6th Cir.1983), liquidated damages paid by a trucking company for violation of state weight laws, which were in addition to admittedly nondeductible fines, were held to be compensatory in nature and hence deductible under Treas. Reg. § 1.162–21(b)(2) (last sentence).

Whether late filing and similar charges are nondeductible penalties is debatable. In *True* the court quoted from the Senate Finance Committee Report, which explained that

> [I]t was not intended that deductions be denied in the case of sanctions imposed to encourage prompt compliance with requirements of law. Thus, many jurisdictions impose "penalties" to encourage prompt compliance with filing or other requirements which are really more in the nature of late filing charges or interest charges than they are fines. . . .

S. Rep. No. 437, 92nd Cong., 1st Sess., reprinted in 1971 U.S. Code Cong. & Admin. News 1918, 1980. Nevertheless, Treas. Reg. § 1.162–21, issued under § 162(f), denies a deduction for all additions to tax and penalties imposed by §§ 6651–6724. Uhlenbrock v. Commissioner, 67 T.C. 818 (1977), followed the regulations in disallowing a deduction for a penalty paid under § 6651 for the delinquent filing of a tax return. Duncan v. Commissioner, 68 F.3d 315 (9th Cir.1995), held that a penalty under § 6672 for failure to withhold and pay over employees' taxes was not deductible but that a similar state tax penalty was deductible. Because the state law penalty, unlike the federal tax penalty, was imposed under a strict liability standard, the court concluded it was compensatory rather than punitive.

In Guardian Industries Corp. v. Commissioner, 143 T.C. 1 (2014), the Tax Court held that fines paid to the European Union in a price fixing case were not deductible under § 162(f). The court interpreted the language of Treas. Reg. § 1.162–21(a) disallowing deductions for fines paid to a foreign government to disallow deductions for fines paid to a collection of foreign governments and determined that the Commission of the European Community serves as an instrumentality of the member states.

2.   PAYMENTS TO PRIVATE PARTIES

Section 162(f) denies deductions only for fines or penalties paid "to a government." Thus, damages or compromise payments made to private parties for violations of law or of the rules of a private organization are deductible. See e.g., Ostrom v. Commissioner, 77 T.C. 608 (1981) (satisfaction of judgment for fraud). Punitive damages are also deductible. In Rev. Rul. 80–211, 1980–2 C.B. 57, for example, the IRS concluded that "X was sued by another corporation for fraudulent acts and contractual violations perpetuated in the ordinary conduct of its business activities. Therefore, payment of the judgment by X, including amounts identified as punitive damages, is an ordinary and necessary cost of doing business."

Deductions have been disallowed for payments to private parties where the circumstances rendered the payment analogous to a fine or similar penalty. In Rev. Rul. 81–151, 1981–1 C.B. 74, a corporation made illegal campaign contributions and as a result was forced to pay a federal fine. A shareholder's derivative action was filed against the taxpayer, the chief executive officer of the corporation, alleging that he had caused the corporation to engage in the criminal act. As a part of the settlement of the case, the officer was required to reimburse the corporation for a portion of the illegal campaign contributions and for the fine paid by the corporation. Deduction was disallowed for the payments to the corporation on the theory that the reimbursements retained the original character of the expenditures to which they related, namely a fine and an illegal payment, and were thus not deductible under § 162(f).

Carrying this analysis one step further, amounts paid to non-government fraud and theft victims by convicted felons as restitution and a condition of probation have been held to be nondeductible on the ground that the restitution requirement served a punitive purpose. Waldman v. Commissioner, 88 T.C. 1384 (1987), aff'd by order, 850 F.2d 611 (9th Cir.1988). Often a settlement is apportioned into deductible compensatory restitution and nondeductible penalties. In Talley Industries, Inc. v. Commissioner, T.C. Memo. 1994–608, remanded, 116 F.3d 382 (9th Cir.1997), on remand, T.C. Memo. 1999–200, aff'd, 18 Fed. Appx. 661 (9th Cir. 2001), the taxpayer paid $1,885 to the United States government pursuant to a guilty plea on criminal charges under the False Claims Act. That amount was held to be nondeductible under § 162(f), even though it clearly was compensatory restitution. It also paid $2.5 million to settle claims based on similar incidents but with respect to which it was not criminally charged. The settlement agreement did not characterize the $2.5 million payment (or any part of it) as either compensation for the government's actual losses or as a civil penalty. The Tax Court held the $2.5 million payment was intended to compensate the Navy for its losses and, thus, was deductible. The Tax Court rejected the IRS's argument that $940,000 of this amount, which was the portion over and above the government's estimated loss of $1.56 million, was intended as punishment and, consequently, not deductible. The IRS's appealed and the Court of Appeals vacated and remanded because it concluded that there was a material issue of fact regarding the purpose of the amount of the settlement, which exceeded the government's actual $940,000 loss.

On remand, the Tax Court held that no part of the settlement was deductible because "the parties did not agree whether the portion of the settlement in excess of the Government's 'singles' damages would constitute compensation to the Government for its losses or a penalty. . . . It thus follows that petitioner has failed to establish entitlement to a deduction for the disputed portion of the settlement." In Fresenius Medical Care Holdings, Inc. v. United States, 763 F.3d 64 (1st Cir. 2014), the First Circuit distinguished the Ninth Circuit's opinion in *Talley* and disagreed with the Government's assertion that *Talley* limited the deductible compensatory damages to the amount of the government's asserted actual damages in a False Claims Act settlement. The court held that some amount in excess of actual damages may be regarded as compensatory, and further rejected the Government's argument that excess damages may be treated as compensatory only when there is a settlement agreement between the parties designating some portion of damages in excess of asserted damages to be compensatory for additional costs incurred by the government (such as costs of litigation) and, therefore, deductible.

In Allied Signal Inc. v. Commissioner, T.C. Memo 1992–204, aff'd by order 54 F.3d 767 (3d Cir.1995), the taxpayer chemical company pled nolo contendere to a criminal indictment charging it with nearly 1000 counts of unlawful discharge of a highly toxic chemical. The sentencing judge imposed a fine of $13.2 million but indicated that he might be willing to reduce that fine under certain conditions. The company, after seeking the advice of counsel on the tax consequences of paying the fine and possible alternatives thereto, established an Endowment Fund to which it contributed $8 million, after which its fine was reduced by the same amount. The Tax Court, citing the restitution cases, (like *Waldman*, discussed above), agreed that § 162(f) applied only to involuntary payments. It then "define[d] a 'voluntary' payment as one made without the expectation of a quid pro quo." Although the judge had made no commitment to reduce the fine, the court found that the company "made the $8 million payment to the Endowment with the virtual guarantee that the sentencing judge would reduce the criminal fine by at least that amount." The court thus found that the primary purpose of the payment in question was "for punishment and deterrence of environmental crimes," so no portion of it was deductible.

3.   LIMITS OF THE PUBLIC POLICY LIMITATION

The Supreme Court considered the legality of the activity to be relevant in determining deductibility only in *Tank Truck* and a companion case, Hoover Motor Express Co. v. United States, 356 U.S. 38 (1958).

In Commissioner v. Tellier, 383 U.S. 687 (1966), the Court held that a securities dealer was entitled to a deduction for legal expenses incurred in an unsuccessful defense to criminal charges for fraud violations under the Securities Act of 1933, and rejected the Commissioner's contention that the deduction was barred on the ground of public policy.

We start with the proposition that the federal income tax is a tax on net income, not a sanction against wrongdoing. That principle has been firmly imbedded in the tax statute from the beginning. One familiar facet of the principle is the truism that the statute does not concern itself with the lawfulness of the income that it taxes. Income from a criminal enterprise is taxed at a rate no higher and no lower than income from more conventional sources. "[T]he fact that a business is unlawful [does not] exempt it from paying the taxes that if lawful it would have to pay." United States v. Sullivan, 274 U.S. 259, 263. * * *

With respect to deductions, the basic rule, with only a few limited and well-defined exceptions, is the same. During the Senate debate in 1913 on the bill that became the first modern income tax law, amendments were rejected that would have limited deductions for losses to those incurred in a "legitimate" or "lawful" trade or business. Senator Williams, who was in charge of the bill, stated on the floor of the Senate:

> [T]he object of this bill is to tax a man's net income; that is to say, what he has at the end of the year after deducting from his receipts his expenditures or losses. It is not to reform men's moral characters; that is not the object of the bill at all. The tax is not levied for the purpose of restraining people from betting on horse races or upon "futures," but the tax is framed for the purpose of making a man pay upon his net income, his actual profit during the year. The law does not care where he got it from, so far as the tax is concerned, although the law may very properly care in another way. 50 Cong.Rec. 3849.

The application of this principle is reflected in several decisions of this Court. As recently as Commissioner v. Sullivan, 356 U.S. 27, we sustained the allowance of a deduction for rent and wages paid by the operators of a gambling enterprise, even though both the business itself and the specific rent and wage payments there in question were illegal under state law. In rejecting the Commissioner's contention that the illegality of the enterprise required disallowance of the deduction, we held that, were we to "enforce as federal policy the rule espoused by the Commissioner in this case, we would come close to making this type of business taxable on the basis of its gross receipts, while all other business would be taxable on the basis of net income. If that choice is to be made, Congress should do it." Id. at 29.

4.   TREBLE DAMAGE PAYMENTS UNDER THE ANTITRUST LAWS

The deductibility of treble damage payments under § 4 of the Clayton Act raises the same kinds of policy issues as the deductibility of fines and penalties. Section 162(g) denies the deduction for two-thirds of treble damage payments made on a judgment or in settlement of an action brought under § 4 of the Clayton Act if the taxpayer has been convicted of, or pleaded guilty or nolo contendere to, criminal charges. Treble damage payments thus will be deductible where the Justice Department decides to institute only civil proceedings. Treas. Reg. § 1.162–22 provides that where a civil judgment has been entered, or a settlement made in the civil case and criminal proceedings are then brought based on the same violation, § 162(g) is applicable even though the criminal action followed rather than preceded the civil matter in which the treble damages payment was made. In addition, an amount "may be considered" as paid in settlement of a treble damages action even though the action is dismissed or otherwise disposed of prior to the settlement, or the complaint is amended to eliminate the claim with respect to the violation. When a suit asserting both antitrust claims and other claims is settled, the portion of the settlement attributable to the antitrust claim, and thus subject to § 162(g), must be determined with reference to the origin and nature of the various claims the payor intended to settle. The regulations also point out that attorney's fees incurred in connection with a treble damages action are not covered by § 162(g) and are deductible if they otherwise meet the tests of § 162.

5. ILLEGAL BRIBES, KICKBACKS AND OTHER PAYMENTS

5.1. *Payments to Government Employees*

Section 162(c)(1) disallows a deduction for any illegal bribe or kickback made to a government official. In the case of a payment to a foreign government official, however, the payment is deductible if it is not unlawful under the Foreign Corrupt Practices Act of 1977.

5.2. *Payments to Others*

Section 162(c)(2) disallows a deduction for an illegal bribe, kickback, or other illegal payment under any federal or state law (if generally enforced) subjecting the payor to a criminal penalty or loss of license. Rev. Rul. 72–236, 1972–1 C.B. 41, held that amounts paid in violation of an Executive Order constituted non-deductible "illegal payments" because the enabling legislation imposed civil and criminal sanctions for violations. On the other hand, in Rev. Rul. 74–323, 1974–2 C.B. 40, an employment agency advertised job opportunities that indicated gender preferences. Although this practice may have been in violation of the Civil Rights Act of 1964, which forbade sex discrimination in advertising, since no criminal penalties or loss of licenses were imposed for violations of the statute, the cost of the advertisements was fully deductible.

Section 162(c)(2) denies deductions only if the state law is "generally enforced." Boucher v. Commissioner, 77 T.C. 214 (1981), aff'd per curiam, 693 F.2d 98 (9th Cir.1982), denied a deduction for illegal rebates on insurance premiums where the statute forbidding such discounts was generally enforced, even though it was not aggressively enforced. The last sentence of § 162(c)(2) puts the burden of proof with respect to the illegality of the payment on the Commissioner, and the Tax Court has held that the burden remains even if the taxpayer is collaterally estopped from denying the illegality of the bribes by virtue of his prior guilty plea in a criminal case. Zecchini v. Commissioner, T.C. Memo. 1992–8.

For the deductibility of legal (but possibly unsavory) bribes, see above.

6. OTHER APPLICATIONS OF THE PUBLIC POLICY LIMITATION

6.1. *Statutory Exclusivity*

The legislative history of § 162(c), (f), and (g), indicates that Congress intended the statutory prohibitions to be exclusive, thereby supplanting the "common law" frustration of public policy limitation on deductions applied in *Tank Truck Rentals* and *Hoover Motor Express*. "The provision for the denial of the deduction for payments in these situations which are deemed to violate public policy is intended to be all inclusive. Public policy, in other circumstances, generally is not sufficiently clearly defined to justify the disallowance of deductions. However, this is not, of course, intended to affect the treatment of lobbying expenditures which are already covered [in § 162(e)]." S.Rep. No. 91–552, 91st Cong., 1st Sess. 274 (1969).

6.2. *Section 61: Cost of Goods Sold*

Costs of goods sold are not part of the tax base because Treas. Reg. § 1.61–3(a) defines gross income from sales activities as total sales less cost of goods sold. The last sentence of § 263A(a) prevents taxpayers from including in inventory (or the basis of any other asset subject to § 263A) any cost that would be nondeductible under any other provision of the Code. Accordingly, illegal bribes, fines, penalties, and similar payments are excluded from the cost of goods sold. Prior to the amendment to § 263A(a) that added the last sentence in 1987, the courts had held that because such costs are not technically deductions *from* gross income, but increase the cost of goods sold (and thereby reduce gross income), they were not subject to disallowance on public policy grounds. See e.g., Max Sobel Wholesale Liquors v. Commissioner, 630 F.2d 670 (9th Cir.1980).

6.3. *Section 212: Nonbusiness Profit-Seeking Activities*

Prior to the enactment of § 162(c), and (f), the public policy limitation had been applied to disallow deductions under § 212, but the legislation that added those provisions did not deal expressly with § 212. Treas. Reg. § 1.212–1(p), however, provides that the "deduction of a payment will be disallowed under section 212 if the payment is of a type for which a deduction would be disallowed under section 162(c), (f) or (g) and the regulations thereunder in the case of a business expense." The negative implication of this position is that, apart from the specific statutory provisions mentioned, no general public policy limitation would be applicable to § 212 expenses. Cf. Treas. Reg. § 1.162–1(a).

6.4. *Section 165: Losses Incurred in Connection with Illegal Activities*

Loss deductions under § 165 may be disallowed on public policy grounds even though § 165 contains no express provisions in this regard. The scope of disallowance of loss deductions under the "common law frustration of public policy doctrine" is broader than the statutory disallowance rules under § 162. See Chapter 15, Section 2.D.

B. LOBBYING ACTIVITIES

INTERNAL REVENUE CODE: Section 162(e).

REGULATIONS: Sections 1.162–20(c)(4); –29.

Cammarano v. United States

United States Supreme Court, 1959.
358 U.S. 498.

■ MR. JUSTICE HARLAN delivered the opinion of the Court.

[A partnership that operated a wholesale beer distributorship contributed to a fund established by the Washington Beer Wholesalers Association to finance a statewide publicity program urging the defeat of an initiative to place the retail sale of beer under state control. The Court denied any deduction for the contribution]

* * *

Since 1918 regulations promulgated by the Commissioner under the Internal Revenue Code have continuously provided that expenditures for the "promotion or defeat of legislation . . .", or for any of the other purposes specified in the "corporate" Regulation now before us, are not deductible from gross corporate income; and since 1938 regulations containing identical language have forbidden such deductions from individual income. * * *

* * *

Petitioners suggest that if the Regulations are construed to deny them deduction, a substantial constitutional issue under the First Amendment is presented. * * * This contention, made by neither petitioner below, is without merit. * * * Petitioners are not being denied a tax deduction because they engage in constitutionally protected activities, but are simply being required to pay for those activities entirely out of their own pockets, as everyone else engaging in similar activities is required to do under the provisions of the Internal Revenue Code. Nondiscriminatory denial of deduction from gross income to sums expended to promote or defeat legislation is plainly not " 'aimed at the suppression of dangerous ideas.' " [Speiser v. Randall,] 357 U.S., at 519. Rather, it appears to us to express a determination by Congress that since purchased publicity can influence the fate of legislation which will affect, directly or indirectly, all in the community, everyone in the community should stand on the same footing as regards its purchase so far as the Treasury of the United States is concerned.

* * *

Affirmed.

DETAILED ANALYSIS

1.   A DIFFERENT SORT OF TAX PENALTY

Note that the rationale of *Cammarano* for disallowing a deduction for political expenditures differs from the tax penalty aspect of the other disallowance rules of § 162 discussed in this section. The Court in *Cammarano* focused on the subsidy that is inherent in reducing the after-tax cost of political expenditures for one group of advocates in political debate, those whose interests are in promoting political causes that affect their business. The disallowance is not intended as a penalty for political speech; disallowance for that reason would violate the First Amendment. Rather, as the Supreme Court later indicated in a slightly different context, in Regan v. Taxation with Representation, 461 U.S. 540 (1983), "Congress has merely refused to pay for the lobbying out of public moneys. This Court has never held that Congress must grant a benefit such as TWR claims here to a person who wishes to exercise a constitutional right."

The Government's brief in *Cammarano* emphasized the equalizing effect of the disallowance:

> At the present time, under the prevailing interpretation of [section 162(a)], any campaigns financed by industry to influence legislation cannot be charged to the Government by taking these expenses as a deduction. The financing is thus entirely out of the pocket of the concerns involved. This is equally true as to any citizens' organizations which might be formed to conduct similar campaigns, since contributions to these campaigns would not qualify as charitable contributions and accordingly are not deductible. The same is true of labor organizations. Thus a tax equilibrium exists. If the expenses of the business community were to become deductible, this tax equilibrium would be upset. While the business community could deduct their expenses, all others could not, *even with respect to the same legislation.* * * *

> Suppose, for example, that a citizens' organization had been established in the State of Washington for the purpose of financing a campaign *supporting* the initiative proposal involved * * * to limit the sale of wine and beer to state-owned stores. Contributions to that organization would not be deductible. But, under taxpayers' construction, the liquor industry could deduct without limit their payments to organizations *opposing* the same measure. * * *

> Stated otherwise, the anomalous result of "public subvention" of such expenditures would be to *increase* the relative-power of business enterprises (especially large ones), *vis-á-vis* private citizens and other taxpayers, to finance the "engineering of consent" on legislative matters. However, the pattern of Congressional action in this area indicates a Congressional purpose to reduce this disparity, not to increase it. In this delicate area, if any changes as above indicated are to be made, we submit that it is Congress—not the courts—which should make them.

2. THE LEGISLATIVE RESPONSE

Congress responded to *Cammarano* with two major pieces of legislation, first in 1962 and then in 1993. Section 162(e), as amended by the 1993 Act, bars deductions of any expense incurred to influence legislation (lobbying), to participate or intervene in a political campaign for or against any individual running for public office, to influence initiatives or referendum campaigns, or to lobby certain executive officials. Thus, the current provision generally is as extensive as the regulations under review in *Cammarano*. However, as originally enacted in 1962, § 162(e) was intended to expand the availability of deductions for expenses incurred in legislative lobbying on matters of direct interest to the taxpayer's business. Neither the Senate nor the House Report provides any specific reason for the 1993 change other than "deficit reduction."

As amended in 1993, § 162(e) denies any deduction for amounts paid or incurred in connection with four categories of politically related expenditures: (1) influencing Federal or state legislation; (2) participating or intervening in any political campaign; (3) attempting to influence the general public with respect to legislative matters or referenda; and (4) any direct communication with the President, Vice-President, Cabinet Secretaries (and their immediate Deputies), various White House employees, as well as certain other high ranking Federal executive branch officials, if the communication is designed to influence their official actions or positions.[3] Section 162(e)(3) backstops the general rule by disallowing deductions for the portion of dues paid to a tax exempt organization but allocable to the organization's lobbying expenses. In addition, although § 162(e) does not expressly so provide, the Committee Reports indicate that Congress intended that, as under prior law, expenses to influence foreign governments should be nondeductible. H.R. Rep. No. 111, 103d Cong., 1st Sess. 659, n. 34 (1993).

Section 162(e)(2) exempts from the disallowance rule expenses to influence any "local council or similar governing body." Thus, lobbying expenses incurred to amend a zoning law or occupational tax at the local level are deductible, even though expenses to lobby the state legislature regarding similar legislation are not deductible. In addition, § 162(e) apparently does not apply to expenses incurred to lobby state executive officers, including governors, except with respect to proposed legislation. The legislative history does not explain the reason for the differing treatment of lobbying at the state and federal levels.

Finally, § 162(e) does not apply to the expenses incurred by lobbyists in conducting their trade or business. I.R.C. § 162(e)(5)(A). It applies to amounts paid to lobbyists by their clients, on whose behalf professional lobbyists seek to influence legislation.

The restrictions on the deductibility of lobbying expenses and campaign contributions contained in § 162(e) are only one part of the federal regulation of the financing of political activity. Legislation also regulates campaign finance, and other tax rules govern the taxation of contributions received by

---

[3]   Deductions for expenses to appear before a legislature under a subpoena are allowed. Treas. Reg. § 1.162–29(b)(3).

individuals and organizations. (See Chapter 5, Section 5.2.). While a coordinated approach to the regulation of political contributions is probably desirable, current law does not achieve that. For a comprehensive analysis of the federal regulation of political activity, *see* Simmons, *An Essay on Federal Income Taxation and Campaign Finance Reform*, 54 FLA. L. REV. 1 (2002).

3.   APPLICATION OF SECTION 162(e)

The regulations provide that influencing legislation means "[a]ny attempt to influence any legislation through a lobbying communication," as well as activities related to making or supporting such a communication. Treas. Reg. § 1.162–29(b)(1)(i). The examples in the regulations make clear that only communications referring to and reflecting a view on specific legislation, or which amplify or support any prior such communication, constitute lobbying communications, although the legislation that is the subject of the communication does not have to have been formally introduced. See Treas. Reg. § 1.162–29(b)(5), (7) (Examples).

Two factors combine to permit deduction of most expenses incurred to contact federal agencies regarding regulations and other administrative rule-making. First, regulations are not treated as legislation (see Treas. Reg. § 56.4911–2(d)(4)), and are therefore not covered by the general prohibition. Second, only contacts with a limited number of executive branch officials are subject to § 162(e). Therefore, efforts to influence administrative regulations are deductible unless the effort involves contact with one of the high-ranking officials described in § 162(e)(6). It is curious that expenses to contact many government officials with respect to promulgation of regulations are deductible, while expenses to lobby government employees who are participating in formulating legislative proposals are not. Distinguishing contacts with government agency lawyers intended to influence future regulations from those intended to influence future legislation may prove to be a formidable task.

It is sometimes difficult to determine where nondeductible attempts to influence the public with respect to legislative matters cease, and deductible public education, institutional advertising, and the like, begin. In Consumers Power Co. v. United States, 427 F.2d 78 (6th Cir.1970), deductions were denied for contributions by a private electric company to a national advertising campaign extolling the virtues of private power, attacking public power, and urging the public to write their representatives to oppose public power, even though no specific legislation was then pending. In Rev. Rul. 78–111, 1978–1 C.B. 41, a corporation printed and distributed to its shareholders its president's statements before the state legislature in opposition to certain proposed legislation. No deduction was allowed even though no request was made of shareholders to contact legislators.

Section 162(e) applies not only to amounts paid to professional lobbyists, but also to the taxpayer's own expenses incurred in connection with the proscribed lobbying activities. Thus, a taxpayer whose employees carry on lobbying activities must allocate a portion of the employees' salaries, fringe benefits, etc., as well as overhead expenses, to nondeductible lobbying activities. Treas. Reg. § 1.162–28 provides methods for making the allocation.

4. OTHER SPECIAL RULES APPLICABLE TO THE COSTS OF POLITICAL ACTIVITY

Section 271 denies a deduction under § 166 (bad debts) and § 165(g) (worthless securities) where a taxpayer's loan to a political party becomes worthless. Its basic purpose is to insure that the restrictions on deductions for political activities are not circumvented by making contributions in the form of "loans" which are subsequently written off.[4] The section is subject to some exceptions dealing with normal commercial transactions. Similarly, § 276 disallows a deduction for the cost of advertising in a political convention program or of admission to any dinner or other program if the proceeds therefrom inure to the use of a political party. Deduction is likewise denied for the cost of admission to an inaugural ball, parade, etc., if the event is identified with a particular political party or candidate.

In Cloud v. Commissioner, 97 T.C. 613 (1991), the taxpayer held a political patronage position in Ohio and the local political party regularly billed him for required "contributions," upon which obtaining and holding the office depended. Even though the payments were not illegal, the court disallowed a deduction because the contributions funded political activities for which § 162(e) or § 276 denied a deduction.

Section 84 treats the transfer of appreciated property to a political organization as a sale, resulting in the recognition of gain by the transferor to the extent the fair market value of the property exceeds its basis. The provision does not apply to property on which a loss would be recognized. Since not recognizing gain on the transfer would be tantamount to recognizing the gain and then taking an offsetting deduction, the forced recognition of gain has the effect of backstopping some of the other restrictions on deductions.

C. OTHER TAX PENALTIES

INTERNAL REVENUE CODE: Sections 162(m)(1)–(3), (m)(4)(A)–(C); 280E; 280G(a), (b)(1)–(2); 4999.

Congress sometimes denies deductions for expenses it wants to discourage for non-tax policy reasons. The provisions discussed here disallow deductions for certain executive compensation and for costs incurred by dealers in illegal drugs.

DETAILED ANALYSIS

1. GOLDEN PARACHUTES

Agreements between top executives and their employer-corporations often provide for the payment of comparatively large amounts in the event

---

[4]   Treas. Reg. § 1.271–1(b) defines a political party as an organization that attempts to influence the election of candidates. Advances to a political organization attempting to influence legislation, such as an initiative campaign, might not be covered by § 271.

that the corporation is acquired. These payments came to be referred to as golden parachutes because of the financially soft landing they afforded executives who might face potential ejection from their pre-acquisition employers. During the early 1980's, Congress became concerned that the need to make such payments could either cause management to favor an acquisition not otherwise beneficial or reduce the amount received by shareholders in the acquisition. To discourage the practice of entering into these so-called golden parachutes, Congress enacted § 280G, which disallows any deduction for an "excess parachute payment," and § 4999, which imposes a non-deductible 20 percent excise tax on the recipient of the payment.

A "parachute payment" is any compensatory amount paid for the benefit of an officer, shareholder, or highly-compensated employee (as defined) of the acquired corporation if the payment is contingent on a change in the ownership or effective control of the corporation or in the ownership of a substantial portion of its assets. Only "excess" parachute payments are disallowed as deductions. An excess exists only if the aggregate present value of payments made (or to be made) under the contract exceeds three times the average annual compensation of the executive over the five years preceding the change in ownership. The "excess parachute payment" amount may be reduced by the amount which the taxpayer establishes by clear and convincing evidence is reasonable compensation for services already rendered or to be rendered after the change in ownership. While generally a payment is treated as contingent on a change in ownership or control only if the payment would not in fact have been made had no change occurred, any contract entered into within one year of a change of ownership or control is presumed contingent on that change unless the taxpayer establishes to the contrary by "clear and convincing evidence."

Special exceptions are provided for payments made by certain corporations with no more than 75 shareholders or corporations the stock of which is publicly traded if at least seventy-five percent of the shareholders have approved the contract.

It is common in corporate acquisition transactions for the change in ownership to be accompanied by the execution of new employment agreements by key officers and employees of the acquired corporation to insure their continued availability. Even though these arrangements may not fall within the category which moved Congress to enact § 280G, they nonetheless appear generally to meet the definition of parachute payments under the presumption and thus the imposition of the penalties would depend on whether the statutory computation described above resulted in an "excess" parachute payment.

The statutory computation of "excess parachute payments" invites the drafting of contracts that carefully skirt but do not fall within the mathematical computation of "excess" payments. Balch v. Commissioner, 100 T.C. 331 (1993), aff'd sub nom. Cline v. Commissioner, 34 F.3d 480 (7th Cir.1994), held that excessive deferred compensation paid to retired executives after their severance pay had been reduced for the purpose of avoiding §§ 280G and 4999 constituted "excess parachute payments" because it was contingent on the change in control of the employer.

If the perceived problem in golden parachute situations is the deductibility of what are essentially capital costs because they are connected to the acquisition of a business, it would have been possible to use normally applicable tax principles to reach the appropriate results. (See discussion of capitalization in Chapter 13.) But Congress clearly intended to impose a tax penalty in golden parachute situations, as evidenced by its denial of basis to the acquiring corporation and by the imposition of the 20 percent excise tax on the recipient of the payments.

2. ONE MILLION DOLLAR LIMIT ON COMPENSATION DEDUCTION

In the late 1980's and early 1990's the amount of compensation received by executives of publicly held corporations was the subject of intense scrutiny and criticism. Congress concluded that many corporate executives were receiving excessive compensation that was nevertheless deductible under § 162(a)(1), and responded with an additional limitation intended to induce corporations to reduce the amount of compensation paid to executives. Section 162(m) imposes a $1,000,000 ceiling on the deduction for annual compensation paid to the chief executive officer and the four other highest compensated officers of any publicly held corporation. The limitation generally applies only to fixed salaries, however. Performance-based contingent compensation, such as stock options and bonuses, earned only if the corporation meets certain performance goals, such as stock price, market share, sales, or earnings per share, is not subject to § 162(m) if the compensation has been approved by outside directors or a majority of the shareholders. For this exception to apply the compensation must be determined under an ascertainable formula that precludes discretion, and a compensation committee must certify attainment of the performance goal. Nor does the limitation apply to any compensation other than compensation paid to executives of publicly traded corporations. Thus, for example, it does not apply to salaries paid to physicians and lawyers by professional service corporations, or compensation paid to athletes and entertainers. Furthermore, the provision does not apply to employees of subsidiaries of publicly traded corporations. Thus it may be possible for a corporation to avoid § 162(m) by forming a publicly traded holding company and having the important officers employed by wholly owned operating subsidiaries rather than by the publicly traded holding company. Whether such avoidance schemes will be successful will turn, in part, on interpretation of certain provisions of the Securities Exchange Act of 1934, which § 162(m)(3) incorporates by reference.

Section 162(m)(5) disallows compensation deductions that would otherwise be available to certain businesses that received financial assistance from the federal government under the Troubled Asset Relief Program (TARP). Under this provision, TARP beneficiaries generally may not deduct annual compensation paid to each of the five most senior executives in excess of $500,000. Unlike the general § 162(m) rule, there is no carve-out for performance-based compensation. In addition, § 162(m)(5) attempts to prevent TARP beneficiaries from circumventing the disallowance by increasing an executive's deferred compensation, which is a common strategy to avoid the general § 162(m) rule.

Section 162(m)(6) is similar in many respects to (m)(5). They both limit compensation deductions to the first $500,000 of compensation, without any carve-out for performance-based compensation, and they both contain rules to prevent taxpayers from using deferred compensation to circumvent the disallowance. However, while (m)(5) applies only to compensation paid to the most senior executives, (m)(6) applies to all persons who provide services to the health insurance provider, regardless of whether the person is an employee or independent contractor. The theory behind the new provision appears to be that, because the new health care law requires individuals to purchase health insurance policies, health insurance providers will receive a windfall by virtue of the increased demand for insurance. If the provision is effective in reducing the amount of compensation paid to service providers, then it will impede the ability of those service providers to capture that windfall.

3.   SECTION 280E: EXPENSES OF TRAFFICKING IN ILLEGAL DRUGS

Section 280E denies any deduction for expenses incurred in the trade or business of trafficking in illegal drugs. Coupled with the last sentence of § 263A, the result is that dealers in illegal drugs are taxed on their gross receipts. However, in Californians Helping to Alleviate Medical Problems, Inc. v. Commissioner, 128 T.C. 173 (2007), and Olive v. Commissioner, 139 T.C. 19 (2012), the IRS conceded that § 280E did not operate to deny the cost of goods sold to the taxpayer. That concession was based on the legislative history of section 280E, which states that "the adjustment to gross receipts with respect to effective costs of goods sold is not affected by [§ 280E]." S. Rept. 97–494 (Vol.1), at 309 (1982), and case law predating the enactment of the last sentence of § 263A(a)(2). See e.g., *Franklin v. Commissioner*, T.C. Memo. 1993–184 (1993). A careful reading of § 280E and the last sentence of § 263A(a)(2) reveals that the concession likely was erroneous, since the last sentence of § 263A(a) was enacted after § 280E.

CHAPTER 13

DEDUCTIBLE PROFIT-SEEKING EXPENSES VERSUS NONDEDUCTIBLE CAPITAL EXPENDITURES

The materials in the preceding Chapter examined the current deduction of ordinary and necessary expenses incurred in the conduct of a trade or business. The current deduction of some expenditures is limited by § 263(a), which applies generally to expenses incurred "for new buildings, or for permanent improvements or betterments made to increase the value of any property or estate." As this chapter illustrates, § 263(a) applies to the acquisition, creation, and improvement to tangible and intangible personal property. These expenditures, referred to as "capital expenditures," are not currently deductible, but they give rise to basis under § 1012 or § 1016. The materials in this Chapter consider whether an expenditure in a profit-seeking activity is an immediately deductible expense under § 162, § 167, or § 212, or whether it is a capital expenditure.

Deductibility of any expenditure involved in the production of income ultimately is a matter of timing. Ordinary and necessary business expenditures are deductible in the year incurred as an offset to income produced in the current year. An item classified as a capital expenditure will be taken into account for tax purposes in a later year, theoretically when income produced by the expenditure is realized. The question becomes when a capital expenditure will be taken into account as a cost of producing current income, not *whether* it will be taken into account. An item classified as a capital expenditure will be added to the basis of an income producing asset and accounted for under one of several cost recovery methods. One of those methods, recovery of capital on the sale or other disposition of an asset, was considered in Chapter 6. The cost of acquiring an asset, or of enhancing its value or useful life, is recoverable as basis on disposition. In addition, as will be discussed in Chapter 14, capital expenditures for some assets are recovered over several taxable years through various cost recovery deductions such as depreciation or amortization. In other instances, capitalized expenditures are recovered through the deductions for losses or bad debts. The distinct concepts of capitalization of expenditures (the disallowance of a current deduction), basis adjustments, and cost recovery (the deduction of a capital expenditure over time) function together to provide tax accounting results that are theoretically intended to match the expenditure with income produced by the expenditure.

The question of timing involved in the capital expenditure limitation is of considerable importance because, given the time value of money, an immediate deduction is worth more to the taxpayer than a deduction in a later year (if the applicable tax rates remain constant). Indeed, as was demonstrated in the discussion of Individual Retirement Accounts, Chapter 8, Section 2, the immediate deduction of a capital expenditure is the equivalent of exempting from tax the income derived from the investment. Moreover, the difference in value becomes greater as the length of time increases. Thus, the significance of the distinction between a current deduction and a capital expenditure is particularly critical in the case of nondepreciable assets such as land and securities because capital costs allocated to these assets cannot be recovered until disposition of the asset. For an economic analysis of the timing of deductions, see Chapter 14, Section 1.C.

Classification of an item as a current expense rather than as a capital expenditure may have consequences other than timing. The classification might affect the treatment of the income offset by the item. Items classified as current expenses generally offset current ordinary income. Expenditures that are capitalized and added to the basis of an asset under § 1012, on the other hand, might offset current ordinary income in future years through depreciation or amortization deductions, but in other cases may reduce capital gains or create a capital loss when the asset is sold.[1]

The terms "ordinary" and "expense" in § 162(a) have been interpreted to include the capital expenditure limitation. Thus, for example, the Supreme Court in Commissioner v. Lincoln Savings & Loan Association, 403 U.S. 345 (1971), resolved a capital expenditure versus current expense issue entirely under § 162(a) without any reference to § 263: "[O]ur only concern here, is whether the payment was an expense and an ordinary one within the meaning of section 162(a) of the Code." More recently, however, the courts have been inclined to look to the tests under § 263 and rely less heavily on the use of the term "ordinary" in § 162(a) to differentiate capital expenditures from immediately deductible expenses.

The body of case law that considers whether an expenditure is a § 263(a) capital expenditure or deductible § 162 or § 212 expenditure is extensive. Traditionally, the analysis of expenditures had to rely solely upon case law, but Treasury has incorporated that case law in regulations. Consequently, the analysis of an expenditure now relies upon rules in regulations to determine whether the expenditure is deductible currently or must be capitalized. Generally, an expenditure is

---

[1]   Deductions of capital losses are limited to the taxpayer's capital gains (plus $3,000 in the case of individuals). I.R.C. § 1211, discussed in Chapter 24, Section 1.3.

allowable as a current deduction unless the regulations require that the expenditure be capitalized. The regulations are divided into rules that require capitalization of costs to acquire or produce tangible property, costs to improve tangible property, and costs to acquire or create intangible property. In rare situations, prior case law may help to inform the analysis, but it primarily provides a backdrop for considering the general purpose of the capitalization rules.

Section 263A is another source of capitalization rules that codifies case law, which requires capitalization of "direct" and "indirect" expenditures incurred to acquire and sell inventory and produce tangible property for use in the taxpayer's trade or business. Direct costs covered by § 263A include costs subject to the capitalization rules predating its enactment. Thus, the cases and regulations identifying direct costs of acquisition and creation of property continue to be relevant to the application of § 263A. Though it applies to direct expenses, § 263A was enacted primarily to deal with the capitalization of "indirect expenses," such as interest, real estate taxes, overhead management costs, and depreciation that generally were not capitalized even though the item may have been related to the creation or acquisition of property.

Finally, a word of caution is in order. It is tempting to assume that if the cost of an asset must be capitalized, the asset is a capital asset. Resist this temptation. Despite the use of the same word, the concepts have little to do with one another. Whether an asset is a capital asset, the gain or loss on which will be classified as capital gain, is a matter governed by statutory definition that is wholly independent of the question whether the cost of acquiring the asset was required to be capitalized. To conclude that the cost of an asset must be capitalized is *only* to conclude that the cost cannot be deducted currently. That conclusion does not necessarily say anything about the character of the asset.

SECTION 1.   JUDICIAL INTERPRETATION OF CAPITAL EXPENDITURE STATUTE

The following two cases do not attempt to provide an overview of the common law governing capital expenditures, but they illustrate issues that courts considered when deciding whether taxpayers must capitalize expenditures. These cases also demonstrate that the application of § 263 extends beyond its plain meaning. Section 263(a) appears to apply to amounts paid (1) for new buildings, (2) permanent improvements or betterments made to increase the value of any property, and (3) restoring property or in making good the exhaustion thereof. That language suggests that the provision applies to both real property (i.e., land and improvements to land that generally cannot be moved) and personal property (i.e., property that is not real property) and only applies to tangible property (i.e., property that can be touched). The cases in this section illustrate, however, that the provision also applies to the acquisition or creation of intangible property.

To apply the capitalization rules correctly, a person must always bear in mind the type of property being considered because different rules apply to different types of property. The rules may also vary depending upon the type of activity involved (i.e., acquiring, constructing, improving, creating), so working with these rules requires identifying the activity at issue. The cases below demonstrate how the courts apply the rules to construction of tangible property and the acquisition of intangible property, while the materials following the cases—beginning in Section 2—discuss the rules that appear in the regulations.

Commissioner v. Idaho Power Co.

U.S. Supreme Court, 1974.
418 U.S. 1.

■ MR. JUSTICE BLACKMUN delivered the opinion of the Court.

Issue ←

This case presents the sole issue whether, for federal income tax purposes, a taxpayer is entitled to a deduction from gross income, under [§ 167(a)] for depreciation on equipment the taxpayer owns and uses in the construction of its own capital facilities, or whether the capitalization provision of [§ 263(a)(1)] bars the deduction.

Procedural History ←

The taxpayer claimed the deduction, but the Commissioner of Internal Revenue disallowed it. The Tax Court . . . upheld the Commissioner's determination. . . . The United States Court of Appeals for the Ninth Circuit . . . reversed. . . . We granted certiorari in order to resolve the apparent conflict between the Court of Claims and the Court of Appeals. . . .

I

Nearly all the relevant facts are stipulated. The taxpayer-respondent, Idaho Power Company, is a Maine corporation organized in 1915, with its principal place of business at Boise, Idaho. It is a public utility engaged in the production, transmission, distribution, and sale of electric energy. * * * The tax years at issue are 1962 and 1963.

FACTS

For many years, the taxpayer has used its own equipment and employees in the construction of improvements and additions to its capital facilities. The major work has consisted of transmission lines, transmission switching stations, distribution lines, distribution stations, and connecting facilities.

During 1962 and 1963, the tax years in question, taxpayer owned and used in its business a wide variety of automotive transportation equipment, including passenger cars, trucks of all descriptions, power-operated equipment, and trailers. Radio communication devices were affixed to the equipment and were used in its daily operations. The transportation equipment was used in part for operation and maintenance and in part for the construction of capital facilities having a useful life of more than one year.

On its books, the taxpayer used various methods of charging costs incurred in connection with its transportation equipment either to current expense or to capital accounts. To the extent the equipment was used in construction, the taxpayer charged depreciation of the equipment, as well as all operating and maintenance costs (other than pension contributions and social security and motor vehicle taxes) to the capital assets so constructed. This was done either directly or through clearing accounts in accordance with procedures prescribed by the Federal Power Commission and adopted by the Idaho Public Utilities Commission.

For federal income tax purposes, however, the taxpayer treated the depreciation on transportation equipment differently. It claimed as a deduction from gross income all the year's depreciation on such equipment, including that portion attributable to its use in constructing capital facilities. The depreciation was computed on a composite life of 10 years and under straight-line and declining-balance methods. The other operating and maintenance costs the taxpayer had charged on its books to capital were not claimed as current expenses and were not deducted.

To summarize: On its books, in accordance with Federal Power Commission-Idaho Public Utilities Commission prescribed methods, the taxpayer capitalized the construction-related depreciation, but for income tax purposes that depreciation increment was claimed as a deduction under § 167(a).

* * *

II

Our primary concern is with the necessity to treat construction-related depreciation in a manner that comports with accounting and taxation realities. Over a period of time a capital asset is consumed and, correspondingly over that period, its theoretical value and utility are thereby reduced. Depreciation is an accounting device which recognizes that the physical consumption of a capital asset is a true cost, since the asset is being depleted. As the process of consumption continues, and depreciation is claimed and allowed, the asset's adjusted income tax basis is reduced to reflect the distribution of its cost over the accounting periods affected. The Court stated in Hertz Corp. v. United States, 364 U.S. 122, 126 (1960): "(T)he purpose of depreciation accounting is to allocate the expense of using an asset to the various periods which are benefited by that asset." *See also* United States v. Ludey, 274 U.S. 295, 300—301 (1927); Massey Motors, Inc. v. United States, 364 U.S. 92, 96 (1960); Fribourg Navigation Co. v. Commissioner of Internal Revenue, 383 U.S. 272, 276—277 (1966). When the asset is used to further the taxpayer's day-to-day business operations, the periods of benefit usually correlate with the production of income. Thus, to the extent that equipment is used in such operations, a current depreciation deduction is an appropriate offset to gross income currently produced. It is clear, however, that different principles are implicated when the consumption of the asset takes place in the construction of other assets that, in the future, will produce income themselves. In this latter situation, the cost represented by depreciation does not correlate with production of current income. Rather, the cost, although certainly presently incurred, is related to the future and is appropriately allocated as part of the cost of acquiring an income-producing capital asset.

The Court of Appeals opined that the purpose of the depreciation allowance under the Code was to provide a means of cost recovery, Knoxville v. Knoxville Water Co., 212 U.S. 1, 13—14 (1909), and that this Court's decisions, e.g., Detroit Edison Co. v. Commissioner of Internal Revenue, 319 U.S. 98, 101 (1943), endorse a theory of replacement through "a fund to restore the property." 477 F.2d, at 691. Although tax-free replacement of a depreciating investment is one purpose of depreciation accounting, it alone does not require the result claimed by the taxpayer here. Only last Term, in United States v. Chicago, B. & Q. R. Co., 412 U.S. 401 (1973), we rejected replacement as the strict and sole purpose of depreciation:

"Whatever may be the desirability of creating a depreciation reserve under these circumstances, as a matter of good business and accounting practice, the answer is . . . '(d)epreciation reflects the cost of an existing capital asset, not the cost of a potential replacement.' " *Id.*, at 415.

Even were we to look to replacement, it is the replacement of the constructed facilities, not the equipment used to build them, with which we would be concerned. If the taxpayer now were to decide not to construct any more capital facilities with its own equipment and employees, it, in theory, would have no occasion to replace its equipment to the extent that it was consumed in prior construction.

Accepted accounting practice and established tax principles require the capitalization of the cost of acquiring a capital asset. In Woodward v. Commissioner of Internal Revenue, 397 U.S. 572, 575 (1970), the Court observed: "It has long been recognized, as a general matter, that costs incurred in the acquisition . . . of a capital asset are to be treated as capital expenditures." This principle has obvious application to the acquisition of a capital asset by purchase, but it has been applied, as well, to the costs incurred in a taxpayer's construction of capital facilities. *See, e.g.,* Southern Natural Gas Co. v. United States, *supra*; Great Northern R. Co. v. Commissioner of Internal Revenue, 40 F.2d 372 (8th Cir.), cert. denied, 282 U.S. 855.

There can be little question that other construction-related expense items, such as tools, materials, and wages paid construction workers, are to be treated as part of the cost of acquisition of a capital asset. The taxpayer does not dispute this. Of course, reasonable wages paid in the carrying on of a trade or business qualify as a deduction from gross income. [§ 162(a)(1).] But when wages are paid in connection with the construction or acquisition of a capital asset, they must be capitalized and are then entitled to be amortized over the life of the capital asset so acquired. Briarcliff Candy Corp. v. Commissioner of Internal Revenue, 475 F.2d 775, 781 (2d Cir. 1973); Perlmutter v. Commissioner, 44 T.C. 382, 404 (1965), *aff'd*, 373 F.2d 45 (10th Cir. 1967); Jaffa v. United States, 198 F.Supp. 234, 236 (N.D.Ohio 1961).

Construction-related depreciation is not unlike expenditures for wages for construction workers. The significant fact is that the exhaustion of construction equipment does not represent the final disposition of the taxpayer's investment in that equipment; rather, the investment in the equipment is assimilated into the cost of the capital asset constructed. Construction-related depreciation on the equipment is not an expense to the taxpayer of its day-to-day business. It is, however, appropriately recognized as a part of the taxpayer's cost or investment in the capital asset. The taxpayer's own accounting procedure reflects this treatment, for on its books the construction-related depreciation was capitalized by a credit to the equipment account and a debit to the capital facility account. By the same token, this capitalization prevents the distortion of income that would otherwise occur if depreciation properly allocable to asset acquisition were deducted from gross income currently realized. *See, e.g.*, Coors v. Commissioner, 60 T.C., at 398; Southern Natural Gas Co. v. United States, 412 F.2d, at 1265, 188 Ct.Cl., at 373—374.

An additional pertinent factor is that capitalization of construction-related depreciation by the taxpayer who does its own construction work maintains tax parity with the taxpayer who has its construction work done by an independent contractor. The depreciation on the contractor's equipment incurred during the performance of the job will be an element of cost charged by the contractor for his construction services, and the entire cost; of course, must be capitalized by the taxpayer having the construction work performed. The Court of Appeals' holding would lead to disparate treatment among taxpayers because it would allow the firm with sufficient resources to construct its own facilities and to obtain a current deduction, whereas another firm without such resources would be required to capitalize its entire cost including depreciation charged to it by the contractor.

* * *

The presence of § 263(a)(1) in the Code is of significance. Its literal language denies a deduction for "(a)ny amount paid out" for construction or permanent improvement of facilities. The taxpayer contends, and the Court of Appeals held, that depreciation of construction equipment represents merely a decrease in value and is not an amount "paid out," within the meaning of § 263(a)(1). We disagree.

The purpose of § 263 is to reflect the basic principle that a capital expenditure may not be deducted from current income. It serves to prevent a taxpayer from utilizing currently a deduction properly attributable, through amortization, to later tax years when the capital asset becomes income producing. The regulations state that the capital expenditures to which § 263(a) extends include the "cost of acquisition, construction, or erection of buildings." Treas. Reg. § 1.263(a)–2(a). This manifests an administrative understanding that for purposes of § 263(a)(1), "amount paid out" equates with "cost incurred." The Internal Revenue Service for some time has taken the position that construction-related depreciation is to be capitalized. Rev. Rul. 59–380, 1959–2 C.B. 87; Rev. Rul. 55–252, 1955–1 Cum. bull. 319.

There is no question that the cost of the transportation equipment was "paid out" in the same manner as the cost of supplies, materials, and other equipment, and the wages of construction workers. The taxpayer does not question the capitalization of these other items as elements of the cost of acquiring a capital asset. We see no reason to treat construction-related depreciation differently. In acquiring the transportation equipment, taxpayer "paid out" the equipment's purchase price; depreciation is simply the means of allocating the payment over the various accounting periods affected. As the Tax Court stated in Brooks v. Commissioner, 50 T.C., at 935, "depreciation—inasmuch as it represents a using up of capital—is as much an 'expenditure' as the using up of labor or other items of direct cost."

Finally, the priority-ordering directive of § 161—or, for that matter, § 261 . . . —requires that the capitalization provision of § 263(a) take precedence, on the facts here, over § 167(a). Section 161 provides that deductions specified in Part VI of Subchapter B of the Income Tax Subtitle of the Code are "subject to the exceptions provided in part IX." Part VI includes § 167 and Part IX includes § 263. The clear import of § 161 is that, with stated exceptions set forth either in § 263 itself or provided for elsewhere (as, for example, in § 404 relating to pension contributions), none of which is applicable here, an expenditure incurred in acquiring capital assets must be capitalized even when the expenditure otherwise might be deemed deductible under Part VI.

The Court of Appeals concluded, without reference to § 161, that § 263 did not apply to a deduction, such as that for depreciation of property used in a trade or business, allowed by the Code even though incurred in the construction of capital assets. We think that the court erred in espousing so absolute a rule, and it obviously overlooked the contrary direction of § 161. To the extent that reliance was placed on the congressional intent, in the evolvement of the 1954 Code, to provide for "liberalization of depreciation," H.R.Rep.No.1337, 83d Cong., 2d Sess., 22 (1954), that reliance is misplaced. The House Report also states that the depreciation provisions would "give the economy added stimulus and resilience without departing from realistic standards of depreciation accounting." *Id.*, at 24. 1954 U.S. Code Cong. & Admin. News, p. 4049. To be sure, the 1954 Code provided for new and accelerated methods for depreciation, resulting in the greater depreciation deductions currently available. These changes, however, relate primarily to computation of depreciation. Congress certainly did not intend that provisions for accelerated depreciation should be construed as enlarging the class of depreciable assets to which § 167(a) has application or as lessening the reach of § 263(a). *See* Note, 1973 Duke L.J. 1386.

We hold that the equipment depreciation allocable to taxpayer's construction of capital facilities is to be capitalized.

→ Holding

* * *

Encyclopaedia Britannica, Inc. v. Commissioner
United States Court of Appeals, Seventh Circuit, 1982.
685 F.2d 212.

■ POSNER, CIRCUIT JUDGE.

Section 162(a) of the Internal Revenue Code of 1954, * * * allows the deduction of "all the ordinary and necessary expenses paid or incurred during the taxable year in carrying on any trade or business . . . ," but this is qualified (see 26 U.S.C. § 161) by section 263(a) of the Code, which forbids the immediate deduction of "capital expenditures" even if they are ordinary and necessary business expenses. We must decide in this case whether certain expenditures made by Encyclopaedia Britannica, Inc. to acquire a manuscript were capital expenditures.

→ Rule

→ Issue

Encyclopaedia Britannica decided to publish a book to be called The Dictionary of Natural Sciences. Ordinarily it would have prepared the book in-house, but being temporarily short-handed it hired David-Stewart Publishing Company "to do all necessary research work and to prepare, edit and arrange the manuscript and all illustrative and other material for" the book. Under the contract David-Stewart agreed "to work closely with" Encyclopaedia Britannica's editorial board "so that the content and arrangement of the Work (and any revisions thereof) will conform to the idea and desires of [Encyclopaedia Britannica] and be acceptable to it"; but it was contemplated that David-Stewart would turn over a complete manuscript that Encyclopaedia Britannica would copyright, publish, and sell, and in exchange would receive advances against the royalties that Encyclopaedia Britannica expected to earn from the book.

FACTS

Encyclopaedia Britannica treated these advances as ordinary and necessary business expenses deductible in the years when they were paid, though it had not yet obtained any royalties. The Internal Revenue Service disallowed the deductions and assessed deficiencies. Encyclopaedia Britannica petitioned the Tax Court for a redetermination of its tax liability, and prevailed. The Tax Court held that the expenditures were for "services" rather than for the acquisition of an

Procedural History

asset and concluded that therefore they were deductible immediately rather than being, as the Service had ruled, capital expenditures. "The agreement provided for substantial editorial supervision by [Encyclopaedia Britannica]. Indeed, David-Stewart's work product was to be the embodiment of [Encyclopaedia Britannica's] ideas and desires. David-Stewart was just the vehicle selected by [Encyclopaedia Britannica] to assist ... with the editorial phase of the Work." Encyclopaedia Britannica was "the owner of the Work at all stages of completion" * * * . The Service petitions for review of the Tax Court's decision * * * .

As an original matter we would have no doubt that the payments to David-Stewart were capital expenditures regardless of who was the "dominating force" in the creation of The Dictionary of Natural Sciences. The work was intended to yield Encyclopaedia Britannica income over a period of years. The object of sections 162 and 263 of the Code, read together, is to match up expenditures with the income they generate. Where the income is generated over a period of years the expenditures should be classified as capital, contrary to what the Tax Court did here. From the publisher's standpoint a book is just another rental property; and just as the expenditures in putting a building into shape to be rented must be capitalized, so, logically at least, must the expenditures used to create a book. It would make no difference under this view whether Encyclopaedia Britannica hired David-Stewart as a mere consultant to its editorial board, which is the Tax Court's conception of what happened, or bought outright from David-Stewart the right to a book that David-Stewart had already published. If you hire a carpenter to build a tree house that you plan to rent out, his wage is a capital expenditure to you. See Commissioner of Internal Revenue v. Idaho Power Co., 418 U.S. 1, 13 (1974).

We are not impressed by Encyclopaedia Britannica's efforts to conjure up practical difficulties in matching expenditures on a book to the income from it. What, it asks, would have been the result if it had scrapped a portion of the manuscript it received from David-Stewart? Would that be treated as the partial destruction of a capital asset,* entitling it to an immediate deduction? We think not. The proper analogy is to loss or breakage in the construction, which are deductible over the useful life of the asset. If the scrapped portion of the manuscript was replaced, the analogy would be perfect. If it was not replaced, the tax consequence would be indirect: an increase or decrease in the publisher's taxable income from the published book.

What does give us pause, however, is a series of decisions in which authors of books have been allowed to treat their expenses as ordinary

---

*   [Ed: Judge Posner's reference to the manuscript as a "capital asset" was erroneous. The manuscript was not a capital asset. Judge Posner apparently fell victim to the temptation against which we warned in the introduction to this chapter; that is, concluding that if the cost of an asset must be capitalized, the asset must be a capital asset.]

and necessary business expenses that are deductible immediately even
though they were incurred in the creation of long-lived assets—the books
the authors were writing. The leading case is Faura v. Commissioner, 73
T.C. 849 (1980); it was * * * relied on heavily by the Tax Court in the
present case.

* * *

[W]e need not decide whether *Faura* is good law * * * . The Tax Court
interpreted *Faura* too broadly in this case. As we interpret *Faura* its
principle comes into play only when the taxpayer is in the business of
producing a series of assets that yield the taxpayer income over a period
of years, so that a complex allocation would be necessary if the taxpayer
had to capitalize all his expenses of producing them. This is not such a
case. The expenditures at issue are unambiguously identified with The
Dictionary of Natural Sciences. * * * This case is like *Idaho Power,* supra.
The expenditure there was on transportation equipment used in
constructing capital facilities that Idaho Power employed in its business
of producing and distributing electricity, and was thus unambiguously
identified with specific capital assets, just as Encyclopaedia Britannica's
payment to David-Stewart for the manuscript of The Dictionary of
Natural Sciences was unambiguously identified with a specific capital
asset.

* * *

There is another point to be noted about the distinction between
recurring and nonrecurring expenses and its bearing on the issue in this
case. If one really takes seriously the concept of a capital expenditure as
anything that yields income, actual or imputed, beyond the period
(conventionally one year, United States v. Wehrli, 400 F.2d 686, 689
(10th Cir.1968)) in which the expenditure is made, the result will be to
force the capitalization of virtually every business expense. It is a result
courts naturally shy away from. * * * It would require capitalizing every
salesman's salary, since his selling activities create goodwill for the
company and goodwill is an asset yielding income beyond the year in
which the salary expense is incurred. The administrative costs of
conceptual rigor are too great. The distinction between recurring and
nonrecurring business expenses provides a very crude but perhaps
serviceable demarcation between those capital expenditures that can
feasibly be capitalized and those that cannot be. Whether the distinction
breaks down where, as in the case of the conventional publisher, the
firm's entire business is the production of capital assets, so that it is
literally true that all of its business expenses are capital in nature, is
happily not a question we have to decide here, for it is clear that
Encyclopaedia Britannica's payments to David-Stewart were of a
nonnormal, nonrecurrent nature.

In light of all that we have said, the contention that really what
David-Stewart did here was to render consulting services to

Encyclopaedia Britannica no different from the services of a consultant whom Encyclopaedia Britannica might have hired on one of its in-house projects, which if true would make the payments more "ordinary" in the *Faura* sense, is of doubtful relevance. * * * This was a turnkey project, remote from what is ordinarily understood by editorial consultation. While maybe some creators or buyers of capital goods—some authors and publishers—may deduct as current expenses what realistically are capital expenditures, they may not do so * * * when the expense is tied to producing or acquiring a specific capital asset.

SECTION 2.   EXPENDITURES TO ACQUIRE OR PRODUCE TANGIBLE PROPERTY

INTERNAL REVENUE CODE: Section 263(a); 263A(a), (b).

REGULATIONS: Sections 1.162–3; –4(a); 1.212–1(k), (n); 1.263(a)–1; –2; –3(e).

The regulations governing capital expenditures include both substantive law and numerous examples. Even though the examples are not substantive law, they can help clarify a difficult area of the law, such that a person trying to understand the substantive law should look to the examples for clarification, most of which reflect the facts and findings of judicial decisions.

In broad terms, the regulations applicable to tangible property require capitalization of an expenditure to acquire, produce, construct, or improve a "unit of property." Any expenditure with respect to a unit of property that is not required by the regulations to be capitalized is deductible as a repair." Treas. Reg. § 1.162–4(a). The rules governing the capitalization of expenditures related to tangible property rely upon the definition of "unit of property." That definition helps determine whether a particular expenditure is made, on the one hand, to acquire, produce, improve, or, on the other hand, to repair a particular item of tangible property. To illustrate, a taxpayer may pay to replace an engine in a ship. If the engine is the unit of property, the expenditure is made to acquire or produce the engine, and will be capitalized. On the other hand, if the ship is the unit of property, the expenditure generally will be a deductible repair unless the expenditure results in an improvement to ship. See Section 3 of this Chapter. Thus, identifying the unit of property is a fundamental part of the analysis of expenditures related to tangible property.

DETAILED ANALYSIS

1.   UNIT OF PROPERTY

As a general matter, the capitalization rules utilize a functional interdependence standard to determine whether something is a unit of property. Special rules apply, however, to buildings, plant property, network assets, leased property, and improvements to property. Treas. Reg.

§ 1.263(a)–3(e)(1). The functional interdependence standard provides that "[c]omponents of property are functionally interdependent if the placing in service of one component by the taxpayer is dependent on the placing in service of the other component by the taxpayer." Treas. Reg. § 1.263(a)–3(e)(3)(i). Thus, personal property such as a locomotive and all of its components, which are functionally interdependent, are a unit of property, but a personal computer and a printer, which are not functionally interdependent, are not a unit of property. Treas. Reg. § 1.263(a)–3(e)(6), Ex. (8), (9).

A building and its structural components are a single unit of property. Treas. Reg. § 1.263(a)–3(e)(2)(i). The capitalization rules incorporate the definitions of building and structural components from the § 48 regulations, but modify that definition of structural component by excluding building systems. Treas. Reg. § 1.263(a)–3(e)(2)(ii)(A). Nonetheless, the capitalization rules treat building systems as part of the building. Treas. Reg. § 1.263(a)–3(e)(2)(ii)(B), (6), Ex. (1), (2). Plant property is functionally interdependent machinery or equipment that performs an industrial process, such as manufacturing, generation, warehousing, distribution, automated materials, or other similar function, but it does not include network assets. Treas. Reg. § 1.263(a)–3(e)(3)(ii)(A). For plant property, a unit of property consists of "each component (or group of components) that performs a discrete and major function or operation within the functionally interdependent machinery or equipment." Treas. Reg. § 1.263(a)–3(e)(3)(ii). Thus, a plant's boiler, turbine, generator, or such can be a unit of property, but other groups of equipment may be functionally interdependent and also comprise a unit of property. Treas. Reg. § 1.263(a)–3(e)(6), Ex. (6), (7).

An improvement to a unit of property generally is not a unit of property separate from the improved unit of property. Treas. Reg. § 1.263(a)–3(e)(4). Nonetheless, a component of a unit of property must be treated as a separate unit of property if the owner of the property treats the component as having a separate class of property for depreciation purposes. Treas. Reg. § 1.263(a)–3(e)(5)(i).

2. EXPENDITURE TO ACQUIRE TANGIBLE PROPERTY

2.1. *General Rule*

Generally, a taxpayer must capitalize the cost to acquire real or tangible personal property. Treas. Reg. § 1.263(a)–2(d)(1). This rule is straightforward, but people who are just beginning to work with the capitalization rules can overlook it as they consider various aspects of the rules. Nonetheless, the rule applies to every unit of property. Consequently, taxpayers generally must capitalize the cost to acquire land, buildings, automobiles, computers, furniture, equipment, and any other piece of property, see e.g., Treas. Reg. § 1.263(a)–2(d)(2), Ex. (1), (3), (5), (6), unless the cost is excluded from the capitalization rules.

Two exceptions apply to the general capitalization rules. First, a taxpayer is not required to capitalize amounts paid for certain materials and supplies. Treas. Reg. § 1.162–3(a). In particular, a taxpayer may deduct amounts paid for incidental materials and supplies that the taxpayer carries on hand and for which the taxpayer does not keep a record of consumption nor a take a physical inventory at the beginning and end of the taxable year. Treas. Reg. § 1.162–3(a)(2). Otherwise, a taxpayer must capitalize the cost of materials and supplies and deduct them in the taxable year when they are used or consumed. Treas. Reg. § 1.162–3(a)(1), (3). The regulations define materials and supplies, Treas. Reg. § 1.162–3(c), but they do not further distinguish between incidental and non-incidental materials and supplies. The examples do not illustrate the application of the rule for incidental materials and supplies, so the regulations do not provide additional guidance regarding the distinction. The rules do, however, allow taxpayers to elect to apply the *de minimis* safe harbor to some purchases of materials and supplies. Treas. Reg. § 1.162–3(f), Treas. Reg. § 1.263(a)–1(f).

Second, a taxpayer may elect not to capitalize (and thus deduct) costs that come within the *de minimis* safe harbor. Treas. Reg. § 1.263(a)–1(f). The *de minimis* safe harbor applies to taxpayers with applicable financial statements if the amount paid for property does not exceed $5,000 per invoice or per time of property substantiated on the invoice, or $2,500 per invoice without applicable financial statement. Treas. Reg. § 1.263(a)–1(f)(1)(i), – 1(f)(7), Ex. (3), (4); Notice 2015–82, 2015–50 I.R.B. 859. The taxpayer must adopt accounting procedures that treat as an expense amounts paid less than a specified amount or amounts paid for tangible property with a useful life of less than twelve months. Treas. Reg. § 1.263(a)–1(f)(1)(i)(B). If the taxpayer does not have an applicable financial statement, the regulations provide that the amount is limited to $500. Treas. Reg. §§ 1.263(a)–1(f)(1)(ii), –1(f)(7), Ex. (1), (2). But the IRS has administratively increased the ceiling under the *de minimis* safe harbor to $2,500. Notice 2015–82, 2015–50 I.R.B. 859.

2.2. *Acquisition Costs*

Amounts paid to acquire property include the invoice price, transaction costs, and costs for work performed before the property is placed in service. Treas. Reg. §§ 1.263(a)–2(d)(1), –2(d)(2), Ex. (10), (11). Transaction costs include amounts paid to facilitate the acquisition of property. Treas. Reg. § 1.263(a)–2(f)(1). An amount is paid to facilitate the acquisition of property if paid in the process of investigating or otherwise pursuing the acquisition. Treas. Reg. § 1.263(a)–2(f)(2)(i). Inherently facilitative payments are incurred in the process of investigating or otherwise pursuing the acquisition of property, which includes a long list of items. Treas. Reg. § 1.263(a)–2(f)(2)(ii). Generally, however, amounts paid for employee compensation and overhead are treated as amounts that do not facilitate the acquisition of property. Treas. Reg. § 1.263(a)–2(f)(2)(iv). Unless a specific exception applies, amounts paid to facilitate the acquisition of property are capital expenditures. Treas. Reg. § 1.263(a)–2(f)(3). The cost of disposing of an asset is similarly a capital cost that reduces gain (or increases loss) on the disposition. Treas. Reg. § 1.263(a)–1(e)(1).

In some situations the question becomes whether an expenditure relates to the acquisition or disposition of an asset. In Woodward v. Commissioner, 397 U.S. 572 (1970), the majority shareholders of a corporation were required by state law to purchase the stock of minority shareholders who dissented from a resolution to extend perpetually the corporate charter. The taxpayers incurred costs for attorneys', accountants', and appraisers' fees in litigation to establish the value of the minority stock interest that they were required to purchase. The taxpayers claimed a deduction for the expenses under § 212 for "ordinary and necessary expenses paid * * * for the management, conservation, or maintenance of property held for the production of income." The Court rejected the taxpayers' argument that the taxpayers' primary purpose for incurring the expense was protecting the value of income producing property, their stock interest. The Court focused instead on "whether the origin of the claim litigated is in the process of acquisition itself." Since the legal fees were incurred in an action having its origin in the acquisition of stock from the minority shareholders, the court required the taxpayers to capitalize the fees into the basis of the acquired stock.

2.3. *Transaction Costs*

Unless subject to one of the exceptions discussed above, a taxpayer must capitalize the expenses incurred to facilitate the acquisition of real or personal property. Treas. Reg. § 1.263(a)–2(f)(1), (3). These expenses include amounts paid to investigate or pursue acquisition of property including transporting the property, determining value, negotiating the acquisition (including tax advice), application fees, bidding costs, document review, title review, securing regulatory approval, finders' fees and brokers' commissions, architectural, engineering, and other inspections. Treas. Reg. § 1.263(a)–2(f)(2)(ii). With respect to real property, expenses that facilitate an acquisition do not include investigation expenses incurred in "the process of determining whether to acquire real property and which real property to acquire." Treas. Reg. § 1.263(a)–2(f)(2)(iii). The cost of acquisition also would not include employee compensation and overhead costs. Treas. Reg. § 1.263(a)–2(f)(2)(iv).

3. EXPENDITURE TO CONSTRUCT TANGIBLE PROPERTY

3.1. *General Rule Regarding Costs to Construct Property*

A taxpayer must capitalize the cost to construct real or personal property. Treas. Reg. § 1.263(a)–2(d)(1). For instance, a taxpayer must capitalize the cost incurred to construct equipment used in a manufacturing process or the cost to construct a building. Treas. Reg. § 1.263(a)–2(d)(2), Ex. (4), (7), (8). Identifying and specifying costs incurred to construct property can be a challenge. For instance, a homebuilder incurs direct costs (e.g., material and labor) as well as overhead costs (e.g., administrative, accounting, and managerial) in its business. Special rules in § 263A help determine which of these costs a taxpayer must capitalize into the construction of property. Treas. Reg. § 1.263(a)–2(f)(2)(iv).

3.2. *Section 263A: The Uniform Capitalization Rules*

Idaho Power provided that if a taxpayer uses its own equipment to construct property, the taxpayer must treat depreciation deductions of equipment as a cost of constructing the property and capitalize those deductions. That case raised the question of whether taxpayers must apportion overhead and other costs to property they construct for purchase for resale. Congress enacted § 263A to help clarify which costs a taxpayer must capitalize.

Section 263A(a) and (b)(1) require capitalization of all direct and indirect costs incurred with respect to real or tangible personal property produced by the taxpayer and property acquired by the taxpayer for resale. Section 263A does not, however, apply to personal-use and certain other types of properties. I.R.C. § 263A(c). Thus, § 263A generally applies to properties that, more than other types of property, require use of a taxpayer's organizational apparatus to construct or acquire. The Senate Finance Committee Report accompanying the enactment of § 263A explains the scope of § 263A as follows:

> In general, the uniform capitalization rules will apply to taxpayers who acquire and hold property for resale in the same manner as they apply to producers. Among the costs "retailers and wholesalers" are required to treat as inventory costs under the bill are the following: costs incident to purchasing inventory (e.g., wages or salaries of employees responsible for purchasing); repackaging, assembly, and other costs incurred in processing goods while in the taxpayer's possession; costs of storing goods (e.g., rent or depreciation, insurance premiums, and taxes attributable to a warehouse, and wages of warehouse personnel); and the portion of general and administrative costs allocable to these functions.

S.Rep. 99–313, 99th Cong., 2d Sess. 142 (1986).

Section 263A requires capitalization of direct costs for labor and materials used in the production of property, thereby incorporating all of the costs required to be capitalized under judicial rules predating § 263A. Treas. Reg. § 1.263A–1(e). Section 263A also applies to indirect costs such as depreciation and maintenance on tools and equipment, indirect labor and contract supervision expenditures, insurance, and general administrative expenses. Treas. Reg. § 1.263A–1(e)(3). Production period interest and taxes also must be capitalized, but Treas. Reg. § 1.263A–8(b) limits the application of the rule to real property, personal property with a class life of 20 years or more, personal property with an estimated production period exceeding two years, or personal property with an estimated production period in excess of one year if the estimated cost of production exceeds $1 million.

Property produced by the taxpayer includes property the taxpayer constructs, builds, installs, manufactures, develops, or improves. I.R.C. § 263A(g)(1). In Von-Lusk v. Commissioner, 104 T.C. 207 (1995), the Tax Court broadly interpreted the scope of the term "produce" in § 263A, and applied that provision to expenses incurred before physical production had commenced. The taxpayer was a partnership that had begun preliminary activities prerequisite to development of 278 acres of raw land. The activities in question included meeting with government officials, obtaining building permits and zoning variances, negotiating permit fees, performing engineering and feasibility studies, and drafting architectural plans. Although the activities undertaken in the year in question might have been considered ancillary to development, the court characterized them "as much a part of a development project as digging a foundation." Because § 263A applied, in addition to the expenses for preliminary development activities, the real estate taxes on the property also were capitalized.

Rev. Rul. 2002–9, 2002–1 C.B. 614, provides that under §§ 263(a) and 263A real estate developers must capitalize "impact fees" as costs allocable to the building. Impact fees are one-time charges imposed by a state or local government with respect to new or expanded real estate developments to finance offsite capital improvements for general public use (such as schools, parks, trunk roads, and utilities), necessitated by the development.

All of the direct and indirect costs of producing, acquiring and storing goods held for resale must be capitalized into inventory. Treas. Reg. § 1.263A–3. The amount capitalized into inventory becomes the basis for determining profits when the goods are sold. Treas. Reg. § 1.61–3. Accounting for inventories is discussed in Chapter 28, Section 4.

4. DEFENSE OR PROTECTION OF TITLE

4.1. *Origin of the Claim Test*

The origin-of-the-claim test of *Woodward, supra*, applies to litigation and related expenses to defend or perfect the title to property. Treas. Reg. §§ 1.212–1(k) and 1.263(a)–2(e). For example, the taxpayer in Boagni v. Commissioner, 59 T.C. 708 (1973), incurred legal costs in two actions. The fees incurred in connection with a declaratory judgment proceeding disputing title to an overriding mineral royalty interest were considered capital expenditures because the "nature and character of the proceeding" involved title to the interest. However, fees incurred in connection with a separate proceeding to determine who was entitled to the income from the interest were deductible since the action involved income that would be taxable to the party entitled to it and did not involve title to the property itself. The Tax Court articulated the application of the rule as follows:

> Quite plainly, the "origin-of-the-claim" rule does not contemplate a mechanical search for the first in the chain of events which led to the litigation but, rather, requires an examination of all the facts. The inquiry is directed to the ascertainment of the "kind of transaction" out of which the litigation arose. * * * Consideration must be given to the issues involved, the nature and objectives of the litigation, the defenses asserted, the purpose for which the claimed deductions were expended, the background of the litigation, and all facts pertaining to the controversy.

In Baylin v. United States, 43 F.3d 1451 (Fed.Cir.1995), the taxpayer appealed a condemnation award of $3,899,000, plus interest, for property taken by the state for a road. On appeal, the taxpayer received a compensatory award of $10,625,850, plus interest of $6,358,418, and paid legal fees of $4,048,424. The taxpayer argued that a proportionate part of the attorney's fees should be attributed to the collection of interest and thus should be deductible against ordinary income rather than reducing the award proceeds taxable as capital gain. Applying the *Woodward* origin of the claim test, however, the court concluded that the origin of the attorney's fees was in the disposition of the land and thus the entire fee was a capital expenditure. The court emphasized that the relative portion of the award labeled interest did not approximate the legal fees attributable to its recovery; there was no evidence that the attorney devoted any effort to increasing the interest portion of the award independently of the compensatory portion of the award.

Examples in the regulations of costs to defend include amounts paid to contest condemnation or to challenge a local agency decision to establish a building line across property owned by the taxpayer. Treas. Reg. § 1.263(a)–2(e)(2), Exs. (1) and (3). On the other hand, expenses incurred to invalidate a local ordinance that would prohibit the taxpayer's business of operating a quarry on land owned by the taxpayer are incurred to protect the on-going business activities and are not required to be capitalized. Treas. Reg. § 1.263(a)–2(e)(2), Ex. (2).

4.2. *Defense of Title Versus Recovery of Property*

The taxpayer in Nickell v. Commissioner, 831 F.2d 1265 (6th Cir.1987), attempted to distinguish legal fees incurred to defend title to property from fees incurred to recover ownership of property. The taxpayer had granted options to her father to purchase stock at a price below fair market value. On the father's death, the executor of his estate attempted to exercise the options, and obtained possession, but not ownership, of the stock certificates. The taxpayer incurred legal fees in a successful action to recover the stock from the executor. The taxpayer also recovered dividends collected by the executor during the period it held the stock.

As support for deducting her legal fees under § 212, the taxpayer relied on language in Treas. Reg. § 1.212–1(k), which provides, "Expenses paid or incurred in defending or perfecting title to property, in recovering property (other than investment property and amounts of income which, if and when recovered, must be included in gross income) . . . constitute a part of the cost of the property and are not deductible expenses." The court interpreted the regulation to mean that the cost of recovering investment property is deductible. But the court also concluded that the language of the regulation referring to recovery is inconsistent with the reference to defending title in the first phrase: to the extent Treas. Reg. § 1.212–1(k) allows a deduction for expenses incurred to recover title to investment property, the regulations are inconsistent with the accepted capitalization requirement with respect to expenses incurred to defend title. However, the court also held that, although the origin of the taxpayer's legal claim was in defense of title to the stock held by the executor, the portion of the taxpayer's expenses allocable to recovery of dividend income were deductible under the language of Treas. Reg. § 1.212–1(k), providing for the deduction of amounts expended to recover property that must be included in gross income.

Contrast *Nickell* with the result in Cruttenden v. Commissioner, 644 F.2d 1368 (9th Cir.1981). In *Cruttenden* the taxpayer incurred legal expenses to obtain the return of securities lent to a brokerage firm under a subordination agreement that allowed the firm to meet its net capital requirements under the stock exchange rules. The court concluded that since there was no question of the taxpayer's title to the securities, the legal fees were not incurred in the defense or protection of title. Expenses for "recovery" of *possession* of property were found to be deductible under Treas. Reg. § 1.212–1(k), based on the following reasoning:

> [T]he term must refer to instances where ownership, having been lost or relinquished, has been restored. An expense in recovering property would thus constitute an expense to secure the right to future income (including appreciation in value) from the property, comparable to an expense of defense or perfection of title, rather than simply an expense to manage or conserve the property in the manner made deductible under section 212(2).

The court concluded that the taxpayer's expense did not involve a "recovery" of *ownership* under the regulation and that the regulation did not, therefore, limit deductibility.

5. LEASING PROPERTY TO AVOID THE CAPITAL EXPENSE LIMITATION

As an alternative to purchasing property for use in a trade or business, with the requirement that the purchase price be capitalized, the taxpayer may acquire the use of property by a lease, and deduct the annual rental payments. Long-term lease arrangements raise the question whether the transaction is a lease of property or a purchase. See Chapter 33.

SECTION 3. AMOUNTS PAID TO IMPROVE TANGIBLE PROPERTY

REGULATIONS: Sections 1.162–4(a); 1.263(a)–1(a), (b); –3

The regulations provide that taxpayers must capitalize amounts paid to improve tangible property. Treas. Reg. § 1.263(a)–3(a). The regulations apply to units of property, discussed above. Treas. Reg. § 1.263(a)–3(e). They further provide that a unit of property is improved if amounts paid by the taxpayer are for a betterment, to restore, or to adapt the unit of property. Treas. Reg. § 1.263(a)–3(d). Thus, if a payment comes under any of those three categories, a taxpayer must capitalize the payment, and to avoid capitalization of a payment, a taxpayer must ensure that it does not come within any of the categories. For instance, a payment may not be a betterment, but it could nonetheless be an improvement under the definition of restoration.

Consequently, the application of the rules generally requires determining whether a cost was for a betterment, restoration, or adaptation of a unit of property. The analysis must also consider whether the cost comes within the routine maintenance safe harbor or whether the taxpayer qualifies for the small taxpayer safe harbor. Treas. Reg. § 1.263(a)–3(h), (i). The regulations also provide rules for costs related to leasehold improvements. Treas. Reg. § 1.263(a)–3(f). The following discussion provides an overview of these topics, but understanding the nuances and application of the rules requires careful study of the substantive rules in the regulations and the examples.

Any expenditure with respect to a unit of property that is not required by the regulations to be capitalized is deductible as a repair. Treas. Reg. § 1.162–4(a).

DETAILED ANALYSIS

1.   BETTERMENTS

A taxpayer must capitalize amounts paid for a betterment to a unit of property. Treas. Reg. § 1.263(a)–3(j)(1). A betterment does one of three things. First, it "[a]meliorates a material condition or defect that either existed prior to the taxpayer's acquisition of the unit of property or arose during the production of the unit of property." Treas. Reg. § 1.263(a)–3(j)(1)(i). The taxpayer's awareness of the condition or defect at the time of acquisition or production is irrelevant. Second, a betterment can be a material addition of a unit of property, which include physical enlargements, expansions, extensions, additions of a major component, and material increases in capacity. Treas. Reg. § 1.263(a)–3(j)(1)(ii). Third, a betterment can be something that "[i]s reasonably expected to materially increase the productivity, efficiency, strength, quality, or output of a unit of property." Treas. Reg. § 1.263(a)–3(j)(1)(iii).

Determining whether an expenditure results in a betterment requires comparing the property after the expenditure to the property immediately prior to the circumstances giving rise to the expenditure. Treas. Reg. § 1.263(a)–3(j)(iv)(A). The comparison further requires knowing whether the expenditure was made to correct normal wear and tear or damage to property. If the expenditure is to correct the effects of normal wear and tear, the comparison point for immediately prior to the circumstances giving rise to the expenditure is either the last time the taxpayer corrected the effects or when the taxpayer placed the property in service. Treas. Reg. § 1.263(a)–3(j)(2)(iv)(B). If the expenditure is to correct damage, the comparison point is the condition of the property immediately prior to the damage. Treas. Reg. § 1.263(a)–3(j)(2)(iv)(C). If only better parts are available to correct the effects of wear and tear or damage, then use of the better part results in a betterment. Treas. Reg. § 1.263(a)–3(j)(2)(iii).

The points of comparison prescribed in the regulations help distinguish between capital and deductible expenditures. For instance, if a taxpayer pays to fix a roof that begins to leak as a result of normal wear and tear, that expenditure will be deductible if it returns the building to the condition it was in when the taxpayer placed the building into service. Treas. Reg. § 1.263(a)–3(j)(3), Ex. (13). On the other hand if a condition, such as a severely leaky roof, exists at the time a taxpayer acquires property, expenditures to ameliorate that pre-existing condition will be a capital expenditure. See e.g., Treas. Reg. § 1.263(a)–3(j)(3), Exs. (1), (5). On the other hand, if the problem is minor or is remedied through routine repairs, the expenditures would not be betterments unless they expanded or materially increased the productivity, efficiency, strength, quality, or output of the unit of property. See e.g., Treas. Reg. § 1.263(a)–3(j)(3), Exs. (3) and (4). Furthermore, if a pre-existing condition was not considered to be a problem at the time the property was acquired, but advances in knowledge, such as the discovery that materials in a building previously thought to be harmless are in fact carcinogenic, require remediation, removal of the carcinogenic might not be a betterment. Treas. Reg. § 1.263(a)–3(j)(3), Ex. (23). Other examples further illustrate expenditures that may or may not be betterments. Treas. Reg. § 1.263(a)–3(j)(3).

2. RESTORATION

Taxpayers must capitalize amounts paid to restore a unit of property. Treas. Reg. § 1.263(a)–3(k)(1). The regulations list six types of expenditures that come within the definition of restoration. The types of expenditures often relate to the useful life of the property or losses incurred with respect to the property. As the list suggests, an expenditure that restores property does not merely repair an item that allows it to operate again as originally intended. First, an expenditure restores property if it replaces "a component of a unit of property for which the taxpayer has properly deducted a loss." Treas. Reg. § 1.263(a)–3(k)(1)(i). Second, an expenditure restores property if it replaces "a component of a unit of property for which the taxpayer has properly taken into account the adjusted basis of the component in realizing gain or loss resulting from the sale or exchange of the component." Treas. Reg. § 1.263(a)–3(k)(1)(ii). Third, an expenditure is considered a restoration if it covers "damage to a unit of property for which the taxpayer is required to make a basis adjustment as a result of casualty loss." Treas. Reg. § 1.263(a)–3(k)(1)(iii). These types of expenditures all replace components or units of property that have either resulted in loss or a downward basis adjustment. See e.g., Treas. Reg. § 1.263(a)–3(k)(7), Exs. (3)–(5). Allowing the taxpayer to deduct the expenditure would provide the taxpayer with a second deduction for the component or unit of property. By requiring the taxpayer to capitalize the expenditure, the rules return the basis of the property to the level it had prior to the basis adjustment.

Fourth, an expenditure restores property if it returns a unit of property "to its ordinary efficient operating condition if the property has deteriorated to a state of disrepair and is no longer functional for its intended use." Treas. Reg. § 1.263(a)–3(k)(1)(iv). Fifth, an expenditure restores property if it "[r]esults in the rebuilding of the unit of property to a like-new condition after the end of its class life." Treas. Reg. § 1.263(a)–3(k)(1)(iv). Dilapidated buildings and old equipment are examples of this type of restoration. See e.g., Treas. Reg. § 1.263(a)–(k)(7), Exs. (6)–(9). Consequently, amounts paid to make an old, unused hotel in a run-down part of town suitable for business as part of a revitalization program is an example of restoration, and the taxpayer would be required to capitalize those amounts.

Sixth, an expenditure restores property if it is "for the replacement part or a combination of parts that comprise a major component or a substantial structural part of a unit of property." Treas. Reg. § 1.263(a)–3(k)(1)(vi). The regulations adopt a facts-and-circumstances test to determine whether something is a major component or substantial structural part of a unit of property. Treas. Reg. § 1.263(a)–3(k)(6)(i). The regulations further define major component as "a part or combination of parts that performs a discrete and critical function in the operation of the unit of property." Treas. Reg. § 1.263(a)–3(k)(6)(i)(A). A substantial structural part "is a part or combination of parts that comprise a large portion of the physical structure of the unit of property." Treas. Reg. § 1.263(a)–3(k)(6)(i)(B). Under this rule, an expenditure, such as replacing an entire roof due to rot, could be a restoration because the roof is a major component of a building, so a taxpayer would have to capitalize the cost of replacing the entire roof. Treas. Reg. § 1.263(a)–3(k)(7), Ex. (14). Even though the same expenditure may not come within the definition of betterment because the condition after replacing the roof is the same as the condition prior to the rotting occurring, the taxpayer must capitalize the expenditure as a restoration cost.

3. ADAPTATION

A taxpayer must capitalize "an amount paid to adapt a unit of property to a new or different use." Treas. Reg. § 1.263(a)–3(l)(1). Generally, an amount is paid to adapt property, if it results in property being adapted to a use that is "not consistent with the taxpayer's ordinary use of the unit of property at the time originally placed in service by the taxpayer." For instance, the owner of a manufacturing building must capitalize the cost to convert the building to a showroom for his business. Treas. Reg. § 1.263(a)–3(l)(3), Ex. (1). Simply preparing a building for sale by repainting it and refinishing the floors does not, however, adapt it to a different use. Treas. Reg. § 1.263(a)–3(l)(3), Ex. (3). Consequently, if such costs do not otherwise come within the definition of an improvement, a taxpayer would not have to capitalize them.

4. ROUTINE MAINTENANCE SAFE HARBOR

Under the safe harbor for routine maintenance, an amount paid for routine maintenance on a unit of property is deemed not to improve the unit of property. Treas. Reg. § 1.263(a)–3(i)(1). The safe harbor has fairly detailed rules that define routine maintenance for both buildings and other property. As a general matter, routine maintenance (for both real property and other property) reflects recurring activities that a taxpayer performs to keep property in its ordinarily efficient operating condition. Examples of routine maintenance are inspection, cleaning, and testing building structures and systems, and the replacement of damaged or worn parts with comparable and commercially available replacement parts. Treas. Reg. § 1.263(a)–3(i)(1)(i), (ii).

To qualify as routine maintenance for buildings, the activities must be ones that the taxpayer reasonably expects to perform more than once during the first 10 years after the taxpayer places the unit of property in service. If a taxpayer does not perform the activity at least twice during the first 10 years, the taxpayer must substantiate that the expectation of performing the service twice was reasonable at the time the property was placed in service. Treas. Reg. § 1.263(a)–3(i)(1)(i), –3(6), Exs. (13)–(15). To be routine maintenance for property other than buildings, the activities must be those that the taxpayer reasonable expects to perform more than once during the class life (as defined in § 168(g)(2), (3)) of the unit of property. If the taxpayer does not perform the activity at least twice during the class life of the unit of property, the taxpayer must substantiate that its expectation was reasonable at the time the property was placed in service. Treas. Reg. § 1.263(a)–3(i)(1)(ii). Additionally, an expenditure can come within the routine maintenance safe harbor, even if the taxpayer incurs the expenditure after the property's class life expires. Treas. Reg. § 1.263(a)–3(i)(6), Ex. (1), (2). Amounts paid in betterments, restoration, or adaptation do not come within the safe harbor for routine maintenance. Treas. Reg. § 1.263(a)–3(i)(3).

SECTION 4. COST TO ACQUIRE OR CREATE INTANGIBLE ASSETS

REGULATIONS: Sections 1.263(a)–4(a)–(b)(4), (d)(7), (9)(i); –5(a).

Intangible assets are assets that an individual cannot touch. They include assets such as copyrights, patents, leases, and contracts. Even though intangible assets may be represented by written words on paper, the tangible paper is not the asset in question. Instead, the asset is the bundle of rights that the law bestows on the owner. Over the years, courts struggled to create rules governing the capitalization and deductibility of costs to acquire or create intangible assets. Most of the common law governing the capitalization and deductibility of intangible assets has been incorporated into the regulations.

DETAILED ANALYSIS

1. REGULATORY FRAMEWORK

The regulations provide generally that a taxpayer must capitalize (1) amounts paid to acquire intangibles, (2) amounts paid to create intangibles, (3) amounts paid to create or enhance separate and distinct intangible assets, (4) amounts paid to create or enhance a future benefit, and (5) amounts paid to facilitate the acquisition or creation of intangibles. Treas. Reg. § 1.263(a)–4(b)(1). Separate rules govern each amount paid with respect to each type of asset (with the exception of amounts paid to create or enhance a future benefit). Notice in the following discussion that the action (acquiring versus creating), rather than the type of asset, may dictate which rules and which exceptions apply. At first blush, some of the rules may be difficult to understand, but the examples in the regulations help clarify the rules.

1.1. *Amounts Paid to Acquire Intangibles*

A taxpayer must capitalize amounts paid to another party to acquire an intangible from that party. Treas. Reg. § 1.263(a)–4(c)(1). Notice that to acquire an intangible asset, the asset must be in existence prior to the acquisition. The regulations provide a non-exhaustive list of the types of assets to which this rule applies, such as ownership interests in corporations and partnerships, debt instruments, financial instruments, contracts, non-functional currency, leases, patents and copyrights, franchises, trademarks, tradenames, assembled workforce, goodwill, and computer software. Treas.

Reg. § 1.263(a) –4(c)(1)(i)–(xv). If the question involved whether the rules applied to a transaction involving a lease, for instance, the rules would only apply if the lease was in existence prior to the transaction. Treas. Reg. § 1.263(a)–4(c)(4) (presenting examples of assets that existed prior to the transaction in question).

1.2. *Amounts Paid to Create Intangibles*

If an intangible comes into existence as part of the transaction in question, then the rules governing the treatment of costs to create an intangible should apply. The regulations provide generally that a taxpayer must capitalize amounts paid to create an intangible. Treas. Reg. § 1.263(a)–4(d)(1). These rules apply to several sub-classes of intangibles. Notice that the list of financial interests to which this rule applies is similar to the list of assets to which the acquisition rules apply (but this list excludes items such as leases, self-created intangibles, going-concern intangibles, and computer software). Treas. Reg. § 1.263(a)–4(d)(2)(i)(A)–(F). The costs to which this rule applies include amounts paid to create, originate, enter into, renew, or renegotiate with the party to whom the taxpayer makes the payment. Treas. Reg. § 1.263(a)–4(d)(2)(i). Thus, a person lending money to another must capitalize the amount of the loan, and a person paying another to enter into an option must capitalize the amount paid for the option. Treas. Reg. § 1.263(a)–4(d)(2)(vi).

Taxpayers must capitalize prepaid expenses, which include items such as prepaid rent and prepaid insurance. Treas. Reg. § 1.263(a)–4(d)(3). Similarly, the amounts paid for membership or privileges in an organization are costs to create an intangible that the taxpayer must capitalize. Treas. Reg. § 1.263(a)–4(d)(4). Taxpayers also must capitalize amounts paid to government agencies to obtain government-granted intangibles, such as copyrights, patents, trademarks, tradenames, and licenses. Treas. Reg. § 1.263(a)–4(d)(5). Prepayment of interest is limited by § 461(g), discussed Chapter 16, Section 3.B., which generally permits an interest deduction only in the period to which the interest relates.

Taxpayers also generally must capitalize amounts paid to create, originate, enter into, renew, renegotiate, and terminate certain contract rights. Treas. Reg. § 1.263(a)–4(d)(6), (7). These types of payments to enter into contracts differ from prepaid expenses. These types of payments appear to be payments made to "sweeten" the deal for the other party. For instance, a tenant may have to pay rent and an additional sum to entice the owner of the property to enter into the lease. Treas. Reg. § 1.263(a)–4(d)(6)(vii). Nonetheless, a taxpayer is not required to capitalize *de minimis* amounts (i.e., amounts that do not exceed $5,000) paid to create, originate, enter into, renew, or renegotiate a contract right. Treas. Reg. § 1.263(a)–4(d)(6)(v). Finally, taxpayers must capitalize amounts paid to defend or perfect title to intangible property. Treas. Reg. § 1.263(a)–4(d)(9).

A 12-month safe-harbor rule excuses from the capitalization requirement amounts paid to create intangibles if the right or benefit does not extend beyond the earlier of the 12 months after the taxpayer realizes the right or benefit, or the taxable year following the year in which the taxpayer pays for the right or benefit. Treas. Reg. § 1.263(a)–4(d)(1), (f)(1). The 12-month rule would apply if a one-year right or benefit extends from the date of payment for 12 months, but it would not apply if the one-year right extended from February of the year following payment until the end of January of the subsequent year. Treas. Reg. § 1.263(a)–(f)(8), Ex. (1), (2).

1.3. *Amounts Paid to Create or Enhance Separate and Distinct Intangibles*

The regulations require taxpayers to capitalize amounts paid to create or enhance separate and distinct intangibles, but they provide little guidance regarding what constitutes separate and distinct assets. A provision provides generally that "separate and distinct assets" reflects a property interest of ascertainable and measurable value that is subject to legal protection, the possession of which is intrinsically capable of being sold, transferred, pledged separate and apart from a trade or business. Treas. Reg. § 1.263(a)–4(b)(3)(i). Presumably such assets would not include the assets governed by the general rule governing amounts paid to create intangibles. The regulations also exclude several other types of assets from the definition, including amounts paid to enter into or terminate agreements that produce rights or benefits for the taxpayer, amounts paid in performing services, amounts paid to create computer software, and amounts paid to develop a package design. Treas. Reg. § 1.263(a)–4(b)(3)(ii)–(v).

1.4. *Amounts Paid to Facilitate the Acquisition or Creation of Intangibles*

Taxpayers must capitalize amounts paid to facilitate the acquisition or creation of intangibles (transaction costs). Treas. Reg. § 1.263(a)–4(b)(1)(v). Such amounts include amounts paid in the process of investigating or otherwise pursuing a transaction. Treas. Reg. § 1.263(a)–4(e)(1)(i). These rules apply even if the taxpayer ultimately does not pay to create the intangible. Treas. Reg. § 1.263(a)–4(e)(2). Transaction costs include amounts paid to attorneys, accountants, appraisers, and others who are not parties to the arrangement that creates the intangible. Treas. Reg. § 1.263(a)–4(e)(5). Employee compensation, overhead, and *de minimis* costs do not come within the purview of this rule. Treas. Reg. § 1.263(a)–4(e)(4). The aggregate amounts incurred to investigate or otherwise pursue a transaction (other than employee compensation and overhead) are *de minimis* if they do not exceed $5,000. Treas. Reg. § 1.263(a)–4(e)(4)(iii). Despite these rules, a taxpayer may elect to treat employee compensation, overhead, or *de minimis* costs as transaction costs and capitalize them. Treas. Reg. § 1.263(a)–4(e)(4)(iv).

2. ADVERTISING EXPENSES

Advertising, particularly advertising that creates brand name recognition, provides a benefit beyond the taxable year. However, Treas. Reg. § 1.162–20(a)(2) specifically provides that expenditures for institutional or goodwill advertising are deductible as ordinary and necessary business expenses "providing that the expenditures are related to the patronage the taxpayer might reasonably expect in the future." In Rev. Rul. 92–80, 1992–2 C.B. 57, the IRS ruled that advertising will be capitalized only in the "unusual circumstance" where the advertising is directed towards future benefits significantly beyond the benefits normally associated with product or goodwill advertising.

Advertising expenses that would be classified as capital expenditures under the separate and distinct asset test, however, always have been treated as nondeductible capital expenditures. Thus, deductible advertising expenses do not include the cost of the tangible or intangible assets used in advertising. Alabama Coca-Cola Bottling Co. v. Commissioner, T.C. Memo. 1969–123 (signs, clocks, and scoreboards emblazoned with trademark and trade name). For example, the cost of producing a television commercial is a capital expense, while the cost of broadcasting it is deductible advertising.

Advertising expenses incurred to obtain an intangible benefit, such as a government permit, might be required to be capitalized. Cleveland Electric Illuminating Co. v. United States, 7 Cl.Ct. 220 (1985) (capitalization required for advertising expenses incurred to reduce public opposition to granting a license to operate a nuclear power plant).

SECTION 5. BUSINESS INVESTIGATION, START-UP AND EXPANSION COSTS

INTERNAL REVENUE CODE: Section 195.

REGULATIONS: Section 1.263(a)–5(a), (b).

Costs of Investigating Business and Investment Opportunities

A current deduction for expenses to investigate whether to purchase or start a new business is disallowed because § 162 allows a deduction for ordinary and necessary business expenses only if the taxpayer is already engaged in a trade or business at the time the expenses are incurred. In Frank v. Commissioner, 20 T.C. 511 (1953), travel expenses and legal fees incurred in a trip to investigate various newspapers or radio stations preliminary to purchasing such a business were held not deductible under § 162 because the investigation was not related to an already existing business. Likewise, the expenses were not deductible under § 212: "There is a basic distinction between allowing deductions for the expense of producing or collecting income, in which one has an existent interest or right, and expenses incurred in an attempt to obtain income by the creation of some new interest. * * * The expenses here involved are of the latter classification."

Similarly, costs of seeking investment opportunities are not currently deductible. In Weinstein v. United States, 420 F.2d 700 (Ct.Cl.1970), the taxpayer traveled throughout the country to investigate potential investment opportunities in order to diversify his portfolio. Some trips resulted in investments and others did not. The court denied a deduction for travel, lodging, meals and other miscellaneous expenses under § 212: "It is well settled that expenditures made in connection with acquiring, rather than retaining or protecting, a business are not deductible as ordinary and necessary business expenses. * * * Similarly, the courts have held that expenses incurred in connection with searching

for or acquiring new investments are nondeductible under section
212 * * * ."

Once a specific acquisition target has been identified, expenses
incurred to continue the investigation thereafter are capitalized. Rev.
Rul. 77–254, 1977–2 C.B. 63. If the acquisition is then abandoned, a
current loss deduction under § 165, discussed in Chapter 15, Section 1,
may be allowed. Rev. Rul. 71–191, 1971–1 C.B. 77 (loss deduction allowed
for costs incurred in unsuccessful attempt to acquire government oil and
gas leases). If, however, the taxpayer is an individual and no potential
acquisition ever is identified, Rev. Rul. 77–254, 1977–2 C.B. 63, holds
that the expenditures of such a general investigatory search for a new
business or investment, including those related to the decisions whether
to enter a transaction and which transaction to enter, are nondeductible
personal expenses. From a policy perspective, this treatment is
questionable; it prevents costs that are profit-seeking in origin from ever
being taken into account for tax purposes.

Pre-Opening Expenditures

Deductions for the start-up or pre-opening expenditures of a new
business long have been subject to strict limitations. Some courts used
the "carrying on any trade or business" language of § 162(a) to deny
deductions for costs incurred prior to the time when the activity became
a "going concern." For example, in Richmond Television Corp. v. United
States, 345 F.2d 901 (4th Cir.1965), vac'd on other grounds, 382 U.S. 68
(1965), a television station incurred costs to train personnel prior to
obtaining an FCC license. The court held that the taxpayer was not
carrying on a trade or business until it received the license and began
broadcasting: "[E]ven though a taxpayer has made a firm decision to
enter into a business and over a considerable period of time spent money
in preparation for entering that business, he still has not 'engaged in
carrying on any trade or business' within the intendment of section
162(a) until such time as the business has begun to function as a going
concern and performed those activities for which it was organized." Thus,
no current deduction was allowed for the training costs. This approach
was followed in Madison Gas and Electric Co. v. Commissioner, 633 F.2d
512 (7th Cir.1980), where three electric utilities agreed to enter into a
joint project to construct and own a nuclear generating plant. Training
and other costs were incurred prior to the opening of the plant. The court
required the capitalization of these costs as pre-opening expenses of a
new business venture.

Statutory Amortization of Start-up Expenditures: Section 195

In 1980, Congress enacted § 195 to deal with the treatment of
business (but not investment) start-up expenditures, which are defined
to include investigation expenses. This provision has significantly
reduced the importance of the controversy over capitalization of start-up
expenditures, but some controversies remain. Section 195(a) expressly
provides that no current deduction will be allowed for business start-up

expenditures, thus codifying the judicial approach reflected in *Frank* and *Richmond Television Corp.* However, § 195(b) ameliorates the disallowance rule of § 195(a). Section 195(b) allows taxpayers to elect to deduct currently up to $5,000 of start-up expenditures, but the deductible amount is reduced by the amount by which the start-up expenditures exceed $50,000. Any amounts in excess of those deducted must be amortized over a 180-month period that begins with the month the trade or business begins. Thus, a taxpayer who incurs $5,000 or less of start-up expenditures is allowed to deduct those expenses in full, but a taxpayer who incurs more than $55,000 of expenses is limited to amortization of the full amount. A taxpayer that incurs more than $5,000 but less than $50,000 in start-up costs will be able to deduct $5,000 in the year incurred but will have to amortize the remainder over a 15-year period.

The excerpt from the Senate Finance Committee Report that follows describes the effect of § 195.

Senate Finance Committee Report, Miscellaneous Revenue Act of 1980

S.Rep. No. 96–1036, 96th Cong., 2d Sess. 11–13 (1980).

Investigatory expenses

Investigatory expenses are costs of seeking and reviewing prospective businesses prior to reaching a decision to acquire or enter any business. Business investigatory expenses may be of either a general or specific nature. The former are related either to businesses generally, or to a category of business; the latter are related to a particular business. * * *

Startup costs

Startup or preopening expenses are costs which are incurred subsequent to a decision to acquire or establish a particular business and prior to its actual operation. Generally, the term "startup costs" refers to expenses which would be deductible currently if they were incurred after the commencement of the particular business operation to which they relate. Such costs may be incurred by a party who is not engaged in any existing business, or by a party with an existing business who begins a new one that is unrelated, or only tangentially related, to his or her existing business.

Startup costs may include expenses relating to advertising, employee training, lining-up distributors, suppliers, or potential customers, and professional services in setting up books and records. * * *

In general

Under [§ 195], business startup expenditures may be amortized, at the election of the taxpayer * * * .

Eligible expenditures

In general, expenditures eligible for amortization must satisfy two requirements. First, the expenditure must be paid or incurred in connection with creating, or investigating the creation or acquisition of, a trade or business entered into by the taxpayer. Second, the expenditure involved must be one which would be allowable as a deduction for the taxable year in which it is paid or incurred if it were paid or incurred in connection with the expansion of an existing trade or business in the same field as that entered into by the taxpayer.

Under [§ 195], eligible expenses consist of investigatory costs incurred in reviewing a prospective business prior to reaching a final decision to acquire or to enter that business. These costs include expenses incurred for the analysis or survey of potential markets, products, labor supply, transportation facilities, etc. Eligible expenses also include startup costs which are incurred subsequent to a decision to establish a particular business and prior to the time when the business begins. For example, startup costs include advertising, salaries and wages paid to employees who are being trained and their instructors, travel and other expenses incurred in lining up prospective distributors, suppliers or customers, and salaries or fees paid or incurred for executives, consultants, and for similar professional services.

In the case of an existing business, eligible startup expenditures do not include deductible ordinary and necessary business expenses paid or incurred in connection with an expansion of the business. As under present law, these expenses will continue to be currently deductible. The determination of whether there is an expansion of an existing trade or business or a creation or acquisition of a new trade or business is to be based on the facts and circumstances of each case as under present law.

Startup expenditures eligible for amortization do not include any amount with respect to which a deduction would not be allowable to an existing trade or business for the taxable year in which the expenditure was paid or incurred. Thus, amounts paid or incurred in connection with the sale of stock, securities, or partnership interests are not within the definition of startup expenditures, e.g., securities registration expenses, underwriters' commissions, etc., are not startup expenditures. In addition, the amortization election for startup expenditures does not apply to amounts paid or incurred as part of the acquisition cost of a trade or business. Also, startup expenditures do not include amounts paid or incurred for the acquisition of property to be held for sale or property which may be depreciated or amortized based on its useful life, including expenses incident to a lease and leasehold improvements. Whether an amount is consideration paid to acquire a business (or an interest therein) depends upon the facts and circumstances of the situation. * * *

Trade or business requirement

Expenditures must relate to the investigation or creation of an active trade or business (within the meaning of code sec. 162). Thus, expenditures attributable to an investment are not eligible for amortization under this provision. For this purpose, an activity with respect to which expenses are deductible only as itemized deductions for individuals (code sec. 212) is not considered to be a trade or business. * * *

Investigatory expenses for acquisition of existing businesses

In addition to the active business requirement applicable to the entity, in the case of investigatory expenditures incurred by a taxpayer with respect to the acquisition of an existing trade or business, the taxpayer will be considered to have entered into a trade or business only if the taxpayer has an equity interest in, and actively participates in the management of, the trade or business. * * *

A sole proprietor would always be considered to have an operator equity interest in the trade or business. In the case of a taxpayer incurring investigatory expenses with respect to the acquisition of common stock, a taxpayer would usually be considered to have acquired an investment interest rather than a qualifying trade or business interest. Thus, investigatory expenses attributable to the acquisition of corporate stock generally will not be eligible for amortization. * * * [A] corporate taxpayer will be considered to have acquired the trade or business assets of an acquired corporation, rather than having made a portfolio investment in stock, if the acquired corporation becomes a member of an affiliated group which includes the taxpayer incurring the investigatory expenses and a consolidated income tax return is filed for that group.[*]

* * *

DETAILED ANALYSIS

1. START-UP EXPENDITURES

1.1. *Application of Section 195*

For purposes of § 195, "start-up expenditures" include both investigatory expenditures, such as those incurred in *Frank, supra,* and preopening expenditures, such as those incurred in *Richmond Television* and *Madison Gas and Electric, supra.* I.R.C. § 195(c)(1). The election to deduct or amortize start-up expenditures under § 195(b) is the exclusive means of recovering start-up expenditures prior to a sale or other termination of the business. Thus, employee training expenses, such as those that were disallowed in *Richmond Television* and *Madison Gas and Electric,* may be recovered under § 195. But items that are capital expenditures because of

---

*   [Ed.: This condition requires that the acquiring corporation owns at least 80 percent of the voting stock and 80 percent of the value of all of the stock (except certain preferred stock) of the acquired corporation. I.R.C. §§ 1502, 1504.]

their relationship to an identifiable asset continue to be nondeductible and nonamortizable. This principle was explained in Rev. Rul. 99–23, 1999–1 C.B. 998, as follows:

> [U]nder § 195(c)(1)(B), expenditures described in § 195(c)(1)(A) that are incurred before the establishment of an active business are deemed to be paid or incurred in the operation of an existing active trade or business (in the same field as the business that the taxpayer is investigating whether to create or acquire), i.e., they are deemed to satisfy the carrying on a trade or business requirement. However, because § 195(c)(1)(B) also requires that an expenditure described in § 195(c)(1)(A) be allowable as a deduction for the taxable year in which paid or incurred, the expenditure still must meet all the other requirements of § 162. Thus, the expenditure must be an ordinary expense under § 162, and not a capital expenditure, to be a start-up expenditure under § 195. "Section 195 did not create a new class of deductible expenditures for existing businesses. . . . [I]n order to qualify under section 195(c)(1)(B), an expenditure must be one that would have been allowable as a deduction by an existing trade or business when it was paid or incurred." FMR Corp. v. Commissioner, 110 T.C. 402 (1998).

The Revenue Ruling went on to hold that expenditures incurred "in the course of a general search for, or an investigation of, an active trade or business, i.e., expenditures paid or incurred in order to determine whether to enter a new business and which new business to enter (other than costs incurred to acquire capital assets that are used in the search or investigation), are investigatory costs that are start-up expenditures under § 195."

The application of § 195 in a start-up situation also is illustrated in Rev. Rul. 81–150, 1981–1 C.B. 119. A limited partnership was organized to acquire an offshore drilling rig and to engage in contract drilling for oil and gas. During the construction period, a manager's fee was paid to the general partner for supervising the construction and financing of the rig, and managing the partnership during the construction period. Citing *Woodward,* the ruling held that the portion of the fee attributable to the supervision of construction and financing of the rig was a capital expenditure not eligible for amortization under § 195. The remainder was a pre-opening expense which, although not deductible because of *Richmond Television,* was eligible for amortization under § 195.

Section 195(c)(1)(A)(iii) includes in the definition of start-up expenditures amounts paid in connection with activities entered into for profit "in anticipation" of the time that the trade or business begins. The purpose of the section is to preclude any possibility of a deduction under § 212 for expenses incurred before the trade or business activity is deemed to begin. However, § 212 deductions for ordinary and necessary expenses paid or incurred in an ongoing non-business, profit-seeking activity are not always disallowed by § 195 just because that activity is subsequently transformed into a trade or business. In Toth v. Commissioner, 128 T.C. 1

(2007), the court allowed the taxpayer to deduct expenses incurred during 1998–2002 in a § 212 activity involving horse boarding, training, and lessons, although by 2004 the activity was conducted on a level that constituted a trade or business.

Treas. Reg. § 1.195–1 provides that a taxpayer is deemed to make the election to amortize start-up or organization expenditures for the year in which the active business, corporate business, or partnership business to which the expenditure relates begins. The regulations provide that a taxpayer may choose to forego the election by affirmatively electing to capitalize the expenditures on a timely filed return for the year in which the business begins.

1.2. *Expenditures to Organize a Business Entity*

Expenses to organize a business entity are capital expenses. Without special rules these costs could not be recovered prior to the disposition of the business involved. Sections 248 and 709(b) permit a current deduction for a limited amount of such organizational expenditures and amortization deductions for the balance, with certain exceptions.

Corporation Organizational Expenditures: Section 248 allows a deduction for up to $5,000 of organizational expenses of a corporation. If organizational expenses exceed $50,000, the deduction is reduced dollar for dollar (and is completely eliminated if organization expenses equal or exceed $55,000). Any organizational expenses that are not deductible must be capitalized and are amortizable over a 180-month period beginning with the month in which the corporation commences business. The provision does not apply to the expenses of issuing stock or to expenditures connected with the reorganization of an existing corporation unless a new corporation is formed.

Partnership Organization Fees: Section 709 is the partnership counterpart of § 248. Section 709(a) disallows any deduction for partnership organization and syndication expenses. Section 709(b) then allows a deduction for up to $5,000 of organizational expenses, but not syndication expenses. If organizational expenses exceed $50,000, the deduction is reduced dollar for dollar (and is completely eliminated if organization expenses equal or exceed $55,000). Any organizational expenses that are not deductible must be capitalized and are amortizable over a 180-month period beginning with the month in which the partnership commences business. If the partnership is liquidated before the end of the 180-month period, the partnership is allowed a loss deduction under § 165 for the unamortized deferred deduction. Syndication expenses are not amortizable. For the differences between the two types of expenses, see Aboussie v. United States, 779 F.2d 424 (8th Cir.1985) and Diamond v. Commissioner, 92 T.C. 423 (1989).

2.   BUSINESS EXPANSION COSTS

2.1. *Historical Background*

For many years before the enactment of § 195 the courts had distinguished cases involving expansion of an already existing business from cases involving expansion of an existing business to a new line of business. Expenses incurred to investigate and implement the expansion of an existing line of business were consistently treated as currently deductible under § 162, while expenses incurred in the start-up of a new line of business were required to be capitalized. The leading case in this area was Briarcliff Candy Corp. v. Commissioner, 475 F.2d 775 (2d Cir.1973), which allowed a deduction to a candy manufacturer for investigating and implementing a new method of retailing its products through different outlets than it had previously utilized. These business expansion cases relied in part on the separate asset test of *Lincoln Savings and Loan* to defeat the Commissioner's claims for capitalization. Several cases allowed banks to deduct the "start-up" costs of introducing a bank credit card program. The courts reasoned that the expenditures did not create a separate property interest; the costs were incurred in the continuing consumer credit business of the bank and simply introduced a more efficient method of conducting an old business. See e.g., Colorado Springs National Bank v. United States, 505 F.2d 1185 (10th Cir.1974).

Distinguishing a new line of business from an existing line of business is not always easy. In NCNB Corporation v. United States, 684 F.2d 285 (4th Cir.1982), the taxpayer incurred a series of expenditures in connection with the expansion of its statewide system of branch banks. The taxpayer capitalized the costs of constructing and equipping new facilities, but deducted as current expenditures amounts paid for market and feasibility studies, staff time devoted to planning and implementing expansion projects, and the costs of obtaining permits from the Comptroller of the Currency to open the new facilities. The Fourth Circuit Court of Appeals allowed the deduction, basing its holding on the language of *Lincoln Savings and Loan* indicating that the presence of an ensuing benefit is not controlling.

On the other hand, in Central Texas Savings & Loan Association v. United States, 731 F.2d 1181 (5th Cir.1984), the Fifth Circuit required capitalization of a bank's expansion expenses under facts similar to *NCNB Corporation*. The taxpayer in *Central Texas Savings & Loan* incurred expenses to investigate and start up new bank branches, including professional fees for economic research and analysis to determine the market potential of new locations, and for permits to expand to new locations. The District Court allowed the taxpayer to deduct the expenditures as costs incurred to accommodate changing business needs. The District Court also found that the expenditures did not create a separate and distinct asset with value that extended beyond the date of approval of the branch offices.

Deductible business expansion expenses do not include the actual cost of business assets or the cost of acquiring the stock of a corporation. Thus, for example, Ellis Banking Corp. v. Commissioner, 688 F.2d 1376 (11th Cir.1982), required capitalization of expenses for office supplies, filing fees, travel, and accounting services in connection with the taxpayer's examination of the books and records of a corporation the purchase of all of the stock of which it was investigating. The examination was performed pursuant to an acquisition agreement for the purchase of target's stock that was contingent on several terms and conditions, such as regulatory approval. The court concluded that the expenses were nondeductible capital expenditures, noting that the requirement that costs be capitalized extends beyond the price payable to include any costs incurred by the buyer in connection with the purchase, such as appraisals of the property or the costs of meeting any conditions of sale. Similarly, in American Stores Co. v. Commissioner, 114 T.C. 458 (2000), the taxpayer was required to capitalize legal fees incurred in defending an antitrust suit challenging the taxpayer's proposed acquisition of another corporation because they were paid in connection with an acquisition.

2.2. Regulations Regarding Current Deductions for Business Expansion Investigation Expenditures

Treas. Reg. § 1.263(a)–5 provides a bright-line rule for determining the point at which expenditures are no longer start-up expenditures subject to § 195 but become inherent capital costs of the acquisition of a particular business. Under the regulations, expenses incurred in the process of pursuing an acquisition of a trade or business—whether the acquisition is structured as an acquisition of stock or of assets (and whether the taxpayer is the acquirer in the acquisition or the target of the acquisition)—must be capitalized only if (1) they are "inherently facilitative" of the acquisition or (2) they relate to activities performed on or after the earlier of (a) the date on which a letter of intent, exclusivity agreement, or similar written communication (other than a confidentiality agreement) is executed by representatives of the acquirer and the target, or (b) the date on which the material terms of the transaction are authorized or approved by the taxpayer's board of directors (or committee of the board of directors) or, if taxpayer is not a corporation, the date on which the material terms of the transaction are authorized or approved by the taxpayer's appropriate governing officials. Expenditures that are "inherently facilitative" include amounts expended to determine the value of the target, drafting transactional documents, or conveying property between the parties. However, a taxpayer is not required to capitalize any portion of its own employee compensation attributable to these activities, and the regulations also provide de minimis rules similar to that applicable to intangibles generally. Treas. Reg. § 1.263(a)–5(d)(2) and (3). The Treasury Decision promulgating the final regulations indicates that amounts that are not required to be capitalized under the regulations may be start-up expenditures under § 195(c)(i). T.D. 9107 (Dec. 31, 2003). Of course, the actual cost of the business itself, whether structured as a stock or asset acquisition, remains a capital expense.

CHAPTER 14

COST RECOVERY MECHANISMS

In Encyclopaedia Britannica v. Commissioner, 685 F.2d 212, 214 (7th Cir.1982) (see Chapter 13, Section 1), the court stated that the purpose of the capitalization requirement is to "match up expenditures with the income they generate." One obvious time to account for capital cost recovery for tax purposes is on the disposition of property, when the cost of the asset may be matched with the proceeds of a sale or exchange. Recoverable capitalized cost reduces taxable gain or creates a deductible loss on the disposition. Disposition of an asset generally is a prerequisite to the application of this return of capital principle. However, where an asset is subject to wear and tear, obsolescence, or exhaustion in the production of income over a period of years, the matching of the capital cost with the income produced by capital investment requires a device to allocate the capitalized cost of the income producing property among those years. From the inception of the income tax, recovery of the capital cost of wasting assets has been provided through deductions for depreciation.[1] In Commissioner v. Idaho Power Co., 418 U.S. 1, 10 (1974), the Supreme Court described the purpose of depreciation as follows:

> Depreciation is an accounting device which recognizes that the physical consumption of a capital asset is a true cost, since the asset is being depleted. As the process of consumption continues, and depreciation is claimed and allowed, the asset's adjusted income tax basis is reduced to reflect the distribution of its cost over the accounting periods affected. The Court stated in Hertz Corp. v. United States, 364 U.S. 122 (1960) * * * , "[T]he purpose of depreciation accounting is to allocate the expense of using an asset to the various periods which are benefited by that asset." * * * When the asset is used to further the taxpayer's day-to-day business operations, the periods of benefit usually correlate to the production of income.

The Court reiterated the cost recovery function of depreciation in a footnote to the above statement, which quoted the Committee on Terminology of the American Institute of Certified Public Accountants, as follows: "These definitions view depreciation, broadly speaking, as describing not downward changes of value regardless of their causes but

---

[1]   The term "depreciation" is generally used to refer to the annual deductions for the costs of tangible assets. The term "amortization" often is used to refer to the annual deductions for the costs of intangible assets. For tax purposes, "depreciation" refers to annual deductions to recover the cost of both tangible and intangible property. In the Internal Revenue Code, "amortization" generally refers to provisions that allow the costs of tangible or intangible assets to be deducted over an arbitrary period of time unrelated to the assets' useful lives. In a different sense, amortization represents any scheme for allocating expenditures or credits to different periods, while depreciation may be thought of as a specific form of amortization.

a money cost incident to exhaustion of usefulness. The term is sometimes applied to the exhaustion itself, but the committee considers it desirable to emphasize the cost concept as the primary if not the sole accounting meaning of the term: thus, *depreciation* means the cost of such exhaustion, as *wages* means the cost of labor" (emphasis in original). 418 U.S. at 10, fn. 7, quoting 2 APB Accounting Principles, Accounting Terminology Bulletin No. 1—Review and Resumé & 48, p. 9512 (1973).

As an alternative to allocating costs to periods of income production without regard to value, the depreciation allowance for a given asset might be based on the actual economic decline in the value of the asset during the year. This "economic depreciation" represents the cost of the "capital" consumed in the period. If the annual decline in value is measured using the initial capital cost as the starting point, the full original cost will be recovered for tax purposes over the useful life of the property. The choice between this "economic depreciation" and other methods of allocating cost over the useful life of an asset has a significant effect upon the rate at which capital costs are recovered. Taxpayers generally will prefer an arbitrary method of capital cost recovery that allows depreciation deductions at a rate that exceeds the rate of economic depreciation (discussed in subsection C of this Section).

The difficulty in determining actual declines in value each year for the wide variety of assets employed in profit-seeking activities has led to a search for methods of depreciation that are reasonable surrogates for economic depreciation. Until 1954 straight line depreciation, which simply allocates the cost of an asset pro-rata over its expected useful life, was used for all assets. However, the IRS often approved a more rapid recovery method, e.g., a 150 percent "declining balance" method, in the case of equipment and machinery, which was presumed to decline in value more in its earlier years than in its later years. Beginning in 1954 the Code allowed accelerated depreciation as a tax incentive for investment rather than using depreciation as a device for the accurate measurement of annual net income. Depreciation deductions have been accelerated by shortening useful lives and/or by increasing depreciation rates to provide an incentive to business to invest in new, or particular types of, depreciable assets. That development culminated in the adoption of the Accelerated Cost Recovery System (ACRS) in 1981, and its modified version in 1986, when the depreciation deduction was separated from the concepts of useful life and salvage value.

Depreciation is not the only form of periodic cost recovery provided by the Code. Specific provisions allow for the periodic amortization or expensing of capital expenditures for which appropriate recovery periods cannot be readily identified, such as the cost of certain intangible business assets (Section 2) and research and development expenditures (Section 3). In addition, as a special incentive to capital investment § 179 allows current expensing of limited amounts of capital investment in equipment by certain small businesses (Section 1.B.).

SECTION 1.   DEPRECIATION

A. ACCELERATED COST RECOVERY SYSTEM

INTERNAL REVENUE CODE: Sections 167(a)–(c); 168(a)–(e)(3), (g)(1)–(3), (i)(1), (4), (6), (8); 1016(a)(2).

REGULATIONS: Sections 1.167(a)–1(a)–(b); –2; –3(a), (b)(1); –4; –6(a); 1.1016–3(a)(1)(i).

Simon v. Commissioner*

Tax Court of the United States, 1994.
103 T.C. 247.

■ LARO, JUDGE:

* * *

[T]he sole issue for decision is whether petitioners are entitled to deduct depreciation claimed under the accelerated cost recovery system (ACRS) for the year in issue. Petitioners claimed depreciation on two 19th-century violin bows that they used in their trade or business as full-time professional violinists. As discussed below, we hold that petitioners may depreciate their violin bows during the year in issue.

FINDINGS OF FACT

* * *

In 1965, Richard Simon joined the New York Philharmonic Orchestra (Orchestra) and began playing in its first violin section. In 1981, he joined and began playing with the New York Philharmonic Ensembles (Ensembles) (hereinafter, the Orchestra and the Ensembles are collectively referred to as the Philharmonic). Since 1965, Richard Simon has maintained two careers, one as a player with the Orchestra (and later with the Philharmonic) and the second as a soloist, chamber music player, and teacher.

* * *

In 1985, Fiona Simon joined the Philharmonic and began playing in its first violin section. Since 1985, Fiona Simon has maintained two careers, one as a full-time player with the Philharmonic and a second as a soloist, chamber music player, teacher, and free-lance performer.

During the year in issue, petitioners were both full-time performers with the Philharmonic, playing locally, nationally, and internationally in the finest concert halls in the world. In 1989, petitioners performed four concerts per week with the Philharmonic, playing over 200 different works, and attended many rehearsals with the Philharmonic that were more demanding and more time-consuming than the concerts. * * *

---

*   [Ed. The decision of the Tax Court was aff'd, 68 F.3d 41 (2d Cir.1995).]

Construction of a Violin Bow

A violin bow consists of a flexible wooden stick, horsehair, a frog, and a ferrule (screw). The stick, which varies in thickness, weight, and balance, is the working part of the bow and is an integral part in the production of sound through vibration. It is designed so that horsehair can be stretched between its ends.

* * *

Old violins played with old bows produce exceptional sounds that are superior to sounds produced by newer violins played with newer bows. The two violin bows in issue were made in the 19th century by Francois Xavier Tourte (1747–1835). Francois Tourte is considered the premier violin bow maker. In particular, he is renowned for improving the bow's design. (Hereinafter, the two bows in issue are separately referred to as Bow 1 and Bow 2, and are collectively referred to as the Tourte bows.)

Purchase of the Tourte Bows

On November 13, 1985, petitioners purchased Bow 1 for $30,000; the bow was purchased from Moes & Moes, Ltd., a dealer and restorer of violins and violin bows. On December 3, 1985, petitioners purchased Bow 2 from this dealer for $21,500. The sticks, frogs, and screws were originals of Francois Tourte at the time of each purchase. No cracks or other defects were apparent in the sticks at the time of each purchase. The frogs and screws, however, were not in playable condition. Therefore, petitioners replaced them.

Petitioners acquired the Tourte bows for regular use in their full-time professional employment as violinists. Petitioners purchased the Tourte bows for their tonal quality, not for their monetary value. In the year of acquisition, petitioners began using the Tourte bows with the original sticks in their trade or business as full-time professional violinists. Petitioners continued to use the Tourte bows with the original sticks during the year in issue.

Depreciation Deductions Claimed for the Tourte Bows

On their 1989 Form 1040, petitioners claimed a depreciation deduction of $6,300 with respect to Bow 1 and $4,515 with respect to Bow 2; these amounts were in accordance with the appropriate ACRS provisions that applied to 5-year property. See sec. 168(b)(1). Respondent disallowed petitioners' depreciation deduction in full * * * .

Conditions Affecting the Wear and Tear of Violin Bows

Playing with a bow adversely affects the bow's condition; when a musician plays with a bow, the bow vibrates up, down, sideways, and at different angles. In addition, perspiration from a player's hands enters the wood of a bow and ultimately destroys the bow's utility for playing. Cracks and heavy-handed bearing down while playing certain pieces of music also create wear and tear to a bow. A player who has a heavy hand may cause the stick to press against the horsehair; in turn, this may cause the bow to curve and warp. * * * Petitioners' use of the Tourte bows during the year in issue subjected the bows to substantial wear and tear.

Frequent use of a violin bow will cause it to be "played out", meaning that the wood loses its ability to vibrate and produce quality sound from the instrument. From the point of view of a professional musician, a "played out" bow is inferior and of limited use. The Tourte bows were purchased by petitioners, and were playable by them during the year in issue, only because the Tourte bows were relatively unused prior to petitioners' purchase of them; the Tourte bows had been preserved in pristine condition in collections. At the time of trial, the condition of the Tourte bows had deteriorated since the dates of their purchase. * * *

Value of the Tourte Bows

On November 21, 1985, Bow 1 was appraised for insurance purposes as having a fair market value of $35,000. On December 3, 1985, Bow 2 was appraised for insurance purposes as having a fair market value of $25,000. Petitioners obtained both appraisals from Moes & Moes, Ltd.

In 1994, at the time of trial, the Tourte bows were insured with the Philharmonic for $45,000 and $35,000, respectively. These amounts are based on an appraisal dated May 14, 1990, from Yung Chin Bowmaker, a restorer and dealer of fine bows. The record does not indicate whether these appraised amounts were the fair market values of the Tourte bows or were their replacement values.

An independent market exists for the Tourte bows and other antique bows. Numerous antique bows (including bows made by Francois Tourte) are regularly bought and sold in this market. The Tourte bows are unadorned; they are not as lavish or decorative as some other bows (including other bows made by Francois Tourte) that are sold in the independent market. Adornments on other bows include engravings, gold, silver, ivory, and mother of pearl.

* * *

OPINION

* * *

The last prerequisite for depreciating personal property under section 168 is that the property must be "of a character subject to the allowance for depreciation". The term "of a character subject to the allowance for depreciation" is undefined in the 1954 Code. Comparing the language that the Congress used in section 167(a) of the 1954 Code immediately before its amendment [in 1981], with the language that it used in section 168 * * * as added to the 1954 Code [in 1981], * * * we conclude that * * * property must suffer exhaustion, wear and tear, or obsolescence in order to be depreciated. Accordingly, petitioners will meet the final requirement under section 168 if the Tourte bows are subject to exhaustion, wear and tear, or obsolescence.

We are convinced that petitioners' frequent use of the Tourte bows subjected them to substantial wear and tear during the year in issue. Petitioners actively played their violins using the Tourte bows, and this active use resulted in substantial wear and tear to the bows. Indeed, respondent's expert witness even acknowledged at trial that the Tourte bows suffered wear and tear stemming from petitioners' business; the witness testified that the Tourte bows had eroded since he had examined them 3 years before, and that wood had come off them. Thus, we conclude that petitioners have satisfied the final prerequisite for depreciating personal property under section 168, and, accordingly, hold that petitioners may depreciate the Tourte bows during the year in issue. Allowing petitioners to depreciate the Tourte bows comports with the text of section 168, and enables them to match their costs for the Tourte bows with the income generated therefrom. Refusing to allow petitioners to deduct depreciation on the Tourte bows, on the other hand, would contradict section 168 and vitiate the accounting principle that allows taxpayers to write off income-producing assets against the income produced by those assets.

With respect to respondent's arguments in support of a contrary holding, we believe that respondent places too much reliance on the fact that the Tourte bows are old and have appreciated in value since petitioners acquired them. Indeed, respondent believes that this appreciation, in and of itself, serves to prevent petitioners from claiming any depreciation on the Tourte bows. We disagree; section 168 does not support her proposition that a taxpayer may not depreciate a business asset due to its age, or due to the fact that the asset may have appreciated in value over time. * * * Respondent incorrectly mixes two well-established, independent concepts of tax accounting, namely, accounting for the physical depreciation of an asset and accounting for changes in the asset's value on account of price fluctuations in the market. Accord Fribourg Navigation Co. v. Commissioner, 383 U.S. at 277 * * *. Moreover, we find merit in petitioners' claim that they should be able to depreciate an asset that receives substantial wear and tear through frequent use in their trade or business. Simply stated, the concept of depreciation is appropriately designed to allow taxpayers to recover the cost or other basis of a business asset through annual depreciation deductions.

We also reject respondent's contention that the Tourte bows are nondepreciable because they have value as collectibles independent of their use in playing musical instruments, and that this value prolongs the Tourte bows' useful life forever. First, it is firmly established that the term "useful life" under pre-[1981] law refers to the period of time in which a particular asset is useful to the taxpayer in his or her trade or business. Fribourg Navigation Co. v. Commissioner, supra at 277; Massey Motors, Inc. v. United States, 364 U.S. 92 (1960) * * *. Thus, the fact that an asset such as the Tourte bows may outlive a taxpayer is not dispositive of the issue of whether that asset has a useful life for depreciation purposes under pre-[1981] law. Second, the same argument concerning a separate, nonbusiness value can be made of many other assets. Such types of assets could include, for example, automobiles, patented property, highly sophisticated machinery, and real property. For the Court to delve into the determination of whether a particular asset has a separate, nonbusiness value would make the concept of depreciation a subjective issue and would be contrary to the Congress' intent to simplify the concept and computation of depreciation.

With respect to respondent's contention that petitioners must prove a definite useful life of the Tourte bows, we acknowledge that the concept of useful life was critical under pre-[1981] law. Indeed, the concept of useful life was necessary and indispensable to the computation of depreciation because taxpayers were required to recover their investments in personal property over the estimated useful life of the property. * * * However, the Congress enacted [section 168], in part, to avoid constant disagreements over the useful lives of assets, to shorten the writeoff periods for assets, and to encourage investment by providing for accelerated cost recovery through the tax law. S.Rept. 97–144, at 47 (1981), 1981–2 C.B. 412, 425. * * * To these ends, the Congress created two short periods of years over which taxpayers would depreciate tangible personal property used in trade or business; the 3-year and 5-year recovery periods, respectively, are the deemed useful life of personal property. * * * Respondent's argument that a taxpayer must first prove the useful life of personal property before he or she may depreciate it over the 3-year or 5-year period would bring the Court back to pre-[1981] law and reintroduce the disagreements that the Congress intended to eliminate by its enactment of [section 168]. This the Court will not do.

Respondent mainly relies on * * * Browning v. Commissioner, T.C. Memo. 1988–293, affd. 890 F.2d 1084 (9th Cir.1989), to support a holding contrary to the one that we reach today. We find * * * [this case] distinguishable. * * *

In Browning, the taxpayer was a musician who performed in nightclubs and bars and for private engagements. Prior to and during 1980 and 1981, the taxable years in issue there, the taxpayer purchased several expensive antique violins, including a Ruggeri, a Stradivarius, and a Gabrielli. The Ruggeri and the Stradivarius violins were purchased in 1978 and 1979, respectively, and were subject to the pre-[1981] rules for depreciation. The Gabrielli violin was purchased in 1981, and was subject to ACRS. During 1980 and 1981, the taxpayer claimed depreciation deductions with respect to the Ruggeri and Stradivarius violins; the taxpayer amended his petition in this Court to claim that section 168 of the 1954 Code, as added [in 1981], allowed him to deduct depreciation on the Gabrielli violin for his 1981 taxable year.

The Court in Browning sustained respondent's determination that the taxpayer was not entitled to any depreciation deductions on the violins. In so doing, the Court first stressed that the taxpayer had presented no credible evidence to support a contrary holding with respect to the Stradivarius violin. * * * With respect to the other two violins (including the one subject to ACRS), we held for respondent because the taxpayer failed to present any evidence with respect to those violins.

The record in the instant case, by contrast to the record in Browning, is replete with evidence showing clearly that the Tourte bows suffered substantial wear and tear while petitioners used them in their trade or business. Accordingly, unlike the taxpayer in *Browning*, petitioners have met their burden of proving wear and tear to their business asset. To state the obvious, violin bows are subject to wear and tear when in use by a professional violinist. Indeed, as stated by Publilius Syrus circa 42 B.C.: "The bow too tensely strung is easily broken." Bartlett, Familiar Quotations 1103 (12th ed. 1951).

* * *

[Seven other judges concurred with the majority opinion.]

■ GERBER, J., DISSENTING: I must, to some extent, agree and disagree with both the majority's view and Chief Judge Hamblen's minority view [that would have disallowed all depreciation deductions]. Both views are thoughtful, but each approach unnecessarily results in taxpayers' being entitled to all or none of the depreciation claimed. Both positions fail to consider that the bows may have two separate attributes—recoverable or depreciable and intrinsic attributes. If both are considered, the results that the majority and minority views advocate could, to some extent, be achieved. As I see this issue, under either section 167, permitting "a reasonable allowance for the exhaustion, wear and tear", or section 168, permitting depreciation for specific categories of "recovery property", a taxpayer should not be entitled to a depreciation deduction for intrinsic value, which is generally not subject to wear and tear and/or makes the life of the object indeterminable. The facts reveal, and neither viewpoint denies, that the bows are being subjected to wear and tear due to their use by professional musicians. It is also factually indisputable that, in spite of their use, the bows continue to increase in value from the original purchase price because of their unique qualities. The crucial point, which has not been addressed, concerns the effect of the wear and tear upon the intrinsic value inherent in the asset.

The majority reaches the conclusion that each entire bow constitutes recovery property as defined in section 168(c)(1). * * * I do not agree, however, that petitioners have shown that all of the property is of a character subject to the allowance for depreciation. Admittedly, some portion of the bows is subject to wear and tear, but not the intrinsic value that may exist even if the bows can no longer be used as bows. The burden is on petitioners to show which portion of the bows is subject to wear and tear * * * .

There are numerous situations in the tax law where property is composed of both depreciable and nondepreciable portions. * * * On several occasions we have delineated the existence of depreciable business use and nondepreciable personal use in the same property. See, e.g., International Artists, Ltd. v. Commissioner, 55 T.C. 94 (1970) * * * . Finally, and by way of analogy, bifurcation of property into depreciable and nondepreciable portions is entrenched in the tax treatment of improvements to realty, which may be depreciable even though the land upon which they rest is not subject to depreciation.

To better illustrate the concept of intrinsic value, let us assume that Elvis Presley had purchased a guitar for $1,000. Due to his fame, however, the value of the guitar immediately increases to $11,000. If Elvis Presley had used the guitar in his business, he would have been entitled to depreciate the $1,000 amount, either over its useful life or in accordance with its section 168 class life, as may have been appropriate. If, however, another musician purchases Elvis' guitar for $11,000, the portion of the guitar which would be subject to wear and tear or be recovery property would be about $1,000, more or less, depending upon how much Elvis had used it and/or the cost of a similar quality guitar at the time of purchase. The fact that it had been Elvis' guitar will sustain a premium value which is attributable to the guitar's intrinsic collector's value. Even if Elvis' guitar became unusable for commercial purposes, collectors would be willing to pay for the intrinsic value because it had belonged to Elvis. Usually, that value increases with time due to increased uniqueness attributable to scarcity or increased popularity. That intrinsic value could be affected by wear and tear, but the wear and tear will not necessarily eliminate the intrinsic value. Accordingly, under section 167 the remaining intrinsic value would be the equivalent of "salvage value". Because section 168 does not consider salvage value, the intrinsic value should not be considered [depreciable].

These same principles apply to the bows under consideration. Some portion of the value and purchase price is attributable to the collector's value and is not [subject to depreciation]. Although Congress, by enacting section 168, intended to simplify the classification of depreciable property and permit shorter periods of writeoff, there was no intent to permit the writeoff of the portion of property attributable to the intrinsic collector's value of unique property. The burden rests with taxpayers to show that portion of the property which is depreciable or recovery property and which portion is intrinsic or investment. Petitioners in this case have not shown the cost portion or value of the bows which is subject to wear and tear and, accordingly, must fail here. Admittedly, it would be unfair to hold that petitioners did not have some depreciation attributable to their use of the bows. It would be equally unfair (to other taxpayers) to permit petitioners to write off the intrinsic value which is unaffected by wear and tear or use.

The majority's holding permits the opportunity for substantial unintended abuse. Taxpayers will be able to depreciate items with current business utility and intrinsic collector's value and, after 3 or 5 years, have the tax benefit of the entire cost, at a time when the value of the item has not decreased or may have increased. The process may be duplicated over and over, providing substantial writeoffs with the cost borne by the public fisc. Ultimately, the taxpayer accumulates numerous of these collector's items which are passed on to future generations because of their intrinsic collector's value, which is likely to have substantially appreciated.

[The dissenting opinions of six other Judges are omitted.]

DETAILED ANALYSIS

1.   ELIGIBLE PROPERTY

1.1. *Property Used in a Trade or Business*

Section 167(a) requires that to be eligible for depreciation deductions property must be used in a trade or business or for the production of income. The reference to property held for the production of income allows depreciation deductions with respect to income producing property that is held in activities that do not rise to the level of a trade or business, such as a single-family residence temporarily leased by the taxpayer. Depreciation deductions are not allowed for property used for personal purposes. In general, if an item of property is used partly for business purposes and partly for personal purposes the basis of the property must be allocated between the business and personal uses, depreciation being allowable only to the extent of the business use. Depreciation with respect to business use of personal use automobiles, computers, and personal residences, is further restricted by §§ 280A and 280F, discussed in Chapter 18, Section 2, and Chapter 19, Section 4. If personal use property is converted to trade or business use, the basis for depreciation purposes is the lesser of the fair market value of the property at the time of the conversion or the property's adjusted basis, and the property is treated as placed in service on the date of the conversion. Treas. Reg. §§ 1.167(g)–1, 1.168(i)–4.

Identification of the depreciation period requires a determination of when the trade or business use begins and ends. Treas. Reg. § 1.167(a)–10(b) provides that the "period for depreciation of an asset shall begin when the asset is placed in service and shall end when the asset is retired from service." Questions regarding the precise date on which depreciable property is placed in service have been mitigated somewhat by § 168(d), which treats most tangible personal property as being placed in service in the middle of the taxable year.

In Brown v. Commissioner, T.C. Memo. 2013–275, the Tax Court held that property is placed in service when the property is ready for full operation in the taxpayer's business on a regular basis. The taxpayer in

Brown took ownership of a $22 million airplane in Portland, Oregon on December 30, 2003. On that date he flew the plane to Seattle and Chicago for what the taxpayer claimed were business meetings, then back to Portland. Shortly thereafter the plane was taken to a plant in Illinois for modifications costing more than $500,000 involving the installation of a conference table and equipment for Power Point presentations that the taxpayer testified were necessary for the taxpayer's business meetings held on the airplane. The modifications were completed in 2004. The court held that the airplane was placed in service in 2004 when the modifications made the airplane fully ready for use in the taxpayer's business.[2]

1.2. *Wasting-Asset Requirement*

As discussed in *Simon*, depreciation is only available for property that is consumed by use in producing income through "exhaustion, wear and tear (including a reasonable allowance for obsolescence)." I.R.C. § 167(a). Tangible personal property that does not lose its value by virtue of the passage of time or use in an income producing activity, such as a work of art or an antique, is not a wasting asset subject to the allowance for depreciation. Associated Obstetricians & Gynecologists, P.C. v. Commissioner, T.C. Memo. 1983–380, aff'd, 762 F.2d 38 (6th Cir.1985), denied depreciation deductions for 70 works of art, ranging in value from $40 to $7,000, used as decor in a professional office. See also Rev. Rul. 90–65, 1990–2 C.B. 677 (property used in a trade or business fashioned out of recoverable precious metal not depreciable).

Liddle v. Commissioner, 103 T.C. 285 (1994), aff'd, 65 F.3d 329 (3d Cir.1995), reached a conclusion similar to *Simon*, permitting depreciation deductions to a professional classical musician with respect to a 300-year-old bass viol because its use value to the taxpayer was diminished over time by virtue of physical deterioration, even though its value as a collectible was increasing. However, in Browning v. Commissioner, 890 F.2d 1084 (9th Cir.1989), discussed in *Simon*, a different taxpayer, who was a member of the New York Philharmonic, was not allowed to claim depreciation on antique violins, including a Stradivarius, used in his trade or business. The IRS has nonacquiesced in *Simon*, 1996–2 C.B. 2, and announced that it will not follow *Simon* and *Liddle*, but instead will continue to disallow depreciation deductions claimed with respect to antique instruments. AOD CC–1996–009.

Land is not a wasting asset and thus is not subject to depreciation allowances. Treas. Reg. § 1.167(a)–2. However, improvements to land, such as buildings, are wasting assets. Although the costs of general land grading are not depreciable, excavation, grading, and removal costs directly associated with the construction of buildings are depreciable capital costs attributable to the buildings. Rev. Rul. 65–265, 1965–2 C.B. 52. The issue thus is one of distinguishing improvements to land that are part of the land

---

[2] The court also expressed some doubt about the business nature of the taxpayer's meetings with insurance clients noting that the flight logs indicated a trip of much shorter duration than the taxpayer's testimony and that the letter from the client thanking the taxpayer for the meetings appeared to have been prepared by the taxpayer's employees and presented to the client for signature after the audit of the taxpayer's returns had commenced.

itself, and thus not depreciable capital expenditures, from improvements that are related to a wasting asset, or are themselves wasting assets. For example, in Rev. Rul. 74–265, 1974–1 C.B. 56, the cost of clearing and grading the land on which an apartment would be built was held to be a nondepreciable improvement to the land itself. But Trailmont Park, Inc. v. Commissioner, T.C. Memo. 1971–212, held that grading and landscaping of a trailer park were depreciable over the useful life of the trailer pads because any other use of the property would require regrading the land. See also Rudolph Investment Corp. v. Commissioner, T.C. Memo. 1972–129 (earthen dams and water tanks found to have limited useful lives). In Rev. Proc. 87–56, 1987–2 C.B. 674, the IRS assigned a 20-year class life, i.e., a 15-year recovery period, to certain improvements to land such as sidewalks, canals, drainage facilities, sewers, docks, bridges, fencing, and landscaping. Maguire/Thomas Partners Fifth & Grand, Ltd. v. Commissioner, T.C. Memo 2005–34, held that the costs incurred to obtain a zoning change with respect to land are not depreciable, but the costs to obtain a zoning variance relating to a specific building to be constructed on a specific parcel of land are depreciable as part of the cost of the building.

The cost of a purchased leasehold interest in land or a premium paid for a long-term lease may be amortized and deducted over the term of the lease. Treas. Reg. § 1.162–11(a). The term of the lease over which the purchase price is amortized must include renewal periods if less than 75 percent of the purchase price is attributable to the lease term remaining on the date of purchase. I.R.C. § 178. However, where a corporation transferred nondepreciable land to its subsidiary, retaining a forty-year estate in the property, no depreciation deduction was permitted with respect to the retained interest; the taxpayer had simply fragmented an asset and had made no additional investment in the term interest that it was entitled to depreciate. Lomas Santa Fe, Inc. v. Commissioner, 693 F.2d 71 (9th Cir.1982).

Inventory also is not considered to be a wasting asset. Thus, Treas. Reg. § 1.167(a)–2 provides that inventory is not subject to the depreciation allowance. The recovery of inventory costs for tax purposes is discussed in Chapter 28, Section 4. In Rev. Rul. 89–25, 1989–1 C.B. 79, the IRS ruled that a homebuilder is not allowed to depreciate model homes. Although the model homes were temporarily used for display purposes, the builder intended to hold the properties for sale to customers.

2. DEPRECIABLE INTEREST

2.1. *General*

Depreciation deductions are allowed only to the owner of property who has a capital investment in the property, that is, the person who bears the economic benefits of ownership and the economic burden of the exhaustion of the asset. Durkin v. Commissioner, 872 F.2d 1271 (7th Cir.1989). In Frank Lyon Co. v. United States, 435 U.S. 561 (1978), discussed in Chapter 33, the taxpayer purchased a building under construction with the proceeds of a nonrecourse loan, and immediately leased the building back to the seller for rental payments designed to match the taxpayer's payment obligations under the nonrecourse loan, plus a return on the relatively small capital investment made by the taxpayer. The Court allowed the taxpayer to claim depreciation deductions as a party whose capital was committed to the property, even though the lessor, by virtue of options to renew the lease and to reacquire ownership of the building, had a growing equity interest in the property. Compare Helvering v. F. & R. Lazarus & Co., 308 U.S. 252 (1939), where the lessee of property under a 99-year lease, with an option to purchase, was held to have a depreciable interest in the leased property even though legal title was vested in a bank as trustee for lenders.

2.2. *As Between Lessor and Lessee*

The lessor of property is allowed depreciation deductions for leased property only if the lessor's interest is subject to wear and tear or exhaustion. Royal St. Louis, Inc. v. United States, 578 F.2d 1017 (5th Cir.1978) (lessors of a hotel were not entitled to depreciation deductions for furniture that they provided to the lessee to equip the hotel when the lease required the lessee to return personal property of equal value to the lessors at the termination of the lease); M. DeMatteo Construction Co. v. United States, 433 F.2d 1263 (1st Cir.1970) (depreciation was denied the purchaser of land and a building subject to a lease where the lessee had built the building and the term of the lease was longer than the useful life of the building; the income-producing asset acquired by the purchaser was the lease, not the building).

Lessee improvements to property that are treated as rental payments to the lessor must be included in income by the lessor. Recognition of income gives the lessor a basis in the improvements that creates a depreciable interest. If lessee improvements are not treated as rental payments, § 109, discussed at Chapter 2, Section 2.5., excludes the value of the improvements from the lessor's income, and § 1019 provides that the lessor receives no basis in the improvements. Thus, the lessor is not allowed any depreciation deductions.

The lessee of property may also have a depreciable interest in improvements made to the leased property. Capital expenditures made by a lessee during the term of the lease are recoverable over the MACRS recovery periods for the specific property, even if the recovery period is longer than the term of the lease. I.R.C. § 168(i)(8). Presumably, if the lease term is shorter than the allowable recovery period, the lessee is allowed a deduction on termination of the lease for unrecovered capital costs.

2.3. *Life Estates and Remainders*

Where interests in property are divided between a life tenant and a remainder interest, § 167(d) allocates all of the depreciation to the interest of the life tenant as if that person were the absolute owner of the property. Depreciation deductions attributable to property held in trust are apportioned between the income beneficiaries and the trust on the basis of the trust income allocable to each. However, if the trust instrument requires or permits the trustee to maintain a reserve for depreciation in any amount, the depreciation deduction is allocated to the trust. Treas. Reg. § 1.167(h)–1(b).

Section 167(e) prohibits depreciation deductions for the declining value of a purchased term interest in income producing property where the remainder interest is held by a related person. However, if the life tenant has a basis in a term interest that would be depreciable but for the restriction of § 167(e),[3] the life tenant's basis in the term interest is decreased by the amount of depreciation or amortization deductions that are disallowed, and the basis is shifted to the remainder interest. I.R.C. § 167(e)(3).

3. ADJUSTED BASIS AND DEPRECIATION

Doyle v. Mitchell Brothers Company, discussed in Chapter 6, Section 1, held that before a taxpayer derives gain from property, the taxpayer is entitled to recover the taxpayer's invested capital tax-free. As described in Chapter 13, the cost of acquiring property and any investment in property that creates a benefit beyond the taxable year is capitalized into the basis of the property. Thus, basis reflects the taxpayer's recoverable capital investment in an asset. In accord with the central role of basis in identifying recoverable capital investment, § 167(c) provides that depreciation is allowed with respect to the property's basis determined under § 1011. Basis under § 1011 generally is cost, § 1012, but the basis of property for depreciation purposes also may be determined from the rules of § 1014 or 1015 (basis of property acquired at death or by gift), or under any of the specific rules of the Code regarding transferred and exchanged basis in nonrecognition transactions (see e.g., § 1031(d), discussed in Chapter 25, Section 1.

Under § 1016, basis is increased for capital expenditures attributable to the property and reduced by depreciation and other recoveries of capital attributable to the property. The resulting figure is defined as the property's "adjusted basis." Basis is reduced annually by the full amount of depreciation *allowable* with respect to the property, even though the taxpayer may have claimed deductions for less than the permissible capital recovery. I.R.C. § 1016(a)(2). Treas. Reg. § 1.167(a)–10(a), complementing § 1016(a)(2), provides that a taxpayer "should deduct the proper depreciation allowance each year and may not increase his depreciation allowances in later years by reason of his failure to deduct any depreciation allowance * * * in prior years."[4] Section 1016(a)(2) provides, however, that if no depreciation method has been adopted under § 167, allowable depreciation shall be determined under the straight line method. If the taxpayer claims depreciation deductions in excess of the amount allowable, the full amount of the claimed deductions is subtracted from basis. Treas. Reg. § 1.1016–3(a)(1) and (e).

Adjusted basis includes indebtedness incurred by the taxpayer to purchase depreciable property or incurred to make improvements to the property. Mortgage indebtedness is includable in basis even though the taxpayer is not personally liable for debt that is merely secured by the property ("nonrecourse debt"). The issues raised with respect to liabilities and basis are discussed in Chapters 6 and 34.

---

[3]   The basis of a term interest acquired by gift or inheritance is zero. I.R.C. § 1001(e).

[4]   If the taxpayer failed to claim allowable depreciation in years closed by the statute of limitations, it may change its accounting method for depreciation to recoup the deductions that were required to reduce basis. See Rev. Proc. 2007–16, 2007–4 I.R.B. 358. The omitted deductions are taken into account in the year of the sale.

Theoretically, the taxpayer's recoverable capital cost should be adjusted for any amount that the taxpayer may be expected to recover on disposition of depreciable property at the end of its useful life, namely its salvage value. However, the accelerated capital recovery system adopted in 1981 ignores salvage value in the calculation of depreciation deductions.

Reductions in basis under § 1016 reflect the taxpayer's recovery of basis through a deduction prior to the disposition of the property, at which time the taxpayer's capital invested in the property is recovered through an offset against the amount realized in calculating gain or loss. Thus, depreciation deductions will increase gain or reduce loss realized on a subsequent disposition. The adjustments to basis for depreciation required by § 1016 ensure that if a taxpayer sells depreciable property in a market transaction the aggregate net deductions taken while the taxpayer held the property will equal its actual depreciation as measured by the market price on disposition. Assume, for example, that a taxpayer purchases equipment for $100, claims $50 of depreciation deductions, and sells the equipment for $70. The taxpayer realizes and recognizes a gain of $20 on the sale, in effect restoring $20 of depreciation deductions to income. The taxpayer effectively has been allowed only the $30 of economic depreciation. Of course the taxpayer has realized the time value of money benefits of being allowed to claimed depreciation in excess of economic depreciation while the taxpayer held the property.

4.   MODIFIED ACCELERATED COST RECOVERY SYSTEM

4.1. *Historical Background*

As the Supreme Court held in Commissioner v. Idaho Power Co. (see Chapter 13, Section 1.2.1.), the purpose of depreciation is "to allocate the expense of using an asset to the various periods which are benefited by that asset." The useful life of any particular asset is difficult to ascertain. Useful life depends upon such factors as the nature of the business, the use of the machine, quality of maintenance, quality of the machine itself, and advances in technology that may make the machine obsolete. See Treas. Reg. § 1.167(a)–(b). In Massey Motors, Inc. v. United States, 364 U.S. 92 (1960), the Court held that the useful life of property used in a trade or business must reflect its useful life to the taxpayer in the taxpayer's *particular* business, rather than the actual physical useful life of the asset itself. Thus, the useful life of automobiles used in a car rental operation was limited to the period of time the automobiles were used in the business before resale (generally fifteen months).[5]

In the 1930's, the Treasury promulgated its so-called "Bulletin F" guidelines, which set forth the useful lives for a large number of assets. Taxpayers could rely on the guidelines of Bulletin F or face the difficult problem of establishing a different useful life under a facts and circumstances approach. In 1962 the Treasury abandoned the asset-by-asset

---

[5]   The taxpayer claimed depreciation deductions for the automobiles based on a 4-year useful life with no salvage value. The Commissioner successfully asserted depreciation based on a 15-month useful life with a salvage value reflecting the sales price of the automobiles at the end of that period, resulting in much smaller depreciation allowances for the taxpayer.

approach and issued guidelines prescribing useful lives for broad classes of assets. Rev. Proc. 62–21, 1962–2 C.B. 418. Treasury's authority to rely on guideline lives was clarified in 1971 with enactment of the statutory Asset Depreciation Range (ADR) system that provided shorter useful lives than the prior guidelines and allowed taxpayers to depreciate assets over a range from 20 percent below, to 20 percent above the ADR midpoint guideline. Business interests continued to pressure for shorter useful lives and more rapid recovery of capital costs than those permitted under ADR.

In 1981, Congress adopted the Accelerated Cost Recovery System (ACRS) of § 168 to simplify the depreciation scheme and divorce capital cost recovery from the concepts of useful life and salvage value. As described in *Simon*, ACRS eliminated reliance on the useful life concept, which was replaced by fixed recovery periods for defined asset classes. As modified by the 1986 Act, §§ 167(b) and 168(a) require that depreciation deductions with respect to tangible property placed in service after 1986 be determined under the Modified Accelerated Cost Recovery System (MACRS). See Treas. Reg. § 1.168(a)–1. Under MACRS, depreciation is computed by applying the *"applicable depreciation method"* to the *"applicable recovery period"* for the property and taking into account the *"applicable convention"* for determining when depreciable property is placed in service.

4.2. *MACRS Applicable Recovery Periods*

Section 168(c) and (e) classify all tangible property into one of seven recovery periods; three, five, seven, ten, fifteen and twenty year recovery periods for tangible personal property, and 27.5 and 39 year recovery periods for real estate. Most property is classified on the basis of ADR midpoint lives assigned by the IRS in Rev. Proc. 87–56, 1987–2 C.B. 674. The Conference Report to the Tax Reform Act of 1986 describes these categories as follows:

Three-year class—ADR midpoints of 4 years or less, except automobiles and light trucks, and adding horses which are assigned to the three-year class * * * .

Five-year class—ADR midpoints of more than 4 years and less than 10 years, and adding automobiles, light trucks, qualified technological equipment, computer-based telephone central office switching equipment, research and experimentation property, and geothermal, ocean thermal, solar, and wind energy properties, and biomass properties that constitute qualifying small power production facilities (within the meaning of § 3(17)(C) of the Federal Power Act).

Seven-year class—ADR midpoints of 10 years and less than 16 years, and adding single purpose agricultural or horticultural structures and property with no ADR midpoint that is not classified elsewhere.

10-year class—ADR midpoints of 16 years and less than 20 years.

15-year class—ADR midpoints of 20 years and less than 25 years, and adding municipal waste water treatment plants, and telephone distribution plant and comparable equipment used for the two-way exchange of voice and data communications.[6]

20-year class—ADR midpoints of 25 years and more, other than section 1250 real property with an ADR midpoint of 27.5 years and more, and adding municipal sewers.

27.5-year class—Residential rental property (including manufactured homes that are residential rental property and elevators and escalators).

[39]-year class—Nonresidential real property (section 1250 real property [buildings] that is not residential rental property and that either does not have an ADR midpoint or whose ADR midpoint is 27.5 years or more, including elevators and escalators).

H.Rep. No. 99–841, 99th Cong., 2d Sess. II–39–40 (1986).

MACRS assigns recovery periods that are generally shorter than the useful lives assigned by the IRS under the ADR guideline tables. However, recovery periods under MACRS are generally longer than the three, five, ten and fifteen year system in place between 1981 and 1987.

4.2.1. *Property Classification*

The classification of property within the guideline categories of Rev. Proc. 87–56 has a significant effect on recovery periods for depreciation and has, therefore, led to significant disputes between taxpayers and the IRS.

In Hospital Corp. of America v. Commissioner, 109 T.C. 21 (1997), the Tax Court held that many items that would generally be considered structural parts of a building for purposes other than income taxation are not structural parts of a building, and thus are not real estate, for tax purposes. Under the test applied by the court, an item is a structural component of a building only if it relates to the operation and maintenance of the building. An item is not a structural component of the building if it is machinery, the sole purpose of which is to meet temperature or humidity requirements essential to the operation of other machinery or processing food or materials. Applying these standards, the court found the following items were not structural components of the building: (1) primary and secondary electrical systems attributable to electrical equipment (on a percentage basis), (2) branch electrical systems serving only equipment (except equipment that related to the operation or maintenance of the building), (3) wiring for the telephones, (4) vinyl wall coverings, i.e., wall paper, (5) vinyl floor covering glued to the floors, kitchen water and steam piping, (6) kitchen exhaust system, (7) movable room "partitions" affixed to the walls and ceilings. These items are tangible personal property subject to cost recovery over a shorter recovery period using an accelerated method under MACRS. Among the items found to be structural components of the building were acoustical ceilings, bathroom fixtures, and steam boilers. See also SuperValu Inc. v. United States, 993 F.Supp. 1243 (D.Minn. 1997)

---

6   Fifteen-year property also includes certain qualified leasehold improvements by a lessor and improvements to a building used as a restaurant that are placed in service before January 1, 2008. I.R.C. § 168(e)(6) and (7).

(centralized refrigeration system to cool rooms in warehouse were tangible personal property, not structural components of the building).

Trentadue v. Commissioner, 128 T.C. 91 (2007), held that wine grape trellises are 10-year class life property under Rev. Proc. 87–56 as "agricultural equipment," which includes machinery and equipment, grain bins, and fences, but no other land improvements. The court analogized the trellises to fences "with the major difference being that one is intended to keep things in or out and the other to support grape growing equipment or train grapevines." The taxpayer's irrigation system and wells, however, were found to constitute land improvements with a 20-year class life. The court noted that components of the drip irrigation system were buried in the ground and that a substantial portion of the system would remain buried until the vines were removed. The court focused to some degree on the fact that the trellises, but not the irrigation pipes (and especially not the well) were movable and in fact were moved on occasion.

In Walgreen Co. v. Commissioner, 103 T.C. 582 (1994), the Tax Court held that leasehold improvements added to a building by the lessee were depreciable by the lessee over the class life for real property because the type of leasehold improvements constituted property that had no ADR class life. The Seventh Circuit reversed, 68 F.3d 1006 (7th Cir.1995), holding that leasehold improvements are not *per se* depreciable only as building improvements. The Court of Appeals concluded that leasehold improvements were implicitly included in ADR system and thus could be subject to depreciation under ACRS under the "Wholesale and Retail Trade" class of property. The crucial issue was whether the particular improvements fell within the "Wholesale and Retail Trade" class or the "Building Services" class. The court described the differences as follows:

> "Building Services," * * * covers "the structural shells of buildings and all integral equipment that services normal heating, plumbing, air conditioning, illumination, fire prevention, and power requirements; equipment for the movement of passengers and freight within the building; and any additions to buildings or their components, capitalized remodeling costs, and partitions both permanent and semipermanent." An alternative interpretation is that the class refers to the shell itself plus the parts that are essential to its functioning as a usable, habitable building, such as elevators and air conditioning, but not to the type of improvements, perhaps largely decorative, necessary to make the building suitable for a particular tenant's use—improvements likely to have a shorter useful life. We do not have any confidence in the alternative interpretation; the references to remodeling costs and to semipermanent partitions cut against it; but we are not prepared to say, the Tax Court not having addressed the issue, that Building Services embraces every improvement to real property and specifically every improvement that Walgreen seeks to classify under Wholesale and Retail Trade. One of those improvements, we were told at argument, is a sign in front of one of Walgreen's

buildings and not attached to it. It is difficult to imagine classifying that sign as an integral part of a structural shell.

In essence, the Court of Appeals appears to have held that under § 168(i)(8) leasehold improvements should be assigned to recovery period classes under the same principles that would apply if the improvements were made by the fee owner. On remand, T.C. Memo. 1996–374, the Tax Court held that leasehold improvements that were not included in Building Services (Class 65.0) were included in the Wholesale and Retail Trade class of property and had a ten-year cost recovery period. The only items fitting into the Wholesale and Retail Trade class of property, however, were decorative items that were not integral parts of any structural shell, e.g., decorative canopies. All interior partitions, ceilings, lighting fixtures, and interior floor finishes were held to be Building Services class property, depreciable as a building.

4.3. *Applicable Conventions*

Under § 168(a)(3) and (d), tangible personal property placed in service at any time during the taxable year is treated for capital recovery purposes as having been placed in service at the mid-point of the taxable year. As a consequence, only one-half of a full year's capital recovery is allowed in the year property is placed in service, regardless of the date on which the property is first used. This also means that the property will produce a one-half year capital recovery deduction in the last year of the recovery period. Thus, for example, seven year property would be depreciated over an eight-year period, with one-half year of depreciation in the first and eighth years.

To prevent taxpayers from taking undue advantage of the half-year convention by acquiring disproportionate amounts of depreciable property in the last month of the taxable year and claiming a full half-year's capital recovery deduction, § 168(d)(3) requires the use of a "mid-quarter convention" in certain circumstances. The mid-quarter convention applies if the aggregate bases of property placed in service during the last three months of the taxable year is greater than 40 percent of the aggregate bases of all tangible personal property placed in service during the taxable year. Under the mid-quarter convention, property placed in service during each quarter of the taxable year is deemed to be placed in service at the mid-point of the quarter.

Real property is subject to a "mid-month convention." I.R.C. § 168(d)(2). Under the mid-month convention, property placed in service during any month of the taxable year is treated as having been placed in service at the mid-point of the month. I.R.C. § 168(d)(4)(B). This requires that the annual capital recovery deductions for real property be computed on a monthly basis.

4.4. *Applicable Depreciation Methods*

Section 168 provides for two methods of capital recovery, straight line and the declining balance method. Straight line requires the taxpayer's recoverable cost basis to be claimed as a deduction against income ratably over each year of the applicable recovery period. For example, if A acquires for $10,000 an income producing machine for use in A's business that has a useful life of 16 years, which is ten-year property under § 168(e)(1), under the straight line method A will be allowed to deduct $1,000 per year over the ten-year period, a recovery rate of 10 percent per year (subject to the mid-year convention, which requires a five-percent rate in the first and eleventh years).

The *declining balance method* of allocating depreciation accelerates depreciation deductions by providing larger depreciation deductions in the early years of an asset's useful life than are available under the straight line method, and smaller annual deductions in the later years of the asset's useful life. The annual allowance is computed by applying a constant rate, determined as a percentage of the straight line rate, to the declining basis of the asset; the basis for each year's deduction is reduced by prior depreciation deductions. The percentage rate is a multiple of the straight line rate, typically 150 or 200 percent. With respect to A's machine with a ten-year recovery period, and thus a straight line depreciation rate of 10 percent, 200 percent declining balance (or "double declining balance") depreciation would use a 20-percent recovery rate (10% × 200%). Under 150 percent declining balance method, the recovery rate would be 15 percent (10% × 150%).

Under the 200 percent declining balance depreciation, the annual depreciation deduction for A's $10,000 machine is computed by multiplying the remaining undepreciated adjusted basis of the machine by 20 percent. Because the annual deduction is always a percentage of the remaining basis, basis is never fully recovered under the declining balance method. For this reason, § 168 provides for a switch to straight line capital recovery when that method would yield a larger allowance. The following table illustrates the annual depreciation deductions from A's $10,000 machine with a ten-year recovery period using the double declining balance method, taking account of the half-year convention, and switching to straight line depreciation in year seven.

Year End	Capital Recovery	Remaining Basis	Recovery Percentage of Original Basis
1	$ 1,000	$9,000	10.00
2	$ 1,800	$7,200	18.00
3	$ 1,440	$5,760	14.40
4	$ 1,152	$4,608	11.52
5	$ 922	$3,685	9.22
6	$ 737	$2,949	7.37
7	$ 655	$2,294	6.55
8	$ 656	$1,638	6.56
9	$ 655	$ 983	6.55
10	$ 655	$ 328	6.55
11	$ 328	$ 0	3.28
Total	$10,000		100.00

The recovery method switches to straight line at the end of six years. At the end of year 6, twenty percent of the remaining $2,949 basis yields a deduction of only $590. Dividing the remaining basis by the remaining 4.5 years of the recovery period produces a deduction of $655.

Under § 168(b), the double declining balance method (200 percent of the straight line rate) is allowed for property with three, five, seven, or ten year recovery periods. Fifteen- and twenty-year property uses the 150 percent declining balance method. Real property is limited to the straight line method. Section 168(b)(5) provides for an irrevocable election to use the straight line method for any class of property.

Much of the computational complexity of the capital recovery provisions is reduced by tables published in Rev. Proc. 87–57, 1987–2 C.B. 687. The tables translate the capital recovery allowance for each taxable year of a recovery period into a percentage of the original adjusted basis. Each year's capital recovery may be ascertained by multiplying the original basis of depreciable property by the appropriate percentage. For example, capital recovery for ten-year property is determined as the percentage of original basis displayed in the last column of the above table. Rev. Proc. 87–57 contains tables for each recovery period and each convention. For real property, the tables provide annual capital recovery percentages related to each month of the taxable year in which the property was placed in service.

4.5. *Alternative Depreciation System*

Section 168(g) provides an alternative depreciation system that requires the use of the straight line method over recovery periods that are longer than those otherwise allowed. The alternative depreciation system is required for tangible personal property that is used predominantly outside of the United States (with specific exceptions for property used in international transportation and space vehicles), property financed with tax-exempt bonds or leased to a tax exempt entity, and property imported from a country that the President has certified engages in discriminatory acts restricting United States commerce. In addition, under § 280F(b)(1), discussed at Chapter 19, Section 4, mixed personal and business use automobiles and personal computers, for which the business use does not exceed 50 percent, must be depreciated under the alternative depreciation system.

4.6. *Additional First Year Recovery*

Section 168(k) allows a first year "bonus depreciation" deduction for a portion of the adjusted basis of qualified property placed in service after December 31, 2007 and before January 1, 2020. For eligible property placed in service before January 1, 2018, the applicable percentage is 50 percent. For eligible property placed in service after 2017, the percentage of the property's adjusted basis that can be deducted in the first year is reduced from 50 percent to 40 percent in 2018 and 30 percent in 2019. The adjusted basis of qualified property for purposes of calculating otherwise allowable depreciation is reduced by the first-year deduction. I.R.C. § 168(k)(1)(B). This basis adjustment is taken into account before computing the otherwise normal annual depreciation allowances.

Section 168(k) was originally added by the 2002 Act as a one-year stimulus for capital investment.[7] The bonus depreciation allowance has been enhanced and regularly extended by Congress. The most recent iteration enacted in December 2015 applies to qualified property placed in service after December 31, 2007 and before January 1, 2020, but if the past is prologue, further extensions can be expected.

Qualified property is defined in § 168(k)(2) as any property the original use of which commences with the taxpayer with a recovery period of 20 years or less (3, 5, 7, 10, 15, and 20 year MACRS property), computer software that is eligible for 36-month capital recovery under § 167(f)(1)(B), water utility property that is defined in § 168(e)(5), and "qualified improvement property." "Qualified improvement property" is defined (subject to certain exceptions) as "any improvement to an interior portion of a building which is nonresidential real property if such improvement is placed in service after the date such building was first placed in service," but does not include an enlargement of the building, elevators or escalators, or the internal structural framework of the building. I.R.C. § 168(k)(3).

---

[7]   The original provision provided a 30-percent first year allowance property placed in service after September 10, 2001, and before May 6, 2003, and a deduction of fifty percent of the adjusted basis of qualified property placed in service after May 5, 2003, and before January 1, 2005.

The first-year deduction is allowed only for qualified property the original use of which commences with the taxpayer. I.R.C. § 168(k)(2)(A)(ii). Staff of the Joint Committee on Taxation, Technical Explanation of the "Job Creation and Worker Assistance Act of 2002" (J.C.T. Rep. No. JCX–12–02, March 6, 2002), explains the original use requirement as follows:

> The term "original use" means the first use to which the property is put, whether or not such use corresponds to the use of such property by the taxpayer. It is intended that, when evaluating whether property qualifies as "original use" the factors used to determine whether property qualified as "new section 38 property" for purposes of the investment tax credit would apply. See Treasury Regulation 1.48–2. Thus, it is intended that additional capital expenditures incurred to recondition or rebuild acquired property (or owned property) would satisfy the "original use" requirement. However, the cost of reconditioned or rebuilt property acquired by the taxpayer would not satisfy the original use requirement. For example, if on February 1, 2002, a taxpayer buys from X for $20,000 a machine that has been previously used by X. Prior to September 11, 2004, the taxpayer makes an expenditure on the property of $5,000 of the type that must be capitalized. Regardless of whether the $5,000 is added to the basis of such property or is capitalized as a separate asset, such amount would be treated as satisfying the "original use" requirement and would be qualified property (assuming all other conditions are met). No part of the $20,000 purchase price would qualify for the additional first year depreciation.

The regulations referred to in the Staff of the Joint Committee explanation contain factors for determining original use under the 10 percent investment tax credit of § 38, which was eliminated in 1986. See also Treas. Reg. § 1.168(k)–1(b)(3).[8]

Qualified property also includes self-constructed tangible property with an estimated production period in excess of two years, or in excess of one year with a cost in excess of $1,000,000, as described in § 263A(f)(1)(B)(ii) and (iii), that has a recovery period of at least 10 years or that is used in the trade or business of transporting persons or property ("transportation property"). I.R.C. § 168(k)(2)(B)(i)(I) and (ii). Property that is required to be depreciated under the alternative depreciation system of § 168(g), supra Part 4.5, is not qualified eligible property for the additional first year write-off of § 168(k).

4.7. *Other Capital Recovery Methods*

Section 168(f)(1) allows an election to exclude property from MACRS rules of § 168 and use an alternative method of depreciation that is not based on a term of years. Property not subject to § 168 is depreciated under § 167. An example is capital recovery based on units of production, miles traveled, or some other method based on units of expected use. Election out of § 168 under § 168(f)(1) is very limited.

---

[8]   The IRS announced that Treas. Reg. § 1.168(k)–1 would apply to property placed in service in 2008 while new guidance is being prepared. I.R. 2008–58, (4/11/2008).

Section 168(f)(3) and (4) exclude films, videos, and sound recordings from the MACRS system under § 168. Capital cost recovery for these items is based on the so-called "income forecast method." Under this approach, the cost of production is allocated over the years the property is expected to produce income in proportion to the anticipated annual income from the film, videotape, or sound recording. This cost recovery method is based on the theory that the decline in productivity of a film, videotape, or sound recording is not dependent upon the mere passage of time. Section 167(g) provides detailed rules regarding the income forecast method of depreciation and limits the use of the income forecast method (and similar methods) of depreciation to copyrights, books, patents, films, videotapes, and sound recordings.

4.8. *General Asset Accounts*

Section 168(i)(4) authorizes aggregation of capital recovery property into one or more "general asset accounts" for purposes of computing capital recovery deductions on an aggregate basis. Treas. Reg. § 1.168(i)–1 allows the taxpayer to elect to group all assets placed in service during a single year that have the same guideline class life into a single account for purposes of computing capital recovery deductions. Capital recovery deductions are computed on the aggregate bases of all assets placed in a general asset account for a particular year. The election to use general asset accounts eliminates the need to compute separately depreciation deductions for each asset used in a trade or business.

To qualify for inclusion in a general asset account, the assets must have the same guideline class life (as specified in Rev. Proc. 87–56, 1987–2 C.B. 674), and must be subject to capital recovery deductions using the same method, recovery period, and convention. A general asset account includes only assets placed in service during the same taxable year. Treas. Reg. § 1.168(i)–1(c)(2)(i)(E).

Treas. Reg. § 1.168(i)–1(e) provides special rules for disposition of assets included in a general asset account. In the event of any disposition of an asset from a general asset account, including retirement or abandonment, the asset is treated as having zero basis. Thus, no loss may be recognized. The full amount realized on disposition is treated as ordinary income to the extent of the total unadjusted bases of all assets in the account, reduced by previously recognized income on dispositions from the account. Any amount realized in excess of the total basis of assets in the account is treated as ordinary or capital gain under special characterization provisions applicable to depreciable property (discussed in Chapter 25). The recoverable basis in the general asset account is not affected by a disposition. Thus, capital recovery deductions continue without alteration. Gain or loss on disposition of all the assets in a general asset account, or on disposition of the last asset in the account, is determined under normal principles. Therefore, basis is recovered on the last disposition from the account. The character of the gain or loss is also determined under generally applicable provisions of the Code for characterizing gain as capital or ordinary.

B. ELECTION TO EXPENSE CERTAIN DEPRECIABLE BUSINESS ASSETS

INTERNAL REVENUE CODE: Section 179(a)–(c), (d)(1).

Section 179 permits a taxpayer (other than an estate or trust) to elect to deduct currently the cost of a limited amount of new or used machinery or equipment and off-the-shelf computer software. The provision allows a taxpayer (other than an estate or trust) to elect to deduct currently the cost of machinery or equipment and off-the-shelf computer software up to $500,000. The deduction is reduced dollar-for-dollar to the extent the cost of property placed in service during the year exceeds $2,000,000. The election under § 179 must be made for each taxable year in which a § 179 expense deduction is claimed. Treas. Reg. § 1.179–5(a).

The deduction under § 179 is limited to the taxpayer's trade or business income for the year, determined prior to the § 179 deduction. Thus, the § 179 deduction allowance can reduce business income to zero but cannot result in a business loss. Any disallowed amount carries over to the following year and is added to the § 179(a) deduction for that year, subject again to the taxable income limitation. I.R.C. § 179(b)(3)(B).

The deduction under § 179 reduces the adjusted basis of property that may be recovered through depreciation under MACRS. To the extent the cost of property for which a § 179 deduction has been allowed exceeds the allowable deduction, MACRS depreciation may be claimed with respect to remaining basis, including the § 168(k) additional first year allowance.

DETAILED ANALYSIS

1. PURCHASE REQUIREMENT

If the purchase price of qualifying property includes both cash and the value of a trade-in, only the amount of the cash payment may be deducted. I.R.C. § 179(d)(3); Treas. Reg. § 1.179–4(d). Under § 179(d)(2), the deduction is not available with respect to property acquired from a related person as defined under § 267, discussed at Chapter 15, Section 2.

2. ELECTION MECHANICS

Under § 179(c) and Treas. Reg. § 1.179–5(a), an election to expense otherwise depreciable assets under § 179 must be made on the taxpayer's first return for the year or on a timely amended return, and cannot be modified without the Commissioner's consent. In Patton v. Commissioner, 116 T.C. 206 (2001), the taxpayer elected to expense a single $4,100 asset. On audit, items that the taxpayer had deducted as "supplies" were reclassified as capital expenditures. The taxpayer attempted to modify the original election to extend it to the capital expenditures determined after the audit, but the court held that the Commissioner did not unreasonably withhold consent to modification of the original election. This is an example of an instance where aggressive reporting on the return foreclosed a subsequent claim of an otherwise available tax benefit that validly could have been claimed at the outset.

A § 179 election must be made on the taxpayer's tax return for the year and must specifically identify the items with respect to which the election applies and the portion of the cost of each of item that is being deducted under § 179. I.R.C. § 179(c)(1) The election is revocable. I.R.C. § 179(c)(2).

3.   THE SUV LIMITATION

Section 179(b)(5) limits the § 179 deduction to $25,000 for the purchase of most sport utility vehicles that have a "gross vehicle weight rating" of not more than 14,000 pounds. This limitation was prompted by concern that vehicles that weigh more than 6,000 pounds, which describes most large sport utility vehicles (some of which appear to have been carefully engineered to have a "gross vehicle weight rating" only slightly in excess of 6,000 pounds), are not subject to the limitations on depreciation deductions for luxury vehicles provided by § 280F, discussed in Chapter 19, Section 4. Because property that is not subject to the § 280F limitations is eligible for § 179 expensing, taxpayers could have reaped a significant tax benefit by purchasing a luxury sport utility vehicle for business use and expensing up to the otherwise applicable § 179 limit of the cost (and applying accelerated depreciation to the remainder of the purchase price in the case of a really expensive SUV, such as a Hummer).

C.   THE FINANCIAL IMPACT OF ACCELERATED COST RECOVERY

Suppose A purchases a machine for $10,000, which A expects will produce $1,500 of income, net of operating expenses, each year for a ten-year period.[9] At the end of the ten-year period, A expects to dispose of the machine for $1,000. Assume that A's marginal tax bracket is 35%, which is the highest marginal rate for both corporations and individuals (in our hypothetical tax system). What is the after-tax impact of various methods of cost recovery?

One useful technique for analyzing the financial impact of A's investment in the machine is to compute the internal rate of return. Internal rate of return is the percentage discount rate on the initial investment that is necessary for A's annual return over the ten-year period (cash flow) to equal the present value of A's $10,000 investment. Comparing the internal rate of return on a before-tax basis and an after-tax basis permits us to determine the actual rate of tax that results from various methods of capital recovery.

Assume for purposes of comparison in the example, that A purchases the machine on the first day of taxable year one, and that the returns are realized on the last day of taxable years one through ten. In the absence

---

[9]   Assuming a constant annual return from an investment presents an unlikely scenario, which, perhaps is useful only to simplify the comparison. Changing the annual returns in each of the examples, while altering after-tax returns to some extent, does not significantly change the comparative reductions in effective tax rates.

of tax, A receives $1,500 each year for the first nine years. In year ten, on the last day of the year, A collects $1,500 of income from the machine and sells the machine for its $1,000 salvage value. Before tax, the internal rate of return on the $10,000 investment is 9.106 percent. In other words, if the present value of A's $1,500 annual cash flow plus the salvage value is to equal A's initial $10,000 investment, the required rate of return on the investment is 9.106 percent.

If A's income from the investment were fully taxed at a 35 percent rate, A's after-tax rate of return would be reduced to 5.919 percent (9.106% − [9.106% × 35%]); the after-tax rate of return under a 35 percent tax would be 65% of the before tax rate of return. The effective rate of tax on income from an asset can be determined by dividing the after-tax internal rate of return by the before-tax internal rate of return and subtracting the result from one, e.g., 1 − (5.919/9.106) = 0.35. Thus, if the effective tax rate is 35 percent, the before-tax rate of return of 9.106 percent produces an after-tax rate of return of 5.919 percent. A capital recovery scheme that provides capital recovery deductions that precisely equal economic depreciation will produce an internal rate of return that is exactly equivalent to the before-tax rate of return reduced by the tax rate.

Expensing

Periodically there are proposals in Congress to dispense with the complexities of depreciation and simply allow taxpayers to fully deduct capital investment in the year property is placed in service.[10] The first year expensing allowed under § 179 and the on-again-off-again fifty percent first year allowance in § 168(k) are moves in this direction. Allowing a deduction for the full cost of capital expenditure obviously will fail to match the cost with the income produced by the investment. The effect is dramatic. In the example above, in the year A's machine is placed in service, A would have a $10,000 deduction that could result in a tax savings of $3,500.[11] The deduction reduces A's after-tax cost of the machine to $6,500 (the $10,000 cost minus A's $3,500 tax savings). At the end of the first year, and at the end of each of the next eight years, the machine returns $1,500 before-taxes. A will have to pay tax on the full $1,500 of income because there is no further capital cost to recover against that income. A's after tax return each year is $975 ($1,500 − [$1,500 × 0.35]). In year ten, after disposition of the machine for $1,000, and paying tax on the gain, A's after-tax return will be $1,625.[12] The internal rate of return on A's initial $6,500 net investment that annually returns $975 after-tax, plus the after-tax salvage value recovered in year

---

[10] This proposal would extend § 179 to all investment in income producing property.

[11] The $3,500 saving comes from the reduction in taxes on $10,000 of income from other sources that is offset by the deduction.

[12] $1,500 of income plus $1,000 of gain on sale. This is assuming that the gain will be taxed as ordinary income at the 35% rate. Capital gains treatment would increase the after-tax return.

ten, is 9.106 percent, the same as the rate of return in a no-tax world. The effective rate of tax on A's income from the machine is zero. In other words, allowing immediate expensing of capital investment is the economic equivalent of exempting the income from the capital investment from taxation.

Straight Line Depreciation

Straight line depreciation over the useful life of an asset that economically depreciates at the same rate as the asset in the example, with salvage value taken into account, will produce an after-tax return that is slightly better than economic depreciation. The straight-line method of depreciation would allocate A's recoverable cost of $9,000 (A's $10,000 cost less $1,000 salvage value) equally to each of the ten years the asset is used in the production of income. Thus A would be allowed a deduction of $900 each year. If the machine annually produces $1,500 of gross income, and thus $600 of taxable income after depreciation is deducted, the annual after-tax return from the machine in years one through nine is $1,290 ($1,500 − [$600 × 0.35]). In year ten, when the machine is sold for $1,000, A receives the annual after-tax return of $1,290 plus $1,000 as the tax-free recovery of basis (salvage value). The after-tax internal rate of return of A's investment using straight line depreciation is 6.106 percent. Compare this to the after-tax internal rate of return of A's investment (9.106%) if the capital cost is expensed in the year incurred. The after-tax internal rate of return under the straight-line method is about 67 percent of the before-tax rate of return. Nevertheless, straight-line depreciation does not match economic depreciation, which, as discussed above, would have produced an internal after-tax rate of return to 5.919 percent, which is 65 percent of the before-tax rate of return, thus reflecting a return that bears the full burden of a 35 percent tax rate. A's effective tax rate using straight-line depreciation is 32.95 percent (1 − (6.106%/9.106%)), slightly lower than the nominal 35 percent rate. The effective tax rate using straight line depreciation is lower than the tax rate with economic depreciation because the straight-line rate tends to provide larger deductions in the early years than would be allowed using economic depreciation rates.

Straight line depreciation calculated by ignoring salvage value, thereby allowing a full $1,000 depreciation deduction each year, increases the internal rate of return to 6.234 percent and would reduce A's effective tax rate to 31.54 percent. On the other hand, if an asset actually suffered greater economic depreciation in the first few years of its useful life than in the later years, straight-line depreciation might result in an effective tax rate higher than the statutory rate.

Double Declining Balance Capital Recovery

Before the 1981 revisions, which shortened useful lives and eliminated salvage value from the computation, the double declining balance method roughly compensated for the assertion that straight-line depreciation was too slow, as well as providing an incentive to capital investment with lower effective tax rates on depreciable business property. As noted in the previous section, the declining balance method provides larger depreciation deductions in the early years of an asset's useful life than are available under the straight line method, and smaller annual deductions in the later years of the asset's useful life, thereby accelerating the rate of capital recovery. Using 200 percent declining balance depreciation, the annual depreciation deduction for A's machine is computed by multiplying the remaining undepreciated adjusted basis of the machine by 20 percent, 200 percent of the ten percent rate allowed with straight line recovery. Salvage value was ignored in computing the annual depreciation allowance under the declining balance method, but an asset could not be depreciated below its salvage value. Table 1 illustrates the annual depreciation deductions from A's $10,000 machine with a ten-year life using the double declining balance method, and the resulting after-tax cash flow.

TABLE 1
Double Declining Balance Depreciation
Ten-Year Useful Life

Year End	Gross Income	Capital Recovery[2]	Remaining Basis	Taxable Income	After-Tax Return
0	($10,000)				($10,000)
1	$ 1,500	$ 2,000	$ 8,000	($ 500)	$ 1,675[4]
2	$ 1,500	$ 1,600	$ 6,400	($ 100)	$ 1,600[4]
3	$ 1,500	$ 1,280	$ 5,120	$ 220	$ 1,423
4	$ 1,500	$ 1,024	$ 4,096	$ 476	$ 1,333
5	$ 1,500	$ 819	$ 3,277	$ 681	$ 1,262
6	$ 1,500	$ 655	$ 2,622	$ 845	$ 1,204
7	$ 1,500	$ 524	$ 2,098	$ 976	$ 1,158
8	$ 1,500	$ 420	$ 1,678	$ 1,080	$ 1,122
9	$ 1,500	$ 336	$ 1,342	$ 1,164	$ 1,093
10	$ 2,500	$ 268	$ 1,074	$ 1,158[5]	$ 2,095
Totals	$ 16,000	$ 8,926		$ 6,000	$ 3,900

Internal Rate of Return   6.6%

Notes to Table 1
1.   All figures are rounded to the nearest dollar.
2.   Depreciation is 20% of the remaining adjusted basis.
3.   Cash income from the machine less tax at the 35% rate.

4.   Includes tax savings on other income because of the loss.

5.   Reflects $1,000 of proceeds on disposition of the machine and a $74 loss deduction.

Note that as compared to straight line depreciation double declining balance depreciation reduces taxable income in the early years of the asset's useful life and increases taxable income in the later years. Acceleration of capital cost recovery into earlier years increases the after-tax rate of return of the investment over the after-tax rate of return that is achieved with straight line depreciation. The after-tax internal rate of return of A's investment using double declining balance depreciation is 6.6 percent, which reduces A's effective rate of tax on income from the machine from the statutory rate of 35 percent to 27.5 percent.

MACRS

The shorter recovery period and provision for recovery of salvage value provided by the modified cost recovery system of the 1986 Act provides a further reduction in the effective tax rate on income from depreciable property. If the ADR midpoint life of A's $10,000 machine is ten years, the machine is classified as seven year property. The midyear convention of § 168(d)(1) and (4), discussed supra at Section 1.A.4.3., requires that the machine be treated as placed in service during the middle of the year, thereby allowing only one-half of a full year's depreciation in the first year, and providing one-half year's depreciation in the eighth year. Depreciating the machine under MACRS, will yield the results set out in Table 2.

TABLE 2
MACRS Depreciation
Seven Year Recovery Period

Year End	Gross Income	Capital Recovery[2]	Remaining Basis	Taxable Income	After-Tax Return
0	($10,000)				($10,000)
1	$ 1,500	$ 1,429[4]	$8,571	$ 71	$ 1,475
2	$ 1,500	$ 2,449	$6,122	($ 949)	$ 1,832
3	$ 1,500	$ 1,749	$4,373	($ 249)	$ 1,587
4	$ 1,500	$ 1,249	$3,124	$ 251	$ 1,412
5	$ 1,500	$ 893[5]	$2,231	$ 607	$ 1,288
6	$ 1,500	$ 892	$1,339	$ 608	$ 1,287
7	$ 1,500	$ 893	$ 446	$ 607	$ 1,288
8	$ 1,500	$ 446	$ 0	$1,054	$ 1,131
9	$ 1,500		$ 0	$1,500	$ 975
10	$ 2,500		$ 0	$2,500	$ 1,625
Totals	$16,000	$10,000		$6,000	$13,900

Internal Rate of Return   6.872%

Notes to Table 2
1. All figures are rounded to the nearest dollar.
2. The depreciation rate is 28.57% (1/7 × 2).
3. The after-tax return is the cash income from the machine less tax at the 35% rate.
4. Accounts for the one-half year convention of § 168(d)(1).
5. Depreciation shifts to straight line in year 5.
6. Includes $1,000 gain on disposition of the machine.

MACRS capital recovery increases the after-tax rate of return on A's investment to 6.87 percent. The effective rate of tax on income from A's machine drops to 24.5 percent.

The added first-year 50-percent allowance of § 168(k), see supra Section 1.C., increases the internal rate of return form A's investment to 7.49 percent and reduces A's effective tax rate to 17.72 percent. This result occurs because allowing 50 percent of the cost to be deducted in the first year, and then allowing depreciation of the remaining 50 percent of the cost, including first year depreciation, results in a system that more nearly approximates expensing, see supra Section 1.A.4.6., than capitalization and depreciation.

As Table 3 demonstrates, accelerating the rate of recovery of capital cost by shortening the recovery period and increasing capital recovery deductions in the early years of an asset's useful life, increases the after-tax return of an investment over the rate of return that would be available if only economic depreciation were allowed.

TABLE 3

Comparison of the Present After-Tax Internal Rates of Return and Effective Tax Rates on A's $10,000 Investment

	Internal Rate of Return	Effective Tax Rate
Economic Depreciation (income fully taxed)	5.919	35.0
Straight Line Depreciation	6.106	32.95
Double Declining Balance	6.600	27.52
MACRS	6.872	24.54
MACRS with § 168(k) allowance	7.493	17.72
Immediate Expensing	9.106	0

Given the increased value of expensing to business investors, it is no wonder that there is a strong lobby for expensing as a subsidy to business investment.

DETAILED ANALYSIS

1. TAX EXPENDITURE ANALYSIS

Tax expenditure analysis provides another method by which accelerated cost recovery methods can be evaluated. As the tax expenditure list indicates (see Chapter 11, Section 1.C.), accelerated depreciation for tangible personal property in excess of the alternative depreciation system[13] results in significant revenue losses to the federal treasury. As the above analysis has shown, acceleration of capital cost recovery results in a deferral of tax liability. Under tax expenditure analysis, this deferral of tax is the equivalent of an interest-free loan by the government to taxpayers who make qualifying investments. The loan is granted in the year(s) in which accelerated depreciation exceeds economic depreciation (or its surrogate) and is repaid in the year(s) in which allowable depreciation is less than economic depreciation, as illustrated in Table 4. The amount of the loan is a function of the taxpayer's marginal tax bracket. Thus, in the examples, if A were allowed to deduct the entire $10,000 cost in year one, A would receive an interest free loan of $3,294 (35% of the excess of $10,000 over $589). The loan would be repaid in years two through ten as A would have no depreciation

---

[13]   The alternative depreciation system is discussed at Section 1.A.4.5.

deductions in those years. At a 9.106 percent discount rate, the present value of A's interest free loan is $1,171, and A's economic cost for the machine cost has been reduced by that amount. A similar analysis can be made of the other methods of accelerated capital cost recovery discussed above. In the case of accelerated depreciation under MACRS, the tax benefit of early deductions is repaid with reduced depreciation in later years. Using MACRS, A receives an interest free loan in years one through five of 35 percent of the amount by which accelerated cost recovery deductions exceed economic depreciation, A repays that loan in years six through ten when economic depreciation is greater than cost recovery allowed under MACRS.

TABLE 4
Comparison of Economic Depreciation and MACRS

Year	MACRS	Economic Depreciation[1]	Difference	Loan (Repayment)[2]
1	$ 1,429	$ 589	$ 840	$294
2	$ 2,449	$ 643	$ 643	$643
3	$ 1,749	$ 702	$1,047	$366
4	$ 1,249	$ 766	$ 483	$169
5	$ 893	$ 835	$ 58	$ 20
6	$ 892	$ 911	($ 19)	($ 7)
7	$ 893	$ 994	($ 101)	($ 35)
8	$ 446	$1,085	($ 639)	($224)
9		$1,184	($1,184)	($414)
10		$1,291	($1,291)	($452)
	$10,000	$9,000	$1,000	($350)[3]

Notes to Table 4

1.   Represents the annual decrease in the present value of the future income stream of $1,500 per year plus $1,000 salvage value in year 10.

2.   35% of the difference in capital recovery representing tax savings or additional tax cost.

3.   This $350 represents tax on realized gain on disposition of the machine. It would be eliminated in year ten by accounting for the tax on disposition in that year when the full loan repayment is $802.

At a 9.106 percent discount rate, the present value of the interest free loan attributable to accelerated recovery under MACRS is $556. Thus the economic cost of A's investment is reduced by that amount.

Since the amount of the interest free loan is a function of a taxpayer's marginal tax rate, a business taxpayer who is in a loss position for tax purposes in the year of investment (such as a startup business) receives no loan in that year. Correspondingly, the value of the loan is much less than A's in the above example since the loan program cannot be taken advantage of until the year in which the year one depreciation deduction can be utilized by means of a net operating loss carryover. Likewise, business taxpayers subject to marginal rates lower than 35 percent will receive smaller loans than A's and hence a lesser subsidy from the government. These results follow even though all the businesses made identical investments which are of equal value to the economy.

The question raised in Chapter 11, Section 1.C.5. must be applied to tax expenditures that are the equivalents of interest free loans. For example, is there a need for the subsidy? Would a comparable direct loan program determine the size of a loan by the size of the taxpayer's taxable income rather than, for example, the size of the investment? Is it appropriate that the tax expenditure loans are unsecured?

2.   IMPLICIT TAX

A sophisticated investor will analyze an investment from the standpoint of its after-tax rate of return. The comparative analysis above assumes that A will bear the full burden of the taxes, and reap the full benefit of the tax subsidy available through accelerated capital recovery. In reality, a taxpayer in a 35 percent tax bracket who might expect to derive a nine percent before-tax rate of return will be motivated to invest in an activity that will provide an after-tax rate of return of anything in excess of 5.85 percent (9% [9% × 35%]). Taxpayer A in the examples in the principal section, expecting a 9.106 percent before tax-return, may be willing to pay a higher price for a machine that produces a slightly better after-tax rate of return than a fully taxed investment. For example, if A were to purchase the machine for $10,800, which would increase A's first year recovery and capital recovery deductions under MACRS on the higher basis, A's after-tax rate of return would be 6.15 percent and A's effective tax rate on the investment would be 32.52 percent. In this case, A has traded a reduction in explicit taxes from 35 to 33 percent for the implicit tax embedded in the $800 purchase price increase.

The benefit of the tax subsidy transferred to the seller/manufacturer of A's machine in the form of a higher price may provide an incentive to the manufacturer to expand its operations by investing more capital in the business and employing more workers (according to supply-side economic theory). In that fashion, the tax expenditure of accelerated capital recovery, as well as other tax incentives for investment, is expected to influence capital investment.

3.   CREDITS

In some instances Congress has provided tax subsidies for investment in specified capital assets by means of tax credits. See Chapter 17.

SECTION 2.   STATUTORY AMORTIZATION OF INTANGIBLE ASSETS

INTERNAL REVENUE CODE: Section 197(a)–(e), (f)(1), (3), (7).

REGULATIONS: Sections 1.167(a)–3; –14(b); 1.197–2(a)–(c).

Revenue Reconciliation Act of 1993, Report of the Committee on Ways and Means, House of Representatives

H.Rep. No. 103–111, 103 Cong., 1st. Sess., 760–762 (1993).

[Pre-1993] Law.

In determining taxable income for Federal income tax purposes, a taxpayer is allowed depreciation or amortization deductions for the cost or other basis of intangible property that is used in a trade or business or held for the production of income if the property has a limited useful life that may be determined with reasonable accuracy. Treas. Reg. sec. 1.167(a)–(3). These Treasury Regulations also state that no depreciation deductions are allowed with respect to goodwill.

The U.S. Supreme Court recently held that a taxpayer able to prove that a particular asset can be valued, and that the asset has a limited useful life which can be ascertained with reasonable accuracy, may depreciate the value over the useful life regardless of how much the asset appears to reflect the expectancy of continued patronage. However, the Supreme Court also characterized the taxpayer's burden of proof as "substantial" and stated that it "often will prove too great to bear." Newark Morning Ledger Co. v. United States, [507 U.S. 546 (1993)] * * * .

Reasons for Change

The Federal income tax treatment of the costs of acquiring intangible assets is a source of considerable controversy between taxpayers and the Internal Revenue Service. Disputes arise concerning (1) whether an amortizable intangible asset exists; (2) in the case of an acquisition of a trade or business, the portion of the purchase price that is allocable to an amortizable intangible asset; and (3) the proper method and period for recovering the cost of an amortizable intangible asset. These types of disputes can be expected to continue to arise, even after the decision of the U.S. Supreme Court in Newark Morning Ledger Co. v. United States, supra.

It is believed that much of the controversy that arises under present law with respect to acquired intangible assets could be eliminated by specifying a single method and period for recovering the cost of most acquired intangible assets and by treating acquired goodwill and going concern value as amortizable intangible assets. It is also believed that there is no need at this time to change the Federal income tax treatment of self-created intangible assets, such as goodwill that is created through advertising and other similar expenditures.

Accordingly, the bill requires the cost of most acquired intangible assets, including goodwill and going concern value, to be amortized ratably over a [15]-year period. It is recognized that the useful lives of certain acquired intangible assets to which the bill applies may be shorter than [15] years, while the useful lives of other acquired intangible assets to which the bill applies may be longer than [15] years.

Explanation of Provision

In General.

The bill allows an amortization deduction with respect to the capitalized costs of certain intangible property (defined as a "section 197 intangible") that is acquired by a taxpayer and that is held by the taxpayer in connection with the conduct of a trade or business or an activity engaged in for the production of income. The amount of the deduction is determined by amortizing the adjusted basis (for purposes of determining gain) of the intangible ratably over a [15]-year period that begins with the month that the intangible is acquired. No other depreciation or amortization deduction is allowed with respect to a section 197 intangible that is acquired by a taxpayer.

In general, the bill applies to a section 197 intangible acquired by a taxpayer regardless of whether it is acquired as part of a trade or business. * * * The bill generally does not apply to a section 197 intangible that is created by the taxpayer if the intangible is not created in connection with a transaction (or series of related transactions) that involves the acquisition of a trade or business or a substantial portion thereof.

Except in the case of amounts paid or incurred under certain covenants not to compete (or under certain other arrangements that have substantially the same effect as covenants not to compete) and certain amounts paid or incurred on account of the transfer of a franchise, trademark, or trade name, the bill generally does not apply to any amount that is otherwise currently deductible (i.e., not capitalized) under present law.

* * *

The term "section 197 intangible" is defined as any property that is included in any one or more of the following categories: (1) goodwill and going concern value; (2) certain specified types of intangible property that generally relate to workforce, information base, know-how, customers, suppliers, or other similar items; (3) any license, permit, or other right granted by a governmental unit or an agency or instrumentality thereof; (4) any covenant not to compete (or other arrangement to the extent that the arrangement has substantially the same effect as a covenant not to compete) entered into in connection with the direct or indirect acquisition of an interest in a trade or business (or a substantial portion thereof); and (5) any franchise, trademark, or trade name.

Certain types of property, however, are specifically excluded from the definition of the term "section 197 intangible." The term "section 197 intangible" does not include: (1) any interest in a corporation, partnership, trust, or estate; (2) any interest under an existing futures contract, foreign currency contract, notional principal contract, interest rate swap, or other similar financial contract; (3) any interest in land; (4) certain computer software; (5) certain interests in films, sound recordings, video tapes, books, or other similar property; (6) certain rights to receive tangible property or services; (7) certain interests in patents or copyrights; (8) any interest under an existing lease of tangible property; (9) any interest under an existing indebtedness (except for the deposit base and similar items of a financial institution); (10) a franchise to engage in any professional sport, and any item acquired in connection with such a franchise; and (11) certain transaction costs.

In addition, the Treasury Department is authorized to issue regulations that exclude certain rights of fixed duration or amount from the definition of a section 197 intangible.

* * *

DETAILED ANALYSIS

1. GENERAL

Congress enacted § 197 to deal comprehensively with the amortization of intangibles. Section 197 both allows and requires taxpayers to amortize the basis of most intangible assets ratably over 15 years, beginning with the month in which the asset was acquired, without regard to whether the asset is a depreciable asset under the standards of § 167. Thus, § 197 allows amortization of the cost basis of purchased goodwill, going concern value, workforce in place, renewable contract and licenses, trademarks, and tradenames, all of which were nondepreciable under prior law. Section 197 is a double-edged sword, however. Intangibles, such as customer lists, bank core deposits, and advantageous contracts, which taxpayers under prior law frequently succeeded in depreciating over a relatively short life, must be amortized over 15 years, even though they actually have a much shorter useful life. Section 197(b) prohibits the use of any cost recovery method other than 15-year amortization for assets to which it applies. In addition to eliminating controversies regarding useful lives, § 197 has reduced controversies regarding allocation of the purchase price among various intangible assets because all the assets have the same amortization period.

2. "AMORTIZABLE SECTION 197 INTANGIBLES"

Subject to an exclusion for certain "self-created intangibles" in § 197(c)(2), any intangible asset listed in § 197(d) that is acquired by the taxpayer and held for use in the taxpayer's trade or business is subject to

15-year amortization. The sweep of § 197(d) is broad, including: (1) goodwill, (2) going concern value, (3) workforce in place, (4) information base assets, such as business books and records and customer lists, (5) technological knowledge and rights, including patents, copyrights, formulae, processes, designs, patterns, know-how, and similar items, (6) customer-based intangibles, such as, market share, contractual relationships, or core deposits of a financial institution, (7) supplier-based intangibles, such as favorable relationships, credit rating, etc., (8) licenses, permits or other rights granted by any governmental authority, (9) covenants not to compete, and (10) franchises, trademarks, and tradenames. This broad list applies only to intangible assets that are acquired by the taxpayer from another person, including certain assets created in the transaction, such as a covenant not to compete.

Section 197(c)(2) generally limits the application of the fifteen-year amortization rule to the following self-created assets: (1) licenses, permits, and other rights granted by a governmental authority such as a liquor license or taxi medallion, (2) franchises (as defined in § 1253(b)(1)), tradenames, or trademarks, and (3) covenants not to complete. If § 197 does not apply, normal depreciation rules govern. Thus for example, because a patent is not listed in § 197(c)(2), any capitalized costs relating to a self-created patent, in contrast to a patent purchased as part of a going business, would be depreciable over the life of the patent under § 167. Likewise, self-created copyrights on computer software are depreciable over 36 months under § 167(f)(1). On the other hand, a covenant not to compete must be amortized over 15 years under § 197, regardless of the term of the covenant or the period over which payments are made, even if the covenant is entered into pursuant to the acquisition of the interest of one of the owners of a business by the remaining owner. See Treas. Reg. § 1.197–2(b)(9); Frontier Chevrolet Co. v. Commissioner, 329 F.3d 1131 (9th Cir.2003) (§ 197 applied to a covenant not to compete entered into when a corporation redeemed the stock of a 75-percent owner). Recovery Group, Inc. v. Commissioner, 652 F.3d 122 (1st Cir. 2011), held that a $400,000 payment by a corporation to a retiring 23 percent shareholder/employee for a one-year covenant not to compete was amortizable over 15 years under § 197 because the covenant was part of an acquisition of an interest in a trade or business. The court rejected the taxpayer's argument that the term "§ 197 intangible" includes covenants not to compete executed in connection with stock purchases only if the stock being purchased comprises a substantial portion of the outstanding stock.

The regulations provide a variety of special rules. For example, Treas. Reg. § 1.197–2(b)(8) provides that § 197 applies to permits and licenses issued by a governmental authority only if the permit or license is for an indefinite period or is reasonably expected to be renewed indefinitely. Permits relating to the use of real property, which otherwise would be subject to fifteen-year amortization, are not subject to § 197. Instead, the cost of such a permit or license is capitalized as part of the basis of the real estate. Treas. Reg. § 1.197–2(c)(3).

3.   EXCLUDED INTANGIBLE ASSETS

3.1. *General*

Section 197(e) in all cases excludes from the fifteen-year amortization rule: (1) financial interests, such as futures contracts, partnership interests and interests in trusts, (2) interests in land, such as easements and life estates, (3) computer software other than custom computer software acquired together with the other assets of a trade or business, (4) interests in leases of tangible property, and (5) interests (whether as a debtor or creditor) in a debt instrument. In addition, § 197(e)(4) provides that certain intangibles are subject to § 197 only if acquired in connection with the acquisition of other assets constituting a trade or business or a substantial portion of a trade or business (under the principles of § 1060). This category includes (1) interests in movies, recordings, videotapes, and books, (2) interests in patents and copyrights, (3) certain government contracts, (4) certain contract rights with a life of less than 15 years, and (5) mortgage servicing contracts.

To depreciate assets that are excluded from § 197, the taxpayer must establish that the asset has a limited useful life or recovery period. The Code and regulations provide special rules for certain intangible assets. Computer software is depreciable over 36 months under § 167(f)(1), and the cost of a lease acquired for a specific sum in addition to periodic rent is recoverable over the term of the lease, Treas. Reg. § 1.162–11(a). Those patents and copyrights excluded from § 197 are depreciable over their useful lives. See Treas. Reg. § 1.167(a)–14(c)(4). Thus, for example, a patent with 12 remaining years that is purchased outright and separately from the seller's business is depreciable over that period; if the patent were acquired as a constituent part of acquiring the seller's business, however, the portion of the purchase price allocated to the patent must be amortized over 15 years under § 197.

3.2. *Safe Harbor Amortization of Intangible Assets Not subject to Section 197*

Treas. Reg. § 1.167(a)–3(b) permits amortization of the basis of most intangibles that do not have readily ascertainable useful lives and for which a specific amortization or depreciation period is not specified in the Code or regulations, and for which amortization or depreciation is not proscribed. Unless the IRS provides a different amortization period by published guidance, the "safe-harbor" amortization period is fifteen years, using a straight-line method with no salvage value. Thus, for example, an amount paid to obtain a trade association membership of indefinite duration would be amortizable over fifteen years. The amortization rule does not apply to intangible assets acquired from another party or to self-created financial interests, but these intangibles may be amortizable under § 197 or under other provisions of the Code or regulations. Intangibles that have a readily ascertainable useful life are amortized over that life. The investment in financial instruments, such as promissory notes, bonds, stock and other securities, however, is never amortizable.

4.   DISPOSITIONS OF SECTION 197 INTANGIBLES

When a taxpayer acquires two or more § 197 intangible assets in a single transaction, § 197(f)(1) disallows any loss deduction under § 165 on the sale or worthlessness of any of the assets as long as the taxpayer retains at least one of them. The purpose of this rule is to eliminate purchase price allocation questions that otherwise would arise when the purchaser of a going business abandons some, but not all, of the intangible assets of the business shortly after the acquisition. For example, if the taxpayer purchases three tradenames, a trademark, and a customer list and immediately abandons all three tradenames, no loss deduction is allowed with respect to the basis allocated to the tradenames. The basis of the abandoned intangibles is reallocated among the remaining intangible assets, in this case the trademark and the customer list. See Treas. Reg. § 1.197–2(g)(1)(i)(A). A special rule applies to covenants not to compete. No loss may be claimed with respect to a covenant not to compete until the taxpayer has disposed of a substantial portion of the trade or business in connection with the acquisition of which the covenant was a part. I.R.C. § 197(f)(1)(B).

5.   ASSESSMENT

Section 197 is an arbitrary solution to difficult problems involved in estimating useful lives and values. In this respect the basis for the provision is similar to that of MACRS, discussed at Section 1.A.4., which was introduced in part to eliminate disputes about useful lives and salvage value. As in the case of § 168, § 197 provides an identical cost recovery period for widely divergent assets, including assets with a useful life so long that for practical purposes the useful life could be called perpetual. Thus the § 197 regime does not reflect optimal economic depreciation. As a result, the effective rate of tax on income from intangible assets may be significantly greater than or less than the nominal tax rate. Furthermore, it gives rise to different cost recovery periods for assets otherwise the same (e.g., patents, copyrights, government contracts) depending on the circumstances of the acquisition. The justification for the approach taken in § 197 is administrative convenience and taxpayer simplicity; it reduces the number of controversies involving basis allocation and useful life issues. Nevertheless, some mundane administrative problems persist. For example, if a taxpayer purchases two or more amortizable § 197 intangibles for a lump sum, each asset still must be allocated a separate basis because gain may be recognized on a subsequent disposition.

SECTION 3.   EXPENSING AND AMORTIZATION PROVISIONS

INTERNAL REVENUE CODE: Sections 169(a); 174(a)(1), (b)(1); 198.

In addition to the basic capital recovery provisions, the Code contains special rules dealing with capital cost recovery in various specific situations. These rules can be divided into two categories. The first category includes provisions that resolve a difficult accounting or technical problem by establishing an arbitrary rule that resolves the treatment of the expenditure involved such as provisions for five-year amortization of start-up expenses and business organization expenditures discussed in Chapter 13, Section 6.

The second category involves special rules that function as tax expenditures for the treatment of certain capital costs. In general, these rules allow a more rapid recovery of the capitalized cost than would be available under normal rules. Sometimes the cost is recovered over an arbitrary period, such as 60 months. In other situations, the capital cost is deductible in full in the year incurred. Treating the capital expenditure as a current expense is the most extreme form of "accelerated" capital cost recovery because, as discussed at Section 1.C., the effective tax rate on income from capital investment that is immediately expensed is zero. The following material discusses various tax expenditures provided for specific types of investment or business activity.

DETAILED ANALYSIS

1.   RESEARCH AND EXPERIMENTAL EXPENDITURES

Section 174 allows the deduction of research and experimental costs that otherwise would have to be capitalized. It also allows an election to recover costs over a period of not less than 60 months in situations in which the costs are capitalized but not otherwise depreciable because a useful life cannot be definitely determined. Section 174(e) specifically limits the election to deduct or amortize research and development expenses to amounts that are reasonable under the circumstances. Expenses which are neither deducted nor amortized under § 174 are capitalized. Treas. Reg. § 1.174–1.

The § 174 option is available only with respect to expenditures incurred in connection with a taxpayer's trade or business. See Best Universal Lock Co., Inc. v. Commissioner, 45 T.C. 1 (1965) (Acq.) (inventor with some 100 patents obtained over a 45-year period is in the trade or business of inventing even where no income has yet been received from the items with respect to which research and development expenses had been incurred); Rev. Rul. 71–162, 1971–1 C.B. 97 (research and experimental expenditures in seeking to develop new products or processes unrelated to the current product lines or manufacturing processes of the taxpayer's trade or business qualify under § 174); Stanton v. Commissioner, 399 F.2d 326 (5th Cir.1968) (expenditures incurred to develop a stormproof door were not deductible under § 174 since the taxpayer's inventing activities were irregular and sporadic).

In Snow v. Commissioner, 416 U.S. 500 (1974), the Supreme Court held that expenditures incurred by a limited partnership involved in the development of a product, but which had not yet made any sales of the product, were "in connection with" a trade or business for purposes of § 174. The Court interpreted the "in connection with" phrase in § 174 as broader in scope than the "carrying on" trade or business phrase in § 162 so that presumably a taxpayer can obtain a deduction under § 174 even though other expenses would be subject to the limits of § 195, discussed in Chapter 13,

Section 6. This liberal interpretation does not seem supported by the legislative history of § 174.

Notwithstanding the broad concept of "business" in *Snow*, deductions under § 174 are not available for mere passive investors in a research venture who expect to receive only royalties because of an exclusive license to exploit the potential of new knowledge that has been granted before development commenced. See e.g., Spellman v. Commissioner, 845 F.2d 148 (7th Cir.1988); Harris v. Commissioner, 16 F.3d 75 (5th Cir.1994) (denying the § 174 deduction because the taxpayer did not prove that the holder of an option to acquire a perpetual exclusive license to exploit the research would not exercise the option).

2.   POLLUTION CONTROL FACILITIES

Section 169 provides that investment in certified pollution control facilities installed in plants in existence before 1976 may be amortized over a period of five years. Facilities must be certified both by applicable state and federal agencies. The facilities for which the funds are expended may not significantly increase the output or capacity, extend the useful life or reduce the total operating costs of the plant, or alter the nature of the manufacturing or production process or facility. The definition of certified pollution control facilities includes facilities that prevent the "creation or emission of" pollutants. Section 169 applies only to tangible personal property, a rule that some pollution control experts have criticized because a "hardware" solution is not always the best response to a pollution problem.

When § 169 was made permanent in 1976, the Senate Finance Committee Report stated that it was reenacting this section because it "is necessary in order to provide a tax incentive for installing pollution control equipment. This equipment is placed in service because public policy now requires that the cost of dealing with pollution be included in the prices of products as a cost of production. This transfers the cost burden of removing pollution created by the production processes to the consumers of the product from the victims of pollution. * * * In recognition of this addition to a businessman's capital costs because of a change in public policy, the committee believes that this additional assistance in reducing the cost burden is appropriate." S.Rep. No. 94–938, 94th Cong., 2d Sess. 418 (1976). The Senate Finance Committee appeared to think it obvious that part of the costs to install pollution control devices should be shifted from consumers of products manufactured by the installing plant to the general taxpaying public. Many economists would question that conclusion.

3.   OTHER PROVISIONS

A number of other provisions provide for the current deduction or amortization of expenditures that would otherwise be required to be capitalized. These include § 173 (current deduction of circulation expenditures of magazines, newspapers and other periodicals); § 175 (current deduction of soil and water conservation costs of farmers); § 190 (current deduction of up to $15,000 of expenses incurred to remove architectural and transportation barriers to the handicapped and elderly);

and § 192 (current deductions for contributions to a trust to fund black lung benefits for employees).

SECTION 4.   CAPITAL RECOVERY FOR NATURAL RESOURCES

Section 611 provides that "[i]n the cases of mines, oil and gas wells, other natural deposits, and timber, there shall * * * be a reasonable allowance for depletion * * * according to the peculiar conditions in each case. * * * " Depletion is the cost recovery mechanism used with respect to the capitalized costs of acquiring an interest in a mineral deposit in the ground. Both the mechanics and policy analysis of depletion are complex, because it comes in two varieties, cost depletion, which permits only ratable recovery of the taxpayer's basis in the mineral deposit, and percentage depletion (under §§ 613 and 613A) which allows deductions in excess of the taxpayer's basis for the mineral deposit. The depletion allowance in a taxable year is the greater of percentage depletion or cost depletion.

Originally, the purpose of the depletion allowance was to allow a taxpayer a tax-free recoupment of the taxpayer's investment in a mineral deposit in recognition of mineral deposits as wasting assets. Depletion often is analogized to depreciation, but it also can be analogized to the cost of goods sold. See United States v. Ludey, 274 U.S. 295, 301 (1927). These analogies are quite true regarding cost depletion, but percentage depletion has an entirely different purpose as acknowledged by the Supreme Court in United States v. Swank, 451 U.S. 571 (1981), where the Court stated: "Because the deduction is computed as a percentage of his gross income from the mining operation and is not computed with reference to the operator's investment, it provides a special incentive for engaging in this line of business that goes well beyond a purpose of merely allowing the owner of a wasting asset to recoup the capital investment in that asset." Thus, percentage depletion is a tax expenditure. See Chapter 11, Section 1.C. Nevertheless, for a taxpayer engaged in extracting and selling minerals, the entire depletion allowance is treated as entering into the cost of goods sold rather than as a deduction. Treas. Reg. § 1.263A–1(e)(3)(ii)(J).

In addition, a number of expenditures that would be capitalized if treated in the same manner as analogous expenditures in other industries may be deducted currently when incurred by taxpayers involved in the extraction of natural resources. Both mining and oil and gas share, although under different but analogous provisions, a preferential deduction for the costs of preparing for extraction. These costs are clearly capital costs and analogous expenditures in other industries are capitalized. Mine exploration costs are currently deductible under § 617, and mine development expenses are currently deducted under § 616. Oil and gas well drilling expenses are largely deducted under § 263(c). None of these provisions is subject to the uniform capitalization rules of § 263A. See I.R.C. § 263A(c)(3). All of these provisions also are tax expenditures.

DETAILED ANALYSIS

1.   THE DEPLETION ALLOWANCE

1.1. *Computing the Depletion Allowance*

Section 613(a) provides that the depletion allowance for a taxable year is the greater of the amount computed under the cost depletion method or percentage depletion method. A separate computation is necessary for each mineral property (as defined in § 614) owned by the taxpayer.

Cost depletion allocates the basis of the mineral deposit over the estimated number of recoverable units, e.g., tons of coal or barrels of oil. The annual cost depletion allowance is the per unit basis, termed the "depletion unit," multiplied by the number of units sold during the year. Treas. Reg. § 1.611–2(a)(1). Adjustments for subsequent years are made if the original estimate proves inaccurate or if subsequent developments change the number of recoverable units. Treas. Reg. § 1.611–2(c)(2).

The taxpayer's basis in the mineral deposit is reduced by the depletion allowance for the year. I.R.C. § 1016(a)(2). When basis has been exhausted, cost depletion ceases.

Percentage depletion is based on very different principles. The annual percentage depletion allowance is a specified percentage of the taxpayer's "gross income from the property." The applicable percentages for various minerals other than oil and gas are set forth in § 613(b) and for oil and gas in § 613A(b)(1). Percentage depletion is available at varying percentages to practically all minerals and natural deposits. Percentage depletion for minerals other than oil and gas is limited to 50 percent of the taxpayer's taxable income from the property, computed without reference to either cost or percentage depletion. I.R.C. § 613(a). Percentage depletion continues to be available after the basis of the mineral property has been reduced to zero, see Rev. Rul. 75–451, 1975–2 C.B. 330 (basis is not reduced below zero), but in some cases corporate taxpayers are required by § 291(a)(2) to reduce the percentage depletion deduction after the basis of the property has been reduced to zero.

Following the dramatic rise in oil prices in the mid-1970s, with accompanying increases in profits for the oil industry, Congress eliminated the percentage depletion allowance for integrated oil or gas companies, primarily the so-called "majors." The percentage depletion allowance was retained for independent domestic oil and gas producers and royalty owners drilling "unproven" wells. I.R.C. § 613A(c). Under this exception percentage depletion may be computed only with reference to 1,000 barrels of average daily production at a rate of 15 percent. In addition, the aggregate depletion allowance for all of the taxpayer's oil and gas properties combined is limited to 65 percent of the taxpayer's net income from all sources. Special rules apply to percentage depletion for "marginal production," as defined in § 613A(c)(6). Special rules also apply for geothermal resources.

1.2. *"Gross Income from the Property"*

Percentage depletion is allowed only with respect to the taxpayer's "gross income from the property." The purpose of this rule is to separate the proceeds from the taxpayer's operations into the portion derived from the extraction of minerals and the portion derived from processing or manufacturing the extracted minerals, permitting percentage depletion to be computed only with respect to the portion or the receipts attributable to extraction activities. For oil and gas wells, gross income from the property is the amount for which the taxpayer sells the oil or gas in the immediate vicinity of the well. If oil or gas is not sold on the premises but is refined or transported prior to sale, the gross income from the property is assumed to equal the "representative market or field price of the oil or gas before conversion or transportation." Treas. Reg. § 1.613–3.

Determining gross income from the property from mining solid minerals is more complex. Section 613(c)(1) provides that gross income from the property is limited to the "amount of income that is attributable to the extraction of the ores or minerals from the ground and the application of mining processes, including mining transportation of up to fifty miles from the point of extraction to the plants or mills where a treatment process considered as mining is applied." Section 613(c)(2)–(4) provide definitions of mining and a list of treatment processes considered as mining. See Treas. Reg. § 1.613–4. If nonmining processes or transportation are applied to the mineral only a portion of the sales price, determined under Treas. Reg. § 1.613–4(c) and (d), will be included in gross income from mining.

1.3. *Eligibility for Claiming Depletion*

1.3.1. *The Economic Interest Concept*

Only a taxpayer with an "economic interest" in the mineral property may claim a depletion allowance. The economic interest concept originated in case law but has been incorporated into Treas. Reg. § 1.611–1(b)(1), as follows:

> An economic interest is possessed in every case in which the taxpayer has acquired by investment any interest in mineral in place * * * and secures, by any form of legal relationship, income derived from the extraction of the mineral * * * to which he must look for a return of his capital. * * * A person who has no capital investment in the mineral deposit * * * does not possess an economic interest merely because through a contractual relation he possesses a mere economic or pecuniary advantage derived from production. For example, an agreement between the owner of an economic interest and another entitling the latter to purchase or process the produce upon production or entitling the latter to compensation for extraction * * * does not convey a depletable economic interest.

This standard does not require that the taxpayer "own" the mineral deposit to claim the depletion allowance. A number of relationships to the deposit may constitute an economic interest. United States v. Swank, 451 U.S. 571 (1981), illustrates how easily this requirement may be met. That case held that a lessee under a mineral lease terminable by the lessor without cause on thirty days prior notice held an economic interest in the deposit. In Gulf Oil Corp. v. Commissioner, 86 T.C. 115 (1986), aff'd, 914 F.2d 396 (3d Cir.1990), the Tax Court stated: "There must be a clear capital interest in the mineral which diminishes as the mineral is extracted, and the taxpayer must share directly in the economic productivity of the minerals and the market risk upon sale of the minerals." Applying this test, the court held that Gulf had an economic interest in certain oil deposits owned by Iran and operated by an Iranian corporation, because Gulf was a member of a consortium that provided funds for exploration, development, and operation in consideration of the right to purchase production at the wellhead and the right to determine the amount of production.

1.3.2. *Specific Examples of Economic Interests*

The holder of a royalty interest in a mineral property who receives royalties from the actual operator has an economic interest and may claim depletion with respect to the royalties whether received with respect to a prime lease or as an overriding royalty on a sublease or assignment of a lease.[14] Burnet v. Harmel, 287 U.S. 103 (1932) (lessor); Palmer v. Bender, 287 U.S. 551 (1933) (sublessor); Commissioner v. Southwest Exploration Co., 350 U.S. 308 (1956) (carved out overriding royalty). The manner in which the royalty is computed is irrelevant. See Burton-Sutton Oil Co. v. Commissioner, 328 U.S. 25 (1946) (percentage of operator's net profits); Bankers' Pocahontas Coal Co. v. Burnet, 287 U.S. 308 (1932) (fixed sum per unit).

A lessee under a mineral lease, who conducts extraction operations, clearly holds an economic interest in the leased mineral deposit. I.R.C. § 611(b)(1); Lynch v. Alworth-Stephens Co., 267 U.S. 364 (1925); *Swank*, supra. Contractors who agree to extract mineral ore for a fixed fee per ton do not have an economic interest. Paragon Jewel Coal Company v. Commissioner, 380 U.S. 624 (1965). But a contractor who has a right to a fixed percentage of the net proceeds of the sale of extracted minerals has an economic interest even if the contract miner never acquires title or the right to sell the mineral for his own account. Rev. Rul. 84–88, 1984–1 C.B. 141.

Licensees permitted to extract mineral deposits owned or leased by another person almost always are denied the right to claim a depletion allowance because their rights are not exclusive. See Missouri River Sand Co. v. Commissioner, 774 F.2d 334 (8th Cir.1985).

2. INTANGIBLE DRILLING AND DEVELOPMENT COSTS (IDC)

2.1. *Election to Deduct*

Section 263(c) and Treas. Reg. § 1.612–4 permit taxpayers to elect to currently deduct "intangible drilling and development costs" (IDC) for domestic oil and gas wells. Absent an election these expenses must be capitalized and recovered through depreciation and depletion. Treas. Reg. § 1.612–4(b). The election must be made on the first return filed after such

---

[14]   The lessor of a coal or domestic iron ore deposit, instead of deducting a depletion allowance, is entitled by § 631(c) to treat royalties as an amount realized on the sale of a § 1231 asset, resulting in capital gains treatment if that treatment is more advantageous.

costs are incurred and is binding with respect to all properties owned by the taxpayer for the year of the election and all subsequent years. Treas. Reg. § 1.614–4(e). Only the holder of an operating interest may deduct IDC. Treas. Reg. § 1.612–4(a). If the taxpayer agrees to pay all or part of the IDC for property in exchange for a grant of a fractional interest in the operating rights, only the IDC attributable to the fractional interest acquired may be deducted. The balance must be capitalized. Treas. Reg. § 1.612–4(a).

In Stradlings Building Materials, Inc. v. Commissioner, 76 T.C. 84 (1981) (Acq.), the Tax Court stated that in order for the taxpayer to claim the IDC deduction, "the payment or incurrence of the costs must occur sufficiently early in the development stage so that the taxpayer is exposed to the unknown risks of development." Administrative practice, however, is to allow a deduction for all eligible drilling costs, even if the property is a proven producer. Nevertheless, a current deduction is allowed only if the taxpayer incurs a liability for the expenditures before the time it has been established that the particular well will be successful. Rev. Rul. 75–304, 1975–2 C.B. 94.

2.2. *Items Subject to Election*

Treas. Reg. § 1.612–4(a) states that the option to deduct IDC includes "all expenditures made by an operator for wages, fuel, repairs, hauling, supplies, etc., incident to and necessary for the drilling of wells and the preparation of wells for the production of oil and gas." This includes such expenditures incurred in "drilling, shooting, and cleaning wells, * * * clearing of ground, draining, road making, surveying, and geological works as are necessary in preparation for the drilling of wells * * * and construction of such derricks, tanks, pipelines, and other physical structures as are necessary for the drilling of wells for the production of oil or gas." Notwithstanding this broad language, expenditures to purchase items that have salvage value are not subject to the election to deduct IDC. Harper Oil Co. v. United States, 425 F.2d 1335 (10th Cir.1970). Costs of labor, fuel and supplies incurred to erect structures on the property and to drill wells, however, do not ordinarily have salvage value. Treas. Reg. § 1.612–4(a). The courts have interpreted the option to deduct IDC very broadly, extending the option to many of the costs of onshore construction of offshore platforms. See e.g., Gulf Oil Corp. v. Commissioner, 87 T.C. 135 (1986). Expenses to install equipment for production are not IDC. IDC include only those costs incident to drilling or development, while production costs are not included. Rev. Rul. 70–414, 1970–2 C.B. 132.

Section 291(b)(1)(A) provides that any corporation that is an integrated oil company may currently deduct only 70 percent of IDC otherwise deductible under § 263(c). The other 30 percent is deducted ratably over 60 months.

3. SOLID MINERAL EXPLORATION AND DEVELOPMENT EXPENSES

Section 617(a) allows a taxpayer to elect to currently deduct expenses to ascertain the existence, location, extent or quality of any deposit of ore or other mineral (other than oil or gas) for which a percentage depletion deduction is allowable. Deductible exploration expenses do not include the cost of the mineral property itself nor the cost of depreciable property used in exploration, but depreciation with respect to property used for exploration is an exploration expense. Treas. Reg. § 1.617–1(b)(3) and (4). Unless the taxpayer elects to deduct mine exploration expenditures under § 617, mine exploration expenses are capital expenditures that are added to the depletable basis of the mine. Treas. Reg. § 1.617–1(c). A taxpayer who elects to deduct mine exploration expenses must recapture the deductions when the mine reaches the producing stage, either by taking such amounts into income or by reducing the amount of the depletion deduction that otherwise would be allowable. This rule is designed to limit the benefit of the tax expenditure to that of an interest free loan.

Section 616(a) provides a current deduction for domestic mine development expenditures, which otherwise are a capital expense. But § 291(b)(1) limits the deduction for corporate taxpayers to only 70 percent of development costs. The remaining 30 percent is deductible ratably over 60 months. Mine development expenses are expenses incurred after deposits of ore or other minerals are shown to exist in sufficient quantity and quality to reasonably justify commercial exploitation by the taxpayer that otherwise would have been added to the depletable basis of the mineral deposit. Treas. Reg. § 1.616–1(a) and (b)(1). Expenditures for the acquisition or improvement of property subject to depreciation are not mine development expenses, but depreciation on equipment used in development work is a development expense. Treas. Reg. § 1.616–1(b)(2).

A mine operator may elect under § 616(b) to capitalize development expenditures and deduct them ratably as the benefited minerals are produced. Capitalized development expenses are added to the basis of the mineral property for purposes of § 1016(a) (i.e., for the purpose of computing gain or loss upon the sale or other disposition of the property), but not for purposes of computing the depletion allowance. I.R.C. § 616(c). Thus, a mine operator may capitalize development expenses, claim percentage depletion, and still receive full benefit of the deferred deduction for mine development expenses.

CHAPTER 15

TRANSACTIONAL LOSSES

Expenditures that are capital in nature and thus not currently deductible by reason of § 263 generally give rise to basis in some tangible or intangible asset, as discussed in Chapter 13. If the asset is a depreciable or amortizable asset, as discussed in Chapter 14, the capital expenditure is taken into account through depreciation deductions, which reduce basis until the entire capital expenditure has been deducted or recovered as part of a sale. When an asset is sold the payment received is not income to the extent of adjusted basis; only the amount by which the payment exceeds the taxpayer's adjusted basis for the property is income.

When property is disposed of for an amount that is less than the taxpayer's adjusted basis for the property, the taxpayer has incurred a loss for which a deduction might be allowed. If the taxpayer receives no consideration on the disposition or destruction of property, the incurred loss would equal the remaining basis in the property. The loss deduction thus is another method to take into account capital costs.

The rules governing loss deductions are intricate and involve a number of Code sections. The computation of the realized loss is essentially the mirror image of gain, involving § 1001 and the various basis provisions, primarily §§ 1011–1016. Subject to only a few exceptions, § 165 allows a deduction for a loss only if the loss was incurred in a trade or business or in a transaction entered into for profit. Thus, for example, a loss on the resale of a taxpayer's personal automobile or personal residence is not deductible. However, § 165(c)(3) does allow a limited deduction for "casualty losses" with respect to individuals' personal-use property. Numerous provisions provide special rules limiting losses otherwise allowable. For example, § 1212 limits deductions for losses on the sale of capital assets (as defined in § 1221) to the amount of the taxpayer's capital gains for the year, plus, in the case of individuals, $3,000; unused capital losses generally may be carried-over to future years.

This chapter is concerned with ascertaining whether a deductible trade or business or profit-seeking loss has occurred and determining the amount of that loss. The term "loss" has two distinct meanings in the Internal Revenue Code. Loss sometimes refers to the excess of expenses over income with respect to a taxpayer or an activity of a taxpayer.[1] Loss also refers to capital costs which are not recovered upon the sale or other disposition of an asset (or otherwise accounted for through specific cost

---

[1]   See § 183, discussed in Chapter 19, Section 1, § 172(c), discussed in Chapter 29, Section 2, § 465(d), in Chapter 35, Section 1, and § 469(a), discussed in Chapter 35, Section 2.

recovery or depletion allowances) and cash expenditures that are neither capital nor ordinary and necessary expenses. The second category of losses is discussed in this chapter. Section 1 is concerned with determining the amount of an allowable loss, the proper year for claiming a loss, and the effect of claims for reimbursement on the allowance of loss deductions. Section 2 discusses limitations on the allowance of losses. Finally, Section 3 explains the special rules that apply to bad debt deductions.[2] Material in subsequent chapters will examine the various limitations on the allowance of losses in special types of transactions and the allowance of personal casualty losses.

SECTION 1.   BUSINESS OR PROFIT-SEEKING LOSSES

INTERNAL REVENUE CODE: Sections 165(a)–(f), (g)(1), (2), (j); 280B; 1001.

REGULATIONS: Sections 1.165–1(a)–(c), (e), –2(a), (b); –4(a); –5(a)–(c); –7(a), (b)(1)–(2); –8; –9.

Section 165 allows a deduction for losses "sustained" during the taxable year. In the case of an individual, realized losses are deductible if incurred in the taxpayer's trade or business or in a "transaction entered into for profit." I.R.C. § 165(c)(1) and (2). If the individual is not engaged in a business or other profit-seeking activity, the loss generally is a nondeductible personal loss.[3] Although § 165(c)(1) and (2) appear to treat all profit-seeking losses identically, the operation of other provisions results in a significant difference between losses incurred in a trade or business and other profit-seeking losses. Section 62(a)(1) permits losses incurred in a trade or business to be deducted in computing adjusted gross income. Section 62(a)(3) applies this rule to losses from the sale or exchange of property. Other nonbusiness profit-seeking losses, however, are deductible only as an itemized deduction under § 63, the deductibility of which is limited. In the case of a corporation, all losses sustained during the year are deductible under § 165(a). A corporation is presumed to be carrying on a trade or business.[4]

Treas. Reg. § 1.165–1(b) states that to be deductible a loss must be evidenced by a closed and completed transaction fixed by an identifiable event. Where property is sold or exchanged, and the taxpayer receives cash or other consideration, the identifiable event is usually clear. Where no consideration is received, however, often there is no event clearly indicating when the loss was sustained. In addition, § 165(a) limits

---

[2]   Bad debts are not governed by § 165; instead, § 166 provides special rules governing the allowance of losses for uncollectible debts.

[3]   Certain personal losses which qualify as "casualty losses" under § 165(c)(3) are nevertheless deductible despite their personal character. See Chapter 21, Section 6.

[4]   In International Trading Co. v. Commissioner, 484 F.2d 707 (7th Cir.1973), the Court of Appeals reversed a Tax Court holding that had disallowed the deduction for a loss sustained by a corporation on the sale of resort property held by the corporation and maintained primarily for the benefit of the shareholders' families. The Court of Appeals found that the "plain words of the statute" could not be read as imposing a trade or business limitation on losses incurred by a corporation. The language of the statute was "neither ambiguous nor vague."

deductions to losses "not compensated by insurance or otherwise." Thus, as long as a compensation claim is pending, a loss deduction may be disallowed.

In a sale or exchange the loss realized is the amount by which the basis of the property exceeds the amount realized, I.R.C. § 1001(a), which reflects the taxpayer's economic loss. But where a loss is realized without a sale or exchange, such as by theft or destruction by fire or other natural calamity, a different question arises, namely whether the loss is properly measured by the basis or fair market value of the property. In such an instance, there has not been what is normally considered to be a "disposition" and, absent insurance reimbursement, there has not been any amount realized. Nevertheless, in a profit-seeking context, it is clear that a recovery of capital should be allowed for tax purposes, and since the property is no longer available for use in the taxpayer's business, a loss deduction in the amount of the unrecovered capital invested in the property is appropriate. Section 165(b), which provides that the basis for determining the deduction for any loss shall be the taxpayer's adjusted basis as provided in § 1011, assures that this occurs, but it also serves a limiting function. The law, in effect, treats the destruction of property as a disposition for no consideration.

Suppose that the taxpayer owns a factory used in the taxpayer's business. When the factory has an adjusted basis of $250,000 and a fair market value of $400,000, it burns to the ground, and no insurance proceeds are collected. What is the amount of the taxpayer's loss? Although the taxpayer clearly must spend $400,000 to replace the factory, allowing a $400,000 loss deduction for tax purposes would be inappropriate. The purpose of § 165 is to assure that the taxpayer is allowed a deduction for amounts previously capitalized under § 263 and not previously deducted. Since only $250,000 of the original basis has not been deducted previously through depreciation deductions, § 165(b) operates to limit the amount of the deduction to $250,000, the taxpayer's adjusted basis for the factory. The $150,000 of unrealized appreciation that was lost is not deductible, because it has never been included in gross income. Section 165(b) also allows and limits the amount of the taxpayer's loss where an event occurs which permanently reduces the value of property but does not result in its total loss.

A loss that is allowable under § 165 may be either an ordinary loss or a capital loss. Section 165(f) provides that losses with respect to capital assets are subject to the limitations in §§ 1211 and 1212. Generally speaking, for individuals § 1211(b) limits capital losses allowable in any year to the amount of capital gains recognized during the year, plus an additional $3,000 deduction against ordinary income. Section 1212(b) permits individuals to carry forward unused capital losses to be deducted in future years. Capital gains and losses are realized on the sale or exchange of assets defined as capital assets in § 1221, discussed in Chapter 24. For example, if in a particular year an individual earned

$50,000 in salary, realized a $10,000 loss on the sale of land held for investment and a $5,000 gain on the sale of marketable securities held for investment, both of which are capital assets, only $8,000 of the loss on the sale of the land would be *currently* deductible ($5,000 of loss equal to the $5,000 of gain, plus $3,000). The remaining $2,000 would be carried forward to the next year, when it could be deducted in full under the special $3,000 rule, even if the taxpayer realized no capital gains that year.

A corporation may deduct capital losses only to the extent of capital gains, and unused capital losses may be carried back three years and forward five years. I.R.C. §§ 1211(a), 1212(a).

Miller v. Commissioner

United States Court of Appeals, Sixth Circuit, 1984.
733 F.2d 399.

■ WELLFORD, CIRCUIT JUDGE, delivering the opinion of the Court.

The Commissioner of Internal Revenue appeals from a decision of the United States Tax Court upholding the taxpayer's claim for a casualty loss deduction. * * *

We are now asked to determine whether a voluntary election not to file an insurance claim for a casualty loss precludes the insured-taxpayer from taking a casualty loss deduction under § 165 * * *. We are not able significantly to distinguish the issue presented in this case from that presented in [Kentucky Utilities v. Glenn, 394 F.2d 631 (6th Cir.1968)], and, to the extent it is contrary to our holding in this case, we overrule that decision and affirm the holding of the Tax Court below.

In *Kentucky Utilities* (K.U.), a steam generator was damaged in an accident. The generator was originally sold to K.U. by Westinghouse Electric Corporation and was under warranty at the time of the accident. Based on an independent investigation, K.U. concluded that Westinghouse was responsible for the loss. Rather than jeopardize a valued business relationship by pursuing a claim against Westinghouse, K.U. sought indemnification from its insurance company, Lloyds of London. The insurance carrier did not dispute either its liability or the amount necessary to indemnify the loss. In fact, Lloyds offered to indemnify K.U. for the full amount of the damage. Because Lloyds insisted upon its right of subrogation against Westinghouse, however, K.U. refused to accept any insurance proceeds. Instead, K.U., Westinghouse, and Lloyds entered into a settlement agreement whereby Westinghouse and Lloyds agreed to compensate K.U. in the amount of $65,550.93 and $37,500.00, respectively. Pursuant to this settlement, K.U. agreed to absorb the remaining cost of repairs and proceeded to deduct the $44,486.77 on its corporate income tax return, either as a § 165 loss or as a[n] "ordinary and necessary" business expense [under § 162]. The district court held that K.U.'s failure reasonably to pursue indemnification from Lloyds barred any casualty loss deduction under [the predecessor of § 165(a)], except to the extent of the $10,000 deductible provision in its insurance policy. Likewise, the district court held that K.U.'s expenditures did not constitute ordinary or necessary business expenses under [the predecessor of § 162]. This Court affirmed.

* * *

Judges and commentators have given differing interpretations of the holding in *Kentucky Utilities*. Generally speaking, *Kentucky Utilities* is said to set forth a two-part transaction view; it looks to the "sustained loss" clause and the "not compensated" clause of § 165. Thus, *Kentucky Utilities* can be interpreted to hold either (a) that a taxpayer must exhaust all reasonable prospects for insurance indemnification before claiming a "sustained loss," or (b) that the phrase "not compensated by" must be equated with the phrase "not covered by" insurance. We now reject both of these interpretations which would preclude Miller's claim of a loss deduction under the circumstances here present.

The former interpretation must be rejected because it renders the "not compensated by" clause mere surplusage. * * * The question of whether a loss has been sustained depends upon the taxpayer's reasonable expectation of recovery from the wrongdoer. Alison v. United States, 344 U.S. 167, 170 (1952). The plain language of § 165(a) supports the proposition that the timing of a loss transaction must be determined independent of insurance consequences. Section 165(a) provides that "[t]here shall be allowed as a deduction any loss sustained . . . and not compensated for by insurance. . . ." (emphasis added). To define a sustained loss with reference to potential indemnification by an insurer strips the language of § 165(a), regarding compensation, of its meaning; any time a loss is sustained it, by definition, would not be "compensated for by insurance." * * * In short, we believe that § 165(a) reflects the intent of Congress that the question of whether a loss is sustained should be resolved independently of any insurance consequences involved. * * * In the instant case, * * * there remained no reasonable prospect of recovery from the wrongdoer. Thus, we conclude that the taxpayer has sustained a loss in a "closed transaction" during the taxable year.

We likewise reject *Kentucky Utilities* for the proposition that "not compensated by" means "not covered by." Such an interpretation of the language of § 165 is inconsistent with the plain meaning of the word "compensated." Absent unusual circumstances, we are bound to apply the plain meaning of a statute. * * * Moreover, legislative history, scant though it is, does not support an interpretation of § 165 that equates "not compensated by" with "not covered by." As the court in [Hills v. Commissioner, 691 F.2d 997, 1000 (11th Cir.1982)] noted:

> The initial House Ways and Means Committee language was "losses . . . not covered by insurance or otherwise and compensated for." The Senate Finance Committee amended the

language to its final and enacted form of "losses . . . not compensated for by insurance or otherwise."

* * *

We agree with the Tax Court's conclusion in Hills v. Commissioner, 76 T.C. 484, 487, after its analysis of the legislative history:

[A]ll losses compensated by insurance are also, as a necessary concomitant, covered by insurance; nonetheless, it should be equally obvious that the converse, i.e. that all losses covered by insurance are also compensated for, is not necessarily true.

* * *

[T]he language of a statute is clear * * * . We conclude that Congress limited the availability of § 165 deductions to "losses not compensated for by insurance or otherwise" to avoid double compensation for taxpayers who in fact had received indemnification from their insurers. * * * Accordingly, our prior decision in *Kentucky Utilities* is overruled * * * and the judgment of the Tax Court is Affirmed.

DETAILED ANALYSIS

1. "NOT COMPENSATED" LIMITATION

1.1. *Generally*

Section 165(a) limits deductions to losses "not compensated by insurance or otherwise." See Callahan v. Commissioner, T.C. Memo. 1996–65, aff'd by order, 111 F.3d 892 (5th Cir.1997) (outright grant from FEMA to victims of hurricane damage was in the nature of insurance compensation for damage). Thus, for example, if a clerk employed in the taxpayer's store steals $5,000 from the cash register, but a bonding company reimburses the taxpayer $4,500, there being a $500 deductible on the insurance policy, the loss deduction is limited to the actual out of pocket loss, $500. The same limitation applies if the taxpayer is reimbursed by a tortfeasor or another person having a contractual liability to make the taxpayer whole, such as the obligor on a warranty.

Often an issue arises regarding whether a claimed loss deduction is premature when the possibility of reimbursement remains open beyond the close of the taxable year in which the loss initially occurred. Treas. Reg. § 1.165–1(d)(2)(i) provides that no loss deduction is allowed as long as there is a reasonable possibility of recovery. This is a factual issue, according to both Treas. Reg. § 1.165–1(d)(2)(i) and Boehm v. Commissioner, 326 U.S. 287 (1945), and the findings of the trial court will not be overturned unless they are clearly erroneous.

In Halliburton Co. v. Commissioner, 93 T.C. 758 (1989), aff'd, 946 F.2d 395 (5th Cir.1991), the taxpayer was allowed a deduction in 1979 with respect to property expropriated by the Iranian government, even though the taxpayer had filed a claim with the Iran-United States Claims Tribunal and in 1984 taxpayer eventually received partial reimbursement for the loss. The taxpayer carried the burden of proof that there was no reasonable possibility of recovery in December 1979 because Iranian-American foreign relations were in such a state of disarray that "a recovery light did not exist at the end of the tunnel of the uncertainties."

The Court of Appeals in *Halliburton Co.* described the applicable principles as follows:

> [T]he standard for determining the year for deduction of a loss is a "flexible, practical . . . realistic" one that varies according to the circumstances of each case. * * * The taxpayer's reasonable and honest belief as to when he sustained the loss is a factor in this determination, but it is not the sole or controlling one. * * * Hindsight plays no role in the totality-of-the-circumstances analysis. The tax law does not require the taxpayer to be an "incorrigible optimist" about the possibility of some eventual recoupment before a loss is deductible. * * *
>
> The Tax Court correctly recognized "that subsequent events should not be given determinative significance." * * * Rather, the existence of a reasonable prospect of recovery "must be determined from the facts and circumstances known or which reasonably could have been known at the end of the year" in which the loss was deducted. * * * Thus, the Tax Court correctly determined that the brightening prospect of recovery late in 1980 and the ultimate recovery by Halliburton of a portion of its loss * * * were not legally significant.

1.2. *Waiver of Claim*

As did Kentucky Utilities v. Glenn, which was overruled by the Sixth Circuit in *Miller,* H.D. Lee Mercantile Co. v. Commissioner, 79 F.2d 391 (10th Cir.1935), denied the taxpayer a loss deduction when it failed to make a claim against the supplier of defective goods. See also Rev. Rul. 78–141, 1978–1 C.B. 58 (barring a deduction for a lawyer who paid a client to compensate the client for erroneous advice and refrained from seeking reimbursement from the malpractice insurance carrier). In contrast, the *Miller* decision indicates that a loss deduction should be allowed if for some business purpose the taxpayer chooses not to seek reimbursement from a third party. There appears to be no sound policy reason for denying deductions when the taxpayer for good business reasons determines not to seek reimbursement from a potentially responsible third party. Even if the expense is not technically a "loss," it would seem to be an ordinary and necessary business expense deductible under § 162.

2. CASUALTY LOSSES TO PROPERTY USED IN A TRADE OR BUSINESS

A "casualty loss" is a loss arising from a fire, storm, shipwreck, or similar event. See Treas. Reg. § 1.165–7(a)(1). Accidents caused by the fault of someone other than the taxpayer or by the fault of the taxpayer not due to the taxpayer's "willful act or willful negligence" also are specifically included. Treas. Reg. § 1.165–7(a)(3). Whether a business or profit-seeking loss is a casualty loss may be relevant with respect to the operation of § 1231, discussed in Chapter 25. See Rev. Rul. 87–59, 1987–2 C.B. 59, amplified by Rev. Rul. 90–61, 1990–2 C.B. 39.

Although personal casualty losses are allowable under the special authority of § 165(c)(3) and therefore subject to the limitations of § 165(h),[5] business and profit-seeking casualty losses are allowable under the authority of § 165(a), and thus are subject only to the basis limitation in § 165(b). Treas. Reg. § 1.165–7 prescribes special rules governing casualty losses. If the casualty results in a total loss, the amount of the loss equals the taxpayer's basis for the property. Treas. Reg. § 1.165–7(b)(1). In the event of a partial loss, the loss is measured by the diminution in the fair market value of the property, but may not exceed the taxpayer's basis in the property. Suppose, for example, that the taxpayer owns a piece of machinery used in its business. When the machine has a basis of $10,000 and a fair market value of $20,000, an accident causes such physical damage to the machine as to reduce its fair market value to $5,000. In a net worth sense, the taxpayer is $15,000 poorer than before the accident occurred, but § 165(b) appropriately limits the loss deduction to the $10,000 adjusted basis in the property. Treas. Reg. § 1.165–7(a)(2) governs valuation and permits the cost of repairs to be used as a proxy for measuring the diminution in fair market value if certain conditions are met.

The basis of damaged property is reduced by the amount of the casualty loss deduction. Expenses for debris removal and repairs to make good a casualty for which a loss deduction has been claimed must be capitalized into the basis of the property, not deducted under § 162. See Rev. Rul. 71–161, 1971–1 C.B. 76. Thus, where the cost of repairs is used as the measure of the casualty loss deduction, the net effect on the property's basis is the same as if the repairs were deducted and the basis of the property were not adjusted, although the timing of future depreciation deductions might be affected.

Treas. Reg. § 1.165–7(b)(2) requires that business and profit-seeking casualty losses be determined with respect to the single identifiable property damaged or destroyed. For example, suppose a hurricane totally destroyed a building, having basis and fair market value of $100,000, located on land having a basis and fair market value (before the hurricane) of $50,000. After the hurricane, the land, which was not otherwise physically affected by the hurricane, fell in value to $40,000 due to market-place fear of another hurricane. The amount of the loss would be limited to the $100,000 basis of the building. In Martin Marietta Corp. v. United States, 3 Cl.Ct. 453 (1983), when ground water flooded part of quarry pit, a casualty loss deduction was allowed for the decreased value of the flooded area, but not for the decreased value of the remainder of the quarry. Similarly, in Trinity Meadows Raceway, Inc. v. Commissioner, 187 F.3d 638 (6th Cir.1999), the taxpayer's racetrack and parking lot were damaged by a flood. No loss deduction was allowed because the taxpayer's calculations were based on the aggregate basis of the racetrack and parking lot and the aggregate diminution in fair market value, and the evidence did not reveal either the basis or the

---

[5]   Whether a loss arises from a casualty or other cause is important in the context of calamitous losses in a nonbusiness or personal context, because § 165(c)(3) limits individual personal losses to "casualty losses."

diminution in the fair market value of each separately identifiable asset damaged by the flood.

3. PROPERTY USED PARTLY FOR BUSINESS OR PROFIT-SEEKING PURPOSE

3.1. *Simultaneous Mixed-Use*

Generally, the amount of loss on a sale or exchange of property is the amount by which basis exceeds the amount realized. However, if a taxpayer uses property only partly for a business or profit-seeking purpose, when the property is sold the transaction is bifurcated. In theory, the computation is a four-step process. First, the unadjusted basis of the property is apportioned between the business (or profit-seeking basis) and the personal (nondeductible) use basis. Second, the previously allowable depreciation is subtracted from the business use basis. Third, the amount realized is allocated between the business use portion of the property and the personal use portion of the property on the basis of the relative percentage of each use. Finally, gain or loss on each aspect of the property is computed. Gains are includable, but only the profit-seeking related loss is deductible. See Sharp v. United States, 199 F.Supp. 743 (D.Del.1961), aff'd per curiam, 303 F.2d 783 (3d Cir.1962); Rev. Rul. 72–111, 1972–1 C.B. 56. This computation is fairly straightforward if the relative percentages of profit-seeking and business use remain constant. Suppose, for example, an airplane is purchased for $100,000. It is used 60 percent for business and 40 percent for personal purposes, and the taxpayer properly has claimed depreciation of $26,000 before the airplane is sold for $50,000. The deductible loss with respect to the 60 percent business portion of the airplane is based on 60 percent of the amount realized, and 60 percent of the basis reduced by the full amount of the depreciation. The deductible loss is $4,000 computed as follows: ($50,000 × 60%)—[($100,000 × 60%)—$26,000] = ($4,000). The nondeductible personal loss is $20,000: ($50,000 × 40%)—[($100,000 40%)] = $20,000. If the airplane had been sold for $70,000, application of these principles would produce an $8,000 gain with respect to sale of the business use portion of the airplane (($70,000 × 60%)—[($100,000 × 60%)—$26,000] = $8,000), and a nondeductible loss of $12,000 with respect to the personal use of the airplane. Where the property is used in varying percentages for business and personal use each year there is no clear-cut method for allocating unadjusted basis and amount realized between business and personal use.

3.2. *Conversion of Property from Personal to Business or Profit-Seeking Use*

From the point of view of the policy underlying §§ 165(c), 212, 167(a)(2) and 168(c)(1), the same test as to the profit-seeking nature of the taxpayer's activities should be used to determine whether expenses and losses are deductible for income tax purposes. Any transactions for which the expenses are deductible should generate a deductible loss if unsuccessful and vice versa. Sections 212, 167(a)(2), and 168(c)(1) (the latter two sections allowing deductions for depreciation and capital cost recovery) express the profit-seeking test in terms of property that is "held for the production of income." Section 165(c)(2) (which allows a deduction for losses), on the other hand, expresses the test in terms of "transaction entered into for profit." Perhaps because of this difference in language, the case law, developed primarily in the context of residence conversion cases, has provided different tests for the deductibility of expenses and the deductibility of losses. In general, although expenses may be deductible while property is being offered for use in an income producing activity, a loss deduction upon disposition of the property is not allowed unless a *transaction* for profit has been *undertaken* prior to sale. However, if the property initially was acquired for the purpose of either use in a profit-seeking activity or in hopes that it could be resold at a profit, and the property was not used for personal purposes, then the initial acquisition is considered to be the requisite "transaction for profit."

3.2.1. *Offering Property for Rent*

In Heiner v. Tindle, 276 U.S. 582 (1928), the taxpayer built a residence in 1892, which he occupied until 1901. He then resided elsewhere, and leased the residence until 1920, when it was sold. The taxpayer claimed a loss on the sale under a provision similar to § 165(c). Treasury Regulations provided that a loss on the sale of an individual's residence was not deductible unless purchased or constructed with a view to subsequent sale for profit. The Court allowed the loss on the ground that at the time of the renting, the property ceased to be held for personal use and became "devoted exclusively to the production of a profit in the form of net rentals."

The factual challenge under the Heiner v. Tindle rule is to determine whether the requisite conversion has occurred. In general, the taxpayer must successfully rent the residence first in order to have its subsequent sale result in a deductible loss. Treas. Reg. § 1.165–9(b)(1). Where property is listed for sale but not rental, a loss upon sale will not be deductible under § 165 because there was no "transaction entered into for profit" even though in some circumstances, offering a residence for sale will permit the taxpayer to deduct expenses and depreciation under §§ 212 and 167 or 168.[6] But if

---

[6]   In Cowles v. Commissioner, T.C. Memo. 1970–198, the taxpayer unsuccessfully listed his residence for sale or rent for over two years and finally sold the property at a loss. Because no rental had actually occurred, the Tax Court upheld the disallowance of the loss under § 165(c)(2), even though the Commissioner conceded that offering the property for rental was enough to establish that the property was "held for the production of income" under §§ 212 and 167. Newcombe v. Commissioner, 54 T.C. 1298 (1970), disallowed deductions under §§ 167 and 212 for depreciation and expenses where the house was not offered for rent and was listed for sale immediately after the taxpayers moved to another city. The court indicated, however, that the absence of offers to rent is not determinative. A residence may be "held for the production of income" if the taxpayer is seeking to realize "postconversion" appreciation. But the court stated: "The placing of the property on the market for immediate sale, at or shortly after the time of its abandonment as a residence, will ordinarily be strong evidence that a taxpayer is not holding the property for postconversion appreciation in value." Quinn v. Commissioner, 65 T.C. 523 (1975), applied *Newcombe* to disallow deductions, but Lowry v. United States, 384 F.Supp. 257 (D.N.H.1974), applied *Newcombe* to permit deductions: "By an immediate listing, plaintiff made the property a visible commodity on a demanding market. He patiently waited until the economic forces pushed the market value of his property up to his list price." The *Lowry* conclusion is questionable. Although the property was first offered in 1967 and ultimately sold in 1973 at its original asking price of $150,000, a prospective purchaser offered to buy the property in 1968 at the asking price but was not approved by the requisite percentage of cooperative stockholders.

Section 280A, discussed in Chapter 18, Section 2., which limits the profit-seeking deductions associated with residences used by the taxpayer during the taxable year, typically

property is never used for personal purposes and is put up for sale immediately upon its acquisition, a loss may be allowed. See Marx v. Commissioner, 5 T.C. 173 (1945) (Acq.) (allowing a taxpayer who promptly sold an inherited yacht to claim a loss deduction).

3.2.2. Determining the Amount of Loss from Property Converted to Business Use

Treas. Reg. §§ 1.165–7(a)(5) (dealing with converted property generally) and 1.165–9(b)(2) (dealing specifically with residences converted to income producing property) limit the adjusted basis used to determine the amount of the loss to the lesser of the property's adjusted basis or fair market value at the time of its conversion, as adjusted for subsequent depreciation. Thus, when property is converted from personal use to business or investment use, the amount of any deductible loss under § 165(c)(1) or (2) from a subsequent disposition is limited to the portion of the loss, if any, incurred while the property was used in the profit-seeking activity. Any economic loss that occurred while the property was used for personal purposes is not appropriately allowable as a loss deduction under § 165.

3.3. Conversion of Property from Business or Profit-Seeking Use to Personal Use

A building originally acquired under conditions satisfying the profit-seeking test may be converted into a non-qualifying residence. Thus, in Gevirtz v. Commissioner, 123 F.2d 707 (2d Cir.1941), the taxpayer purchased a lot with the intention of erecting an apartment house. Learning that other such houses sufficient to satisfy the demand were being built, she then built a 12-room $90,000 residence, constructed with three separate wings so that it could be converted into a three-family dwelling. She lived in the house for five years, vacated it, unsuccessfully attempted to sell or rent it, and suffered foreclosure. The loss was held not deductible: there was a definite abandonment of her original profit motive and a definite devotion of the property to a personal residence; and the prospect of a future business use was subsidiary, taxpayer's attitude being "not unlike that of the White Knight who carried a mouse-trap on his horse because, he said, 'it's well to be provided for everything.' " A temporary residential use, however, will not necessarily disqualify property acquired with a profit motive. See Jefferson v. Commissioner, 50 T.C. 963 (1968) (Acq.).

4. WORTHLESS SECURITIES

Section 165(g) allows a deduction for losses sustained in connection with an investment in securities when the securities become "worthless." A mere decline in value, even if substantial, is not sufficient to establish a loss deduction. Treas. Reg. § 1.165–4(a). This statutory provision provides the "closed and completed transaction" with respect to such property. Furthermore, because § 165(g) creates a deemed sale or exchange on the last day of the year in which the security becomes worthless, losses from worthless securities generally are capital losses, subject to the limitations of

---

will not limit the §§ 212 and 167 or 168 deductions otherwise allowable under the above test. See I.R.C. § 280A(d)(4).

§§ 1211 and 1212.[7] Absent § 165(g), the technical lack of a sale or exchange on worthlessness could arguably produce an ordinary loss. As a result of § 165(g), however, either a sale or the establishment of worthlessness without sale produces the same tax result for corporate securities within the definition of § 165(g)(2).[8]

Pinpointing the year of worthlessness of securities in a corporation successively experiencing, for example, business reverses, then financial difficulties, then institution of receivership proceedings, then operation by the receiver, and then reorganization or final liquidation, is clearly a difficult task. The Supreme Court held in Boehm v. Commissioner, 326 U.S. 287 (1945), that the year of worthlessness is not fixed by a subjective test turning on the taxpayer's reasonable and honest belief as to worthlessness, but by a practical approach under which all pertinent facts and circumstances are open to consideration regardless of their objective or subjective nature. The question is one of fact and the standard of its determination is thus "a flexible, practical one, varying according to the circumstances of each case." The taxpayer and the Commissioner are each likely to choose the year that fits their respective approaches to the taxpayer's tax liabilities and dispute over the "question of fact" is thus bound to emerge. Compare Mahler v. Commissioner, 119 F.2d 869 (2d Cir.1941), holding that common stock in a company became worthless prior to 1934, but that the preferred stock in the company became worthless in 1934, with G.E. Employees Securities Corp. v. Manning, 137 F.2d 637 (3d Cir.1943), holding, with respect to the same company stock, that the stock did not become worthless prior to 1936. A sale for a nominal amount will not prevent a finding of worthlessness prior to the sale. De Loss v. Commissioner, 28 F.2d 803 (2d Cir.1928).

The relevant measure of worthlessness is whether the corporation has liquidation value (i.e., whether the security holders would receive anything upon the liquidation of the corporation); the absence of going concern value will not by itself render securities of the corporation worthless. Byrum v. Commissioner, 58 T.C. 731 (1972) (Acq.). Conversely, if a corporation's liabilities exceed its assets, its stock will be considered worthless unless there is a reasonable prospect of improved conditions sufficient for the corporation to regain solvency. See Thompson v. Commissioner, 115 F.2d 661 (2d Cir.1940); McCurdy v. United States, 467 F.2d 285 (6th Cir.1972).

In United States v. S.S. White Dental Mfg. Co., 274 U.S. 398 (1927), the taxpayer owned all of the stock of a German subsidiary whose assets were taken over by the German government in 1918. The taxpayer claimed a deduction for 1918 in the amount of its investment in the German corporation. In 1920 the assets were returned to the corporation but had diminished substantially in value and were sold in 1922 for a nominal

---

[7] Section 1244(d) allows an ordinary deduction for losses with respect to common stock in certain small corporations. Only an individual who purchased the stock directly from the corporation is eligible for ordinary loss treatment under this provision.

[8] For debt obligations this definition requires either interest coupons or registration. See Treas. Reg. § 1.165–5(a)(3). Debt securities which do not meet this definition result in bad debt deductions under § 166. See I.R.C. § 166(e). However, a "retirement" of such securities is treated under § 1271 as an exchange which may result in a capital loss. This disparity results from a lack of coordination of the two provisions.

amount. The Supreme Court allowed the deduction in 1918: "The * * * regulations, consistently with the statute, contemplate that a loss may become complete enough for deduction without the taxpayer's establishing that there is no possibility of an eventual recoupment. It would require a high degree of optimism to discern in the seizure of enemy property by the German government in 1918 more than a remote hope of ultimate salvage from the wreck of the war. The Taxing Act does not require the taxpayer to be an incorrigible optimist."

Section 6511(d) provides a seven-year statute of limitations, in lieu of the normal three-year period, for refund claims based on deductions under § 165(g) for worthless securities or under § 166 for worthless debts. This seven-year statute of limitations considerably diminished litigation turning on the year of worthlessness. Much of the prior litigation had been forced by the fact that the "proper year," as urged by the Commissioner, turned out to be a year barred by the statute of limitations.

5. "CLOSED AND COMPLETED TRANSACTION" REQUIREMENT APPLIED TO PERSONAL PROPERTY

5.1. *Abandonment of Depreciable Business Property*

Personal property generally is subject to the rule that a loss must be evidenced by a closed and completed transaction fixed by an identifiable event. The taxpayer must either (1) show both (a) an intention to abandon the asset, and (b) an affirmative act of abandonment, or (2) prove that an identifiable event rendering the property worthless has occurred. See e.g., Echols v. Commissioner, 935 F.2d 703 (5th Cir. 1991) (a partner tendered his partnership interest to another partner "gratis"). However, Treas. Reg. § 1.167(a)–8(a)(4) and Prop. Reg. § 1.168–6(a)(2) (1984) permit a loss deduction where a taxpayer physically abandons depreciable business property and intends neither to use the property again nor to retrieve it for sale, exchange, or other disposition. See e.g., Lockwood v. Commissioner, 94 T.C. 252 (1990) (master recording tapes were physically abandoned in the year they were stored in a nonclimate-controlled room).

5.2. *Goodwill and Other Intangible Assets*

Generally no deduction is allowed for a decline in value of goodwill until the disposition of the entire business. When a taxpayer has purchased two or more § 197 intangibles, such as goodwill and a tradename, in a single transaction, § 197(f)(1) disallows any loss deduction under § 165—even as a result of a sale—until all of the intangible assets so purchased have been disposed of or become worthless. See Chapter 14, Section 2.4.

Establishing abandonment of intangible property is difficult if title has not been surrendered. In such a case the taxpayer generally must either (1) prove that an identifiable event has occurred that rendered the property worthless or (2) demonstrate an affirmative act of abandonment. For example, Rev. Rul. 2004–58, 2004–1 C.B. 1043, held that a movie studio could not deduct as a loss under § 165 its basis in a copyright to a movie script merely because its executives decided not to set it for production and wrote it off for financial accounting purposes. There was no affirmative act of abandonment or identifiable event evidencing a closed and completed transaction establishing worthlessness. However, the movie studio could deduct the basis of its rights in the year the rights expired without production.

A taxpayer may abandon property and deduct the loss as ordinary, even if the property has value. Citron v. Commissioner, 97 T.C. 200 (1991), permitted a limited partner to claim a 165 loss deduction for the abandonment of a partnership interest in a partnership that was continued by the remaining partners. Rev. Rul. 93–80, 1993–2 C.B. 239, reached the same result where the partnership has no liabilities. In *Pilgrim's Pride Corp. v. Commissioner*, 779 F.3d 311 (5th Cir. 2015), the court denied the IRS's claim that the abandoned securities should be treated as worthless and the loss treated as a capital loss. In that case, the taxpayer held stock that it could have sold for $20 million, but the taxpayer stood to gain more from the tax benefits of abandoning the stock and taking an ordinary deduction than it did from selling the stock for $20 million and recognizing capital loss. Because both the taxpayer and IRS agreed that the stock was worth $20 million at the time the taxpayer abandoned it, the court held that the worthless-securities rule did not apply and the loss from abandoning the stock was ordinary.

However, the holding in *Pilgrim's Pride* is relevant with respect to the abandonment of "securities" only to abandonments of securities before March 13, 2008. Treas. Reg. § 1.165–5(i), effective after March 12, 2008, provides that the abandonment of a security generally will be treated as a loss from a worthless security under § 165(g), giving rise to a sale or exchange on the last day of the taxable year of a capital asset.

5.3. *Theft Losses*

Section 165(e) provides a specific rule as to theft, which includes embezzlement, larceny, etc., selecting the year of discovery as the year of loss. Where the victim has a reasonable prospect of recovery either through insurance or from the malefactor, however, the timing and amount of the loss are limited by the "not compensated" requirement. For example, if a solvent embezzler promises to repay misappropriated funds, a current loss may be denied because the debt obligation represents a reasonable prospect of recovery. If the debt subsequently is not paid, a bad debt deduction may be allowed under § 166, discussed in Section 3 of this Chapter. See Douglas County Light & Water Co. v. Commissioner, 43 F.2d 904 (9th Cir.1930). However, not all losses arising from a malefactor's actions are deductible. Paine v. Commissioner, 63 T.C. 736 (1975), aff'd by order, 523 F.2d 1053 (5th Cir.1975), denied a loss deduction under § 165(c)(3) to an investor who purchased publicly traded stock at a price that was inflated by fraudulent financial statements; no "theft" had occurred under state law because the taxpayer failed to prove a causal connection between the misrepresentations and the loss.

A theft loss deduction is allowed with respect to criminally fraudulent Ponzi schemes. Rev. Rul. 2009–9, 2009–14 I.R.B. 735, provides that defrauded investors may claim a theft loss deduction under § 165(c)(2). The amount of the deductible theft loss is equal to the excess of the investor's contributions over the sum of (i) the investor's withdrawals or other recoveries and (ii) the amount of any of the investor's claims as to which there is a reasonable prospect of future recovery. For this purpose, fictitious "earnings" on an investor's account that were previously reported as income by investor are treated as contributions by the investor. Thus, for example, if an investor originally contributed $100 of cash to a Bernie Madoff account, in Year 2 made an additional cash contribution of $20, in Year 3 withdrew $30 of cash from the account, and reported fictitious earnings of $60 in the years before becoming aware of the nature of Madoff's fraudulent activities, the investor could claim a theft loss deduction of $150 in the year he became aware of the Ponzi scheme, assuming that he has no reasonable prospect of any future recovery. The IRS also ruled that, because the investors opened their investment accounts with the intent to enter into a transaction for profit, their theft losses were deductible under § 165(c)(2) (rather than § 165(c)(3)) and, accordingly, the limitations in § 165(h) did not apply to these losses.

6. "CLOSED AND COMPLETED TRANSACTION" REQUIREMENT APPLIED TO REAL PROPERTY

6.1. *Generally*

Historically, a loss deduction could be obtained for worthless real property if an identifiable event fixed the year of worthlessness; divestiture of legal title was not necessary. See Helvering v. Gordon, 134 F.2d 685 (4th Cir.1943) (tenants vacated and building closed); Commissioner v. Hoffman, 117 F.2d 987 (2d Cir.1941) (owners, who had not assumed mortgage, advised mortgagee they were abandoning their interests). See also Treas. Reg. § 1.165–2. Furthermore, upon abandonment of mortgaged property, the transaction technically is a sale of the property and the amount of the mortgage debt is the amount realized. See Yarbro v. Commissioner, 737 F.2d 479 (5th Cir.1984). Thus, the loss deduction is limited to the amount by which the basis exceeds the mortgage debt. See Lockwood v. Commissioner, 94 T.C. 252 (1990) (abandonment of property to lienholder resulted in loss measured by excess of basis over lien).

It is more difficult to obtain an abandonment loss with respect to land than with respect to buildings if title is not abandoned. In Selig v. Commissioner, T.C. Memo. 1967–253, the taxpayer surveyed and improved land he owned in Brazil, planning to develop it as a new city. It subsequently became impossible to get governmental approval for the project and it was abandoned. The land, however, was still usable for farming. The taxpayer attempted to take a loss for the abandonment of the city project. The Tax Court held that no loss deduction was available: "There can be no deductible loss arising out of a partial abandonment of land. The taxpayer is not free to abandon some shafts of his bundle of rights in the land while retaining others." A leasehold interest can be abandoned and a loss allowed for any remaining adjusted basis in the leasehold. Gulf Oil Corp. v. Commissioner, 914 F.2d 396 (3d Cir.1990), held that no loss deduction was allowed to the lessee of a mineral lease who continued to pay rent after drilling dry holes and discontinued efforts to develop the property. Some "overt act of abandonment," such as surrender of the lease or ceasing to pay rents, was required as a prerequisite to claiming the loss.

6.2. *Disallowance of Loss Deductions Under Section 280B*

Under § 280B the demolition of a building does not give rise to a loss deduction; instead the remaining basis of the building is added to the basis of the now-vacant land. Prior to enactment of § 280B in 1984 a taxpayer could deduct the adjusted basis of a building when it was demolished, unless the taxpayer had acquired the property intending to demolish the structure, in which event the entire cost was allocated to the taxpayer's basis in the land. Congress enacted § 280B, because prior law relied on the taxpayer's unascertainable subjective intent and "operated as an undue incentive" for the demolition of existing buildings. See Staff of Joint Comm. on Taxation, 98th Cong., 2d Sess., General Explanation of the Tax Reform Act of 1984, at 1178 (1985). Section 280B does not, however, necessarily deny all abandonment losses. In De Cou v. Commissioner, 103 T.C. 80 (1994), the Tax Court held that § 280B did not apply to bar a deduction for the unrecovered adjusted basis of a building upon its abnormal retirement due to a casualty or unexpected obsolescence. The court reasoned that the loss was sustained before the building's demolition, by virtue of its retirement from service, not upon its demolition, and that § 280B applies only to losses attributable to the demolition itself. Under this reasoning, if a building has any salvage value upon retirement, the loss deduction is limited to the excess of the building's adjusted basis over the salvage value; § 280B bars any loss deduction for the salvage value upon the subsequent demolition. In *De Cou,* the taxpayer proved that the building had no salvage value. The direct cost of the demolition, nonetheless, was held to be subject to § 280B and was added to the basis of the land. See also Schroeder v. Commissioner, T.C. Memo. 1996–336 (cost of demolition and debris removal with respect to farm outbuildings no longer used in farming business was nondeductible under § 280B).

On the other hand, in Gates v. United States, 81 A.F.T.R.2d 98–1622 (M.D.Pa.1998), aff'd by order, 168 F.3d 478 (3d Cir.1998), the court applied § 280B to deny the taxpayer a loss with respect to the demolition of a building three years after it was vandalized and found to contain asbestos. The taxpayer had purchased and held the building as a speculative investment, never having leased it out. The court held that to avoid the disallowance rule of § 280B, the taxpayer must demonstrate either sudden obsolescence or an affirmative act of abandonment. If the building had become suddenly worthless by virtue of vandalism and the discovery of asbestos, the proper year for a deduction would have been the year in which those events occurred, not the subsequent year in which it was demolished. The taxpayer never demonstrated an act of abandonment prior to the building's demolition.

Suppose that instead of completely demolishing a building, the taxpayer renovates the building totally, so that only the exterior walls, or perhaps only the street-facing facade, are retained—a not uncommon practice in historic parts of older cities. At what point do such "renovations" become so extensive that for practical purposes the original building has been demolished and replaced? Rev. Proc. 95–27, 1995–1 C.B. 704, provides a safe harbor under which a renovation modification that retains in place at least 75 percent of both the interior and exterior walls is not "demolition" as long as the building is not a certified historic structure. If the building is a certified historic structure, the same 75 percent of walls test must be met and the project must be part of a certified rehabilitation as defined in § 47(c)(2)(C).

In contrast to § 280B, § 168(i)(8) expressly allows a loss deduction to the lessor of a building for the remaining adjusted basis of leasehold improvements made by the lessor that are abandoned by the lessor upon the termination of the lease. If the lessee compensates the lessor for the improvements, however, the loss deduction must be reduced or gain must be recognized.

7.   GAMBLING LOSSES

Section 165(d) limits gambling losses to "gains" from gambling. This limitation is applied by comparing aggregate winnings and losses for the year. Mack v. Commissioner, 429 F.2d 182 (6th Cir.1970). In Libutti v. Commissioner, T.C. Memo. 1996–108, the taxpayer lost approximately $8 million over a three-year period gambling at a casino in Atlantic City. In order to induce the taxpayer's continued patronage, the casino provided the taxpayer with complementary goods and services ("comps") worth over $2.5 million. Most of the comps were in the form of new automobiles that the taxpayer resold for cash that was used for gambling. (The transactions were structured in this manner to evade a state law prohibiting cash comps.) Rejecting the Commissioner's argument that § 165(d) permits the deduction of gambling losses only against wagering "winnings," the court allowed the taxpayer to deduct his losses up to the amount of the comps, reasoning that the comps were "gains" from gambling against which § 165(d) permits gambling losses to be deducted.

Section 165(d), which appears to be based on the idea that gambling expenses are personal, but nevertheless should be set off against winnings, applies to professional gamblers as well as casual gamblers. See Winkler v. United States, 230 F.2d 766 (1st Cir.1956). The § 165(d) limitation can apply in some surprising situations. Miller v. Quinn, 792 F.2d 392 (3d Cir.1986), held that a lottery ticket dealer who was required by the lottery sponsor to bear the cost of unsold tickets could deduct the cost of the unsold tickets only to the extent of the ticket dealer's gambling winnings, which did not include commissions from selling winning lottery tickets to others.

SECTION 2.   LOSS DISALLOWANCE RULES

The "closed and completed transaction" that is necessary for the recognition of a loss assumes that the taxpayer has completely terminated any relationship to the asset in question. A taxpayer may, however, seek to recognize a loss and at the same time retain the asset directly or indirectly. Among the techniques employed are selling the property to a related party, selling the property and reacquiring it at a later date, and exchanging the property for similar property.

The following materials explore the situations under which, although a loss has been realized in form, a deduction nevertheless may be disallowed.

A. Sales to Related Persons: Section 267

Internal Revenue Code: Section 267(a)(1)–(2), (b)–(e), (g).

Regulations: Section 1.165–1(b).

Section 267 prohibits deductions for losses from sales or exchanges of property, directly or indirectly, between persons who are "related" as determined by § 267(b) and (c).

In McWilliams v. Commissioner, 331 U.S. 694 (1947), a husband and wife each claimed losses from various sales of stock executed by a broker through a stock exchange. In each case, the broker was instructed to sell stock from the account of one spouse and to buy the same number of shares of that stock for the account of the other. The Court held that these losses were disallowed by the predecessor of § 267:

> [Section 267] states an absolute prohibition—not a presumption—against the allowance of losses on any sales between the members of certain designated groups. The one common characteristic of these groups is that their members, although distinct legal entities, generally have a near-identity of economic interests. It is a fair inference that even legally genuine intra-group transfers were not thought to result, usually, in economically genuine realizations of loss, and accordingly that Congress did not deem them to be appropriate occasions for the allowance of deductions.
>
> * * *
>
> We conclude that the purpose of [§ 267] was to put an end to the right of taxpayers to choose, by intra-family transfers and other designated devices, their own time for realizing tax losses on investments which, for most practical purposes, are continued uninterrupted.
>
> We are clear as to this purpose too, that its effectuation obviously had to be made independent of the manner in which an intra-group transfer was accomplished. Congress, with such purpose in mind, could not have intended to include within the scope of [§ 267] only simple transfers made directly or through a dummy, or to exclude transfers of securities effected through the medium of the Stock Exchange, unless it wanted to leave a loophole almost as large as the one it had set out to close.

Where a loss is disallowed under § 267, the purchaser's basis for loss purposes is the purchaser's cost and not the seller's basis; the loss deduction is thus permanently denied to the seller. But if the related purchaser realizes a gain on a resale, the gain is recognized only to the extent it exceeds the disallowed loss. I.R.C. § 267(d). Thus in the gain situation, the capital cost attributable to the original seller's disallowed loss is recovered by the related purchaser. For example, assume a mother sells stock with a basis in her hands of $800 to her child for $500. Under § 267, the $300 loss is not deductible by the mother. If the child sells the stock for $300, the child is entitled to a loss deduction of only $200 ($500 minus $300). If the child sells the stock for $1,000, the $500 gain is reduced by the disallowed $300 loss and the child thus recognizes only a $200 gain. If the child sells the stock for any price between $500 and $800, the child recognizes neither gain nor loss.

Section 1041 provides a special nonrecognition rule applying to all sales between spouses after 1983. See I.R.C. § 267(g). Neither gain nor loss is recognized, and the purchaser spouse's basis in the property is the same as the selling spouse's basis. Section 1041 is discussed in detail in Chapter 38, Section 3.A.

DETAILED ANALYSIS

1. INVOLUNTARY SALES

Section 267(b) has been strictly construed. Miller v. Commissioner, 75 T.C. 182 (1980), applied § 267 to disallow a loss on the sale of stock and real estate by one brother to another in accordance with the decision of arbitrators hired to resolve a dispute between the brothers. Family hostility was held to be irrelevant in the application of § 267.

Section 267 has been applied to disallow losses even where the sale was involuntary. In Merritt v. Commissioner, 400 F.2d 417 (5th Cir.1968), stock owned by the taxpayer was seized and sold at public auction at a loss to pay an income tax deficiency. The taxpayer's wife, the sole bidder at the auction, bought the stock. The court held that § 267 applied to the transaction. Although the legislative history of § 267 indicated an intention to prevent taxpayers from voluntarily realizing tax losses through sales to related parties, that history "does not alter the broad sweep of the language [of § 267] which outlines a far more general coverage." In Hassen v. Commissioner, 599 F.2d 305 (9th Cir.1979), a lender foreclosed on a hospital owned by the taxpayers that had been pledged as security for the loan. Prior to the foreclosure, the lender had indicated to the taxpayers that if it acquired the hospital through foreclosure, they could reacquire the hospital for the unpaid balance of the loan plus foreclosure costs. The lender purchased the hospital at the foreclosure sale and shortly thereafter sold it to a corporation wholly owned by the taxpayers and members of their family. The court held that § 267 disallowed the loss.

In some situations, however, § 267 has been found inapplicable to involuntary sales. In McNeill v. Commissioner, 251 F.2d 863 (4th Cir.1958), the taxpayers' land was seized and held for nonpayment of taxes by state tax authorities for six years, at which time it was sold to a corporation controlled by the taxpayers. The sale by the state authorities was considered to be a sufficiently separate and independent action which precluded the transactions from being considered an indirect sale by the taxpayers to their controlled corporation. In McCarty v. Cripe, 201 F.2d 679 (7th Cir.1953), the taxpayer's farm was sold at public auction. Twenty-five bids were received. The purchaser acquired the farm with money furnished by the taxpayer and subsequently sold the farm to a corporation controlled by the taxpayer. The court concluded that "[i]t is difficult to conceive that the purpose [of § 267 as stated in *McWilliams*] could encompass an involuntary sale or transfer."

2.   NETTING OF GAINS AND LOSSES

In Morris Investment Corp. v. Commissioner, 156 F.2d 748 (3d Cir.1946), a corporation sold various blocks of stock, some at a gain and others at a loss, to a stockholder owning more than 50 percent of its stock. The gains were all held to be taxable, but the losses were disallowed under § 267. The court rejected the taxpayer's contention that only the net of losses over gains should be disallowed. Accord, Estate of Johnson v. Commissioner, 42 T.C. 441 (1964), aff'd per curiam, 355 F.2d 931 (6th Cir.1965); Rev. Rul. 76–377, 1976–2 C.B. 89.

3.   LOSS NOT BONA FIDE

Section 267(b) applies only when one of the specified relationships exists. However, if a loss is incurred in a transaction that is not *bona fide*, it may be disallowed without reliance on § 267. Treas. Reg. § 1.165–1(b) provides that "[o]nly a bona fide loss is allowable. Substance and not mere form shall govern in determining a deductible loss." Similarly, Treas. Reg. § 1.267(a)–1(c) provides that no deduction for losses "arising in a transaction which is not bona fide will be allowed even though section 267 does not apply to the transaction."

Losses have been disallowed where the taxpayer "sold" property at a loss to a party who was not related under § 267(b) and, pursuant to an oral understanding, subsequently reacquired the property. See Du Pont v. Commissioner, 118 F.2d 544 (3d Cir.1941) (disregarding purported sale of stock between two business associates who were social intimates, followed by subsequent resale of the stock to each other a short time later); Fender v. United States, 577 F.2d 934 (5th Cir.1978) (disregarding a sale of unrated municipal bonds from a trust to a corporation under an arrangement whereby the seller was expected to repurchase the bonds more than 30 days later); Paccar, Inc. v. Commissioner, 849 F.2d 393 (9th Cir.1988) (denying a loss deduction to a manufacturer that sold surplus inventory to an unrelated warehouse pursuant to an unconditional written contract, but with an oral agreement that the warehouse would not resell to anyone other than taxpayer; although legal title was transferred, dominion and control had not been surrendered).

In Higgins v. Smith, 308 U.S. 473 (1940), relating to a tax year prior to the adoption of the forerunner of § 267, the Supreme Court disallowed a deduction where an individual sold securities to a wholly-owned corporation at a loss on the ground that, while the form of the investment had changed, there was no change in the taxpayer's "continued domination and control" over the securities and hence no "loss" was sustained.

Given the relative specificity of the statutory language in § 267, some courts refuse to apply the more generalized approach in *Higgins* to disallow losses in situations not specifically covered by the statute. In Joseph E. Widener, Trust No. 5 v. Commissioner, 80 T.C. 304 (1983) (Acq.), losses from sales between two trusts formed 23 years apart were permitted where the grantor of one trust was the father of the grantor of the second trust and each trust had the same current income beneficiary but different contingent beneficiaries. The Tax Court rejected the Commissioner's contention that *Higgins* applied and held the sale to be bona fide. Scully v. United States, 840 F.2d 478 (7th Cir.1988), reached a contrary result. That case involved the sale of leased farmland at a loss from one trust to another. Both trusts had the same trustee and the terms of the trusts were substantially similar. Even though the court found that § 267 did not apply because none of the relationships in § 267(b) were present, the loss was disallowed. The evidence indicated that, although the sale itself was motivated by the need of the trust to raise cash, the sale to the other trust was motivated by a desire to maintain equitable ownership in the same persons. Furthermore, the actual operation of the trusts and the leasing were unaffected by the sale. Accordingly, the loss was not *bona fide*. Northern Pacific Railway Co. v. United States, 378 F.2d 686 (Ct.Cl.1967), disallowed a loss on a sale of stock from a parent corporation to its wholly-owned subsidiary (in a year prior to the amendment of § 267 to apply to such sales) where the court found no "business purpose" for the sale: "[T]he design was to have everything remain as before. Despite the form of a loss-sale, that is the actuality and the substance."

Where a loss is disallowed under Treas. Reg. § 1.165–1(b), rather than under § 267, the purchaser's basis is its cost and the relief provisions of § 267(d) are not applicable to mitigate the amount of gain recognized upon a subsequent sale.

B. WASH SALES

INTERNAL REVENUE CODE: Section 1091.

Section 1091 disallows the loss in the case of a "wash sale," a sale preceded or followed by a purchase within a 30-day period of substantially identical stock, securities, or options either to buy or sell stock or securities. Under § 1091(d) the purchased stock has the same basis as the stock sold, adjusted for differences in the sales and purchase prices, so that the loss deduction is postponed and not permanently lost. Section 1091 disallows only losses and not gains. Hence a taxpayer who has realized capital losses in excess of capital gains is free to execute a wash sale of the appreciated stock at a gain, which gain will be offset by the losses, and thereby secure a step-up in the basis of the wash sale stock to current value.

The scope of § 1091 is quite limited. Suppose a taxpayer holds a 10 percent Massachusetts general obligation bond that was purchased when issued at its face amount of $10,000. The taxpayer exchanges the bond for a 10 percent general obligation bond issued by California. Suppose further that interest rates have increased since the bonds were issued so that each is currently valued at $9,500. Apart from the possible application of limitations on the deductibility of capital losses, the taxpayer may deduct a loss of $500. Because the issuers are different, § 1091 does not apply as the bonds are not "substantially identical." The purpose of § 1091 would be better served if the section disallowed losses from the exchange of bonds of the same general type, such as long-term tax-exempt bonds. Another possibility would be to provide a rule similar to § 1092, described below; losses would be allowed only to the extent they exceeded unrecognized gains from similar property.

C. TAX STRADDLES

Section 1092 limits the recognition of loss from positions in "straddles." A straddle refers to an investment consisting of two or more parts which, although individually increasing or decreasing in value, are collectively offsetting or "balanced," thereby reducing or eliminating the overall economic risk of the two transactions. One of the uses of straddles was to defer income by creating a current loss and an equivalent amount of income that would be recognized in the next year. The following example illustrates how taxpayers sought to defer income through a straddle in commodity futures, although other contracts such as options also were used.

Prior to the enactment of § 1092, a taxpayer would acquire a contract to buy a commodity in one month (the long position) and a contract to sell the same quantity of the same commodity in a different month (the short position). The two positions, or "legs," would generally move in opposite directions but with approximately equal absolute changes, thereby significantly reducing any economic risk of overall loss. For example, in 1975 a taxpayer simultaneously purchased silver futures for delivery in March 1976, and sold an equal quantity of silver futures for delivery in July 1976. Three days later, the March contracts were sold for a loss and an identical number of May contracts were purchased in order to "lock in" the gain on the July contracts. The May and July contracts were closed out in 1976. The taxpayer reported a loss for 1975 and a nearly identical gain in 1976. Although under certain conditions the loss might fail to qualify under § 165(c)(2), there was no clear rule generally providing for disallowance. Compare Rev. Rul. 77–185, 1977–1 C.B. 48, and Smith v. Commissioner, 78 T.C. 350 (1982), aff'd by order, 820 F.2d 1220 (4th Cir.1987). The loss was not disallowed by § 1091 because commodities futures contracts were not "stock or securities." See Rev. Rul. 71–568, 1971–2 C.B. 312.

The legislative response in 1981, which was expanded in subsequent years, included § 1092. This section generally allows a loss with respect to a position in a straddle only to the extent the loss exceeds the unrecognized gain on the offsetting position. Thus in the above example, if the taxpayer closed out the March contracts in December 1975 at a "loss" of $100,000 and on December 31, 1975, there was unrealized gain on the May and July contracts of $101,000, no loss would have been allowed in 1975, the loss deduction being deferred until the entire transaction was closed out in 1976. On the other hand, if the realized loss in 1975 had been $110,000, the taxpayer would have been allowed a $9,000 loss in 1975.

Section 1092(d)(3) provides that actively traded stock (or stock of a corporation formed or availed of for straddle transactions) is included in the types of personal property subject to the straddle rules. Thus, § 1092 applies to offsetting positions comprised of a position in actively traded stock and an offsetting position, such as a put option, with respect to the stock.

Any loss incurred with respect to a leg of an "identified straddle," is totally disallowed, and the amount of the disallowed loss is added to the taxpayer's basis in the offsetting position of the straddle. I.R.C. § 1092(a)(2)(A). Section 1092(a)(2)(B) defines "identified straddles" to include only straddles identified by the taxpayer pursuant to regulations (or which should have been identified pursuant to the regulations), and provides that the definition will be limited, to the extent provided in the regulations, to straddles in which the value of each position is not less than its basis at the time the straddle was created.

Section 1092 is based on the theory that the entire straddle is the relevant property; closing out the loss leg represents a bona fide loss only to the extent there has been an overall loss on the entire straddle. Section 1092 applies only to straddles not subject to § 1256, which accounts for gains and losses from certain futures and options contracts traded on specified exchanges using an annual mark-to-market system that dispenses with realization as a prerequisite to recognition of gains and losses. See Chapter 6, Section 2.B.3.

D. PUBLIC POLICY LIMITATION

In Mazzei v. Commissioner, 61 T.C. 497 (1974), a taxpayer was denied a loss deduction under § 165(c)(2) and (3) on the ground that allowance of the deduction would frustrate public policy. The taxpayer suffered a loss in 1965 as a result of being victimized by participating in what he thought was a plan or conspiracy to produce counterfeit money, but in fact was designed to swindle him out of $20,000 ("the sting"). On the applicability of the public policy limitation, a majority of the court stated:

> Not only was the result sought by the petitioner contrary to such policy, but the conspiracy itself constituted a violation of law. The petitioner conspired with his co-victim to commit a criminal act, namely, the counterfeiting of U.S. currency and his theft loss was directly related to that act. If there was a transaction entered into for profit, as petitioner argues, it was a conspiracy to counterfeit. * * *

The ultimate question for decision in this case is whether considerations of public policy should enter into the allowance of a theft loss under section 165(c)(3). Where there is a "theft"—and the loss by the petitioner of his money would certainly qualify as such—the statute imposes no limitation of the deductibility of the loss. Nevertheless, in Luther M. Richey, Jr., [33 T.C. 272], this Court held that the deduction of an admitted theft was properly disallowed on grounds of public policy in a factual situation which we find indistinguishable. We would follow that case.

Judge Tannenwald, in a concurring opinion, stated:

* * * It is inconceivable to me that Congress intended that a taxpayer should be allowed to deduct a payment *voluntarily made,* which is part and parcel of the very act believed by him to constitute a crime and involving a type of conduct proscribed by sharply defined "national or state policies evidenced by some governmental declaration" (see Commissioner v. Tellier, 383 U.S. 687, 694 (1966)). To put a more extreme case, could there be any doubt that no deduction would be allowable where the taxpayer, desiring to have a particular person murdered, pays a sum of money for that purpose to a thug who pockets the cash without intending to carry out the deed?

* * *

Clearly, *Tellier* did not preclude the application of public policy considerations under any and all circumstances. Similarly, in enacting the amendments to section 162, dealing with the deduction of various items involving such considerations, Congress left the door open by recognizing that '[p]ublic policy, in other circumstances, *generally* is not sufficiently clearly defined to justify the disallowance of deductions.' See S.Rept. No. 91–552, 91st Cong., 1st Sess., p. 274 (1969); emphasis added. The reference to legislative retention of control over deductions in the Senate committee report accompanying the Revenue Act of 1971 was limited to situations involving bribes and kickbacks. See S.Rept. No. 92–437, 92nd Cong., 1st Sess., p. 72 (1971).

Judge Sterrett, dissenting, stated:

* * * Congress as part of the Tax Reform Acts of 1969 and 1971 attempted to set forth categories of expenditures within the purview of section 162 which were to be denied on the grounds of public policy. The Senate Finance Committee Report for the 1969 Tax Reform Act states "The provision for the denial of the deduction for payments in these situations which are deemed to violate public policy is intended to be *all inclusive.* Public policy, in other circumstances, generally is not

sufficiently clearly defined to justify the disallowance of deductions." [Emphasis added] S.Rept. No. 91–552, 91st Cong., 1st Sess. (1969), 1969–3 C.B. 597. In expanding the category of nondeductible expenditures, the legislative history of the 1971 Tax Reform Act states, "The committee continues to believe that the determination of when a *deduction* should be *denied* should remain under the *control of Congress.*" [Emphasis added] S.Rept. No. 92–437, 92nd Cong., 1st Sess. (1971), 1972–1 C.B. 599.

While the above statements have direct effect under § 162, where most of the public policy decisions have arisen, it seems to call for judicial restraint in other areas where Congress has not specifically limited deductions.

SECTION 3.   BAD DEBTS

INTERNAL REVENUE CODE: Sections 166(a)–(e); 271.

REGULATIONS: Sections 1.166–1(c), (d)(1), (e); 1.166–2(a), (b), (c).

In the case of both corporations and individuals, debts which become worthless during the taxable year are deductible from gross income under § 166. The section excludes securities covered by § 165(g)(2)(C), i.e., registered securities and securities with interest coupons attached, but otherwise covers a wide variety of debts. Although bad debts are a form of loss, the rules of § 166 are significantly different from the § 165 rules governing losses generally, and § 166 displaces § 165 as far as deductions for losses arising from worthless debts are concerned. See Spring City Foundry Co. v. Commissioner, 292 U.S. 182 (1934). In the following materials consider whether there are good reasons for treating bad debts differently from other losses and, if not, whether the bad debt rule or the general loss rule is the more appropriate.

Business Debts: Both *corporations* and *individuals* may deduct business debts that are worthless. In addition, they may deduct such debts when only partially worthless to the extent of the amount charged off for financial accounting purposes during the year. This allowance for partial worthlessness is a deviation from the general rule that no loss can be deducted until a sale or complete worthlessness, demonstrated by an identifiable event, has occurred.

The standard in § 166—"becomes worthless"—is the same as in § 165(g) respecting securities, and hence cases concerning when a security becomes worthless are applicable to bad debt situations, except that a charge-off requirement exists as to partially worthless debts. Treas. Reg. § 1.166–2(a)–(c) provides some guidelines regarding evidence of worthlessness.

Nonbusiness Debts: An *individual* not engaged in trade or business nevertheless may claim a deduction for worthless debts, whether incurred in a profit-seeking enterprise or whether incurred in a purely personal activity such as a loan to a relative or friend, although proving that the transaction was not actually a gift may be difficult in the latter case. The debt must be wholly worthless, since a deduction for partial worthlessness is not allowed as in the case of business debts. The losses on these nonbusiness debts, however, are deducted only as short-term capital losses and their utilization as a deduction is restricted by §§ 1211 and 1212 to offsetting capital gains, plus in the case of individuals $3,000 of other income annually until the loss has been used up. If the debt was created or acquired in the course of the taxpayer's business, it is not treated as a nonbusiness debt regardless of the lack of relation to a business at the time of worthlessness. If the debt became worthless in the taxpayer's business, it is not treated as a nonbusiness debt regardless of the lack of relation to a business when it was created. See Treas. Reg. § 1.166–5(b)(2).

DETAILED ANALYSIS

1.   EXISTENCE OF A BONA FIDE DEBT

A worthless debt deduction is allowed only for a "bona fide debt * * * which arises from a valid and enforceable promise to pay a fixed or determinable sum of money." Treas. Reg. § 1.166–1(c). It thus cannot represent what is really a gift or a contribution to capital of a corporation, rather than a loan. It is difficult, but not impossible, for a taxpayer to claim a nonbusiness bad debt deduction for a worthless loan to a relative. Intrafamily transactions are scrutinized and purported loans to spouses or children will be presumed to be gifts. To overcome the presumption the taxpayer must prove the existence of a real expectation of repayment and intent to enforce collection at the time the transaction arose. See e.g., Estate of Van Anda v. Commissioner, 12 T.C. 1158 (1949), aff'd per curiam, 192 F.2d 391 (2d Cir.1951) (finding a gift); Rodgers v. Commissioner, T.C. Memo. 1985–220 (finding valid loans).

Whether a purported debt is a bona fide debt depends on all of the facts. For example, in Hunt v. Commissioner, T.C. Memo. 1989–335, Nelson Bunker Hunt and his wife lent over $150 million to several of their children in connection with the Hunt family's attempt to corner the world silver market in 1979 and 1980. When the children were unable to repay the loans, largely as a result of the collapse of silver prices, Mr. and Mrs. Hunt claimed bad debt deductions. Based on all of the facts and circumstances the court concluded that some of the loans were bona fide loans, but that others, those made when the children were insolvent, were gifts. In Bowman v. Commissioner, T.C. Memo. 1995–259, advances to the taxpayer's daughter to capitalize her business were respected as loans because the taxpayer noted on each check that it was a loan, stopped making advances when his daughter's business proved to be unprofitable, and refrained from attempting to collect the debts only because the daughter was insolvent and employed only part-time after her business failed.

2.   WORTHLESSNESS

Whether a debt is "worthless" is a question of fact. Treas. Reg. § 1.166–2 comprehensively discusses relevant evidentiary factors. In addition, if a significant modification of a debt instrument is treated as a recognition event under Treas. Reg. § 1.1001–3, discussed Chapter 6, Section 2.B.3., the creditor generally is deemed to have charged off during the year a portion of the debt equal to the cancellation of indebtedness income realized by the debtor. See Treas. Reg. § 1.166–3(a)(3).

In Cox v. Commissioner, 68 F.3d 128 (5th Cir.1995), the taxpayer lent money to his wholly owned corporation. When the corporation was reorganized in bankruptcy, the taxpayer refrained from filing a claim with respect to the debt for the purpose of facilitating the reorganization. The taxpayer claimed a bad debt deduction and argued that the bankruptcy evidenced the worthlessness of the debt. The court held that the loan was not wholly worthless because if the taxpayer had filed a claim in bankruptcy, he would have received partial repayment; thus the deduction was disallowed.

In Canelo v. Commissioner, 53 T.C. 217 (1969) (Acq.), aff'd per curiam, 447 F.2d 484 (9th Cir.1971), a lawyer advanced amounts to clients in personal injury litigation, repayment to be made only out of the recovery obtained. The Tax Court disallowed the advances as business expenses in the years paid out on the ground that they were loans. No bad debt deduction was allowed for advances where litigation was still outstanding since the contingency requiring repayment, i.e., successful recovery, had not yet taken place. A deduction was allowed for unrepaid advances in connection with cases that had been closed without recovery.

In Rendall v. Commissioner, 535 F.3d 1221 (10th Cir. 2008), the taxpayer lent $2 million to a publicly traded corporation. In 1997, the corporation declared bankruptcy and arranged the sale of most of its assets. However, the corporation retained rights to certain patents, and at the close of the year it was trading over-the-counter for $3 per share. The court affirmed the Tax Court's denial of a deduction for a worthless debt in 1997. The court held that the taxpayer had not established that the debt was worthless, which requires "identifiable events that form the basis of reasonable grounds for abandoning any hope of recovery." Quoting Roth Steel Tube Co. v. Commissioner, 620 F.2d 1176, 1182 (6th Cir. 1980), the court stated: " 'Where a debtor company continues to operate as a going concern the courts have often concluded that its debts are not worthless for tax purposes despite the fact that it is technically insolvent.' "

3.   NONBUSINESS DEBTS

3.1. *Profit-Seeking Nonbusiness Debts*

The distinction drawn by § 166 between business and nonbusiness bad debts necessitates a categorization of an individual taxpayer's trade or business and profit-seeking activities. The categorization is the same as that required with respect to other deduction sections, such as §§ 162 and 212, and 165(c)(1) and (2). And, as with those sections, §§ 62 and 63 will then operate to allow trade or business deductions in all events but generally allow profit-seeking deductions only to taxpayers who itemize deductions. In the case of bad debts an additional limitation is imposed in the nonbusiness situation. While a business bad debt generates an ordinary loss, a nonbusiness bad debt is allowed only as a capital loss. Capital losses are deductible only to the extent of capital gains (plus $3,000 for individuals).

In Whipple v. Commissioner, 373 U.S. 193 (1963), the taxpayer was denied a business bad debt deduction for unpaid advances to a company that he had formed and to which he had leased property he owned: "Absent substantial additional evidence, furnishing management and other services to corporations for a reward not different from that flowing to an investor in those corporations is not a trade or business under [the predecessor of § 166(d)]." Although, as was observed by the court in Bell v. Commissioner, 200 F.3d 545 (8th Cir.2000), "[t]axpayers have been litigating this theory for decades," taxpayer victories in these contests are few and far between. In *Bell* the taxpayer failed to establish that he was engaged in the trade or business of "buying, rehabilitating, and reselling corporations" because he did not provide any services to the companies that might result in a return exceeding a typical investor's return and there was no pattern of sales indicating that profits on resale were attributable to the taxpayer's work to rehabilitate corporations. There is something of a "Catch 22" in the taxpayer's situation in these cases. The courts are prone to state that to prove that the taxpayer was in the trade or business of "buying, rehabilitating, and reselling corporations" the taxpayer must introduce evidence that the sales of the corporations occurred "in a manner that confirms that the taxpayer's profits were * * * 'received directly for his own service' " or evidence of " 'an early and profitable sale' of the corporation." *Id.* The fact that a loan to the corporation has turned into a bad debt generally is factually inconsistent with either of these possibilities, unless the loan has continued to be outstanding for long after the sale. But see Farrar v. Commissioner, T.C. Memo. 1988–385 (an attorney who bought and sold 31 businesses over a fourteen year period was a "promoter," and was allowed a business bad debt deduction for worthless loans to some of the corporations).

If an employee is required to make loans to a corporate employer as a condition of employment, a business bad debt deduction is available if the loan subsequently becomes worthless; the business character of the bad debt arises from its connection with the taxpayer's "trade or business" as a corporate employee. Trent v. Commissioner, 291 F.2d 669 (2d Cir.1961).

Difficult problems of characterization arise where the taxpayer is a sole or principal stockholder of a corporation, an officer in the corporation, is active in its affairs, and has lent money on obligations that are not "securities." Treas. Reg. § 1.166–5(b) provides that a loan proximately related to the taxpayer's trade or business is a business bad debt. In United States v. Generes, 405 U.S. 93 (1972), the Supreme Court interpreted the regulations to require that the business motive be the dominant motive for the loan in situations where an investment motive is also present. The Court explained the reason for applying a dominant motive test as follows: "By making the dominant motivation the measure, the logical tax consequence ensues and prevents the mere presence of a business motive, however small and however insignificant, from controlling the tax result at the taxpayer's convenience. This is of particular importance in a tax system that is so largely dependent on voluntary compliance." Applying the dominant motive test to the facts in *Generes,* the Court found the debt in question to be a nonbusiness bad debt. The taxpayer owned a substantial amount of stock in the corporation and was only a part time employee; the amount of his compensation from employment by the corporation was significantly less than his investment in its stock.

If the transaction relates to a profit-seeking activity but not to a business, the taxpayer may urge loss characterization to avoid the § 166(d) limitations on nonbusiness bad debts. In Stahl v. United States, 441 F.2d 999 (D.C.Cir.1970), the taxpayer "loaned" securities to a brokerage house to enable it to meet its capital requirements, the taxpayer being paid a quarterly percentage of the value of the securities advanced as compensation for the use of the securities. The brokerage house went into bankruptcy and the taxpayer claimed a loss deduction. The court held for the taxpayer, finding that the relationship with the brokerage house was not a debtor-creditor relationship; the loss involved was deductible under § 165, not under § 166.

3.2. *Personal Nonbusiness Debts*

A capital loss deduction is allowed for nonbusiness bad debts under § 166(d) even where the purpose of the loan was a personal and not a profit-seeking one. In Levin v. United States, 597 F.2d 760 (Ct.Cl.1979), the taxpayer made an interest free loan to a stockholder and member of the board of directors of a corporation in which the taxpayer had an investment. The dominant motive was held to be personal, and the debt was deductible only as a nonbusiness bad debt.

Because personal losses generally are not deductible, the different treatment of bad debts in some situations encourages the taxpayer to attempt to characterize a transaction as a bad debt rather than as a loss. For example, in Rev. Rul. 69–457, 1969–2 C.B. 32, the taxpayer made a deposit on a personal residence. The construction company which had contracted to build the residence subsequently became insolvent and the taxpayer was unable to recover his deposit. The taxpayer was allowed a nonbusiness bad debt deduction in the year in which the claim against the construction company became worthless. If the deduction in Rev. Rul. 69–457 depended on § 165, it would not be allowed under § 165(c) because it did not arise in a transaction entered into for profit. Under a technical reading of § 166(d) nonbusiness bad debts are not deductible under § 166, but instead are "considered" as a loss from the sale of a capital asset. A loss from the sale of a capital asset is deductible, if at all, under § 165, and § 165(c) does not permit a deduction for a loss relating to personal consumption (other than casualty losses). As illustrated by *Levin,* however, the courts treat § 166(d) as an independent basis for a deduction apart from § 165, and generally do not apply § 262 to disallow the deduction. Allowing a deduction for worthless "personal loans" finds some support in the legislative history of § 166(d). The House committee report gives as an example of a nonbusiness bad debt "an unrepaid loan to a friend or relative" and then goes on to state that "the effect of [§ 166(d)] is to take the loss fully into account, but to allow it to be used only to reduce capital gains." H.Rep. No. 75–2333, 75th Cong., 1st Sess. (1942), reprinted in 1942–1 C.B. 372, 408–09.

As long as a loan, even if made from personal motives, bears interest, it fairly may be characterized as profit-seeking and a bad debt deduction will be proper. However, there does not appear to be any policy justification for permitting bad debts arising from noninterest-bearing personal loans to be deducted as a capital loss or otherwise. In this respect § 166(d) departs from the general principle that income available for personal use ought to be taxed. Allowing the deduction permits the taxpayer to pay for what is essentially consumption with after tax dollars. This issue has been largely mooted, however, by the enactment in 1984 of § 7872, discussed in Chapter 37, Section 4, which imputes an interest charge on most below market interest rate loans. In situations in which § 7872 applies, a loan made wholly for personal motives becomes profit-seeking by virtue of the requirement that the lender report the imputed interest as income.

3.3. *"Wholly" Worthless Requirement*

The "wholly" worthless requirement does not limit the deduction for nonbusiness bad debts to debts on which no payments have been made. It merely delays the deduction for the unpaid balance until there is a certainty that no further payments will be forthcoming. See Alexander v. Commissioner, 26 T.C. 856 (1956) (Acq.) (allowing a deduction of $5,500 after only $500 of $6,000 nonbusiness debt was collected); Nash v. Commissioner, 31 T.C. 569 (1958) (allowing a deduction for unpaid balance of partially repaid nonbusiness bad debts). But Buchanan v. United States, 87 F.3d 197 (7th Cir.1996), disallowed a claimed § 166(d) deduction for the unpaid balance of a worthless nonbusiness bad debt on the ground that only nonbusiness bad debts on which no payment ever is received can give rise to a nonbusiness bad debt deduction.

4. UNPAID SALARY AND ACCOUNTS RECEIVABLE

Treas. Reg. § 1.166–1(e) provides that no bad debt deduction is allowed for any worthless debt relating to unpaid wages, rents, fees, and a similar item unless the item previously had been included in income. This rule reflects the basis limitation in § 166(b). Wage earners, lessors, individual investors, and many small service businesses use the cash method of accounting. As discussed in Chapter 28, Section 2.A., under the cash method of accounting income is not includable until actually received. If an account receivable has not been included in income, the taxpayer has no basis in the receivable. Thus, no deduction should be allowed if the debt is not collected. See Alsop v. Commissioner, 290 F.2d 726 (2d Cir.1961) (accounts receivable). Accrual method taxpayers, on the other hand, must include accounts receivable when the right to receive the item arises, even if it is not yet due. Upon inclusion of the claim in income, the taxpayer acquires a basis in the item equal to amount included. If the debt is not collected, a deduction is allowed.

5. LOSSES FROM SATISFYING LOAN GUARANTEES

In Putnam v. Commissioner, 352 U.S. 82 (1956), the Supreme Court held that a guarantor's payment of a debt upon the principal's default gave rise to a bad debt deduction under § 166 because the guarantor's claim against the primary debtor acquired by subrogation was worthless at the time it was acquired. Because the guaranty in *Putnam* was not proximately related to the taxpayer's trade or business but was related to a transaction entered into for profit, the deduction was allowed only as a short-term capital loss under § 166(d). Horne v. Commissioner, 523 F.2d 1363 (9th Cir.1975), held that a guarantor who paid the primary obligor's debt was entitled to a bad debt deduction even though there was no right of subrogation.

Because the guarantor's deduction is a bad debt deduction, it may be claimed only upon the worthlessness of the guarantor's right of subrogation against the primary obligor. Thus, in Intergraph Corp. v. Commissioner, 106 T.C. 312 (1996), aff'd by order, 121 F.3d 723 (11th Cir.1997), the taxpayer's deduction for paying a guarantee of its Japanese subsidiary's debt was denied because the subrogation right was not worthless, even though the corporate primary obligor was insolvent at the time the guarantee was satisfied; the subsidiary continued to conduct business as a going concern.

Bad debts arising from loan guarantees based on a personal motivation, such as the guarantee of an automobile loan for a friend or relative, are not deductible. Treas. Reg. § 1.166–9 provides that a bad debt deduction is allowable for a payment by a guarantor only if the agreement was entered into in the course of the taxpayer's trade or business or in a transaction entered into for profit and the taxpayer received reasonable consideration for making the guarantee (or the guarantee was in accordance with normal business practice). Where the debtor is the taxpayer's spouse, dependent, or other close relative, however, cash (or other property) consideration must be received for providing the guarantee. In Lair v. Commissioner, 95 T.C. 484 (1990), the Tax Court upheld these regulations, stating as follows: "The regulation was obviously intended to make unavailable a bad debt deduction * * * where the guarantor was in substance gratuitously benefitting * * * persons who could reasonably be considered as natural objects of the guarantor's bounty." This aspect of Treas. Reg. § 1.166–9 is inconsistent with the allowance of a bad debt deduction for a noninterest-bearing loan directly to a relative or friend even though no interest may be imputed under the *de minimis* rules of § 7872, but is consistent with the rule of § 262 that no deductions are allowed for personal living expenses, including gifts.

6.   SECURED DEBTS

If a debt is secured by a mortgage on real property or a security interest in personal property and upon the debtor's default the property is sold pursuant to the security arrangement, the net amount realized by the creditor is treated as recovery of basis of the debt, and if the remaining unpaid balance is uncollectible, it can be deducted under § 166. Treas. Reg. § 1.166–6(a)(1). If the creditor buys the property upon foreclosure, the amount of the bad debt deduction is the amount by which the debt exceeds the bid price (less expenses). Section 1038 provides special rules where a vendor-mortgagee forecloses a purchase money lien and reacquires title. Generally speaking, no bad debt deduction is allowed under § 166, and the lienholder takes a basis in the property equal to its basis in the debt.

Where a nonbusiness debt is secured by collateral, a creditor who finds its debtor unable to pay is not required to charge off the excess of the debt over the value of the collateral and take a deduction in that amount for worthlessness of the debt; instead, the creditor may wait and obtain a deduction for the unpaid debt when the collateral is finally sold even though the delay is motivated solely by a desire to postpone the deduction. Loewi v. Ryan, 229 F.2d 627 (2d Cir.1956).

7. BAD DEBT VERSUS CANCELLATION OF DEBT AS A MEDIUM OF PAYMENT

A creditor may obtain a bad debt deduction where the cancellation results from the debtor's inability to pay the debt. Where a debtor is solvent and may be able to pay, so that a bad debt deduction would not be justified, but the creditor cancels the debt for business motivations, the creditor may be allowed a deduction for the canceled debt either as an ordinary and necessary business expense or as a loss. In Rev. Rul. 69–465, 1969–2 C.B. 27, an employer was allowed a deduction for compensation paid in the year in which it forgave loans that it had previously made to employees to cover personal and traveling expenses. See also Lab Estates, Inc. v. Commissioner, 13 T.C. 811 (1949) (Acq.) (involving a cancellation of accrued rents induced by a motivation to retain a desirable tenant who might otherwise have left if forceful steps to obtain full payment had been taken); West Coast Securities Co. v. Commissioner, 14 T.C. 947 (1950) (Acq.) (involving the creditor's acceptance of 60 percent of the face amount of the debtor's notes, its action being based on a need for immediate cash).

Lidgerwood Manufacturing Co. v. Commissioner, 229 F.2d 241 (2d Cir.1956), applied the rule in Treas. Reg. § 1.61–12(a) that a shareholder's cancellation of the corporation's debt is a contribution to capital to deny a bad debt deduction to the shareholder even where the debt was worthless; the amount of the debt cancellation would increase the basis of the shareholder's stock. See Treas. Reg. § 1.166–1(c). Giblin v. Commissioner, 227 F.2d 692 (5th Cir.1955), allowed the deduction stating that Treas. Reg. § 1.61–12(a) relates only to treatment of the debtor to determine whether it realized income on the cancellation of the debt. *Lidgerwood Manufacturing Co.* was followed in W.A. Krueger Co. v. Commissioner, T.C. Memo. 1967–192, involving the cancellation of accounts receivable for which the shareholder received additional shares of stock. *Giblin* was distinguished on the ground that in that case no shares of stock were received back on the cancellation.

CHAPTER 16

INTEREST AS A PROFIT-SEEKING EXPENSE

INTERNAL REVENUE CODE: Section 163(a)

Interest—the cost of using money—is a common expense of profit-seeking activities and is specifically deductible under § 163(a). Before the Tax Reform Act of 1986, § 163(a) also permitted a deduction for interest on debt incurred to finance personal consumption, such as car loans and credit card interest. Under current law, personal interest—except for certain home mortgage interest and "qualified educational loan interest"—is not deductible. I.R.C. § 163(h).

Interest relating to profit-seeking activities presumably would be deductible under §§ 162 or 212 even if § 163(a) were not in the Code. Nevertheless, under various subsections of § 163 and certain other related provisions, the limitations governing the deductibility of interest in connection with profit-seeking activities are significantly different than those governing most other profit-seeking costs. In some respects, the deductibility of interest might be less restricted than the deductibility of other business expenses. Interest is not expressly subject to the "ordinary and necessary" limitation of §§ 162 and 212 to the extent this designation represents a substantive limitation in addition to those found in §§ 263 and 263A. In addition, interest payments are not generally subject to capitalization under §§ 263 and 263A; interest must be capitalized only in narrow circumstances.

While most questions about the interest deduction involve the proper characterization of the application of loan proceeds for purposes of applying one or more of the various statutory limitations on the deductibility of interest discussed in Section 3 of this Chapter, in many cases the threshold question of distinguishing interest expense from some other profit-seeking expense must be answered.

SECTION 1.   WHAT IS INTEREST?

Albertson's, Inc. v. Commissioner[*]
Tax Court of the United States, 1990.
95 T.C. 415.

■ RUWE, JUDGE:

FINDINGS OF FACT

* * * Petitioner is an accrual basis taxpayer.

Prior to the fiscal year in issue, petitioner established nonqualified deferred compensation arrangements (DCAs) for eight "key" executives (Employee DCAs) * * * . The executives * * * participating in the DCAs will be referred to as DCA Participants. The DCAs were unfunded and represented the unsecured contractual obligations of petitioner to pay a specified sum, determined in accordance with the terms of each DCA, to each DCA Participant at or after a specified time. * * *

Under the DCAs, petitioner and the DCA Participants agreed to defer payments for future personal services the DCA Participants would otherwise have been entitled to receive in the year they performed said services.

* * *

Petitioner maintained bookkeeping accounts to calculate the deferred personal service compensation of each DCA Participant. The accounts for each DCA Participant reflected the amount of compensation that was originally deferred plus an amount designated as "interest." * * * Participants' rights to receive payments under the DCAs could not be commuted, encumbered, assigned, or otherwise disposed of.

* * * On its Federal income tax return for the year in issue, petitioner claimed an interest expense deduction in the amount of $667,142 for the DCAs' interest component accruing during the year.

* * * [The Commissioner] disallowed the deduction petitioner claimed with respect to the DCAs' interest component for the year in issue because no interest was actually paid during the year.

OPINION

We must now * * * address whether the amount designated as interest under the DCAs is "interest" within the meaning of section 163. If it is interest, we must also decide whether it is deductible in the year accrued.

[The Commissioner] argues that the amount designated as interest under the DCAs is not interest. Instead, respondent contends that the amounts in question represent additional deferred compensation for personal services, deductible only as permitted by section 404(a)(5) or (d).

---

[*]   The decision of the Tax Court was aff'd on other grounds, 42 F.3d 537 (9th Cir.1994).

Respectively, that section permits deduction of deferred compensation only when the compensation is includable in the income of an employee or independent contractor. * * *

Petitioner concedes that if the amounts in issue represent compensation for personal services, section 404(a)(5) and (d) controls, and the amounts in question are deductible only in the year they are actually paid to the DCA Participants. Petitioner argues, however, that the amounts in question are not deferred compensation for personal services. Instead, petitioner contends that these amounts represent interest within the meaning of section 163. * * *

Our first inquiry is whether the amounts in question represent interest or compensation for personal services. In answering this question, we must consider all relevant facts and circumstances and make our determination based on the substance of the transaction and not the form in which it is cast. Commissioner v. Court Holding Co., 324 U.S. 331, 334 (1945); Gregory v. Helvering, 293 U.S. 465 (1935).

Interest is "the amount which one has contracted to pay for the use of *borrowed* money." (Emphasis added.) Old Colony Railroad Co. v. Commissioner, 284 U.S. 552, 560 (1932). Interest is also commonly defined as "compensation for the use or *forbearance* of money." (Emphasis added.) Deputy v. du Pont, 308 U.S. 488, 498 (1940). Interest is the equivalent of "rent" for the use of funds. Dickman v. Commissioner, 465 U.S. 330, 339 (1984). Implicit in these three definitions of interest is the concept that interest is a payment for the use of money that the lender had the legal right to possess, prior to relinquishing possession rights to the debtor.

One of the principal advantages of deferred compensation plans is that participants are allowed to defer taxes on the deferred compensation until the year of actual receipt. Contracts deferring the right to receive compensation that are entered into prior to the performance of the services for which the compensation is being paid have been recognized for purposes of determining when income is received for Federal income tax purposes. In such cases, the contract controls the employee's right to receive payment. It is the absence of any legal right to receive compensation in the year in which the DCA Participants rendered services that precludes recognition of income in that year. Basila v. Commissioner, 36 T.C. 111, 116–117 (1961) * * * .

The participants in petitioner's deferred compensation plans agreed to defer either a portion of their salary, or a bonus, or both. * * * They entered into these agreements prior to rendering any services for petitioner and, therefore, never had a legal right to be paid any of the deferred compensation in the year they rendered services. Likewise, petitioner was not under, and never had been under, any legal requirement to pay the deferred amounts to the DCA Participants in the year they performed services or during any subsequent year prior to their retirement, termination, or attainment of a specified age. Petitioner was always the "owner" of the money involved in these plans. * * *

The amounts recorded in the bookkeeping accounts as "interest" do not represent payments made by petitioner for the use of money "borrowed" from its employees and director. Nor do these amounts constitute liabilities owed to the DCA Participants for the "forbearance" of money whose payment had become due. In determining the effect of a transaction for income tax purposes, formalities such as nomenclature and bookkeeping entries are not controlling. Gregory v. Helvering, supra * * * . The important consideration is substance, not form. * * * . The fact that certain amounts are described as interest by the parties to an agreement and are calculated by applying a percentage rate per annum to some principal amount does not mean that the amounts will be deductible as interest for income tax purposes. * * *

DCA Participants never had any legal basis to demand payment of the deferred amounts, and petitioner never had an obligation to pay deferred compensation in the year in issue. Petitioner could not have "borrowed" something from the DCA Participants that the DCA Participants never had the right to possess. One cannot forgo something to which one *never* had a right. One cannot lend that which one *never* had a right to possess, and petitioner cannot *borrow* money that it *always* had the right to possess. Petitioner cannot properly characterize its accruals as "interest."

Petitioner's purpose in offering to defer compensation was to remain competitive within the executive and director recruitment marketplace. Executives and directors are paid compensation in return for services and are free to enter into contracts specifying the timing and amounts of compensation.[7] The amount of deferred compensation to be paid an employee can, and often is, related to the date on which the employee is entitled to payment. Under such an arrangement, the time value of money affects the amount of compensation to be paid under the contract. * * * The fact that these same economic considerations are used to determine interest rates cannot transform a portion of the deferred payment into "interest." Likewise, an amount computed on the basis of interest rates does not automatically transform the amount being computed into "interest." * * * For the same reasons, a deferred compensation plan that uses interest rates to compute the amount of deferred compensation plan benefits does not result in the accrual of deductible "interest."

In holding that petitioner incurred no liability for "interest," we do not mean to infer that petitioner had not incurred a bona fide obligation to compensate the DCA Participants. However, as the Supreme Court stated in Deputy v. du Pont, 308 U.S. at 497, "although an indebtedness

---

[7]   We doubt that the opportunity to lend one's employer money at market rates would normally be considered a recruitment device.

is an obligation, an obligation is not necessarily an 'indebtedness' within the meaning of [the predecessor of section 163]." In Deputy v. du Pont, the taxpayer had borrowed shares of stock and had agreed to return the shares within ten years and to pay the lender an amount equivalent to all dividends on the stock during the period of the loan, plus any taxes incurred by the lender as a result of the arrangement. The taxpayer sought to deduct these latter amounts as interest. In holding that the amounts in issue were not interest, the Court stated:

> In Old Colony Railroad Co. v. Commissioner, 284 U.S. 552, this Court had before it the meaning of the word "interest" as used in the comparable provision of the 1921 Act, (42 Stat. 227). It said, at p. 560, " * * * as respects 'interest,' the usual import of the term is the amount which one has contracted to pay for the use of borrowed money." It there rejected the contention that it meant "effective interest" within the theory of accounting or that "Congress used the word having in mind any concept other than the usual, ordinary and everyday meaning of the term." page 561. It refused to assume that the Congress used the term with reference to "some esoteric concept derived from subtle and theoretic analysis." page 561.
>
> We likewise refuse to make that assumption here. It is not enough, as urged by respondent, that "interest" or "indebtedness" in their original classical context may have permitted this broader meaning. We are dealing with the context of a revenue act and words which have today a well-known meaning. In the business world "interest on indebtedness" means compensation for the use or forbearance of money. * * *

[Deputy v. du Pont, supra at 497–498. Fn. refs. omitted.]

For reasons previously explained, petitioner did not borrow money from the DCA Participants. At the time the DCAs were entered into, the DCA Participants had no right to money which could be the subject of their forbearance. After they performed services called for by the DCAs, they still had no money or immediate right to receive money which could have been the subject of their forbearance during the year in issue. Rather, the amounts accrued as "interest" were an integral part of the method used by petitioner to calculate the total amount of deferred compensation to be paid to the DCA Participants. As compensation, deductibility is governed by the provisions of section 404 relating to employee benefit plans.

[The court went on to hold that under section 404 the taxpayer could deduct the " 'interest' factor" in the deferred compensation only in the year the participants received payments and included the amounts in income.]

DETAILED ANALYSIS

1.   DEFINITION OF INTEREST

1.1. *General*

The Tax Court's opinion in *Albertson's* is grounded on the view that interest is "rent" for borrowed money. Thus, if the "lender" has no current claim or interest in the "borrowed" funds, an additional amount paid to the putative lender for forbearance is not interest but simply a greater amount of an otherwise characterized payment. From an economic perspective, however, any increase in the amount of a payment that compensates the obligee for deferral should be viewed as interest. Other cases have defined interest as "compensation for the use or forbearance of money." Deputy v. du Pont, 308 U.S. 488, 498 (1940). This definition, which is routinely applied in transactions involving sales of property for a deferred payment, can lead to a different result than that in *Albertson's*.

Suppose that A buys Blackacre from B for $100,000. A and B agree from the outset that A will not pay B the $100,000 in cash when B tenders the deed, but instead A will deliver to B a promissory note for $100,000, due in one year, together with interest at 10 percent. One year from the closing date, A pays B $110,000 pursuant to the note. Under § 1274, discussed in Chapter 32, A is treated as having paid B $10,000 of interest on a $100,000 debt for the purchase price, even though A never "borrowed" any cash. One way to view the transaction is that A made an imputed cash payment of $100,000 to B, who then lent that same amount to A. Indeed, consistent with this analysis, a purchaser of property who gives a seller a promissory note is always treated as having borrowed the purchase price from the seller, and incurring an interest expense, for purposes of characterizing the nature of the payments made by the buyer to the seller. Thus, in the preceding example A has incurred an interest expense.

Starker v. United States, 602 F.2d 1341, 1356 (9th Cir.1979), is consistent with this theory of the definition of interest. In *Starker*, the taxpayer transferred real property to another in exchange for a promise that the transferee would convey other real property, as of then unidentified, to the taxpayer within five years. The value of the property that the taxpayer was entitled to receive was to be increased by 6 percent for every year between the original conveyance and the exchange conveyance to the taxpayer. The court upheld the Commissioner's determination that the "growth factor" was interest. Under this view, any compensation for deferred payment can be viewed as interest. The distinction may appear to be slight, but it is important because in many cases interest expense deductions are subject to different limitations than are deductions for other kinds of expenses.

Perhaps the different result can be justified on the grounds that under generally accepted tax principles, the employees in *Albertson's* are not considered to have "realized" the deferred compensation and it is not taxable to them until receipt.[1] In contrast, upon the sale of property for a deferred

---

[1]   See Chapter 30, Section 1.

payment, the seller is considered to have an amount realized equal to the principal amount of the deferred payment, and unless a specific nonrecognition rule applies, gain generally must be recognized at that time.[2]

Nevertheless, even if an expense is characterized as interest, the deduction may be disallowed or deferred by another provision. Indeed, in affirming the Tax Court's decision in Albertson's v. Commissioner, 42 F.3d 537 (9th Cir.1994), the Court of Appeals did not adopt the Tax Court's reasoning that the additional amounts were not interest, but instead concluded that regardless of whether the additional amounts were classified as interest owed under a deferred compensation contract or simply as deferred compensation itself, § 404 (discussed in Chapter 28, Section 3) nevertheless applied to defer the obligor's deduction.

Although many deferred payments bear express interest or are subject to being increased through an interest-like formula, in many other deferred payment situations, the parties simply agree on a greater price to reflect the deferral. The price increase serves the same function as interest but is not as precisely time sensitive. In some cases, such as the preceding example, the Code attempts to identify disguised interest when a price is increased to reflect deferred payment, but in many cases it does not.

1.2. *Points and Loan Origination Fees*

As a prerequisite for making a loan, lenders frequently charge borrowers either a fixed sum regardless of the amount of the loan or "points"—an amount equal to a fixed percentage of the loan—in addition to stated periodic interest. Rev. Rul. 69–188, 1969–1 C.B. 54, addressed the deductibility of such payments as interest:

> It is not necessary that the parties to a transaction label a payment made for the use of money as interest for it to be so treated. * * * The mere fact that the parties [agree] to call the [payment] a "loan processing fee" does not in itself preclude this payment from being interest under section 163(a) of the Code. * * *
>
> The method of computation also does not control its deductibility, so long as the amount in question is an ascertainable sum contracted for the use of borrowed money. * * * The fact that the amount paid * * * is a flat sum paid in addition to a stated annual interest rate does not preclude a deduction under section 163 of the Code.
>
> To qualify as interest for tax purposes, the payment, by whatever name called, must be compensation for the use or forbearance of money per se and not a payment for specific services which the lender performs in connection with the borrower's account. For example, interest would not include separate charges made for investigating the prospective borrower and his security, closing costs of the loan and papers drawn in connection therewith, or fees paid to a third party for servicing and collecting that

---

[2]   This analysis is not consistently applied however, because § 453, discussed in Chapter 31, often permits the seller to defer recognition of gain on the sale until the note is paid.

particular loan. * * * Also, even where service charges are not stated separately on the borrower's account, interest would not include amounts attributable to such services. * * * .

Although "points" or a "loan origination fee" may qualify as deductible interest under § 163(a), such interest is a prepaid expense. As such it should be capitalized and deducted over the life of the loan. This result is mandated for both cash and accrual method taxpayers by § 461(g).

Fees that are not interest incurred to obtain a loan are capital expenditures in connection with the loan and are amortizable over the life of the loan if the loan is incurred in a business or profit-seeking activity. See Goodwin v. Commissioner, 75 T.C. 424 (1980), aff'd per curiam, 691 F.2d 490 (3d Cir.1982); Rev. Rul. 81–160, 1981–1 C.B. 312 (fees are amortized ratably over the life of the loan).

2. BONA FIDE INDEBTEDNESS REQUIREMENT

2.1. *General*

For a taxpayer to have paid "interest," the amount must be paid with respect to an obligation to pay an enforceable debt expressed in money terms, i.e., a dollar amount (even though the obligation so fixed might be dischargable by a transfer of property). An interest factor that accrues on a conditional obligation generally is not interest for tax purposes until the obligation becomes enforceable. In Midkiff v. Commissioner, 96 T.C. 724 (1991), aff'd sub nom. Noguchi v. Commissioner, 992 F.2d 226 (9th Cir.1993), the taxpayer acquired an option to purchase certain real estate through a condemnation proceeding. The price was fixed as of a certain date, subject to increase at the rate of five percent per year from the date the option arose until the date of exercise. The base price was $473,000, but the taxpayer paid $611,287 due to the "interest" factor. The Tax Court held that the additional $138,287 was not deductible interest because the taxpayer was not "unconditionally obligated to pay" the purchase price until he accepted the offer to sell. Similarly, in Kaempfer v. Commissioner, T.C. Memo. 1992–19, the Tax Court held that an additional $250 per day payable by the purchaser of property for each day that the closing was delayed beyond a specified date was not deductible interest, because prior to the closing there was no legally enforceable obligation to pay a principal amount.

In Halle v. Commissioner, 83 F.3d 649 (4th Cir.1996), rev'g, Kingstowne L.P. v. Commissioner, T.C. Memo. 1994–630, the taxpayer agreed to purchase all of the stock of a corporation for $29,000,000 (for the purpose of acquiring the corporation's sole asset, over 1,000 acres of undeveloped land) and paid a deposit of $3,000,000. The contract permitted the taxpayer to postpone the closing for up to five months by paying the buyer $225,000 per month (prorated daily). In the event of default, the seller could retain the $3,000,000 deposit as liquidated damages. The taxpayer elected to defer the closing four months and paid the seller $900,000 as required by the contract. The Court of Appeals held that the executory contract created an unconditional obligation and allowed an interest deduction for the $900,000 paid to postpone the closing. Because the amount of liquidated damages was very large, both absolutely and as a percentage of the contract price, and exceeded the seller's actual damages in the event of the buyer's default, the agreement did not resemble an option. The court bolstered its opinion by describing the taxpayer-buyer as having assumed the burdens of ownership based on the taxpayer having assumed the obligation after the date of the contract and before the closing to bear the expenses of seeking rezoning, the actual grant of which the court found was a foregone conclusion. The Court of Appeals attempted to distinguish Kaempfer v. Commissioner, supra, in which the Tax Court held that an additional $250 per day that was to be paid by the taxpayer for each day closing was delayed beyond a specific date, was not deductible as interest because prior to the closing there was no legally enforceable obligation to which the $250 per day amount could attach. It also distinguished Midkiff v. Commissioner, supra, on the grounds that in *Midkiff* the taxpayer-buyer would have sacrificed only a nominal amount, 1.2 percent of the price, by defaulting.

Notwithstanding the attempt by the Court of Appeals in *Halle* to distinguish *Kaempfer*, the cases are not actually distinguishable. The Tax Court's analysis in *Kaempfer* and *Midkiff* is more persuasive than the Fourth Circuit's analysis in *Halle*. The taxpayer in *Halle* never really had an unconditional obligation to purchase the property and pay a principal sum. Furthermore, once the closing was deferred, the additional amounts paid by the buyer were due regardless of whether or not the closing ever occurred. Thus, the payments did not relate to an obligation to pay a principal amount. In International Paper Co. v. United States, 33 Fed.Cl. 384 (1995), the taxpayer was the purchaser of property under a contract that provided for the payment to the seller of "interest" from the date of the contract until the date of the closing, in addition to the stated purchase price. Because the benefits and burdens of ownership did not pass until the closing, the additional payments were not interest for tax purposes but were an increase in the purchase price.

The "no valid indebtedness" analysis also has been applied to intra-familial income shifting schemes involving gifts to family members followed by an immediate loan of the funds from the donee to the donor. In Muserlian v. Commissioner, 932 F.2d 109 (2d Cir.1991), the taxpayer made a number of "gifts" to his adult children over a two-year period. The taxpayer contemporaneously borrowed from each donee almost all of the amount of each "gift." Deductions for interest on the loans were disallowed on the ground that there was no valid indebtedness, because the taxpayer had no intent actually to transfer a beneficial interest in the money to the children at the time the cash originally was transferred to them.

2.2. *Nonrecourse Debt*

Treas. Reg. § 1.163–1(b) provides that interest paid on a real estate mortgage by the legal or equitable owner of the property is deductible as interest under § 163(a) notwithstanding the absence of personal liability. Thus, interest on a nonrecourse mortgage is deductible only by the owner of the property subject to the nonrecourse mortgage. If the owner of mortgaged property sells it, regardless of whether the buyer assumes the obligation or takes the property subject to the debt, the buyer is entitled to claim a deduction for interest subsequently paid. A seller who remains secondarily liable after the transfer is in effect a guarantor and cannot deduct interest payments made following the buyer's default. Dean v. Commissioner, 35 T.C. 1083 (1961).

Where a taxpayer purchases property subject to a nonrecourse mortgage debt that substantially exceeds the fair market value of the property, a question arises regarding the extent to which the indebtedness should be considered bona fide. If the debtor is a cash method taxpayer who deducts interest only as paid, this question rarely arises because it is unlikely that interest would be paid if the debt were not bona fide. But an accrual method taxpayer may claim interest deductions when the obligation to pay interest arises, even though both the principal and interest obligations are nonrecourse. In this case the bona fides of the transaction are important. The courts have reached differing results in dealing with this problem. Estate of Franklin v. Commissioner, 544 F.2d 1045 (9th Cir.1976), discussed in Chapter 34, Section 3, disallowed any accruals whatsoever where the indebtedness far exceeded the fair market value of the property, holding that the transaction did not create a bona fide indebtedness. However, Pleasant Summit Land Corp. v. Commissioner, 863 F.2d 263 (3d Cir.1988), held that interest accruals could be deducted on the portion of the indebtedness that did not exceed the fair market value of the encumbered property. The proper time to compare the fair market value of the collateral and the amount of the debt is at the time the debt is incurred.

2.3. *Indebtedness of the Taxpayer Requirement*

A fundamental requirement of § 163 is that the item sought to be deducted is in fact interest on an indebtedness of the taxpayer. In Simon v. Commissioner, 36 B.T.A. 184 (1937), the taxpayer, the president of a corporation, individually agreed to pay interest on a note of the corporation as part of an agreement between the corporation and a third-party obligee to extend maturity and reduce interest rates. The taxpayer's interest deduction was disallowed on the ground that the interest paid was not interest on the taxpayer's indebtedness.

This result also has been reached where taxpayers, both shareholders and officers of a corporation, made payments to a third-party lender in connection with the guarantee of the corporation's obligation. See Golder v. Commissioner, 604 F.2d 34 (9th Cir.1979); Nelson v. Commissioner, 281 F.2d 1 (5th Cir.1960); Rev. Rul. 74–592, 1974–2 C.B. 47. The guarantor is treated as making a loan to the primary obligor, which may be deductible as a bad debt under § 166, discussed in Chapter 15, Section 3, if not repaid.

3.   INTEREST VERSUS LOAN PRINCIPAL OR PURCHASE PRICE

As long as a debt instrument bears stated interest (and, if the instrument is issued in exchange for property the interest rate is at least the applicable federal rate, the interest rate on U.S. government obligations of a similar term) and is not issued at a discount, the allocation of payments between interest and nondeductible principal usually is determined by Treas. Reg. § 1.446–2(e), which provides that payments are to be treated as consisting first of accrued but unpaid interest, with any balance being treated as a principal payment. If a debt instrument is issued at a discount (even if it bears stated interest) or if a debt instrument is issued in exchange for property and the stated interest is not at least equal to the applicable federal rate, the rules for determining whether amounts paid or accrued on loans or deferred payment sales represent interest or principal are found in §§ 483 and 1272–1275, discussed in Chapter 32.

SECTION 2.   ALLOCATION OF INTEREST

INTERNAL REVENUE CODE: Section 163(a), (d)(3), (h)(1).

TEMPORARY REGULATIONS: Section 1.163–8T(a)(1), (a)(3), (a)(4), (b), (c)(1), (c)(2)(i), (ii), (c)(3), (c)(4)(i)–(iii), (c)(5), (m).

The Internal Revenue Code treats interest differently depending on the use of the loan proceeds on which the interest is paid. Section § 163(h) denies any deduction for most "personal interest." At the other extreme, most interest incurred in the course of a trade or business (other than the trade or business of being an employee) is currently deductible without any restrictions. However, some trade or business interest is subject to one or more restrictions on deductibility. Deductions for interest incurred in a business that is a "passive activity" subject to the rules of § 469—a category that includes most interest with respect to rental real estate— are subject to limitations, discussed in Chapter 35, Section 2. Investment interest, which, generally speaking, is interest allocable to purchasing property held for investment, such as stocks, bonds, or undeveloped land, is subject to special limitations in § 163(d), which limits deductions to the amount of investment income. Interest on loans incurred to purchase or carry state and local bonds, the interest income from which is tax exempt under § 103, is wholly nondeductible under § 265(a)(2). Finally, § 264(a)(2) disallows a deduction for interest on indebtedness incurred or continued to purchase or carry a single premium life insurance, endowment, or annuity contract.[3]

Thus, determining the deductibility of interest often requires a fact specific analysis of the use of the borrowed funds on which the interest is paid, and application of the particular section or judicial doctrine applying to the specific transaction.

Because application of the myriad limitations on the deductibility of interest turns on the use of the funds on which the interest was paid, interest expense generally is allocated to one of six broad categories: (1) active business interest, which generally is deductible, (2) passive activity business interest, which is subject to the loss limitations of § 469, (3) investment interest, which is subject to limitations under § 163(d),[4] (4) tax-exempt bond interest, which is nondeductible under § 265, (5) interest incurred to purchase or carry single life insurance,

---

[3]   There are myriad other limitations on the deduction of interest allocable to certain types of activities that are beyond the scope of this text.

[4]   Section 1277 imposes further limitations on deductions for interest on debt incurred to purchase or carry discount bonds. See Chapter 32, Section 2.

endowment, and annuity contracts, deductions for which deductions are limited by § 264,[5] and (6) personal interest, which is nondeductible under § 163(h) except for certain home mortgage interest and qualified educational loan interest.[6] Interest classified as either active business interest or passive activity interest may be further categorized as "production period" interest, subject to capitalization under § 263A(f). Only active business interest that is not "production period" interest is unqualifiedly deductible currently under § 163(a). This hierarchy of limitations on interest deductions requires an allocation of interest to different uses of loan proceeds.

The Code and regulations provide elaborate, sometimes overlapping, rules for determining the use of borrowed funds. These rules rely primarily on tracing the use of funds. They are totally artificial because money is fungible. If individual A has $100 in cash, borrows $100 from B and $100 from C, and buys a truck for $100 for use in his business, 100 shares of corporate stock for $100, and a recreational boat for $100, the correct economic answer is that each asset was acquired equally using A's equity, funds borrowed from B, and funds borrowed from C. Furthermore, if the next day A earned another $100 and purchased a building, thereafter it would be proper to conclude that each of the four assets was one-half equity financed and one-quarter financed with loan proceeds from each of B and C. Nevertheless, to a significant extent, A is permitted to trace the application of borrowed funds to the most tax-favored uses.

DETAILED ANALYSIS

1. CLASSIFICATION OF INTEREST

The statute itself is generally silent regarding the method for determining the use of loan proceeds so as to identify the proper Code section for determining the extent of the deductibility of the interest, and there is no single principle that is universally applied. Temp. Reg. § 1.163–8T requires tracing the use of the borrowed funds as the basic rule. Under the tracing approach, actual use is determinative. The presence or absence of a security interest for the loan is not relevant (except in the case of certain home mortgages). Temp. Reg. § 1.163–8T(c). Thus, for example, interest on a loan secured by a second mortgage on an apartment building owned by the taxpayer is investment interest if the borrowed funds are used to buy corporate stock, active business interest if the proceeds are used to buy equipment for a sole proprietorship business to which the taxpayer devotes full time, and passive activity interest if used to improve the apartment building (see § 469(c)(2)). Interest on loans used to pay interest on other loans is allocated to the use of the original loan principal. Temp. Reg. § 1.163–8T(c)(6)(ii).

---

[5]   See Section 3.D. of this Chapter.

[6]   Home mortgage interest is discussed in Chapter 21, Section 5, and qualified educational loan interest is discussed in Chapter 22.

Loan proceeds are easily traced where the borrower does not receive any cash and the loan proceeds are transferred directly to the seller of property (or vendor of services). Tracing becomes more difficult and arbitrary conventions must be applied when the taxpayer receives cash loan proceeds and then purchases several assets. Suppose that a taxpayer has $100,000 in cash, borrows another $100,000, purchases an office building for use in the taxpayer's dental practice for $100,000, and purchases shares of corporate stock for $100,000. If the borrowed $100,000 were disbursed directly from the lender to the seller of the office building, the interest on the loan is active business interest. Conversely, if the loan proceeds were disbursed directly to the stockbroker, the interest is investment interest. If the taxpayer also acquired an apartment building by assuming an existing mortgage debt, the interest on that loan is traced to the apartment building and is thus passive activity interest.

If, however, the taxpayer received the $100,000 loan proceeds in cash and commingled the loan proceeds with the taxpayer's original $100,000 by depositing all $200,000 in the same bank account, Temp. Reg. § 1.163–8T(c)(4) provides that subsequent expenditures from the bank account are treated as being first from borrowed funds. (Proceeds of multiple loans are deemed to be expended in the order that the loan proceeds are deposited.) Thus, if the taxpayer purchased the office building first, paying with a check drawn on the account, the interest would be business interest. But if the taxpayer purchased the stock before purchasing the office building, the interest would be investment interest. To obviate the need for taxpayers to plan carefully the exact order in which checks are written, the regulations permit the taxpayer arbitrarily to designate the order of checks written on the same day—perhaps because taxpayers in all likelihood would do so anyway—and further permit the taxpayer to designate any expenditure made within fifteen days after the borrowed funds were deposited as the use of the borrowed funds. Temp. Reg. § 1.163–8T(c)(4)(iii)(B). Suppose that on September 1 the taxpayer in the prior example had a bank account balance of $100,000, none of which was borrowed. On September 2, the taxpayer borrowed the additional $100,000 and deposited it in the bank account. On September 2, the taxpayer bought the corporate stock with a $100,000 check and on September 16 he bought the office building with a $100,000 check. Under the normal rule, the loan is traced to the stock purchase and the interest is investment interest. However, the taxpayer may elect to trace the loan to the building, thereby treating the interest as active business interest.

When the proceeds of a single loan are used for several purposes, repayment presents tracing questions if the interest is subject to different limitations on deductibility. Suppose, for example, that a taxpayer borrows $300,000 in cash and purchases a new building for her medical practice for $200,000 and corporate stock for $100,000. If in year 1 the taxpayer pays $30,000 of interest, $20,000 would be active business interest and $10,000 would be investment interest. At the end of year 1 the taxpayer repays $60,000 of principal, and in year 2 the taxpayer pays $24,000 of interest on the remaining $240,000 of principal. How should this interest be characterized? Did the taxpayer repay the portion of the loan that financed the building, the portion that financed the stock, or a proportionate part of each? In this situation actual tracing is impossible. Generally speaking, Temp. Reg. § 1.163–8T(d) deems repayment to be attributable to loan proceeds used for expenditures in the following order: (1) personal expenditures, (2) pro rata between investments and passive business activities, and (3) active trade or business expenditures. Thus, the taxpayer is deemed to have repaid $60,000 of the loan used to purchase the stock; $20,000 of the interest in year 2 is active business interest and $4,000 is investment interest. Special rules deal with borrowing and repayment under a line of credit, refinancing, and the reallocation of a loan if property purchased with loan proceeds is transferred but the loan is not paid or assumed by the transferee.

For most taxpayers who incur debt to purchase property, lenders distribute funds directly to sellers, and tracing is uncomplicated. The tracing principle for determining the deductibility of borrowed money is highly favorable, however, for taxpayers with liquid assets and sufficient income and wealth to borrow funds without the lender disbursing directly to a third-party seller. By carefully segregating funds from different sources in separate bank accounts, such taxpayers have virtually unfettered discretion to determine the purchase to which any loan proceeds will be traced. This freedom permits these taxpayers to minimize the effect of the various restrictions on the deductibility of interest.

Tracing is based on the idea that individuals analyze transactions at the margin to determine whether to finance an expenditure with equity or debt. On the theory that money is fungible, it would seem appropriate to treat each expenditure as being financed with a proportionate part of the taxpayer's total indebtedness. This allocation would require treating the taxpayer as refinancing all assets held during the year. This recomputation should be made with respect to the fair market value of all of the taxpayer's assets and expenses, but for administrative ease, allocations might be made with reference to the basis of assets, to avoid annual revaluation. This allocation approach relates interest deductions to all income producing activities and assets of the taxpayer for purposes of determining U.S. source income and foreign source income from international business activities. See Temp. Reg. § 1.861–9T. Apparently, the Treasury Department adopted the tracing rules to avoid the administrative complexities of an allocation system, even though the tracing rules are easy to manipulate and allow some taxpayers to allocate debt to business and investment activities.

Alternatively, the Treasury Department could have adopted stacking rules that would have arbitrarily treated loan proceeds as being used for certain categories of purchases in a designated order. Stacking rules could be either restrictive or permissive. Restrictive stacking rules would classify borrowings first as used for purposes for which the interest deduction is most limited, while permissive stacking rules would classify borrowings first as used for purposes for which the interest deduction is unlimited. Section 263A(f), discussed in Section 3.B., applies a stacking approach to override the tracing rules of the temporary regulations in some cases.

Seymour v. Commissioner, 109 T.C. 279 (1997), held that the interest on a promissory note from a husband to a wife given as part of the property settlement in a divorce should be allocated, pursuant to Temp. Reg. § 1.163–8T, among the various properties in which the wife transferred her interests to the husband as part of the property settlement. To the extent that principal of the note was in exchange for the wife's interest in corporate stock transferred to the husband, the interest was deductible as investment interest, subject to the limitations in § 163(d). To the extent the note was in exchange for the wife's interest in rental real estate, the interest was deductible, subject to the passive activity loss rules of § 469. Because the note was secured by the taxpayer's principal residence, to the extent the note was in exchange for the wife's interest in the residence, interest was deductible as qualified residence interest under § 163(h)(3), but to the extent that the note was in exchange for the wife's interest in personal use property, such as home furnishings, the interest was nondeductible personal interest under § 163(h)(1). The court rejected the Commissioner's argument that because the obligation originated in the taxpayer's personal affairs all the interest should be nondeductible.

Temp. Reg. § 1.163–9T(b)(2)(i)(A) treats interest on any noncorporate income tax deficiency as nondeductible personal interest, even if the underlying tax liability relates to a trade or business. The courts uniformly have upheld the validity of these regulations in the face of taxpayer challenges. Allen v. United States, 173 F.3d 533 (4th Cir.1999); McDonnell v. United States, 180 F.3d 721 (6th Cir.1999); Kikalos v. Commissioner, 190 F.3d 791 (7th Cir.1999); Redlark v. Commissioner, 141 F.3d 936 (9th Cir.1998); Miller v. United States, 65 F.3d 687 (8th Cir.1995); Robinson v. Commissioner, 119 T.C. 44 (2002); Alfaro v. Commissioner, 349 F.3d 225 (5th Cir.2003).

2.   DISTINCTION BETWEEN DEDUCTIBLE TRADE OR BUSINESS INTEREST AND OTHER NON-INVESTMENT PROFIT-SEEKING INTEREST

For an individual, interest paid or incurred in a trade or business (other than the trade or business of being an employee) is deductible from gross income in computing adjusted gross income under § 62, rather than as an itemized deduction. Dorminey v. Commissioner, 26 T.C. 940 (1956). Interest paid or incurred in the trade or business of being an employee—for example, interest on a car loan paid by a salaried traveling salesperson who uses the car exclusively for business—is nondeductible personal interest. I.R.C. § 163(h)(2)(A). See McKay v. Commissioner, 102 T.C. 465 (1994), vac'd by order on other grounds, 84 F.3d 433 (5th Cir.1996) (interest on loan to pay attorney's fees in connection with suit for wrongful discharge from employment is nondeductible personal interest); German v. Commissioner, T.C. Memo. 1993–59 (1993), aff'd by order, 46 F.3d 1141 (9th Cir.1995) (interest on loans traced to educational expenses is personal interest unless the educational expenses are deductible as nonemployee business expenses). Other non-business profit-seeking interest, such as interest allocable to loans to purchase investment securities (e.g., stocks and taxable bonds), is deductible only as an itemized deduction under § 63. See Skoglund v. United

States, 230 Ct.Cl. 833 (Ct.Cl.1982). Taxpayers generally cannot net interest expense with interest receipts and report only net interest as gross income. Murphy v. Commissioner, 92 T.C. 12 (1989). Section 171(e) provides a limited exception to this rule in the case of amortizable bond premium.

SECTION 3.   LIMITATIONS ON THE INTEREST DEDUCTION

A.   INVESTMENT INTEREST LIMITATION

INTERNAL REVENUE CODE: Section 163(d).

Prior to 1969, the Code imposed no special limitations on the deduction of interest incurred to purchase investment property. The absence of any limitation on the deduction of investment interest permitted taxpayers to currently deduct against ordinary income the carrying costs of investment property, defer recognition of gain until the sale of the property in a future year, and convert the recoupment of the deducted carrying costs into capital gain, taxed at a lower rate than the ordinary income against which the interest deductions had been claimed.[7]

To deal with these problems, Congress enacted § 163(d) as part of the Tax Reform Act of 1969, limiting the deductibility of investment interest. Congress revised § 163(d) in 1976, and again in 1986, as explained in the following materials.

General Explanation of the Tax Reform Act of 1986
Staff of the Joint Committee on Taxation 262–265 (1987).

[Pre-1987] Law.

In general

Under [pre-1987] law (Code sec. 163(d)), in the case of a noncorporate taxpayer, deductions for interest on indebtedness incurred or continued to purchase or carry property held for investment were generally limited to $10,000 per year, plus the taxpayer's net investment income. Under prior and present law, investment interest paid or accrued during the year which exceeds the limitation on investment interest is not permanently disallowed, but is subject to an unlimited carryover and

---

[7]   Assume, for example, that in Year 1, A borrowed $10,000 at 10 percent interest to buy stock that paid no current dividends. A paid $1,000 interest in each of Years 1 through 5, selling the stock at the beginning of Year 6 for $15,000. Apart from taxes, A realized no profit—the $15,000 sales proceeds less total costs of $15,000 ($10,000 acquisition price plus $5,000 interest cost). Allowing the interest to be deducted currently in full resulted in tax savings in Years 1 through 5 equal to $5,000 multiplied by the ordinary income tax rate. Assuming a tax rate of 40 percent, the tax savings would have been $2,000. Those tax savings were not fully offset by the $5,000 gain realized in Year 6 because of the preferential rate accorded to capital gains. Assuming a 15-percent rate on capital gains, the tax in Year 6 would have been $750. Thus, wholly apart from the time value of money advantage to the taxpayer, the overall transaction produced a profit of $1,250 after taxes.

may be deducted in future years (subject to the applicable limitation) (prior-law sec. 163(d)(2)). * * *

Investment Income and Expenses

Investment income.—Investment income under prior law was income from interest, dividends, rents, royalties, short-term capital gains arising from the disposition of investment assets, and any amount of gain treated as ordinary income pursuant to the depreciation recapture provisions (secs. 1245, 1250, and 1254), but only if the income was not derived from the conduct of a trade or business (sec. 163(d)(3)(A)).

Investment expenses.—In determining net investment income, the investment expenses taken into account were trade or business expenses, real and personal property taxes, bad debts, depreciation, amortizable bond premiums, expenses for the production of income, and depletion, to the extent these expenses were directly connected with the production of investment income.

* * *

Explanation of Provisions
* * *

In general

The Act provides that the deduction for investment interest is limited to the amount of net investment income. Interest disallowed under the provision is carried forward and treated as investment interest in the succeeding taxable year. Interest disallowed under the provision is allowed in a subsequent year only to the extent the taxpayer has net investment income in such year. Interest expense that is paid or incurred in carrying on a trade or business is not subject to the interest deduction limitations under the Act but may be subject to the passive loss limitation [section 469, discussed in Chapter 35, Section 2.] in some circumstances.

Definition of investment interest

Investment interest is defined to include interest paid or accrued on indebtedness incurred or continued to purchase or carry property held for investment. * * *

Investment interest does not include any interest that is taken into account in determining the taxpayer's income or loss from a passive activity. * * * Investment interest also does not include any qualified residence interest, as described [in § 163(h)(3)].

Net investment income

Investment income includes gross income from property held for investment, gain [other than long-term capital gain] attributable to the disposition of property held for investment, and amounts treated as gross portfolio income under the passive loss rule. Investment income also includes income from interests in activities, involving a trade or business, in which the taxpayer does not materially participate, if that activity is not treated as a passive activity under the passive loss rule.

Net investment income is investment income net of investment expenses. Investment expenses are deductible expenses (other than interest) directly connected with the production of investment income. Under the Act, if depreciation or depletion deductions are allowed with respect to assets that produce investment income, investment expense is determined utilizing the actual depreciation or depletion deductions allowable. In determining other deductible investment expenses, it is intended that investment expenses be considered as those allowed after application of the rule limiting deductions for miscellaneous expenses to those expenses exceeding two percent of adjusted gross income. In computing the amount of expenses that exceed the 2-percent floor, expenses that are not investment expenses are intended to be disallowed before any investment expenses are disallowed.

* * * The investment interest limitation is not intended to disallow a deduction for interest expense which in the same year is required to be capitalized (e.g., construction interest subject to sec. 263A) or is disallowed (e.g., under sec. 265 (relating to tax-exempt interest)).

DETAILED ANALYSIS

1.   ANALYSIS

In certain important respects the rules in § 163(d) are more generous to taxpayers than if capitalization of investment interest were required. The rules permit investment interest to offset investment income from all assets, not just the investment income from the asset to which the interest relates under the tracing rules of Temp. Reg. § 1.163–8T. A capitalization approach would require at least that the interest in excess of the income from the investment asset be capitalized. Although current law avoids some of the administrative difficulties of relating the indebtedness to particular assets, the aggregation approach to some extent may limit the effectiveness of § 163(d) in dealing with problems of timing and conversion.

The 1976 version of § 163(d) allowed *no* interest deduction (in excess of the $10,000 floor) except in years in which ordinary net investment income was realized. Investment income did not include long-term capital gains. Thus, the 1976 version of § 163(d) was both a deferral and, to the extent a taxpayer realized income as capital gains rather than ordinary income, a disallowance provision. In principle, to the extent long-term capital gains are taxed, they should be included in investment income for purposes of § 163(d). The exclusion of long-term capital gains from the definition of investment income against which investment interest may be deducted is a draconian rule that would not exist under a capitalization approach.

Because the 1986 Act taxed long-term capital gains at the same rate as ordinary income, the 1986 Act revision of § 163(d) included long-term capital gains as investment income. As a result of the reintroduction of a significant capital gains preference in subsequent tax acts, the conversion problem addressed in the 1969 Act reappeared. This situation led Congress to amend § 163(d) in 1993 to eliminate net long-term capital gains from the investment income computation, as they were prior to 1986. However, § 163(d) also permits taxpayers to take long-term capital gains into account in computing investment income under § 163(d) if they forgo the preferential rate in any given year.

2.　INTERPRETATIVE ISSUES

2.1. *Investment Versus Trade or Business*

Section 163(d) applies only to investment interest; it does not apply to interest incurred in a trade or business. The principles for drawing the line are similar to those used to distinguish § 162 expenses from § 212 expenses, see Chapter 12, Section 1. Compare King v. Commissioner, 89 T.C. 445 (1987), holding that § 163(d) did not apply to interest paid by a commodity trader to carry gold futures contracts, and Morley v. Commissioner, 87 T.C. 1206 (1986), holding that interest on loans to purchase real property held for resale by a real estate broker was not investment interest, with Polakis v. Commissioner, 91 T.C. 660 (1988), holding that interest incurred by a physician to acquire undeveloped real property was investment interest.

In Rev. Rul. 93–68, 1993–2 C.B. 72, the Service held that, under the definition of investment in § 163(d)(5)(A), interest incurred with respect to the purchase of corporate stock for the purpose of protecting the individual's employment with the corporation is investment interest unless the individual is a dealer or trader in securities. In Russon v. Commissioner, 107 T.C. 263 (1996), the Tax Court sustained the Commissioner's position in Rev. Rul. 93–68 and held that § 163(d) applies to interest allocable to any investment in property that produces interest, dividends, annuities, or royalties not derived in the ordinary course of a trade or business. The statutory standard is an objective test based on the type of income "normally" produced by property of the type in question, and the taxpayer's particular intent in acquiring the property is not relevant. Applying this objective test, interest that the taxpayer incurred on a loan to purchase stock of a closely held corporation was investment interest even though his intent in purchasing the stock was to secure employment and earn a salary from a corporation that had never paid any dividends.

2.2. *Investment Income*

The 2003 Act added § 1(h)(11), which, as subsequently amended, provides that dividends received by taxpayers other than corporations generally will be taxed at the same rate as long-term capital gains: zero percent for capital gains and dividends that would have been taxed in the 10 and 15 percent brackets if they had been taxed at ordinary income rates, 15 percent for capital gains and dividends that would have been taxed in the tax brackets higher than 15 percent but below the 39.6 percent bracket if they had been taxed at ordinary income rates, and 20 percent for capital gains and dividends that would have been taxed in the 39.6 percent bracket if they had been taxed at ordinary income rates. See Chapter 8, Section 3. The existence of this preferential rate for dividends gives rise to tax arbitrage possibilities similar to those that arise when an interest deduction is allowed with respect to investments that produce only tax-favored capital gains. Accordingly, the 2003 Act also amended § 163(d)(4) to exclude from the definition of net investment income any dividends that are taxed at preferential rates under § 1(h). However, §§ 1(h)(11)(D)(i) and 163(d)(4)(B) allow taxpayers to elect to forgo the preferential rates for dividends and to treat the dividends as investment income for purposes of § 163(d). If a taxpayer does not have other investment income against which investment interest may be deducted under § 163(d), it is to the taxpayer's advantage to elect not to have the preferential rates under § 1(h) apply to an amount of dividend income equal to the amount of investment interest that otherwise would be nondeductible by virtue of § 163(d).

2.3. *Investment Expenses*

The § 212 investment expenses taken into account in computing net investment income under § 163(d) are limited to the amount deductible after applying § 67. See Chapter 21, Section 7. See also Keating v. Commissioner, 89 T.C. 1071 (1987) (Acq.) (nonbusiness bad debts were treated as investment expenses under § 163(d) only to extent they were currently deductible under § 166(d)).

B. CAPITALIZATION OF INTEREST

INTERNAL REVENUE CODE: Sections 263A(f); 461(g).

Profit-seeking interest historically was considered to be deductible without regard to the limitation on capital expenditures applicable to most other profit-seeking expenditures. While this result does not seem to have been required by the explicit statutory structure of the Code, the courts were unwilling to apply the capital expenditure limitation of § 263 to the interest deduction. See e.g., Commissioner v. Idaho Power Co., 418 U.S. 1 (1974). In addition, prior to 1976, Congress, in enacting various rules requiring capitalization in specific circumstances, seems to have assumed that § 263 is inapplicable to interest. In 1976, Congress enacted former § 189, requiring the capitalization of interest incurred by individuals during the construction period of a building. The capitalization of interest requirement was expanded when the more comprehensive interest capitalization rules of § 263A(f) were enacted.

Under § 263A(f), interest must be capitalized if it is paid or incurred by any taxpayer, not just an individual, during the production period of (1) any real property, (2) any personal property to be held for use in the taxpayer's (or a related party's) trade or business and having a class life of twenty years or more under § 168, or (3) any personal property with an estimated production period exceeding two years (one year if construction costs exceed $1 million). The production period is defined in § 263A(f)(4)(B) as beginning when production starts and ending when the property is ready to be placed in service or to be held for sale. Thus interest expense incurred to carry inventory after it is constructed is currently deductible.

DETAILED ANALYSIS

1.   "AVOIDED COST" METHOD OF INTEREST ALLOCATION

Section 263A(f) applies not only to interest traced to production expenses under Temp. Reg. § 1.163–8T, but also to other interest incurred by the taxpayer "to the extent that the taxpayer's interest costs could have been reduced if production expenditures were limited to those paid from borrowings directly attributable to the expenditures." The latter allocation, referred to as the "avoided cost" method of attributing interest expense, reflects a stacking approach to classifying interest. Its operation is explained by the following excerpt from Staff of the Joint Committee on Taxation, General Explanation of the Tax Reform Act of 1986, 511 (1987):

> Under [these] rules, any interest expense that the taxpayer would have avoided if production expenditures had been used to repay debt of the taxpayer is treated as allocable to production of property. Accordingly, under [§ 263A(f)(2)(A)(i)], any debt that can be specifically traced to production expenditures is first allocated to production and interest on such debt is capitalized. If production expenditures exceed the amount of the specifically traceable debt, interest on other debt of the taxpayer must be capitalized [under § 263A(f)(2)(A)(ii)] to the extent of the excess. For this purpose, the assumed interest rate is an average of the rates on the taxpayer's outstanding debt, excluding debt specifically traceable to production or construction.

Thus, for example, if a taxpayer borrows $500,000 specifically to construct a building that costs $800,000, not only is production period interest on the $500,000 loan capitalized, but during the production period of the building, interest on $300,000 of other indebtedness of the taxpayer also is capitalized. Furthermore, if the taxpayer owns construction equipment that is used in the construction of a building, as in *Idaho Power,* interest on any of the taxpayer's outstanding debt allocable to that equipment must be capitalized into the basis of the building. I.R.C. § 263A(f)(3).

Section 263A(f) does not apply to property produced for the taxpayer's use other than in a trade or business or an activity conducted for profit, for example, a personal residence. See Treas. Reg. § 1.263A–8(b)(3)(ii). Nor does the avoided cost attribution of interest apply to any of the taxpayer's personal interest, whether nondeductible under § 163(h) or deductible as qualified residence interest. Treas. Reg. § 1.263A–9(a)(4)(iv) and (v). This rule prevents a deferred deduction for interest that would be nondeductible under § 163(h), while preserving the preferential treatment of home mortgage interest expense accorded by § 163(h)(3).

2.   PREPAID INTEREST

Taxpayers on the accrual method of accounting may only deduct interest for the year to which the interest relates. Section 461(g) extends this rule to prepaid interest of taxpayers on the cash receipts and disbursements method of accounting by requiring that prepaid interest be capitalized and treated as paid in the year to which it is allocable. For a discussion of this provision see Chapter 28, Section 2.B.(2).4.

3.   CAPITALIZATION OF INTEREST ALLOCABLE TO "STRADDLES"

Section 263(g) addresses a special application of the situation that generally is the focus of § 163(d)—transactions producing a current interest deduction and income taxable as capital gains in a later year. "Straddle transactions" involve the ownership of offsetting positions in financial market investment property, and typically involve options, such as simultaneously holding put and call options with respect to the same corporate stock. As one leg of the option increases in value the other leg declines in value. The transactions are designed to eliminate almost all economic risk and thus involve exclusively the sale of tax benefits. Section 263(g) addresses this problem by requiring capitalization of any interest expenses attributable to straddle transactions.

4.   ELECTION TO CAPITALIZE INTEREST

Apart from the special rules *requiring* the capitalization of construction period interest and taxes, a taxpayer who for some reason cannot utilize the allowable deductions for interest and taxes may *elect* to capitalize the expenditures under § 266.

C.   INTEREST ON LOANS TO ACQUIRE OR CARRY TAX-EXEMPT BONDS

INTERNAL REVENUE CODE: Section 265(a)(2).

Revenue Procedure 72–18
1972–1 C.B. 740.

Sec. 1.   Purpose.

The purpose of this Revenue Procedure is to set forth guidelines for taxpayers and field offices of the Internal Revenue Service for the application of section [265(a)(2)] of the Internal Revenue Code of 1954 to certain taxpayers holding state and local obligations the interest on which is wholly exempt from Federal income tax. * * *

Sec. 2.   Background.

* * * It is clear from the legislative history of [section 265(a)(2)] and of subsequent unsuccessful efforts to amend [the section] that Congress intended to disallow interest under section [265(a)(2)] of the Code only upon a showing of a purpose by the taxpayer to use borrowed funds to purchase or carry tax-exempt securities. * * *

Sec. 3.   General Rules.

.01 Section [265(a)(2)] of the Code is only applicable where the indebtedness is incurred or continued for the purpose of purchasing or carrying tax-exempt securities. Accordingly, the application of section [265(a)(2)] of the Code requires a determination, based on all the facts and circumstances, as to the taxpayer's purpose in incurring or continuing each item of indebtedness. Such purpose may, however, be established either by direct evidence or by circumstantial evidence.

.02 Direct evidence of a purpose to *purchase* tax-exempt obligations exists where the proceeds of indebtedness are used for, and are directly traceable to, the purchase of tax-exempt obligations. Wynn v. United States, 411 F.2d 614 (1969) * * * . Section [265(a)(2)] does not apply, however, where proceeds of a bona fide business indebtedness are temporarily invested in tax-exempt obligations * * * .

.03 Direct evidence of a purpose to *carry* tax-exempt obligations exists where tax-exempt obligations are used as collateral for indebtedness. "[O]ne who borrows to buy tax-exempts and one who borrows against tax-exempts already owned are in virtually the same economic position. Section [265(a)(2)] makes no distinction between them." Wisconsin Cheeseman v. United States, [388] F.2d 420, at 422 (1968).

.04 In the absence of direct evidence linking indebtedness with the purchase or carrying of tax-exempt obligations as illustrated in paragraphs .02 and .03 above, section [265(a)(2)] of the Code will apply only if the totality of facts and circumstances supports a reasonable inference that the purpose to purchase or carry tax-exempt obligations exists. Stated alternatively, section [265(a)(2)] will apply only where the totality of facts and circumstances establishes a "sufficiently direct relationship" between the borrowing and the investment in tax-exempt obligations. See *Wisconsin Cheeseman,* 388 F.2d 420, at 422. The guidelines set forth in sections 4, 5, and 6 shall be applied to determine whether such a relationship exists.

.05 Generally, where a taxpayer's investment in tax-exempt obligations is insubstantial, the purpose to purchase or carry tax-exempt obligations will not ordinarily be inferred in the absence of direct evidence as set forth in sections 3.02 and 3.03. In the case of an individual, investment in tax-exempt obligations shall be presumed insubstantial only where during the taxable year the average amount of the tax-exempt obligations (valued at their adjusted basis) does not exceed 2 percent of the average adjusted basis of his portfolio investments (as defined in section 4.04) and any assets held in the active conduct of a trade or business. * * *

Sec. 4.　Guidelines for Individuals.

.01 In the absence of direct evidence of the purpose to purchase or carry tax-exempt obligations (as set forth in sections 3.02 and 3.03), the rules set forth in this section shall apply.

.02 An individual taxpayer may incur a * * * mortgage [debt] to purchase or improve a residence or other real property which is held for personal use. Generally, section [265(a)(2)] of the Code will not apply to indebtedness of this type, because the purpose to purchase or carry tax-exempt obligations cannot reasonably be inferred where a personal purpose unrelated to the tax-exempt obligations ordinarily dominates the transaction. For example, section [265(a)(2)] of the Code generally will not apply to an individual who holds salable municipal bonds and takes out a mortgage to buy a residence instead of selling his municipal bonds to finance the purchase price. Under such circumstances the purpose of incurring the indebtedness is so directly related to the personal purpose of acquiring a residence that no sufficiently direct relationship between the borrowing and the investment in tax-exempt obligations may reasonably be inferred.

.03 The purpose to purchase or carry tax-exempt obligations generally does not exist with respect to indebtedness incurred or continued by an individual in connection with the active conduct of trade or business (other than a dealer in tax-exempt obligations) unless it is determined that the borrowing was in excess of business needs. However, there is a rebuttable presumption that the purpose to *carry* tax-exempt obligations exists where the taxpayer reasonably could have foreseen at the time of purchasing the tax-exempt obligations that indebtedness probably would have to be incurred to meet future economic needs of the business of an ordinary, recurrent variety. * * * The presumption may be rebutted, however, if the taxpayer demonstrates that business reasons, unrelated to the purchase or carrying of tax-exempt obligations, dominated the transaction.

.04 Generally, a purpose to *carry* tax-exempt obligations will be inferred, unless rebutted by other evidence, wherever the taxpayer has outstanding indebtedness which is not directly connected with personal expenditures (see section 4.02) and is not incurred or continued in connection with the active conduct of a trade or business (see section 4.03) and the taxpayer owns tax-exempt obligations. This inference will be made even though the indebtedness is ostensibly incurred or continued to purchase or carry other portfolio investments.

Portfolio investment for the purposes of this Revenue Procedure includes transactions entered into for profit (including investment in real estate) which are not connected with the active conduct of a trade or business. * * * A substantial ownership interest in a corporation will not be considered a portfolio investment. * * *

A sufficiently direct relationship between the incurring or continuing of indebtedness and the purchasing or carrying of tax-exempt obligations will generally exist where indebtedness is incurred to finance portfolio investment because the choice of whether to finance a new portfolio investment through borrowing or through the liquidation of an existing investment in tax-exempt obligations typically involves a purpose either to maximize profit or to maintain a diversified portfolio. This purpose necessarily involves a decision, whether articulated by the taxpayer or not, to incur (or continue) the indebtedness, at least in part, to purchase or carry the existing investment in tax-exempt obligations.

A taxpayer may rebut the presumption that section [265(a)(2)] of the Code applies in the above circumstances by establishing that he could not have liquidated his holdings of tax-exempt obligations in order to avoid incurring indebtedness. The presumption may be overcome where, for example, liquidation is not possible because the tax-exempt obligations cannot be sold. * * *

The provisions of this paragraph may be illustrated by the following example:

> Taxpayer A, an individual, owns common stock listed on a national securities exchange, having an adjusted basis of $200,000; he owns rental property having an adjusted basis of $200,000; he has cash of $10,000; and he owns readily marketable municipal bonds having an adjusted basis of $41,000. A borrows $100,000 to invest in a limited partnership interest in a real estate syndicate and pays $8,000 interest on the loan which he claims as an interest deduction for the taxable year. Under these facts and circumstances, there is a presumption that the $100,000 indebtedness which is incurred to finance A's portfolio investment is also incurred to carry A's existing investment in tax-exempt bonds since there are no additional facts or circumstances to rebut the presumption. Accordingly, a portion of the $8,000 interest payment will be disallowed under section [265(a)(2)] of the Code.

See section 7 concerning the amount to be disallowed. * * *

Sec. 7.   Procedures.

.01 When there is direct evidence under sections 3.02 and 3.03 establishing a purpose to purchase or carry tax-exempt obligations (either because tax-exempt obligations were used as collateral for indebtedness or the proceeds of indebtedness were directly traceable to the holding of particular tax-exempt obligations) no part of the interest paid or incurred on such indebtedness may be deducted. However, if only a fractional part of the indebtedness is directly traceable to the holding of particular tax-exempt obligations, the same fractional part of the interest paid or incurred on such indebtedness will be disallowed. For example, if A borrows $100,000 from a bank and invests $75,000 of the proceeds in tax-exempt obligations, 75 percent of the interest paid on the bank borrowing would be disallowed as a deduction.

.02 In any other case where interest is to be disallowed in accordance with this Revenue Procedure, an allocable portion of the interest on such indebtedness will be disallowed. The amount of interest on such indebtedness to be disallowed shall be determined by multiplying the total interest on such indebtedness by a fraction, the numerator of which is the average amount during the taxable year of the taxpayer's tax-exempt obligations (valued at their adjusted basis) and the denominator of which is the average amount during the taxable year of the taxpayer's total assets (valued at their adjusted basis) minus the amount of any indebtedness the interest on which is not subject to disallowance to any extent under this Revenue Procedure.

DETAILED ANALYSIS

1.   TRACING VERSUS FORMULAIC ALLOCATION

Section 265(a)(2), dealing specifically only with interest expenses that are related to tax-exempt interest income, in general reflects a tracing approach but one that is somewhat broader than the general tracing rules of Temp. Reg. § 1.163–8T. Section 265(a)(2) requires a showing of a *purpose* by the taxpayer to use the borrowed funds to *purchase or carry* tax-exempt securities. The requirement of purpose establishes the connection between the borrowing and the tax-exempt securities. Thus, interest that under the general rules is traced to a particular expenditure other than the purchase of tax-exempt bonds, for example, taxable investment securities, nevertheless may be traced to *carrying* tax-exempt bonds under § 265(a)(2). Temp. Reg. § 1.163–8T(m)(2). For example, in E.F. Hutton Group, Inc. v. United States, 811 F.2d 581 (Fed.Cir.1987), § 265(a)(2) was applied to disallow a deduction for a portion of the interest (determined under Rev. Proc. 72–18, § 5.03) on debt incurred to enable a brokerage house to meet the net capital requirements of the New York Stock Exchange because the borrowing enabled the taxpayer to continue to hold tax-exempt bonds.

In some situations, Rev. Proc. 72–18 allocates interest expense between tax-exempt and taxable income. Where there is no direct evidence of a connection between the borrowing and the tax-exempt securities, there is nonetheless a presumption that the borrowing relates to all portfolio investments, both taxable and tax-exempt (§ 4.04). If the presumption cannot be overcome, the interest expense is allocated on the basis of asset bases (§ 7.02). In addition, § 265(b) provides a special rule requiring allocation rather than tracing in all cases when § 265 is applied to disallow interest expense deductions for financial institutions.

In contrast to the general tracing approach in § 265(a)(2), § 265(a)(1) in general adopts an allocation approach that applies to all expenses, including interest, which are allocable to tax-exempt income other than interest. See Chapter 12, Section 4.

2.   BUSINESS AND PERSONAL INDEBTEDNESS

Section 265(a)(2) generally does not apply to indebtedness incurred or continued in connection with the active conduct of a trade or business. Rev. Proc. 72–18, §§ 4.02, 4.03. Substantial litigation has arisen regarding whether indebtedness has the business connection claimed by the taxpayer.

The active trade or business exception does not apply where the borrowing is in excess of business needs. Thus, Indian Trail Trading Post, Inc. v. Commissioner, 60 T.C. 497 (1973), aff'd per curiam, 503 F.2d 102 (6th Cir.1974), held § 265(a)(2) applicable where the taxpayer borrowed funds in excess of its business needs and invested the funds some eight months later in tax-exempt bonds: "Under these circumstances, it might be said that there is a sufficient degree of tracing present to justify the inference that, whatever petitioner's original purpose may have been, it became so diffused by the act of allowing the funds to lie fallow that the actual use of the funds for the acquisition of the bonds provided the necessary purposive connection with the earlier borrowing." 60 T.C. at 501. On the other hand, Handy Button Machine Co. v. Commissioner, 61 T.C. 846 (1974), distinguished *Indian Trail Trading Post* where the purchase by the business of the tax-exempt bonds had preceded the borrowing. The Government argued that the taxpayer had made a conscious choice to incur the subsequent borrowings rather than to liquidate its tax-exempt holdings and this combination of facts brought § 265(a)(2) into play. The Government also argued that a conscious choice was made in subsequent years as evidenced by taxpayer's failure to prepay the indebtedness. The Tax Court rejected the application of such a "mechanical" rule in holding that the requisite purpose was not present.

Although personal interest generally is not deductible, § 163(h)(3) permits individuals to deduct interest on "home equity indebtedness," e.g., second mortgage interest, without regard to the use to which the loan proceeds are traced under Temp. Reg. § 1.163–8T. See Temp. Reg. § 1.163–10T(b). Section 265(a)(2) can override § 163(h)(3), however, and disallow a deduction for interest on home equity indebtedness if the proceeds are used to buy tax-exempt bonds. Mariorenzi v. Commissioner, T.C. Memo. 1973–141, aff'd per curiam, 490 F.2d 92 (1st Cir.1974), held 265(a)(2) applicable where the taxpayers took out a loan secured by their personal residence shortly before substantially increasing their investment in tax-exempt bonds; in making the investments they were following the advice given them by an investment advisor prior to taking out the mortgage loan.

3.   INVESTMENT INDEBTEDNESS

Rev. Proc. 72–18 indicates that a purpose to carry tax-exempt obligations will be inferred, absent evidence to the contrary, whenever the taxpayer owns tax-exempt obligations and has outstanding indebtedness not directly connected with personal expenditures or an active trade or business. Thus, under the Internal Revenue Service view, if the taxpayer borrows or continues an indebtedness in connection with a portfolio investment (defined to include investments in real estate) and at the same time holds municipal bonds, § 265(a)(2) presumptively will apply. In such a situation, the presumption can be overcome only by showing that a liquidation of the tax-exempt obligations was not possible; it is not sufficient to show simply that the tax-exempt obligations could have been liquidated with difficulty or at a loss.

In Ball v. Commissioner, 54 T.C. 1200 (1970) (Nonacq.), the Tax Court refused to follow this approach. The taxpayer, while holding tax-exempt bonds, incurred obligations that were related to various other investment activities. The Commissioner argued that § 265(a)(2) should operate to disallow the interest deduction on those obligations since the taxpayer held the tax-exempt bonds at the same time he borrowed to make the other investments. No new investments were made in tax-exempt bonds during the years in question. The Tax Court refused to apply § 265, holding that a "sufficiently direct relationship" between the borrowing and the tax-exempt bonds was not established.

4. POLICY ASPECTS

Section 265 reflects the traditional tax policy view that the costs of producing tax-exempt income, including interest, should be disallowed if administratively feasible. Similarly, costs of producing tax-favored income should be proportionately disallowed. The justification for allowing costs of producing income is to measure net income; if the gross receipts are not included in gross income under § 61, then, under this view, no costs of producing that income should be allowed.

Tax-preferred income generally bears an "implicit tax." See discussion of tax-exempt bonds at Chapter 8, Section 4. Viewed from this perspective, deduction of expenses associated with tax-preferred income should arguably be allowed to the extent that the expenses relate to income that is subject to an implicit tax. The data, however, indicate that the "implicit tax" on tax-exempt state and local bonds is significantly less than the tax that would have been incurred if the income had been fully taxable.[8] Thus, the limitation in § 265 remains necessary to restrain tax shelter activities involving tax-exempt bonds and to prevent the realization of tax arbitrage profits.

D. INTEREST INCURRED IN CONNECTION WITH INSURANCE CONTRACTS

INTERNAL REVENUE CODE: Section 264(a)(2)–(4).

Section 264(a)(2) through (a)(4) disallow deductions for interest incurred with respect to life insurance policies. Since 1954, § 263(a)(2) has disallowed a deduction for interest on indebtedness incurred or continued to purchase or carry a single premium life insurance, endowment, or annuity contract. Since 1963, § 264(a)(3) has disallowed a deduction for interest on indebtedness incurred or continued to purchase other life insurance, endowment, or annuity contracts pursuant to a plan of purchase contemplating the systematic borrowing of cash value.

Since 1997, § 264(a)(4) has disallowed any deduction for interest on indebtedness with respect to life insurance, endowment, or annuity contracts owned by any taxpayer insuring any individual. This rule applies to interest allocable to insurance policies carried for personal estate planning or investment motives, as well as to insurance policies carried in the course of the taxpayer's trade or business, but § 264(e)(1) provides an exception for $50,000 of "key person" insurance carried by a business. Section 264(a)(4) almost completely subsumes the situations covered by § 264(a)(2) and (a)(3).

Section 264(f) disallows any deduction for interest allocable to the unborrowed cash surrender value of life insurance policies owned by the

---

8   See McMahon, Simplifying the Interest Deduction for Individual Taxpayers, 91 Tax Notes 1371, 1406–1409 (May 28, 2001).

taxpayer. In applying this rule, interest paid or accrued during the year is allocated among all of the taxpayer's assets in proportion to their adjusted bases, except for life insurance policies, which are taken into account at the value of their cash reserves. Section 264(f) does not generally apply to individuals except with respect to any insurance policies held by an individual in the conduct of a trade or business. See S. Rep. No. 105–33, 105th Cong., 1st Sess. 186–187 (1997).

CHAPTER 17

BUSINESS TAX CREDITS

SECTION 1. INTRODUCTION

A taxpayer's tax liability may be reduced by tax credits. The business tax credits considered in this section are used primarily by corporations, but they are also available to other forms of business operations such as limited liability companies, partnerships, and sole proprietorships. Before examining the business tax credits in detail, it is helpful to consider some general characteristics and issues involved in the use of tax credits.

Credits Versus Deductions. As the preceding materials have indicated, trade or business deductions are subtracted from gross income. As a result, the financial benefit of a deduction is a function of the taxpayer's marginal tax rate. For example, a $100 deduction produces a $35 benefit to a taxpayer in the 35 percent rate bracket and a $15 benefit for a taxpayer in the 15 percent rate bracket. A tax credit, on the other hand, is subtracted from the taxpayer's tentative tax liability on a dollar-for-dollar basis.

Types of Credits. Some tax credits are part of the basic structure of the income tax. An example in this category is the credit for income taxes paid to foreign countries; the credit accommodates the U.S. income tax system to those of other countries when U.S. taxpayers are subject to tax both in the United States and foreign jurisdictions. Other tax credits are accounted for as tax expenditures, and provide an incentive for a particular activity or to relieve hardship. The low income housing credit, the credit for increased research expenses, and credits for education expenditures, discussed in Chapter 23, are examples of tax credits in the tax expenditure category. A tax credit can be employed where Congress wishes to limit the dollar amount of the tax benefit provided by a tax expenditure so as to replicate dollar limitations on direct grants.

Credits in Excess of Tax Liability. The amount of the tax credit for which a taxpayer is eligible may exceed the amount of tax owed. Two techniques can be used to insure that taxpayers in this situation do not lose the amount of credit that exceeds tax liability. One method "refunds" the taxpayer the portion of the credit in excess of tax liability. The payment is not literally a refund since it does not represent taxes actually paid by the taxpayer (as is the case of withheld income taxes, for example). Rather, the payment is a direct payment by the government to the taxpayer. A second technique permits the taxpayer to carry back and/or carry forward the excess credit, and apply it against tax liabilities in past or future years.

The Tax Treatment of Tax Expenditure Tax Credits. As discussed in earlier chapters, the value of a tax expenditure provided through an exclusion from income or a special deduction varies with the marginal tax bracket of the taxpayer—the higher the bracket the greater the value of the tax expenditure. A tax credit can avoid this result in certain circumstances. A tax expenditure tax credit is the equivalent of a direct government grant. If a direct grant had been employed, the proper income tax treatment of the grant would have to be determined. The grant either should be included in income or accompanied by a reduction in the basis of an asset (thus, in effect, including the credit in income over time through reduced depreciation deductions or through increased gain or reduced loss upon disposition of the property). A similar determination must be made when the government grant is supplied through a tax credit. Failure to include a credit in income (either immediately or over time) means that the value of the credit will vary with a taxpayer's marginal rate bracket. In recognition of this fact, Congress has in some instances required inclusion of a tax credit in income or, more frequently, achieved the same result by disallowing deductions for the expenses for which the tax credit is provided or by requiring that the basis of assets be reduced.

Ordering of Tax Credits. There are numerous tax credits included in the Code. Some are refundable and others are not; some are limited to a percentage of tax liability and others are not; some may be carried to other tax years and others may not; some are taxable and others are not. For a taxpayer qualifying for more than one tax credit, the order in which the various tax credits are to be taken may affect the benefit derived from one or more of the credits. For example, if one credit cannot be carried over if it exceeds tax liability, but a second credit may be carried over, the taxpayer would prefer to claim the non-carryover credit first since its benefit might otherwise be lost. Therefore, rules establish the order in which credits are claimed, set forth as follows:

1.   The nonrefundable personal credits in §§ 21–26.

2.   The foreign tax credit and certain business credits in §§ 27, 30A–30D.

3.   The nonrefundable business credits in §§ 38–50, 51A, 52–54F, 54AA.

4.   The refundable credits in §§ 31–36, 36B.

The following material discusses the history, technical issues and policy questions presented by the most important business credits. As you will see, Congress has enacted many of these credits as non-permanent Code provisions with expiration or "sunset" dates, mostly to avoid long-term budgetary impacts of the tax expenditures. As you will also see, as a credit's expiration date approaches, Congress may extend its application, allow it to expire but remain in the Code with no further application until subsequent Congressional action, or repeal it altogether. Such unpredictable and unreliable policymaking can adversely influence the incentive effects of these tax credits, particularly for those credits that Congress enacts or extends only at the very end of a calendar year. The personal credits are considered in Chapter 22, Section 2, and Chapter 23.

SECTION 2.   GENERAL BUSINESS CREDIT

The § 38 general business credit includes numerous separate tax credits. These credits are grouped as the general business credit under § 38 for purposes of determining the order of allowance, limitations on allowance, and carryover of unused credits. All of these credits are tax expenditure credits, and the various credits that comprise the general business credit are subject to wide variation, almost on a year-to-year basis, as Congress responds to economic and social issues that it wishes to address.

Section 38(c) provides a complex formula requiring that the credits allowed under §§ 21–30C be taken into account before determining the amount of the allowable general business credit. It also limits the extent to which the general business credit can offset alternative minimum tax liability in excess of regular tax liability. In any year in which the amount of the general business credit exceeds the applicable limits, § 39 provides for a 1-year carryback and a 20-year carryforward of the excess credit. Under § 39, the excess credit is used on a first-in, first-out (FIFO) basis; i.e., credit earned first is applied first. Thus, in a given year, the taxpayer will first apply any carryover credit from a prior year, then the credit for the current year, and finally any credit carried back to the current year from a succeeding year. If, after the 22-year period comprised of the 1-year carryback, current year, and 20-year carryover, the taxpayer has been unable to utilize the credit for a given year, § 196 allows the taxpayer to deduct in the twentieth carryover year the unused credit amount attributable to some, but not all, of the various credits that comprise the general business credit. If the limitation applies, § 38(d) provides the ordering rules for determining which credits have been used.

Many of the components of the general business credit are not permanent provisions but are reenacted from time to time, sometimes after a lapse, with specific sunset dates. When a provision sunsets, it generally is not removed from the Code, but simply becomes inoperative until it is revived in response to a particular perceived need for government intervention.

DETAILED ANALYSIS

1.   INVESTMENT CREDIT

1.1. *General*

The investment credit allowed by § 46 is itself the sum of six different credits. For most of the period from 1962 to 1985, the investment credit broadly allowed a credit equal to 10 percent of the cost of machinery and equipment used in the taxpayer's business. However, the investment credit no longer applies to the cost of machinery and equipment.

1.2. *Rehabilitation Credit*

The rehabilitation credit in § 47 is 10 percent of qualified rehabilitation costs incurred in rehabilitating certain buildings used in the taxpayer's trade or business that were built before 1936 (whether by the taxpayer or another taxpayer), and 20 percent of the rehabilitation costs incurred in rehabilitating certified historic buildings. The cost of the building itself is not included in calculating the credit. Because the purpose of the credit is to encourage historic preservation, at least 75 percent of the building's internal structural framework and external walls must remain in place, while at least 50 percent of the building's external walls must remain in place. See Nalle v. Commissioner, 99 T.C. 187 (1992) (pursuant to Treas. Reg. § 1.48–12(b)(5) the credit was not allowed for a structure that was relocated because exterior walls were not "retained in place"), rev'd, 997 F.2d 1134 (5th Cir.1993) (Treas. Reg. § 1.48–12(b)(5) is invalid because revitalization of "distressed areas" was not the sole goal of the rehabilitation credit and the regulation is inconsistent with the "plain language" of the statute).

1.3. *Energy Credit*

Section 48 provides a tax credit for placing in service equipment or property that utilizes non-traditional energy producing resources (e.g., solar energy). See § 48(a)(3). The allowable credit is the "energy percentage" multiplied by the basis of the energy property placed in service during the taxable year. The "energy percentage" is 30 percent for described categories of energy property and 10 percent for the balance. See § 48(a)(2).

1.4. *Qualifying Advanced Coal Project Credit and Qualifying Gasification Project Credit*

Sections 48A and 48B provide tax credits for investments in high technology projects to produce coal and gas pursuant programs to be developed by the Secretary of the Treasury (in the case of § 48B credit) in consultation with the Secretary of Energy.

1.5. *Basis Reduction and Recapture*

Section 50(c) requires that the basis of investment credit property be reduced by the full amount of the credit claimed, thus reducing future depreciation deductions. The effect of this rule is to include the amount of the credit in the taxpayer's income over the recovery period of the property.

Section 50(a) provides that if property is disposed of or ceases to be investment credit property in the hands of the taxpayer within five years all or part of the credit will be "recaptured" by inclusion of the amount of the credit in the taxpayer's income. Within the first year, 100 percent of the credit is recaptured; for each full year the property is held, recapture is reduced by 20 percentage points. See Rev. Rul. 89–90, 1989–32 C.B. 3 (conveyance of historical facade easement results in partial recapture of rehabilitation credit); Rome I, Ltd. v. Commissioner, 96 T.C. 697 (1991) (same).

1.6. *At-Risk Rule*

Section 49 provides that a taxpayer may claim an investment credit only if "at-risk" with respect to its investment. The at-risk concept is discussed in Chapter 35, Section 1.

2. WORK OPPORTUNITY AND EMPOWERMENT ZONE EMPLOYMENT WAGES CREDITS

2.1. *Work Opportunity Credit*

In 1971, Congress enacted a Work Incentive Program tax credit intended "to open up job opportunities for welfare recipients." The credit was available to employers who hired employees from the program and was equal to a specified percentage of their wages. The credit was revised in 1978 to provide a tax credit for wages paid to persons who were in one of the targeted groups of chronically unemployed, while Congress revised various technical aspects of the credit in succeeding years. Periodically, Congress acted to extend the credit, most recently until December 31, 2019.

The work opportunity tax credit under § 51 equals 40 percent of the first $6,000 of qualified first year wages. Employees' eligibility must be certified by a designated local employment agency, and they must work a minimum of 400 hours during the first year of employment. Wages paid to employees who work at least 120 hours but less than 400 hours are eligible for the credit at only 25 percent.

Eligible employees include certain "qualified" members of families receiving Temporary Assistance for Needy Families (TANF), recipients of the Supplemental Nutrition Assistance Program (SNAP, previously known as Food Stamps), veterans (for disabled veterans, the $6,000 ceiling is increased to $12,000), ex-felons, "designated community residents" (who must reside in an empowerment zone or enterprise community), vocational rehabilitation referrals, summer youth employees, and qualified long-term unemployment recipients," defined as persons who have been certified by local unemployment agencies as having been unemployed for at least 27 consecutive weeks, and as having received unemployment compensation for at least a portion of that period.

Under § 280C(a), the employer's deduction (or capitalization under § 263A) for wages must be reduced by the amount of the targeted jobs tax credit claimed. This requirement has the same effect as if the amount of the tax credit were treated as gross taxable income to the employer, and makes the credit equivalent to a taxable direct grant.

The efficacy of the credit in achieving its objective at a reasonable cost is doubtful. A 1993 report by the Inspector General of the Labor Department concluded that the program simply provided federal funds to employers who would have hired the targeted employees in any event. See Targeted Jobs Tax Credit Program, State of Alabama, October 1, 1990—September 30, 1991, LEXIS, 93 TNT 177–1. The Treasury estimated that in 1983 nine out of ten eligible targeted workers found employment without the benefit of the tax credit. See Subcommittee on Select Revenue Measures, Committee on Ways and Means, Hearings on Extension of the Targeted Jobs Tax Credit,

98th Cong., 2d Sess. (1984) (statement of Deputy Assistant Secretary of the Treasury for Tax Policy Charles E. McLure, Jr.).

2.2. *Empowerment Zone Employment Wages Credit*

Section 1396 allows employers a credit for wages paid to certain employees who work in an "empowerment zone." Empowerment zones are geographic zones designated by the Departments of Housing and Urban Development and Agriculture that suffer from pervasive poverty, unemployment, and general economic distress. A zone may be designated only if a state or local government requests designation and has a strategic plan for redevelopment.

The credit equals 20 percent of qualified zone wages with only the first $15,000 of wages qualifying for the credit paid to an employee who both works and resides in the empowerment zone. Thus the maximum credit is $3,000 per qualifying employee. Wages paid to individuals employed at golf courses, country clubs, massage parlors, tanning salons, gambling establishments, liquor stores, and farms with more than $500,000 of assets do not qualify; nor do wages that are taken into account in computing the work opportunity credit. Part-time employees qualify, but employees who are employed for less than 90 days do not qualify. Designated relatives of the employer or a 5 percent owner-employee do not qualify. Finally, § 280C(a) reduces the employer's deduction for wages paid by the amount of the credit claimed.

Analyses of similar legislation adopted by several states and in the United Kingdom conclude that such tax subsidies are ineffective in increasing aggregate employment among members of poor, unemployed, and economically distressed communities. See Ellen P. Aprill, Caution Enterprise Zones, 66 S. Cal. L. Rev. 1341 (1993). One obvious problem with the efficacy of these tax subsidies is that any job created within an empowerment zone may be at the expense of a formerly employed (and similarly poor) worker living outside the zone.

3. CREDIT FOR INCREASING RESEARCH EXPENDITURES

In 1981, Congress added the predecessor of § 41 to provide a 20 percent tax credit for qualified research expenses. Until 2016, the credit was not a permanent provision of the Code, and required periodic reenactment. In 2015, Congress made the credit permanent.

The qualified research credit is incremental in that it applies only to current-year expenditures in excess of the taxpayer's "base amount." In general, the "base amount" is a moving figure that reflects the percentage of the company's gross receipts expended for research from 1984 through 1988, but not more than 16 percent, multiplied by the company's average annual receipts for the preceding four years. Section 41(c)(3)(B) provides special rules for computing the base amount for "start-up" companies and companies that did not have gross receipts for at least three years during the 1984–1988 period. Section 41(c)(4) provides a complex, elective, alternative computation of the credit.

Section § 41(c)(5) provides an "alternative simplified credit." If a taxpayer elects to claim the "alternative simplified credit," rather than apply the regular § 41(a)(1) rules, the credit is 12 percent of the amount by which the qualified research expenses for the current year exceed 50 percent of the average qualified research expenses for the three preceding taxable years. For a taxpayer who has not had research expenses in each of the three preceding years, the credit is limited to 6 percent.

The definition of "qualified research" in § 41(d) is detailed and more restrictive than under § 174. In addition to qualifying as research under § 174, the research must be focused on discovering information that is "technological" in nature. Treas. Reg. § 1.48–4(a)(3). Research is technological if the process of experimentation relies on the physical or biological sciences, engineering, or computer science. Research in the social sciences, arts, and humanities does not qualify. See TSR, Inc. v. Commissioner, 96 T.C. 903 (1991) (credit was not available for research and development of the game "Dungeons and Dragons"). Moreover, it must relate to a new or improved function, performance, or reliability or quality. Surveys and similar studies do not qualify. The research is not required to succeed, but obtaining a patent is conclusive evidence that the research qualifies. The credit is available not only for "in-house" expenditures but also for certain amounts paid to independent research firms or universities. Governmentally funded research, however, is not eligible for the credit, nor is research conducted outside the United States.

The research expenses must be paid or incurred by the taxpayer "in carrying on any trade or business of the taxpayer." The congressional Committee Reports stated that the "carrying on" test for purposes of the credit "generally is the same as for purposes of § 162." Thus, it appears that research expenditures otherwise meeting the definitional requirements of § 41(b) might qualify for the § 174 immediate expensing deduction under the interpretation given by the Supreme Court in *Snow* (see Chapter 14, Section 3.1.), but not qualify for the research and experimentation credit under § 41. To limit the potential use of the credit in tax shelter transactions, § 41(g) provides that in certain circumstances individuals may claim the credit only against taxes on income generated by the business carrying on the research and experimentation activity.

Section 280C(c) disallows a deduction for an amount of research expenditures for which the credit is claimed equal to the amount of the credit, thereby effectively including the amount of the credit in gross income. Alternatively, a taxpayer may elect to claim a reduced credit, and deduct the full amount of the research expenditures.

The incremental aspect of the credit is intended to reward only increased levels of expenditure on research and development by a given taxpayer. However, the interaction of the incremental feature and the rolling base, when applied to dissimilar patterns of research and development expenditures over several years, can result in two companies qualifying for differing amounts of credits, even though each company spent the same amount on research and development during a given period.

4.   LOW-INCOME HOUSING CREDIT

4.1. *General*

The low-income housing credit provided in § 42 was enacted in 1986 to encourage private investment in low-income housing projects.

Only residential rental property that meets one of two tests for a "qualified low-income housing project" is eligible for the credit. Under the first alternative, at least 20 percent of the rental units must be "rent restricted" and occupied by individuals whose incomes are no greater than 50 percent of the area median income during a fifteen-year period beginning with the year the credit is first allowed. Alternatively, at least 40 percent of the units must be "rent restricted" and occupied by individuals whose incomes are no greater than 60 percent of the area median gross income. For a unit to be "rent restricted," the maximum rent that may be charged is 30 percent of the qualifying income of a family deemed to have a size of 1.5 persons per bedroom. For example, a two-bedroom unit has a rent limitation based on the qualifying income for a family of three.

The credit is not available for the acquisition of an existing building unless the building is substantially rehabilitated and certain other conditions have been met. This rule is intended to prevent churning of low-income housing properties among owners to multiply credits without the construction of additional low-income housing. Finally, the credit is available only to the extent the relevant state housing credit agency allocates a credit to the building. Each state housing credit agency is allocated an aggregate credit of $1.25 per resident per year. The state housing credit agency allocates that amount among low-income housing buildings that the owner has agreed to commit to low-income housing use for 30 years.

The credit is allowed in ten annual installments. The amount allowable each year is the "applicable percentage" of the "qualified basis." The applicable credit percentage is determined monthly by the Treasury, and generally set at an amount that results in the credit having a present value of 70 percent of the cost of the low-income housing units. For low-income housing that receives additional Federal subsidies (e.g., tax-exempt bond financing) and for the acquisition costs (e.g., costs other than rehabilitation expenditures) of existing housing that is substantially rehabilitated, the credit percentage is set to produce a credit having a present value equal to 30 percent of the qualified basis. Qualified basis is a fraction of the original cost of the building plus rehabilitation expenses; the fraction is the lower of (1) the ratio of the number of low-income units in the building to all units or (2) the ratio of the floor space of the low-income units to the floor space of all units in the building. Qualified basis is limited to the amount the taxpayer has "at risk" in the building (see Chapter 35, Section 1).

Generally, any disposition of a building within fifteen years of the first year for which a credit is allowed results in recapture of part of the credit. Recapture can be avoided if the selling taxpayer posts a bond with the Treasury Department and it can reasonably be expected that the building will continue to be operated as a qualified low-income building for the remainder of the fifteen-year period. If a building does not remain a qualified low-income project for fifteen years, a portion of all credit claimed is recaptured with interest. In addition, even though the building remains part of a qualified low-income project, if the number of qualified low income units is reduced, there is recapture, with interest, of the credit claimed for all previous years on the amount of the reduction in qualified basis. If a recapture is triggered by failure to comply with the low-income housing unit set-aside requirement, the taxpayer may correct the noncompliance within a reasonable period and avoid recapture.

4.2. *Policy Analysis*

Because credits are very clearly tax expenditures, Congress analyzes the economic and social effect of a credit in much the same manner that it analyzes direct spending programs. In this regard, tax credits are just one of several possible options for delivering the subsidy, and the effect of using a tax credit as opposed to a different delivery mechanism, or different tax expenditure, must be considered. The following excerpt from Staff of the Joint Committee on Taxation, Description and Analysis of Tax Provisions Expiring in 1992 (Comm. Print 1992), discusses some of the economic policy aspects of using the tax system to subsidize low-income housing. Its analysis applies equally to other tax credits discussed in this chapter.

Demand subsidies versus supply subsidies

As is the case with direct expenditures, the tax system may be used to improve housing opportunities for low-income families either by subsidizing rental payments (increasing demand) or by subsidizing construction and rehabilitation of low-income housing units (increasing supply).

Provision of Federal Section 8 housing vouchers is an example of a demand subsidy. Exclusion of the value of such vouchers from taxable income is an example of a demand subsidy in the Internal Revenue Code. By subsidizing a portion of rent payments, these vouchers enable beneficiaries to rent more or better housing than they might otherwise be able to afford. The low-income housing credit is an example of a supply subsidy. By offering a credit worth 70 percent of construction costs, it is hoped that the credit induces investors to provide housing which otherwise would not be built.

A demand subsidy can improve the housing opportunities of a low-income family by increasing the family's ability to pay for improved housing. * * * An increase in the demand for housing, however, may increase rents in the short run as families bid against one another for available housing. Consequently, while a family which receives the subsidy may benefit by being able to afford more or better housing, the resulting increase in market rents may reduce the well-being of other families. In addition, higher rents increase the income of owners of existing rental housing, and therefore may be expected to make rental housing a more attractive investment. Thus, in the long run, investors should supply additional housing ameliorating the current increase in market rents and expanding availability.

A supply subsidy can improve the housing opportunities of a low-income family by increasing the available supply of housing from which the family may choose. Generally speaking, a supply subsidy increases the investor's return to investment in rental housing. An increased after-tax return should induce investors to provide more rental housing. As the supply of rental housing increases, the market rents investors charge should decline as investors compete to attract tenants to their properties. Consequently, not only should qualifying low-income families benefit from an increased supply of housing, but other renters should also benefit. In addition, owners of existing housing should experience declines in income or declines in property values as rents fall.

Efficiency of tax subsidies

In principle, a demand or supply subsidy of equal size should lead to equal changes in improved housing opportunities.

However, both direct expenditures and tax subsidies for rental payments may not increase housing consumption dollar for dollar. One study of the Federal Section 8 Existing Housing Program suggests that, for every $100 of rent subsidy, a typical family increases its expenditure on housing by $22 and increases its expenditure on other goods by $78. * * *

The theory of subsidizing demand assumes that, by providing low-income families with more spending power, their increase in demand for housing will ultimately lead to more or better housing being available in the market. However, if the supply of housing to these families does not respond to the higher market prices that rent subsidies ultimately cause, the result will be that all existing housing costs more, the low-income tenants will have no better living conditions than before, and other tenants will face higher rents. The benefit of the subsidy will accrue primarily to the property owners because of the higher rents.

Supply subsidy programs can suffer from similar inefficiencies. If a developer had planned to build low-income rental units before enactment of the low-income housing credit, the developer may now find that the project qualifies for the credit. That is, the subsidized project may displace what otherwise would have been an unsubsidized project with no net gain in number of low-income housing units. If this is the case, the tax expenditure of the credit will result in little or no benefit except to the extent that the credit's targeting rules may force the developer to serve lower-income individuals than otherwise would have been the case. In addition, by depressing rents the supply subsidy may displace privately supplied housing.

One study of government-subsidized housing starts between 1961 and 1977 suggests that as many as 85 percent of the government-subsidized housing starts may have merely displaced unsubsidized housing starts. This figure is based on both moderate- and low-income housing starts, and therefore may overstate the potential inefficiency of tax subsidies solely for low-income housing.

* * *

Some believe that tax-based supply subsidies do not produce significant displacement within the low-income housing market because they believe that low-income housing is unprofitable and the private market would not otherwise build new housing for low-income individuals. In this view, tax-subsidized low-income housing starts would not displace unsubsidized low-income housing starts. However, the bulk of the stock of low-income housing consists of older, physically depreciated properties which once may have served a different clientele. Subsidies to new construction could make it no longer economic to convert some of these older properties to low-income use, thereby displacing potential low-income units.

The tax subsidy for low-income housing construction also could displace construction of other housing. Constructing rental housing requires specialized resources. A tax subsidy may induce these resources to be devoted to the construction of low-income housing rather than other housing. If most of the existing low-income housing stock originally was built to serve non-low-income individuals, a tax subsidy to newly constructed low-income housing could displace some privately supplied low-income housing in the long run.

Supply subsidies for low-income housing may be subject to some additional inefficiencies. As noted above much of the low-income housing stock consists of older structures. Subsidies to new construction may provide for units with more amenities or units of a higher quality than low-income individuals would be willing to pay for if given an equivalent amount of funds. That is, rather than have $100 spent on a newly constructed apartment, a low-income family may prefer to have consumed part of that $100 in increased food and clothing. In this sense, the supply subsidy may provide an inefficiently large quantity of housing services. If the supply subsidy involves fixed costs, such as the cost of obtaining a credit allocation under the low-income housing credit, a bias may be created towards large projects in order to amortize the fixed cost across a larger number of units. This may create an inefficient bias in favor of large projects. On the other hand, the construction and rehabilitation costs per unit may be less for large projects than for small projects. Lastly, unlike demand subsidies which permit the beneficiary to seek housing in any geographic location, supply subsidies may lead to housing being located in areas which, for example, are farther from places of employment than the beneficiary would otherwise choose. In this example, some of benefit of the supply subsidy is being dissipated through increased transportation cost.

Targeting the benefits of tax subsidies

* * *

Targeting the recipient of a demand-side tax subsidy does not necessarily result in targeting the benefit of the subsidy. As discussed above, if market supply does not respond to the increase in demand which the subsidy creates, the benefit of the subsidy would flow to landlords in the form of higher rents. Even if, as a result of the subsidy, recipients can successfully buy more or better housing, some of the benefit of the subsidy will not be spent on housing because demand subsidies are rarely fully efficient (this is because money is fungible and can be spent on many types of consumption).

On the other hand, a supply subsidy to housing will be spent on housing; although, as discussed above, this may not be in addition to housing spending that would have occurred in the absence of the subsidy. Further, to insure that the housing, once built, serves low-income families, income and rent limitations for tenants must be imposed as is the case for demand subsidies. While an income limit may be more effective in targeting the benefit of the housing to lower income levels than would an unrestricted market, it may best serve only those families at or near the income limit.

If, as with the low-income housing credit, rents are restricted to a percentage of targeted income, the benefits of the subsidy may not accrue equally to all low-income families. Those with incomes beneath the target level may pay a greater proportion of their income in rent than does a family with a greater income. On the other hand, to the extent that any new, subsidy-induced housing draws in only the highest of the targeted low-income families it should open units in the privately provided low-income housing stock for others.

Even though the subsidy may be directly spent on housing, targeting the supply subsidy, unlike a demand subsidy, does not necessarily result in targeting the benefit of the subsidy to recipient tenants. Not all of the subsidy will result in net additions to the housing stock. The principle of a supply subsidy is to induce the producer to provide something he or she otherwise would not. Thus, to induce the producer to provide the benefit of improved housing to low-income families, the subsidy must provide benefit to the producer.

5. HEALTH INSURANCE CREDIT

The Patient Protection and Affordable Care Act of 2010 enacted § 45R, which added to the § 38 general business credit a new credit for health insurance expenses of certain small business employers, effective for taxable years after 2010. Congress intended this provision to encourage small employers not required by the Act to provide health insurance to offer such insurance to their employees.

SECTION 3.   OTHER BUSINESS CREDITS

There are a number of other business tax credits that Congress has enacted, most with a very narrow set of beneficiaries. The following material provides a brief description of some of these credits. Each is a discrete spending program run through the tax system and is subject to the analysis and tradeoffs described in Chapter 11. Generally speaking, these credits can be grouped into three broad categories: (1) energy-related credits; (2) employment-related credits; and (3) additional research and investment-related credits.

DETAILED ANALYSIS

1.   ENERGY-RELATED CREDITS

1.1. *Alternative Fuel Vehicle Refueling Property Credit*

Section 30C provides a credit equal to 30 percent of the cost of any qualified alternative fuel vehicle refueling property placed in service by the taxpayer. Qualifying fuels are ethanol, natural gas, compressed natural gas, liquefied natural gas, liquefied petroleum gas, hydrogen, and mixtures of diesel and biodiesel containing at least 20 percent biodiesel. For a business taxpayer, the credit generally may not exceed $30,000 with respect to all qualified property placed in service by the taxpayer during the taxable year at a particular location. The credit's application to qualified business property is part of the § 38 general business credit. The credit is also available to a taxpayer installing a refueling facility on the grounds of his personal residence for personal use, but the maximum amount of the nonbusiness credit is $1,000. The credit is temporary and has been extended many times. It will expire after December 31, 2016, unless it is extended again.

1.2. *Alcohol Fuels Credit*

The alcohol fuels credit in § 40 was enacted in 1980 as an incentive to develop gasohol as a fuel alternative to gas produced from crude oil. The amount of the credit was includable in gross income under § 87. The alcohol fuels credit consisted of (1) the alcohol mixture credit, (2) the alcohol credit, (3) the small ethanol producer credit, and (4) the second generation biofuel producer credit. The first three credits expired at the end of 2011, while the second-generation biofuel producer credit will expire on December 31, 2016.

1.3. *Biodiesel Fuels Credit*

Section 40A provides a biodiesel fuels credit that is the sum of two separately computed credits: the biodiesel fuel mixture credit and the biodiesel credit. The biodiesel fuel mixture credit generally is 50 cents for each gallon of biodiesel fuel used by the taxpayer in the production of a qualified biodiesel mixture; a qualified biodiesel mixture is a mixture of biodiesel and diesel fuel that is sold by the taxpayer for use as fuel or is used as fuel by the taxpayer in the taxpayer's trade or business. The biodiesel credit is 50 cents for each gallon of biodiesel that is not in a mixture with diesel fuel and which the taxpayer either uses as fuel in a trade or business or is sold at retail by the taxpayer to someone who places it in the fuel tank of a vehicle (as would occur in a gas station). The credit amount is increased to $1.00 per gallon for "agri-biodiesel," which is defined as "biodiesel derived solely from virgin oils, including esters derived from virgin vegetable oils from corn, soybeans, sunflower seeds, cottonseeds, canola, crambe, rapeseeds, safflowers, flaxseeds, rice bran, and mustard seeds, and from animal fats." A producer of agri-biodiesel that does not otherwise qualify for a credit under § 40A can qualify for the "small agri-biodiesel credit," equal to 10 cents per gallon of qualified agri-biodiesel production (which is limited to 15 million gallons per year) for producers with an annual productive capacity of no more than 60 million gallons. Unlike most other credits, the taxpayer's deductions or basis with respect to the biodiesel or biodiesel mixture is unaffected by the credit, nor is the credit included in the taxpayer's gross income. The § 40A credit will expire at the end of 2016.

1.4. *Low Sulfur Diesel Fuel Production Credit*

Section 45H provides a credit of 5 cents for each gallon of low sulfur diesel fuel produced by small business refiners. The credit is limited to 25 percent of the qualified capital costs incurred by the refiner with respect to the facility, reduced by the aggregate § 45H credits claimed in prior years with respect to that facility. Amounts credited under this provision cannot increase the taxpayer's basis in the facility. Qualified capital costs are those necessary to comply with certain EPA regulations after January 1, 2003 and before the earlier of one year after the date on which the taxpayer must be in compliance with the regulations, or December 31, 2009. Section 280C(d) disallows any deduction with respect to the production of low-sulfur diesel fuel in an amount equal to the credit.

1.5. *Credit for Producing Oil and Gas from Marginal Wells*

Section 45I provides a credit of $3 per barrel of qualified crude oil production and 50 cents per 1,000 cubic feet of qualified natural gas production from a domestic "qualified marginal well" (defined in § 45I(c)(3)(A). The credit amounts are reduced as oil and gas prices increase. If the production also qualifies for the § 45K credit, infra, the credit under § 45I is not allowed unless the taxpayer waives the § 45K credit. Unlike most other credits, the taxpayer's deductions or basis with respect to the production is unaffected by the credit, nor is it included in the taxpayer's gross income.

1.6. *Advanced Nuclear Power Facility Credit*

Section 45J provides a credit of 1.8 cents per kilowatt-hour of electricity produced at a qualifying advanced nuclear power facility during the eight-year period beginning on the date the facility is placed in service. To qualify, the taxpayer must have received an allocation of megawatt capacity from the IRS and the facility must have been placed in service before January 1, 2021.

1.7. *New Energy Efficient Home Credit*

Section 45L provides a credit, in the amount of either $2,000 or $1,000, to an eligible contractor (including the producer of a manufactured home) who constructs and sells an energy efficient home to a person who will use the home as a residence. The credit for any qualified new energy efficient home is set to expire at the end of 2016.

1.8. *Qualifying Advanced Coal Project Credit*

Section 48A provides a credit for investments in "qualifying advanced coal projects," defined as projects using integrated gasification combined cycle (IGCC) and other advanced coal-based technologies for generating electricity. The credit is available only for projects certified by the IRS, in consultation with the Department of Energy.

1.9. *Qualifying Gasification Project Credit*

Section 48B provides a 20 percent credit for investments in "qualifying gasification projects," defined as projects involving the conversion of coal, petroleum residue, biomass, or certain other materials into a synthesis gas composed primarily of carbon monoxide and hydrogen. The credit is available only for projects certified by the IRS, in consultation with the Department of Energy.

2.   EMPLOYMENT-RELATED CREDITS

2.1. *Employer Social Security Credit*

Section 45B allows an employer an elective credit in lieu of a deduction for a portion of the social security taxes paid by the employer with respect to tip income of employees serving food or beverages.

2.2. *Credit for Small Employer Pension Plan Startup Costs*

Section 45E provides a tax credit to small business employers (100 or fewer employees) to help cover the start-up administrative costs incurred in setting up or administering an eligible employer pension plan or in providing retirement-related education for employees regarding the plan. The maximum credit is $500 for the first year and each of the next two taxable years. The deduction for the start-up costs for which a credit is taken is reduced by the amount of the credit, thus, in effect, treating the amount of the credit as taxable.

2.3. *Employer-Provided Child Care Credit*

Section 45F provides a credit of up to $150,000 to an employer for 25 percent of the employer's "qualified child care expenditures" and 10 percent of the employer's "qualified child care resource and referral expenditures." The credit is available with respect to a broad range of expenditures incurred to provide childcare facilities and services for the taxpayer-employer's employees. Myriad special rules are imposed on qualification for the credit, including a recapture of a credit if a facility ceases to be used for child care after the credit is allowed with respect to the facility. The basis of the facility is reduced by the amount of the credit, thus, in effect, including the credit in income over time. In general, the benefits received by the employees as a result of the expenses for which the employer receives the credit are excludable from gross income under § 129 (see Chapter 3, Section 3.B.4.).

2.4. *Indian Employment Credit*

Section 45A allows an employer a credit of 20 percent for increased wages and the cost of health benefits for certain enrolled members of Indian tribes. The base year is 1993. Only the first $20,000 of wages is taken into account and the credit does not apply to any wages paid to an employee who makes more than $30,000 per year. The credit applies only if the employee Indian lives and works "within an Indian reservation." Section 280C(a) disallows a deduction for an amount of the wages equal to the credit. The credit is scheduled to expire at the end of 2016.

3.   ADDITIONAL RESEARCH AND INVESTMENT RELATED CREDITS

3.1. *Disabled Access Credit*

To further the goals of the Americans With Disabilities Act of 1990 (ADA), § 44 allows a taxpayer that operates an "eligible small business" to claim an elective credit equal to 50 percent of any capital expenditures incurred to provide access to disabled individuals (as defined in the ADA). Generally, only expenditures incurred to comply with the ADA are taken into account in computing the credit. However, certain expenditures are taken into account in all cases, including removal of architectural, communication, physical, or transportation barriers as well as expenditures to modify or acquire equipment for disabled individuals. Expenses for new construction that complies with the ADA are not eligible for the credit. To qualify, as an "eligible small business," the business either (1) must have had gross receipts of $1 million or less in the preceding year or (2) during the preceding year must not have employed more than thirty full-time employees. Only aggregate annual expenditures of more than $250 and not more than $10,250 are taken into account; thus the maximum credit is $5,000. No repair deduction or adjustment (increase) to the basis of the affected property is allowed for any expenditure taken into account in computing the credit.

3.2. *Credit for Clinical Testing Expenses*

Section 45C provides an elective tax credit for qualified human clinical testing expenditures incurred to obtain approval by the Food and Drug Administration for the commercial sale of a drug used to treat a "rare disease," and is sometimes referred to as the "orphan drug credit." The amount of the credit is equal to 50 percent of the qualified expenses. Expenses taken into account under § 45C cannot also be taken into account for purposes of determining the research tax credit under § 41. If the taxpayer elects to utilize the § 45C credit, § 280C(b) reduces by the amount of the credit any deductions for current expenses that are used to qualify for the credit. If the expenditures that qualify for the credit are capital in nature, then, in effect, basis must be reduced by the amount of the credit.

3.3. *New Markets Credit*

Section 45D provides a tax credit for a cash investment in a qualified community development entity (CDE). A CDE is an entity that uses the investment to provide capital for investment by or for low-income persons or communities. The maximum nationwide aggregate annual credit amount is $3.5 billion for 2010 through 2019. The Secretary of the Treasury allocates among qualified CDEs nationwide the amount of the total allowable credits. An investor who purchases stock in a CDE is entitled to a tax credit (if so designated from the CDE's allocation of the national tax credit amount) equal to 5% of the investment for each of the first three years and 6% for each of the next four years of holding the stock. Thus, if an investor purchases $100,000 of stock of a CDE on January 1, 2008, she receives a $5,000 tax credit on that date as well as on January 1, 2009 and 2010. She also receives a $6,000 tax credit on January 1, 2011, 2012, 2013, and 2014. If, during the 7-year period beginning on the date of the original stock purchase, the entity ceases to be a qualified CDE, stops using the invested funds for the prescribed purposes, or the stock is redeemed, all prior credits taken are recaptured with interest. The basis of the stock is reduced by the amount of the credit.

3.4. *Railroad Track Maintenance Credit*

Section 45G provides a credit for certain qualified railroad track maintenance. The basis of the track is reduced by the amount of the credit. The credit is scheduled to expire at the end of 2016.

SECTION 4.   ADDITIONAL RECENTLY ENACTED CREDITS

In recent years, Congress has extended the effective dates of most existing business credits while simultaneously creating new, complicated credits. Contributing to the complexity, these new credits include their own sunset dates, some of which are subsequently extended, allowed to expire, or repealed altogether. For example, as part of the Energy Improvement and Extension Act of 2008, Congress added a carbon sequestration credit (§ 45Q) to the § 38 general business credit, enacted credits for plug-in electric vehicles (§ 30D), new clean renewable energy bonds (§ 54C), and energy conservation bonds (§ 54D), and extended the effective dates of many existing credits. Furthermore, in the American Recovery and Reinvestment Act of 2009, Congress added the making work pay credit (§ 36A, repealed on December 19, 2014), the qualifying advanced energy product credit (§ 48C), the qualified school construction bond credit (§ 54F, effective only for years 2009 and 2010), the Build America bond credit (§ 54AA, effective only for bonds issued before 2011), and the recovery zone bond credit (§§ 1400U–1 to U–3). In addition, the Patient Protection and Affordable Care Act of 2010 added § 48D, which provides a credit to eligible taxpayers (mostly small businesses) equal to 50 percent of "qualifying investment" with respect to any "qualifying therapeutic discovery project," aimed at developing a product, process, or therapy to diagnose, treat, or prevent diseases or afflictions.

PART IV

DUAL PURPOSE EXPENSES

CHAPTER 18

DETERMINING WHEN A TAXPAYER IS ENGAGING IN A BUSINESS OR PROFIT-SEEKING ACTIVITY

In this Chapter, as in all of the Chapters in this Part, we are concerned with distinguishing the deductible profit-seeking expenses of an individual—the costs incurred to produce income—from the individual's nondeductible personal expenses—the costs of personal consumption. An individual is regarded for tax purposes as having two personalities: one, a seeker of profit entitled to deduct the expenses incurred in that search; the other, as a seeker of pleasure and comfort satisfying personal and family needs through consumption and related expenditures. Since consumption is part of income, amounts spent on consumption must remain in the tax base. The line between profit-seeking and personal expenses is therefore fundamental in determining the tax base.

The inquiry begins by determining when the taxpayer is engaged in a profit-seeking activity and when the taxpayer is engaged in a non-deductible personal pursuit. This distinction is sometimes difficult to make but two statutory provisions, §§ 183 and 280A, contain rules designed to facilitate that task. The first section of this Chapter considers activities that can have a significant consumption element—for example, horse racing, dog breeding, art collecting, or sailboat chartering. These activities tend to produce expenses that exceed the income they generate and therefore result in an overall loss. This excess of deductions over income is sometimes dubbed a "hobby loss." In these cases, if the taxpayer were found to be engaged in a trade or business or a profit-seeking activity the expenses would be deductible under § 162 or § 212, but the analysis must still determine whether the taxpayer is engaging in a business or profit-seeking activity. Section 183 addresses this problem. Meanwhile, the second section of this Chapter considers the analogous and equally difficult problem of whether a taxpayer who is engaged in business is using a residence for business or personal purposes, which is addressed by § 280A.

SECTION 1.   IS THERE A PROFIT-SEEKING MOTIVE?

INTERNAL REVENUE CODE: Section 183.

REGULATIONS: Sections 1.183–1(a), (b), (d)(1); –2.

Peacock v. Commissioner

United States Tax Court, 2002.
T.C. Memo 2002–122.

■ LARO, JUDGE. * * * Respondent determined for the respective years deficiencies of $132,801, $40,330, and $97,992 and accuracy-related penalties of $26,560, $8,066, and $19,598. Respondent also determined for 1997 a $24,498 addition to tax under section 6651(a)(1).

* * *

FINDINGS OF FACT

* * *

Petitioners organized Profitable Management Services, Inc. (PMSI), an S corporation, on December 2, 1993. PMSI's president and only shareholder was Ms. Peacock. Both she and Mr. Peacock were paid employees of PMSI. But for services connected with the fishing activity, the only service that Ms. Peacock performed for PMSI was answering its telephones. * * *

On its tax return, PMSI reported its principal business activity as providing consultation on automobile dealerships, and, during the relevant years, it had a consulting arrangement with approximately three automobile dealerships. For 1994 through 1997, PMSI's primary activity involved petitioners' participation in numerous deep-sea fishing tournaments (the tournaments). Petitioners decided together after consulting with other members of their tournament team that they and the team would participate in the tournaments through PMSI. Petitioners have fished recreationally since their childhood and began tournament fishing for pleasure sometime in 1988 or 1989.

The tournaments were mostly part of the Billfish (in this case, blue or black marlin) Series, a series of tournaments held throughout the world with contestants representing a wide range of countries. The Billfish Series tournaments generally awarded trophies and cash prizes to the contestants who within an allotted time caught at the tournament one of the four largest billfish and/or the four contestants who within that time caught the most billfish. The total purse of each of the Billfish Series tournaments generally ranged from $100,000 to $2.5 million, and the individual prizes awarded to the contestants generally ranged from $150,000 to $1.2 million. PMSI did not win any cash prizes in 1994 but won two cash prizes in 1997. PMSI won one or two cash prizes in each of 1995 and 1996.

* * *

PMSI's claimed losses from the fishing activity were $168,042 for 1994, $270,755 for 1995, $307,016 for 1996, and $249,181 for 1997. In late 1997, PMSI stopped participating in the tournaments because Ms. Peacock suffered a knee injury that caused her to decide to discontinue her participation.

* * *

OPINION

* * *

1. Fishing Activity

Section 183, which applies to activities engaged in by individuals or S corporations, generally limits the deductions for an "activity not engaged in for profit" to the amount of income received from the activity. Sec. 183(a) and (b). Section 183(c) defines an "activity not engaged in for profit" as "any activity other than one with respect to which deductions are allowable for the taxable year under section 162 or under paragraph (1) or (2) of section 212." An activity is engaged in for profit if the taxpayer entertained an actual and honest, even though unreasonable or unrealistic, profit objective in engaging in the activity. * * *

Section 1.183–2(b), Income Tax Regs., sets forth a nonexclusive list of factors to be considered when ascertaining a taxpayer's intent. These factors are: (1) The manner in which the taxpayer carries on the activity; (2) the expertise of the taxpayer or his advisers; (3) the time and effort expended by the taxpayer in carrying on the activity; (4) the expectation that assets used in the activity may appreciate in value; (5) the success of the taxpayer in carrying on other similar or dissimilar activities; (6) the taxpayer's history of income or losses with respect to the activity; (7) the amount of occasional profits, if any; (8) the financial status of the taxpayer; and (9) elements of personal pleasure or recreation. All facts and circumstances must be taken into account, and no single factor or mathematical preponderance of factors is determinative. * * *

Petitioners rely solely on their testimony to establish all of their proposed findings of disputed facts. As to the issue at hand concerning the fishing activity, petitioners testified that they aimed to earn money from that activity and that they could win millions of dollars in the activity. According to petitioners, PMSI would have reported a profit for each subject year except that two fish got away and one did not. As to the first fish, Mr. Peacock testified that they would have won $300,000 in 1995 had it not got away. Mr. Peacock animatedly described the events surrounding this fish as follows during his direct testimony at trial:

* * *

A. So about two or three o'clock, we hook up with this fish and it just takes off running. And Myrtice gets in the chair and gets strapped down. We get the cockpit clear, meaning you have to take in all other lines, all the teasers, and all the time, this fish is running and taking line. You've got your drag backed all the way off.

* * *

This fish takes off and he's running and he jumps and we know it's a 400-pound fish. I mean, we've caught enough fish, we know. * * * An[d] Myrtice works on the fish and works on the fish and works on the fish and we're backing down on the fish and he takes off for his last run and everything went slack. And we said, you know, what * * * happened? Well, when we reel it in, the dead line, the hook, the knot came untied.*

* * *

We give petitioners' uncorroborated testimony little weight in determining whether PMSI had the requisite profit objective. Petitioners testified that they had a profit objective as to the fishing activity. Mr. Peacock, in particular, as a successful businessperson, showed some appreciation for making a profit. In determining whether PMSI's participation in the fishing activity was permeated with the honest and actual profit objective, however, we give greater weight to the nine objective factors set forth above than we do to petitioners' expressions of subjective intent. * * * We turn to those factors and discuss them seriatim.

i.   Manner in Which the Activity Is Conducted

The fact that a taxpayer carries on an activity in a businesslike manner and maintains complete and accurate records on the activity may indicate that the activity is engaged in for profit. Sec. 1.183–2(b)(1), Income Tax Regs. A change in operating procedures, adoption of new techniques, or the abandonment of unprofitable methods may also indicate a profit motive. Id.

Petitioners argue that this factor weighs in their favor. We disagree. PMSI neither carried on the fishing activity in a businesslike manner nor maintained complete and accurate records for the activity. PMSI never set forth a statement of corporate purpose as to the fishing activity in, for example, its articles of incorporation, by-laws, or board minutes. Nor did PMSI ever prepare a business plan, budget, balance sheet, income projection, or other financial statement. We also are unable to find that petitioners kept a separate set of books and records on the fishing activity. Petitioners did keep invoices, receipts, canceled checks, and a ledger on and for the activity. Petitioners, however, never used those records or the data reflected therein to evaluate or improve the fishing activity's financial performance. * * * Nor did petitioners ever undertake a meaningful effort to make the fishing activity more profitable. Mr.

---

*   [Ed.: Mr. Peacock went on to describe, with equivalent detail and animation, the circumstances surrounding two more fish that got away; one fish would have allowed the taxpayers to win $350,000 and the other, $150,000].

Peacock is an accomplished and successful businessperson who for many years has been directly involved with the requirements of business, including the need to keep complete and accurate records. As an individual who had the skills necessary to make his automobile dealerships profitable and successful, we believe that he was, or should have been, sufficiently familiar with business practices to allow him to conduct the fishing activity in a manner evidencing a profit objective had he had one. Instead, the manner in which he and Ms. Peacock fished at the tournaments suggests that they were participating in the tournaments recreationally. * * * This factor favors respondent.

ii. Petitioners' Expertise

A taxpayer's expertise, research, and study of an activity, as well as his or her consultation with experts, may be indicative of a profit intent. Sec. 1.183–2(b)(2), Income Tax Regs.

Petitioners argue that this factor weighs heavily in their favor. We disagree. Although petitioners studied tournament fishing and competitions from the point of view of a contestant, and were very good fishers at that, they never undertook a basic investigation of the factors that affected the profitability of the fishing activity. * * * Petitioners were aware of the large cash prizes which could be won at the tournaments and believed that they could win many of those prizes because their skills were superior to those of other contestants. Petitioners, however, never seriously studied tournament fishing from a businessperson's point of view; e.g., they never researched or solicited advice on the magnitude of expenses which they were likely to incur in attempting to win the prizes. In fact, we are unable to find in the record that petitioners ever performed any meaningful economic study on the profit potential of tournament fishing. * * * Petitioners' expertise and experience in fishing is counterweighed by their lack of knowledge on the economics of tournament fishing. This factor is neutral.

iii. Time and Effort Spent Conducting the Activity

The fact that a taxpayer devotes much of his or her personal time to an activity may indicate a profit intent, especially where the activity does not involve substantial personal or recreational aspects. Also, a taxpayer's withdrawal from another occupation to devote his or her time and effort to an activity may indicate a profit motive. * * * sec. 1.183–2(b)(3), Income Tax Regs.

Petitioners argue that this factor weighs in their favor. We disagree. Although petitioners devoted their time to the activity during the tournaments, they spent only approximately 3 months of the year on that activity. Moreover, not all of that time was devoted to the fishing activity. The record reveals that contestants at the tournaments spent much of their time frolicking and reveling with family and friends, and we are unable to find in the record credible evidence that would indicate that such was not the case with petitioners. We also note that Mr. Peacock's stated reason for leaving the automobile industry in 1993 was to spend more time with his wife rather than to devote his time to another business. This factor is neutral.

iv. Expectation That Assets Will Appreciate in Value

"Profit" encompasses appreciation in the value of assets. Sec. 1.183–2(b)(4), Income Tax Regs. Therefore, in evaluating a taxpayer's intent, we also look to the taxpayer's expectation that the assets used in an activity may appreciate in value. The potential for asset appreciation is usually associated with land and other tangible assets.

Petitioners make no argument as to this factor. Nor have they offered any evidence that indicates that any assets used in the fishing activity would appreciate in value. This factor favors respondent.

v. Taxpayer's Success in Similar or Dissimilar Activities

Although an activity is unprofitable, the fact that a taxpayer has previously converted similar activities from unprofitable to profitable enterprises may show a profit intent with respect thereto. Sec. 1.183–2(b)(5), Income Tax Regs.

Petitioners argue that this factor weighs in their favor. We disagree. Although Mr. Peacock has been a successful entrepreneur in the automobile industry, the record does not reveal that his work in that industry had any bearing on petitioners' ability to conduct PMSI's fishing activity profitably. Moreover, the record reveals that petitioners conducted the fishing activity as a means to participate jointly in a recreational and social pursuit. In fact, PMSI terminated the activity when Ms. Peacock was no longer able to participate in it. This factor favors respondent.

vi. An Activity's History of Income and/or Losses

A series of losses beyond the startup stage may be indicative of the absence of a profit motive unless the losses can be blamed on unforeseen or fortuitous circumstances beyond the taxpayer's control. Sec. 1.183–2(b)(6), Income Tax Regs.

Petitioners argue that this factor weighs in their favor. We disagree. Notwithstanding that their tournament winnings totaled almost $500,000 in 1994 through 1997, PMSI reported losses from the fishing activity of $168,042 for 1994, $270,755 for 1995, $307,016 for 1996, and $249,181 for 1997. In total, PMSI incurred almost $1.5 million of expenses to win approximately $500,000, producing an approximate loss of $1 million. The record, moreover, contains no credible evidence to suggest that PMSI ever expected to recoup any of these losses. The fact that the fishing activity suffered losses year after year and that petitioners took no meaningful action to reverse the tide supports a finding that they were indifferent as to whether the losing trend could be reversed. * * * Although it is true that petitioners aspired in the tournaments to win large cash prizes, the mere fact that they so aspired and were qualified to win those prizes does not mean that PMSI entered into the fishing activity with the requisite profit objective. This factor favors respondent.

vii. Amounts of Occasional Profits

Occasional profits may indicate a profit motive. The absence of profits, however, is not determinative of a lack of profit motive. Petitioners need only have an actual and honest profit objective. Absent actual profits generated from the activity, an opportunity to earn a substantial ultimate profit in a highly speculative venture may be sufficient to indicate that the activity is engaged in for profit. Sec. 1.183–2(b)(7), Income Tax Regs. "Profit" means economic profit independent of tax consequences. * * *

The fishing activity has never earned a profit, and petitioners have not persuaded us that PMSI had a chance either to make a profit or to recoup their losses. Whereas petitioners testified that the nonoccurrence of three misfortunes would have resulted in PMSI's reporting a profit for each subject year, we are unpersuaded that such would have been the case. Among other things, we are unpersuaded that petitioners would have won the claimed amounts of money had the misfortunes not occurred. The record lacks any objective evidence to establish the specific prizes which petitioners would have won had those misfortunes not occurred, or the net amount of those prizes which would have ultimately been realized by PMSI. This factor favors respondent.

viii. Taxpayer's Financial Status

Substantial income from sources other than the activity (particularly if the losses from the activity generate substantial tax benefits) may indicate that the activity is not engaged in for profit. This is especially true where there are personal or recreational elements involved. Sec. 1.183–2(b)(9), Income Tax Regs.

Petitioners argue that this factor weighs in their favor. We disagree. Petitioners had substantial income and cash receipts from activities other than PMSI, and their net worth exceeded $1 million. Petitioners' financial status allowed them to finance the fishing activity and to use the activity's losses to reduce significantly their income tax liability. To be sure, but for those losses, PMSI would have reported (and Ms. Peacock would have been required to recognize) large amounts of ordinary income in each subject year. By participating in the fishing activity, however, petitioners aim to reduce their income while, at the same time, participating jointly in an expensive activity that they both enjoy with a subsidy from the fisc. This factor favors respondent.

ix. Elements of Personal Pleasure

Although the mere fact that a taxpayer derives personal pleasure from a particular activity does not mean that he or she lacks a profit intent with respect thereto, the presence of personal motives may indicate that the activity is not engaged in for profit. This is especially true where there are recreational elements involved. Id. "[T]he fact that the taxpayer derives personal pleasure from engaging in the activity is not sufficient to cause the activity to be classified as not engaged in for profit if the activity is in fact engaged in for profit as evidenced by other factors." Id.

Petitioners argue that this factor weighs in their favor. We disagree. Petitioners began tournament fishing for pleasure sometime in the late 1980s and focused their participation in tournaments on ones held in exotic, resortlike locations. Although a taxpayer's participation in a tournament fishing activity may sometimes qualify as an activity engaged in for profit, e.g., Busbee v. Commissioner, T.C. Memo. 2000–182, such is not the case here. Petitioners' pursuit of competitive excellence was not motivated primarily by the pursuit of profit. On the basis of our evaluation of the record as a whole, including our viewing of an approximately 1-hour video on the 1994 World Billfish Series, a segment of which was devoted to petitioners and their team, we conclude that petitioners participated in the tournaments for pleasure and recreation rather than the pursuit of business. This factor favors respondent.

x.   Conclusion

On the basis of our careful review of the record and our evaluation of the nine aforementioned factors, we conclude that PMSI did not engage in the fishing activity with an actual and honest objective of making a profit. We sustain respondent's determination.

* * *

3.   Accuracy-Related Penalties and Addition to Tax

Respondent determined that petitioners are liable for accuracy-related penalties under section 6662(a) for, among other things, negligence and intentional disregard of rules or regulations. Petitioners argue that they reasonably believed that the fishing activity was a business and that they reasonably relied upon their tax return as prepared by their accountant.

Section 6662(a) and (b)(1) imposes a 20-percent accuracy-related penalty on the portion of an underpayment that is due to negligence or intentional disregard of rules or regulations. Negligence includes a failure to attempt reasonably to comply with the Code. Sec. 6662(c). Disregard includes a careless, reckless, or intentional disregard. Id. An underpayment is not attributable to negligence or disregard to the extent that the taxpayer shows that the underpayment is due to the taxpayer's having reasonable cause and acting in good faith. Secs. 1.6662–3(a), 1.6664–4(a), Income Tax Regs.

Reasonable cause requires that the taxpayer have exercised ordinary business care and prudence as to the disputed item. United States v. Boyle, 469 U. S. 241 (1985) * * * . The good faith reliance on the advice of an independent, competent professional as to the tax treatment of an item may meet this requirement. United States v. Boyle, 469 U.S. 241, supra; sec. 1.6664–4(b), Income Tax Regs. Whether a taxpayer relies on advice and whether such reliance is reasonable hinge on the facts and circumstances of the case and the law applicable thereto. Sec. 1.6664–4(c)(1)(I), Income Tax Regs. The taxpayer must prove that: (1) The adviser was a competent professional who had sufficient expertise to justify reliance, (2) the taxpayer provided necessary and accurate information to the adviser, and (3) the taxpayer actually relied in good faith on the adviser's judgment. Ellwest Stereo Theatres, Inc. v. Commissioner, T.C. Memo. 1995–610 * * * .

We are unable to conclude that petitioners have met their burden of proof as to this issue. First, we are unable to find that petitioners reasonably believed that the fishing activity was actually a business. Mr. Peacock, a successful businessperson, knew, or at least should have known, that the manner in which he conducted the fishing activity was dramatically different from the manner in which he conducted his automobile ventures. Nor do we believe that petitioners can escape the reach of the accuracy-related penalties by asserting baldly that they relied reasonably upon their accountant. Petitioners never called their accountant to testify as to the preparation of any of the returns. Petitioners also never attempted to meet any of the requirements of the *Ellwest* test. We sustain respondent's determination of the accuracy-related penalties under section 6662(a).

DETAILED ANALYSIS

1. DEVELOPMENT OF THE NINE-FACTOR TEST

Prior to the enactment of § 183, a substantial body of case law articulated the factors to be taken into consideration in determining whether a taxpayer's activities qualified as profit-seeking. The factors set forth in Treas. Reg. § 1.183–2, discussed in *Peacock*, are derived principally from the prior case law. As the *Peacock* opinion shows, and as Treas. Reg. § 1.183–2(b) expressly provides, no single factor is controlling. All of the facts and circumstances must be taken into account to determine an overall impression of whether or not the taxpayer had the "requisite greed."

Under the facts and circumstances approach in the regulations and cases, a continuing activity may be found to have a profit motive in some years but to lack a profit motive in other years. Kartrude v. Commissioner, T.C. Memo. 1988–498, aff'd on this issue, rev'd on other issues, 925 F.2d 1379 (11th Cir.1991). But Landry v. Commissioner, 86 T.C. 1284, 1306 (1986), held that § 183 does not apply where there is a good faith intention to make a long-run profit, even though there was no good faith intention that a profit would be made during the particular taxable year.

2. APPLICATION OF THE NINE-FACTOR TEST

Others have been more successful than the taxpayers in *Peacock* in proving the existence of a profit motive. In Churchman v. Commissioner, 68

T.C. 696 (1977), the court found that an artist, sculptor and author was engaged in profit-seeking activities despite a 20-year history of losses and the "inherently recreational" nature of the activities. The taxpayer engaged in significant promotional efforts in order to sell her artwork, organized her activities in a "businesslike" manner, and had the requisite training to become a successful artist. As to the argument that the taxpayer was really seeking fame and not profit, the Tax Court made the following observation: "It is abundantly clear from her testimony and from the objective evidence that petitioner is a most dedicated artist, craves personal recognition as an artist, and believed that selling her work for a profit represents the attainment of such recognition. Therefore, petitioner intends and expects to make a profit. For § 183 purposes, it seems to us irrelevant whether petitioner intends to make a profit because it symbolizes success in her chosen career or because it is the pathway to material wealth. In either case, the essential fact remains that the petitioner does intend to make a profit from her artwork and she sincerely believes that if she continues to paint she will do so." Compare Hollander v. Commissioner, T.C. Memo. 1975–157 (activities as an artist did not amount to a trade or business where they were conducted in a haphazard manner, no "inventory" of works was maintained, and no efforts to sell beyond occasional parties for "friends" where the paintings were exhibited).

Taxpayers who convince the court that an activity consuming large amounts of time was not pleasurable usually manage to avoid § 183. Christensen v. Commissioner, T.C. Memo. 1988–484, involved a part-time inventor who "spent all of his available funds and long hours of hard, dirty work" on various invention projects over a long period of time. The court concluded that he engaged in the inventing activity with a profit motive despite continual losses. In Engdahl v. Commissioner, 72 T.C. 659 (1979), an orthodontist and his wife sought a business investment to supplement their income after he retired from his practice. They consulted with a number of people knowledgeable about horse breeding. They ran the subsequently acquired breeding operations in a business-like manner, keeping separate records that were reviewed periodically by an accountant. The taxpayers also advertised their operations in various trade publications and made changes in the operating methods in an effort to increase profitability. The court rejected the government's contention that the taxpayers entered into the activities for personal pleasure: "For a number of years, petitioners have spent an average of 35 to 55 hours per week caring for the horses, mucking out stalls, and maintaining the horse facilities. Activities of this nature could hardly be called pleasurable. Moreover, petitioners do not ride, nor do they use their ranch for social activities." On the other hand, merely because an activity is pleasurable does not necessarily subject it to § 183. In Shane v. Commissioner, T.C. Memo. 1995–504, a computer programmer who bred and raced horses on the side was found to have been engaged in a profit-seeking activity even though his enjoyment of the activity was among the reasons he engaged in it. The court stated: "It is human nature to undertake those activities which we enjoy and to avoid those activities which we find less appealing. * * * Even though petitioner derived personal pleasure from his labor intensive horse activity, this is not sufficient to cause the activity to be classified as not engaged in for profit if the activity is, in fact, engaged in for profit as evidenced by other factors."

In Eastman v. United States, 635 F.2d 833 (Ct.Cl.1980), the taxpayer purchased riding horses for his daughters. As the costs of maintaining the horses increased, the taxpayer decided to generate income by breeding the horses, then training and selling the foals. Thereafter, he attempted to deduct all of the expenses generated in connection with the horses. The court held that, although the taxpayer was attempting to minimize his costs, this did not constitute a profit motive so as to transform what was basically a hobby into a trade or business. See also Purdey v. Commissioner, T.C. Memo. 1989–657, aff'd by order, 922 F.2d 833 (3d Cir.1990) (even though taxpayer's thoroughbred horse-breeding activity was conducted in a business-like manner with competent professional assistance, § 183 applied because the taxpayer's motive was pleasure and his other income was sufficient to allow him to pursue the activity for personal pleasure); Golanty v. Commissioner, 72 T.C. 411 (1979), aff'd by order, 647 F.2d 170 (9th Cir.1981) (no deduction for horse breeding expenses where taxpayer incurred losses of over $129,000 in a seven-year period, had substantial income from other sources, and sought no advice regarding the business side of the operation beyond consulting a work entitled the "Horsemen's Tax Guide").

The multi-factor test generally is applied by examining objective evidence of the manner in which the business is conducted. On occasion, however, testimony of the taxpayer and the taxpayer's family regarding attitudes toward the activity is important. For example, in Novak v. Commissioner, T.C. Memo 2000–234, losses associated with a physician's Arabian horse breeding activity were disallowed, despite the taxpayer's own expertise in horse breeding and the fact that he had hired additional experts. The taxpayer admitted that he became a doctor instead of a teacher because his father advised him, "if you ever want to have horses you can't be a school teacher, you've got to find a job where you can make some money, be a doctor or a dentist." Conversely, in Morley v. Commissioner, T.C. Memo 1998–312, a dentist who also engaged in Arabian horse breeding and sales was found to have a profit seeking motive. The court noted:

> Mr. Morley's work on the farm was difficult, and it often precluded him from- spending time with his family. Mrs. Morley credibly testified that she and her children missed her husband and that she would have preferred it if Mr. Morley had been at home instead of working on the horse-breeding activity. Mr. Moley arrived home after dark, very tired, in a bad mood, and dirty with a "certain aroma" from his work on the farm. It appeared to the Court that Mrs. Morley resented the amount of time Mr. Morley spent on the horse-breeding activity and that she was unhappy that her husband came home every night dirty and smelly. We are not convinced that Mr. Morley would subject himself to such rigors solely for recreation or pleasure.

In some cases the taxpayer makes the factual determination of whether there was an actual and honest profit objective almost too easy. O'Connell v. Commissioner, T.C. Memo. 2001–158, involved an insurance agent who avidly fished in billfish (e.g., marlin and sailfish) tournaments. He owned and occasionally chartered out an ocean-going fishing yacht that he used primarily for his own sport fishing activities. Over seven years he lost approximately $1.4 million due to his ownership of the yacht. In disallowing the losses under § 183, the court quoted an interview that the taxpayer gave for MARLIN magazine, in which he stated:

> You have to be in competitive offshore fishing for the sport * * * not the money. What you win could never cover the expenses. (That's just a drop in the bucket!) * * * If you're in tournament fishing for the money, you'll go broke. * * *

> In my mind, it is inconceivable to make any money at tournament fishing * * *. This is strictly a sport. If a guy only fished one or two tournaments in a year and he won one of them, then he might end up in the black for that year * * *. If you fish them a lot, though, it is really tough.

An activity need not be one that has the earmarks of a hobby for § 183 to apply. Elliott v. Commissioner, 90 T.C. 960 (1988), aff'd by order, 899 F.2d 18 (9th Cir.1990), applied § 183 to a husband and wife who conducted an "Amway" distributorship part-time. They had other full-time jobs, records were kept in a cursory and sloppy fashion, and the taxpayers "did not record how many products they sold to customers making it impossible to determine the success of their sales efforts." The court concluded that the taxpayers "offered scant evidence that their Amway activity required them to do anything other than maintain an active social life." Conversely, activities that most people would view as a hobby may escape § 183 if the taxpayer can establish a bona fide profit motive even though the chances of profit are slim. For example, Kimbrough v. Commissioner, T.C. Memo. 1988–185, held that a high school teacher's golfing activities while in the PGA apprenticeship program and serving as an unpaid assistant to the pro at a golf course were profit-motivated.

3. HAVING A PROFIT OBJECTIVE VERSUS HAVING THE EXPECTATION OF PROFIT

3.1. *Generally*

In Dreicer v. Commissioner, 665 F.2d 1292 (D.C. Cir.1981), the taxpayer was a wealthy individual who spent many years and much money gathering information for a commercially unsuccessful book titled, *The Diner's Companion*. For the tax years in question, the taxpayer conducted extensive and expensive research for a book titled *My 27 Year Search for the Perfect Steak—Still Looking*, which was rejected by publishers. The Tax Court held that he could not deduct the expenses incurred gathering information for the book because he did not have a "bona fide expectation" of profit. The Court of Appeals reversed and remanded, explaining that the test was not whether the taxpayer *expected* to make a profit but rather whether the taxpayer had the *objective* of making a profit. Based on the legislative history of § 183, the court explained that the difference was that a taxpayer who engaged in an activity with the objective of making a profit should be allowed to deduct the associated expenses even if it was not reasonable for the taxpayer to expect to make a profit. In particular, the Senate Finance Committee had considered "a bona fide inventor or a person who invests in a wildcat oil well." S.Rep. No. 552, 91st Cong. 1st Sess. 104 (1969). On remand in *Dreicer,* the Tax Court stated that the term "bona fide expectation of profit" used in the earlier opinion "was intended [to] have the same meaning as an actual and honest profit objective" and again disallowed the deductions:

> Mr. Dreicer would have us find that he was like the wildcat driller or the inventor (see sec. 1.183–2(c), Examples 5 and 6, Income Tax Regs.), continuing his endeavors in the face of adverse results in the hope of one day reaping a large profit. However, such statement of intent is not supported by the objective facts of this case. For many years, he sustained large losses; there was no realistic possibility that he could ever earn sufficient income from his activity to offset such losses (sec. 1.183–2(b)(6) and (7), Income Tax Regs.) * * * he was able to continue to bear such losses only because of his large resources (sec. 1.183–2(b)(8), Income Tax Regs.); * * * a review of the entire record fails to convince us that Mr. Dreicer conducted his activities in a businesslike manner calculated to earn a profit (sec. 1.183–2(b)(1), (2), (5), (6), Income Tax Regs.) * * * Rather, there is a strong indication that he enjoyed his life of travel. Sec. 1.183–2(b)(8) and (9), Income Tax Regs. * * * In conclusion, we find and hold that Mr. Dreicer failed to meet his burden of proving that in carrying on his activity as a writer and lecturer, he had an actual and honest objective of making a profit. 78 T.C. 642, 645–646 (1982).

3.2. *Relevance of Scope of "Activity"*

Whether a taxpayer has a bona fide profit objective with respect to an activity may depend on how broadly or narrowly a single activity is defined. For example, a taxpayer who owns farmland and operates a hopelessly unprofitable horse breeding operation may have a very strong probability of making a profit on the sale of the land some years later in an amount that more than recoups the losses. If holding the land for appreciation and operating the horse farm are a single activity, § 183 may not apply, but if they are separate activities, § 183 applies to the expenses related to current operation of the farm, but not to those expenses related solely to holding the land for speculative investment. Treas. Reg. § 1.183–1(d) deals with the scope of an "activity." On the hypothesized facts, the regulations provide that farming and holding the land for investment will be treated as one activity only if the farming income exceeds the deductions which would have been incurred if the land had merely been held as an investment, e.g., mortgage interest, property taxes, and depreciation.

The scope of an activity is a factual issue, and the presentation of the taxpayer's case can make all of the difference in the resolution of the issue. For example, in Topping v. Commissioner, T.C. Memo. 2007–92, the Tax Court held that the taxpayer's unprofitable equestrian activities were an integral part of her profitable home and barn design business, even though she reported her equestrian and design activities separately on her tax return. The court found convincing the taxpayer's testimony that she used the equestrian activities to make contacts with potential "extraordinarily wealthy" clients while she competed in events at an elite private equestrian club. The taxpayer did not advertise her interior design business through advertising media, because "the ethos of the Jockey Club and its members perceive that kind of generic advertising of a personal service business as tacky or gauche," and she instead "relie[d] on her exposure and reputation as both a rider and owner, and also her popularity among the members of the Jockey Club." Furthermore, the taxpayer "use[d] her general knowledge of horses and specifically her knowledge of the idiosyncrasies of each of her client's horses to evolve her barn designs." Thus, based on the totality of the evidence, she was involved in a single activity.

Compare Engdahl v. Commissioner, 72 T.C. 659 (1979) (Acq.) (holding land acquired to conduct the activity of breeding, raising, and selling horses, and the horse activity, were a single activity) with Power's Estate v. Commissioner, 736 F.2d 826 (1st Cir.1984) (horse farm activity and holding land were separate activities because the land was not acquired to operate the farm; it had been held many years previously); see also Keanini v. Commissioner, 94 T.C. 41 (1990) (dog-breeding and dog-grooming business were a single activity because they were integrated and breeding activity generated goodwill for grooming business).

4. APPLICATION OF SECTION 183 TO TAX-MOTIVATED INVESTMENT TRANSACTIONS

Throughout the 1970's and the first half of the 1980's there was a proliferation of tax shelters, largely investments financed with nonrecourse borrowing and unlikely to produce any before-tax profit. Because of the generous capital cost recovery provisions in effect at that time, the tax savings from interest and depreciation deductions and other capital cost recovery allowances were so heavily loaded toward the front-end of the venture's lifetime, that on an after-tax basis these transactions could produce a profit. The Internal Revenue Service urged the application of § 183 to disallow the deductions claimed with respect to investments that showed no hope of realizing any before-tax gain, and after some initial hesitancy, the courts ultimately followed this lead. See Rose v. Commissioner, 88 T.C. 386 (1987), aff'd, 868 F.2d 851 (6th Cir.1989); Baron's Estate v. Commissioner, 83 T.C. 542 (1984), aff'd, 798 F.2d 65 (2d Cir.1986). Building upon this initial extension of the situations to which § 183 applies, subsequent decisions indicate that the factors in Treas. Reg. § 1.183–2 are applicable generally in determining whether a profit motive, which is a prerequisite to a trade or business or a transaction entered into for profit, exists whenever trade or business deductions are claimed. See Krause v. Commissioner, 99 T.C. 132 (1992), aff'd sub nom. Hildebrand v. Commissioner, 28 F.3d 1024 (10th Cir.1994) (§ 183 applies to determine whether the deduction for research and experimentation expenses under § 174 is available).

5. RESULTS OF APPLICATION OF SECTION 183

5.1. *Allowable Deductions*

Assuming that the activity in question does not fall on the profit-seeking side of the line under the tests discussed above, the deductions attributable to the activity are then controlled by § 183. Further assuming that the taxpayer does not meet the statutory requirements of § 183(d) such that the activity is presumed to be engaged in for profit (generally, by demonstrating that gross income from the activity exceeds expenses for three of five consecutive years), the taxpayer must turn to § 183(b) for assistance, which permits deductions in certain circumstances.

Computing the amount of allowable deductions under § 183(b) is a multi-step process. Section 183(b)(2) allows the taxpayer to offset expenses against any income generated by the activity, despite the fact that the activity is by definition not profit seeking. First, however, the section requires that deductions that would be allowable independent of any connection with profit-seeking activities, such as interest and taxes, be offset against the income generated by the activity before other deductions are considered. Suppose, for example, that the taxpayer has a yacht that is rented occasionally but does not qualify as an activity entered into for profit. If the yacht owner receives $1,000 in rent and incurs $400 of *ad valorem* personal property tax expense (deductible under § 164) and $700 maintenance expenses, only $600 of the maintenance expenses would be deductible against the rental income (i.e., $1,000 in gross income from the activity less $400 in "otherwise allowable" deductions). The taxpayer is forced to "use up" the taxes, which would be deductible in any event, before deducting the maintenance expenses. In this case, no depreciation deductions would be allowed. If, on the other hand, property taxes were only $200, and allowable depreciation apart from § 183 were $1,000, then all $700 of the maintenance expense would be deductible, along with $100 of depreciation ($1,000 less $200 leaves $800 for other offsetting deductions). Treas. Reg. § 1.183–1(d)(2) provides detailed rules for determining when the "otherwise allowable" deductions are deemed to be related to the non-profit-seeking activity.

Section 163(h) limits the deduction of interest to business and profit seeking activities and mortgages on the taxpayer's primary residence and one secondary residence. Therefore, unless the "activity" subject to § 183 is something like a weekend farm that may be characterized as the taxpayer's second home, mortgage interest is not treated as an "otherwise allowable" expense, but rather as an expense fully subject to § 183 limitations.

The overall effect of § 183 is to allow a taxpayer who realizes some incidental income from a hobby (e.g., stamp collecting) to offset that income with the associated expenses.

5.2. *Presumption of For-Profit Activity*

With careful timing of deductions and income, the taxpayer often will be able to qualify for the presumption in § 183(d) concerning profit-seeking activity. Failure to qualify under the pro-taxpayer presumption results in the taxpayer bearing the normal burden of proof by the preponderance of the evidence that an activity was conducted for profit. To avoid this burden in the early years of the conduct of a new venture—when start-up losses may be incurred—the taxpayer may elect to defer the determination of whether the activity was conducted for profit and seek shelter in the retrospective presumption provided by § 183(e). To do so however, the taxpayer must agree to extend the normal three year statute of limitations.

SECTION 2.   BUSINESS USE OF RESIDENCE

INTERNAL REVENUE CODE: Section 280A.

Expenses associated with a personal residence (utilities, maintenance, and depreciation) generally are not deductible. Suppose, however, an individual uses a portion of the individual's personal residence in connection with business activities. Arguably, a portion of the expenses of the personal residence should be deductible because of its partial use as a business. Rev. Rul. 62–180, 1962–2 C.B. 52, took the position that a deduction was allowed to an employee in this situation only if the employee was required by the person's employer as a condition of employment to provide the employee's own work space and facilities. The "voluntary, occasional, or incidental use" of a part of the residence in connection with employment activities did not qualify any portion of the cost with respect to the residence as a business expense deduction. But Newi v. Commissioner, 432 F.2d 998 (2d Cir.1970), rejected the strict "condition of employment" test and affirmed a Tax Court decision allowing a deduction of 25 percent of the household rental, cleaning, and lighting costs where there was a finding that the use by the taxpayer of his personal residence to perform some of his duties as an employee was "appropriate and helpful." In the *Newi* case, the taxpayer was a salesman of television time and spent three hours every evening in his den reviewing his notes on the day's work and watching commercials on television.

Under the liberalized tests applied by the Tax Court, almost every employee who took work home would be allowed to deduct some portion of the cost of maintaining a personal residence. In 1976, Congress, concerned with the expansion of the deduction, eliminated the "appropriate and helpful" test, and made the business use of the taxpayer's residence subject to § 280A.

Another situation in which the problem of distinguishing between personal and profit-seeking activities arises is a summer house or ski lodge that is used by the taxpayer personally and also is rented for some period of time. Before 1983, the allowability of deductions turned on whether the rental activity was conducted "for profit," and the Regulations under § 183 gave some guidance in determining whether the profit-seeking activity test was met. Congress found these standards too vague, and introduced more definitive rules in the area in § 280A. In general, § 280A limits deductions for any claimed business use of a "dwelling unit" that the taxpayer uses as a residence. Use as a residence is deemed to occur if the taxpayer uses the property for personal purposes for the greater of 14 days or 10 percent of the number of days for which the property is rented.

Hamacher v. Commissioner

Tax Court of the United States, 1990.
94 T.C. 348.

■ GERBER, JUDGE: * * *

[P]etitioner was employed by the Alliance Theatre in Atlanta, Georgia, as an independent contract actor to perform in plays on its main stage and studio stage. * * * Although most of petitioner's contract employment * * * was through the Alliance Theatre, petitioner also worked as an actor doing radio and television commercials. * * *

[Petitioner also taught] acting at Alliance Theatre's acting school, and [was] the administrator of the school. * * *

Petitioner utilized two offices in connection with his acting and administrative activities. One was provided by the Alliance Theatre from which petitioner performed his duties as administrator of the acting school. * * * However, due to space and equipment limitations at the theater, this office was not used by petitioner exclusively. * * * [O]ther theater employees used petitioner's office to telephone students of the acting school regarding enrollment, to do various paperwork related to the theater, and to use his typewriter. * * *

Petitioner's home office was in one of the six rooms in his apartment and measured approximately 10 by 15 feet. * * * [A]pproximately half of petitioner's time rehearsing and developing his contract stage roles was spent in his home office and the remainder was spent at the Alliance Theatre rehearsal hall. Petitioner also used his home office to receive calls regarding acting roles, prepare for auditions, and rehearse parts for commercials. Because he was regularly interrupted at his theater office by telephone calls and employees with questions, petitioner used his home office to do whatever "creative thinking" was needed to direct the theater school. Petitioner also used his home office to develop the school's curriculum, select plays for the theater, and otherwise perform some of his duties as administrator of the Alliance Theatre acting school. The Alliance Theatre did not require that petitioner have a home office.

Petitioner spent the largest portion or percentage of his working hours at the theater office, not his home office. * * *

Respondent disallowed the claimed home office deductions because petitioners "failed to establish that the office was used exclusively on a regular basis as [petitioner's] principal place of business and that as an employee, [he] maintained this office for the convenience of [his] employer," as required under section 280A(c)(1)(A). * * *

Section 280A, in general, provides that no deduction is allowed with respect to the business use of a taxpayer's personal residence * * * . Section 280A(c) contains some limited and specific exceptions to this general rule * * * .

[F]or a deduction to be allowed under section 280A(c)(1), the provision petitioners rely upon, the taxpayer must establish that a portion of his dwelling unit is (1) exclusively used, (2) on a regular basis, (3) for the purposes enumerated in subparagraphs (A), (B), or (C) of section 280A(c)(1), and (4) if the taxpayer is an employee, the office is maintained for the convenience of the employer. * * *

The parties agree that petitioner regularly used his home office in connection with two separate and independent business activities * * *. Petitioner was both an independent contract actor and a salaried employee of the Alliance Theatre, responsible for administering its acting school.

* * * [T]his case presents a unique question: When a taxpayer uses one home office for two separate and distinct business activities, whether both business uses must be of the types described in section 280A(c)(1) in order to satisfy the exclusive use requirement of that section. * * *

Section 280A was added to the Internal Revenue Code by the Tax Reform Act of 1976 to provide "definitive rules relating to deductions for expenses attributable to the business use of homes." S. Rept. 94–1236 (1976), 1976–3 C.B. (Vol. 3) 807, 839. Congress was responding to cases (particularly those decided by this Court) in which a more liberal standard than that applied by the Internal Revenue Service for the deduction of home office expenses was held to be appropriate. Under these decisions, expenses connected to a home office were held deductible on the grounds that the maintenance of such office was "appropriate and helpful" to the taxpayer's business under the circumstances. See * * * Newi v. Commissioner, T.C. Memo. 1969–131, affd. 432 F.2d 998 (2d Cir.1970). * * * Congress was concerned that under this "appropriate and helpful" standard, expenses which were otherwise personal in nature would be allowed as business deductions:

> In many cases the application of the appropriate and helpful test would appear to result in treating personal living, and family expenses which are directly attributable to the home (and therefore not deductible) as ordinary and necessary business expenses, even though those expenses did not result in additional or incremental costs incurred as a result of the business use of the home. Thus, expenses otherwise considered nondeductible personal, living, and family expenses might be converted into deductible business expenses simply because, under the facts of the particular case, it was appropriate and helpful to perform some portion of the taxpayer's business in his personal residence. * * * [S.Rept. 94–938 (1976), 1976–3 C.B. (Vol. 3) 49, 185.]

Section 280A, therefore, was enacted to preclude the deduction of expenses attributable to the business use of a home office except under certain limited conditions, which are provided in section 280A(c).

Congress intended that only expenses which were clearly ordinary and necessary business expenses would be deductible.

Congress, in 1981, amended section 280A(c) * * * to permit a business expense deduction for taxpayers having more than one trade or business. Prior to the amendment, the Internal Revenue Service allowed home office deductions only if the taxpayer was using his residence as the principal place of business of his *main* business activity. * * *

In light of the above statutory framework and legislative history, we conclude that expenses attributable to the use of a home office in conducting two or more separate business activities may be deductible. Section 280A was not intended to compel a taxpayer to physically segregate his different business activities when it would otherwise be unnecessary, * * * or to discourage an industrious individual from conducting more than one business activity out of his home. * * * Therefore, the exclusive use requirement of section 280A(c)(1) does not demand that a home office be used exclusively in connection with only one business or only one of the types of uses enumerated in subparagraphs (A), (B), and (C). * * *

We also conclude, however, that when a taxpayer utilizes one home office in conducting numerous business activities, each and every business use must be the type(s) described in section 280A(c)(1). Otherwise, the exclusive use requirement of that section will not be satisfied and the general nondeductibility provision of section 280A(a) will apply. Therefore, if only one of a number of uses qualifies under subparagraph (A), (B), or (C) of section 280A(c)(1), the expenses attributable to the business use of a home office will not be allowable as deductions even if the other uses are business related. For example, if the taxpayer uses his home office in conducting two business activities, one which qualifies under section 280A(c)(1)(A), (B), or (C) and one which does not, the expenses attributable to the business use of the home office are not allowable as deductions. The taxpayer in this situation does not use the home office exclusively for one or more of the purposes described in section 280A(c)(1) and the expenses are not deductible to any extent. For purposes of sec. 280A(c)(1), where a home office is put to both qualified and nonqualified uses, we are precluded from allocating expenses between those uses for purposes of their deductibility. The exclusive use requirement of sec. 280A(c)(1) is an all-or-nothing standard which was specifically imposed by Congress to put an end to any previous rules containing allocation methods. * * *

Petitioner argues that, [as administrator of the Alliance Theatre acting school], he satisfies section 280A(c)(1)(A) because his home office was his "principal place of business" and his use of the home office for that purpose was "for the convenience of his employer." Respondent argues to the contrary. We agree with respondent.

In the case of an employee, section 280A(c)(1) will apply only if the home office is used "for the convenience of his employer." Sec. 280A(c)(1).

Neither the statute nor the proposed regulations provide us with any guidance as to when an office will be considered used for the convenience of the employer. * * * Such use, however, has been found where the employee must maintain the office as a condition of his employment, Green v. Commissioner, 78 T.C. 428, 430 (1982), revd. on other grounds 707 F.2d 404 (9th Cir.1983), or when the home office was necessary for the functioning of the employer's business, or necessary to allow the employee to perform his duties properly. See Frankel v. Commissioner, 82 T.C. 318, 325–326 (1984); Drucker v. Commissioner, 715 F.2d 67, 70 (2d Cir.1983), rev'g. 79 T.C. 605 (1982). However, the home office cannot be "purely a matter of personal convenience, comfort, or economy" with respect to the employee. See Sharon v. Commissioner, 66 T.C. 515, 523 (1976), aff'd. 591 F.2d 1273 (9th Cir.1978).

The record in this case does not support petitioners' contention that the home office was used for the convenience of the Alliance Theatre acting school. It is apparent from the facts in this case that petitioner's Alliance Theatre home office use was for his own convenience, comfort, or economy. His employer did not require or expect him to do any of his work at his home. To the contrary, petitioner's employer provided him with a suitable office which was accessible to petitioner at all times, including during nonbusiness hours, the same hours petitioner used his home office. * * * Many people engaged in businesses and professions may find it helpful to take work home with them, but that does not automatically establish that the home office is maintained for the convenience of their employer.

Accordingly, * * * petitioner's use of his home office in connection with his employment as administrator of the acting school was * * * personal use. Consequently, petitioner's use of his home office does not comply with section 280A(c)(1). Thus, petitioner has not satisfied the exclusivity requirement of section 280A(c)(1), and, pursuant to section 280A(a), petitioner's home office deductions are not allowed except as provided in section 280A(b). * * *

DETAILED ANALYSIS

1.   ALLOWABLE HOME OFFICE DEDUCTIONS

1.1. *Generally*

Although § 280A(a) denies all deductions attributable to the use of a portion of the taxpayer's home as an office, important exceptions allow some deductions. First, the effect of § 280A(b) is to allow a deduction of the entire amount of real estate taxes (deductible under § 164) and home mortgage interest that is deductible under § 163(h). Second, as discussed in *Hamacher,* § 280A(c) provides limited exceptions to the general rule. Deductions for the business use of a home are permitted if a portion of the residence is used "exclusively"[1] on a "regular basis" as (a) the taxpayer's principal place of business for conducting any trade or business, whether it is the taxpayer's principal or a secondary business, (b) a place of business that is used by patients, clients, or customers in meeting or dealing with the taxpayer, or (c) is an unattached separate structure used only in connection with a trade or business. For employees, expenses meeting the above tests must also be incurred for the convenience of the employer.

The several requirements for meeting one of these exceptions raise numerous technical issues.

1.2. *"Residence"*

Section 280A applies to any "dwelling unit" used by the taxpayer as a "residence" during the year for more than the greater of (a) 14 days or (b) ten percent of the number of days that the unit is rented out at fair rental value. I.R.C. § 280A(d). This test can catch taxpayers who live and work in the same building even though the living and working areas are physically distinct. Cunningham v. Commissioner, T.C. Memo. 1996–141, held that § 280A applied to disallow deductions with respect to a two story building in which the taxpayer maintained an art gallery on the first floor because the taxpayer lived in a second floor apartment that had a stairway with an interior door to the first floor gallery.

On the other hand, in Kurzet v. Commissioner, T.C. Memo. 1997–54, rev'd in part and aff'd in part on other issues, 222 F.3d 830 (10th Cir. 2000), the taxpayer owned a mobile home located on a farm that was the taxpayer's secondary place of business. The mobile home included both living quarters and office space and the taxpayer lived in the mobile home only while working at the farm; none of the time the taxpayer spent at the farm was recreational. The court held that the mobile home was not a "residence" for purposes of § 280A because all of taxpayer's time on the farm was work related.

1.3. *"Exclusive" and "Regular" Use*

Sengpiehl v. Commissioner, T.C. Memo. 1998–23, illustrates the line-drawing questions that must be faced in applying § 280A. The taxpayer was a lawyer who worked exclusively from his home office. Based on his credible testimony that he and his wife "usually did not entertain at home," their children "never had guests," and they used only the bedrooms, kitchen, bathroom, hallway, and occasionally the dining room for personal purposes, he carried the burden of proof that his living room was used exclusively as a conference room for his legal practice, even though it contained a piano. No deduction was allowed with respect to the dining room even though it was used exclusively for the taxpayer's legal practice during working hours, because it was also used occasionally for family meals after working hours.

In Hewett v. Commissioner, T.C. Memo. 1996–110, a piano teacher kept a grand piano used exclusively for teaching in an alcove off her living room. The Tax Court held that the "portion" of the dwelling unit used "exclusively"

---

[1]   A limited exception to the exclusivity requirement is made for child care services provided in the home. § 280A(c)(4).

for the exempted purpose is not required to be a separate room or to be partitioned off from the remainder of a room that is used for personal living in order to qualify under an exception to the general disallowance rule under § 280A. Notwithstanding the result in *Hewett*, so long as a taxpayer uses any portion of the taxpayer's building as a personal residence, § 280A continues to apply even though there may be significant and distinct separation of the business and residential portions of the building.

1.4. *Principal Place of Business*

1.4.1. *Requirement of a "Trade or Business"*

Curphey v. Commissioner, 73 T.C. 766 (1980), involved a physician who maintained a home office used exclusively to manage several rental buildings that he owned. A deduction for the home office was allowed because the rental activities constituted a trade or business, as distinguished from mere investment activities, and his home office was the principal place of business for the rental business. In contrast, managing a substantial investment portfolio which constitutes the taxpayer's principal source of income is not a trade or business. Thus, in Moller v. United States, 721 F.2d 810 (Fed.Cir.1983), the taxpayer was denied a home office deduction where the office was exclusively used to manage investments.

1.4.2. *Requirement of "Principal" Place of Business*

The standard for determining whether a home office constitutes the taxpayer's "*principal* place of business" has been subject to considerable controversy. For many years, the IRS and Tax Court applied a "focal point" test, looking to the location where the taxpayer delivered goods or services. See e.g., Baie v. Commissioner, 74 T.C. 105 (1980) (proprietress of "Gay Dog," a hot dog stand, cooked some of the food in her own kitchen and did all her bookkeeping in another room; the hot dog stand, not her home, was the place of business). The Courts of Appeals have applied a more liberal facts and circumstances test. Compare Weissman v. Commissioner, 751 F.2d 512 (2d Cir.1984) (college professor's principal place of business was his home office and not his office at the university, because he spent 80 percent of his time at home, his college office was shared with several other persons, was not available outside of working hours, and was not a safe place to leave teaching, writing, or research materials) and Drucker v. Commissioner, 715 F.2d 67 (2d Cir.1983) (concert musician's principal place of business was his home practice studio and not the Metropolitan Opera where he performed, the court indicating that the case presented a "rare situation") to Cadwallader v. Commissioner, 919 F.2d 1273 (7th Cir.1990) (disallowing a home office deduction for a university professor who performed most of his research in a home office used exclusively for that purpose; because the university provided him with three adequate offices on campus, the home office was for the taxpayer's convenience, not the employer's convenience).

In Commissioner v. Soliman, 506 U.S. 168 (1993), the taxpayer was an anesthesiologist who did not have an office at the hospital where he worked, but had a home office used exclusively to perform office functions relating to his medical practice. The Supreme Court disallowed the deduction. After concluding that the statutory phrase "principal place of business" is not synonymous with "principal office," it fashioned a facts and circumstances test which the taxpayer failed because he spent substantially more time treating patients at the hospital than performing office functions at home.

Congress found the *Soliman* standard to be too harsh, and in 1997 amended § 280A(c)(1) to add the last sentence of that subsection. The provision allows home office deductions to a taxpayer who uses the office for the "administrative and management activities" of a trade or business if the trade or business does not have any other "fixed location" at which the taxpayer conducts "substantial" administrative or management activities. This amendment reversed the result in cases like *Soliman*, where the taxpayer had no other office.

The legislative history of the amendment indicates that Congress intended to apply an extraordinarily lax standard to allow home office deductions for self-employed taxpayers. The House Report stated that the taxpayer's right to the home office deduction is not affected by the fact that the taxpayer performs substantial "non-administrative or non-management business activities at a fixed location of the business outside the home (e.g., meeting with, or providing services to customers, clients, or patients at a fixed location of the business away from home)." Furthermore, the test is satisfied even though the taxpayer could have used an office outside his home to perform administrative or management functions but simply chose not to do so. See H. Rep. No. 148, 105th Cong., 1st Sess. 407–408 (1997).

In addition, the House Committee Report states that the home office deduction will be allowed to a taxpayer "who does not conduct substantial administrative or management activities at any other fixed location of the trade or business, regardless of whether administrative or management activities connected with his trade or business (e.g., billing activities) are performed by others at other fixed locations of the trade or business." The somewhat ambiguous "others" in this sentence might be read to encompass only independent contractors, but if the Treasury and the IRS, or the courts, interpret "others" to encompass the taxpayer's own employees as well, the disallowance rule of § 280A effectively will have been repealed in large part. If "others" whose administrative activities are not imputed to the taxpayer include his employees, every doctor, dentist, lawyer, and accountant in the country can obtain a home office deduction by *personally* avoiding "*substantial*" billing and substantial management activities while in the office that is used to meet patients and clients, even though employees perform nearly all of such work at that office.

The 1997 amendment to § 280A(c)(1) has little impact on employees because an employee's home office still cannot qualify unless it is maintained "for the convenience of the employer" a test that is very difficult to satisfy. In marked contrast to the treatment of self-employed taxpayers, the House Report states that an employee's failure to use suitable office space provided by the employer will be taken into account in determining whether the home office is maintained for the convenience of the employer. See H. Rep. No. 148, 105th Cong., 1st Sess. 407–408 (1997).

1.5. *Meeting or Dealing with Clients*

Green v. Commissioner, 707 F.2d 404 (9th Cir.1983), held that the "meeting or dealing with clients" exception in § 280A(c)(1)(B) was not satisfied where the manager of seven condominiums used a room in his home exclusively to receive telephone calls on business matters for some two and one-half hours each night, five nights a week. The court found that Section 280A(c)(1)(B) requires an in-person appearance by those dealing with the taxpayer, and proposed regulations are consistent with that. Prop. Reg. § 1.280A–2(c) (1983). Crawford v. Commissioner, T.C. Memo. 1993–192, held that an emergency room physician who saw some patients at a home office did not qualify for the exception because incidental or occasional meetings with patients are not sufficient to qualify.

1.6. *Computing Allowable Deductions*

Even if the taxpayer can meet the tests of one of the exceptions to the disallowance rule of § 280A(a), the expenses incurred in connection with the residence must be allocated between business and personal use and are subject to an overall limitation under § 280A(c)(5). Prop. Reg. § 1.280A–2(I) (1983) explains how these rules work.

Suppose that the taxpayer used one room of her house exclusively as the principal place of a business, which earned $3,500, and during the year incurred the following expenses with respect to the home: mortgage interest, $6,000; real estate taxes, $2,400; utilities, $1,200; real property casualty insurance, $600; roof repairs, $1,800; business telephone, $1,000; residence telephone, $500. Assume that if the building had been used one-hundred percent for business, depreciation would have been $3,600. The residence telephone is entirely nondeductible under § 262(b). The business telephone is deductible under § 162, without regard to § 280A. Section 280A(b) allows a complete deduction for the $6,000 home mortgage interest under § 163(h), and the real estate taxes under § 164, both of which are deductible without regard to trade or business use of the property.

Deductibility of the remainder of the expenses requires that they be apportioned between the business and personal use of the residence. This is done on a relative square footage basis, although if the rooms are roughly equal in size, the calculation may be based on the relative number of rooms devoted to business and personal use. If the home were 2400 square feet and the office were 400 square feet, then one-sixth (or $1,200) of the remaining expenses would be deductible: utilities, $200; real property casualty insurance, $100; roof repairs, $300; and depreciation, $600. The total amount of these deductions allowed may not exceed the income from the business ($3,500), reduced by both business expenses (telephone—$1,000), and the portion of the mortgage interest and real estate taxes attributable to the business use of the property (interest—$1,000; taxes—$400). Since the income was $3,500 and these always allowable deductions equal $2,400, only $1,100 of the remaining deductions are allowable. In determining which of the remaining deductions are allowed, depreciation is taken into account last. Thus, the $200 for utilities, $100 for insurance, and $300 for repairs, totaling $600, are fully allowable; but only $500 of the $600 depreciation is allowable. Section 280A(c)(5) permits the $100 of disallowed depreciation deduction to be carried over for deduction in future years, subject to certain limitations .

2. VACATION HOMES

2.1. *Computing the Limitations*

Section 280A limits the deductibility of expenses attributable to a vacation home that is used for personal purposes any time during the taxable year, even if personal use is insufficient for the dwelling unit to be a "residence" as defined in § 280A(d). By virtue of § 280A(c)(3), however, the complete disallowance rule of § 280A(a) never applies to vacation homes that are rented out some of the time. Instead, § 280A(e) requires a proration of expenses between the personal and business aspects of the vacation home. In addition, if personal use of the dwelling unit is sufficient to meet the "residence" definition, § 280A(c)(5) provides that the deductions attributed to the residence are allowed only to the extent of the excess of the gross income from the property reduced by the allocable share of deductions which are "otherwise allowable," such as interest and taxes. Thus, where the rental income is sufficient to cover both the mortgage interest and taxes allocable to the rental activity, but not all of the maintenance expenses, some maintenance expenses are disallowed and no depreciation will be allowed. Depreciation deductions will be allowed only to the extent gross income exceeds all other expenses attributable to the rental use of the property.

In allocating the "otherwise allowable" expenses to the income from the property, the Commissioner takes the position that the allocation must be based on the ratio of the number of days the property is rented to the total number of days the property is used, the same approach that is used in § 280A(e)(1) for maintenance deductions. However, Bolton v. Commissioner, 694 F.2d 556 (9th Cir.1982), allowed the taxpayer to allocate interest and taxes on the basis of the total number of days in the year, thus substantially increasing the taxpayer's ability to offset maintenance and depreciation deductions against the income from the property.

The difference between the two approaches is illustrated by the following example. Assume that A owns a vacation home that is rented for 60 days and used by A for another 30 days per year; the home is vacant for the remaining 275 days. Gross rental receipts are $8,000. Expenses include $1,000 rental broker's commission; $6,000 mortgage interest (deductible in any event under § 163(h)(3)); $900 real estate taxes (deductible in any event under § 164); and $1,200 insurance and maintenance. If the property had been used solely for rental activity, depreciation would have been $3,600.

Section 280A does not affect the deductibility of the rental broker's commissions, mortgage interest (assuming that the residence qualifies as the taxpayer's second home under § 163(h)(3)), or real estate taxes, but it does limit the deductions for insurance, maintenance, and depreciation. Initially, § 280A(e) provides that only two thirds (60 rental days/90 total use days) of the $1,200 insurance and maintenance ($800) and two thirds of the $3,600 depreciation ($2,400) may be deducted.

In applying § 280A(c)(5), the $1,000 broker's commission is deducted against $8,000 of rents, leaving $7,000 of gross rental income. See Prop. Reg. § 1.280A–3(d)(2) (1983). Next, although the $900 of real estate taxes are deductible in any event, as is the $6,000 mortgage interest, in determining how much of the insurance, maintenance, and depreciation is deductible, the Internal Revenue Service would reduce the $7,000 of rents by two thirds (60 days/90 days) of the taxes and interest, or $4,600, thereby leaving only $2,400 of remaining deductions. The $800 of maintenance and insurance would be deductible, but only $1,600 of depreciation would be deductible.

Comparatively, under *Bolton,* only 16.5 percent (60 rental days/365 days) of the taxes ($148.50) and interest ($990) would be subtracted from the rental income to derive the ceiling on deductions for maintenance, insurance and depreciation. Thus, the full $2,400 of depreciation would be allowable.

2.2. *Personal Use*

Section 280A(d)(2) defines "personal use" of a dwelling unit so broadly that § 280A can apply even though the taxpayer and the taxpayer's immediate family never physically occupy the property. Personal use includes use by any other person (except an employee subject to § 119, see Chapter 3, Section 3.A.9.) unless a fair rental is charged. See Rev. Rul. 89–51, 1989–1 C.B. 89 (one week use of residence donated to charity and sold in a fund-raising auction is personal use); Colbert v. Commissioner, T.C. Memo. 1992–30 (1992) (charitably motivated rental for full year to a low-income family at less than fair rental value is personal use). Furthermore, rental to a family member (as defined in § 267(c)(4)), such as a brother or sister, is considered personal use, even though the rental is for fair value, unless the relative uses the premises as her principal residence. I.R.C. § 280A(d)(3).

Taxpayers sometimes engage in transactions designed to manipulate the residence test in § 280A(d). In Razavi v. Commissioner, 74 F.3d 125 (6th Cir.1996), the taxpayer owned a condominium unit that he used for 27 days during the year and leased it to a management company for the remainder of the year. The rent paid by the management company reflected a contingent percentage of the rents that it collected from subleases to actual users of the condominium, with a guaranteed minimum of $21,000. The management company rented the condominium to third parties for only 200 days and received $48,327. Using the 200 days of actual rentals would have caused the taxpayer to fail the 10 percent test, as he had used the unit for 27 days. Nevertheless the court held that the lease to the management company for the full year allowed the taxpayer to treat all 365 days of the year, minus the taxpayer's personal use days, as rental days. Under that calculation, the 27 days of personal use did not exceed 10 percent of rental days.

If a taxpayer converts a principal residence to rental property, or rental property to a principal residence, the mechanical tests of § 280A could disallow deductions in excess of income in the year of conversion. Section 280A(d)(4) provides a special rule to deal with such situations and allows the deductions in full if its tests are met.

2.3. *Exceptions and Interaction with Section 183*

A special rule provides that if the property is rented for less than 15 days during the taxable year, the rental income is excludable and no deductions (except for interest, taxes, etc.) are allowed. I.R.C. § 280A(g). The Tax Court has held that § 280A(g) does not provide an exclusion for *de minimis* amounts of income if the rental period exceeds fourteen days; the number of rental days is determinative, not the amount of rental income. See Roy v. Commissioner, T.C. Memo 1998–125 (1998). If for any year § 280A applies to any dwelling unit, § 183 does not apply, but the year counts as a year in applying the five-year presumption of § 183(d). I.R.C. § 280A(f)(3). If § 280A does not apply, § 183 still may be applicable.

Thus, the statute in effect creates specific rules for four different situations: (1) If the *rental* use is less than 15 days, there is no income inclusion and no deduction (except for qualified home mortgage interest, etc.); (2) if the *rental* use is 15 days or more and the *personal* use is greater than 14 days or 10 percent of the rental period, then expenses are prorated between rental and personal use *and* deductions are limited to the income which the property generates; (3) if the *rental* use is 15 days or more and the *personal* use is insufficient to trigger § 280A, then expenses are prorated between rental and personal use, but deductions in excess of income may be allowed; and (4) if the *rental* use is 15 days or more and there is no *personal* use, all deductions are fully allowable, subject only to limitation under § 183 if a profit-seeking motive is not present, an unlikely occurrence.

CHAPTER 19

EXPENSES INVOLVING BOTH PERSONAL AND BUSINESS PURPOSES

Although many expenditures may be classified as either profit-seeking or personal, a wide variety of expenditures involve varying degrees of both profit-seeking and personal elements. When an individual who is clearly engaged in business incurs expenses for items like travel, a meal, or entertainment, it is difficult to determine how much of the expense served business purposes and how much provided personal consumption. For example, an individual may take a business client to an enjoyable sporting event, may fly to Europe to conduct business but may also have a few good meals and visit a museum, or may buy an evening gown to attend an event at which she will receive a professional achievement award. Ideally, the precise amount of profit-seeking and personal satisfaction costs should be identified in each case, but that calculation is administratively impossible. Congress has responded to this problem in a variety of ways.

One response treats the activity as inherently personal and disallows a deduction regardless of the circumstances. For example, even though commuting expenses have a clear profit-seeking connection, they are considered to be the result of the personal choice of where to live and are not deductible. An alternative response treats the expense as purely business in nature. Under this approach, nearly all business travel—even if it contains personal elements—is deductible. Yet another response provides statutory rules that allow partial deductibility. Detailed statutory provisions govern the deductibility of meals and moving expenses and render some of those expenses deductible.

As you encounter each type of expense throughout this chapter, try to fit the current tax treatment into one of the categories described above, and consider whether a different treatment would be more effective or appropriate. Also consider whether applying the rules in a mechanical versus flexible manner achieves the best results.

SECTION 1.   GENERAL PRINCIPLES

INTERNAL REVENUE CODE: Sections 162(a); 212(1), (2); 262; 274(a)(1).

Moss v. Commissioner

United States Court of Appeals, Seventh Circuit, 1985.
758 F.2d 211.

■ POSNER, CIRCUIT JUDGE: The taxpayers, a lawyer named Moss and his wife, appeal from a decision of the Tax Court disallowing federal income tax deductions of a little more than $1,000 in each of two years, representing Moss's share of his law firm's lunch expense at the Café Angelo in Chicago. The Tax Court's decision in this case has attracted some attention in tax circles because of its implications for the general problem of the deductibility of business meals. * * *

Moss was a partner in a small trial firm specializing in defense work, mostly for one insurance company. Each of the firm's lawyers carried a tremendous litigation caseload, averaging more than 300 cases, and spent most of every working day in courts in Chicago and its suburbs. The members of the firm met for lunch daily at the Café Angelo near their office. At lunch the lawyers would discuss their cases with the head of the firm, whose approval was required for most settlements, and they would decide which lawyer would meet which court call that afternoon or the next morning. Lunchtime was chosen for the daily meeting because the courts were in recess then. The alternatives were to meet at 7:00 a.m. or 6:00 p.m., and these were less convenient times. There is no suggestion that the lawyers dawdled over lunch, or that the Café Angelo is luxurious.

The framework of statutes and regulations for deciding this case is simple, but not clear. Section 262 of the Internal Revenue Code (Title 26) disallows, "except as otherwise expressly provided in this chapter," the deduction of "personal, family, or living expenses." Section 119 excludes from income the value of meals provided by an employer to his employees for his convenience, but only if they are provided on the employer's premises; and section 162(a) allows the deduction of "all the ordinary and necessary expenses paid or incurred during the taxable year in carrying on any trade or business, including— * * * (2) traveling expenses (including amounts expended for meals * * *) while away from home." * * * "Since Moss was not an employee but a partner in a partnership not taxed as an entity, since the meals were not served on the employer's premises, and since he was not away from home (that is, on an overnight trip away from his place of work, see United States v. Correll, 389 U.S. 299 (1967)), neither section 119 nor section 162(a)(2) applies to this case. The Internal Revenue Service concedes, however, that meals are deductible under section 162(a) when they are ordinary and necessary business expenses (provided the expense is substantiated with adequate records, see section 274(d)) even if they are not within the express permission of any other provision and even though the expense of commuting to and from work, a traveling expense but not one incurred away from home, is not deductible. Treasury Regulations on Income Tax § 1.262–1(b)(5) * * * .

The problem is that many expenses are simultaneously business expenses in the sense that they conduce to the production of business income and personal expenses in the sense that they raise personal welfare. This is plain enough with regard to lunch; most people would eat lunch even if they didn't work. Commuting may seem a pure business expense, but is not; it reflects the choice of where to live, as well as where to work. Read literally, section 262 would make irrelevant whether a business expense is also a personal expense; so long as it is ordinary and necessary in the taxpayer's business, thus bringing section 162(a) into play, an expense is (the statute seems to say) deductible from his income tax. But the statute has not been read literally. There is a natural reluctance, most clearly manifested in the regulation disallowing deduction of the expense of commuting, to lighten the tax burden of people who have the good fortune to interweave work with consumption. To allow a deduction for commuting would confer a windfall on people who live in the suburbs and commute to work in the cities; to allow a deduction for all business-related meals would confer a windfall on people who can arrange their work schedules so they do some of their work at lunch. → Application

Although an argument can thus be made for disallowing *any* deduction for business meals, on the theory that people have to eat whether they work or not, the result would be excessive taxation of people who spend more money on business meals because they are business meals than they would spend on their meals if they were not working. Suppose a theatrical agent takes his clients out to lunch at the expensive restaurants that the clients demand. Of course he can deduct the expense of their meals, from which he derives no pleasure or sustenance, but can he also deduct the expense of his own? He can, because he cannot eat more cheaply; he cannot munch surreptitiously on a peanut butter and jelly sandwich brought from home while his client is wolfing down tournedos Rossini followed by soufflé au grand marnier. No doubt our theatrical agent, unless concerned for his longevity, derives personal utility from his fancy meal, but probably less than the price of the meal. He would not pay for it if it were not for the business benefit; he would get more value from using the same money to buy something else; hence the meal confers on him less utility than the cash equivalent would. The law could require him to pay tax on the fair value of the meal to him; this would be (were it not for costs of administration) the economically correct solution. But the government does not attempt this difficult measurement; it once did, but gave up the attempt as not worth the cost, see United States v. Correll, supra, 389 U.S. at 301 n. 6. The taxpayer is permitted to deduct the whole price, provided the expense is "different from or in excess of that which would have been made for the taxpayer's personal purposes." Sutter v. Commissioner, 21 T.C. 170, 173 (1953).

Because the law allows this generous deduction, which tempts people to have more (and costlier) business meals than are necessary, the Internal Revenue Service has every right to insist that the meal be shown to be a real business necessity. This condition is most easily satisfied when a client or customer or supplier or other outsider to the business is a guest. Even if Sydney Smith was wrong that "soup and fish explain half the emotions of life," it is undeniable that eating together fosters camaraderie and makes business dealings friendlier and easier. It thus reduces the costs of transacting business, for these costs include the frictions and the failures of communication that are produced by suspicion and mutual misunderstanding, by differences in tastes and manners, and by lack of rapport. A meeting with a client or customer in an office is therefore not a perfect substitute for a lunch with him in a restaurant. But it is different when all the participants in the meal are coworkers, as essentially was the case here (clients occasionally were invited to the firm's daily luncheon, but Moss has made no attempt to identify the occasions). They know each other well already; they don't need the social lubrication that a meal with an outsider provides—at least don't need it daily. If a large firm had a monthly lunch to allow partners to get to know associates, the expense of the meal might well be necessary, and would be allowed by the Internal Revenue Service. See Wells v. Commissioner, 36 T.C.M. 1698, 1699 (1977), aff'd without opinion, 626 F.2d 868 (9th Cir.1980). But Moss's firm never had more than eight lawyers (partners and associates), and did not need a daily lunch to cement relationships among them.

It is all a matter of degree and circumstance (the expense of a testimonial dinner, for example, would be deductible on a morale-building rationale); and particularly of frequency. Daily—for a full year—is too often, perhaps even for entertainment of clients, as implied by Hankenson v. Commissioner, 47 T.C.M. 1567, 1569 (1984), where the Tax Court held nondeductible the cost of lunches consumed three or four days a week, 52 weeks a year, by a doctor who entertained other doctors who he hoped would refer patients to him, and other medical personnel.

We may assume it was necessary for Moss's firm to meet daily to coordinate the work of the firm, and also, as the Tax Court found, that lunch was the most convenient time. But it does not follow that the expense of the lunch was a necessary business expense. The members of the firm had to eat somewhere, and the Café Angelo was both convenient and not too expensive. They do not claim to have incurred a greater daily lunch expense than they would have incurred if there had been no lunch meetings. Although it saved time to combine lunch with work, the meal itself was not an organic part of the meeting, as in the examples we gave earlier where the business objective, to be fully achieved, required sharing a meal.

The case might be different if the location of the courts required the firm's members to eat each day either in a disagreeable restaurant, so that they derived less value from the meal than it cost them to buy it, * * * or in a restaurant too expensive for their personal tastes, so that, again, they would have gotten less value than the cash equivalent. But so far as appears, they picked the restaurant they liked most. Although it must be pretty monotonous to eat lunch the same place every working day of the year, not all the lawyers attended all the lunch meetings and there was nothing to stop the firm from meeting occasionally at another restaurant proximate to their office in downtown Chicago; there are hundreds.

An argument can be made that the price of lunch at the Café Angelo included rental of the space that the lawyers used for what was a meeting as well as a meal. There was evidence that the firm's conference room was otherwise occupied throughout the working day, so as a matter of logic Moss might be able to claim a part of the price of lunch as an ordinary and necessary expense for work space. But this is cutting things awfully fine; in any event Moss made no effort to apportion his lunch expense in this way.

Affirmed.

DETAILED ANALYSIS

1.   GENERAL THEORY

In *Moss,* Judge Posner states that the economically correct result would be for the taxpayer to include in the tax base the fair value of the meals to him. This statement may appear somewhat puzzling since the issue in the case is whether the cost of the meals should be deducted, not whether a receipt should be included in income. But not allowing a deduction is the same as including an amount in income; if Moss deducts the cost of the meals from his otherwise taxable income, then the cost of the meals is eliminated from the tax base. Disallowing the deduction ensures that the amount remains in the tax base.

The value of a meal to a taxpayer is generally measured by the amount paid. Thus, where a meal has no connection to a profit-seeking activity, the amount paid is presumed to represent the value to the taxpayer.[1] But the value of the meal to Moss may have been less than its cost because of its connection to a profit-seeking activity. It is at least possible that Moss would have preferred to eat a yogurt for lunch and that the cuisine at Café Angelo provided little or no value to him. Expenditures containing both profit-seeking and personal elements thus present difficult valuation problems arising from the presence of restricted choice. These problems closely parallel the problems previously encountered regarding employee fringe benefits, discussed in Chapter 3. The relationship between mixed profit-seeking and

---

[1]   This amount actually measures the minimum value to the taxpayer since the taxpayer might have been willing to pay more for the meal if the restaurant had set its prices higher. Unfortunately, there is no way to measure this consumer surplus.

personal expenditures and fringe benefits can perhaps be seen more clearly by asking how an associate of the law firm should be taxed where the firm provides lunch at no cost to the associate at the Café Angelo daily meetings. See I.R.C. § 132(d).

The relationship between the inclusion of the value of the meal in the tax base and the general principle that the costs of producing income are deductible requires further illustration. These two basic principles could be reconciled if a deduction were allowed for the amount by which the cost of the meal exceeds the personal value of the meal to the taxpayer. Thus, if Moss would have only paid $10 for the lunch apart from any business considerations, and the lunch in fact cost $15, then the $5 of excess cost would be allowed as a business deduction. This would leave $10 as a nondeductible personal expense. The $10 of gross income which was used to pay for the personal value of the lunch would thus be included in the tax base; the $5 of the gross income used to pay the profit-seeking portion would be offset by the $5 deduction.

But suppose that Moss would have paid $15 for the lunch even if it had no connection to a profit-seeking activity and that Moss also would have paid $5 solely because of the profit-seeking value even if he derived no personal value. This resembles the fringe benefit situation except that the taxpayer is acting as both employer and employee. In the fringe benefit situation, the employer would be entitled to a $15 deduction and the employee would have $15 of income (the exclusions provided by § 132 would not appear to apply). The employee who pays for the meal thus should be entitled to a $15 deduction and be required to include $15 of income. This result is achieved in the context of the self-employed taxpayer like Moss by simply denying the deduction and not requiring income inclusion. The net result is that the $15 of gross income used to pay for lunch is not offset by any deduction and is included in the tax base.

The statement in *Moss* thus correctly focuses upon the personal aspect of the expense. As stated by Professor Daniel I. Halperin:

> The position that a deduction ought to be allowed for all income-generating expenses, while quite correct, is really beside the point. If such expenditures actually provide personal satisfaction, the amount of such satisfaction ought to be included in income. The fairest income tax would take account of income from "whatever source derived." On-the-job entertainment, traveling expenses and other expenditures which but for their connection with income-generating activities would be considered to provide personal satisfaction should not be distinguished from other forms of enjoyment.
>
> An indirect way of taxing these benefits is to deny a deduction to the extent personal satisfaction has been obtained from the expenditure. If satisfaction were equal to cost, this approach would suggest complete disallowance.

Daniel Halperin, *Business Deduction for Personal Living Expenses: A Uniform Approach to an Unsolved Problem*, 122 U.PA.L.REV. 859, 862–63 (1974).

Section 274(n), which generally limits the deduction for business meals and entertainment to 50 percent of the expense, in effect applies this technique by arbitrarily treating the personal benefit as one-half of the cost.

2. APPLICATIONS OF THE *MOSS* PRINCIPLE

Note the relatively limited scope of *Moss*. The restaurant in which the necessary business meetings were held was not particularly expensive. Also, because of the general absence of clients from the lunches the choice of restaurants was the collective choice of the partners and was convenient to them. As the court concludes, "[i]t is all a matter of degree and circumstance" so that different facts might well justify deductibility.

In Christey v. United States, 841 F.2d 809 (8th Cir.1988), Minnesota state troopers were required to eat meals at roadside restaurants within their patrol areas. Because the purpose of the requirement was public visibility of the troopers for purposes of promoting public safety, they were not permitted to pack their own lunches and eat in their vehicles. On these facts, the court found that the troopers were required to purchase restaurant meals "for the convenience of the employer," and they were allowed to deduct the cost of the meals. A dissenting opinion argued that this result is inconsistent with the Supreme Court's decision in *Kowalski,* discussed in Chapter 3, Section 3.A.9.3.

Business entertainment expenses raise the same basic issues as business-related meals and business travel. The fundamental task is to identify the amount that represents personal consumption. But in this context the question arises somewhat differently. Suppose A, a business person, purchases two $60 tickets for a baseball game and takes an important client to the game. What portion of the $120 should be deductible?

With regard to A's ticket, the analysis is similar to that for the cost of the lunch in *Moss:* A should be allowed a deduction only to the extent the cost of the ticket exceeds the personal value to A. Although it is possible that A hates baseball and only invites B because A is aware of B's desire to attend the game, in most situations it is likely that the value to A approximates the $60 cost. It would therefore be appropriate to deny any deduction for the cost of A's ticket.

The analysis for the cost of B's ticket is somewhat different. In principle, A should deduct the $60 cost of B's ticket as a purely profit-seeking expense. B should include in income the value of the benefit received. At the same time, we might not want to use the full $60 cost of the ticket as the value to be included in income by B. While theoretically the ticket might be worth less than $60 to B because it was subject to the condition that B attend the game with A on a particular night not necessarily of B's choosing, the difficulties of quantifying these factors and their relative insignificance in relation to the clear personal benefit of the ticket argue for full inclusion. Yet, it is difficult as an administrative matter to assure that the $60 deducted by A for B's ticket is in fact included in income by B. Thus, once again, a "second best" solution would deny a deduction for the cost of B's ticket to A, assuring that non-inclusion would be matched by nondeductibility. On the basis of this analysis, total disallowance of deductions for entertainment can be justified. Statutory provisions that limit the deductibility of some entertainment expenses sometimes provide such a result.

SECTION 2.   TRAVEL AND RELATED EXPENSES

INTERNAL REVENUE CODE: Sections 162(a)(2); 274(n); 217(a)–(f); 82.

REGULATIONS: Sections 1.162–2; 1.212–1(f); 1.217–2(a)–(f); 1.262–1(b)(5); 1.274–5(c)(2)(iii); 1.274–5T(a), (b)(1), (2), (c)(1)–(3)(i).

Commissioner v. Flowers

Supreme Court of the United States, 1946.
326 U.S. 465.

[The taxpayer, an attorney, resided in Jackson, Mississippi. All of his legal work consisted of acting as general counsel for the Gulf, Mobile & Ohio Railroad. The main office of the railroad was in Mobile, Alabama, but the taxpayer had accepted the position on the understanding that he could continue to reside in Jackson, and that he would pay the cost of traveling between Jackson and Mobile as well as his living expenses in both places. In 1939 he worked 203 days in Jackson and 66 days in Mobile, making 33 trips between the cities. In 1940, he worked 168 days in Jackson and 102 in Mobile, making 40 trips. The distance is between 231 and 329 rail miles depending on the route, and required roughly 11 hours of travel time. The taxpayer claimed a deduction for 1939 and 1940 for traveling expenses from Jackson to Mobile, and for meals and hotel accommodations while in Mobile.]

■ MR. JUSTICE MURPHY delivered the opinion of the Court. * * *

The portion of [the predecessor of section 162(a)(2)] authorizing the deduction of "traveling expenses (including the entire amount expended for meals and lodging) while away from home in the pursuit of a trade or business" is one of the specific examples given by Congress in that section of "ordinary and necessary expenses paid or incurred during the taxable year in carrying on any trade or business." It is to be contrasted with the provision of [the predecessor of section 262], disallowing any deductions for "personal, living, or family expenses." And it is to be read in light of the interpretation given it by [the predecessor of Treas. Reg. § 1.162–2(a) and (e)]. * * *

Three conditions must thus be satisfied before a traveling expense deduction may be made under [section 162(a)(2)].

(1) The expense must be a reasonable and necessary traveling expense, as that term is generally understood. This includes such items

as transportation fares and food and lodging expenses incurred while traveling.

(2) The expense must be incurred "while away from home."

(3) The expense must be incurred in pursuit of business. This means that there must be a direct connection between the expenditure and the carrying on of the trade or business of the taxpayer or of his employer. Moreover, such an expenditure must be necessary or appropriate to the development and pursuit of the business or trade. * * *

The meaning of the word "home" in [section 162(a)(2)] with reference to a taxpayer residing in one city and working in another has engendered much difficulty and litigation. * * * The Tax Court and the administrative rulings have consistently defined it as the equivalent of the taxpayer's place of business. See Barnhill v. Commissioner, 4 Cir. [148 F.2d 913]. On the other hand, the decision below and Wallace v. Commissioner, 9 Cir., 144 F.2d 407, have flatly rejected that view and have confined the term to the taxpayer's actual residence. * * *

We deem it unnecessary here to enter into or to decide this conflict. The Tax Court's opinion, as we read it, was grounded neither solely nor primarily upon that agency's conception of the word "home." Its discussion was directed mainly toward the relation of the expenditures to the railroad's business, a relationship required by the third condition of the deduction. Thus even if the Tax Court's definition of the word "home" was implicit in its decision and even if that definition was erroneous, its judgment must be sustained here if it properly concluded that the necessary relationship between the expenditures and the railroad's business was lacking. Failure to satisfy any one of the three conditions destroys the traveling expense deduction.

Turning our attention to the third condition, this case is disposed of quickly. There is no claim that the Tax Court misconstrued this condition or used improper standards in applying it. And it is readily apparent from the facts that its inferences were supported by evidence and that its conclusion that the expenditures in issue were nondeductible living and personal expenses was fully justified.

The facts demonstrate clearly that the expenses were not incurred in the pursuit of the business of the taxpayer's employer, the railroad. Jackson was his regular home. Had his post of duty been in that city the cost of maintaining his home there and of commuting or driving to work concededly would be non-deductible living and personal expenses lacking the necessary direct relation to the prosecution of the business. The character of such expenses is unaltered by the circumstance that the taxpayer's post of duty was in Mobile, thereby increasing the costs of transportation, food and lodging. Whether he maintained one abode or two, whether he traveled three blocks or three hundred miles to work, the nature of these expenditures remained the same.

The added costs in issue, moreover, were as unnecessary and inappropriate to the development of the railroad's business as were his personal and living costs in Jackson. They were incurred solely as the result of the taxpayer's desire to maintain a home in Jackson while working in Mobile, a factor irrelevant to the maintenance and prosecution of the railroad's legal business. The railroad did not require him to travel on business from Jackson to Mobile or to maintain living quarters in both cities. Nor did it compel him, save in one instance, to perform tasks for it in Jackson. It simply asked him to be at his principal post in Mobile as business demanded and as his personal convenience was served, allowing him to divide his business time between Mobile and Jackson as he saw fit. Except for the federal court litigation, all of the taxpayer's work in Jackson would normally have been performed in the headquarters at Mobile. The fact that he traveled frequently between the two cities and incurred extra living expenses in Mobile, while doing much of his work in Jackson, was occasioned solely by his personal propensities. The railroad gained nothing from this arrangement except the personal satisfaction of the taxpayer.

Travel expenses in pursuit of business within the meaning of [section 162(a)(2)] could arise only when the railroad's business forced the taxpayer to travel and to live temporarily at some place other than Mobile, thereby advancing the interests of the railroad. Business trips are to be identified in relation to business demands and the traveler's business headquarters. The exigencies of business rather than the personal conveniences and necessities of the traveler must be the motivating factors. Such was not the case here.

It follows that the court below erred in reversing the judgment of the Tax Court.

Reversed.

■ MR. JUSTICE RUTLEDGE, dissenting.

I think the judgment of the Court of Appeals should be affirmed. When Congress used the word "home" in [section 162(a)(2)] I do not believe it meant "business headquarters." And in my opinion this case presents no other question. * * *

Congress gave the deduction for traveling away from home on business. The commuter's case, rightly confined, does not fall in this class. One who lives in an adjacent suburb or city and by usual modes of commutation can work within a distance permitting the daily journey and return, with time for the day's work and a period at home, clearly can be excluded from the deduction on the basis of the section's terms equally with its obvious purpose. But that is not true if "commuter" is to swallow up the deduction by the same sort of construction which makes "home" mean "business headquarters" of one's employer. If the line may be extended somewhat to cover doubtful cases, it need not be lengthened to infinity or to cover cases as far removed from the prevailing connotation of commuter as this one. Including it pushes "commuting" too far, even for these times of rapid transit. * * *

By construing "home" as "business headquarters"; by reading "temporarily" as "very temporarily" into [section 162(a)(2)]; by bringing down "ordinary and necessary" from [the first part] into [paragraph (2)]; by finding "inequity" where Congress has said none exists; by construing "commuter" to cover long-distance, irregular travel; and by conjuring from the "statutory setting" a meaning at odds with the plain wording of the clause, the Government makes over understandable ordinary English into highly technical tax jargon. There is enough of this in the tax laws inescapably, without adding more in the absence of either compulsion or authority. * * *

Hantzis v. Commissioner

United States Court of Appeals, First Circuit, 1981.
638 F.2d 248.

■ CAMPBELL, CIRCUIT JUDGE, delivered the opinion of the Court.

The Commissioner of Internal Revenue (Commissioner) appeals a decision of the United States Tax Court that allowed a deduction under 26 U.S.C. § 162(a)(2) (1976) for expenses incurred by a law student in the course of her summer employment. The facts in the case are straightforward and undisputed.

In the fall of 1973 Catharine Hantzis (taxpayer) * * * entered Harvard Law School in Cambridge, Massachusetts, as a full-time student. During her second year of law school she sought unsuccessfully to obtain employment for the summer of 1975 with a Boston law firm. She did, however, find a job as a legal assistant with a law firm in New York City, where she worked for ten weeks beginning in June 1975. Her husband, then a member of the faculty of Northeastern University with a teaching schedule for that summer, remained in Boston and lived at the couple's home there. At the time of the Tax Court's decision in this case, Mr. and Mrs. Hantzis still resided in Boston.

On their joint income tax return for 1975, Mr. and Mrs. Hantzis reported the earnings from taxpayer's summer employment ($3,750) and deducted the cost of transportation between Boston and New York, the cost of a small apartment rented by Mrs. Hantzis in New York and the cost of her meals in New York ($3,204). The deductions were taken under 26 U.S.C. § 162(a)(2) (1976), which provides:

"§ 162. Trade or business expenses

(a) In general. There shall be allowed as a deduction all the ordinary and necessary expenses paid or incurred during the taxable year in carrying on any trade or business, including

(2) traveling expenses (including amounts expended for meals and lodging other than amounts which are lavish or

extravagant under the circumstances) while away from home in the pursuit of a trade or business. . . ."

The Commissioner disallowed the deduction on the ground that taxpayer's home for purposes of section 162(a)(2) was her place of employment and the cost of traveling to and living in New York was therefore not "incurred . . . while away from home." The Commissioner also argued that the expenses were not incurred "in the pursuit of a trade or business." Both positions were rejected by the Tax Court, which found that Boston was Mrs. Hantzis' home because her employment in New York was only temporary and that her expenses in New York were "necessitated" by her employment there. The court thus held the expenses to be deductible under section 162(a)(2).

In asking this court to reverse the Tax Court's allowance of the deduction, the Commissioner has contended that the expenses were not incurred "in the pursuit of a trade or business." We do not accept this argument; nonetheless, we sustain the Commissioner and deny the deduction, on the basis that the expenses were not incurred "while away from home."

I.

Section 262 of the Code, 26 U.S.C. § 262 (1976), declares that "except as otherwise provided in this chapter, no deductions shall be allowed for personal, living, or family expenses." Section 162 provides less of an exception to this rule than it creates a separate category of deductible business expenses. This category manifests a fundamental principle of taxation: that a person's taxable income should not include the cost of producing that income. * * * "(O)ne of the specific examples given by Congress" of a deductible cost of producing income is travel expenses in section 162(a)(2). Commissioner v. Flowers, 326 U.S. 465, 469 (1946). * * *

The test by which "personal" travel expenses subject to tax under section 262 are distinguished from those costs of travel necessarily incurred to generate income is embodied in the requirement that, to be deductible under section 162(a)(2), an expense must be "incurred . . . in the pursuit of a trade or business." In *Flowers* the Supreme Court read this phrase to mean that "(t)he exigencies of business rather than the personal conveniences and necessities of the traveler must be the motivating factors." 326 U.S. at 474. Of course, not every travel expense resulting from business exigencies rather than personal choice is deductible; an expense must also be "ordinary and necessary" and incurred "while away from home." 26 U.S.C. § 162(a)(2) (1976) * * * . But the latter limitations draw also upon the basic concept that only expenses necessitated by business, as opposed to personal, demands may be excluded from the calculation of taxable income.

* * *

III.

As already noted, *Flowers* construed section 162(a)(2) to mean that a traveling expense is deductible only if it is (1) reasonable and necessary, (2) incurred while away from home, and (3) necessitated by the exigencies of business. Because the Commissioner does not suggest that Mrs. Hantzis' expenses were unreasonable or unnecessary, we may pass directly to the remaining requirements. Of these, we find dispositive the requirement that an expense be incurred while away from home. As we think Mrs. Hantzis' expenses were not so incurred, we hold the deduction to be improper.

The meaning of the term "home" in the travel expense provision is far from clear. When Congress enacted the travel expense deduction now codified as section 162(a)(2), it apparently was unsure whether, to be deductible, an expense must be incurred away from a person's residence or away from his principal place of business. * * * This ambiguity persists and courts, sometimes within a single circuit, have divided over the issue. Compare Six v. United States, 450 F.2d 66 (2d Cir.1971) (home held to be residence) and Rosenspan v. United States, 438 F.2d 905 (2d Cir.), cert. denied, 404 U.S. 864 (1971) and Burns v. Gray, 287 F.2d 698 (6th Cir.1961) and Wallace v. Commissioner, 144 F.2d 407 (9th Cir.1944) with Markey v. Commissioner, 490 F.2d 1249 (6th Cir.1974) (home held to be principal place of business) and Curtis v. Commissioner, 449 F.2d 225 (5th Cir.1971) and Wills v. Commissioner, 411 F.2d 537 (9th Cir.1969).[10] It has been suggested that these conflicting definitions are due to the enormous factual variety in the cases. * * * Brandl v. Commissioner, 513 F.2d 697, 699 (6th Cir.1975) ("Because of the almost infinite variety of the factual situations involved, the courts have not formulated a concrete definition of the term 'home' capable of universal application.") We find this observation instructive, for if the cases that discuss the meaning of the term "home" in section 162(a)(2) are interpreted on the basis of their unique facts as well as the fundamental purposes of the travel expense provision, and not simply pinioned to one of two competing definitions of home, much of the seeming confusion and contradiction on this issue disappears and a functional definition of the term emerges.

We begin by recognizing that the location of a person's home for purposes of section 162(a)(2) becomes problematic only when the person lives one place and works another. Where a taxpayer resides and works at a single location, he is always home, however defined; and where a taxpayer is constantly on the move due to his work, he is never "away" from home. (In the latter situation, it may be said either that he has no residence to be away from, or else that his residence is always at his place of employment. See Rev. Rul. 60–16, 1960–1 C.B. 58, 62.) However, in

---

[10]   The Tax Court has, with a notable exception, consistently held that a taxpayer's home is his place of business. See Daly v. Commissioner, 72 T.C. 190 (1979); Foote v. Commissioner, 67 T.C. 1 (1976); Montgomery v. Commissioner, 64 T.C. 175 (1975), aff'd, 532 F.2d 1088 (6th Cir.1976); Blatnick v. Commissioner, 56 T.C. 1344 (1971). The exception, of course, is the present case.

the present case, the need to determine "home" is plainly before us, since the taxpayer resided in Boston and worked, albeit briefly, in New York.

We think the critical step in defining "home" in these situations is to recognize that the "while away from home" requirement has to be construed in light of the further requirement that the expense be the result of business exigencies. The traveling expense deduction obviously is not intended to exclude from taxation every expense incurred by a taxpayer who, in the course of business, maintains two homes. Section 162(a)(2) seeks rather "to mitigate the burden of the taxpayer who, *because of the exigencies of his trade or business, must* maintain two places of abode and thereby incur additional and duplicate living expenses." *Kroll*, supra, 49 T.C. at 562 (emphasis added). * * * Consciously or unconsciously, courts have effectuated this policy in part through their interpretation of the term "home" in section 162(a)(2). Whether it is held in a particular decision that a taxpayer's home is his residence or his principal place of business, the ultimate allowance or disallowance of a deduction is a function of the court's assessment of the reason for a taxpayer's maintenance of two homes. If the reason is perceived to be personal, the taxpayer's home will generally be held to be his place of employment rather than his residence and the deduction will be denied. See, e.g., *Markey*, supra, 490 F.2d at 1252–55. If the reason is felt to be business exigencies, the person's home will usually be held to be his residence and the deduction will be allowed. See, e.g., Frederick v. United States, 603 F.2d 1292 (8th Cir.1979). We understand the concern of the concurrence that such an operational interpretation of the term "home" is somewhat technical and perhaps untidy, in that it will not always afford bright line answers, but we doubt the ability of either the Commissioner or the courts to invent an unyielding formula that will make sense in all cases. The line between personal and business expenses winds through infinite factual permutations; effectuation of the travel expense provision requires that any principle of decision be flexible and sensitive to statutory policy.

Construing in the manner just described the requirement that an expense be incurred "while away from home," we do not believe this requirement was satisfied in this case. Mrs. Hantzis' trade or business did not require that she maintain a home in Boston as well as one in New York. Though she returned to Boston at various times during the period of her employment in New York, her visits were all for personal reasons. It is not contended that she had a business connection in Boston that necessitated her keeping a home there; no professional interest was served by maintenance of the Boston home as would have been the case, for example, if Mrs. Hantzis had been a lawyer based in Boston with a New York client whom she was temporarily serving. The home in Boston was kept up for reasons involving Mr. Hantzis, but those reasons cannot substitute for a showing by Mrs. Hantzis that the exigencies of her trade or business required her to maintain two homes.[11] Mrs. Hantzis' decision to keep two homes must be seen as a choice dictated by personal, albeit wholly reasonable, considerations and not a business or occupational necessity. We therefore hold that her home for purposes of section 162(a)(2) was New York and that the expenses at issue in this case were not incurred "while away from home."

We are not dissuaded from this conclusion by the temporary nature of Mrs. Hantzis' employment in New York. Mrs. Hantzis argues that the brevity of her stay in New York excepts her from the business exigencies requirement of section 162(a)(2) * * * . The Tax Court here held that Boston was the taxpayer's home because it would have been unreasonable for her to move her residence to New York for only ten weeks. At first glance these contentions may seem to find support in the court decisions holding that, when a taxpayer works for a limited time away from his usual home, section 162(a)(2) allows a deduction for the expense of maintaining a second home so long as the employment is "temporary" and not "indefinite" or "permanent." See, e.g., *Frederick*, supra, 603 F.2d at 1294 * * * This test is an elaboration of the requirements under section 162(a)(2) that an expense be incurred due to business exigencies and while away from home. * * * Thus it has been said,

> "Where a taxpayer reasonably expects to be employed in a location for a substantial or indefinite period of time, the reasonable inference is that his choice of a residence is a personal decision, unrelated to any business necessity. Thus, it is irrelevant how far he travels to work. The normal expectation, however, is that the taxpayer will choose to live near his place of employment. Consequently, when a taxpayer reasonable (sic) expects to be employed in a location for only a short or temporary period of time and travels a considerable distance to the location from his residence, it is unreasonable to assume that his choice of a residence is dictated by personal convenience. The reasonable inference is that he is temporarily making these travels because of a business necessity."

Frederick, supra, 603 F.2d at 1294–95 (citations omitted).

The temporary employment doctrine does not, however, purport to eliminate any requirement that continued maintenance of a first home have a business justification. We think the rule has no application where the taxpayer has no business connection with his usual place of residence. If no business exigency dictates the location of the taxpayer's usual residence, then the mere fact of his taking temporary employment

---

[11]   In this respect, Mr. and Mrs. Hantzis' situation is analogous to cases involving spouses with careers in different locations. Each must independently satisfy the requirement that deductions taken for travel expenses incurred in the pursuit of a trade or business arise while he or she is away from home. See Chwalow v. Commissioner, 470 F.2d 475, 477–78 (3d Cir.1972) ("Where additional expenses are incurred because, for personal reasons, husband and wife maintain separate domiciles, no deduction is allowed.") * * * .

elsewhere cannot supply a compelling business reason for continuing to maintain that residence. Only a taxpayer who lives one place, works another and has business ties to both is in the ambiguous situation that the temporary employment doctrine is designed to resolve. In such circumstances, unless his employment away from his usual home is temporary, a court can reasonably assume that the taxpayer has abandoned his business ties to that location and is left with only personal reasons for maintaining a residence there. Where only personal needs require that a travel expense be incurred, however, a taxpayer's home is defined so as to leave the expense subject to taxation. * * * Thus, a taxpayer who pursues temporary employment away from the location of his usual residence, but has no business connection with that location, is not "away from home" for purposes of section 162(a)(2). See Cockrell v. Commissioner, 321 F.2d 504, 507 (8th Cir.1963); Tucker v. Commissioner, 55 T.C. 783, 786–88 (1971).

On this reasoning, the temporary nature of Mrs. Hantzis' employment in New York does not affect the outcome of her case. She had no business ties to Boston that would bring her within the temporary employment doctrine. By this holding, we do not adopt a rule that "home" in section 162(a)(2) is the equivalent of a taxpayer's place of business. Nor do we mean to imply that a taxpayer has a "home" for tax purposes only if he is already engaged in a trade or business at a particular location. Though both rules are alluringly determinate, we have already discussed why they offer inadequate expressions of the purposes behind the travel expense deduction. We hold merely that for a taxpayer in Mrs. Hantzis' circumstances to be "away from home in the pursuit of a trade or business," she must establish the existence of some sort of business relation both to the location she claims as "home" and to the location of her temporary employment sufficient to support a finding that her duplicative expenses are necessitated by business exigencies. This, we believe, is the meaning of the statement in *Flowers* that "(business) trips are to be identified in relation to business demands and the traveler's business headquarters." 326 U.S. at 474 (emphasis added). On the uncontested facts before us, Mrs. Hantzis had no business relation to Boston; we therefore leave to cases in which the issue is squarely presented the task of elaborating what relation to a place is required under section 162(a)(2) for duplicative living expenses to be deductible.

Reversed.

Wilbert v. Commissioner

United States Court of Appeals, Seventh Circuit, 2009.
553 F.3d 544.

■ POSNER, CIRCUIT JUDGE, delivered the opinion of the Court.

The question presented by this appeal is whether an employee who uses "bumping" rights to avoid or postpone losing his job can deduct the living expenses that he incurs when he finds himself working far from home as a result of exercising those rights. The Tax Court ruled against the taxpayer, * * * and he appeals.

Hired by Northwest in 1996, Wilbert worked for the airline at the Minneapolis airport for some years. He lived with his wife in Hudson, Wisconsin, across the Mississippi River from Minneapolis. * * *

Facing financial pressures and a decline in airline traffic in the wake of the terrorist attacks of September 11, 2001, Northwest laid off many employees, including, in April 2003, Wilbert. But Northwest's mechanics each had a right to bump a more junior mechanic employed by the airline, that is, to take his job. Wilbert was able to bump a mechanic who worked for the airline in Chicago, but he worked there for only a few days before being bumped by a more senior mechanic. A few days later he was able to bump a mechanic in Anchorage, Alaska, and he worked there for three weeks before being himself bumped. He was soon able to bump a mechanic who worked in New York, at LaGuardia Airport, but he worked there for only a week before he was bumped again. At this point, he had exhausted his bumping rights. But for reasons that the parties have not explained, three weeks later the airline hired him back, outside the bumping system, to fill an interim position (maximum nine months) in Anchorage. He occupied that position for several months before being laid off again, this time for good. * * *

He did not sell or rent his home in Hudson, where his wife continued to live, while working intermittently in 2003. Because he was working too far from home to be able to live there, he incurred living expenses (amounting to almost $ 20,000) that he would not have incurred had he remained working in Minneapolis, and those are the expenses he deducted from the taxable income shown on his 2003 return.

The Internal Revenue Code allows the deduction, as part of "the ordinary and necessary expenses . . . incurred during the taxable year in carrying on any trade or business," of "traveling expenses . . . *while [the taxpayer is] away from home* in the pursuit of a trade or business." 26 U.S.C. § 162(a)(2) (emphasis added). There is an exception for "personal, living, or family expenses." § 262(a). The phrase we have italicized is critical. It is by an interpretation of that phrase that commuting expenses are disallowed because of "a natural reluctance . . . to lighten the tax burden of people who have the good fortune to interweave work with consumption. To allow a deduction for commuting would confer a windfall on people who live in the suburbs and commute to work in the cities." Moss v. Commissioner, 758 F.2d 211, 212 (7th Cir. 1985). The length of the commute is thus irrelevant. If Wilbert had had a permanent job in Anchorage but decided to retain his home in Minneapolis and return there on weekends and during the week live in a truck stop in Wasilla, Alaska, he could not have deducted from his taxable income the expense of traveling to and fro between Minnesota and Alaska or his room and board in Wasilla. (We ignore for the moment the possibility that Mrs. Wilbert had a job in Minneapolis, and if so its relevance.)

Similarly, he could not have deducted his traveling expenses if he had had no home separate from the places he traveled to—if he had been, in the language of the cases, an "itinerant" worker, for then he would never have been "away from home" on his travels. E.g., Fisher v. Commissioner, 230 F.2d 79 (7th Cir. 1956); Henderson v. Commissioner, 143 F.3d 497 (9th Cir. 1998) * * *. He would have been like someone whose only residence is a recreational vehicle, or a truck driver who lives in the cab of his truck, or the taxpayer in the *Fisher* case—"an itinerant professional musician, [who] traveled from city to city performing, solo, in various hotel dining rooms and cocktail lounges. These engagements varied in duration from three to four weeks, or as long as seven or eight months. His wife and child traveled and lived with taxpayer wherever he was situated." 230 F.2d at 80.

With our hypothetical Wilbert the long-distance commuter, compare a lawyer whose home and office are both in Minneapolis but who has an international practice and as a result spends more time on the road than he does at home. Nevertheless he can deduct his traveling expenses. His work requires him to maintain a home within normal commuting distance of Minneapolis because that is where his office is, but his work also requires him to travel, and the expenses he incurs in traveling are necessary to his work and he cannot offset them by relocating his residence to the places to which he travels because he has to maintain a home near his office. And likewise if, as in Andrews v. Commissioner, 931 F.2d 132 (1st Cir. 1991), the taxpayer has to make such frequent trips to a particular site that it is more economical for him to rent or buy a second residence, at that site, than to live there in a hotel.

Wilbert's case falls in between our two hypothetical cases. Unlike the lawyer, he did not have to live near Minneapolis after the initial layoff because he had no work there (ignoring for the moment his real estate business). But unlike the imaginary Wilbert who has a permanent job in Alaska and so could readily relocate his home there, the real Wilbert had jobs of indefinite, unpredictable duration in Alaska (and Chicago, and New York). It would hardly have been realistic to expect him to pull up stakes and move to Anchorage and then to Chicago and then to New York and then back to Anchorage. Remember that his first stint after the initial layoff lasted only days, his second only weeks, and the third only one week. His situation was unlike that of the employee of a New York firm who, if he chooses to live in Scarsdale rather than on Fifth Avenue, is forbidden to deduct from his taxable income the commuting expense that he incurs by virtue of his choice; it is a personal choice—suburban over urban living—rather than anything necessitated by his job.

The Tax Court, with some judicial support, has tried to resolve cases such as this by asking whether the taxpayer's work away from home is "temporary" or "indefinite," and allowing the deduction of traveling expenses only if it is the former. E.g., Peurifoy v. Commissioner, 358 U.S. 59, * * * (1958) (per curiam); Kasun v. United States, 671 F.2d 1059 (7th Cir. 1982) * * * . The Internal Revenue Code does not explicitly adopt the distinction, but does provide (with an immaterial exception) that "the taxpayer shall not be treated as being temporarily away from home during any period of employment if such period exceeds 1 year." 26 U.S.C. § 162(a).

The problem with the Tax Court's distinction is that work can be, and usually is, both temporary and indefinite, as in our lawyer example. A lawsuit he is trying in London might settle on the second day, or last a month; his sojourn away from his office will therefore be both temporary *and* indefinite. Indeed *all* work is indefinite and much "permanent" work is really temporary. An academic lawyer might accept a five-year appointment as an assistant professor with every expectation of obtaining tenure at the end of that period at that or another law school; yet one would not describe him as a "temporary" employee even if he left after six months and thus was not barred from claiming temporary status by the one-year rule. Our imaginary Wilbert who has a permanent job in Anchorage but is reluctant to move there from Minneapolis might argue (at least until he had worked a year, the statutory cutoff for "temporary" work) that no job is "permanent"—he might be fired, or he might harbor realistic hopes of getting a better job back in Minneapolis. That possibility would not permit him to deduct the expense of commuting from Minnesota to Alaska.

So "temporary versus indefinite" does not work well as a test of deductibility and neither does "personal choice versus reasonable response to the employment situation," tempting as the latter formula is because of its realism. If no reasonable person would relocate to his new place of work because of uncertainty about the duration of the new job, his choice to stay where he is, unlike a choice to commute from a suburb to the city in which one's office is located rather than live in the city, is not an optional personal choice like deciding to stay at a Four Seasons or a Ritz Carlton, but a choice forced by circumstances. Wilbert when first notified that he was being laid off could foresee a series of temporary jobs all across the country and not even limited, as we know, to the lower 48 states, and the costs of moving his home to the location of each temporary job would have been prohibitive. It would have meant moving four times in one year on a mechanic's salary to cities hundreds or (in the case of Anchorage versus Minneapolis, Chicago, or New York) thousands of miles apart.

The problem with a test that focuses on the reasonableness of the taxpayer's decision not to move is that it is bound to prove nebulous in application. For it just asks the taxpayer to give a good reason for not moving his home when he gets a job in a different place, and if he gave a good reason then his traveling expenses would be deductible as the product of a reasonable balancing of personal and business considerations. In the oft-cited case of Hantzis v. Commissioner, 638 F.2d 248 (1st Cir. 1981), the question was whether a law student who lived in Boston with her husband during the school year could deduct her traveling expenses when she took a summer job in New York. Given the temporary nature of the job, it made perfectly good sense for her to retain her home in Boston and just camp out, as it were, in New York. What persuaded the court to reject the deduction was that she had no *business* reason to retain the house in Boston. Id. at 255. Stated differently, she had no business reason to be living in two places at once, id. at 256, unlike the lawyer in our example. And so the expenses she incurred living in New York could not be thought "ordinary and *necessary* expenses . . . incurred . . . in carrying on any trade or business."

If this seems rather a mechanical reading of the statute, it has the support not only of the influential precedent of *Hantzis* but also of the even more influential precedent of Commissioner v. Flowers, 326 U.S. 465, 474, * * * (1946), where the Supreme Court said that "the exigencies of business rather than the personal conveniences and necessities of the traveler must be the motivating factors" in the decision to travel. The "business exigencies" rule, though harsh, is supported by compelling considerations of administerability. To apply a test of reasonableness the Internal Revenue Service would first have to decide whether the taxpayer should have moved to his new place of work. This might require answering such questions as whether the schools in the area of his new job were far worse than those his children currently attend, whether his elderly parents live near his existing home and require his attention, and whether his children have psychological problems that make it difficult for them to find new friends. Were it decided that it was reasonable for the taxpayer to stay put, it would then become necessary to determine whether the expenses he incurred in traveling to and from his various places of work for home visits had been reasonable—whether in other words such commutes, in point of frequency, were "ordinary and necessary" business expenses. The Internal Revenue Service would have to establish norms of reasonable home visits that presumably would vary with such things as distance and how many of the taxpayer's children were living at home and how old they were.

We are sympathetic to Wilbert's plight and recognize the artificiality of supposing that, as the government argues, he made merely a personal choice to "commute" from Minneapolis to Anchorage, and Chicago, and New York, as if Minneapolis were a suburb of those cities. But the statutory language, the precedents, and the considerations of administerability that we have emphasized persuade us to reject the test of reasonableness. The "temporary versus indefinite" test is no better, so we fall back on the rule of *Flowers* and *Hantzis* that unless the taxpayer has a business rather than a personal reason to be living in two places he cannot deduct his traveling expenses if he decides not to move. Indeed, Wilbert's situation is really no different from the common case of the construction worker who works at different sites throughout the country, never certain how long each stint will last and reluctant therefore to relocate his home. The construction worker loses, as must Wilbert. E.g., *Yeates v. Commissioner*, 873 F.2d 1159 (8th Cir. 1989).

We might well have a different case if Wilbert had had a firm, justified expectation of being restored to his job at the Minneapolis airport within a short time of his initial layoff. Suppose the airline had said to him, "We must lay you off, but you will be able to bump a less senior employee in Anchorage for a few weeks, and we are confident that by then, given your seniority, you will be able to return to Minneapolis." His situation would then be comparable to that of a Minneapolis lawyer ordered by his senior partner to spend the next month trying a case in Anchorage. But that is not this case.

* * * As explained in *Andrews*, "The guiding policy must be that the taxpayer is reasonably expected to locate his 'home,' for tax purposes, at his 'major post of duty' so as to minimize the amount of business travel away from home that is required; a decision to do otherwise is motivated not by business necessity but by personal considerations, and should not give rise to greater business travel deductions." 931 F.2d at 138. If Wilbert had had to travel back to Minneapolis from his new tax "homes" from time to time in order to attend to his real estate business, the travel expense (if the business was really the reason for the travel home), and conceivably even some of his living expenses at his home (his "secondary" home, in a tax sense, since his primary home for tax purposes would follow his work), might have been deductible, just as his expenses for the office equipment that he purchased in his real estate business were. * * * But he does not argue for such a deduction.

For completeness we note that if Wilbert's wife had a business in Minneapolis, this would make it all the more reasonable for Wilbert not to move away from Minneapolis. But it would not permit him to deduct his traveling expenses, because his decision to live with his wife (if only on occasional weekends) would (setting aside any considerations relating to his real estate sideline) be a personal rather than a business decision. *Hantzis v. Commissioner, supra,* 638 F.2d at 254 and n. 11 ("in this respect, Mr. and Mrs. Hantzis' situation is analogous to cases involving spouses with careers in different locations. Each must independently satisfy the requirement that deductions taken for travel expenses incurred in the pursuit of a trade or business arise while he or she is away from home"); *Chwalow v. Commissioner,* 470 F.2d 475, 477–78 (3d Cir. 1972) * * * .

Affirmed.

DETAILED ANALYSIS

1.   BUSINESS-RELATED TRAVEL

1.1. *Generally*

The treatment of business-related travel expenses raises difficult income measurement issues. As the court in *Flowers* stated, it is well established that costs incurred in commuting between a taxpayer's residence and place of business are nondeductible personal expenses. Treas. Regs. §§ 1.212–1(f) and 1.262–1(b)(5) specifically disallow any deduction for commuting expenses. This result can be justified on the ground that the commuting costs reflected the taxpayer's personal decision concerning where to live and that the value of personal satisfaction from that decision equals or exceeds the commuting costs. Nonetheless, distinctions still need to be made, particularly when a job is not permanent, as in *Hantzis*.

At the opposite end of the spectrum from the commuter in *Flowers* is a lawyer whose only office is in Atlanta but who travels from Atlanta to Chicago for the day to try a case. That lawyer incurs fully deductible transportation expenses because there is no personal benefit involved in the travel and it would be unreasonable for the lawyer to move to Chicago under those circumstances. Between these polar cases, a host of factual variations must be resolved. Suppose the lawyer in the above example spends only half a day in court and the other half visiting a museum. Or suppose that the trial lasts one week and meals and lodging costs are incurred for the duration. Suppose further that the lawyer is so successful that the law firm decides to open an office in Chicago to which the lawyer is assigned for one year and the lawyer is required to rent an apartment. Suppose that the stay in Chicago is extended to three years. Suppose that after the lawyer's return to Atlanta, the lawyer continues to travel to Chicago one day a week. In these situations, various types of costs are incurred and the conceptual task involves determining for each item whether the cost exceeds the value of the personal satisfaction derived by the taxpayer from the expenditure. Such an administrative task is nearly impossible, and only made manageable by statutory or judicial rules that can be applied by taxpayers and tax administrators alike. The following materials consider the technical rules applicable to various travel-related costs and then proceeds to evaluate those rules.

1.2. *Distinguishing Commuting from Business Travel*

Expenses incurred in going from the taxpayer's home to her regular place of business are considered nondeductible commuting expenses. But expenses incurred in traveling to other places of business may be deductible, particularly if the other location is a temporary place of business. Rev. Rul. 90–23, 1990–1 C.B. 28, provides the following helpful example:

> [D]aily transportation expenses incurred by a doctor in going between the doctor's residence and one or more offices, clinics, or hospitals at which the doctor works or performs services on a regular basis are nondeductible commuting expenses. However, daily transportation expenses incurred by the doctor in going

between a clinic and a hospital or between the doctor's residence and a temporary work location are deductible business expenses.

Rev. Rul. 99–7, 1999–1 C.B. 361, which modified and superseded Rev. Rul. 90–23, supra, summarized and expanded on prior guidance to hold as follows:

> In general, daily transportation expenses incurred in going between a taxpayer's residence and a work location are nondeductible commuting expenses. However, such expenses are deductible under the circumstances described in paragraph (1), (2), or (3) below.
>
> (1) A taxpayer may deduct daily transportation expenses incurred in going between the taxpayer's residence and a *temporary* work location *outside* the metropolitan area where the taxpayer lives and normally works. However, unless paragraph (2) or (3) below applies, daily transportation expenses incurred in going between the taxpayer's residence and a *temporary* work location *within* that metropolitan area are nondeductible commuting expenses.
>
> (2) If a taxpayer has one or more regular work locations away from the taxpayer's residence, the taxpayer may deduct daily transportation expenses incurred in going between the taxpayer's residence and a *temporary* work location in the same trade or business, regardless of the distance. * * *
>
> (3) If a taxpayer's residence is the taxpayer's principal place of business within the meaning of section 280A(c)(1)(A), the taxpayer may deduct daily transportation expenses incurred in going between the residence and another work location in the same trade or business, regardless of whether the other work location is *regular* or *temporary* and regardless of the distance.
>
> For purposes of paragraphs (1), (2), and (3), the following rules apply in determining whether a work location is temporary. If employment at a work location is realistically expected to last (and does in fact last) for 1 year or less, the employment is temporary in the absence of facts and circumstances indicating otherwise. If employment at a work location is realistically expected to last for more than 1 year or there is no realistic expectation that the employment will last for 1 year or less, the employment is not temporary, regardless of whether it actually exceeds 1 year. If employment at a work location initially is realistically expected to last for 1 year or less, but at some later date the employment is realistically expected to exceed 1 year, that employment will be treated as temporary (in the absence of facts and circumstances indicating otherwise) until the date that the taxpayer's realistic expectation changes, and will be treated as not temporary after that date.

The one-year rule to which Rev. Rul. 99–7 refers originated as an administrative principle, but in 1992 Congress codified the one-year rule by amending § 162(a) (flush language) to limit deductions to cases where the temporary employment does not exceed one year. In Rev. Rul. 93–86, 1993–2 C.B. 71, the IRS ruled that if a taxpayer realistically expects work in a different city to last more than one year before the taxpayer returns to her permanent place of employment, but the job actually ends in less than one year, the job in the new city is "indefinite," not "temporary." On the other hand, if the job in the new city originally was reasonably expected to last for only nine months, but after eight months the taxpayer was asked to stay in the new city for another seven months, away from home deductions are allowable for the first eight months, the period during which the taxpayer reasonably expected the work at the new location to last for less than one year. Like the deduction for travel away from home, the exception for temporary employment is generally grounded on the fact that the taxpayer who is away from the principal place of business for a short period of time incurs duplicate expenses.

1.3. *Transportation of Tools*

The fact that an individual is required to transport tools to her place of work does not convert nondeductible commuting expenses into deductible travel costs. Fausner v. Commissioner, 413 U.S. 838 (1973), denied the deduction when the taxpayer used the same mode of transportation and incurred the same costs whether or not work tools had to be transported. Nevertheless, it left open the possibility of a deduction for the excess transportation costs required by the need to carry the tools. In Rev. Rul. 75–380, 1975–2 C.B. 59, the IRS explained this rule as follows:

> A taxpayer commuted to and from work by public transportation before the taxpayer had to carry necessary work implements. It cost $2.00 per day to commute to and from work. When it became necessary to carry the implements to and from work, it cost $3.00 per day to drive a car and an additional $5.00 per day to rent a trailer in which the implements were carried. The allowable deduction would be the $5.00 per day additional expenses that the taxpayer incurred in renting the trailer to carry the work implements.

1.4. *Where Is the Taxpayer's "Home"?*

As the court in *Hantzis* explains, identifying the location of the taxpayer's home has long divided the IRS and some courts. The Tax Court and the IRS, in analyzing travel expense cases, start from the proposition that "home" in § 162(a)(2) means the taxpayer's principal place of business. Kroll v. Commissioner, 49 T.C. 557 (1968). The Tax Court's position that the term "home" refers to the taxpayer's principal place of business has been adopted by several Courts of Appeals. See e.g., Markey v. Commissioner, 490 F.2d 1249 (6th Cir.1974); Curtis v. Commissioner, 449 F.2d 225 (5th Cir.1971).

On the other hand, several Courts of Appeals have refused to follow this vocational interpretation of the word "home" and have concluded that the term should be given its ordinary meaning as referring to the taxpayer's residence. When this approach is adopted, the inquiry then shifts to the third test enunciated in *Flowers,* i.e., whether the expense was incurred in the pursuit of business. The "business exigencies" approach to § 162(a)(2) was developed in Rosenspan v. United States, 438 F.2d 905 (2d Cir.1971), where the taxpayer was a traveling salesman with no permanent residence. His employer's headquarters was in New York and he made five or six trips to New York every year, spending the rest of the time on the road in his sales territory. The taxpayer deducted the expenses for meals and lodging while in his sales territory, arguing that New York was his business headquarters and hence his tax home from which he was "away" while traveling. The court held that the taxpayer had no "home" even in the ordinary sense of the word and hence was not "away from home" for purposes of § 162(a)(2). Where the taxpayer has a home, the court indicated that the question should be whether the taxpayer's "failure to move his home was for his personal convenience and not compelled by business necessity."

The differences in the tests adopted by the Tax Court, the Second Circuit in *Rosenspan*, and the First Circuit in *Hantzis* may be illustrated by applying each test to the facts in *Hantzis.* Under the Tax Court's approach, the taxpayer's home for tax purposes was in New York where her business activities were located; accordingly, her expenses in New York were nondeductible. Similarly, the costs of maintaining the Boston home were personal and therefore nondeductible. Under the *Rosenspan* approach, the taxpayer's home was in Boston. She was thus away from home while in New York but the expenses of traveling to and residing in New York were not incurred because of business necessity but because her personal choice was to live in Boston. Furthermore, the Boston expenses were not incurred "away from home." The *Hantzis* approach examined whether the expenses incurred in the maintenance of two homes were required by business exigencies and, concluding that they were not, labeled New York as the taxpayer's home. At that point the analysis paralleled that of the Tax Court.

In Lyseng v. Commissioner, T.C. Memo 2011–226, the Tax Court found that a travelling taxpayer's home was the personal residence that he shared with his father and his fiancé. The taxpayer was a contract laborer who performed maintenance work on nuclear plants and other utilities at temporary job sites that required travel away from his residence. The taxpayer's employment at any particular job site lasted less than a year and often only a few months. Applying its tests from *Hantzis,* the Tax Court allowed the taxpayer's travel expense deductions, holding that the taxpayer incurred duplicate expenses because the temporary nature of the work meant that the taxpayer had no principal place of business, the taxpayer had personal and historic connections to the "home," and the taxpayer had a business justification for maintaining his home in the city where the union hall through which he obtained employment was located.

1.5. *When Is the Taxpayer "Away" from Home*

In United States v. Correll, 389 U.S. 299 (1967), the taxpayer was a traveling salesman who customarily left home early each morning, taking two meals on the road, and returning home in time for dinner. The Commissioner disallowed the deduction for meals on the theory that since the taxpayer was not required to sleep or rest on his trips, he was not "away from home" for purposes of § 162(a)(2). The Supreme Court sustained the Commissioner's "sleep or rest" rule:

> Any rule in this area must make some rather arbitrary distinctions, but at least the sleep or rest rule avoids the obvious inequity of permitting the New Yorker who makes a quick trip to Washington and back, missing neither his breakfast nor his dinner at home, to deduct the cost of his lunch merely because he covers more miles than the salesman who travels locally and must finance all his meals without the help of the Federal Treasury. And the Commissioner's rule surely makes more sense than one which would allow the respondent in this case to deduct the cost of his breakfast and lunch simply because he spends a greater percentage of his time at the wheel than the commuter who eats breakfast on his way to work and lunch a block from his office.

> The Court of Appeals nonetheless found in the "plain language of the statute" an insuperable obstacle to the Commissioner's construction. 369 F.2d 87, 89. We disagree. The language of the statute—'meals and lodging * * * away from home'—is obviously not self-defining. And to the extent that the words chosen by Congress cut in either direction, they tend to support rather than defeat the Commissioner's position, for the statute speaks of 'meals and lodging' as a unit, suggesting—at least arguably—that Congress contemplated a deduction for the cost of meals only where the travel in question involves lodging as well. Ordinarily, at least, only the taxpayer who finds it necessary to stop for sleep or rest incurs significantly higher living expenses as a direct result of his business travel, and Congress might well have thought that only taxpayers in that category should be permitted to deduct their living expenses while on the road. In any event, Congress certainly recognized, when it promulgated § 162(a)(2), that the Commissioner had so understood its statutory predecessor. This case thus comes within the settled principle that "Treasury regulations and interpretations long continued without substantial change, applying to unamended or substantially re-enacted statutes, are deemed to have received congressional approval and have the effect of law".

The Tax Court has held that the "sleep or rest" rule requires a period of sufficient duration to justify deductible expenses for lodging. In Strohmaier v. Commissioner, 113 T.C. 106 (1999), the court disallowed a deduction for meal expenses of a taxpayer who traveled between client locations but had a medical condition which required him to take long breaks during the day; he claimed the breaks extended his work day and required that he eat on the road. However, the "sleep or rest" rule does not necessarily require "overnight" rest or incurring lodging expenses. Bissonnette v. Commissioner, 127 T.C. 124 (2006), allowed a deduction for meal expenses incurred by a ferryboat captain during six- to seven-hour layovers in harbor during single-day, 15- to 17-hour sea voyages, because the taxpayer's very demanding job required sleep or rest (on a cot on the ferry boat) during the layovers. The length of the layovers increased his meal expenses. However, meal expenses incurred during one-hour layovers (and occasional longer layovers) during which the taxpayer did not rest were not deductible.

The "sleep or rest" rule does not mean that all non-overnight costs are always nondeductible. If a lawyer with an office in Boston flies to New York and spends the day on business, the transportation costs are fully deductible under § 162(a) since they are not commuting expenses. Moreover, if the lawyer has lunch with a client under circumstances that satisfy the "business entertainment" requirements (see Section 3.2. of this Chapter) fifty percent of the cost of the meal would be deductible. Failure to satisfy the overnight test simply means that the expenditures for meals are not deductible as traveling expenses under § 162(a)(2) and, if a deduction is sought, the basis for the deduction must be found in other Code provisions.

1.6. *The Taxpayer with No Principal Place of Business*

Although *Rosenspan* and cases like it suggest that some taxpayers have no home from which they can be away, there are situations in which a taxpayer who travels extensively may be able to establish his place of abode as his tax "home" even if he has no place of business. Rev. Rul. 75–432, 1975–2 C.B. 60, drew the distinction as follows:

> In the rare case in which the employee has no identifiable principal place of business, but does maintain a regular place of abode in a real or substantial sense in a particular city from which the taxpayer is sent on temporary assignments, the tax home will be regarded as being that place of abode. This should be distinguished from the case of an itinerant worker with neither a regular place of business nor a regular place of abode. In such case, the home is considered to go along with the worker and therefore the worker does not travel away from home for purposes of section 162(a)(2) of the Code, and may not deduct the costs of meals or lodging.

In Johnson v. Commissioner, 115 T.C. 210 (2000), the taxpayer was the captain of a merchant ship that sailed worldwide. The Tax Court rejected the Commissioner's argument that the taxpayer was an itinerant with no tax home from which to be away, and held that his permanent residence, where he resided with his wife and their daughter, was his tax home. The court explained that:

> According to respondent, an employee such as petitioner can never have a tax home because he continually travels to different cities during his employment. We disagree that such continual travel, in and of itself, serves to disqualify a taxpayer from having a tax home for purposes of section 162(a). Regardless of where a taxpayer performs most of his or her work, the fact that he or she maintains financially a fixed personal residence generally means that he or she has a tax home someplace. See James v. United States, 308 F.2d 204 (9th Cir.1962) (a taxpayer's permanent residence is his or her tax home if the taxpayer has no principal place of employment, is currently working away from that

residence, and incurs substantial continuing living expenses at the residence).

In Sapson v. Commissioner, 49 T.C. 636 (1968), the taxpayer, who was a traveling salesman, was allowed a deduction for meals and lodging while away from San Antonio, where he spent about one month out of the year and paid $50 a month in rent for use of a room. The court held that the taxpayer had his principal place of business and a personal residence in San Antonio and rejected the argument that the deductions should be disallowed because there was no substantial duplication of expense.

1.7. *The Taxpayer with Two Places of Business*

Where a taxpayer resides and engages in an income producing activity in one city and also engages in an income producing activity in another city, it is well established that the meals and lodging while away from home and the travel expenses incurred in traveling between the two cities are deductible. The difficulty in this situation is to ascertain which city is the taxpayer's home. The IRS's position is stated in Rev. Rul. 63–82, 1963–1 C.B. 33:

> Where a taxpayer has two occupations, or is carrying on a single occupation at two continuing posts of duty which require him to spend a substantial amount of time in each of two cities, his "home" is held to be at his *principal* place of business. A taxpayer can deduct his expenses for meals and lodging while his duties require him to be at his minor place of business and away from his principal post of duty at least overnight. A taxpayer may also deduct the cost of transportation on all trips made between such locations for business reasons, whether or not they are overnight trips.

In Rev. Rul. 75–432, 1975–2 C.B. 60, the Internal Revenue Service acknowledged that these principles apply to permit a deduction for meals and lodging expense at the taxpayer's minor post of duty even where the taxpayer had two "seasonal" jobs between which the taxpayer alternated year after year.

In Markey v. Commissioner, 490 F.2d 1249 (6th Cir.1974), the taxpayer was a consultant who had conducted a sole proprietorship in his hometown in Ohio. He entered into a consulting contract with General Motors to perform consulting work in Michigan. He spent five days per week for fifty weeks each year at the Michigan location and returned to Ohio on the weekends to attend to his business affairs there. His business and investment activities in his residence city produced little or no net income. The taxpayer deducted his travel costs between the two cities and costs for meals and lodging while he was in the Michigan location. The court held that the Michigan location was the taxpayer's "home," finding: "[W]hen a taxpayer has two places of business or employment at a considerable distance from one another, his designation of one as his abode, if different from the place where he spends more of his time, engages in greater business activity, and derives a greater proportion of his income, is not dispositive of the question which location is his home for the purpose of deducting traveling expenses."

In any event, only the meals and lodging attributable to the period of time the taxpayer is at the minor post of duty for business reasons are deductible. Rev. Rul. 55–604, 1955–2 C.B. 49.

1.8. *The Two-Worker Family*

Foote v. Commissioner, 67 T.C. 1 (1976), involved the travel expense deduction for a two-worker family. The taxpayers argued that in denying a deduction for the travel expenses the tax laws were penalizing married couples for living together, but the Tax Court was unsympathetic: "If both spouses are employed, it is often impossible for them to reside near the place of employment of both so that one spouse necessarily will incur commuting expenses. Regardless of the distance traveled, the nature of these expenditures remains the same. * * * The personal considerations involved in [taxpayers'] situation do not alter the fact that [the husband's] expenses of traveling to the ranch are nondeductible commuting expenses."

The courts have uniformly held that each spouse in a two-worker married couple has a tax home and, where one of the spouses is required to travel some distance to the place of employment, the fact that the other spouse has a tax home in the locality where they reside does not convert the first spouse's travel costs into deductible travel expenses. See e.g., Daly v. Commissioner, 662 F.2d 253 (4th Cir.1981); Mitchell v. Commissioner, 74 T.C. 578 (1980).

1.9. *Local Lodging*

Treas. Reg. § 1.162–32 allows a deduction for local lodging—i.e., lodging while the taxpayer is not away from home—in carrying on a taxpayer's trade or business (whether or not as an employee) under a "facts and circumstances" test. One factor to consider involves whether the taxpayer incurs the expense because of a bona fide condition or requirement of employment imposed by the taxpayer's employer. To the extent an employer reimburses an employee for local lodging expenses, the reimbursement may be excluded from the employee's gross income if the expense allowance arrangement satisfies the requirements of an accountable plan under § 62(c). The regulations provide a safe harbor for local lodging at business meetings and conferences. A taxpayer's local lodging expenses that do not satisfy the safe harbor may still be deductible depending on the taxpayer's facts and circumstances. The examples indicate that there must be a bona fide business reason for the overnight stay, and, if provided by an employer, there must be a substantial noncompensatory reason.

2.   TRAVEL EXPENSES CONNECTED WITH INVESTMENT ACTIVITY

Taxpayers who are engaged in a profit-seeking activity that is not a trade or business may incur travel costs in connection with the activity. In such cases, the issue under § 212 is whether there is a sufficiently close relationship between the travel and the profit-seeking activity. Rev. Rul. 56–511, 1956–2 C.B. 170, denied a deduction for transportation expenses incurred in attending stockholders' meetings of corporations in which the taxpayer owned stock on the ground that the expenses were "not sufficiently related to the taxpayer's investment activities."

Section 274(h)(7) disallows any deductions under § 212 for attending seminars, conventions, or similar meetings. Section 274(h)(7) is strictly applied and disallows deductions even where no entertainment or recreational activities are involved. Jones v. Commissioner, 131 T.C. 131 (2008), denied a deduction for a stock day trader who incurred approximately $6,000 of expenses to attend a 5-day one-on-one course consisting of 37 hours of instruction. The seminar was held in a small town in northwest Georgia, approximately 750 miles from the taxpayer's home in Florida. He stayed in a modest hotel and did not participate in any recreational activities. Citing Merriam-Webster's Collegiate Dictionary, which defines a seminar as a "meeting for giving and discussing information," the court concluded that the course was a seminar or a similar meeting within the scope of § 274(h)(7).

3. ADDITIONAL LIMITATIONS

When the cost of meals is deductible under § 162(a)(2), the deduction is limited by § 274(n) to fifty percent of the cost (see Section 3.4. of this Chapter).

Some forms of travel, such as foreign travel and travel involving spouses, are subject to special statutory limitations in § 274 (see Section 3.5.4. of this Chapter),

Section 274(d) imposes rigorous substantiation requirements for claiming traveling expense deductions (see Section 3.6. of this Chapter).

4. MOVING EXPENSES

Section 217 provides a limited deduction for moving expenses. Under § 217, the *direct* expenses of a move are fully deductible, e.g., the cost of transporting the individual, members of the family, and household effects to the location of the new employment. Expenses for meals incurred while moving are not deductible.

The deductibility of moving expenses is subject to geographical and time tests. The deduction is allowed only if (a) the new place of work is at least fifty miles farther from the individual's former residence than was his former place of work, and (b) the individual is employed full-time for at least thirty-nine weeks during the twelve-month period following the move.

Under Treas. Reg. § 1.217–2(a)(3), the deduction is allowable whether the taxpayer is beginning work for the first time, for a different employer, or for the same employer at a new location, and is also available to self-employed individuals. But an individual who has been in a trade or business at his former residence cannot deduct moving expenses if no trade or business is conducted at the new location. See Taylor v. Commissioner, 71 T.C. 124 (1978) (after completing military duty, an individual moved in order to resume work on his graduate degree; deduction for moving expenses disallowed because the taxpayer was not an employee of the university).

An individual cannot obtain a deduction both for moving expenses under § 217 and for travel expenses while "away from home" under § 162(a)(2). See Treas. Reg. § 1.217–1(c)(3)(iii); Rev. Rul. 74–242, 1974–1 C.B. 69; Goldman v. Commissioner, 497 F.2d 382 (6th Cir.1974) (disallowing moving expenses for Kentucky law school professor who spent one year working for the federal government in Washington, D.C. and allowing a deduction of expenses for travel "away from home").

To the extent that the taxpayer's employer pays or reimburses the taxpayer for moving expenses that otherwise would be deductible under § 217, the payment or reimbursement is a tax free fringe benefit under § 132(a)(6) (see Chapter 3, Section 3.A.6.).

SECTION 3.   BUSINESS MEALS AND ENTERTAINMENT

INTERNAL REVENUE CODE: Section 274(a), (c)–(g), (h)(1), (2), (4), (k), (l), (n).

REGULATIONS: Sections 1.62–2; 1.162–2(d); 1.274–2(b)–(d); 1.274–5T(a), (b)(3), (4), (c)(1)–(3)(i), (f)(2), (3).

Churchill Downs, Inc. v. Commissioner*
Tax Court of the United States, 2000.
115 T.C. 279.

■ LARO, JUDGE: * * * Respondent determined deficiencies in petitioners' 1994 and 1995 Federal income tax of $51,872 and $20,658, respectively. The sole issue we must decide is whether petitioners' claimed deductions for expenses for parties and other entertainment are limited by section 274(n)(1). We hold they are. * * *

BACKGROUND

* * * Petitioners own the Churchill Downs racetrack in Louisville, Kentucky, and three other race tracks.

Petitioners conduct live horse races, including the Kentucky Derby, at their facilities. The races produce revenues through pari-mutual wagering (including simulcast pari-mutual wagering), admissions and seating, concession commissions, sponsorship revenues, licensing rights, and broadcast fees. The main source of petitioners' revenues is wagers placed on horse races.

Petitioners do not directly compete with other racetracks for local patrons because of the separation of facilities and the differences in the seasonal timing of meets. However, petitioners operate in a highly competitive industry. They compete for patrons with other sports, entertainment, and gaming operations, including land-based, riverboat, and cruise ship casinos and State lotteries.

Petitioners' biggest race is the Kentucky Derby. The Kentucky Derby is held each year on the first Saturday in May. Petitioners' Kentucky Derby events include: The Sport of Kings Gala, a brunch following the post position drawing for the Derby race, a week long hospitality tent with coffee, orange juice, and donuts for the press open from 4 a.m. to 9 a.m., the Derby race, and the Kentucky Derby Winner's Party.

---

*   [Ed.: The judgment of the Tax Court was aff'd, 307 F. 3d 423 (6th Cir.2002).]

The Sport of Kings Gala includes a press-reception cocktail party followed by a dinner and entertainment on the Thursday evening of Derby week. The costs of the Sport of Kings Gala, including those for food, beverages, and entertainment, are borne by petitioners. Petitioners' employees were in attendance at the Sport of Kings Gala in 1994 and in 1995. * * *

The Breeders' Cup race rotates among several racetracks. In 1994, petitioners hosted the Breeders' Cup race, the Breeders' Cup press-reception cocktail party and dinner, and the Breeders' Cup press breakfast. Under petitioners' contract with Breeders' Cup Limited (BCL) they were obligated to conduct certain promotional activities designed to enhance the significance of the Breeders' Cup day of races as a national and international championship event for the sport of racing. Included in these required promotional activities are the Breeders' Cup press-reception cocktail party and dinner and the Breeders' Cup press breakfast.

* * *

Petitioners allocated blocks of tickets to the Sport of Kings parties to horsemen, sponsors, staff, city/county VIP's, racing VIP's, racing officials, media representatives, and others. More tickets were allocated to the media than to any other category.

* * *

DISCUSSION

Respondent concedes that all of the expenses at issue [$397,193] meet the requirements for deductions as ordinary and necessary business expenses of petitioner under section 162 for the years in issue. However, respondent argues that these deduction[s] are limited by section 274.

Petitioners argue they are in the entertainment business, and accordingly, they should not be subject to the restrictions of section 274(n) with respect to expenses they incur in the course of providing that entertainment. Alternatively, petitioners argue the expenses at issue are excluded from the provisions of section 274 by application of section 274(e), paragraphs (7) and (8), and section 274(n)(2)(A).

Section 162(a) allows a deduction for all ordinary and necessary expenses paid or incurred during the taxable year in carrying on a trade or business. Section 274 disallows a deduction in certain instances for expenses which would otherwise be deductible under section 162. Section 274(a) provides in part:

SEC. 274(a). Entertainment, Amusement, or Recreation.—

(1) In general.—No deduction otherwise allowable under this chapter shall be allowed for any item—

(A) Activity.—With respect to an activity which is of a type generally   considered   to   constitute   entertainment, amusement, or recreation, unless the taxpayer establishes that the item was directly related to, or, in the case of an item directly preceding or following a substantial and bona fide business discussion (including business meetings at a convention or otherwise), that such item was associated with, the active conduct of the taxpayer's trade or business, * * *

Respondent does not dispute that the expenses at issue are directly related to the active conduct of petitioners' business. There is also no dispute that the events were critical to the success of the Kentucky Derby and the Breeders' Cup. Some of the expenses at issue were required to be provided under the contract between petitioners and BCL.

Respondent argues that the deductions of the expenses at issue are → *Commissioner's Argument* limited by section 274(n). Section 274(n) allows only a portion of entertainment expense to be deducted. That section provides:

SEC. 274(n). Only 50 Percent of Meal and Entertainment → *Rule* Expenses Allowed as Deduction.—

(1) In general.—The amount allowable as a deduction under this chapter for—

(A) any expense for food or beverages, and

(B) any item with respect to an activity which is of a type generally considered to constitute entertainment, amusement, or recreation, or with respect to a facility used in connection with such activity,

shall not exceed 50 percent of the amount of such expense or item which would (but for this paragraph) be allowable as a deduction under this chapter.

The Secretary was granted authority to promulgate regulations to carry out the purposes of section 274. See sec. 274(o). Regulations were promulgated to clarify what type of activity would be considered → *Analysis* entertainment. In pertinent part they provide:

Objective test. An objective test shall be used to determine whether an activity is of a type generally considered to constitute entertainment. Thus, if an activity is generally considered to be entertainment, it will constitute entertainment for purposes of this section and section 274(a) regardless of whether the expenditure can also be described otherwise, and even though the expenditure relates to the taxpayer alone. This objective test precludes arguments such as that "entertainment" means only entertainment of others or that an expenditure for entertainment should be characterized as an expenditure for advertising or public relations. However, in applying this test the taxpayer's trade or business shall be considered. Thus, although attending a theatrical performance would generally be considered entertainment, it would not be so considered in the case of a professional theater critic, attending in his professional capacity. Similarly, if a manufacturer of dresses conducts a fashion show to introduce his products to a group of store buyers, the show would not be generally considered to constitute entertainment. However, if an appliance distributor conducts a fashion show for the wives of his retailers, the fashion show would be generally considered to constitute entertainment. [Treas. Reg. § 1.274–2(b)(1)(ii)].

Petitioners argue that they are in the entertainment business and that the Derby expenses, Breeders' Cup expenses, and miscellaneous expenses are all part of their entertainment product and therefore should be fully deductible. Petitioners conduct live horse races, including the Kentucky Derby, at their facilities. The races produce revenues through pari-mutual wagering (including simulcast pari-mutual wagering), admissions and seating, concession commissions, sponsorship revenues, licensing rights, and broadcast fees. Petitioners' main source of revenues is wagers placed on horse races.

In determining whether the expenses in question are entertainment expenses petitioners' trade or business must be considered. We would agree petitioners are in the entertainment business. However, applying the objective test mandated by section 1.274–2(b)(1)(ii), Income Tax Regs., the Derby, Breeders' Cup, and miscellaneous expenses all constitute entertainment expenses and cannot be properly categorized as "part of the entertainment product". Thus the Derby, Breeders' Cup, and miscellaneous expenses are subject to the restrictions imposed by section 274(n)(1) unless they fall within one of the exceptions set out in section 274(n)(2).

Petitioners alternatively argue that the Derby, Breeders' Cup, and miscellaneous expenses are excluded from the operation of section 274(n)(1) by paragraphs (7) and (8) of section 274(e). Those paragraphs provide as follows:

(7) Items available to public.—Expenses for goods, services, and facilities made available by the taxpayer to the general public.

(8) Entertainment sold to customers.—Expenses for goods or services (including the use of facilities) which are sold by the taxpayer in a bona fide transaction for an adequate and full consideration in money or money's worth.

Petitioners provide entertainment to all of the public through their different events. The Kentucky Derby and the Breeders' Cup Championship are open to the general public as are other races during Derby Week and Breeders' Cup week. In contrast, the events that give rise to the Derby, Breeders' Cup, and miscellaneous expenses are invitation-only events that are attended by selected horsemen, petitioners' employees, media officials, and local dignitaries. They may be entertainment events designed to make the Derby and Breeders' Cup more prestigious events and to heighten public awareness of the upcoming events as petitioners claim. However, we can see no meaningful difference between the expenses at issue here and normal entertainment of selected clients and suppliers, which is limited by section 274(n). The expenses at issue are not expenses for goods, services, and facilities made available by petitioners to the general public. The events at issue provide goods and services to persons petitioner selects to entertain. We therefore hold that the Derby, Breeders' Cup, and miscellaneous expenses are not excluded by section 274(e)(7) and (n)(2).

We find no evidence in the record that the Derby, Breeders' Cup, and miscellaneous expenses for goods and services were sold by petitioners in a bona fide transaction for an adequate and full consideration in money or money's worth. Indeed, the record indicates that the expenses were borne by petitioner and goods and services were given without cost to the parties that were entertained. We therefore hold that the Derby, Breeders' Cup, and miscellaneous expenses are not excluded by section 274(e)(8) and (n)(2).

We hold that petitioners' claimed deductions for Derby, Breeders' Cup, and miscellaneous expenses are limited by section 274(n)(1) as determined by respondent. In reaching the holdings in this opinion, we have considered all arguments for contrary holdings, and have rejected all arguments not discussed as without merit or irrelevant.

* * *

DETAILED ANALYSIS

1.   PURPOSE AND COVERAGE OF SECTION 274

As *Churchill Downs* illustrates, § 274 disallows a deduction for certain expenses even if § 162 or § 212 has been satisfied. It is important to remember that § 274 is a *disallowance* section. If an expense is not deductible under either § 162 or § 212 to start with, § 274 need not be considered.

Section 274 was added to the Code in 1962. The legislative history explains its origins as follows.

> The Treasury brought to the attention of Congress that widespread abuses have developed through the use of the expense account. In his tax message to the Congress [President Kennedy] stated his conviction that entertainment and related expenses, even though having a connection with the needs of business, confer substantial tax-free personal benefits on the recipients, and that in many instances deductions are obtained by disguising personal expenses as business expenses. He recommended that the cost of such business entertainment and the maintenance of entertainment facilities be disallowed in full as a tax deduction and that

restrictions be imposed on the deductibility of business gifts and travel expenses.

S.Rep. No. 1881, 87th Cong., 2nd Sess. (1962). Although the provision Congress enacted was not quite as draconian as the President urged, it nevertheless placed very substantial restrictions on the deductibility of many items, and its reach has expanded substantially since then.

Section 274 provides specific rules for a wide variety of meal and entertainment situations:

(1) Section 274(a)(1)(A) denies a deduction for entertainment expenses unless the item is "directly related" to the taxpayer's trade or business, or, in the case of an item directly preceding or following a substantial bona fide business discussion, the item is "associated with" the taxpayer's trade or business. Section 274(e) contains exceptions to the general rules of § 274(a) designed to cover situations in which Congress did not see a significant potential for abuse or for personal consumption by the person paying the expense; mostly the items are related to compensation, fringe benefits, or conditions of employment for the taxpayer's employees.

(2) Section 274(a)(1)(B) disallows deductions for expenses incurred with respect to a "facility" such as a yacht or hunting lodge that is used in connection with entertainment or recreational activities. This provision disallows deductions for dues or fees paid to social, athletic, and sporting clubs as well as for expenses of owning or leasing a facility. I.R.C. § 274(a)(3).

(3) Section 274(c) requires an allocation of all costs for foreign travel between business and personal expenses, unless the trip is one week in duration or less, or where the personal component of the travel does not exceed 25 percent of the time away from home. Before 1964, § 274(c) applied to all travel, but in 1964 it was amended to apply only to foreign travel. The Senate Finance Committee gave as its reason that the provision "was too little understood by the general public," S.Rep. No. 830, 88th Cong., 2d Sess. 82 (1964), but the real pressure for the change came from businesses in domestic resort areas who understood the allocation rules all too well. See Hearings on Travel and Entertainment Expenditures Before the Senate Finance Committee, 88th Cong., 1st Sess. 10–20, 60–63 (1963).

(4) Section 274(d) imposes rigorous substantiation requirements as a prerequisite for claiming any deduction for travel expenses, entertainment, gifts, and listed property.

(5) Section 274(h) sets forth rules dealing with foreign conventions, and meetings on cruise ships.

(6) Section 274(k) limits deductions for "lavish or extravagant" meals, and § 274(n) generally limits the deduction for business meals or entertainment to 50 percent of the expenditure. This limitation does not apply to most (but not all) of the situations listed in § 274(e).

(7) Section 274(*l*) limits deductions for entertainment tickets to their face value. It further limits any deduction for athletic stadium skybox tickets to an amount equal to the cost of box seats.

(8) Section 274(m) limits deductions for luxury water travel, forbids deductions for travel as a form of education, and for travel expenses attributable to a spouse or dependent, except in narrow circumstances.

Section 274(e) provides a number of exceptions to the limitations in § 274(a), which include:

(1) Food and beverages furnished on the employer's business premises primarily for employees.

(2) Expenses treated as compensation. In Sutherland Lumber-Southwest, Inc. v. Commissioner, 114 T.C. 197 (2000), *aff'd* 255 F.3d 495 (8th Cir.2001) (Acq.), the court found that § 274 did not apply to a corporation that allowed its officers to take private nonbusiness flights on the company's jet, but it also treated the fair market value of the flights as taxable compensation to the employees.

(3) Section 274 provides specific rules for reimbursed expenses (see Section 3.7. of this Chapter).

(4) Expenses for recreational, social, or similar activities primarily for the benefit of employees, so long as the primary beneficiaries are not highly compensated employees.

(5) Expenses directly related to business meetings of the taxpayer's employees, stockholders, agents, or directors.

(6) Expenses necessary for attendance at meetings of business leagues, chambers of commerce, and similar organizations.

(7) Expenses for items made available to the general public.

(8) Expenses for goods or services sold to customers (even if the good or service is entertainment).

(9) Expenses includable in the income of the recipient who is not an employee of the taxpayer.

The regulations define the term entertainment in a relatively straightforward way: "[A]ny activity which is of a type generally considered to constitute entertainment, amusement, or recreation, such as entertaining at night clubs, cocktail lounges, theaters, country clubs, golf and athletic clubs, sporting events, and on hunting, fishing, vacation and similar trips, including activity relating solely to the taxpayer or the taxpayer's family." Treas. Reg. § 1.274–2(b)(1)(i). The term also includes the provision of food and beverages, or anything else that satisfies personal needs, such as the provision of hotel rooms or cars. As suggested in *Churchill Downs*, the taxpayer's business is relevant to the definition of entertainment; the regulations explain that for a theater critic, attending a theatrical performance in his professional capacity is not entertainment. Treas. Reg. § 1.274–2(b)(1)(ii).

2. ENTERTAINMENT "DIRECTLY RELATED" OR "ASSOCIATED WITH" BUSINESS

Treas. Reg. § 1.274–2(c) delineates the standards for determining if entertainment is "directly related" to the active conduct of the taxpayer's trade or business. The standards for determining if entertainment is "associated with" the active conduct of the taxpayer's trade or business are in Treas. Reg. § 1.274–2(d)(2). Except in the narrow circumstances where the business purpose of the expenditure is unambiguous, in order to satisfy either test, the taxpayer (or the taxpayer's employees) must have engaged in a bona fide business meeting or discussion with the person being entertained. Eating a meal alone (or with coworkers) while traveling away from home on business is not entertainment and is not subject to § 274(a). See H.Rep. No. 99–841, 99th Cong., 2d Sess. II–27 (1986).

In *Churchill Downs* the Commissioner conceded that the expenses in question were directly related or associated with the taxpayer's business, but taxpayers have not always been so fortunate. One significant difficulty is that the regulations make it clear that entertainment expenses designed merely to generate goodwill do not qualify as directly related to the taxpayer's business, and many entertainment expenses fall precisely within that category.

In St. Petersburg Bank & Trust Co. v. United States, 362 F.Supp. 674 (M.D.Fla.1973), aff'd by order, 503 F.2d 1402 (5th Cir.1974) the court explained this principle as follows:

> The statute clearly creates two classes of entertainment expenses which are measured by separate tests in determining deductibility. One class is general, the other is specific. Entertainment expense in general must be "directly related" to "the active conduct of the taxpayer's trade or business." On the other hand, in the case of an expense incurred for entertainment "directly preceding or following a substantial and bona fide business discussion," it need only be "associated with" the taxpayer's business in order to qualify for deduction.

In *St. Petersburg* a bank claimed deductions for expenses it incurred in connection with cocktail and dinner parties, dove shoots, and barbecues held at the home and ranch of the president of the bank. The expenditures failed the "directly related" test because, although they were "motivated primarily by business considerations," it was "equally clear that the benefit enjoyed by the Bank was of the goodwill variety derived from a purely social setting and, as such, was precisely the type of expense deduction that Congress intended to eliminate by way of the 'directly related' test." The court also held that the bank did not meet the "associated with" test because the expenditures involved did not immediately precede or follow a substantial and bona fide business discussion.

In Townsend Industries v. United States, 342 F.3d 890 (8th Cir.2003), an Iowa corporation succeeded in convincing the Court of Appeals that annual fishing trips it held for its employees in a Canadian resort were directly related or associated with its business. Although the taxpayer had lost at trial, it won on appeal by pointing to a trial record replete with employee testimony on specific business insights obtained during the trips and demonstrating that it stopped inviting employees of a particular division when the activities of that division diverged from the mainstream business of the others and reduced the likelihood that discussions between the employees of that division and others would produce specific benefits for the corporation. The court also noted that spouses and children were not invited, thus making the trips unlike vacations for the employees.

Once the directly related or associated with tests are met, taxpayers have an additional obstacle to deductibility. Section 274(k)(1)(B) provides that no deduction is allowed for food or beverages unless the taxpayer or an employee of the taxpayer is present when the food or beverages are provided. The apparent intent of the provision is to disallow deductions for restaurant meals and beverages provided as a gift for the client to enjoy unencumbered by the taxpayer's presence.

The IRS generally allows taxpayers to deduct the costs attributable to their own meals and entertainment, subject to the 50 percent limitation of § 274(n), when the requirements of § 274 have been met. In "abuse cases" where taxpayers attempt to deduct "substantial amounts of personal living expenses," the IRS follows judicial decisions and disallows deductions for meals exceeding what a typical taxpayer "would normally spend." Rev. Rul. 63–144, 1963–2 C.B. 129.

3.   ENTERTAINMENT FACILITIES

Section 274(a)(1)(B) completely disallows deductions for entertainment facilities. This strict rule applies to any personal or real property owned, rented, or used by a taxpayer during the taxable year for or in connection with any entertainment. Examples of entertainment facilities include yachts, hunting lodges, fishing camps, swimming pools, tennis courts, bowling alleys, automobiles, airplanes, apartments, hotel suites, and vacation homes. Treas. Reg. § 1.274–2(e)(2)(i). Thus, rental payments on leased facilities as well as interest, depreciation, and repairs on owned facilities, are all nondeductible. Section 274(a)(3) extends this complete disallowance rule to dues paid to any club organized for business, pleasure, recreation, or other social purpose. Treas. Reg. § 1.274–2(a)(2)(iii) applies this limitation to any membership organization that is organized with a principal purpose to provide entertainment activities or access to entertainment. The regulations exclude from the disallowance rule dues to trade associations, business leagues, chambers of commerce, boards of trade, professional associations, and civic and public service organizations unless the organization has a principal purpose of providing entertainment.

Harrigan Lumber Co. v. Commissioner, 88 T.C. 1562 (1987), aff'd by order, 851 F.2d 362 (11th Cir.1988), illustrates the application of § 274(a)(1)(B) and the difference between entertainment activities (which can be deductible subject to the limitations in § 274(a)(1)(A)), and facilities (nondeductible pursuant to § 274(a)(1)(B)). The taxpayer leased for ten years exclusive hunting rights on a 6,000 acre tract of land located near a hunting lodge it owned. The hunting lodge was conceded to be a facility, but the taxpayer claimed that the $10,000 annual rental payment for the hunting rights was an item with respect to an entertainment activity. After considering the legislative history of § 274(a), the court concluded that the distinction between an "activity" and a "facility" turned on whether the taxpayer acquired exclusive use of and unfettered access to particular real or personal property for the specific period of time during which the entertainment occurs. If the taxpayer has such use and access, the property is a facility. But if the taxpayer's use is not exclusive or the taxpayer's access is limited, the taxpayer may be engaged in an activity. Applying this standard, the court held that because the hunting rights were exclusive as to the tract of land, the rental payments were incurred with respect to a facility, not an activity, and disallowed the deduction.

Courts strictly apply § 274(a)(1)(B). In Ireland v. Commissioner, 89 T.C. 978 (1987), the taxpayer was a stockbroker who used a beachfront house for business meetings with customers and business associates. Because the customers' and business associates' families often accompanied them and engaged in recreation, the property was treated as used for entertainment, and depreciation deductions were disallowed. The court held that "any use of the facility, no matter how small, in connection with entertainment is fatal to the claimed deduction."

4.   FIFTY PERCENT LIMITATION ON MEALS AND ENTERTAINMENT

As illustrated by *Churchill Downs*, § 274(n)(1) provides that if a business pays for meals and entertainment of its employees, the 50 percent limitation applies unless one of the exceptions in § 274(n)(2) applies.

The exception in § 274(n)(2)(B) permits the employer to deduct the entire cost of the meal if it is excludable by the employee under § 132(e) as a *de minimis fringe*. In the case of meals excluded under § 119 (see Chapter 3, Section 3.A.9.), § 132(e)(2) provides that the employees are deemed to have paid an amount equal to the direct cost of the meal. This in turn renders the meals a *de minimis fringe* benefit under § 132(e) and allows the employer to deduct the full cost of the meals. This rule, coupled with § 119(b)(4), which provides that if more than one-half of the meals furnished to employees on an employer's business premises satisfy the "convenience of the employer test" all meals furnished to all employees on those premises are deemed to have been provided for the convenience of the employer, assures that the employer may deduct the full cost (and all the employees may exclude from income the full value) of all the meals as long as the employer can substantiate that more than half of them were for its convenience.

Section 274(n)(3) allows a deduction for more than 50 percent of the meal expenses incurred by individuals who while away-from-home on business are subject to Department of Transportation hours-of-service limitations. This provision applies to persons such as airline crews and mechanics, air traffic controllers, interstate truck and bus drivers, railroad crews, and merchant mariners. The rationale for the greater deduction is that these types of workers are subject to greater than normal compulsion to eat meals away from home in high cost locales. See S. Rep. No. 105–33, 105th Cong., 1st Sess. 106 (1997).

5.   LIMITATIONS ON DEDUCTIONS FOR TRAVEL

5.1. *Domestic Business Travel*

Suppose a taxpayer who normally lives and works in Chicago travels to Orlando in January, and spends three days in a business meeting (or convention) and another three days touring Disney World. To what extent are the taxpayer's transportation, meals, and lodging deductible? Treas. Reg. § 1.162–2(b) provides that the transportation expense is fully deductible if the primary purpose of the trip was business and wholly nondeductible if the primary purpose of the trip was pleasure. All of the facts and circumstances must be taken into account, although the relative amount of time devoted to business and pleasure is the most important factor. Nevertheless, even if the primary purpose of the trip is pleasure, meals and lodging attributable to business purpose days remain deductible.

Section 274(m)(1)(A) imposes additional limitations on the amount of the deduction for luxury water transportation. With some exceptions, expenses incurred for transportation by water are only allowed to the extent that they do not exceed twice the highest per diem rate allowable to employees of the executive branch serving domestically.

5.2. *Foreign Travel*

Section 274(c) imposes special restrictions on the deductibility of foreign travel expenses. If a trip outside the United States exceeds seven consecutive days *and* the days attributable to nonbusiness activities are twenty five percent or more of the total days of the trip, only a portion of transportation costs are deductible. This rule does not apply if the taxpayer did not have "substantial control over the arranging of the business trip" or obtaining a personal vacation or holiday was not a major consideration in determining to make the trip. Treas. Reg. § 1.274–4(f)(5).

5.3. *Conventions*

The costs of attending business conventions and meetings generally are deductible under § 162 as travel away from home expenses. Treas. Reg. § 1.162–2(d). If the convention is held outside the "North American Area," the taxpayer also must meet the tests of § 274(h). That provision contains detailed rules under which the taxpayer must establish that the meeting is "directly related" to business activities and that, taking into account the circumstances involving the meeting, it is "as reasonable" for the meeting to be held outside of North America as within North America. Section 274(h)(2) denies a deduction for the expenses of a meeting held on a cruise ship unless detailed reporting requirements are satisfied and the vessel calls only at ports in the United States or its possessions. This provision was enacted in response to a number of widely publicized "educational" cruises taken by bar and medical associations.

Section 274(h)(7), disallows any deductions under § 212 for attending seminars, conventions, or similar meetings.

5.4. *Expenses for Spouses*

Section 274(m)(3), enacted in 1993, disallows any deduction for expenses of a spouse or a dependent accompanying a business traveler on a trip unless the deductibility of the spouse's or dependent's travel expenses is independently established. Prior to the enactment of § 274(m)(3), Treas. Reg. § 1.162–2(c) permitted a deduction if the spouse's presence on the trip had a "bona fide business purpose."

6.   SUBSTANTIATION REQUIREMENTS

6.1. *Travel and Entertainment Expenses Generally*

Treas. Reg. § 1.274–5(c)(2) and Temp. Reg. § 1.274–5T(b) and (c) set forth detailed rules dealing with the substantiation of travel and entertainment expenses. Generally speaking, the taxpayer must substantiate travel and entertainment expenses with "adequate records" or "sufficient evidence corroborating his own statement." To satisfy the "adequate records" standard involves keeping a complete and accurate diary or record of the expenses. The diary must generally include the date, amount, place and business purpose of each item of expense. The entries in the diary must be contemporaneous with the expense. Where entertainment is involved, the person entertained and the business relationship to the taxpayer must be shown. See Recklitis v. Commissioner, 91 T.C. 874 (1988) (expense statements that failed to state the business purpose for entertainment were inadequate). Where the expenditure is for $75 or more, or where lodging expenses are involved while the taxpayer is traveling, documentary evidence such as bills, receipts and other evidence of the expenditure must be retained to substantiate the diary entries. Treas. Reg. § 1.274–5(c)(2)(iii)(B). In Alter v. Commissioner, 50 T.C. 833 (1968), a salesman was denied deduction for entertainment expenses in excess of $25—then the threshold for the receipt requirement—where he kept a "pocket diary" but maintained no receipts or other documentary evidence.

A taxpayer who does not meet the "adequate records" requirements can provide the missing elements with an oral or noncontemporaneous written statement *and* other corroborative evidence. Temp. Reg. § 1.274–5T(c)(3). The taxpayer's statement must provide "specific information in detail" to substantiate the required information with respect to the expense; generalized statements as to the business relation or amount are not sufficient. LaForge v. Commissioner, 434 F.2d 370 (2d Cir.1970). Corroborative evidence, such as the written or oral statement of the person entertained or other witnesses is required. In Dowell v. United States, 522 F.2d 708 (5th Cir.1975), the taxpayer did not substantiate his expenses under § 274(d) by submitting "a virtual blizzard of bills, chits and other papers," while in Durgom v. Commissioner, T.C. Memo. 1974–058, testimony by the taxpayer's wife satisfied the substantiation requirement. In Newi v. Commissioner, T.C. Memo. 1969–131, aff'd on another issue, 432 F.2d 998 (2d Cir.1970), deductions were denied for Christmas tips to office hands, delivery boys, doormen, elevator operators, and maître d's. Although no documentary evidence was required because the gifts were small, the taxpayer was still required to show business purpose, business relationship, and time and place of the expenses, which he failed to do.

6.2. *Special Rules for Travel Expenses*

Treas. Reg. § 1.274–5(c)(2)(iii) sets forth the rules governing substantiation of expenses for travel away from home. Nevertheless, in lieu of complying with the detailed record keeping rules (which always apply to entertainment expenses, even if incurred while traveling away from home), a taxpayer may forgo deducting actual expenses for automobile travel, meals, and lodging, and instead deduct a standard mileage allowance for automobile travel and a per diem allowance for meals and lodging. Treas. Reg. § 1.274–5(g). See e.g., Notice 2015–63, 2015–40 I.R.B. 464 (meals and lodging); Notice 2016–1, 2016–2 I.R.B. 265 (mileage).

Special substantiation rules for automobiles and other listed property, while less rigorous than those for entertainment, nevertheless are more rigorous than for other business expenses. See Temp. Reg. § 1.274–6T.

7.   REIMBURSED EXPENSES

If an employee incurs deductible expenses on behalf of his employer for which he is reimbursed, the regulations allow the employee to net the deductions and the reimbursements on his tax return rather than use the more cumbersome method of including the reimbursements in gross income and then taking the deductions. Temp. Reg. § 1.274–5T(f)(2). This rule applies only if the employee is required to make an "adequate accounting" to the employer for his expenses, and the regulations define adequate accounting as a submission to the employer of the documentary evidence required generally to substantiate travel and entertainment expense deductions. Treas. Reg. § 1.274–5(f)(4). Rev. Rul. 2003–106, 2003–2 C.B. 936, allows electronic receipts provided by a credit card company that has issued business credit cards to the company's employees to be used to satisfy the substantiation requirements. The netting method may also be used in connection with a per diem method of reimbursement, subject to certain limitations. Treas. Reg. § 1.274–5(g).

Treas. Reg. § 1.62–2(f) conditions application of the netting rule on the employee being required to return excess advances to the employer. Namyst v. Commissioner, T.C. Memo 2004–263, aff'd, 435 F.3d 910 (8th Cir. 2006), required the taxpayer to include expense reimbursements in gross income because, although he was required to and did account to the employer for his expenses, the taxpayer was not obligated to return any excess advances to the employer. Rev. Rul. 2005–52, 2005–2 C.B. 423, held that a set amount for each hour worked paid as a "tool allowance" by an automobile repair business to an employee-mechanic, who was required to purchase his own tools, was includable in employee's gross income and could be deducted by the employee only as a miscellaneous itemized deduction, because the employee was not required to provide any substantiation of expenses incurred for tools and the employer did not require the employee to return any portion of the tool allowances that exceeded his actual expenses.

If the plan otherwise qualifies as an accountable plan, but the employee fails to return excess advances or reimbursements within a reasonable time, the employee must include the excess in income. Treas. Reg. § 1.62–2(c)(3)(ii); Temp. Reg. § 1.274–5T(f)(2)(ii). Conversely, excess expenses that the employee can substantiate are deductible as an itemized deduction, subject to the limitations of § 67. Temp. Reg. § 1.274–5T(f)(2)(iii).

When an employee is reimbursed for meals or entertainment under an accountable plan, the burden of the 50 percent disallowance rule in § 274(n) is shifted to the employer.

SECTION 4.   STATUTORY LIMITATIONS ON DEDUCTIONS FOR CERTAIN PROPERTY

INTERNAL REVENUE CODE: Section 280F.

Automobiles, airplanes, computers, and similar property used by a taxpayer who is engaged in business present the same problem as meals, travel, and entertainment because they provide both business and personal utility. It is therefore not surprising that Congress has responded to the problem much as it has in the area of travel, meals and entertainment, by limiting available deductions.

Section 280F contains two separate rules limiting depreciation and lease rental payment deductions (expenses) for passenger automobiles and so-called "listed property," including all vehicles, airplanes, boats, computers, and certain other similar property. First, § 280F(a) limits the amount of depreciation (or lease rental) deduction allowed for any passenger automobile to a stated maximum annual amount. Second, for any listed property that is not used *more than* fifty percent for business, § 280F(b) requires that depreciation be computed under § 168(g) rather than the usual MACRS rules (see Chapter 14, Section 1 for § 168 and MACRS). Deductions under § 179 (see Chapter 14, Section 1.B.) are treated as depreciation for this purpose. I.R.C. § 280F(d)(1). These limitations are in addition to the usual proration of the basis for computing allowable depreciation on mixed-use property.

General Explanation of the Revenue Provisions of the Tax Reform Act of 1984

Staff of the Joint Committee on Taxation, 559–60 (1984).

Congress believed that the investment incentives afforded by * * * accelerated cost recovery should be directed to encourage capital formation, rather than to subsidize the element of personal consumption associated with the use of very expensive automobiles. The transportation necessary for conducting a business can be obtained from a luxury car or another car. To the extent an automobile is required for this necessary transportation, the generally allowable tax benefits should be available. Beyond that point, however, the extra expense of a luxury automobile provides, in effect, a tax-free personal emolument which Congress believed should not qualify for tax credits or acceleration of depreciation deductions because such expenditures do not add significantly to the productivity which these incentives were designed to encourage.

Congress was also concerned that many taxpayers claimed the advantage of * * * accelerated depreciation with respect to automobiles and other property used primarily for personal or investment use rather than in the conduct of a trade or business. The incentives of * * * ACRS were designed to encourage investment in new plant and equipment rather than to subsidize the purchase of personal property that is used incidentally or occasionally in the taxpayer's business. Therefore, Congress decided not to allow the incentive portion of tax benefits for property whose predominant use is personal or investment-related, rather than in the conduct of a trade or business.

Congress was also concerned that some taxpayers acquired automobiles and other property very late in the taxable year and claimed a very high percentage of business use for that portion of the year. Business use in subsequent years would often be minimal. Taxpayers could nonetheless claim full ACRS deductions for that first year and not be subject to recapture by reason of greatly diminished business use in the subsequent years.

DETAILED ANALYSIS

1.   DEPRECIATION CEILING ON "LUXURY AUTOMOBILES"

Section 280F limits the maximum annual depreciation, § 179 deduction (see Chapter 14, Section 1.B.), and rental payment deductions for passenger automobiles, whether or not used exclusively for business purposes. The statutory annual ceilings on depreciation, which are adjusted for inflation, are: $2,560 for the year the automobile is placed in service, $4,100 for the second year in the recovery period, $2,450 for the third year, and $1,475 for each succeeding year until the basis has been fully recovered.[2] The limitations apply to any passenger automobile that costs more than $12,800 (before the inflation adjustment). If a passenger automobile is used for both business and personal purposes, these limitations are applied before any limitations based on personal use. I.R.C. § 280F(a)(2)(A). Because § 280F(d)(5)(A)(ii) limits the definition of passenger automobile to vehicles that weigh 6,000 pounds or less, these limitations do not apply to heavy sport utility vehicles. Under Temp. Reg. § 1.280F–6T(c)(3), the depreciation limitation of § 280F also does not apply to a truck or van that is by its nature not likely to be used more than a *de minimis* amount for personal purposes, as defined in Temp. Reg. § 1.274–5T(k). This includes trucks or vans that have been specially modified so that they serve only a business function such as a delivery truck or ambulance.

Suppose that a sole proprietor paid $30,000 for an automobile used solely for business, and capitalized and depreciated the cost (rather than claiming a deductions under § 179).[3] Under § 168, the depreciation deductions allowable with respect to the automobile over six years (for five-year property using the half-year convention) would be $6,000, $9,600,

---

[2]   As adjusted for inflation, the limitations for 2016 (and not accounting for the § 168(k) additional first year depreciation deduction) are as follows: for cars placed in service in 2016, the limit is $3,160 for the first year, $5,100 for the second year, $3,050 for the third year, and $1,875 for each succeeding year; for trucks and vans placed in service in 2016 the limit is $3,560 for the first year, $5,700 for the second year, $3,350 for the third year, and $2,075 for each succeeding year. Rev. Proc. 2016–23, 2016–16 I.R.B. 581.

[3]   Section 280F limits both § 179 deductions and depreciation. See I.R.C. § 280F(d)(1). For calculation of the limitations on § 179 deductions for the cost of luxury automobiles, see Temp. Reg. § 1.280F–2T(b)(1), (4) and (c)(1)(ii)(B), (3).

$5,760, $3,456, $3,456, and $1,728 and equal the full cost of the car. Under § 280F(a)(1), however, the annual ceilings would allow only $13,535 of depreciation to have been deducted at the end of six years. The remaining $16,465 of basis would be depreciated over the next 12 years at a rate of $1,475 per year (slightly less in the twelfth year).

Leases present a special problem. Without special rules that apply to leases, taxpayers could circumvent the limitations imposed by § 280F(a) by simply leasing, instead of buying, property. Since § 280F(a) does not apply to taxpayers regularly engaged in the business of leasing, (I.R.C. § 280F(c)(1)), the lessor could depreciate the property without restriction and pass the savings on to the lessee in the form of reduced lease payments. To prevent such avoidance, § 280F(c)(2) requires that rental deductions be limited if the lease term is thirty days or longer. The regulations implement this policy by allowing the deduction but requiring an offsetting income inclusion. Treas. Reg. § 1.280F–7. The pattern of imputation of income specified in the regulations is designed to replicate in leasing transactions the economics of slower depreciation deductions in the case of directly owned listed property; its operation is more stringent for "passenger automobiles" than for other listed property.

2.   LIMITATIONS ON "LISTED PROPERTY" NOT USED PRIMARILY FOR BUSINESS

2.1. *Generally*

Section 280F(b) limits the allowable depreciation or rental payment deduction with respect to "listed property." Such designated property includes passenger automobiles (whether or not subject to § 280F(a)), other means of transportation (such as an airplane or boat), property used for entertainment, recreation, or amusement, certain computers and peripheral equipment. I.R.C. § 280F(d)(4). The Treasury is authorized to expand this list by regulation.

If the business use of any listed property is not more than fifty percent, depreciation must be computed on the straight-line method over the extended cost recovery period prescribed by § 168(g). (For automobiles, however, a special rule provides that the recovery period remains five years.) Thus, for example, if a $10,000 automobile were used exactly fifty percent for business, depreciation deductions (at one-half of the full amount to reflect the apportioned business use) would be $500 in the first year, $1,000 for each of the next four years, and $500 in the sixth year, rather than $1,000, $1,600, $960, $576, $576, and $288.

In the case of leases of listed property, as in the case of automobiles, Temp. Reg. § 1.280F–5T requires the lessee to include in gross income an amount computed under a formula designed to reflect the reduction in depreciation that would have occurred as a result of the mixed use if the property had been purchased, but the precise reduction differs from that applicable to automobiles.

Section 280F operates to limit or eliminate the tax expenditure provided by accelerated depreciation for listed property. As in the case of automobiles, the leasing rules are necessary to prevent taxpayers from obtaining the benefits of accelerated depreciation indirectly, through reduced rental costs. In tax expenditure terms, Congress is unwilling to provide interest free loans with respect to purchases of the types of property to which § 280F applies.

To claim any deduction with respect to listed property, the taxpayer must meet the rigorous substantiation requirements of § 274(d) (see Section 3.6. of this Chapter). See Temp. Reg. §§ 1.274–5T and –6T. See also Matlock v. Commissioner, T.C. Memo. 1992–324 (depreciation deduction on computer disallowed because taxpayer did not have a log book detailing use of computer time).

2.2. *Employee Ownership and Use of Listed Property*

Employees are subject to even more stringent restrictions. Section 280F(d)(3) provides that an employee's use of listed property does not count as a business use in determining the employee's deductions for depreciation or rental payments unless the use is for the employer's convenience and is required as a condition of employment. These terms have the same meaning for these purposes as they do under § 119. Temp. Reg. § 1.280F–6T(a)(2)(i). To meet the "condition of employment" test, the listed property must be necessary for the employee to perform the employee's duties properly, but the employer need not explicitly require that the employee provide the listed property. Temp. Reg. § 1.280F–6T(a)(2)(ii). In Cadwallader v. Commissioner, T.C. Memo. 1989–356, aff'd on other issues, 919 F.2d 1273 (7th Cir.1990), a computer purchased by a college professor and used in his home office (which qualified under § 280A(c)(1)) to do research necessary to attain tenure was held not to be subject to § 280F under this standard because the college did not provide him either an adequate office or a computer. Nevertheless, because of § 280F(d)(3), in most cases, an employee who purchases a computer and uses it one-hundred percent for business would likely be denied any depreciation deductions, even if the computer is kept at the employee's office rather than at her home.

2.3. *Use of Listed Property in Nonbusiness Profit-Seeking Activities*

Mixed-use property that is used for the production of income in a business activity (e.g., analysis of the taxpayer's investment portfolio) is depreciable under § 168. But under § 280F, profit-seeking non-business use of listed property is not counted in determining whether the property is eligible for the normal ACRS cost recovery period and rates. Because a profit-seeking use supports a deduction even though it does not count in applying the "predominant use" test of § 280F(b), the rule has a "cliff" effect. Assume, for example, that a taxpayer used an airplane 51 percent for business travel, 44 percent for nonbusiness income-producing activities, such as travel to shareholder meetings of corporations in which he owned stock, and five percent for recreational activities. The more-than-fifty-percent-business-use test is met, and § 280F does not apply. Depreciation under the normal § 168 rules is allowed based on 95 percent of the taxpayer's depreciable basis for the airplane. But if the percentage of use allocated to the business and non-business profit-seeking activities are reversed (i.e., 44 percent business and 51 percent profit-seeking), the test is not met. Although 95 percent of the basis qualifies for depreciation, § 280F applies, and the deductible amount must be computed using the straight-line method over the longer life as prescribed by § 168(g).

2.4. *Recapture*

To deal with the problem of taxpayers acquiring listed property and claiming deductions (often expensing under § 179) based on business use in the year of purchase, Congress enacted the recapture rules in § 280F(b)(2). For application of these rules, see Temp. Reg. § 1.280F–3T. In addition, the property never again can meet the predominantly business use rule, even if the taxpayer ceases using it for personal purposes.

SECTION 5.   CLOTHING

Pevsner v. Commissioner

United States Court of Appeals, Fifth Circuit, 1980.
628 F.2d 467.

■ JOHNSON, CIRCUIT JUDGE:

This is an appeal by the Commissioner of Internal Revenue from a decision of the United States Tax Court. The tax court upheld taxpayer's business expense deduction for clothing expenditures in the amount of $1,621.91 for the taxable year 1975. We reverse. — Holding

Since June 1973 Sandra J. Pevsner, taxpayer, has been employed as the manager of the Sakowitz Yves St. Laurent Rive Gauche Boutique located in Dallas, Texas. The boutique sells only women's clothes and accessories designed by Yves St. Laurent (YSL), one of the leading designers of women's apparel. Although the clothing is ready to wear, it is highly fashionable and expensively priced. Some customers of the boutique purchase and wear the YSL apparel for their daily activities and spend as much as $20,000 per year for such apparel.

As manager of the boutique, the taxpayer is expected by her employer to wear YSL clothes while at work. In her appearance, she is expected to project the image of an exclusive lifestyle and to demonstrate to her customers that she is aware of the YSL current fashion trends as well as trends generally. Because the boutique sells YSL clothes exclusively, taxpayer must be able, when a customer compliments her on her clothes, to say that they are designed by YSL. In addition to wearing YSL apparel while at the boutique, she wears them while commuting to and from work to fashion shows sponsored by the boutique, and to business luncheons, where she represents the boutique. During 1975, the taxpayer bought, at an employee's discount, the following items: four blouses, three skirts, one pair of slacks, one trench coat, two sweaters, one jacket, one tunic, five scarves, six belts, two pairs of shoes and four necklaces. The total cost of this apparel was $1,381.91. In addition, the sum of $240 was expended for maintenance of these items.

Although the clothing and accessories purchased by the taxpayer were the type used for general purposes by the regular customers of the boutique, the taxpayer is not a normal purchaser of these clothes. The taxpayer and her husband, who is partially disabled because of a severe heart attack suffered in 1971, lead a simple life and their social activities are very limited and informal. Although taxpayer's employer has no objection to her wearing the apparel away from work, taxpayer stated that she did not wear the clothes during off-work hours because she felt that they were too expensive for her simple everyday lifestyle. Another reason why she did not wear the YSL clothes apart from work was to make them last longer. Taxpayer did admit at trial, however, that a number of the articles were things she could have worn off the job and in which she would have looked "nice."

On her joint federal income tax return for 1975, taxpayer deducted $990 as an ordinary and necessary business expense with respect to her purchase of the YSL clothing and accessories. However, in the tax court, taxpayer claimed a deduction for the full $1381.91 cost of the apparel and for the $240 cost of maintaining the apparel. The tax court allowed the taxpayer to deduct both expenses in the total amount of $1621.91. The tax court reasoned that the apparel was not suitable to the private lifestyle maintained by the taxpayer. This appeal by the Commissioner followed.

The principal issue on appeal is whether the taxpayer is entitled to deduct as an ordinary and necessary business expense the cost of purchasing and maintaining the YSL clothes and accessories worn by the taxpayer in her employment as the manager of the boutique. This determination requires an examination of the relationship between Section 162(a) of the Internal Revenue Code of 1954, which allows a deduction for ordinary and necessary expenses incurred in the conduct of a trade or business, and Section 262 of the Code, which bars a deduction for all "personal, living, or family expenses." Although many expenses are helpful or essential to one's business activities—such as commuting expenses and the cost of meals while at work—these expenditures are considered inherently personal and are disallowed under Section 262. See, e.g., * * * Commissioner v. Flowers, 326 U.S. 46 (1946).

The generally accepted rule governing the deductibility of clothing expenses is that the cost of clothing is deductible as a business expense only if: (1) the clothing is of a type specifically required as a condition of employment, (2) it is not adaptable to general usage as ordinary clothing, and (3) it is not so worn. Donnelly v. Commissioner, 262 F.2d 411, 412 (2d Cir.1959).[3]

In the present case, the Commissioner stipulated that the taxpayer was required by her employer to wear YSL clothing and that she did not wear such apparel apart from work. The Commissioner maintained, however, that a deduction should be denied because the YSL clothes and

---

[3]   When the taxpayer is prohibited from wearing the clothing away from work a deduction is normally allowed. See Harsaghy v. Commissioner, 2 T.C. 484 (1943). However, in the present case no such restriction was placed upon the taxpayer's use of the clothing.

accessories purchased by the taxpayer were adaptable for general usage as ordinary clothing and she was not prohibited from using them as such. The tax court, in rejecting the Commissioner's argument for the application of an objective test, recognized that the test for deductibility was whether the clothing was "suitable for general or personal wear" but determined that the matter of suitability was to be judged subjectively, in light of the taxpayer's lifestyle. Although the court recognized that the YSL apparel "might be used by some members of society for general purposes," it felt that because the "wearing of YSL apparel outside work would be inconsistent with * * * [taxpayer's] lifestyle," sufficient reason was shown for allowing a deduction for the clothing expenditures.

What the tax court said →

In reaching its decision, the tax court relied heavily upon Yeomans v. Commissioner, 30 T.C. 757 (1958). In *Yeomans,* the petitioner was employed as fashion coordinator for a shoe manufacturing company. Her employment necessitated her attendance at meetings of fashion experts and at fashion shows sponsored by her employer. On these occasions, she was expected to wear clothing that was new, highly styled, and such as "might be sought after and worn for personal use by women who make it a practice to dress according to the most advanced or extreme fashions." 30 T.C. at 768. However, for her personal wear, Ms. Yeomans preferred a plainer and more conservative style of dress. As a consequence, some of the items she purchased were not suitable for her private and personal wear and were not so worn. The tax court allowed a deduction for the cost of the items that were not suitable for her personal wear. Although the basis for the decision in *Yeomans* is not clearly stated, the tax court in the case *sub judice* determined that

> [a]   careful reading of *Yeomans* shows that, without a doubt, the Court based its decision on a determination of Ms. Yeomans' lifestyle and that the clothes were not suitable for her use in such lifestyle. Furthermore, the Court recognized that the clothes Ms. Yeomans purchased were suitable for wear by women who customarily wore such highly styled apparel, but such fact did not cause the court to decide the issue against her. Thus, *Yeomans* clearly decides the issue before us in favor of the petitioner.

T.C. Memo. 1979–311 at 9–10.

Notwithstanding the tax court's decision in *Yeomans,* the Circuits that have addressed the issue have taken an objective, rather than subjective, approach. Stiner v. United States, 524 F.2d 640, 641 (10th Cir.1975); Donnelly v. Commissioner, 262 F.2d 411, 412 (2d Cir.1959). An objective approach was also taken by the tax court in Drill v. Commissioner, 8 T.C. 902 (1947). Under an objective test, no reference is made to the individual taxpayer's lifestyle or personal taste. Instead, adaptability for personal or general use depends upon what is generally accepted for ordinary street wear.

The principal argument in support of an objective test is, of course, administrative necessity. The Commissioner argues that, as a practical matter, it is virtually impossible to determine at what point either price or style makes clothing inconsistent with or inappropriate to a taxpayer's lifestyle. Moreover, the Commissioner argues that the price one pays and the styles one selects are inherently personal choices governed by taste, fashion, and other unmeasurable values. Indeed, the tax court has rejected the argument that a taxpayer's personal taste can dictate whether clothing is appropriate for general use. See Drill v. Commissioner, 8 T.C. 902 (1947). An objective test, although not perfect, provides a practical administrative approach that allows a taxpayer or revenue agent to look only to objective facts in determining whether clothing required as a condition of employment is adaptable to general use as ordinary streetwear. Conversely, the tax court's reliance on subjective factors provides no concrete guidelines in determining the deductibility of clothing purchased as a condition of employment.

In addition to achieving a practical administrative result, an objective test also tends to promote a substantial fairness among the greatest number of taxpayers. As the Commissioner suggests, it apparently would be the tax court's position that two similarly situated YSL boutique managers with identical wardrobes would be subject to disparate tax consequences depending upon the particular manager's lifestyle and "socio-economic level." This result, however, is not consonant with a reasonable interpretation of Sections 162 and 262.

For the reasons stated above, the decision of the tax court upholding the deduction for taxpayer's purchase of YSL clothing is reversed. Consequently, the portion of the tax court's decision upholding the deduction for maintenance costs for the clothing is also reversed.

DETAILED ANALYSIS

The test for deductibility of clothing set out in *Pevsner* represents long-standing IRS policy. See Rev. Rul. 70–474, 1970–2 C.B. 34. It has been applied in a number of factual situations. For example, deductions have been allowed for the costs of purchasing and cleaning waitress uniforms, Owens v. Commissioner, T.C. Memo. 1977–319; for clothing designed to tear readily in the event it should be caught in the machinery around which an electronic technician worked daily, Bushey v. Commissioner, T.C. Memo. 1971–149; and for protective smocks worn by an art teacher, Kellner v. Commissioner, T.C. Memo. 1976–72, aff'd by order 553 F.2d 93 (2d Cir.1977). Genck v. Commissioner, T.C. Memo, 1998–105 (1998), held that the cost of a jazz singer's stage clothes and makeup were deductible. Meanwhile, deductions have been disallowed for the wardrobe and dry cleaning costs of a television newsman, Hynes v. Commissioner, 74 T.C. 1266 (1980).

The costs of military uniforms that can be worn off the base without restriction are nondeductible since they are considered to take the place of ordinary civilian clothing. However, expenses for fatigues, which military regulations prohibit from being worn when off duty, and for the uniforms of reservists that cannot be worn off duty, are deductible to the extent they exceed the clothing allowance. Rev. Rul. 67–115, 1967–1 C.B. 30; Treas. Reg. § 1.262–1(b)(8).

Not all uniforms satisfy the tests imposed by the IRS and courts for deductibility. To obtain a deduction, the taxpayer must prove that the uniform is not suitable for ordinary wear. In Mortrud v. Commissioner, 44 T.C. 208 (1965) (Acq.), the Commissioner conceded that expenses for a milkman's shirt, jacket, and cap that had the milk company insignia on them were deductible, but did not allow a deduction for the expenses attributable to the milkman's pants. The Tax Court allowed the pants deduction, finding that they were not adaptable for general wear. Bradley v. Commissioner, T.C. Memo. 1996–461, denied a deduction for the cost of a nurse's uniforms because the taxpayer did not introduce evidence that they were not suitable for ordinary wear. Changing tastes in clothing thus may deny a deduction to a taxpayer who in fact uses a uniform only for business purposes merely because others decide that a particular uniform garment, such as surgical scrubs worn as casual wear, is in fashion.

SECTION 6.   CHILD AND DEPENDENT CARE

Smith v. Commissioner*
Board of Tax Appeals, 1939.
40 B.T.A. 1038.

OPINION

■ OPPER: Respondent determined a deficiency of $23.62 in petitioner's 1937 income tax. This was due to the disallowance of a deduction claimed by petitioners, who are husband and wife, for sums spent by the wife in employing nursemaids to care for petitioner's young child, the wife, as well as the husband, being employed. The facts have all been stipulated and are hereby found accordingly.

Petitioners would have us apply the "but for" test. They propose that but for the nurses the wife could not leave her child; but for the freedom so secured she could not pursue her gainful labors; and but for them there would be no income and no tax. This thought evokes an array of interesting possibilities. The fee to the doctor, but for whose healing service the earner of the family income could not leave his sickbed; the cost of the laborer's raiment, for how can the world proceed about its business unclothed; the very home which gives us shelter and rest and the food which provides energy, might all by an extension of the same proposition be construed as necessary to the operation of business and to the creation of income. Yet these are the very essence of those "personal" expenses the deductibility of which is expressly denied.

---

*   [Ed.: The decision was affirmed per curiam, 113 F.2d 114 (2d Cir.1940).]

We are told that the working wife is a new phenomenon. This is relied on to account for the apparent inconsistency that the expenses in issue are now a commonplace, yet have not been the subject of legislation, ruling, or adjudicated controversy. But if that is true it becomes all the more necessary to apply accepted principles to the novel facts. We are not prepared to say that the care of children, like similar aspects of family and household life, is other than a personal concern. The wife's services as custodian of the home and protector of its children are ordinarily rendered without monetary compensation. There results no taxable income from the performance of this service and the correlative expenditure is personal and not susceptible of deduction. Rosa E. Burkhart, 11 B.T.A. 275. Here the wife has chosen to employ others to discharge her domestic function and the services she performs are rendered outside the home. They are a source of actual income and taxable as such. But that does not deprive the same work performed by others of its personal character nor furnish a reason why its cost should be treated as an offset in the guise of a deductible item.

We are not unmindful that, as petitioners suggest, certain disbursements normally personal may become deductible by reason of their intimate connection with an occupation carried on for profit. In this category fall entertainment, Blackmer v. Commissioner, 70 Fed.(2d) 255 (C.C.A., 2d Cir.), and traveling expenses, Joseph W. Powell, 34 B.T.A. 655; affd., 94 Fed.(2d) 483 (C.C.A., 1st Cir.) * * * . The line is not always an easy one to draw nor the test simple to apply. But we think its principle is clear. It may for practical purposes be said to constitute a distinction between those activities which, as a matter of common acceptance and universal experience, are "ordinary" or usual as the direct accompaniment of business pursuits, on the one hand; and those which, though they may in some indirect and tenuous degree relate to the circumstances of a profitable occupation, are nevertheless personal in their nature, of a character applicable to human beings generally, and which exist on that plane regardless of the occupation, though not necessarily of the station in life, of the individuals concerned. See Welch v. Helvering, 290 U.S. 111.

In the latter category, we think, fall payments made to servants or others occupied in looking to the personal wants of their employers. David Sonenblick, 4 B.T.A. 986. And we include in this group nursemaids retained to care for infant children.

Decision will be entered for the respondent.

DETAILED ANALYSIS

1.   SUBSEQUENT LEGISLATIVE RESPONSE

As the *Smith* decision indicates, in the absence of a statutory provision, courts concluded that child care expenses were primarily personal in nature and were nondeductible. Section 21 now allows a tax credit of between 20 and 35 percent of the taxpayer's employment related dependent care expenses. Dependent care expenses include the costs of caring for children under the age of 13, dependents physically or mentally incapable of caring for themselves regardless of age, and a physically or mentally disabled spouse, provided the dependent shares the taxpayer's principal place of abode for a majority of the year. (Dependents are discussed in Chapter 22, Section 1.B.). The exact credit amount is based on the taxpayer's adjusted gross income. Taxpayers with adjusted gross incomes of $15,000 or less are entitled to a 35-percent credit with the credit falling one percentage point for every additional $2,000 of adjusted gross income (or fraction thereof) such that taxpayers with adjusted gross incomes exceeding $43,000 receive a 20-percent credit. In addition, only $3,000 of expenses are taken into account for one child and $6,000 for two or more children, but never an amount of expenses in excess of gross income. Thus, the maximum credit under any circumstances is $2,100 (i.e., $6,000 x 0.35). The credit is not refundable and only offsets the taxpayer's tax liability. I.R.C. § 26. As a result, families with incomes insufficient to generate a positive tax liability do not benefit from the credit. Section 24 (see Chapter 22, Section 2.A.) provides a refundable credit for a taxpayer's qualifying children irrespective of the taxpayer's expenses for household and dependent care services.

2.   POLICY ASPECTS

The fundamental tax policy issue regarding child care expenses involves whether they should be treated as personal expenses or the costs of producing income. In turn, part of that determination relates to whether the costs should be viewed as incurred due to the personal decision to have children or the decision to work outside the home (which might include some consideration of the voluntariness of both decisions). If all or part of child care costs are deemed to be related to the production of income, a deduction from gross income, rather than a tax credit, would be required as a structural matter. Between 1954 to 1976, taxpayers were allowed a limited deduction for child care costs. The Treasury Department accounted for the provision as a tax expenditure, reflecting the courts' view that these expenses were primarily personal in nature.

Some commentators see the failure to provide a full deduction for the costs of child care as adversely affecting the decision of women to enter the workforce because child care is still provided primarily by women, who are often secondary earners and whose decision to enter the workforce has been viewed historically as more discretionary than men's. Others see it as disproportionately affecting poor women, who must use a greater portion of their income for child care than richer women and who, moreover, might be forced to work as an economic necessity. Since racial and ethnic minorities are disproportionately represented among the ranks of the poor, the burden of nondeductibility also falls disproportionately on these groups. Still other observers suggest that if child care were fully deductible, the use of cheaper, unlicensed child care providers would decline and the wages of child care workers might rise. Proposals for reforming the treatment of child care range from indexing the current tax credit or converting it to a more granularly graduated deduction to taxing the value of housework as a way of valuing women's non-market contributions. Debate over the proper tax treatment of child and dependent care expenses will continue to evolve as baby boomers age, and concern over caring for dependents encompasses not only the costs of caring for young children but also the cost of caring for aging parents, who can become their children's legal dependents.

CHAPTER 20

EXPENDITURES INVOLVING BOTH PERSONAL AND CAPITAL ASPECTS

SECTION 1.   LEGAL EXPENSES

REGULATIONS: Section 1.212–1(k)–(m); 1.262–1(b)(7).

United States v. Gilmore

Supreme Court of the United States, 1963.
372 U.S. 39.

■ MR. JUSTICE HARLAN delivered the opinion of the Court.

In 1955 the California Supreme Court confirmed the award to the respondent taxpayer of a decree of absolute divorce, without alimony, against his wife Dixie Gilmore, 45 Cal.2d 142. The case before us involves the deductibility for federal income tax purposes of that part of the husband's legal expense incurred in such proceedings as is attributable to his successful resistance of his wife's claims to certain of his assets asserted by her to be community property under California law. The claim to such deduction, which has been upheld by the Court of Claims, 154 Ct.Cl. 365, 290 F.2d 942, is founded on [the predecessor of section 212], which allows as deductions from gross income

> " * * * ordinary and necessary expenses * * * incurred during
> the taxable year * * * for the * * * conservation * * * of property
> held for the production of income."

Because of a conflict of views among the Court of Claims, the Courts of Appeals, and the Tax Court regarding the proper application of this provision,[4] and the continuing importance of the question in the administration of the federal income tax laws, we granted certiorari on the Government's petition. * * *

At the time of the divorce proceedings, instituted by the wife but in which the husband also cross-claimed for divorce, respondent's property consisted primarily of controlling stock interests in three corporations, each of which was a franchised General Motors automobile dealer. As president and principal managing officer of the three corporations, he received salaries from them aggregating about $66,800 annually, and in recent years his total annual dividends had averaged about $83,000. His

---

[4]   Compare Lewis v. Commissioner, 253 F.2d 821 (C.A.2d Cir.), and Douglas v. Commissioner, 33 T.C. 349, with Gilmore v. United States, 154 Ct.Cl. 365, 290 F.2d 942—the present case—and Baer v. Commissioner, 196 F.2d 646 (C.A.8th Cir.1952).

total annual income derived from the corporations was thus approximately $150,000. His income from other sources was negligible.

As found by the Court of Claims, the husband's overriding concern in the divorce litigation was to protect these assets against the claims of his wife. Those claims had two aspects: *first,* that the earnings accumulated and retained by these three corporations during the Gilmores' marriage (representing an aggregate increase in corporate net worth of some $600,000) were the product of respondent's personal services, and not the result of accretion in capital values, thus rendering respondent's stockholdings in the enterprises *pro tanto* community property under California law; *second,* that to the extent that such stockholdings were community property, the wife, allegedly the innocent party in the divorce proceeding, was entitled under California law to more than a one-half interest in such property.

The respondent wished to defeat those claims for two important reasons. *First,* the loss of his controlling stock interests, particularly in the event of their transfer in substantial part to his hostile wife, might well cost him the loss of his corporate positions, his principal means of livelihood. *Second,* there was also danger that if he were found guilty of his wife's sensational and reputation-damaging charges of marital infidelity, General Motors Corporation might find it expedient to exercise its right to cancel these dealer franchises.

The end result of this bitterly fought divorce case was a complete victory for the husband. He, not the wife, was granted a divorce on his cross-claim; the wife's community property claims were denied in their entirety; and she was held entitled to no alimony. 45 Cal.2d 142.

Respondent's legal expenses in connection with this litigation amounted to $32,537.15 in 1953 and $8,074.21 in 1954—a total of $40,611.36 for the two taxable years in question. The Commissioner of Internal Revenue found all of these expenditures "personal" or "family" expenses and as such none of them deductible. * * * In the ensuing refund suit, however, the Court of Claims held that 80% of such expense (some $32,500) was attributable to respondent's defense against his wife's community property claims respecting his stockholdings and hence deductible under [section 212] as an expense "incurred * * * for the * * * conservation * * * of property held for the production of income." In so holding the Court of Claims stated:

> "Of course it is true that in every divorce case a certain amount of the legal expenses are incurred for the purpose of obtaining the divorce and a certain amount are incurred in an effort to conserve the estate and are not necessarily deductible under section [212] but when the facts of a particular case clearly indicate [as here] that the property, around which the controversy evolves, is held for the production of income and without this property the litigant might be denied not only the property itself but the means of earning a livelihood, then it

must come under the provisions of section [212] * * * . The only question then is the allocation of the expenses to this phase of the proceedings." 154 Ct.Cl., at 373, 290 F.2d, at 947.

The Government does not question the amount or formula for the expense allocation made by the Court of Claims. Its sole contention here is that the court below misconceived the test governing [section 212] deductions, in that the deductibility of these expenses turns, so it is argued, not upon the *consequences* to respondent of a failure to defeat his wife's community property claims but upon the *origin* and *nature* of the claims themselves. So viewing Dixie Gilmore's claims, whether relating to the existence or division of community property, it is contended that the expense of resisting them must be deemed nondeductible "personal" or "family" expense under [section 262] not deductible expense under [section 212]. For reasons given hereafter we think the Government's position is sound and that it must be sustained.

I.

For income tax purposes Congress has seen fit to regard an individual as having two personalities: "one is [as] a seeker after profit who can deduct the expenses incurred in that search; the other is [as] a creature satisfying his needs as a human and those of his family but who cannot deduct such consumption and related expenditures."[11] The Government regards [section 212] as embodying a category of the expenses embraced in the first of these roles.

Initially, it may be observed that the wording of [section 212] more readily fits the Government's view of the provision than that of the Court of Claims. For in context "conservation of property" seems to refer to operations performed with respect to the property itself, such as safeguarding or upkeep, rather than to a taxpayer's retention of ownership in it. But more illuminating than the mere language of [section 212] is the history of the provision.

Prior to 1942 [the predecessor of section 162] allowed deductions only for expenses incurred "in carrying on any trade or business," the deduction presently authorized by [section 162(a)]. In Higgins v. Commissioner, 312 U.S. 212, this Court gave that provision a narrow construction, holding that the activities of an individual in supervising his own securities investments did not constitute the "carrying on of a trade or business," and hence that expenses incurred in connection with such activities were not tax deductible. * * * The Revenue Act of 1942 (56 Stat. 798, § 121), by adding what is now [section 212], sought to remedy the inequity inherent in the disallowance of expense deductions in respect of such profit-seeking activities, the income from which was nonetheless taxable.

As noted in McDonald v. Commissioner, 323 U.S. 57, 62, the purpose of the 1942 amendment was merely to enlarge "the category of incomes

---

[11]   Surrey and Warren, Cases on Federal Income Taxation, 272 (1960).

with reference to which expenses were deductible." And committee reports make clear that deductions under the new section were subject to the same limitations and restrictions that are applicable to those allowable under [section 162(a)].[14] Further, this Court has said that [section 212] "is comparable and *in pari materia* with [section 162(a)]," providing for a class of deductions "coextensive with the business deductions allowed by [section 162(a)], except for" the requirement that the income-producing activity qualify as a trade or business. Trust of Bingham v. Commissioner, 325 U.S. 365, 373, 374.

A basic restriction upon the availability of a [section 162(a)] deduction is that the expense item involved must be one that has a business origin. That restriction not only inheres in the language of [section 162(a)] itself, confining such deductions to "expenses * * * incurred * * * in carrying on any trade or business," but also follows from [section 262], expressly rendering nondeductible "in any case * * * [p]ersonal, living, or family expenses." * * * In light of what has already been said with respect to the advent and thrust of [section 212], it is clear that the "[p]ersonal * * * or family expenses" restriction of [section 262] must impose the same limitation upon the reach of [section 212]—in other words that the only kind of expenses deductible under [section 212] are those that relate to a "business," that is, profit-seeking, purpose. The pivotal issue in this case then becomes: was this part of respondent's litigation costs a "business" rather than a "personal" or "family" expense?

The answer to this question has already been indicated in prior cases. In Lykes v. United States, 343 U.S. 118, the Court rejected the contention that legal expenses incurred in contesting the assessment of a gift tax liability were deductible. The taxpayer argued that if he had been required to pay the original deficiency he would have been forced to liquidate his stockholdings which were his main source of income, and that his legal expenses were therefore incurred in the "conservation" of income-producing property and hence deductible under [section 212]. The Court first noted that the "deductibility [of the expenses] turns wholly upon the nature of the activities to which they relate" (343 U.S., at 123), and then stated:

> "Legal expenses do not become deductible merely because they are paid for services which relieve a taxpayer of liability. That argument would carry us too far. It would mean that the expense of defending almost any claim would be deductible by a taxpayer on the ground that such defense was made to help him keep clear of liens whatever income-producing property he might have. For example, it suggests that the expense of defending an action based upon personal injuries caused by a

---

14   H.R.Rep. No. 2333, 77th Cong., 2d Sess. 75: "A deduction under this section is subject, except for the requirement of being incurred in connection with a trade or business, to all the restrictions and limitations that apply in the case of the deduction under section [162(a)] of an expense paid or incurred in carrying on any trade or business." See also S.Rep. No. 1631, 77th Cong., 2d Sess. 88.

taxpayer's negligence while driving an automobile for pleasure should be deductible. [Section 212] never has been so interpreted by us. * * *

"If, as suggested, the relative size of each claim, in proportion to the income-producing resources of a defendant, were to be a touchstone of the deductibility of the expense of resisting the claim, substantial uncertainty and inequity would inhere in the rule. * * * It is not a ground for * * * [deduction] that the claim, if justified, will consume income-producing property of the defendant." 343 U.S., at 125–126.

In Kornhauser v. United States, 276 U.S. 145, this Court considered the deductibility of legal expenses incurred by a taxpayer in defending against a claim by a former business partner that fees paid to the taxpayer were for services rendered during the existence of the partnership. In holding that these expenses were deductible even though the taxpayer was no longer a partner at the time of suit, the Court formulated the rule that "where a suit or action against a taxpayer is directly connected with, or * * * proximately resulted from, his business, the expense incurred is a business expense * * *." 276 U.S., at 153. Similarly, in a case involving an expense incurred in satisfying an obligation (though not a litigation expense), it was said that "it is the origin of the liability out of which the expense accrues" or "the kind of transaction out of which the obligation arose * * * which [is] crucial and controlling." Deputy v. du Pont, 308 U.S. 488, 494, 496.

The principle we derive from these cases is that the characterization, as "business" or "personal," of the litigation costs of resisting a claim depends on whether or not the claim *arises in connection with* the taxpayer's profit-seeking activities. It does not depend on the *consequences* that might result to a taxpayer's income-producing property from a failure to defeat the claim, for, as *Lykes* teaches, that "would carry us too far"[15] and would not be compatible with the basic lines of expense deductibility drawn by Congress.[16] Moreover, such a rule would lead to capricious results. If two taxpayers are each sued for an automobile accident while driving for pleasure, deductibility of their litigation costs would turn on the mere circumstance of the character of the assets each happened to possess, that is, whether the judgments against them stood to be satisfied out of income- or nonincome-producing property. We should be slow to attribute to Congress a purpose producing

---

[15]   The Treasury Regulations have long provided: "An expense (not otherwise deductible) paid or incurred by an individual in determining or contesting a liability asserted against him does not become deductible by reason of the fact that property held by him for the production of income may be required to be used or sold for the purpose of satisfying such liability." Treas. Reg. (1954 Code) § 1.212–1(m); see Treas. Reg. § 118 (1939 Code) § 39.23(a)–15(k).

[16]   Expenses of contesting tax liabilities are now deductible under § 212(3) of the 1954 Code. This provision merely represents a policy judgment as to a particular class of expenditures otherwise non-deductible, like extraordinary medical expenses, and does not cast any doubt on the basic tax structure set up by Congress.

such unequal treatment among taxpayers, resting on no rational foundation.

* * *

For these reasons, * * * the origin and character of the claim with respect to which an expense was incurred, rather than its potential consequences upon the fortunes of the taxpayer, is the controlling basic test of whether the expense was "business" or "personal" and hence whether it is deductible or not under [section 212]. * * *

We turn then to the determinative question in this case: did the wife's claims respecting respondent's stockholdings arise in connection with his profit-seeking activities?

II.

In classifying respondent's legal expenses the court below did not distinguish between those relating to the claims of the wife with respect to the *existence* of community property and those involving the *division* of any such property. * * * Nor is such a breakdown necessary for a disposition of the present case. It is enough to say that in both aspects the wife's claims stemmed entirely from the marital relationship, and not, under any tenable view of things, from income-producing activity. This is obviously so as regards the claim to more than an equal division of any community property found to exist. For any such right depended entirely on the wife's making good her charges of marital infidelity on the part of the husband. The same conclusion is no less true respecting the claim relating to the existence of community property. For no such property could have existed but for the marriage relationship. Thus none of respondent's expenditures in resisting these claims can be deemed "business" expenses, and they are therefore not deductible under [section 212].

In view of this conclusion it is unnecessary to consider the further question suggested by the Government: whether that portion of respondent's payments attributable to litigating the issue of the existence of community property was a capital expenditure or a personal expense. In neither event would these payments be deductible from gross income.

The judgment of the Court of Claims is reversed and the case is remanded to that court for further proceedings consistent with this opinion.

DETAILED ANALYSIS

1.   LEGAL EXPENSES GENERALLY

1.1. *Application of "Origin" Test*

The origin-of-the-claim test operates both to distinguish deductible legal expenses from nondeductible legal expenses and to distinguish capital legal expenses from current legal expenses. An interesting consequence of this dualistic application is that personal legal expenses may be capitalized, thereby reducing gain on the subsequent sale of an asset, even though personal legal expenses are nondeductible.

In United States v. Patrick, 372 U.S. 53 (1963), a companion case to *Gilmore,* the Supreme Court denied a deduction for legal expenses incurred by a husband in connection with a property settlement agreement made pursuant to an uncontested divorce proceeding. The "origins" test is routinely applied to deny deductions for legal expenses incurred in situations in which the taxpayer is seeking to preserve income-producing ability. See Lewis v. Commissioner, 253 F.2d 821 (2d Cir.1958) (involving fees to defend incompetency proceeding); West v. Commissioner, 71 T.C. 532 (1979) (pertaining to legal expenses incurred by doctor seeking to avoid active duty in the Navy under a military deferral agreement he signed while in medical school); and Kurkjian v. Commissioner, 65 T.C. 862 (1976) (involving legal expenses incurred in defending actions brought against taxpayer by his church for breach of fiduciary duty with respect to certain fund raising activities and dealings in real estate; although the taxpayer was an investor and real estate developer, the origin of the legal expenses was in the church association).

Legal fees incurred to defend against criminal charges or civil disciplinary proceedings arising out of the conduct of the taxpayer's trade or business generally are deductible. For example, Commissioner v. Tellier, 383 U.S. 687 (1966), allowed a deduction by a securities dealer for legal expenses incurred in the unsuccessful defense of criminal fraud charges brought under the Securities Act of 1933. O'Malley v. Commissioner, 91 T.C. 352 (1988), allowed a deduction for legal expenses incurred by a trucking company executive in the unsuccessful defense of criminal charges of attempted bribery of a United States senator in connection with legislation deregulating the trucking industry. The "origins" test was also held to allow the deduction of legal expenses incurred by a state judge in obtaining a dismissal of a charge of judicial misconduct before a state commission where the allegations were based on a misuse of office and hence arose out of the taxpayer's duties as a judge. Rev. Rul. 74–394, 1974–2 C.B. 40.

On the other hand, expenses to defend criminal charges that may result in loss of employment are not deductible if the conduct leading to the charges did not originate in the course of business. See Nadiak v. Commissioner, 356 F.2d 911 (2d Cir.1966) (airline pilot charged with criminal assault and battery and grand larceny could not deduct legal expenses of successful defense even though conviction on either charge would have resulted in revocation of pilot's license, since charges arose out of "exacerbated" relations with his former wife); Harden v. Commissioner, T.C. Memo. 1991–454 (legal fees to defend criminal sexual assault charge were not deductible merely because taxpayer's employer may have discharged him as a result of conviction).

The origin of particular litigation expenses in profit seeking activity is not always clear. In re Collins, 26 F.3d 116 (11th Cir.1994), the taxpayer attempted to deduct a settlement payment and attorney fees incurred to resist a bankruptcy trustee's post-discharge attempt to set aside pre-bankruptcy conveyances to a family trust. Although the original bankruptcy originated from debts to business creditors, the court disallowed the deductions on the basis of its finding that the taxpayer's subsequent litigation costs and settlement originated in the taxpayer's attempts to protect the assets of a family trust. See also Accardo v. Commissioner, 942 F.2d 444 (7th Cir.1991) (expenses incurred to successfully defend an asset forfeiture suit under RICO were nondeductible; dictum suggests that the fees would have been deductible under § 162 and *Tellier* if taxpayer's defense had been unsuccessful and he had been found to be engaged in the racketeering business).

On occasion, legal expenses that might appear unitary can be allocated between the business and personal aspects. Cox v. Commissioner, T.C. Memo. 1981–552, allocated an attorney's fee for filing a bankruptcy petition between amounts deductible under § 162 and the nondeductible personal amount in proportion of the taxpayer's business debts to total debts. Even though the consequences of bankruptcy discharge were to protect the taxpayer's household goods and home equity, and thus personal, the cause of the bankruptcy, and hence the origin of the claim, was business.

The determination of whether a profit-seeking expense is deductible under § 162 or, on the other hand, under § 212, and thereby subject to the myriad of more restrictive ancillary rules, turns on the "origin and character of the claim for which the expense was incurred and whether the claim bears a sufficient nexus to the taxpayer's business." See Guill v. Commissioner, 112 T.C. 325, 329 (1999). Thus legal fees incurred by a sole proprietor or independent contractor to recover damages for conversion of business profits (and also any punitive damages awarded in addition to the compensatory damage) are deductible under § 162, but legal fees to recover taxable damages for personal defamation are deductible only under § 212.

1.2. *Presence of an Income Item*

Legal fees incurred to collect income from a nonbusiness profit-seeking activity are deductible under § 212(1). In Barr v. Commissioner, T.C. Memo. 1989–420, legal expenses incurred by a trust beneficiary to pursue a claim against the trustee were deductible to the extent the fees were allocable to a claim for recovery of lost income, rather than corpus; legal fees attributable to an action to replace the trustee were deductible because the purpose was to improve management of the trust assets. In Leonard v. Commissioner, 94 F.3d 523 (9th Cir.1996), the taxpayers received interest on a condemnation award with respect to their personal residence. Only the interest portion of the award was includable in gross income. The taxpayers paid their lawyers both an hourly fee and a 25-percent contingency fee. They were allowed to deduct the hourly fees directly attributable to the interest award plus a portion of the contingency fee equal to 25 percent of the interest award.

Treas. Reg. § 1.262–1(b)(7) states that legal expenses are deductible under § 212 if incurred in connection with a divorce proceeding and properly attributable to the production or collection of an item includable in income under § 71. In Elliott v. Commissioner, 40 T.C. 304 (1963) (Acq.), a wife was permitted to deduct legal fees incident to collecting alimony payments. In

Wild v. Commissioner, 42 T.C. 706 (1964) (Acq.) (three dissents), a wife was permitted to deduct the legal expenses of a divorce proceeding allocable to negotiating for alimony payments. In *Wild,* the Commissioner argued that the above-cited regulation was no longer applicable after *Gilmore* and *Patrick.* The majority concluded that the regulation was not affected and that it controlled this case. The dissenters argued that the regulation had been superseded by the Supreme Court decisions and that there should be a distinction between expenses incurred to secure alimony (nondeductible) and expenses incurred to collect alimony already awarded (deductible). The majority opinion in *Wild* has been followed subsequently and is accepted by the IRS. See Hesse v. Commissioner, 60 T.C. 685 (1973) (Acq.), aff'd by order, 511 F.2d 1393 (3d Cir.1975).

1.3. *Capital Expenditure Aspects*

The regulations specifically provide that legal expenses to defend title to property must be capitalized. Treas. Reg. § 1.212–1(k). See Nickell v. Commissioner, 831 F.2d 1265 (6th Cir.1987) (legal fees paid by an optionor of stock to resist attempted exercise of the option must be capitalized). This specific provision in the regulations does not limit operation of the general principle that if legal expenses are incurred in the taxpayer's business or profit-seeking activity, they are subject to capitalization under the rules of §§ 263 and 263A, discussed in Chapter 13. Thus, in Barrett v. Commissioner, 96 T.C. 713 (1991), the legal fees incurred by a stockbroker to defend a Securities and Exchange Commission proceeding to suspend his broker's license on grounds of insider trading in stock were required to be capitalized into the basis of the stock. Dana Corp. v. United States, 174 F.3d 1344 (Fed.Cir.1999), held that legal fees paid by applying an annual retainer against fees due in connection with the purchase of corporate stock were capital expenses. The court reasoned that the origin-of-the-claim test must be applied year-by-year, based on the purpose for which the retainer was applied in that year—its application in other years for purposes that resulted in a current § 162 deduction was not relevant.

In Gilmore v. United States, 245 F.Supp. 383 (N.D.Cal.1965) (*Gilmore* #2), the legal expenses disallowed in *Gilmore* #1 (see supra Section 1 of this Chapter) were allowed to be added to the basis of the assets involved in the divorce action, thereby reducing the gain or increasing the loss on a subsequent sale. The result in *Gilmore* #2 is arguably correct if the opinion in *Gilmore* #1 can be read as leaving open the issue whether expenditures were capital. On the other hand, the Court's opinion focused principally on the personal nature of the expenditures and the opinion in *Woodward* so characterized the *Gilmore* #1 holding. If that is viewed as the ground for the disallowance of the deduction, then capitalization is incorrect, because the resulting increase in basis eventually will offset the amount realized on the sale of the stock, thereby reducing the gain or increasing the loss realized.

In *Wild* (see Section 1.1.2 of this Chapter), assuming that the legal expenses to obtain alimony constituted a cost of producing income, to accurately reflect annual income, the expenses should have been capitalized and recovered ratably over the years in which the alimony payments were received and included in income. Nevertheless, the practice has been to allow a current deduction.

1.4. *Receipt of Taxable Damage Award Net of Plaintiff's Attorney's Fees*

When a plaintiff in a tort suit receives a judgment or settlement, the plaintiff must include the full amount of the recovery in gross income to the extent that it is not excludable under § 104 (or in the amount realized if the suit relates to property) and then claim any deduction allowed under § 162 or § 212 for the attorney's fees, which might be limited by § 67 (see Chapter 21, Section 7). Commissioner v. Banks, 543 U.S. 426 (2005). However, § 62(a)(21), which was enacted in 2004, provides that attorney fees in statutorily specified unlawful discrimination cases are deductible in computing adjusted gross income. Thus, the *Banks* principle does not affect the plaintiff-taxpayer's tax liability in cases in which the underlying claim for damages arose from one of the civil rights type actions to which § 62(a)(21) applies. The attorney's fees are deductible in all events and are not subject to any of the restrictions or limitations normally imposed on § 212 deductions. Nevertheless, the *Banks* decision has continuing importance with respect to contingent attorney's fees in the types of suits not covered by § 62(a)(21), which excludes from its ambit all nonphysical personal injury tort suits. Thus, for example, if a plaintiff in a tort suit for libel is awarded compensatory damages of $2,000,000 but receives only $1,200,000 net of a 40-percent contingent attorney's fee, the plaintiff taxpayer nevertheless must include the full $2,000,000 in gross income and may deduct the $800,000 attorneys' fee, subject to the various limitations that might apply.

2. TAX MATTERS

2.1. *In General*

Paragraph (3) of § 212 was added in 1954 to provide a deduction for individuals for expenses incurred in connection with the determination, collection, or refund of any tax, whether it be a federal, state, or local tax or an income, estate, gift, property, or other tax.

2.2. *Scope of Section 212(3)*

The IRS initially took the position that § 212(3) applied only in cases of contested tax liability, and not in cases of tax and estate planning. It has since abandoned this position, falling in line with judicial decisions in the area. See Treas. Reg. § 1.212–1(*l*).

In Merians v. Commissioner, 60 T.C. 187 (1973) (Acq.), the taxpayers incurred a legal fee for estate planning services. The services included the preparation of wills and trusts, the transfer of corporate stock, the dissolution of a corporation, and the creation of a partnership. Gift tax returns were prepared with respect to the transfers to the trusts. The Commissioner conceded that "there is a probability that some of the legal fee represented services which are deductible under § 212(3)," but asserted that the taxpayer had failed to sustain the burden of proving what amount could properly be allocated to these services. Based on vague testimony by the attorney, whose bill did not allocate the amount attributable to the tax advice, the court allowed the taxpayer to deduct only 20 percent of the fee as a deductible cost of tax advice. The IRS now accepts that § 212(3) applies to expenses for tax planning. See Rev. Rul. 89–68, 1989–1 C.B. 82 (allowing deduction for legal fees, as well as user fees paid to IRS, in connection with seeking private letter ruling regarding deductibility under § 212 of medical expenses); Rev. Rul. 72–545, 1972–2 C.B. 179 (tax advice incident to divorce is deductible).

2.3. *Capital Expenditure Aspects*

Some cases have stated or suggested that the capital expenditure limitation does not apply to § 212(3). For example, in footnote 16 of the *Gilmore* opinion, the Court implied that the § 212(3) deduction was akin to an itemized personal deduction, in which case the capital expenditure limitation might be applicable. Sharples v. United States, 533 F.2d 550 (Ct.Cl.1976), involved legal expenses that the taxpayer incurred in resisting foreign tax claims asserted against him in connection with the liquidation of a corporation of which he was a shareholder. The government argued that since the "origin of the claim" involved a capital transaction the legal expenses should be capitalized. The Court of Claims rejected this argument and allowed a deduction under § 212(3): "The short answer to [the government's] argument is that the statute, the regulations, and the legislative history of subsection 212(3) provide *no different treatment* for expenses incurred in fighting a tax which arose from a capital transaction as opposed to expenses for contesting a tax which arose from a non-capital transaction." Similarly, in Collins v. Commissioner, 54 T.C. 1656 (1970) (Acq.), the taxpayer, on the advice of his accountant, purchased an apartment building in order to reduce his tax liability. The IRS denied a deduction for the accounting fees on the basis that the expenses were capital costs of acquiring the building. The Tax Court formulated the issue as follows: "The issue presented as to the fee * * * paid to the C.P.A. * * * is whether it is to be deducted that year as an ordinary and necessary expense under the above statute [212(3)] or whether it is a capital expenditure under sec. 263(a)(1) * * * ." The court then held that fees for the accountant's services were deductible under § 212(3), even though his services related to the drawing of the documents for the purchase, as well as for tax advice and preparing the tax return, because the services all related to acquiring "tax advantages," in contrast to the nondeductible attorney's fees that were incurred to effect a "legal acquisition" of the building. In contrast, Honodel v. Commissioner, 722 F.2d 1462 (9th Cir.1984), held that expenses paid for tax advice in connection with investments must be capitalized. It distinguished *Sharples* on the ground that *Sharples* involved expenses in contesting a tax liability rather than for tax advice directly related to a capital acquisition.

2.4. *Significance of Origin of Tax Claim*

Not all items deductible under § 212(3) are treated identically. A significant distinction exists between expenses with respect to a tax liability related to a trade or business (other than as an employee) and expenses incurred with respect to tax liability relating to other items. Expenses for preparing the portion of a tax return relating to the taxpayer's trade or business and to contest tax deficiencies arising from the trade or business are deductible under § 162 and are taken into account in computing adjusted gross income, pursuant to § 62. See Estate of Henry N. Brawner, Jr., 36 B.T.A. 884 (1937). Any other expenses relating to the determination of an individual's tax liability are deductible only as itemized deductions under § 63. Rev. Rul. 92–29, 1992–1 C.B. 20.

3.   ALLOCATION ISSUES

In many situations, it will be difficult to distinguish the deductible and nondeductible portions of a legal expense. The attorney's allocation of the fee among the client's matters, including allocation between the individual client and a corporation the client owns or other business interests involved, generally will be decisive as a practical matter, though not controlling, if contested by the Commissioner. The difficulty of allocating fees does not excuse the attorney from doing so honestly. To assist a client in the preparation of documents designed to mislead the IRS is unethical. See ABA Comm. on Ethics and Professional Responsibility, Informal Opinion 1517 (1988) (if a corporation is billed for both services to the corporation and personal services to individuals, the bill must disclose the existence (but not the nature) of the personal services and the portion of the bill allocable to the personal services). See also ABA Comm. on Ethics and Professional Responsibility, Formal Opinion 85–352 (1985) (pertaining to tax return advice); 31 C.F.R. §§ 10.0–10.93 (2014) (Practice Before the IRS, particularly §§ 10.22 (diligence as to accuracy), 10.33(a)(4) (acting fairly and with integrity in practice before the IRS), and 10.34 (standards pertaining to tax returns and other documents).

SECTION 2.   EXPENSES FOR EDUCATION AND SEEKING EMPLOYMENT

INTERNAL REVENUE CODE: Section 274(m)(2).

REGULATIONS: Section 1.162–5.

Prior to 1958, educational expenses incurred by individuals in attending schools or in other activities to qualify for, or improve, their professional position generally were disallowed as personal expenses or as capital expenditures. On the other hand, expenses incurred to maintain skills in an established trade or business were deductible. The line between deductibility and nondeductibility was difficult to draw given the variety of possible factual situations. In 1958, revised regulations introduced a "primary purpose" test, permitting deduction if the educational expenses were incurred primarily to maintain or improve skills in a present trade or business or were required by the taxpayer's employer. A deduction was denied if the education was undertaken to qualify for a new position, to obtain a substantial advancement, or to satisfy the general educational aspirations of the taxpayer. The "primary purpose" test in the 1958 regulations proved equally difficult to apply.

In 1967, the regulations were revised to abandon the "primary purpose" test in favor of a more objective standard. The test under Treas. Reg. § 1.162–5 contains two parts. First, the education must maintain or improve skills used in the taxpayer's trade or business (or be required by

[Handwritten margin note: When a taxpayer went to continue education in relation to trade or business it is deductible, if it was not in relation or for a new trade or business then it was not deductible]

the employer). Second, if educational expenses in fact qualify an individual for a new trade or business, no deduction is allowed regardless of the taxpayer's motive in obtaining the education. In addition, the regulations disallow a deduction for expenses incurred to enable the taxpayer to meet the "minimum educational requirements" of a trade or business. These regulations have raised a number of interpretive questions.

Wassenaar v. Commissioner

Tax Court of the United States, 1979.
72 T.C. 1195.

■ SIMPSON, JUDGE: The Commissioner determined a deficiency of $521 in the petitioner's Federal income tax for 1973. The issues for decision are: (1) Whether the petitioner may deduct as an ordinary and necessary business expense the cost of his masters of law degree in taxation; [and] (2) whether such expenses are deductible under section 212(3) of the Internal Revenue Code of 1954, as ordinary and necessary expenses paid in connection with the determination of tax liability * * * .

Findings of Fact

* * *

The petitioner graduated from Wayne State University Law School (Wayne State) in Detroit, Mich., in June 1972. He served on law review while at Wayne State in both 1971 and 1972, and although he was a member of the board of editors, his services were no different from those of any other law review member. His duties included editing legal material, checking sources of legal articles, and writing legal articles. He received compensation for such services from Wayne State in the amounts of $845 in 1971 and $1,314 in 1972.

From June to September 1971, the petitioner worked for the law firm of Warner, Norcross & Judd (Warner firm). He prepared legal memorandums, drafted legal documents, and consulted with clients in the presence of an attorney from the firm. He received $2,920 from the Warner firm as compensation for his services that summer.

The petitioner was not employed during the summer following his graduation from law school; instead, he prepared for the Michigan bar, which he took in July 1972. However, he continued to search for employment with a law firm during such period. In October 1972, he passed the bar exam, but he was not formally admitted to the Michigan bar until May of 1973.

In September 1972, the petitioner began courses in the graduate law program in taxation at New York University (NYU), and he graduated with a masters degree in taxation in May 1973.

* * * Following his graduation from NYU, the petitioner returned to Detroit to commence employment with the law firm of Miller, Canfield, Paddock & Stone (Miller firm).

* * *

On his Federal income tax return for 1973, the petitioner deducted the expenses he incurred while attending NYU as an employee business expense. In his notice of deficiency, the Commissioner disallowed the deduction on the ground that such expenses were not ordinary and necessary expenses paid or incurred in connection with any trade or business. * * *

Opinion

The first issue for decision is whether the petitioner may deduct as an ordinary and necessary expense incurred in his trade or business the expense for tuition, books, meals, lodging, and other miscellaneous items paid by him while he obtained his masters degree in taxation.

The petitioner contends that for more than 10 years prior to 1973, he was in a trade or business of "rendering his services to employers for compensation." He contends that he was engaged in the trade or business of "analyzing and solving legal problems for compensation" while he worked on the law review at Wayne State, while he worked for the Warner firm, and later while he worked for the Miller firm. He maintains that the graduate courses in taxation helped maintain and improve his skills in that work. On the other hand, the Commissioner takes the position that the petitioner never began the practice of law until the summer of 1973 and that his attendance at NYU was merely the completion of his program of education preparatory to the practice of law. * * *

Section 162(a) allows a deduction for all the ordinary and necessary expenses of carrying on a trade or business, including amounts expended for education. Deductible educational expenses under section 162(a) may include expenditures for tuition and books as well as amounts for travel and meals and lodging while the taxpayer is away from home. (Sec. 1.162–5(e)(1), Income Tax Regs.) Section 1.162–5(a)(1), Income Tax Regs., expressly allows a deduction for those educational expenditures which maintain or improve skills "required by the individual in his employment or other trade or business." Whether education maintains or improves skills required by the taxpayer in his trade or business is a question of fact (Baker v. Commissioner, 51 T.C. 243, 247 (1968)). * * * Moreover, the taxpayer must be established in the trade or business at the time he incurs an educational expense to be able to deduct such expense under section 162. See Jungreis v. Commissioner, 55 T.C. 581, 588 (1970).

The petitioner artfully attempts to characterize his trade or business as "analyzing and solving legal problems for compensation," and he received compensation for the performance of such services.

Nevertheless, it is clear that the petitioner's intended trade or business at the time he attended NYU was that of an attorney, with an emphasis on the law of taxation. We observe that he enrolled in the masters in taxation program at NYU directly from law school, and there was thus an uninterrupted continuity in his legal education. * * * Although the work the petitioner performed before his graduation from law school and NYU was admittedly of a legal nature, such work in no way constituted his being engaged in the practice of law. Before his admission to the bar in May of 1973, he was not authorized to practice law as an attorney. Therefore, his expenses at NYU were not incident to the trade or business of practicing law, and thus, he was not maintaining or improving the skills of that profession within the purview of section 1.162–5(a)(1), Income Tax Regs. See, e.g., Fielding v. Commissioner, 57 T.C. 761 (1972) (medical school graduate was denied a business expense deduction for tuition cost of his residency since expenses were not incident to any profession that he previously practiced); Horodysky v. Commissioner, 54 T.C. 490 (1970) (taxpayer who had been a lawyer in Poland was denied a business expense deduction for cost of obtaining an American law school degree since he had no previous employment as a lawyer in this country).

Moreover, although the petitioner completed the requirements for admission to the bar in 1972, he was not formally admitted until May of 1973, and until that time, he could not engage in the practice of law. It is a well-established principle that being a member in good standing of a profession is not tantamount to *carrying on* that profession for the purpose of section 162(a). Ford v. Commissioner, 56 T.C. 1300, 1304 (1971), affd. per curiam 487 F.2d 1025 (9th Cir.1973) * * *.

Because the petitioner had not practiced law as an attorney before his attendance at NYU, his situation is not analogous to that of other professionals who have been allowed educational expense deductions under section 162(a). In such cases, the taxpayer was already firmly established in his profession and was truly taking courses or attending a seminar for the purpose of maintaining or improving the skills of his profession. See Coughlin v. Commissioner, 203 F.2d 307 (2d Cir.1953), revg. and remanding 18 T.C. 528 (1952) (attorney allowed business deduction for expenses incurred in attending NYU Tax Institute seminar); Bistline v. United States, 145 F.Supp. 802 (D.Idaho 1956), affd. per curiam on another issue 260 F.2d 80 (9th Cir.1958) (attorney allowed a business deduction for expenses incurred in attending 2-week course in Federal taxation at the Practicing Law Institute); Watson v. Commissioner, 31 T.C. 1014 (1959) (doctor specializing in internal medicine allowed deduction under earlier regulations for courses in psychiatry since such courses helped him to better understand psychosomatic illnesses); * * * see also sec. 1.162–5(c), Income Tax Regs.

In addition, the petitioner is also denied a deduction for his expenses at NYU by section 1.162–5(b)(3), Income Tax Regs., which provides that educational expenses are not deductible if the education "is part of a program of study being pursued by him which will lead to qualifying him in a new trade or business." The petitioner's attendance at NYU was part of his "program of study" of becoming a lawyer, a trade or business in which he was not previously engaged before his attendance there. After his admission to the bar in May of 1973 and his completion of the program at NYU, he was authorized to and began the practice of law, a wholly different trade or business from any in which he had been previously engaged. * * *

* * *

Conclusion + Holding →

Accordingly, we hold that the petitioner's expenses in obtaining a masters of law degree in taxation are not deductible as an ordinary and necessary business expense since he was not engaged in the trade or business of being an attorney at the time such expenses were incurred and since, therefore, he was not maintaining or improving the skills of such trade or business. Such expenses are nondeductible personal expenses. (Sec. 262.) Therefore, it is unnecessary to consider the Commissioner's alternative argument that the petitioner's expenses for travel and meals and lodging are not deductible since he was not "away from home" while attending NYU.

* * *

[The court also held that the expenses were not deductible under § 212(3).]

DETAILED ANALYSIS

1.   EDUCATION EXPENSES

1.1. *Existence of a Trade or Business*

As *Wassenaar* illustrates, the taxpayer must be engaged in a trade or business at the time the expenses are incurred in order for educational expenses to be deductible. Contrast Ruehmann v. Commissioner, T.C. Memo. 1971–157, which allowed a deduction for the expenses of obtaining a Master of Law degree where the taxpayer was admitted to the bar and employed as a lawyer in the period June–September following his graduation from law school. But in Link v. Commissioner, 90 T.C. 460 (1988), aff'd by order, 869 F.2d 1491 (6th Cir.1989), the Tax Court confined *Ruehmann* to its particular facts and denied the deduction. The taxpayer in *Link* graduated from college in June with a bachelor's degree in operations research and commenced a fulltime job as a market research analyst. He quit work in September to pursue an MBA degree on a fulltime basis. On these facts, the taxpayer had not established a trade or business before seeking the MBA degree.

Even if the taxpayer has at one time been in a trade or business, that trade or business can be "lost" if it is not actively pursued for some period of time. In Furner v. Commissioner, 393 F.2d 292 (7th Cir.1968), a junior high school teacher resigned in order to spend a year doing graduate work. She obtained her masters degree and returned to teaching. The court allowed the deduction over the IRS's contention that the taxpayer was not on leave and hence was not engaged in a trade or business. The IRS will follow *Furner* where the suspension of active employment is temporary, generally for one year or less. Rev. Rul. 68–591, 1968–2 C.B. 73. An example of a situation not meeting this one-year rule was presented in Wyatt v. Commissioner, 56 T.C. 517 (1971), where a deduction was disallowed to a former teacher, employed as a secretary from 1963–1967, for expenses of graduate education preparatory to the resumption of employment as a teacher in 1967. The deduction also will not be allowed if the hiatus is "indefinite." Thus, in Rev. Rul. 77–32, 1977–1 C.B. 38, an anesthesiologist who suspended his practice indefinitely because of high medical insurance premium costs was denied a deduction for the costs of attending meetings and other educational events during the self-imposed cessation.

1.2. *Maintain or Improve Skills*

Expenses to attend a professional continuing educational course are the prototypical education expenses meeting the maintenance or improvement of skills test. Treas. Reg. § 1.162–5(c)(1). See Coughlin v. Commissioner, 203 F.2d 307 (2d Cir.1953) (lawyer's cost of attending NYU Institute on Federal Taxation). Education that improves skills required by current employment also can be deducted. Beatty v. Commissioner, T.C. Memo. 1980–196, allowed an aeronautical engineer to deduct the cost of an MBA program because his duties required management skills. Nevertheless, a factual issue may arise regarding the relevance of the course to the taxpayer's job responsibilities. The test is whether the course of study is "appropriate, helpful, or needed." See Rev. Rul. 60–97, 1960–1 C.B. 69, declared obsolete by Rev. Rul. 72–619, 1972–2 C.B. 650.

In Takahashi v. Commissioner, 87 T.C. 126 (1986), the taxpayers were high school science teachers in Los Angeles. In order to be promoted and receive raises, they were required to take courses in "multicultural studies." The taxpayers took a ten-day trip to Hawaii, and on nine of the ten days attended a seminar program, lasting between one and six hours, on Polynesian culture. They deducted all of their expenses, claiming that the seminars "enabled them to better understand their minority students [and] maintained or improved skills required by them to teach science to minority students." The court denied the deduction, finding that attending the particular seminar neither improved their skills as science teachers nor was required by their employer. To be deductible, the court stated, the taxpayer "must demonstrate a connection between the course of the study and his particular job skills." The Hawaiian culture course was "simply not sufficiently germane to the teaching of science to bring the course within the category of expenditures for education which maintains or improves skills required by the individual in his employment."

Occasionally, expenses for an activity not normally considered to be education may qualify. Iglesias v. Commissioner, 76 T.C. 1060 (1981) (Acq.), allowed a hospital resident physician in psychiatry to deduct the cost of his own psychoanalysis because it maintained or improved skills required in his treatment of psychiatric patients. Meanwhile, Voigt v. Commissioner, 74 T.C. 82 (1980) (Nonacq.), allowed a clinical social worker to deduct psychoanalysis expenses because it improved diagnostic and treatment skills.

1.3. *Minimum Education Requirements*

Expenses incurred in meeting the minimum educational requirements for the taxpayer's trade or business are nondeductible even if the taxpayer has begun employment. This limitation appears to apply primarily to teachers who are provisionally hired on the condition that they obtain a requisite college degree (either undergraduate or advanced) within a relatively brief period in order to retain their position. See Treas. Reg. § 1.162–5(b)(2). In Jungreis v. Commissioner, 55 T.C. 581 (1970), the taxpayer was denied a deduction for the costs of obtaining a Ph.D. degree while he was working as a graduate teaching assistant at a university. Since he could not become a regular faculty member without a Ph.D. degree, the minimum educational requirement was not met. On the other hand, in Toner v. Commissioner, 623 F.2d 315 (3d Cir.1980), the taxpayer who had only a high school diploma was hired by a parochial elementary school. The school required only a high school diploma for its teachers although teachers without a bachelor's degree were required to agree to take courses to obtain that degree. After initial appointment, the teachers without bachelor's degrees were treated in all respects as full members of the faculty. The court allowed a deduction for the costs of the courses taken to obtain the bachelor's degree since the taxpayer already met the minimum educational requirements for an initial faculty appointment.

1.4. *Qualifying for a New Trade or Business*

If the education qualifies the taxpayer for a new trade or business, Treas. Reg. § 1.165–5(b)(3) disallows a deduction for the expenses even though the education is in fact related to the taxpayer's existing trade or business and the taxpayer has no intention of pursuing the new trade or business. Thompson v. Commissioner, T.C. Memo. 2007–174, held that an aeronautical engineer could not deduct flight school expenses leading to a commercial pilot's license, even though the taxpayer did not thereafter become a commercial pilot. Although commercial pilot training improved his engineering skills, the education qualified him for a new trade or business as a pilot. Treas. Reg. § 1.162–5(b)(3)(iii), Ex. (2), treats educational expenses that qualify the taxpayer for a new trade or business as nondeductible, even if the individual does not engage in the new activity. The mere capacity to engage in a new trade or business is sufficient to disqualify the expenses for the deduction.

The regulations eliminate some of the classification problems that might otherwise arise by treating all teaching and related duties as part of the same trade or business. Thus, the change from classroom teaching to school administration does not constitute entering a new trade or business. Treas. Reg. § 1.162–5(b)(3)(i). But in Diaz v. Commissioner, 70 T.C. 1067 (1978), aff'd by order, 607 F.2d 995 (2d Cir.1979), a paraprofessional teaching assistant was not a "teacher" and thus did not come within the rule that all teaching and related duties are the same trade or business. The costs of obtaining a Bachelor of Arts degree therefore were not deductible.

Allemeier v. Commissioner, T.C. Memo. 2005–207, allowed an orthodontic appliance salesman who was promoted to a management position after starting an MBA program to deduct the cost of pursuing the MBA, because the education merely improved pre-existing skills. The MBA was not a "minimum requirement" because the taxpayer's promotion was not contingent on beginning or completing the MBA program. Nor did the MBA qualify the taxpayer for a new trade or business, because the basic nature of the taxpayer's work activities did not change as a result of obtaining the additional education, even though the taxpayer was awarded new titles and positions and advanced more rapidly than he would have had he not pursued the MBA.

Much of the litigation in this area has involved the costs of obtaining a law degree, with taxpayers suffering repeated losses. In O'Donnell v. Commissioner, 62 T.C. 781 (1974), aff'd by order, 519 F.2d 1406 (7th Cir.1975), a certified public accountant was not allowed a deduction for the costs of attending law school at night. The taxpayer argued that he was already in the trade or business of being in the "tax accounting profession" to which both lawyers and accountants belong and, as a result, the law degree merely maintained and improved his skills. The court rejected the argument, pointing out that as an attorney the taxpayer would be free to establish himself in any area of the practice of law and hence a new trade or business was involved. Vetrick v. Commissioner, 628 F.2d 885 (5th Cir.1980), denied a deduction for law school costs of an attorney who was qualified to practice in the federal courts and in one state before going to law school; the law degree enabled him to sit for the bar exam in other states and hence qualified him for "substantially different tasks and activities."

Glenn v. Commissioner, 62 T.C. 270 (1974), disallowed the deduction for expenses incurred by a public accountant in taking a review course to qualify him for the Certified Public Accountant examination required of all candidates for a CPA license. The court stated that the test for determining when the acquisition of "new titles or abilities constitutes the entry into a new trade or business" for purposes of the education expense regulations requires "that a comparison be made between the types of tasks and activities which the taxpayer was qualified to perform before the acquisition of a particular title or degree, and those which he is qualified to perform afterwards." Since the differences in potential scope of practice between a public accountant and a CPA were significant, the taxpayer's expenses were disallowed as incurred in attempting to qualify for a new trade or business.

As to other occupations, see Johnson v. Commissioner, 77 T.C. 876 (1981) (real estate broker held to be a different trade or business from real estate agent and expenses to qualify as broker were not deductible); Burnstein v. Commissioner, 66 T.C. 492 (1976) (teacher of learning-disabled children denied deduction for costs of obtaining a master's degree in social work since the degree qualified her for a new trade or business); Reisinger v. Commissioner, 71 T.C. 568 (1979) ("physician's assistant" a different trade or business from licensed practical nurse); Robinson v. Commissioner, 78 T.C. 550 (1982) ("registered nurse" was a new trade or business for a licensed practical nurse). Compare Rev. Rul. 74–78, 1974–1 C.B. 44 (deduction allowed for expenses in training in orthodontics by a dentist engaged in general practice).

1.5. *Travel as Education*

Prior to 1987 the cost of trips simply to visit foreign countries sometimes was treated as a deductible education expense on the ground that the travel was itself "a form of education." See Treas. Reg. § 1.162–5(d). Because this situation presented excessive opportunity for abuse, Congress foreclosed deducting foreign travel itself as education by enacting § 274(m)(2). Nevertheless, travel expenses (transportation, meals, and lodging) incurred primarily to attend a course of study that qualifies as deductible education under the regulations remain deductible. Treas. Reg. § 1.162–5(e).

1.6. *Capitalization of Educational Expenses*

In Denman v. Commissioner, 48 T.C. 439 (1967) (Acq.), the taxpayer attempted to capitalize the total estimated cost of the expenses he incurred in obtaining an engineering degree. He claimed a useful life for the degree by utilizing a retirement age of 65. On this basis, the taxpayer claimed a deduction for amortization of the costs of the degree for the years in question. The Tax Court held that the degree did not constitute property within § 167, but instead constituted a nondeductible personal expense. Thus, if a taxpayer is not able to obtain a deduction under Treas. Reg. § 1.162–5, there is never any cost recovery of the education expenses for tax purposes.

Sharon v. Commissioner, 66 T.C. 515 (1976), aff'd per curiam, 591 F.2d 1273 (9th Cir.1978), followed *Denman* in denying the taxpayer's attempt to capitalize and amortize his college and law school expenses. With respect to the cost of gaining admission to the State bar, the court similarly disallowed a deduction of $230 paid for a bar review course on the ground that this was a nondeductible educational expense. The court did permit the other expenses of obtaining a license to practice law in California to be amortized over the taxpayer's life expectancy.[1] The taxpayer's testimony that he would retire at age 65 if he were financially able to do so was not sufficient to establish a shorter useful life for the amortization. The taxpayer was similarly allowed to amortize the cost of admission to the Supreme Court bar over his life expectancy.

Duecaster v. Commissioner, T.C. Memo. 1990–518, held that the cost of a legal education was not amortizable under § 195 (see Chapter 13, Section 3).

1.7. *Educational Assistance Fringe Benefits*

If the cost of education is funded by the taxpayer's employer through an educational assistance program under § 127 (see Chapter 3, Section 3.B.3.1.), the taxpayer-employee realizes no gross income even if the cost of the education would not have been deductible under Treas. Reg. § 1.162–5 if the employee had borne the cost. Section 127 is broad enough to permit the exclusion of law school tuition paid for the benefit of an employee. The rules

---

[1]   Treas. Regs. §§ 1.263(a)–4(d)(5) and 1.167(a)–3(b) specifically require capitalization and amortization over fifteen years of fees paid to the state for bar admission, but do not clearly address bar review course expenses.

of Treas. Reg. § 1.162–5, and § 127 play very different roles. The regulations seek to resolve difficult structural problems involved in classifying an expenditure as personal or profit-seeking. Section 127 is a tax expenditure that helps subsidize the cost of education, whether personal or business, for qualifying employees. Whether that policy is wise or unwise is open to debate, but unrelated to resolution of the issues in Treas. Reg. § 1.162–5.

1.8. *Deduction for "Qualified Tuition"*

Section 222 provides a special deduction for qualified tuition and related expenses, subject to ceilings based on the taxpayer's adjusted gross income. This provision operates independently of the rules of Treas. Reg. § 1.162–5, and was intended primarily to provide a deduction for parents who pay college tuition for their dependent children. Nevertheless, deductions under § 222 are available to all taxpayers whose income is under the ceiling. Section 222 is discussed in Chapter 23.

1.9. *Policy Aspects of the Treatment of Educational Expenditures*

The tax treatment of certain educational expenditures requires two distinct levels of analysis. First, a rule must be developed to distinguish between profit-seeking and personal aspects. Second, with respect to the profit-seeking aspects, currently deductible expenses must be separated from capital expenditures. The current regulations address the profit-seeking-personal question by generally focusing on whether the educational expenses maintain or improve skills required in the taxpayer's trade or business. Here the question turns on the relationship between the educational expense and the particular taxpayer's profit-seeking activities. Thus, a course in French literature may be a deductible expense for a teacher of foreign languages but not for a tax attorney. As to profit-seeking expenditures, the distinction between currently deductible expenditures and capital expenditures is addressed by disallowing a deduction where the expenses are part of the initial qualification for business activity. But unlike capital expenditures involving physical assets and many intangible assets, there is no mechanism under current law that allows for the recovery of these costs. The costs may not be amortized over their useful life and no deduction is allowed when skills acquired with the educational expenses are "disposed of" or become worthless at death. The taxpayer whose income is generated by professional activities is thus taxed on more than her economic income over her lifetime. While the cost of most other investments is ultimately recovered for tax purposes (through depreciation deductions, as an offset to sales proceeds, or through a loss deduction on disposition), a similar investment in "human capital" generally is not recovered.

There are conflicting views on whether an income tax should provide a capital cost recovery system for appropriate educational expenses. Difficult questions must be addressed in resolving the issue. What types of education should qualify? Post-graduate professional education? College degree? High school? Vocational? Should the deduction be limited to earned income or should it be available against all income that the taxpayer ultimately generates? Over what period should the capitalized educational expenditures be recovered? What should be the relation between the treatment of scholarships and fellowships and the amortization of educational expenses?

In addition, the preceding questions focus on the proper treatment of educational expenditures under an *income* tax. A number of provisions enacted in the last 15 to 20 years provide new and expanded tax expenditures for the cost of education, which are discussed in Chapter 23.

2.   EXPENSES OF SEEKING EMPLOYMENT

Treas. Reg. § 1.212–1(f) provides that expenses "incurred in seeking employment or in placing oneself in a position to begin rendering services for compensation" are not deductible. Consistently, in McDonald v. Commissioner, 323 U.S. 57 (1944), the Supreme Court held that a state judge could not deduct campaign expenses in seeking reelection because they "were not expenses incurred in being a judge but in trying to be a judge for the next ten years."

This "reelection principle" does not apply to ordinary employees. The IRS has adopted the position that an individual may deduct expenses involved in searching for employment if the taxpayer is already established in the same trade or business in which the employment is being sought. If the individual is seeking employment for the first time, or if there is a "lack of continuity" between the time of past employment and the efforts to obtain new employment, the IRS disallows the deductions. Rev. Rul. 75–120, 1975–1 C.B. 55. Under the approach taken in Rev. Rul. 75–120, the employee need not succeed in securing the new employment, a position that departed from the IRS's prior distinction between expenses of an employee *securing* new employment (deductible) and expenses of unsuccessfully *seeking* new employment (nondeductible). The Tax Court has rejected this distinction. See e.g., Cremona v. Commissioner, 58 T.C. 219 (1972) (Acq.). Currently, the determinative issue is whether the taxpayer is seeking employment in the same trade or business. See e.g., McKinley v. Commissioner, T.C. Memo. 1978–428 (electrical construction worker allowed deduction for costs of driving 17,400 miles to various union halls seeking jobs; although currently unemployed, petitioner was still engaged in the electrical construction trade); Rev. Rul. 77–16, 1977–1 C.B. 37 (traveling expenses incurred by a corporate executive while interviewing for a new position were deductible; the taxpayer was seeking new employment in the same trade or business of being a corporate executive); and Rev. Rul. 78–93, 1978–1 C.B. 38 (an attorney who was a part-time law school instructor secured a full-time teaching position; deduction of expenses for career counseling was allowed since the taxpayer was not changing his trade or business by seeking a full-time teaching position).

Whether there exists the requisite "continuity" in the taxpayer's conduct of the taxpayer's trade or business is determined under the same standards applied in *Furner* and Rev. Rul. 68–591 (see Section 2.1.1. of this Chapter), and involves whether the taxpayer has abandoned the taxpayer's trade or business due to a hiatus between jobs to obtain an education.

In Estate of Rockefeller v. Commissioner, 762 F.2d 264 (2d Cir.1985), a deduction was disallowed for expenses incurred by Nelson Rockefeller in connection with his confirmation by Congress as Vice President. The estate of Mr. Rockefeller argued that he was in the business of being "a government executive" and that the expenses were incurred in connection with seeking employment in that trade or business. The court, relying on cases involving educational expenses, found that the various public positions which Mr. Rockefeller had held over his career did not represent the continuation of the same trade or business. The Vice Presidency was a separate trade or business, distinguishable from other posts that Mr. Rockefeller had held, such as Governor of New York, and therefore the expenses were not deductible.

For the related situation where a taxpayer incurs expenses to investigate new business opportunities, see Chapter 12, Section 4.

PART V

DEDUCTIONS AND CREDITS FOR PERSONAL LIVING EXPENSES

CHAPTER 21

ITEMIZED PERSONAL DEDUCTIONS

SECTION 1. INTRODUCTION—THE ADJUSTED GROSS INCOME CONCEPT AND ITEMIZED DEDUCTIONS

INTERNAL REVENUE CODE: Sections 62(a), (d); 63(a), (d), (e)(1)–(2); 262.

Chapters 18 through 20 demonstrate the difference between deductible costs related to profit-seeking activities and the individual's personal, living, or family costs, which generally are not deductible and thus included in the tax base. Nonetheless personal costs play a role in determining an individual's tax liability. A certain portion of an individual's income always has been exempted from income taxation, although the amount and mechanics of determining the exemption have changed over the years. The current rules account for a multiplicity of factors in determining the exempt amount.

For individuals (but not for other taxpayers), computing taxable income involves a two-step process. First, the taxpayer subtracts from total gross income the total amount of deductions specified in § 62. Section 62 does not by itself allow any deductions; rather, it specifies which deductions allowed by other sections are taken into account in computing "adjusted gross income." These specified deductions generally account for the cost of earning income, but some of them reduce gross income for other policy-related reasons. The resulting amount of income after these deductions is termed "adjusted gross income" ("AGI").

The next step in deriving taxable income involves accounting for certain personal expenses. These deductions, termed "itemized deductions," are subtracted from AGI to determine taxable income under § 63. Although these itemized deductions for personal expenses are officially classified as tax expenditures (discussed in Chapter 11), one could argue that items such as the deduction for medical expenses, personal casualty losses, and state and local income taxes should be considered structural provisions of the income tax rather than governmental subsidies delivered through the tax system, because they generally represent involuntary expenses that reduce consumption and net worth. Furthermore, the deductions reflect the ability to pay federal income tax rather than tax subsidies that promote specific economic or social objectives. In some situations, the deductions relate to expenses that are always personal in nature, such as the deduction for home mortgage interest. In other situations, the deductions relate to expenses that could be incurred either in a profit-seeking or personal activity. For example, state and local income and property taxes are deductible under § 164 without regard to whether ownership of property reflects a profit-seeking activity or a personal activity.

A second way in which personal expenses affect tax liability is that a certain minimal level of such expenditures is exempted from tax through various statutory mechanisms. Taxpayers who do not itemize deductions may shield an amount of income from tax through the standard deduction under § 63(c), which taxpayers claim in lieu of itemized deductions. If the standard deduction exceeds the taxpayer's itemized personal deductions, the taxpayer will take the standard deduction rather than electing to itemize deductions.[1] In addition, every taxpayer is entitled to a "personal exemption" for the taxpayer personally, as well as additional exemptions for dependents, such as minor children. Thus, a married couple with two children filing a joint return would receive four personal exemptions: two for the taxpaying spouses and two for the children. In this fashion, the concept of ability-to-pay is adjusted for family size.

Finally, personal costs also affect tax liability through personal income tax credits targeted to certain taxpayers.

This chapter examines the itemized deductions allowed for certain personal living expenses. The next chapter examines the standard deduction, personal exemptions, and personal credits.

DETAILED ANALYSIS

1. DEDUCTIONS ALLOWABLE IN COMPUTING ADJUSTED GROSS INCOME

1.1. *In General*

Section 62 specifies which deductions allowed by other sections are taken into account in computing adjusted gross income. All remaining deductions—the "itemized deductions"—are taken into account in computing taxable income under § 63. In general, the deductions taken into account in computing adjusted gross income are those incurred in profit-seeking activities, while the itemized deductions are those reflecting personal living expenses. However, § 62 lists some deductions that are not related to profit seeking, such as the deduction for alimony paid (discussed at Chapter 38, Section 3.B.). Meanwhile, § 212 expenses related to the production of income and unreimbursed employee business expenses, which clearly are profit-seeking expenses, are not specified as deductible in computing adjusted gross income, except for § 212 expenses incurred in connection with rents and royalty income. Most § 212 expenses and unreimbursed employee business expenses are taken into account only as itemized deductions under § 63. Thus, the standard deduction serves as an alternative to itemized deductions

---

[1]   The adjusted gross income concept was enacted at the same time as the standard deduction. The purpose of the adjusted gross income concept is to distinguish those deductions that are allowed in all events from those deductions allowable only if the taxpayer itemizes deductions instead of claiming the standard deduction.

for certain profit-seeking expenses as well as for itemized personal deductions. As a result, if the taxpayer's itemized deductions do not exceed the standard deduction, these costs of producing income are not taken into account in reducing gross income to taxable income. The standard deduction in effect serves as a floor for deductions for these profit-seeking expenses. The legislative history of the various tax acts that have shaped the provisions dealing with categorizing deductions offers no principled policy reason for treating certain profit-seeking expenses as itemized deductions.

1.2. *Reimbursed Employee Business Expenses*

Expenses incurred by an employee in the trade or business of being an employee are deductible under § 162 (see Chapter 12). But unlike most other § 162 deductions, employee business deductions are not always deductible in computing adjusted gross income. Section 62(a)(2)(A) generally allows employee business expenses that are deductible under § 162 to be deducted in computing adjusted gross income only when the expenses have been reimbursed by the employer. All other employee business expenses, with the exception of those listed in § 62(a)(2)(B) through (D) for certain limited professions, are deductible only as itemized deductions. Section 62(c) imposes rules that limit the applicability of § 62(a)(2)(A) to instances in which the employee provides the employer detailed substantiation of the expenses.

SECTION 2.   MEDICAL EXPENSES

INTERNAL REVENUE CODE: Section 213.

REGULATIONS: Section 1.213–1(e)(1), (2).

Section 213 allows an itemized deduction for certain uncompensated medical expenses of an individual, spouse, or dependent. When enacted in 1942, the deduction was limited to medical expenses exceeding 5 percent of adjusted gross income. The floor has varied over the years. Currently, the deduction for medical expenses (including prescriptions and qualifying medical and long-term care insurance) is limited to the amount in excess of 10 percent of the taxpayer's adjusted gross income. In general, the restrictions on the deduction are due to congressional concern that the deduction for medical expenses was "creating an incentive for further health care spending and exacerbating the problem of rising medical expenditures." S.Rep. No. 494, Cong., 2d Sess., vol. 1, 113 (1982).

Deductible medical expenses must be distinguished from other nondeductible consumption expenditures. Rules to deal with expenditures that have both a medical and a normal consumption component also are necessary. Thus, the medical expense deduction raises issues similar to those presented by expenditures having both personal and profit-seeking elements.

Revenue Ruling 99–28
1999–1 C.B. 1269.

ISSUE

Are uncompensated amounts paid by taxpayers for participation in a smoking-cessation program, for prescribed drugs designed to alleviate nicotine withdrawal, and for nicotine gum and nicotine patches that do not require a prescription, expenses for medical care that are deductible under § 213 of the Internal Revenue Code?

FACTS

Taxpayers A and B were cigarette smokers. A participated in a smoking-cessation program and purchased nicotine gum and nicotine patches that did not require a prescription. A had not been diagnosed as having any specific disease, and participation in the program was not suggested by a physician. B purchased drugs that required a prescription of a physician to alleviate the effects of nicotine withdrawal. A's and B's costs were not compensated for by insurance or otherwise.

LAW AND ANALYSIS

Section 213(a) allows a deduction for uncompensated expenses for medical care of an individual, the individual's spouse or a dependent to the extent the expenses exceed [10] percent of adjusted gross income. Section 213(d)(1) provides, in part, that medical care means amounts paid for the diagnosis, cure, mitigation, treatment, or prevention of disease, or for the purpose of affecting any structure or function of the body.

Under § 213(b), a deduction is allowed for amounts paid during the taxable year for medicine or a drug only if the medicine or drug is a prescribed drug or insulin. Section 213(d)(3) defines a "prescribed drug" as a drug or biological that requires a prescription of a physician for its use by an individual.

Section 1.213–1(e)(1)(ii) of the Income Tax Regulations provides, in part, that the deduction for medical care expenses will be confined strictly to expenses incurred primarily for the prevention or alleviation of a physical or mental defect or illness. An expense that is merely beneficial to the general health of an individual is not an expense for medical care.

Section 262 provides that, except as otherwise expressly provided by the Code, no deduction is allowed for personal, living, or family expenses.

Rev. Rul. 79–162, 1979–1 C.B. 116, holds that a taxpayer who has no specific ailment or disease may not deduct as a medical expense under § 213 the cost of participating in a smoking-cessation program. However, the IRS has held that treatment for addiction to certain substances qualifies as medical care under § 213. See Rev. Rul. 73–325, 1973–2 C.B. 75 (alcoholism); Rev. Rul. 72–226, 1972–1 C.B. 96 (drug addiction).

A report of the Surgeon General, The Health Consequences of Smoking: Nicotine Addiction (1988), states that scientists in the field of drug addiction agree that nicotine, a substance common to all forms of tobacco, is a powerfully addictive drug. Other reports of the Surgeon General have concluded, based on numerous studies, that a strong causal link exists between smoking and several diseases. See, e.g., Tobacco Use Among U.S. Racial/Ethnic Minority Groups (1998); Preventing Tobacco Use Among Young People (1994); The Health Benefits of Smoking Cessation (1990). Scientific evidence has thus established that nicotine is addictive and that smoking is detrimental to the health of the smoker.

Under the facts provided, the smoking-cessation program and the prescribed drugs are treatment for A's and B's addiction to nicotine. Accordingly, A's costs for the smoking-cessation program and B's costs for prescribed drugs to alleviate the effects of nicotine withdrawal are amounts paid for medical care under § 213(d)(1). However, under § 213(b), A's costs for nicotine gum and nicotine patches are not deductible because they contain a drug (other than insulin) and do not require a prescription of a physician.

HOLDING

Uncompensated amounts paid by taxpayers for participation in a smoking-cessation program and for prescribed drugs designed to alleviate nicotine withdrawal are expenses for medical care that are deductible under § 213, subject to the [10] percent limitation. However, amounts paid for drugs (other than insulin) not requiring a prescription, such as nicotine gum and certain nicotine patches, are not deductible under § 213.

EFFECT ON OTHER DOCUMENTS

Rev. Rul. 79–162 is revoked.

Revenue Ruling 2002–19
2002–1 C.B. 778.

ISSUE

Are uncompensated amounts paid by individuals for participation in a weight-loss program as treatment for a specific disease or ailment (including obesity) diagnosed by a physician and for diet food items expenses for medical care that are deductible under § 213 of the Internal Revenue Code?

FACTS

Taxpayer A is diagnosed by a physician as obese. A does not suffer from any other specific disease. Taxpayer B is not obese but suffers from hypertension. B has been directed by a physician to lose weight as treatment for the hypertension.

A and B participate in the X weight-loss program. A and B are required to pay an initial fee to join X and an additional fee to attend periodic meetings. At the meetings participants develop a diet plan, receive diet menus and literature, and discuss problems encountered in dieting. A and B also purchase X brand reduced-calorie diet food items. Neither A's nor B's costs are compensated by insurance or otherwise.

LAW

* * *

Rev. Rul. 79–151 (1979–1 C.B. 116) holds that a taxpayer who participates in a weight reduction program to improve the taxpayer's appearance, general health, and sense of well-being, and not to cure a specific ailment or disease, may not deduct the cost as a medical expense under § 213.

Rev. Rul. 55–261 (1955–1 C.B. 307) holds that medical care includes the cost of special food if (1) the food alleviates or treats an illness, (2) it is not part of the normal nutritional needs of the taxpayer, and (3) the need for the food is substantiated by a physician. However, special food that is a substitute for the food the taxpayer normally consumes and that satisfies the taxpayer's nutritional needs is not medical care.

ANALYSIS

Amounts paid for the primary purpose of treating a disease are deductible as medical care. Obesity is medically accepted to be a disease in its own right. The National Heart, Lung, and Blood Institute, part of the National Institutes of Health, describes obesity as a "complex, multifactorial chronic disease." Clinical Guidelines on the Identification, Evaluation, and Treatment of Overweight and Obesity in Adults (1998), page vii. This report is based on an evaluation by a panel of health professionals of scientific evidence published from 1980 to 1997.

Other government and scientific entities have reached similar conclusions. For example, in a preamble to final regulations the Food and Drug Administration states "obesity is a disease." 65 Fed. Reg. 1027, 1028 (Jan. 6, 2000). The World Health Organization states that "[o]besity is now well recognized as a disease in its own right. . . ." Press Release 46 (June 12, 1997).

In the present case, a physician has diagnosed A as suffering from a disease, obesity. Therefore, the cost of A's participation in the X weight-loss program as treatment for A's obesity is an amount paid for medical care under § 213(d)(1). Although B is not suffering from obesity, B's participation in X is part of the treatment for B's hypertension. Therefore, B's cost of participating in the program is also an amount paid for medical care. A and B may deduct under § 213 (subject to the limitations of that section) the fees to join the program and to attend periodic meetings. These situations are distinguishable from the facts of Rev. Rul. 79–151, in which the taxpayer was not suffering from any specific disease or ailment and participated in a weight-loss program merely to improve the taxpayer's general health and appearance. However, A and B may not deduct any portion of the cost of purchasing reduced-calorie diet foods because the foods are substitutes for the food A and B normally consume and satisfy their nutritional requirements.

HOLDING

Uncompensated amounts paid by individuals for participation in a weight-loss program as treatment for a specific disease or diseases (including obesity) diagnosed by a physician are expenses for medical care that are deductible under § 213, subject to the limitations of that section. The cost of purchasing diet food items is not deductible under § 213.

EFFECT ON OTHER DOCUMENTS

Rev. Rul. 79–151 and Rev. Rul. 55–261 are distinguished.

Detailed Analysis

1. DEFINITION OF MEDICAL EXPENSES

1.1. *General*

Section 213(d)(1)(A) defines "medical care" as including amounts paid "for the diagnosis, cure, mitigation, treatment, or prevention of disease, or for the purpose of affecting any structure or function of the body." Treas. Reg. § 1.213–1(e) provides examples of medical expenses that qualify as deductible "medical care," while court cases and IRS rulings have helped further define the statutory phrase. It is not necessary that medical expenses be incurred for the taxpayer's own benefit or for that of a dependent, as long as the expenditures relate to a qualified person. Rev. Rul. 73–189, 1973–1 C.B. 139, held that a kidney donor and a rejected prospective donor could deduct as medical expenses amounts paid for laboratory fees, hospitalization, and the actual donor's surgery, as well as transportation in connection with a kidney transplant operation for a third party.

The "medical care" standard under § 213(d) requires a causal relationship between an underlying medical condition or defect and the taxpayer's expenses. Moreover, the expenses must be incurred for the purpose of affecting a structure or function of the taxpayer's body. Magdalin v. Commissioner, T.C. Memo. 2008–293, denied a medical expense deduction for the costs incurred in fathering children through unrelated gestational carriers via in vitro fertilization of an anonymous donor's eggs using the taxpayer's sperm. According to the court, there was no causal relationship between an underlying medical condition or defect because taxpayer's sperm count and motility were found to be within normal limits, and the expenses at issue were not incurred to affect a structure or function of the taxpayer's body.

Deductible medical expenses can include amounts paid to persons other than licensed physicians and health care professionals or hospitals. Rev. Rul. 55–261, 1955–1 C.B. 307, allowed a deduction for costs of treatment by a

Christian Science practitioner; Rev. Rul. 72–593, 1972–2 C.B. 180, allowed a deduction for acupuncture; and Tso v. Commissioner, T.C. Memo. 1980–399, allowed a deduction for the cost of traditional Navajo "sings." On the other hand, Ring v. Commissioner, 23 T.C. 950 (1955), denied deduction for a trip for spiritual aid to a shrine at which the performance of miracles in the cure of physical ailments had been officially recognized by church authorities. There was no medical advice at the shrine or medical recommendation for the trip being involved. Likewise, Brown v. Commissioner, 62 T.C. 551 (1974), aff'd per curiam, 523 F.2d 365 (8th Cir.1975), held that Scientology "auditing" (i.e., counseling through which "a person is enabled to see the truth about himself") is not in the nature of psychotherapy, especially in light of the Church of Scientology's specific disclaimer of its "ability or intent to heal ailments of the body or the mind." Thus, such treatments did not qualify under § 213.

On the other hand, the fact that expenses are incurred based on a doctor's recommendation does not automatically qualify them as deductible medical expenses. In Thoene v. Commissioner, 33 T.C. 62 (1959), doctors recommended dancing lessons for a taxpayer who had undergone both an abdominal operation and psychiatric treatment. The court denied the deduction:

> The fact that dancing was included in the list of activities, along with table tennis, recommended by the medical doctor, and included in the list of activities, along with community activities and church work, which the psychiatrist felt would be beneficial, does not mean the dance lessons can be characterized as medical care. Actually, what the doctors were recommending were purely personal activities: postoperative mild exercise activity and engagement in social activity. The fact that petitioner secured both activities in the dancing studio does not mean the activities can be characterized as anything but personal in nature. The instructresses in the dance studio had no training in physical or psychiatric therapy. The fact that the dance lessons were beneficial to petitioner is not determinative of the issue. Conceivably the same benefits might have been derived from petitioner's taking up golf and participating in the social activity of a country club but it could hardly be argued the expenditures therefor would be deductible as medical care.

As noted above, "medical care" under § 213(d)(1)(A) also includes amounts paid "for the purpose of affecting any structure or function of the body." Thus a deduction is allowable for an abortion or vasectomy. Rev. Rul. 73–201, 1973–1 C.B. 140. The fact that the taxpayer undergoes a procedure on the taxpayer's own initiative rather than on the advice of a physician is not relevant. This otherwise broad aspect of the definition of medical care is limited by § 213(d)(9), which denies any deduction for cosmetic surgery or similar procedure unless necessary to ameliorate a congenital deformity or one arising from a personal injury or disfiguring disease. Thus, Rev. Rul. 2003–57, 2003–1 C.B. 959, held that expenses incurred for breast reconstruction surgery following a mastectomy and laser eye surgery to correct myopia are deductible medical expenses. The expenses ameliorate a deformity that relates to a disease or corrects a dysfunction of the body. Expenses incurred for teeth whitening are not deductible, however, because the procedure merely improves a person's appearance rather than treats a physical or mental disease. In O'Donnabhain v. Commissioner, 134 T.C. 34 (2010), the Tax Court held that the costs of hormone therapy and male-to-female sex reassignment surgery to treat gender identity disorder—a condition recognized in medical reference texts—were deductible as medical expenses, reasoning that the procedure was not "cosmetic surgery" as defined by the statute. However, the cost of breast augmentation was not deductible, because it constituted cosmetic surgery whose only purpose was to alter the taxpayer's appearance.

Disabled taxpayers have been allowed to deduct as medical expenses the cost of special items and equipment needed even when these are ordinarily used for personal and family purposes. The amount of the deduction for medical care is "the excess of the cost of the special form over the normal cost of the item." See Rev. Rul. 75–318, 1975–2 C.B. 88 (Braille books and magazines for taxpayer's blind child); Rev. Rul. 80–340, 1980–2 C.B. 81 (special audio-display equipment which prints subtitles on television screen for deaf person); Randolph v. Commissioner, 67 T.C. 481 (1976) (organic foods required to prevent taxpayer's allergic reaction to chemically treated foods). But see Rev. Rul. 76–80, 1976–1 C.B. 71, which disallowed the cost of a vacuum cleaner purchased by a taxpayer allergic to dust, because it was not "readily apparent" that a vacuum cleaner prevents or alleviates any disease or disability.

Several cases have involved whether expenses for special schools that deal with medical problems qualify as deductible medical expenses. In Greisdorf v. Commissioner, 54 T.C. 1684 (1970) (Acq.), the taxpayer's child had psychological problems and on the recommendation of a psychiatrist was placed in a special school that handled students with emotional problems of this type. The court found that the educational purpose of the school was only "incidental" to the medical care function and allowed the deduction for the tuition. On the other hand, if a school does not qualify as a "special school," a deduction generally will be disallowed. Nevertheless, in Fay v. Commissioner, 76 T.C. 408 (1981), the court allowed a medical expense deduction for the additional tuition for the taxpayer's two learning disabled children paid to a Montessori school for a special program to remedy learning disabilities. The court held that since the school was primarily a Montessori school and the learning disabilities program was merely supplemental, only the additional cost of the special program qualified as a medical expense.

In Ochs v. Commissioner, 195 F.2d 692 (2d Cir.1952), the taxpayers incurred expenses to send their children to boarding school after the wife had surgery for throat cancer. They had been advised by a "reputable physician . . . that if the children were not separated from [their mother] she would not improve and her nervousness and irritation might cause a recurrence of the cancer." The purpose of sending the children to boarding school was "to alleviate [the wife's] pain and suffering in caring for the children by reason of her inability to speak above a whisper and to prevent a recurrence of the cancer which was responsible for the condition of her voice." Even though the court found no reason to doubt the taxpayers' good faith in their decision to send the children to boarding school, it held that the boarding school costs were not deductible medical expenses:

> In our opinion the expenses incurred by the taxpayer were nondeductible family expenses within the meaning of [§ 262] rather than medical expenses. Concededly the line between the two is a difficult one to draw, but this only reflects the fact that expenditures made on behalf of some members of a family unit frequently benefit others in the family as well. The wife in this case had in the past contributed the services—caring for the children— for which the husband was required to pay because, owing to her illness, she could no longer care for them. If, for example, the husband had employed a governess for the children, or a cook, the wages he would have paid would not be deductible. Or, if the wife had died, and the children were sent to a boarding school, there would certainly be no basis for contending that such expenses were deductible. The examples given serve to illustrate that the expenses here were made necessary by the loss of the wife's services, and that the only reason for allowing them as a deduction is that the wife also received a benefit. We think it unlikely that Congress intended to transform family expenses into medical expenses for this reason.

1.2. *Food, Lodging, Transportation, and Other Incidental Expenses*

Treas. Reg. § 1.213–1(e)(1)(v) expressly treats the cost of in-patient hospital care, including meals and lodging, as a medical expense. In addition, § 213(d)(2) allows a deduction for lodging expenses incurred while away from home to obtain medical treatment from a licensed physician or in a hospital, subject to a limit of $50 a night. Urbauer v. Commissioner, T.C. Memo. 1992– 170, disallowed a deduction for parents' lodging expenses near their child's boarding school to enable them to participate in holistic drug rehabilitation therapy sessions because the treatment was not provided by a physician. Lodging expenses are not deductible under § 213(d)(2) if the taxpayer merely travels to a location of moderate climate to alleviate a chronic ailment and while there receives medical care that is only incidental to the primary purpose of the trip. Polyak v. Commissioner, 94 T.C. 337 (1990). This result is consistent with Commissioner v. Bilder, 369 U.S. 499 (1962), in which the Supreme Court held that the definition of "medical care" does not include meals and lodging incurred while away from home to convalesce in a salubrious climate. See also Treas. Reg. § 1.213–1(e)(1)(iv).

Section 213(d)(1)(B) expressly includes transportation expenses incurred primarily for and essential to medical care in the definition of medical expenses. Although § 213(d) does not embrace meals as medical expenses, some cases have allowed a deduction for meals, even though they were not provided in an institutional setting, on the ground that they were nonetheless necessary to obtain medical treatment. See Montgomery v. Commissioner, 428 F.2d 243 (6th Cir.1970) (meals while in transit between Kentucky and the Mayo Clinic in Minnesota were deductible as "transportation" under § 213(d)(1)(B)); Kelly v. Commissioner, 440 F.2d 307 (7th Cir.1971) (meals and lodging in hotel while convalescing from emergency surgery while away from home on business).

Some other incidental expenses incurred with respect to obtaining medical treatment may also qualify as "medical care." In Rev. Rul. 71–281, 1971–2 C.B. 165, the IRS indicated that it would follow Gerstacker v. Commissioner, 414 F.2d 448 (6th Cir.1969), allowing a deduction under § 213 for expenses incurred for legal services relating to a guardianship proceeding for the taxpayer's wife where compulsory confinement was a necessary part of the wife's treatment for mental problems. On the other hand, Jacobs v. Commissioner, 62 T.C. 813 (1974) denied deduction for legal expenses involved in a divorce that was recommended by the taxpayer's psychiatrist. The taxpayer failed to show that the expenses would not otherwise have been incurred for nonmedical reasons.

1.3. *Capital Expenditures*

The full cost of capital expenditures that otherwise qualify as medical expenses are eligible for deduction unless they represent permanent improvements which increase the value of the taxpayer's property. Rev. Rul. 59–411, 1959–2 C.B. 100. In Rev. Rul. 87–106, 1987–2 C.B. 67, the IRS promulgated an extensive, but nonexclusive, list of improvements for the primary purpose of accommodating a personal residence to the disabled condition of the taxpayer, the taxpayer's spouse, or the taxpayer's resident dependents that generally do not increase the value of the property. If the improvements do increase the value of property, the deduction is limited to the difference between the cost of improvement and the increase in value. Treas. Reg. § 1.213–1(e)(1)(iii). In Rev. Rul. 70–606, 1970–2 C.B. 66, a wheelchair-bound taxpayer was allowed a medical deduction for the amount by which the cost of a car specially designed for the taxpayer exceeded the cost of a comparable ordinary automobile. Rev. Rul. 83–33, 1983–1 C.B. 70, allowed a deduction for the cost of constructing a swimming pool, prescribed by a physician, to the extent the cost exceeded the amount by which the value of the home was increased. In Ferris v. Commissioner, 582 F.2d 1112 (7th Cir.1978), the taxpayer's doctor recommended the construction of a swimming pool in order that the taxpayer could swim as part of treatment for a spinal disorder. The taxpayer spent $172,160 on a pool and deducted one-half of that amount based on an appraisal that indicated that the value of the residence would increase by roughly one-half of the amount expended on the pool. The court found that a substantial amount of the expense was attributable to the "grand and luxurious style" in which the pool was constructed and remanded the case for a determination of the "minimal reasonable cost of a functionally adequate pool" and the impact which such a pool would have had on the value of the property.

1.4. *Medicine and Drugs*

Section 213(b) allows a medical expenses deduction for prescription drugs and insulin. To be deductible, medicine or drugs must be "legally procured." Treas. Reg. § 1.213–1(e)(2). Rev. Rul. 97–9, 1997–1 C.B. 77, held that the cost of marijuana purchased upon a physician's recommendation was not deductible under § 213, even though the taxpayer purchased and used the marijuana in a state in which the purchase and possession of marijuana for medicinal purposes were legal, because the purchase and possession were criminal under federal law. Rev. Rul. 2003–58, 2003–1 C.B. 959, distinguished expenses incurred for nonprescription drugs and expenses for other medical equipment. The taxpayer had injured his leg and purchased crutches to enhance his mobility and bandages to cover torn skin. On a doctor's recommendation, he also purchased aspirin to relieve pain. The cost of the aspirin was not deductible because it was a non-prescription drug, but the limitation in § 213(b) did not apply to the crutches and bandages.

2.   MEDICAL INSURANCE PREMIUMS

Although most taxpayers may deduct medical insurance premiums and qualified long-term care insurance premiums only as medical expenses subject to the limitations of § 213, a special rule applies to self-employed taxpayers. Section 162(*l*), allows self-employed individuals to deduct both medical insurance premiums and qualified long-term care insurance in computing adjusted gross income. The purpose of the special deduction under § 162(*l*) is to extend to self-employed taxpayers substantially the same benefit that owner-employees of small corporations obtain by excluding employer paid medical insurance premiums as a tax-free fringe benefit under § 105, and thus reduce the tax incentive to incorporate a business that would otherwise remain unincorporated.

3.   QUALIFIED LONG-TERM CARE SERVICES AND INSURANCE

Section 213(d)(1) includes "qualified long-term care services" as deductible medical expenses. Qualified long-term care services are defined in § 7702B(c) as necessary diagnostic, preventive, therapeutic, curing, treating, mitigating, and rehabilitative services, and maintenance or personal care services required by a "chronically ill individual" that are provided pursuant to a plan of care prescribed by a licensed health care professional. No deduction is allowed for long-term care expenses paid to certain relatives or businesses owned in whole or in part by the taxpayer or the taxpayer's relatives unless the service is performed by a relative who is a licensed health care professional. I.R.C. § 213(d)(11).

Section 213(d)(1)(D) allows a medical expense deduction for premiums paid for "qualified long-term care insurance," as defined in § 7702B(b). Such insurance provides qualified long-term care (defined in § 7702B(c)) that meets certain conditions, including lack of any cash surrender value. Amounts received under a qualified long-term care insurance contract are not includable in gross income to the extent that they do not exceed the greater of long-term care service expenses or $175 per day (adjusted for inflation; in 2016, the per diem limitation was $340). Long-term care expenses paid with excludable benefits are not deductible.

4.   PROBLEMS OF "COMPENSATION" AND TIMING

4.1. *Compensation*

The § 213 deduction is allowed only for expenses not compensated by insurance or otherwise and it is thus necessary to coordinate § 213 and §§ 104–106. Sections 104 and 105(b) limit tax-free receipt of medical insurance benefits to payments that are not "attributable to" deductions allowed under § 213 for any prior taxable year.

In Rev. Rul. 75–230, 1975–1 C.B. 93, the taxpayer received a lump-sum settlement for a personal injury suit. The payment was otherwise excludable from gross income under § 104(a)(2), but in prior tax years the taxpayer had deducted medical expenses attributable to the accident. The settlement agreement did not specifically allocate any portion to the taxpayer's medical expenses. The ruling held that in such situations the amounts received in settlement are attributable first to the prior medical expenses deducted and are thus includable in income to the extent of the previous deductions. If the parties in the settlement specifically allocate an amount to medical expenses, the IRS will accept the correctness of that allocation unless it is unreasonable in light of all the facts. See also Treas. Reg. § 1.213–1(g).

4.2. *Timing*

The 10 percent limitation encourages taxpayers to "bunch" medical expenses. The Tax Court has denied a deduction where the taxpayer made an advance payment for medical services to be rendered the following year, Bassett v. Commissioner, 26 T.C. 619 (1956). Presumably, making delayed rather than advance payments in cooperation with the doctor or hospital would not run afoul of the statute. Furthermore, the portion of a lump sum fee paid by the taxpayer to a retirement home for lifetime care that is attributable to medical care is deductible in the year it is paid. Rev. Rul. 75–302, 1975–2 C.B. 86, clarified by Rev. Rul. 93–72, 1993–2 C.B. 77. The ruling distinguished *Bassett* on the ground that the obligation to pay in advance was imposed by the institution undertaking the medical care. See also Estate of Smith v. Commissioner, 79 T.C. 313 (1982) (Acq.), which allowed a deduction for that part of the entrance fee to a retirement community allocable to the cost of providing residents free days of nursing care in its convalescent center.

When medical expenses are paid with borrowed funds, the "amount paid" is deductible when the taxpayer becomes indebted to the third party, not when the loan is actually repaid. See Rev. Rul. 78–39, 1978–1 C.B. 73 (expenses of hospital bill paid by bank credit card held deductible when taxpayer used credit card, not the following year when he repaid bank); Rev. Rul. 78–173, 1978–1 C.B. 73 (taxpayer's parents paid medical bill for which taxpayer issued them a promissory note; deduction allowed for the year in which parents paid the doctor, not the following year in which taxpayer repaid the parents).

5.   RELATIONSHIP OF SECTIONS 213 AND 162

In situations where disabled taxpayers require special services in connection with their work, it is necessary to distinguish among business, medical, and personal expenses. In Rev. Rul. 75–316, 1975–2 C.B. 54, the cost of the services of readers needed by a blind employee in connection with the taxpayer's work was deductible as a business expense and not as a medical expense. The ruling set forth the following test: "Where it is questionable whether an expense is deductible as a business expense rather than as a medical expense, such expense may be deducted as a business expense under § 162 of the Code if all three of the following elements are present: (1) the nature of the taxpayer's work clearly requires that he incur a particular expense to satisfactorily perform such work, (2) the goods or services purchased by such expense are clearly not required or used, other than incidentally, in the conduct of the individual's personal activities, and (3) the Code and regulations are otherwise silent as to the treatment of such expenses." Rev. Rul. 75–317, 1975–2 C.B. 57, held that amounts paid by a wheelchair-bound taxpayer for the travel, meals and lodging expenses of a neighbor who accompanied him on a business trip to assist him with his wheelchair, luggage, driving, daily removal and replacement of his prosthesis, and administration of medication were deductible as medical expenses and not as business expenses. These services were used by the taxpayer in his personal activities and only incidentally in his business activities.

6.   MEDICAL SAVINGS ACCOUNTS

Section 220 allows a current deduction for contributions by eligible individual taxpayers to an "Archer MSA," or a "medical savings account," named after a former chairman of the House Ways & Means Committee. If a taxpayer does not itemize deductions, the taxpayer may still deduct contributions to an MSA. I.R.C. § 62(a)(16). Only self-employed individuals and employees of certain "small employers" (see Chapter 3, Section 3.B.1.) covered under a "high deductible" medical insurance plan are eligible to make contributions to a qualified MSA. High deductible plans are plans (1) with an annual deductible of (a) not less than $1,500 or more than $2,250 for an individual or (b) not less than $3,000 or more than $4,500 for a family, and (2) with a maximum out-of-pocket expense requirement of not more than $3,000 for an individual and $5,500 for a family. These deductibles and thresholds are adjusted for inflation. In 2016, the deductible range was $2,250 to $3,350 for individuals and $4,450 to $6,700 for families. Meanwhile, the maximum out-of-pocket expense ceiling was $4,450 for individuals and $8,150 for families.) The maximum deduction per month is 1/12 of 65 percent of the annual deductible under a single coverage insurance plan or 1/12 of 75 percent of the annual deductible under a family plan.

An MSA must be maintained by a trustee or custodian. Earnings of the MSA are not taxed currently, and distributions are not taxable to the extent that they are used for medical expenses of the taxpayer or the taxpayer's dependents. Medical expenses include expenses described in § 213(d), excluding medical insurance other than long-term care, continuation of health insurance between jobs (if continuation is required by Federal law, such as COBRA coverage), and insurance while on unemployment. No medical expense deduction under § 213 is allowed for expenses paid with distributions from an MSA. Distributions that are not used for medical expenses are subject to a 15 percent penalty unless made after the taxpayer becomes disabled, dies, or turns 65.

Section 223 allows taxpayers who have a "high deductible" health insurance plan to establish "health savings accounts" (HSAs). The tax treatment of HSAs is almost identical to the treatment of MSAs, with the principal difference being that unlike MSAs, HSAs are available to employees of employers of any size.

7.   POLICY ASPECTS

The following excerpt from Feld, Abortion to Aging: Problems of Definition in the Medical Expense Tax Deduction, 58 B.U.L.Rev. 165 (1978), discusses the policy issues raised by the medical expense deduction in § 213, but which are equally applicable to other tax expenditures for health and medical care:

> Some commentators see the medical expense deduction as an appropriate adjustment in determining the taxpayer's ability to pay income tax. In this view, medical expenditures differ radically from a taxpayer's other personal consumption choices and should not be taxed similarly:
>
>> What distinguishes medical expenses from other personal expenses at bottom is a sense that large differences in their magnitude between people in otherwise similar circumstances are apt to reflect differences in need rather than choices among gratifications.[5]
>
> Others, however, criticize the medical expense deduction as a poorly framed tax subsidy which, like any deduction or other tax expenditure, is far more valuable to high-bracket than low-bracket taxpayers and carries no benefit for those too poor to fall within the tax system.[6] * * *
>
> Under both views, questions of line drawing arise. We might suppose that so fundamental a question as whether the deduction is regarded as an adjustment to income reflecting actual ability to pay or as a subsidy should affect resolution of definitional problems. But these divergences in view are directed to the wisdom of including the deduction in the statute. Once the legislative decision has been made, it becomes necessary under both views to reconcile the deduction with the general prohibition against the deduction of personal expenditures. All agree that it would be wrong to extend the medical deduction to expenditures that enhance the taxpayer's well-being rather than restore it after a mishap. If the deduction serves as a subsidy, the statute should be construed to address medical emergencies, not personal frolics. If, on the other hand, the deduction is viewed as an adjustment

---

[5]   [Andrews, Personal Deductions in an Ideal Income Tax, 86 Harv. L. Rev. 309, 336 (1972).]

[6]   See Surrey, Tax Incentives as a Device for Implementing Government Policy: A Comparison with Direct Government Expenditures, 83 Harv.L.Rev. 705, 720 (1970). In noting the inequities inherent in a deduction as opposed to a direct subsidy, Professor Surrey remarked:

> What HEW Secretary would propose a medical assistance program for the aged that cost $200 million, and under which $90 million would go to persons with incomes over $50,000, and only $8 million to persons with incomes under $5,000? The tax proposal to remove the 3% floor under the medical expense deductions of persons over 65 [Tax Reform Bill of 1969, H.R. 13,270, 91st Cong., 1st Sess. § 914] would have had just that effect. Id. at 722.

necessary to assess an individual's true income—that amount available for consumption and accumulation—then the statute should be narrowly construed to cover only those expenditures dictated by medical need.

These two views of the medical expense deduction have substantially different policy implications. If the deduction is viewed as a tax expenditure, as it is classified by official tax expenditure budgets, the medical expense deduction represents a payment by the government to the taxpayer to help defray the costs of private medical care. As such, it must be analyzed as part of the nation's overall health care program. On the other hand, such considerations are irrelevant if the deduction is viewed as a necessary part of the definition of the tax base. Under either approach, the definitional problems as to what constitutes a qualifying medical expense are essentially the same.

8.   IMPACT OF PATIENT PROTECTION AND AFFORDABLE CARE ACT OF 2010

The far-reaching Patient Protection and Affordable Care Act of 2010 (commonly called the "ACA") affects the tax treatment of medical expenses. The ACA amended § 213 to increase the 7.5 percent adjusted gross income limitation for deducting unreimbursed medical expenses to 10 percent for taxable years beginning after December 31, 2012. The increased threshold did not apply for years 2013 through 2016 if either the taxpayer or the taxpayer's spouse turned 65 before the end of the year. The 10 percent AGI threshold for deducting medical expenses under the alternative minimum tax is unaffected by the ACA.

The primary purpose of the ACA is to reduce the number of uninsured individuals. With more health care expenses presumably will be covered by insurance, the importance of § 213, which applies only to unreimbursed expenses, should be reduced. To encourage people to purchase health insurance, the ACA imposes a "penalty" through the Internal Revenue Code on persons who fail to acquire "minimum essential health insurance coverage." The penalty imposed under new § 5000A phased in starting January 2014 and becomes fully effective in 2016. The penalty applies month-by-month with a once-per-year exception for a coverage gap of less than three consecutive months. The monthly penalty is 1/12 of an annualized penalty amount. Beginning in 2016, the annualized penalty is the greater of: (1) 2.5 percent of the amount by which the taxpayer's household income for the taxable year exceeds the threshold amount of income requiring a tax return to be filed, or (2) $695 per uninsured adult in the household (indexed for inflation after 2016). The penalty for an uninsured individual under age 18 is one-half of the penalty for an adult. There are limits on the aggregate household penalty that can be imposed. The penalty is due upon notice and demand, and is subject to normal assessment procedures. At the same time, the penalty cannot be collected by lien and levy. There are no criminal or civil penalties for failure to pay, and interest does not accrue on late payments. In 2013, the U.S. Supreme Court upheld the constitutionality of the "individual mandate" under Congress's taxing power. See National Federation of Independent Business v. Sebelius, 132 S.Ct. 2566 (2012).

The ACA included two additional new taxes. Section 4980I imposes an excise tax on insurers who provide so-called "Cadillac plans"; that is, health insurance plans that provide lower co-pays than other plans, lower deductibles, and more flexibility, all of which—at least in theory—encourage overuse of medical services that, in turn, lead to increased prices for the services. The tax is equal to 40 percent of the "excess benefit" to the employee. Notably, however, the tax does not take effect until 2020. In addition (and somewhat anomalously), § 5000B imposes a 10 percent excise tax on the amount paid for tanning services in order to fund the ACA's subsidies that help lower-income persons purchase health insurance. The tax became effective on July 1, 2010, and is collected by the service provider and remitted to the IRS quarterly.

SECTION 3.   CHARITABLE CONTRIBUTIONS

INTERNAL REVENUE CODE: Sections 170(a)–(e), (f)(8), (h)–(i), (j), (*l*); 162(b); 1011(b).

REGULATIONS: Sections 1.170A–1(b), (c)(1)–(2), (g); –4(a), (b)(1)–(3), (c), (h); –8(a)–(e); –13(f).

A deduction has been allowed for contributions to charitable organizations since 1917. The current provision, § 170, reflects a highly complex pattern for determining the deduction allowed for charitable contributions. Prospective donors, and their tax advisors, may have to take into account as many as six different factors to determine the amount of a charitable contribution deduction:

1.   The nature of the contribution—whether cash, tangible or intangible assets, or services;

2.   The nature of the recipient—whether the object of charity is an organization, gifts to which qualify for deduction up to fifty percent of the taxpayer's contribution base, or an organization, such as a private foundation, subject to a more stringent limitation;

3.   The tax attributes of any donated property—whether the property, if sold, would have produced ordinary income or capital gain;

4.   The use to which the recipient puts the property—i.e., exempt versus nonexempt purposes;

5.   The legal form of the transfer—i.e., outright transfers versus transfers in trust, split interest gifts versus gifts of undivided interests, and transfers with possession retained versus complete dispositions.

6.   Substantiation—section 170(f)(17) requires a donor to have a bank record or written communication from the donee acknowledging a donation of money to substantiate any deduction; section 170(f)(8) makes receipt of a contemporaneous

written acknowledgment from the donee organization a substantive prerequisite for claiming a deduction for a contribution of $250 or more; and sections 170(f)(11) and (12) provide additional substantiation requirements for contributions of property for which the taxpayer claims a deduction of more than $500

In addition, donors who are individuals must be mindful that the deduction for charitable contributions under § 170 currently is allowed only to taxpayers who itemize their deductions. This has not always been true, and the issue is revisited from time to time by Congress.

In all cases, however, the threshold question is whether a transfer of money or property to a charitable organization is a "contribution" in the first place.

Hernandez v. Commissioner

Supreme Court of the United States, 1989.
490 U.S. 680.

■ MR. JUSTICE MARSHALL delivered the opinion of the Court.

Section 170 of the Internal Revenue Code of 1954 (Code), 26 U.S.C. § 170, permits a taxpayer to deduct from gross income the amount of a "charitable contribution." The Code defines that term as a "contribution or gift" to certain eligible donees, including entities organized and operated exclusively for religious purposes. We granted certiorari to determine whether taxpayers may deduct as charitable contributions payments made to branch churches of the Church of Scientology (Church) in order to receive services known as "auditing" and "training." We hold that such payments are not deductible.

Scientology was founded in the 1950's by L. Ron Hubbard. It is propagated today by a "mother church" in California and by numerous branch churches around the world. The mother church instructs laity, trains and ordains ministers, and creates new congregations. Branch churches, known as "franchises" or "missions," provide Scientology services at the local level, under the supervision of the mother church. * * *

Scientologists believe that an immortal spiritual being exists in every person. A person becomes aware of this spiritual dimension through a process known as "auditing."[2] Auditing involves a one-to-one encounter between a participant (known as a "preclear") and a Church official (known as an "auditor"). An electronic device, the E-meter, helps the auditor identify the preclear's areas of spiritual difficulty by measuring skin responses during a question and answer session. Although auditing sessions are conducted one on one, the content of each

---

[2]   Auditing is also known as "processing," "counseling," and "pastoral counseling." 83 T.C. 575, 577 (1984), aff'd, 822 F.2d 844 (C.A.9 1987).

session is not individually tailored. The preclear gains spiritual awareness by progressing through sequential levels of auditing, provided in short blocks of time known as "intensives." * * *

The Church also offers members doctrinal courses known as "training." Participants in these sessions study the tenets of Scientology and seek to attain the qualifications necessary to serve as auditors. Training courses, like auditing sessions, are provided in sequential levels. Scientologists are taught that spiritual gains result from participation in such courses. * * *

The Church charges a "fixed donation," also known as a "price" or a "fixed contribution," for participants to gain access to auditing and training sessions. These charges are set forth in schedules, and prices vary with a session's length and level of sophistication. In 1972, for example, the general rates for auditing ranged from $625 for a 12½-hour auditing intensive, the shortest available, to $4,250 for a 100-hour intensive, the longest available. Specialized types of auditing required higher fixed donations: a 12½-hour "Integrity Processing" auditing intensive cost $750; a 12½-hour "Expanded Dianetics" auditing intensive cost $950. This system of mandatory fixed charges is based on a central tenet of Scientology known as the "doctrine of exchange," according to which any time a person receives something he must pay something back. * * * In so doing, a Scientologist maintains "inflow" and "outflow" and avoids spiritual decline. * * *

The proceeds generated from auditing and training sessions are the Church's primary source of income. The Church promotes these sessions not only through newspaper, magazine, and radio advertisements, but also through free lectures, free personality tests, and leaflets. The Church also encourages, and indeed rewards with a 5% discount, advance payment for these sessions. * * * The Church often refunds unused portions of prepaid auditing or training fees, less an administrative charge.

Petitioners in these consolidated cases each made payments to a branch church for auditing or training sessions. They sought to deduct these payments on their federal income tax returns as charitable contributions under § 170. Respondent, * * * Internal Revenue Service (IRS), disallowed these deductions, finding that the payments were not charitable contributions within the meaning of § 170.

Petitioners sought review of these determinations in the Tax Court. * * * Before trial, the Commissioner stipulated that the branch churches of Scientology are religious organizations entitled to receive tax-deductible charitable contributions under the relevant sections of the Code. This stipulation isolated as the sole statutory issue whether payments for auditing or training sessions constitute "contribution[s] or gift[s]" under § 170.

The Tax Court * * * upheld the Commissioner's decision. 83 T.C. 575 (1984). It observed first that the term "charitable contribution" in § 170 is synonymous with the word "gift," which case law had defined "as a voluntary transfer of property by the owner to another without consideration therefor." * * * It then determined that petitioners had received consideration for their payments, namely, "the benefit of various religious services provided by the Church of Scientology." * * * The Tax Court also rejected the taxpayers' constitutional challenges.

The Court of Appeals * * * affirmed. The First Circuit rejected Hernandez's argument that under § 170, the IRS' ordinary inquiry into whether the taxpayer received consideration for his payment should not apply to "the return of a commensurate *religious* benefit, as opposed to an *economic or financial* benefit." 819 F.2d, at 1217 (emphasis in original). The court found "no indication that Congress intended to distinguish the religious benefits sought by Hernandez from the medical, educational, scientific, literary, or other benefits that could likewise provide the quid for the quo of a nondeductible payment to a charitable organization." * * * The court also rejected Hernandez's argument that it was impracticable to put a value on the services he had purchased, noting that the Church itself had "established and advertised monetary prices" for auditing and training sessions, and that Hernandez had not claimed that these prices misstated the cost of providing these sessions. * * *

Hernandez's constitutional claims also failed. * * *

We now affirm.

II

For over 70 years, federal taxpayers have been allowed to deduct the amount of contributions or gifts to charitable, religious, and other eleemosynary institutions. * * * Section 170, the present provision, * * * requires a taxpayer claiming the deduction to satisfy a number of conditions. The Commissioner's stipulation in this case, however, has narrowed the statutory inquiry to one such condition: whether petitioners' payments for auditing and training sessions are "contribution[s] or gifts[s]" within the meaning of § 170.

The legislative history of the "contribution or gift" limitation, though sparse, reveals that Congress intended to differentiate between unrequited payments to qualified recipients and payments made to such recipients in return for goods or services. Only the former were deemed deductible. The House and Senate Reports on the 1954 tax bill, for example, both define "gifts" as payments "made with no expectation of a financial return commensurate with the amount of the gift." S.Rep. No. 1622, 83d Cong., 2d Sess., 196 (1954); H.R.Rep. No. 1337, 83d Cong., 2d Sess., A44 (1954). Using payments to hospitals as an example, both Reports state that the gift characterization should not apply to "a payment by an individual to a hospital *in consideration* of a binding obligation to provide medical treatment for the individual's employees. It would apply only if there were no expectation of any quid pro quo from the hospital." S.Rep. No. 1622, supra, at 196 (emphasis added); H.Rep. No. 1337, supra, at A44 (emphasis added).

In ascertaining whether a given payment was made with "the expectation of any quid pro quo," * * * the IRS has customarily examined the external features of the transaction in question. This practice has the advantage of obviating the need for the IRS to conduct imprecise inquiries into the motivations of individual taxpayers. The lower courts have generally embraced this structural analysis. See, e.g., Singer Co. v. United States, 449 F.2d 413, 422–423 (Ct.Cl.1971) * * * . We likewise focused on external features in United States v. American Bar Endowment, [477 U.S. 105 (1986)], to resolve the taxpayers' claims that they were entitled to partial deductions for premiums paid to a charitable organization for insurance coverage; the taxpayers contended that they had paid unusually high premiums in an effort to make a contribution along with their purchase of insurance. We upheld the Commissioner's disallowance of the partial deductions because the taxpayers had failed to demonstrate, at a minimum, the existence of comparable insurance policies with prices lower than those of the policy they had each purchased. In so doing, we stressed that "the sine qua non of a charitable contribution is a transfer of money or property *without adequate consideration*." Id., at 118 (emphasis added in part).

In light of this understanding of § 170, it is readily apparent that petitioners' payments to the Church do not qualify as "contribution[s] or gift[s]." As the Tax Court found, these payments were part of a quintessential quid pro quo exchange: in return for their money, petitioners received an identifiable benefit, namely, auditing and training sessions. The Church established fixed price schedules for auditing and training sessions in each branch church; it calibrated particular prices to auditing or training sessions of particular lengths and levels of sophistication: it returned a refund if auditing and training services went unperformed; it distributed "account cards" on which persons who had paid money to the Church could monitor what prepaid services they had not yet claimed; and it categorically barred provision of auditing or training sessions for free. Each of these practices reveals the inherently reciprocal nature of the exchange.

Petitioners do not argue that such a structural analysis is inappropriate under § 170, or that the external features of the auditing and training transactions do not strongly suggest a quid pro quo exchange. * * * Petitioners argue instead that they are entitled to deductions because a quid pro quo analysis is inappropriate under § 170 when the benefit a taxpayer receives is purely religious in nature. Along the same lines, petitioners claim that payments made for the right to participate in a religious service should be automatically deductible under § 170.

We cannot accept this statutory argument for several reasons. First, it finds no support in the language of § 170. * * * Congress has specified that a payment to an organization operated exclusively for religious (or other eleemosynary) purposes is deductible only if such a payment is a "contribution or gift." 26 U.S.C. § 170(c). The Code makes no special preference for payments made in the expectation of gaining religious benefits or access to a religious service. * * * The House and Senate Reports on § 170, and the other legislative history of that provision, offer no indication that Congress' failure to enact such a preference was an oversight.

Second, petitioners' deductibility proposal would expand the charitable contribution deduction far beyond what Congress has provided. Numerous forms of payments to eligible donees plausibly could be categorized as providing a religious benefit or as securing access to a religious service. For example, some taxpayers might regard their tuition payments to parochial schools as generating a religious benefit or as securing access to a religious service; such payments, however, have long been held not to be charitable contributions under § 170. [Foley v. Commissioner, 844 F.2d 94 (C.A.2 1988), citing Winters v. Commissioner, 468 F.2d 778 (C.A.2 1972)]. * * *

Accordingly, we conclude that petitioners' payments to the Church for auditing and training sessions are not "contribution[s] or gift[s]" within the meaning of that statutory expression.

III

[The Court then held that there was no merit to the taxpayer's claim that denying their requested charitable contribution deduction violated the Establishment Clause of the Constitution.]

IV

We turn, finally, to petitioners' assertion that disallowing their claimed deduction is at odds with the IRS' longstanding practice of permitting taxpayers to deduct payments made to other religious institutions in connection with certain religious practices. * * *

[Petitioners' claim that] * * * the IRS has accorded payments for auditing and training disparately harsh treatment compared to payments to other churches and synagogues for their religious services: Recognition of a comparable deduction for auditing and training payments is necessary to cure this administrative inconsistency.

* * * A 1971 ruling, still in effect, states: "Pew rents, building fund assessments, and periodic dues paid to a church . . . are all methods of making contributions to the church, and such payments are deductible as charitable contributions within the limitations set out in section 170 of the Code." Rev. Rul. 70–47, 1970–1 Cum.Bull. 49 * * * . We also assume for purposes of argument that the IRS also allows taxpayers to deduct "specified payments for attendance at High Holy Day services, for

tithes, for torah readings and for memorial plaques." Foley v. Commissioner, 844 F.2d, at 94, 96.

The development of the present litigation, however, makes it impossible for us to resolve petitioners' claim that they have received unjustifiably harsh treatment compared to adherents of other religions. The relevant inquiry in determining whether a payment is a "contribution or gift" under § 170 is, as we have noted, not whether the payment secures religious benefits or access to religious services, but whether the transaction in which the payment is involved is structured as a quid pro quo exchange. * * *

Perhaps because the theory of administrative inconsistency emerged only on appeal, petitioners did not endeavor at trial to adduce from the IRS or other sources any specific evidence about other religious faiths' transactions. The IRS' revenue rulings, which merely state the agency's conclusions as to deductibility and which have apparently never been reviewed by the Tax Court or any other judicial body, also provide no specific facts about the nature of these other faiths' transactions. In the absence of such facts, we simply have no way * * * to appraise accurately whether the IRS' revenue rulings have correctly applied a quid pro quo analysis with respect to any or all of the religious practices in question. We do not know, for example, whether payments for other faiths' services are truly obligatory or whether any or all of these services are generally provided whether or not the encouraged "mandatory" payment is made.

The IRS' application of the "contribution or gift" standard may be right or wrong with respect to these other faiths, or it may be right with respect to some religious practices and wrong with respect to others. It may also be that some of these payments are appropriately classified as partially deductible "dual payments." * * * Only upon a proper factual record could we make these determinations. Absent such a record, we must reject petitioners' administrative consistency argument.

■ JUSTICE O'CONNOR, with whom JUSTICE SCALIA joins, dissenting.

The Court today acquiesces in the decision of the Internal Revenue Service (IRS) to manufacture a singular exception to its 70-year practice of allowing fixed payments indistinguishable from those made by petitioners to be deducted as charitable contributions. Because the IRS cannot constitutionally be allowed to select which religions will receive the benefit of its past rulings, I respectfully dissent.

* * *

The stipulations * * * established that Scientology was at all relevant times a religion; [and] that each Scientology branch to which payments were made was at all relevant times a "church" within the meaning of § 170(b)(1)(A)(i). * * *

It must be emphasized that the IRS' position here is not based upon the contention that a portion of the knowledge received from auditing or training is of secular, commercial, nonreligious value. Thus, the denial of a deduction in these cases bears no resemblance to the denial of a deduction for religious-school tuition up to the market value of the secularly useful education received. * * * Here the IRS denies deductibility solely on the basis that the exchange is a quid pro quo, even though the quid is exclusively of spiritual or religious worth. * * *

When a taxpayer claims as a charitable deduction part of a fixed amount given to a charitable organization in exchange for benefits that have a commercial value, the allowable portion of that claim is computed by subtracting from the total amount paid the value of the physical benefit received. If at a charity sale one purchases for $1,000 a painting whose market value is demonstrably no more than $50, there has been a contribution of $950. The same would be true if one purchases a $1,000 seat at a charitable dinner where the food is worth $50. An identical calculation can be made where the quid received is not a painting or a meal, but an intangible such as entertainment, so long as that intangible has some market value established in a noncontributory context. Hence, one who purchases a ticket to a concert, at the going rate for concerts by the particular performers, makes a charitable contribution of zero even if it is announced in advance that all proceeds from the ticket sales will go to charity. The * * * audience has paid the going rate for a show.

It becomes impossible, however, to compute the "contribution" portion of a payment to a charity where what is received in return is not merely an intangible, but an intangible * * * that is not bought and sold except in donative contexts so that the only "market" price against which it can be evaluated is a market price that always includes donations. Suppose, for example, that the charitable organization that traditionally solicits donations on Veterans Day, in exchange for which it gives the donor an imitation poppy bearing its name, were to establish a flat rule that no one gets a poppy without a donation of at least $10. One would have to say that the "market" rate for such poppies was $10, but it would assuredly not be true that everyone who "bought" a poppy for $10 made no contribution. Similarly, if one buys a $100 seat at a prayer breakfast—receiving as the quid pro quo food for both body and soul—it would make no sense to say that no charitable contribution whatever has occurred simply because the "going rate" for all prayer breakfasts (with equivalent bodily food) is $100. The latter may well be true, but that "going rate" includes a contribution.

Confronted with this difficulty, and with the constitutional necessity of not making irrational distinctions among taxpayers, and with the even higher standard of equality of treatment among religions that the First Amendment imposes, the Government has only two practicable options with regard to distinctively religious quids pro quo: to disregard them all, or to tax them all. Over the years it has chosen the former course.

[I]n A.R.M. 2, 1 Cum.Bull. 150 (1919), the IRS gave its first blessing to the deductions of fixed payments to religious organizations as charitable contributions:

> "The distinction of pew rents, assessments, church dues, and the like from basket collections is hardly warranted by the act. The act reads 'contributions' and 'gifts.' It is felt that all of these come within the two terms.

> "In substance it is believed that these are simply methods of contributing although in form they may vary. Is a basket collection given involuntarily to be distinguished from an envelope system, the latter being regarded as 'dues'? From a technical angle, the pew rents may be differentiated, but in practice the so-called 'personal accommodation' they may afford is conjectural. It is believed that the real intent is to contribute and not to hire a seat or pew for personal accommodation. In fact, basket contributors sometimes receive the same accommodation informally."

The IRS reaffirmed its position in 1970, ruling that "pew rents, building fund assessments and periodic dues paid to a church . . . are all methods of making contributions to the church and such payments are deductible as charitable contributions." Rev. Rul. 70–47, 1970–1 Cum.Bull. 49. Similarly, notwithstanding the "form" of Mass stipends as fixed payments for specific religious services, * * * the IRS has allowed charitable deductions of such payments. See Rev. Rul. 78–366, 1978–2 Cum.Bull. 241.

* * *

[T]he IRS recently explained in a "question and answer guidance package" to tax-exempt organizations that "in contrast to tuition payments, religious observances generally are not regarded as yielding private benefits to the donor, who is viewed as receiving only incidental benefits when attending the observances. The primary beneficiaries are viewed as being the general public and members of the faith. Thus, payments for saying masses, pew rents, tithes, and other payments involving fixed donations for similar religious services, are fully deductible contributions." * * * Although this guidance package may not be as authoritative as IRS rulings, * * * it does reflect the continuing adherence of the IRS to its practice of allowing deductions for fixed payments for religious services.

There can be no doubt that at least some of the fixed payments which the IRS has treated as charitable deductions, or which the Court assumes the IRS would allow taxpayers to deduct, * * * are as "inherently reciprocal," * * * as the payments for auditing at issue here. In exchange for their payment of pew rents, Christians receive particular seats during worship services. * * * Similarly, in some synagogues attendance at the worship services for Jewish High Holy Days is often predicated upon the purchase of a general admission ticket or a reserved seat ticket. * * * Religious honors such as publicly reading from Scripture are purchased or auctioned periodically in some synagogues of Jews from Morocco and Syria. * * * Mormons must tithe their income as a necessary but not sufficient condition to obtaining a "temple recommend," i.e., the right to be admitted into the temple. * * * A Mass stipend—a fixed payment given to a Catholic priest, in consideration of which he is obliged to apply the fruits of the Mass for the intention of the donor—has similar overtones of exchange. According to some Catholic theologians, the nature of the pact between a priest and a donor who pays a Mass stipend is "a bilateral contract known as *do ut facias.* One person agrees to give while the other party agrees to do something in return." * * * A finer example of a quid pro quo exchange would be hard to formulate.

This is not a situation where the IRS has explicitly and affirmatively reevaluated its longstanding interpretation of § 170 and decided to analyze all fixed religious contributions under a quid pro quo standard. There is no indication whatever that the IRS has abandoned its 70-year practice with respect to payments made by those other than Scientologists. In 1978, when it ruled that payments for auditing and training were not charitable contributions under § 170, the IRS did not cite—much less try to reconcile—its previous rulings concerning the deductibility of other forms of fixed payments for religious services or practices. See Rev. Rul. 78–189, 1978–1 Cum.Bull. 68 (equating payments for auditing with tuition paid to religious schools).

Nevertheless, respondent now attempts to reconcile his previous rulings with its decision in these cases by relying on a distinction between direct and incidental benefits in exchange for payments made to a charitable organization. * * * As long as the benefits remain "incidental" and do not indicate that the payment was actually made for the "personal accommodation" of the donor, the payment will be deductible. It is respondent's view that the payments made by petitioners should not be deductible under § 170 because * * * "the rigid connection between the provision of auditing and training services and payment of the fixed price" indicates a quid pro quo relationship and "reflect[s] the value that petitioners expected to receive for their money." * * *

There is no discernible reason why there is a more rigid connection between payment and services in the religious practices of Scientology than in the religious practices of the faiths described above. Neither has respondent explained why the benefit received by a Christian who obtains the pew of his or her choice by paying a rental fee, a Jew who gains entrance to High Holy Day services by purchasing a ticket, a Mormon who makes the fixed payment necessary for a temple recommend, or a Catholic who pays a Mass stipend, is incidental to the real benefit conferred on the "general public and members of the faith," * * * while the benefit received by a Scientologist from auditing is a personal accommodation.

* * *

In my view, the IRS has misapplied its longstanding practice of allowing charitable contributions under § 170 in a way that violates the Establishment Clause. It has unconstitutionally refused to allow payments for the religious service of auditing to be deducted as charitable contributions in the same way it has allowed fixed payments to other religions to be deducted. * * *

DETAILED ANALYSIS

1. DONATIVE INTENT—BENEFIT TO THE DONOR

1.1. *Subsequent Developments Regarding the Church of Scientology*

Rev. Rul. 93–73, 1993–2 C.B. 75, obsoleted Rev. Rul. 78–189, 1978–1 C.B. 68, which denied a charitable contribution deduction for auditing payments to the Church of Scientology and which led to the *Hernandez* decision. In light of the decision in favor of the IRS in *Hernandez,* the ruling presumably was based on changes made by the Church of Scientology with respect to payments for auditing sessions and contributions.

1.2. *Donative Intent and Benefit to the Donor Generally*

Taxpayers often mix public spirit and self-interest in nominally donative transactions. In such cases, where the private benefit to the contributor is significant, the charitable deduction is reduced or disallowed altogether. The IRS and the courts have dealt extensively with the variety of mixed-motive situations.

In the cases involving the receipt of a benefit by the donor, the issue may be phrased in terms of whether the donor has made a "gift" under the test enunciated in Commissioner v. Duberstein (see Chapter 4, Section 1.B.). See e.g., Winters v. Commissioner, 468 F.2d 778 (2d Cir.1972); Dowell v. United States, 553 F.2d 1233 (10th Cir.1977). However, in Singer Co. v. United States, 449 F.2d 413 (Ct.Cl.1971), the court took the position that the *Duberstein* test "has no relevance to the definition of a 'gift' in respect to a charitable contribution." Oppewal v. Commissioner, 468 F.2d 1000 (1st Cir.1972), likewise rejected an inquiry into the donor's motive: "The more fundamental objective test is—however the payment was designated, and whatever motives the taxpayer had in making it, was it, to any substantial extent, offset by the cost of services rendered to taxpayers in the nature of tuition?"

This issue was first addressed by the Supreme Court in United States v. American Bar Endowment, 477 U.S. 105 (1986), a case that involved the treatment of dividends paid on group insurance policies purchased through the American Bar Endowment by its member lawyers. The members paid premiums and assigned to the ABE the dividends paid by the insurers to reflect the members' favorable mortality and morbidity experience. The members claimed a charitable deduction for the dividends. The Court concluded: "The *sine qua non* of a charitable contribution is a transfer of money or property without adequate consideration. The taxpayer, therefore, must at a minimum demonstrate that he purposely contributed money or property in excess of the value of any benefit he received in return. The most logical test of the value of the insurance respondents received is the cost of similar policies." Applying this principle, the Court held that the insurance benefits obtained by the members were worth at least the amount of the premiums paid by them without any reduction for the dividends, and denied the deduction.

Treas. Reg. § 1.170A–1(h) incorporates the test of the *American Bar Endowment* case to determine the extent to which a payment to a charity that is partly in consideration for goods or services is deductible as a charitable contribution. A deduction is allowed only to the extent that the payment exceeds the fair market value of any goods or services received from the charity (whether received in the year of the contribution or in another year). Furthermore, no deduction is allowed unless the taxpayer *intends* to make a payment to the charity that exceeds the fair market value of the goods or services received. Goods or services have been received "in consideration for" the taxpayer's payment to the charity if the taxpayer either receives or *expects* to receive goods or services as a result of making the payment. Treas. Reg. § 1.170A–13(f)(6). A donor generally is treated as expecting to receive a *quid pro quo* if a contribution is in response to an express promise of a benefit or if the donor makes a contribution knowing that the charitable donee has conferred a benefit on other donors making comparable contributions. This standard disallows deductions where the facts and circumstances indicate that the donor expected, at the time of making the payment to the charity, that there would be a *quid pro quo*, even though there was no explicit promise by the charity. On the other hand, if the taxpayer expressly refuses to accept any consideration for the payment to the charity, a deduction is allowed even though a *quid pro quo* was available. See T.D. 8690, 1997–1 C.B. 68, 69, citing Rev. Rul. 67–246, 1967–2 C.B. 104. Items of insubstantial value, such as coffee mugs, pins, and other low-cost token items, as well as other unordered benefits the value of which is not more than the lesser of 2 percent of the contribution or $10.60 (for 2016) may be disregarded for these purposes and a deduction allowed for the full amount paid. See Rev. Proc. 2015–53 2015–44 I.R.B. 615. The regulations also ignore membership benefits received in exchange for a payment of $53.00 (for 2016) or more, if the benefits consist of either (1) rights or privileges that can be exercised frequently during the membership period, such as free admission to facilities or events, discounts at a museum shop, etc.; or (2) free admission to members-only events with a per-person cost to the charity that is no higher than the standard for low-cost articles under § 513(h)(2)(C), which is a very nominal amount ($10.60 for 2016). Treas. Reg. § 1.170A–1(h)(3); Rev. Proc. 2015–53 2015–44 I.R.B. 615. In valuing any consideration received from the charity, a taxpayer may rely on a contemporaneous written acknowledgment provided by the charity that either states no consideration has been provided in exchange for the contribution or values the *quid pro quo*, unless the taxpayer knows or has reason to know that the charity's determination is unreasonable. Treas. Reg. § 1.170A–1(h)(4).

Prior to the promulgation of Treas. Reg. § 1.170A–1(h), Rev. Rul. 67–246, 1967–2 C.B. 104, held that a deduction is allowed for the amount paid for admission to fund-raising events such as charity balls, bazaars, banquets, shows, and athletic events only to the extent the amount paid exceeds the fair market value of the privileges or other benefits received by the taxpayer. This result is consistent with the regulation. See also Goldman v. Commissioner, 388 F.2d 476 (6th Cir.1967) (no deduction for cost of raffle tickets despite taxpayer's claim that he intended to make a gift); Rev. Rul. 83–130, 1983–2 C.B. 148 (no deduction for $100 ticket in raffle for a house worth $100,000; 2,000 tickets were sold and the chance to win was full consideration).

If the fair market value of the benefit received by the donor cannot readily be determined, the fair market value received is presumed to be equal to the value of the contribution and the charitable contribution is disallowed in its entirety. The issue is usually phrased in terms of whether the donor has received a "substantial economic benefit" in return for the contribution. Sklar v. Commissioner, 282 F.3d 610 (9th Cir.2002), upheld the denial of a deduction for any portion of tuition payments to Orthodox Jewish Day schools that provided both religious and secular instruction to their children, because taxpayers failed to prove that their payments for tuition exceeded the tuition charged by other private schools (i.e., the value of the secular education), citing *American Bar Endowment*. Subsequently, in Sklar v. Commissioner, 125 T.C. 281 (2005), involving the same issue for the same taxpayers in a different year, the Tax Court held that even if tuition could be prorated between the portion attributable to the secular education and the portion attributable to religious education, or the taxpayer could demonstrate that the tuition exceeded the value of the secular education, no charitable contribution deduction was allowed for the portion of the tuition allocable to religious instruction because the taxpayers did not demonstrate any charitable intent in paying the tuition. The Tax Court's decision in *Sklar* was affirmed on appeal. Sklar v. Commissioner, 549 F.3d 1252 (9th Cir. 2008). The Ninth Circuit followed its earlier decision and denied the taxpayers' claimed deductions of a portion of the tuition and fees paid to the schools. The court held that under *Hernandez*, tuition paid for religious education is a payment for services and not deductible as a charitable contribution. The taxpayer failed to establish that the payments included an amount in excess of the value of the education benefit provided by the schools. The court reasoned that any attempt to distinguish payments for religious benefits from secular services would involve the court in impermissible entanglements between church and state.

The presumption of equal value often is applied to deny deductions to real estate developers who "donate" land within or adjacent to a subdivision or industrial park for public purposes, such as a park or schools. See e.g., Ottawa Silica Co. v. United States, 699 F.2d 1124 (Fed.Cir.1983) (no deduction where a corporation gave land to a city for a school and rights of way for access roads to the school because the corporation received a substantial economic benefit from the access roads in the form of increased value of its remaining land). But McLennan v. United States, 994 F.2d 839

(Fed.Cir.1993), allowed a deduction for the value of a contributed scenic conservation easement even though the easement incidentally benefited the donor by maintaining the aesthetic value of the donor's property.

In a few instances, Congress has enacted specific provisions to deal with the issue of valuing the benefits received by a contributor. Rev. Rul. 86–63, 1986–2 C.B. 88, held that payments to a college football scholarship program which entitled the contributor to preferential ticket purchase rights were deductible only to the extent the payment exceeded the value of the right to purchase the tickets, which were separate and distinct from the face value purchase price of the tickets. Congress responded by enacting § 170(*l*), specifically allowing a deduction for 80 percent of such payments, even though the quid pro quo is explicit and the tickets would have been unobtainable without payment of the full amount of the contribution.

1.3. *Substantiation*

No deduction for a contribution of money is allowed unless the donor "maintains as a record of such contribution a bank record or written communication from the donee showing the name of the donee organization, the date of the contribution, and the amount of the contribution."[2]

In addition to this general substantiation requirement, for any contribution of $75 or more, § 6115 requires the charitable donee to provide the donor-taxpayer with a written statement regarding the value of the goods or services received in consideration of the contribution and informing the taxpayer that only the amount in excess of the value of the consideration received is deductible. If the contribution is $250 or more, § 170(f)(8) denies a deduction if the taxpayer does not have such a receipt. See Treas. Reg. § 1.170A–13(f). Section 170(f)(8) is strictly applied. Even if the donor receives nothing in return for the contribution, the deduction will be disallowed in its entirety unless the receipt states that the donor received nothing in return. Kendrix v. Commissioner, T.C. Memo 2006–9, denied a deduction for contributions in excess of $250 to a church for which the taxpayer had a receipt that did not state whether or not the church had provided any goods or services to the taxpayer. See also Durden v. Commissioner, T.C. Memo. 2012–140 (denying a charitable contribution deduction of over $250, where the letter from the donee church failed to indicate that no goods or services were provided to the taxpayer). Section 170(f)(17) imposes stringent substantiation requirements for contributions of money.

2.   NATURE OF RECIPIENT

Only gifts to organizations of the type described in § 170(c) qualify for the deduction. Most charitable contributions are to organizations intended to qualify under § 170(c)(2), which has elaborate restrictions on the permissible range of activities in which the organization may engage. In no event can a donation directly to an individual or to a trust for an individual qualify, however needy that individual may be. Thus, where a taxpayer and others contributed sums to a fund to provide a musical education for a girl who did not have means of her own to obtain the education, the amount

---

[2]   Notice 2006–110, 2006–2 C.B. 1127, provides special rules for substantiating contributions made by payroll deduction.

contributed was not allowed as a charitable deduction. Tilles v. Commissioner, 38 B.T.A. 545 (1938), aff'd on other issues, 113 F.2d 907 (8th Cir.1940).

The IRS publishes a "Cumulative List of Organizations Described in § 170(c) of the Internal Revenue Code of 1986," which sets forth organizations that have obtained a ruling from the IRS that they meet the criteria of § 170(c). While "cumulative," the list is not exclusive. Taxpayers may deduct contributions to any organization that meets the statutory definition. See Rev. Proc. 2011–33, 2011–25 I.R.B. 887, for how a taxpayer can rely on the cumulative list in claiming a charitable contribution deduction.

The nature of the recipient organization also determines whether contributions by donors are subject to the 50-percent limitation in § 170(b)(1)(A), or the 30-percent and 20-percent limitations in, respectively, § 170(b)(1)(B) and (D).

3. OVERALL PERCENTAGE LIMITATION

3.1. *General*

Section 170(b) imposes complex limitations on the total amount of charitable contributions that may be deducted in any year. The limitations are so generous, however, that they usually affect the deduction only in the case of extraordinarily large gifts. For individuals, a four-tier set of limitations applies based on varying percentages of the taxpayer's "contribution base." The taxpayer's contribution base is adjusted gross income, as defined in § 62 (see Section 1 of this Chapter) without taking into account net operating loss carryovers under § 172. In general, the 50-percent limitation applies where the recipient organization is a publicly supported charity or a private operating foundation. In the case of private non-operating foundations—typically foundations involved only in grant making—contributions of cash and ordinary income property are limited to 30 percent of the donor's contribution base. Gifts of capital gain property made to such organizations may be deducted only up to 20 percent of the donor's contribution base. More specifically:

(1) Cash contributions (and contributions measured by the basis of donated property) to "50 percent charities"—churches, schools, hospitals, charities receiving most of their support from the government or the public, governments,[3] and certain private foundations (generally speaking those that currently distribute all of their income to other charities)—are deductible in an amount up to fifty percent of the taxpayer's contribution base. I.R.C. § 170(b)(1)(A).

(2) Cash contributions to any other charity—primarily private nonoperating foundations—and contributions "for the use of" but not directly to a charity are deductible only up to the lesser of thirty percent of the taxpayer's contribution base or fifty percent of the contribution base minus the amount of cash contributions to "50 percent charities."

---

[3] Voluntary cash contributions to reduce the national debt are tax deductible!

(3) Contributions to "50 percent charities" of appreciated long term capital gain property, taken into account at fair market value, can be deducted only to the extent the amount does not exceed the lesser of thirty percent of the contribution base or the portion of the fifty percent base remaining after deducting all cash gifts. I.R.C. § 170(b)(1)(C). Taxpayers may elect to deduct only the basis of long term capital gain property contributed to charity in order to deduct contributions against the 50 percent base. I.R.C. § 170(b)(1)(C)(iii). This election may be advantageous when the basis of the property exceeds fifty percent of the taxpayer's contribution base and the property has not appreciated substantially.

(4) Contributions to any other charity of appreciated long term capital gain property, taken into account at fair market value, can be deducted only to the extent the amount does not exceed the lesser of twenty percent of the contribution base or the excess of thirty percent of the contribution base minus the amount of contributions of long term capital gain property to 50 percent charities. I.R.C. § 170(b)(1)(D).

3.2. *Carryforward of Excess Contributions*

If a taxpayer makes contributions that exceed the applicable 50 percent, 30 percent, or 20 percent limitations in a year, the excess may be carried forward and deducted in each of the succeeding 5 years. I.R.C. §§ 170(d), 170(b)(1)(B) (last sentence), 170(b)(1)(C)(ii), 170(b)(1)(D)(ii). For example, if a taxpayer makes a cash contribution of $200,000 to a fifty percent charity in a year in which the taxpayer's contribution base is $120,000, only $60,000 is deductible in the year of the contribution and $140,000 carries forward. If the taxpayer's contribution base the following year is $110,000 (and the taxpayer makes no other contributions), $55,000 of the $140,000 carried forward will be deductible, with the remaining $85,000 carried forward to the next available year. If the taxpayer's contribution base is zero in each of the next three years, the carryforward expires and the remaining $85,000 will not be deductible.

In a carryforward year, the taxpayer takes deductions in the following order: (1) 50-percent contributions actually made during the year; (2) carryforwards of excess 50-percent contributions from the preceding five years; (3) 30-percent cash contributions made during the year; (4) carryforward of excess 30-percent cash contributions from the preceding five years; (5) 30-percent long-term-capital-gain property contributions made during the year; (6) carryforward of excess 30-percent long-term-capital-gain property contributions from the preceding five years; (7) 20-percent contributions made during the year; and (8) carryforwards of excess 20-percent contributions from the preceding five years. Treas. Reg. § 1.170A–10 illustrates the complex computations necessary to apply the carryforward rules to the various limitations.

4. FORM OF THE CONTRIBUTION

4.1. *Personal Services*

Treas. Reg. § 1.170A–1(g) provides that no deduction is allowed for the contribution of services. This rule may be justified on the ground that the imputed income from the services performed will never be included in the contributor's tax base. Compare taxpayer A, who renders services to a charity, with taxpayer B, who renders services to a third party for cash which is then contributed to the charity. B will include the cash in gross income and will be entitled to an offsetting charitable deduction. Denying a deduction for services contributed by A will put A in the same position as B. The rule should also be compared with the rules governing contributions of appreciated property (see Section 3.5. of this Chapter). Both situations involve the question of whether a deduction should be allowed for items (services and capital appreciation) that will never be included in income.

For examples of situations held to involve services, see Rev. Rul. 53–162, 1953–2 C.B. 127 (furnishing blood to a blood bank is analogous to the rendering of a personal service); Rev. Rul. 67–236, 1967–2 C.B. 103 (radio station which provided free broadcast time to religious and other public affairs organizations was denied a charitable deduction).

Actual out-of-pocket expenses, such as the costs of operating an automobile, incurred in connection with charitable activities qualify for the charitable contribution deduction, Rev. Rul. 69–645, 1969–2 C.B. 37. In Orr v. United States, 343 F.2d 553 (5th Cir.1965), the taxpayer was denied a charitable contribution deduction for depreciation (it did not constitute a "payment"), and for automobile insurance premiums and costs of repairs attributable to his personal automobile and airplane that he used part time in connection with his activities on behalf of a church (only expenses "solely for the use of" charity may be deducted). In Rev. Rul. 73–597, 1973–2 C.B. 69, a woman incurred child care expenses while she performed volunteer services for a charitable organization. The ruling stated that in order for out-of-pocket expenses incurred in connection with performance of volunteer services for charitable organizations to be deductible, the expenditures must be "*nonpersonal* and *directly connected with* and solely attributable to the rendition of such services." The ruling held that, since child care expenses had been found by the courts to be personal (see Chapter 19, Section 6) and the expenditures in question had only an indirect and tenuous connection to the performance of the charitable services, no charitable contribution deduction was allowed.

To be deductible the expenses connected with the contribution of services must be paid by the person who contributed the services. A third party who pays the expenses incurred by another in performing services for a charity is not entitled to a deduction. In Davis v. United States, 495 U.S. 472 (1990), the taxpayers, as requested by the Mormon church, paid the living and proselytizing expenses incurred by their sons during the sons' two year long Mormon missions. The Supreme Court disallowed the deduction, upholding the validity of Treas. Reg. § 1.170A–1(g), which allows a deduction for unreimbursed expenses as a contribution to a charity only for expenditures made in connection with the payor's own contribution of services.

4.2. *The "To or for the Use of" Test*

Section 170(c) requires that a contribution or gift be "to or for the use of" a qualified charitable organization. The test performs two functions.

First, only gifts "to" a qualified charitable organization qualify for the 50 percent limit; gifts "for the use of" a charitable organization are subject to the 30-percent limit in § 170(b)(1)(B). Second, the test is used to determine whether the charitable organization has in fact benefited from a purported contribution.

The first function of the "to or for the use of" test was involved in Rockefeller v. Commissioner, 676 F.2d 35 (2d Cir.1982). The taxpayer had deducted as charitable contributions unreimbursed expenses incurred in providing services to charitable organizations. These expenses included salaries of employees of the taxpayer and travel, entertainment, and miscellaneous expenses. The court held that the unreimbursed expenses constituted contributions "to" rather than "for the use of" the charitable organizations since the latter term was intended to mean "in trust for." The court found that the Congressional purpose in making the distinction was to limit deductions for gifts which "do not reach the charitable beneficiaries for a long period of time." The IRS follows the *Rockefeller* decision, Rev. Rul. 84–61, 1984–1 C.B. 39.

The second function of the test was involved in Davis v. United States, supra. In addition to upholding Treas. Reg. § 1.170A–1(g), the Court also held that in order to qualify under the "for the use of" provision a qualified donee must have the same degree of control over contributed funds that a beneficiary would have over a trust res. Thus a taxpayer may not claim a deduction for a contribution to another individual who performs services for a charitable organization unless the funds are placed under the charitable organization's control. In Babcock v. Commissioner, T.C. Memo. 1996–89, foster parents were permitted to deduct unreimbursed out-of-pocket expenses of caring for foster children as contributions for the benefit of the governmental agency that placed the foster children with the foster parents.

5. APPRECIATED PROPERTY

5.1. *Generally*

Many of the complexities of the charitable contribution provisions result from the various approaches taken to contributions of property in which there is unrealized appreciation or other potential tax gain. The general rule is that the charitable contribution deduction is based upon the value of the property contributed, not its adjusted basis. Treas. Reg. § 1.170A–1(c)(2). See also Withers v. Commissioner, 69 T.C. 900 (1978) (deduction for property that has depreciated in value is limited to fair market value). Where this rule applies, the contribution is not treated as a realization event and the deduction generally includes any unrealized gain on the contributed property even though that gain is never included in the contributor's income. See Rev. Rul. 55–410, 1955–1 C.B. 297 (a contribution of appreciated property to satisfy a dollar denominated charitable pledge is not a realization event). This treatment provides a considerable advantage to donors contributing highly appreciated property because it substantially reduces the "cost" of making a charitable contribution. The after-tax cost of the contribution is the value of the contributed property reduced by the taxes avoided by not selling the property and the taxes saved as a result of the contribution. Conversely, the cost to the Treasury is the sum of the foregone taxes on the appreciation of the property and the taxes saved by deducting its fair market value.

Consider the following excerpt from Goode, The Individual Income Tax 167–168 (1976):

> There seems to be no good reason for favoring those who contribute appreciated property over those who give other property or cash. The present provision, moreover, gives rise to difficulties in valuing gifts of art objects, books and manuscripts, and other items and apparently tempts some donors to place excessive values on their gifts, occasionally with the collusion of recipient institutions. The inequalities and administrative difficulties could be avoided by limiting deductions for gifts of property to an amount equal to the cost (or other basis). Another approach, which would be less simple but which would deal with the inequities and abuses and lessen the valuation problems, would be to treat a gift as a constructive realization of a capital gain for tax purposes * * *. Either of these reforms would reduce the special tax incentives for making gifts of appreciated property but would leave unimpaired the general incentives for contributions.

5.2. *Reduction of the Allowable Deduction*

In many cases, as suggested by Goode, the general rule is displaced by § 170(e), which limits the amount of the deduction to the basis of certain property. Section 170(e)(1)(A) reduces the amount of the deduction by any amount that would not have been long-term capital gain if the property had been sold. Long-term capital gain results from the sale of a "capital asset" held for *more* than one year. Stated differently, the reduction is any amount that would have been ordinary income or short-term capital gain if the property had been sold. The definition of a capital asset is complex and is discussed in Chapter 24. Suffice it to say that property held for investment generally is a capital asset and property held for sale to customers, such as inventory and works of art owned by the creator, are not capital assets. See Chronicle Publishing Co. v. Commissioner, 97 T.C. 445 (1991), which denied any deduction to a newspaper that contributed its clippings library to a state historical society, because the clippings had no basis and under Treas. Reg. § 1.1221–1(c)(2) were denied capital asset status. Capital gains also may be realized on the sale of real estate used in a business, such as an office building or apartment house. In Jones v. Commissioner, 560 F.3d 1196 (10th Cir. 2009), one of Timothy McVeigh's lawyers in the criminal trial stemming from the 2000 bombing of the Oklahoma City Federal Building donated to a university copies of documents that he received from the government in the course of his representation of McVeigh, and claimed a charitable contribution deduction for their appraised value. The Tenth Circuit denied the deduction because the discovery material was not a capital asset and the taxpayer had no basis in the documents. More specifically, the discovery material—which was compiled by the government to assist in its investigation and copies of which were made, organized, and categorized by the government and delivered to the taxpayer for the benefit of the taxpayer and his client—did not constitute a capital asset because it amounted to letters, memoranda, or similar property "prepared or produced" for the taxpayer within the meaning of § 1221(a)(3)(B).

Section 170(e)(1)(A) does not affect the amount of the deduction if, for example, investment real estate or corporate stock held for more than one year is contributed to charity; rather, the full fair market value is deductible. But the deduction for a contribution of corporate stock held for one year or less or real estate held for sale by a dealer generally will be limited to the basis for the property. The effect of the limitation in § 170(e)(1)(A) is to reduce the donor's tax savings so that the after-tax effect of the contribution is the same as if the taxpayer sold the property and gave the *gross* proceeds to the charity, paying the taxes out of other funds.

Section 170(e)(3) imposes a smaller reduction in the amount of the deduction for contributions by a corporation of inventory or property used in the business to a charity if the charity will use the property for the care of the ill, the needy, or infants. Sections 170(e)(4) and (6) provide similar rules with respect to scientific equipment contributed to a charitable organization for use by the donee in research and experimentation or research training and for contributions of computer software, equipment, and peripherals to educational institutions for use in kindergarten through twelfth grade education, or to a public library. In these cases, the amount of the deduction is limited to the lesser of (1) twice the basis of the property or (2) the basis of the property plus one-half of the unrealized appreciation.

The deduction for some contributions of long-term capital gain property is limited to basis. Section 170(e)(1)(B) limits to basis the deduction for contributions of *tangible personal* property that the donor does not reasonably expect will be used by the donee charity to further its exempt purpose. Thus, for example, if an art collector donates to a charity, the exempt function of which is medical research, a work of art for which she paid $1,000 but which is worth $1,000,000, the deduction would be limited to $1,000; but if the work of art were contributed to an art museum, § 170(e)(1)(B) would not apply and as long as it had been held for more than one year, the deduction would be $1,000,000. The purpose of this limitation is to prevent avoidance of tax where the real object of the contribution is to put cash in the hands of the charity through a post-contribution sale, rather than provide the property for the continuing use of the charity. In the former situation, the donor should be treated in the same manner as if she sold the property and contributed the cash proceeds. These limitations are bolstered by § 170(e)(1)(B)(i)(II), which generally disallows a deduction in excess of basis in tangible personal property if the donee disposes of the property before the end of the year in which the contribution was made. Furthermore, § 170(e)(7) generally requires recapture of the deduction for unrealized appreciation in tangible personal property, through an inclusion in ordinary income, if the donee disposes of the property after the year in which the donor made the contribution and before three years from the date of the donation. These limitations can be avoided if the donee organization certifies to the IRS (under penalties of perjury) that either (1) its use of the property was related to its exempt purposes, or (2) it originally intended to use the property in connection with its exempt purpose, but that such use later become impossible or infeasible.

In addition, § 170(e)(1)(B)(ii) limits the deduction for capital gain property donated to a private foundation. Again, the deduction must be reduced by the amount the taxpayer would have included in income had the property been sold. Section 170(e)(5), however, allows a deduction for the full fair market value of publicly traded securities donated to a "non-operating" private foundation—a narrowly defined type of organization.

Even if a property contribution escapes limitation under § 170(e), the relevant overall limitation on the amount of deductible contributions is lower than for contributions of cash (see Section 3.3. in this Chapter).

5.3. *Bargain Sales*

If property is sold to a charity at a discount, the transaction is treated as part-gift and part-sale. The amount by which the fair market value of the property exceeds the sales price is a contribution, which may be deducted subject to the various limitations. The sale aspect of the transaction is a recognition event, with the sales price being the amount realized. In computing gain, § 1011(b) requires that the donor allocate the property's basis between the gift and the sale parts of the transaction, taking into account only that portion of the basis which is the same percentage of total basis as the sales price is the percentage of fair market value. Suppose that a taxpayer sells corporate stock with a basis of $3,000 and a fair market value of $24,000 to a charity for $8,000. The amount of the contribution is $16,000. The gain on the sale is the amount realized of $8,000 less the adjusted basis of $1,000 (i.e., one-third of the total $3,000 in basis to reflect the ratio of the $8,000 sales price to the $24,000 fair market value), which equals $7,000. Hodgdon v. Commissioner, 98 T.C. 424 (1992) held that Treas. Reg. § 1.1011–2(a)(2) required application of the basis apportionment rules of § 1011(b) even though the taxpayer was unable to deduct fully the contribution due to the percentage limitations of § 170(b)(1)(C)(i) (see Section 3.3. in this Chapter).

Similar principles apply where the taxpayer transfers encumbered property to a charity. In Guest v. Commissioner, 77 T.C. 9 (1981) (Acq.), the taxpayer contributed to a religious organization real property subject to nonrecourse indebtedness in excess of his basis in the property. The court held that the taxpayer realized gain to the extent that the mortgage exceeded the basis for the property. The taxpayer was entitled to a charitable contribution deduction for the value of the property in excess of the mortgage. The court also held that the debt to which the property was subject constituted the amount realized on the disposition of the property. And it made a basis calculation under § 1011(b) to derive the amount taxable on the transaction.

In Douglas v. Commissioner, T.C. Memo. 1989–592, the taxpayer contributed encumbered real estate to a charity. Even though the taxpayer promised to make the mortgage payments as they fell due, the current deduction was limited to the value of the property net of the mortgage lien.

The promise to make the mortgage payments was treated as a charitable pledge, which does not give rise to a deduction until payment.

5.4. *Valuation Issues*

Treas. Reg. § 1.170A–1(c)(2) provides the general rule that the deduction for a contribution of property is equal to the fair market value of the property at the time of transfer. Fair market value is defined as the price at which the property would change hands in an arm's-length transaction. Generally speaking this is "the sales price of the item in the market 'in which such item is most commonly sold to the public.' " Goldstein v. Commissioner, 89 T.C. 535 (1987). If the donated property is real estate, the fair market value is based on the highest and best use for the land. Stanley Works v. Commissioner, 87 T.C. 389 (1986). However, the valuation must reflect any legal obstacles limiting the property's monetary potential. McMurray v. Commissioner, 985 F.2d 36 (1st Cir.1993), held that the valuation of a peat bog donated to a conservation group could not reflect the commercial value of harvesting peat because the appraiser failed to consider the substantial opposition which would be encountered in obtaining a variance and permit to harvest the peat.

In Rolfs v. Commissioner, 668 F.3d 888 (7th Cir. 2012), the Seventh Circuit considered whether a charitable deduction was allowed when the taxpayers donated their house to the local fire department so that firefighters could burn it down in a training exercise. The taxpayers, who sought the demolition in order to build another house on the property, claimed a $76,000 charitable deduction based on before-and-after appraisals of the property. The court rejected the taxpayers' valuation approach, concluding that, "[w]hen property is donated to a charity on the condition that it must be destroyed, that condition must be taken into account when valuing the gift." As a result, the value of the gift by the taxpayers did not exceed the fair market value of the benefit (i.e., the demolition of the house) that they received in return and thus no charitable deduction was allowed.

Subsequently, in Patel v. Commissioner, 138 T.C. 395 (2012), the Tax Court also denied a deduction for the donation of a home to a local fire department for firefighting training exercises, although it used a different rationale. The court found that under controlling state law the taxpayers had merely granted the fire department a license to conduct training exercises on their property and to destroy the structure. As a matter of law, the taxpayers were not entitled to any charitable contribution deduction because they did not convey a complete interest in the structure to the fire department. Instead, they conveyed only a partial interest in the property (i.e., "a mere license to use the property"), and § 170(f)(3) barred any charitable contribution deduction for the donation of partial interests. Thus, while *Rolfs* and *Patel* reach the same conclusion, *Rolfs* was fact-based while *Patel* was decided as a matter of law.

Various schemes have been developed to try to obtain inflated charitable contribution deductions. For example, in Anselmo v. Commissioner, 757 F.2d 1208 (11th Cir.1985), the taxpayer's deduction for a contribution of gemstones to the Smithsonian Institution based on a claimed retail value that was approximately five times the wholesale amount paid for the stones was disallowed; the wholesale price was the appropriate valuation, particularly given the fact that because of their poor quality the Smithsonian used the stones as study or laboratory pieces rather than as exhibits. See also Sammons v. Commissioner, 838 F.2d 330 (9th Cir.1988) (value of Indian artifacts purchased just long enough before contribution to qualify for fair market value deduction was limited to purchase price, which was considered better evidence of value than appraisals).

In response to the problems created by the overvaluation of property contributed to charity, overstatements of the value of charitable contributions now are subject to the "substantial valuation misstatement" penalty in § 6662(b)(3). If the value of the property shown on the return exceeds 200 percent of the amount ultimately determined to be the correct value of the property and the underpayment of tax attributable to such overvaluation is at least $5,000, a penalty is imposed equal to 20 percent of the tax underpayment attributable to the overvaluation. If the overvaluation is 400 percent or more the penalty is increased to 40 percent. Section 6050L, and Treas. Reg. § 1.6050L–1 impose additional reporting requirements with respect to contributions to charity of property with a value in excess of $5,000 for any single item of property ($10,000 in the case of non-publicly traded stock) or $5,000 in the aggregate for similar items of property contributed to one or more donees. In these situations, the donor must obtain and retain a qualified written appraisal by an independent appraiser and must attach a signed appraisal summary to the return on which the deduction is claimed. As a backstop to the appraisal requirement, the donee charity must also file a report if it sells within two years property donated to it with a value in excess of $5,000.

More relaxed substantiation requirements apply to smaller gifts. Section 170(f)(8) requires that any contribution of more than $250 be substantiated by a contemporaneous written acknowledgment from the donee charity that describes, but need not value, the contributed property. Addis v. Commissioner, 374 F.3d 881 (9th Cir. 2004), held that the substantiation requirements of § 170(f)(8) and Treas. Reg. § 1.170A–13(f)(7) are not met unless the charitable organization's estimate of the value of the benefits provided to the contributor was made in good faith. The court concluded that "[t]he deterrence value of section 170(f)(8)'s total denial of a deduction comports with the effective administration of a self-assessment and self-reporting system."

In recent years, Congress added additional substantiation requirements with respect to contributions of property for which the taxpayer claims a deduction of more than $500. Section 170(f)(11) applies a series of increasingly stringent substantiation requirements to contributions of property, excluding motor vehicles, which are subject to the even more stringent requirements of new § 170(f)(12), and readily valued property such as cash, publicly traded stock, and inventory. If the claimed deduction is between $501 and $5,000, the taxpayer's return (other than certain corporate returns) must include a description of the property and such other information as is required by regulations. If the claimed deduction is between $5,001 and $500,000 the taxpayer must also obtain a qualified appraisal of the property and attach to the return whatever information is required by regulations. If the claimed deduction is more than $500,000 the qualified appraisal must also be attached to the return. To prevent taxpayers from dividing property into component parts in an attempt to avoid the dollar thresholds, § 170(f)(11)(F) provides that similar items of property donated to one or more donees are treated as one property.

In Mohamed v. Commissioner, T.C. Memo. 2012–152, the Tax Court applied strict adherence to the substantiation requirements. The taxpayer claimed over $3,000,000 of charitable contribution deductions on the transfer of real property to a charitable remainder trust for which the taxpayer was the trustee. The taxpayer was a real estate broker and certified real estate appraiser. The taxpayer prepared his own tax returns and, although the taxpayer attached statements to his return for the year describing the donated property, the taxpayer did not attach a qualified appraisal as required by Treas. Reg. § 1.170A–13(c). The Tax Court granted summary judgment to the IRS upholding the validity of the substantiation regulations, finding that the taxpayer failed to satisfy the "substantial compliance doctrine" which allows minor deviations from the substantiation requirements but which cannot substitute for the absence of the qualified appraisal. In addition, a subsequent independent appraisal prepared for the taxpayer in the course of the audit showing valuations slightly higher than those claimed by the taxpayer did not substitute for the qualified appraisal required to be filed with the taxpayer's return claiming the deductions.

Another relatively new substantiation provision, § 170(d)(12), applies to donations of used motor vehicles, boats and airplanes if the claimed deduction is more than $500. Its enactment was prompted by congressional concern that taxpayers who were donating used cars to charities were claiming deductions that far exceeded the amounts that the charities were receiving following the sale (often at auction) of the cars. Section 170(d)(12) provides different rules depending on what the donee charity does with the vehicle. If the donee uses the vehicle or materially improves it, the taxpayer must obtain from the donee, and include with the tax return, a contemporaneous written acknowledgment that provides certain identifying information and certifies the intended use or material improvement of the vehicle, states the intended duration of the use, and certifies that the vehicle will not be transferred or exchanged for money before the termination of such use or improvement. In this case the amount of the deduction is not affected. However, if the donee sells the vehicle without any significant intervening use or material improvement, the deduction cannot be more than the gross proceeds received from the sale, and other substantiation requirements apply. In addition to the other requirements, the donee's contemporaneous written acknowledgment must certify that the vehicle was sold in an arms-length transaction to unrelated parties, state the gross proceeds from the sale, and inform the donor taxpayer that the deductible amount may not exceed the gross proceeds. Donees that fail to furnish the required acknowledgment or furnish a false or fraudulent acknowledgment are subject to a penalty under § 6720.

5.5. *Split Interest Gifts*

Special problems arise in the context of gifts to charities which involve contributions of fractional interests in property or transfers with interests split between charitable and noncharitable beneficiaries.

5.5.1. *Fractional Interests*

A donor may deduct the value of an undivided fractional interest in property transferred to a charity. See I.R.C. § 170(f)(3)(B)(ii). Zable v. Commissioner, T.C. Memo. 1990–55 (1990), held that the fair market value of a fractional interest in property should be discounted from the proportionate share of the value of a 100 percent interest. Winokur v. Commissioner, 90 T.C. 733 (1988) (Acq.), allowed a charitable contribution deduction for a gift to an art museum of an undivided interest in works of art in the year the interest was deeded to a museum even though the museum did not obtain possession until the next year. The museum's right to possession of the art was sufficient to support the deduction.

Section 170(*o*) limits deductions for the contribution of an undivided interest in tangible personal property, such as a gift to an art museum of a fractional interest in a painting, in several ways. First, a deduction is generally disallowed unless, immediately before the contribution, all of the interests in the property are held by the taxpayer or by the taxpayer and the donee. Second, if a taxpayer contributes a fractional interest in one year, and an additional fractional interest in the property in a later year, the fair market value of the property will be determined with reference to the lesser of the value of the property at the time of the first contribution or its value at the time of the later contribution. Third, if a taxpayer contributes a fractional interest, but does not contribute the taxpayer's entire interest in the property to the donee before the earlier of ten years from the date of the initial contribution or the date of the donor's death, the initial deduction is recaptured, with interest and a 10-percent penalty. The recapture rules also apply if the donee does not both acquire "substantial physical possession of the property" and use the property in connection with its exempt purposes within the earlier of ten years from the date of the initial contribution or the donor's death.

5.5.2. *Gifts in Trust*

An individual can create an irrevocable trust with the income payable to a member of his family and the remainder to go to a charity at a designated time. Similarly, a donor may create a trust with an income interest for the charity and the remainder to a noncharitable beneficiary. In both situations the question is how to determine the present value of the interest created in favor of the charity, a determination that requires the selection of the appropriate discount rate for valuation. Section 170(f)(2) imposes substantial restrictions on the use of split-interest trusts in order to insure that the amount ultimately received by the charity bears some reasonable relationship to the amount claimed as an income tax deduction by the creator of the split-interest trust. In general, for the donor to obtain a current tax deduction for a split-interest gift in trust, the trust must take the form of either a *charitable remainder annuity trust* or a *charitable remainder unitrust,* as defined in § 664(d). In a charitable remainder annuity trust, the noncharitable income beneficiary must be entitled to receive annually a specified dollar amount. In a charitable remainder unitrust, the noncharitable income beneficiary must receive an annual payment equal to a specified percentage of the trust corpus valued annually. Thus, the investment policy of the trustee cannot have an adverse effect on the charitable remainder. In the case of the annuity trust, any gain or loss due to changes in value would inure to the remainder interest since the amount payable to the noncharitable beneficiary is fixed at the time the trust is established. In the case of the charitable remainder unitrust, the charitable and noncharitable beneficiaries would share alike in increases or decreases in the value of the trust corpus.

Section 170(f)(2)(A) provides a third mechanism through which split-interest gifts can be made. Under a so-called *pooled income fund* (defined in § 642(c)), a trust or other fund is maintained by a charitable organization to which the donor transfers property. Under the terms of the transfer the remainder interest in the property is irrevocably assigned to the charity and the donor retains a life estate for herself or others. The charitable institution invests the funds, along with other funds contributed by other donors under similar transfers, and pays out a proportionate share of the total income earned by the fund to each of the donors to the fund. As each life income interest terminates, the remainder interest is separated from the pooled fund and goes to the charity for its unrestricted use. Methods for valuing the charitable and non-charitable interests are set forth in Treas. Reg. § 1.642(c)–6.

5.5.3. *Nontrust Life Estates and Remainders*

Section 170(f)(3) imposes the same limitations on nontrust split interest transfers as are imposed in transfers in trust. Thus, no deduction is generally allowed for a transfer of either a life estate (or estate for years) or a remainder if the other interest is held by a noncharitable beneficiary. Similarly, no deduction is allowed for permitting a charity the rent-free use of the taxpayer's property. Rev. Rul. 70–477, 1970–2 C.B. 62. Rev. Rul. 2003–28, 2003–11 C.B. 594 (no deduction is allowed for a contribution of a license to use a patent, if the taxpayer retains any substantial right in the patent, e.g., a right to license to others). This restriction does not apply to a remainder interest in a personal residence or farm. I.R.C. § 170(f)(3)(B)(i). Special valuation rules for real property are prescribed in § 170(f)(4). Section 170(f)(3)(B)(iii) exempts from the disallowance rule certain conservation easements, such as easements for greenbelts around real estate development or historic building facade easements. I.R.C. § 170(h) defines qualified conservation contributions. Glass v. Commissioner, 471 F.3d 698 (6th Cir. 2006), held that the contribution of a perpetual conservation easement that restricted development of certain portions of the taxpayers' lakefront residential lot, but which did not otherwise affect the taxpayers' use or enjoyment of the property, was a qualified conservation contribution under § 170(h) because it protected a relatively natural habitat of specifically identified wildlife, including bald eagles, and plants. Kaufman v. Commissioner, 134 T.C. 182 (2010), held that no charitable contribution deduction is allowable for the conveyance of an otherwise qualifying transfer of a facade conservation easement if the property is subject to a mortgage and the mortgagee has a prior claim to condemnation and insurance proceeds. Because the mortgage has priority over the easement, the easement is not protected in perpetuity, which is required by § 170(h)(5)(A). The First Circuit Court of Appeals reversed the Tax Court's decision, 687 F.3d 21 (1stCir. 2012), reasoning, a "grant that is absolute against the owner-donor" is sufficient "and almost the same as an absolute one where third-party claims (here, the bank's or the city's) are contingent and unlikely." In subsequent cases, the Tax Court has continued to follow its own holding in *Kaufman*, and both the Ninth and Tenth Circuits have agreed with the Tax Court. See Mitchell v. Commissioner, 138 T.C. 324 (2012), supplemented by T.C. Memo. 2013–204, aff'd, 775 F.3d 1243 (10th Cir. 2005); Minnick v. Commissioner, T.C. Memo. 2012–345, aff'd 796 F.3d 1156 (9th Cir. 2015).

A number of cases have held that façade easements restricting changes to the exterior of buildings that were located in designated historic districts and subject to local law restrictions on architectural changes did not give rise to a charitable contribution deduction on the ground that the contribution did not result in any diminution in the value of the property. Scheidelman v. Commissioner, 755 F.3d 148 (2d Cir. 2014), aff'g T.C. Memo. 2013–18; Kaufman v. Commissioner, 784 F.3d 56 (1st Cir. 2015), aff'g T.C. Memo. 2014–52, aff'd, 784 F.3d 56 (1st Cir. 2015).

Section 170(a)(3) provides that a contribution of a remainder interest in tangible personal property occurs only when all intervening interests have lapsed.

5.6. *Donations of Intellectual Property*

Section 170(e)(1)(B) limits the amount of the deduction for contributions of intellectual property to the lesser of fair market value or the donor's basis in the property. However, because intellectual property often has no basis in the hands of its creator, to retain an incentive for donations of valuable intellectual property, § 170(m) allows the donor an additional deduction equal to a portion of the income recognized by the donee with respect to the donated intellectual property over a period of up to 12 years, reduced by the amount allowable as a deduction in the year the property was donated. The intellectual property with respect to which the additional deduction under § 170(m) is allowed generally includes patents, certain copyrights, trademarks, trade names, trade secrets, know-how, some software and applications or registrations for such property but excludes property donated to many private foundations. The donor must inform the donee at the time of the contribution that the donor intends to use this provision. Congress enacted this regime over concern that "taxpayers with intellectual property are taking advantage of the inherent difficulties in valuing such property and are preparing or obtaining erroneous valuations. In such cases, the charity receives an asset of questionable value, while the taxpayer receives a significant tax benefit." H.R. Rep. No. 108–548, pt. 1, 108th Cong., 2d Sess. 351 (2004).

5.7. *Donations of "Junk"*

Long after Bill Clinton's infamous claimed deduction for a donation of used underwear to the Salvation Army, but possibly in reaction to the publicity surrounding the event, Congress enacted § 170(f)(16) in 2006 to disallow any deduction for a contribution of clothing or a household item unless the clothing or item is in "good used condition or better," or the claimed deduction for a single item exceeds $500 and the taxpayer attaches a qualified appraisal to the tax return. Donations of food, paintings, antiques, other art objects, jewelry, gems, and collections are not subject to § 170(f)(16).

6.   CONTRIBUTION TREATED AS A SECTION 162(a) DEDUCTION

Section 162(b) prevents a deduction under § 162(a) if a deduction under § 170 would have been available but for the percentage limitation. Where § 170 is not available, as where a foreign donee is involved, a corporation may obtain a deduction under § 162(a) if the contribution bears a direct relationship to its business and the contribution is made with the expectation of financial return. See e.g., B. Manischewitz Co. v. Commissioner, 10 T.C. 1139 (1948) (Acq.), allowing a deduction for a contribution to a theological school in Palestine whose graduates aided in convincing European Jews that the company's machine-made matzos complied with Jewish dietary laws.

In Marquis v. Commissioner, 49 T.C. 695 (1968) (Acq.), a travel agent made substantial cash payments to church-related organizations (in none of which she was a member) that patronized her travel agency and deducted the payments as business expenses for promotions. The Commissioner asserted a deficiency on the grounds that the payments were charitable contributions, and that when added to the other contributions claimed on her return, the 50-percent ceiling had been exceeded. The Tax Court allowed the deduction as a business expense, finding that the payments were directly keyed to the amount, character, and profitability of the business the taxpayer obtained from the organizations. These facts indicated that the payments were not "contributions."

In Rev. Rul. 73–113, 1973–1 C.B. 65, a retail business located in a resort city suffered substantial adverse business consequences as a result of an oil well blow-out that occurred off the city's coastline, causing pollution of waters and beaches. The city council created a special fund to help protect local business by conducting scientific research on oil pollution, preserving the city's beaches, and advertising to counteract the damaging publicity resulting from the pollution. A retail business organization contributed to the fund and the ruling held that, since the business expected a financial return commensurate with the amount contributed, § 162(a) rather than § 170 was the controlling section for purposes of determining deductibility. The expenses were held ordinary and necessary and deduction was allowed under § 162(a).

Section 170(f)(9) bars any deduction for contributions to an organization that conducts lobbying activities on matters of direct financial interest to the taxpayer's trade or business if the principal purpose of the contribution was to avoid the disallowance of deductions for lobbying activities under § 162(e) (see Chapter 12, Section 5.B.2.).

7. POLICY ASPECTS OF THE DEDUCTION FOR CHARITABLE CONTRIBUTIONS

The charitable contribution deduction is usually viewed as a tax expenditure designed to encourage private contributions to charity. In 2016, § 170 reduced federal revenues by nearly $48 billion. Joint Committee on Taxation, Estimates of Federal Tax Expenditures for Fiscal Years 2015–2019 36 & 38 (2015). The Report of the House Ways and Means Committee on the Revenue Act of 1938 described the purpose of the deduction, first enacted in 1917, as follows: "The exemption from taxation of money or property devoted to charitable and other purposes is based upon the theory that the Government is compensated for the loss of revenue by its relief from financial burden which would otherwise have to be met by appropriations from public funds, and by the benefits resulting from the promotion of the general welfare." H.Rep. No. 75–1860, 75th Cong., 3d Sess. 19 (1939), reprinted in 1939–1 (Part 2) C.B. 738, 742.

Some commentators have argued that charitable contributions do not constitute "consumption" and thus should not be included in the tax base. Under this view the deduction is justified in order to measure income correctly. But this position requires a narrow view of consumption. Moreover, a gift should be included in the income of either the donor or donee to track increases in net worth (see Chapter 4, Section 1). In the case of charitable organizations that provide consumption benefits to individuals, it would be difficult administratively to tax the benefits to recipients.[4]

The deduction for charitable contributions may be viewed as a tax expenditure program by which the federal government matches a portion of an individual donor's contribution to charity. Under this view, a donor's contribution to charity represents two separate contributions: one, that of the U.S. Treasury equal to the value of the deduction and two, the donor's own after-tax gift. As with other tax expenditures provided through the deduction mechanism, the federal portion of the contribution is a function of the donor's marginal tax bracket. The higher the marginal tax bracket, the higher the taxpayer's monetary benefit and the government's revenue loss. But donors who do not itemize personal deductions (a group that includes nearly 70 percent of all taxpayers), as well as those whose incomes do not require them to file tax returns, make their charitable contributions entirely from after-tax funds; that is, they receive no federal matching contribution. The distributive and other effects of utilizing the tax deduction mechanism as the vehicle for providing federal support for charities, coupled with a proposal to substitute a direct matching grant system in lieu of the charitable contributions deduction, are considered in McDaniel, Federal Matching Grants for Charitable Contributions: A Substitute for the Income Tax Deduction, 27 Tax L.Rev. 377 (1972).

---

[4]   However, it would be feasible to impose a tax on charitable organizations providing such benefits as a proxy for taxing the organizations' beneficiaries. See McDaniel, The Charitable Contributions Deduction (Revisited), 59 S.M.U. L.Rev. 773 (2006).

When the top marginal rates were reduced from 70 percent to 50 percent in 1981, some studies found that the amounts received by charitable organizations were less than they would have been had the rate reduction not taken place, presumably because the federal matching share for high income donors was reduced and donors did not increase their own after-tax contributions to compensate for the reduced federal grant. See Fullerton and Goodman, The Economic Recovery Tax Act of 1981: Implications for Charitable Giving, 16 Tax Notes 1027 (1982); Clotfelter and Salamon, The Impact of the 1981 Tax Act on Individual Charitable Giving, 35 Nat'l Tax J. 171 (1982). Studies conducted after the 1986 Act further reduced the top marginal rates confirmed these results. Charles T. Clotfelter, The Impact of Tax Reform on Charitable Giving: A 1989 Perspective, in Joel Slemrod, ed., Do Taxes Matter? (MIT Press 1990).

8.   THE CHARITABLE DEDUCTION AND SOCIAL PROBLEMS

Many non-profit organizations address social problems and issues. These organizations seek tax-exempt status primarily to insure the deductibility of contributions by interested citizens or organizations. The resulting expanded administrative roles for the IRS and the courts involve policing, evaluating, and, in some cases, determining the nature of societal efforts to respond to social problems.

For example, education has been considered a traditional charitable activity with contributions to educational facilities generally being deductible. But what if the recipient is a segregated private school? In Green v. Connally, 330 F.Supp. 1150 (D.D.C.1971), aff'd without opinion sub nom., Coit v. Green, 404 U.S. 997 (1971), the court entered a declaratory judgment that no deduction for a contribution to a segregated private school was allowed under § 170. The court issued an injunction prohibiting the IRS from approving the application for tax-exempt status of any private school located in Mississippi unless the school demonstrated that it had an established and publicized policy of racial nondiscrimination as to students, faculty, admissions, scholarship and loan programs, and athletic and extracurricular programs. After noting that there existed a serious question as to whether, under the common law of trusts, a segregated educational institution could qualify as a charitable organization, the court rested its decision on an interpretation of § 501(c)(3) based on the federal policy against racially segregated schools:

> The Internal Revenue Code provisions on charitable exemptions and deductions must be construed to avoid frustrations of Federal policy. Under the conditions of today they can no longer be construed so as to provide to private schools operating on a racially discriminatory premise the support of the exemptions and deductions which Federal tax law affords to charitable organizations and their sponsors.

> We are fortified in our view * * * by the consideration that a contrary interpretation of the tax laws would raise serious constitutional questions * * * . Clearly the Federal Government could not under the Constitution give direct financial aid to schools

practicing racial discrimination. But tax exemptions and deductions certainly constitute a Federal Government benefit and support. While that support is indirect, and is in the nature of a matching grant rather than an unconditional grant, it would be difficult indeed to establish that such support can be provided consistently with the Constitution.

In Bob Jones University v. United States, 461 U.S. 574 (1983), the Supreme Court reaffirmed this position.

The issue whether an organization qualifies for tax exemption and hence for deductible contributions has also arisen in cases involving segregated social organizations, property tax exemptions to religious organizations, tax benefits for parents of parochial school children, and sex discrimination. See e.g., Nationalist Movement v. Commissioner, 102 T.C. 558 (1994), aff'd per curiam, 37 F.3d 216 (5th Cir.1994) (tax exemption denied to white supremacist organization on the basis of findings that its activities were neither charitable nor educational).

If, in contrast, an otherwise eligible public charitable organization seeks to influence the solution of social problems through political activities, such as attempting to influence elections or lobbying the legislature, in most cases it is not an eligible recipient of charitable contributions for purposes of § 170. I.R.C. §§ 170(c)(2)(D), 501(c)(3). A charitable organization other than a church may elect to maintain its status by limiting lobbying expenditures to a specified percentage of its exempt purpose expenditures, but never more than $1,000,000. I.R.C. § 501(h). The ceilings are based on a decreasing percentage as the organization incurs greater exempt purpose expenditures. See § 4911(c). Limitations on the right to engage in political activities of organizations seeking tax exempt status under § 501(c)(3), which is linked to the definition of a public charity in § 170(c)(2), were upheld against Constitutional challenge in Regan v. Taxation with Representation, 461 U.S. 540 (1983).

SECTION 4. STATE AND LOCAL TAXES

INTERNAL REVENUE CODE: Sections 164; 275.

REGULATIONS: Sections 1.164–1(a); –2; –3; –4(a).

Section 164 allows a deduction for certain taxes, including domestic state and local real property, personal property, and income taxes. Foreign real property and income taxes are also deductible. Section 275 denies deductions for certain other taxes including federal income taxes. Prior to 1987, § 164 also allowed a deduction for state and local general sales taxes, but the deduction for sales taxes was repealed by the Tax Reform Act of 1986, an action that was partially reversed in 2004.

The deduction for taxes under § 164 is not limited to profit-seeking transactions so that, for example, a deduction is allowed for *ad valorem* personal property taxes on a vehicle used solely for personal purposes. Individuals, however, may deduct taxes that are not incurred in a trade or business only as itemized deductions under § 63. Taxes paid in the course of the taxpayer's trade or business are deductible in computing adjusted gross income. Brown v. United States, 434 F.2d 1065 (5th Cir.1970) (ad valorem taxes); Dorminey v. Commissioner, 26 T.C. 940 (1956) (Acq.). Furthermore, taxes incurred in trade or business, such as the employer's share of the FICA tax, are deductible under § 162, even though not enumerated in § 164, unless the employee's salary itself must be capitalized under § 263A (discussed in Chapter 13). Similarly, state and local sales taxes paid in the course of a trade or business are capitalized as part of the purchase price of the property, unless the cost of the property itself was deductible. Section 263A also requires the capitalization of real property taxes incurred during the construction period of property to be held for use in a trade or business. Treas. Reg. § 1.263A–2(a)(3)(ii) requires real estate developers to capitalize all real estate taxes paid with respect to any property if, at the time the taxes are incurred, it is reasonably likely that the property will be developed, even though no "production activities" of any sort have yet occurred. See Reichel v. Commissioner, 112 T.C. 14 (1999).

DETAILED ANALYSIS

1. DEFINITION OF "TAX"

To qualify for deduction under § 164, a levy must constitute a "tax." For purposes of § 164, a "tax" is "an enforced contribution, exacted pursuant to legislative authority in the exercise of the taxing power, and imposed and collected for the purpose of raising revenue to be used for public or governmental purposes." Rev. Rul. 75–444, 1975–2 C.B. 66, 67. Levies that relate to improvements that enhance the value of the assessed property, such as sewer or sidewalk assessments, are not deductible taxes. I.R.C. § 164(c)(1); Treas. Reg. § 1.164–4(a). The courts and the IRS have considered what constitutes a "tax" under § 164 in myriad situations, including: a "utility user tax" equal to 5 percent of charges for certain utilities was not a real property or general sales tax, Fife v. Commissioner, 73 T.C. 621 (1980); a sewer tap fee required to be paid to hook up to a city sewer system was a nondeductible user fee, Noble v. Commissioner, 70 T.C. 916 (1978); state law that divided a tenant's monthly payments to the landlord into a "renter's tax" and a basic rental payment did not convert nondeductible rent into a property tax on the tenant where the landlord remained liable for the full property tax, Rev. Rul. 79–180, 1979–1 C.B. 95; amounts inserted in parking meters are not deductible taxes, Rev. Rul. 73–91, 1973–1 C.B. 71; amounts withheld from employee's wages for a compulsory contribution to a state disability fund were deductible as a state "income tax," McGowan v. Commissioner, 67 T.C. 599 (1976); contributions required to be made by both employees and employers to a state supplemental worker's compensation fund constituted a "tax," Rev. Rul. 75–444, 1975–2 C.B. 66.

Only taxes imposed on the payor are deductible; a person who pays a tax assessed against another is not entitled to a deduction. For example, Tuer v. Commissioner, T.C. Memo. 1983–441, denied a daughter living in her father's house a deduction for her payment of property taxes on the house. Treas. Reg. § 1.162–11(a) provides that where a tenant pays real estate taxes imposed on the landlord, the tax payment is treated as an additional rental payment, which is income to the landlord who is, in turn, entitled to a deduction for the taxes paid.

2.   ELECTION TO DEDUCT STATE SALES TAXES

Section 164(b)(5) allows taxpayers to elect to deduct state sales taxes in lieu of deducting state income taxes. This provision primarily affects taxpayers living in states with a sales tax but no income tax, but it also affects taxpayers who itemize deductions and pay state and local sales tax that exceed state and local income taxes. Only a "general sales tax," defined as a tax imposed at a single rate on the retail sale of a broad range of classes of items, is deductible. Exemptions or lower rates for certain types of items are disregarded in making this determination. On the other hand, if an item (other than a motor vehicle) is taxed a rate higher than the general rate, no deduction is allowed for taxes with respect to that item. Taxpayers may claim deductions based on their receipts, or they may elect to claim deductions based on tables promulgated by the IRS. I.R.C. § 164(b)(5)(H)(i). The tables take into account filing status, number of dependents, adjusted gross income, and state-specific sales tax rates. A taxpayer who elects to use the tables, may claim additional deductions for actual taxes paid with respect to motor vehicles, boats, and certain items specified by the IRS. See Notice 2005–31, 2005–1 C.B. 830, for the list of additional items, which includes aircraft, homes (including mobile and prefabricated homes), and materials to build a home.

3.   POLICY ASPECTS

The deduction for state and local taxes raises difficult policy issues, both with respect to income tax policy and tax expenditure analysis.

3.1. *Income Tax Policy*

As a matter of income tax policy, the issue generally focuses on the relationship between the taxes paid to the state and local governments and the benefits received by the taxpayer from these governmental units. The classic work on this inquiry was conducted by Professor Richard Musgrave who concluded that, based on his ideal model of allocation of fiscal functions between the federal government and the state and local governments, the deduction for state and local taxes should not be allowed. Under Musgrave's model, state and local taxes are "benefit" taxes that provide goods and services to taxpayers equal in value to the taxes paid. See Musgrave, The Theory of Public Finance: A Study in Public Economy (1959); Musgrave and Musgrave, Public Finance in Theory and Practice 345 (5th ed. 1989). President Reagan's 1985 tax proposals recommended eliminating the deduction for all state and local income taxes and for other state and local taxes not incurred in carrying on a profit-seeking activity. The proposal relied in part on the benefit theory.

The Musgrave model has been criticized on the ground that the level of state and local taxes paid by a given individual is not always (and often is not) correlated to the level of benefits received. Denying a federal income tax deduction for state and local taxes paid by the individual when those taxes exceed the benefits received results in over taxation. See Billman and Cunningham, Nonbusiness State and Local Taxes: The Case for Deductibility, 28 Tax Notes 1107, 1110–1113 (1985):

Even if a state or local tax is redistributive, it is possible that those taxpayers from whom income is distributed receive intangible benefits (such as the personal satisfaction of aiding less fortunate residents) in addition to the value of economic goods and services for which their taxes pay. To account for this possibility, some commentators have suggested methods for estimating the consumption value associated with state and local services, and then permitting a deduction for state and local taxes paid only to the extent they exceed the value of a taxpayer's consumption of public goods. See Due, Personal Deductions, in Comprehensive Income Taxation 37, 51–52 (J. Pechman ed. 1977).

3.2. Tax Expenditure Aspects

Apart from the income definitional aspects, the deduction for state and local taxes is often justified in terms of the aid it gives state and local governments. The deductibility of state taxes effectively reduces the tax cost on a state's residents, and theoretically allows state governments more flexibility in financing their public services. In this way, the deduction for state and local taxes can be viewed as a form of revenue sharing, with the federal government subsidizing the states. In 2015, the cost of this subsidy reduced federal tax receipts by $100 billion ($65 billion for state and local incomes, sales, and personal property taxes, and $35 billion for state and local real property taxes). Joint Committee on Taxation, Estimates of Federal Tax Expenditures for Fiscal Years 2015–2019 32 & 40 (2015).

SECTION 5. QUALIFIED HOME MORTGAGE INTEREST

INTERNAL REVENUE CODE: Section 163(h) (omitting (h)(3)(D)).

REGULATIONS: Sections 1.163–8T(a)(1), (3), (4), (b), (c)(1), (2)(i), (ii), (3), (4)(i)–(iii), (5), (m)(3); –9T(a), (b).

General Explanation of the Tax Reform Act of 1986

Staff of the Joint Committee on Taxation 263–266 (1987).

[Pre-1987] Law.

Under [pre-1987] law, no limitation was imposed * * * on the deductibility of interest on indebtedness incurred for [noninvestment] purposes, e.g. to purchase or carry consumption goods. * * *

Reasons for Change

* * *

Personal interest

Prior law excluded or mismeasured income arising from the ownership of housing and other consumer durables. Investment in such goods allowed consumers to avoid the tax that would apply if funds were invested in assets producing taxable income and to avoid the cost of renting these items, a cost which would not be deductible in computing tax liability. Thus, the tax system under prior law provided an incentive to invest in consumer durables rather than assets which produce taxable income and, therefore, an incentive to consume rather than save.

Although Congress believed that it would not be advisable to subject to income tax imputed rental income with respect to consumer durables owned by the taxpayer, it nevertheless concluded that it is appropriate and practical to address situations where personal expenditures are financed by borrowing. By phasing out the present deductibility of personal interest, Congress intended to eliminate from the prior tax law a significant disincentive to saving.

While Congress recognized that the imputed rental value of owner-occupied housing may be a significant source of untaxed income, the Congress nevertheless determined that encouraging home ownership is an important policy goal, achieved in part by providing a deduction for residential mortgage interest. Therefore, the personal interest limit does not affect the deductibility of interest on debt secured by the taxpayer's principal residence or second residence [within the permissible ceilings on the amount of eligible debt]. * * *

Explanation of Provisions

* * *

Personal interest

Under [section 163(h)], personal interest is not deductible. Personal interest is any interest, other than interest incurred or continued in connection with the conduct of a trade or business (other than the trade or business of performing services as an employee),[59] investment interest, or interest taken into account in computing the taxpayer's income or loss from passive activities for the year. Thus, personal interest includes, for example, interest on a loan to purchase an automobile, interest on a loan to purchase a life insurance policy, and credit card interest, where such interest is not incurred or continued in connection with the conduct of a trade or business. Personal interest also includes interest on underpayments of individual Federal, State or local income taxes notwithstanding that all or a portion of the income may have arisen in a trade or business, because such taxes are not considered derived from the conduct of a trade or business.[60] * * *

Personal interest does not include qualified residence interest of the taxpayer * * * .

---

[59]   Thus, for example, interest on debt to finance an employee business expense is not deductible, under this rule.

[60]   Personal interest does not include interest on taxes, other than income taxes, that are incurred in connection with a trade or business. (For the rule that taxes on net income are not attributable to a trade or business, see Treas. Reg. sec. 1.62–1(d), relating to nondeductibility of State income taxes in computing adjusted gross income.) * * *

Qualified residence interest

Under [section 163(h)(3)], qualified residence interest is not subject to the limitation on personal interest. Qualified residence interest generally means interest on debt secured by a security interest valid against a subsequent purchaser under local law on the taxpayer's principal residence or a second residence of the taxpayer.[61] Qualified residence interest [is limited to interest on (1) debt, or refinancing of debt, to acquire or substantially improve a principal or second residence, up to a total debt of $1,000,000, plus (2) other debt (home equity indebtedness), not in excess of $100,000, secured by a principal or second residence]. * * * Qualified residence interest does not include interest on any portion of [home equity indebtedness] in excess of the fair market value of the residence [reduced by qualified acquisition indebtedness]. * * * Qualified residence interest is not subject to the limitation on personal interest even though the borrowed funds are used for personal expenditures.

* * *

DETAILED ANALYSIS

1. DISTINGUISHING PERSONAL INTEREST FROM PROFIT-SEEKING INTEREST

As indicated in the excerpt from the General Explanation of the Tax Reform Act of 1986, prior to 1987 interest on debt incurred to finance personal consumption was deductible as an itemized deduction. Disallowance of such a deduction under current law requires a method for allocating interest expense to different expenditures of the taxpayer. As discussed in Chapter 16, dealing with interest incurred in profit-seeking activities, Temp. Reg. § 1.163–8T adopts complex tracing rules. Under the tracing rules, individuals with significant liquid capital are able to structure transactions to trace equity to personal expenditures and debt to business and investment expenditures. Thus the burden of the disallowance of personal interest as a deduction falls on individuals who do not possess significant amounts of liquid capital.

2. QUALIFIED RESIDENCE INTEREST

2.1. *Acquisition Indebtedness*

2.1.1. *General*

Interest on up to $1,000,000 of indebtedness to buy, build, or improve the taxpayer's principal residence and one other residence is deductible. This rule does not necessarily allow a deduction for interest on two residences. For example, if the taxpayer's principal residence is a rented apartment on Park Avenue, and the taxpayer purchases a $600,000 vacation home in Palm Springs and a $400,000 vacation home in Aspen, the taxpayer must choose whether to deduct the interest on the Aspen or Palm Springs vacation home

---

[61]   Generally, under local law such a security interest must be recorded.

mortgage. The interest on the other vacation home mortgage loan is treated as nondeductible personal interest.

Acquisition or improvement indebtedness must be secured by a mortgage on the residence. Thus, for example, interest paid on a bona fide but unsecured loan from a family member to provide the down payment for a young couple's first house is not deductible under § 163(h)(3). If, however, the purchasers gave the family member from whom they borrowed the downpayment a valid junior mortgage on the residence, the interest paid on the junior mortgage would be deductible.

In Sophy v. Commissioner, 138 T.C. 204 (2012), rev'd sub nom, 796 F.3d 1051 (9th Cir. 2015), two unmarried individuals who were registered as domestic partners under California law, co-owned two residences. At issue was how the $1,000,000 limitation on acquisition indebtedness and the $100,000 limitation on home equity indebtedness were to be applied. The taxpayers argued that the aggregate $1.1 million limitation was to be applied on a per-taxpayer basis with respect to residence co-owners who are not married to each other. Based on its parsing of the language in § 163(h)(3), the Tax Court disagreed, concluding that Congress intended the limitation to be applied on a per-residence basis. Accordingly, the taxpayers' aggregate deductions for mortgage interest were limited to the interest that they paid on $1.1 million of the loans secured by the two residences.

On appeal, the Ninth Circuit reversed the Tax Court, holding that the debt limit provisions of § 163(h)(3) apply on a per-taxpayer basis to unmarried co-owners of a qualified residence and remanded the case for a determination of the proper amount of interest that each taxpayer was entitled to deduct. *Voss*, 796 F.3d 1051. The opinion focused principally on the parentheticals in § 163(h)(3)(B)(ii) and (C)(ii) that halve the debt ceilings "in the case of a married individual filing a separate return." If Congress had wanted to draft the parentheticals in per-residence terms, it could have done so. "The per-taxpayer wording of the parentheticals, considered in light of the parentheticals' use of the phrase 'in the case of,' thus suggests that the wording of the main clause—in particular, the phrase 'aggregate amount treated'—should likewise be understood in a per taxpayer manner." Furthermore, "the very inclusion of the parentheticals suggests that the debt limits apply per taxpayer." The holding in *Voss* means that unmarried co-owners of a home secured by a mortgage are *each* entitled to deduct mortgage and home equity interest up to $1.1 million on their own tax returns. In 2016, the IRS acquiesced to the decision in *Voss*. See A.O.D. 2016–02, 2016–31 I.R.B. 193.

2.1.2. *Mortgage Debt in Excess of $1,000,000 Ceiling*

Where the total acquisition and improvement indebtedness on qualified residences exceeds $1,000,000, only the interest on $1,000,000 is deductible. If there is only one mortgage loan, the amount of the interest paid on $1,000,000 of principal is not difficult to determine. But where the taxpayer has incurred two or more mortgage loans to acquire and improve the residences and the loans bear different rates of interest, the determination is more complex. Suppose for example, that the taxpayer owes $800,000 on a mortgage loan at 4 percent interest to purchase a principal residence and an additional $400,000 on a mortgage loan at 5 percent interest incurred to improve the residence (or to purchase a second residence). The taxpayer pays $32,000 of interest on the first mortgage and $20,000 of interest on the second mortgage. One method of determining the allowable deduction is to pro rate the $1,000,000 ceiling. Under this method, five-sixths (1,000,000/1,200,000) of the interest on each mortgage loan, $26,666.67 on the first mortgage and $16,666.67 on the second mortgage for a total of $43,333.34, would be deductible. Alternatively, a stacking principle based on mortgage priorities might be applied. Under this rule, all $32,000 of interest on the first mortgage would be deductible, and interest on only $200,000 (1,000,000 ceiling minus $800,000 first mortgage) of the second mortgage (i.e., $10,000) would be deductible, for a total of $42,000.

2.1.3. *Principal Residence*

Section 163(h)(4)(A)(i)(I) defines the taxpayer's principal residence through a cross reference to § 121, the exclusion for gain realized on the sale of a principal residence. Treas. Reg. § 1.121–1(b)(2) provides that whether a property is the taxpayer's principal residence depends upon all the facts and circumstances, but the residence used a majority of the time during the year ordinarily will be considered the taxpayer's principal residence. The regulations also have a nonexclusive list of factors that are relevant in identifying a property as a taxpayer's principal residence. Among the factors considered when the taxpayer has two or more residences are the location of the taxpayer's business or employment, the state or locality where the taxpayer files income tax returns, the address for voter registration and driver's licensure, and the location of the taxpayer's place of worship (see Chapter 6, Section 4.4.). A taxpayer cannot have more than one principal residence at a time. Temp. Reg. § 1.163–10T(p)(2).

2.1.4. *Second Residence*

Section 163(h)(4)(A)(i)(II) permits interest on one residence other than the taxpayer's principal residence to be deducted. The definition of residence for this purpose, as well as for the principal residence interest deduction, is broad enough to include mobile homes, recreational vehicles, and boats that have sleeping, cooking, and toilet facilities. See Temp. Reg. § 1.163–10T(p)(3)(ii). Thus interest on a loan to purchase a cabin cruiser may qualify for the deduction, depending on how the boat is outfitted, but interest on a loan to buy a less expensive open boat never may qualify. The House version of the Omnibus Budget Reconciliation Act of 1987 would have prohibited recreational vehicles and boats from qualifying as second residences for purposes of § 163(h)(3), but this provision was not enacted as part of the final legislation. See also Rev. Rul. 96–32, 1996–1 C.B. 5 (after destruction of principal residence by casualty, interest on purchase money mortgage continues to qualify for deduction during period before sale of land and purchase of replacement residence or reconstruction of new residence on original land).

If the taxpayer has rented the second residence to others for any period during the year, to qualify under § 163(h)(4)(A)(i)(II), the residence must be used by the taxpayer during the year for more than the greater of fourteen days or ten percent of the number of days it is rented. The purpose of this rule is to assure that interest paid with respect to property that is actually a rental property will be subject to the passive activity loss rules of § 469 (see Chapter 35, Section 2).

When the taxpayer owns two residences in addition to a principal residence, the taxpayer may elect which of the other residences is the second residence for purposes of § 163(h)(3). The election may be changed from year to year. Temp. Reg. § 1.163–10T(p)(3)(iv).

2.1.5. *Deductibility of Mortgage Insurance Premiums*

Mortgage lenders sometimes require borrowers to purchase mortgage insurance, which protects the lender in the event the borrower is unable to repay the loan in full. Historically, while the tax treatment of mortgage insurance premium payments by the borrower was not entirely clear, it was generally believed that the premiums were not deductible under § 163(h)(3) because they are not, as a technical matter, interest payments (i.e., payments made to the lender for the use of money).

In 2006, Congress enacted § 163(h)(3)(E), which treats mortgage insurance premiums as qualified residence interest (provided that the underlying loan qualifies as acquisition indebtedness with respect to a qualified residence). As a result, these premium payments are deductible for a taxpayer whose income is below a specified threshold. The deduction is phased out for taxpayers with adjusted gross incomes in excess of $100,000 ($50,000 for married persons filing separate returns), and the deduction is entirely disallowed for taxpayers with adjusted gross incomes above $110,000 ($55,000 for married persons filing separate returns). This deduction is set to expire on December 31, 2016.

2.2. *Home Equity Indebtedness*

Section 163(h)(3)(C) allows an individual to deduct interest on up to $100,000 of home equity indebtedness regardless of the use to which the loan proceeds are traced under Temp. Reg. § 1.163–8T. Thus, interest on a loan secured by a second mortgage on the taxpayer's home is deductible even though the loan proceeds are used to buy an automobile for personal use or to pay for a Caribbean vacation. Temp. Reg. § 1.163–8T(m)(3). This treatment has led banks to expand home equity mortgage loans where individual borrowers are given a line of credit secured by a mortgage on their home and a checkbook linked to the line of credit rather than a bank account; in some cases the borrower receives a credit card, such as a VISA or Master Card, to use to draw on the line of credit. These transactions significantly undermine the policy of disallowing a deduction for interest on loans that finance personal consumption.

If a home equity mortgage exceeds $100,000, interest paid on the excess principal amount is not necessarily nondeductible. The use of the loan proceeds must be traced under Temp. Reg. § 1.163–8T. See Temp. Reg. § 1.163–10T(e)(4). For example, if the excess principal amount were used to buy investment securities, the interest on the excess principal amount would be deductible as investment interest, subject to the limitations of § 163(d).

But if the proceeds were used to buy an automobile for personal use the interest would be nondeductible.

If a purchase money mortgage on the taxpayer's principal residence exceeds $1,000,000, Pau v. Commissioner, T.C. Memo. 1997–43, held that the taxpayer may not use the "home equity indebtedness" provision to deduct interest on the acquisition indebtedness exceeding $1,000,000. According to the Pau decision, only interest on $1,000,000 is deductible because "home equity indebtedness" does not include excess acquisition costs. Whether the statutory language supports this interpretation is not clear. However, in Rev. Rul. 2010–25, 2010–44 I.R.B. 571, the IRS backed off of its victory in *Pau*, concluding that "home equity indebtedness" (within the meaning of § 163(h)(3)(C)(i)) includes acquisition indebtedness exceeding $1,000,000.

2.3. *Application of Section 265*

Although Temp. Reg. § 1.163–8T(m)(3) provides that qualified residence interest is deductible without regard to the use to which the loan proceeds are traced, § 265 nevertheless may apply to disallow a deduction for qualified residence interest in two contexts. First, if the proceeds of a home equity loan are used to purchase tax-exempt bonds, § 265(a)(2) may disallow the deduction. Temp. Reg. § 1.163–10T(b). For § 265(a)(2), see Chapter 16, Section 3.C.

Second, § 265(a)(1) may be applied to disallow a deduction for interest on acquisition indebtedness if the taxpayer receives a tax-exempt housing allowance. Induni v. Commissioner, 990 F.2d 53 (2d Cir.1993), involved an employee of the United States Immigration and Naturalization Service who received a tax-exempt "living quarters allowance" while stationed abroad. The court sustained the disallowance of an interest deduction, finding the interest payments "allocable" to the living quarters allowance. The enactment in 1986 of § 265(a)(6), providing that § 265 shall not be applied to disallow home mortgage interest deductions in the case of tax-exempt parsonage and military housing allowances, was cited as evidence that Congress intended § 265(a)(1) to disallow home mortgage interest deductions allocable to other tax-exempt housing allowances.

3. "POINTS" PAID IN CONNECTION WITH MORTGAGES ON QUALIFIED RESIDENCES

Section 461(g) generally defers deductions for prepaid interest. Home mortgages typically involve the payment of prepaid interest in the form of a flat percentage of the loan principal, commonly termed "points" at the closing. Consistent with the preferred status that Congress has accorded home mortgage interest, § 461(g)(2) allows a current deduction for "points" paid with respect to a mortgage loan incurred to purchase or improve the taxpayer's principal residence if the payment of points is an established local business practice and does not exceed the amount generally charged in the area. See Rev. Proc. 92–12, 1992–1 C.B. 663, providing guidelines used by the IRS to identify the amount, if any, of currently deductible points. Schubel v. Commissioner, 77 T.C. 701 (1981), held that "points" withheld from the loan principal disbursement rather than separately collected from the borrower's own funds, were not "paid" as required by § 461(g)(2). Thus, no current deduction was allowed.

The IRS has ruled that the special rule in § 461(g)(2) does not apply to points paid to refinance an existing mortgage loan on the taxpayer's principal residence. Rev. Rul. 87–22, 1987–1 C.B. 146. In Huntsman v. Commissioner, 91 T.C. 917 (1988), the Tax Court held that points paid to refinance a mortgage on a principal residence were not currently deductible but instead were deductible ratably over the life of the loan. The Court of Appeals reversed and allowed a current deduction, reasoning that because the original mortgage loan was for only three years, its replacement two years later with a permanent thirty-year mortgage met the "in connection with" requirement of § 461(g)(2). 905 F.2d 1182 (8th Cir.1990). Subsequently, in Kelly v. Commissioner, T.C. Memo. 1991–605, the Tax Court disallowed a current deduction for points paid in connection with refinancing an original thirty-year mortgage, distinguishing *Huntsman* as involving a short-term original loan.

Points for which a current deduction is disallowed under § 461(g), but which are deductible under § 163(h)(3) are deducted over the life of the loan. Under certain conditions the borrower may deduct the points ratably over the term of the loan. Otherwise, the deduction is allowed at the rate at which the interest economically accrues. Rev. Proc. 87–15, 1987–1 C.B. 624.

4. POLICY ASPECTS OF THE DEDUCTION FOR PERSONAL INTEREST

Whether personal interest unrelated to profit-seeking activities should be deductible has been a topic of considerable debate. One view is that under an income tax only expenses incurred in connection with profit-seeking activities should be deductible. Thus, interest paid on a consumption-related loan, such as a loan to enable a taxpayer to take a vacation, is not connected with any profit-seeking activity and therefore should not be deductible.

Others maintain that the deduction for personal interest can be justified on theoretical grounds. Under the Schanz-Haig-Simons definition of income, amounts which are expended for consumption admittedly should be nondeductible and therefore taxable. But, it does not necessarily follow that interest costs incurred in connection with borrowing for personal consumption are also consumption. The interest costs reflect a preference for current consumption; but the absolute amount of consumption remains the same whether an individual borrows for personal consumption in year 1 or defers consumption until year 2 when non-borrowed funds are available for consumption. Under this view, consumption-related interest should be deductible since it represents only a payment for time preference and not additional consumption. The response to this argument, is that if the taxpayer is willing to pay the additional interest to accelerate the consumption, the value of the consumption to the taxpayer includes the interest and thus no deduction should be available.

5. POLICY ASPECTS OF THE DEDUCTION FOR INTEREST AND PROPERTY TAXES ALLOCABLE TO PERSONAL RESIDENCES

Allowing deductions for qualified residence acquisition interest and real property taxes on personal residences raises a special tax policy issue because the personal residence is a consumer durable. A taxpayer purchasing a consumer durable acts as both investor and consumer. It is as if the taxpayer purchased the item as investor and leased it to himself as consumer. The imputed rent *received* should produce gross income to the taxpayer as investor; the imputed rent *paid* should be a nondeductible personal expense. Sales or property taxes, interest, depreciation, and maintenance expenses with respect to the asset relate to the profit-seeking aspect of the transaction and should be deductible. Under present law, however, the imputed rent received is not included in gross income. The interest and taxes are thus costs of producing tax-exempt income. Although § 265 (discussed in Chapter 12, Section 4 and Chapter 16, Section 3.C.) disallows the deduction for interest and other items related to tax-exempt income in some circumstances, this section has never been extended to disallow a deduction where the income to which it related was imputed income. As a result, the interest deduction and property tax deduction are allowed for taxpayers with imputed income from property ownership.

The problems presented by the current treatment of not taxing the imputed income from living in a personal residence while allowing a deduction for certain expenses of acquiring and holding a personal residence are discussed in the following excerpt from Aaron, Income Taxes and Housing, 60 Am.Econ.Rev. 789 (1970):

> The Internal Revenue Code contains massive tax subsidies for housing. The largest accrue to homeowners through exemption from taxation of net imputed rent and deductibility of mortgage interest and property taxes paid. Smaller benefits accrue to owners of rental housing to the extent that accelerated depreciation exceeds true depreciation on real estate by a greater margin than accelerated depreciation on other properties.

> These tax subsidies affect resource allocation, income distribution, and the form of legal tenure in which housing is held. Consumption of housing services is considerably greater than it would be in the absence of tax benefits, particularly by homeowners. The magnitude of this effect is difficult to gauge, but is about 20 percent in the aggregate, and much greater for some groups.[32]

---

[32]   This estimate presumes a mean marginal tax rate among homeowners of 22 percent (in 1966 the mean marginal rate among all taxpayers was 19 percent), that imputed rent plus deductible expenses average five-eighths of gross rent and that the price elasticity of demand for housing is 1.5. [Ed.: Subsequent studies have found a somewhat lesser impact of the tax preferences on the extent of home ownership, generally in the 5 percent to 8 percent range. These studies are summarized in Congressional Budget Office, The Tax Treatment of Home Ownership: Issues and Options 27 (Sept. 1981). Other studies, however, have found that housing capital in general is 25 percent higher than it would be if federal tax policy treated all capital equally. Staff of the Joint Committee on Taxation, Overview of Entitlement Programs 1044, n. 29 (Comm. Print 1992).]

The impact on income distribution is large. In an accounting sense the benefits accrue primarily to upper income homeowners. These tax benefits are formally equivalent to direct housing subsidies combined with a tax system which treats income from housing as other income from capital is treated. * * *

With respect to any conceivable policy objective, the pattern of tax benefits seems to be capricious and without rationale. Apart from the alleged, but unsubstantiated, benefits accruing to the community when households come to own their own homes, there appears to be no reason for subsidizing homeownership rather than other investments or the consumption of owned rather than rented housing services or of other commodities.[33] Even if one were to acknowledge that homeownership benefits society by making homeowners more stable or less antisocial than they otherwise would have been, the pattern of tax benefits is ill suited to that objective. Tax benefits provide largest benefits to recipients of larger than average income whose experience with wealth is typically not limited to their own houses. They provide negligible aid to low income households, most of whom have not been vouchsafed the salutary discipline of property management.

The obvious remedy for the problems * * * is that homeowners be required to report gross imputed rent and expenses on their residence as other businesses must report gross income and expenses generated in producing other goods.

The implementation of such a procedure would raise some serious administrative problems. It would be necessary through appraisal to establish net imputed rent. At least two approaches could be used. First, direct appraisals of gross imputed rent could be prepared by appraisers, much as appraisals of fair market value are now made by property tax offices, and for banks, insurance companies, savings and loan associations and other financial intermediaries. From these estimates maintenance expense, depreciation, and interest would be deducted to reach net rent. Alternatively, the owner's equity interest could be estimated by deducting the balances of outstanding debt secured by the house from the appraised fair market value of the house. Net imputed income could be estimated by multiplying owners equity by a rate of return equal to that on alternative investments the homeowner could have made, such as the interest rate on long-term government bonds, high grade corporate bonds, * * * or rates on some other form of security.

---

[33] A vast literature exists which purports to show the beneficent effects of good housing or of homeownership or the harmful effects of slums on households or on society. * * * In this author's opinion, no study has shown both of the following: (a) that the beneficial effects of housing are due to the housing itself rather than adequate income, i.e., that the composition, rather than the level, of consumption matters; (b) that correlations between homeownership and socially or personally desirable characteristics (or the absence of antisocial characteristics) are not the joint results of other psychological, sociological or economic characteristics. The issue of which way causation runs also is frequently troublesome.

On balance, the latter method seems preferable since under the first procedure the homeowner, by discretionary behavior, could keep net rent artificially low. Each dollar spent for maintenance or noncapital improvements would reduce tax liability, thereby encouraging homeowners, particularly high bracket taxpayers, to make improvements in excess of those which they would choose to make apart from tax considerations. Moreover, since capital gains on owner occupied homes are treated even more favorably than are capital gains on other assets, the chance of even partial recovery through capital gains taxation at time of sale would be far from certain. This avenue of avoidance would be narrowed under the latter procedure. While the administrative problems are not trivial, they do not appear insuperable. The reliance which financial intermediaries place on property appraisals, suggests that appraisals of sufficient accuracy to support estimates of imputed rent can be made. The additional costs of making such appraisals would be substantial, however, unless appraisals for federal income tax and local property taxes could be joined. Such a course would generate major collateral benefits through improvement in the administration of the property tax.

Alternatively, deductions could be disallowed for mortgage interest, property taxes, or both. If deductions for mortgage interest were disallowed, homeowners would be encouraged to substitute borrowing on other assets for borrowing on their homes. To the extent that homeowners could substitute other credit instruments for home mortgages or had already paid off their mortgages, disallowance of deductions for mortgage interest would have no tax consequences. However, the impact would be severe on markets for financial assets. Clearly, deductions for mortgage interest could not be disallowed in practice without major changes in laws regulating savings and loan associations.

None of the preceding problems would arise if deductions for property taxes paid were disallowed. No valuation problems would arise, nor would any tendencies to distort asset choice. Rather significant political consequences would ensue, however. Property tax increases would generate greater net costs for homeowners and aggravate the already sharp discontent over property taxation. Disallowance of property tax deductions would not appear to be politically acceptable unless it were combined with financial aid, through revenue sharing or other fiscal devices, for the municipal governments and school districts, thereby permitting large reductions in property tax rates. If complete reform in the taxation of homeowners is not adopted, then disallowance of deductions for property taxes should be included as part of any large scale program of revenue sharing, block grants, or other fiscal devices designed to strengthen revenues of local governments.

In summary, the program of complete reform seems the most attractive course, particularly if it were introduced as part of an overall tax reduction to offset the tax increases which homeowners would otherwise experience. The reform would develop a common interest between the federal government, municipal governments, and school districts in accurate property tax appraisal. It would reduce the substantial horizontal inequality resulting from the anomalous treatment of homeowners. And, at given tax rates, it would cause the personal income tax to generate substantially larger revenues which could support direct expenditures for housing or other purposes, reductions in tax rates, or lower interest rates.

It sometimes has been suggested that tenants should be provided with a special deduction in order to equalize their position with homeowners who are able to deduct property taxes. As the analysis in the foregoing excerpt indicates, however, the owner of a residence is both a tenant and an investor. As a tenant she gets no deduction for her rent and thus is in precisely the same position as a renter from a third party. It is as an investor that the homeowner may be in an advantaged position compared to the tenant. The homeowner-investor not only realizes tax-free income from the net imputed rental value, but also is entitled to deduct the costs associated with producing that income. By contrast, the tenant who invests, for example, in municipal bonds may be barred by § 265 from deducting the costs associated with the production of that exempt income.

In addition to the inequities and inefficiencies associated with tax subsidies for housing, the provisions cost a considerable amount of money. Even if we consider just the three most costly tax expenditures for housing— the deduction for mortgage interest, the exclusion of gain on the sale of a principal residence, and the deduction for real property taxes—the annual revenue loss to the national treasury is close to $145 billion (respectively, for the three tax expenditures: $77 billion, $32.4 billion, and $34.7 billion in 2016). Joint Committee on Taxation, Estimates of Federal Tax Expenditures for Fiscal Years 2015–2019 32 (2015). If we further include the exclusion for net imputed rental income—which the Office of Management and Budget includes in its tax expenditure budget—that figure jumps another $100 billion. Office of Management and Budget, Analytical Perspectives: Budget of the United States Government, Fiscal Year 2017 243 (2016). All told (and including the exclusion for net imputed rental income), tax expenditures for housing reduce federal tax receipts every year by more than $275 billion, or one-fifth of the entire tax expenditure budget.

SECTION 6.   CASUALTY LOSSES

INTERNAL REVENUE CODE: Section 165(b), (c)(3), (h).

REGULATIONS: Sections 1.165–7(a), (b); –8.

Section 165(c)(3) allows a deduction for losses that are not connected with a profit-seeking activity if those losses arise from "fire, storm, shipwreck, or other casualty, or from theft" and exceed various thresholds. As in the case of the medical expense deduction, the involuntary and unexpected nature of the loss is the principal justification for the deduction. Nevertheless, the casualty loss deduction is classified as a tax expenditure. In the case of property, this classification is appropriate because the deduction is given despite the fact that the imputed income from the property involved is not included in income. Meanwhile, where the loss involves cash, the appropriateness of classifying the deduction as a tax expenditure item is not nearly as clear.

The principal issue arising under § 163(c)(3) is whether the losses are attributable to a qualifying "casualty."

Chamales v. Commissioner

United States Tax Court, 2000.
T.C. Memo. 2000–33.

■ NIMS, J.

* * *

FINDINGS OF FACT

* * *

Gerald and Kathleen Chamales (petitioners) are married and resided in Los Angeles, California, at the time of filing their petition in this case. In the spring of 1994, petitioners became interested in purchasing a residence in Brentwood Park, an exclusive Los Angeles neighborhood. They were attracted to the beautiful, parklike setting and the quiet peacefulness of the area. Subsequently, on June 2, 1994, petitioners opened escrow on property located in Brentwood Park, at 359 North Bristol Avenue. They were represented in this transaction by Jay Solton (Solton), a real estate agent with more than 20 years of experience. Solton's work focused on sales of properties in the Westwood, Brentwood, Palisades, and Santa Monica areas of Los Angeles.

At the time petitioners opened escrow, O.J. Simpson (Simpson) owned and resided at the property located directly west of and adjacent to that being purchased by petitioners. Simpson's address was 360 North Rockingham Avenue. Both parcels were corner lots, bounded on the north by Ashford Street. The rear or westerly side of petitioners' land abutted the rear or easterly side of the Simpson property.

During the escrow period, on June 12, 1994, Nicole Brown Simpson and Ronald Goldman were murdered at Ms. Brown Simpson's condominium in West Los Angeles. Simpson was arrested for these murders shortly thereafter. Following the homicides and arrest, the Brentwood Park neighborhood surrounding the Simpson property became inundated with media personnel and equipment and with individuals drawn by the area's connection to the horrific events. The media and looky-loos[1] blocked streets, trespassed on neighboring residential property, and flew overhead in helicopters in their attempts to get close to the Simpson home. Police were summoned to the area for purposes of controlling the crowds, and barricades were installed at various Brentwood Park intersections to restrict traffic. This police presence, however, had little practical effect. Significant media and public attention continued throughout 1994 and 1995. Although Simpson was acquitted on October 4, 1995, civil proceedings in 1996 reignited public interest.

Petitioners closed escrow on June 29, 1994, purchasing the residence on North Bristol Avenue for $2,849,000. * * *

Petitioners' 1994 tax return was prepared by Ruben Kitay (Kitay), a certified public accountant. In the course of preparing this return, Kitay and petitioner discussed the possibility of claiming a deduction for casualty loss. After preliminary research in the regulations addressing casualty loss, Kitay spoke with two area real estate agents regarding the amount by which petitioners' property had decreased in value. The agents estimated the decline at 30 to 40 percent. Kitay and petitioner decided to use the more conservative 30 percent figure in calculating the deduction to be taken on petitioners' return. An expert appraisal was not obtained at this time, as Kitay felt that a typical appraisal based on values throughout the Brentwood Park area would be inconclusive as to the loss suffered by the few properties closest to the Simpson home.

Kitay and petitioner also recognized and discussed the fact that there existed a substantial likelihood of an audit focusing on petitioners' 1994 return. Hence, to clarify the position being taken and the reasons underlying petitioners' deduction [which they valued at $751,427], an explanatory supplemental statement labeled "Casualty Loss" was attached to the return. After indicating the location of petitioners' property in relation to that of Simpson, it stated that the casualty loss was premised on "the calamity of the murder & trial, which was sudden & unavoidable & which resulted in a permanent loss to value of property." A table enumerating instances of minor physical damage to petitioners' property, such as damage to lawn and sprinklers, was also attached to the return, but no valuation was placed upon the harm caused thereby.

* * *

As of early 1999, the area surrounding the former Simpson home was no longer inundated with media personnel or equipment. The police barricades restricting traffic in the immediate vicinity of petitioners'

---

[1]　As explained by petitioners' counsel, "looky-loo" is a term developed in Hollywood to describe individuals who gather at places and events in hopes of glimpsing celebrities. The phrase is apparently used in California to denote those who frequent a location not because of its status as a conventional tourist sight but because of its association with a famous or notorious person. We adopt the terminology and spelling as used in petitioners' briefs and by the witnesses at trial.

property had been removed. Looky-loos, however, continued to frequent the neighborhood, often advised of the location of Simpson's former residence by its inclusion on "star maps" published for the Los Angeles area. Anniversaries of the murders were also typically accompanied by periods of increased media and public attention.

OPINION

We must decide whether petitioners are entitled to a casualty loss deduction based upon a postulated decline in the value of their residential property and, if not, whether they are liable for the section 6662(a) accuracy-related penalty.

* * *

Petitioners contend that the media and onlooker attention following the murders and focusing on Simpson's home has decreased the value of their adjacent property. They argue that because the homicides were a sudden, unexpected, and unusual event, and because aspects of the public interest precipitated thereby continued at least to the time of trial in this case, they have suffered a permanent casualty loss. Petitioners further allege that the proximity of their residence to that of Simpson has stigmatized their property and rendered it subject to permanent buyer resistance.

Conversely, respondent asserts that public attention over the course of a lengthy murder trial is not the type of sudden and unexpected event that will qualify as a casualty within the meaning of the Code. Respondent additionally contends that the Court of Appeals for the Ninth Circuit, to which appeal in this case would normally lie, has limited the amount that may be claimed as a casualty loss deduction to the loss suffered as a result of physical damage to property. According to respondent, since petitioners have failed to substantiate any such damage, they are entitled to no deduction. In respondent's view, any decline in market value represents merely a temporary fluctuation and not a permanent, cognizable loss.

We agree with respondent that petitioners have not established their entitlement to a casualty loss deduction. * * *

As interpreted by case law, a casualty loss within the meaning of section 165(c)(3) arises when two circumstances are present. First, the nature of the occurrence precipitating the damage to property must qualify as a casualty. * * * Second, the nature of the damage sustained must be such that it is deductible for purposes of section 165. * * * At issue here then are whether the events surrounding the alleged Simpson murders and affecting petitioners' property can properly be termed a casualty and whether the type of loss suffered by petitioners as a consequence of these events is recognized as deductible. We conclude that both inquiries must be answered in the negative.

A. Nature of Occurrence Constituting a Casualty

The word "casualty" as used in section 165(c)(3) has been defined, through application of the principle of ejusdem generis, by analyzing the shared characteristics of the specifically enumerated casualties of fire, storm, and shipwreck. * * * As [previously] explained by this Court:

> wherever unexpected, accidental force is exerted on property and the taxpayer is powerless to prevent application of the force because of the suddenness thereof or some disability, the resulting direct and proximate damage causes a loss which is like or similar to losses arising from the causes specifically enumerated in section 165(c)(3). * * * [*White v. Commissioner, supra* at 435.]

Hence, casualty for purposes of the Code denotes " 'an undesigned, sudden and unexpected event' ", Durden v. Commissioner, [3 T.C. 1, 3 (1944)] (quoting Webster's New International Dictionary), or " 'an event due to some sudden, unexpected or unusual cause' ", *id.* * * * . Conversely, the term " 'excludes the progressive deterioration of property through a steadily operating cause.' " *Id.* * * * . The sudden and unexpected occurrence, however, is not limited to those events flowing from forces of nature and may be a product of human agency. See *id.* at 4.

Here, we cannot conclude that the asserted devaluation of petitioners' property was the direct and proximate result of the type of casualty contemplated by section 165(c)(3). While the stabbing of Nicole Brown Simpson and Ronald Goldman was a sudden and unexpected exertion of force, this force was not exerted upon and did not damage petitioners' property. Similarly, the initial influx of onlookers, although perhaps sudden, was not a force exerted on petitioners' property and was not, in and of itself, the source of the asserted decrease in the home's market value. Rather, petitioners base their claim of loss on months, or even years, of ongoing public attention. If neither media personnel nor looky-loos had chosen to frequent the Brentwood Park area after the murders, or if the period of interest and visitation had been brief, petitioners would have lacked grounds for alleging a permanent and devaluing change in the character of their neighborhood. Hence, the source of their difficulties would appear to be more akin to a steadily operating cause than to a casualty. Press and media attention extending for months bears little similarity to a fire, storm, or shipwreck and is not properly classified therewith as an "other casualty".

B. Nature of Damage Recognized as Deductible

With respect to the requisite nature of the damage itself, this Court has traditionally held that only physical damage to or permanent abandonment of property will be recognized as deductible under section 165. * * * In contrast, the Court has refused to permit deductions based upon a temporary decline in market value. * * *

For example, in *Citizens Bank v. Commissioner*, [28 T.C. 717, 720 (1957), aff'd, 252 F.2d 425 (1st Cir.1957)], the Court stated that "physical damage or destruction of property is an inherent prerequisite in showing a casualty loss." When again faced with taxpayers seeking a deduction premised upon a decrease in market value, the Court further explained in *Pulvers v. Commissioner*, [48 T.C. 245 (1967), aff'd 407 F.2d 838 (9th Cir.1969)] (quoting *Citizens Bank v. Commissioner*, 252 F.2d at 428): " 'The scheme of our tax laws does not, however, contemplate such a series of adjustments to reflect the vicissitudes of the market, or the wavering values occasioned by a succession of adverse or favorable developments.' " Such a decline was termed "a hypothetical loss or a mere fluctuation in value." * * * This rule was reiterated yet again in *Kamanski v. Commissioner*, [T.C. Memo 1970–352, aff'd, 477 F.2d 452 (9th Cir.1973)] when the Court observed:

> In the instant case there was likewise relatively small physical damage to petitioner's property and the primary drop in value was due to buyer resistance to purchasing property in an area which had suffered a landslide. If there had been no physical damage to the property, petitioner would be entitled to no casualty loss deduction because of the decrease in market value resulting from the slide. * * *
>
> * * *
>
> * * * the only loss which petitioner is entitled to deduct is for the physical damage to his property
>
> * * *

Given the above decisions, we conclude that petitioners here have failed to establish that their claimed casualty loss is of a type recognized as deductible for purposes of section 165(c)(3). They have not proven the extent to which their property suffered physical damage, and their attempt to base a deduction on market devaluation is contrary to existing law.

With respect to physical damage and assuming arguendo that petitioners' loss stemmed from an occurrence that could properly be deemed a casualty, they would be entitled to a deduction for physical harm to their property. Nonetheless, although petitioners attached to their return a list of minor instances of physical damage and mentioned several other items at trial, they have neither offered evidence of the monetary value of nor provided any substantiation for such losses. We therefore have no basis for determining what, if any, portion of the claimed deduction might be allowable, and we cannot sustain a $751,427 deduction on the grounds of damage to a lawn or a sprinkler system.

As regards decrease in property value, petitioners' efforts to circumvent the established precedent repeatedly rejecting deductions premised on market fluctuation, through reliance on *Finkbohner v. United States*, 788 F.2d 723 (11th Cir.1986), are misplaced. In

Finkbohner, the Court of Appeals for the Eleventh Circuit permitted a deduction based on permanent buyer resistance in absence of physical damage. The Finkbohners lived on a cul-de-sac with 12 homes, and after flooding damaged several of the houses, municipal authorities ordered 7 of the residences demolished and the lots maintained as permanent open space. Such irreversible changes in the character of the neighborhood were found to effect a permanent devaluation and to constitute a casualty within the meaning of section 165(c)(3).

However, as explicated above, this Court has long consistently held that an essential element of a deductible casualty loss is physical damage or, in some cases, physically necessitated abandonment. * * *

Moreover, we further note that petitioners' circumstances do not reflect the type of permanent devaluation or buyer resistance which would be analogous to that held deductible in *Finkbohner v. United States, supra.* The evidence in the instant case reveals that media and onlooker attention has in fact lessened significantly over the years following the murders. Access to petitioners' property is no longer restricted by media equipment or police barricades. Residents of Brentwood Park have continued to invest substantial funds in remodeling and upgrading their homes [including the petitioners, who, in 1995 and 1996, made capital improvements to their property of nearly $2 million]. Hence, petitioners' difficulties are more akin to a temporary fluctuation in value, which no court has found to support a deduction under section 165(c)(3). We therefore hold that petitioners have failed to establish their entitlement to a casualty loss deduction. * * *

Issue 2: Accuracy-Related Penalty

Section 6662(a) and (b)(1) imposes an accuracy-related penalty in the amount of 20 percent of any underpayment that is attributable to negligence or disregard of rules or regulations. "Negligence" is defined in section 6662(c) as "any failure to make a reasonable attempt to comply with the provisions of this title," and "disregard" as "any careless, reckless, or intentional disregards." Case law similarly states that "Negligence is a lack of due dare or the failure to do what a reasonable and ordinarily prudent person would do under the circumstances." Freytag v. Commissioner, 89 T.C. 849, 887 (1987) (quoting Marcello v. Commissioner, 380 F.2d 499, 506 (5th Cir. 1967), affg. on this issue 43 T.C. 168 (1964) and T.C. Memo 1964–299), affd. 904 F.2d 1011 (5th Cir. 1990), affd. 501 U.S. 868 (1991).

An exception to the section 6662(a) penalty is set forth in section 6664(c)(1) and provides: "No penalty shall be imposed under this part with respect to any portion of an underpayment if it is shown that there was a reasonable cause for such portion and that the taxpayer acted in good faith with respect to such portion." The taxpayer bears the burden of establishing that this reasonable cause exception is applicable, and the Commissioner's determination of an accuracy-related penalty is presumed correct. * * *

Regulations interpreting section 6664(c) state:

> The determination of whether a taxpayer acted with reasonable cause and in good faith is made on a case-by-case basis, taking into account all pertinent facts and circumstances. * * * Generally, the most important factor is the extent of the taxpayer's effort to assess the taxpayer's proper tax liability. * * * [Sec. 1.6664–4(b)(1), Income Tax Regs.]

Furthermore, reliance upon the advice of an expert tax preparer may, but does not necessarily, demonstrate reasonable cause and good faith in the context of the section 6662(a) penalty. See id.; see also Freytag v. Commissioner, supra at 888. Such reliance is not an absolute defense, but it is a factor to be considered. See Freytag v. Commissioner, supra at 888. In order for this factor to be given dispositive weight, the taxpayer claiming reliance on a professional such as an accountant must show, at minimum, that (1) the accountant was supplied with correct information and (2) the incorrect return was a result of the accountant's error. See e.g., Ma-Tran Corp. v. Commissioner, 70 T.C. 158, 173 (1978); Pessin v. Commissioner, 59 T.C. 473, 489 (1972); Garcia v. Commissioner, T.C. Memo 1998–203, affd. without published opinion 190 F.3d 538 (5th Cir. 1999).

Applying these principles to the instant case, we conclude that petitioners have sustained their burden of establishing reasonable cause and good faith for the deduction taken on their return. Petitioner first inquired of his real estate agent, an experienced broker, regarding the potential decline in value as a result of events stemming from the alleged Simpson murders. He then sought advice from his accountant Kitay concerning the propriety of a casualty loss deduction. Kitay, in turn, discussed devaluation with two additional real estate brokers. Kitay's opinion that a typical appraisal would be inconclusive as to petitioners' property also appears to have played a significant role in the decision not to seek such an evaluation.

Moreover, the explanatory statement prepared by Kitay and attached to petitioner's return indicates, on the part of petitioners, both communication to the accountant of relevant information and good faith. Petitioners supplied Kitay with factual data related to the nature of the loss, and they chose to make full disclosure rather than to obscure the reasons for their deduction. We therefore conclude that petitioners did not exhibit the type of unreasonableness or imprudence that would support imposition of the section 6662(a) accuracy-related penalty. * * *

DETAILED ANALYSIS

1.   MEANING OF "CASUALTY" AND THEFT

1.1. *Casualty*

Chamales illustrates the necessity of distinguishing a casualty loss from an unrealized decrease in property value. If a taxpayer owned real estate that substantially increased in value because of development of adjacent property, the gain unquestionably would not be realized. *Chamales* essentially provides a parallel rule for losses.

Casualty losses also must be distinguished from gradual deterioration. Application of this distinction to termite damage has proven to be particularly troublesome. In Rosenberg v. Commissioner, 198 F.2d 46 (8th Cir.1952), the court allowed a casualty loss deduction for termite damage where the property was inspected in September 1946 and found free of termites, but the damage was subsequently discovered in April 1947. The IRS will not follow the *Rosenberg* case. As a result of extensive study it has determined that termite damage is not sufficiently "sudden" for a casualty loss. Rev. Rul. 63–232, 1963–2 C.B. 97.

Losses involving automobiles have also required courts and the IRS to distinguish between normal deterioration and a casualty. Casualty losses have been allowed for automobiles wrecked in accidents, Shearer v. Anderson, 16 F.2d 995 (2d Cir.1927), and which unexpectedly fell through the ice while the taxpayer was ice fishing, Rev. Rul. 69–88, 1969–1 C.B. 58. But a loss was disallowed for the "burned out" motor of the taxpayer's automobile which was due to progressive deterioration. Newton v. Commissioner, 57 T.C. 245 (1971) (Acq.).

The requirement of suddenness has also applied in situations involving property damage caused by adverse weather. For example, a casualty loss was allowed for the destruction of trees and shrubs caused by an unusually late spring freeze, Pantzer v. United States, 64–2 U.S.T.C. ¶ 9641 (S.D.Ind.1964), but a loss was disallowed for damage to ornamental trees and shrubs resulting from prolonged drought, Rev. Rul. 66–303, 1966–2 C.B. 55.

The fact that a casualty loss was caused by the taxpayer's own negligence does not bar a deduction. But where the loss is caused by the taxpayer's willful act of gross negligence, no deduction will be allowed. In Blackman v. Commissioner, 88 T.C. 677 (1987), aff'd by order, 867 F.2d 605 (1st Cir.1988), during an argument with his wife the taxpayer placed some of his wife's clothing on the kitchen stove and turned it on, igniting the clothing. The fire spread and the house was destroyed. The taxpayer was convicted of arson and his homeowners' insurance carrier refused to pay the claim. Because the house fire was a foreseeable consequence of setting the clothing on fire, and the taxpayer did not make sufficient effort to extinguish the fire, the court concluded that he had been grossly negligent and denied the deduction.

In contrast, a deduction was allowed for the loss of a diamond when a husband inadvertently slammed a car door on his wife's hand thereby dislodging the stone from its setting. The sudden, violent nature of the event that caused the loss was significant. White v. Commissioner, 48 T.C. 430 (1967) (Acq.). Following *White* the IRS altered its position that no deduction ever was available for an accidental loss of property. Rev. Rul. 72–592, 1972–2 C.B. 101, held that a casualty loss deduction was available for the loss of property due to an "identifiable event," "damaging the property," that was "sudden, unexpected, and unusual." But where jewelry wrapped in tissue paper overnight by a woman was thrown away by her husband while disposing of soiled tissue paper used by him for his cold, no deduction was allowed, Keenan v. Bowers, 91 F.Supp. 771 (E.D.S.C.1950).

A loss from confiscation or seizure by governmental authority is not a casualty or theft loss. Powers v. Commissioner, 36 T.C. 1191 (1961) (confiscation of taxpayer's automobile by former East German authorities). But Popa v. Commissioner, 73 T.C. 130 (1979) (Acq.), allowed a casualty deduction with respect to the loss of the personal property of an American citizen living in South Vietnam who was unable to recover his possessions at the time of its fall to the North Vietnamese. The only circumstances under which a deduction was not warranted was if the property had been confiscated under color of law. Under the circumstances, the court did "not think it fair or reasonable to require that the taxpayer eliminate all possible noncasualty causes of his loss," and the court found the most reasonable conclusion to be that the property was either destroyed or pilfered with criminal intent.

The casualty loss is limited to the decline in value of the property involved (not to exceed adjusted basis) and does not include additional expenses incurred because of the casualty. Tarsey v. Commissioner, 56 T.C. 553 (1971) (no casualty loss for out-of-pocket expenses for legal fees and amounts paid in settlement to injured party in connection with an automobile accident in which the taxpayer's automobile was destroyed); Cornelius v. Commissioner, 56 T.C. 976 (1971) (Acq.) (no deduction for the amount paid for a fence built around the destroyed property in order to protect the taxpayer from potential tort claims).

1.2. Theft

Treas. Reg. § 1.165–8(d) provides that the meaning of "theft" includes but is not limited to larceny, embezzlement, and robbery. Rev. Rul. 72–112, 1972–1 C.B. 60, states that for purposes of § 165(c)(3) "theft" includes "any theft, or felonious taking of money or property by which a taxpayer sustains a loss, whether defined and punishable under the penal codes of the states as larceny, robbery, burglary, embezzlement, extortion, kidnapping for ransom, threats, or blackmail." A theft loss is allowable as a deduction only if the taking was criminal under the applicable state law. Citron v. Commissioner, 97 T.C. 200 (1991) (denying a deduction because the mere refusal of another person to return the taxpayer's property was not embezzlement). Thus, commercial fraud and misrepresentation are not theft under the statute unless the act is criminal. Compare Kreiner v. Commissioner, T.C. Memo. 1990–587 (allowing a theft deduction for money voluntarily paid to a fortune-teller, because under state law mere receipt of funds for fortune-telling was criminal theft) with Bellis v. Commissioner, 540 F.2d 448 (9th Cir.1976) (denying a deduction to a purchaser of unregistered stock even though the sale was a crime under state corporation law, because absent intent to deprive purchasers of their property there was not "theft" under the state penal code).

Where property is merely lost but not stolen so as to qualify as a loss from "theft," a deduction is not available. Thus, in Smith v. Commissioner, 10 T.C. 701 (1948), a casualty loss deduction was disallowed for the disappearance of the taxpayer's prize-winning dog, "Waddell's Proud Bum," while being exercised. The taxpayer was unable to prove theft. But in Jones v. Commissioner, 24 T.C. 525 (1955) (Acq.), a loss was allowed for jewelry which disappeared from a house under circumstances supporting a reasonable inference that a theft had occurred.

Section 165(e) provides a special rule regarding the proper year for claiming a theft loss deduction. The loss is deductible in the year of discovery, not the year the theft actually occurred. Thus taxpayers are relieved of the burden of proving the actual year of the theft.

2. DETERMINATION OF THE AMOUNT OF THE CASUALTY LOSS

Where the value of a residence or other property held for personal use is in excess of its adjusted basis (usually its original cost), the amount of the loss is the difference between the value of the property immediately prior to the casualty and its value after the damage. However, § 165(b) limits the amount of the loss to the adjusted basis of the property. The adjusted basis is thereafter reduced by the amount of the deduction. Treas. Reg. § 1.165–7(b). The result of this rule is that where property has appreciated, a deduction is allowed even though the value of the property after the casualty still exceeds the adjusted basis prior to the casualty. For example, if a personal residence with an adjusted basis of $80,000 and a fair market value of $200,000 is subject to an uninsured casualty loss of $70,000 (after application of the various thresholds), the entire $70,000 qualifies as a casualty loss deduction even though the value of the house is $130,000, substantially more than the taxpayer's original investment. The basis of the house is reduced from $80,000 to $10,000. This rule in effect allocates all of the loss to the basis of the asset.

Where the value of the property prior to the casualty is less than the adjusted basis, the casualty loss is limited to the fair market value of the property. Helvering v. Owens, 305 U.S. 468 (1939). Without such a limitation, a casualty loss would have been allowed for the decline in value of the property attributable to normal wear and tear which took place prior to the casualty. Contrast this rule with the rule allowing a deduction for the entire basis of completely destroyed property held for use in a profit-seeking activity. See Chapter 15, Section 1.2.

3. REIMBURSEMENT FOR LOSS

A deduction for a loss that otherwise qualifies under § 165(c)(3) is not allowed if the loss is "compensated for by insurance or otherwise." If the taxpayer deducts the casualty loss and in a subsequent year receives reimbursement for the loss, the tax in the year of loss is not recomputed. Instead, the taxpayer includes in income the amount of the reimbursement in the taxable year in which it is received. If the casualty loss and the reimbursement occur in the same year, the casualty loss must be reduced accordingly since, to that extent, the casualty loss has been "compensated" under the terms of the statute. Treas. Reg. § 1.165–1(d)(2)(iii). Rev. Rul. 64–

329, 1964–2 C.B. 58, held that a gift to disaster victims by relatives is not compensation for purposes of § 165(c)(3). On the other hand, Shanahan v. Commissioner, 63 T.C. 21 (1974), found that the cancellation of indebtedness with respect to a disaster loan which was related to a previously deducted casualty loss constituted "compensation."

Section 165(h)(4)(E) denies any deduction for a personal casualty loss that may be covered by insurance if the insured-taxpayer fails to file a timely claim with the insurance carrier with respect to the loss. The rationale for this rule is that by refraining from filing a claim the taxpayer is attempting to avoid increased insurance premiums that would be nondeductible personal expenses.

When a casualty loss is reimbursed, the limitation on the loss deduction to the taxpayer's basis for the property must be coordinated with the limitation to unreimbursed losses. Suppose, for example, a personal residence with an adjusted basis of $50,000 and a fair market value of $100,000 is subject to a casualty loss of $70,000 (after application of the various thresholds), and the taxpayer receives insurance reimbursement of $40,000. In this case, the reimbursement is first applied against the $50,000 basis of the property, reducing the basis to $10,000, and then $10,000 of the uninsured $30,000 loss is allowed. See Treas. Reg. § 1.165–7(a)(3), Ex. (2).

4. FLOOR FOR CASUALTY LOSS DEDUCTIONS

Two floors limit casualty loss deductions. First, each individual loss is itself subject to a $100 floor. This floor eliminates *de minimis* losses, and for many years served as the only floor on the amount of loss deductions. In addition, casualty loss deductions are subject to a percentage floor that is similar to that applicable to medical expense deductions. Aggregate personal casualty losses are allowable only to the extent they exceed 10 percent of the taxpayer's adjusted gross income. Thus, if a taxpayer with $20,000 of adjusted gross income suffers two casualty losses to personal property, one in the amount of $1,100 and another in the amount of $1,400, each loss is first reduced by the $100 floor. Of the remaining $2,300, of casualty losses only $300 would be deductible (i.e., the amount of loss exceeding 10 percent of the taxpayer's adjusted gross income).

5. CASUALTY GAINS

If personal casualty gains (insurance and other reimbursement in excess of basis) in any year exceed personal casualty losses, the gains and the losses are treated as gains and losses from the sale or exchange of capital assets. I.R.C. § 165(h)(2)(B). This rule prevents taxpayers from reporting capital gains and ordinary losses. It also permits the losses to be deducted from gross income under § 62(a)(3) by a taxpayer who does not itemize deductions under § 63(e). If a taxpayer has a net loss from personal casualties during the year, both the gains and losses are ordinary income and deduction items, and the net loss is treated as an itemized deduction.

SECTION 7.   LIMITATIONS ON ITEMIZED DEDUCTIONS

INTERNAL REVENUE CODE: Sections 67(a)–(b); 68.

Section 67

Section 67 allows a deduction for "miscellaneous itemized deductions" only to the extent the aggregate amount of such deductions exceeds two percent of the taxpayer's adjusted gross income. "Miscellaneous itemized deductions" are defined in § 67(b) to include all itemized deductions other than deductions for interest, taxes, casualty and wagering losses, charitable gifts, medical expenses, and a few other less important deductions. After all of these exceptions, § 67 applies primarily to unreimbursed employee business expenses deductible under § 162 and investment expenses deductible under § 212. For example, due to § 67 a taxpayer whose only income is a salary of $50,000, who itemizes deductions, and has no deductions taken into account in computing adjusted gross income, may not deduct the first $1,000 of unreimbursed employee business expenses. This distinction in the treatment of employee business expenses and nonemployee business expenses has led to extensive litigation regarding whether certain business expenses were incurred while acting as an employee versus as a sole proprietor or an independent contractor. See e.g., Weber v. Commissioner, 103 T.C. 378 (1994), aff'd per curiam, 60 F.3d 1104 (4th Cir.1995) (a United Methodist minister was treated as an employee and therefore not allowed to deduct expenses related to his professional activity as business expenses on a schedule C; the expenses were treated as miscellaneous itemized deductions); McKay v. Commissioner, 102 T.C. 465 (1994), vac'd by order on other grounds, 84 F.3d 433 (5th Cir.1996) (attorney's fees incurred to recover damages for breach of employment contract are employee business expenses); Kovacevich v. Commissioner, 177 Fed.Appx. 561 (9th Cir. 2006) (amount paid by an attorney to settle a lawsuit against him by a former client was an unreimbursed employee business expense, and thus a miscellaneous itemized deduction, because the attorney was a statutory employee of his wholly owned legal professional corporation through which he practiced).

Section 67 was enacted because Congress believed that "the prior-law treatment of employee business expenses, investment expenses, and other miscellaneous itemized deductions fostered significant complexity, and that some of these expenses have characteristics of voluntary personal expenditures." Staff of the Joint Committee on Taxation, General Explanation of the Tax Reform Act of 1986, 78 (1987). Specifically, Congress believed that the record keeping burden was excessive relative to the amount of the expenditures, and the deductibility of these items presented significant administrative and enforcement problems, particularly because taxpayers frequently made mistakes with respect to such deductions. Accordingly, Congress concluded that these expenses should be deductible only if they significantly affect the taxpayer's disposable income.

To the extent that it disallows deductions for actual profit-seeking expenses, § 67 reflects a dubious tax policy decision. A simple example illustrates the impact of these rules. Assume that A, a single individual, earns $50,000, incurs expenses of $4,000 to earn that amount, and makes no other deductible payments during the year. If the earnings were from a trade or business, for example, being a sole practitioner lawyer, under § 62 the expenses would be fully deductible against gross income and §§ 63 and 67 would not limit the deductibility of the expense. Thus, before taking into account personal exemptions and the standard deduction, A's taxable income would be $46,000. Assume now that B, another single individual and an associate in a law firm, receives $50,000 of salary and incurs unreimbursed employee business expenses (e.g., education expenses to obtain an LL.M. degree).[5] Section 62 treats B's expenses as an itemized deduction. As such, although § 212 allows a deduction, § 67 would limit B's deduction to the amount by which the expenses exceeded $1,000 (i.e., 2 percent of $50,000). Thus only $3,000 of the $4,000 in expenses is potentially deductible under § 162. Next, under § 63(c)(2)(C), unless B has aggregate itemized deductions in excess of $3,000 (reflecting the basic standard deduction for individuals, adjusted for inflation; in 2016, the figure was $6,300), B cannot deduct any itemized deductions, and must claim the standard deduction. Accordingly, before taking into account personal exemptions and the standard deduction, B's taxable income would be $50,000. Therefore, even though A and B have identical gross incomes and expenses associated with profit-seeking activities, A's taxable income is $4,000 less than B's, because the tax system only treats A as having incurred those expenses in a business activity that is tax-favored.

Section 68

Section 68 limits the total amount of certain itemized deductions for high-bracket taxpayers. The limitation applies to all itemized deductions except medical expenses, investment interest, wagering losses and casualty losses. When adjusted gross income exceeds $250,000 for individuals and $300,000 for married couples filing joint returns (adjusted for inflation; the 2015 figures were $258,250 and $309,900, respectively), the allowable itemized deductions are reduced by the lesser of 3 percent of the excess (I.R.C. § 68(a)(1)) or 80 percent of the allowable itemized deductions (I.R.C. § 68(a)(2)). Thus, for an individual taxpayer with adjusted gross income of $300,000 and itemized deductions subject to limitation of $20,000, the amount of disallowed deductions would be $1,500 (calculated as $50,000, the amount of AGI exceeding the applicable amount, multiplied by 3 percent), because that figure is less

---

[5]   The same principles apply to C, another single individual who received $50,000 of income from interest and incurred $4,000 of expenses deductible under § 212 to earn that interest.

than 80 percent of the $20,000 in allowable deductions, or $16,000. Section 68 applies after all other limitations on itemized deductions have been applied (including the 2 percent floor of § 67).

It is worth noting that § 68, by limiting itemized deductions and exposing more income to tax, effectively raises taxes on high-income taxpayers without actually raising statutory marginal rates. In this way, Congress has not only added complexity to the income tax but has significantly reduced its transparency. Far better—both from the standpoint of simplicity and transparency—simply to raise (or lower) rates on the targeted taxpayers.

CHAPTER 22

STANDARD DEDUCTION, PERSONAL AND DEPENDENCY EXEMPTIONS, AND PERSONAL CREDITS

INTERNAL REVENUE CODE: Sections 63(a); 262.

Taxpayers who do not elect to claim the itemized deductions (discussed in Chapter 21) under § 63(a), (d), or (e), are entitled to claim the standard deduction. If the amount of the standard deduction under § 63(c) exceeds the taxpayer's itemized personal deductions, the taxpayer will take the standard deduction rather than elect to itemize. The standard deduction varies in size by filing status (e.g., married couples filing a joint return are entitled to a standard deduction twice that for single taxpayers).

In addition to claiming either itemized deductions or the standard deduction under § 63, under § 151, every taxpayer is entitled to a "personal exemption" for the taxpayer, for a spouse, and for dependents (such as minor children).

After reducing gross income to taxable income in the steps prescribed in §§ 62 and 63 by claiming all allowable deductions, the taxpayer calculates the taxpayer's tax liability by applying the appropriate rate schedule in § 1 to the amount of taxable income. That tax liability can be further reduced by personal income tax credits. Some credits provide an allowance for basic living expenses, including § 32, the refundable "earned income credit" (EIC) for low-wage workers that Congress designed and subsequently expanded to eliminate tax liability for the working poor. Meanwhile, other credits, such as the § 23 credit for certain adoption expenses, serve different functions by providing economic incentives or furthering social goals.

SECTION 1.   PERSONAL EXEMPTIONS AND THE STANDARD DEDUCTION

All individual taxpayers, except certain minor children and dependents of other taxpayers, are allowed to claim the standard deduction and personal exemption. If a taxpayer has dependent children under age 17, in addition to the dependency exemption under §§ 151 and 152, the taxpayer may be allowed a per-child fixed-dollar credit against tax owed.

A. THE STANDARD DEDUCTION

INTERNAL REVENUE CODE: Sections 62(a), (d); 63(a), (c).

The standard deduction performs two separate functions in the tax structure. First, together with the personal exemptions, the standard deduction provides a tax-free or "zero-bracket" amount above which positive tax rates begin to apply. Second, the standard deduction constitutes a floor that itemized personal expenses must exceed if they are to be allowed as deductions. For any given year, less than one-third of all taxpayers itemize deductions, while more than two-thirds take the standard deduction. See Internal Revenue Service, Statistics of Income, Individual Tax Returns, Tax Year 2013 Preliminary Data, Table 1 (2015) (reporting figure of 30 percent). That does not mean that the considerably large group of taxpayers taking the standard deduction have not incurred personal costs otherwise deductible under the income tax, such as home mortgage interest or charitable contributions. But they do not get credit for these expenses under the current tax system. One might argue that these taxpayers are, in fact, receiving *more* than their fair share from the income tax, because the standard deduction shields a larger portion of their income from tax than the total amount of their nondeductible personal expenses. But such an argument erroneously conflates the two distinct functions of the standard deduction: (1) as a tax-free threshold that every taxpayer receives and (2) as a floor that allows only a minority of taxpayers to receive tax subsidies for personal expenses.

DETAILED ANALYSIS

1. AMOUNT OF STANDARD DEDUCTION

Section 63(c)(2) provides a "basic standard deduction" in a statutory amount that is indexed for inflation every year using 1987 as a base. Currently, § 63(c)(2)(C) provides a statutory basic standard deduction of $3,000 (adjusted for inflation, $6,300 in 2016) applicable to all unmarried taxpayers other than surviving spouses and heads of household. For married taxpayers filing a joint return and surviving spouses, the standard deduction is twice the $3,000 amount, or $6,000 ($12,600 in 2016), while heads of household (generally, individual taxpayers with dependents) receive a standard deduction between that of the other two groups of taxpayers, or $4,400 ($9,300 in 2016). If married taxpayers file separate returns and one spouse itemizes deductions, the other spouse may not claim the standard deduction. For taxpayers who are dependents of another taxpayer, primarily minor children and college students, the standard deduction is limited to the greater of (a) $500 ($1,050 in 2016) or (b) the dependent's earned income plus $250 ($350 in 2016). Thus, if a taxpayer is a dependent of another taxpayer and has less than $250 of unearned income and a total income equal to or less than the normal standard deduction, the taxpayer will not be required to file a return.

The actual dollar amount of the various standard deductions after indexing for inflation pursuant to § 63(c)(4) is announced annually by the IRS in a revenue procedure. See Rev. Proc. 2015–53, 2015–44 I.R.B. 615.

Sections 63(c)(1)(B) and (f) provide an additional standard deduction for taxpayers who are blind or over age 65. For unmarried individuals other than a surviving spouse (as defined in § 2(a)), the additional standard deduction is $750 (adjusted for inflation, $1,550 in 2016); for married individuals it is $600 ($1,250 in 2016).

B. PERSONAL EXEMPTIONS

INTERNAL REVENUE CODE: Sections 151(a), (b), (c)(1)–(4), (d)–(e); 152; 153(1).

REGULATIONS: Sections 1.152–1(a)(2); 1.151–3.

The basic personal exemption amount for each individual is set by § 151(d) at $2,000 (adjusted for inflation, $4,050 in 2016). Section 151(b) grants the basic exemption for each taxpayer. If spouses file a joint return, each claims a personal exemption, even if one had no gross income. Section 151(c) adds additional exemptions for dependents, as defined in § 152. Section 152(a) limits the dependency exemptions to qualifying children, as defined in § 152(c), and qualifying relatives, as defined in § 152(d). The dependent's gross income may not exceed the amount of the exemption, except in the case of children under the age of 19 or full-time students under the age of 24.

Section 151(d)(2) denies the personal exemption to any taxpayer who is a dependent of another taxpayer entitled to claim a dependency exemption. This limitation affects primarily minor children with unearned income and college students who are supported primarily by their parents but who also work part-time.

A number of themes run through the personal exemption sections. First, the personal exemption allowed to the taxpayer can be viewed as a structural provision which plays a role in defining the point at which positive tax rates begin to apply. Under this approach, the personal exemption provides a bracket of income taxed at a zero rate. On the other hand, some view the personal exemption as freeing from tax the necessary subsistence expenses for those taxpayers who have no taxpaying capacity after incurring these expenses. These two views of the personal exemption lead to different evaluations of the current statutory scheme. If a taxpayer's personal exemption is viewed as defining an amount of income taxed at a zero rate, then the same level of personal exemption should be provided to each taxable unit regardless of income. This was the approach prior to 1986. On the other hand, if the personal exemption is viewed as a mechanism for exempting a subsistence level of income from tax, then that need decreases and, at some point, disappears altogether as the taxpayer's income increases. Under this view—reflected in current law, which phases out the personal exemption for high-income taxpayers—granting a flat exemption to all taxpayers provides an undue windfall for high-income households.

The exemption for dependents raises the question of how family size should be taken into account in allocating tax burdens. Under one view, family configurations should be irrelevant in determining tax liability and no special account should be taken of the expenses incurred by the taxpayer in providing support for dependents. Rather, expenses for dependents are like any other consumption expense and should not be relevant in determining taxable income. Alternatively, the cost of supporting the taxpayer's dependents could be viewed as pertinent in helping define the point at which positive tax rates begin or in determining the appropriate subsistence level of income below which the taxpayer should not be required to pay tax. Under the latter approach, the exemptions for dependents should be phased out as the taxpayer's income increases and the need to exempt subsistence amounts from tax diminishes. On the other hand, one might simply take the position that dependent exemptions provide a rough adjustment to account for taxpayers' ability to pay in structuring effective tax rates.

Current law views family size as relevant in determining the point at which positive tax rates begin. Thus, the current tax expenditure budget does not treat the dependency exemptions as tax expenditures. At the same time, the income of dependents is not included in the income of the family unit. Granting dependency exemptions without requiring income aggregation seems incorrect as a structural matter. See Chapter 38, Section 2.

DETAILED ANALYSIS

1. QUALIFYING CHILDREN AND DEPENDENTS

Section 152(a) allows a taxpayer dependency exemptions for two categories of dependents: (1) qualifying children, defined in § 152(c), and (2) qualifying relatives, defined in § 152(d).

1.1. *Qualifying Child*

Four conditions are required to qualify a child for the dependency exemption: (1) the child must bear a special relationship to the taxpayer, as provided by § 152(c)(2); (2) the child must have the same principal place of abode as the taxpayer for more than one-half the year; (3) the child must be either (a) under 19, (b) if a full-time student, under 24, or (c) permanently and totally disabled; and (4) the child must not have provided over one-half of his or her own support.[1] Note that this last requirement does not necessarily mean that the taxpayer claiming the dependency exemption have provided more than one-half of the child's support. The relationships

---

[1]   The definition of qualifying child in § 152(c) applies not only for purposes of the dependency exemption, but with some modifications it also applies for purposes of the child credit (see Section 2.A.(2) of this Chapter), the earned income tax credit (see Section 2.A.(1) of this Chapter), the dependent care credit (see Section 2.B.1. of this Chapter), and head of household filing status (see Chapter 38, Section 1.2.).

prerequisite to meeting the definition of a qualified child under § 152(c)(2) include a child of the taxpayer, or a descendant of such child, or a brother, sister, stepbrother or stepsister of the taxpayer or a descendant of any of them. Legally adopted children and children lawfully placed with the taxpayer by a placement agency or court of competent jurisdiction are treated as children by blood, and foster children placed with the taxpayer by an authorized placement agency or court of competent jurisdiction are treated as the taxpayer's children as well. See I.R.C. § 152(f)(1). In addition, a qualifying child (1) must not have filed a joint return with a spouse (other than to claim a refund) and (2) must be younger than the taxpayer.

Various tie-breaker rules apply when more than one person might otherwise be entitled to claim a qualifying child as a dependent and both claim the dependency exemption. In the case of parents (other than divorced parents) who do not file a joint return, § 152(c)(4)(B)(i) awards the dependency exemption to the parent with whom the child resided for the longest period during the year. If the child resided with both parents for an equal amount of time during the year, § 152(c)(4)(B)(ii) awards the dependency exemption to the parent whose adjusted gross income is higher. If the child might otherwise be a qualifying child of both a parent and another person, § 152(c)(4)(A)(i) awards the dependency exemption to the parent. If the child might otherwise be a qualifying child of two different persons neither of whom is a parent, § 152(c)(4)(A)(ii) awards the dependency exemption to the person whose adjusted gross income is higher.

Section 152(e) deals with the problems of allocating dependency exemptions between divorced or separated parents. Under § 152(e), the parent who has custody of the child for the greater portion of the year generally is deemed to have provided over one-half of the child's support and is thus entitled to the exemption. However, under § 152(e)(2) the noncustodial parent is entitled to the deduction if the parties so agree. The custodial parent must sign a written declaration on Form 8332 that he or she will not claim the child as a dependent for the taxable year and the noncustodial parent must attach that declaration to the tax return. The personal signature of custodial parent is critical to the shifting of the dependency exemption; a court order alone will not suffice. In Armstrong v. Commissioner, 745 F.3d. 890 (8th Cir. 2014), the wife who had custody of the child failed to provide the required waiver notwithstanding a court order in divorce proceedings that the husband would be entitled to the dependency exemption and ordering the wife to execute the Form 8332. While the court expressed sympathy for non-custodial parents whose former spouses violate court ordered or contractual obligations to provide necessary documents, it held that § 152(e)(2) precludes remedying such wrongs in federal tax proceedings. Section 152(e) also applies to determine which of the unmarried parents of a minor child is entitled to the dependency exemption if the parents were never married. See I.R.C. § 152(e)(1)(A)(iii). In King v. Commissioner, 121 T.C. 245 (2003), the father and mother were both married to other persons. The child lived with her mother and her mother's husband, who provided more than one-half of the child's support. However, because the custodial mother had signed a written release of her claim to exemption, the non-custodial father was entitled to claim the dependency exemption for the child.

Under Treas. Reg. § 1.152–4, for purposes of § 152(e) the custodial parent is the parent with whom the child spends the greatest number of nights during the taxable year. A child who is temporarily away is treated as spending the night with the parent with whom the child would have resided. If another person is entitled to custody for a night, the child is treated as spending the night with neither parent. On a school day, the child is treated as residing at the primary residence registered with the school. The regulations also provide that the required written declaration to surrender the exemption to the noncustodial parent must contain an *unconditional* statement that the custodial parent will not claim the exemption for the specified year or years; a declaration that conditions the custodial parent's release of the right to claim to the exemption on the noncustodial parent meeting a support obligation is not valid. A copy of the written declaration must be attached to the tax return for each year the noncustodial parent claims the exemption. The custodial parent may revoke a revocation by providing written notice to the non-custodial parent specifying the years of the revocation. Once a child reaches the age of majority under state law, generally age 18, the child is not in the custody of either parent (or anyone else) for purposes of § 152. Boltinghouse v. Commissioner, T.C. Memo. 2007–324.

1.2. *Qualifying Relative*

To be classified as a "qualifying relative" under § 152(d), a person must (1) bear one of the relationships to the taxpayer specified in § 152(d)(2), (2) have gross income that is less than the exemption amount, and (3) receive over one-half of his support from the taxpayer. The list of qualifying relatives in § 152(d)(2) includes children or descendants of children, brothers, sisters, stepbrothers or stepsisters, fathers and mothers or an ancestor of either, stepfathers and stepmothers, nieces and nephews, aunts and uncles, various in-laws, regardless of their place of abode, as well any individual (other than a spouse) who lived with the taxpayer and was a member of the taxpayer's household for the taxable year. A person will not be considered a member of the taxpayer's household if the relationship between the taxpayer and the person is in violation of local law. I.R.C. § 152(f)(3).

2.   DETERMINATION OF SUPPORT

2.1. *In General*

In addition to the other prerequisites for claiming dependency exemptions, § 152 requires that a qualifying child cannot have provided over one-half of his or her own support and that the taxpayer must have provided over one-half of the support for a qualifying relative other than a qualifying child. Thus, determinations must be made as to what constitutes support and who provided the support. For example, premiums for medical insurance constitute support provided by the policyholder, but the payments under the policy are not treated as support. Rev. Rul. 64–223, 1964–2 C.B. 50.

The cases do not attempt to define the exact parameters of what is considered in determining support, but courts have examined a wide range of items, categories, and activities. See e.g., Sauer v. Commissioner, T.C. Memo. 1953–394 (music lessons, gifts, and pets); McKay v. Commissioner, 34 T.C. 1080 (1960) (singing, dancing and dramatic lessons); Toponce v. Commissioner, T.C. Memo. 1968–101 (horseback riding); and Shapiro v. Commissioner, 54 T.C. 347 (1970) (Acq.) (summer camp). Flowers v. United States, 57–1 U.S.T.C. ¶ 9655 (W.D.Pa.1957), drew the line at a $1,400 boat, a $130 rifle and a $104 power lawnmower for a thirteen-year-old boy. Revenue Rulings are also liberal in their interpretation of support. See e.g., Rev. Rul. 76–184, 1976–1 C.B. 44 (expenses for wedding and wedding reception included as support); Rev. Rul. 77–282, 1977–2 C.B. 52 (television and automobile used principally by the dependent).

Governmental public assistance payments are included in support and are attributed to the dependent rather than to the parent to whom the payment is made on behalf of the dependent. Lutter v. Commissioner, 514 F.2d 1095 (7th Cir.1975); see also Williams v. Commissioner, T.C. Memo. 1996–126, aff'd by order, 119 F.3d 10 (11th Cir.1997) (after taking into account welfare payments and food stamps received by custodial mother for children, parents did not provide over one-half of support). On the other hand, Turecamo v. Commissioner, 554 F.2d 564 (2d Cir.1977), held that amounts paid to the dependent under Medicare were not taken into account in the support computation, distinguishing them from general welfare payments on the dubious basis that the recipient "purchases" the Medicare coverage either through mandatory employment taxes or through voluntary contributions for supplementary Medicare benefits.

2.2. Value of Support

Treas. Reg. § 1.152–1(a)(2) generally uses the amount of expenses incurred as the value of support provided by the one furnishing the support, but uses market value with respect to property or lodging furnished as support. The value of services provided to the dependent by the taxpayer cannot be considered in determining the amount of the taxpayer's support. Bartsch v. Commissioner, 41 T.C. 883 (1964); Markarian v. Commissioner, 352 F.2d 870 (7th Cir.1965). If the dependent owns the dependent's residence, the imputed rental value of the residence must be considered as support provided by the dependent. Snyder v. United States, 321 F.Supp. 661 (D.Colo.1970), aff'd per curiam, 445 F.2d 319 (10th Cir.1971).

2.3. Multiple Support Agreements

Under § 152(d)(3), a taxpayer who does not contribute over one-half of the support of a person in one of the relationships described in § 152(d)(2), but who contributes at least 10 percent of such support, may claim an exemption for that person as a qualifying relative if the taxpayer is a member of a group that together supplies the required support and agrees that the taxpayer may claim the exemption, provided that the statutory tests are met. This rule allows a group of individuals to allocate to one of its members the dependency exemption that otherwise would be lost because none of the individuals who provided support provided at least half of the support.

3. PHASEOUT OF EXEMPTIONS

Section 151(d)(3) phases out the personal and dependency exemptions for taxpayers with adjusted gross incomes above a threshold amount. For married couples filing jointly, the threshold amount is $300,000 ($150,000 for married couples filing separate returns) (adjusted for inflation; in 2016, the figures were $311,300 and $155,650, respectively). For unmarried taxpayers, the threshold amount is $250,000 ($259,400 in 2016). Section 151(d)(3) reduces the taxpayer's personal and dependency exemptions by 2 percentage points for each $2,500 (or fraction thereof) of adjusted gross income above these threshold amounts. Thus, an unmarried individual's personal exemptions will phase out completely at AGI exceeding $381,900 (in 2016). The effect of phasing out personal and dependency exemptions under § 151(d)(3) creates a rate "bubble" that subjects the first $122,500 of taxable income above the phaseout threshold to a marginal rate exceeding the maximum statutory rate. As a result, taxpayers with larger numbers of dependents can face higher marginal rates (but not necessarily higher average rates) than taxpayers in the same marginal statutory bracket with fewer dependents.

4. TAXPAYER IDENTIFICATION NUMBER REQUIREMENT

Section 151(e) denies a taxpayer a dependency exemption for any person for whom a taxpayer identification number (TIN), typically the taxpayer's Social Security number, is not included on the return. This provision prevents taxpayers from claiming personal exemptions for fictional dependents, and further prevents more than one person from claiming an individual as a dependent. The denial of the dependency exemption also may result in denial of head of household filing status (see Chapter 38, Section 1.2.).

SECTION 2. PERSONAL CREDITS

A. CREDITS FOR BASIC LIVING EXPENSES

(1) EARNED INCOME CREDIT

INTERNAL REVENUE CODE: Section 32.

Section 32 allows a refundable tax credit to certain low-income taxpayers, depending on the taxpayer's earned income and the number of children in the taxpayer's household. The earned income credit (EIC) phases in over a range of income, then plateaus at that credit amount for another range of income, and, finally, phases out before going to zero. For an eligible individual with one qualifying child, the credit is 34 percent of the earned income credit base (defined in § 32(c)(2)). For taxpayers with two or more qualifying children, the credit is 40 percent of the credit base. For low-income workers with no qualifying children, the credit is 7.65 percent of the credit base, a figure that perfectly reflects an employee's payroll tax obligation comprised of 6.2 percent for Social Security taxes and 1.45 percent for Medicare taxes. In 2009, Congress added a fourth category of qualifying EIC claimants, taxpayers with three or more qualifying children, for whom the credit is 45 percent of the credit base. The "earned income" base for the credit is limited to earned income that is included in gross income.

If the taxpayer's adjusted gross income exceeds a ceiling amount, the credit is phased out by a percentage of the income in excess of the ceiling. The phaseout percentage for a taxpayer with one qualifying child is 15.98 percent, 21.06 percent for a taxpayer with two or more qualifying children, and 7.65 percent for low-income workers with no qualifying children.

Section 32(b) specifies the earned income and phaseout amounts as well as the credit and phaseout percentages. Sections 32(b)(2)(B) and (b)(3)(B) provide higher thresholds for triggering the phaseout for married claimants of the EIC who also file joint returns, a provision designed to mitigate "marriage tax penalties" for EIC recipients (discussed below). The phaseout portion of the credit begins $5,000 later for these taxpayers. The baseline statutory amounts are adjusted for inflation as provided in § 32(j).

The inflation adjusted credit base and phaseout thresholds for 2016 are as follows.

Item	Number of Qualifying Children			
	One	Two	Three or More	None
Earned Income Amount	$ 9,920	$13,930	$13,930	$ 6,610
Maximum Amount of Credit	$ 3,373	$ 5,572	$ 6,269	$ 506
Threshold Phaseout Amount (single, surviving spouse, or head of household)	$18,190	$18,190	$18,190	$ 8,270
Completed Phaseout Amount (single, surviving spouse, or head of household)	$39,296	$44,648	$47,955	$14,880
Threshold Phaseout Amount (married filing jointly)	$23,740	$23,740	$23,740	$13,820
Completed Phaseout Amount (married filing jointly)	$44,846	$50,198	$53,505	$20,430

Rev. Proc. 2015–53, 2015–44 I.R.B. 615.

Even though the threshold for the phaseout is higher for married couples filing a joint return than it is for heads of households and childless persons, the phaseout rules result in a significant "tax penalty" to marriage for low-income individuals eligible to claim the earned income credit. The penalty is not associated with the rate structure or tax brackets (a phenomenon discussed in Chapter 38, Section 1). Rather, it is the function of a previously eligible EIC recipient phasing out of the credit upon marriage due to the combined income of the new family unit reflected on a "married filing jointly" tax return rather than on two "unmarried" tax returns.

Consider the following example. Family A is a father with two children and earned income of $15,000. After accounting for personal exemptions (three at $4,050 in 2016) and the standard deduction ($9,300 for head of household status in 2016), Family A has no taxable income (because its tax-free threshold of $21,450 exceeds earned income by $6,450). In addition, this family qualifies for an earned income credit of

$5,572, which the family receives in the form of a cash subsidy (recall that the EIC is refundable). Meanwhile, Family B is a single person with earned income of $36,000. After accounting for one personal exemption ($4,050) and the standard deduction ($6,300), Family B has taxable income of $25,650 and tax liability of $3,383.75. Now consider that the two adults in Family A and Family B get married, creating Family C. Together, Family C's combined earned income of $51,000 disqualifies it from receiving the earned income credit, because the credit phases out altogether at $50,198 filing jointly). Family C loses the entire $5,572 cash subsidy that Family A enjoyed from the EIC, and it pays a positive tax liability of $2,866.25 (after accounting for personal exemptions and the standard deduction). All told, Family C pays $5,054.50 more in taxes—a marriage tax penalty of nearly 10 percent of its total earned income—than the combined tax liability of Family A and Family B prior to marriage (i.e., the difference between a net subsidy of $2,188.25—or Family A's $5,572 cash subsidy and Family B's $3,383.75 tax bill—and Family C's tax liability of $2,866.25).

DETAILED ANALYSIS

1. ADDITIONAL QUALIFYING CONDITIONS

To claim the credit based on qualifying children, each "qualifying child" must have the same principal place of abode as the taxpayer. Section 32(c)(3) defines "qualifying child" by cross reference to § 152(c), the uniform definition of qualifying child (see Section 1.B.1. of this Chapter), with some modifications. For purposes of the credit, it does not matter if the child provided over one-half of his or her own support, and the special provisions applicable to divorced or separated parents (I.R.C. § 152(e)) do not apply. In addition, if the child is married, the child will not be a qualifying child for purposes of the credit unless the taxpayer can claim the child as a dependent (or could have claimed the child if the special rule in § 152(e) awarding the exemption to a noncustodial spouse had not been applicable). Furthermore, children whose principal place of abode is outside the United States will not qualify.

Section 32(c)(1)(E) denies the earned income credit to any individual who fails to include on her return her taxpayer identification number (typically a taxpayer's Social Security number) and, if married, her spouse's taxpayer identification number. This provision effectively denies the credit to illegal aliens, even though they are required to pay both income taxes and social security taxes. Section 32(c)(1)(F) denies the earned income credit if the taxpayer fails to include on his tax return the taxpayer identification number of any qualifying children that influence the computation of the credit. This provision is designed to discourage fraudulent claims, and operates to deny the credit completely to a taxpayer without a qualifying child if the taxpayer falsely claims to have a qualifying child.

For a childless taxpayer to qualify for the credit, the taxpayer must be over the age of 25 and under the age of 65, and may not be claimed as a dependent on another's tax return.

A taxpayer who otherwise qualifies for the earned income credit is not eligible if she has more than $2,200 of "disqualified income" (adjusted for inflation, $3,400 in 2016). I.R.C. § 32(i). Disqualified income includes: (1) taxable interest and dividends, (2) tax-exempt interest, (3) net rent and royalty income, (4) net capital gains, and (5) net passive-activity income that is not subject to the self-employment tax.

2.   DISALLOWANCE BASED ON PRIOR ERRONEOUS CLAIMS

Section 32(k)(1) denies the earned income credit to a taxpayer for two years following any year for which there has been a determination in a deficiency proceeding that the taxpayer's erroneous claim of the earned income credit was due to reckless or intentional disregard of the rules or regulations applicable to the credit. If the taxpayer's claim was fraudulent, the disallowance period is extended to 10 years. These disallowance penalties are in addition to the regular statutory penalties for negligence and fraud (see Chapter 1, Section 3.D(6)). See H. Rep. No. 148, 105th Cong., 1st Sess. 445 (1997).

3.   POLICY ISSUES

Congress enacted the earned income credit in 1975 to mitigate a series of increases in Social Security taxes, which fell most heavily on low-wage workers. Over the next forty years, Congress expanded the EIC to serve additional functions. While the credit still refunds Social Security taxes on wages for millions of recipients, it also offsets income taxes and provides a cash benefit for any portion of the credit that exceeds tax liability.

Congress could have offset the regressive effects of the Social Security tax by providing a low-income allowance within the Social Security tax structure rather than the income tax structure. Alternatively, Congress could have provided financial assistance to low income individuals through direct cash payments (after all, low-income individuals most obviously suffer from deficiencies in income). Instead, Congress chose to deliver government benefits through the income tax system for the purpose of encouraging work and reducing welfare dependency. See S.Rep. No. 36, 94th Cong., 1st Sess. 33 (1975). As structured, the earned income credit provides income maintenance for individuals with small amounts of earned income, and has had the effect of supplementing wages, increasing labor force participation, and drastically reducing poverty for low-wage workers and their families. See Center on Budget and Policy Priorities, EITC and Child Tax Credit Promote Work, Reduce Poverty, and Support Children's Development (2015).

As Congress continues to expand both the amount and coverage of the earned income credit, however, the credit begins to resemble a traditional welfare program. Indeed, in 2016, the EIC offset $2.82 billion in taxes for eligible claimants, but it also paid out $63.37 billion in cash subsidies; in other words, nearly 95 percent of benefits represented cash outlays. Office of Management and Budget, Analytical Perspectives: Budget of the United States Government, Fiscal Year 2017 231–32 (2016). Lest the EIC be labeled "welfare for the middle class," a charge that prior critics of the program used in attempting to derail the EIC, policymakers should be mindful of targeting the program to its intended and most sympathetic beneficiaries: the working poor and their families. For a history of the EIC, negative income taxation, and the policymaking tradeoffs in delivering social welfare benefits through the tax system, see Dennis J. Ventry, Jr., The Collision of Tax and Welfare Politics: The Political History of the Earned Income Tax Credit, 1969–1999, 53 National Tax Journal 983 (2000); Dennis J. Ventry, Jr., Welfare By Any Other Name: Tax Transfers and the EITC, 56 American University Law Review 1261 (2007).

The earned income credit presents some unusual compliance issues. Because of its refundability, a person can obtain a refund by declaring more income than was earned, the opposite of the usual compliance problem faced by the IRS (that is, where taxpayers attempt to reduce or hide income from the tax authorities). In 1997, Congress enacted Section 32(k)(1) pertaining to improper claims for the EIC as a response to this problem. (see Section 2.A.(1)2. of this Chapter).

(2) THE CHILD CREDIT

INTERNAL REVENUE CODE: SECTION 24.

Section 24 provides a credit of up to $1,000 with respect to each of a taxpayer's qualifying children. Section 24(a) requires that the taxpayer be eligible to claim the child as a dependent under § 151 as a prerequisite to claiming the credit. The definition of a qualifying child is the same as the definition that applies for purposes of the dependency exemption in § 152(c) (see Section 1.B.1. of this Chapter), except that the child must be under 17 years of age and cannot be a noncitizen nonresident. I.R.C. § 24(c). A taxpayer may not claim the credit if the child's taxpayer identification number is not included on the return. I.R.C. § 24(e). (An "individual taxpayer identification number" (ITIN), see Treas. Reg. § 301.6109(d)(3), may be used in lieu of a Social Security number. Undocumented immigrants who are ineligible for social security numbers but who still pay U.S. income taxes by using an ITIN may claim the child credit.) Nonresident children who are not citizens do not qualify. I.R.C. § 24(c)(2). Thus, for example, many resident migrant workers who pay U.S. income taxes but whose children do not reside in the United States cannot claim the credit.

As originally enacted, the child credit generally was not refundable to the extent that it exceeded the taxpayer's income tax liability. I.R.C. § 26. Currently, § 24(d) allows partial refundability of the child credit. The credit is refundable to the extent of 15 percent of the taxpayer's earned income in excess of $3,000. I.R.C. § 24(d)(1)(B)(i) and (d)(4). In the case of a taxpayer with three or more children, § 24(d) provides that the child credit is refundable to the extent that the taxpayer's Social Security taxes exceed the sum of any other nonrefundable credits plus the taxpayer's earned income credit, if that amount exceeds the amount otherwise refundable. I.R.C. § 24(d)(1)(B)(ii). Generally, this rule means that otherwise unusable child credits can be used to obtain a refund of Social Security taxes.

The child credit was intended by Congress to benefit the "middle class" rather than high-income taxpayers. As such, it phases out quickly for taxpayers with adjusted gross income over the "threshold amount." Section 24(b)(1) and (2) reduce the credit by $50 for each $1,000 (or fraction thereof) by which the taxpayer's "modified adjusted gross income" exceeds $110,000 in the case of joint returns ($55,000 in the case of married taxpayers filing separately) and $75,000 for unmarried taxpayers (typically heads of household). The narrow phaseout ranges can create extraordinarily high marginal tax rates for taxpayers phasing out of the credit. For example, Family A, a husband and wife with two children and a modified AGI of $121,001 would receive a credit of $450; this couple's modified AGI exceeds the threshold amount of $110,000 by $10,001, so its $1,000 credit is reduced by $550, i.e., $50 for every $1,000 exceeding the threshold amount, including the $1 "fraction thereof." Meanwhile, Family B, a husband and wife with two children and a modified AGI of exactly $121,000—$1 less than Family A—would be eligible for a credit of $500. Family A's additional $1 in income results in a tax increase of $50, a marginal tax rate (albeit over an extremely narrow range of income) of 5,000 percent!

B. TAX CREDITS FOR PERSONAL COSTS

INTERNAL REVENUE CODE: Sections 21; 22; 23; 26.

Deductions for personal expenditures that further some social or economic goal rather than refine the concept of net income (including the deductions for medical expenses, charitable contributions, and home mortgage interest) frequently are criticized as "upside-down subsidies"; that is, they provide disproportionate tax savings to high-income taxpayers, because their value is tied to a taxpayer's marginal tax rate rather than to actual dollars expended.[2] For example, a deduction for $10,000 of home mortgage interest is worth $3,500 to a high-income taxpayer in the 35 percent bracket, but only $1,500 to a taxpayer in the 15 percent bracket. Furthermore, taxpayers who do not itemize their deductions—i.e., low- and middle-income taxpayers—receive no subsidy even though they incur expenses that the tax system subsidizes for high-income taxpayers. The "upside down" feature of delivering subsidies through tax deductions could be mitigated by using tax credits in lieu of deductions for certain personal expenses that Congress wished to subsidize. For example, the deduction for home mortgage interest could be replaced by a 20 percent credit for qualifying interest paid. Thus, a payment of $10,000 of home mortgage interest would generate a $2,000 tax benefit for *all* taxpayers, without regard to their marginal tax rates, even to taxpayers whose marginal rate is less than 20 percent. Also, unlike personal deductions, which are available only to taxpayers with total itemized deductions exceeding the standard deduction, credits are available to all taxpayers, including those who claim the standard

---

2   See Surrey, Pathways to Tax Reform (1973).

deduction. In addition to providing the same benefit, dollar for dollar, to all taxpayers, tax credits allow policymakers to better target the subsidy to the neediest beneficiaries. By phasing out the earned income credit, for example, Congress has ensured that the program benefits only low-to middle-income taxpayers. In a similar manner, Congress structured the child tax credit to target the middle class and to prevent benefits from flowing to upper-income taxpayers less in need of assistance.

Over the last 20 to 30 years, Congress has used tax credits to deliver important targeted subsidies through the tax system, including the dependent care credit (§ 21), the credit for the elderly and disabled (§ 22), the credit for adoption expenses (§ 23), the mortgage interest credit (§ 25), and the Hope and lifetime learning credits (§ 25A, discussed in Chapter 23). Other credits include credits for energy efficiency improvements to a taxpayer's principal residence (I.R.C. § 25C, scheduled to expire after December 31, 2016), for expenditures on residential energy efficient property (I.R.C. § 25D), and a credit for certain vehicles purchased for personal use (I.R.C. § 30B). Section 26 limits all but one of the credits that may be taken under §§ 21–25D to the taxpayer's tax liability for the year. By contrast, the earned income credit is refundable to the extent the available credit exceeds the taxpayer's tax liability (after taking into account the other credits for which the taxpayer qualifies under §§ 21–30).

DETAILED ANALYSIS

1. CREDIT FOR HOUSEHOLD AND DEPENDENT CARE EXPENSES

1.1. *Technical Aspects of the Dependent Care Credit*

As discussed in Chapter 19, Section 6, judicial decisions historically denied the deduction for child care costs on the ground that they were personal expenditures. In 1954, Congress provided a limited deduction for child care costs that was extended by subsequent legislation. In 1976, the deduction for child care costs was eliminated and replaced by a tax credit.

Section 21 provides a tax credit equal to 35 percent of employment-related dependent care expenses paid by an individual who maintains a household that includes one or more qualifying individuals. The 35 percent credit is reduced by one percentage point (but not below 20 percent) for each $2,000 (or fraction thereof) of adjusted gross income above $15,000. Thus, a taxpayer with more than $44,000 of adjusted gross income is entitled to a credit equal to 20 percent of employment-related expenses.

The amount of employment-related expenses that qualify for the credit is limited to $3,000 if there is only one qualifying individual or $6,000 if there are two or more qualifying individuals in the household. The maximum dependent care credit is thus $1,050 ($3,000 × .35) in the case of one qualifying individual and $2,100 ($6,000 × .35) in the case of two or more qualifying individuals. The credit may not exceed the taxpayer's tax liability. Married couples must file a joint return to claim the credit.

Although the § 21 credit is most often claimed with respect to the taxpayer's children, the categories of dependents for whose care the credit is available are much broader. A qualifying individual is (1) a dependent of the taxpayer, as defined in § 151(a) (discussed at Section 1.B.1. of this Chapter), who is under the age of 13 and for whom the taxpayer may claim a dependency exemption; (2) a physically or mentally incapacitated dependent; or (3) a physically or mentally incapacitated spouse who lives with the taxpayer for most of the year. I.R.C. § 21(b)(1). Section 21(e)(1) disqualifies expenses incurred with respect to any individual if at any time "the relationship between the individual and the taxpayer is in violation of local law."

The employment-related expenses that are taken into account for purposes of the credit generally may not exceed the earned income of an unmarried individual or the earned income of the lesser-earning spouse in the case of a married couple. Employment-related expenses include costs for household services and expenses for the care of a qualified individual which are incurred to enable the taxpayer to be employed. Eligible expenses include the employer's share of Social Security taxes paid with respect to a baby sitter employed to permit the parent to work. Employment-related expenses which are incurred inside the taxpayer's household may also qualify for the credit if they are for the care of a physically or mentally incapacitated spouse or dependent of the taxpayer who regularly spends at least eight hours each day in the taxpayer's household, i.e., effectively someone who lives with the taxpayer. In addition, expenses incurred for services provided outside the taxpayer's household by a dependent care center (which meets the statutory definition in § 21(b)(2)(D)) can be taken into account if the center complies with all applicable state and local laws and regulations. I.R.C. § 21(b)(2)(C).

Section 21(e)(9) disallows the credit if the taxpayer's return does not report the name, address, and taxpayer identification number of the person to whom qualified expenses were paid. This requirement is intended to reduce false claims and to provide information to the IRS regarding income of self-employed child-care providers.

In Brown v. Commissioner, 73 T.C. 156 (1979), a mother took her son out of public school and placed him in a private boarding school because she feared for his physical safety and was concerned about the quality of his education. She felt she could not work, and she did not work, while he remained in public school. A majority of the court held that a portion of the costs of the boarding school were incurred to enable the taxpayer to be "gainfully employed":

> Since one of petitioner's reasons for sending her son to boarding school was to be able to take a job, and since she could not have taken a job without such child care arrangement, she is entitled to a child care deduction for some part of the cost of sending him to [the private school]. We adopt, in other words, a "but for" test. If the care was required to permit the taxpayer to work, and if *one* motive for obtaining the care was to permit gainful employment, the concurrent existence of other motives will not

cause the expenditure to fail the statutory test. The employment motive must be present. It need not be exclusive or even dominant.

There is the further question whether a subjective or objective test of necessity is applicable. Petitioner considered herself unable to work while her son was at [the public school]. However, no doubt many [of the public school] students did have working mothers. It was not objectively impossible to be employed while a child was at [the public school]. However, we do not believe that the statute requires us to test the correctness of the parent's conclusion that child care is required to obtain employment, but only the sincerity of that conclusion. Different parents will apply different standards for what risks they are willing to put their children to. One parent may feel a 13-year-old boy could be left alone at home after school hours; another would disagree. The statute requires the prescribed purpose; it does not impose a test of objective necessity.

In Zoltan v. Commissioner, 79 T.C. 490 (1982) (Acq.), the credit was allowed for a portion of the costs of a summer day camp for the taxpayer's son as incurred for the "care" of the child. Congress responded by adding the last sentence of § 21(b)(2)(A) excluding the cost of overnight camps from the definition of employment related expenses.

Expenses to transport a child to a qualified day care facility do not qualify for the credit. Warner v. Commissioner, 69 T.C. 995 (1978). Perry v. Commissioner, 92 T.C. 470 (1989), aff'd by order, 912 F.2d 1466 (5th Cir.1990), held that transportation costs to send children to stay with grandparents for the purpose of allowing a parent to work were not eligible for the credit.

In Rev. Rul. 83–1, 1983–1 C.B. 3, the taxpayer was reimbursed for qualified child care costs by a State welfare agency and the payments were excluded from his income as social welfare payments. The credit was not allowed for the reimbursed portion since the taxpayer incurred no economic detriment or expense to that extent.

1.2. *Policy Aspects of the Dependent Care Credit*

Working parents with incomes below the poverty level are excluded from receiving financial benefits under § 21 because the credit is not refundable. In addition, since the credit is a function of expenses incurred rather than of income levels, its benefits are not primarily directed to lower income taxpayers. Over the years, proposals to make the child care credit refundable have been adopted by the Senate, but opposed by the House, and consistently resisted by the Treasury on the ground that refundability imposes a significant burden on tax administration. In addition, like most personal credits, the amount of the credit is not included in gross income. As a result, the value of the credit is a function of the taxpayer's marginal rate, with high-bracket taxpayers saving more in taxes than low-income taxpayers on the same amount of excluded credit.

2.   CREDIT FOR THE ELDERLY AND DISABLED

Individuals who are age 65 or over or who have retired because of a permanent and total disability are entitled to a tax credit under § 22. The value of the credit is equal to 15 percent of the first $7,500 of retirement income for a married couple where both spouses are eligible for the credit, $5,000 for a married couple where only one spouse is eligible for the credit, and $5,000 for a single person. Earned income as well as investment income is eligible for the credit. To confine the tax benefits of the credit to lower-income and middle-income taxpayers, the maximum amount on which the credit is computed is reduced by one-half of the amount by which adjusted gross income exceeds $7,500 for a single person and $10,000 for married couples. As a result of this phaseout, no credit is allowed to a single taxpayer with adjusted gross income in excess of $17,500 or to a married taxpayer filing jointly with adjusted gross income in excess of $25,000.

The tax credit for the elderly and disabled is intended to provide a benefit roughly comparable to the exclusion from gross income of Social Security benefits. Accordingly, the base on which the credit is computed is reduced by the portion of the taxpayer's social security benefits that are exempt from tax under § 86 as well as certain other tax-exempt income. Because of this function, the credit has been changed from time to time to correspond with changes in the levels of Social Security benefits.

3.   CREDIT FOR ADOPTION EXPENSES

Section 23 provides a nonrefundable credit of up to $10,000 (adjusted for inflation, $13,460 in 2016) per child for qualified adoption expenses paid or incurred by individual taxpayers. Qualified adoption expenses include reasonable and necessary adoption fees, court costs, attorney's fees and other expenses to legally adopt an "eligible child," other than the child of the taxpayer's spouse. To be "eligible," a child must be under 18 years of age or physically or mentally incapable of caring for himself. If the adopted child is a "special needs child" (as defined in I.R.C. § 23(d)(3)), a full $10,000 credit (adjusted for inflation, $13,600 in 2016) is allowed even if no qualified adoption expenses have been incurred. I.R.C. § 23(a)(3). Married taxpayers must file a joint return to claim the credit and are jointly subject to the dollar limitation ceiling. I.R.C. § 23(f)(1). Section 23(i) authorizes the IRS to promulgate regulations under which unmarried taxpayers adopting a child apportion the ceiling between them.

The credit is allowed in the year following the year in which adoption expenses are paid, except for expenses paid in or after the year in which the adoption is final, which are creditable in the year paid. (In the case of adoptions of foreign children, the credit is available only in the year the adoption is final.) No credit is allowed for expenses that are deductible or creditable under another provision or for expenses for which the taxpayer is reimbursed. See I.R.C. § 23(b)(3), (d)(1)(D). Although the credit is not refundable, if the otherwise allowable credit exceeds the taxpayer's tax liability, the excess may be carried forward for up to five years. I.R.C. § 23(c). The credit is phased out ratably for taxpayers whose adjusted gross income (with certain modifications) exceeds $150,000 (adjusted for inflation, $201,920 in 2016), and it is completely phased out (without regard to the inflation adjustment) when adjusted gross income reaches $190,000 ($241,920 in 2016). See I.R.C. § 23(b)(2).

4.   MORTGAGE INTEREST CREDIT

Section 25 allows a credit for a portion of the interest paid on a mortgage to purchase a principal residence if the taxpayer has received a mortgage credit certificate from the appropriate state agency. Only taxpayers who otherwise could not afford to purchase a principal residence are eligible to receive a mortgage credit certificate. The credit formula can vary, but it generally is between 20 and 50 percent of the amount of the interest paid. If the percentage exceeds 20 percent, the maximum credit is capped at $2,000. The home mortgage interest deduction under § 163(h), discussed in Chapter 21, Section 5), is reduced by the amount of the credit, thereby effectively including the amount of the credit in income for taxpayers who itemize deductions.

5.   RESIDENTIAL ENERGY EFFICIENT PROPERTY CREDIT

Section 25D provides a nonrefundable credit for certain expenditures on certain residential energy efficient property, including photovoltaic property (which uses solar energy to generate electricity), solar water heating property, and fuel cell property (which converts a fuel into electricity using electrochemical means). The property must be installed in a dwelling unit located in the United States and used by the taxpayer as a residence. Expenditures relating to swimming pools and hot tubs are not eligible.

6.   "GREEN" VEHICLE CREDITS

Section 30B provides a complex, multi-faceted credit for certain "alternative motor vehicles" in the year a qualifying vehicle is placed in service either for business or personal use by the taxpayer. This credit has applied to purchases of "hybrid" vehicles with rechargeable batteries, as well as to other "green" technology vehicles. A taxpayer claiming the credit must reduce the taxpayer's basis in the vehicle by the amount of the credit. The credit has expired or is expected to expire with respect to several of the originally targeted vehicles, including: fuel cell motor vehicles (scheduled to expire on December 31, 2016); advanced lean burn technology vehicles (December 31, 2010); hybrid motor vehicles, other than passenger automobiles and light trucks (December 31, 2009); alternative fuel motor vehicles (December 31, 2010); and plug-in electric drive motor vehicles (December 31, 2011).

CHAPTER 23

TAX EXPENDITURES FOR EDUCATION

INTERNAL REVENUE CODE: Sections 25A; 108(f); 135; 221; 222; 529; 530(a)–(c), (d)(1)–(4), (6), (g), (h); 4973(a), (e).

The number of tax expenditures for education adopted at the federal level has grown at an accelerating pace since the mid-1990s. Many would support increased federal financial support for education. In most other industrialized countries, education through all levels is generally free (paid for by tax revenues). To get a sense of how a variety of tax expenditures affect a particular activity, the tax expenditures for education are brought together in this chapter for descriptive and evaluative purposes. Two points should be kept in mind. First, a complete picture of federal financial support for education would have to include direct spending programs as well. Such a task is beyond the scope of this book. Second, a similar undertaking could be set forth for any number of other budget areas in which multiple tax expenditures have been enacted (for instance, housing and social welfare). We have selected education because it is a topic in which we and our students share a common interest. The type of education referred to in this chapter is "foundational" education that is not otherwise deductible as a business expense (see Chapter 20, Section 2).

Overview of Present Law and Economic Analysis Relating to Tax and Savings Incentives for Education*

Staff of the Joint Committee on Taxation (JCX–1–01).
February 12, 2001.

OVERVIEW OF PRESENT-LAW TAX INCENTIVES FOR EDUCATION

A. General Tax Treatment of Education Expenses

Individual taxpayers generally may not deduct their education and training expenses. However, a deduction for education expenses generally is allowed under Internal Revenue Code ("the Code") section 162 if the education or training (1) maintains or improves a skill required in a trade or business currently engaged in by the taxpayer, or (2) meets the express requirements of the taxpayer's employer, or requirements of applicable law or regulations, imposed as a condition of continued employment (Treas. Reg. sec. 1.162–5). * * *

---

*   [Ed.: Material in brackets reflects changes enacted in 2001 and later years.]

B.   Exclusion for Employer-Provided Educational Assistance

A special rule allows an employee to exclude from gross income for income tax purposes and from wages for employment tax purposes up to $5,250 annually paid by his or her employer for educational assistance (secs. 127 and 3121(a)(18)). This provision covers undergraduate as well as [graduate-level] courses. In order for the exclusion to apply, certain requirements must be satisfied. The educational assistance must be provided pursuant to a separate written plan of the employer. The employer's educational assistance program must not discriminate in favor of highly compensated employees. In addition, no more than 5-percent of the amounts paid or incurred by the employer during the year for educational assistance under a qualified educational assistance program can be provided for the class of individuals consisting of more than 5-percent owners of the employer and the spouses or dependents of such more than 5-percent owners. * * *

For purposes of the exclusion, educational assistance means the payment by an employer of expenses incurred by or on behalf of the employee for education of the employee including, but not limited to, tuition, fees, and similar payments, books, supplies, and equipment. Educational assistance also includes the provision by the employer of courses of instruction for the employee (including books, supplies, and equipment). Educational assistance does not include (1) tools or supplies that may be retained by the employee after completion of a course, (2) meals, lodging, or transportation, and (3) any education involving sports, games, or hobbies. * * *

C.   Qualified Scholarships

Present law provides an exclusion from gross income for amounts received as a qualified scholarship by an individual who is a candidate for a degree and used for tuition and fees required for the enrollment or attendance (or for fees, books, supplies, and equipment required for courses of instruction) at a primary, secondary, or post-secondary educational institution (sec. 117). This tax-free treatment does not extend to scholarship amounts covering regular living expenses, such as room and board. In addition to the exclusion for qualified scholarships, present law provides an exclusion from gross income for qualified tuition reductions for certain education provided to employees of certain educational organizations (and their spouses and dependents) (sec. 117(d)).

The exclusion for qualified scholarships and qualified tuition reductions does not apply to any amount received by a student that represents payment for teaching, research, or other services by the student required as a condition for receiving the scholarship or tuition reduction.

D. HOPE and Lifetime Learning Credits

1. HOPE credit

[Under sec. 25A], [i]ndividual taxpayers are allowed to claim a nonrefundable credit, the "HOPE" credit, against Federal income taxes of up to [$2,500 in 2016] per student per year for qualified tuition and related expenses paid for the first two years of the student's post secondary education in a degree or certificate program. The HOPE credit rate is 100 percent on the first [$2,000] of qualified tuition and related expenses, and [25] percent on the next [$2,000] of qualified tuition and related expenses [in 2016].[1]

The qualified tuition and related expenses must be incurred on behalf of the taxpayer, the taxpayer's spouse, or a dependent of the taxpayer. The HOPE credit is available with respect to an individual student for two taxable years, provided that the student has not completed the first two years of post-secondary education before the beginning of the second taxable year. The HOPE credit that a taxpayer may otherwise claim is phased out ratably [in 2016] for taxpayers with modified AGI between [$80,000] and [$90,000] ([$160,000] and [$180,000] for married taxpayers filing a joint return). For taxable years beginning after 2001, the * * * maximum HOPE credit amount and the AGI phase-out ranges are indexed for inflation.

The HOPE credit is available in the taxable year the expenses are paid, subject to the requirement that the education is furnished to the student during that year or during the first three months of the next year. Qualified tuition and related expenses paid with the proceeds of a loan generally are eligible for the HOPE credit. The repayment of a loan itself is not a qualified tuition or related expense.

A taxpayer may claim the HOPE credit with respect to an eligible student who is not the taxpayer or the taxpayer's spouse (e.g., in cases in which the student is the taxpayer's child) only if the taxpayer claims the student as a dependent for the taxable year for which the credit is claimed. * * *

The HOPE credit is available for "qualified tuition and related expenses," which include tuition and fees required to be paid to an eligible educational institution as a condition of enrollment or attendance of an eligible student at the institution. Charges and fees associated with meals, lodging, insurance, transportation, and similar personal, living, or family expenses are not eligible for the credit. The expenses of education involving sports, games, or hobbies are not qualified tuition

---

[1]   Thus, an eligible student who incurs [$2,000] of qualified tuition and related expenses is eligible (subject to the AGI phaseout) for a [$2,000 HOPE] credit. If an eligible student incurs [$4,000] of qualified tuition and related expenses, then he or she is eligible for the maximum [$2,500] HOPE credit. [Ed: The American Opportunity Tax Credit under § 25A(i), enacted in 2008 and made permanent in 2015, increases the HOPE credit to these levels; that is, to 100 percent of the first $2,000 of qualified tuition and related expenses and to 25 percent on the next $2,000 of qualified tuition and related expenses.]

and related expenses unless this education is part of the student's degree program.

Qualified tuition and related expenses generally include only out-of-pocket expenses. Qualified tuition and related expenses do not include expenses covered by employer-provided educational assistance and scholarships that are not required to be included in the gross income of either the student or the taxpayer claiming the credit. Thus, total qualified tuition and related expenses are reduced by any scholarship or fellowship grants excludable from gross income under section 117 and any other tax-free educational benefits received by the student (or the taxpayer claiming the credit) during the taxable year. The HOPE credit is not allowed with respect to any education expense for which a deduction is claimed under section 162 or any other section of the Code.

An eligible student for purposes of the HOPE credit is an individual who is enrolled in a degree, certificate, or other program (including a program of study abroad approved for credit by the institution at which such student is enrolled) leading to a recognized educational credential at an eligible educational institution. The student must pursue a course of study on at least a half-time basis. * * * To be eligible for the HOPE credit, a student must not have been convicted of a Federal or State felony consisting of the possession or distribution of a controlled substance.

[Ed: The American Recovery and Reinvestment Tax Act of 2009 temporarily increased the Hope Scholarship Credit to the sum of (1) 100 percent of the first $2,000 of tuition, fees, and course materials paid during the taxable year, and (2) 25 percent of the next $2,000. The maximum credit is $2,500 (not indexed for inflation), whereas the maximum original Hope credit was $1,500 (indexed for inflation after 2001). The "new" Hope credit has been renamed the "American Opportunity Tax Credit" and is reflected in § 25A(i). The credit is allowed with respect to any of the first four years of post-secondary education (in lieu of the first two years rule under the HOPE credit). Thus, the credit can be claimed with respect to a student for whom the credit already had been claimed for two years. Further, the cost of "course materials," in addition to tuition and fees, is now eligible for the credit. The revised credit can also be claimed against the alternative minimum tax. Forty percent of the allowable credit is refundable, unless the taxpayer is a child subject to the § 1(g) "kiddie tax" (see Chapter 38, Section 2). The American Opportunity Tax Credit gradually phases out for taxpayers with adjusted gross incomes in excess of $80,000 ($160,000 for married couples filing jointly; these amounts are not adjusted for inflation), under the same formula as the Hope Scholarship Credit. In 2015, Congress made the credit permanent.]

2. Lifetime Learning Credit

Individual taxpayers are allowed to claim a nonrefundable credit, the Lifetime Learning credit, against Federal income taxes equal to 20 percent of qualified tuition and related expenses incurred during the taxable year on behalf of the taxpayer, the taxpayer's spouse, or any dependents. [Section 25A(c)] related expenses per taxpayer return are eligible for the Lifetime Learning credit. * * * For expenses paid after December 31, 2002, up to $10,000 of qualified tuition and related expenses per taxpayer return will be eligible for the Lifetime Learning credit (i.e., the maximum credit per taxpayer return will be $2,000).

In contrast to the HOPE credit, a taxpayer may claim the Lifetime Learning credit for an unlimited number of taxable years. Also in contrast to the HOPE credit, the maximum amount of the Lifetime Learning credit that may be claimed on a taxpayer's return will not vary based on the number of students in the taxpayer's family—that is, the HOPE credit is computed on a per student basis, while the Lifetime Learning credit is computed on a family-wide basis. The Lifetime Learning credit amount that a taxpayer may otherwise claim is phased out ratably for taxpayers with modified AGI between [$55,000] and [$65,000] ([$110,000 and $130,000] for married taxpayers filing a joint return) [in 2016].

The Lifetime Learning credit is available in the taxable year the expenses are paid, subject to the requirement that the education is furnished to the student during that year or during the first three months of the next year. Qualified tuition and related expenses paid with the proceeds of a loan generally are eligible for the Lifetime Learning credit. As with the HOPE credit, repayment of a loan is not a qualified tuition expense.

As with the HOPE credit, a taxpayer may claim the Lifetime Learning credit with respect to a student who is not the taxpayer or the taxpayer's spouse (e.g., in cases in which the student is the taxpayer's child) only if the taxpayer claims the student as a dependent for the taxable year for which the credit is claimed. * * *

A taxpayer may claim the Lifetime Learning credit for a taxable year with respect to one or more students, even though the taxpayer also claims a HOPE credit for that same taxable year with respect to other students. If, for a taxable year, a taxpayer claims a HOPE credit with respect to a student, then the Lifetime Learning credit is not available with respect to that same student for that year (although the Lifetime Learning credit may be available with respect to that same student for other taxable years).

The Lifetime Learning credit is available for "qualified tuition and related expenses," which include tuition and fees required to be paid to an eligible educational institution as a condition of enrollment or attendance of a student at the institution. Charges and fees associated with meals, lodging, insurance, transportation, and similar personal, living or family expenses are not eligible for the credit. The expenses of education involving sports, games, or hobbies are not qualified tuition expenses unless this education is part of the student's degree program.

In contrast to the HOPE credit, qualified tuition and related expenses for purposes of the Lifetime Learning credit include tuition and fees incurred with respect to undergraduate or graduate-level (and professional degree) courses.

* * * Undergraduate and graduate students are eligible for the Lifetime Learning credit. Moreover, in contrast to the HOPE credit, the eligibility of a student for the Lifetime Learning credit does not depend on whether or not the student has been convicted of a Federal or State felony consisting of the possession or distribution of a controlled substance.

[D–1. Deduction for Qualified Higher Education Expenses]

[Section 222] permits taxpayers an above-the-line deduction for qualified higher education expenses paid by the taxpayer during a taxable year. Qualified higher education expenses are defined in the same manner as for purposes of the HOPE credit.

* * * [T]axpayers with adjusted gross income that does not exceed $65,000 ($130,000 in the case of married taxpayers filing joint returns) are entitled to a maximum deduction of $4,000 and taxpayers with adjusted gross income that does not exceed $80,000 ($160,000 in the case of married taxpayers filing joint returns) are entitled to a maximum deduction of $2,000. [Section 222 is set to expire on December 31, 2016.]

Taxpayers are not eligible to claim the deduction and a HOPE or Lifetime Learning Credit in the same year with respect to the same student. A taxpayer may claim in the same year the deduction, the exclusion for distributions from [a Coverdell savings] account [§ 530], and the exclusion for interest on education savings bonds [sec. 135], as long as the deductions and exclusion are not claimed with respect to the same expenses. A taxpayer may also claim, in the same year, both the deduction and an exclusion for distributions from a qualified tuition program [under sec. 530]. Additionally, a taxpayer may claim the deduction with respect to the same expenses that are used to claim an exclusion for a distribution from a qualified tuition program, but only to the extent of the amount of the distribution representing a return of contributions.]

E. Provisions Relating to Student Loans

1. Deduction for student loan interest

Certain individuals who have paid interest on qualified education loans may claim an above-the-line deduction for such interest expenses, subject to a maximum annual deduction limit (sec. 221). * * * No deduction is allowed to an individual if that individual is claimed as a dependent on another taxpayer's return for the taxable year.

A qualified education loan generally is defined as any indebtedness incurred solely to pay for the costs of attendance (including room and board) of the taxpayer, the taxpayer's spouse, or any dependent of the taxpayer as of the time the indebtedness was incurred in attending on at least a half-time basis [a qualified educational institution, i.e., post-secondary education (including internships and residencies in educational institutions, hospitals, and health care facilities) leading to a degree, certificate, or other recognized educational credential]. The maximum allowable deduction per year is $2,500. The deduction is phased out ratably for single taxpayers with AGI of [between $65,000 and $80,000] and [between $130,000 and $160,000] for married taxpayers filing a joint return [in 2016]. The income phase-out ranges are indexed for inflation.

2. Exclusion of income from student loan forgiveness

Gross income generally includes the discharge of indebtedness of the taxpayer. Under an exception to this general rule, gross income does not include any amount from the forgiveness (in whole or in part) of certain student loans, provided that the forgiveness is contingent on the student's working for a certain period of time in certain professions for any of a broad class of employers (sec. 108(f)).

Student loans eligible for this special rule must be made to an individual to assist the individual in attending an educational institution that normally maintains a regular faculty and curriculum and normally has a regularly enrolled body of students in attendance at the place where its education activities are regularly carried on. Loan proceeds may be used not only for tuition and required fees, but also to cover room and board expenses. The loan must be made by [a governmental or tax exempt entity].

* * *

F.   Qualified Tuition Programs

[Section 529] provides tax-exempt status to "qualified tuition programs," meaning certain programs established and maintained by a State (or agency or instrumentality thereof) [or by private colleges and universities] under which persons may (1) purchase tuition credits or certificates on behalf of a designated beneficiary that entitle the beneficiary to a waiver or payment of qualified higher education expenses of the beneficiary, or (2) [in the case of State programs only] make contributions to an account that is established for the purpose of meeting qualified higher education expenses of the designated beneficiary of the account. The term "qualified higher education expenses" * * * includes expenses for tuition, fees, books, supplies, and equipment required for the enrollment or attendance at an eligible educational institution, as well as certain room and board expenses * * * .

[Section 529] also provides that no amount shall be included in the gross income of a contributor to, or beneficiary of, a qualified State tuition program with respect to any distribution from, or earnings under, such program, except that (1) amounts distributed * * * to a beneficiary * * *

will be included in the beneficiary's gross income (unless excludable under another Code section) to the extent such amounts or the value of the [distribution exceeds the amount paid for qualified higher education expenses], and (2) amounts distributed to a contributor or another distributee (e.g., when a parent receives a refund) will be included in the contributor's/distributee's gross income to the extent such amounts exceed contributions made on behalf of the beneficiary.

A qualified tuition program is required to provide that purchases or contributions only be made in cash. Contributors and beneficiaries are not allowed to direct the investment of contributions to the program (or earnings thereon). The program is required to maintain a separate accounting for each designated beneficiary. A specified individual must be designated as the beneficiary at the commencement of participation in a qualified tuition program (i.e., when contributions are first made to purchase an interest in such a program), * * *

No amount is includible in the gross income of a contributor to, or beneficiary of, a qualified tuition program with respect to any contribution to or earnings on such a program [to the extent the distribution is used to pay qualified higher education expenses]. However, to the extent that a distribution from a qualified * * * tuition program is used to pay for qualified tuition and related expenses (as defined in sec. 25A(f)(1)) [and] the distributee (or another taxpayer claiming the distributee as a dependent) * * * claim[s] the HOPE credit or Lifetime Learning credit under section 25A with respect to such tuition and related expenses [the exclusion under § 530 is unavailable] * * * .

G. Exclusion of Interest Earned on Education Savings Bonds

Interest earned on a qualified U.S. Series EE savings bond issued after 1989 is excludable from gross income if the proceeds of the bond upon redemption do not exceed qualified higher education expenses paid by the taxpayer during the taxable year (sec. 135). "Qualified higher education expenses" include tuition and fees (but not room and board expenses) required for the enrollment or attendance of the taxpayer, the taxpayer's spouse, or a dependent of the taxpayer at certain eligible higher educational institutions (defined in the manner as for the HOPE and Lifetime Learning credits). The amount of qualified higher education expenses taken into account for purposes of the exclusion provided by section 135 is reduced by the amount of such expenses taken into account in determining the HOPE or Lifetime Learning credits claimed by any taxpayer, or an exclusion from gross income for a distribution from an education IRA, with respect to a particular student for the taxable year.

The exclusion provided by section 135 is phased out for certain higher-income taxpayers, determined by the taxpayer's modified AGI during the year the bond is redeemed. For [2016], the exclusion is phased out for single taxpayers with modified AGI between [$77,550] and

[$92,550] ([$116,300] and [$146,300] for married taxpayers filing a joint return). To prevent taxpayers from effectively avoiding the income phase out limitation through issuance of bonds directly in the child's name, present law provides that the interest exclusion is available only with respect to U.S. Series EE savings bonds issued to taxpayers who are at least 24 years old.

H.   [Coverdell] Education [Savings Accounts]

1.   In general

Taxpayers may establish [Coverdell education savings accounts] created exclusively for the purpose of paying qualified higher education expenses of a named beneficiary * * * (sec. 530). Annual [cash] contributions to [Coverdell education savings accounts] may not exceed [$2,000] per designated beneficiary and may not be made after the designated beneficiary reaches age 18 [except for special needs children]. The contribution limit is phased out for taxpayers with modified AGI between $95,000 and $110,000 ([($190,000 and $220,000] for married taxpayers filing a joint return); the AGI of the contributor not the beneficiary controls whether a contribution is permitted by the taxpayer. No contribution may be made to [a Coverdell education savings account] during any year in which any contributions are made by anyone to a qualified State tuition program on behalf of the same beneficiary.

Earnings on contributions to [a Coverdell education savings account] generally are subject to tax when withdrawn. However, distributions from [a Coverdell education savings account] are excludable from the gross income of the distributee (i.e., the student) to the extent that the distribution does not exceed the qualified education expenses incurred by the beneficiary during the year the distribution is made (provided that a HOPE credit or Lifetime Learning credit is not claimed with respect to the beneficiary for the same taxable year). The earnings portion of [a Coverdell education savings account] distribution not used to pay qualified education expenses is includible in the gross income of the distributee and generally is subject to an additional 10-percent tax.

Tax-free (and penalty-free) transfers or rollovers of account balances from [a Coverdell education savings account] benefiting one beneficiary to another [Coverdell education account] benefiting another beneficiary (as well as redesignations of the named beneficiary) are permitted, provided that the new beneficiary is a member of the family of the old beneficiary.

The term "qualified education expenses" includes [qualified higher education expenses and qualified elementary and secondary education expenses, including] tuition, fees, books, supplies, and equipment required for the enrollment or attendance of the designated beneficiary at an eligible education institution, regardless of whether the beneficiary is enrolled at an eligible educational institution on a full-time, half-time, or less than half-time basis. Moreover, qualified * * * education expenses include certain room and board expenses for any period during which the beneficiary is at least a half-time student. Qualified higher education expenses include expenses with respect to undergraduate or graduate-level courses. [A taxpayer can claim a HOPE credit or Lifetime Learning credit and exclude amounts distributed from a Coverdell education savings account] for the same student so long as the qualified education expenditures for the year equal or exceed the sum of the [Coverdell distribution and the Section 25A credit base amount.]

Qualified higher education expenses generally include only out-of-pocket expenses. Such qualified higher education expenses do not include expenses covered by employer-provided educational assistance or scholarships for the benefit of the beneficiary that are excludable from gross income. Thus, total qualified higher education expenses are reduced by scholarship or fellowship grants excludable from gross income under section 117, as well as any other tax-free educational benefits, such as employer-provided educational assistance, that are excludable from the employee's gross income under section 127.

2.   Coordination with HOPE and Lifetime Learning credits

If an exclusion from gross income under section 530 is allowed for a particular student, then neither the HOPE credit nor the Lifetime Learning credit will be available in the same taxable year with respect to the same student. However, if a student elects to waive the exclusion from gross income under section 530, then either the student or a parent (if the student is claimed as a dependent by the parent) may claim the HOPE credit or the Lifetime Learning credit.

I.   Individual Retirement Arrangements ("IRAs")

1.   In general

In general, [see Chapter 8, Section 2), there are two types of IRAs under present law: traditional IRAs, to which both deductible and nondeductible contributions may be made, and Roth IRAs.

* * *

2.   Traditional IRAs

Deductible IRA contributions

* * *

Amounts held in a deductible IRA are includible in income when withdrawn (except to the extent the withdrawal is a return of nondeductible contributions). Includible amounts withdrawn prior to attainment of age 59–1/2 are subject to an additional 10-percent early withdrawal tax, unless the withdrawal is * * * used for education expenses, * * * . Education expenses that qualify for the exception to the early withdrawal tax are qualified higher education expenses (as defined under the rules relating to qualified * * * tuition programs) of the taxpayer, the taxpayer's spouse, or any child or grandchild of the taxpayer and his or her spouse, at an eligible educational institution. The amount of education expenses is reduced by certain scholarships and similar payments.

* * *

3. Roth IRAs

Individuals with AGI below certain levels may make nondeductible contributions to a Roth IRA. * * * Amounts held in a Roth IRA that are withdrawn as a qualified distribution are not includible in income, nor subject to the additional 10-percent tax on early withdrawals. * * *

Distributions from a Roth IRA that are not qualified distributions are includible in income to the extent attributable to earnings, and subject to the 10-percent early withdrawal tax (unless an exception applies). * * * [A] withdrawal from a Roth IRA that is not a qualified distribution and that is used for educational expenses is includible in gross income to the extent attributable to earnings, but is not subject to the 10-percent early withdrawal tax.

J. Tax Benefits for Certain Types of Bonds for Educational Facilities and Activities

1. Tax-exempt bonds

In general

Interest on debt incurred by States or local governments is excluded from income if the proceeds of the borrowing are used to carry out governmental functions of those entities or the debt is repaid with governmental funds (sec. 103). Like other activities carried out and paid for by State and local governments, the construction, renovation, and operation of public schools is an activity eligible for financing with the proceeds of tax-exempt bonds.

Interest on bonds that nominally are issued by States or local governments, but the proceeds of which are used (directly or indirectly) by a private person and payment of which is derived from funds of such a private person is taxable unless the purpose of the borrowing is approved specifically in the Code or in a non-Code provision of a revenue Act. These bonds are called "private activity bonds." * * *

[Qualified public educational facilities bonds.—State and local governments may issue tax-exempt private activity bonds to finance elementary and secondary school facilities that are owned by private for-profit corporations pursuant to a public-private partnership agreement with a State or local educational agency (sec. 142(k)).]

Qualified student loan bonds.—States and local governments may issue tax-exempt private activity bonds to finance certain student loans. Eligible student loans include Federally guaranteed loans under the Higher Education Act of 1965 ("GSL loans") and other loans financed as part of a program of general application approved by the State (sec. 144(b)(1)). * * *

2. Qualified zone academy bonds

As an alternative to traditional tax-exempt bonds, certain States and local governments are given the authority to issue "qualified zone academy bonds." [Section 1397E, which expired as to new bond issuances after October 3, 2008, at which point § 54E became effective.] Under present law, a total of $400 million of qualified zone academy bonds may be issued in each of 1998 through [2008, $1.4 billion in 2009 and 2010, and $400 million in 2011 through 2016]. The $400 million aggregate bond authority is allocated each year to the States according to their respective populations of individuals below the poverty line. Each State, in turn, allocates the credit to qualified zone academies within such State. A State may carry over any unused allocation for up to two years. * * * [Section 54E is set to expire on December 31, 2016 as to new issuances.]

Certain financial institutions (i.e., banks, insurance companies, and corporations actively engaged in the business of lending money) that hold qualified zone academy bonds are entitled to a nonrefundable tax credit in an amount equal to a credit rate (set daily by the Treasury Department) multiplied by the face amount of the bond (sec. 1397E). A taxpayer holding a qualified zone academy bond on the credit allowance date (i.e., each one-year anniversary of the issuance of the bond) is entitled to a credit. The credit amount is includible in gross income (as if it were a taxable interest payment on the bond) * * * .

"Qualified zone academy bonds" are defined as bonds issued by a State or local government, provided that: (1) at least [100] percent of the proceeds is used for the purpose of [rehabilitating or repairing], providing equipment to, developing course materials for use at, or training teachers and other school personnel in a "qualified zone academy" and (2) private entities have promised to contribute to the qualified zone academy certain equipment, technical assistance or training, employee services, or other property or services with a value equal to at least 10 percent of the bond proceeds.

A school is a "qualified zone academy" if (1) the school is a public school that provides education and training below the college level, (2) the school operates a special academic program in cooperation with businesses to enhance the academic curriculum and increase graduation and employment rates, [and to better prepare students for the rigors of college and the increasingly complex workforce, through a comprehensive education plan approved by the local education agency that subjects students to the same academic standards and assessments as other students in the local education system], and (3) either (a) the school is located in a designated empowerment zones or a designated enterprise community, or (b) it is reasonably expected that at least 35 percent of the students at the school will be eligible for free or reduced-cost lunches.

DETAILED ANALYSIS

1. GENERAL

The sheer number of tax expenditures for education poses numerous issues ranging from the impact of the programs on efficiency, equity, administrability, and simplicity, to the policy and structural justifications of the individual programs and their interaction with each other.

The following materials explore these issues.

2. EDUCATION POLICY

The United States employs direct spending programs to provide financial aid to students. The most well-known forms of assistance include Pell Grants for low-income families and the Federal Direct Loan program, the latter of which is comprised of Subsidized Stafford Loans, Unsubsidized Stafford Loans, PLUS loans, and Consolidation Loans. For Fiscal 2015, federal aid for higher education through Pell grants was estimated to reach $30 billion, while new Federal Direct Loans were expected to approach $130 billion ($27 billion in Consolidation Loans and $102 billion in the other three programs combined). See Department of Education, Student Financial Assistance, Fiscal Year 2015 Budget Request (2014), Q–17; Department of Education, Student Loans Overview, Fiscal Year 2015 Budget Proposal (2014), S–4.

Meanwhile, the tax expenditures for education in 2015 that provided subsidies most directly for family education expenses cost over $26 billion. These tax expenditure items included: (i) the HOPE credit in § 25A (called the American Opportunity Tax Credit for tax years after 2008), which provided tax offsets of $15.7 billion as well as cash subsidies of nearly $6 billion through its refundable feature; (ii) the Lifetime Learning credit in § 25A ($2.43 billion in tax benefits); (iii) the deduction for interest paid on student loans in § 221 ($1.8 billion); (iv) the deduction for qualified tuition and related expenses in § 222 ($400 million); (v) the exclusion for qualified scholarships in § 117 ($2.98 billion); (vi) the exclusion of employer-provided education assistance in § 127 ($800 million); (vii) the exclusion of interest on savings bonds redeemed to finance educational expenses in § 135 ($30 million); (viii) the exemption for qualified tuition programs in § 529 ($1.95 billion); and (ix) the exemption for Coverdell education savings accounts in § 530 ($60 million). Office of Management and Budget, Analytical Perspectives: Budget of the United States Government, Fiscal Year 2016 224–225, 227 (2015). Thus, tax expenditures for higher education, though costing less than the amount of direct assistance, reflect a sizeable portion of total federal financial assistance for education. Given their importance in education financing, the tax expenditures for education, like all federal expenditure programs, should be examined regularly to determine whether they are, in fact, reaching the target beneficiaries (primarily middle-income families and their children) in an efficient and constructive manner. As a separate though related issue, policymakers should consider the extent to which tax subsidies for education have in fact made higher education more affordable for the target population or simply resulted in colleges and universities raising tuition and fees; that is, whether the subsidy has helped or hindered the target beneficiaries from acquiring access to higher education.

3. ECONOMIC ISSUES

The tax expenditures for education may be classified in two broad groupings. The first category creates incentives to save for education (e.g., qualified tuition programs and Coverdell education savings accounts), while the second category provides cost sharing for educational expenses (e.g., HOPE credit).

The tax expenditures for savings for education raise several issues. On the one hand, the federal government subsidizes direct loans for higher education for which virtually any student can qualify. Thus, the savings from these programs occur as the student pays off the loans from income presumably generated as a result of the education, however, the tax incentives to save for education are directed at parents to save for their children's education in advance of the education itself. It is unclear whether this advance saving model—or, for that matter, using the tax system to encourage such saving in the first place—provides a good complement or alternative to the traditional real-time loan model. A second problem with the savings incentives is that they may not actually increase saving for higher education. Parents who have been saving or plan to save for their children's higher education on an after-tax basis simply may shift their savings from taxable to the tax-preferred methods, but not actually increase savings for education. There is evidence that this behavioral response occurred after the introduction of traditional IRAs, and there is little reason to believe the response would be different for education savings accounts that provide similar tax-favored saving models. To the extent this phenomenon occurs, the revenue cost of the tax expenditure amounts to a waste of federal funds.

In general, economists disapprove of subsidies aimed at encouraging certain kinds of behavior, because such intervention distorts choices and causes funds to be shifted from their highest and best use to activities that are made more profitable solely because of the subsidies. At the same time, economists recognize that subsidies may be appropriate under one of two conditions: (1) to correct a market failure, or (2) when they produce benefits for both the general public and the individual who uses the subsidy to make a purchase or investment.

There are people for whom borrowing to pay for education is not an option. If borrowers cannot provide the necessary security for financing education in real time, then there might be a market failure that justifies tax subsidies for saving. Still, this assumes that the benefit of the tax subsidies is not captured by educational institutions through higher tuition, and, furthermore, that taxpayers actually receive the benefit of the subsidies. It also assumes that the persons who need the subsidy have positive tax liability against which to apply the tax credit or deduction, or, alternatively, that the tax benefit is refundable. Currently, the only refundable tax subsidy for education is the American Opportunity Tax Credit under § 25A(i).

The cost-sharing tax expenditures for education could be justified on efficiency grounds if they produce benefits for society as a whole. There is a good deal of evidence that a college education benefits individual students in the form of higher earnings. But, if the student captures the entire benefit of the college education—either through higher earnings or otherwise—then society does not necessarily share in the benefits of education (ignoring higher tax revenues from an educated person's higher income), and the subsidy results in efficiency losses.

On the other hand, if positive societal benefits are achieved through a better-educated citizenry or if innovation resulting from education is not fully compensated by the market (so that the public derives the benefit of below-market returns), a subsidy may be justified. In these instances, subsidies (including tax subsidies) for the costs of education could improve overall efficiency for society. Even so, other issues remain. First, the fact that a subsidy can be justified on grounds of generating societal benefits does not help in determining the proper amount of the subsidy or the optimal form of delivering the subsidy (e.g., loans versus grants, tax expenditures versus direct spending programs). Needless to say, as Congress has enacted additional tax subsidies for education, it has not considered in any rigorous fashion whether new subsidies on top of old subsidies provide social value exceeding the costs or whether tax expenditures (some equivalent to outright grants and some equivalent to interest-free loans) provide the best method for delivering the financial assistance.

Economists view the costs of higher education as a combination of investment in human capital (getting a degree in chemistry, for example) and personal consumption (the chemistry major takes a course in art history or attends the school's football games). If the subsidies for investment in human capital are effective such that they expand, there may be a resultant reduction in investment in tangible capital (although, as the materials in Chapters 14 and 17 demonstrate, such investments are also heavily subsidized by tax expenditures). At that point, the question becomes whether the capital reallocation increases or decreases overall efficiency in society.

4.   EQUITY ISSUES

4.1. *Spending Equity Issues*

There are two major equity issues raised by the tax expenditures for education. First, the programs generally provide very few benefits to individuals with insufficient taxable income or tax liability; that is, very few of the provisions, including most of the credits, have a refundability feature. Second, the value of the benefits is a function of the beneficiary's marginal tax rate. As a result, the value of any benefit starts at zero for non-taxpayers and rises to equal the taxpayer's highest marginal rate. It is difficult to imagine that a direct spending program for education would involve either of these implicit program designs; that is, little or no benefit to low-income taxpayers and disproportionate benefit to high-income taxpayers.

Neither problem is an inevitable result of using the tax system to extend federal financial assistance for education. The first problem can be solved by utilizing tax credits instead of deductions or exclusions and making the tax credit refundable. As noted above, however, only the American Opportunity Tax Credit is currently refundable. Thus, the current structure of the tax expenditure program overwhelmingly excludes low-income families and students them from its benefits.

The upside down aspect of current tax expenditures could also be avoided by including the tax benefits in taxable income or, in the case of tax deferral provisions, by imposing an interest charge on the tax deferred. Neither technique is novel. For example, § 87 requires that the amount of the alcohol fuels and biodiesel fuels credits be included as gross income. Meanwhile, among the tax expenditures for education only the tax credit for qualified zone academy bonds is included as gross income. For another example, § 453A imposes the interest charge on tax deferral in the cases of large amounts of installment sales transactions and distributions from foreign trusts. While both of these techniques can eliminate the upside down features of tax expenditures by including their value in income, using tax credits in lieu of exclusions or deductions can eliminate the upside-down effect of tax expenditures only in the case of refundable credits that include the cash subsidy in income. Consider a $100 tax credit and an identical $100 cash grant. The cash subsidy should be included in the gross income of the recipient lest a high-income taxpayer in the 35-percent tax bracket benefits from the full face value of the $100 without having to pay $35 in tax on the windfall. A low-income taxpayer in the 15-percent bracket receives the same treatment, but saves only $15 in tax compared to $35 for the high-bracket taxpayer. In a similar way, failure to include in income the $100 tax credit creates an upside-down distribution of the subsidy (although this adverse effect can be mitigated by phasing out credits for higher levels of adjusted gross income).

4.2. *Tax Policy Equity Issues*

Apart from the foregoing subsidy issues, the current treatment of education expenses raises tax policy issues. Students who attend public schools get the benefit of the taxes used to finance those schools. It is as if the students received the funds directly and then used them to pay for their education. This same analysis could be used for every type of publicly financed service paid for with tax revenues, such as fire and police protection or parks, roads, and courts. In theory, users of these public goods could be required to include their value in income, net of any taxes paid to provide those goods. But such an exercise would be administratively impossible.

Students also incur opportunity costs in deciding to pursue education by foregoing income from jobs. The situation can be viewed as if each student worked and received an imputed wage, which the students immediately spent on the cost of education. Under a "pure" income tax model, the imputed wage should be included in income, and the education expenditures should be allowed as an offset to any taxes levied on that income.

As noted above, economists view costs of education as comprising two components: investment in human capital and personal consumption. The former should be taken into account for income tax purposes, the latter should not. While it would be difficult to draw the line between the two categories, if such a line were drawn, then the expenditure to increase human capital should be capitalized and deducted against the future income resulting from the education. Current tax rules do not permit the amortization of expenditures for education to increase an individual's store of human capital.

Somewhat counterintuitively, the current tax system favors education costs. By excluding from gross income both the benefit of public financed education and imputed income in the opportunity cost scenario, current law effectively gives an immediate deduction for the education costs associated with that income. To illustrate, suppose a student receives $1,000 in education benefits from attending a public state university. Excluding the $1,000 from gross income and providing no tax effects for the corresponding expenditure, produces the same result as including it in gross income and giving an immediate deduction for the full $1,000. This result (that is, either no inclusion and no deduction or inclusion and immediate deduction) is more favorable than a model in which the $1,000 is included in income and the costs associated with generating human capital are recovered over time through future amortization deductions (the consumption component being completely disallowed).

At the end of the day, the current treatment of education benefits and costs can be justified on administrative grounds. Additionally, it results in more rather than less favorable treatment of education expenses than would "proper" treatment under a comprehensive income tax.

4.3. *Interest on Student Loans*

As a general rule, under § 163, interest on loans used for personal consumption is not deductible, either because it is not a cost of producing income or because it is a cost of producing tax-exempt income (imputed rental income on consumer durables, for example). Investment interest is deductible only against investment income. And interest attributable to tax-exempt income is nondeductible. Under this rubric, it can be difficult to determine into which category interest paid on student loans should fall.

Some commentators argue that just because consumption expenditures should not be deductible in an income tax, it does not follow that interest on loans to finance consumption should also be nondeductible. Borrowing to finance consumption in year 1 rather than saving and waiting to consume in year 2 represents a timing preference for consumption but no increase in total consumption by the taxpayer. Under this view, the general disallowance of the interest deduction in § 163 is improper. It follows that to the extent education costs constitute personal consumption, allowance of the § 221 deduction for student loan interest represents the correct rule.

To the extent education costs represent an investment in human capital, the § 221 deductions should not be allowed until the taxpayer has generated income from that capital against which to deduct the interest expense.

The proper treatment of interest expense in an income tax is a source of considerable and ongoing controversy. The treatment of interest on student loans represents simply one element of that controversy.

5. ADMINISTRABILITY AND SIMPLICITY ISSUES

5.1. *General*

Each of the tax expenditures for education is complex in its own right. But the interaction of the provisions creates even more complexity. Some of those interactions are discussed below.

5.2. *Differing Definitions*

The definition of "qualified" education expenses varies among the different provisions. Some definitions cover only tuition and related costs; others cover room and board; still others cover transportation expenses. The definition of qualified institutions differs as well. Some provisions cover only costs of higher education, while others include vocational education or elementary and secondary education. The lack of definitional uniformity forces parents and students to grapple with and understand all the tax expenditure provisions for education before selecting the one or two provisions with the broadest and most appropriate coverage and the most generous financial benefits. The current web of tax expenditures for education and its unique and varying qualifying criteria creates undue complexity for taxpayers as well as efficiency losses from the time (and expense) expended in making sense of the process.

5.3. *Phaseouts*

Perhaps a source of even greater complexity among tax expenditures for education is that they phase out benefits over specified (and often narrow) ranges of income. In general, phaseouts are justified on one of two grounds: (1) targeting benefits to lower- and middle-class households (although the programs provide different definitions of what it means to be "middle class"), and (2) controlling cost. The validity of these justifications notwithstanding, the use of different phaseouts multiplies many times over the inherent complexity of the individual provisions and produces anomalous effects on the nominal marginal rate structure.

5.3.1. *Effects of Phaseouts in Marginal Tax Rates*

The use of a phaseout provision always produces a higher marginal tax rate in the phaseout range than confronts the taxpayer whose income is either below or above the phaseout range. This phenomenon can be illustrated by analyzing the phaseout of the benefits of the HOPE credit (as currently reflected in § 25A(i)). Suppose that a single taxpayer incurs $5,000 of qualified educational expenses, thus generating a $2,500 HOPE credit. The taxpayer has adjusted gross income of $80,000 and taxable income of $70,000, thus placing the taxpayer in the 25 percent marginal tax bracket. The phaseout range for the HOPE credit for a single person in 2016 is between $80,000 and $90,000 of modified AGI. Therefore, this taxpayer is unaffected by the phaseout and receives the benefit of the full tax credit. Now suppose that the taxpayer earns an additional $1,000 of AGI. As a result, the HOPE tax credit must be reduced by the phaseout formula in § 25A(i)(4). Application of the formula reduces the taxpayer's HOPE credit by $250. Thus, increasing the taxpayer's AGI by $1,000 costs the taxpayer $250 in lost HOPE credit plus $250 of increased regular tax (i.e., $1,000 × .25). Prior to entering the phaseout range, the taxpayer's marginal rate was 25 percent.

But in the phaseout range, the taxpayer incurred a 50% marginal tax rate—11.4 percentage points higher than the highest marginal rate of 39.6 percent—rather than the 25 percent before entering the phaseout range as well as the 25 percent that the taxpayer will incur after the taxpayer's AGI rises above $90,000.

Of course, the taxpayer is better off with some credit in the phase-out range as compared to no credit. But, as we have seen, the marginal tax rate is the one that counts when assessing the effects of incentive-based type subsidies, whether tax or direct. This taxpayer thus will benefit more from other tax expenditure subsidies while in the phase-out range than when below or above the range.

The complexity created by the varying phaseout amounts and ranges in the education tax expenditures (as well as other interactions) is analyzed in Albert J. Davis, Choice Complexity in Tax Benefits for Higher Education, 60 Nat'l Tax J. 509 (2002).

5.4. *Planning and Compliance Complexity*

The greatest complexity facing taxpayers involves choosing among the various tax subsidies for education while not losing benefits that might otherwise be available. The number of overlapping provisions, almost all of which are mutually exclusive as pertaining to individual students—at least with respect to any particular dollar of qualifying educational expenses—as well as the welter of detail in the provisions makes it easy to lose sight of the crucial differences in determining which program to choose. The Staff of the Joint Committee on Taxation has made the following observations about the complex program design of education tax expenditures:

> Although the existence of a variety of tax incentives for education may mean that more taxpayers are able to take advantage of one or more education incentives, understanding the tax benefits provided by the different provisions, the various eligibility requirements, the interaction between different incentives and provisions within each incentive, and as well as the recordkeeping and reporting requirements, may be time consuming and confusing for taxpayers who are interested in reducing their current educational expenses or saving for future expenses.

* * *

> Because the HOPE and Lifetime Learning credits have differing credit percentages applied to different base amounts of qualifying expenses, families eligible for both credits must complete separate calculations to calculate their total education credits. Additionally, * * * certain families with a child eligible for the HOPE credit will need to calculate separately the value of the Lifetime Learning credit to see if it exceeds that of the value of the HOPE credit. The complexity involved in maximizing available credits is compounded for families with more than one student in college at the same time. The complexities associated with multiple credits make it difficult for taxpayers to take into account the value of the credits in budgeting for college expenses. The income-related phase-outs of

the credits create both computational and transactional complexity for taxpayers.

* * *

The interactions among various education provisions create transactional complexity for taxpayers. Although it is possible for taxpayers to take advantage of many or even all of the education tax benefits at some point, taxpayers must be careful about which incentives are selected in any particular year so as to avoid losing eligibility for other incentives. The interactions may lead to inadvertent errors because more than one taxpayer may be involved. For example, an excise tax is triggered if a grandparent contributes to a State tuition plan on behalf of a grandchild whose father makes a contribution to [a Coverdell education savings account]. In some cases, taxpayers may not be aware that others have taken action that results in denial of penalty for using a benefit.

* * *

In general, the present law education tax incentives generate complexity as a result of the numerous education tax provisions that may impact a given taxpayer. Each of the various provisions has its own eligibility criteria and definition of qualified expenses. Because of this variation in the provisions with respect to definitions of qualified expenses and eligibility criteria (and interact[ion] with one another with regard to eligibility), taxpayers are confronted with a confusing array of choices with respect to federal tax incentives for financing education.

With respect to saving for future education expenses, taxpayers are confronted with a choice of at least three tax-favored vehicles, as described above. With respect to qualified State tuition programs, taxpayers may choose to purchase either tuition credits that entitle the beneficiary to the waiver or payment of qualified higher education expenses or to invest in accounts established for the purpose of meeting qualified higher education expenses of the beneficiary.

Multiple tax-favored savings vehicles present planning complexities for the taxpayer who seeks to maximize the likely after-tax economic return to savings. Because the savings vehicles differ with respect to the tax benefit offered and have differing rules on qualified expenses, contribution limits, income limits, and interactions with other education benefits, such as the HOPE credit much complexity results in choosing the right approach to saving for education. A taxpayer seeking tax-favored saving for education may choose to invest in only one vehicle, or choose to allocate funds among all the vehicles, provided, however, that investments in qualified State tuition programs and [Coverdell education savings accounts] are not made in the same year on behalf of the same beneficiary. Furthermore, once a saving plan is adopted, a taxpayer must be careful in how the savings are spent in order to get the intended tax result. For example, if the [Coverdell education savings account] is used in a year in which a HOPE credit can be claimed, the value of the [Coverdell education savings account] exclusion is lost. The well-advised taxpayer would use such funds for educational expenses after the HOPE credit is no longer available.

Staff of the Joint Committee on Taxation, Study of the Overall State of the Federal Tax System and Recommendations for Simplification Pursuant to section 8022(3)(B) of the Internal Revenue Code of 1986, Vol. 2, 122, 129–131, 135–136 (2001).

5.5. *Education Institution Reporting Requirements*

Section 6050S imposes extensive information reporting requirements on colleges and universities for every student qualifying for a HOPE credit or a Lifetime Learning credit under § 25A. The costs of complying with the requirements are significant and reduce the value of any benefits that may be generated by the tax credits. These additional costs could explain, at least in part, why tuition across all higher-education institutions increased in response to enactment of the tax credits. The financial burden imposed by the compliance and reporting requirements under § 6050S is detailed in Thomas R. Wolonin, "Rhetoric and Reality: Effects and Consequences of the HOPE Scholarship," The New Millennium Project on Higher Education Costs, Pricing, and Productivity Working Paper, April, 2001. The IRS estimates that colleges and universities must spend an aggregate 2.4 million hours annually to supply the government and students with the required information.

PART VI

CHARACTERIZATION OF GAINS AND LOSSES

CHAPTER 24

CAPITAL GAINS AND LOSSES

SECTION 1.   SPECIAL TREATMENT OF CAPITAL GAINS AND LOSSES

INTERNAL REVENUE CODE: Sections 1(h)(1)–(6); 1201(a); 1211; 1212(a)(1), (b); 1221(a); 1222.

Favorable tax rates apply to gains realized by individuals on the "sale or exchange of a capital asset" that is held for more than 1 year. This form of income is referred to as "long-term capital gain." Gain realized on the sale or exchange of a capital asset held for one-year or less, "short-term capital gain," is not subject to preferential tax rates. Also, there are no special capital gains rates for corporations.

Loss on the sale or exchange of a capital asset, if otherwise deductible under § 165, is deductible only to the extent that the taxpayer has offsetting capital gain. Individual taxpayers are also allowed to deduct up to $3,000 of capital loss against ordinary income each year. I.R.C. § 1211(b). Gains and losses that are not capital gains or losses are referred to as ordinary income or loss. I.R.C. §§ 64 and 65.

Section 1(h) provides preferential tax rates for long-term capital gains by prescribing maximum rates for such gains.[1] In general, for taxpayers other than corporations, the maximum rate of tax on regular long-term capital gain is 20 percent. Long-term capital gain of taxpayers in the 10 percent or 15 percent tax bracket is taxed at a zero rate, which effectively makes it exempt from tax.

Net investment income is also subject to an additional 3.8 percent "surtax" under § 1411 when it is earned by certain higher-income individuals. This tax applies to many types of long-term capital gain, but generally does not apply to gain from the sale of business-use property. While the tax imposed by § 1411 is technically an employment tax provision, it operates as an income tax "surtax." The surtax applies to the lesser of (1) net investment income or (2) the excess of adjusted gross income over a threshold amount. The threshold amount is $250,000 for spouses filing a joint return and $200,000 for single taxpayers (neither amount is adjusted for inflation). Investment income includes capital gains, so the effective federal tax rate for these gains is 3.8 percentage points higher when the surtax applies. Thus, the effective marginal federal tax rate on long-term capital gains recognized by individuals in

---

[1]   The tax due on capital gain is the income tax due as reflected in § 1 of the Code. Despite many references that suggest otherwise, there is no such thing as a "capital gains tax." Capital gains are merely income subject to a reduced maximum tax rate.

the 39.6 percent tax bracket is now at least 23.8 percent; that is, the 20 percent tax on long-term capital gains plus the 3.8 percent surtax).

Certain types of long-term capital gain are subject to special preferential rates. Gain realized on the sale or exchange of "collectibles" is subject to a 28 percent rate (unless the taxpayer is otherwise in a tax bracket lower than 28 percent). Collectibles include such items as works of art, rugs, antiques, metals, gems, stamps, coins, and alcoholic beverages. Long-term capital gain on the sale of real estate that is attributable to depreciation is taxed at a 25 percent rate. Section 1202 contains a special rule for long-term gain on the sale of small business stock. Subject to a complex ceiling formula, at least $10,000,000 of any such gain can be excluded from gross income, which provides an effective tax rate of zero.

In tabular form, the rate schedule (excluding the tax on net investment income) for long-term capital gain is as follows—

Application	Rate
Long-term capital gain if otherwise taxable at 39.6%.	20%
Long-term capital gain if otherwise taxable at 25% or higher, but less than 39.6%.	15%
Long-term capital gain if otherwise taxable below 25%.	0%
Net gain on the sale of collectibles held for more than 1 year if otherwise taxable at 28% or higher.	28%
Long-term gain on real estate to the extent of prior depreciation if otherwise taxable at 25% or higher.	25%

The use of maximum rates—rather than by a parallel but uniformly proportional lower rate schedule for each income tax bracket—makes the benefits of the preferential rates disproportionate for taxpayers in different tax brackets. The rate reduction generally, though not always, inures to taxpayers in higher tax brackets, who also disproportionately realize capital gains. Using the quotient of dividing the rate differential (i.e., the difference between the long-term capital gain rate and the applicable marginal ordinary rate) by the applicable marginal ordinary rate as a measurement of the benefit helps illustrate this point. The benefit of a 5 percent long-term capital gains rate to a taxpayer who would normally be subject to the 10 percent marginal tax bracket is 50 percent of the applicable marginal ordinary income. The following table illustrates the randomness of the benefit.

Randomness of Capital-Gains Benefit

Marginal Rate	Long-Term-Capital-Gain Rate	Differential	Benefit
15%	0%	15	100%
25%	15%	10	40%
28%	15%	13	46%
33%	15%	18	55%
35%	15%	20	57%
39.6%	20%	19.6	49%

Capital losses from the sale or exchange of a capital asset, whether short or long term, are limited as deductions against ordinary income. For individuals, regardless of the period for which the property was held, capital losses are deductible only to the extent of capital gains recognized during the year, plus $3,000. I.R.C. § 1211(b). Excess capital losses may be carried forward indefinitely until they are used. I.R.C. § 1212(b). The rules are more restrictive for corporations, with capital losses only deductible against capital gains. I.R.C. § 1211(a). Any excess losses generally may be carried back three years and forward five years. I.R.C. § 1212(a). After five years, any unused capital losses expire. Corporations thus have significant motivation to avoid capital loss characterization and, alternatively, to achieve ordinary loss characterization.

There has never been agreement among tax experts or policymakers as to why capital gains should be taxed at lower rates than other income. The most commonly asserted rationale for preferential treatment is to alleviate the bunching of income caused by the realization in one year of gains that accrued over a number of years. Subjecting bunched income to progressive tax rates can be viewed as unfair. At the same time, capital gains treatment seems too broad a response to this perceived problem. Many gains do not cause bunching, and those taxpayers regularly at or near the top marginal tax bracket are not pushed into a higher bracket through bunching. Meanwhile, other taxpayers with relatively regular capital gains do not suffer from bunching. To the extent bunching is a problem, it more reasonably could be addressed by an income averaging provision.

Another rationale advanced for preferential treatment—particularly when the preference took the form of a deduction of a portion of capital gain as was the law prior to 1987—is that it compensates for the absence of an inflation adjustment. Current law measures gains in nominal rather than real dollars and thus taxes inflationary gains. While not accounting for inflation is a real problem, preferential treatment for capital gains is a blunt instrument to address a precise problem. Suppose, for example, that three taxpayers each have $100,000 of accumulated wealth invested in vacant land. Each holds the land for 10 years over which period the price level due to inflation has doubled. A then sells A's parcel for $100,000; B sells B's parcel for $200,000; and C sells C's parcel for $900,000. In real terms (after accounting for inflation), A has experienced a loss. Although prices in general have doubled, A's investment has not. Yet, under current law, because A does not have even a nominal gain, the capital gains preference provides no relief. B, while receiving some relief, is not adequately compensated for inflation by the preferential rate. B has no real gain since B's investment has only kept pace with inflation. Yet B still has a tax gain on which B must pay tax, although at a reduced rate. For C, on the other hand, the capital gains preference overcompensates for inflation. C is entitled under current law to a preferential rate with respect to the real gain as well as the inflationary gain. Because most of C's gain is real, the preference reduces C's tax by more than an inflation adjustment would provide. If C paid the normal maximum rate of 39.6 percent on C's real gain of $700,000, the tax would be $277,200, while the tax on the nominal $800,000 capital gain at a 20 percent rate under § 1(h) is only $160,000. A preference in the form of a maximum rate, as is provided under current law, is even more difficult to justify as a surrogate for an inflation adjustment because it does not apply proportionally to all taxpayers who realize capital gains.

Another popular rationale for preferential treatment is to provide an economic incentive for investment in order to increase aggregate savings. At the same time, many people question the need or desirability for any subsidy to encourage savings and investment. Moreover, the economic evidence to support the claim that preferential treatment for capital gains increases aggregate investment and savings is inconclusive. Even if the capital gains preference did increase savings and investment, it is difficult to justify the preference. Assets differ in their mix of current returns in the form of dividends, interest or rent as compared with anticipated capital appreciation. There appears to be no logical basis for favoring "growth" stocks with low current dividends over corporate bonds or rental real estate having a higher current return but less chance of capital appreciation. Indeed, by favoring investment in certain assets, investment capital is diverted from more productive uses thereby producing a less efficient allocation of capital.

Another asserted justification for preferential treatment is to reduce the disparity in treatment between realized and unrealized gains. Under this theory, inequity results from taxing realized gains and failing to tax unrealized gains (especially if the realized gains are reinvested). A reduced rate of tax on realized gains reduces this perceived inequity. Similarly, inefficiency results from the incentive to retain appreciated assets in order to defer (or, if held until death, eliminate) income tax. This "lock-in" effect reduces mobility of capital and prevents investment capital from moving to its most efficient use. Again, a reduced rate of tax is urged as a solution. A more direct approach to this problem would be to tax gains annually as they accrue without imposing a realization requirement.

Even if one were to accept as valid one or more of the above justifications, none would lead to the complex, irrational, and inequitable scheme that is set forth in § 1(h). The rules in § 1(h) have no justification in policy and are the arbitrary result of political compromises.

In studying the following materials, consider how each rationale bears upon the appropriate scope of the capital gain and loss provisions. It also is important to understand that the present capital gain and loss treatment is merely the currently prevailing treatment. Because it has no firm anchorage in either policy or rationality, it is likely to change in the future. Historically, Congress has devised other methods for taxing capital gains. For several years in the late 1980s, capital gains enjoyed no preference while capital losses were subject to the same limitations as under current law. For many years prior to 1986, the capital gain preference was in the form of a deduction of a percentage of net capital gain (60 percent in the late 1970s and early 1980s, 50 percent before that); capital loss deductions were limited as now, but individuals deducting capital losses against ordinary income under the $3,000 allowance rule, were required to use $2 of net long-term capital loss to acquire a $1 deduction. Still earlier, the capital gain preference was either a deduction equal to 50 percent of net capital gain or a maximum rate of 25 percent (at a time when the maximum rate on ordinary income was 70 percent or higher), whichever was more advantageous to the taxpayer; capital losses were deductible against ordinary income only to the extent of $1,000 per year. Over the last forty years the requisite holding period has moved back and forth between six-months, one-year, and eighteen months. In the mid to late 1930s, varying percentages of capital gain were excluded depending on how long the taxpayer held the property prior to sale. The smallest preference was a 20 percent exclusion for assets held more than one year but less than two years; the maximum preference was a 70 percent exclusion for assets held for more than ten years. Capital losses were subject to varying rules. And in the beginning of the income tax, there were no capital gain preferences whatsoever.

DETAILED ANALYSIS

1.   CAPITAL ASSET REQUIREMENT IN GENERAL

Section 1222 defines "capital gain" and "capital loss" in terms of "the sale or exchange of a capital asset," which, in turn, requires defining "capital asset," currently reflected in § 1221. Reading that provision reveals only a small part of the enormity of the problem. Section 1221 commences by defining "capital asset" as "property held by the taxpayer (whether or not connected with his trade or business)," and then lists eight exceptions, each of which is subject to interpretive questions. In the main, these exceptions relate to business assets, such as merchandise, accounts receivable, depreciable property and land used in trade or business, assets of a literary or artistic nature, and certain financial transactions that are inherently related to a trade or business. But the problem is compounded by the fact that the courts have not read literally the word "property" in § 1221, and sometimes have excluded from the definition of capital asset property items or rights other than those enumerated in the list of exceptions. The definition of a capital asset is considered in detail in Section 2 of this Chapter.

Furthermore, § 1231 partially reverses the exclusion of depreciable property and land used in a trade or business by providing that net gains recognized with respect to such property held for more than one year will be treated as capital gain. Technically, if the taxpayer's gains from sales or exchanges of such property exceed the taxpayer's losses, both gains and losses are treated as long-term capital gain and loss. At the same time, §§ 1245 and 1254 "recapture" as ordinary income (rather than capital gain) gains that result solely from basis reductions attributable to depreciation (or certain other cost recovery provisions) on property other than buildings. Section 1231 does not apply if during the year the taxpayer realizes a net loss from sales or exchanges of depreciable property and land used in a trade or business. Thus, due to the exclusion of such assets from the definition of capital asset in § 1221(a)(2), all gains and losses for such a year remain ordinary.

Finally, a number of other Code sections—for example, §§ 165(g), 1235, 1237, and 1271—specially provide or deny capital gain and loss treatment.

2. THE STATUTORY CALCULATION OF CAPITAL GAINS ELIGIBLE FOR PREFERENTIAL RATES

2.1. *General*

Application of the preferential rates to regular long-term capital gain requires working through the calculations in §§ 1(h) and 1222. The most preferential rates of § 1(h) apply only to "adjusted net capital gain." In general, adjusted net capital gain is "net capital gain," which is defined in § 1222(11), reduced by certain long-term capital gains on depreciable real estate and "collectibles" taxed at higher preferential rates, and § 1202 gain, i.e., gain on certain corporate stock that is effectively taxed at an even lower preferential rate. Under § 1222 net capital gain is the result of the netting of long-term and short-term gains and losses.

Section 1222(1) and (2) define "short-term capital gain" and "short-term capital loss" as gain or loss from the sale or exchange of a capital asset held for 1 year or less. "*Net* short-term capital gain" and "*net* short-term capital loss" are defined as the excess of short-term gain over short-term loss, and the excess of short-term loss over short-term gain, respectively. I.R.C. § 1222(5) and (6).

Long-term capital gains and losses are defined as gains and losses recognized on the sale or exchange of a capital asset held for *more than* one year. I.R.C. § 1222(3) and (4). "*Net* long-term capital gain" is the excess of long-term gain over long-term loss, and, conversely, "*net* long-term capital loss" is the excess of long-term capital loss over long-term capital gain. I.R.C. § 1222(7) and (8).

"Net capital gain," the stuff that is given preferential treatment, is the excess of net long-term capital gain over net short-term capital loss. I.R.C. § 1222(11). Thus, net short-term loss reduces the gains available for preferential tax rates. If the taxpayer has both net long-term capital gain and net short-term capital gain, only the net long-term capital gain meets the statutory definition of "net capital gain" eligible for the preference. Net short-term capital gain is taxed at the rates applicable to ordinary income.

Recognize that while any taxpayer can have both short-term gain and loss and long-term gain and loss in any given year, no single taxpayer can have net gains and losses that meet all of the definitions found in § 1222(5) through (8). The various permutations are necessary, however, to cover all possible situations of diverse taxpayers.

Once it has been determined that the taxpayer has a "net capital gain" for the year, the different rates of § 1(h) apply to different categories of net capital gains. In general, the most preferential rates under § 1(h) are applied to gains from certain capital assets held more than one year. Gains from such assets are termed "adjusted net capital gains," and are taxed at a 20 percent rate if the taxpayer is in the 39.6 percent marginal tax bracket, a rate of 15 percent if the taxpayer is otherwise in the 25 percent or higher marginal tax bracket up to the 39.6 percent bracket, and at a zero rate if the taxpayer is in a marginal tax bracket below 25%. "Adjusted net capital gain" does not include: (1) "unrecaptured § 1250 gain," generally speaking, gain on real estate held for more than one year attributable to prior depreciation deductions,[2] which is taxed at a 25 percent rate, and (2) "28-percent rate gain." The term "28-percent rate gain" is defined as the excess of the sum of (a) gains on "collectibles"[3] over the sum of (c) collectibles losses, (d) net-short term capital loss, and (e) long-term capital loss carryovers to the year in question.

2.2. *Applying the Preferential Rates*

Application of the varied preferential rates is determined under the statutory formula of § 1(h), which has six steps—

First, under § 1(h)(1)(A), the taxpayer's "normal" statutory rate is applied to the greater of (1) taxable income minus "net capital gain" (i.e., long-term capital gains minus long-term capital losses and net short-term capital losses), or (2) the lesser of (a) the amount of income that ordinarily would be taxed below 25 percent or (b) taxable income minus "adjusted net capital gain." Adjusted net capital gain for this purpose is net capital gain minus unrecaptured § 1250 gain and gain that is taxed at the 28 percent rate (collectible gain and § 1202 gain). In effect, this first step calculates the taxpayer's regular tax liability on income other than the gains taxable at preferential rates. For taxpayers in a 25 percent bracket or higher, that means taxable income less adjusted net capital gain, unrecaptured § 1250

---

[2]   Unrecaptured § 1250 gain is defined in § 1(h)(6) and is discussed in Chapter 25, Section 1.3.

[3]   I.R.C. § 1(h)(4). Collectibles are defined by § 1(h)(5)(A), through a cross reference to § 408(m), to include works of art, antiques, rugs, gems, metals, stamps, coins, and alcoholic beverages.

gain, collectibles gain, and § 1202 gain. For taxpayers in the 10 percent or 15 percent brackets, it means taxable income less adjusted net capital gain.

The second step under § 1(h)(1)(B) is to exempt from tax adjusted net long-term capital gains of a taxpayer whose income, other than adjusted net capital gain, is below the threshold for the 25 percent marginal rate bracket. The exemption under this step applies to the portion of the taxpayer's adjusted net capital gain that does not exceed an amount equal to the threshold for the 25 percent bracket minus the taxpayer's income other than *adjusted* net capital gain. In this calculation, net capital gain is reduced by unrecaptured § 1250 gain and 28—percent rate gain. For the taxpayer in the 25 percent tax bracket or below, net short-term capital gain, net long-term capital gain from collectibles, unrecaptured § 1250 gain, and ordinary income are taxed at the taxpayer's regular rates.

The third step applies the 15 percent rate of § 1(h)(1)(C) to any remaining adjusted net long-term capital gains (or, if less, the taxpayer's taxable income) of a taxpayer whose income, other than adjusted net capital gain, is at the 25 percent marginal rate bracket but less than the 39.6 percent rate bracket.

The fourth step applies the 20 percent rate of § 1(h)(1)(D) to any remaining adjusted net long-term capital gains.

The fifth step adds the 25 percent rate tax on "unrecaptured section 1250 gain" under § 1(h)(1)(E).

The sixth and final step, under § 1(h)(1)(F), is to apply a 28 percent rate to any remaining taxable income. After the first five steps, this amount only will include 28 percent rate gains, i.e. gain on collectibles and § 1202 gains (after the 50% exclusion).

The following simple example illustrates the application of these steps. Each taxpayer situation presents the opportunity for the effect of various types of income to affect the application of various rates to various types of income. Consequently, the only way to accurately determine what rates will apply to income often requires working through the steps for each particular situation.

Taxpayer A is a single taxpayer subject to the § 1(c) rates (assuming approximate thresholds). In taxable year 2015 Taxpayer A realized $700,000 of taxable income, consisting of the following:

Salary	$200,000
Sale of NYSE traded securities held for less than one year (short-term capital gain)	$250,000
Sale of collectibles held for several years	$100,000
Gain from publicly traded securities held for more than one year (adjusted net long-term capital gain)	$150,000

(1)   Under step 1, A's $200,000 of salary and the $250,000 of short-term capital gains are taxed under the taxpayer's ordinary rates. In terms of the statute, A's $700,000 taxable income minus $250,000 net capital gain ($100,000 collectibles gain plus $150,000 long-term capital gain on securities), $450,000, is greater than the *lesser* of the threshold for the 25% bracket, assume $37,000 (as prevailed for tax year 2015), or taxable income minus adjusted net capital gain ($700,000 − $150,000 = $550,000). Since before taking into account A's capital gains, A is in the 39.6 percent marginal bracket (assuming a $415,000 threshold), the $150,000 long-term gain on the exchange-traded securities and the $100,000 of gain on the collectible are taxed at preferential rates.

(2)   A has no income exempt from tax under § 1(h)(1)(B). The exemption only applies to the extent that adjusted net capital gain, here $150,000 ($250,000 net capital gain less $100,000 collectible gain), does not exceed the excess of the amount of taxable income that would be taxed at a rate below 25 percent, assume $37,000, over taxable income reduced by adjusted net capital gain, here $550,000 ($700,000 − $150,000). In A's case, taxable income is greater than the threshold for the 25 percent bracket and A's adjusted net capital gain exceeds the limit of amounts taxed below the 25 percent rate.

(3)   The third step taxes A's adjusted net capital gain, $150,000, at the preferential 15% tax rate only to the extent that A's amounts taxed at less than 39.6 percent exceed the amounts taxed under the first two steps. The amounts taxed at less than 39.6 percent do not exceed those amounts, so no portion of A's adjusted net capital gain will be taxed at 15% under § 1(h)(1)(C).

(4)   The fourth step taxes A's adjusted net capital gain, $150,000 at the preferential 20% tax rate under § 1(h)(1)(D).

(5)   A has no unrecaptured § 1250 gain taxable at the 25 percent rate under § 1(h)(1)(E).

(6)   A's remaining taxable income, $700,000 minus salary, the short-term capital gain, and the adjusted net capital gain, which are taxed in the preceding steps, is $100,000 representing the long-term capital net gain on A's sales of collectibles. Under § 1(h)(1)(F) the remaining $100,000 is taxed at 28%.

Section		Income	Rate	Tax[4]
1(h)(1)(A)	Salary and	$2,000		
	Short-term capital gain	$250,000	10%–39.6%	$178,200
1(h)(1)(B)		0	0%	
1(h)(1)(C)		0	15%	
1(h)(1)(D)	Adjusted net capital gain	$150,000	20%	$ 30,000
1(h)(1)(E)	Unrecaptured § 1250 gain	0	25%	
1(h)(1)(F)	28% rate gain on collectibles	$100,000	28%	$ 28,000
Total Tax				$236,200

2.3. *Netting of Capital Losses*

If the taxpayer's "net capital gain" for the year consists of gains that are in part offset by losses, it is necessary to determine the order in which losses are subtracted from gains before applying the various rates under § 1(h). Generally speaking, losses are netted first against gains of a like character (by tax rates), with net losses in any grouping being applied to reduce net gains in other rate groupings, moving from the highest rate to the lowest rate, in order, although the statutory mechanics are not particularly straightforward.

Assume, for example, that in the current taxable year individual B, who is otherwise in the 39.6 percent rate bracket, recognized the following long-term capital gains and losses: $2,500 loss on a collectible, a $2,000 gain on a collectible, a $2,300 gain on exchange-traded stock, a $300 loss on exchange-traded stock, and a $2,000 gain on the sale of an apartment building, all of which was unrecaptured § 1250 gain. B's net capital gain (as defined in § 1222(11)) is $4,500, computed as follows:

Capital Gain / Loss Character	Amount of Gain/Loss
Collectible #1	($2,500)
Collectible #2	$3,000
Exchange-traded Stock	$2,300
Exchange-traded Stock	($ 300)
Unrecaptured § 1250 Gain	$2,000
Net Capital Gain (§ 1222(11))	$4,500

---

[4]   The tax in this example is calculated using the rates applicable under § 1(c) using simplifying convention of multiplying the entire ordinary income by 39.6%. An accurate computation of the tax requires applying the applicable rate to each tranche of income.

The first step in determining B's "adjusted net capital gain," as defined in § 1(h)(3), is to determine the amount of B's net 28-percent gain. This amount is $500—the $3,000 gain on Collectible #1 minus the $2,500 loss on Collectible #2—because the collectible gain and loss are both in the "28-percent rate gain" category under § 1(h)(4). Under § 1(h)(3), both the $500 28-percent rate gain and the $2,000 unrecaptured § 1250 gain (totaling $2,500) are then subtracted from the $4,500 net capital gain to leave $2,000 of adjusted net capital gain.

Net Capital Gain		$4,500
Minus:		
28 Percent Gain		
Collectible Gain	$3,000	
Collectible Loss	($2,500)	$ 500
Unrecaptured § 1250 Gain	$2,000	$2,000
Adjusted Net Capital Gain		$2,000

This process has effectively netted the $300 long-term capital loss on exchange-traded stock against the $2,300 gain on exchange-traded stock.

In addition to netting collectible losses against 28-percent rate gains, § 1(h)(4) also applies to net short-term capital losses, as defined in § 1222(8), and all capital loss carryforwards under § 1212, regardless of the rate category of property that generated the loss in the year it was recognized, against 28—percent rate gains before netting such losses against gains taxed at a lower rate. If a taxpayer recognizes net losses in the 28-percent rate category, § 1(h)(6) provides for the reduction of unrecaptured § 1250 gain, taxable at 25 percent, by the amount of those losses, thereby applying these losses against gain that otherwise would be taxed at 25 percent before they are applied against losses that otherwise would be taxed at 20 percent.

Assume, for example, that in the current year individual C recognized a $4,000 short-term capital loss on the sale of exchange-traded stock, a $5,000 unrecaptured § 1250 gain, and a $6,000 long-term capital gain on the sale of exchange-traded stock. C's net capital gain is $7,000, consisting of $1,000 of unrecaptured § 1250 gain ($5,000 – $4,000) taxed at 25 percent and $6,000 of adjusted net capital gain taxed at 20 percent. If, however, the short-term capital loss on the sale of exchange-traded stock had been $7,000, then C would have recognized a net capital gain of only $4,000, taxed at 20 percent. Under § 1(h)(6), the $7,000 short-term capital loss would completely offset the $5,000 net unrecaptured § 1250 gain. Under § 1(h)(3), which uses net capital gain as a starting point for determining adjusted net capital gain, the remaining $2,000 of the short-term capital loss effectively would be netted against the $6,000 long-term capital gain on the stock.

If an individual recognizes a net loss with respect to property in the 20 percent rate category and recognizes gains with respect to property in both the 25 percent category (unrecaptured § 1250 gain) and the 28 percent category, the statutory rules result in offsetting the losses against the gains on the 28-percent rate property before offsetting them against the unrecaptured § 1250 gain.

Assume that D recognized a $5,000 long-term capital loss on the sale of exchange-traded stock, a $10,000 gain on the sale of an apartment building, all of which is unrecaptured § 1250 gain, and a $3,000 long-term capital gain on the sale of a collectible. D's net capital gain (as defined in § 1222(11)) is $8,000 (($10,000 + $3,000) − $5,000). G's 28-percent rate gain (as defined in § 1(h)(5)) is $3,000; D's unrecaptured § 1250 gain under the calculation in § 1(h)(6) is $10,000, but D has only $8,000 of taxable capital gains. This is the maximum amount that can be taxed at 25 percent under § 1(h)(1)(D), and there is no remaining taxable income to be taxed at 28 percent under § 1(h)(1)(E).

3. CAPITAL LOSS LIMITATION

Under § 1211, deductions of capital losses are limited to capital gain for the year, except that taxpayers other than corporations are permitted to deduct up to $3,000 of capital loss in excess of capital gain in each year. Section 1212 provides non-corporate taxpayers an unlimited carryover of unused capital losses. Corporate taxpayers are permitted to carryback capital loss to the three preceding years, and forward to the five succeeding years.

No analog of the refined computation used to ascertain net capital gain is necessary in applying the limitation on capital losses in § 1211. Short-term capital losses are subject to the same limitations as long-term capital losses. Section 1212, however, distinguishes between short-term and long-term capital losses in determining which losses are used in the current year and which losses are carried over if the taxpayer has both net short-term and net long-term capital losses. In the case of individuals, § 1212 results in net short-term loss being used before net long-term loss. When capital losses are carried over, in applying the rules of § 1(h) to determine the rate at which gains are taxed in the year to which the losses are carried, the character of the capital assets that generated the carried-over capital loss is irrelevant. All long-term capital loss carryovers, as well as short-term capital loss carryovers in excess of short-term capital gains for the year to which they are carried, are deducted first against long-term capital gains taxed at the 28 percent rate, see I.R.C. § 1(h)(4)(B), then against long-term capital gains taxed at the 25 percent rate (unrecaptured § 1250 gain), see I.R.C. § 1(h)(6)(A), then against gains taxed at the 15 percent rate, and finally against gains taxable at the 5 percent rate. In the case of corporations, all carried-over capital losses are treated as short-term losses in the carryover years.

The capital loss limitation has been justified on two grounds. First, a limitation on capital losses is arguably a corollary to the preference accorded capital gains. It prevents taxpayers from receiving the preference for gains in one year while fully deducting losses carefully realized in the preceding or subsequent year. This justification suffers from at least two shortcomings: (i) taxpayers who receive the benefit of the preference for gains are not necessarily the same taxpayers who suffer the limitation on losses; and

(ii) the limitation applies to both short-term and long-term losses, while the preference extends only to long-term gains. In addition, net long-term capital losses freed of the limitation (by the $3,000 rule) are deductible dollar-for-dollar against ordinary income, even though gains are taxed at rates that may be only 30 to 40 percent of the rate applied to ordinary income.

The second justification for the limitation on the deduction for capital losses is that it is necessitated by the realization requirement. Section 1211 reflects the policy judgment that full deductibility of capital losses would be inappropriate in light of the discretion that taxpayers have regarding when to realize gains and losses. An unrestricted right to deduct realized property losses would permit taxpayers to dispose of depreciated assets selectively to offset the resulting losses against other income while retaining appreciated assets and avoiding tax on the appreciation. For example, a taxpayer owning ABC stock that has appreciated in value by $10,000, and XYZ stock that has decreased in value by $10,000, might choose to sell only the XYZ stock to have the loss to offset other income. Under the Haig-Simons income definition, the $10,000 unrealized gain and the $10,000 unrealized loss offset one another, but in a system based on realization of gains and losses, they are not offsetting. Section 1211 prevents the taxpayer from selecting to realize losses and offsetting other income except to the extent of $3,000 a year. This justification suffers from its own shortcomings, with disparate positions depending on one's view of the function and propriety of the realization requirement itself. Nevertheless, at the end of the day, the limitation on the deduction for capital losses represents a reasonable limitation as long as most taxpayers with net realized losses have unrealized gains of at least an equal amount.

4.   RELATIONSHIP TO OTHER PROVISIONS

4.1. *Capital Loss Provisions and Section 165*

It is important to keep in mind that the provisions of § 1222, which net capital gains and losses, and §§ 1211 and 1212, determining the extent to which recognized capital losses will be allowed in any particular year, do not independently allow a deduction for a loss that is not first deductible under § 165 or some other provision. Rather, they limit the amount of otherwise allowable deductible losses. Thus, for example, a loss incurred in the sale of a personal residence may not be deducted against capital gain recognized from the sale of stock held for investment or even against gain from the sale of a second personal residence, which is taxable. Since a loss on the sale of a personal residence is not deductible under § 165, the loss cannot be utilized by the taxpayer, even though the residence is a capital asset and § 1211 would permit the offset if the loss were initially deductible.

4.2. *Passive Activity Loss Rules*

Capital gain or loss also may be classified as passive activity income or deduction under § 469, discussed in Chapter 35, Section 2. Such classification does not affect the preferential treatment of capital gain, but a capital loss that is allowable under §§ 165 and 1211 nevertheless may be nondeductible in the current year if it arises in a passive activity and the taxpayer has insufficient income from passive activities for the year.

4.3. *Preferential Rates for Dividends*

Under § 1(h)(11), dividends received by taxpayers other than corporations generally are taxed at the same rate as long-term capital gains. Section 1(h)(11) treats dividends as "adjusted net capital gain" under § 1(h)(3), even though the dividend itself (in contrast to the stock on which a dividend is paid) is not a capital asset as defined in § 1221, and dividends are not taken into account in the calculation of "net capital gain" under § 1222. The principal effect of this statutory construction is to extend the preferential maximum rates under § 1(h), including the zero tax rate for taxpayers otherwise in the 10 and 15 percent rate brackets, to dividends, without permitting capital losses to be deducted against dividend income, except to the extent allowed by §§ 1211 and 1212. For more on the taxation of dividends, see Chapter 8, Section 3.

4.3.1. *Minimum Holding Period*

The preferential rates for dividends, coupled with short-term holding of stock purchased in anticipation of receiving a dividend, creates inappropriate tax arbitrage benefits. Section 1(h)(11)(B)(iii) is aimed at preventing taxpayers from obtaining unwarranted tax benefits in such situations. Section 1(h)(11)(B)(iii) provides that the preferential rate for dividends does not apply to any dividends on any share of stock that is held for less than 60 days during the 121 day period beginning on the date that is 60 days before the date on which the stock becomes ex-dividend. (Under stock exchange rules, stock generally becomes ex-dividend three business days before the "record date" for paying dividends.) For preferred stock, if the dividends received are attributable to a period in excess of 366 days, the holding period is extended to 90 days during the 181-day period beginning on the date that is 90 days before the date on which the stock becomes ex-dividend. See I.R.C. § 246(c)(2).

Suppose, in the absence of § 1(h)(11)(B)(iii), that during the current tax year individual A realized a $200,000 short-term capital gain on the sale of X Corporation stock and no offsetting capital loss. Absent any other transactions, at a 39.6 percent marginal tax rate this $200,000 gain would result in a tax of $79,200. Now suppose that shortly before the end of the taxable year, A purchases 100,000 shares of Y Corporation stock for $5,000,000. Before the close of the taxable year, A (1) receives a $200,000 dividend on the Y Corporation stock, and (2) sells the Y Corporation stock for $4,800,000 (the value of the shares having declined as a result of the dividend). A realizes a $200,000 loss on disposition of the Y Corporation shares, because the basis in the stock was not reduced as a result of the dividend. This transaction is uneconomic, because the dividend income is exactly offset by the resulting capital loss. However, at the 20 percent preferential rate, A pays a tax of $40,000 on the $200,000 dividend received from Y Corporation, while using the $200,000 capital loss on the sale of the Y Corporation stock to offset the $200,000 short-term capital gain on the X Corporation stock that otherwise would have been taxed at the rate of 39.6 percent, saving $79,200 of tax. Thus, the transaction produces an after-tax benefit of $39,200, even though it produced a break-even before tax cash flow. Under § 1(h)(11)(B)(iii), because the minimum holding period had not been met, the dividend would be taxed at 39.6 percent, instead of at 20 percent—resulting in a $79,200 tax—and the $39,200 tax arbitrage benefit is eliminated.

4.3.2. *Loss Recharacterization*

Congress considered § 1(h)(11)(B)(iii) to be adequate to deal with only some of the tax avoidance possibilities created by the availability of the preferential rate for dividends as applied to extraordinarily large dividends. If an extraordinarily large dividend was expected to be paid on stock of a corporation, the investor owning the stock would be willing to hold the stock for the period required to avoid the limitation in § 1(h)(11)(B)(iii). Thus, § 1(h)(11)(D)(i) imposes another limitation when the preferential rate has been claimed with respect to an "extraordinary dividend," as defined in § 1059(c). If an individual receives an extraordinary dividend taxed at the preferential rate, any loss on the sale of the stock on which the dividend was paid is treated as a long-term capital loss to the extent of the dividend, even if the actual holding period of the stock was short-term.

Section 1059(c) defines an extraordinary dividend in terms of the size of the dividend in relation to the shareholder's adjusted basis in its stock, subject to an alternative test that, at the taxpayer's election, uses fair market value instead of basis. A dividend is extraordinary if aggregate dividends received in any 85-day period exceed 10 percent of the basis of common stock, or 5 percent of the basis of preferred stock, with respect to which the dividends were paid. Furthermore, if aggregate dividends paid with respect to stock in any one-year period exceed 20 percent of the corporate shareholder's basis for the stock, then all such dividends are aggregated and considered to be an extraordinary dividend.

Congress seems to have intended that under §§ 1222 and 1(h)(11)(D)(ii) the long-term capital loss on the sale of the stock with respect to which the dividend was received would reduce the amount of the dividend in determining adjusted capital gain eligible for the 20 percent rate preference. That treatment is not how the language of the statute applies, however. Section 1(h)(11) provides that "net capital gain" means "net capital gain (determined without regard to this paragraph) increased by qualified dividend income." Under § 1222(11), "net capital gain" is the excess of net long-term capital gain over net short-term capital loss. Treating loss on the sale of stock with respect to which an extraordinary dividend is paid as a long-term capital loss may eliminate "net capital gain" (and indeed may create a "net capital loss"), but there is no provision in the Code for a negative "net capital gain." Net capital gain is either a positive number or non-existent. As a result, treating a loss as a long-term capital loss will reduce long-term capital gain, but once long-term capital gain is exhausted, the "net capital gain" remains zero. Under § 1(h)(11), that zero amount is increased by the amount of a qualified dividend, which remains subject to tax at preferred capital gains rates. For example, if an individual has no other capital gains or losses but has $1,000 of loss attributable to the sale of stock that paid an extraordinary dividend of $1,000, such individual would have no net capital gain (determined without regard to § 1(h)(11)(A)), but would have $1,000 of qualified dividend income that would be taxable at the preferential 20 percent rate. The individual would still have a net capital loss of $1,000 and that capital loss could offset short-term capital gain and up to $3,000 of ordinary income. To accomplish its purpose, Congress should have provided that qualified dividend income must be reduced by the amount of any loss attributable to the sale of stock that paid extraordinary dividends.

5.   ADDITIONAL PREFERENCE FOR "QUALIFIED SMALL BUSINESS STOCK"

Section 1202 provides a special preference for gain recognized by a noncorporate taxpayer on a sale or exchange of "qualified small business stock." If the stock is held for more than five years, a portion of the gain is excluded from gross income, thus reducing the effective tax rate, possibly to zero. *See* I.R.C. § 1202(a)(4). Section 1202(b)(1) limits the "amount . . . of gain taken into account" under § 1202(a) with respect to the stock of a particular corporation in any year to the greater of (a) $10,000,000 ($5,000,000 for married taxpayers filing separately), minus any amount excluded with respect to that corporation's stock in prior years, or (b) ten times the aggregate basis of stock of the qualified corporation sold during the year. The phrase, "the amount of gain . . . taken into account" is ambiguous. The phrase may refer to the amount of gain that may be excluded from income under § 1202(a), but might refer, on the other hand, to the total amount of gain with respect to which the excludable amount is calculated. Under the first interpretation, the maximum amount of gain that may be excluded from gross income is the greater of $10,000,000 or 10 times basis; under the latter interpretation, the maximum amount of the exclusion is limited to $5,000,000 or five times basis, one-half of the gain eligible for exclusion under § 1202(a). There has been no formal clarification.

Suppose an investor paid $3,000,000 for 300,000 shares in a qualified small business and six years later sold the stock for $35,000,000, realizing a gain of $32,000,000. The ten-times-basis limitation is $30,000,000, and the $10,000,000 limitation thus is not applicable. Thus, $30,000,000 is excludable and the investor must include only $2,000,000. Suppose now that the investor paid only $300,000 for the stock. The gain would be $24,700,000. Ten times the taxpayer's basis is $3,000,000, and thus the maximum exclusion is $10,000,000. The investor must include $14,700,000.

A special basis rule applies solely for determining the exclusion and the limitation if qualifying stock is acquired in exchange for property rather than cash. I.R.C. § 1202(i). The purpose of this rule is to limit the exclusion to gain accruing after the issuance of the stock. Suppose, for example, if a taxpayer contributes property with a basis of $1,000,000 and a fair market value of $5,000,000 to a qualified small business corporation in exchange for stock and six years later sells the stock for $9,000,000, the gain for purposes of § 1202 is only $4,000,000. The exclusion is $2,000,000.

Section 1202 is intended to encourage investment in small businesses. Thus, only newly-issued stock acquired from a domestic corporation (or through an underwriter) in exchange for money, property other than stock or securities, or services (except services as an underwriter of the stock) qualifies. The original-issue limitation is backstopped by a number of special rules to prevent its circumvention. Stock acquired by gift or inheritance may qualify under a special rule. I.R.C. § 1202(h)(2).

Stock qualifies only if the corporation is a "qualified small business" at the time the stock is issued *and* for substantially all of the taxpayer's holding period is engaged in an "active business." Generally, to be a qualified small business the aggregate gross assets of the corporation (measured by tax basis, not fair market value) on or before the date the stock is issued may not exceed $50,000,000.[5] In addition the corporation must meet certain reporting requirements. Gain realized with respect to stock of a corporation that was a qualified small business when the stock was issued is eligible for the exclusion even though in future years the corporation has more than $50,000,000 in gross assets.

Finally, the corporation also must satisfy an "active business" requirement. I.R.C. § 1202(e). This test excludes businesses performing certain services, including most professional services, dealing in real estate, banking, insurance, leasing, investment, or other financial activities, farming, forestry, natural resource extraction, and operating a hotel, motel, restaurant, or similar business. If more than 10 percent of a corporation's assets consist of either portfolio securities or real estate not used in its trade or business, the corporation automatically fails the active business requirement.

SECTION 2.   DEFINITION OF "CAPITAL ASSET"

INTERNAL REVENUE CODE: Section 1221.

Capital gains and losses are derived only from the sale or exchange of a "capital asset." Section 1221 initially defines a "capital asset" as "property held by the taxpayer (whether or not connected with his trade or business)." In one sense, "property" includes everything that the taxpayer holds. The broad definition is followed by eight specific statutory exclusions.

Under the broad definition of a capital asset as "property," any money received by a taxpayer could readily be regarded as the result of the surrender of "property" in the form of either tangible assets or intangible property such as claims to money.[6] Under this definition, unless a particular item of property is expressly excluded, it will remain in the residual category of capital asset and the income arising on its disposition will be capital gain. Given the disparity between capital gain rates and ordinary income rates, this definition advantages taxpayers'

---

[5]   Evidently, members of Congress define "small business" more expansively than their constituents!

[6]   Thus, since a claim to salary is "property" in one sense of the term, the claim to salary would in that sense be a capital asset. While payment of the salary would not produce a capital gain because of the "sale or exchange" requirement under the existing interpretation of "exchange," a sale of the claim would produce a capital gain under such an interpretation of property. And, if this interpretation were adopted, a national brokerage business might conceivably develop through which employees sold salary claims. In effect, the "sale or exchange" requirement would not suffice to restrict favorable capital gain treatment if "capital asset" were all-inclusive.

desire to convert or classify all income as capital gain. As a result, the courts in some cases have felt obliged to interpret the term "property" more narrowly than in the normal, all-inclusive sense in which it is used elsewhere in the Code and, in other cases, to create additional exceptions. These judicial concepts have in turn generated problems of their own.

The breadth of the definition of "capital asset" disguises significant differences in the sources of "capital gain." An increase in the value of an asset can result from many causes. In the case of shares of stock, for example, an increase in value may come from accumulated corporate earnings, from innovations or discoveries, such as the development of a new product or market, from the maturation of the business organization or the efforts of the shareholder-managers, from the weaknesses of competitors, from an improvement in the general level of economic activity, from inflation, from a change in the tax laws, and so on. The value of property may be increased through the effects of the expected and planned or the unexpected and erratic, through the effects of inflation, war, depression, invention, the vagaries of public taste. An increase in the value of land may result from the discovery of new resources in the land, from the development of new uses for its resources, from the growth of population, from the growth of crops on the land, such as timber, over the passage of time, or from subdivision of the land and sale of small pieces. The value of a bond may increase through a change in general interest rates. When Congress defined "capital asset" to include all property, it regarded all of these increases in value as "capital gains," but did not at the same time identify exclusions essentially related to the causes of the increase in value. Consequently, the additional value imparted to a taxpayer's stock investment through factors within the taxpayer's control, such as the accumulation of corporate earnings or her personal efforts as corporate president, was regarded in the definition of a capital asset as no different from increases in value caused by forces beyond the taxpayer's control. Taxpayers were quick to perceive the enormous range of possibilities in planning for capital gain under such a definitional approach.

As a result, the process of defining capital asset has become one of examining a great many transactions and reaching a policy decision in each case as to whether it is desirable to give to the transaction the form of preferential treatment known as capital gain (or the form of adverse treatment known as capital loss). If so, the transaction is then considered a capital gain transaction. The process becomes even more complicated by the fact that there is no consensus as to the grounds upon which this preferential treatment should be granted.

In dividing the whole range of income between capital gain and ordinary income, Congress attempted to draw some basic distinctions. Essentially it attempted to meet the following problems: (1) the problem of distinguishing investment gain from recurring business receipts; (2) the problem of distinguishing investment gain from the rewards for personal efforts; (3) the problem of classifying transactions involving the sale of recurring receipts; and (4) the problem of distinguishing investment and speculation. These problems are considered in this Section, while special statutory provisions providing capital status to some types of assets but not others are considered in Section 5 of this Chapter.

A. THE STATUTORY EXCLUSIONS

(1) INVESTMENT PROPERTY VERSUS PROPERTY HELD FOR SALE TO CUSTOMERS

INTERNAL REVENUE CODE: Sections 1221(a)(1); 1231(b)(1).

The first exclusion from "capital assets," in § 1221(a)(1) applies to:

> stock in trade of the taxpayer or other property of a kind which would properly be included in the inventory of the taxpayer if on hand at the close of the taxable year, or property held by the taxpayer primarily for sale to customers in the ordinary course of his trade or business.

This exclusion attempts to articulate a division between "investment" property and other property. The main objective of § 1221(a)(1) is reasonably clear, but the scope of the problem is masked by this deceptively short definition. Congress is attempting to exclude from "capital gain" all of those profits that it regards as the everyday profits of the business and commercial world. Thus, the daily profits of the corner grocery store, the shopping mall, the department store, and the large manufacturing concern are treated as ordinary income even though they arise from the sale of "property."[7] So too are the profits of admitted "dealers" in real estate, persons who stand ready to buy and sell property, and perform the function of go-betweens analogous to dealers in other assets. On the other hand, gains from a sale of stock on a stock exchange by the average investor, a sale of undeveloped land purchased as an investment, or a sale of a residence (if the gain is recognized) are clear examples of capital gains.

Beyond the obvious examples remain areas of great uncertainty. The problem has been to determine at what point the act of selling property to a potential purchaser—i.e., the customer—changes from an "investment activity" to a "business activity." More specifically, at what point is property "held for sale to customers in the ordinary course of [a] trade or business?" For example, Wendy Wilson is an attorney who occasionally buys unimproved land with the purpose of resale. The purchases and sales are not regular, but over the years the number of transactions accumulate. Do Wendy's real estate activities place her in a "business" and, furthermore, is her property for sale to customers in that

---

[7]   Even a bulk sale of inventory to a single purchaser does not produce capital gain. Grace Bros., Inc. v. Commissioner, 173 F.2d 170 (9th Cir.1949).

business? At what point do "investment activities" become "recurring business activities?"[8]

To realize the increase in value, investors generally must sell the investment. The process of maximizing profits on the liquidation of an investment may take on many of the characteristics found in the activity of the everyday business person whose profits from sales are regarded as excluded from capital gains. John Jones bought a tract of land many years ago as an investment and now he desires to sell. To find buyers he may have to engage in such activities as improving the property, advertising, hiring an agent, and subdividing. Jones is a college classics professor and does not think of himself as a real estate dealer. Yet he may have more land or more desirable land to sell than everyday real estate dealers, such that "John Jones, classics professor" has become the biggest real estate operator in the area due to land that he bought years ago as an investment that the IRS now considers "property held by the taxpayer primarily for sale to customers in the ordinary course of his trade or business."

Suppose that the land is not even initially acquired as an investment. Thus, Tom Taylor acquires a million acres of land to use in a cattle-raising business. The cattle-raising business is unsuccessful, and Tom Taylor must now dispose of a million acres. He does so by selling some land every year for twenty years, employing a large sales force and making every effort to attract buyers. Is Tom Taylor now holding the land primarily for sale in his business? What about Sally Smith, who decides to invest her money in rental housing and builds 200 houses? She had at first sought a return on her capital in the form of rent, but after several years she desires to sell those houses and retire. She now has more houses for sale than many real estate brokers. Is Sally Smith holding the houses primarily for sale in her business?

These issues are not restricted to land—the estate of Richard is disposing of an inventory of $1 million in furs he inherited from a decedent who owned a fur shop; Robert is selling a large quantity of antiques previously collected by him; the estate of Mary is selling a large number of items of valuable jewelry that she had accumulated during her life; Jane conducts a truck or automobile rental business and sells the cars after a period of use in the rental activities. Consider, on the flip side, the businessperson whose inventory greatly appreciates because of unforeseen conditions, such as war or shortages due to strikes or other factors, such that the inventory starts to look like an investment in capital assets.

Sometimes there is a dual purpose with respect to an asset. Harold Hughes develops property for rental purposes but is prepared to sell at any time if that appears more profitable. Before completing the

---

[8]   Persons in the "recurring business" category may be denominated as "dealers" or as "traders." For the distinction, see Section 2.A.6. in this Chapter.

development, Harold sells the property such that it is difficult to tell for tax purposes if Harold was holding the property primarily for *use* in his business or *primarily for sale* in the course of his business.

In Malat v. Riddell, 383 U.S. 569 (1966), the Supreme Court attempted to clarify the statute with its pronouncement that:

> The purpose of the statutory provision with which we deal is to differentiate between the "profits and losses arising from the everyday operation of a business" on the one hand (Corn Products Co. v. Commissioner, 350 U.S. 46, 52) and "the realization of appreciation in value accrued over a substantial period of time" on the other. (Commissioner v. Gillette Motor Co., 364 U.S. 130, 143.)

The opinion in *Malat* adds that the use of the term "primarily" in § 1221(a)(1) "means 'of first importance' or 'principally.' " As the following materials demonstrate, the application of these principles is challenging to say the least.[9]

Suburban Realty Co. v. United States

United States Court of Appeals, Fifth Circuit, 1980.
615 F.2d 171.

■ GOLDBERG, CIRCUIT JUDGE:

We must today answer the riddle at once adumbrated and apparently foreclosed by the false dichotomy created by the United States Supreme Court in Malat v. Riddell, 383 U.S. 569, 572 (1966) (per curiam): when profits have "aris[en] from the [ordinary] operation of a business" on the one hand and are *also* "the realization of appreciation in value over a substantial period of time" on the other, are these profits treated as ordinary income or capital gain? Lacking any clear guidance but the language of the capital asset statute itself, we turn to that language for the answer. Before we can arrive at this interesting and important question, however, we must once again tramp along (but not trample on) that time-and precedent-worn path which separates capital gains from ordinary income. By the time we emerge into the light at the far edge of the forest, we will find that the *Riddell* riddle has seemingly answered itself, and all that will remain will be a brief reassessment of our answer. In our peregrinations, we of necessity wander into virgin territory. We hope that we shed new light onto this murky terrain; at the least, we think we have neither riddled the cases nor muddled the issues.

---

[9]   Section 1231(b), discussed in Chapter 25, Section 1, distinguishes between land and depreciable property held for use in a trade or business and "recurring business" property. Because of the similarity in structure between §§ 1221(a)(1) and 1231(b)(1), the courts apply the precedents under the sections interchangeably. See Cottle v. Commissioner, 89 T.C. 467 (1987) (holding that the last phrase of § 1221(a)(1) and § 1231(b)(1)(B) have identical meaning). Thus, in a number of the cases discussed in the following material, the courts treat cases arising under § 1231(b) as precedent for cases involving only § 1221(a)(1), and vice versa. Many of the cases discussed in this Section involved an interpretation of § 1231(b)(1) rather than § 1221(a)(1).

I.

[Ed.: In 1937 Suburban Realty Company ("Suburban") acquired an undivided one-fourth interest in 1,742.6 acres of land located in Harris County, Texas ("the property") in exchange for its stock. Between 1939 and 1971, Suburban sold some 244 individual parcels of real estate, making at least one sale each year. In the late 1950's and early 1960's, Suburban's officers, directors and shareholders began discussing the possibility of selling off its real estate holdings and liquidating the corporation. These discussions did not lead to any action. Between 1968 and 1971, Suburban sold six parcels of unimproved real estate in five different transactions. Suburban initially reported the gain on the sales as ordinary income but subsequently filed claims for refund asserting that it was entitled to long-term capital gain treatment. The court discussed the facts surrounding the parcels sold between 1968 and 1971.]

Our analysis of this case must begin with Biedenharn Realty Co., Inc. v. United States, 526 F.2d 409 (5th Cir.) (en banc), cert. denied, 429 U.S. 819 (1976). Biedenharn is this Court's latest (and only) *en banc* pronouncement concerning the characterization of profits of a real estate business as ordinary income or capital gain. The decision answers the characterization question by evaluating certain "factors" often present in cases of this ilk.[16] *Biedenharn* attempts to guide the analysis in this area by assigning different levels of importance to various of the "factors." Substantiality and frequency of sales is called the most important factor. * * * Improvements to the land, solicitation and advertising efforts, and brokerage activities also play an important part in the *Biedenharn* analysis.

The question before us today, put into the *Biedenharn* framework, can be stated as follows: when a taxpayer engages in frequent and substantial sales over a period of years, but undertakes no development activity with respect to parts of a parcel of land, and engages in no solicitation or advertising efforts or brokerage activities, under what circumstances is income derived from sales of undeveloped parts of the parcel ordinary income?

The *Biedenharn* framework allows us to ask the question, but gives us little guidance in answering it. In the principal recent cases, there has always been a conjunction of frequent and substantial sales with development activity relating to the properties in dispute. See, e.g., Houston Endowment, Inc. v. United States, 606 F.2d 77, 82 (5th

---

[16]   In the United States v. Winthrop, 417 F.2d 905, 910 (5th Cir.1969), the following factors were enumerated:

> (1) the nature and purpose of the acquisition of the property and the duration of the ownership; (2) the extent and nature of the taxpayer's efforts to sell the property; (3) the number, extent, continuity and substantiality of the sales; (4) the extent of subdividing, developing, and advertising to increase sales; (5) the use of a business office for the sale of the property; (6) the character and degree of supervision or control exercised by the taxpayer over any representative selling the property; and (7) the time and effort the taxpayer habitually devoted to the sales.

Cir.1979), *Biedenharn,* 526 F.2d at 417 * * * . The conjunction of these two factors "will usually conclude the capital gains issue against [the] taxpayer." *Biedenharn,* 526 F.2d at 418. Judge Wisdom has recently written that "ordinary income tax rates usually apply when dispositions of subdivided property over a period of time are continuous and substantial rather than few and isolated." *Houston Endowment,* 606 F.2d at 81. Also, it has been explicitly stated that the factor which will receive greatest emphasis is frequency and substantiality of sales over an extended time period. See *Biedenharn,* 526 F.2d at 417. However, substantial and frequent sales activity, standing alone, has never been held to be automatically sufficient to trigger ordinary income treatment. In fact, we have continual reminders of the fact that "specific factors, or combinations of them are not necessarily controlling," *Biedenharn,* 526 F.2d at 415, quoting Thompson v. Commissioner, 322 F.2d 122, 127 (5th Cir.1963), quoting Wood v. Commissioner, 276 F.2d 586, 590 (5th Cir.1960).

* * *

Today, we must go into territory as yet unmapped in this Circuit. Suburban's case is at once more favorable to the taxpayer than Biedenharn's and less so. It is more favorable because, *with respect to the particular parcels of land here at issue,* it is undisputed that Suburban undertook no development or subdivision activity. It is less favorable because Biedenharn was continually engaged in business activities other than real estate sales, whereas Suburban was for many years doing little else. Following the *Biedenharn* framework alone, we would be left with yet another essentially *ad hoc* decision to be made. We could justify a decision for either party, yet remain confident that we were being fully consistent with the analysis in *Biedenharn.* However, although there will always remain a certain irreducible *ad hoc*-ishness in this area, we are now firmly convinced that the uncertainty can be substantially reduced by turning to the divining rod of capital gains versus ordinary income—the statute itself.

III.

The jurisprudence of the "real estate capital gains-ordinary income issue" in this Circuit has at times been cast somewhat loose of its statutory mooring. The ultimate inquiry in cases of this nature is whether the property at issue was "property held by the taxpayer primarily for sale to customers in the ordinary course of his trade or business." 26 U.S.C.A. § 1221(1) (West 1967).* In our focus on the "tests" developed to resolve this question, we have on occasion almost lost sight entirely of the statutory framework. The "tests" or "factors," whether they be counted to number seven, see *Winthrop,* 417 F.2d at 910, or to number four, see *Houston Endowment,* 606 F.2d at 81, have seemingly acquired

---

*   [Ed. Prior to 2000 the language of § 1221(a)(1) was in § 1221(1).]

an independent meaning of their own, only loosely tied to their statutory pier. Some years ago, Judge Brown cautioned us against this tendency:

> Essential as they are in the adjudication of cases, we must take guard lest we be so carried away by the proliferation of tests that we forget that the statute excludes from capital assets "property held by the taxpayer primarily for sale to customers in the ordinary course of his trade or business."

Thompson, 322 F.2d at 127. * * *

The tendency to overemphasize the independent meaning of the "factors" has been accompanied by, perhaps even caused by, a tendency to view the statutory language as posing only one question: whether the property was held by the taxpayer "primarily for sale to customers in the ordinary course of his trade or business." This determination was correctly seen as equivalent to the question whether the gain was to be treated as ordinary or capital. However, probably because the question "is the gain ordinary" is a single question which demands an answer of yes or no, the courts have on occasion lost sight of the fact that the statutory language requires the court to make not one determination, but several separate determinations. In statutory construction cases, our most important task is to ask the proper questions. In the context of cases like the one before us, the principal inquiries demanded by the statute are:

> (1) was taxpayer engaged in a trade or business, and, if so, what business?

> (2) was taxpayer holding the property primarily for sale in that business?

> (3) were the sales contemplated by taxpayer "ordinary" in the course of that business?[19] * * *

In fact, once the inquiry is redirected towards the statutory inquiries, the ultimate relevance of the *Biedenharn* factors becomes apparent. It will remain true that the frequency and substantiality of sales will be the most important factor. But the reason for the importance of this factor is now clear: the presence of frequent and substantial sales is highly relevant to each of the principal statutory inquiries listed above. A taxpayer who engages in frequent and substantial sales is almost inevitably engaged in the real estate business. The frequency and substantiality of sales are highly probative on the issue of holding purpose because the presence of frequent sales ordinarily belies the contention that property is being held "for investment" rather than "for

---

[19]   In other types of cases, or even in real estate cases with different factual patterns, other questions may be crucial. For example, whether the contemplated purchasers were "customers" of the taxpayers, or whether business activity is to be imputed to taxpayer so as to be considered "taxpayer's business," could be an important inquiry. Yet other inquiries may be demanded by the statutory language in other contexts. Here, the key questions are those set out above.

sale." And the frequency of sales may often be a key factor in determining the "ordinariness" question.

The extent of development activity and improvements is highly relevant to the question of whether taxpayer is a real estate developer. Development activity and improvements may also be relevant to the taxpayer's holding purpose, but, standing alone, some degree of development activity is not inconsistent with holding property for purposes other than sale.[22] The extent of development activity also seems to be only peripherally relevant to the "ordinariness" question. Thus, under the statutory framework, as under *Biedenharn,* the extent of development activity and improvements, although an important factor, is less conclusive than the substantiality and frequency of sales.

Solicitation and advertising efforts are quite relevant both to the existence of a trade or business and to taxpayer's holding purpose. Thus, their presence can strengthen the case for ordinary income treatment. See *Biedenharn,* 526 F.2d at 418. However, in cases like *Biedenharn,* their absence is not conclusive on either of these statutory questions for, as we noted there, "even one inarguably in the real estate business need not engage in promotional exertions in the face of a favorable market." Id.

We need not comment individually on each of the other *Biedenharn-Winthrop* factors. It should be apparent that each factor is relevant, to a greater or lesser extent, to one or more of the questions posed by the statute along the path to the ultimate conclusion.[24]

First, a taxpayer who has made only a few sales involving fairly modest dollar amounts may argue that he is not in the real estate business. The taxpayer's claim to capital gain treatment is likely to be weaker if he can point to no other business activities; i.e., if close to 100 percent of his income is derived from sales of real estate. Conversely, if the taxpayer is also engaged in extensive activities other than real estate sales, the presence of another trade or business may make it less likely that he will be found to be in the real estate business. However, frequent real estate sales activity substantial in dollar amount will likely conclude the "trade or business" question against taxpayer. He will be held to be engaged in both the real estate business and his other business. See *Biedenharn,* 526 F.2d at 419 & n. 35.

---

[22]   For example, a taxpayer might clear trees and conduct some grading and filling activities in preparation for farming the land.

[24]   We will here attempt to clear up some of the confusion relating to the relevance of the percentage of taxpayer's average annual income attributable to real estate sales. This percentage has often been mentioned in the real estate cases; its significance has never been clear. See, e.g. Houston Endowment, 606 F.2d at 81 n. 3; *Biedenharn,* 526 F.2d at 419; * * * *Winthrop,* 417 F.2d at 907. Rather, these decisions have referred to the percentage, often compared it to the comparable percentage in another case, and perhaps noted that the percentage in the case being decided was like or unlike the percentage in another case. Once the percentage is related to the statutory inquiries, it can easily be seen that the percentage may or may not be relevant depending on the facts of the case and the taxpayer's claims. * * *

The taxpayer's next argument will likely be that the property is held "primarily" for use in his other business (e.g., farming) rather than "for sale." If a large percentage of his income *derived from the land in dispute* is earned other than by sale, his claim that his primary holding purpose is for use in his other business is buttressed. This would clearly be the case if a few small tracts of land were sold from a large active farm. Conversely, if most of the income derived from the land in dispute is earned from real estate sales, it is more likely that the taxpayer's primary holding purpose is "for sale."

In *Biedenharn,* the percentage offered was real estate sales as compared to total income. The fact that this percentage was low (11.1%), see 526 F.2d at 419, demonstrated that Biedenharn was engaged in businesses other than real estate (e.g., securities investments). These other businesses did not relate to the property in dispute. Thus, the percentage offered was not relevant to Biedenharn's holding purpose. The relevant percentage would have been real estate sales profits compared to total income from the land (which would include, e.g., income from farming or leasing the land).

A second situation in which a percentage is relevant involves a taxpayer attempting to demonstrate that certain parcels of land were held for purposes other than for sale. This taxpayer could concede that he was in the real estate development business, but would argue that certain specific parcels of land were not held "primarily for sale." See, e.g., Wood v. Commissioner, 276 F.2d 586 (5th Cir.1960); Maddux Construction Co., 54 T.C. 1278 (1970) * * * . These specific properties, he would argue, were held for other purposes. In this situation, a relevant percentage would be profits from (or number of) sales from property held primarily for sale as compared to profits from (or number of) all sales. If many of taxpayer's sales, or much of his profit, emanated from properties he claimed to hold for purposes other than "for sale," the taxpayer would be highly unlikely to establish capital gain treatment. Conversely, if a taxpayer who engaged in a high volume subdivision business sold one clearly segregated tract in bulk, he might well prevail in his claim to capital gain treatment on the segregated tract.

IV.

Having laid the framework for the requisite analysis, we must now apply that framework to the facts here. We must decide whether Suburban was engaged in a trade or business, and, if so, what business; whether Suburban was holding the properties at issue here primarily for sale; and whether Suburban's contemplated sales were "ordinary" in the course of Suburban's business.

* * *

A.   Was Suburban in the real estate business?

This is a relatively simple issue. The question is whether taxpayer has engaged in a sufficient quantum of focused activity to be considered to be engaged in a trade or business. The precise quantum necessary will be difficult to establish, and cases close to the line on this issue will arise.

Happily, we need not here define that line. It is clear to us that Suburban engaged in a sufficient quantity of activity to be in the business of selling real estate. Suburban's sales were continuous and substantial. It completed at least 244 sales transactions over the 33-year period 1939–1971. This averages to over 7 transactions per year. Proceeds from these sales exceeded 2.3 million dollars.

Suburban does not claim to have been engaged in any business other than real estate; rather, it claims that during the periods at issue it simply "did not carry on a trade or business." * * * Were additional support necessary for our conclusion, we would point to Suburban's own statements on its tax returns over the years that its principal business activity was "development and sales of real estate." * * *

B. What was Suburban's primary purpose for holding the properties whose characterization is here in dispute?

Put into the framework being used here, Suburban's contention concerning holding purpose is two-fold. Principally, it argues that, at the time of the sales in dispute, the properties were not being held for sale. Alternatively, it contends that it "originally acquired its property as an investment * * *, and it continued to hold it for investment purposes." * * *

We reject Suburban's statement of the legal principle upon which its first argument is premised. It simply cannot be true that "the decisive question is the purpose for which [the property] 'primarily' was held when sold." * * * At the very moment of sale, the property is certainly being held "for sale." The appropriate question certainly must be the taxpayer's primary holding purpose at some point before he decided to make the sale in dispute.

There is language in the cases that supports the proposition we are here rejecting. For example, the Tax Court has stated explicitly that "the determining factor is the purpose for which the property is held at the time of sale." Eline Realty Co., 35 T.C. 1, 5 (1960). * * *

The "holding purpose" inquiry may appropriately be conducted by attempting to trace the taxpayer's primary holding purpose over the entire course of his ownership of the property. See Malat v. Riddell, 383 U.S. 569 (1966) * * *.[36] Thus, the inquiry should start at the time the

---

[36]　It is not clear to us from the *Malat* decision whether "primarily" means "predominates at a certain point of time" or "predominates over the life of taxpayer's ownership of the asset." This could be critical if, for example, a taxpayer held a piece of property primarily for sale over many years, but then, shortly but not immediately before sale, switched his primary holding purpose to one of investment. If the appropriate measure of "primarily" is at a fixed instant of time, this taxpayer would be entitled to capital gain treatment if the other requirements of § 1221 are met. However, taxpayer's "primary holding purpose" over the length of his ownership of the asset would still be "for sale," and, if this is the proper test, ordinary income treatment would be mandated.

property is acquired. We seek to divine the taxpayer's primary purpose for acquiring the property. In this case, we are willing to assume, as Suburban argues, that the property was acquired principally as an investment. We then seek evidence of a change in taxpayer's primary holding purpose. Here, such evidence is plentiful and convincing.

* * *

[The extent of development activity and extent of sales activity] convince us that, by the mid-1940's at the latest, and probably much earlier, Suburban's primary holding purpose was "for sale." We need not decide the precise moment. Were it necessary to our decision, we quite likely would be unwilling to accept Suburban's contention that the property was initially acquired for investment. * * *

With its primary holding purpose through the 1940's and 1950's fixed at "for sale," Suburban is then entitled to show that its primary purpose changed to, or back to, "for investment." Suburban claims that this shift occurred either in 1959, when its officers and directors discussed liquidation; in 1961, when Rice University became a stockholder of Suburban; further liquidation discussions were held, and the plats were withdrawn; or, at the latest, in 1966, when further liquidation discussions were held and Suburban began investing in securities.

We view this determination to be a closer call than any of the others in this case. The frequency of sales did drop off after the late 1950's. Suburban had discontinued its development activities. Also, 1961 was the year the plats for [one of the parcels were withdrawn].

This withdrawal of plats could be quite significant. Unlike liquidation discussions,[39] which were apparently a dime a dozen for Suburban, withdrawal of the plats was an action taken by Suburban which may evince a different relationship to its land. The critical question is whether this withdrawal indicated that henceforth the land was being held principally as an investment or simply showed that Suburban was attempting to maximize sales profits by selling to commercial users.

* * * Suburban uses the term "liquidation" to refer to discussions about winding up Suburban as a corporate entity and distributing its assets, as well as discussions about converting its investments into cash. Discussions about each of these matters may evidence a change in holding purpose, but a corporation's actions may speak louder than "its"

We express no opinion on the resolution of this issue, for it is unnecessary to our decision. We find Suburban's primary holding purpose to be "for sale" both at the relevant moment of time, if the first proposed test is appropriate, and over most of the period of Suburban's ownership of the property, if the second proposed test is appropriate. * * *

[39]　We attach no independent significance to "liquidation discussions." As we said in *Biedenharn,* "a taxpayer's claim that he is liquidating a prior investment does not really present a separate theory but rather restates the main question * * * under scrutiny." *Biedenharn,* 526 F.2d at 417.

words. The latter is the case here. When investigating a corporation's intent, courts must be skeptical of words spoken at board meetings.

Although Suburban uses the word "liquidation" in an effort to place itself in *Biedenharn's* "liquidation niche," *Biedenharn,* 526 F.2d at 417, that concept is not applicable here. Rather, it refers to the possibility that a holding purpose other than "for sale" might be found to continue through a period of relatively substantial sales activity when "unanticipated, externally induced factors * * * make impossible the continued pre-existing use of the realty." Id. at 421.

The continuing sales activity is strong evidence that the latter interpretation is the correct one. Moreover, the trial court found that the withdrawal evinced "an attempt to maximize profits from the sale of real estate and to capitalize on the new [expressway] which would cross [Suburban's] property." Thus, we conclude that Suburban's primary purpose for holding the property remained "for sale" at the time of the transactions here disputed.[42]

Suburban does not explicitly contend that its primary purpose for holding the specific parcels at issue here was different from its purpose for holding the property as a whole. However, it does attempt to rely to some degree on the lack of development activity relating to the parcels here at issue. Although in some circumstances a taxpayer in the real estate business may be able to establish that certain parcels were held primarily for investment, see n. 24, supra and cases cited; the burden is on the taxpayer to establish that the parcels held primarily for investment were segregated from other properties held primarily for sale. The mere lack of development activity with respect to parts of a large property does not sufficiently separate those parts from the whole to meet the taxpayer's burden. Cf. *Houston Endowment,* 606 F.2d at 81 (pattern of sales activity with respect to entire tract determines characterization of individual sales). The lack of development activity with respect to the parts of the property here at issue is at least equally consistent with a primary motivation to maximize immediate sales profits as it is with a primary motivation to hold for investment.

C.   Were the sales contemplated by Suburban "ordinary" in the course of Suburban's business?

We need say no more on this question than quote from the discussion of this issue in *Winthrop* supra:

---

[42]   Some of our skepticism over Suburban's claim to have changed its holding purpose stems from the fact that it points to so many separate times when its purpose may have changed. This leads us to believe that Suburban was merely gradually shifting its strategies as market conditions changed in an effort to maximize sales profits. We do not reject outright the possibility that a sequence of events separate in time may indicate a gradual change in holding purpose from "for sale" to "for investment." However, we would be more likely to find a "change of purpose" argument convincing if a discrete event were followed by a string of zeros in the annual sales column figures, especially if this were followed by a sale of the remainder of taxpayer's property in a small number of transactions.

The concept of normalcy requires for its application a chronology and a history to determine if the sales of lots to customers were the usual or a departure from the norm. History and chronology here combine to demonstrate that [taxpayer] did not sell his lots as an abnormal or unexpected event. [Taxpayer] began selling shortly after he acquired the land; he never used the land for any other purpose; and he continued this course of conduct over a number of years. Thus, the sales were * * * ordinary.

417 F.2d at 912. The same is true here.

V.

Having relied on the language of § 1221 itself to determine that the assets here at issue were not capital assets, we must return for a moment to the query posed at the outset. In this case, as we have demonstrated, sales of the type here in dispute were precisely what Suburban's business was directed towards. In other words, the profits garnered from these sales arose from the ordinary operation of Suburban's business.

At the same time, however, these profits did not arise principally from the efforts of Suburban. Rather, they arose from the same historical, demographic, and market forces that have caused the City of Houston to grow enormously during the years Suburban held the land. Shrewdly, Suburban held on to much of its land. It only sold relatively small portions year by year. Thus, by 1968, market forces and the location of the [expressway] had driven up the value of Suburban's land.[43] We must decide whether the policies motivating lower tax rates on capital gains and the controlling precedents expressing those policies require that we ignore the plain language of § 1221 and hold for Suburban.

The key cases we must explore here number three. First is Malat v. Riddell, 383 U.S. 569 (1966) (per curiam). It lends us no aid. As we have previously stated, it suggests that profits cannot arise from both "the [ordinary] operation of a business" and "appreciation in value accrued over a substantial period of time." Yet here we have profits which fall squarely into both categories.

We thus turn to the two cases from which the *Malat* court quotations are taken, Commissioner v. Gillette Motor Transport, Inc., 364 U.S. 130 (1960), and Corn Products Refining Company v. Commissioner, 350 U.S. 46 (1955). In *Gillette,* the Supreme Court said:

This Court has long held that the term "capital asset" is to be construed narrowly in accordance with the purpose of Congress to afford capital-gains treatment only in situations typically

---

[43]   Suburban's evidence demonstrated that the normal net profit on sales by a developer is approximately thirty-three percent, whereas Suburban's profit on the sales here in issue approximated ninety-five percent. Since Suburban did nothing to enhance the value of the parcels here at issue, and since we can take notice of the often rapid rise in real estate prices as cities expand, we accept Suburban's contention that its profits on these sales emanated from market forces and Suburban's patience rather than any other value-enhancing activities performed by Suburban.

involving the realization of appreciation in value accrued over a substantial period of time, and thus to ameliorate the hardship of taxation and the entire gain in one year.

364 U.S. at 134. We note that the quoted language does not state that all gains emanating from appreciation in value over a substantial period of time are to be treated as capital gains. Rather, it states the logical converse of that proposition; i.e., that capital gain treatment will be proper only if the gain emanates from appreciation in value. Instances of gain emanating from appreciation being treated as ordinary income are not inconsistent with this proposition.

We also note the Supreme Court's recognition of the attempt by Congress to avoid taxing income earned over a period of years in one year. In Suburban's case, although it is true that with respect to each individual parcel of land there is a "bunching" effect, taxation of the overall gains from the property as a whole has been spread over a long period of years. Thus, the "bunching" effect has been minimized. Last, we note the Supreme Court's admonition to construe the term "capital asset" narrowly. Id.

Further support for a narrow construction of the term "capital asset" and a broad interpretation of its exclusions comes from *Corn Products,* the third key case in this area. * * * More importantly, the Supreme Court in *Corn Products* squarely stated:

> Congress intended that profits and losses arising from the everyday operation of a business be considered as ordinary income or loss rather than capital gain or loss.

It is this type of profit that is before us today.

We thus conclude that § 1221(1) should be construed in accord with its plain meaning, and that, if the other requirements of § 1221(1) are met, when the ordinary business of a business is to make profits from appreciation in value caused by market forces, those profits are to be treated as ordinary income. Such is the case here.

VI.

Our journey over, we have nothing more to add. The decision of the district court dismissing Suburban's complaint is Affirmed.

DETAILED ANALYSIS

1.　GENERAL

The *Suburban Realty Co.* case is typical of the situations in which the courts, with little statutory guidance, have been required to classify transactions into the categories of "business" or "investment." Although some courts have attempted to reduce the inquiry to a list of factors, *Suburban Realty Co.* correctly observes that the questions that should be asked in the cases are: whether the taxpayer is engaged in a trade or business; if so, whether the taxpayer was holding the property primarily for sale to customers in that business; and whether the sales were in the "ordinary" course of that business. The factors ought not take on independent significance; they are merely relevant to answering the above questions.

As the opinion in *Suburban Reality Co.* suggests, application of the multiple factors analyzed by the courts interpreting § 1221(a)(1) has led to divergent results in a multitude of cases. That is to be expected with respect to questions that are dependent on subjective application of a facts and circumstances analysis, but the cases do not provide the precision desirable for the sound administration of the tax law. Nonetheless, the cases in the area may be divided into three groups.

(1) In one group of cases, the issue is whether the nature and purpose of the taxpayer's dealings in property, usually real estate, generally put it in the business of holding the property primarily for sale to customers—i.e., result in classification of the taxpayer as a "dealer"—so that the sales of the property presumptively are in the ordinary course of that business. Situations of this type are discussed in Section 2.A.2. of this Chapter.

(2) In a second group of cases, the taxpayer originally acquired the property for investment but the purpose following that decision changed; here, the issue is whether that change in purpose resulted in holding the property in a business primarily for sale to customers in the ordinary course of that business. Situations of this type are considered in Section 2.A.3. of this Chapter.

(3) The third group of cases are the "dual purpose" situations. In some of these cases the taxpayer acquired the property with no clear plans for it other than to make money, whether that resulted from appreciation in value over time or from selling off the property to customers. In other such cases the taxpayer acquired the property with an eye to using it in a manufacturing or rental business but also had in mind the resale of the property, often within a relatively short period of time. Cases of this type are considered in Section 2.A.5. of this Chapter.

Notwithstanding these categorizations, the inquiry is complex and multi-faceted. A taxpayer may have more than one trade or business. Identical types of property may be acquired primarily for sale to customers in one business and for use as rental property in another business or for long-term investment. The taxpayer's intention with respect to the property may change. Fact questions predominate in the cases.

2. NATURE AND PURPOSE OF THE HOLDING

2.1. *Persons Not Otherwise Dealers*

The frequency and continuity of sales are important factors in determining dealer status; they are relevant in determining whether the taxpayer was engaged in a trade or business, the taxpayer's purpose in holding the property, and whether the sales were "ordinary."

In Goodman v. United States, 390 F.2d 915 (Ct.Cl.1968), the taxpayer was a lawyer specializing in real estate law. He participated in various real estate ventures in which his clients were involved. During the three years at issue, the taxpayer sold 32 different realty interests averaging over $48,000 per year in income from the disposition of real estate. This amount was in excess of his average annual net income from the practice of law during the same years. The court found ordinary income from the sales:

> Individuals may conduct more than one business at a time and each will be taxed accordingly. Crosswhite v. United States, 369 F.2d 989, 177 Ct.Cl. 671 (1966), collecting cases. Clearly, buying and selling realty was *one* of the businesses of the partners. Moreover, it was their biggest business, and the primary purpose of it was not investment but sales for profit in the ordinary course of business. We emphasize in particular the frequency and continuity of sales in reaching this conclusion. * * * The fact that plaintiffs also practiced law and had income from investments and other sources does not disturb the character of their real estate activity as a separate business, nor does it affect the tax treatment to be given that separate business.

While frequency of sales is an important factor, the absence of frequent sales does not necessarily establish capital asset status for the property involved. Dealer status may be established, for example, by the nature of improvements or other development activity. For example, in S & H, Inc. v. Commissioner, 78 T.C. 234 (1982), the taxpayer was in the business of acquiring improved real estate and leasing or operating the property. It constructed a building and, pursuant to a pre-existing contract, immediately sold the building to a third party. The court concluded that the only purpose in constructing the building was to sell it and therefore the property was held primarily for sale to a customer in the ordinary course of business. The court stressed the pre-existing contract, but the level of activities by the taxpayer would seem to have justified the court's conclusion even if the contract had been entered into after construction had begun or had been completed.

In other cases, property has been regarded as held for sale to customers in the ordinary course of business if the taxpayer's intention on purchase was immediate resale at a profit. In Zack v. Commissioner, 25 T.C. 676 (1955), aff'd per curiam, 245 F.2d 235 (6th Cir.1957), a joint venture was formed to dispose of bomb hoists that had been purchased earlier by one of the members and which he had not been able to sell. The court found ordinary income: "The only purpose in buying the bomb hoists was to resell them at a higher price. There was no 'investment' such as might be made in other types of property, but on the contrary there was a general public offering and sales in such a manner that the exclusion of the statute cannot be denied." A similar result obtained in Brady v. Commissioner, 25 T.C. 682 (1955) (Acq.), involving a joint venture to buy and then dispose of improved residential lots encumbered with liens for delinquent taxes: "We are impelled to conclude also that the 68 lots were acquired with a view to producing profits on a quick turnover, as soon as the obstructing liens could be removed, and that they were not acquired for investment purposes. The lots were not income producing, and none of the associates intended either to use them personally or to build upon them. Also, until buildings were constructed, there could be no reasonable expectation of any substantial appreciation in value, for the lots had already been fully improved with streets, paving, curbs, sewers and utilities, and an active market for improved lots of such character had existed for several years."

While the courts often assert that frequency of sales is the most important element in determining the taxpayer's purpose in holding property, it is nonetheless quite possible to engage in a substantial number of sales transactions and still obtain capital gain treatment. For example, in Byram v. United States, 705 F.2d 1418 (5th Cir.1983), capital gain treatment was accorded a taxpayer who made no effort to initiate sales, had no sales office, did not use a broker, did not improve or develop the property, and devoted a minimal amount of time to the sales transactions, even though the taxpayer sold 22 parcels in a 3-year period and held some parcels for as short a period as 6 months.

The absence of frequent sales may negate the existence of a trade or business if there are no substantial development activities as well. In Mitchell v. Commissioner, 47 T.C. 120 (1966), a businessman purchased a hospital building at auction. He subsequently entered into a joint venture with two others which, after exploring several proposals, ultimately sold the property in two portions over a year later. The court found capital gain on the sale:

> Regarding the acquisition of the property, the evidence is clear and uncontroverted that petitioner bought the property as an investment. He realized the bidding was low and felt that the property, if it could be purchased at this price, would make a good investment. There is clear evidence in the record that he did not buy with the aim of immediately reselling the property. This is shown by his refusal to take a possible profit on the property seconds after the bidding ceased. However, under the circumstances of this case, if petitioner had acquired the property with an intention to resell immediately, that intent alone would not put petitioner in the real estate business. * * *
>
> As to the continuity and frequency of sales, the joint venturers bought one piece of property and sold one piece of property. This was the only purchase and sale, not only for the venture, but also for petitioner. Clearly, this does not show the necessary continuity or frequency to establish a "trade or business." * * *
>
> Petitioner's business was not that of a real estate agent, broker, or dealer. * * * The business of all three of the joint venturers was that of being a corporation executive. The purchase and sale of the Old Sinai Hospital property were nothing more than isolated transactions in the lives of these individuals.

2.2. Investments by Dealers

An admitted dealer in real estate may hold particular property as investment property and not for sale. The problem is one of identifying the character of the particular holdings and naturally the difficulty is intensified by the existence of other holdings as a dealer or trader. In Scheuber v. Commissioner, 371 F.2d 996 (7th Cir.1967), the taxpayer was a dealer in real estate. The transaction in question involved two tracts of real estate. One was purchased by the taxpayer in 1950 and sold in two portions in 1958 and 1959. The property was never advertised for sale and the buyer initiated contact with the taxpayer-seller. The second tract was acquired in 1945 at which time the taxpayer testified that the property was purchased to provide an annuity in old age because of its expected long-term appreciation in value. In 1954 the taxpayer sold a portion of the property because of a change in zoning. The remaining property was ultimately condemned by the city in 1959. The Tax Court found the gains taxable as ordinary income and suggested that a dealer in real estate had a "more stringent" burden of proof to show that capital gain treatment was proper. The Court of Appeals reversed, relying on Malat v. Riddell, 383 U.S. 569 (1966):

> [*Malat* held] that the purpose of [§ 1221(a)(1)] was to differentiate between the profits and losses arising from everyday operation of a business and the realization of appreciation in value accrued over a substantial period of time. In seeking to distinguish *Malat*, the Commissioner stresses the existence of a dual purpose there, viewing the Supreme Court's decision as limited to interpreting "primary" purpose, where there is more than one, as that which is first in order of importance. Thus the Commissioner contends that the Scheubers had no dual purpose; that they always intended to sell the parcels some time in the future, and that they have shown no effort to demark or isolate these properties from those in their usual inventory. We think that this represents a very strained interpretation of *Malat* and a misapplication of its principles to the facts of this case. * * * [T]his real estate was purchased and held for realization of appreciation in value to be accrued over a substantial period of time, with no intensive effort to improve or sell it. It was always intended ultimately to be disposed of to provide the "annuity" of which Mr. Scheuber spoke, but not to be disposed of to customers in the ordinary course of trade.

2.3. *Attribution of Activities of Dealers*

Some cases have taken into account the activities of corporations controlled by an individual taxpayer in order to determine if the individual is in the real estate business. See e.g., Brown v. Commissioner, 54 T.C. 1475 (1970), aff'd, 448 F.2d 514 (10th Cir.1971). In the case of a partnership, gain or loss is characterized by the activities of the partnership rather than the individual partners. I.R.C. § 702(b). Thus, holding a partnership interest in a partnership that is characterized as a dealer in property does not, by itself, cause the partner to be treated as a dealer, although the non-dealer partner's share of partnership gain on disposition of property held for sale to customers is characterized as ordinary income. Conversely, sales of property by a business entity in which an admitted dealer in real estate is a significant investor are evaluated on their own merits. Phelan v. Commissioner, T.C. Memo 2004–206, held that sales of unimproved land by a limited liability company, one of the principal members of which was a commercial real estate developer, resulted in capital gain because the land was held for long-term appreciation and the LLC did not advertise parcels for sale or hire sales agents. In Riddell v. Scales, 406 F.2d 210 (9th Cir.1969), the taxpayers entered into a joint venture with a real estate dealer to purchase and dispose of property. The court rejected the Government's contention that the taxpayers became real estate dealers by virtue of their association in a joint venture with the dealer and found that they realized capital gain on the disposition of the property, characterizing the transaction as "the acquisition and sale of a parcel of property as a speculative investment." The Commissioner apparently did not argue that the joint venture was a partnership thereby characterizing the taxpayer's share of the gain as partnership ordinary income.

3.   "LIQUIDATION" OF AN INVESTMENT—CHANGE OF PURPOSE

Where a taxpayer has invested in a large tract of land and later decides to sell it, the taxpayer often finds that the sale of the tract in a single transaction is not possible. The taxpayer then turns to subdividing the land, possibly developing it, and then selling portions over a period of time. Two main problems emerge in the cases when the taxpayer changes activities in the above-described situations. First, a court must determine whether the nature and volume of the development activities and the sales activities were sufficient to place the taxpayer in the business of selling land, such that the property can be regarded as held primarily for sale in the ordinary course of that business. And second, a court must evaluate whether, despite the nature and volume of activities, the original investment character of the holding persisted over time such that the properties should not be regarded as held primarily for sale in the ordinary course of the taxpayer's business.

In some cases, the nature and volume of the activities has been considered sufficient to warrant ordinary income treatment. For example, in Bynum v. Commissioner, 46 T.C. 295 (1966), the taxpayer owned farmland for eighteen years. A portion of the land was used to grow plants and shrubs for the taxpayer's landscaping business. The taxpayer's bank, which held a mortgage on the farm, wanted the taxpayer to sell part of the farm to pay off the mortgage. At the urging of the bank, the taxpayer decided to improve and subdivide a portion of the farm, and install sewers, water, curb breaks and other improvements. The taxpayer sold 38 lots in 1960 and 17 in 1962. The lots were advertised in newspapers and listed with realtors. The Tax Court found ordinary income:

> The record facts indicate that the value of the raw land of petitioner's farm had appreciated very little since 1942, such appreciation amounting to about $35 per acre, yet the gain on approximately 13 acres sold during the years at issue amounted to almost $4000 per acre. * * * We do believe that the gain here was generated by petitioners' actions and activities with regard to this property [citing cases] and as such it is taxable as ordinary income.

A somewhat different approach to the liquidation-type situation was adopted in Daugherty v. Commissioner, 78 T.C. 623 (1982). The taxpayer held land that, immediately prior to the receipt of a condemnation notice from the state, was held primarily for sale to customers in the ordinary course of business. Relying on the analysis in *Raytheon Production Corp.* (see

Chapter 9, Section 1), the court held that the gain realized upon receipt of the condemnation proceeds was ordinary income since the condemnation award replaced proceeds that would have been ordinary income if the property had been sold.

Other cases have stressed the "liquidation" aspect of the transaction to avoid characterizing what otherwise appeared to be an extensive real estate business as such. This result is most likely to follow where sales, although frequent in number, were not preceded by significant development activity. For example, in Farley v. Commissioner, 7 T.C. 198 (1946) (Acq.), the taxpayer's sale of 25 lots out of a tract previously used in its nursery business but which had become more desirable as residential property was held not to be a sale of property held for sale to customers. Since the taxpayer made no active efforts to sell and did not develop the property, the court described the sales as "in the nature of a gradual and passive liquidation of an asset."

Other cases have focused on the fact that the asset was not acquired for sale but was inherited. For example, in Estate of Ferber v. Commissioner, 22 T.C. 261 (1954) (Acq.), in three auction sales executors disposed of about $200,000 in furs, representing the inventory of furs held by the decedent in his retail fur store. The court held that the losses sustained were capital losses, since the nature of the decedent's holding of the property did not carry over to the estate and the sale of the furs after the executors had disposed of the retail store was consistent with the duty to liquidate the estate.

4. SECTION 1237

Section 1237 provides safe harbor capital gain treatment for individuals not otherwise holding real property for sale to customers who are engaged in minimal subdivision activities with respect to a tract held for investment for at least five years. Under this provision, the taxpayer may sell five lots and report the profits as capital gain. After five lots are sold, however, any gain on subsequent lots is ordinary income to the extent of 5 percent of the selling price, with gains reduced by expenses associated with the sales. Section 1237 is rather restrictive. "No substantial improvement that substantially enhances" the value of the lot sold can be made, although some improvements are permitted if the property has been held for ten years. Section 1237 is not applicable if factors other than the subdivision activities are present to show that the taxpayer is holding the property for sale to customers. Such factors include subdivision activities respecting other property in prior years, the taxpayer's intention at the time of purchase of the particular tract and the current subdivision of other tracts. A taxpayer failing to meet the requirements of § 1237 may nevertheless show that the particular property was not held for sale to customers. A taxpayer making such a showing can obtain complete capital gain treatment for the property rather than the special treatment under § 1237. The section has no application to a loss. See generally Treas. Reg. § 1.1237–1(a).

5. "DUAL PURPOSE" CASES

In Malat v. Riddell, 383 U.S. 569 (1966), discussed in *Suburbon Reality*, the taxpayers purchased property with the asserted intention to develop and operate an apartment complex on the land. Zoning and other obstacles resulted in sales of the properties. The District Court found that the taxpayer held the property "for development *or sale* depending on which course appeared to be the most profitable." The Government characterized this situation as involving a "dual purpose," as opposed to the "change of purpose" analysis urged by the taxpayer. Similar "dual purpose" situations arise under § 1231(b)(1) where the taxpayer purchases property that it then either leases or sells depending on the desires of its customers. A related situation involves the successive rental and then sale of property. A number of earlier cases had found ordinary income in situations such as these reasoning that the property was held "primarily" for sale to customers where the sales were "substantial" or an "essential" part of the business. See Rollingwood Corp. v. Commissioner, 190 F.2d 263 (9th Cir.1951); American Can Co. v. Commissioner, 317 F.2d 604 (2d Cir.1963). The Court in *Malat* rejected this approach holding that " 'primarily' means 'of first importance' or 'principally.' " On remand the District Court found that the "purpose of first importance of the [taxpayers] was to develop and hold [the property] for rental." Accordingly, the property was not held primarily for sale to customers in the ordinary course of trade or business and the taxpayers were entitled to capital gain treatment. 275 F.Supp. 358 (S.D.Cal.1966).

The holding in *Malat* has its greatest impact in cases where the taxpayer's purpose for holding property is both investment or use in a trade or business, and for sale to customers in favorable circumstances. In Continental Can Co. v. United States, 422 F.2d 405 (Ct.Cl.1970), the taxpayer sold cans to canners and leased can-closing machines to its customers. As part of an antitrust decree, the taxpayer was required to offer to sell the already installed machinery to its present lessees and in the future to offer the machines for sale or rent. Substantially all of the users purchased the machinery and the taxpayer made additional sales of new machinery. The taxpayer treated the additional income from the sales of new machinery as ordinary income but returned as capital gain the amount realized from the sale of machinery to the lessees-in-possession. The taxpayer argued that capital gain treatment was justified since the property had been held for an extended period of time for rental, not sale, and hence was not held "primarily" for sale as defined by *Malat*. The taxpayer also stressed the fact that the sales were not made in the "ordinary" course of the business. The majority of the court found the sales to result in ordinary income. They stressed the fact that, at the time of sale, the taxpayer was in the business of *both* selling and leasing the machines and was therefore in effect in a second business of selling machines after the date of the decree: "[W]here a company is, at [the date of the sale], regularly engaged in the dual business of selling and renting its machines then income resulting from either activity satisfies the 'primarily' concept." Three judges dissented, stressing the long period of rental use of the property prior to the sale and the unusual nature of the circumstances surrounding the sale.

In International Shoe Machine Corp. v. United States, 491 F.2d 157 (1st Cir.1974), the court found that the taxpayer realized ordinary income on gain from sales of shoe machinery equipment. Though the sales income was substantially less than the rental income from the leasing of the same type of equipment, it was a steady source of income for the taxpayer. Since the equipment could still have been leased at a profit at the time of sale, the taxpayer was unable to bring itself within the cases allowing capital gain treatment on the liquidation of an investment.

In Guardian Industries Corp. v. Commissioner, 97 T.C. 308 (1991), a photograph developer regularly extracted silver compound waste from photograph-processing solution and sold substantially all of it in bulk to a single refiner. During the two years at issue the taxpayer operated so as to maximize the efficiency of its extraction process and made 228 shipments of waste silver. On the other hand, the sales proceeds represented only a small percentage of the taxpayer's revenues, and environmental pollution laws would have required taxpayer to remove the silver waste from its processing compounds even if the waste had been valueless. The court held that each shipment was a separate sale and that the silver waste was property held primarily for sale to customers. Sales were frequent, substantial, and an integral part of the taxpayer's business operations.

6. STOCK EXCHANGE SALES AND SIMILAR TRANSACTIONS

Section 1221(a)(1) requires that the property be held primarily for sale "to customers." A person selling securities on a stock exchange, even though his activities are considerable, is not regarded as selling to customers; hence his gains and losses are capital even if he is a "trader" engaged in a trade or business. Commissioner v. Burnett, 118 F.2d 659 (5th Cir.1941); Kemon v. Commissioner, 16 T.C. 1026 (1951) (Acq.). On the other hand, if he is a "dealer" selling to customers, the gains and losses will then be ordinary. A similar distinction applies to those engaged in commodities futures transactions. See Faroll v. Jarecki, 231 F.2d 281 (7th Cir.1956) (finding capital losses on the sales of commodities futures since the taxpayer was a trader); Commissioner v. Covington, 120 F.2d 768 (5th Cir.1941) (distinguishing dealers from traders in commodities futures). The capital gain treatment for sales of stock and securities, even by investors whose activities may be so numerous as to qualify them as traders, stems from the Congressional desire in 1933 to deny ordinary treatment for stock losses, because of the great decline in stock values in that period.

A dealer may, however, hold some securities for investment purposes and others for sale to customers thus presenting a problem of identification similar to that involved in some of the real property cases. Since the problems of classification and the opportunities for manipulation are more serious in the case of securities, § 1236 supplies classification rules. A security held by a dealer in securities may not qualify for capital gain treatment unless, before the close of the day on which it was acquired, it is clearly identified in the dealer's records as an investment and is not at any time thereafter held for sale to customers. A security may not qualify for ordinary loss treatment if at any time it was clearly identified as a security held for investment.

(2) SECTION 1221(a)(2): REAL PROPERTY AND DEPRECIABLE PROPERTY HELD FOR USE IN THE TAXPAYER'S TRADE OR BUSINESS

The problem of distinguishing sales of assets in the "investment" context from sales in the "recurring business" context also arises with respect to business assets other than inventory, such as the building and land on which the business is conducted or the machinery used in the business operations. Since many businesses buy large numbers of such assets, use them for a period, and then retire and sell them, sales often are expected and recurring in the ordinary course of the business.

Depreciable business assets originally were treated as capital assets. Gains enjoyed preferential treatment while losses were deductible only against capital gains. During the 1930s, when losses were more common than gains, pressure developed to ease the limitation on the deductibility of losses from dispositions of depreciable property. Capital asset characterization was impeding the disposition of depreciable property because, rather than encounter the capital loss limitations, businesses would retain the property to remain entitled to depreciation deductions until the end of its useful life. Congress responded in 1938 with the predecessor of § 1221(a)(2), excluding depreciable property from the definition of capital assets.

Several years later, in 1942, when gains once again became common, businesses now complained that it was the absence of preferential treatment that was deterring dispositions of depreciable property. Ever responsive, Congress created the special regime of § 1231: capital gain treatment if § 1231 gains exceeded losses; but ordinary loss if § 1231 losses exceeded gains. To avoid the problems of allocation of sales proceeds between the land and the buildings and machinery on it, § 1221(a)(2) and § 1231 both included real property used in the taxpayer's trade or business. Section 1231 raised its own set of problems because much of the gain realized on the sale of depreciable property represents adjustments to basis for depreciation deductions that exceed actual economic depreciation, not appreciation in value. To address this situation, Congress stepped in once more and enacted § 1245 and other "recapture" provisions that restore to ordinary income status much of the gain originally converted to capital gain by § 1231. The statutory complexities engendered by § 1231, which in effect creates a third type of asset for tax purposes, are considered in Chapter 25.

(3) SECTION 1221(a)(3): INVESTMENT PROFITS VERSUS REWARDS FOR PERSONAL SERVICES

INTERNAL REVENUE CODE: Section 1235.

REGULATIONS: Section 1.1221–1(c).

Payments received for personal services represent the paradigm of ordinary income treatment. But "property" is often created by personal efforts. Such property can take the form of a patent, copyright, work of art, etc. Some such self-created "property" can qualify as a capital asset with resulting capital gain treatment upon disposition, but other such property is excluded from capital asset status.

DETAILED ANALYSIS

1. AUTHORS, COMPOSERS, AND COMPUTER PROGRAMMERS

Section 1221(a)(3) specifically excludes from the definition of capital assets copyrights, literary, musical or artistic compositions, and letters and memoranda held by the taxpayer whose personal efforts created the property. This section, first adopted in 1950, was necessary because the courts and the IRS appear to have thought that a copyright could be considered "property" even though substantial personal efforts were involved. Although § 1221(a)(3) originally applied primarily to books and music, more recently (and increasingly) it has applied to computer programs (i.e., software) subject to copyright protection. Prior to the adoption of § 1221(a)(3), the tax classification of a copyright or book upon sale by the author depended on the status of the author. If the author was deemed to be an amateur, then the literary effort was not property held primarily for sale to customers in the ordinary course of a trade or business and the sale resulted in capital gain. If the author was a professional writer then a sale resulted in ordinary income. As it turns out, the tax law has known some famous amateurs, including President Dwight Eisenhower, who sold all the rights in his war memoirs for a lump sum of $635,000 and received a favorable ruling that the sales proceeds represented capital gain.

Under § 1221(a)(3), the status of the author is not an issue; the literary product, musical composition, or computer program is excluded from the capital asset definition whether the author, composer, or programmer is an amateur or a professional. Moreover, both copyrighted and uncopyrighted literary works, musical compositions, and computer programs are subject to § 1221(a)(3). Meanwhile, the exclusion applies only to persons whose personal efforts created the property or persons who receive such property as a gift. For purchasers and resellers of literary, musical, or computer software property, the characterization question turns on whether the property is held primarily for sale to customers in the ordinary course of a trade or business. See e.g., Martin v. Commissioner, 50 T.C. 341 (1968) (Acq.).

Congress has expressed a special affinity for the creators of musical works. At the election of the taxpayer, § 1221(b)(3) provides capital gains treatment to the sale or exchange of musical compositions or copyrights to musical works by the creator of the musical work. The legislative history provides no explanation for this tax preference other than to assert that "it is appropriate to allow taxpayers to treat as capital gain the income from a sale or exchange of musical compositions or copyrights in musical works the taxpayer created." H.R. Rept 109–304, 109th Cong. 2d Sess. (2006).[10]

---

[10]   The exclusion from capital gains treatment does not apply to charitable contributions of musical works by the creator, however, which remain deductible only to the extent of the creator's basis in the work. I.R.C. § 170(e)(1)(A).

The exclusion in § 1221(a)(3)(B) extends to letters, memoranda or similar property held by a taxpayer for whom such property was prepared or produced. This provision was added in 1969 in response to the problem of public figures donating collections of letters and memoranda to charitable institutions and obtaining a charitable deduction for the fair market value of the material. After the 1969 amendment, the sale of the collections would give rise to ordinary income and, under the charitable deduction rules (see Chapter 21, Section 3.5.2.), the deduction would be limited to the cost basis of the collection, which in most cases would be zero.[11] The amendment achieved substantial publicity when it was learned that President Nixon's donation of papers to the National Archives involved a deed of gift allegedly "backdated" to predate the effective date of the provision.

Treas. Reg. § 1.1221–1(c)(1) gives broad, but not unlimited, sweep to the term "similar property" in § 1221(a)(3). In Stern v. United States, 164 F.Supp. 847 (E.D.La.1958), aff'd per curiam, 262 F.2d 957 (5th Cir.1959), the court held that the taxpayer, the creator of the character "Francis, The Talking Mule," the beloved hero in several novels written by the taxpayer, received ordinary income when he sold the rights to the character to a motion picture company. The court found the character to be a "literary composition," despite the fact that it was not subject to copyright, and the sale of the rights was excluded from capital asset treatment by the predecessor of § 1221(a)(3). The court also suggested that the character, standing alone, might not be "property" within the meaning of § 1221. See also Glen v. Commissioner, 79 T.C. 208 (1982) (tapes of interviews with famous scientists were "similar property" and thus not capital assets in the hands of the interviewer-taxpayer); Levy v. Commissioner, T.C. Memo. 1992–471 (an uncopyrighted computer program eligible for copyright protection was not a capital asset in the hands of the programmer who created it). In Kurlan v. Commissioner, 343 F.2d 625 (2d Cir.1965), the court held that a radio and TV program format and method of character presentation that the taxpayer had developed was excluded from capital asset status by § 1221(a)(3)(A).

Chronicle Publishing Co. v. Commissioner, 97 T.C. 445 (1991), held that the clippings library of a corporate newspaper publisher was a corporate archive under Treas. Reg. § 1.1221–1(c)(2), and thus was "similar property" denied capital asset status by § 1221(a)(3). Because the corporate taxpayer had no established basis in the clippings, it was not entitled to any charitable contribution deduction for donating the clippings library to a state historical society.

2. PATENTS AND KNOW-HOW

2.1. *Patents Generally*

Section 1221(a)(3) does not cover patents. As long as the taxpayer is able to establish that he is not in the business of developing and selling patents, the sale of a patent can qualify for capital gain treatment despite the fact that it was created through the taxpayer's personal efforts. In addition, § 1235 allows any inventor, including a professional inventor in the business

---

[11]   The exclusion in § 1221(a)(5) has a similar objective.

of developing and selling patents, to receive capital gain treatment in certain circumstances.

The principal issue in the "common law" of patent transfers is whether there has been a sale or exchange of a patent, or whether the transaction is a license of patented technology. Sale treatment requires transfer of all substantial rights to the patent. If the transfer meets this test, the "sale" of the patent receives capital gains treatment, even where the payments take the form of royalties and are contingent on use or productivity. Rev. Rul. 58–353, 1958–2 C.B. 408; Rev. Rul. 69–482, 1969–2 C.B. 164. In general, the transfer of all substantial rights requires that the transaction transfers exclusive rights to the purchaser that are not limited by time or territory. Nonetheless, in E.I. du Pont de Nemours & Co. v. United States, 432 F.2d 1052 (3d Cir.1970), the court found a transfer of all substantial rights, and hence a sale, despite the fact that the licensor had retained the right to import the product into the territory, to control subsequent sublicensing, and to use the patent with respect to a related product. Bell Intercontinental Corp. v. United States, 381 F.2d 1004 (Ct.Cl.1967), upheld seven of nine agreements transferring patent rights and other intangibles as sales qualifying for capital gain treatment, despite the retention of control over subsequent assignments, the right of the licensor to cancel on failure of the licensee to make minimum payments or in the case of the licensee's insolvency, and the right to bring enforcement actions in its own name. In the other two transfers, no sale was found because the taxpayer retained the right to terminate the agreement at will.

In *Cooper v. Commissioner*, 143 T.C. 194 (2014), the Tax Court held that the transferor of patents to a corporation, in which the transferor held 24 percent of the stock with the remaining stock held by his wife's sister and a friend, in exchange for a royalty did not transfer all substantial rights to the patent and, thus, the royalty receipts constituted ordinary income. The court found that substantially all of the corporation's decisions regarding the patents were made either by the transferor or at his direction. The court reasoned that the transferor's control over the corporation that held the patents prevented the transfer of all substantial rights to the patents.[12]

2.2. *Inventors*

Section 1235 provides capital asset treatment for individuals who are otherwise in the business of developing and selling patents and for whom the patents would normally receive ordinary treatment under § 1221(a)(1). In addition, the section provides sale or exchange treatment for transactions in which contingent or periodic payments are involved, and it allows long-term capital gain treatment regardless of the holding period of the patent.

These favorable results apply only if there has been a transfer of "all substantial rights to a patent or an undivided interest therein which includes a part of all such rights." For cases dealing with the effects of limited

---

[12]   The related party rules of §§ 267(b) and 1235(c), barring capital gain treatment for transfers to related parties, did not apply because the taxpayer's 24 percent stock ownership was below the 25 percent threshold in those provisions.

transfers, see Kueneman v. Commissioner, 68 T.C. 609 (1977); Fawick v. Commissioner, 436 F.2d 655 (6th Cir.1971).

2.3. *Know-How and Other Protected Property*

Patent licensing transactions are frequently accompanied by transfer of nonpatentable know-how, secret formulas, and trade secrets. An initial question is whether the know-how qualifies as "property" for purposes of the capital gain section. Ofria v. Commissioner, 77 T.C. 524 (1981) (Nonacq.), held that industrial data developed under a government contract constituted a capital asset. In an analogous situation, in Rev. Rul. 64–56, 1964–1 C.B. 133, involving transfers of know-how to foreign corporations under § 351, the IRS ruled that know-how was "property" for purposes of § 351 if the information transferred was entitled to substantial legal protection against disclosure under the law of the foreign country. Even if the know-how qualifies as property for capital gain purposes, the transfer must constitute a "sale" to qualify for capital gains treatment. In E.I. Du Pont De Nemours & Co. v. United States, 288 F.2d 904 (Ct.Cl.1961), the taxpayer transferred certain secret processes to a third party, but retained the right to further disclose the process to others. The court, drawing on the patent law analogies, found no sale had taken place where the licensee did not receive the right to prevent the licensor from further disclosure. Commercial Solvents Corp. v. Commissioner, 42 T.C. 455 (1964) (Acq.), and Taylor-Winfield Corp. v. Commissioner, 57 T.C. 205 (1971), aff'd per curiam, 467 F.2d 483 (6th Cir.1972), reached the same result. Pickren v. United States, 378 F.2d 595 (5th Cir.1967), found no sale of trade secrets where the transfer was limited to 25 years and it appeared that the secrets would have a longer useful life.

3. OTHER INTANGIBLE PROPERTY RIGHTS

Prior to the adoption of § 1221(a)(3), the issue arose whether a performer, such as a television star, selling her interest in her show, could obtain capital gain treatment for the portion of the price paid for the show itself apart from the performer's services. The Tax Court had allowed capital gain treatment, stating that the problem was one of ascertaining whether no more than fair value was paid for the capital asset component. Thus, in Benny v. Commissioner, 25 T.C. 197 (1955) (Acq.), capital gain resulted on the sale by Jack Benny to CBS of the stock of a corporation owning the Jack Benny show; Benny's personal services as an entertainer were governed by a separate contract with the sponsor. In Marx v. Commissioner, 29 T.C. 88 (1957) (Acq.), Groucho Marx received capital gain on the sale to NBC of his interest in the "You Bet Your Life" show; Marx had required CBS and NBC to submit sealed bids itemizing the amounts to be paid for the show, for Marx's services as performer, and for Marx's services as a consultant for five years after his services as a performer had ended.

In Runyon, Jr. v. United States, 281 F.2d 590 (5th Cir.1960), the taxpayer, a son of the writer Damon Runyon, received $25,000 for his agreement that a motion picture could be made based on the life of his deceased father and portraying the taxpayer's life as well. The taxpayer claimed that the right of privacy in both his and father's life was "property" and thus a capital asset that he had sold. The court held that under applicable state law, the right of privacy was not a property right, and that, in any event, there was no "sale." A similar result was reached in Miller v. Commissioner, 299 F.2d 706 (2d Cir.1962), involving amounts received by the widow of Glen Miller from a motion picture company in connection with the production of "The Glen Miller Story." The court found the taxpayer had no "property" in the "public image" of the late Mr. Miller.

(4) SECTION 1221(a)(4): ACCOUNTS RECEIVABLE

Section 1221(a)(4) excepts from capital asset classification accounts or notes receivable acquired in the ordinary course of business for services rendered or from the sale of inventory and other property under § 1221(a)(1). As far as cash method taxpayers are concerned, the section serves as a backstop to §§ 1221(a)(1) and (3), preventing a taxpayer from converting a noncapital asset into a claim that arguably could be a capital asset. For accrual method taxpayers, it provides ordinary loss treatment upon the sale of accounts receivable at less than face value.

The courts and IRS have interpreted § 1221(a)(4) to treat loans made by banks and other lending institutions as ordinary assets. Burbank Liquidating Corp. v. Commissioner, 39 T.C. 999 (1963), acq. sub nom. United Associates, Inc., aff'd in part and rev'd in part on other grounds, 335 F.2d 125 (9th Cir. 1964). The more significant aspect of this treatment is that it results in an ordinary, rather than capital loss, if the full amount of the loan is not recovered by the lender, see Rev. Rul. 73–558, 1973–2 C.B. 298 (loss allowed on the exchange of mortgage notes by a savings and loan was ordinary), although it also results in ordinary income treatment in the much less common situation when a loan is sold for more than its basis, see Rev. Rul. 72–238, 1972–1 C.B. 65 (gain realized by bank pursuant to the exchange of defaulted note for the real property is ordinary income).

(5) SECTION 1221(a)(5): GOVERNMENT DOCUMENTS

Section 1221(a)(5) excepts from capital asset classification any publication of the United States Government that is obtained other than by purchase. The exclusion applies to any person who received the publication or whose basis in the publication is determined in whole or in part from the basis of the person who originally received the publication, i.e., through a gift transfer. Thus, receipt and resale of U.S. government publications results in ordinary income. The exclusion does not apply to a taxpayer who acquired governmental publications by purchase at a price for which the publication is offered for sale to the public.

The major impact of § 1221(a)(5) is to limit charitable contribution deductions under § 170(e)(1)(A), which limits the deduction for contribution of capital assets to basis. Thus, a taxpayer who receives a tax-free copy of a U.S. government document cannot claim a charitable contribution deduction for the full value of the document on contribution to a library. See S. Rep. No. 94–938 (Part 2), 1976–3 (Vol. 3) C.B. 643,719. However, in Private Letter Ruling 8240009 (6/23/1982), the IRS ruled that unclassified copies of strike orders for the atomic bomb missions of World War II that the taxpayer recovered from the trash were not capital assets under § 1.1221(a)(5). The IRS reasoned that because the documents were unique and not offered for sale to the general public they were not publications within the meaning of the statute.

(6) SECTION 1221(a)(6): DEALER-HELD COMMODITIES DERIVATIVE FINANCIAL INSTRUMENTS

Section 1221(a)(6) excepts from capital asset classification any "commodities derivative financial instrument" held by a commodities derivatives dealer, unless (1) it is established to the satisfaction of the Commissioner that the particular instrument in question had no connection to the activities of the dealer as a dealer, and (2) the instrument was clearly identified in the dealer's records as having no connection to the dealer activities before the close of the day on which it was acquired, originated, or entered into. The enactment of this section is part of an effort by Congress and the Treasury to deal with innovative Wall Street financial transactions designed to convert ordinary income into capital gains.

(7) SECTION 1221(a)(7): HEDGING TRANSACTIONS

REGULATIONS: Section 1.1221–2.

Section 1221(a)(7) excepts from capital asset classification any "hedging transaction" that is "clearly identified" as such by the taxpayer before the end of the close of the day on which the transaction is entered into. Section 1221(b)(2) defines a hedging transaction as a transaction entered into in the normal course of the taxpayer's trade or business primarily to manage the risk of price changes, currency fluctuations, or interest rate changes with respect to ordinary income producing property held by the taxpayer. Thus, for example, a manufacturer of baked goods fearing an increase in the price of flour may purchase a futures contract for the delivery of one ton of baking flour in six months for a price established in the contract. If the price of flour increases above the price called for in the contract, the manufacturer may take delivery of the flour in-kind, or may sell the contract at a profit. The contract is "property" and its sale would produce gain from the sale of a capital asset absent the exclusion of § 1221(a)(7). If the price of flour should decline, the manufacturer would either pay the contract price for the flour, which is higher than the current market price, or sell the contract at a loss. The loss would be a capital loss, deductible only against capital gain, unless the contract is not treated as a capital asset.

Under the so-called *"Corn Products* doctrine" courts held that property acquired as part of the ordinary course of business as insurance for inventory, or as a substitute for inventory, was not a capital asset. Although this doctrine applied both to gains and losses, assuring ordinary loss treatment was the principal reason for avoiding capital asset status for a hedging contract. In the absence of identification of the contract as a hedging transaction under the terms of § 1221(a)(7), a loss will be treated as a capital loss. Under the regulations, risk management includes transactions entered into to manage an aggregate risk of interest rate changes, price changes, and/or currency fluctuations with respect to ordinary property, ordinary obligations, or borrowings. Treas. Reg. § 1.1221–2(c)(3). Risk management also includes transactions entered into to offset the risk of another hedging transaction. Treas. Reg. § 1.1221–2(d)(3).

Regulations provide that while hedging transactions include any transaction entered into to manage risk, including options and short sales, hedging transactions generally do not include acquisition or sale of a debt instrument, equity security, or annuity contract even if the effect of the transaction is to manage risk. Treas. Reg. § 1.1221–2(a)(2) and (d)(5)(i). The regulations leave open the possibility of future published guidance that would treat some such transactions as hedging transactions.

DETAILED ANALYSIS

1. IDENTIFYING A HEDGING TRANSACTION

Section 1221(a)(7) applies to a hedging transaction that is identified by the close of the day on which the transaction is entered into. Treas. Reg. § 1.1221–2(f)(1). Treas. Reg. § 1.1221–2(f)(2)(i) requires that the taxpayer entering into a hedging transaction also identify the items, or aggregate risk, being hedged, and specify the type of risk that is being hedged. Although identification of the risks being hedged must be made "substantially contemporaneously" with the hedging transactions, the regulations provide that identification within 35 days of entering into the hedging transaction will be considered substantially contemporaneous. Treas. Reg. § 1.1221–2(f)(2)(ii). Treas. Reg. § 1.1221–2(f)(4) sets forth record-keeping requirements for identified hedging transaction.

Identification of a transaction as a hedging transaction is binding on the taxpayer with respect to gain realized on the transaction, which will be treated as ordinary gain. Treas. Reg. § 1.1221–2(g)(1)(i). The regulations provide for capital gain treatment, however, in the case of an "inadvertent" identification of a transaction as a hedging transaction if the identification was due to inadvertent error and all similar transactions are treated consistently by the taxpayer. Treas. Reg. § 1.1221–2(g)(1)(ii). On the loss side, if a transaction that is identified by the taxpayer as a hedging transaction does not meet the definition of a hedging transaction, the character of loss will be determined without regard to whether the transaction is a surrogate for ordinary business transactions; in other words, the loss may be treated as a capital loss under other provisions of § 1221(a).

In this respect, case law predating enactment of § 1221(a)(7) may be relevant in identifying transactions that qualify as hedging transactions.

Failure to identify a transaction as a hedging transaction is binding on the taxpayer, and thus the transaction will be treated as resulting in capital gain or loss on disposition of the position. Treas. Reg. § 1.1221–2(g)(2)(i). Treas. Reg. § 1.1221–2(g)(2)(ii) provides some relief in the case of an inadvertent failure to identify a transaction that qualifies under the definition of a hedging transaction. A transaction not so identified will be treated as a hedging transaction if the transaction meets the definition of a hedging transaction, the taxpayer's failure to identify the transaction as a hedging transaction was due to inadvertent error, and the taxpayer consistently treats such transactions as hedging transactions in all open tax years.

The regulations also contain an anti-abuse provision that treats as ordinary income any gain on transactions that fit within the definition of a hedging transaction, but which are not identified by the taxpayer, where the taxpayer "has no reasonable grounds for treating the transaction as other than a hedging transaction." Reasonable grounds are determined by taking into consideration the nature of the transaction as risk management, the taxpayer's treatment of the transaction for financial accounting or other purposes, and the taxpayer's identification of similar transactions as hedging transactions. Treas. Reg. § 1.1221–2(g)(2)(iii).

Prior to the enactment of § 1221(a)(7), Supreme Court decisions had caused confusion regarding the treatment of hedging transactions. Corn Products Refining Company v. Commissioner, 350 U.S. 46 (1955), held that gains recognized on disposition of futures contracts entered into to protect the taxpayer's source of supplies were to be treated as ordinary gain because the gains were derived from ordinary business activities as an integral part of the business.[13] Taxpayers immediately took advantage of this holding to assert ordinary loss treatment on the sale of property that otherwise clearly constituted a capital asset. See e.g. Booth Newspapers, Inc. v. United States, 303 F.2d 916 (Ct.Cl. 1962), where the taxpayer was allowed to deduct loss on stock of a paper manufacturer purchased to insure a source supply of newsprint. In Arkansas Best Corp. v. Commissioner, 485 U.S. 212 (1988), the Court limited the *Corn Products* doctrine to its facts by interpreting *Corn Products* merely as a broad reading of the inventory exclusion of § 1221(a)(1), meaning that the futures contracts in *Corn Products* were excluded from capital asset status only because the contracts were "surrogates for the stored inventory of raw corn." *Arkansas Best* held that, "The broad definition of the term 'capital asset' explicitly makes irrelevant any consideration of the property's connection with the taxpayer's business." The Court added that the statutory exceptions to the definition of a capital asset are exclusive.

---

[13]   The Court said that, "Congress intended that profits and losses arising from the everyday operation of a business be considered as ordinary income or loss rather than capital gain or loss. The preferential treatment provided by [the capital gain sections] applies to transactions in property which are not the normal source of business income. It was intended 'to relieve the taxpayer from * * * excessive tax burdens on gains resulting from a conversion of capital investments, and to remove the deterrent effect of those burdens on such conversions.' "

After enactment of § 1221(a)(7), the *Corn Products* doctrine largely is an historical footnote, except to the extent that the case law identifying hedging transactions may be relevant to the definition of risk management under § 1221(a)(7). Treas. Reg. § 1.1221–2(a)(3) states that if a transaction is not a hedging transaction as defined in the regulations, "gain or loss from the transaction is not made ordinary on the grounds that property involved in the transaction is a surrogate for a noncapital asset, that the transaction serves as insurance against a business risk, that the transaction serves a hedging function, or that the transaction serves a similar function or purpose." The regulation is consistent with legislative history that indicates that § 1221(a)(7) is intended to supplant the judicially developed doctrines. S. Rep. No. 106–120, 106th Cong., 1st Sess. 196 (1999).

(8) SECTION 1221(a)(8): NON-INVENTORY SUPPLIES

Section 1221(a)(8) excludes supplies of a type regularly used or consumed by the taxpayer in the ordinary course of a trade or business of the taxpayer. In a number of cases, supplies consumed by the taxpayer or the taxpayer's customer in the course of providing services were held not to be inventory for purposes of accounting method rules. See e.g., Osteopathic Medical Oncology and Hematology, P.C. v. Commissioner, 113 T.C. 376 (1999). These cases raised the question of whether such supplies, which have been expensed upon purchase, are capital assets. Section 1221(a)(1) does not expressly exclude stocks of previously expensed supplies used in the course of providing services, and neither does § 1221(a)(2). Section 1221(a)(8) eliminates any question in this regard, relegating supplies to ordinary asset characterization. Section 1221(a)(8) also interacts with § 1221(a)(7) to assure that ordinary gain and loss is realized with respect to hedges of prices for supplies, such as an airline's transactions in jet fuel futures.

B. JUDICIAL LIMITATIONS ON CAPITAL ASSET CLASSIFICATION

Suppose the owner of a building leases the building for 3 years to a tenant. The owner then sells to a third party the right to receive the rent under the lease. A literal application of § 1221 would suggest that the amounts received for the lessor's interest in the lease would qualify for capital gain treatment. The right to receive the rentals is literally "property" and none of the exclusions would by their terms apply. If capital gain treatment could be achieved in this type of situation, taxpayers could convert almost all payment streams into capital gain.

In a slightly different context, suppose that the taxpayer holds only the right to interest payments from a bond (the right to principal being held by another person) and the taxpayer sells the right to the interest to a third party. The right to future interest also is "property" and sale may convert the right to receive ordinary income for a lump sum payment that is capital gain. What if the taxpayer has won a state lottery and receives the right to payments over a term of years, which the taxpayer sells to a third party. Again the right to the future ordinary income is property. Does sale of this "property" generate capital gain? In the absence of adequate statutory treatment, it has fallen to the courts to deal with the problem.

Situations of the type described above generally are governed by the judicial principle that capital gain treatment is not available where the payment is "essentially a substitute for what would otherwise be received at a future time as ordinary income."[14] But this principle proves too much, because the value of property often represents the present value of the stream of anticipated future earnings it will generate and any sale of a capital asset thus reflects in one sense a transfer of those earnings. Suppose that a corporation with increased earnings decides to increase its dividend rate and this decision results in an increase in the value of the stock. If the stock is not sold, the receipt of the increased dividends must remain ordinary income, because otherwise capital gain treatment would be given to current investment income.[15] But a sale of the stock at a profit due to that increase in value produces a capital gain, because otherwise there could hardly be a capital gain concept. This conclusion prevails even though the amount received represents the present value of ordinary income that the recipient would otherwise obtain in the future. Thus, some means must be established to distinguish "investment profit" from "investment income." The extremes may be clear but the area in between offers only gradations, as the subsequent cases indicate.

Hort v. Commissioner

Supreme Court of the United States, 1941.
313 U.S. 28.

■ MR. JUSTICE MURPHY delivered the opinion of the Court.

We must determine whether the amount petitioner received as consideration for cancellation of a lease of realty in New York City was ordinary gross income as defined in [the former version of § 61(a)], and whether in any event, petitioner sustained a loss through cancellation of the lease which is recognized in [the former version of § 165(c)].

Petitioner acquired the property, a lot and ten-story office building, by devise from his father in 1928. At the time he became owner, the premises were leased to a firm which had sublet the main floor to the Irving Trust Co. In 1927, five years before the head lease expired, the Irving Trust Co. and petitioner's father executed a contract in which the latter agreed to lease the main floor and basement to the former for a

---

14   Commissioner v. P.G. Lake, Inc., in Section 2.B. of this Chapter.

15   Since 2003, "qualified" dividends on corporate stock are taxed at the same preferential rates as capital gain. See Chapter 8, Section 3. Nevertheless, dividends technically remain ordinary income and there are other significant differences between ordinary income and capital gains.

term of fifteen years at an annual rental of $25,000, the term to commence at the expiration of the head lease.

In 1933, the Irving Trust Co. found it unprofitable to maintain a branch in petitioner's building. After some negotiations, petitioner and the Trust Co. agreed to cancel the lease in consideration of a payment to petitioner of $140,000. Petitioner did not include this amount in gross income in his income tax return for 1933. On the contrary, he reported a loss of $21,494.75 on the theory that the amount he received as consideration for the cancellation was $21,494.75 less than the difference between the present value of the unmatured rental payments and the fair rental value of the main floor and basement for the unexpired term of the lease. He did not deduct this figure, however, because he reported other losses in excess of gross income.

The Commissioner included the entire $140,000 in gross income, disallowed the asserted loss, made certain other adjustments not material here, and assessed a deficiency. * * * [We have] granted certiorari limited to the question whether, "in computing net gain or loss for income tax purposes, a taxpayer [can] offset the value of the lease canceled against the consideration received by him for the cancellation".

Petitioner apparently contends that the amount received for cancellation of the lease was capital rather than ordinary income and that it was therefore subject to [the provisions] which govern capital gains and losses. Further, he argues that even if that amount must be reported as ordinary gross income he sustained a loss which [§ 165(c)] authorizes him to deduct. We cannot agree.

The amount received by petitioner for cancellation of the lease must be included in his gross income in its entirety. [The former version of § 61(a)] * * * expressly defines gross income to include "gains, profits, and income derived from * * * rent, * * * or gains or profits and income from any source whatever". Plainly this definition reached the rent paid prior to cancellation just as it would have embraced subsequent payments if the lease had never been canceled. It would have included a prepayment of the discounted value of unmatured rental payments whether received at the inception of the lease or at any time thereafter. Similarly, it would have extended to the proceeds of a suit to recover damages had the Irving Trust Co. breached the lease instead of concluding a settlement. Compare United States v. Safety Car Heating Co., 297 U.S. 88; Burnet v. Sanford & Brooks Co., 282 U.S. 359. That the amount petitioner received resulted from negotiations ending in cancellation of the lease rather than from a suit to enforce it cannot alter the fact that basically the payment was merely a substitute for the rent reserved in the lease. So far as the application of [the former version of § 61(a)] is concerned, it is immaterial that petitioner chose to accept an amount less than the strict present value of the unmatured rental payments rather than to engage in litigation, possibly uncertain and expensive.

The consideration received for cancellation of the lease was not a return of capital. We assume that the lease was "property", whatever that signifies abstractly. Presumably, the bond in Helvering v. Horst, 311 U.S. 112, and the lease in Helvering v. Bruun, 309 U.S. 461, were also "property", but the interest coupon in Horst and the building in Bruun nevertheless were held to constitute items of gross income. Simply because the lease was "property" the amount received for its cancellation was not a return of capital, quite apart from the fact that "property" and "capital" are not necessarily synonymous [in the statute] or in common usage. Where, as in this case, the disputed amount was essentially a substitute for rental payments which [the former version of § 61(a)] expressly characterizes as gross income, it must be regarded as ordinary income, and it is immaterial that for some purposes the contract creating the right to such payments may be treated as "property" or "capital".

For the same reasons, that amount was not a return of capital because petitioner acquired the lease as an incident of the realty devised to him by his father. Theoretically, it might have been possible in such a case to value realty and lease separately and to label each a capital asset. * * * . But that would not have converted into capital the amount petitioner received from the Trust Co. since [the former version of § 102] would have required him to include in gross income the rent derived from the property, and that section, like [§ 61(a)], does not distinguish rental payments and a payment which is clearly a substitute for rental payments.

We conclude that petitioner must report as gross income the entire amount received for cancellation of the lease without regard to the claimed disparity between that amount and the difference between the present value of the unmatured rental payments and the fair rental value of the property for the unexpired period of the lease. The cancellation of the lease involved nothing more than relinquishment of the right to future rental payments in return for a present substitute payment and possession of the leased premises. Undoubtedly it diminished the amount of gross income petitioner expected to realize, but to that extent he was relieved of the duty to pay income tax. Nothing in [the former version of § 165(c)] indicates that Congress intended to allow petitioner to reduce ordinary income actually received and reported by the amount of income he failed to realize. * * * We may assume that petitioner was injured insofar as the cancellation of the lease affected the value of the realty. But that would become a deductible loss only when its extent had been fixed by a closed transaction. United States v. White Dental Mfg. Co., 274 U.S. 398.

The judgment of the Circuit Court of Appeals is affirmed.

Commissioner v. P.G. Lake, Inc.

Supreme Court of the United States, 1958.
356 U.S. 260.

■ MR. JUSTICE DOUGLAS delivered the opinion of the Court.

* * * Lake is a corporation engaged in the business of producing oil and gas. It has a seven-eighths working interest[1] in two commercial oil and gas leases. In 1950 it was indebted to its president in the sum of $600,000 and in consideration of his cancellation of the debt assigned him an oil payment right in the amount of $600,000, plus an amount equal to interest at 3 percent a year on the unpaid balance remaining from month to month, payable out of 25 percent of the oil attributable to the taxpayer's working interest in the two leases. At the time of the assignment it could have been estimated with reasonable accuracy that the assigned oil payment right would pay out in three or more years. It did in fact pay out in a little over three years.

In its 1950 tax returns Lake reported the oil payment assignment as a sale of property producing a profit of $600,000 and taxable as a long-term capital gain [under the 1939 code]. The Commissioner determined a deficiency, ruling that the purchase price (less deductions not material here) was taxable as ordinary income, subject to depletion. * * *

First, as to whether the proceeds were taxable as long term taxable gains under [the predecessors of sections 1221, 1222] or as ordinary income subject to depletion. The Court of Appeals started from the premise, laid down in Texas decisions, see especially Tennant v. Dunn, 130 Tex. 285, 110 S.W.2d 53, that oil payments are interests in land. We too proceed on that basis; and yet we conclude that the consideration received for these oil payment rights (and the sulphur payment right) was taxable as ordinary income, subject to depletion.

The purpose of [the capital gain sections] was "to relieve the taxpayer from * * * excessive tax burdens on gains resulting from a conversion of capital investments, and to remove the deterrent effect of those burdens on such conversions." See Burnet v. Harmel, 287 U.S. 103, 106. And this exception has always been narrowly construed so as to protect the revenue against artful devices. See Corn Products Refining Co. v. Commissioner, 350 U.S. 46, 52.

We do not see here any conversion of a capital investment. The lump sum consideration seems essentially a substitute for what would otherwise be received at a future time as ordinary income. The payout of

---

[1]   An oil and gas lease ordinarily conveys the entire mineral interest less any royalty interest retained by the lessor. The owner of the lease is said to own the "working interest" because he has the right to develop and produce the minerals.

In Anderson v. Helvering, 310 U.S. 404, * * * , we described an oil payment as "the right to a specified sum of money, payable out of a specified percentage of the oil, or the proceeds received from the sale of such oil, if, as and when produced." * * * A royalty interest is "a right to receive a specified percentage of all oil and gas produced" but, unlike the oil payment, is not limited to a specified sum of money. The royalty interest lasts during the entire term of the lease. * * *

these particular assigned oil payment rights could be ascertained with considerable accuracy. Such are the stipulations, findings, or clear inferences. In the O'Connor case, the pay-out of the assigned oil payment right was so assured that the purchaser obtained a $9,990,350 purchase money loan at 3½ percent interest without any security other than a deed of trust of the $10,000,000 oil payment right, he receiving 4 percent from the taxpayer. Only a fraction of the oil or sulphur rights were transferred, the balance being retained. * * * Cash was received which was equal to the amount of the income to accrue during the term of the assignment, the assignee being compensated by interest on his advance. The substance of what was assigned was the right to receive future income. The substance of what was received was the present value of income which the recipient would otherwise obtain in the future. In short, consideration was paid for the right to receive future income, not for an increase in the value of the income-producing property.

These arrangements seem to us transparent devices. Their forms do not control. Their essence is determined not by subtleties of draftsmanship but by their total effect. See Helvering v. Clifford, 309 U.S. 331 * * * . We have held that if one, entitled to receive at a future date interest on a bond or compensation for services, makes a grant of it by anticipatory assignment, he realizes taxable income as if he had collected the interest or received the salary and then paid it over. That is the teaching of Helvering v. Horst, 311 U.S. 112, and Harrison v. Schaffner, [312 U.S. 579 (1941)]; and it is applicable here. As we stated in Helvering v. Horst, supra, 311 U.S. at 117, "The taxpayer has equally enjoyed the fruits of his labor or investment and obtained the satisfaction of his desires whether he collects and uses the income to procure those satisfactions, or whether he disposes of his right to collect it as the means of procuring them." There the taxpayer detached interest coupons from negotiable bonds and presented them as a gift to his son. The interest when paid was held taxable to the father. Here, even more clearly than there, the taxpayer is converting future income into present income.

Lattera v. Commissioner

United States Court of Appeals, Third Circuit, 2006.
437 F.3d 399.

■ AMBRO, CIRCUIT JUDGE. Lottery winners, after receiving several annual installments of their lottery prize, sold for a lump sum the right to their remaining payments. They reported their sale proceeds as capital gains on their tax return, but the Internal Revenue Service (IRS) classified those proceeds as ordinary income. The substitute-for-ordinary-income doctrine holds that lump-sum consideration substituting for something that would otherwise be received at a future time as ordinary income should be taxed the same way. We agree with the Commissioner of the IRS that the lump-sum consideration paid for the right to lottery payments is ordinary income.

I.   Factual Background and Procedural History

In June 1991 George and Angeline Lattera turned a one-dollar lottery ticket into $9,595,326 in the Pennsylvania Lottery. They did not then have the option to take the prize in a single lump-sum payment, so they were entitled to 26 annual installments of $369,051.

In September 1999 the Latteras sold their rights to the 17 remaining lottery payments to Singer Asset Finance Co., LLC for $3,372,342. * * *

On their joint tax return, the Latteras reported this sale as the sale of a capital asset held for more than one year. They reported a sale price of $3,372,342, a cost or other basis of zero, and a long-term capital gain of the full sale price. The Commissioner determined that this sale price was ordinary income. In December 2002 the Latteras were sent a notice of deficiency of $660,784.

In March 2003 the Latteras petitioned the Tax Court for a redetermination of the deficiency. The Court held in favor of the Commissioner. The Latteras now appeal to our Court.

* * *

III. Discussion

The lottery payments the Latteras had a right to receive were gambling winnings, and the parties agree that the annual payments were ordinary income. * * * (calling a state lottery "public gambling" in a case treating gambling winnings as ordinary income). But the Latteras argue that when they sold the right to their remaining lottery payments, that sale gave rise to a long-term capital gain.

Whether the sale of a right to lottery payments by a lottery winner can be treated as a capital gain under the Internal Revenue Code is one of first impression in our Circuit. But it is not a new question. Both the Tax Court and the Ninth Circuit Court of Appeals have held that such sales deserve ordinary-income treatment. United States v. Maginnis, 356 F.3d 1179, 1181 (9th Cir.2004) ("Fundamental principles of tax law lead us to conclude that [the] assignment of [a] lottery right produced ordinary income."); Davis v. Comm'r, 119 T.C. 1 * * * .

The Ninth Circuit's reasoning has drawn significant criticism, however. See Matthew S. Levine, Case Comment, Lottery Winnings as Capital Gains, 114 Yale L.J. 195, 197–202 (2004); Thomas G. Sinclair, Comment, Limiting the Substitute-for-Ordinary Income Doctrine: An Analysis Through Its Most Recent Application Involving the Sale of Future Lottery Rights, 56 S.C. L.Rev. 387, 421–22 (2004). In this context, we propose a different approach. We begin with a discussion of basic concepts that underlie our reasoning.

A.   Definition of a capital asset

A long-term capital gain (or loss) is created by the "sale or exchange of a capital asset held for more than 1 year." I.R.C. § 1222(3). Section 1221 of the Internal Revenue Code defines a capital asset as "property held by the taxpayer (whether or not connected with his trade or business)." This provision excludes from the definition certain property categories, none of which is applicable here.

A 1960 Supreme Court decision suggested that this definition can be construed too broadly, stating that "it is evident that not everything which can be called property in the ordinary sense and which is outside the statutory exclusions qualifies as a capital asset." Comm'r v. Gillette Motor Transp., Inc., 364 U.S. 130, 134 * * * (1960). The Court noted that it had "long held that the term 'capital asset' is to be construed narrowly in accordance with the purpose of Congress to afford capital-gains treatment only in situations typically involving the realization of appreciation in value accrued over a substantial period of time, and thus to ameliorate the hardship of taxation of the entire gain in one year." Id. But the Supreme Court's decision in Arkansas Best Corp. v. Commissioner, 485 U.S. 212 * * * (1988), at least at first blush, seems to have reversed that narrow reading. *Arkansas Best* suggests instead that the capital-asset definition is to be broadly construed. See id. at 218 * * * ("The body of § 1221 establishes a general definition of the term 'capital asset,' and the phrase 'does not include' takes out of that broad definition only the classes of property that are specifically mentioned.").

B.   The substitute-for-ordinary-income doctrine

The problem with an overly broad definition for capital assets is that it could "encompass some things Congress did not intend to be taxed as capital gains." *Maginnis*, 356 F.3d at 1181. An overly broad definition, linked with favorable capital-gains tax treatment, would encourage transactions designed to convert ordinary income into capital gains. * * * For example, a salary is taxed as ordinary income, and the right to be paid for work is a person's property. But it is hard to conceive that Congress intends for taxpayers to get capital-gains treatment if they were to sell their rights (i.e., "property held by the taxpayer") to their future paychecks. See 2 Boris I. Bittker & Lawrence Lokken, Federal Taxation of Income, Estates and Gifts ¶ 47.1 (3d ed.2000).

To get around this problem, courts have created the substitute-for-ordinary-income doctrine. This doctrine says, in effect, that " 'lump sum consideration [that] seems essentially a substitute for what would otherwise be received at a future time as ordinary income' may not be taxed as a capital gain." *Maginnis*, 356 F.3d at 1182 (quoting *Comm'r v. P.G. Lake, Inc.*, 356 U.S. 260, 265 * * * (1958)) (alteration in original).

The seminal substitute-for-ordinary-income case is the 1941 Supreme Court decision in Hort v. Commissioner, 313 U.S. 28 * * * (1941). * * * The Supreme Court bolstered the doctrine in *Lake*. P.G. Lake, Inc. was an oil-and gas-producing company with a working interest in two oil and gas leases. 356 U.S. at 261–62 * * *

* * *

But there is a tension in the doctrine: in theory, all capital assets are substitutes for ordinary income. See, e.g., William A. Klein et al., Federal Income Taxation 786 (12th ed. 2000) ("A fundamental principle of economics is that the value of an asset is equal to the present discounted value of all the expected net receipts from that asset over its life."); see also *Lake,* 356 U.S. at 266 * * * (noting that the lump-sum consideration-held to be ordinary income-paid for an asset was "the present value of income which the recipient would otherwise obtain in the future"). For example, a stock's value is the present discounted value of the company's future profits. See, e.g., *Maginnis,* 356 F.3d at 1182 * * * . "[R]ead literally, the [substitute-for-ordinary-income] doctrine would completely swallow the concept of capital gains." Levine, supra, at 196; accord 2 Bittker & Lokken, supra, ¶ 47.9.5, at 47–68 ("Unless restrained, the substitute-for-ordinary-income theory thus threatens even the most familiar capital gain transactions."). Also, an "overbroad 'substitute for ordinary income' doctrine, besides being analytically unsatisfactory, would create the potential for the abuse of treating capital losses as ordinary."[3] Levine, supra, at 197. The doctrine must therefore be limited so as not to err on either side.

C. The lottery cases

Even before the Ninth Circuit decided *Maginnis,* the Tax Court had correctly answered the question of whether sales of lottery winnings were capital gains. In *Davis v. Commissioner,* lottery winners had sold their rights to 11 of their total 14 future lottery payments for a lump sum. * * * The Tax Court found that the lump-sum payment to the lottery winners was the "discounted value of certain ordinary income which they otherwise would have received during the years 1997 through 2007." * * * The Court held, therefore, that (1) the purchaser of the lottery payment rights paid money for "the right to receive future ordinary income, and not for an increase in the value of income-producing property"; (2) the lottery winners' right to their future lottery payments was not a capital asset; and (3) the lump-sum payment was to be taxed as ordinary income. Id.; see also *Watkins,* 88 T.C.M. (CCH) at 393 (following *Davis,* in a post-*Maginnis* decision); *Clopton,* 87 T.C.M. (CCH) at 1219 (citing Tax Court cases following *Davis*).

In 2004 the Ninth Circuit decided *Maginnis,* the first * * * appellate opinion to deal with this question. Maginnis won $9 million in a lottery and, after receiving five of his lottery payments, assigned all of his remaining future lottery payments to a third party for a lump-sum payment of $3,950,000. Maginnis * * * . The Ninth Circuit held that Maginnis's right to future lottery payments was not a capital asset and that the lump-sum payment was to be taxed as ordinary income.

---

[3]   Note that our holding in this case does not consider the substitute-for-ordinary-income doctrine in loss transactions.

The Court relied on the substitute-for-ordinary-income doctrine, but it was concerned about taking an "approach that could potentially convert all capital gains into ordinary income [or] one that could convert all ordinary income into capital gains." * * * The Court opted instead for "case-by-case judgments as to whether the conversion of income rights into lump-sum payments reflects the sale of a capital asset that produces a capital gain, or whether it produces ordinary income." * * * It set out two factors, which it characterized as "crucial to [its] conclusion," but not "dispositive in all cases": "Maginnis (1) did not make any underlying investment of capital in return for the receipt of his lottery right, and (2) the sale of his right did not reflect an accretion in value over cost to any underlying asset Maginnis held." * * *

* * *

[W]hile we agree with *Maginnis's* result, we do not simply adopt its reasoning. And it is both unsatisfying and unhelpful to future litigants to declare that we know this to be ordinary income when we see it. The problem is that, "[u]nless and until Congress establishes an arbitrary line on the otherwise seamless spectrum between *Hort-Lake* transactions and conventional capital gain transactions, the courts must locate the boundary case by case, a process that can yield few useful generalizations because there are so many relevant but imponderable criteria." 2 Bittker & Lokken, supra, ¶ 47.9.5, at 47–69 (footnote omitted).

We therefore proceed to our case-by-case analysis, but in doing so we set out a method for analysis that guides our result. At the same time, however, we recognize that any rule we create could not account for every contemplated transactional variation.

D.   Substitute-for-ordinary-income analysis

In our attempt to craft a rubric, we find helpful a Second Circuit securities case and a recent student comment. The Second Circuit dealt with a similarly "seamless spectrum" in 1976 when it needed to decide whether a note was a security for purposes of section 10(b) of the 1934 Securities and Exchange Act. See *Exch. Nat'l Bank of Chi. v. Touche Ross & Co.*, 544 F.2d 1126, 1138 (2d Cir.1976). The Court created a "family resemblance" test, (1) presuming that notes of more than nine months' maturity were securities, (2) listing various types of those notes that it did not consider securities, and (3) declaring that a note with maturity exceeding nine months that "does not bear a strong family resemblance to these examples" was a security. * * * The Supreme Court, adopting this test in 1990, added four factors to guide the "resemblance" analysis: the motivations of the buyers and sellers, the plan of distribution, the public's reasonable expectations, and applicable risk-reducing regulatory schemes. *Reves v. Ernst & Young*, 494 U.S. 56, 65–67 * * * (1990).

We adopt an analogous analysis. Several types of assets we know to be capital: stocks, bonds, options, and currency contracts, for example. See, e.g., *Arkansas Best*, 485 U.S. at 222–23 * * * (holding-even though, as noted above, the value of a stock is really the present discounted value of the company's future profits-that "stock is most naturally viewed as a capital asset"); see also id. at 217 n. 5* * * (distinguishing "capital stock" from "a claim to ordinary income"); *Simpson v. Comm'r*, 85 T.C.M. (CCH) 1421, 1423 n. 7 (2003) (distinguishing "currency contracts, stocks, bonds, and options" from a right to receive lottery payments). We could also include in this category physical assets like land and automobiles.

Similarly, there are several types of rights that we know to be ordinary income, e.g., rental income and interest income. In *Gillette Motor*, the Supreme Court held that ordinary-income treatment was indicated for the right to use another's property-rent, in other words. See 364 U.S. at 135 * * * . Similarly, in *Midland-Ross*, the Supreme Court held that earned original issue discount should be taxed as ordinary income. See *United States v. Midland-Ross Corp.*, 381 U.S. 54, 58 * * * (1965). There, the taxpayer purchased non-interest-bearing notes at a discount from the face amount and sold them for more than their issue price (but still less than the face amount). * * * . This gain was conceded to be equivalent to interest, and the Court held it taxable as ordinary income. * * *

For the "family resemblance" test, we can set those two categories at the opposite poles of our analysis. For example, we presume that stock, and things that look and act like stock, will receive capital-gains treatment. For the in-between transactions that do not bear a family resemblance to the items in either category, like contracts and payment rights, we use two factors to assist in our analysis: (1) type of "carve-out" and (2) character of asset.

1.   Type of carve-out

The notion of the carve-out, or partial sale, has significant explanatory power in the context of the *Hort-Lake* line of cases. As Marvin Chirelstein writes, the " 'substitute' language, in the view of most commentators, was merely a short-hand way of asserting that carved-out interests do not qualify as capital assets." Marvin A. Chirelstein, *Federal Income Taxation* ¶ 17.03, at 369–70 (9th ed.2002).

There are two ways of carving out interests from property: horizontally and vertically. A horizontal carve-out is one in which "temporal divisions [are made] in a property interest in which the person owning the interest disposes of part of his interest but also retains a portion of it." Sinclair, supra, at 401. In lottery terms, this is what happened in *Davis*, *Boehme*, and *Clopton*-the lottery winners sold some of their future lottery payment rights (e.g., their 2006 and 2007 payments) but retained the rights to payments further in the future (e.g., their 2008 and 2009 payments). See *Clopton*, 87 T.C.M. (CCH) at 1217–18 (finding that the lottery winner sold only some of his remaining lottery payments); *Boehme*, 85 T.C.M. (CCH) at 1040 (same); *Davis*, 119 T.C. at 3 (same). This is also what happened in *Hort* and *Lake*; portions of the total interest (a term of years carved out from a fee simple and a three-year payment right from a working interest in a [*sic*] oil lease, respectively) were carved out from the whole.

A vertical carve-out is one in which "a complete disposition of a person's interest in property" is made. * * * In lottery terms, this is what happened in *Watkins* and *Maginnis*—the lottery winners sold the rights to all their remaining lottery payments. * * *

Horizontal carve-outs typically lead to ordinary-income treatment. See, e.g., *Maginnis*, 356 F.3d at 1185–86 ("Maginnis is correct that transactions in which a tax-payer transfers an income right without transferring his entire interest in an underlying asset will often be occasions for applying the substitute for ordinary income doctrine."). This was also the result reached in *Hort* and *Lake*. * * *

Vertical carve-outs are different. In *Dresser Indust*, for example, the Fifth Circuit distinguished Lake because the taxpayer in *Dresser* had "cut [ ] off a 'vertical slice' of its rights, rather than carv[ed] out an interest from the totality of its rights." *Dresser Indus.*, 324 F.2d at 58. But as the results in *Maginnis* and *Watkins* demonstrate, a vertical carve-out does not necessarily mean that the transaction receives capital-gains treatment. See, e.g., *Maginnis*, 356 F.3d at 1185 (holding "that a transaction in which a taxpayer sells his entire interest in an underlying asset without retaining any property right does not automatically prevent application of the substitute for ordinary income doctrine" (emphasis in original)) * * * .

Because a vertical carve-out could signal either capital-gains or ordinary-income treatment, we must make another determination to conclude with certainty which treatment should apply. Therefore, when we see a vertical carve-out, we proceed to the second factor-character of the asset-to determine whether the sale proceeds should be taxed as ordinary income or capital gain.

2. Character of the asset

The Fifth Circuit in *Dresser Industries* noted that "[t]here is, in law and fact, a vast difference between the present sale of the future right to earn income and the present sale of the future right to earned income." *Dresser Indus.*, 324 F.2d at 59 (emphasis in original). The taxpayer in Dresser Industries had assigned its right to an exclusive patent license back to the patent holder in exchange for a share of the licensing fees from third-party licensees. * * * The Court used this "right to earn income"/"right to earned income" distinction to hold that capital-gains treatment was applicable. It noted that the asset sold was not a "right to earned income, to be paid in the future," but was "a property which would produce income." * * * Further, it disregarded the ordinary nature of the income generated by the asset; because "all income-producing property" produces ordinary income, the sale of such property does not result in ordinary-income treatment. * * * (This can be seen in the sale of stocks or bonds, both of which produce ordinary income, but the sale of which is treated as capital gain.)

Sinclair explains the concept in this way: "Earned income conveys the concept that the income has already been earned and the holder of the right to this income only has to collect it. In other words, the owner of the right to earned income is entitled to the income merely by virtue of owning the property." * * * He gives as examples of this concept rental income, stock dividends, and rights to future lottery payments * * * ; see also *Rhodes' Estate v. Comm'r*, 131 F.2d 50, 50 (6th Cir.1942) (*per curiam*) (holding that a sale of dividend rights is taxable as ordinary income). For the right to earn income, on the other hand, "the holder of such right must do something further to earn the income [because] mere ownership of the right to earn income does not entitle the owner to income." Sinclair, supra, at 406. Following *Dresser Industries*, Sinclair gives a patent as an example of this concept. * * *

Assets that constitute a right to earn income merit capital-gains treatment, while those that are a right to earned income merit ordinary-income treatment. Our Court implicitly made this distinction in *Tunnell v. United States*, 259 F.2d 916 (3d Cir.1958). Tunnell withdrew from a law partnership, and he assigned his rights in the law firm in exchange for $27,500. * * * When he withdrew, the partnership had over $21,000 in uncollected accounts receivable from work that had already been done. Id. We agreed with the District Court that "the sale of a partnership is treated as the sale of a capital asset." * * * . The sale of a partnership does not, in and of itself, confer income on the buyer; the buyer must continue to provide legal services, so it is a sale of the right to earn income. Consequently, as we held, the sale of a partnership receives capital-gains treatment. The accounts receivable, on the other hand, had already been earned; the buyer of the partnership only had to remain a partner to collect that income, so the sale of accounts receivable is the sale of the right to earned income. Thus, we held that the portion of the purchase price that reflected the sale of the accounts receivable was taxable as ordinary income. * * *

Similarly, when an erstwhile employee is paid a termination fee for a personal-services contract, that employee still possesses the asset (the right to provide certain personal services) and the money (the termination fee) has already been "earned" and will simply be paid. The employee no longer has to perform any more services in exchange for the fee, so this is not like Dresser Industries's "right to earn income." These termination fees are therefore rights to earned income and should be treated as ordinary income. See, e.g., *Elliott v. United States*, 431 F.2d 1149, 1154 (10th Cir.1970); *Holt v. Comm'r*, 303 F.2d 687, 690 (9th Cir.1962) * * * .

* * * *

E.   Application of the "family resemblance" test

Applied to this case, the "family resemblance" test draws out as follows. First, we try to determine whether an asset is like either the "capital asset" category of assets (e.g., stocks, bonds, or land) or like the "income items" category (e.g., rental income or interest income). If the asset does not bear a family resemblance to items in either of those categories, we move to the following factors.

We look at the nature of the sale. If the sale or assignment constitutes a horizontal carve-out, then ordinary-income treatment presumably applies. If, on the other hand, it constitutes a vertical carve-out, then we look to the character-of-the-asset factor. There, if the sale is a lump-sum payment for a future right to earned income, we apply ordinary-income treatment, but if it is a lump-sum payment for a future right to earn income, we apply capital-gains treatment.

Turning back to the Latteras, the right to receive annual lottery payments does not bear a strong family resemblance to either the "capital assets" or the "income items" listed at the polar ends of the analytical spectrum. The Latteras sold their right to all their remaining lottery payments, so this is a vertical carve-out, which could indicate either capital-gains or ordinary-income treatment. But because a right to lottery payments is a right to earned income (i.e., the payments will keep arriving due simply to ownership of the asset), the lump-sum payment received by the Latteras should receive ordinary-income treatment.

This result comports with *Davis* and *Maginnis*. It also ensures that the Latteras do not "receive a tax advantage as compared to those taxpayers who would simply choose originally to accept their lottery winning in the form of a lump sum payment," something that was also important to the *Maginnis* Court. * * * .[6]

IV. Conclusion

The lump-sum consideration paid to the Latteras in exchange for the right to their future lottery payments is ordinary income.[7] We therefore affirm.

---

[6]   We do not decide whether Singer, who purchased the right to lottery payments from the Latteras, would receive ordinary income or capital gain if it later decided to sell that right to another third party. * * * Such a determination would need to be made on the specific facts of the transaction. * * *

[7]   The Latteras appear to argue that their lottery ticket was itself a capital asset. We do not need to address this issue, as we note that the Latteras did not sell their winning ticket to Singer. Instead, they relinquished it in 1991 to the Pennsylvania State Lottery so they could claim their prize. They sold Singer eight years later not the physical lottery ticket but their right to the annual lottery payments.

DETAILED ANALYSIS

1. THE RELEVANCE OF A VERTICAL VERSUS A HORIZONTAL CARVE-OUT

The result in *Hort* is clear enough, even though some aspects of the analysis are somewhat obscure: amounts received for the cancellation of a lease are ordinary income with no reduction for any basis that might be attributable to the lease. The Court stressed the fact that rental payments that would have been paid in the absence of the cancellation would have been ordinary income and therefore required that the proceeds on cancellation be treated in the same fashion. The payment was "merely a substitute for the rent reserved in the lease." *P.G. Lake* and *Hort* are similar in that in both situations the taxpayers disposed of a portion of the property while retaining the balance. As in *Hort*, the Court in *P.G. Lake* stressed that the payments were a substitute for what would have otherwise been received at a future time as ordinary income. However, the Court's reasoning in *P.G. Lake*, unlike in *Hort*, makes no reference to the fact that an interest in the leasehold was retained; the analysis is based solely on the "substitute for ordinary income" line of reasoning.

Suppose that the taxpayer in *P.G. Lake* had sold its entire leasehold interest. The sales price would have included the current value of the future oil payments. In that instance, the Supreme Court's analysis likely would have been different. In *McAllister v. Commissioner*, 157 F.2d 235 (2d Cir.1946), the Second Circuit Court of Appeals accorded capital gain treatment to a taxpayer who sold her entire life estate in a trust. Because the taxpayer in *McAllister* transferred everything she owned, the court distinguished *Hort*, reasoning that "the distinction seems logically and practically to turn upon anticipation of income payments over a reasonably short period of time and an out-and-out transfer of a substantial and durable property interest, such as a life estate at least is."

The Third Circuit's *Lattera* opinion dismissed *McAllister* in a footnote, calling it "an aberration" that it did "not find it persuasive." The *Lattera* court reasoned that although McAllister sold a vertical carve-out, potentially susceptible to either capital gain or ordinary income treatment under the *Lattera* analysis, the sale proceeds should have received ordinary-income treatment because McAllister gave up her right to earned income, since she would have continued receiving payments simply by holding the life estate. However, if the taxpayer in *P.G. Lake* had sold its entire leasehold interest, despite the fact that the payment received for the leasehold interest would have been a substitute for the ordinary income payments that would have been received in the normal course, unlike the situation in *Lattera* and *McAllister*, had the taxpayer in *P.G. Lake* retained the leasehold, it would not have produced income merely by continuing to hold the leasehold. Thus, unlike in *Lattera* and *McAllister*, the income stream in *P.G. Lake* would not have already been "earned" at the time of the sale under the *Lattera* analysis.

Unlike *Lattera*, the opinions of every other court that has considered the treatment of the taxpayer who sells an interest in future lottery winnings for a lump-sum payment has simply read *P.G. Lake* as requiring ordinary treatment under the "substitute for ordinary income" principle, regardless of whether the taxpayer sold the right to all or some of the payments.

In Prebola v. Commissioner, 482 F.3d 610 (2d Cir. 2007), the Second Circuit Court of Appeals—the circuit that decided *McAllister*—held that the sale of all a lottery winner's rights to future installments gave rise to ordinary income rather than capital gain, relying on the reasoning of *Davis* and *Maginnis*. The court stated: "We recognize that there are contexts in which the substitute-for-ordinary-income doctrine does not or should not apply. . . . But whatever the doctrine's outer limits, this case falls squarely within them." The court largely ignored *McAllister* as a precedent, but specifically noted that *McAllister* was decided before the Supreme Court decided *P.G. Lake*. The *Prebola* opinion thus appears to have completed the consignment of *McAllister* to the dust bin of history, and for the most part to have rendered moot the distinction between vertical and horizontal carve-outs.

2.   OTHER CONTRACTUAL ARRANGEMENTS

2.1. *Generally*

A contract right may constitute "property" in a general sense but still not rise to the dignity of a "capital asset" despite the language of § 1221. In Commissioner v. Gillette Motor Transport, Inc., 364 U.S. 130 (1960), the taxpayer received an award from the Motor Carrier's Commission representing compensation for a taking of "property" as a result of the Government having taken over the operation of taxpayer's transportation business during World War II. The Court held that the payment constituted ordinary income in the nature of rent for the right to use the taxpayer's transportation facilities:

> While a capital asset is defined in [§ 1221] as "property held by the taxpayer," it is evident that not everything which can be called property in the ordinary sense and which is outside the statutory exclusions qualifies as a capital asset. This Court has long held that the term "capital asset" is to be construed narrowly in accordance with the purpose of Congress to afford capital gains treatment only in situations typically involving the realization of appreciation in value accrued over a substantial period of time, and thus to ameliorate the hardship of taxation of the entire gain in one year.

The IRS has applied the *Gillette Motor Transport* principle to employment contracts, ruling that payments received from an employer in consideration of the cancellation of an employment contract are ordinary income, and not capital gain, because the amount is not received as a "payment for property." Rev. Rul. 2004–110, 2004–2 C.B. 960.

In Commissioner v. Ferrer, 304 F.2d 125 (2d Cir.1962), the court attempted to distinguish between disposition of different kinds of contract rights for future payments of ordinary income. Jose Ferrer acquired the rights to produce a play from the novel "Moulin Rouge" from its author, Pierre LaMure, which included the right to prevent disposition of motion picture rights until the play had run for a specified period of time. Before he produced the play, Ferrer agreed to a disposition of the motion picture rights to a company created by the director John Huston for the purpose of making the film. As provided in his original contract with LaMure, Ferrer received an interest in the net profits of the film as consideration for release of his rights. Ferrer also was hired as an actor in the film for a specified salary. Ferrer reported the payments received under his net profits interest as long-term capital gain. The court identified three separate bundles of rights transferred by Ferrer, two of which produced capital gains. First, Ferrar transferred a "lease" of the play itself. The court analogized this property interest to a lease of property that was transferable at capital gains rates.

> We see no basis for holding that amounts paid Ferrer for surrender of his lease of the play are excluded from capital gain treatment because receipts from the play would have been ordinary income. The latter is equally true if a lessee of real property sells or surrenders a lease from which he is receiving business income or subrentals; * * * . Likewise we find nothing in the statute that forbids capital gain treatment because the payment to Ferrer might be spread over a number of years rather than coming in a lump sum.

Second, Ferrer was found to possess a negative power to prevent disposition of motion picture, radio, and television rights until after production of the play. The court concluded that this right, which was enforceable in equity, represented an equitable interest in a portion of the author's copyright. As an equitable interest in property, the contract right also was transferable as a capital asset. Third, Ferrer was found to possess a right to a percentage of the proceeds of the motion picture if he produced the play. Here the court concluded that Ferrer had no rights in the motion picture itself, other than a right to receive a share of the proceeds:

> Ferrer [never] had, or ever would have, an affirmative equitable interest in the motion picture or other rights, as distinguished from his temporary negative "encumbrance" on them.

> It follows that if Ferrer had produced the play and LaMure had sold the motion picture, radio and television rights for a percentage of the profits, Ferrer's 40% of that percentage would have been ordinary income and not the sale or exchange of a capital asset. The decisions in *Hort* * * * point to what would seem the inevitable corollary that if, on the same facts, Ferrer had then sold his rights to a percentage of the profits for a lump sum, that, too, would have been ordinary income * * * .

Thus, as distinguished from what the court considered to be sale of an interest in "property," payment for the contract right to future income was taxable as ordinary income.

Ferrer started out on his tax journey with the right to expend personal efforts to produce a play; if carried to fruition, this activity would have produced ordinary income. Under the contract that Ferrer signed with the motion picture company, he ended his tax journey rendering personal services as an actor in a motion picture. Somewhere in this process, despite the pervasive aura of personal services, the Court of Appeals converted a significant portion of the receipts into capital gain.

The approaches in the cases addressing the capital asset status of contract rights may be grouped into three broad categories, although many of these cases contain elements of several different theories. First, is the asset "property" considered a "capital asset" under § 1221? The court in *Ferrer* adopted this definitional approach. Second, do the amounts received by the taxpayer upon the assignment or release of contract rights represent a substitute for future ordinary income that would otherwise have been received by the taxpayer? Cases adopting this approach follow the holding in *Hort*, including *Ferrer*, which hints at this doctrine when discussing the third interest transferred by the taxpayer. Third, does the transaction constitute a "sale or exchange?"[16] The sale or exchange requirement, which is largely though not entirely moribund as a result of § 1243A in 1997, is considered in Section 3 of this chapter.

The substitute for ordinary income principle is not rigorously applied to gains from the sale of life insurance policies. Rev. Rul. 2009–13, 2009–21 I.R.B. 1029, held that if a life insurance contract with a cash surrender value is sold by the insured to an unrelated person who would not suffer loss if the beneficiary died, only the portion of the gain realized on the sale that reflects the inside build-up of the cash surrender value immediately prior to the sale is ordinary income, and any excess amount is capital gain, even though if the entire policy were surrendered to the insurer for cash, all of the gain would be ordinary income. (The amount of gain realized on a sale is the amount received on the sale minus the adjusted basis in contract, which is the amount of premiums paid minus an amount to properly reflect "cost of insurance.") If a term life insurance contract with no cash surrender value is sold, the entire amount recognized is long-term capital gain; because the cost of insurance each month is presumed to be equal to the premiums paid, there is no inside build-up under the contract. Rev. Rul. 2009–14, 2009–21 I.R.B. 1031, held that all of the gain recognized on sale of a life insurance policy by a taxpayer who had purchased the policy as an investment from the insured, to whom the policy had originally been issued, and who had no insurable interest is capital gain, notwithstanding that the full amount of the proceeds minus the basis in the contract is ordinary income if the purchaser holds the contract until the insured's death and collects the death benefit.

2.2. *Is the Contract Right "Property" Qualifying as a Capital Asset?*

In Martin v. Commissioner, 50 T.C. 341 (1968) (Acq.), the taxpayer, a Broadway producer, entered into a contract with his playwrights, entitling him to receive a share in the motion picture proceeds from the play "Guys and Dolls" if the motion picture rights to the play itself were sold by the playwrights. The court held that amounts received by the taxpayer upon sale of the motion picture rights by the playwrights were ordinary income. The court found that there was no sale or exchange of any asset because the

---

16   This classification system is based on that developed by Professor Eustice in his analysis of the *Ferrer* decision and the cases decided prior to it. See Eustice, Contract Rights, Capital Gain and Assignment of Income—The Ferrer Case, 15 Tax L.Rev. 1 (1964).

taxpayer at no time had any interest in the underlying movie rights. On the other hand, where the taxpayer purchased dramatization rights in other plays, and subsequently sold the movie rights himself, amounts received were held to constitute capital gain since there was a substantial capital investment by the taxpayer.

In Bellamy v. Commissioner, 43 T.C. 487 (1965), an actor entered into an employment agreement to perform a television series. Under his contract, the taxpayer had the right to prevent the showing of reruns after a specified period. He released those rights for $89,000. The court held that he realized ordinary income, emphasizing that his interest exclusively involved his personal services. The Tax Court distinguished *Ferrer* on the ground that Ferrer had an investment in the "lease" of the play. Anderson v. United States, 468 F.Supp. 1085 (D.Minn.1979), aff'd by order, 624 F.2d 1109 (8th Cir.1980), involved a taxpayer who had a 30-day right of refusal that had been granted to him by a franchised hotel organization (Holiday Inn). The hotel organization agreed not to grant anyone else a franchise in the area without first giving the taxpayer an opportunity to obtain the franchise. Subsequently, the hotel organization paid the taxpayer $100,000 for the release of his right. The court found that the payment qualified for capital gain treatment. It analogized the right of first refusal to the contractual right in *Ferrer* allowing Ferrer to prevent any disposition of the motion picture rights for a specified period of time. The taxpayer's "negative power" to prevent the hotel organization from establishing an additional franchise in the area was enforceable in equity and was "property in the nature of a capital asset."

The taxpayers in Foy v. Commissioner, 84 T.C. 50 (1985), sold contract rights in a janitorial and building maintenance franchise organization that they had developed. The Commissioner argued that the payment for the transfer of the rights was not entitled to capital gain treatment because the rights only represented the ability to receive ordinary income in the future. The court held for the taxpayers finding that the taxpayers owned an "equity" interest in the franchising network. In addition to assuming financial and business risks, the taxpayers had the right to veto new franchises and the right to share in sale proceeds if the "owner" sold his interests. These rights and risks are not typically granted to or assumed by mere employees or salesmen.

2.3. *Substitute for Future Income*

Some courts, relying on *Hort* and *P.G. Lake,* deny capital gain treatment on the transfer or relinquishment of contractual rights on the ground that the amount received is a substitute for future ordinary income that would have been earned by the taxpayer through exercise of those rights. In Bisbee-Baldwin Corp. v. Tomlinson, 320 F.2d 929 (5th Cir.1963), the court held that the taxpayer realized ordinary income upon the transfer of mortgage servicing contracts to the extent that payments were allocable to such contracts. The amounts received for the contracts represented the right to receive future income. The court disagreed with a contrary result by a different panel of the same Circuit in Nelson Weaver Realty Co. v. Commissioner, 307 F.2d 897 (5th Cir.1962), also involving mortgage servicing contracts, which concluded that the amounts received were payments for goodwill because they bore no relationship to the amounts that would have been collected and thus were not a substitute for future ordinary income. Other cases finding ordinary income on the substitution for future income theory include Flower v. Commissioner, 61 T.C. 140 (1973), aff'd by order, 505 F.2d 1302 (5th Cir.1974), which involved the receipt of a payment for termination of a contract under which the taxpayer had the right to perform personal services in the future, and Buena Vista Farms v. Commissioner, 68 T.C. 405 (1977), in which the taxpayer sold contract rights to obtain water, since if the water had been obtained and sold directly, the income from the sales would have been ordinary under § 1221(a)(1).

If a court cannot predict for certain what the future income will be, it might rule that the right that will confer that income is a capital asset. In Long v. Commissioner, 772 F.3d 670 (11th Cir. 2014), rev'g T.C. Memo 2013–233, the court declined to apply the "substitute for future ordinary income" doctrine. In that case, the taxpayer had the right to purchase land from another party under a purchase and sale agreement. He planned to build a condominium on the land. The seller refused to perform, and the taxpayer sued the seller and obtained a court order for specific performance. Rather than purchasing the property, the taxpayer "sold his position as plaintiff" in the suit for $5,750,000. The Tax Court held that the proceeds of the sale of the contract were ordinary income, but the Eleventh Circuit reversed, holding that the proceeds were capital gain. According to the Court of Appeals, the Tax Court erred by treating the land itself, which the taxpayer intended to develop and sell in the ordinary course of business, as the property that the taxpayer sold, when it was clear that he "did not sell the land itself, but rather his right to purchase the land, which is a distinct contractual right that may be a capital asset." Thus, "[t]he dispositive inquiry [was] not 'whether Long intended to sell the land to customers in the ordinary course of his business,' but whether Long held the exclusive right to purchase the property 'primarily for sale to customers in the ordinary course of his trade or business.'" Because there was no evidence that the taxpayer had any "intent to assign his contractual rights in the ordinary course of business," or to obtain the judgment for the purpose of selling it in ordinary course of business, the gain was capital gain. Furthermore, the gain was long-term capital gain because the "property" that was sold was the right to purchase the land, which originally arose from the purchase contract, not the state court judgment in the specific performance suit. Finally, the court rejected the IRS's argument that the sales proceeds were ordinary income under the "substitute for ordinary income" doctrine. The court reasoned as follows:

> It cannot be said that the profit Long received from selling the right to attempt to finish developing a large residential project that was far from complete was a substitute for what he would have received had he completed the project himself. Long did not have a future right to income that he already earned. By selling his position in the litigation, Long effectively sold Ferris his right to finish the project and earn the income that Long had hoped to earn

when he started the project years prior. Taxing the sale of a right to create—and thereby profit—at the highest rate would discourage many transfers of property that are beneficial to economic development.

Long possessed a "bundle of rights [that] reflected something more than an opportunity . . . to obtain periodic receipts of income." Comm'r v. Ferrer, 304 F.2d 125, 130–31 (2d Cir.1962). . . . Long's profit was not "simply the amount [he] would have received eventually, discounted to present value." . . . Rather, Long's rights in the . . . property represented the potential to earn income in the future based on the owner's actions in using it, not entitlement to the income merely by owning the property. . . . We have already held that selling a right to earn future undetermined income, as opposed to selling a right to earned income, is a critical feature of a capital asset. United States v. Dresser Indus., Inc., 324 F.2d 56, 59 (5th Cir. 1963). The fact that the income earned from developing the project would otherwise be considered ordinary income is immaterial.

In King Broadcasting Co. v. Commissioner, 48 T.C. 542 (1967), the taxpayer sold its business of transmitting Muzak music programs to another corporation. Pursuant to the sale, the taxpayer canceled its exclusive franchise from Muzak so that the franchise could be reassigned to the purchaser. In addition, the taxpayer sold directly its program servicing agreements. No part of the purchase price was allocated by the parties to the franchise cancellation. The court held that the taxpayer realized ordinary income on the entire amount received since, although the franchise cancellation might be considered a sale or exchange of a capital asset under *Ferrer* principles, the parties had not allocated any portion of the purchase price to it. Since the program servicing contracts constituted "mere [contractual] opportunities * * * to obtain periodic receipts of income," ordinary income resulted on the transfer of these agreements. The parties were bound by their allocation of the purchase price.

2.4. *Leases and Distribution Agreements*

The holder of a primary lease to real property will derive ordinary income from rental payments received from leases. Nonetheless, the lessee's rights to the primary lease have been treated as "property" and disposition of a lease results in capital gain. Commissioner v. Golonsky, 200 F.2d 72 (3d Cir.1952); Metropolitan Bldg. Co. v. Commissioner, 282 F.2d 592 (9th Cir.1960). In Miller v. Commissioner, 48 T.C. 649 (1967) (Acq.), the taxpayer had purchased the primary lease on commercial property and in turn subleased it. He received a payment from the sublessee in exchange for canceling the sublease and transferring the primary lease to the sublessee. The court held that the amounts received on the transaction constituted capital gain. Although the parties had assigned the entire amount of the consideration received to the cancellation of the sublease that, standing alone, clearly would have resulted in ordinary income, the court treated the transaction as a transfer of the prime lease and allowed capital gain treatment.

Section 1241 provides that amounts received by a lessee from a lessor for cancellation of a lease or by a distributor of goods for cancellation of a distribution agreement shall be treated as amounts received in exchange for the lease or distribution agreement, thus satisfying the sale or exchange requirement for the lease or distribution agreement, the sale of which clearly could result in capital gain treatment.

3.   BASIS ASPECTS

The taxpayer's argument in *Hort,* that he actually incurred a loss on the transaction, confuses value and basis, which the Court in its opinion did nothing to clarify. The taxpayer claimed a basis in the inherited lease under § 1014 equal to its fair market value on the date of death of his father. He calculated the value of the lease by comparing the discounted value of the rents to be received over the remaining lease term under the favorable lease with the lower amounts that he would be able to receive at current rental rates. The claimed loss was the difference between this amount and the consideration received on the lease cancellation. All the taxpayer's calculations of value have no relevance to the real issue, which is whether the taxpayer had a basis in the lease that could be used to offset the proceeds received on the cancellation. The *Hort* decision, with no real analysis of the question, in effect denied the taxpayer a separate basis for the lease and instead treated the lease as an element of the fair market value of the property that the taxpayer received at his father's death. Thus, the basis established under § 1014 related only to the underlying property and no part was allocated to the lease as a separate asset. The principle that no portion of the basis of the underlying property is allocable to the owner-lessor's interest in a lease is now reflected in § 167(c)(2).

Unlike *Hort,* there was no basis issue in *P.G. Lake,* presumably because the taxpayer had already recovered its basis in the lease through depletion deductions. Nonetheless, rather than treating the transaction as a disposition of the production payment, the court in *P.G. Lake* treated the taxpayer as receiving an anticipatory assignment of its future income.

Prior to 1969, it was not clear what basis should be used by the life beneficiary in computing gain or loss on the sale of a life estate. In 1969, Congress added § 1001(e), which provides that upon the sale of a term interest, such as a life estate, that portion of the taxpayer's basis that is determined by § 1014 or § 1015 is to be disregarded unless both the term interest and remainder are sold in a single transaction. Thus, in the case of the sale of an inherited life estate, the taxpayer's basis will be zero and the entire amount realized will constitute capital gain. See Treas. Reg. § 1.1001–1(f).

For depreciation purposes, a similar rule applies to the acquisition of a favorable lease. Section 167(c)(2) provides that no portion of the basis of property acquired subject to a lease may be allocated to a favorable lease; the entire basis must be allocated to the tangible property.

SECTION 3.   SALE OR EXCHANGE REQUIREMENT

A. TERMINATION OF TAXPAYER'S INTEREST WITHOUT A "SALE OR EXCHANGE"—THE CREDITOR'S SITUATION

INTERNAL REVENUE CODE: Sections 1234A; 1241; 1271(a)(1), (b).

REGULATIONS: Sections 1.1241–1; 1.1275–1(d).

Under § 1222, capital gain or loss treatment is predicated upon a "sale or exchange" of a capital asset. "Sale or exchange" is not defined in the Code. Although early cases differed as to whether "sale or exchange" was synonymous with or more restrictive than "sale or other disposition," the restrictive interpretation prevailed. But case law development proved too restrictive for both taxpayers and the government. Consequently, certain other transactions were characterized by statute as dispositions that "shall be considered as a sale or exchange." Thus, a disposition of a capital asset by a sale, exchange, or another method artificially characterized as a sale or exchange, will produce capital treatment; any other disposition will produce ordinary gain or loss. Since 1997, the realm of dispositions for ordinary gain or loss has been reduced to insignificance by virtue of the operation of § 1234A, which expanded the scope of deemed exchanges to include virtually all dispositions, as discussed in the following excerpt from a report of the House Ways and Means Committee.

Taxpayer Relief Act of 1997, Report of the Committee on Ways and Means, House of Representatives

H. Rep. No. 105–148, 105th Cong., 1st Sess. 451–455 (1997).

[Pre-1987] Law

Treatment of gains and losses.—Gain from the "sale or other disposition" is the excess of the amount realized therefrom over its adjusted basis; loss is the excess of adjusted basis over the amount realized. The definition of capital gains and losses in section 1222 requires that there be a "sale or exchange" of a capital asset. The U.S. Supreme Court has held that the term "sale or exchange" is a narrower term than "sale or other disposition."[5] Thus, it is possible from [sic] there to be a taxable income from the sale or other disposition of an asset without that gain being treated as a capital gain.

* * *

Court decisions interpreting the "sale or exchange" requirement.— There has been a considerable amount of litigation dealing with whether modifications of legal relationships between taxpayers is be treated as a

---

[5]   Helvering v. William Flaccus Oak Leather Co., 313 U.S. 247 (1941).

"sale or exchange." * * * Several court decisions interpreted the "sale or exchange" requirement to mean that a disposition, that occurs as a result of a lapse, cancellation, or abandonment, is not a sale or exchange of a capital asset, but produces ordinary income or loss. * * *

Extinguishment treated as sale or exchange—The Internal Revenue Code contains provisions that deem certain transactions to be a sale or exchange and, therefore, any resulting gain or loss is to be treated as a capital gain or loss. These rules generally provide for "sale or exchange" treatment as a way of extending capital gain or loss treatment of those transactions. Under one special provision, gains and losses attributable to the cancellation, lapse, expiration, or other termination of a right or obligation with respect to certain personal property are treated as gains or losses from the sale of a capital asset (sec. 1234A). Personal property subject to this rule is (1) personal property of a type that is actively traded[6] and that is, or would be on acquisition, a capital asset in the hands of the taxpayer (other than stock that is not part of straddle or of a corporation that is not formed or availed of to take positions that offset positions in personal property of its shareholders) and (2) a "section 1256 contract"[7] that is capital asset in the hands of the taxpayer.[8] Section 1234A does not apply to the retirement of a debt instrument.

Retirement of debt obligations treated as sale or exchange.—Amounts received on the retirement of any debt instrument are treated as amounts received in exchange therefore (sec. 1271(a)(1)). In addition, gain on the sale or exchange of a debt instrument with OID[9] generally is treated as ordinary income to the extent of its OID if there was an intention at the time of its issuance to call the debt instrument before maturity (sec. 1271(a)(2)). These rules do not apply to (1) debt issued by a natural person * * * . As a result of this exemption, the character of gain or loss realized on retirement of an obligation issued by a natural person under present law is governed by case law.

Reasons for Change

Extinguishment treated as sale or exchange.—In general, the Committee believes that present law is deficient since it (1) taxes similar economic transactions differently, (2) effectively provides some, but not

---

6   Treasury Regulations generally define "actively traded" as any personal property for which there are an established financial market. * * * Treas. Reg. sec. 1.1092(c)–1(c).

7   A "section 1256 contract" means (1) any regulated futures contract, (2) foreign currency contract, (3) nonequity option, or (4) dealer equity option.

8   The present law provision (sec. 1234A) * * * was added by Congress in 1981* * * . There are two components or "legs" to a straddle, where the value of one leg changes inversely with the value of the other leg. Without a special rule, taxpayers were able to "leg-out" of the loss leg of the straddle, while retaining the gain leg, resulting in the creation of an ordinary loss. * * *

9   The issuer of a debt instrument with OID generally accrues and deducts the discount, as interest, over the life of the obligation even though the amount of such interest is not paid until the debt matures. The holder of such a debt instrument also generally includes the OID in income as it accrues as interest on an accrual basis. * * * [Ed.: See Chapter 32.]

all, taxpayers with an election, and (3) its lack of certainty makes the tax laws unnecessarily difficult to administer.

The Committee believes that some transactions, such as settlements of contracts to deliver a capital asset, are economically equivalent to a sale or exchange of such contracts since the value of any asset is the present value of the future income that such asset will produce. In addition, to the extent that present law treats modifications of property rights as not being a sale or exchange, present law effectively provides, in many cases, taxpayers with an election to treat the transaction as giving rise to capital gain, subject to more favorable rates than ordinary income, or an ordinary loss that can offset higher-taxed ordinary income and not be subject to limitations on use of capital losses. The effect of an election can be achieved by selling the property right if the resulting transaction results in a gain or providing for the extinguishment of the property right if the resulting transaction results in a loss.

Courts have given different answers as to whether transactions which terminate contractual interests are treated as a "sale or exchange." This lack of uniformity has caused uncertainty to both taxpayers and the Internal Revenue Service in the administration of the tax laws.

Accordingly, the Committee bill treats the cancellation, lapse, expiration, or other termination of a right or obligation with respect to property which is (or on acquisition would be) a capital asset in the hands of the taxpayer to all types of property as a "sale or exchange." A major effect of the Committee bill would be to remove the effective ability of a taxpayer to elect the character of gains and losses from certain transactions. Another significant effect of the Committee bill would be to reduce the uncertainty concerning the tax treatment of modifications of property rights.

Character of gain on retirement of debt obligations issued by natural persons.—Similar objections can be raised about the rule which exempts debt of natural persons from the deemed sale or exchange rule applicable to debt of other taxpayers. The Committee believes that the debt of natural persons and other taxpayers is sufficiently economically similar to be similarly taxed upon their retirement. Accordingly, the Committee believes that the exception to the deemed sale or exchange rule on retirement of debt of a natural person should be repealed.

Explanation of Provision

Extension of relinquishment rule to all types of property.—The bill extends to all types of property the rule which treats gain or loss from the cancellation, lapse, expiration, or other termination of a right or obligation with respect to property which is (or on acquisition would be) a capital asset in the hands of the taxpayer.

By definition, the extension of the "sale or exchange rule" of present law section 1234A to all property will only affect property that is not personal property which is actively traded on an established exchange.

Thus, the Committee bill will apply to (1) interests in real property and (2) non-actively traded personal property. An example of the first type of property interest that will be affected by the Committee bill is the tax treatment of amounts received to release a lessee from a requirement that the premise be restored on termination of the lease.[10] An example of the second type of property interest that is affected by the Committee bill is the forfeiture of a down payment under a contract to purchase stock.[11] The Committee bill does not affect whether a right is "property" or whether property is a "capital asset."

Character of gain or loss on retirement of debt obligations issued by natural persons.—The Committee bill repeals the provision that exempts debt obligations issued by natural persons from the rule which treats gain or loss realized on retirement of the debt as gain or loss realized on an exchange. Thus, under the bill, gain or loss on the retirement of such debt will be capital gain or loss. * * *

DETAILED ANALYSIS

1. STATUTORY RULES GOVERNING COLLECTION OR RETIREMENT OF DEBT INSTRUMENTS

Section 1271 generally provides that amounts received by the holder upon retirement of any debt instrument are considered to have been received in "exchange" for the obligation. McClain v. Commissioner, 311 U.S. 527 (1941), held under the predecessor to § 1271 that "retirement" included the surrender and payment prior to maturity of about one-half the principal amount of the obligation. Treas. Reg. § 1.1275–1(d) broadly defines the term "debt instrument" to include any right to payment under an instrument or contract.

In economic terms, gain realized on the collection of any debt purchased at a discount is in reality interest income and ought to be taxable as ordinary income. The treatment as interest or as other ordinary income, under §§ 1272 through 1278, of the gain attributable to the purchase of a debt instrument, either upon its original issuance or on the secondary market, at a discount below its face amount is discussed in Chapter 32. Because the original issue discount and market discount rules generally tax the excess of the redemption price of a bond over its issue price or purchase price as ordinary income, the importance of § 1271 has been reduced. If the amount collected is less than the amount paid for a debt—i.e., its basis—a bad debt deduction may be allowed under § 166, which has its own characterization rules (see Chapter 15, Section 3). But if the debt is a security, as are most bonds, then § 165(g), discussed below, applies.

---

[10]   See Billy Rose's Diamond Horseshoe, Inc. v. United States, 448 F.2d 549 (1971), where the Second Circuit held that payments were not entitled to capital gain treatment because there was no sale or exchange. See also Sirbo Holdings, Inc. v. Commissioner, 509 F.2d 1220 (2d Cir.1975).

[11]   See U.S. Freight Co. v. U.S. 422 F.2d 887 (Ct.Cl.1970), holding that forfeiture was an ordinary loss.

2. WORTHLESSNESS

2.1. *Stocks and Other Corporate Securities—Section 165(g)*

Section 165(g) provides that losses incurred when stock and other corporate securities that are capital assets become worthless are considered as losses arising from a sale or exchange on the last day of the taxable year. Absent this provision, the technical lack of a sale or exchange on worthlessness arguably would produce an ordinary loss. As a result of § 165(g), either a sale or the establishment of worthlessness without sale produces the same tax result for corporate securities, as defined in § 165(g)(2).[17] This definition, as to debt obligations, requires either interest coupons or registration. As to securities that do not meet this definition, an ordinary loss is available upon worthlessness. See I.R.C. § 166(e). However, a "retirement" of such security that is a "debt instrument" may be treated by § 1271 as an exchange, which may result in a capital loss. This disparity results from a lack of coordination of the two provisions. See Treas. Reg. § 1.1275–1(d), which very broadly defines "debt instrument" for purposes of § 1271 to include "any instrument or contractual arrangement that constitutes indebtedness."

2.2. *Nonbusiness Obligations Held by an Individual—Section 166(d)*

Section 166(d) treats the worthlessness of nonbusiness bad debts as the sale or exchange of a capital asset. This provision covers debts that are generally personal in nature, such as loans to friends and associates. See Chapter 15, Section 3.3.2.

3. INVOLUNTARY CONVERSIONS: DESTRUCTION AND CONDEMNATION

Section 1231 prescribes special rules for gain or loss from the compulsory or involuntary conversion through destruction, theft, condemnation or sale under threat or imminence of condemnation, of property used in the trade or business, or capital assets held for more than one year in connection with a trade or business or a transaction entered into for profit. If the recognized gains from all § 1231 transactions for the year exceed recognized losses, the difference is treated as a long-term capital gain. If recognized losses exceed recognized gains, the difference is treated as an ordinary loss. See Chapter 25, Section 1. Consequently, the question of whether these transactions constitute sales or exchanges is not in issue, except for capital assets held for one year or less.

While the case law prior to the adoption of the rule of § 1231 treated condemnation as a sale (see Hawaiian Gas Products v. Commissioner, 126 F.2d 4 (9th Cir.1942)), it did not regard destruction in the same manner, even if the taxpayer received insurance proceeds as result of the casualty. Helvering v. William Flaccus Oak Leather Co., 313 U.S. 247 (1941). The

---

[17]   Treas. Reg. § 1.165–5(i) provides that a security that has been abandoned is treated as a worthless security. To abandon a security, a taxpayer must permanently surrender and relinquish all rights in the security and receive no consideration in exchange for it. Thus, if the abandoned security is a capital asset, the resulting loss is a capital loss incurred on the last day of the taxable year. All the facts and circumstances determine whether the transaction is properly characterized as an abandonment or other type of transaction, such as an actual sale or exchange, contribution to capital, dividend, or gift.

principle of *William Flaccus Oak Leather Co.*, which is retained in § 1231(a)(4)(C) for property used in the taxpayer's trade or business, appears to be one of the few remaining situations in which the sale or exchange requirement continues to result in ordinary as opposed to capital characterization of gains and losses.

For the elective postponement of tax on a gain resulting from an involuntary conversion, see § 1033, covered in Chapter 27, Section 1.

4. ABANDONMENT

Abandonment of an unencumbered capital asset of questionable value is another situation that resulted in ordinary loss because there has been no sale or exchange. However, under § 1234A, abandonment may constitute a "termination" of the taxpayer's rights to property. In Citron v. Commissioner, 97 T.C. 200 (1991), the taxpayer was a limited partner in a partnership organized to produce a movie. At a time when the partnership had no net assets, other than the partially completed movie, and no liabilities, the general partner called for additional contributions to complete the movie. The taxpayer, along with the other limited partners, decided not to advance funds, voted to dissolve the partnership, and disavowed any interest in the movie negative, which the general partner thereafter attempted to develop into an X-rated movie. Although § 731 treats receipt of distributions in liquidation of a partnership as received in an exchange for the disappearing partnership interest, in this case nothing was received and thus the court held that there was no sale or exchange. Accordingly, ordinary loss treatment was allowed for the taxpayer's basis in the partnership interest. Section 1234A might overrule the holding of *Citron* and treat abandonment of property that is a capital asset as resulting in a loss from the sale or exchange of a capital asset.

In Pilgrim's Pride Corp. v. Commissioner, 141 T.C. 533 (2013), rev'd 779 F.3d 311 (5th Cir. 2015), the taxpayer purchased preferred stock issued by another corporation for $98.6 million. Subsequently, the issuer offered to redeem the stock for only $20 million, while the taxpayer wanted approximately $39 million. The negotiations ended without an agreement and the taxpayer "abandoned" the securities and claimed a $98.6 million ordinary loss deduction. The Tax Court held that § 1234A required capital loss treatment upon the abandonment of a capital asset. The court reasoned that "[s]hares of stock are intangible interests or rights that the owner has in the management, profits, and assets of a corporation, while the certificate of stock is tangible evidence of the stock ownership of the person designated therein and of the rights and liabilities resulting from such ownership," and that Congress intended "section 1234A to [apply to] terminations of all rights and obligations with respect to property that is a capital asset in the hands of the taxpayer or would be if acquired by the taxpayer, including not only derivative contract rights but also property rights arising from the ownership of the property." The Tax Court's decision was reversed by the Fifth Circuit Court of Appeals, 779 F.3d 311 (5th Cir. 2015), which held that § 1234A(1) by its express terms applies only to the termination of contractual or derivative rights, and not to the abandonment of capital assets. The court also reasoned that "[t]he Commissioner's interpretation of § 1234A(1) would render superfluous § 1234A(2), which requires capital gain or loss treatment for the termination of "a section 1256 contract . . . not described in paragraph (1) which is a capital asset in the hands of the taxpayer," violating the rule of statutory interpretation that 'we are obliged to give effect, if possible, to every word Congress used.'"

The holding in *Pilgrim's Pride* appears to be relevant only to abandonments of securities before March 13, 2008. Treas. Reg. § 1.165–5(i), effective after March 12, 2008, provides that if a security is abandoned and otherwise satisfies the requirements for a deductible loss under § 165 (and is not described in § 165(g)(3), the resulting loss is treated as a loss from the sale or exchange, on the last day of the taxable year, of a capital asset.

As discussed in the next section, abandonment of property encumbered by debt is treated as an exchange of the property for the amount of the liability. See Treas. Reg. § 1.1001–2(a), which includes liabilities in amount realized; see also Yarbro v. Commissioner, 737 F.2d 479 (5th Cir.1984).

B. SATISFACTION OF A CLAIM—THE DEBTOR'S SITUATION

If a debtor satisfies an obligation by paying cash in an amount less than the amount borrowed, the taxpayer realizes discharge of indebtedness income under § 61(a)(12). Unless excluded by § 108, such income is recognized currently as ordinary income. This result is consistent with the treatment of the creditor discussed above; the transaction is not considered a "sale or exchange" to either party because the debtor is viewed as having received nothing.

Where a taxpayer transfers property in satisfaction of a claim, the transfer can be viewed as two separate transactions: (1) a sale of the property by the debtor for cash, and (2) the payment of that cash by the debtor in discharge of the obligation. Although the second transaction is not a sale or exchange, the property transfer is considered to be a sale or exchange. Thus, in Kenan v. Commissioner, 114 F.2d 217 (2d Cir.1940), the transfer of appreciated securities by testamentary trustees in satisfaction of a $5,000,000 bequest qualified as the sale or exchange of capital assets. Similar results were reached in Rev. Rul. 66–207, 1966–2 C.B. 243, and Rev. Rul. 67–74, 1967–1 C.B. 194.

The same principle has been applied in transactions involving mortgaged property. Helvering v. Hammel, 311 U.S. 504 (1941), held that a loss sustained by an owner of real estate resulting from a foreclosure was a capital loss; the involuntary nature of the transaction did not make it any less a "sale." This rule was extended to nonrecourse liabilities in Helvering v. Nebraska Bridge Supply & Lumber Co., 312 U.S. 666 (1941).

The voluntary conveyance or abandonment to a mortgagee of a capital asset also has been held to be a sale or exchange. Yarbro v. Commissioner, 737 F.2d 479 (5th Cir.1984), and Middleton v. Commissioner, 77 T.C. 310 (1981), aff'd per curiam, 693 F.2d 124 (11th Cir.1982), held that a loss from the abandonment of property subject to nonrecourse debt resulted from the sale or exchange of a capital asset and thus was subject to the limitations of § 1211. The *Yarbro* court found abandonment followed by foreclosure to be no different in substance than quit-claiming the mortgaged property to the mortgagee, which had been held in Freeland v. Commissioner, 74 T.C. 970 (1980), to be a sale.

In Lockwood v. Commissioner, 94 T.C. 252 (1990), the taxpayer abandoned depreciable § 1231 property encumbered by nonrecourse debt in an amount less than the taxpayer's basis for the property. Although the abandonment was an exchange, because the property was depreciable an ordinary loss was allowed under Treas. Reg. § 1.167(a)–8(a)(2) and (4), for the amount by which the property's basis exceeded the encumbrance.

SECTION 4.   HOLDING PERIOD REQUIREMENT

INTERNAL REVENUE CODE: Sections 1222; 1223(1), (2), (9).

REGULATIONS: Section 1.1223–1(a), (b), (i).

The function of the holding period requirement is best understood against the background of stock market transactions. The capital gain provisions distinguish among three groups who make their profits in the stock market: the dealer in securities, the speculator, and the investor. The "dealer in securities" is regarded similar to the grocer who maintains an inventory for sale to customers except that the dealer's inventory consists of securities and not groceries. The securities are thus not capital assets. The "investor" who holds securities for their appreciation in value is the prototypical capital gain taxpayer. The investor's securities are therefore capital assets. Even here a problem is presented when a taxpayer is both a "dealer" and an "investor," and § 1236 helps classify securities of the dual status taxpayer. The profits of the "speculator" were not regarded as worthy of preferential treatment. Congress, however, could see no way to distinguish the "speculator" from the "investor" by reference to the nature of the assets held. So it resorted to another criterion and added a "holding period" requirement under which a capital asset had to be held a certain length of time to obtain preferential treatment. That period is now one year, with property being held "long term" if it has been held for *more than* one year.

But the double test—capital asset and holding period—produces some strange results. Most "traders," particularly speculators seeking an eighth or a quarter of a point on trades and whose turnover of securities generally involves a period of hours or days rather than months, are relegated to nonpreferential treatment. But the other market participants are all grouped together—the professional speculator whose purchases and sales are substantial and frequent but involve more than a one-year holding period, the large investor who is constantly perfecting the investor's portfolio through changes in its composition, the modest investor who occasionally changes the investor's portfolio, and the amateur speculator who takes an occasional chance. These market participants generally fall safely on the preferential gain side because of the short length of the required holding period.

DETAILED ANALYSIS

1.   DETERMINATION OF COMMENCEMENT AND TERMINATION OF HOLDING PERIOD

The calculation of the holding period is made with reference to calendar months and fractions thereof, excluding the day acquired and including the day sold, rather than to days. Thus a purchase on May 1, 2016 and a sale on May 1, 2017 result in a holding period that is *not more* than one year. But a sale on May 2, 2017 would result in a long-term transaction. See Rev. Rul. 70–598, 1970–2 C.B. 168; Rev. Rul. 66–7, 1966–1 C.B. 188.

Section 1223(9) provides a special holding period rule for property transferred at death that is included in the decedent's gross estate. Under this provision, the person taking from the decedent, such as an executor, administrator, or surviving joint tenant, is deemed to have held the property for more than one year, thereby qualifying gains for the applicable preferential rate under § 1(h) accorded long-term capital gains, even though sale of the property occurs within one year of the date of death of the decedent.

The commencement or termination of the holding period is not determined solely by passage of title. The applicable dates are established when the taxpayer acquires or disposes of the burdens and benefits of ownership. See Bradford v. United States, 444 F.2d 1133 (Ct.Cl.1971); Hoven v. Commissioner, 56 T.C. 50 (1971); Boykin v. Commissioner, 344 F.2d 889 (5th Cir.1965).

In the case of the exercise of an option to purchase property, the holding period of the acquired property commences with its acquisition and not with the date of acquisition of the option. See Helvering v. San Joaquin Fruit & Investment Co., 297 U.S. 496 (1936); Molbreak v. Commissioner, 61 T.C. 382 (1973), aff'd per curiam, 509 F.2d 616 (7th Cir.1975). In Becker v. Commissioner, 378 F.2d 767 (3d Cir.1967), the court held that a taxpayer's holding period for stock acquired under a restricted stock option began on the date he mailed notice of his election to exercise the option to the corporation, and not on the date that the corporation received it.

Where shares of stock in the same corporation have been purchased at different dates, on later sale of some of the stock the taxpayer is permitted to identify the shares sold if such identification is possible. If not, in general the stock sold is charged against the earliest purchases on a first-in, first-out basis. Treas. Reg. § 1.1223–1(i).

The holding period of a newly-constructed building sold shortly after completion is determined ratably in relation to the cost expended and does not start only when the building is completed. Paul v. Commissioner, 206 F.2d 763 (3d Cir.1953); Aagaard v. Commissioner, 56 T.C. 191 (1971); Rev. Rul. 75–524, 1975–2 C.B. 342. Where a taxpayer, having leased property to explore for oil, then discovers oil, a new property interest in effect arises and the holding period commences with discovery of the oil. Petroleum Exploration v. Commissioner, 193 F.2d 59 (4th Cir.1951). See also Rev. Rul. 62–140, 1962–2 C.B. 181 (involving convertible debentures) and Rev. Rul. 67–309, 1967–2 C.B. 263 (involving undivided interests in real property) for additional situations involving split holding periods.

2. POLICY ISSUES

Congress reduced the holding period for long-term capital gains from twelve to six months in the Tax Reform Act of 1984. Its reasoning was that "investors are 'locked-in' to investments because they do not desire to realize short-term gains," a result that "reduced capital market efficiency because investors hold assets longer than they otherwise might in the absence of tax considerations." Staff of Joint Committee on Taxation, General Explanation of the Revenue Provisions of the Deficit Reduction Act of 1984 at 1083 (1984). Subsequently, the "more than one year" holding period required for long-term treatment was restored for assets acquired after 1987 and an even more preferential rate for assets held more than 18 months was added in 1997. The 18-month holding period was replaced in 1998 with the current one-year holding period. From 1998 through May 2003 there were more preferential rates for certain capital assets held for more than five years.

Lock-in is inherent in an income tax system with a realization requirement, no deferral charge, and no taxation of gains at death. There is tension between any positive tax rate on realized gains and capital market efficiency. The use of any particular holding period is arbitrary and changes in the holding period that have occurred over a number of years appear more to reflect shifting attitudes in Congress regarding the general desirability of preferential capital gains treatment than any specific concerns about market efficiency.

SECTION 5. SPECIAL STATUTORY TREATMENT OF PARTICULAR GAINS AND LOSSES

INTERNAL REVENUE CODE: Sections 1234; 1253.

As the preceding materials have indicated, there are three building blocks involved in the preferential treatment for capital gains: (i) the capital asset definition, (ii) the sale or exchange requirement (although this building block has been largely eliminated by § 1234A), and (iii) the holding period requirement. In a series of special statutory provisions, Congress has modified the results that would have occurred under the general statutory tests. As noted previously, in the case of depreciable property held for use in the taxpayer's trade or business, § 1231 provides a hybrid treatment under which net gains are taxed as capital gains and net losses are ordinary in character. In other cases, Congress has provided capital asset status for items that otherwise would fall within the exceptions in § 1221(a)(1)–(8). In yet other cases, Congress has created a sale or exchange where one would not otherwise exist; and for still others, it has waived the holding period requirements. Finally, having provided preferential treatment for some kinds of assets,

Congress has enacted other special rules to limit the scope of capital gain treatment. These special statutory provisions have encumbered an already detailed area of the tax law with an additional level of complexity. This section discusses these special rules, with the exception of § 1231, which is discussed in Chapter 25.

DETAILED ANALYSIS

1.   OPTIONS TO PURCHASE AND SELL STOCK-PUTS AND CALLS

An option that entitles the holder of the option to *purchase* a specific amount of stock or securities at a designated price (the "strike price") on or before a specified date is known as a "call." An option that gives the holder of the option the right to *sell* a specified quantity of stock or securities at a strike price on or before a specified date is known as a "put." Options not exercised by the specified date automatically lapse, but prior to that date may be sold and resold.

Section 1234 governs the tax treatment of such options. In very general terms (and assuming the underlying assets are capital assets), the holder of a "call" treats the cost of the call as a capital expenditure and any *sale* or *exchange* of the call prior to the expiration date results in long-term or short-term capital gain or loss, depending on the period of time the call option has been held. The *lapse* of a call option is treated as a sale or exchange by § 1234 and capital gain or loss results accordingly. If the call is *exercised,* the cost of the option is added to the basis of the stock purchased. Section 1234 does not apply to option writers who are dealers in options. Dealers realize ordinary income or loss on all option transactions they enter into in their capacity as dealers.

As to the writer of the call option—that is, the person obligated to sell the property—the amount received for writing the call (the "premium") does not constitute income at the time it is received. The tax consequences are deferred until the call option expires, is exercised, or is canceled in a closing transaction. See Rev. Rul. 78–182, 1978–1 C.B. 265, for a comprehensive discussion of the tax treatment of options. A call option may lapse and the writer will retain the premium. Alternatively, the writer of an option may enter into a "closing transaction" under which the writer terminates the obligation under the option by reacquiring it or by purchasing a call from an Options Exchange equal to the value of the option originally granted. Section 1234(b) provides that gain or loss on a closing transaction and gain from a lapse of an option on stock, securities, or commodities constitutes short-term capital gain or loss to the writer of the option. Section 1234A (discussed in Section 3 of this Chapter) treats the lapse of an option as a sale or exchange for the holder.

Similar issues arise when a taxpayer closes out a position in a straddle transaction covered by § 1092 or in a futures contract covered by § 1256. Section 1234A provides that gain or loss attributable to the cancellation, lapse, expiration, or the termination of such positions is treated as a gain or loss from the sale of a capital asset.

2. SHORT SALES OF STOCK AND OTHER ASSETS

In a short sale, the short seller agrees to sell stock or a commodity, which the seller generally does not own, to another at a fixed price on a future date. The short sale contract itself is an option that may be sold before the closing date resulting in capital gain or loss (assuming the option contract is a capital asset in the hands of the taxpayer.) If the taxpayer acquires property to meet the requirements of the short sale contract, in general, gain or loss on the transfer of the property is treated as gain or loss on the sale or exchange of a capital asset to the extent that the property used to close the short sale is a capital asset in the taxpayer's hands. I.R.C. § 1233(a). The short sale is deemed to be consummated on delivery of the property. Treas. Reg. § 1.1233–1(a)(1). The holding period of the property is measured from the date of the seller's acquisition of the property. Treas. Reg. § 1.1233–1(a)(3).

Short sales can be used to "lock-in" gains on stock held by the taxpayer while extending the holding period of the property. For example, on February 1, 2017, the taxpayer acquires stock of X Corp. for $100. On November 1, the stock has appreciated to $120. The taxpayer can be protected from further price fluctuation without actually selling the stock by entering a short sale of the stock to close with delivery of the stock on February 15, 2018.[18] In the absence of statutory restriction, the taxpayer has increased the taxpayer's holding period for the X stock beyond one year, thereby converting the gain to long-term gain. Two rules prevent this result. First, § 1259 provides that where a taxpayer enters into a short sale of property that is substantially identical to appreciated property held by the taxpayer when the short sale contract is entered into, the transaction will be treated as a constructive sale of the appreciated property for its fair market value. Thus, in the example, the taxpayer will be treated as selling the X Corp. stock for $120 on November 1, the date the short sale contract is acquired. The gain will be short-term capital gain. Section 1259 applies to holdings of appreciated stock, debt instruments, or partnership interests, but does not apply to non-publicly traded property. I.R.C. § 1259(b)(1) and (c)(2). Section 1233(b) provides, in addition, that if on the date the taxpayer enters into a short sale, the taxpayer holds substantially identical property that has been held for less than one year, gain or loss recognized on the closing of the short sale will be treated as short-term capital gain or loss. Section 1233 applies to stocks, securities, and commodity futures that are capital assets in the hands of the taxpayer. I.R.C. § 1233(e)(2)(A).

A second rule of § 1233(b) provides that the holding period of substantially identical property held by the taxpayer as of the date of a short sale, or of substantially identical property acquired by the taxpayer between the date of the short sale and the closing of the short sale contract, will be deemed to commence as of the date of the closing of the short sale. For example, the taxpayer purchases 100 shares of X stock on February 1, 2017,

---

[18]   This transaction is referred to as a "short sale against the box." If the price of the stock goes down, the taxpayer is protected by an identical increase in the value of the short sale contract, and conversely, if the price of the stock goes up, the value of the short sale contract will decrease by the same amount.

for $10 per share. On March 1, 2018, the taxpayer sells short 100 shares of X stock for $16 dollars per share. Section 1259 would require recognition of $600 of long-term capital gain on the constructive sale of X stock. The first rule of § 1233(b)(1) does not apply because the taxpayer had held the X stock for more than one year at the time of the short sale. The taxpayer closes the short sale on November 1, 2018, with 100 shares of X stock purchased on that date for $18 per share. The taxpayer's $200 loss on the short sale is a short-term capital loss. On February 1, 2019, the taxpayer sells the original 100 shares of X stock, purchased on February 1, 2017, for $18 per share. Because under § 1223(b)(2) the taxpayer's holding period for these shares is deemed to commence on November 1, 2018, the date the short sale is closed, the taxpayer's $200 of gain is treated as short-term capital gain. See Treas. Reg. § 1.1233–1(c)(6), ex. (2), on which this illustration is based.

The third rule of § 1233 prevents use of a short sale to convert long-term capital loss into short-term capital loss. Under § 1233(d), if substantially identical property has been held by the taxpayer for more than one year on the date of a short sale, any loss on closing the short sale will be treated as a long-term capital loss.

3. FRANCHISES, TRADEMARKS AND TRADE NAMES

The extent of franchising operations in the United States created pressure on the capital gain issue. In some cases, the pressure was on the sale or exchange requirement, i.e., whether the retention of powers, rights or a continuing interest in the franchise agreement itself would cause the agreement to be treated as a license rather than as a sale of a franchise. The courts divided on this issue. Even if a franchise agreement constituted a sale, the question then turned to whether capital gain treatment was precluded because the sales were made in the ordinary course of the taxpayer's business, thus falling under the exclusion in § 1221(a)(1).

Congress resolved the matter by enacting § 1253(a), which provides that the transfer of a franchise, trademark, or trade name shall not be treated as a sale or exchange of a capital asset if the transferor retains any significant power, right, or continuing interest with respect to the subject matter of the franchise, trademark, or trade name. Section 1253(b)(2) sets forth a series of rights that automatically constitute a "significant" power or right with respect to the transfer if the right is coextensive with the duration of the transferred interest. The statutory list is not exclusive, however, and considering all the facts and circumstances, other retained rights may be a significant continuing interest, right, or power, whether or not coextensive with the duration of the transferred interest. See Stokely USA, Inc. v. Commissioner, 100 T.C. 439 (1993) (prohibition on assignment of one transferred trademark for 5 years was not "significant" but transfer to vegetable packer of a trade name subject to the restriction that it not be used to sell pork and beans product for 20 years was "significant"). Even if the tests of § 1253(b)(2) are met, § 1253(c) provides that any amount received by the transferor that is contingent on the productivity, use or disposition of the franchise, trademark, or trade name is treated as ordinary income.

Section 1253(d) provides rules to limit the franchisee's ability to claim a current deduction for amounts paid to secure a franchise to those cases of continuing payments analogous to rent. Under § 197 the franchise is an amortizable intangible asset and thus a § 1231 asset in the hands of the franchisee. See I.R.C. § 197(f)(7).

4. SMALL BUSINESS CORPORATION STOCK

Section 1244 provides a special rule for losses on certain "small business corporation" stock. Under this provision an individual shareholder may claim an ordinary loss on the sale or exchange or worthlessness of qualifying stock. The amount allowed as an ordinary loss in any taxable year is limited to $50,000, or $100,000 for married taxpayers filing a joint return, even if all of the stock was owned by one of the spouses. To qualify the stock must have been acquired directly from the corporation upon original issuance for money or property other than stock or securities. Only stock issued before the corporation has invested equity capital of more than $1,000,000 qualifies. In addition, the corporation must have derived more than 50 percent of its income from operating an active business for the five years prior to the year the loss was realized.

5. FINANCIAL "CONVERSION TRANSACTIONS"

Suppose that on June 1, 2017, A, an investor who is not a dealer, purchases a quantity of precious metal for $100,000. On July 31, 2017, A enters into a contract to sell the precious metal to B for $110,000 on August 1, 2019. Applying ordinary principles, A arguably would recognize a $10,000 long-term capital gain when the sale was closed on August 1, 2019, the holding period having commenced on June 1, 2017. In reality, however, A locked-in A's $10,000 gain on July 31 after holding the precious metal for only two months, and thereafter A is exposed only to the type of risk normally associated with being a lender.

Section 1258 is designed to address this problem as well as more complex financial transactions designed to convert ordinary income into capital gain. Generally speaking, § 1258 applies to any transaction that consists of two or more offsetting positions—i.e., a "long leg" and a "short leg"—with regard to the same or similar property acquired substantially contemporaneously if substantially all of the taxpayer's return is attributable to the time value of the net investment in the transaction. In addition to applying to transactions like that in the above example, § 1258 also applies to a straddle, as defined in § 1092, the return from which is substantially attributable to the time value of the investment or any transaction marketed as being based on the economic characteristics of a loan but with the tax-benefits of capital gain treatment.

Under § 1258 a portion of the gain realized from the sale of a position in a conversion transaction is recharacterized as ordinary income. The ordinary income amount equals the interest income that would have accrued on the taxpayer's net investment in the transaction at 120 percent of the applicable Federal rate under § 1274(d)(2)(A), or if the straddle has an indefinite term, the Federal short term rate under § 6621(b). The portion of the gain treated as ordinary income is reduced by any amount previously included as ordinary income as a result of the prior disposition or termination of another leg of the same transaction.

The effect of § 1258 on the above example is as follows. As of July 31, 2017, A has entered into a conversion transaction with a definite term. When A realizes the $10,000 gain on August 1, 2019, § 1258 recharacterizes part of the gain as ordinary income. Assuming that the applicable federal rate on July 31, 2017 was 5 percent, the applicable rate for § 1258 is 6 percent (5% × 120%). Assuming further that A paid nothing to B as part of the transaction, A's net investment was $100,000. Thus $6,090 of the gain ($100,000 × 6 percent [compounded semi-annually]) is ordinary income; the remaining $3,910 is capital gain.

Transactions of options dealers and commodities traders in the normal course of their activities are not subject to § 1258. This exception is not generally available for limited partners or limited entrepreneurs in an options dealer or a commodities trader.

SECTION 6. TRANSACTIONAL PROBLEMS OF CAPITAL GAINS AND LOSSES RELATED TO SUBSEQUENT EVENTS

Sound tax administration requires that the annual tax return should be based on the events occurring during that year. Subsequent events in general do not permit the taxpayer to recalculate income; any adjustments must be made for the year in which the subsequent events take place. But many factors may cause the aggregate tax liability to be greater than it would have been if the original year's return were adjusted. The perceived inequities of a strict annual accounting concept have resulted in some relaxation of these rules.

The following materials discuss the problems resulting from the interaction of the annual accounting concept and transactions affecting two or more years that involve capital gains and losses. There are two basic patterns of transactions. First, there is the situation where the initial transaction is capital in nature and a related transaction occurs in a subsequent year. For example, property is sold and a capital gain is recognized. If for some reason a portion of the amount realized is paid back to the purchaser in a subsequent year, is the repayment ordinary or capital? The second situation is the converse of the first. Thus, suppose that a deduction, such as for a bad debt, is claimed against ordinary income. Under what circumstances will a later related gain, such as from the sale of the debt, otherwise qualifying as a capital gain, be considered an ordinary gain because of the prior transaction?

The annual accounting concept is discussed more thoroughly in Chapter 29.

Arrowsmith v. Commissioner

Supreme Court of the United States, 1952.
344 U.S. 6.

■ MR. JUSTICE BLACK delivered the opinion of the Court.

This is an income tax controversy growing out of the following facts as shown by findings of the Tax Court. In 1937 two taxpayers, petitioners here, decided to liquidate and divide the proceeds of a corporation in which they had equal stock ownership. Partial distributions made in 1937, 1938, and 1939 were followed by a final one in 1940. Petitioners reported the profits obtained from this transaction, classifying them as capital gains. They thereby paid less income tax than would have been required had the income been attributed to ordinary business transactions for profit. About the propriety of these returns, there is no dispute. But in 1944 a judgment was rendered against the old corporation * * * . [The litigation had grown out of a dispute over the operation of a joint trading account by the old corporation.] The two taxpayers were required to and did pay the judgment for the corporation, of whose assets they were transferees. * * * Classifying the loss as an ordinary business one, each took a tax deduction for 100% of the amount paid. Treatment of the loss as a capital one would have allowed deduction of a much smaller amount. * * * The Commissioner viewed the 1944 payment as part of the original liquidation transaction requiring classification as a capital loss, just as the taxpayers had treated the original dividends as capital gains. Disagreeing with the Commissioner the Tax Court classified the 1944 payment as an ordinary business loss. 15 T.C. 876. The Court of Appeals reversed, treating the loss as "capital." 193 F.2d 734. * * *

[Section 165] treats losses from sales or exchanges of capital assets as "capital losses" and [§ 331(a)] requires that liquidation distributions be treated as exchanges. The losses here fall squarely within the definition of "capital losses" contained in these sections. Taxpayers were required to pay the judgment because of liability imposed on them as transferees of liquidation distribution assets. And it is plain that their liability as transferees was not based on any ordinary business transaction of theirs apart from the liquidation proceedings. It is not even denied that had this judgment been paid after liquidation, but during the year 1940, the losses would have been properly treated as capital ones. For payment during 1940 would simply have reduced the amount of capital gains taxpayers received during that year.

It is contended, however, that this payment which would have been a capital transaction in 1940 was transformed into an ordinary business transaction in 1944 because of the well-established principle that each taxable year is a separate unit for tax accounting purposes. United States v. Lewis, 340 U.S. 590 * * * . But this principle is not breached by considering all the 1937–1944 liquidation transaction events in order properly to classify the nature of the 1944 loss for tax purposes. Such an examination is not an attempt to reopen and readjust the 1937 to 1940 tax returns, an action that would be inconsistent with the annual tax accounting principle.

* * *

Affirmed.

* * *

DETAILED ANALYSIS

1. *ARROWSMITH* EXPANDED TO RELATED SITUATIONS

In United States v. Skelly Oil Co., 394 U.S. 678 (1969), the Supreme Court, relying on *Arrowsmith,* required the taxpayer to reduce the deduction taken for overcharges that it was required to repay by the amount of the depletion deduction which it had taken in earlier years when it included the overcharges in income:

> The rationale for the *Arrowsmith* rule is easy to see; if money was taxed at a special lower rate when received, the taxpayer would be accorded an unfair tax windfall if repayments were generally deductible from receipts taxable at the higher rate applicable to ordinary income. The Court in *Arrowsmith* was unwilling to infer that Congress intended such a result. This case is really no different.

In Lowe v. Commissioner, 44 T.C. 363 (1965) (Acq.), the taxpayer sold all the shares in a wholly-owned corporation. The buyer made a downpayment on the purchase price and gave a note secured by a pledge of the shares for the balance. Subsequently, the buyer defaulted on the remaining purchase price and the taxpayer received back the shares, keeping as liquidated damages $22,500 of the downpayment. The gain was held under *Arrowsmith* to be capital since it involved an "adjustment" or "revision" of the prior sale. In contrast, in Smith v. Commissioner, 50 T.C. 273 (1968), aff'd per curiam, 418 F.2d 573 (9th Cir.1969), the taxpayer entered into an executory contract to sell all the stock of a corporation for $9,500,000 with $500,000 to be paid immediately in escrow and the balance to be paid on a specified date, at which time the stock would be transferred. The buyer paid the initial $500,000 but did not meet the deadline for the final payment. The buyer subsequently sued, alleging certain defaults on the part of the seller. As part of the settlement in the case, the sellers kept a portion of the downpayment. The Tax Court held that the retained amount was taxable as ordinary income since there was no sale or exchange to which to relate the payment, distinguishing *Lowe* on the basis that in that case the sale had actually been consummated. Binns v. United States, 385 F.2d 159 (6th Cir.1967); Mittleman v. Commissioner, 56 T.C. 171 (1971), aff'd per curiam, 464 F.2d 1393 (3d Cir.1972); and Handelman v. Commissioner, 509 F.2d 1067 (2d Cir.1975), all held that receipt of liquidated damages upon a default of an executory purchase contract results in ordinary income.

2. THE *ARROWSMITH* PATTERN: INITIAL CAPITAL GAIN—LATER LOSS

Arrowsmith has been followed in a variety of situations involving an initial capital gain and a later loss. For example, in Estate of Shannonhouse v. Commissioner, 21 T.C. 422 (1953), a taxpayer who sold real property at a capital gain, and who later reimbursed the purchaser for expenses caused by a defect in title, was allowed only a capital loss. Similarly, in Rev. Rul. 67–331, 1967–2 C.B. 290, a taxpayer who realized a capital gain under § 1231 as a result of the involuntary conversion of business property but was subsequently required to repay a portion of the proceeds received was limited to a capital loss in the year of restoration.

A number of cases have involved the application of *Arrowsmith* to payments required by § 16(b) of the Securities Exchange Act of 1934 prohibiting the buying and selling (or selling and buying) within six months of the stock of a corporation by an "insider." In case of violation, the corporation must be paid the difference between the sales price and purchase price (or purchase price and sales price) of the stock. The Courts of Appeals have applied *Arrowsmith* to these payments although the Tax Court has found the relationship between the payment and sale to be insufficient to require capital characterization.

In Mitchell v. Commissioner, 428 F.2d 259 (6th Cir.1970), the taxpayer, a vice-president of General Motors, sold General Motors stock and realized a capital gain. Within six months he exercised a stock option and acquired new General Motors shares. General Motors, on learning of the transactions, advised the taxpayer that he had violated § 16(b). The taxpayer, although asserting that he had not violated the statute, made the payment required under the Securities Exchange Act and treated it as an ordinary and necessary business expense deductible under § 162. The Court of Appeals held that *Arrowsmith* and *Skelly Oil* required the gain and subsequent repayment to be given the same treatment and limited the taxpayer to a capital loss deduction. In Anderson v. Commissioner, 56 T.C. 1370 (1971), involving a similar situation, the Tax Court allowed the deduction, stressing that the capital gain realized on the sale transaction was realized by the taxpayer in his capacity as a shareholder, while his obligation to make the repayment arose out of his status as an employee of the corporation; the "integrality" of relationship between the two transactions required by *Arrowsmith* thus was not present. The Court of Appeals reversed, finding "unpersuasive" the distinction between the various capacities in which the taxpayer realized the gain and made the repayment. 480 F.2d 1304 (7th Cir.1973). The Court of Appeals decision in *Anderson* was followed in Brown v. Commissioner, 529 F.2d 609 (10th Cir.1976). Cummings v. Commissioner, 506 F.2d 449 (2d Cir.1974), also held that *Arrowsmith* principles required § 16(b) repayments be treated as capital losses, stressing the "windfall" that the taxpayer would receive if he were allowed to treat the income as capital gain while able to deduct the repayment against ordinary income.

In evaluating the relationship between the payment required under § 16(b) and the earlier sale of stock, it has been pointed out on many occasions that the payment has no necessary relationship to the tax gain recognized on the sale. Indeed, it is possible that the sale produced a tax loss but was followed by a repurchase at a lower price. But it does not appear that this aspect is inconsistent with *Arrowsmith,* as the cases in part 3 indicate.

3. INITIAL CAPITAL LOSS—LATER FURTHER LOSS

Where a stockholder of a bank obtained a capital loss deduction for worthless stock, but was later required to make a payment under his statutory liability, the stockholder was limited to a capital loss for the payment. Commissioner v. Adam, Meldrum & Anderson Co., 215 F.2d 163 (2d Cir.1954).

In Wener v. Commissioner, 242 F.2d 938 (9th Cir.1957), the taxpayer sold an interest in a partnership, the purchase price to be paid in installments, and realized a capital loss. A later prepayment to the taxpayer of the purchase price at a lower amount resulted in a further capital loss representing a reduction in the purchase price rather than an ordinary loss on the obligation of the buyer.

4. THE *ARROWSMITH* CONVERSE-GAINS RELATED TO A PRIOR ORDINARY DEDUCTION TRANSACTION

4.1. *General*

In Bresler v. Commissioner, 65 T.C. 182 (1975), the taxpayer reported a $729,584 ordinary loss under § 1231 on the sale of property used in its trade or business. Three years later the taxpayer recovered $150,000 as a reimbursement on the sale of its business assets in a settlement of an antitrust claim against a competitor. The taxpayer reported the receipt as a recovery for loss of goodwill taxable as long-term capital gain. The Tax Court treated the recovery as ordinary income under *Arrowsmith* principles.

> [The taxpayer] reported an ordinary loss in 1964 when it sold its section 1231 assets. If it had received the antitrust settlement in that year, any portion representing compensation for the loss on the sale of its section 1231 property would have merely reduced its ordinary loss since the losses from the sales or exchanges of section 1231 assets would have exceeded the gains from such sales or exchanges including such compensation. *Arrowsmith* requires that the gain realized in 1967 be treated in the same manner as if it had been received in 1964.

> Since the gain, if received in 1964, would have resulted in an increase in ordinary income, it is not transformed into capital gain by a mere delay in receipt. The subsequent gain is part and parcel of the original loss transaction and cannot be segregated for tax purposes. The gain in 1967 is merely an adjustment of the prior sale price; it is not a new and independent sale or exchange of section 1231 property. * * * The receipt of the payment in 1967 was merely the completion of a prior transaction. *Arrowsmith* requires us to treat both events as a unified transaction. * * * Accordingly, we hold that the portion of the antitrust settlement attributable to

the loss incurred when [the taxpayer] sold its section 1231 property is ordinary income and not capital gain.

4.2. *Situations Where Capital Gains Are Permitted*

In what circumstances should the *Arrowsmith* doctrine as interpreted in *Bresler* apply to restrict capital gains? A transaction otherwise qualifying for capital gain treatment is not disqualified solely because ordinary deductions in connection with the asset have been claimed previously. Indeed, there are numerous situations where capital gains are permitted notwithstanding earlier ordinary deductions. For example, gain from the sale of vacant land or other assets not currently productive will not be disqualified from capital gain treatment because mortgage interest was paid and deducted in prior years. Gain from the sale of self-created goodwill is also treated as capital gain, even though it is typically generated through ordinary deductions such as advertising.

Rev. Rul. 85–186, 1985–2 C.B. 84, provides that gain realized on the sale of technology, the costs of which had previously been deducted under § 174(a), was not required to be reported as ordinary income to the extent of those deductions by reason of the tax benefit rule (see Chapter 29, Section 1.B.). Pursuant to the test in Hillsboro National Bank v. Commissioner, 457 U.S. 1103 (1982) (see Chapter 29, Section 1.B.), the Ruling concluded that the sale was not "fundamentally inconsistent" with the earlier deductions; if the sale had occurred in the year the expenditures were incurred, they would still have been deductible given the purpose and function of § 174(a).

In Allan v. Commissioner, 856 F.2d 1169 (8th Cir.1988), an accrual method taxpayer claimed deductions for unpaid interest on a nonrecourse mortgage. When the interest was not paid, the lender added it to the unpaid principal amount due on the note. Upon default, the taxpayer conveyed the property to the lender in lieu of foreclosure. The taxpayer reported the full amount of the debt, including the portion representing accrued interest as amount realized in computing gain, and the court sustained this treatment. It refused to bifurcate the transaction as urged by the Commissioner to treat as ordinary income that portion of the gain attributable to the previously deducted interest added to the mortgage principal.

4.3. *Situations Where Previous Ordinary Deduction Prevents Capital Gain*

4.3.1. *Bad Debts in General*

In First National Bank of Lawrence County v. Commissioner, 16 T.C. 147 (1951), a bank had charged off bonds as worthless, thereby recognizing an ordinary loss under a special Code provision. Subsequently, the bonds were redeemed. The taxpayer claimed a capital gain under the predecessor of § 1271(a)(1), but the court held that after the charge-off the bonds ceased to be capital assets.[19] A similar result was reached in Merchants National Bank of Mobile v. Commissioner, 199 F.2d 657 (5th Cir.1952), involving the sale of a note previously charged off as worthless:

---

[19]   Capital gains are of reduced significance to a corporate taxpayer for which there is no preferential tax rate. Characterization of gains as capital gain remains important, however, to a corporate taxpayer with capital losses that are only deductible against capital gain.

When these notes were charged off as a bad debt in the first instance, the bank deducted the amount thereof from its ordinary income, thus escaping taxation on that portion of its income in those years. The amount subsequently recovered on the notes restores *pro tanto* the amount originally deducted from ordinary income, and is accordingly taxable as income, not as a capital gain. When the notes were charged off, and the bank recouped itself for the capital loss by deducting the amount thereof from its current income, the notes were no longer capital assets for income tax purposes. To permit the bank to reduce its ordinary income by the amount of the loss in the first instance, thus gaining a maximum tax advantage on that basis, and then permit it to treat the amount later recovered on the notes as a capital gain, taxable on a much lower basis than ordinary income, would afford the bank a tax advantage on the transaction not contemplated by the income tax laws.

4.3.2. *Mortgage Foreclosures*

The *Arrowsmith* principle has been applied to limit the potential for creating ordinary deductions and capital gains upon the foreclosure of mortgages. When a mortgage is foreclosed and the property is acquired by the mortgagee, the transaction is treated as an exchange by the mortgagee of the mortgage obligation for the property. The mortgagee thus recognizes gain or loss on the difference between the fair market value of the property received and the basis of the obligation used to satisfy the bid price. Treas. Reg. § 1.166–6(b). To the extent that indebtedness remains unsatisfied, a bad debt deduction is available if the deficiency is uncollectible. This deduction will be ordinary unless the limitations of §§ 165(g) or 166(d) apply. Because the mortgagee often controls the bid price, an individual mortgage holder could in some instances bid a low amount for the property in an attempt to achieve both a bad debt deduction and a capital gain. Suppose, for example, that property with a fair market value of $750,000 is encumbered with a $1,000,000 mortgage on which the owner has defaulted. The mortgagee, rather than bidding $750,000 and claiming a $250,000 bad debt deduction (if the $250,000 is uncollectible), might bid $500,000 in an attempt to achieve a $500,000 bad debt deduction and a $250,000 capital gain. Treas. Reg. § 1.166–6(b)(2) provides that the property's fair market value is presumed to equal the bid price, although this presumption can be overcome by "clear and convincing proof."

The IRS took the position in Rev. Rul. 80–56, 1980–1 C.B. 154, that the artificially-created gain in such situations is ordinary in character. Citing *Merchants National Bank of Mobile,* supra, the Ruling held that any such gain is ordinary to the extent it offsets a bad debt deduction. The foregoing issues generally do not arise where the foreclosure relates to real property that was seller-financed. Section 1038 generally treats the foreclosure as a tax-free exchange with recognition postponed until the property's subsequent disposition.

CHAPTER 25

SALES OF ASSETS HELD FOR USE IN A TRADE OR BUSINESS

SECTION 1. SECTION 1231 PROPERTY

INTERNAL REVENUE CODE: Sections 1231; 1239(a)–(c); 1245(a)(1)–(3); 1245(b)(1)–(4); 197(f)(7). See also Section 1(h)(1)(E), (h)(6).

REGULATIONS: Sections 1.1231–1; 1.1245–1(a)(1), (b); 1.1245–2(a)(1)–(4); 1.1245–3(a)(1); 1.1245–4(a)–(c); 1.1245–6(a).

Taxpayers who dispose of real estate and depreciable property used in a trade or business want to avoid capital asset treatment so that the loss may be deducted against ordinary income. On the other hand, where the asset is likely to be sold at a gain, such as real estate, the taxpayer wants capital gain treatment. These conflicting interests have been resolved by Congress through the interaction of §§ 1221 and 1231. Section 1221(a)(2) excludes depreciable property and real property used in the taxpayer's trade or business from classification as capital assets. Ordinary gains and losses would thus result on disposition of assets specified in § 1221(a)(2). Section 1231(a) and (b), however, pick up the property excluded in § 1221(a)(2) and restore that property to capital asset status for *gain* purposes if the more than one-year holding period requirement is met. The restoration to grace under § 1231(a) is not absolute. Section 1231(a) does not apply to the property described in § 1231(b)(1)(A), (B), (C), and (D). This statutory arrangement results in maintaining the noncapital status of inventory items (§§ 1231(b)(1)(A) and 1221(a)(1)), property sold to customers in the ordinary course of business (§§ 1231(b)(1)(B) and 1221(a)(1)), copyrights and assets created by the personal efforts of the taxpayer (§§ 1231(b)(1)(C) and 1221(a)(3)), and supplies (§ 1221(a)(8)). Thus, only depreciable property used in a trade or business and real property used in a trade or business generally qualify as "section 1231 property."

Section 1231 has another aspect. By virtue of § 1231(a)(3)(A)(ii) and (a)(4)(B), it provides special treatment for gains or losses with respect to involuntary conversions that, absent any special rules, would be ordinary because technically no sale or exchange is present.

Section 1231 thus applies to two distinct types of transactions:

(1) Sales or exchanges of "property used in the trade or business." This expression is defined in § 1231(b) to include property, used in trade or business that is either depreciable property or real property (in both cases only if held for more than one year), other than stock in trade,

inventories, or property held primarily for sale to customers (essentially the same exclusion as § 1221(a)(1)). In addition, certain assets that otherwise would not qualify—cut timber, coal, iron ore and timber royalties, certain livestock, and unharvested crops—are defined in § 1231(b)(2)–(4) as "property used in the trade or business," thus qualifying under § 1231(a), even though they might otherwise be treated as ordinary items under one of the exceptions specified in § 1221 and preserved under § 1231(b)(1).

(2) The compulsory or involuntary conversion of property by destruction, theft, seizure, condemnation, or threat of condemnation (including, under § 1231(a)(4)(B), a loss without conversion into money or property). The property must be used in a trade or business or consist of capital assets held for more than one year that are held in connection with a trade or business or a transaction entered into for profit.[1]

As to these two categories, the rule of § 1231 is that:

(a) If the aggregate § 1231 gains for the year exceed the aggregate § 1231 losses, all of the gains and losses are considered as arising on the sale or exchange of capital assets held for more than one year, i.e., the net amount is treated as long-term capital gain that enters into the calculation in determining net capital gain (§ 1222(11)).

(b) If § 1231 losses equal or exceed the § 1231 gains, all of the gains and losses are ordinary, i.e., the net loss offsets ordinary income in calculating taxable income.

Assume, for example, that in the current year taxpayer A sold two parcels of real estate, Blackacre and Whiteacre, used in A's trade or business and held for more than one year. On the sale of Blackacre, A realized a $50,000 gain and on the sale of Whiteacre, A realized a $35,000 loss. The $50,000 gain and the $35,000 loss will be treated as long-term capital gain and loss, respectively. Taxpayer B, on the other hand, realized a $70,000 gain on the sale of a patent used in B's trade or business, and held for more than one year, and a $90,000 loss on the sale of an airplane used in B's trade or business and held for more than one year. Both the $70,000 gain and the $90,000 loss will be treated as ordinary.

Section 1231(c) Recapture. Section 1231(c) prevents manipulation of the netting rules to maximize capital gain and ordinary loss. Under § 1231(c), any net § 1231 gain in a year is taxed as ordinary income to the extent of the sum of the net § 1231 ordinary losses incurred by the

---

[1]   As a result, the section does not apply to personal casualty losses. Section 165(h)(2) requires that personal casualty gains and losses be separately netted. If the netting results in a gain, then all gains and losses are treated as capital gains or losses. Conversely, if the netting results in a loss, the loss is ordinary but for individuals is subject to the 10 percent of adjusted gross income floor on casualty losses, as discussed Chapter 21, Section 6.

taxpayer in the five preceding taxable years. For example, if an individual held two parcels of business property, one of which could be sold at a gain of $50,000 and the other at a loss of $40,000, a sale of both in the same year would produce under § 1231 a net gain of $10,000 qualifying for capital gain treatment. Assuming that the taxpayer was an individual in the 39.6 percent tax bracket and had no other capital gains or losses, if the properties had been held for more than one year, the 20 percent maximum rate on adjusted net long-term capital gains in § 1(h) results in a tax liability of $2,000.[2] But if the assets were sold in separate years and the taxpayer had ordinary income against which to claim the loss, the transactions would produce a combined *tax savings* of $5,840. A sale of the loss asset in taxable year one would result in an ordinary loss of $40,000, resulting in tax savings of $15,840. A sale of the gain asset in taxable year two would produce a capital gain of $50,000 resulting in a tax liability of $10,000. Section 1231(c) prevents this tax arbitrage by treating the subsequent gain as ordinary, thus eliminating the tax savings. The sale of the gain asset in one year followed by a later sale of the loss asset does not trigger the limitation of § 1231(c).

Section 1245 Recapture. The treatment of gains from depreciable property used in the business as capital gain under § 1231 causes a significant problem when the capital cost recovery provisions and the reduction of basis rules under § 1016 are considered. If a taxpayer can claim ordinary deductions through depreciation or other cost recovery rules and then sell the property at a tax profit (resulting from basis reductions) in a transaction qualifying for capital gain treatment, the combination could allow the taxpayer an after-tax profit in a transaction that involved no economic gain. Suppose, for example, that a 35-percent bracket taxpayer purchased a depreciable asset for $100 and took depreciation deductions of $100, resulting in $35 of tax saving. If the asset were then sold for $100 and the $100 of gain qualified for the most beneficial long-term capital gain treatment, the resulting tax would be $20. The taxpayer would then have had $15 of after-tax profit despite the fact that the asset was sold for the same price at which it was purchased. To prevent this rate arbitrage § 1245 provides that gains on dispositions of certain depreciable property are taxed as ordinary income to the extent of prior deductions for depreciation. In general, § 1245 applies to depreciable personal property regardless of the method of depreciation adopted. It generally does not apply to depreciable real property.[3] The principal effect of § 1245 is to override, to the extent of the recapture, the

---

[2]　　A somewhat higher, but nevertheless preferential, tax liability would result if any of the gain were attributable to reductions in basis resulting from depreciation deductions. See infra.

[3]　　For corporate taxpayers, § 291(a) treats as ordinary income 20 percent of the gain realized on depreciable real estate that would have been § 1245 recapture gain if § 1245 applied to depreciable real estate.

capital gain treatment that otherwise would be accorded by § 1231. As far as depreciable personal property is concerned, the circle is thus complete. Section 1221 denominates certain items as capital assets but excludes certain types of property from capital gain treatment; § 1231 restores some, but not all, of the property described in the exceptions to the capital gain category; § 1245 restores to ordinary income that portion of the gain on many § 1231 items that represents prior depreciation deductions, and excludes that ordinary income from the § 1231 netting process. Treas. Reg. § 1.1245–6(a). Section 1245 never comes into play if a § 1231 asset is sold for a loss.

The interaction between §§ 1231 and 1245 may be illustrated by the following example. Assume a taxpayer purchases a machine for $1,000 and claims $400 of depreciation deductions. The taxpayer then sells the machine for $800. Section 1245 requires that the $200 of gain ($800–$600) be "recaptured" as ordinary income, thus overriding § 1231. If the taxpayer sold the machine for $1,000, the full amount of the depreciation deductions previously taken would be ordinary income under § 1245. If, however, the machine were sold for $1,100, the gain would be segmented: $400 would be recaptured as ordinary income under § 1245 and the remaining $100 (that portion of the gain not representing prior depreciation deductions) would be taken into account in the netting process under § 1231 and could qualify for capital gain treatment.

The "recapture" provided in § 1245 performs several functions. First, it prevents the conversion of ordinary income into capital gain where the depreciation deductions have been taken against ordinary income but under § 1231 the gain reflecting those deductions would qualify for capital gain treatment on the disposition of the property. Second, viewed purely from the perspective of depreciation rules, applying § 1245 to the disposition may be seen as imposing a requirement that a taxpayer ultimately be allowed only economic depreciation with respect to the property, although significant timing advantages remain. Third, from the perspective of tax expenditure analysis, § 1245 operates as the mechanism by which the government receives full rather than partial repayment (which would result if preferential capital gain treatment were allowed) of the interest-free loan that it granted through the accelerated depreciation provisions.

The treatment of depreciable real estate is markedly different from that accorded depreciable personal property (whether tangible or intangible), used in a trade or business. Depreciable real estate placed in service after 1986 is not subject to any recapture if it has been held for more than one year.[4] Thus, taxpayers may claim depreciation as an

---

[4]   Depreciable real estate placed in service before 1981 is subject to the limited recapture rules of § 1250, which generally do not apply to straight-line depreciation. Depreciable real estate placed in service between 1981 and 1986 is subject to § 1245 if accelerated depreciation

ordinary deduction and receive capital gain treatment, albeit in part at a preferential rate higher than the most preferential capital gain rate, for the entire gain realized on a subsequent sale. As a result, owners of depreciable real estate can realize an after-tax profit on a transaction that merely breaks even, or in some cases loses money, before taxes. Stated differently, the Code provides no mechanism to assure that over the life of an investment in real estate total depreciation is limited to economic depreciation. Or from the tax expenditure perspective, taxpayers who receive "accelerated" depreciation for real estate are required to repay only a portion of the resulting interest-free loan from the government.

DETAILED ANALYSIS

1. SECTION 1231 ASSETS

1.1. *"Used" in the "Trade or Business"*

When an asset is sold at a loss, the main problem under § 1231 is to determine whether a "trade or business" exists and whether the asset has been "used" in that business. The first question—does a "trade or business" exist—is an issue only for individuals since corporations organized for profit are presumed to be in business. The second question—"used" in the business—can arise for both corporations and individuals.

The "trade or business" issue typically arises in the case of rental real estate. Section 1231 ordinary loss treatment applies only to trade or business property and not to investment property. The courts generally treat any rental activity as a trade or business. In Fackler v. Commissioner, 133 F.2d 509 (6th Cir.1943), the taxpayer, who was an attorney, sold his interest in a six-story office building that he held, rented, and managed under a 99-year lease. The court held that the taxpayer was engaged in a trade or business. Accordingly, because the case arose prior to the enactment of § 1231, the gain was ordinary under the rules then applicable.

In Crawford v. Commissioner, 16 T.C. 678 (1951) (Acq.), the taxpayer inherited a residence; the taxpayer did not use it as a residence but unsuccessfully attempted to rent it, and the property was treated as a § 1231 asset. On the other hand, in Grier v. United States, 120 F.Supp. 395 (D.Conn.1954), aff'd per curiam, 218 F.2d 603 (2d Cir.1955), the taxpayer, who was a securities advisor and salesman, inherited a house that had been rented to the same tenant for some years. The taxpayer continued to rent the house until it was sold some 14 years later. During the time the taxpayer owned the house, he provided, either by himself or through an agent, services in the nature of upkeep and repair. The court held, under the predecessor of § 1221(a)(2), that the taxpayer's activities with respect to the single house were so minimal in nature that the property, although used for the

---

was claimed under a prior version of § 168, but to no recapture if straight-line depreciation was claimed.

production of income, was not used in the taxpayer's trade or business. Accordingly, the loss was a capital loss.

The decision in *Grier* is an anomaly. Except for *Grier*, the courts have held that renting of a residence or other property constitutes a trade or business. In Alvary v. United States, 302 F.2d 790 (2d Cir.1962), the same Court of Appeals that affirmed the *Grier* decision found a trade or business to exist where the taxpayer owned two apartment houses managed by an agent and upheld an ordinary loss for the taxpayer. In contrast, if property is inherited and the new owner sells it without any effort first to rent it, the property will be treated as a capital asset, thereby precluding ordinary loss characterization under § 1231. Estate of Assmann v. Commissioner, 16 T.C. 632 (1951).

1.2. *Intangible Assets*

Under § 197, discussed in Chapter 14, Section 3, virtually all purchased intangibles, including goodwill, are amortizable. Section 197(f)(7) provides that amortizable § 197 intangibles are treated as property subject to the allowance for depreciation under § 167, thereby providing that § 197 intangibles are treated as § 1231 property. Historically, both self-created and separately purchased intangible assets with a determinable useful life were treated as depreciable property and as § 1231 assets, while such assets without a determinable useful life, particularly goodwill, were treated as capital assets. Since enactment of § 197 in 1993, purchased goodwill, tradenames, trademarks, and customer lists, etc., are § 1231 assets. A number of important frequently encountered self-created intangibles— specifically, licenses, and other governmental permits, franchises, tradenames, and trademarks—also are amortizable § 197 intangibles and thus are § 1231 property. See I.R.C. § 197(c)(2), (d)(1)(D)–(F). For the same reasons that amortizable § 197 intangibles are § 1231 property, any gain recognized on the disposition of an amortizable § 197 intangible is subject to depreciation recapture under § 1245. Section 1245(b)(9) provides that if a taxpayer disposes of several § 197 intangibles in one transaction, or in a series of related transactions, all the intangibles are treated as a single asset for purposes of calculating § 1245 recapture.

Self-created business goodwill and other self-created intangibles without any ascertainable useful life, such as customer lists, that are not amortizable § 197 intangibles (i.e., self-created intangible assets not described in § 197(d)(1)(D), (E), or (F)) continue to be characterized as capital assets, rather than § 1231 assets. Because these self-created intangibles are not amortizable § 197 assets, § 197(f)(7) does not apply to treat them as depreciable property, and thus there is no link to § 1231(b) from the standpoint of the seller. As nondepreciable capital assets they never enter into the § 1231 computation and are not subject to § 1245 depreciation recapture. In the hands of the purchaser, however, those intangible assets that were self-created by the seller become amortizable § 197 intangibles and thus are § 1231 assets in the hands of the purchaser.

While goodwill is "property" under §§ 1221 and 1231—and thus a capital asset, if it was self-created, or a § 1231 asset if it was purchased—a sale of goodwill must be distinguished from a sale of similar "rights" that do not arise to "property" for tax purposes. A number of cases and rulings have addressed this issue. Rev. Rul. 71–583, 1971–2 C.B. 312, held that amounts received by the existing clubs of a professional football league as consideration for the granting of a franchise to a new club in connection with a merger of two leagues was entitled to capital gain treatment since "the creation of a new * * * league franchise is a portioning out of the reputation (goodwill) that the existing teams have." In Franklin v. Commissioner, T.C.Memo 1947–273, the Mrs. Franklin, Inc. corporation, owned by Mrs. Franklin, sold its assets. The buyer separately paid Mrs. Franklin for the use of her name. The Tax Court held the payment represented a payment for the business goodwill associated with her name. A similar result was reached in Reid v. Commissioner, 26 T.C. 622 (1956) (Acq.), involving the right to use the taxpayer's name in connection with the transfer of certain patents. On the other hand, the sale of the right to exploit the taxpayer's name, not connected with any business or commercial product, results in ordinary income. Rev. Rul. 65–261, 1965–2 C.B. 281.

1.3. *Specially Treated Property*

1.3.1. *Livestock*

Cattle and horses first held for draft, breeding, dairy or sporting purposes before being sold qualify for § 1231 treatment only if held for more than twenty-four months. I.R.C. § 1231(b)(3)(A). Other livestock qualifies if held for the prescribed purposes for more than one year. I.R.C. § 1231(b)(3)(B). Livestock qualifies even though at the outset sale was intended after a period of use for the specified purpose and even though the sales constitute a regular source of profit. Since the cost of raising the animal is currently deductible from ordinary income if the taxpayer is on the cash method of accounting, the provision allows the conversion of ordinary income into capital gain. But livestock is neither fish nor fowl, at least for purposes of the Internal Revenue Code. See I.R.C. § 1231(b)(3) (flush language) and Treas. Reg. § 1.1231–2(a)(3).

1.3.2. *Timber*

Under § 631(a), the cutting of timber is treated as a sale of timber and the "sale" receives § 1231(a) treatment by § 1231(b)(2). The result is that the increase in value of the standing timber due to normal growth or any other factor generally receives capital gain treatment even though the cut timber is then sold to customers in the ordinary course of business. Only the profit in excess of the value when cut is ordinary income when the cut timber is sold. (A Christmas tree tax expenditure: timber includes evergreen trees that are more than six years old at the time severed from the roots and are sold for ornamental purposes.) Under § 631(b) the disposal of timber under a contract by which an economic interest is retained by the owner or a person having cutting rights is similarly accorded § 1231 treatment.

2.   TECHNICAL ASPECTS OF DEPRECIATION RECAPTURE

2.1. *Section 1245 Property*

Section 1245 applies to property depreciable under §§ 167 and 168, amortizable § 197 intangibles (via § 197(f)(7)), and property the cost of which is deducted under § 179 or amortized under certain specified sections. See I.R.C. § 1245(a), (c)(3). Thus, § 1245 recapture applies to almost all tangible and intangible § 1231 property held by the taxpayer for use in a trade or business. Section 1245 recapture does not extend to sales of property the cost of which has been expensed if no statutory provision specifically designates the property as subject to § 1245. Thus, gain on the sale of a self-developed patent, the cost of which was deducted as research and development expense under § 174, is not subject to ordinary income recapture. See Rev. Rul. 85–186, 1985–2 C.B. 84.

With respect to depreciable real estate, § 1250 provides for depreciation recapture as ordinary income to the extent of the excess of cumulative accelerated depreciation over straight-line depreciation. Before 1964 the recapture rules did not apply to depreciable real estate. In the 1986 Act, Congress limited depreciation on all real estate to the straight-line method. Thus, for real estate placed in service after 1986, there is no depreciation recapture (unless the property is sold within one year, in which case the gain is ordinary income rather than § 1231 gain in any event, since the one year holding period requirement has not been met). For corporate taxpayers on the sale of depreciable real property, § 291(a) treats as ordinary income 20 percent of the gain realized that would have been § 1245 recapture gain if § 1245 applied to depreciable real property.

2.2. *Triggering Dispositions*

On its face, § 1245 applies to all property dispositions, including those that otherwise would be tax-free under other provisions of the Internal Revenue Code. I.R.C. § 1245(a) (last sentence). Section 1245(b), however, carves out an exception for most of the common nonrecognition transactions. When one of these exceptions applies, depreciation recapture is not completely forgiven; instead the recapture potential attributable to the transferor's depreciation deductions continues to inure in the property in the hands of the transferee. This results from the phrase "or to any other person" in § 1245(a)(2)(A). For example, although a gift is not a "disposition" for purposes of § 1245, the § 1245 potential carries over with the property and the donee, upon a subsequent disposition to which § 1245 applies, must recapture the depreciation taken by the donor. Treas. Reg. § 1.1245–3(a)(3).

3.   "UNRECAPTURED SECTION 1250 GAIN" ON SALES OF DEPRECIABLE REAL PROPERTY

Except in the narrow circumstances in which § 1245 or § 1250 characterizes gain from the sale of depreciable real estate as ordinary income, gains from the sale of real estate used in a trade or business always are § 1231 gains. Not all § 1231 gains from the sale of real estate, however, are entitled to the most advantageous capital gains preference under § 1(h), even if the taxpayer's gains from the sale of § 1231 assets during the year exceed the § 1231 losses from the sale of § 1231 assets. In general, § 1231 gains that are characterized as capital gains are eligible for taxation at the 15 and 20 percent maximum rates that normally apply to adjusted net capital gains. However, to the extent that § 1231 gains characterized as capital gains are attributable to prior depreciation deductions claimed with respect to the property (which have not been recharacterized as ordinary income under § 1245 or § 1250), the gain is termed "unrecaptured section 1250 gain" by I.R.C. § 1(h)(6) and subjected to a special rule.[5] Section 1(h)(1)(E) sets the maximum tax rate for capital gains that are "unrecaptured section 1250 gain" at 25 percent, not the more favorable 20 percent rate otherwise available for gains on § 1231 assets held for more than one year by a taxpayer in the 39.6 percent bracket.[6]

This differentiated preferential rate does not affect the characterization of the gains as § 1231 gains for purposes of the § 1231 netting process. Assume, for example, that a taxpayer, generally subject to the 39.6 percent marginal tax rate, sold Blackacre, with a basis of $50,000, for $30,000, thereby recognizing a $20,000 loss, and sold Whiteacre, with a basis of $40,000 for $75,000, thereby recognizing a $35,000 gain. Both properties were held for rental. Since § 1231 gains exceed § 1231 losses (there is a net gain of $15,000), the loss on Blackacre and gain on Whiteacre are both capital. If the taxpayer previously had claimed $12,000 of straight-line depreciation deductions with respect to Whiteacre, $12,000 of the gain would be taxed at 25 percent, and the remaining gain would be eligible for the 20 percent maximum rate (although if the taxpayer had no other capital or § 1231 gains or losses the remaining gain and loss offset). On the other hand, if the taxpayer previously had claimed $30,000 of depreciation deductions with respect to Whiteacre, § 1(h)(1)(E) would limit the amount of gain taxed at the 25 percent rate to the $15,000 net § 1231 gain.

Notwithstanding that the § 1(h)(1)(E) "recapture" reduces the amount of § 1231 gain eligible for the 20 percent rate, the loss on Whiteacre remains capital. This treatment contrasts with the result when §§ 1245 and 1250 interact with § 1231; in those cases, the recharacterized income is excluded from the § 1231 netting process. Thus, for example, if $30,000 of the gain on Whiteacre had been § 1245 gain, the remaining $5,000 gain on Whiteacre and the $20,000 loss on Blackacre would have been characterized as

---

[5]　Notwithstanding the deceptively similar terminology of "unrecaptured § 1250 gain" under § 1(h)(7) and "§ 1250 recapture," the two concepts are as different as apples and cabbages. Unrecaptured § 1250 gain covers all depreciation on real estate to which it applies and is subject to preferential capital gains rate. Section 1250 recapture generally applies to only limited amounts of depreciation; for real property placed in service after 1980, § 1250 applies only to sales of depreciable property held for one year or less, and when it applies, § 1250 treats the recaptured gain as ordinary income (which it would be in any event since the § 1231 holding period requirement has not been met).

[6]　If the taxpayer is in a tax bracket below 39.6 percent, the maximum rate on § 1231 gains is less than 25 percent, and the "unrecaptured § 1250 gain" provision thus has no effect.

ordinary, because the § 1231 losses ($20,000) exceeded the § 1231 gains ($5,000).

4.   OTHER RECAPTURE PROVISIONS

4.1. *Natural Resources Recapture Rules*

The recapture technique is extended to natural resources cost recovery deductions in § 1254. Section 1254 recaptures as ordinary income on the disposition of any mineral property (both solid mineral and oil and gas) the sum of the following items: (1) depletion allowed under § 611 to the extent that depletion reduced the basis of the property; (2) solid mineral exploration expenses deducted under § 617 with respect to the property and that were not included in the basis of the property; (3) solid mineral development expenses that were deducted under § 616; and (4) in the case of oil and gas properties, all intangible drilling and development costs (IDC) deducted under § 263(c). Recapture also applies to any expenses deducted over the optional ten-year period provided in § 59(e). Section 1254 recapture is subject to the same exceptions that apply to § 1245 recapture.

4.2. *Miscellaneous Recapture Rules*

Section 1252 requires recapture upon the sale of farmland of amounts previously deducted under § 175 for soil and water conservation expenses. Section 1255 provides for the recapture of amounts excluded from income under § 126, discussed in Chapter 4, Section 5.A.2., upon sale of property acquired with funds obtained through various federal cost-sharing conservation programs.

5.   SALE OF DEPRECIABLE PROPERTY TO A CONTROLLED ENTITY

Section 1239 treats as ordinary income all gain recognized on a sale or exchange of property subject to depreciation in the hands of the transferee to any of certain related taxpayers, even though the gain otherwise would be § 1231 or capital gain. Treas. Reg. § 1.1239–2 extends this rule to property that can be amortized under certain other provisions. By virtue of § 197(f)(7), § 1239 applies to amortizable § 197 intangibles. The purpose of § 1239 is to prevent a taxpayer from selling depreciable assets to a corporation or partnership controlled by her, and reporting the profit as long-term capital gain while her controlled corporation acquires a stepped up basis to support larger depreciation deductions against ordinary income. Section 1239 is relatively narrowly focused, applying to sales and exchanges between an individual and a "controlled entity," primarily a corporation or partnership that is more than 50 percent owned by the taxpayer, or between a taxpayer and a trust of which the taxpayer (or the taxpayer's spouse) is a beneficiary.

SECTION 2.   SALE OF AN ENTIRE BUSINESS

INTERNAL REVENUE CODE: Section 1060

REGULATIONS: Sections 1.1060–1(a), (b)(1)–(7), (c)–(e); 1.338–6(b).

Williams v. McGowan

United States Circuit Court of Appeals, Second Circuit, 1945.
152 F.2d 570.

[Williams, the taxpayer, and one Reynolds had been engaged as partners in the hardware business, Williams having a two-thirds interest and Reynolds a one-third interest in the profits. On Reynolds' death in 1940, Williams agreed to buy Reynold's share of the partnership's business. Later in 1940 Williams sold the entire business to the Corning Building Company. On this sale, Williams suffered a loss upon his original two-thirds of the business but made a small gain on the one-third he had bought from Reynolds' executrix. Williams treated both the loss and gain as ordinary items. The Commissioner asserted a deficiency on the ground that the sale related to a capital asset so that the loss was a capital loss. The District Court stated that the "question is whether the assets sold were 'capital assets' within the meaning of [the former version of § 1221]."]

■ L. HAND, CIRCUIT JUDGE. * * * When Williams bought out Reynolds' interest, he became the sole owner of the business, the firm had ended upon any theory, and the situation for tax purposes was no other than if Reynolds had never been a partner at all, except that to the extent of one-third of the "amount realized" on Williams' sale to the Corning Company, his "basis" was different. * * * We have to decide only whether upon the sale of a going business it is to be comminuted into its fragments, and these are to be separately matched against the definition in [§ 1221], or whether the whole business is to be treated as if it were a single piece of property.

Our law has been sparing in the creation of juristic entities; it has never, for example, taken over the Roman "universitas facti";[1] and indeed for many years it fumbled uncertainly with the concept of a corporation. One might have supposed that partnership would have been an especially promising field in which to raise up an entity, particularly since merchants have always kept their accounts upon that basis. Yet there too our law resisted at the price of great and continuing confusion; and, even when it might be thought that a statute admitted, if it did not demand, recognition of the firm as an entity, the old concepts prevailed. Francis v. McNeal, 228 U.S. 695. And so, even though we might agree

---

[1]   "By universitas facti is meant a number of things of the same kind which are regarded as a whole; e.g., a herd, a stock of wares." Mackeldey, Roman Law § 162.

that under the influence of the Uniform Partnership Act a partner's interest in the firm should be treated as indivisible, and for that reason a "capital asset" within [§ 1221], we should be chary about extending further so exotic a jural concept. Be that as it may, in this instance the section itself furnishes the answer. It starts in the broadest way by declaring that all "property" is "capital assets," and then makes three exceptions. The first is "stock in trade * * * or other property of a kind which would properly be included in the inventory"; next comes "property held * * * primarily for sale to customers"; and finally, property "used in the trade or business of a character which is subject to * * * allowance for depreciation." In the face of this language, although it may be true that a "stock in trade," taken by itself, should be treated as a "universitas facti," by no possibility can a whole business be so treated; and the same is true as to any property within the other exceptions. Congress plainly did mean to comminute the elements of a business; plainly it did not regard the whole as "capital assets."

As has already appeared, Williams transferred to the Corning Company "cash," "receivables," "fixtures" and a "merchandise inventory." "Fixtures" are not capital because they are subject to a depreciation allowance; the inventory, as we have just seen, is expressly excluded. So far as appears, no allowance was made for "good-will"; but, even if there had been, we held in Haberle Crystal Springs Brewing Company v. Clarke, Collector, 2 Cir., 30 F.2d 219, that "good-will" was a depreciable intangible. It is true that the Supreme Court reversed that judgment—280 U.S. 384; but it based its decision only upon the fact that there could be no allowance for the depreciation of "good-will" in a brewery, a business condemned by the Eighteenth Amendment. There can of course be no gain or loss in the transfer of cash; and, although Williams does appear to have made a gain of $1072.71 upon the "receivables," the point has not been argued that they are not subject to a depreciation allowance.* That we leave open for decision by the district court, if the parties cannot agree. The gain or loss upon every other item should be computed as an item in ordinary income.

Judgment reversed.

DETAILED ANALYSIS

1.   BACKGROUND

Williams v. McGowan established a "comminution rule" that the sale of an entire business by the owner, whether a sole proprietor, partnership, or corporation, is not a unitary transaction permitting classification of the business as a capital asset. Rather, the purchase price must be allocated among the various assets sold with the character of the gain or loss

---

*   [Ed.: Section 1221(a)(4) was not then in the statute.]

recognized on the sale of the business determined by that allocation. Note that it was the Government that was arguing for a unitary approach in Williams v. McGowan since the business treated as a unit had been sold for a loss, which would have been a capital loss, a deduction from which was limited by § 1211.

The Williams v. McGowan rule requires an allocation of the purchase price among the assets sold. The allocation may be made by the parties in the purchase and sale agreement or, if no specific allocation is made in the agreement, then buyer and seller each will independently determine the allocation of the purchase price that will be reflected in their tax treatment of the sale. Historically, the buyer's and seller's interests with respect to the allocation have diverged significantly. From the seller's side, inventory and depreciable equipment are likely to produce ordinary gain; real estate and intangibles are likely, after considering § 1231, to produce capital gain. Thus, the seller was interested in maximizing the portion of the price allocated to the latter, minimizing the portion allocated to the former. From the buyer's side, a higher basis in inventory and depreciable equipment was more desirable because those capitalized costs would be recovered more rapidly than the basis of real property and goodwill. Indeed, prior to 1993, goodwill was not depreciable or amortizable at all. The result often was inconsistent treatment by the buyer and seller, each allocating the purchase price in a relatively more advantageous manner.

2.   STATUTORY COMMINUTION

2.1. *Allocation of Purchase Price*

The comminution rule of Williams v. McGowan now is required by statute. Section 1060, enacted in 1986, requires both the seller and the buyer to allocate the purchase price paid among the assets pursuant to regulations. This provision was designed to prevent inconsistent and artificial allocations that were a problem under prior law.

Section 1060 refers to preexisting regulations under § 338(b)(5), which contain a detailed set of rules for allocating the purchase price among the assets sold and purchased. Treas. Reg. § 1.1060–1 (through a cross reference to Treas. Regs. § 1.338–6 and § 1.338–7, which provide the substantive details) requires that the assets of the purchased business be divided into seven classes and the purchase price allocated first among the classes and then among the assets in each class. Class I includes cash and general deposit accounts (not including certificates of deposit). Class II includes actively traded personal property (as defined in § 1092(d)), such as marketable stock and securities, certificates of deposit, and foreign currency. Class III includes all debt instruments, including accounts receivable, mortgages, and credit card receivables that arise in the ordinary course of business, as well as property that the taxpayer must mark-to-market annually for tax purposes (see e.g., § 475). Class IV includes stock in trade of the taxpayer or other property of a kind that would properly be included in the inventory of the taxpayer if on hand at the close of the taxable year, and property held by the taxpayer primarily for sale to customers in the ordinary course of the taxpayer's trade or business. Class V includes all assets not included in Class I, II, III, IV, VI, or VII; this class includes all machinery and equipment, as well as land and buildings (and, if the taxpayer is a corporation, stock of any of its subsidiaries). Class VI includes all § 197 intangibles (as defined in § 197(d)) except goodwill or going concern value. The term "§ 197 intangibles" is broader than the term "amortizable § 197 intangibles" and includes, for example, § 197 intangibles that are amortizable by the buyer but not by the seller, such as self-created customer lists, employment contracts, supply contracts, etc., as well as business licenses, trademarks and tradenames, and covenants not to compete, even if the covenant is created in the purchase and sale transaction, and patents and copyrights (whether depreciable or amortizable to the seller). Finally, Class VII, which is the residual basis category, includes only goodwill and going concern value.

The consideration paid for the business is allocated first to Class I assets based on their fair market value, then seriatim to Class II, Class III, Class IV, Class V, Class VI, and Class VII assets. Within each class, the price is allocated among the assets relative to their fair market values. Since each asset in Classes I through VI generally will be allocated a portion of the price equal to its fair market value, any premium is allocated to Class VII, goodwill and going concern value. Conversely, if a business is purchased for less than its liquidation value, the Class VI (and in some cases, possibly the Class V) assets are allocated an amount less than their individual fair market values.

The seller and buyer have a variety of conflicting tax interests in the allocations. From the buyer's side, since all § 197 intangibles are amortized over 15 years, the division of § 197 amortizable intangibles between two classes for purposes of determining basis is significant only if some, but not all, of the amortizable intangibles acquired in a single transaction are subsequently sold at a gain, necessitating calculation of individual bases of the intangibles that were sold. From the seller's side, § 1245 recapture may apply with respect to both Class V assets and Class VI assets, because Class VI contains both amortizable self-created intangibles and purchased intangibles, both of which are subject to § 1245 recapture on sale. But § 1245 applies to Class VII assets only if the goodwill and going concern value were purchased and amortized; self-created goodwill and going concern value, on the other hand, always produce capital gain. Furthermore, the allocation of price between Classes VI and VII on the one hand and between assets within Class V itself can be important. The parties can have differing interests. Class V contains both depreciable assets, such as buildings and equipment, and nondepreciable assets, such as land. Purchasers will want to establish as high a fair market value as is possible first for inventory and then for depreciable property, but for the seller such an allocation may give rise to ordinary income (including § 1245 recapture income) instead of capital gain via § 1231. Sellers generally will want to assign as high a value as possible first to land and § 1231 assets that are not subject to any recapture rule, and then to ordinary income. The impact of § 1(h)(1)(E), limiting the capital gain preference for depreciable real estate also must be taken into account. Further generalizations as to whether the seller or purchaser is benefitted by an allocation to Class V versus Class VI are impossible because the analysis is fact specific. Class V contains many assets for which cost recovery under § 168 is more rapid than is cost recovery under § 197 for Class VI and Class VII assets, but it also contains important assets, e.g., buildings and other improvements to real property, for which cost recovery under § 168 is not as rapid as cost recovery for intangibles under § 197.

2.2. Covenants Not to Compete

2.2.1. Historical Background

The sale of business assets is often accompanied by an agreement that the seller will not compete with the buyer in the field of business involved. Payments received under such covenants not to compete generally are treated as ordinary income. Hamlin's Trust v. Commissioner, 209 F.2d 761 (10th Cir.1954); Rev. Rul. 69–643, 1969–2 C.B. 10. But if a covenant not to compete included in a purchase and sale agreement was not separately bargained and was included as a mere incident to the transfer of goodwill, then the seller sometimes has succeeded in obtaining capital gain treatment for the payments received under the covenant. See General Insurance Agency, Inc. v. Commissioner, 401 F.2d 324 (4th Cir.1968) (involving the sale of an insurance agency, in which the court held that the covenant was not separable from the transfer of goodwill).

From the seller's point of view, payments received for a covenant not to compete are ordinary income while amounts received for goodwill produce either capital gain or § 1231 gain, which can result in capital gain treatment. Before the enactment of § 197, on the buyer's side, payments attributable to a covenant not to compete were amortized over the life of the covenant while payments for goodwill purchased a nondepreciable asset. These tax considerations led sellers to seek an allocation of price to goodwill and buyers to seek an allocation to a covenant not to compete. The enactment of § 197 in 1993 significantly reduced this tension. Individual sellers generally prefer allocations to goodwill, which result in either capital gain or § 1231 gain (subject to § 1245 recapture if the sold goodwill had been previously purchased).[7] Purchasers, however, are indifferent regarding the allocation because under § 197 both goodwill and covenants not to compete are amortizable by the buyer over fifteen years.

Because of the tension between the buyer and seller, mutually agreed upon allocations between a covenant not to compete and goodwill historically were given deference. The Third Circuit generally gave the most weight to the agreement, holding the parties to their contract allocation except in cases of "fraud, duress, or undue influence." Commissioner v. Danielson, 378 F.2d

---

[7]   Because there is no preferential capital gains rate for corporations, a corporation that sells a business is indifferent with regard to the allocation unless the corporation has capital losses, which are deductible only against capital gains.

771 (3d Cir.1967). In Thomas v. Commissioner, 67 Fed.Appx. 582 (11th Cir.2003), the Eleventh Circuit refused to allow the taxpayer to re-classify payments as capital gain after a revision of a stock sale agreement that originally allocated a significant portion of the purchase price to a covenant not to compete. The agreement was modified as part of the settlement of a subsequent dispute over the taxpayer's competition with the purchaser. The subsequent agreement did not contain the non-competition agreement. Applying *Danielson*, the court held that the taxpayer was bound by the initial allocation of purchase price to the covenant not to compete.

Where the Commissioner, and not the taxpayer, was arguing that the allocation made in the agreement should be ignored, the "fraud" rule of *Danielson* was not applied. In Lemery v. Commissioner, 52 T.C. 367 (1969), aff'd per curiam, 451 F.2d 173 (9th Cir.1971), the taxpayer purchased stock in a corporation. The stock purchase agreement contained a covenant by the seller that he would not compete with the purchaser for five years; $200,000 of the purchase price was allocated to the covenant. The taxpayer took amortization deductions for payments on the covenant which the Commissioner disallowed. The Tax Court found for the Commissioner, holding that the allocation to the covenant was not the result of an arm's length bargain. Since the vendor had held the stock for less than the long-term holding period, it was immaterial to him whether the payments were considered as relating to the covenant not to compete or the sale of the stock, and hence the parties' tax interests were not adverse. See also Dixie Finance Co., Inc. v. United States, 474 F.2d 501 (5th Cir.1973); O'Dell & Co. v. Commissioner, 61 T.C. 461 (1974) (parties' allocation sustained).

Where the agreement of sale makes no allocation between goodwill and the covenant not to compete, the courts will review the allocation, based on normal standards of burden of proof. For example, in Kinney v. Commissioner, 58 T.C. 1038 (1972), the contract for the sale of a business provided for a covenant not to compete but made no specific allocation because of a disagreement among the parties as to the amount to be allocated. The seller treated the entire purchase price as allocable to the assets transferred but the court found that one-third of that amount should be allocated to the covenant not to compete. Peterson Machine Tool, Inc. v. Commissioner, 79 T.C. 72 (1982), aff'd, 84–2 U.S.T.C. ¶ 9885 (10th Cir.1984), reached a similar result. On the other hand, in Better Beverages, Inc. v. United States, 619 F.2d 424 (5th Cir.1980), where no allocation was made to the covenant not to compete, the court refused to follow a subsequent allocation made by the buyer.

2.2.2. *Effect of Section 1060*

Section 1060 did not completely address the problem of artificial allocations between goodwill and covenants not to compete. A covenant not to compete, even though created in the sale transaction and ancillary to the sale of goodwill, is a Class VI asset, Treas. Reg. § 1.1060–1(b)(7), (d), Ex. 2, while goodwill is assigned to Class VII. As far as the buyer is concerned, this allocation is of little consequence because § 197 provides for the amortization of *all* purchased intangible assets over 15 years, and § 197(d)(1)(E) treats the covenant not to compete as an amortizable § 197 intangible. Thus, under § 197, both a covenant not to compete and purchased goodwill must be amortized over 15 years. No loss deduction is allowed for the basis allocated to one as long as the other is retained. I.R.C. § 197(f)(1). The seller, on the other hand, is not indifferent on the sale of goodwill that qualifies for capital gain treatment. Due to the preferential rates accorded capital gains, an individual seller will want as much as possible of the purchase price that exceeds the liquidation value of other assets to be allocated to goodwill rather than to a covenant not to compete. Although in many cases the buyer's business need for an enforceable covenant not to compete will prevent the parties from omitting a covenant not to compete from the transaction entirely, artificial allocations will continue to be a problem.

2.3. *Safeguards Against Whipsaw and Artificial Allocations*

Section 1060 provides mechanisms for the IRS to police artificial allocations. Although nothing in § 1060 requires that the buyer and seller agree on a price allocation, § 1060(b) requires both the buyer and seller to file information returns regarding their respective price allocations. Section 1060(e) authorizes the IRS to require any 10 percent or more owner who sells assets or an interest in a business in a sale subject to § 1060 to report information regarding any associated employment or noncompetition agreements. Thus the IRS has available information to prevent a whipsaw. Furthermore, § 1060(a) provides that if the seller and buyer do agree in writing on the allocation of the purchase price or the fair market value of any assets, the agreement generally is binding on both parties. Treas. Reg. § 1.1060–1(c)(4) provides that the agreement will be binding on both parties unless a party is able to refute the allocation under the standards of Commissioner v. Danielson, 378 F.2d 771 (3d Cir.1967), supra. See also H.Rep. 101–964, 101st Cong., 2d Sess. 95 (1990). Thus, a taxpayer can avoid an agreed-upon allocation only with proof admissible in an action to show unenforceability because of mistake, undue influence, fraud, or duress. The IRS, however, is not restricted from challenging the taxpayers' allocations. Treas. Reg. § 1.1060–1(c)(4); see also S.Rep. No. 99–313, 99th Cong., 2d Sess. 255 (1986). Where the parties do not have adverse interests with respect to the allocation of an agreed-upon total amount, the IRS is more likely to scrutinize the allocation, even though there is no whipsaw per se. See Heritage Auto Center, Inc. v. Commissioner, T.C. Memo. 1996–21 (agreed upon allocation between sales price and covenant not to compete/consulting agreement was redetermined because the buyer and seller did not have adverse tax interests and consulting agreement lacked economic significance).

3.   PROFESSIONAL BUSINESSES

Whether goodwill arising in a professional business ever qualifies as a separate asset upon sale of the business has been the subject of substantial controversy. The IRS tried for some time to limit the allocation of sales proceeds to goodwill in this situation, arguing that professional goodwill was not transferable. The courts, however, consistently held otherwise. See e.g., Watson v. Commissioner, 35 T.C. 203 (1960) (accounting practice); Brooks v. Commissioner, 36 T.C. 1128 (1961) (Acq.) (orthodontic practice). In Rev. Rul. 64–235, 1964–2 C.B. 18, the IRS conceded that the sale of a professional business, even a one-person business, could involve goodwill but refused to find a transfer of goodwill where the professional person, rather than selling the practice, merely admitted new partners. Subsequently, Butler v. Commissioner, 46 T.C. 280 (1966), held to the contrary, allowing an accountant who took in a new partner to treat the entering partner's payment as capital gain. In Rev. Rul. 70–45, 1970–1 C.B. 17, the IRS retreated from its earlier position indicating that "the question of whether there has been a partial transfer of goodwill or merely an anticipatory assignment of future earnings of the practice will be treated as a question of fact."

4. CORPORATE STOCK AND PARTNERSHIP INTERESTS

4.1. *Corporate Stock*

Williams v. McGowan and § 1060 do not apply to the sale of corporate stock, whether the sale is of only a portion of the outstanding stock of a corporation or all of the stock. The stock is a capital asset, and no attempt is made to "look through" the stock to the character of the assets owned by the corporation. Where an owner sells ten percent or more of the outstanding stock of a corporation and enters into an employment agreement, covenant not to compete, lease, or other similar agreement, § 1060(e) may require that an information return be filed and the IRS may challenge the allocation between the stock and the contractual arrangement.

If a corporation sells all of the assets of a line of business, Williams v. McGowan and § 1060 apply in computing the gain and loss recognized by the corporation. United States Mineral Products Co. v. Commissioner, 52 T.C. 177 (1969) (Acq.) (transfer of assets by corporation to wholly owned subsidiary); Rev. Rul. 67–192, 1967–2 C.B. 140.

A question sometimes arises regarding the identity of the owner and seller of business goodwill when the assets of a business owned by a closely held corporation are sold. In most cases, the business goodwill clearly is owned by the corporation and not by the shareholders. In a few cases, however, shareholders who were the primary entrepreneurs and key employees argued that some or all of the business goodwill was owned by them individually. In Martin Ice Cream Co. v. Commissioner, 110 T.C. 189 (1998), Häagen-Dazs repurchased the rights to distribute Häagen-Dazs ice cream in the United States from the business that had been distributing Häagen-Dazs under an oral agreement between Häagen-Dazs and the majority shareholder. The IRS treated the amounts received in consideration of the distributorship rights as an amount realized by the corporation, but the corporation and its majority shareholder argued that the amounts were received directly by the shareholder. The Tax Court agreed with the taxpayers, holding that the shareholder, rather than the corporation, owned the distribution rights and sold them back to Häagen-Dazs, reasoning that the rights were based on the shareholder's personal relationships with supermarket chains and the shareholder's personal oral agreement with the founder of Häagen-Dazs, which never became a corporate asset.

The Tax Court reached a similar result in Norwalk v. Commissioner, T.C. Memo 1998–279, which involved a CPA professional services corporation that dissolved and distributed its assets to its two CPA shareholders, who in turn contributed the assets to a partnership that they joined in that year. The IRS asserted that in addition to the tangible assets expressly distributed, the corporation distributed various customer-based intangible assets, including goodwill, which resulted in a gain to the corporation under § 336, which requires a distributing corporation to recognize gain when appreciated assets are distributed to shareholders in the same manner as if the corporation had sold the assets for fair market value. The Tax Court agreed with the taxpayer's contention that the corporation's earnings were entirely attributable to the CPA-shareholders— any clients would have followed the individual CPAs—and that the corporation, therefore, owned no goodwill that could be sold separately. The court reasoned that on the facts clients sought the personal ability, personality, and reputation of the individual CPAs, and these assets did not belong to the corporation; the corporation's name and its business location did not contribute to goodwill.

Martin Ice Cream and *Norwalk* were distinguished in Solomon v. Commissioner, T.C. Memo. 2008–102. Solomon Colors, Inc. sold one of its businesses to another corporation. In connection with the sale, the Solomons (father and son), who were majority shareholders and key employees, entered into covenants not to compete. Provisions in the contracts described payments received by the taxpayers as consideration for their execution of the covenants not to compete, but other documents allocating the purchase price and payments among assets described those payments as consideration for the shareholder's ownership interest in the customer list for the business that was sold. The court rejected the taxpayers' argument that, as in *Martin Ice Cream Co.*, the payments were consideration for the sale of goodwill owned by the shareholders. The *Solomon* court found that the value of the Solomon Colors' business was not attributable to the quality of service and customer relationships developed by the shareholders, which distinguished the facts from *Martin Ice Cream Co.* Because the Solomon Colors' business involved processing, manufacturing, and sale of a product, rather than the provision of services, the corporation's success did not depend entirely on the personal goodwill of its shareholder/employees. Furthermore, the fact that the purchaser did not require the shareholders to enter into employment or consulting agreements made it unlikely that it was purchasing their personal goodwill. Accordingly, the payments were entirely consideration for the shareholders' covenants not to compete and thus were ordinary income, not capital gain.

The court in Muskat v. United States, 554 F.3d 183 (1st Cir. 2009), reached a similar result. The taxpayer was the chief executive officer and owner of 37 percent of the outstanding stock of a corporation, all of which was acquired by another corporation. In connection with the acquisition, the taxpayer entered into an employment agreement and a noncompetition agreement. The noncompetition agreement provided for payments over thirteen years, and the payments would survive the taxpayer's death. The taxpayer claimed that the payments under the noncompetition agreement were in fact payments for personal goodwill, and thus should have been taxed as capital gains rather than ordinary income. The court held that when the parties to a transaction have executed a written instrument allocating the purchase price to particular items, and one party thereafter seeks to alter the written allocation for tax purposes, that party "must adduce 'strong proof' that, at the time of execution of the instrument, the contracting parties actually intended the payments to compensate for something different. . . . The party] seeking to alter a written allocation must demonstrate an actual meeting of the minds with respect to some other allocation." Strong proof would require evidence having "persuasive power closely resembling the 'clear and convincing' evidence required to reform a written contract on the ground of mutual mistake." The record did not contain any evidence of discussions of the taxpayer's personal goodwill during the negotiations, and none of the transaction documents (including drafts) mentioned his personal goodwill. Furthermore, the purchaser's president testified that "he could not imagine that any goodwill other than [the corporation's] was material to the transaction." The court held for the government because the taxpayer "had failed to adduce strong proof that the contracting parties intended the challenged payment to be compensation for personal goodwill."

4.2. *Partnership Interests*

Sections 741 and 751 provide that the sale by a partner of his partnership interest receives capital asset treatment unless the partnership holds unrealized receivables (which include built-in gains subject to the various recapture rules considered above, as well as cash-method accounts receivable) or inventory, in which case the sale is treated on an asset-by-asset basis with respect to those items, but otherwise remains a sale of a capital asset. A sale by the partnership itself of its assets is governed by *Williams v. McGowan* and § 1060. United States v. Woolsey, 326 F.2d 287 (5th Cir.1963).

CHAPTER 26

LIKE-KIND EXCHANGES

As discussed in Chapter 6, *realized* gain or loss from the disposition of property is determined first by identifying the amount realized, then subtracting adjusted basis. Section 1001(c) requires that the entire amount of gain or loss realized on the disposition of property be *recognized*, that is, taken into account in determining taxable income, unless otherwise provided in the Code. The next step in the analysis is to determine whether a particular transaction falls within one of the Code's nonrecognition provisions. Finally, as discussed in Chapter 24, recognized gain or loss is then classified as ordinary or capital gain to fully determine the tax consequence of the property disposition.

Under specific provisions of the Code, gain or loss on certain dispositions of property is not recognized, even though gain or loss is realized under § 1001. Unrecognized gain or loss does not enter into the calculation of taxable income. Some of these nonrecognition provisions, such as § 1031 dealing with like-kind exchanges of property, are based upon the theory that, although the form of investment has changed, there has been an insufficient change in the substance of the investment to break its continuity and justify a reckoning for tax purposes. These provisions, which apply to both gain and loss, may be viewed as an elaboration of the realization requirement. Other nonrecognition provisions, such as the treatment of involuntary conversions under § 1033, discussed in Chapter 27, are elective relief provisions that apply only to gains. Section 1041, discussed in Chapter 37, which treats a transfer between spouses as a nonrecognition event is a hybrid in that it treats the marital unit as a single taxpayer in the case of transfers between spouses and it provides relief from the hardship of tax liability on property divisions in divorce. Section 1041, like § 1031 and unlike § 1033, applies to both gains and losses and is not elective.

Nonrecognition provisions are timing rules. The inclusion of the gain or the deduction of the loss is postponed until a subsequent recognition event. Although nonrecognition provisions generally are not intended to produce forgiveness of the tax or permanent disallowance of the loss, as long as it remains the law, § 1014 will make the nonrecognition permanent if the replacement property is retained by the taxpayer until death.

Postponement of income recognition is accomplished through the basis provisions. If the basis of property received in a nonrecognition disposition reflects the basis of the transferred property, then proper reckoning of gain or loss will occur when the property is subsequently disposed of in a taxable transaction. Thus, if a taxpayer exchanges property with a basis of $10,000 and a value of $90,000 for other property worth $90,000 in a nonrecognition transaction, then assigning the original $10,000 basis to the newly acquired property still leaves the taxpayer with a potential $80,000 gain. This "exchanged basis," is contrasted with "cost basis," which would result if the transaction had produced recognition of gain.

SECTION 1.   LIKE-KIND EXCHANGES IN GENERAL

INTERNAL REVENUE CODE: Section 1031 (omitting (g) and (h)).

REGULATIONS: Sections 1.1031(a)–1; –2(a), (b)(1)–(3), (c)(1), (2); 1.1031(b)–1; 1.1031(c)–1; 1.1031(d)–1; –2; 1.1031(j)–1(a)–(c).

Section 1031 provides for the nonrecognition of gain or loss where property held for productive use or investment is exchanged *solely* for property of a "like-kind" that is held for productive use or for investment. Three tests are included in this language. First, there must be an "exchange" of property for property (not cash). Second, the properties involved must be of "like-kind." Third, both the property exchanged and the property received must be held for productive use in a trade or business or for investment.

While § 1031(a) provides for nonrecognition of gain or loss on the exchange of property *solely* for property of like-kind, § 1031(b) allows for the receipt of money or property that is not of like-kind, commonly referred to as "boot." Realized gain must be recognized to the extent of the amount of money or the fair market value of the other, non-like-kind, property (the boot). The amount recognized as gain will not exceed the amount of gain realized. Loss is not recognized in any event.

Gain or loss that is not recognized in an exchange is deferred until disposition of the replacement property in a taxable transaction through operation of the exchanged basis rules of § 1031(d). The basis of property acquired in a § 1031 exchange will be the same as the basis of property given up in the exchange, decreased by the amount of any money received, and increased by the amount of any gain recognized. This basis rule is similar to the definition of basis developed by the court in *Philadelphia Park Amusement Co. v. United States*, and discussed in Chapter 6, Section 3.B. The basis formulation ensures that gain or loss that is not recognized on a like-kind exchange remains built-in to the basis of the property received. Thus, for example, if A exchanges property with a fair market value of $100 and a basis of $30 for property worth $80, plus $20 of cash, then A realizes $70 of gain ($100 – $30) and must recognize the $20 of the gain that is attributable to receipt of $20 of cash. A's basis in the new property will be $30, consisting of A's $30 basis in the property given up, decreased by the $20 of cash received, and increased by $20 of gain recognized. If A were later to sell the new property for $80, then A would recognize $50 of gain. A's $50 of deferred gain, plus the $20 of gain recognized on the initial exchange, fully accounts for the $70 of gain realized on A's disposition of the exchange property.

Section 1031(d) also provides that if more than one property is received, a portion of the basis will be allocated to any non-like-kind property received in an amount equal to the fair market value of the non-like-kind property. This rule, in effect, treats the non-like-kind property in same manner as cash. The basis of the nonrecognition property is reduced by the fair market value of property received as boot.

DETAILED ANALYSIS

1. QUALIFYING PROPERTY

1.1. *Property of a Like-Kind*

In determining whether property is of a "like-kind," three categories of property first must be differentiated: (a) excluded property; (b) real property; and (c) personal property (other than excluded property).

1.1.1. *Excluded Property*

Certain types of property are not eligible for nonrecognition treatment under § 1031 in any circumstance. Stock in trade (inventory) and property held primarily for sale, stock, securities, evidences of indebtedness, partnership interests, certificates of trust, and choses in action are all specifically excluded by § 1031(a)(2). Although § 1031 does not apply to the exchange of stock for stock, bonds for bonds, or stock for bonds, other provisions may provide nonrecognition treatment. Section 1036, for example, provides nonrecognition for gains and losses in exchanges of common stock of the same corporation.

Stock in trade or other property "held primarily for sale" is specifically excluded from § 1031. I.R.C. § 1031(a)(2)(A). The statutory standard here is different from that utilized in § 1221(a)(1), discussed in Chapter 24, Section 2.A.(1), in that the phrase "to customers in the ordinary course of his trade or business" is omitted. Thus, for example, in Black v. Commissioner, 35 T.C. 90 (1960), where a taxpayer, who was not in the real estate business, exchanged desert land for residential property, repaired the acquired house, and sold it eight months later, the court denied § 1031 treatment upon a finding that the property received in the exchange was held primarily for sale.

1.1.2. *Real Property*

In the case of real property, the term "like-kind" refers to "the nature or character of the property and not to its grade or quality." Treas. Reg. § 1.1031(a)–1(b). Thus, no distinction is made between improved and unimproved real estate. An exchange of city real estate for a ranch or farm, or an exchange of a 30-year or more real estate leasehold for a fee, are considered to be of a like-kind. Treas. Reg. § 1.1031(a)–1(c). The extraordinarily broad scope given to "like-kind" as that term is applied to real estate was underscored in Commissioner v. Crichton, 122 F.2d 181 (5th Cir.1941), which held an exchange of an improved city lot for a mineral interest in unimproved country land to be within § 1031(a), stating that the distinction intended by the statute is a "broad one between classes and characters of properties, for instance, between real and personal property. It was not intended to draw any distinction between parcels of real property however dissimilar they may be in location, in attributes and in capacities for profitable use." However, under § 1031(h), real property located within the United States and real property located in another country are not treated as like-kind property.

The broad application of § 1031 to real estate has raised issues, such as in *Crichton,* as to whether various limited interests in real estate have the same character as a fee interest. In Commissioner v. P.G. Lake, Inc., 356 U.S. 260 (1958), an exchange of oil production payments, restricted to a specified dollar value of production, for real estate was held not to qualify as a like-kind exchange. Rev. Rul. 68–331, 1968–1 C.B. 352, held an exchange of a leasehold interest in a producing oil lease extending over the life of the deposit for a fee interest in an improved ranch to be a like-kind exchange. The distinction is dependent on various characterizations of interests in oil and gas as real property interests.

In Koch v. Commissioner, 71 T.C. 54 (1978) (Acq.), the transfer of real estate for an interest in real estate subject to a 99-year lease was treated as a like-kind exchange. The Commissioner had argued that the taxpayers received an interest in an income stream in exchange for the property that was not like-kind. The Tax Court concluded that the taxpayer's right to rent was part of the bundle of rights incident to the fee interest. But in Oregon Lumber Co. v. Commissioner, 20 T.C. 192 (1953) (Acq.), an exchange of timber land for the right to cut and remove timber from other lands was held not to come under § 1031, the exchange being one of realty for personalty under local law.

In Peabody Natural Resources Co. v. Commissioner, 126 T.C. 261 (2006), the taxpayer exchanged a gold mine for a coal mine encumbered with contracts to be the exclusive provider of coal to a power plant. The Commissioner argued that the supply contracts were separate property that should be treated as boot. The court found the contracts were real property under state law. While stating that an exchange involving interests characterized as real property does not automatically qualify as an exchange of like-kind property, following *Koch,* the court held that the taxpayer's right to mine coal and the payment rights under the supply contracts represent parts of the bundle of rights incident to ownership of the real property. The court explained its rationale as follows:

> The underlying rationale for allowing nonrecognition of gain or loss under section 1031 is the concept that a taxpayer's economic situation following the exchange is essentially the same as it had been before the transaction. This is expressed in the following quote from the committee report underlying the predecessor statute to section 1031: "if the taxpayer's money is still tied up in the same kind of property as that in which it was originally invested, he is not allowed to compute and deduct his theoretical loss on the exchange, nor is he charged with a tax upon his theoretical profit". H. Rept. 704, 73d Cong., 2d Sess. (1934), 1939–1 C.B. (Part 2) 554,

564 * * * . The underpinning supporting section 1031(a) is that the new property is substantially a continuation of the old investment which remains unliquidated. * * *

In determining whether the like-kind requirement of section 1031 had been met, we found it significant in Koch v. Commissioner, 71 T.C. at 65, that section 1031(a) refers to property of a like, not an identical, kind. The required comparison of the old and new exchanged properties, we reasoned, should be directed to whether the taxpayer, in making the exchange, has used its property to acquire a new kind of asset or has merely exchanged its property for an asset of like nature or character. Id. Examining the exchanged properties in Koch with those principles in mind, we held the taxpayer's exchange of fee simple land for other fee simple land subject to 99-year condominium leases qualified for nonrecognition treatment under section 1031(a) because those exchanged properties were property of a like kind. * * * .

Rev. Rul. 55–749, 1955–2 C.B. 295, provides that an exchange of a perpetual water right, regarded as real property under local law, for land qualified for nonrecognition under § 1031; the legal classification of both assets as real property was not in itself enough, since a substantial difference in the rights involved may make the properties not of like-kind. But Wiechens v. United States, 228 F.Supp.2d 1080 (D. Ariz. 2002), held that an exchange of water rights to a limited quantity of water for a duration of 50 years, which under state law were real property, for a fee simple interest in land did not qualify for nonrecognition under § 1031. The water rights and a fee simple interest in land were not "like-kind," even under the broad standard of Treas. Reg. § 1.1031(a)–1(b), because the water rights were not perpetual. The court rejected the taxpayer's argument that the 50-year water rights were analogous to the 30-year lease that qualified as like-kind with a fee simple in real estate under Treas. Reg. § 1.1031(a)–1(c).

A similar issue arises in an exchange of partial interests. Compare Rev. Rul. 72–601, 1972–2 C.B. 467 (neither a transfer of a life estate in one parcel of real estate in exchange for a remainder interest in another, nor a transfer of a remainder interest in one parcel for a life estate in another, qualified under § 1031) with Rev. Rul. 78–4, 1978–1 C.B. 256 (transfer of a remainder interest in one-half of one tract of farm land for a remainder interest in one-half of another tract of farm land, both interests measured by the same life, qualified under § 1031).

1.1.3. *Personal Property*

The definition of like-kind personal property attends to the specific characteristics and qualities of the properties involved. Treas. Reg. § 1.1031(a)–2(a) and (b) provides that depreciable tangible personal property will be treated as like-kind if it is within the same General Asset Class specified in Rev. Proc. 87–56, 1987–2 C.B. 674, which describes asset class guidelines for depreciation purposes. For example, like-kind exchanges include "a truck for a new truck or a passenger automobile for a new passenger automobile to be used for a like purpose." Treas. Reg. § 1.1031(a)–

1(c). Depreciable property not so classified will be classified, if possible, under the six-digit product coding system in Sectors 31 through 33 of North American Industry Classification System, United States (NAICS) published by the Executive Office of the President, Office of Management and Budget (as updated from time to time). Treas. Reg. § 1.1031(a)–2(b)(3)–(6). Under this rule, for example, a road grader and a road scraper are like kind, Treas. Reg. § 1.1031(a)–2(b)(7), Ex. (3), as are a computer and a printer. Treas. Reg. § 1.1031(a)–2(b)(7), Ex. (4). These rules permit wide varieties of properties to be considered like-kind. For example, dairy equipment and haying equipment are like-kind. T.D. 9151, 2004–2 C.B. 489. But there are limits, including where an airplane and a heavy-duty truck are not considered like-kind. Treas. Reg. § 1.1031(a)–2(b)(7), Ex. (4). The IRS reserves the right to modify the rules for the classification of property through published guidance of general applicability. Treas. Reg. § 1.1031(a)–2(b)(5). For example, the IRS could decide not to follow a general asset class or product class for purposes of identifying property of like-kind or might determine that other properties not listed within the same or in any product class or general asset class nevertheless are of a like kind. T.D. 9151, 2004–2 C.B. 489, 490.

Whether intangible properties are like-kind is determined with reference to the specific nature of the rights and the underlying property. For example, a copyright on a novel and a copyright on a song are not like-kind. Treas. Reg. § 1.1031(a)–2(c)(3), Ex. (2). Furthermore, Treas. Reg. § 1.1031(a)–2(c)(2) specifically provides that goodwill and going concern value of two businesses are never like-kind. The rationale for this rule is that the business goodwill and going concern value of any particular business operation are inherently unique and inseparable from the business.

The regulations do not specifically prescribe how to apply the like-kind standard to nondepreciable property and depreciable property not covered by the safe-harbor rules. Prior law applied the general principles discussed above on a case-by-case basis, and prior precedents are relevant. Thus an exchange of numismatic-type gold coins for bullion-type gold coins is not of a like-kind. Rev. Rul. 79–143, 1979–1 C.B. 264. Similarly, an exchange of gold bullion for silver bullion is not within § 1031; silver bullion is essentially an industrial commodity while gold bullion is primarily utilized as an investment. Rev. Rul. 82–166, 1982–2 C.B. 190.

Section 1031(e) specially provides that livestock of different sexes are not like-kind property.

1.2. *Use of Property*

The transferred property must have been held by the taxpayer for productive use in a trade or business or for investment. In addition, the property of a like-kind received must be property that "is to be held" by the taxpayer either for productive use in a trade or business or for investment. Property held for productive use in a trade or business may be exchanged under § 1031 for investment property and vice versa. Treas. Reg. § 1.1031(a)–1(a).

If either exchanged property is held for personal use, then nonrecognition under § 1031 is not available. An exchange does not qualify under § 1031 because of the mere expectation that property used as a residence will appreciate. In Moore v. Commissioner, T.C. Memo. 2007–134, the taxpayer exchanged land and a mobile home, which the taxpayer used as a vacation residence, for another vacation property, and claimed the transaction qualified for nonrecognition under § 1031. There was no evidence that the taxpayer made either property available for rent, but the taxpayer argued that both vacation properties were "investment" property because they were acquired and held with the expectation that they would appreciate in value. The court found no evidence that the taxpayer held either property primarily for sale at a profit.

Shortly after the Tax Court decided *Moore*, the IRS promulgated Rev. Proc. 2008–16, 2008–1 C.B. 547, providing safe-harbor guidance regarding whether a residential property that the taxpayer held or intends to hold for mixed uses, e.g. personal vacation use and rental/investment purposes, qualifies as property held for productive use in a trade or business or for investment under § 1031. Under the revenue procedure, the relinquished property qualifies if (1) the property was owned by the taxpayer for at least 24 months immediately before the exchange, and (2) within that period, in each of the two 12-month periods immediately preceding the exchange (a) the taxpayer rented the property to another person at a fair rental for 14 days or more, and (b) the taxpayer's personal use of the property did not exceed the greater of 14 days or 10 percent of the number of days during each 12-month period that the dwelling unit was rented at fair rental. The replacement property qualifies if (1) the property is owned by the taxpayer for at least 24 months immediately after the exchange, and within that period in each of the two 12-month periods immediately after the exchange (a) the taxpayer rents the property to another person at a fair rental for 14 days or more, and (b) the taxpayer's personal use of the property does not exceed the greater of 14 days or 10 percent of the number of days during each 12-month period that the property is rented at a fair rental. Personal use of a dwelling unit occurs on any day on which a taxpayer is deemed to have used the dwelling unit for personal purposes under § 280A(d)(2) (taking into account § 280(d)(3) but not § 280(d)(4)).

Whether property received "is to be held" for the requisite use is based upon the taxpayer's intention at the time of the exchange. Thus, in Wagensen v. Commissioner, 74 T.C. 653 (1980), an exchange of like-kind properties was held to qualify under § 1031 even though the property received was given by the taxpayer to his children nine months after the exchange. The court held that the taxpayer had no concrete plans at the time of the exchange to make the gift. On the other hand, in Click v. Commissioner, 78 T.C. 225 (1982), an exchange of investment farm land for two residences was held not to qualify where the taxpayer's two children and their families moved into the residences immediately after the exchange and the residences were given to the children seven months later. The court held the taxpayer never had the requisite intent to hold the property for investment.

In Reesink v. Commissioner, T.C. Memo 2012–118, the taxpayer converted the property received in an exchange into a personal residence eight months after the exchange but succeeded in convincing the Tax Court that the property was held for investment. The court was persuaded by evidence that the taxpayer made efforts to rent the property after the exchange and that the taxpayer did not sell his principal residence in another city for six months after the exchange over the objections of his spouse, as well as the testimony of the taxpayer's estranged brother that the taxpayer did not intend to relocate from his former residence until his son finished high school several years after the transaction.

Some cases have held that an exchange will qualify even where the taxpayer retained only momentarily the property transferred or received. Magneson v. Commissioner, 753 F.2d 1490 (9th Cir.1985), found an exchange of like-kind property qualified under § 1031 even though property received was immediately contributed to a partnership. However, the court's holding in *Magneson* was based on the fact that the taxpayer's general partnership interest represented an indirect ownership interest in real property of like-kind within the partnership.[1] Similarly, Bolker v. Commissioner, 760 F.2d 1039 (9th Cir.1985), held an exchange of real estate qualified even though the transferred property had been acquired upon liquidation of taxpayer's wholly-owned corporation several months earlier and the taxpayer had agreed to the exchange prior to receiving the property. A similar result was reached in Maloney v. Commissioner, 93 T.C. 89 (1989) (valid like-kind exchange by a corporate taxpayer followed by a distribution of the exchange property in complete liquidation). Rev. Rul. 77–337, 1977–2 C.B. 305, is to the contrary. In each of these cases, under the then applicable law, the taxpayers had an exchanged basis in all of the property involved.

1.3. *Exchange of Multiple Assets*

Rev. Rul. 89–121, 1989–2 C.B. 203, held that an exchange of one television broadcasting business for another was not a unitary like-kind exchange. The exchange had to be analyzed on an asset-by-asset basis. This approach is required under Treas. Reg. § 1.1031(j)–1. When multiple assets are exchanged, whether or not the assets constitute a going business, the recognized gain and basis of the assets in the exchange are computed by dividing the assets eligible for § 1031 nonrecognition into "exchange groups" based on the classes to which they are assigned. Gain realized with respect to any exchange group is recognized only to the extent that the fair market value of the transferred group exceeds the fair market value of the corresponding exchange group received (which presumes that other property, boot, is received to make up the difference in values). The basis of each asset received in the exchange is its proportionate share of the basis assigned to its exchange group, increased by a proportionate portion of gain recognized on the transfer of the corresponding exchange group. Property ineligible for nonrecognition is aggregated in a residual group, and the exchange of assets in the residual group is taxable. Because almost all businesses include goodwill or going concern value, which never will be of

---

[1]   Magneson exchanged a wholly owned interest in real estate for a 10 percent interest in an apartment building. The apartment building was contributed to a partnership in exchange for a 10 percent partnership interest. Thus, the taxpayer's percentage ownership interest in the contributed real property was unchanged.

like-kind, it generally will be impossible to exchange going businesses in a transaction accorded complete nonrecognition under § 1031.

The application of the exchange groups is illustrated in Yates III v. Commissioner, T.C. Memo 2012–251. The taxpayer exchanged a property qualified as a principal residence under § 121 (discussed in Chapter 6, Section 4) and a business property for a new principal residence and two business properties. The business properties were put in the exchange group and the residential properties were put in the residual group. Where the fair market value of the property transferred in the exchange group exceeded the fair market value of the property received in the exchange group, the resulting "exchange group deficiency," which comes from the residual group, is treated as boot and recognized to the extent of realized gain in the residual group. The court was required to ascertain the relative fair market values of the transferred properties accounted for in the exchange and residual groups. A higher value allocated to the business property in the exchange group (and a concurrent lower value allocated to the property in the residual group) decreased the amount of realized gain that the taxpayer had to recognize as boot. Ultimately the court accepted allocations of value in the purchase agreement for the transferred property and rejected the IRS claim that the taxpayer overstated the value of the business property to avoid gain recognition.

2. IDENTIFYING THE DEFERRED GAIN AND LOSS IN LIKE-KIND EXCHANGES

2.1. *Generally*

The interaction of the subsections of § 1031 is important to the operation of the provision. Assume that A exchanges the Clearview Apartments, whose adjusted basis is $170,000 and whose fair market value is $200,000, for the Tower Apartments owned by B, with an adjusted basis in B's hands of $135,000 and a fair market value of $180,000, and $20,000 cash to be paid by B. A's gain is the amount realized, here $200,000 (a $180,000 building plus $20,000 cash) less the basis of the asset given in exchange, here $170,000, giving a gain realized of $30,000. Section 1031(a) does not apply because the exchange on A's side is not solely for like property; A received the $20,000 cash. But § 1031(b) applies, so that while gain is recognized, it cannot exceed the value of the other property or money received. Since part of A's investment in Clearview has been converted into cash, a tax reckoning to that extent must be made and hence gain is taxed to the extent of such boot.[2] The recognized gain is thus $20,000.

---

[2]   If boot is received in the form of an installment note, or other deferred payment obligation, recognition of gain may be deferred under the installment method of § 453. See Chapter 31, Section 2. Under § 453(f)(6), in applying the installment method, gross profit includes only gain required to be recognized under § 1031(b), and the payments and total contract price are determined by excluding the value of like-kind property permitted to be received under § 1031 without recognition of gain.

Amount Realized

Tower Apartment	$180,000
Cash	$ 20,000
	$200,000

Basis of Property Transferred

Clearview Apartment	$170,000
Gain Realized	$ 30,000
Gain Recognized	$ 20,000

The basis of Tower in A's hands is determined under § 1031(d) is as follows:

Basis of Property Exchanged	$170,000
Decreased by Money Received	$ 20,000
Increased by Gain Recognized	$ 20,000
Decreased by Loss Recognized	$ 0
Ending Basis	$170,000

The $170,000 basis for the property received is the anticipated figure. A's overall "tax investment" in terms of the dollar amount that has been accounted for as income has increased from A's original $170,000 investment to $190,000 in view of the $20,000 recognized as taxable gain. The money now represents $20,000 of this investment, which can be viewed as having a basis of $20,000,[3] and the balance, $170,000, is represented by A's continued investment in Tower. Because Tower's fair market value is $180,000 at the time of the exchange, the adjusted basis of $170,000 preserves the $10,000 unrecognized appreciation from A's investment in Clearview.

Section 1031(a) applies to B, who has received only the Clearview Apartments. "Solely" refers to the property received, not the property given up, and B is regarded as having made a like-kind exchange plus paying cash in addition. B's realized gain is $45,000—the amount by which B's amount realized, the $200,000 fair market value of Clearview, exceeds $135,000 basis in Tower plus the $20,000 of cash paid.[4] But none of this gain is recognized under § 1031(a).

---

[3]   The basis of the cash is $20,000, its face value. Although cash is not generally thought of as having a basis, that is only because by definition the basis of money in U.S. currency is equal to its face.

[4]   Gain is amount realized less the basis of the property given up. I.R.C. § 1001(a). In this case G gives up two different assets in exchange for Clearview, Tower Apartments and the cash.

Amount Realized	For Tower	For Cash
Clearview Apartment	$180,000	$ 20,000
Basis of Property Transferred		
Tower Apartment	$135,000	
Cash		$ 20,000
Gain Realized	$ 45,000	$ 0
Gain Recognized	$ 0	

The basis of Clearview in B's hands under § 1031(d) is:

Basis of Property Exchanged	
Tower Apartments	$135,000
Cash	$ 20,000
Decreased by Money Received	$ 0
Increased by Gain Recognized	$ 0
Decreased by Loss Recognized	$ 0
Ending Basis	$155,000

The $155,000 basis is the anticipated figure as B's "tax investment" in an apartment building has been increased to $155,000. Also, the $45,000 unrecognized appreciation of Tower is preserved by the spread between the $200,000 fair market value of Clearview and its $155,000 basis to B.

If, instead of the $20,000 cash, B had transferred to A stock worth $20,000 with a basis in B's hands of $1,000, then the tax results would have been as follows: As to A, the gain recognized would have still been $20,000, because the stock is not like-kind property.

Amount Realized	
Tower Apartment	$180,000
Stock	$ 20,000
Basis of Property Exchanged	
Clearview Apartment	$170,000
Gain Realized	$ 30,000
Gain Recognized	$ 20,000

The basis of the property acquired—Tower and the stock—would be $170,000 less any money received, zero, plus gain recognized, $20,000, or a total of $190,000. This basis is allocated between Tower and the stock by assigning to the stock basis equal to the fair market value of the stock, $20,000, and the balance, $170,000, to Tower. I.R.C. § 1031(d) (second sentence). This is the correct theoretical result because A's "after-tax investment" of $170,000 has been increased by the $20,000 recognized gain. The increased after-tax investment is now attributed to the stock and Tower.

Basis of Property Transferred	
Clearview Apartment	$170,000
Gain (Loss) Realized	$ 30,000
Gain (Loss) Recognized	$ 20,000
Basis of Property Received	
Property Transferred Clearview Apartment	$170,000
Plus Gain Recognized	$ 20,000
Minus Money	$ 0
Minus Loss Recognized	$ 0
Basis Tower	$170,000
Basis Stock (FMV)	$ 20,000

As to B, there would be a realized gain of $19,000 on the disposition of the stock; gain realized is $20,000 of the value of Clearview Apartment, less $1,000 basis in the stock. This gain is recognized in full, since § 1031(a) does not apply to the stock because the stock was not exchanged for like property, and also since § 1031(a) does not apply to stock. The basis of Clearview is $155,000 as above. If B's basis for the stock had been $25,000, then B would have had a recognized loss of $5,000 on the disposition of the stock. The basis of Clearview would still be $155,000: basis of property exchanged ($135,000 plus $25,000) less $5,000 recognized loss.

Amount Realized	For Tower Apartment	For Stock Basis = $1,000	For Stock Basis= $25,000
Clearview Apartment FMV = $200,000	$180,000	$20,000	$20,000
Basis of Property Transferred			
Tower Apartment	$135,000		
Stock		$ 1,000	$25,000
Gain (Loss) Realized	$ 45,000	$19,000	($ 5,000)
Gain (Loss) Recognized	$ 0	$19,000	($ 5,000)
Basis of Property Received			
Basis of Property Transferred			
Tower Apartment		$135,000	$135,000
Stock		$ 1,000	$ 25,000
Gain (Loss) Recognized		$ 19,000	($ 5,000)
Basis Clearview		$155,000	$155,000

Suppose one of the parties to the transaction realizes a loss on a like-kind exchange. If A's basis for Clearview had been $210,000, so that A realized a loss of $10,000, having received a total value of only $200,000, then the loss would not be recognized despite the presence of the $20,000 boot. Section 1031(c) prohibits recognition of loss even where boot is received. A's basis in Tower would be $190,000—the $210,000 basis of Clearview minus the $20,000 of boot. Because Tower has a fair market value of $180,000 this $190,000 of basis preserves the $10,000 unrecognized loss.

2.2. *Mortgaged Property*

Debt on one or both sides of a transaction is common, particularly where real estate is involved. Where mortgaged property is transferred in exchange for unmortgaged property, the amount realized by the person transferring the mortgaged property generally includes the amount of the mortgage. Treas. Regs. §§ 1.1001–2 and 1.1031(d)–2, Exs. (1) and (2). Net release from liability is treated as cash received, thus as boot, for purposes of § 1031(b), whether the mortgage is assumed by the other party or the property is taken subject to a nonrecourse mortgage. Treas. Regs. §§ 1.1031(b) and 1.1031(d). The person receiving the mortgaged property is considered to have received property in the amount of its unencumbered value and the consideration given for that property is regarded as including the amount of the liability assumed or to which the property is subject. For tax purposes the transaction is thus considered to be the equivalent of an exchange of unmortgaged property for unmortgaged property plus cash (going to the person transferring the mortgaged property). See Brons Hotels, Inc. v. Commissioner, 34 B.T.A. 376 (1936), an early like-kind exchange case that addressed the question of mortgage release as boot, where the court states,

"We are not unmindful of the fact that the assumption of a mortgage is not money in a true legal sense. It is, however, part of the consideration received; it is the equivalent of money, and in our opinion must be treated as money for the purposes of this case."

Assume C purchased land for $50,000 with $20,000 of C's own funds and $30,000 from a nonrecourse loan secured by a mortgage on the property. If C subsequently exchanges the property subject to the mortgage when the property's unencumbered value is $130,000, for unencumbered like-kind property owned by D worth $100,000, then C's amount realized is $130,000, the $100,000 fair market value of D's property plus the mortgage debt relief of $30,000. The transaction is thus treated as if C had received the $100,000 property from D plus $30,000 cash to discharge the liability. C's realized gain is $80,000 ($130,000 minus $50,000), recognition of which is limited to $30,000, the amount of the boot. Under the last sentence of § 1031(d), which treats the release of debt as cash received, C's basis in the acquired property is $50,000: the basis of the transferred property ($50,000) less the money received (the liability of $30,000) plus the gain recognized ($30,000). C's unrecognized gain of $50,000 is reflected by the difference between the value of the property, $100,000, and the basis of $50,000.

Amount Realized	
FMV of Property Received From D	$100,000
Release from Mortgage	$ 30,000
Total	$130,000
Basis of C's Property Transferred	$ 50,000
Gain Realized	$ 80,000
Gain Recognized	$ 30,000
Basis in New Property	$ 50,000

C's basis in the property received is $50,000, computed as follows:

Basis of Property Transferred	$50,000
Decreased by Release of Liabilities[5]	−$30,000
Increased by Gain Recognized	+$30,000
	$50,000

As to D, § 1031(a) applies to the exchange. If D's basis in the property transferred were $50,000, D realizes $50,000 of gain, none of which is recognized.

---

[5]   The new indebtedness is included in the basis of the property received. It is a cost of the acquisition of the new property. For this purpose, the obligation to pay the new indebtedness may be viewed as a deferred cash investment in the new property and thus part of the property given up in the exchange.

Amount Realized	
FMV of Property Received From C	$130,000
Basis of D's Property Given in Exchange	$ 50,000
Assumption of Mortgage	$ 30,000
Gain Realized	$ 50,000
Gain Recognized	$ 0

D's basis in the property received is $80,000: D's $50,000 basis in the property transferred plus the $30,000 mortgage that encumbered the property received.

Where there are mortgages on both sides of the exchange, the difference between the amounts of the mortgages becomes, for the purpose of determining how much gain is recognized, the money or other property received by the party transferring the property with the larger mortgage. If, in addition, cash is actually received, then any gain realized by the recipient must be recognized at least to the extent of the cash received. For the purpose of recognizing gain the cash cannot be offset by any liabilities that the taxpayer assumes or receives property subject to (or by the net of such liabilities over liabilities of which the taxpayer is relieved). The complexities of this computation demonstrate the value of analyzing the transaction as a series of steps beginning with amount realized. For example, if E exchanged Blackacre, in which E's basis is $25,000, and which is worth $55,000 but subject to a $20,000 mortgage, for Greenacre from F worth $65,000, but subject to a $40,000 mortgage, plus $10,000 cash, then the gain realized by E is determined under Treas. Reg. § 1.1031(d)–2, Ex. (2), as follows:

Amount Realized		
FMV of Greenacre	$65,000	
Mortgage Release	$20,000	
Cash	$10,000	
Total		$95,000
Basis of Property Transferred		
Basis of Blackacre	$25,000	
New Mortgage	$40,000	$65,000
Gain Realized		$30,000

The gain recognized by E is limited to the $10,000 cash received. E is taking subject to a $40,000 mortgage while being relieved of only a $20,000 mortgage, thus the net of the mortgages does not result in any "money received" for the purpose of recognizing gain. (Note that if the cash and mortgages were netted together, there would be no net boot as to E, since E is assuming a $40,000 mortgage but receiving only $10,000 cash and an assumption of a $20,000 mortgage. However, the $10,000 cash, being actual cash, is regarded as boot per se that cannot be eliminated by an adverse net of the mortgages.) E's basis in the new property is $45,000:

Basis of Transferred Property	$25,000
Increased by Liability Assumed	$40,000
Decreased by Cash Received	$10,000
Decreased by Liability Release (Treated as Cash)	$20,000
Increased by Gain Recognized	$10,000
Basis of Property Received	$45,000

If F has a basis of $45,000 in Greenacre, then the gain realized by F is determined as follows:

Amount Realized		
FMV of Blackacre	$55,000	
Mortgage Release	$40,000	
Total		$95,000
Basis of Property Transferred		
Basis of Greenacre	$45,000	
Cash Paid	$10,000	
New Mortgage	$20,000	
Total		$75,000
Gain Realized		$20,000

F must recognize $10,000 of the gain: the net of the $40,000 mortgage less the $20,000 mortgage and the $10,000 cash, since the cash *transferred* may be subtracted from the net of the mortgages to reduce the boot that would otherwise result from the net of the mortgages. F's basis in the new property is $45,000;

Basis of Transferred Property	$45,000
New Mortgage	$20,000
Cash Paid	$10,000
Decreased by Cash Received	$10,000
Decreased by Liability Relief (Treated as Cash)	$40,000
Increased by Gain Recognized	$10,000
Basis of Property Received	$45,000

For additional illustrations of these principles, see Treas. Reg. § 1.1031(d)–2, Exs. (1) and (2).

2.3. *Character of Recognized Gain and Holding Period*

After identifying gain recognized in an exchange, the final step in the analysis of a property disposition is to determine whether the gain is characterized as capital gain or ordinary gain. (See Chapters 24 and 25.) Capital gain is derived from the sale or exchange of a capital asset. Thus, recognized gain in a like-kind exchange will be subject to the preferential tax rates for long-term capital gain if the exchanged property is a capital asset held for more than one year. Gain recognized on the exchange of property used in a trade or business held for more than one year may be characterized as § 1231 gain, discussed in Chapter 25, Section 1. Most like-kind exchanges involve § 1231 property.

Gain recognized on an exchange may be subject to recapture under § 1245 (discussed in Chapter 25, Section 1.2.). Section 1245(a) broadly requires ordinary income treatment of gain realized on a disposition of property to the extent of the lesser of the difference between the amount realized (or fair market value) and adjusted basis, or the difference between basis recomputed by adding back adjustments for capital recovery items and adjusted basis; i.e. the provision recaptures past capital recovery deductions. Section 1245(b)(4) contains an exception from the broad recapture rule of § 1245(a) for like-kind exchanges under § 1031. Under § 1245(b)(4), recapture gain is limited to the amount of gain recognized on the exchange plus the fair market value of any property not treated as boot which is not depreciable property used in a trade or business or held for the production of income (§ 1245) property.

Under § 1223(1) the holding period for property permitted to be received without recognition in a like-kind exchange includes the taxpayer's holding period for the property given up in the exchange. If boot property is received as partial consideration in an exchange that otherwise qualifies under § 1031, the holding period of the boot property starts anew with the exchange.

2.4. *Depreciation of the Property Received*

Treas. Reg. § 1.168(i)–6 provides specific rules for the application of MACRS depreciation to replacement MACRS property received in a like-kind exchange for relinquished property subject to MACRS depreciation. To the extent the taxpayer's basis in the acquired MACRS property does not exceed the taxpayer's adjusted basis in the relinquished MACRS property and the relinquished and replacement properties have the same recovery periods and depreciation methods, the acquired property is depreciated over the remaining recovery period of, and using the same depreciation method and convention as that of the relinquished property. Treas. Reg. § 1.168(i)–6(c)(3)(ii). If the replacement property has a shorter recovery period, or is subject to a less accelerated recovery method, then the replacement property is depreciated at the same rate as the relinquished property. Treas. Reg. § 1.168(i)–6(c)(4)(ii), (iv). If the replacement property has a longer recovery period than the relinquished property, the depreciation allowances beginning with the taxable year of the exchange are determined as if the replacement property had been placed in service by the taxpayer in the same taxable year as the relinquished property. Treas. Reg. § 1.168(i)–6(c)(4)(i). Similarly, if the replacement property is subject to a less accelerated recovery method than that of the relinquished property, depreciation deductions based on the exchange basis of the replacement property for the year of the exchange, and thereafter, are determined as if the taxpayer had placed the replacement property in service in the same year as the relinquished property and had calculated depreciation using the slower recovery method. Treas. Reg. § 1.168(i)–6(c)(4)(iii)(A). Any additional basis in the replacement property is treated as newly purchased MACRS property placed in service in the year of the exchange. Treas. Reg. § 1.168(i)–6(d)(1). Thus, depreciation is separately determined with respect to any basis increase attributable to gain recognized on the exchange. Alternatively, Treas. Reg. § 1.168(i)–6(i) allows an election to treat the replacement property as placed in service in the year of the exchange with depreciation then calculated on the sum of the exchange basis and any increase to the basis as of the year of the exchange.

3. RELATED PARTY RESALE

Section 1031(f) provides that if a taxpayer exchanges property with a related person (as defined in § 267(b)) in a § 1031 transaction and either the related person or the taxpayer disposes of the property involved in the exchange within two years after the exchange, the taxpayer is required to include the amount of the deferred gain in income in the year in which the disqualifying disposition takes place. The provision does not apply to dispositions at death, pursuant to an involuntary conversion, or with respect to which it is established that the disposition did not have tax avoidance as one of its principal purposes. The two-year period is suspended during any period of time that either holder of the exchanged property is protected against risk of loss by a put, call, short sale or any other arrangement. I.R.C. § 1031(g). As discussed below, § 1031(f)(4) extends the related-party prohibition to transactions designed to circumvent the general § 1031(f) rules.

4. SALE-LEASEBACK TRANSACTIONS

Century Electric Co. v. Commissioner, 192 F.2d 155 (8th Cir.1951), held that a sale of real estate coupled with a long-term leaseback was a like-kind "exchange" of a fee interest for a long-term leasehold interest, thereby preventing the taxpayer from recognizing a loss on sale of the property. The taxpayer in *Century Electric* transferred business property to a tax-exempt educational institution in exchange for cash plus the long-term leaseback. The long-term leaseback was treated as like-kind property received in exchange for the transferred real property. Jordan Marsh Co. v. Commissioner, 269 F.2d 453 (2d Cir.1959), involved a similar transaction in which the taxpayer transferred business property to a bank in exchange for cash and a long-term leaseback. However, the transfer in *Jordan Marsh* was held to be a sale solely for the cash, rather than an exchange for the cash and leaseback and the taxpayer was permitted to recognize its loss on the transaction. The court in *Jordan Marsh Co.* distinguished *Century Electric* on the ground that the consideration received for the sale in *Century Electric*, other than the leaseback, was less than the fair value of the exchanged property and that the lease in that case was, therefore, a favorable lease having capital value.

A below-market "sale" price with the bargain element offset by reduced rentals on the leaseback is significant for two reasons. First, where the stated sale price is less than fair market value, the stated price, if used as the amount realized, would artificially create a loss or increase the loss that otherwise would be realized upon sale. In this respect, the contract price was not the true sale price. Second, where the lease is for fair rental value as in *Jordan Marsh*, it is difficult to view receipt of the lease as part of an "exchange;" the fee interest in the property would appear to be sold for cash only. If the lease had capital value, then the transaction could be viewed as an "exchange" of the fee for a lease plus cash boot. Under § 1031(c), no loss is recognized even where boot is received. See also Rev. Rul. 76–301, 1976–2 C.B. 241 (transfer of leasehold interest in a 20 story building for a sublease of the first five floors was a like-kind exchange; no loss deduction allowed).

Other aspects of sale and leaseback transactions are discussed in Chapter 33.

5. POLICY ASPECTS

In Jordan Marsh Co. v. Commissioner, 269 F.2d 453 (2d Cir.1959), the Court of Appeals explained the rationale for the like-kind exchange provision as follows: "[I]f the taxpayer's money is still tied up in the same kind of property as that in which it was originally invested, he is not allowed to compute and deduct his theoretical loss on the exchange, nor is he charged with a tax upon his theoretical profit." The *Jordan Marsh* court also recognized that difficulty of valuation does not justify § 1031. Under § 1031(b) the receipt of any "boot" by the taxpayer requires that the property in the exchange be valued in order to ascertain the amount of gain realized. Furthermore, most like-kind exchanges are multiparty exchanges (discussed below), so parties know the value of both the relinquished and replacement properties. The concern over imposing tax where taxpayers have their money tied up in the same kind of property also does not satisfactorily explain § 1031. Taxpayers selling property for cash and immediately reinvesting in similar property are not protected by § 1031, even if they have substantial liquidity problems.

Another principal justification for § 1031 found in many cases is that the change in the form of the investment in the like-kind exchange is not sufficient to break the essential continuity of the investment. However, the broad definition of "like-kind," at least with respect to real estate, is not consistent with this view. The exchange of improved city real estate for a ranch or farm or the exchange of property held for productive use in the taxpayer's trade or business for investment property appears to be a sufficient change in economic situation to justify recognition of gain or loss. A possible response would be to restrict the scope of § 1031 to property "similar or related in service or use" to the property exchanged as is done in § 1033, discussed in Chapter 27, Section 1.

Section 1031 represents a consumption tax provision in the income tax. As such, it is classified as a tax expenditure. See Chapter 11. The provision is an interest-free loan to the reinvesting taxpayer and has a revenue cost of $87.7 billion for the period 2015–2019. Staff of the Joint Committee on Taxation, Estimates of Federal Tax Expenditures for Fiscal Years 2015– 2019 32 (JCX–141R–15) (Dec. 2015). Despite these policy deficiencies, § 1031 enjoys the support of an industry group of exchange facilitators who aggressively advocate for its continuance.

SECTION 2. MULTIPARTY AND DEFERRED EXCHANGES

INTERNAL REVENUE CODE: Section 1031(a)(3).

REGULATIONS: Sections 1.1031(b)–2; 1.1031(k)–1(a), (b), (d)(1), (f)(1)–(2), (g)(1), (3), (4).

The language of § 1031(a) contemplates that a taxpayer will exchange a property held by the taxpayer with another party for property of like-kind that the taxpayer desires to hold. As a practical matter most transactions are not that simple. The person who wishes to acquire the taxpayer's property generally is not the owner of the property desired by the taxpayer. The owner of the property desired by the taxpayer may want cash rather than the taxpayer's property. The solution has been the multiparty exchange, which, in numerous variations, involves acquisition of the replacement property for cash by a third party who exchanges the replacement property with the taxpayer for the taxpayer's relinquished property. Often the third party is a qualified intermediary to whom the exchanging taxpayer transfers the relinquished property, the person acquiring the taxpayer's property transfers cash, and the intermediary uses the cash to acquire the replacement property from its seller and then transfers the replacement property to the taxpayer. As a general proposition, these three-way, or multiparty, exchanges have qualified for nonrecognition under § 1031 as long as the exchanging taxpayer receives property in exchange and does not control cash in the interim (with the exception of cash treated as boot). While approving a multiparty exchange, the Tax Court in Barker v. Commissioner, 74 T.C. 555 (1980), described the issues as follows:

> This case involves another variant of the multiple-party, like-kind exchange by which the taxpayer, as in this case, seeks to terminate one real estate investment and acquire another real estate investment without recognizing gain. The statutory provision for nonrecognition treatment is section 1031. The touchstone of section 1031, at least in this context, is the requirement that there be an *exchange* of like-kind business or investment properties, as distinguished from a cash sale of property by the taxpayer and a reinvestment of the proceeds in other property.

> The "exchange" requirement poses an analytical problem because it runs headlong into the familiar tax law maxim that the substance of a transaction controls over form. In a sense, the

substance of a transaction in which the taxpayer sells property and immediately reinvests the proceeds in like-kind property is not much different from the substance of a transaction in which two parcels are exchanged without cash. * * * Yet, if the exchange requirement is to have any significance at all, the perhaps formalistic difference between the two types of transactions must, at least on occasion, engender different results. Accord, Starker v. United States, 602 F.2d 1341, 1352 (9th Cir.1979).

The line between an exchange on the one hand and a nonqualifying sale and reinvestment on the other becomes even less distinct when the person who owns the property sought by the taxpayer is not the same person who wants to acquire the taxpayer's property. This means that multiple parties must be involved in the transaction. In that type of case, a like-kind exchange can be effected only if the person with whom the taxpayer exchanges the property first purchases the property wanted by the taxpayer. This interjection of cash, especially when the person who purchases the property desired by the taxpayer either uses money advanced by the taxpayer or appears to be acting as his agent, or both, makes the analysis that much more difficult.

* * *

We begin by observing that there is nothing inherent in a multiple-party exchange that necessarily acts as a bar to section 1031 treatment. Thus, it is not a bar to section 1031 treatment that the person who desires the taxpayer's property acquires and holds another piece of property only temporarily before exchanging it with the taxpayer. * * * Similarly, it is not fatal to section 1031 treatment that the person with whom the taxpayer exchanges his property immediately sells the newly acquired property. * * *

Difficulties arise, however, when the transaction falls short of the paradigm in which transitory ownership is the only feature distinguishing the transaction from two-party exchanges. Still, the courts (and by and large the Commissioner), in reviewing these transactions, have evinced awareness of business and economic exigencies.

* * *

Notwithstanding those deviations from the standard multiple-party exchanges which have received judicial approval, at some point the confluence of some sufficient number of deviations will bring about a taxable result. Whether the cause be economic and business reality or poor tax planning, prior cases make clear that taxpayers who stray too far run the risk of having their transactions characterized as a sale and reinvestment.

For example, in Carlton v. United States, 385 F.2d 238 (5th Cir.1967), the parties intended to enter into an *Alderson* like-kind exchange (i.e., the person who wanted the taxpayer's property was to temporarily acquire and hold the property wanted by the taxpayer), but to avoid unnecessary duplication in the transfer of money and titles, the third party conveyed his property directly to the taxpayer, and the buyer paid money to the taxpayer, intending that the taxpayer pay this money to the third party. Focusing on the taxpayer's receipt of cash rather than real property, the court held that the transaction was a sale.

The court in *Barker* also observed that the taxpayer and the prospective purchaser of the taxpayer's exchange property will enter into an agreement for the acquisition of the taxpayer's property before the taxpayer has located a replacement property. In Starker v. United States, 602 F.2d 1341 (9th Cir. 1979), the court rejected the Commissioner's position that a simultaneous exchange of properties is required for nonrecognition under § 1031. The taxpayer in *Starker* entered into an agreement with Crown Zellerbach to transfer timber property in exchange for property to be located and acquired by Crown Zellerbach for transfer to Starker within five years of the transfer of Starker's original property. Crown Zellerbach was obligated to pay cash if replacement property was not located within the five-year period. Starker located and received several properties within two years of his original transfer to Crown Zellerbach. The court held that the deferred acquisition of the exchange property was not a bar to nonrecognition under § 1031. The court pointed out that "the central concept of § 1031 is that an exchange of business or investment assets does not trigger recognition of gain or loss, because the taxpayer in entering into such a transaction does not 'cash in' or 'close out' his or her investment. To impose a tax on the event of a deed transfer upon a signing of an exchange agreement could bring about the very result § 1031 was designed to prevent: 'the inequity * * * of forcing a taxpayer to recognize a paper gain which was still tied up in a continuing investment of the same sort.' " Quoting from Jordan Marsh v. Commissioner, 269 F.2d 453, 456 (2d Cir.1959), supra. The Commissioner also argued in *Starker* that the possibility that the taxpayer might receive cash if replacement property were not found disqualified the exchange from nonrecognition treatment. The court held that the "mere possibility at the time of agreement that a cash sale might occur does not prevent the application of section 1031. * * * In this case the taxpayer claims he intended at the outset of the transaction to get nothing but like-kind property, and no evidence to the contrary appears on the record. Moreover, the taxpayer never handled any cash in the course of the transactions."

The long period in *Starker* between the taxpayer's transfer of the exchange property and receipt of the replacement property created procedural problems with respect to keeping the taxpayer's return for the year of exchange open under the statute of limitations to properly account for recognized gain in the event the taxpayer received any boot on the transaction or ultimately failed to acquire suitable replacement property. This problem was addressed with the enactment of § 1031(a)(3), which requires that, for the exchange to qualify under § 1031, the taxpayer must identify the replacement property within 45 days of the date on which the taxpayer transfers the relinquished property, and the taxpayer must receive the replacement property not later than 180 days after the taxpayer transfers the relinquished property or, if earlier, the due date for the taxpayer's tax return (including extensions) for the taxable year in which the taxpayer transferred the relinquished property.

DETAILED ANALYSIS

1.   THE "EXCHANGE" REQUIREMENT

Section 1031(a) requires that the new property be acquired through an exchange and not a sale and purchase. As *Barker* and *Starker* illustrate, the principle is firmly established that an "exchange" occurs even though the party acquiring the taxpayer's property was willing to pay cash. The test, rather, is the more technical one of whether an exchange has in fact taken place. If the taxpayer has identified available like-kind property, a carefully structured, multiparty transaction can usually be arranged to qualify under § 1031.

The cases that result in litigation have generally involved transactions that through circumstance or lack of care raise the possibility that what occurred was a sale and not an exchange. In *Barker*, the Commissioner challenged the transaction because a fourth party simultaneously acquired both the relinquished property from the taxpayer and the replacement property from a third party then immediately re-transferred the properties to the intended recipients. The court rejected this argument:

> At first blush, the transitory nature of Covington Bros.' ownership of the Demion property on the one hand and the Casa El Camino property on the other seems to lend itself to a step-transaction argument; that is, Covington Bros.' ownership of the properties could be viewed as nothing more than an unnecessary and formalistic step of no legal or economic significance which should be ignored in determining the character of the transaction for tax purposes. But, as indicated above, the Commissioner accedes to transitory ownership in the three-party context (Rev. Rul. 77–297, supra [1977–2 C.B. 304]), and we can perceive no reason why the four-party context should be treated any differently. In other four-party exchanges previously considered by the courts and decided in favor of the taxpayer, the fourth party has held title to the properties for no longer than a transitory

period. We do not understand respondent's attack on four-party exchanges to be so broad-based that he thinks none qualify for section 1031 treatment. * * * Indeed, respondent has not made such an argument here. To the complaint that this treatment places undue emphasis on a formalistic step of no substance, we repeat what we have already said: that the conceptual distinction between an exchange qualifying for section 1031 on the one hand and a sale and reinvestment on the other is largely one of form.

The court in *Barker* relied heavily on its conclusion that the mutual interdependence of the multiple transfers represented an exchange of properties by the taxpayer without the receipt of cash.

As in *Barker,* the courts often overlook technical defects as long as the taxpayer clearly intended to effect a § 1031 exchange, received like-kind property through various interdependent steps, and received no cash (other than cash intended as "boot"). Thus, a like-kind exchange was found to qualify under § 1031 in Biggs v. Commissioner, 632 F.2d 1171 (5th Cir.1980), even though the taxpayer had advanced funds for the replacement property ultimately acquired and title to that property was never transferred to the party ostensibly transferring it to the taxpayer. The court held that an "exchange" occurred even though it "could have been more artfully accomplished and with a greater economy of steps." A similar arrangement was held to qualify in Garcia v. Commissioner, 80 T.C. 491 (1983) (Acq.), when the court stated:

> The petitioners desired to effect a section 1031 exchange, their actions were consistent with that expressed intent, the conditions required to effect that intent were met, the contracts providing for the necessary series of transfers were interdependent, no cash proceeds from the sale of the original property were actually or constructively received by the petitioners, and, when the dust had settled, we are persuaded that an integrated plan for an exchange of like-kind property was conceived and implemented.

In Rev. Rul. 90–34, 1990–1 C.B. 154, the IRS conceded that an exchange qualifies for nonrecognition under § 1031 even though the party acquiring the exchange property from the taxpayer never held title to the replacement property. Under the facts of the ruling, X transferred property to Y, in exchange for property acquired with proceeds provided by Y, but which was transferred directly to X from Z. The Ruling concluded that since § 1031 treatment clearly would be available if Z had transferred the replacement property to Y who in turn transferred the property to X, "section 1031(a) does not require that Y hold legal title to [the replacement property], but merely that X receive solely property of a like-kind to the property transferred in order for the exchange to qualify for nonrecognition of gain or loss."

Cases rejecting taxpayer claims that a § 1031 exchange occurred generally have involved the receipt of cash. For example, Swaim v. United States, 651 F.2d 1066 (5th Cir.1981), held that § 1031 did not apply where the taxpayer sold real estate to individuals for cash, notes, and the assumption of a mortgage followed several months later by the transfer of real estate by those individuals to the taxpayer also for cash, notes and the assumption of a mortgage. See also Bezdjian v. Commissioner, 845 F.2d 217 (9th Cir.1988) (taxpayer purchased property followed by sale of other property for cash, § 1031 treatment denied). In Estate of Bowers v. Commissioner, 94 T.C. 582 (1990), like-kind exchange treatment was denied because there had been "substantial implementation" of the taxpayer's acquisition and use of the replacement property before the taxpayer's disposition of the exchange property. These cases serve as a warning that, although opinions in cases such as *Barker* and *Biggs* allow considerable latitude in the execution of a multiparty exchange, the form of the transaction remains important.

It is particularly important to the success of these transactions that the intermediary not be found to be the taxpayer's agent. If that is the case, the taxpayer will be in constructive receipt of cash received by the intermediary. Treas. Reg. § 1.1031(b)–2 provides a safe harbor for "qualified intermediaries," as defined in Treas. Reg. § 1.1031(k)–1(g)(4)(iii), who are deemed not to be the taxpayer's agent. Any person who is related to the taxpayer under § 267(b) or 707(b) or who has acted generally as the taxpayer's employee, attorney, accountant, investment banker or broker, or real estate agent or broker within two years of the exchange is ineligible to be a "qualified intermediary." Treas. Reg. § 1.1031(k)–1(k)(2) and (3). Blangiardo v. Commissioner, T.C. Memo. 2014–110, disqualified exchange treatment where the taxpayer used his lawyer-son as a qualified intermediary because the son was a related person as defined in § 267(b). The result was not changed by the fact that the son was an attorney, the funds from the relinquished property were held in an attorney trust account, and the documents described the transaction as a § 1031 exchange.

On occasion, a taxpayer may try to structure a transaction that ordinarily would be a like-kind exchange as a sale and purchase in order to avoid the operation of § 1031. In Redwing Carriers, Inc. v. Tomlinson, 399 F.2d 652 (5th Cir.1968), a parent corporation in the trucking business arranged to have its subsidiary buy new trucks while the parent sold its old trucks to the manufacturer. The parent treated the transaction as a separate sale and purchase in order to obtain a high basis for depreciation of the new trucks. The court held that the transaction constituted a § 1031 like-kind exchange. It was essentially a trade-in cast in the form of a separate purchase and sale. Rev. Rul. 61–119, 1961–1 C.B. 395, reaches the same conclusion. Compare Bell Lines, Inc. v. United States, 480 F.2d 710 (4th Cir.1973), in which the taxpayer purchased 148 tractors from Mack Trucks, Inc., and sold 143 old tractors to Horner Service Corporation. Mack had advanced money to Horner to purchase the tractors, guaranteed Horner it would not lose money on any tractors, and ultimately purchased most of the tractors. The court held the transactions to be separate purchases and sales, principally because the taxpayer was unaware of Mack's arrangement with Horner.

2.   DEFERRED EXCHANGES

As discussed above, § 1031(a)(3) provides that to qualify a deferred exchange under § 1031 the property received by the taxpayer must be

(1) identified within 45 days of the date on which the taxpayer transfers the property given up in the exchange, and (2) received by the taxpayer within 180 days or, if earlier, the date the tax return is due. Treas. Reg. § 1.1031(k)–1(c)(2) requires that the replacement property be unambiguously identified in a written document sent to a participant in the transaction, other than the exchanging seller, before the end of the forty-five day identification period. Treas. Reg. § 1.1031(k)–1(c)(4) allows the identification of a limited number of alternate replacement properties.

Treas. Reg. § 1.1031(k)–1 contains detailed rules to implement § 1031(a)(3) in the case of deferred exchanges. Treas. Reg. § 1.1031(k)–1(a) warns that the actual or constructive receipt of money or other non like-kind property in the full amount of the consideration for the relinquished property will cause the transaction to be treated as a sale. Constructive receipt occurs if money or other property is made available for the taxpayer's use. Treas. Reg. § 1.1031(k)–1(f)(2). Treas. Reg. § 1.1031(k)–1(g) provides safe harbors, however, to allow the exchanging taxpayer to protect its interest in money or property during the identification and exchange periods. Constructive receipt of money or other property will not be deemed to occur because of guarantees, security interests or letters of credit, the fact that money or other property is held in a "qualified escrow account" or "qualified trust," or is held by a "qualified intermediary." Treas. Reg. § 1.1031(k)–1(g)(2)–(4). In addition, Treas. Reg. § 1.1031(k)–1(g)(6) allows the arrangement to provide access to the money or other property after the exchange period has lapsed without identification of replacement property, or after all of the replacement property has been received by the exchanging taxpayer. If a properly structured deferred exchange ultimately fails to qualify because the taxpayer receives cash instead of like-kind property, installment reporting under § 453, see Chapter 31, may be available. Treas. Reg. § 1.1031(k)–1(j)(2). Most deferred exchanges are carried out as multiparty exchanges, as in *Barker,* using as an intermediary (particularly to hold cash) a person who is a "qualified intermediary" under Treas. Reg. § 1.1031(k)–1(g)(4).

Treas. Reg. § 1.1031(k)–1(g)(6) provides that an "exchange" under § 1031 occurs if the requisite form is followed even though the party acquiring the taxpayer's property was willing to pay cash. This aspect of § 1031 is perhaps understandable as a technical rule designed to provide certainty. But this approach permits the multiparty transaction, the form of which is designed solely to comply with the exchange requirement. There appears to be little justification for permitting gain to be deferred through these arrangements, which by their very nature involve situations where cash is available to the taxpayer. The original purpose of § 1031 would be served and certainty maintained if these transactions were excluded from the coverage of § 1031. Alternatively, given the option to receive cash in the event suitable replacement property is not located, Congress could vastly simplify this provision by allowing nonrecognition in the case of reinvestment of cash into like-kind property within a limited time period. See Staff of the Joint Committee on Taxation, Study of the Overall State of the Federal Tax System and Recommendations for Simplification, Pursuant to Section 8022(3)(B) of the Internal Revenue Code of 1986, 300–305 (1986) (recommending enactment of such a "rollover" replacement for § 1031); McMahon, Rollover—Better than Section 1031, But Why Stop There, 92 Tax Notes 1111 (Aug. 20, 2001).

3. REVERSE EXCHANGES

On some occasions a taxpayer who wishes to engage in a like-kind exchange locates the replacement property before locating a person who wants to acquire the taxpayer's old property. The case law has long recognized that § 1031 can apply when a taxpayer receives replacement property before transferring the relinquished property. In Rutherford v. Commissioner, T.C. Memo 1978–505, the taxpayer-farmer entered into an agreement with another farmer under which the second farmer would transfer twelve half-blood heifers to the taxpayer, who would have the heifers artificially inseminated at his expense. The taxpayer, in exchange, would transfer to the other farmer the first twelve three-quarter-blood heifers born as a result of the artificial insemination. The taxpayer received the half-blood heifers in 1973 and satisfied his obligation by delivering the three-quarter-blood heifers to the farmer over a period beginning in 1975 and ending in 1977. The Tax Court held that the taxpayer had engaged in a § 1031 like-kind exchange by his transfer of the relinquished property (the three-quarter blood heifers) for the replacement property (the half-blood heifers). In this "reverse deferred exchange," the taxpayer received the replacement property before the relinquished property even existed.

A number of cases have involved exchanges of real estate in somewhat similar, but more complex transactions. In J.H. Baird Publishing Co. v. Commissioner, 39 T.C. 608 (1962) (Acq.) and Coastal Terminals, Inc. v. United States, 320 F.2d 333 (4th Cir.1963), the courts found a like-kind exchange to have occurred where, at the taxpayer's direction, the replacement property was acquired by another person who proceeded to make significant improvements. After completion of the taxpayer-directed construction, the taxpayer acquired the newly constructed property as replacement property in exchange for the relinquished property. Biggs v. Commissioner, 632 F.2d 1171 (5th Cir.1980), supra, reached a similar result on similar facts. In all of these cases, however, the courts found that the other party was acting as a principal, not as the taxpayer's agent, in acquiring and improving the property, even though the acquisition and improvement were pursuant to an agreement between the taxpayer and that party. Thus, in form, if not in substance, the exchanges were simultaneous rather than reverse deferred exchanges.

Neither § 1031(a)(3) nor Treas. Reg. § 1.1031(k)–1 expressly deals with reverse deferred exchanges. The juxtaposition of the *Rutherford* case and the cases involving real estate raise the question of the extent to which the taxpayer can "park" property with a third party who will improve the property to the taxpayer's specifications, possibly with financing provided by the taxpayer, and still have the entire transaction treated as a like-kind exchange. Rather than develop the parameters of permissible "parking" arrangements in reverse deferred like-kind exchanges by litigation and regulations, the IRS issued safe-harbor guidance. Rev. Proc. 2000–37, 2000–2 C.B. 308, facilitates like-kind exchange treatment for "parking" reverse deferred exchanges when the replacement property is received by an "exchange accommodation titleholder" (EAT) before the taxpayer transfers the relinquished property. Under the revenue procedure, the EAT will be treated as the owner of the property if the property is held in a "Qualified Exchange Accommodation Arrangement" (QEAA). The EAT must hold either legal or beneficial title to the property, termed "qualified indicia of ownership." Moreover, the EAT and the taxpayer must enter into a QEAA in writing within five days of the EAT acquiring qualified indicia of ownership of the replacement property, the relinquished property must be identified (consistently with the rules of § 1031(a)(3) and Treas. Reg. § 1.1031(k)–1(g)(4)) within 45 days of the EAT acquiring qualified indicia of ownership to the replacement property, and the EAT can hold the qualified indicia of ownership in the property for no more than 180 days of the EAT acquiring the qualified indicia of ownership. The taxpayer may guarantee any debt incurred by the EAT to improve the property, advance funds to the EAT to pay the purchase price, lease the property from the accommodation party, supervise the property or construction, and protect the accommodation party against risk of loss from fluctuations in value. An EAT may, but need not, be a qualified intermediary (as defined in Treas. Reg. § 1.1031(k)–1(g)(4)), but may not be a disqualified party (as defined in Treas. Reg. § 1.1031(k)–1(k)). If the EAT holds both properties simultaneously for a period not in excess of 180 days and the EAT is a qualified intermediary, the transaction can qualify under both the revenue procedure safe harbor and § 1031(a)(3). Rev. Proc. 2004–51, 2004–2 C.B. 294, modifies Rev. Proc. 2000–37 by providing that the safe-harbor does not apply if the taxpayer owns the replacement property within the 180-day period preceding the transfer to the EAT.

Outside of the safe harbor of Rev. Proc. 2000–37, reverse deferred like-kind exchanges will not qualify if not structured correctly. In DeCleene v. Commissioner, 115 T.C. 457 (2000), the taxpayer purchased a parcel of land that he wanted to improve and use in his business to replace a property that he wanted to relinquish. The taxpayer located a buyer for the property he wanted to relinquish and entered into the following plan. The taxpayer sold the recently purchased replacement property to the buyer at a price equal to its adjusted basis, with payment deferred. The buyer held the property while a new building, financed by the taxpayer, was constructed on it, and then transferred it to the taxpayer in exchange for the relinquished property. The taxpayer claimed that the transaction was a direct reverse exchange, without the participation of any accommodation party, but the Tax Court held that there was a taxable sale of property, not a like-kind exchange. The buyer had never acquired the benefits and burdens of ownership of the replacement property because the taxpayer and the buyer had agreed at the outset that the relinquished property and the replacement property were of equal value. The court held that Bloomington Coca-Cola Bottling Co. v. Commissioner, 189 F.2d 14 (7th Cir.1951), which held that no § 1031 exchange occurs when a taxpayer constructs a building on already-owned property, was indistinguishable.

4. APPLICATION OF SECTION 1031(f) TO MULTIPARTY EXCHANGES

Rev. Rul. 2002–83, 2002–2 C.B. 927, dealt with the application of § 1031(f) to a multiparty exchange effected through a qualified intermediary. Individual A owned highly appreciated real property held for investment (Property 1), and individual B, who was related to individual A, owned real property (Property 2), which was not appreciated. A and B each transferred their properties to an unrelated intermediary, and C, an unrelated purchaser of Property 1, transferred cash to the intermediary; the intermediary then transferred Property 1 to C, Property 2 to A, and the cash to B. The IRS ruled that pursuant to § 1031(f), A was not entitled to nonrecognition treatment under § 1031(a) because the purpose of § 1031(f) is to deny nonrecognition treatment for transactions in which related parties make like-kind exchanges of high basis property for low basis property in anticipation of the sale of the low basis property. Section 1031(f)(4) applied because the multiparty exchange "was part of a transaction (or a series of transactions) structured to avoid the purposes of § 1031(f)(1)."

The IRS has been successful challenging exchanges under § 1031(f)(4) anytime the exchanger acquires replacement property from a related party. See e.g., North Central Rental & Leasing, LLC v. United States, 779 F3d 738 (8th Cir. 2015); Ocmulgee Fields, Inc. v. Commissioner, 613 F.3d 1360 (11th Cir. 2010); Teruya Brothers, Ltd. v. Commissioner, 580 F.3d 1038 (9th Cir. 2009). The rulings in this line of cases suggest that courts will apply § 1031(f)(4) anytime an exchanger acquires replacement property from a related party.

PART VII

DEFERRED RECOGNITION OF GAIN FROM PROPERTY

CHAPTER 27

INVOLUNTARY CONVERSIONS AND OTHER DEFERRED RECOGNITION TRANSACTIONS

SECTION 1. INVOLUNTARY CONVERSIONS

INTERNAL REVENUE CODE: Section 1033(a), (b), (g).

Section 1033(a) provides for nonrecognition of gain where property is destroyed, stolen, seized, condemned, or sold under threat or imminence of condemnation, and replaced with property "similar or related in service or use" to the former property. For certain involuntary conversions of real property, gain will not be recognized if the "like-kind" test of § 1031 is met, even though the generally applicable "similar or related in service or use" test has not been met. I.R.C. § 1033(g)(1). Generally, the taxpayer will use the insurance or condemnation proceeds to purchase the new property. To the extent that the proceeds are not invested in the new property within a specified time period—generally by the end of the second taxable year after the year of the involuntary conversion—any gain realized is recognized to the extent the proceeds received exceed the cost of the new property. Under § 1033(b), the basis of the new property is the cost of the new property purchased with proceeds of the involuntary conversion, less any gain not recognized; this rule carries over the basis of the former property adjusted for any gain recognized and any additional investment. In the case of an exchange of involuntarily converted property for the replacement property, § 1033(b) provides that the basis of replacement property is the same as the basis of the converted property, reduced by the amount of money received by the taxpayer that was not reinvested in the replacement property, and increased by gain recognized. Section 1033 applies to gain only; it does not restrict recognition of loss.

Unless the property is converted directly into similar property without first receiving proceeds, an election is required for § 1033 to apply. Although an election can be revoked as a practical matter by not acquiring similar property, a formal revocation is not permitted. See McShain v. Commissioner, 65 T.C. 686 (1976) (revocation in order to report gain on installment method and to depreciate replacement property using a higher cost basis not allowed).

Section 1033 is available only if the replacement is made by the taxpayer or the taxpayer's representative. Compare Morris v. Commissioner, 454 F.2d 208 (4th Cir.1972) (§ 1033 available where replacement completed by the estate of a deceased taxpayer), with Estate of Jayne v. Commissioner, 61 T.C. 744 (1974) (§ 1033 not available where replacement made by decedent's spouse).

Willamette Industries, Inc. v. Commissioner

United States Tax Court, 2002.

118 T.C. 126.

OPINION

■ Gerber, J.

* * * The parties filed cross-motions for partial summary judgment. The controversy concerns whether petitioner is entitled to defer gain resulting from the salvage (processing and sale) of damaged trees under section 1033. The parties have agreed on the salient facts. The controverted issue involves a legal question that is ripe for summary judgment.

Background

Petitioner is an Oregon corporation with its principal office in Portland, Oregon. Petitioner operates a vertically integrated forest products manufacturing business, which includes the ownership and processing of trees (raw materials) at various types of manufacturing plants, including lumber mills, plywood plants, and paper mills. The raw materials used in the manufacturing process are derived from petitioner's trees and from trees grown by others. Approximately 40 percent of petitioner's timber needs is acquired from petitioner's timberland, which comprises 1,253,000 acres of forested land.

Petitioner suffered damage to some of its standing trees during each of the years in issue, 1992–95. The damage was caused by wind, ice storms, wildfires, or insect infestations. The damage left part of petitioner's damaged trees standing and part of them fallen. The intended use of the trees was continued growth and cultivation until maturity, at which time the trees would have been systematically and efficiently harvested. The damage occurred prior to the intended time for harvest.

Petitioner salvaged its damaged trees to avoid further loss (from decay, insects, etc.) by means of the following steps: (1) Taking down damaged trees that remained standing; (2) cutting damaged trees into standard length logs; (3) stripping the branches from the logs; (4) dragging the logs to a pickup point; (5) grading and sorting the logs; (6) stacking the logs at a landing point; and (7) loading the logs onto trucks for further use or processing.

Petitioner chose to take the seven steps described in the preceding paragraph, rather than attempting to sell the damaged trees in place to a third party. Once it performed the seven steps, its options were to (1) attempt to sell the partially processed damaged trees to a third party; or (2) complete the processing of the damaged trees in its own plants in the ordinary course of its business. Petitioner chose the latter and completed the processing itself.

Petitioner relies on section 1033 for involuntary conversion treatment (deferral of gain). Petitioner did not realize income from harvesting and processing the damaged trees until it sold the products it manufactured from the damaged trees. Petitioner is seeking to defer only that portion of the gain attributable to the difference between its basis and the fair market value of the damaged trees as of the time its salvage of them began; that is, the value petitioner contends would have been recognized if it had sold the damaged trees on the open market instead of further processing and/or milling the damaged trees into finished products. Petitioner further contends that it is not attempting to defer any portion of the gain attributable to the processing, milling, or finishing of products.[5] Respondent determined that petitioner understated income by improperly deferring gain from the sale of the end product of the damaged trees, as follows: 1992—$647,953; 1993—$2,276,282; 1994—$3,592,035; and 1995—$4,831,462.

Discussion

The specific question we consider is whether petitioner is disqualified from electing deferral of gain under section 1033 because it processed damaged trees into end or finished products rather than being compelled simply to sell the damaged trees.[6]

Respondent contends that under section 1033 the realization of gain must stem directly or solely from the damage and the involuntary conversion. More particularly, respondent asserts that petitioner's conversion was not "involuntary" because damaged trees were processed into end products in the ordinary course of its business. Respondent points out that section 1033 is a relief provision which does not or should not include petitioner's situation; i.e., where the damaged trees are processed in the same manner as undamaged trees. Finally, respondent contends that section 1033 was not intended for the long-term deferral of profits from petitioner's timber processing and manufacturing business.[7]

---

[5]　Based on a hypothetical example presented by petitioner, the majority of the gain deferred would appear to be attributable to the difference between the fair market value of the damaged trees and petitioner's basis. Petitioner posed a hypothetical example which included the premises that the damaged trees had a $100 basis and a $475 selling price if sold in place. If the damaged trees were processed into logs, the processing cost would be $25 resulting in a $500 selling price. Petitioner further posits that the cost of milling timber is $100 and that a finished product would have a $610 selling price, resulting in $10 of gain from milling. Petitioner argues that, under this hypothetical, respondent would have allowed a deferral of the $375 gain if petitioner had sold the damaged trees in place. Petitioner contends that respondent has denied any deferral whatsoever, even though the milling of timber into a final product adds only $10 of additional gain in the context of petitioner's hypothetical. We consider here only whether petitioner is entitled to use sec. 1033. The parties have left to another day the question of the amount of gain to be deferred if petitioner's motion for partial summary judgment is granted. See infra note 6.

[6]　The parties have isolated this issue from other unresolved issues, including petitioner's substantiation of the quantity and value of the damaged trees; the amount of gain realized from sale of damaged trees; the amount of gain that may be deferred; and the determination of the correct year(s) for deferring the gain.

[7]　Respondent's contention appears to address the possibility that petitioner reinvested the proceeds (and deferred gains) from the sale of the damaged trees in replacement property in the form of relatively young trees, thereby resulting in lengthy deferral of the subject gains.

Petitioner argues that its factual situation complies literally with the requirements of section 1033 allowing deferral of gain realized from salvaging its damaged trees. Specifically, petitioner contends that it was compelled (in order to avoid further damage or loss) to salvage (process) the damaged trees resulting in an involuntary conversion within the meaning of section 1033. Petitioner also points out that the conversion was "involuntary" because the damaged trees were not scheduled for harvest at the time of the damage. In response to respondent's argument, petitioner contends that its choices for salvaging the damaged trees should not preclude deferral of the portion of the gain that it was compelled to realize on account of the damage to its trees. Petitioner emphasizes that it is not attempting to defer gain from processing and/or milling the damaged trees. Petitioner seeks to defer only that portion of the gain attributable to the difference between its basis in the damaged trees and their fair market value at the time the process of salvaging the trees began.

Section 1033 provides, under certain prescribed circumstances, for relief from taxpayer's gains realized from involuntary conversion of property. The relief provided for under section 1033 is deferral of the gain from involuntary conversion, so long as the proceeds are used to acquire qualified replacement property.

The purpose of section 1033 was described, as follows:

> The purpose of the statute is to relieve the taxpayer of unanticipated tax liability arising from involuntary * * * [conversion] of his property, by freeing him from such liability to the extent that he re-establishes his prior commitment of capital within the period provided by the statute. The statute is to be liberally construed to accomplish this purpose. On the other hand, it was not intended to confer a gratuitous benefit upon the taxpayer by permitting him to utilize the involuntary interruption in the continuity of his investment to alter the nature of that investment tax free. * * *

Filippini v. United States, 318 F.2d 841, 844 (9th Cir.1963).

* * *

Only a limited amount of legislative history has accompanied the enactment of the various involuntary conversion relief provisions since 1921. The House and Senate reports issued in connection with section 214(a)(12) of the 1921 Act explained that the relief "permits the taxpayer to omit or deduct the gains involuntarily realized, when he proceeds forthwith in good faith to invest the proceeds of such conversion in the acquisition of similar property or in establishment of a replacement fund therefor." H. Rept. 350, 67th Cong., 1st Sess. 12 (1921), 1939–1 C.B. (Part

---

Respondent's contention, however, is more properly directed at the question of whether petitioner reinvested the proceeds in qualified replacement property, a question which is not at issue in the cross-motions for partial summary judgment.

2) 168, 177; accord S. Rept. 275, 67th Cong., 1st Sess. 15 (1921), 1939–1 C.B. (Part 2) 181, 191.

From that limited legislative history, it can be gleaned that Congress intended relief from involuntary conversions only to the extent of the "proceeds of such conversion", and expected taxpayers to acquire replacement property within a reasonable time. Obviously, relief was intended only where the conversion was involuntary. Although Congress was concerned about the timeliness and "good faith" of efforts in seeking replacement property, there was no explanation or particular focus upon the use of damaged assets in the taxpayer's business.

Where the complete destruction or loss of property has occurred, there has been only a limited amount of litigation about whether a taxpayer should be allowed to defer the attendant gain. Where the destruction or loss to property is partial, however, additional questions have arisen.

In C.G. Willis, Inc. v. Commissioner, 41 T.C. 468 (1964), affd. 342 F.2d 996 (3d Cir.1965), the taxpayer's ship was damaged in a 1957 collision, and the insurance company paid $100,000 to the taxpayer. The insurance payment was approximately $9,000 less than the taxpayer's basis in the ship, and, accordingly, no gain was realized for 1957. In 1958, however, the taxpayer sold the damaged, but unrepaired, ship for an amount which exceeded the remaining basis by approximately $86,000. Under those circumstances, it was held that the 1958 sale was not an "involuntary conversion" within the meaning of section 1033 so that the gain had to be recognized and could not be deferred. In so holding, it was explained that the damage to the taxpayer's ship was insufficient to compel the taxpayer to sell and, accordingly, the sale was not involuntary. * * * In that setting, "involuntary conversion" under section 1033 was defined to mean "that the taxpayer's property, through some outside force or agency beyond his control, is no longer useful or available to him for his purposes." * * *

In S.H. Kress & Co. v. Commissioner, 40 T.C. 142 (1963), we held that condemnation of the taxpayer's property was imminent and unavoidable, and that the only realistic alternatives were to either await condemnation or to sell to an appropriate buyer. We found that those circumstances met the "compulsorily or involuntarily converted" requirement of section 1033, (citing Masser v. Commissioner, 30 T.C. 741 (1958)). Accordingly, even though a taxpayer has choices or alternatives a disposition may be deemed involuntary so that section 1033 relief remains available.

Masser v. Commissioner, supra, involved section 112(f)(1) of the Internal Revenue Code of 1939 (another predecessor of section 1033). In *Masser,* the taxpayer operated an interstate trucking business from two proximately positioned pieces of business realty that were used as part of a single economic unit. One of the properties was subject to imminent condemnation, but the taxpayer sold both parcels. In that circumstance, we held that both pieces of realty were involuntarily converted and the gain from both could be deferred.

Those cases reveal two general elements as being necessary to qualify for deferral of gain under section 1033. First, a taxpayer's property must be involuntarily damaged, and second the property must no longer be available for the taxpayer's intended business purposes for the property.

The Commissioner issued a revenue ruling that specifically focused on whether gain from the sale of trees damaged by a hurricane qualified under section 1033. In that ruling it was held that the gain on sale of uprooted trees was "voluntary" and, in addition, that there was no direct conversion into money in the circumstances expressed in the ruling. See Rev. Rul. 72–372, 1972–2 C.B. 471. The principal rationale for the holding of Rev. Rul. 72–372, supra, was that the hurricane did not cause the conversion of the trees into cash or other property directly resulting in gain from the damage.

In a second ruling, however, the 1972 ruling was revoked. See Rev. Rul. 80–175, 1980–2 C.B. 230. The 1980 ruling permitted deferral of gain from the sale of damaged trees. The factual predicate for both rulings was as follows:

> the taxpayer was the owner of timberland. As a result of a hurricane, a considerable number of trees were uprooted. The timber was not insured, and once downed, was subject to decay or being rendered totally worthless by insects within a relatively short period of time. The taxpayer was, however, able to sell the damaged timber and realized a gain from such sale. The proceeds of the sale were used to purchase other standing timber.

The rationale articulated in Rev. Rul. 80–175, is that gain is "postponed on the theory that the taxpayer was compelled to dispose of property and had no economic choice in the matter" and that the taxpayer "was compelled by the destruction of the timber to sell it for whatever the taxpayer could or suffer a total loss." * * * Accordingly, the taxpayer in the 1980 ruling was found to have met the two part test; i.e., that the damage was involuntary and the timber was no longer available for the taxpayer's intended business purpose. Most significantly, the 1980 ruling eliminated the requirement that the damage-causing event convert the property directly into cash or other property.

The 1980 ruling also contained a comparison with the holding in C.G. Willis, Inc. v. Commissioner, supra, as follows:

> In the present case, the downed timber was not repairable and was generally no longer useful to the taxpayer in the context of its original objective. The destruction caused by the hurricane forced the taxpayer to sell the downed timber for whatever price it could get. Unlike the situation in *Willis,* the sale of the downed

timber was dictated by the damage caused by the hurricane.
[Rev. Rul. 80–175, *supra,* 1980–2 C.B. at 232.]

The taxpayer in the 1980 ruling apparently intended to grow trees
and/or hold timberland for sale at a particular maturity. The hurricane
caused the taxpayer to involuntarily sell/use the trees prior to the time
intended for harvest or sale. The taxpayer's intended purpose or use was
only affected as to timing, and the sale was prior to the time the taxpayer
intended to sell or harvest.

Returning to the disagreement here, petitioner contends that, at the
time of the damage, it did not intend to harvest the damaged trees, so
that the conversion was involuntary and within the meaning of the
statute. Petitioner argues that a taxpayer may not have a choice as to
whether to dispose of damaged property, but a taxpayer may have a
choice as to *how* to dispose of damaged property.

Respondent contends that petitioner should not be entitled to such
deferral because of its choice to further process the trees into logs or
finished products, its original intention. Respondent's position in this
case is a reversion to the requirement of the 1972 ruling that the sale
(conversion to cash) be the direct result of the damage-causing event. For
more than 21 years, the Commissioner's ruling position has permitted
section 1033 deferral even though the conversion is not directly into cash.

Petitioner in this case is effectively no different from the taxpayer in
the 1980 ruling.[11] Petitioner's conversion was involuntary, and petitioner
was forced to act or suffer complete loss of the damaged trees. Section
1033 could be interpreted to permit either a direct or an indirect
conversion. The case law permits indirect conversion, but the
Commissioner's 1972 ruling denied relief because the trees damaged by
the hurricane were sold by the taxpayer. The Commissioner, in revoking
the 1972 ruling has permitted, since 1980, section 1033 relief where there
is a sale (a voluntary act) of the damaged property. Respondent has
denied relief here because petitioner processed rather than sold the
damaged trees.

The critical factor is that petitioner was compelled to harvest the
damaged trees prior to the time it had intended. The possibility that the
partial damage to petitioner's trees might have been relatively small or
resulted in a nominal amount of reduction in gain is not a reason to deny
relief. In addition, if petitioner's salvage efforts were more successful
than other taxpayers that is not a reason for denial of relief under section
1033.

Petitioner's circumstances fulfill the statutory purpose and intent.
There was unanticipated tax liability due to various casualties that
damaged the trees. Petitioner seeks to defer the gain that was occasioned

---

[11]   Respondent has not argued that the 1980 ruling was not in accord with sec. 1033 or
the case law. Respondent's position in this case, however, does not comport with the outcome or
reasoning of the 1980 ruling.

by the damage and which it had reinvested in like property. Petitioner had not planned to harvest the damaged trees. Identical to the taxpayer's situation in the 1980 ruling, petitioner's trees were damaged by forces without its control, and petitioner was compelled to salvage its damaged trees prior to the intended date for harvest, sale, and/or processing into end products. Unlike the taxpayer in C.G. Willis v. Commissioner, supra, petitioner was forced to salvage (process or sell) the damaged trees or suffer a total loss.

Respondent's attempt to distinguish petitioner's situation from the ruling does not reconcile with the rationale of the 1980 ruling, the underlying statute, and case law. The taxpayer in the ruling and petitioner were both forced to salvage the damaged trees or suffer the imminent and total loss of the damaged trees. The taxpayer in the ruling and petitioner were prematurely forced to salvage (sell or use) the damaged trees. The damaged trees were used in their businesses, but not in the same manner as they would normally have done. In the 1980 ruling, the taxpayer was forced to sell the trees under unintended business conditions. Likewise, petitioner was forced to use the damaged trees, albeit in its manufacturing process, under unintended business conditions; i.e. before maturity and/or before the time at which the trees would normally be ready for efficient harvest.

* * *

Finally, respondent contends that section 1033 was intended to provide relief for taxpayers who experience "destruction [of property] in whole or in part". Although respondent agrees that petitioner had a casualty, damage to the trees, and petitioner was compelled to salvage them, respondent infers that petitioner's situation is somehow not directly affected by the destruction. Respondent contends that petitioner's gain is voluntary or not caused by the damage because petitioner is able to process the logs into finished products.

Admittedly, petitioner's circumstances may appear more favorable than might have been expected after a "casualty", but the statute does not have a quantitative threshold. Petitioner is not seeking a windfall in the form of the deferral of gain from processing and/or making the finished products. Nor is petitioner attempting to "utilize the involuntary interruption in the continuity of his investment to alter the nature of that investment tax free." Filippini v. United States, 318 F.2d at 844. Petitioner is seeking to defer the unexpected gain that resided in trees that it had not, at the time of the damage, intended to harvest and to reinvest that gain in trees that will fulfill petitioner's intended purpose. Such deferral was the intended purpose for the enactment of section 1033.

* * *

Petitioner was growing its trees for harvest when they reached a certain maturity. The damage occurred outside of petitioner's control and forced petitioner to salvage its trees earlier than intended. That situation is indistinguishable from the circumstances set forth in Rev. Rul. 80–175, 1980–2 C.B. 230, where the taxpayer's trees were felled by a hurricane. The fact that the damage was sufficiently partial so as to result in a substantial amount of deferral is not a reason, under the statute, to deny relief.

* * *

DETAILED ANALYSIS

1. THE MEANING OF "INVOLUNTARY CONVERSION"

1.1. *Conversions Other than Condemnations*

Willamette Industries is a large timber operation. Every year some percentage of its trees will fall victim to windstorm, fire, and insect damage, and consequently will be harvested and processed before their peak maturity. Notwithstanding that Willamette Industries may have intended to harvest all of its trees at maturity an "involuntary conversion" may not have occurred to extent the harvesting of the trees before their optimal maturity was a predictable event. Although the Tax Court did not consider the predictability of the "casualties" suffered by Willamette—presumably because the Commissioner did not raise the issue—the predictability and regularity of the events arguably should have been relevant in determining whether Willamette did indeed suffer a "casualty loss" in the form of an involuntary conversion. The Tax Court emphasized that Willamette "was growing its trees for harvest when they reached a certain maturity. The damage occurred outside of [Willamette's] control and forced [it] to salvage its trees earlier than intended." To the extent premature harvesting is predictable and occurs regularly, no one year is any different from any other year; as far as sales revenues and before-tax income are concerned, every year is a normal year. To that extent, nonrecognition of any portion of the gain on the trees is inappropriate.

In situations other than condemnations, the courts and the Internal Revenue Service generally have strictly interpreted the requirement that the conversion be involuntary. The requisite element of involuntariness was not present in the following situations: Thorpe Glass Mfg. Corp. v. Commissioner, 51 T.C. 300 (1968) (sale of property as requirement of obtaining a Small Business Administration loan); Rev. Rul. 69–654, 1969–2 C.B. 162 (real estate developer voluntarily consented to subsequent conversion of part of development property for a school in order to get zoning approval for remainder of property); Rev. Rul. 82–74, 1982–1 C.B. 110 (taxpayer hired someone to burn down his building in order to collect insurance proceeds); Rev. Rul. 74–532, 1974–2 C.B. 270 (sale by corporation of rental housing project because of extensive and recurring vandalism); Rev. Rul. 78–377, 1978–2 C.B. 209 (sale of shopping center partially destroyed by fire).

In contrast, Rev. Rul. 96–32, 1996–1 C.B. 177, held that the sale of land on which a taxpayer's personal residence was located and was destroyed by casualty would be treated as part of the involuntary conversion because the land underlying a personal residence and the residence itself are considered to be a unitary property.

1.2. *Condemnations*

A condemnation has been defined as a taking by a public authority for the use of the taker. For example, § 1033 was held not to apply to a sale of stock by a public utility under an SEC order. American Natural Gas Co. v. United States, 279 F.2d 220 (Ct.Cl.1960). Similarly, sale of a stock interest in settlement of a stockholder's dispute pursuant to a state deadlock statute was held not to be a condemnation. Dear Publication & Radio, Inc. v. Commissioner, 274 F.2d 656 (3d Cir.1960).

Some situations have involved the required nexus between the condemnation and the sale. Thus, a sale of a fishing lodge on the shores of a lake qualified where the sale followed the enactment of federal legislation prohibiting motorboats with greater than 25 horsepower from the lake, thus rendering the property unsuitable for its intended commercial use. Rev. Rul. 82–147, 1982–2 C.B. 191. Where the taxpayer owned two pieces of property used as an economic unit and one was condemned, thereby making use of the other commercially impractical, sale of the other lot to a third party qualified as an involuntary conversion. Masser v. Commissioner, 30 T.C. 741 (1958) (Acq.); Rev. Rul. 59–361, 1959–2 C.B. 183 (lack of suitable replacement property is prerequisite). But where a corporation rented a warehouse from the taxpayer and a manufacturing plant on the adjacent lot from a third party, the taxpayer did not qualify under § 1033 where he voluntarily sold his warehouse property after the adjoining plant had been condemned. Rev. Rul. 69–53, 1969–1 C.B. 199.

1.3. *Threat of Condemnation*

A sale of property to a party other than the governmental authority threatening condemnation qualifies as an involuntary conversion if the taxpayer has reasonable grounds to believe the property eventually will be condemned. In S & B Realty Co. v. Commissioner, 54 T.C. 863 (1970) (Acq.), a taxpayer owned property located in an urban renewal area that was under threat of condemnation. The taxpayer had several options: he could improve the property in compliance with the urban renewal plan; he could sell the property either to a third party or to the urban renewal agency; or he could do nothing and let the property be condemned. The taxpayer elected to sell the property to a third person and the court held that § 1033 applied; as a relief provision § 1033 is to be "liberally construed."

The sale of property to a non-profit organization for resale to a Federal agency constituted an involuntary conversion where the agency had notified the taxpayer that the land would be condemned when funds became available. Rev. Rul. 69–303, 1969–1 C.B. 201; Rev. Rul. 71–567, 1971–2 C.B. 309. The sale of property to a party other than the threatening authority was treated as an involuntary conversion where the city had the taxpayer's property appraised, a newspaper report quoted a city official who stated the city intended to acquire the property, and the official confirmed the report in writing. Rev. Rul. 81–180, 1981–2 C.B. 161. The subsequent sale by the acquiring party to the city also qualified. Rev. Rul. 81–181, 1981–2 C.B. 162.

2. IDENTIFYING PROCEEDS FROM INVOLUNTARY CONVERSIONS

2.1. *Severance Damages*

Where part of the property is taken in condemnation proceedings there may be damage to the land not taken; amounts awarded for such damage are severance damages and are not part of the gain for § 1033 purposes. The severance damages reduce the basis of the remaining land, and the taxpayer recognizes gain only if the severance damages exceed that basis. Vaira v. Commissioner, 444 F.2d 770 (3d Cir.1971); Rev. Rul. 68–37, 1968–1 C.B. 359. But where the severance damages resulted from a condemnation that destroyed the retained property's usefulness, so that the retained property itself had to be sold, nonrecognition under § 1033 was applicable to the gain resulting from the condemnation proceeds, the severance damages, and the sale proceeds of the retained property. Rev. Rul. 73–35, 1973–1 C.B. 367.

2.2. *Other Proceeds*

Suppose a business whose property is condemned agrees to move the fixtures and machinery to its new location instead of transferring them to the state. The question arises as to whether the proceeds received to compensate the business for moving the property qualify as proceeds for an involuntary conversion. In Graphic Press, Inc. v. Commissioner, 523 F.2d 585 (9th Cir.1975), the state acquired the corporation's land, building and machinery which had a combined fair market value of $317,808. The corporation also agreed to move certain other machinery so that the state would be relieved of its statutory obligation to purchase this machinery. The corporation received a total of $725,000 from the state that it reinvested in property similar to that transferred or moved. The court held that the excess of the amount received over the fair market value of the property transferred constituted relocation costs attributable to the condemnation and not, as urged by the Commissioner, a payment for the corporation's waiver of its right to require the state to purchase the machinery: "We believe compensation in excess of land and building payments in this case qualifies for section 1033 treatment. From the taxpayer's viewpoint, he is being compensated for a loss due to the condemnation of his property. Whatever payment the taxpayer receives is attributable to the involuntary conversion. Where, as here, a payment is made for relocation costs in addition to land and building costs, as long as the condemnee reinvests the total award into other property similar or related in service or use within the statutory period, both the language and spirit of the statute have been met." The Ninth Circuit reversed the Tax Court's decision in this case (60 T.C. 674 (1973)).

Proceeds of an insurance policy insuring against loss of business profits do not qualify. Treas. Reg. § 1.1033(a)–2(c)(8).

3. "SIMILAR IN SERVICE OR USE"

3.1. *General*

Replacement property generally must be "similar * * * in service or use" for § 1033 to apply. Three different tests have been employed depending on the circumstances: (1) the "functional use" test has been applied where trade or business property is involved; (2) the "nature of the investment" test is applied where the taxpayer is an investor-lessor; and (3) the "like-kind" test is used for condemnations of certain real estate.

3.2. *"Functional Use" Test for Trade or Business Property*

Under the "functional use" test, the end use of the replacement property must be substantially similar to that of the replaced property. Thus, for example, McCaffrey v. Commissioner, 275 F.2d 27 (3d Cir.1960), held that a public parking lot replaced by warehouse space did not qualify. Similarly, proceeds compensating a taxpayer for inventory and reinvested in plant and inventory qualified only with respect to the reinvested inventory. Maloof v. Commissioner, 65 T.C. 263 (1975). See also Rev. Rul. 83–70, 1983–1 C.B. 189 (proceeds received as a result of condemnation of leasehold used in storage business to acquire fee interest in a warehouse qualifies); Rev. Rul. 76–319, 1976–2 C.B. 242 (billiard center acquired to replace bowling center destroyed by fire does not qualify).

3.3. *Investor-Lessors*

Where the taxpayer is an investor-lessor, a different test is applied. In this situation, following Liant Record, Inc. v. Commissioner, 303 F.2d 326 (2d Cir.1962), the Service looks at the relationship that the taxpayer has to the service or use of the replacement property rather than the functional use to which the replacement property is put. Thus, the inquiry is into whether there is a similarity of demands on the taxpayer for management, services, and relations to tenants; the nature of the business risks; and whether the replacement property performs a similar service to the taxpayer. Rev. Rul. 64–237, 1964–2 C.B. 319.

The taxpayer in *Liant Record* was allowed to defer gain recognized on the condemnation of an office building rented to numerous tenants that the taxpayer replaced with three apartment buildings, also rented to numerous tenants. Although the office and apartment buildings did not serve the same functional uses, the Court of Appeals determined that the replacement property was nonetheless similar in service or use to the taxpayer.[1] The court described the test as follows:

> Since in enacting this section Congress intended the taxpayer-owner to maintain continuity of interest and not to alter the nature of his investment tax-free, it is the service or use which the properties have to the taxpayer-owner that is relevant. Thus when the taxpayer-owner himself uses the converted property, the Tax Court is correct in comparing the actual physical service or use which the end user makes of the converted and the replacement properties. However, if the taxpayer-owner is an investor rather than a user, it is not the lessee's actual physical use but the nature of the lessor's relation to the land which must be examined. For example, if the taxpayer-owner himself operated a retail grocery business on the original land and operated an automobile sales

---

[1]   The condemnation occurred before the effective date of § 1033(g).

room on the replacement land, it would be obvious that by changing his own end use he had so changed the nature of his relationship to the property as to be outside the nonrecognition provision. However, where the taxpayer is a lessor, renting the original land and building for a retail grocery store and renting the replacement land and building for an automobile sales room, the nature of the taxpayer-owner's service or use of the property remains similar although that of the end user changes. There is, therefore, a single test to be applied to both users and investors, i.e., a comparison of the services or uses of the original and replacement properties to the taxpayer-owner. In applying such a test to a lessor, a court must compare, inter alia, the extent and type of the lessor's management activity, the amount and kind of services rendered by him to the tenants, and the nature of his business risks connected with the properties.

The following authorities are illustrative of the results reached in investor-lessor situations under the *Liant Record* test: Rev. Rul. 70–399, 1970–2 C.B. 165 (replacement of resort hotel leased under net lease with owner-operated resort hotel did not qualify); Rev. Rul. 70–466, 1970–2 C.B. 165 (replacement of rental residence with personal residence did not qualify); Rev. Rul. 71–41, 1971–1 C.B. 223 (replacement of land and rental warehouse with rental gas service station on land already owned by taxpayer qualified); Rev. Rul. 79–261, 1979–2 C.B. 295 (replacement of leased office building with office building that was partially leased and partially occupied by taxpayer in its banking business qualified to the extent leased).

3.4. *Section 1033(g)—"Like-Kind" Real Estate*

Section 1033(g)(1) provides that the "similar or related in service or use" requirement is satisfied in the case of a seizure, requisition or condemnation of real estate (or the threat or imminence thereof) if the replacement property is of a like-kind to the converted property. "Like-kind" under § 1033(g) has the same meaning as under § 1031. Section 1033(g) was enacted in 1958 to extend to condemned real estate the standards for replacement property applicable to voluntary exchanges. See S.Rep. No. 1983, 85th Cong., 2d Sess., reprinted in 1958–3 C.B. 922, 993–94. Paralleling § 1031, § 1033(g) applies only to property held for productive use in trade or business or for investment.

Rev. Rul. 67–255, 1967–2 C.B. 270, held that the investment of the proceeds from an involuntary conversion of land held for investment to construct an office building on land already owned by the taxpayer did not qualify as a like-kind replacement of the converted property under § 1033(g). The IRS reasoned, "Land is not of the same nature or character as a building." Rev. Rul. 76–390, 1976–2 C.B. 243, is to the same effect. In Davis v. United States, 411 F.Supp. 964 (D.Hawaii 1976), the court refused to follow Rev. Rul. 67–255 and treated improvements to land in the form of storm drainage and water systems, grading of the land, and excavation of a roadway, as like-kind to various condemned unimproved land. There is no indication that the Service has attempted to apply the broad principle of these rulings in cases arising under § 1031, and the failure to do so might indicate that the Service itself does not apply the reasoning except on the narrow specific fact pattern of the rulings, i.e., the use of proceeds from an involuntary conversion of unimproved land to construct a building on land already owned by the taxpayer.

Although § 1033(g) was adopted to expand the availability of § 1033, the development of the broad standard under § 1033(a) in the investor-lessor situation has resulted in the latter provision being broader in scope than § 1033(g). See Rev. Rul. 71–41, 1971–1 C.B. 223 (failure to qualify under § 1033(g) did not preclude qualification under the test for investor-lessors enunciated in Rev. Rul. 64–237 for § 1033(a)).

3.5. *Replacement with Corporate Stock*

In lieu of purchasing related property with the proceeds of an involuntary conversion, § 1033(a)(2)(A) permits the acquisition of control (80 percent stock ownership) of a corporation that owns related property. In Taft Broadcasting Co. v. United States, 929 F.2d 240 (6th Cir.1991), the taxpayer disposed of two radio stations in a transaction that qualified as an involuntary conversion. The taxpayer entered into a contract to acquire radio stations in a different locale and transferred the contract to a wholly owned subsidiary that the taxpayer formed to purchase the replacement property. The taxpayer also transferred money to the subsidiary to permit its acquisition of the radio stations. The court held that nonrecognition under § 1033 was not available if the subsidiary did not own and operate the radio stations at the time of the taxpayer's acquisition of the subsidiary's stock and remanded the case for a finding on that issue.

If a taxpayer satisfies the requirements of § 1033 by purchasing stock of a corporation holding property similar or related in service or use to the involuntarily converted property, then § 1033(b)(3)(A) requires the corporation also to reduce the basis of its property (but not below zero) by an amount identical to the amount by which the taxpayer reduced the basis of the purchased stock, i.e., the amount of realized but unrecognized gain. This provision ensures that the deferred gain ultimately is recognized through reduced depreciation deductions, as would occur if the taxpayer had directly purchased the replacement property.

3.6. *Special Rule for Presidentially Declared Disaster Areas*

Section 1033(h)(2) provides an important special rule for involuntary conversions resulting from an event declared by the President to be a disaster. If tangible property held for productive use in a trade or business (or for investment) is involuntarily converted as a result of a Presidentially declared disaster, any tangible property held for productive use in a trade or business (or for investment) will be treated as qualifying replacement property. This section permits the replacement of real property with personal property, and vice versa, as well as the replacement of property used in one type of business with property used in an entirely different type of business. For example, if a taxpayer engaged in a retail clothing store business using a leased building lost all of her inventory and fixtures in a tornado that was declared by the President to be a disaster, use of the insurance proceeds to purchase a restaurant building to be held for rental purposes would qualify under § 1033.

4. TIME LIMITATION ON REPLACEMENT

Qualified reinvestment generally must be made within two years of the close of the taxable year in which any gain is realized. The time period for conversions under § 1033(g) is three years. The following cases are illustrative of the problems taxpayers may encounter regarding the time limitation. In Fort Hamilton Manor, Inc. v. Commissioner, 445 F.2d 879 (2d Cir.1971), the court held that entering into an agreement to purchase qualifying replacement property within the period specified is not sufficient; the taxpayer must either acquire ownership by deed or by a transfer of the burdens and benefits of ownership. Where the condemnation proceeds are deposited in court without any restrictions as to the disposition or use by the taxpayer, the time period begins running at that point even though the award may be subsequently reversed or modified on appeal. Boyce v. United States, 405 F.2d 526 (Ct.Cl.1968); Aldridge v. Commissioner, 51 T.C. 475 (1968). In R.A. Stewart and Co. v. Commissioner, 57 T.C. 122 (1971), the taxpayer received $70,000 in 1965 with respect to condemned property; a final payment of $104,570.95 was made in 1968, pursuant to a court determination. In 1965, the taxpayer's adjusted basis for the property was $55,005.53. The court held that the replacement time began to run in 1965 since the taxpayer had realized gain in that year.

5. ACQUISITION OF REPLACEMENT PROPERTY FROM RELATED PARTY

Section 1033(i) denies § 1033 nonrecognition if the gain realized on the involuntarily converted property exceeds $100,000 and the replacement property is purchased from a person related to the taxpayer within the meaning of § 267(b) or § 707(b), such as a close family member or a controlled corporation. If the taxpayer is a C corporation or a partnership in which one or more of the partners is a C corporation, § 1033(i) applies without regard to the $100,000 gain threshold.

6. INVOLUNTARY CONVERSIONS OF PRINCIPAL RESIDENCES

Section 121, discussed in Chapter 6, provides nonrecognition of up to $250,000 gain ($500,000 on a joint return) realized on the involuntary conversion of a taxpayer's principal residence through destruction, theft, seizure, requisition, or condemnation. I.R.C. 121(d)(5)(A). If the taxpayer replaces an involuntarily converted principal residence, then the rules of §§ 121 and 1033 must be coordinated. Section 121(d)(5)(B) provides that in applying § 1033, the amount realized "is determined without regard to this section, reduced by the amount of gain not included in gross income pursuant to this section." This language requires the application of § 121 before the application of § 1033. Thus, as long as the gain realized as a result of an involuntary conversion does not exceed the applicable dollar ceiling on the amount excludable under § 121 the entire gain is excluded under § 121, § 1033 does not apply, and the replacement property has a basis equal to its actual cost. If, however, the gain realized on the involuntary conversion exceeds the amount excludable under § 121, § 1033 comes into play.

Assume, for example, that a single taxpayer owned a home with a basis of $50,000, which was condemned for highway construction, and the taxpayer received an award of $370,000, thereby realizing a $320,000 gain. If the taxpayer met the tests of § 121, then $250,000 of the gain would not be recognized under that provision. In applying § 1033 to determine the extent to which the remaining $70,000 gain realized on the involuntary conversion must be recognized, for purposes of § 1033(a)(2)(A) the amount realized will be reduced from $370,000 to $120,000. Thus, if the taxpayer purchases a new principal residence for $120,000, complies with the other requirements of § 1033, and so elects, no gain will be recognized. As a result, the taxpayer's basis in the replacement residence determined under § 1033(b)(2) would be $50,000—the $120,000 purchase price of the replacement residence minus the $70,000 gain that was not recognized under § 1033. The phrase in § 1033(b)(2) reducing the basis of the replacement property by the "gain not so recognized" should be construed to refer only to gain not recognized under § 1033, and not to gain that was excluded from gross income by virtue of § 121. Thus, if the taxpayer purchased a new principal residence for $125,000, the basis of the new residence would be $55,000—its $125,000 cost minus the $70,000 excluded under § 1033.

Although § 121 excludes up to $250,000 of gain ($500,000 for certain married taxpayers filing a joint return), § 1033 does not always provide nonrecognition of any remaining gain. Assume that in the above example the taxpayer paid only $75,000 for the replacement residence. Section 121 still excludes $250,000 of gain realized on the original residence. Under § 1033 an additional $25,000 of gain would not be recognized. But $45,000 of gain, the excess of the deemed amount realized for purposes of § 1033(a)(2)(A) after the application of § 121(d)(5)(B), $120,000, over the $75,000 cost of the replacement residence, must be recognized. The replacement residence would take a basis of $50,000—the $75,000 cost of the replacement residence minus the $25,000 gain that was not recognized under § 1033. The $250,000 of gain that was excluded under § 121, does not affect the basis of the replacement residence.

In either of these cases, because the taxpayer's basis in the new principal residence is determined, in whole or in part, with reference to the basis of the old principal residence, the taxpayer is treated as having owned and used the new principal residence for a period that includes the period that the taxpayer owned and used the old principal residence. I.R.C. § 121(d)(5)(C).

SECTION 2.   MISCELLANEOUS NONRECOGNITION PROVISIONS

Several nonrecognition rules are included in the Code to facilitate transactions that change the form of ownership of property while representing a continued ownership of transferred assets. Examples include the transfer of assets to a corporation in exchange for corporate stock by a person or persons in control of the resulting corporation, or the transfer of assets to a partnership by a person who is or becomes a partner. Nonrecognition is provided for the exchange of stock of one corporation for the stock of a different corporation in certain qualified corporate reorganizations. In these nonrecognition transactions, the transferor of property typically maintains a continuing interest in the property through an investment in a different form.

DETAILED ANALYSIS

1.   ORGANIZATION OF CORPORATIONS AND PARTNERSHIPS

A number of provisions affecting the organization and reorganization of corporations are based on principles similar to the like-kind exchange rules of § 1031. Under § 351, a taxpayer who transfers property to a corporation in exchange for stock of the corporation does not recognize gain or loss if the taxpayer (and other transferors) own 80 percent or more of the stock of the transferee corporation ·immediately after the transfer. Section 358, a provision similar to § 1031(d), provides for an exchanged basis in the stock received in a § 351 exchange. Under § 721, the transfer of property to a partnership in exchange for a partnership interest is also a nonrecognition transaction.

The nonrecognition treatment provided in corporate reorganizations, as defined in § 368, operate in a similar fashion. Sections 354 and 361 provide for the nonrecognition of gain or loss on an exchange of stock of corporations that are party to a reorganization by the shareholders and by the corporations. Deferred gain or loss is preserved for the shareholders by the exchanged basis rules of § 358. Similar nonrecognition rules are applicable under § 355 to transactions that divide a corporation, such as a corporate spin-off in which a corporation distributes a trade or business to its shareholders in the form of a distribution of the stock of a corporation formerly owned by the distributing corporation.

2.   QUALIFIED LESSEE CONSTRUCTION ALLOWANCES

Section 110, which is applicable to both individuals and corporations, operates in a manner analogous to § 118 with respect to the relationship of income exclusion and basis, although its triggering conditions differ from those of § 118. In general, § 110 excludes amounts received by lessees from lessors, whether received in cash or as a rent reduction, that are applied by the lessee to the construction of leasehold improvements that will be used in the lessee's trade or business. The provision applies only if the lease is for the use of retail space for 15 years or less, and the leasehold improvements must revert to the lessor at the end of the lease. Any leasehold improvements constructed with an excludable qualified leasehold construction allowance are treated as the lessor's property rather than as the lessee's property.

3.   ROLLOVER OF GAIN ON "QUALIFIED SMALL BUSINESS STOCK"

Section 1045(a) provides for elective nonrecognition of capital gain on the sale of "qualified small business stock," as defined in § 1202(c), to the extent that the amount realized is reinvested in other qualified small business stock within 60 days of the sale. The stock that is sold must have been held by the taxpayer for more than six months. See I.R.C. § 1045(b)(4).

In general, only newly issued stock in a domestic C corporation that was acquired from the corporation (or through an underwriter) in exchange for money, property, or services qualifies. At the time the stock is issued, the aggregate gross assets of the corporation (measured by tax basis, not fair market value) may not exceed $50,000,000, and for substantially all of the taxpayer's holding period the corporation must be engaged in an "active business" as defined in § 1202(e). This test excludes business performing certain services, including most professional services, dealing in real estate, banking, insurance, leasing, investment, or other financial activities, farming, forestry, natural resource extraction, and operating a hotel, motel, restaurant, or similar business. If more than ten percent of a corporation's assets consist of either portfolio securities or real estate not used in its trade or business, then the corporation automatically does not qualify.

The basis of the replacement stock is its purchase price minus the unrecognized gain on the first sale. I.R.C. § 1045(b)(3). If the taxpayer makes more than one purchase of qualified replacement stock within the sixty-day period following the nonrecognition sale, then the basis reduction applies to the earliest purchases.

When the replacement qualified small business stock is sold, the gain realized but previously not recognized on the sale of the original small business stock must be recognized whether or not the first replacement stock is in turn replaced. The remaining gain also is taxed unless the taxpayer again purchases replacement qualified small business stock within sixty days, in which case the gain on the replacement stock in excess of the gain on the original stock (which was rolled over the first time) can be rolled over without recognition. If the gain on the second sale—the sale of the first replacement stock—is rolled over to another replacement stock, the basis of that stock is its cost minus the unrecognized gain on the second sale.

Under § 1223(13), the holding period of the replacement stock includes the holding period of the original stock. Thus, any gain recognized on the sale of the replacement stock, whether economically attributable to the original stock or the replacement stock, is eligible for the § 1202 exclusion, discussed in Chapter 24, if the combined holding periods of the original stock and the replacement stock meet the 5-year holding period requirement of § 1202(b)(2). In any event, recognized includable gains are taxed at the preferential capital gains rates, discussed in Chapter 24, although gains with respect to which the § 1202 exclusion have been claimed are not eligible for the lowest preferential rates.

Assume for example, that on October 1, 2010, the taxpayer purchased stock of X Corp., a qualified small business, for $10,000. On October 15, 2015, the taxpayer sold the X Corp. stock for $100,000 and purchased stock of Y Corp., another qualified small business, for $90,000. Section 1045 provides nonrecognition for $80,000 of gain, and § 1202 excludes the remaining $10,000 of gain. Taxpayer's basis for the Y Corp. stock is $10,000. On March 1, 2016, taxpayer sells the Y Corp. stock for $140,000, realizing a $130,000 gain, and purchases at original issue stock of Z Corp., another qualified small business, for $120,000. The $80,000 deferred gain on the sale of the X Corp. stock now must be recognized, but that gain is excluded under § 1202. Of the remaining $50,000 gain, $20,000, the excess of the amount realized on the sale of the Y Corp. stock over the purchase price of the Z Corp. replacement stock, would be recognized, but because § 1223(13) provides a tacked holding period, that gain is excluded under § 1202. The remaining $30,000 of gain is eligible for nonrecognition under § 1045 because it was rolled over into the Z Corp. stock. The Z Corp. stock takes a $90,000 basis, its purchase price ($120,000) minus the unrecognized gain on the Y Corp. stock ($30,000).

4.   OTHER NONRECOGNITION PROVISIONS

Sections 1035 through 1038 provide that neither gain nor loss is recognized in various circumstances where the continuity of the investment has in some measure been maintained although the requirements of § 1031 are not met. Section 1035 provides for nonrecognition upon the exchange of certain life insurance, endowment, and annuity policies. Section 1036 accords nonrecognition status to exchanges of common stock for common stock and preferred stock for preferred stock in the same corporation. Nonrecognition upon the exchange of certain U.S. bonds for other U.S. bonds is provided in § 1037. Certain reacquisitions of real estate in satisfaction of purchase money indebtedness secured by the property are nonrecognition events under § 1038.

PART VIII

TIMING OF INCOME AND DEDUCTIONS

CHAPTER 28

TAX ACCOUNTING METHODS

SECTION 1. GENERAL PRINCIPLES

INTERNAL REVENUE CODE: Sections 441(a)–(e), (g); 442; 446; 448(a), (b).

REGULATIONS: Sections 1.441–1(a), (c), (e); 1.446–1(a)(1), (2), (b).

A. TAX ACCOUNTING METHODS IN GENERAL—CASH AND ACCRUAL METHODS

The income tax is an annual tax based on the income of a particular year. The taxable year of a taxpayer is either a calendar year, ending on December 31, or a fiscal year, ending on the last day of any month other than December (e.g., July 1 to June 30), depending on the annual accounting period used by the taxpayer in keeping its books.[1] The various items involved in the computation of taxable income thus must be allocated to an annual period. It is the function of the tax accounting methods to make this allocation.

A taxpayer is required to report income for federal income tax purposes in accordance with the method of accounting regularly employed in the taxpayer's business or personal record keeping. That method, however, must "clearly reflect income." I.R.C. § 446(b). There are two principal methods of accounting for income and deductions, the cash method and the accrual method. The cash method is used by most individuals, including small proprietorships and partnerships, and some small corporations. The accrual method is used by a few individuals, many partnerships, and most corporations. In general, all corporations having more than $5,000,000 a year of gross receipts are required to use the accrual method. I.R.C. § 448.

Most individuals not engaged in a trade or business do not maintain accounting books, other than perhaps a checkbook or other cash record book. Even many small proprietors keep only simple cash books. Their "accounting method" therefore turns on cash receipts and disbursements. An item is includable in income when received, including salary, wages, rent from a tenant, interest on a bank account, etc. Meanwhile, expenses—such as state and local taxes, business expenses, home mortgage interest, etc.—are deductible when paid. Thus, the cash method easily reflects the taxpayer's way of judging the taxpayer's financial position and budget. It also usually reflects the taxpayer's taxable income for the year with sufficient accuracy. However, the cash method is not as simple as merely adding receipts and subtracting

---

[1] In some instances, a 52–53 week accounting period, always ending on the same day of the week, is permitted. I.R.C. § 441(f).

disbursements. As illustrated in Section 2 of this chapter, multiple questions arise when cash is not actually received but is made available to the taxpayer, or the taxpayer receives a promise or instrument that may be the economic equivalent of a cash receipt. On the deduction side, an actual disbursement of cash may not be necessary where the taxpayer issues a check or other form of immediately enforceable promise to pay. Alternatively, payment of cash in one year for an amount due in a later year, or payment of cash for a benefit in a later year may not create an immediate deduction.

As business or other income-producing activity reaches more complex levels, the cash method ceases to be a sufficiently accurate reflection of income to justify its utilization for tax or other purposes. Inventories must be used to determine the cost of goods sold. Large expenses are incurred in one year though they may not be paid until a year or two later. Large amounts of income may be earned in one year, although the actual cash will be received in the future. The cash method is not always adequate to reflect the taxable income attributable to such items in a particular year. Instead, many business organizations, and some individuals, employ the accrual method of accounting. Under this method, an item of income is includable in gross income in the year in which there is a right to payment, and an item of deduction generally is subtracted in the year in which the obligation to pay the expense arises. As a result, income and the expenses incurred in producing it are largely linked together to determine the net income during the year, even though the actual receipt of income and payment of expenses may occur in other years.

An income item is generally accrued when there is an unconditional right to receive the item. Numerous situations arise in which it must be determined whether a right to an item is sufficient to require accrual. The right to receive income may be limited by the use of an escrow account, the right to the item is acknowledged but its amount is uncertain or in dispute, a claim may be contested by the other party, or a liability is acknowledged by the other party but its financial condition makes payment unlikely. Also, cash may be received before it has been earned, as where a magazine receives a payment for a three-year subscription. All of these situations raise questions regarding whether the essential right to payment has arisen.

Similar questions occur on the deduction side. Historically, the rule was that an expense was accrued when its amount could be determined with reasonable accuracy and there was an unconditional liability to pay the expense. When does this unconditional liability exist? Liabilities may be contingent or contested. Payment of acknowledged liabilities may be unlikely because the taxpayer is in a precarious financial condition. In some cases, income might be received but there is a probability that a part of the income will be required to be returned in the future and the taxpayer finds it prudent to set up a reserve to meet these future obligations, as in the case of commissions received on sales which will have to be partially returned if the buyer cancels the transaction in the next two years. In some cases, the taxpayer may make a cash payment before the liability has definitely been incurred, as where a tax is paid but a refund claimed. In some cases the existence of the liability may be clear but the liability will not be paid until far in the future The test for deductibility of accrual method expenses is further complicated by § 461(h), which provides that even though the amount and existence of a liability is certain, the expenses may not be accrued as a deduction until "economic performance" has occurred.

The materials in Section 3 consider the issues that arise in the application of the accrual method for tax purposes. Often an accountant would have to answer these questions even if an income tax were not involved, since many other matters turn on the answer, such as reports to stockholders and creditors, earnings for rate-fixing purposes, profits for wage negotiations, etc. In many situations, the accountant's method of handling income and expense items for the regular business purposes of his client is also satisfactory for tax purposes. But in some situations, the answer given by the accountant for business purposes is not always the answer accepted by the IRS or sustained by the courts for tax purposes. Policies specifically relevant to taxation properly force a departure from the accountant's method.

B. THE FUNCTION OF TAX ACCOUNTING

A recurring theme in the discussion of accounting methods is the relationship of tax accounting to other tax principles. Many timing questions under the federal income tax laws are governed by rules of general application not involving the tax accounting provisions and not dependent upon the taxpayer's method of accounting. For example, the question when income from casual sales of property is accounted for is generally answered by the principles of realization and recognition. Similarly, the timing of the deductions for losses and bad debts is fixed in terms of "losses sustained" and debts "becoming worthless" and not by the tax accounting provisions. Still other examples include the questions regarding capital expenditures versus current expenses and the various cost recovery mechanisms applicable to capital expenditures. Moreover, as the materials in this Chapter indicate, there are some timing questions where it is not clear whether the tax accounting rules or other rules control.

In a number of situations, the sections prescribing the conditions regarding the inclusion or deduction of an item also specify rules governing timing. In these instances, the specific timing rule, rather than the general timing rules, controls the year of inclusion or deduction. For example, many of the personal expense deductions and credits, such as for charitable contributions, medical expenses, alimony, and child care,

are allowed only when "paid." In those instances, the special rules control over the general rules.

Both the tax accounting rules and other timing provisions in the federal income tax laws can be viewed as attempts to balance conflicting interests. In principle, timing rules seek to ascertain the point at which economic income arises. Accrual accounting is generally best suited to this task because it more accurately matches items of income and expense than does cash method accounting. But accrual taxation raises a number of difficulties. Accrual by its very nature requires periodic valuations and allocates income to periods when cash may not be available to taxpayers. This result may impose liquidity problems for taxpayers when the tax is imposed prior to the receipt of cash or collection difficulties for the government when cash is received prior to accrual. Furthermore, to reflect economic income accurately accrual accounting should take both income and deduction items into account only at their discounted present value, not the nominal amount of the item. In practice, however, accrual accounting always has taken the full amount of items into account, even if they would not be received or paid until future years. This treatment can cause the accrual method of accounting to distort income in ways that the cash method does not, a distortion that has occasioned Congressional response.

The similarity in goals of the tax accounting rules and other timing provisions has produced similar results in a number of situations. For example, prepaid expenditures by a cash method taxpayer have been disallowed as current deductions because they must be capitalized under § 263 or, alternatively, because they do not clearly reflect income. On the other hand, the results under tax accounting often differ from the results under financial accounting. It is in these situations that it becomes important to define more precisely the scope of the tax accounting provisions.

C. THE ACCOUNTING METHOD STANDARD: CLEAR REFLECTION OF INCOME

While taxpayers are required to report income for tax purposes in accordance with a method of accounting that "clearly reflects income," there are no precise standards for determining whether an accounting method meets this standard. Indeed, the requirement is circular in that the accounting method must clearly reflect taxable income which in turn is computed by reference to accounting methods.

In practice, some inaccuracies in measuring income are tolerated in the name of simplicity—through the general acceptance of the cash method for individuals, for instance—but the inaccuracies in some circumstances become too substantial and the method ceases clearly to reflect income. For example, the requirement that taxpayers maintaining inventories use the accrual method appears to be based upon the policy that the cash method would produce an unacceptable level of inaccuracy in those circumstances. Treas. Reg. § 1.446–1(c)(2)(i).

Consistency is also a factor in clearly reflecting income. Treas. Reg. § 1.446–1(c)(2)(ii) provides: "No method of accounting will be regarded as clearly reflecting income unless all items of gross profit and deductions are treated with consistency from year to year. The IRS may authorize a taxpayer to adopt or change to a method of accounting permitted by this chapter although the method is not specifically described in the regulations in this part if, in the opinion of the IRS, income is clearly reflected by the use of such method. Further, the IRS may authorize a taxpayer to continue the use of a method of accounting consistently used by the taxpayer, even though not specifically authorized by the regulations in this part if, in the opinion of the IRS, income is clearly reflected by the use of such method." Inconsistent treatment of items from year to year can result in the total omission of income or in double deductions. As a result, the IRS generally must approve changes in accounting methods with its consent typically conditioned on the taxpayer agreeing to transitional adjustments to prevent such distortions.

Yet consistency by itself is no insurance against inaccuracy. In Electric & Neon, Inc. v. Commissioner, 56 T.C. 1324 (1971), aff'd per curiam, 496 F.2d 876 (5th Cir.1974), a corporation was in the business of manufacturing, installing, and leasing commercial signs. Although the signs were ordinarily leased for a period of five years, the taxpayer deducted the entire costs of constructing the signs as current expenses. The accounting practice in the industry was to capitalize the costs of the signs and depreciate those expenditures over the period of the original lease. Under § 446(b), the Commissioner determined that the taxpayer's method of accounting did not clearly reflect income, and the Tax Court upheld the Commissioner's determination:

> [T]he error in the petitioner's accounting method was not simply one of concept, but rather, was one which demonstrably produced serious inaccuracies in the year-by-year computation of income. As a result of its use of an improper method, E & N's taxable income would be seriously understated in a year when many new signs were constructed for lease, and just as seriously overstated in a year when very few signs were constructed, with the result of making the corporation's financial fortunes appear to be sinking when in fact it was enjoying great success, and rising when in fact its business was seriously diminished. * * *

> [W]e point out next that while consistency is highly desirable when combined with some acceptable method of accounting, it is not a substitute for correctness; the respondent is justified in requiring a change in a taxpayer's method of accounting which, although consistently used over a period of years, is erroneous, and does not clearly reflect income.

Although the Commissioner's power to require a taxpayer to change its method of accounting is strong, it is not unlimited. In RLC Industries Co. v. Commissioner, 98 T.C. 457 (1992), aff'd, 58 F.3d 413 (9th Cir.1995), the court rebuffed the Commissioner's attempt to require a taxpayer to switch to a method that "more clearly reflected income":

> Section 446 vests the Commissioner with broad discretion in determining whether a particular method of accounting clearly reflects income. * * * The Commissioner's determination is entitled to more than the usual presumption of correctness. * * * Respondent's interpretation of the "clear-reflection standard [of § 446(b)] 'should not be interfered with unless clearly unlawful.' " Thor Power Tool Co. v. Commissioner, 439 U.S. 522, 532 (1979) (quoting Lucas v. American Code Co., 280 U.S. 445, 449 (1930)). The taxpayer bears "a heavy burden of [proof]" to show that the Commissioner abused her discretion, and the Commissioner's determination "is not to be set aside unless shown to be 'plainly arbitrary.' " Thor Power Tool Co. v. Commissioner, supra at 532–533 (quoting Lucas v. Kansas City Structural Steel Co., 281 U.S. 264, 271 (1930)). * * *

> Although the Commissioner has broad discretion, she cannot require a taxpayer to change from an accounting method which clearly reflects income because the Commissioner considers an alternate method to more clearly reflect income. * * * If a taxpayer's method of accounting is specifically authorized by the Internal Revenue Code or the underlying regulations and has been applied on a consistent basis, respondent has not been allowed to arbitrarily require a change or reject the taxpayer's method. * * *

These two cases are merely a sampling of the cases addressing the issue of "clear reflection." The general power of the IRS to require a taxpayer to adopt a method of accounting which clearly reflects income is involved either explicitly or implicitly in many of the cases discussed in the following materials.

D. DIFFERENCES BETWEEN TAX ACCOUNTING AND FINANCIAL ACCOUNTING

Financial or book accounting generally refers to accounting systems used to maintain the books and records of a business and to prepare financial statements to provide information regarding its operations and financial situation. They are usually prepared in accordance with generally accepted accounting principles (GAAP) which in turn employ principles of accrual accounting.

Despite some general similarity between tax accounting and financial accounting rules, there are significant differences in the approach of the two systems particularly with respect to timing issues.

Differences between tax accounting and financial accounting reflect fundamental differences between the goals of tax accounting and financial accounting. Some of these differences were discussed by the Supreme Court in Thor Power Tool Co. v. Commissioner, 439 U.S. 522 (1979):

> * * * The primary goal of financial accounting is to provide useful information to management, shareholders, creditors, and others properly interested; the major responsibility of the accountant is to protect these parties from being misled. The primary goal of the income tax system, in contrast, is the equitable collection of revenue; the major responsibility of the Internal Revenue Service is to protect the public fisc. Consistently with its goals and responsibilities, financial accounting has as its foundation the principle of conservatism, with its corollary that "possible errors in measurement [should] be in the direction of understatement rather than overstatement of net income and net assets."[18] In view of the Treasury's markedly different goals and responsibilities, understatement of income is not destined to be its guiding light. Given this diversity, even contrariety of objectives, any presumptive equivalency between tax and financial accounting would be unacceptable.

> This difference in objectives is mirrored in numerous differences of treatment. Where the tax law requires that a deduction be deferred until "all the events" have occurred that will make it fixed and certain, United States v. Anderson, 269 U.S. 422, 441 (1926), accounting principles typically require that a liability be accrued as soon as it can reasonably be estimated. Conversely, where the tax law requires that income be recognized currently under "claim of right," "ability to pay," and "control" rationales, accounting principles may defer accrual until a later year so that revenues and expenses may be better matched. Financial accounting, in short, is hospitable to estimates, probabilities, and reasonable certainties; the tax law, with its mandate to preserve the revenue, can give no quarter to uncertainty. This is as it should be. Reasonable estimates may be useful, even essential, in giving shareholders and creditors an accurate picture of a firm's overall financial health; but the accountant's conservatism cannot bind the Commissioner in his efforts to collect taxes. * * *

> Finally, a presumptive equivalency between tax and financial accounting would create insurmountable difficulties of tax administration. Accountants long have recognized that

---

[18] AICPA Accounting Principles Board, Statement No. 4, Basic Concepts and Accounting Principles Underlying Financial Statements of Business Enterprises § 171 (1970), reprinted in 2 APB Accounting Principles 9089 (1973). * * *

"generally accepted accounting principles" are far from being a canonical set of rules that will ensure identical accounting treatment of identical transactions. "Generally accepted accounting principles," rather, tolerate a range of "reasonable" treatments, leaving the choice among alternatives to management. * * * Variances of this sort may be tolerable in financial reporting, but they are questionable in a tax system designed to ensure as far as possible that similarly situated taxpayers pay the same tax. If management's election among "acceptable" options were dispositive for tax purposes, a firm, indeed, could decide unilaterally—within limits dictated only by its accountants—the tax it wished to pay. Such unilateral decisions would not just make the Code inequitable; they would make it unenforceable.

SECTION 2.   THE CASH METHOD

A. INCOME ITEMS

INTERNAL REVENUE CODE: Sections 446(a), (c), (d); 451(a).

REGULATIONS: Sections 1.61–2(d)(4); 1.446–1(a)(3), (c)(1)(i); 1.451–1(a); –2.

The cash method of accounting does not depend solely on the amount of cash received. Cash received must first represent an item of income; items such as loans or returns of capital are not includable in income. Furthermore, the cash method taxpayer may have income without the actual receipt of cash. For example, income from forgiveness of indebtedness by its very nature does not involve the current receipt of cash.

There are other important respects in which the cash method does not depend on the actual reduction of income to cash. Treas. Reg. § 1.446–1(c)(1)(i) provides that income items received in the form of property or services as well as cash are to be included in income in the taxable year in which received. Here tax accounting conforms to the basic principles of income inclusion regarding non-cash payments discussed in Chapter 3, Section 1. Special problems arise, however, where the property that the cash method taxpayer receives is a claim against another party such as a check, promissory note, or open account indebtedness. If all property of this type were required to be included in income upon receipt, the difference between cash and accrual methods would be reduced or eliminated. Historically some courts limited the literal language of the regulations and required income inclusion by a cash method taxpayer only in situations in which the intangible "property" received was "equivalent to cash." Subsequent legislative developments have reduced the scope of this limitation.

A similar but related doctrine has been applied where money (or other property) is irrevocably placed in trust for the benefit of a cash method taxpayer even though the taxpayer has no right to receive the money until a subsequent year. Courts often have found that the taxpayer's equitable interest in the trust is currently taxable either because of the economic benefit conferred or because the interest in the trust is a receipt of "property."

The third situation in which a cash method taxpayer's income does not depend on the actual receipt of cash involves the principle of "constructive receipt." If tax liability turned on the actual receipt of the income, a cash method taxpayer could determine the year of income inclusion simply by failing to collect income due. To forestall this possibility, the regulations provide: "Income although not actually reduced to a taxpayer's possession is constructively received by him in the taxable year during which it is credited to his account, set apart for him, or otherwise made available so that he may draw upon it at any time * * * . However, income is not constructively received if the taxpayer's control of its receipt is subject to substantial limitations or restrictions." Treas. Reg. § 1.451–2(a). See also Treas. Reg. § 1.446–1(c)(1)(i). Much case law has developed around the question of when income is "made available" to the taxpayer. In most cases, the doctrine of constructive receipt determines when an item must be taken into income, but in some cases the constructive receipt doctrine affects whether an item is included or excludable.

These three principles that may result in the realization of income by a cash method taxpayer prior to actual receipt of payment in cash can be interrelated. When a taxpayer voluntarily postpones receipt of cash, the constructive receipt doctrine may apply. But even if the constructive receipt doctrine is inapplicable, the right to payment itself may require current inclusion.

DETAILED ANALYSIS

1. CONSTRUCTIVE RECEIPT

1.1. *In General*

Perhaps the most common application of constructive receipt is the taxation of interest on bank accounts in the year it is posted to depositor's account. Because the interest can be withdrawn at any time, it is taxable. In Loose v. United States, 74 F.2d 147 (8th Cir.1934), bond coupons representing interest were held to be taxable as they matured even though the taxpayer and his wife, the only ones having access to the safe deposit box in which the bonds were kept, were unable because of illness to clip the coupons. Menard, Inc. v. Commissioner, T.C. Memo. 2004–207, involved facts analogous to bank deposit accounts. In *Menard*, a president/controlling shareholder of a corporation made a demand loan to the corporation. Though interest was due in 1998, it was not paid or received until 1999. The court held that the interest had been constructively received.

Hornung v. Commissioner, 47 T.C. 428 (1967) (Acq.), illustrates the significance of both legal rights and geographical distance in application of the constructive receipt doctrine. In *Hornung,* the taxpayer was awarded an automobile for his performance in the NFL championship football game played on Sunday, December 31, 1961 in Green Bay, Wisconsin. The prize was announced immediately after the game. The car was actually presented to the taxpayer on January 3, 1962 in New York and was in the possession of a dealer in New York on December 31, 1961. Hornung argued that he had constructively received the car in 1961, but the court found the doctrine of constructive receipt was not applicable. The constructive receipt doctrine requires "essentially unfettered control by the recipient over the date of actual receipt." On the facts, it was doubtful that the car could have been transferred to Hornung before January 2 of the next year and delivery was not solely dependent on Hornung's volition.

Baxter v. Commissioner, 816 F.2d 493 (9th Cir.1987), refused to find constructive receipt with respect to a check that the taxpayer could have driven 40 miles on Saturday, December 30 to pick up, but chose to let the payor mail to him. The Tax Court had found that the taxpayer had constructively received the check because he could have picked it up had he so chosen. T.C. Memo. 1985–378. Compare United States v. Hancock Bank, 400 F.2d 975 (5th Cir.1968) (constructive receipt found despite the fact that payor refused on demand to make payment to the taxpayer, the court finding the refusal "wholly without legal basis").

1.2. *Receipt by Agent*

An amount received by the taxpayer's agent is considered as received by the taxpayer in applying cash method accounting rules. In Gale v. Commissioner, T.C. Memo. 2002–54, the taxpayer's lawyer received the proceeds from settling a lawsuit, but the proceeds were held in the attorney's escrow account pending resolution of a fee dispute between the taxpayer and the attorney with respect to that case and other matters. The court held that the full amount of the proceeds was constructively received by the cash method taxpayer in the year the proceeds were paid over to the taxpayer's lawyer by the defendant.

1.3. *Arrangements to Postpone Income*

The doctrine of constructive receipt does not apply merely because the obligor is solvent and would have been willing to pay immediately. An important consideration may be whether a deferral agreement is made before or after the taxpayer performs on the underlying contract.

In Amend v. Commissioner, 13 T.C. 178 (1949) (Acq.), a wheat farmer had since 1942 followed the practice of selling his wheat in August or December of the year it was produced but under contracts calling for delivery and payment in January of the succeeding year. The buyer would have agreed to delivery and payment in the production year, but the taxpayer believed the method followed would make his income more uniform. The wheat was actually shipped in the production year. The court held that the amounts were not constructively received in the production year (as respects

1944 and 1945) since under the contracts the taxpayer could not have demanded payment in that year.

Rev. Rul. 60–31, 1960–1 C.B. 174, accepts the principle that there is no constructive receipt when an employee receives unfunded nonforfeitable rights to deferred compensation even though the employer would have been willing to pay cash immediately and the deferral arrangement had no independent business purpose beyond the tax deferral of the payments. See Chapter 30, Section 1.

In United States v. Ingalls, 399 F.2d 143 (5th Cir.1968), the taxpayer had borrowed over $200,000 from a corporation with which he also had a long-term employment contract. A dispute developed and, as part of the settlement in 1961, the taxpayer and the corporation agreed that he would repay the debt to the corporation ratably over a ten-year period. The corporation agreed to pay him the same amount in discharge of his claims for salary, the parties exchanging checks in identical amounts each year. The arrangement, if effective, would have deferred the taxpayer's income from the discharge of the indebtedness. The court found for the Commissioner: "The taxpayer here set up the installment arrangement to reduce his taxes and for no other purpose. Hence, no sufficient business purpose appearing for the installment aspect of the contract compromise agreement, the substance of the transaction must be given effect. The substance of the transaction is that a disputed claim was settled, with payment being made by way of a discharge of indebtedness. The discharge was complete for income tax purposes in 1961."

A complex web of special rules governs the year in which compensation for services that is deferred by contract must be reported. Deferred compensation arrangements are discussed in detail in Chapter 30.

1.4. *Substantial Restrictions—Forfeiture Provisions*

Treas. Reg. § 1.451–2(a) provides that "income is not constructively received if the taxpayer's control of its receipt is subject to substantial limitations or restrictions." Rev. Rul. 80–300, 1980–2 C.B. 165, concluded that stock appreciation rights were not income to an employee when the stock appreciated. Under the arrangement, the employee was entitled to a cash payment upon exercise of the right equal to the excess of the fair market value of the stock on the exercise date over the fair market value on the date the right was granted to the employee. The employee, to receive the amount of increase in value, had to exercise the right, thus relinquishing the right to benefit from further appreciation. The forfeiture of a valuable right prevented the employee from being in constructive receipt of the increase in value prior to exercise. On the other hand, fulfillment of a ministerial condition as a prerequisite to receiving payment is not a substantial restriction on the right to payment. In Rev. Rul. 80–177, 1980–2 C.B. 109, a shareholder who received a liquidating distribution in 1979, when he surrendered his stock certificate to receive payment, was held to be in constructive receipt in 1978, the time the distribution first became payable. The shareholder was entitled to receive payment at any time after March 1, 1978 by surrendering his certificate, and there was no likelihood that the liquidation would not be consummated; the requirement that stock certificates had to be presented was not a substantial restriction.

1.5. *Cash Option Payoffs of Lottery Annuity Prizes*

Winners of state lotteries and other contests that typically offer an annuity for a term of years as a prize frequently are given the option to take a lump-sum payoff approximating the net present value of the annuity. Ordinarily, the constructive receipt doctrine would require a prizewinner who is given such an option to include currently an amount equal to the lump-sum option, even if the taxpayer chose to receive the annuity. On the other hand, if prior to the declaration of a winner, for example, at the time a lottery ticket is purchased, the taxpayer designates in advance whether the taxpayer will take a lump-sum distribution or an annuity in the event that the taxpayer wins, the constructive receipt doctrine does not apply. In 1998, Congress addressed this dichotomy by enacting § 451(h), which, if the qualifying conditions are met, ameliorates the application of the constructive receipt doctrine when lottery winners chose to take their winnings in the form of an annuity, even if the lottery winner makes the election after the winner of the drawing is announced.

2. CASH EQUIVALENCY AND ECONOMIC BENEFIT

2.1. *In General*

A recurring issue is whether a cash method taxpayer who receives property that represents a right to receive money at a future date realizes gross income upon receipt of the property. The property may take the form of a note or check or may be a bare contract right (a chose in action). The property may be negotiable or transferable, or may be transferable only at a substantial discount from its face amount. The promise to pay may be guaranteed through the use of an escrow, third-party guarantee, or security arrangement. The promise may arise from an employment arrangement, sale of property, or other transaction. In Pulsifer v. Commissioner, 64 T.C. 245 (1975), three minor children and their father were co-owners of a government-sponsored lottery ticket that won $48,000. The children's winnings of $36,000 ($12,000 each) were withheld and deposited in a bank in accordance with governing law prohibiting distribution of winnings to minors unless approved by a court order. The issue was whether the children were required to include the prize in income in the year it was deposited in the bank for their benefit. The Tax Court held that the economic-benefit doctrine applied, thereby requiring recognition of the prize money in that year: "Under the economic-benefit theory, an individual on the cash receipts and disbursements method of accounting is currently taxable on the economic and financial benefit derived from the absolute right to income in the form of a fund which has been irrevocably set aside for him in trust and is beyond the reach of the payor's debtors. * * * Petitioners had an absolute, nonforfeitable right to their winnings on deposit with the * * * court."

Cowden v. Commissioner, 289 F.2d 20 (5th Cir.1961), held that the nonnegotiable note of a solvent obligor received by a cash method taxpayer in payment of an obligation due under a mineral lease would be a cash equivalent if it was "unconditional and assignable, not subject to set-offs, and

* * * of a kind that is frequently transferred to lenders or investors at a discount not substantially greater than the generally prevailing premium for the use of money * * * ," and remanded the issue to the Tax Court for the application of this standard to the facts of the case.

Treas. Reg. § 1.61–2(d)(4) generally requires that a cash method taxpayer currently include the fair market value of a promissory note received in consideration of services. Rev. Rul. 76–135, 1976–1 C.B. 114, applied this regulation in a situation in which a cash method lawyer received a promissory note from a client in payment of a legal fee and immediately discounted the note at a bank. The ruling held the lawyer taxable on the discounted value of the note in the year in which the note was received; the reasoning of the ruling relies on the fact that the note was discounted only to provide evidence of its value, not as the basis for holding that the lawyer realized income currently. A few cases have reached contrary conclusions on their peculiar facts.

Williams v. Commissioner, 28 T.C. 1000 (1957) (Acq.), held that the receipt by a cash method taxpayer of an unsecured note evidencing an amount owed to him for services rendered was not payment, and thus not includable, where the maker of the note was incapable of payment at the time the note was delivered. Dial v. Commissioner, 24 T.C. 117 (1955) (Acq.), reached a similar result where promissory notes in the amount of past due salary were held to have been delivered to provide additional security for the past-due debt rather than in payment of the past due debt. The difference is difficult to discern.

2.2. *Unfunded Contract Rights Involving Sales of Property*

Historically, much of the controversy regarding the application of the cash equivalency doctrine was with respect to transactions involving sales of property. Some early cases allowed cash method taxpayers to defer recognition of gain on property sales where the buyer's obligation was not freely negotiable. See e.g., Ennis v. Commissioner, 17 T.C. 465 (1951) (no gain recognized currently on receipt of buyer's note which was not freely tradeable). Later cases focused on the question of the fair market value of the buyer's obligation, regardless of the form it took or whether it could be characterized as a "cash equivalent." See e.g., Warren Jones Co. v. Commissioner, 524 F.2d 788 (9th Cir.1975). Under current law, Treas. Reg. § 1.1001–1(g) provides that the amount realized on any sale of property is the adjusted issue price of the debt obligation (even if only contractual) under the original issue discount rules, discussed in Chapter 32. Generally speaking, if adequate interest is charged, the adjusted issue price of the debt obligation equals the stated principal amount. The effect of Treas. Reg. § 1.1001–1(g) is to apply the cash equivalency doctrine to all sales of property. Deferred recognition may be available under § 453, discussed in Chapter 31.

2.3. *Contractual Obligations in Connection with Services—Economic Benefit*

Rev. Rul. 60–31, 1960–1 C.B. 174, Chapter 30, Section 1, held that a cash method taxpayer is not required to include in income the mere contractual obligation of an employer to make a deferred compensation payment in the future, regardless of the employer's financial strength.

Conversely, if an employee's nonforfeitable claim against the employer is "funded" (i.e., amounts are set aside in a trust or escrow account for the benefit of the employee and beyond the reach of the employer's creditors), so that the employee is no longer relying solely on the financial resources of the employer, the amount is currently includable wholly apart from the cash equivalence or economic benefit doctrines. If the payment is made to a trust, § 402(b) requires that the payments be treated under § 83, discussed in Chapter 30, Section 2, which, in general, includes in income the fair market value of all property received as compensation for services, except for "an unfunded and unsecured promise to pay money or other property in the future." Treas. Reg. § 1.83–3(e).

3.   YEAR-END CHECKS

The treatment of checks received by a cash method taxpayer illustrates some interesting problems in the relation between the doctrine of constructive receipt and the problem of cash equivalence. On the constructive receipt theory, the receipt of a check would be income to a cash method taxpayer since it would "make available" to him the funds that he could obtain by cashing the check. On the cash equivalence theory, the check itself would be property received by the taxpayer which, by virtue of its negotiability, was equivalent to cash. The difference between the two theories would be significant for checks received that could not for one reason or another be cashed or otherwise transferred during the taxable year. Lavery v. Commissioner, 158 F.2d 859 (7th Cir.1946), held that a check received on December 30 but not deposited until January 2 of the following year was includable in the year received, stressing the fact that the taxpayer could have cashed the check in the year it was received. Subsequently, Kahler v. Commissioner, 18 T.C. 31 (1952), held that a check received after banking hours on December 31 was includable in income in that year because property having a fair market value had been received. This case indicates that the cash equivalency test applies. But the reasoning of Bright v. United States, 926 F.2d 383 (5th Cir.1991), indicates that constructive receipt notions are important. *Bright* held that a check received and deposited on December 30 was taxable in the year received even though, when the check was deposited in the taxpayer's bank, the bank placed a hold on the deposited funds until the next year. The court reasoned that the taxpayer could have obtained the funds immediately by presentation to the drawee bank. See also Premji v. Commissioner, T.C. Memo. 1996–304 (receipt of check that would not be honored due to insufficient funds in drawer's account did not result in constructive receipt), aff'd by order, 139 F.3d 912 (10th Cir.1998).

Questions also can arise regarding whether a check itself has been constructively received. In Rev. Rul. 68–126, 1968–1 C.B. 194, the taxpayer's retirement check from a state agency for December was not mailed until January. However, the check was available on the last working day of December if the taxpayer had personally picked it up. The ruling provides that the income was constructively received in the earlier year. Rev. Rul. 68–126 notes, however, that if a check is mailed in December but not received until January, the payment is not includable until actually received, unless the taxpayer could have received the payment in December by appearing in person and claiming the check. In Rev. Rul. 76–3, 1976–1 C.B. 114, a check was mailed by certified mail and the Post Office attempted to deliver the check on December 31, 1974. The taxpayer was not home to sign the receipt necessary to receive the check. The ruling held that the income was nonetheless taxable in 1974. The fact that the taxpayer was not home when the check was delivered was not a "limitation or restriction on receipt of the payment on that day" and thus did not bar constructive receipt. Davis v. Commissioner, T.C. Memo. 1978–12, expressly declined to apply Rev. Rul. 76–3 in a case that was factually identical, holding that the check was not includable in the year of attempted delivery.

Treas. Reg. § 1.451–2(b) provides that where corporate dividends are declared payable on December 31 but the corporation as a matter of practice pays the dividends by check mailed so that the shareholders do not receive them until January, the dividends are not considered to have been constructively received in December.

B. DEDUCTION ITEMS

INTERNAL REVENUE CODE: Sections 446; 461(a), (g); 7701(a)(25).

REGULATIONS: Section 1.461–1(a)(1), (3).

(1) CONSTRUCTIVE PAYMENT AND THE EQUIVALENCE OF CASH—HAS AN ITEM BEEN "PAID"

Treas. Reg. § 1.446–1(c)(1)(i) provides that for cash method taxpayers "[e]xpenditures are to be deducted for the taxable year in which actually made." Unlike the corresponding provision dealing with income items, there is no reference to expenditures "constructively" made and the courts have been unwilling to fashion a constructive payment doctrine as a companion to the constructive receipt concept discussed in the previous material. In Vander Poel, Francis & Co. v. Commissioner, 8 T.C. 407 (1947), a corporation on the cash method credited its officers' salaries on the corporation's books but did not pay the salaries until the following year. The court held that the corporation was not entitled to a deduction for salaries in the year in which they were credited to the officers, notwithstanding that the officers were authorized to sign checks on the corporate bank accounts and there was sufficient cash to pay the salaries. The court refused to apply a doctrine of constructive payment.

Apart from the problem of constructive payment, an item must be "paid" for a cash method taxpayer to secure a deduction and it is necessary to determine whether a transaction involves a "payment" or some other legal relationship between the parties.

DETAILED ANALYSIS

1.   CHECKS

Payment by check generally is treated as occurring upon delivery of the check. In Estate of Spiegel v. Commissioner, 12 T.C. 524 (1949) (Acq.), the court allowed the taxpayer to deduct as a charitable contribution for 1942 the amount of a check given on December 30, 1942, but not cashed until January, 1943. Commissioner v. Bradley, 56 F.2d 728 (6th Cir.1932), allowed a deduction in the period ending with the decedent's death where the check was paid by the bank after the decedent's death. In Estate of Hubbell v. Commissioner, 10 T.C. 1207 (1948), the decedent gave his check to the state in payment of taxes. After his death 10 days later, on presentation of the check, the bank, on account of such death, refused payment. The court disallowed the deduction for the tax period ending with the decedent's death. Griffin v. Commissioner, 49 T.C. 253 (1967), held that no deduction was allowed in 1962 for a check mailed on December 31, 1962, but postdated January 1, 1963; the postdated check was in effect a promissory note.

Rev. Rul. 80–335, 1980–2 C.B. 170, held that a taxpayer maintaining a "pay by phone" account with a financial institution, under which the taxpayer could authorize the institution by telephone to make payments to the taxpayer's creditors, paid the creditors when the institution mailed a check to creditors, transferred funds to creditors' accounts, or actually delivered checks to creditors.

2.   PROMISSORY NOTES

In Helvering v. Price, 309 U.S. 409, 413 (1940), the Supreme Court held that a secured note given in final payment of the taxpayer's liability on an obligation did not support a deduction, since there "was no cash payment and * * * the giving of the taxpayer's own note was not the equivalent of cash to entitle the taxpayer to the deduction."

The *Price* holding has two consequences. First, the test for whether a note is a payment deductible by a cash method taxpayer differs from the test for whether a note is income to a cash method taxpayer. Thus, in Rev. Rul. 76–135, 1976–1 C.B. 114, supra, a cash method client paid a cash method lawyer for legal services with a negotiable promissory note. The lawyer immediately discounted the note at a bank, and the client subsequently made payments to the bank. The ruling held the client was entitled to a deduction only as the payments on the note were made to the bank. The lawyer was taxable on the discounted value of the note in the year in which the note was received.

Second, as a result of *Price,* tax consequences often depend upon the method of financing. In *Price,* for example, the deduction would have been allowed currently had Price borrowed money from a bank in order to pay his liability under the guaranty obligation.

3.   CREDIT CARDS

Payment for goods or services with a credit card might be considered the equivalent of a cash payment, on the one hand, or a mere promise to pay in the future as in *Price.* The IRS has concluded that because the credit cardholder immediately becomes indebted to the bank and cannot prevent the payee from receiving payment, the situation is analogous to the cardholder's borrowing money from a bank and making an immediate payment to the payee. Rev. Rul. 78–38, 1978–1 C.B. 67, revoking Rev. Rul. 71–216. This logic does not apply to purchases made with two-party credit cards issued by retail stores and oil companies, which are more analogous to giving a promissory note.

4. INTEREST BORROWED FROM LENDER

Suppose a cash method taxpayer borrows $100,000 from the X Bank for a term of ten years with interest of 10 percent per year due on each December 31st. One year later the borrower, having insufficient cash to make the interest payment, borrows $10,000 from the Z Bank and pays the X Bank. As indicated by Rev. Rul. 78–38, supra, there is no doubt that the taxpayer has "paid" the interest due to X Bank, even though it was paid with funds borrowed from Z Bank. See Crown v. Commissioner, 77 T.C. 582 (1981) (Acq.).

Now suppose that instead of borrowing from Z Bank to pay the interest, the taxpayer borrows the $10,000 due to X Bank from X Bank. Has the taxpayer "paid" X Bank the interest, or has the taxpayer simply delivered a note promising to pay in the future, which does not support a current deduction? Burgess v. Commissioner, 8 T.C. 47 (1947), held that a cash method taxpayer had "paid" the interest and was entitled to a deduction where the taxpayer executed a new note, received the funds, which were commingled with the taxpayer's other funds, and then issued its check to the bank. A contrary result was reached in Battelstein v. I.R.S., 631 F.2d 1182 (5th Cir.1980), where the bank did not issue its check representing the new loan proceeds until after it had received the borrower's check for the interest. The court characterized the transaction as the issuance of a new note accompanied by a meaningless exchange of checks. Accordingly, the decision in *Price,* supra, applied to bar a deduction.

The key distinction is whether the taxpayer acquires unrestricted control over the funds borrowed from the lender prior to using the funds to pay interest due to the lender. If so, the interest has been "paid." Noble v. Commissioner, 79 T.C. 751 (1982) (rejecting Commissioner's argument that a borrower does not obtain unrestricted control of funds deposited to the borrower's account in the lender bank because of the existence of a state law right of set-off). In Davison v. Commissioner, 107 T.C. 35 (1996), aff'd per curiam, 141 F.3d 403 (2d Cir.1998), a cash method partnership (in which the taxpayer was a partner) borrowed $1,587,310 from an insurance company to which it owed over $20,000,000. The newly borrowed funds were deposited in the partnership's bank account, and the partnership immediately paid $1,587,310 of interest and $7,007 of principal to the insurance company, which had approved the $1,587,310 loan for the specific purpose of paying the interest on the first loan. The taxpayer argued that a deduction was allowable because by depositing the funds to the partnership account the partnership acquired "unrestricted control" over the loan proceeds. Applying a substance over form analysis, the court rejected the notion that "unrestricted control" refers to physical control of the funds and denied the deduction. The funds used to pay the interest were borrowed for that purpose from the lender to whom the interest was owed. If the partnership had not paid the interest, it would have defaulted on the loan and gone out of business. Thus, the partnership never effectively had unrestricted control over the funds.

Where the taxpayer executes a promissory note for more than the amount disbursed by the lender, the amount retained by the lender is treated as prepaid interest subject to the rules of § 461(g), discussed below, Rubnitz v. Commissioner, 67 T.C. 621 (1977), or as original issue discount, taken into account as interest over the term of the loan. See Chapter 32.

(2) ADVANCE PAYMENTS—WHEN MUST DEDUCTION OF AN ITEM BE DEFERRED EVEN THOUGH ACTUALLY PAID

REGULATIONS: Sections 1.162–3; 1.263(a)–4(d)(3), (f); 1.461–1(a).

The cash method does not permit deductions of all items in the year paid. It is clear, for example, that if a taxpayer on the cash method purchases stock, the purchase price may not be deducted in the year of payment but rather must be treated as a capital expenditure. The regulations impose the capital expenditure limitation on the accounting methods sections by providing: "Under the cash receipts and disbursements method of accounting, amounts representing allowable deductions shall, as a general rule, be taken into account for the taxable year in which paid * * * . If an expenditure results in the creation of an asset having a useful life which extends substantially beyond the close of the taxable year, such an expenditure may not be deductible, or may be deductible only in part, for the taxable year in which made." Treas. Reg. § 1.461–1(a).

While the application of this regulation to stock, land, buildings, and most equipment is clear, situations involving the prepayment of what typically are current expense items such as salary, rent, and insurance premiums historically had not always been treated consistently. In addition to the possible application of the above-quoted regulation to these situations, the question could arise whether the use of cash method to deduct these prepaid items in the year of payment clearly reflects income under § 446(b). Since 2014, however, as discussed in Chapter 13, the capitalization regulations provide extensive guidance regarding the deductibility of prepaid items. Treas. Reg. § 1.263(a)–4(d)(3) requires that prepaid expenses generally be capitalized. Thus, taxpayers on the cash method who prepay expenses generally cannot immediately deduct the full amount of expenditures but are instead required to prorate the deduction over the taxable years to which the benefits flowing from the expenditure relate. However, Treas. Reg. § 1.263(a)–4(f) provides that an expenditure to create or enhance intangible rights or benefits, such as prepaid insurance or prepaid rent, that do not extend for more than twelve months after the expenditure is incurred may be currently deducted in full. Amounts paid to create rights or benefits that extend beyond the twelve months must be capitalized and deducted ratably over the period benefited.

DETAILED ANALYSIS

1. DEPOSIT VERSUS DEDUCTIBLE PREPAYMENT

Businesses in which the production or sale of merchandise is significant must generally use the accrual method and maintain inventories. These rules have the effect of postponing deductions relating to the sale of the costs of the merchandise until the income from its sale is realized. Businesses that use the cash method, however, often have a tax incentive to prepay expenses—usually in the last month of the taxable year—due early in the next taxable year.

An expenditure must be a "payment" as opposed to a mere "deposit" before it can be deducted. In Rev. Rul. 79–229, 1979–2 C.B. 210, the IRS summarized the factors relevant for distinguishing deposits from payments:

> Whether a particular expenditure is a deposit or a payment depends on the facts and circumstances of each case. When it can be shown that the expenditure is not refundable and is made pursuant to an enforceable sales contract, it will not be considered a deposit. The following factors, although not all inclusive, are indicative of a deposit rather than a payment: the absence of specific quantity terms; the right to a refund of any unapplied payment credit at the termination of the contract * * *; the treatment of the expenditure as a deposit by the seller; and the right to substitute other goods or products for the [goods] specified in the contract. * * * The fact that adjustment is made to the contract price to reflect market value at the date of delivery, is not, standing alone, conclusive of a deposit.

The principles in this area largely have been developed in cases involving farmers, because farmers are permitted to use the cash method without maintaining inventories—ostensibly because of the more complex bookkeeping that otherwise would be required—and farmers generally are entitled to treat the cost of feed as an immediately deductible expense rather than as a capital expenditure.[2] Treas. Reg. § 1.162–12(a). The IRS employs three tests that must be met before a prepayment for feed may be deducted currently. The expenditure must be a payment for the purchase of feed and not a deposit; there must be a business purpose for the prepayment and not merely a tax avoidance objective; and the deduction in the year of prepayment must not materially distort income. Rev. Rul. 79–229, 1979–2 C.B. 210.

The courts often focus on the issue of payment versus deposit in terms of business purpose. For example, in Cravens v. Commissioner, 272 F.2d 895 (10th Cir.1959), a taxpayer on the cash method paid for feed grain to be delivered and used over the next two years. By means of the prepayment, the

---

[2] A number of statutory provisions prevent the special rules for farmers from being used by large corporations, farming syndicates, and tax shelters. See I.R.C. §§ 447, 461(i), and 464.

taxpayer was able to obtain preferential delivery treatment and avoid a distress liquidation of his herd. The court allowed the deduction of the full amount of the prepayment in the year paid despite the fact that the taxpayer conceded that the tax implications of the prepayment influenced his conduct. On the other hand, in Shippy v. United States, 308 F.2d 743 (8th Cir.1962), a deduction for prepaid feed was disallowed because the taxpayer could obtain a refund of the advance payment at any time prior to delivery. In Schenk v. Commissioner, 686 F.2d 315 (5th Cir.1982), the taxpayer paid $25,000 to a cooperative of which he was a member for fertilizer and "general supplies." Although he could not receive a cash refund, he could apply the payment to totally different goods in the future. The payment was held to be a nondeductible deposit.

The principles developed in the context of farm expenses have been applied to prepayments of other business expenses. See e.g., Bonaire Development Co. v. Commissioner, 679 F.2d 159 (9th Cir.1982) (real estate management fees).

Under § 461(i) prepaid expenses of certain "tax shelters" are never deductible in the year of payment. Deductions are allowed only as the activities are performed.

2. RESERVES

In Sebring v. Commissioner, 93 T.C. 220 (1989), a bail bondsman made payments to an indemnity fund maintained by a surety company underwriting the bail bonds. The purpose of the indemnity fund was to reimburse the surety company if any of the defendants on whom the taxpayer had written a bail bond defaulted. Payments were a fixed percentage of each bail bond and were required for every bond written. The surety company acted as the trustee of the indemnity funds, and without notice to the taxpayer could withdraw funds from the account to satisfy any forfeiture. If the bail bondsman ceased doing business, the balance of the indemnity fund was refundable. The court disallowed a current deduction for payments to the indemnity fund:

> * * * [T]he case law has long followed the principle that a contribution to a reserve for future liabilities is not deductible; only actual payment out of the reserve to satisfy a definite liability can give rise to a deductible expense. * * * Whether the reserve payments are mandatory is not dispositive of the issue of their deductibility. * * * Until payment is made of an actual liability that is due, no deductible expense exists. This rule has been followed for more than 60 years. E.g., Commercial Liquidation Co. v. Commissioner, [16 B.T.A. 559 (1929)] (collection agency contractually required to set aside a portion of its receipts in a reserve fund held by a surety to protect against contingent liabilities not allowed a deduction).
>
> Even if, as in this case, the reserve is more than a bookkeeping entry, and payments are actually made to a third party, payments to a reserve are not deductible because they are in the nature of a security deposit held for payment of future liabilities. * * * Indeed,

petitioner's liability for expenses associated with a bond forfeiture does not arise prior to his obligation to indemnify the surety. * * *

Importantly, on termination of an Agreement, the insurance company is contractually required to return the balance of petitioner's * * * account to petitioner after satisfaction of any outstanding liability. Although the insurance companies manage the * * * accounts for the duration of their business relationship with him, the benefits of each account inure to petitioner. Petitioner ultimately retains the benefit of the reserve payments plus any investment income earned.

In Rev. Rul. 2007–47, 2007–30 I.R.B. 127, the taxpayer paid a premium on an insurance policy that insured the taxpayer against future environmental remediation costs up to a specified limit. The amount of the premium equaled the estimated net present value of the future remediation costs. The IRS ruled that the taxpayer could not deduct the premium based on its conclusion that economically the arrangement was merely a prefunding of the taxpayer's future costs and not an insurance transaction.

3. INTEREST AND TAXES

3.1. *Interest*

Section 461(g) permits an interest deduction only in the period to which the interest relates. There is a limited exception for "points" in connection with certain principal residence financings. The effect of § 461(g) is to put the cash method taxpayer on the accrual method for the interest deduction. The rule applies whether or not the allowance of a deduction for prepaid interest would materially distort the taxpayer's income in the year of the payment. See S.Rep. No. 94–938, 94th Cong., 2d Sess. 104 (1976). The proper period for accrual of the interest deduction is determined under the original issue discount rules, discussed in Chapter 32. See Treas. Reg. § 1.1273–2(g).

The IRS has ruled that the exception to § 461(g) for points paid in connection with the acquisition of a principal residence does not apply to refinancing. Rev. Rul. 87–22, 1987–1 C.B. 146. The Tax Court has sustained the IRS's position, but some other courts have applied the exception to points paid in connection with refinancing. See Huntsman v. Commissioner, 91 T.C. 917 (1988) (points paid on loan to refinance mortgage on principal residence were not deductible in year paid because the loan did not finance improvements), rev'd, 905 F.2d 1182 (8th Cir.1990) (refinancing of original three-year balloon purchase-money mortgage debt with permanent 30-year mortgage two years later meets the "in connection with" requirement of § 461(g)(2)); Kelly v. Commissioner, T.C. Memo. 1991–605 (points paid to refinance original 30-year mortgage were not currently deductible under § 461(g)(2); *Huntsman* was distinguished as involving refinancing of a short-term purchase-money debt).

3.2. *State and Local Taxes*

The IRS takes the position that a current deduction is not allowable for prepaid or estimated state income taxes unless the payment is required. See Rev. Rul. 82–208, 1982–2 C.B. 58, disallowing a deduction for estimated state income taxes paid in December where there was no reasonable basis for believing payment was required. The Tax Court has been more liberal in allowing a current deduction. Glassell v. Commissioner, 12 T.C. 232 (1949) (Acq.), allowed a cash method taxpayer a deduction for prepayment of state income taxes as long as the taxes were actually paid and not merely deposited with the state. See also Estate of Cohen v. Commissioner, T.C. Memo. 1970–272 (prepayment of estimated state income taxes was in "good faith").

Hradesky v. Commissioner, 540 F.2d 821 (5th Cir.1976), held that real estate taxes paid by a cash method taxpayer in escrow are not deductible until the escrow agent makes a payment out of the escrow to satisfy the taxpayer's tax liability.

SECTION 3.   THE ACCRUAL METHOD

The preceding material has dealt with the cash method of accounting. The major virtue of the cash method is simplicity. There is little attempt, except in the case of capital and prepaid expenditures, to match receipts and payments with the time period of the activities to which the receipts and payments are attributable. The accrual method achieves considerable refinement in the attribution of income and deductions to the appropriate taxable year. The differing goals of the tax laws and accounting rules, however, make the conventions of the accountant unsuitable in a number of respects to the similar time assignments required under the income tax.

A.   INCOME ITEMS

INTERNAL REVENUE CODE: Sections 446; 448(d)(5); 451(a).

REGULATIONS: Sections 1.446–1(c)(1)(ii); 1.451–1(a).

(1)   INCLUSION PRIOR TO RECEIPT—THE CONCEPT OF ACCRUAL

For taxpayers using the accrual method of tax accounting, the determination of when an item is included in income turns on the taxpayer's right to receive the amount in question. The regulations provide: "Under an accrual method of accounting, income is includable in gross income when all the events have occurred which fix the right to receive such income and the amount thereof can be determined with reasonable accuracy." Treas. Reg. § 1.451–1(a). The creation of the unconditional right to receive the income is the crucial event for the accrual method taxpayer and the fact that actual payment is received later is not relevant to the issue of income inclusion. The problem of accrued items that are included in income but subsequently not paid is handled by the bad debt provisions in § 166 (see Chapter 15, Section 3).

In finding that all the events have occurred to fix income, courts distinguish between conditions precedent and subsequent. Thus, in Charles Schwab Corporation v. Commissioner, 107 T.C. 282 (1996), the Tax Court required a securities broker to accrue commission income on the trade date of securities, not the settlement date. The court reasoned as follows:

> In applying the all events test, this and other courts have distinguished between conditions precedent, which must occur before the right to income arises, and conditions subsequent, the occurrence of which will terminate an existing right to income, but the presence of which does not preclude accrual of income. Central Cuba Sugar Co. v. Commissioner, 198 F.2d 214, 217–218 (2d Cir.1952), affg. in part and revg. in part 16 T.C. 882 (1951); Wien Consol. Airlines, Inc. v. Commissioner, 60 T.C. 13, 15 (1973), affd. 528 F.2d 735 (9th Cir.1976); Buckeye Intl., Inc. v. Commissioner, T.C. Memo. 1984–668 * * * .[6]

> We think the above factors indicate that petitioner's execution of a trade for a customer is a condition precedent that fixes petitioner's right to receive the commission income. The functions that remain to be performed by petitioner after the trade date are of a ministerial nature to effectuate the mechanics of the transfer and confirm the trade executed. Although failure to perform these functions may ultimately divest petitioner of its right to the commission income, we think that these functions are conditions subsequent and, therefore, do not preclude accrual of commission income on the trade date.

> Nor does the possibility that an executed trade may not settle due to cancellation of an entire public offering make petitioner's right to the commission income too indefinite or contingent for accrual. See Brown v. Helvering, 291 U.S. 193, 199–200 (1934) (holding that overriding commissions received by a general agent for policies written must be accrued even though there was a contingent liability to return a portion of the commission in the event the policy was canceled); Georgia School-Book Depository, Inc. v. Commissioner, 1 T.C. 463, 468–470 (1943) (holding that a book broker that represented publishers in sales of school books to the State of Georgia must accrue commission income, despite the fact that the State was obligated to pay for the books only out of a particular fund, and, during the years in issue, the fund was insufficient to pay for the books in full). The possibility that a trade might not finally be settled is, if anything, a condition subsequent to the execution of the trade, which was the event that fixed petitioner's right to the commission. See Central Cuba Sugar

---

[6]   Although Central Cuba Sugar Co. v. Commissioner, 198 F.2d 214, 217–218 (2d Cir.1952), affg. in part and revg. in part 16 T.C. 882 (1951), Wien Consol. Airlines, Inc. v. Commissioner, 60 T.C. 13, 15 (1973), affd. 528 F.2d 735 (9th Cir.1976), and Buckeye Intl., Inc. v. Commissioner, T.C. Memo. 1984–668, involved the accrual of deductions rather than the proper reporting of income, this Court has recognized that similar considerations apply with respect to both issues. See Simplified Tax Records, Inc. v. Commissioner, 41 T.C. 75, 79 (1963) * * * .

Co. v. Commissioner, supra at 217–218 (holding that sales commission expenses were deductible in the year the taxpayer entered the contract for sale even though they were not payable until delivery, and even though the commission expenses were subject to adjustment in accordance with final weighing before shipment and forfeiture if the contract were not carried out).

* * *

While we appreciate the differences in the services provided by full-commission and discount brokers, we cannot agree that ministerial acts that constitute conditions subsequent to a customer's obligation to pay commissions are converted to conditions precedent merely because they may comprise a significant percentage of the overall activities conducted by the broker.

* * *

Accordingly, we uphold respondent's determination that petitioner must accrue commission income for the purchase or sale of securities on the trade date as opposed to the settlement date.

DETAILED ANALYSIS

1.   DOUBT AS TO THE COLLECTIBILITY OF THE PAYMENT

1.1. *Generally*

In Spring City Foundry Co. v. Commissioner, 292 U.S. 182 (1934), a taxpayer on the accrual method sold goods in 1920 on open account. In the latter part of the year, the vendee was in financial straits and a receiver was appointed in December. In 1922 and 1923, the taxpayer received payments totaling 27.5 percent of the amount due. Under the statute applicable to the year 1920, a bad debt deduction was available only for debts that were completely worthless and not merely partially worthless, as were the debts in the instant case:

> Petitioner [taxpayer] first contends that the debt, to the extent that it was ascertained in 1920 to be worthless, was not returnable as gross income in that year, that is, apart from any question of deductions, it was not to be regarded as taxable income at all. We see no merit in this contention. Keeping accounts and making returns on the accrual basis, as distinguished from the cash basis, import that it is the *right* to receive and not the actual receipt that determines the inclusion of the amount in gross income. When the right to receive an amount becomes fixed, the right accrues. When a merchandizing concern makes sales, its inventory is reduced and a claim for the purchase price arises. * * *

> If such accounts receivable become uncollectible, in whole or part, the question is one of the deduction which may be taken according to the applicable statute. * * * That is the question here.

It is not altered by the fact that the claim of loss relates to an item of gross income which had accrued in the same year.

Subsequent cases have considered the likelihood of collectability. Koehring Co. v. United States, 421 F.2d 715 (Ct.Cl.1970), held that royalties under a license agreement that were not paid when due because of the licensee's financial problems nonetheless were properly accruable since there was no real doubt about the ultimate ability of the licensee to pay and because some "start up" difficulties had been anticipated by the taxpayer when the agreement was consummated. But Commercial Solvents Corp. v. Commissioner, 42 T.C. 455 (1964) (Acq.), held that management fees were not accruable where the taxpayer agreed not to press its right to payment against a financially embarrassed debtor in order to enable the debtor to get a bank loan. Income items must be accrued if there is a reasonable likelihood of receiving payment even if the claim is not legally enforceable. Flamingo Resort, Inc. v. United States, 664 F.2d 1387 (9th Cir.1982) (accrual method gambling casino was require to accrue gambling winnings from customers on credit in the year the gambling occurred even though the credit obligations were not enforceable under state law); Rev. Rul. 83–106, 1983–2 C.B. 77. If the income item is uncollectible at the time it arises, in contrast to becoming uncollectible after it arises but before the end of the taxable year, accrual is not required. Rev. Rul. 80–361, 1980–2 C.B. 164.

Doubt as to collectability generally is not found to exist merely because a government appropriation is required to pay the obligation. In Georgia School-Book Depository, Inc. v. Commissioner, 1 T.C. 463 (1943), the taxpayer earned commissions on the sale of textbooks to the state of Georgia, but payment of the commissions was not to be made until the publisher was paid by the State of Georgia. The State's payment was required by law to be made only from funds derived from a beer tax. The commissions were held accruable for the year of sale even though the beer tax fund was not adequate to permit full payment for the books, because there was no expectation the sums would not be paid: "Georgia is a state possessing great resources and a fine record of fiscal probity, and undoubtedly it can and will meet its obligations." In Rev. Rul. 70–151, 1970–1 C.B. 116, the taxpayer won a suit against the United States in the Court of Claims in 1968 and the Government applied for certiorari. Certiorari was denied in 1969, but there was no Congressional appropriation in that year to pay the claim. The ruling held that the amount of the judgment was includable in the taxpayer's gross income in 1969 since at that time it represented "an acknowledged liability of the United States." The absence of an appropriation did not prevent inclusion.

Where the prerequisite government action is not a forgone conclusion, however, the results differ. Thus, where no appropriation was made by the Cuban Government to pay for transportation services rendered it by the taxpayer, and where "collection was apparently at the mercy of the political whims of future Cuban administrations," accrual was not required. Cuba Railroad Company v. Commissioner, 9 T.C. 211 (1947) (Acq.). See also Doyle, Dane, Bernbach, Inc. v. Commissioner, 79 T.C. 101 (1982) (Nonacq.) (state tax refund claim arising in one year did not accrue until refund was approved in a subsequent year by state revenue department).

1.2. *Statutory Rule for Accounts Receivable for Services*

Section 448(d)(5) allows service providers to reduce the accruals by the amount that experience indicates will not be collected. Section 448(d)(5) applies only to amounts accrued for the performance of certain services or for other services provided by certain small businesses. Qualified services (as defined in § 448(d)(2)) include only services in the fields of health, law, engineering, architecture, accounting, actuarial science, performing arts, or consulting. Section 448(d)(5) also is available with respect to non-qualified services if the taxpayer's average annual gross receipts (as defined in § 448(c)) do not exceed $5 million. For example, if an accrual method surveyor's experience indicates that only $96,000 is collected from $100,000 of billings, when services are provided and invoiced to a particular customer for $100, only $96 must be accrued. The remaining $4 will be included in income upon receipt of payment.

2.   IMPOSSIBILITY OF ESTIMATING AMOUNT

In United States v. Harmon, 205 F.2d 919 (10th Cir.1953), the taxpayer in 1943 completed construction work performed on a cost plus fixed-fee basis under which the balance of the contract price after completion of the work would be paid after an audit of costs by the government. The audit was completed in 1944, disallowing about $1,200 of costs in a balance of about $18,000. The court held that the taxpayer could not be required to accrue in 1943 the amount claimed to be due. Similarly, in Gar Wood Industries, Inc. v. United States, 437 F.2d 558 (6th Cir.1971), the taxpayer entered into government contracts that had a clause allowing "price redetermination" at the end of the contract. The Government, without authority and in breach of the contract, withheld amounts in anticipation of future price redetermination. The dispute was subsequently settled and the withheld amounts were paid over in part. The court, citing *Harmon,* did not require the accrual of the withheld amount during the earlier years.

3.   ESCROW AND SECURITY RESERVES

Amounts held in escrow generally are not includable in income by an accrual method taxpayer if the amounts will not be paid until requirements upon which the sale or other transaction is conditioned have been met. For example, in Leedy-Glover Realty & Insurance Company, Inc. v. Commissioner, 13 T.C. 95 (1949) (Acq.), aff'd on other issues, 184 F.2d 833 (5th Cir.1950), the commissions of an insurance agency to be paid by the insurance company were placed in escrow with a bank, under arrangements providing for pro rata payment over the life of the policy, generally five years. The insurance agency was required to service the policies during their lives. The court sustained the contention of the insurance agency that the commissions did not accrue when the insurance was written but only when it became entitled to withdraw the commissions from the escrow holder.

On the other hand, conditions of an escrow or security arrangement will not prevent accrual of income where they are for the benefit of third parties. These conditions do not make the arrangement contingent as between the payor and the taxpayer; they are tantamount to a reserve fund established by the taxpayer with funds received from the payor. In Commissioner v. Hansen, 360 U.S. 446 (1959), the Supreme Court required an automobile dealer to accrue the full amount for which he sold customers' installment paper to finance companies. The dealer unsuccessfully contended that a portion of such amount withheld by the finance companies and credited to "dealer's reserve account" as security for the dealer's guarantees was not includable in income until paid. Bolling v. Commissioner, 357 F.2d 3 (8th Cir.1966), involved a taxpayer who sold homes under financing arrangements requiring it to pledge a portion of the sales proceeds to a lender in order to induce the lender to make loans to the taxpayer's purchasers. The amounts pledged were released to the seller as the principal of the loans to the purchasers was reduced. Following *Hansen,* the court held that the seller had to include the full amount of the sales price in income despite the security deposits. Stendig v. United States, 843 F.2d 163 (4th Cir.1988), involved a taxpayer who was required by a mortgage lender to deposit a portion of rental receipts in an interest bearing bank account that could be drawn upon only for limited purposes prior to repayment of mortgage indebtedness. The taxpayer was currently taxed on payments to the reserve account.

In Johnson v. Commissioner, 108 T.C. 448 (1997), the taxpayers were motor vehicle dealers who entered into multi-year vehicle service contracts with customers and received a flat fee in advance for work to be performed under the contracts. If a customer canceled the contract, any refund was based on the period of time the contract had been in force and the number of miles the vehicle had been driven; the amount of repairs performed on the vehicle generally was not a factor in determining the refund. The court applied *Hansen* to require accrual of amounts that were paid into an escrow account to guarantee the taxpayer's own future performance of the contract under which the amounts were received. Amounts would be released only as the dealers fulfilled obligations under the contracts or when the period of the contract had expired.

4.   SALE OF GOODS

Treas. Reg. § 1.446–1(c)(1)(ii)(C) provides that "a taxpayer engaged in a manufacturing business may account for sales of the taxpayer's product when the goods are shipped, when the product is delivered or accepted, or when title to the goods passes to the customer, whether or not billed, depending upon the method regularly employed in keeping the taxpayer's books." Passage of title is not determinative for accruing income from continuous sales of inventory. In United States v. Utah-Idaho Sugar Co., 96 F.2d 756 (10th Cir.1938), the taxpayer, which manufactured and sold sugar at wholesale, executed contracts for the sale of sugar with delivery to be in thirty days and payment to be made seven days after delivery. The taxpayer accrued its profit at the time of execution of the contract. The court held the accrual was proper, whether or not the contracts passed title before segregation and shipment. In Pacific Grape Products Co. v. Commissioner, 219 F.2d 862 (9th Cir.1955), a fruit-canner, according to trade practice, billed all ordered goods still unshipped as of December 31st each year and accrued its income accordingly. This method of accounting was proper whether or not title had passed on the billing date, though the court found title had passed.

In Hallmark Cards, Inc. v. Commissioner, 90 T.C. 26 (1988), a greeting card manufacturer shipped Valentine's Day cards to purchasers before January 1st pursuant to contracts providing that title and risk of loss passed on January 1st and it accrued the sales on that date. The taxpayer accrued income with respect to all other sales as of the shipping date. The court allowed a different method of accrual for cards relating to a particular holiday.

5. CONTESTED CLAIMS

Rev. Rul. 2003–10, 2003–1 C.B. 288, addresses the accrual of income from the sale of goods when an accrual method taxpayer's customer disputes its liability. A taxpayer is not required to accrue income in the taxable year of sale if, during that year, the customer disputes the liability because the taxpayer shipped incorrect goods. If the taxpayer overbills a customer due to a clerical mistake in an invoice, the customer discovers the error and, in the following taxable year, disputes its liability for the overbilled amount, then the taxpayer must accrue income in the taxable year of sale for only the correct amount.

In Continental Tie & Lumber Co. v. United States, 286 U.S. 290 (1932), the taxpayer had a claim against the federal government for profits on the operation of its railroads during 1917 and 1918. Congress, in the Transportation Act of 1920, had authorized the Interstate Commerce Commission to make awards to carriers in the taxpayer's situation. The Court found that the taxpayer's right to the award was fixed by the passage of the Transportation Act, although payment was not made until 1923. The Commission's function was only ministerial and had no bearing on the right to the award. Since, on the basis of data available to it, the taxpayer could have estimated the amount of the award in the year of the passage of the Act, the income was properly accruable in that year.

The taxpayer in Maryland Shipbuilding & Drydock Co. v. United States, 409 F.2d 1363 (Ct.Cl.1969), was not required to accrue amounts claimed under an insurance policy where, in order to receive the insurance company's proposed settlement, it would have had to forego its rights to pursue claims under another policy: "When the cases speak of 'a fixed right to receive' an amount as the touchstone of its accruability for federal tax purposes, they plainly comprehend a 'right' that is enforceable without strings attached—not a 'right' the exercise of which must be purchased by the beneficiary with the surrender of some other related and valuable right * * * ."

In Snyder Air Products Inc. v. Commissioner, 71 T.C. 709 (1979), the taxpayer, with a May 31 fiscal year, received a court judgment for a condemnation award in 1968. Prior to May 31, 1970, the lower court decision was upheld on appeal, further appeal was denied, and the state issued a voucher for the amount owing. Completion of state administrative procedures delayed the mailing of a check until June. The court held that the gain accrued in the fiscal year ended May 31, 1970, even though the administrative procedures to issue the check had not yet been completed. In

Schlumberger Technology Corp. v. United States, 195 F.3d 216 (5th Cir.1999), the taxpayer was not required to accrue a Swiss arbitral award until the period for appeal had expired. Under Swiss law, the arbitral award required judicial confirmation before becoming enforceable and the unappealed award was not judicially confirmed until the period for appeal had lapsed.

In Trinity Industries, Inc. v. Commissioner, 132 T.C. 6 (2009), the taxpayer built barges for customers and part of the payment of the purchase price was contractually deferred until 18 months after delivery of each barge. Before having completed payment for some barges, the purchasers claimed there were defects in other previously purchased barges and asserted a common law right to offset their claimed damages against the deferred payments. When the customer withheld payment, the taxpayer included only the payments actually received and excluded the deferred payments, which ordinarily would have been accrued as income. The Tax Court held that the full contract price was includable in the year the barges were delivered, and the amount that should have been accrued as income could not be reduced by amounts withheld by the purchasers under their asserted right to offset claimed damages. The customer's offset affected only the timing of the taxpayer's receipt of the sales proceeds, not its right to receive the proceeds, because the taxpayer subsequently "received" the withheld amounts when, pursuant to a settlement agreement, the withheld amounts were applied in compromise of the purchaser's claims for damages.

(2) ADVANCE RECEIPTS—MAY INCLUSION OF AN ACTUAL RECEIPT BE DEFERRED

INTERNAL REVENUE CODE: Sections 455; 456.

REGULATIONS: Section 1.451–5.

In the case of the cash method taxpayer, actual receipt of funds for services or goods will ordinarily constitute income in the year of receipt. For an accrual method taxpayer, however, it may be possible to receive funds in advance of the time the income item would otherwise be properly accruable for financial accounting purposes. Should this fact allow the accrual method taxpayer to defer inclusion of the income item until the time of proper accrual under financial accounting concepts?

Schlude v. Commissioner
Supreme Court of the United States, 1963.
372 U.S. 128.

■ MR. JUSTICE WHITE delivered the opinion of the Court.

This is still another chapter in the protracted problem of the time certain items are to be recognized as income for the purposes of the federal income tax. The Commissioner of Internal Revenue increased the 1952, 1953 and 1954 ordinary income of the taxpayers by including in gross income for those years amounts received or receivable under contracts executed during those years despite the fact that the contracts obligated taxpayers to render performance in subsequent periods. * * *

Taxpayers, husband and wife, formed a partnership to operate ballroom dancing studios (collectively referred to as "studio") pursuant to Arthur Murray, Inc., franchise agreements. Dancing lessons were offered under either of two basic contracts. The cash plan contract required the student to pay the entire down payment in cash at the time the contract was executed with the balance due in installments thereafter. The deferred payment contract required only a portion of the down payment to be paid in cash. The remainder of the down payment was due in stated installments and the balance of the contract price was to be paid as designated in a negotiable note signed at the time the contract was executed.

Both types of contracts provided that (1) the student should pay tuition for lessons in a certain amount, (2) the student should not be relieved of his obligation to pay the tuition, (3) no refunds would be made, and (4) the contract was noncancelable.[2] The contracts prescribed a specific number of lesson hours ranging from five to 1,200 hours and some contracts provided lifetime courses entitling the student additionally to two hours of lessons per month plus two parties a year for life. Although the contracts designated the period during which the lessons had to be taken, there was no schedule of specific dates, which were arranged from time to time as lessons were given.

Cash payments received directly from students and amounts received when the negotiable notes were discounted at the bank or fully paid[3] were deposited in the studio's general bank account without segregation from its other funds. The franchise agreements required the studio to pay to Arthur Murray, Inc., on a weekly basis, 10% of these cash receipts as royalty and 5% of the receipts in escrow, the latter to continue until a $20,000 indemnity fund was accumulated. Similarly, sales commissions for lessons sold were paid at the time the sales receipts were deposited in the studio's general bank account.

The studio, since its inception in 1946, has kept its books and reported income for tax purposes on an accrual system of accounting. In addition to the books, individual student record cards were maintained showing the number of hours taught and the number still remaining under the contract. The system, in substance, operated as follows. When a contract was entered into, a "deferred income" account was credited for

---

[2]   Although the contracts stated they were noncancelable, the studio frequently rewrote contracts reducing the number of lessons for a smaller sum of money. Also, despite the fact that the contracts provided that no refunds would be made, and despite the fact that the studio discouraged refunds, occasionally a refund would be made on a canceled contract.

[3]   Notes taken from the students were ordinarily transferred, with full recourse, to a local bank which would deduct the interest charges and credit the studio with approximately 50% of the face amount. The remaining 50% was held in a reserve account, unavailable to the studio, until the note was fully paid, at which time the reserved amount was transferred to the studio's general bank account.

the total contract price. At the close of each fiscal period, the student record cards were analyzed and the total number of taught hours was multiplied by the designated rate per hour of each contract. The resulting sum was deducted from the deferred income account and reported as earned income on the financial statements and the income tax return. In addition, if there had been no activity in a contract for over a year, or if a course were reduced in amount, an entry would be made canceling the untaught portion of the contract, removing that amount from the deferred income account, and recognizing gain to the extent that the deferred income exceeded the balance due on the contract, i.e., the amounts received in advance. The amounts representing lessons taught and the gains from cancellations constituted the chief sources of the partnership's gross income. The balance of the deferred income account would be carried forward into the next fiscal year to be increased or decreased in accordance with the number of new contracts, lessons taught and cancellations recognized.

Deductions were also reported on the accrual basis except that the royalty payments and the sales commissions were deducted when paid irrespective of the period in which the related receipts were taken into income. Three certified public accountants testified that in their opinion the accounting system employed truly reflected net income in accordance with commercial accrual accounting standards.

* * *

The question * * * for decision, * * * is this: Was it proper for the Commissioner, exercising his discretion under * * * § 446(b), * * * to reject the studio's accounting system as not clearly reflecting income and to include as income in a particular year advance payments by way of cash, negotiable notes and contract installments falling due but remaining unpaid during that year? We hold that it was since we believe the problem is squarely controlled by *American Automobile Association,* 367 U.S. 687.

* * *

The *American Automobile Association* case rested upon an additional ground which is also controlling here. Relying upon Automobile Club of Michigan v. Commissioner, 353 U.S. 180, the Court rejected the taxpayer's system as artificial since the advance payments related to services which were to be performed only upon customers' demands without relation to fixed dates in the future. The system employed here suffers from that very same vice, for the studio sought to defer its cash receipts on the basis of contracts which did not provide for lessons on fixed dates after the taxable year, but left such dates to be arranged from time to time by the instructor and his student. Under the contracts, the student could arrange for some or all of the additional lessons or could simply allow their rights under the contracts to lapse. But even though the student did not demand the remaining lessons, the contracts permitted the studio to insist upon payment in accordance with the obligations undertaken and to retain whatever prepayments were made without restriction as to use and without obligation of refund. At the end of each period, while the number of lessons taught had been meticulously reflected, the studio was uncertain whether none, some or all of the remaining lessons would be rendered. Clearly, services were rendered solely on demand in the fashion of the *American Automobile Association* and *Automobile Club of Michigan* cases.[9]

Moreover, percentage royalties and sales commissions for lessons sold, which were paid as cash was received from students or from its note transactions with the bank, were deducted in the year paid even though the related items of income had been deferred, at least in part, to later periods. In view of all these circumstances, we hold the studio's accrual system vulnerable under * * * § 446(b) with respect to its deferral of prepaid income. Consequently, the Commissioner was fully justified in including payments in cash or by negotiable note in gross income for the year in which such payments were received. If these payments are includible in the year of receipt because their allocation to a later year does not clearly reflect income, the contract installments are likewise includible in gross income, as the United States now claims, in the year they become due and payable. For an accrual basis taxpayer "it is the *right* to receive and not the actual receipt that determines the inclusion of the amount in gross income," Spring City Co. v. Commissioner, 292 U.S. 182, 184; Commissioner v. Hansen, 360 U.S. 446, and here the right to receive these installments had become fixed at least at the time they were due and payable.

* * *

■ MR. JUSTICE STEWART, with whom MR. JUSTICE DOUGLAS, MR. JUSTICE HARLAN, and MR. JUSTICE GOLDBERG join, dissenting.

* * *

The Court's decision can be justified, * * * only upon the basis that the system of accrual accounting used by the taxpayers in this case did not "clearly reflect income" in accordance with the command of [section 446(b)]. In the *Automobile Club of Michigan* case the taxpayer allocated yearly dues ratably over 12 months, so that only a portion of the dues received during any fiscal year was reported as income for that year. In the absence of any proof that services demanded by the Automobile Club members were distributed in the same proportion over the year, the Court held that the system used by the taxpayer did not clearly reflect income. In the *American Automobile Association* case the taxpayer

---

[9]   The treatment of "gains from cancellations" underlines this aspect of the case. These gains, representing amounts paid or promised in advance of lessons given, were recognized in those periods in which the taxpayers arbitrarily decided the contracts were to be deemed canceled. The studio made no attempt to report estimated cancellations in the year of receipt, choosing instead to defer these gains to periods bearing no economic relationship to the income recognized. * * *

offered statistical proof to show that its proration of dues reasonably matched the proportion of its yearly costs incurred each month in rendering services attributable to those dues. The Court discounted the validity of this statistical evidence because the amount and timing of the services demanded were wholly within the control of the individual members of the Association, and the Court thought that the Association could not, therefore, estimate with accuracy the costs attributable to each individual member's demands.

In the present case the difficulties which the Court perceived in *Automobile Club of Michigan* and *American Automobile Association* have been entirely eliminated in the accounting system which these taxpayers have consistently employed. The records kept on individual students accurately measured the amount of services rendered—and therefore the costs incurred by the taxpayer—under each individual contract during each taxable year. But, we are told, there is a fatal flaw in the taxpayers' accounts in this case too: The individual contracts did not provide "for lessons on fixed dates * * * , but left such dates to be arranged from time to time by the instructor and his student." Yet this "fixed date of performance" standard, it turns out, actually has nothing whatever to do with those aspects of the taxpayers' accounting system which the Court ultimately finds objectionable.

There is nothing in the Court's opinion to indicate disapproval of the basic method by which income earned by the rendition of services was recorded. On the contrary, the taxpayers' system was admittedly wholly accurate in recording lessons given under each individual contract. It was only in connection with lessons which had not yet been taught that the taxpayers were "uncertain whether none, some or all" of the contractual services would be rendered, and the condemned "arbitrariness" therefore is limited solely to the method by which cancellations were recognized. It is, of course, true of all businesses in which services are not rendered simultaneously with payment that the number and amount of cancellations are necessarily unknown at the time advances are received. But surely it cannot be contended that a contract which specified the times at which lessons were to be given would make any more certain how many of the remaining lessons students would in fact demand. Indeed, the Court does not suggest that a schedule fixing the dates of all future lessons would, if embodied in each contract, suffice to make petitioners' accounting system "clearly reflect income."

Instead, the cure suggested by the Court for the defect which it finds in the accounting system used by these taxpayers is that estimated cancellations should be reported as income in the year advance payments are received. I agree that such estimates might more "clearly reflect income" than the system actually used by the taxpayers. But any such estimates would necessarily have to be based on precisely the type of statistical evaluations which the Court struck down in the *American Automobile Association* case. Whatever other artificialities the exigencies of revenue collection may require in the field of tax accounting, it has never before today been suggested that a consistent method of accrual accounting, valid for purposes of recognizing income, is not equally valid for purposes of deferring income. Yet in this case the Court says that the taxpayers, in recognizing income, should have used the very system of statistical estimates which, for income deferral purposes, the *American Automobile* decision held impermissible.

It seems to me that this decision, the third of a trilogy of cases purportedly decided on their own peculiar facts, in truth completes the mutilation of a basic element of the accrual method of reporting income—a method which has been explicitly approved by Congress for almost half a century.

I respectfully dissent.

DETAILED ANALYSIS

1. *SCHLUDE* IN CONTEXT

Prior to the decision in *Schlude,* the Supreme Court had considered the treatment of prepaid income in two cases. In Automobile Club of Michigan v. Commissioner, 353 U.S. 180 (1957), an automobile club received annual dues from its members in return for various services, such as emergency road services and furnishing maps. The Commissioner had required the inclusion of the dues in the years received, arguing that the claim of right doctrine was applicable. The Court avoided consideration of the claim of right doctrine by holding that the Commissioner did not abuse his discretion under section 446(b) in requiring the current inclusion of the prepaid amounts in order clearly to reflect income. The taxpayer's allocation of the membership dues in monthly amounts was "purely artificial" and bore no relation to the services that the taxpayer might be called on to perform. In American Automobile Association v. United States, 367 U.S. 687 (1961), involving the same type of factual situation, the taxpayer tried to cure the "artificiality" of its accounting system by more specific evidence correlating the performance of member services and the period of time over which the dues were credited. Again, the Supreme Court held the accounting method to be "artificial." The method rested on general statistical data as to when services would be performed and did not attempt to establish the cost attributable to each individual member's demands for service.

In *AAA,* the Court also found significant the legislative history of the prepaid income question. In 1954, § 452 was enacted which permitted taxpayers using the accrual method to elect to defer the inclusion of prepaid income. Under this election, the taxpayer could prorate prepayments over the years to which they related, except that the amounts could not be spread over more than the five succeeding taxable years without permission. The provision was repealed retroactively in 1955, primarily because the failure to provide transitional rules resulted in a substantial revenue loss. Though the legislative history of the repeal indicated that no inference was to be drawn regarding the state of the law apart from the special statutory provision, the Court in *AAA* found the repeal of the provision significant:

"[T]he repeal of the section * * * upon the insistence of the Treasury that the proposed endorsement of such tax accounting would have a disastrous impact on the Government's revenues, was just as clearly a mandate from the Congress that petitioner's system was not acceptable for tax purposes."[3]

In *Schlude,* the Court again upheld the Commissioner's discretion to require the inclusion of prepaid income, even when accounting was made for individual contracts, where it was still impossible to determine whether and when the remaining lessons would be given. As the dissent points out, if the taxpayer had attempted to provide statistical evidence as to the likelihood of the remaining lessons being given, the evidence would have been inconsistent with the rejection of statistical estimates in *AAA.* The thrust of the Court's decisions is thus to give the Commissioner very broad discretion in dealing with prepaid income situations. This emphasis in the Supreme Court cases on the Commissioner's discretion is reflected in subsequent appellate court decisions. See e.g., RCA Corp. v. United States, 664 F.2d 881 (2d Cir.1981), where the court stated that its function was "not to determine whether in its own opinion RCA's method of accounting for prepaid service income 'clearly reflect[ed] income' but to determine whether there is an adequate basis in law for the Commissioner's that it did not."

In a few prepaid income cases courts have not deferred to the Commissioner's discretion. In Artnell Co. v. Commissioner, 400 F.2d 981 (7th Cir. 1968), the Chicago White Sox sold advance tickets to baseball games and did not report the income from the advance tickets in the year of the sales, but instead reported the income as the games were played. The Seventh Circuit distinguished *Artnell* from *Schlude,* noting that while the latter involved future performance that was uncertain in time and extent, White Sox games were played according to fixed schedule. As a result, notwithstanding the Commissioner's claims to the contrary, the Seventh Circuit concluded that the taxpayer's deferral treatment could reflect income clearly. See also Artnell Co. v. Commissioner, T.C. Memo 1970–85 (concluding on remand that the taxpayer's treatment clearly reflected income).

Similarly, in Tampa Bay Devil Rays, Ltd. v. Commissioner, T.C. Memo 2002–248, the Tampa Bay Devil Rays collected advance ticket payments in 1995 and 1996 for the 1998 baseball season, the first season of major league play for the Devil Rays. In the earlier years, the Devil Rays were conducting minor league baseball activities and deducted the expenses, but did not include the advance season ticket receipts. Because the receipts would have to be refunded if the Devil Rays did not play the 1998 season, the court rejected the Commissioner's argument that under *Schlude* the receipts for the 1998 season were includable when received in 1995 and 1996. See also Boise Cascade Corp. v. United States, 530 F.2d 1367 (Ct. Cl. 1976) (concluding that deferral treatment of advance receipts was permitted

---

[3]   Following the *AAA* decision, Congress enacted § 456 permitting membership organizations that do not issue capital stock and do not distribute any earnings to their members to elect to defer income from prepaid dues ratably over the period in which there is liability to perform services. Deferral is available only for dues covering a period of time that does not exceed 36 months.

because the taxpayer "had a fixed obligation to perform its services without the uncertainty as to performance so prominent in" the *Automobile Club*, *AAA*, and *Schlude* trilogy of cases).

2. PREPAID INCOME AND THE CLAIM OF RIGHT DOCTRINE

As discussed in Chapter 5, as a general rule, amounts received under a claim of right and without restriction as to their use are income in the year of receipt without regard to the taxpayer's accounting method. Indeed, in North American Oil Consolidated v. Commissioner, Chapter 5, Section 2, the Supreme Court did not even mention the taxpayer's accounting method in holding that an unrestricted receipt was income under the claim of right doctrine. As indicated above, the Commissioner initially argued that claim of right principles controlled the treatment of prepaid income of an accrual method taxpayer. The Supreme Court, on the other hand, has rejected the application of the claim of right doctrine in these situations, resting its holdings instead on the Commissioner's discretion with respect to the clear reflection of income. The dissent in *AAA* stated somewhat cryptically that the claim of right doctrine was only applicable in situations in which the income had been "fully earned." In the typical claim of right case, the income is as "earned" as it ever will be in the year of receipt and the only question is whether restrictions on the receipt are so substantial that it does not constitute income at all. On the other hand, in the prepaid income cases the taxpayer by definition has a continuing obligation to perform services or deliver goods in the future and to incur the expenditures necessary to complete its performance. This aspect distinguishes the prepaid income cases from the typical claim of right situations and may explain why the courts have approached the prepaid income cases from the perspective of accounting rules rather than as a question of income definition.

3. LIMITED DEFERRAL FOR CERTAIN ADVANCE PAYMENTS

After many years of litigation to establish the principle that prepaid income must be included in gross income in the year of receipt, the IRS carved out a significant exception to the general rule for certain advance receipts. Rev. Proc. 2004–34, 2004–1 C.B. 991, allows taxpayers in certain specified circumstance to elect to defer the inclusion of some or all of an advance receipt until the taxable year following the year of receipt. The most significant category of advance payments to which the revenue procedure applies involves those received in exchange for services. Rev. Proc. 2004–34 also applies to advance payments received in exchange for (1) the sale of goods (other than those to which the general rules applicable to advance payments for goods in Treas. Reg. § 1.451–5 apply), (2) the use of intellectual property (e.g., copyrights, patents, trademarks, etc.), (3) the occupancy or use of property if the occupancy is ancillary to the provision of services (e.g., advance receipts for hotel rooms), (4) the sale, lease, and license of computer software, (5) guaranty or warranty contracts ancillary to the above items, (6) subscriptions (if an election under § 455 is not in effect), (7) memberships in an organization (if an election under § 456 is not in effect), and (8) a combination of the foregoing items.[4] Taxpayers who make the election under Rev. Proc. 2004–34 must include the advance receipt in gross income for the taxable year of receipt to the extent that it is included in revenues in its applicable financial statements for that year. The balance of the receipt must be included in the next succeeding taxable year regardless of how the balance is treated for financial accounting purposes. For example, consider a taxpayer who receives in 2016 an advance payment for services in the amount of $160,000 for services to be performed in 2016, 2017, 2018, and 2019. For financial accounting purposes, the taxpayer recognizes $40,000 in revenues in each of the four years. Under the revenue procedure, for tax purposes the taxpayer may include $40,000 in gross income in 2016 and the remaining $120,000 in 2017. Alternatively, the taxpayer could, consistent with *Schlude*, include the entire $160,000 in 2016.

4.   ADVANCE PAYMENTS FOR GOODS

In Hagen Advertising Displays, Inc. v. Commissioner, 407 F.2d 1105 (6th Cir.1969), advance payments for goods were held taxable when received on the basis of *Schlude*. Shortly thereafter, Treas. Reg. § 1.451–5 was promulgated to provide that certain advance payments for goods may be deferred by the taxpayer. The regulation applies to advance payments received with respect to (i) goods held for sale in the ordinary course of the taxpayer's business, and (ii) items built, installed, manufactured, or constructed by the taxpayer. The taxpayer may defer the inclusion of such advance receipts until they are property accruable under the accrual method of accounting (i.e., without regard to the rule in *Schlude*); however, the taxpayer may not defer the inclusion beyond the time in which the advance receipt is included in revenues in its financial statements. Note that unlike the rule relating to services (and other specified transactions) in Rev. Proc. 2004–34, Treas. Reg. § 1.451–5 may allow for deferral beyond the taxable year following the year in which the advance payment is received.

Treas. Reg. § 1.451–5 does not apply to amounts allocable to services that are to be performed in connection with goods for which advance payment is received unless the services are integrated with the sale or manufacture of the goods. Therefore, where the services are separable the portion of the payments attributable to services must be analyzed under Rev. Proc. 2004–34. However, if the amount allocable to services is less than 5 percent of the total contract price, that amount may be treated as an advance payment for goods. Special rules are provided for inventory goods that limit the extent of the deferral in certain cases.

5.   PREPAYMENT VERSUS SECURITY DEPOSIT

If a receipt is characterized as a security deposit rather than as a prepayment, the taxpayer is not required to accrue income until the deposit is forfeited. The standards for distinguishing security deposits from prepaid income are discussed in Commissioner v. Indianapolis Power & Light Co., Chapter 5, Section 4.

---

[4]   Certain advance receipts are specifically exempted from the scope of Rev. Proc. 2004–34. For example, the revenue procedure does not apply to insurance premiums, payments with respect to financial instruments, or most rental arrangements.

6. IN SEARCH OF A RATIONALE

As the previous material indicates, accrual method taxpayers generally have been required by the courts to include advance payments in income for tax purposes in the year of receipt. This general rule and the significant administrative and legislative exceptions raise important tax policy issues.

The general rule in effect places an accrual method taxpayer on the cash method with respect to advance payments. The rule may seem questionable when one considers that the accrual method generally achieves the best measurement of economic income; changes in net worth are, after all, what the accrual method is designed to measure. But the accurate measurement of economic income for tax purposes often must be subordinated to tax administration considerations. For example, the realization requirement, examined in Chapter 2, which defers taxation of gains from property until the property has been sold or exchanged instead of taxing such gains as they economically accrue, illustrates that the pragmatic concerns of taxpayer liquidity and the difficulties of property valuation can be given precedence over the accurate measurement of economic income. The principle that advance payments must generally be included in the income of accrual method taxpayers can be viewed as the mirror image of the realization requirement. Accrual accounting for income from advance payments, while potentially the most accurate method, is more difficult to apply and imposes the tax liability after the year the cash is received. In such circumstances, administrative considerations and revenue concerns prevail over income measurement concerns.

Although the policy issue typically is posed as a conflict between accuracy of income measurement and tax administration, the implementation of the accrual method by taxpayers has not always suggested that accuracy of income measurement is the end being sought. Consider, for example, how in *Schlude* the taxpayer, while meticulously allocating only the "earned" portion of the prepayment to income, nevertheless deducted its payments to Arthur Murray, Inc. in their entirety, even though a significant portion was attributable to the deferred income. Deferral of income was apparently considered by the taxpayer to be more important than deferral of an expense.

Advance payments received by accrual method taxpayers is but one situation where the goals of accurate income measurement and sound tax administration are in conflict.

B. DEDUCTION ITEMS

INTERNAL REVENUE CODE: Sections 446(a)–(d); 461(a), (c), (f); 7701(a)(25).

REGULATIONS: Sections 1.446–1(c)(1)(ii); 1.461–1(a)(2), (3).

The historic general rule controlling the accrual of expenses for tax purposes is that expenses are deductible in the year in which all the events occur that create an unconditional obligation to pay. United States v. Anderson, 269 U.S. 422 (1926). *Anderson* involved a federal tax imposed on the taxpayer's profits on munitions sales made in 1916. The tax became due and was paid by the taxpayer in 1917. The taxpayer claimed a 1917 deduction for income tax purposes. The Supreme Court held the expense of the tax should have been accrued in 1916 since it was in that year that all the events occurred which fixed the amount of the liability and determined the liability of the taxpayer to pay it.

Following financial accounting conventions, the tax accrual method of accounting for expenses historically has not required any discounting of deductions to reflect the fact that payment would not be made until some time in the future. That is, the accrual accounting method rules did not take into account the time value of money concept. Taxpayers exploited this omission, sometimes to an extreme degree. To deal with these situations, in 1984 Congress added § 461(h), which imposes the additional requirement of "economic performance" in order for the all events test to be satisfied.

The current regulations reflect the historic principles (see below), as modified by § 461(h): "Under an accrual method of accounting, a liability * * * is incurred, and is generally taken into account for Federal income tax purposes, in the taxable year in which all the events have occurred that establish the fact of the liability, the amount thereof can be determined with reasonable accuracy, and economic performance has occurred with respect to the liability." Treas. Reg. § 1.461–1(a)(2).

(1) THE HISTORIC ALL EVENTS TEST

The historic "all events" test requires only that the liability be fixed and owed, not that it actually be payable. For example, in Newhouse Broadcasting Corp. v. Commissioner, T.C. Memo. 2000–244, the taxpayer's book publishing subsidiary business was contractually obligated to pay book authors royalties on all books sold and not returned, even if payment for the books was never received by the publisher. The taxpayer accrued deductions for royalties on all the books it sold during the year. However, the taxpayer did not currently pay to the authors the full amount of the royalties earned on the books that had been sold but set up a "reserve" against returns and held back payment for the portion of the royalties attributable to books expected to be returned. The Tax Court rejected the Commissioner's argument that as a result of this arrangement the all events test had not been satisfied with respect to the amount of royalties equal to the additions to the reserve and not paid. The royalties were legally "owed" to the authors until the books were returned, which was a subsequent event, even if they were not yet payable and might never be payable due to those subsequent events. Thus, the full amount of the royalties was deductible because the liability was fixed and owed.

However, the possibility of a substantial time lag between the time a liability becomes fixed and owed and the time at which it becomes payable can present difficult questions. In Mooney Aircraft, Inc. v. United

States, 420 F.2d 400 (5th Cir. 1969), an aircraft manufacturer issued a "Mooney Bond" with each aircraft that it manufactured and sold that unconditionally promised that the taxpayer would pay to the bearer the sum of $1,000 when the corresponding aircraft should be permanently retired from service. The taxpayer sought to deduct from gross income the face value of the Mooney Bonds in the year the instruments were issued, even though they might not be redeemed for 20 or more years. The court upheld the Government's position that the Mooney Bonds could be deducted only in the year the aircraft to which they relate were permanently retired from service. The taxpayer's "accrual" system of accounting was unacceptable for tax purposes. The court rejected the government's argument that the obligation was contingent upon the happening of a future event; although the timing was uncertain, there was no contingency regarding the *fact* of liability. Nevertheless, the court upheld the disallowance of the deduction under § 446(b) on the ground that the taxpayer's accounting method did not clearly reflect income, citing both *AAA* and *Schlude*. The expenses that the taxpayer sought to currently deduct would not actually be paid for "15, 20 or even 30 years." Thus, the IRS had a reasonable basis for disallowing the deduction as not clearly reflecting income. "The longer the time the less probable it becomes that the liability, though incurred, will ever in fact be *paid*. * * * Indeed, the very purpose of the "all events test" is to make sure that the taxpayer will not deduct expenses that might never occur. * * * In the present case the taxpayer could in good faith use the monies it has received as capital to expand its business; if one day it became insolvent the expense might never be paid, yet the money would have been used as tax-free income." We repeat that because of the inordinate length of time involved in this case the Commissioner was clearly within his discretion in disallowing deduction of the "Mooney Bonds" as a *current* expense.

DETAILED ANALYSIS

1.   THE ECONOMICS OF THE *MOONEY AIRCRAFT* TRANSACTION

What was the taxpayer trying to accomplish in *Mooney Aircraft?* Assume that Mooney Aircraft paid taxes at a 40 percent rate, a Mooney Bond would not be redeemed for twenty years, and Mooney Aircraft could earn 10 percent before taxes on invested funds. If Mooney Aircraft had been permitted a current deduction for the $1,000 Mooney Bond to be redeemed in 20 years, it would have saved $400 of taxes that year. If that $400 could have been invested at 10 percent interest, after paying taxes on the interest as it was earned, at the end of 20 years the $400 would have grown to be $1,283. Thus, on an after-tax basis, after paying off the Mooney Bond, Mooney Aircraft would have earned $283 more than if it had never promised to pay the $1,000 rebate.

2.   THE ALL EVENTS TEST—GENERALLY

2.1. *Doubt as to the Taxpayer's Ability to Make Payment*

Zimmerman Steel Co. v. Commissioner, 130 F.2d 1011 (8th Cir.1942), held that interest was properly accruable even though it might not be paid by the taxpayer: "[W]here interest actually accrues on a debt of a taxpayer in a tax year the statute plainly says he may deduct it. That he has no intention or expectation of paying it, but must go into bankruptcy as this taxpayer was obliged to do, can not of itself justify denial of deduction in computing the taxpayer's net income." The Tax Court has qualified the *Zimmerman* rule. In Cohen v. Commissioner, 21 T.C. 855 (1954) (Acq.), the court allowed accrual where the taxpayer, in uncertain financial condition, continued to conduct his business and did make some payments: "There may have been doubt as to the ultimate ability of the petitioner to pay the accrued interest in full, but there was no certainty that he would be unable to do so." In re West Texas Marketing Corp., 54 F.3d 1194 (5th Cir.1995), reached a result contrary to *Zimmerman Steel*. *West Texas Marketing Corp.* involved the deductibility by a bankruptcy trustee of accrued post-petition interest on claims that would be payable under § 726(a)(5) of the Bankruptcy Code only if sufficient assets remained after payment of other claims. Although the amount of the liability was found to be fixed, the court held that the liability itself was contingent and therefore the deduction could not be accrued.

2.2. *Contested Liabilities*

If a taxpayer contests a claim asserted against it, the amount of the liability is not properly accruable since the liability remains contingent on the happening of a future event, that is, the outcome of the dispute. Dixie Pine Products Co. v. Commissioner, 320 U.S. 516 (1944) (contested tax liability).

The fact that a liability is contested will prevent its accrual even where the income to which the liability relates is required to be included in income for the taxable year. Security Flour Mills Co. v. Commissioner, 321 U.S. 281 (1944). In *Security Flour Mills*, the taxpayer contested a tax liability to the United States but passed the tax on to its customers in the form of higher sales prices which it collected and included in income. The Supreme Court rejected the taxpayer's argument that accrual of the deduction should be allowed in the year in which the income was earned, despite the fact of the contest, in order to match the income and expenses from the same transaction.

State law may require the payment of a contested tax liability as a prerequisite to disputing its validity. United States v. Consolidated Edison Co. of New York, 366 U.S. 380 (1961), held that payment of a tax under protest did not allow the accrual of the contested liability. The significance of this decision, however, was short-lived. Section 461(f), added in 1964, provides in general for the deduction of disputed items in the year paid, when the taxpayer after making the payment continues to contest the liability. This provision applies both to payments made in the same year and to those made in a year later than that to which the contested liability relates. If, after the deduction is taken, there is a final determination that the liability is less than what had been previously paid, the taxpayer would treat the difference as income.

Section 461(f) applies only if the taxpayer has "transferred" property in satisfaction of the asserted liability. Treas. Reg. § 1.461–2(c)(1) interprets this requirement as being met by a transfer to a trust or escrow account only if the transfer is pursuant to a government or court order or if the claimant is a party to the trust or escrow agreement. The requirement that the claimant be a party to the agreement was enforced in Poirier & McLane Corp. v. Commissioner, 547 F.2d 161 (2d Cir.1976). But in several other cases a deduction has been allowed for transfers to a trust or escrow account even though the claimant was not a party. Varied Investments, Inc. v. United States, 31 F.3d 651 (8th Cir.1994) (securities were transferred to an escrow account to secure an appeal bond in a contract suit even though the claimant was not a party to the escrow and the taxpayer was entitled to withdraw the accumulated interest); Chem Aero, Inc. v. United States, 694 F.2d 196 (9th Cir.1982) (same). Treas. Reg. § 1.461–2(c)(1) provides that the transfer to a trust of the transferor's debt instrument or stock, or the stock or indebtedness of a related person or corporation, does not give rise to a deduction under § 461(f) with respect to a contested liability.

2.3. *Accrual of Taxes*

In general, state and local taxes accrue in the year in which all the events (under state law) fixing the amount of tax and determining the liability to pay it have occurred. Some taxes, including real property taxes, are accrued on a particular date, such as the date on which a tax becomes a lien.

Several statutory provisions provide special rules regarding the accrual of taxes. Section 461(c)(1) permits taxpayers to elect to accrue real property taxes ratably over the local tax period. Section 461(d) prevents taxpayers from accruing in a single year the taxes relating to two years as a result of a change in the accrual date by local taxing authorities by disregarding the change in dates for purposes of accruing the tax.

2.4. *Prepaid Expenses*

Treas. Reg. § 1.461–1(a)(2) prevents the accrual of prepaid expenses, and Treas. Reg. § 1.263(a)–4(d)(3) reinforces Treas. Reg. § 1.461–1(a)(2) by generally requiring that prepaid expenses be capitalized. However, Treas. Reg. § 1.263(a)–4(f) adopts the holding of U.S. Freightways Corp. v. Commissioner, 270 F.3d 1137 (7th Cir.2001), in which an accrual method trucking company paid over $4,000,000 to state and local governments for licenses and permits for a one-year period straddling two taxable years, and provides that an expenditure to create or enhance intangible rights or benefits that do not extend for more than twelve months after the expenditure is incurred is not required to be capitalized. Furthermore, the deduction will not be deferred under the "clear reflection of income" standard of § 446(b). Thus, only amounts paid to create rights or benefits that extend beyond twelve months must be capitalized in full and deducted ratably over the period benefitted. However, a taxpayer may elect to capitalize and amortize prepaid expenses that cover a period of twelve months or less. Treas. Reg. § 1.263(a)–4(f)(7).

2.5. *Executory Contracts*

Rev. Rul. 2007–3, 2007–1 C.B. 350, held that the mere execution of a contract, without more, does not establish the fact of a taxpayer's liability under the all events test. For example, consider a taxpayer who executes a contract on December 15, 2016 that calls for services to be provided to the taxpayer from January 15 through January 31, 2017 and payment by the taxpayer on January 15, 2017. According to Rev. Rul. 2007–3, the fact of liability is not established until 2017, even though the taxpayer executed the service contract in 2016.

3. OTHER ASPECTS OF THE ALL EVENTS TEST PRIOR TO SECTION 461(h)

3.1. *Contingencies and Unidentifiable Recipients*

Many cases dealing with the all events test have involved liabilities where the amount of the liability is known but some contingency exists. Although in some cases, taxpayers attempted to accrue liabilities many years before they would be paid, while other cases involved situations in which a contingency was likely to be satisfied in the next taxable year.

United States v. Hughes Properties, Inc., 476 U.S. 593 (1986), involved accruals for guaranteed jackpots on progressive slot machines that had not been paid during the year because no patron in fact won the jackpot. Under the rules of the state gaming commission, the guaranteed jackpot could not be rolled back, but the casino was completely free to set any odds it wanted. Evidence indicated that the average period between payoffs on progressive slot machines was 4½ months, but one machine went 13 months and another 45 months without paying a jackpot. For the remainder of the machines the payoff period varied between 1.9 months and 14.3 months. The government argued that the liability was not fixed and certain until "some fortunate gambler" had pulled the lever to win the jackpot. Concluding that the effect of state law prohibiting rolling back the jackpot was the same as requiring payment into an escrow, the Court allowed the deduction. The possibility that the jackpot would not be paid due to the casino going out of business was rejected on the grounds that this possibility exists with respect to every business that uses the accrual method.

United States v. General Dynamics Corp., 481 U.S. 239, 244 (1987), decided by the Supreme Court the year after *Hughes Properties*, presented another situation involving both unascertained payees and contingencies. The Supreme Court upheld the IRS's disallowance of a deduction of a year-end estimate of the taxpayer obligations under a self-insured health plan for medical care for employees who had not yet filed claims, even though the number and amount of the claims could be estimated with reasonable accuracy. The decision was based on the fact that the taxpayer was obligated to reimburse employees for medical care claims only if properly documented claims were filed. Since the claims had not been filed, "all events" had not occurred: "[F]iling is not a mere technicality. It is crucial to the establishment of liability on the part of the taxpayer." The court rejected the taxpayer's argument that the likelihood of employees failing to file claims was "extremely remote and speculative," distinguishing *Hughes Properties* in which the Court had held that a remote possibility of nonpayment did not render the liability contingent.

3.2. *Reserves*

Because accrual method taxpayers are required to include prepaid income in the year received, they often have sought to accelerate deductions for the estimated costs of producing that income into the year the income is included. The accounting method employed is the maintenance of reserves for estimated expenses. For financial accounting purposes, the future expenses are charged against income in the year in which the prepaid income is received, and in the year the expenses are incurred, they are charged against the reserve rather than against income. Following this method, taxpayers have attempted to currently deduct additions to those reserves.

Deductions for estimated expenses for which there was no legal basis for liability generally have not been allowed. In Brown v. Helvering, 291 U.S. 193 (1934), deduction was denied for a reserve attempted to be established against insurance commissions to take into account possible cancellations in future years. Accrual of deductions was not permitted "since the events necessary to create the liability do not occur during the taxable year."

Creating a reserve for estimated expenses has generally been viewed as an "artificial" accounting method, akin to the deferral of prepaid income rejected by the Supreme Court in *AAA* and *Schlude*. In Commissioner v. Milwaukee & Suburban Transport Corp., 367 U.S. 906 (1961), the Court of Appeals had permitted the taxpayer to create a reserve for estimated liabilities for tort claims growing out of its operations (283 F.2d 279 (7th Cir.1960)). The Supreme Court reversed and remanded the case for reconsideration in light of the *AAA* decision. On remand the Court of Appeals affirmed the original Tax Court decision and disallowed the reserve. 293 F.2d 628 (7th Cir.1961).

(2) THE ECONOMIC PERFORMANCE REQUIREMENT

INTERNAL REVENUE CODE: Section 461(a), (h).

REGULATIONS: Sections 1.461–4(a)–(g); –5(a)–(c), (e).

Suppose an oil company installed an offshore oil production platform in 2016. Federal law requires the oil company to remove the platform when production ceases. The removal expenditures, although a fixed and definite legal obligation of the company, are not expected to be performed until 2036, when oil production is expected to cease. Other situations involving liabilities which, although arguably fixed, will not be satisfied for a significant number of years, include the expenses relating to reclaiming surface mines, the decommissioning of nuclear power plants, workers' compensation claims, tort claims, and plant closing expenses. For a substantial time following the Supreme Court decisions in *AAA* and *Schlude* there were no cases permitting the use of reserves. Later cases such as Ohio River Collieries v. Commissioner, 77 T.C. 1369 (1981), held that the all events test was satisfied with regard to such future expenditures.

Allowing a current deduction for estimated future expenses, even if a correct interpretation of the then existing all events test, failed to account for the time value of money. A deduction of $1,000,000 in 2016 with respect to a liability to be satisfied with $1,000,000 in 2036 provides the taxpayer with a windfall. The value of a $1,000,000 deduction in 2016, assuming a 6 percent discount rate, is more than three times the value of a $1,000,000 deduction in 2036 (assuming the marginal tax bracket of the taxpayer is the same in both years). In fact, as illustrated in the discussion of *Mooney Aircraft*, supra, if a taxpayer is allowed a $1,000,000 current deduction for an amount that will not be paid for twenty years, the after tax earnings for twenty years on the tax savings realized through the deduction might be more than the liability. In such a case, on an after-tax basis the taxpayer would be better off as a result of the liability.

There are two possible approaches to this problem. It would be possible to postpone the $1,000,000 deduction until 2036. Alternatively, the taxpayer could be allowed a current deduction limited to the *present value* of the liability to pay $1,000,000 in 2036, or $311,805 at a discount rate of 6 percent. As explained in the following, excerpt from the General Explanation of the 1984 Act, in enacting § 461(h), Congress has chosen to follow the former route.

General Explanation of the Tax Reform Act of 1984

Staff of the Joint Committee on Taxation, 258–267 (1984).

[Pre-1984] Law.

General

Prior law provided that, under the accrual method of accounting, an expense was deductible for the taxable year in which all the events had occurred which determined the fact of the liability and the amount thereof could be determined with reasonable accuracy (the so-called "all events test") (Treas. Reg. sec. 1.461–1(a)(2)). If the "all events" test was satisfied, an accrual basis taxpayer generally could deduct the full face amount of the liability (ignoring any discounting of the amount to reflect the time value of money).

Fact of liability

In a number of early cases, the courts held that expenditures are deductible only when the activities that the taxpayer is obligated to perform are in fact performed, not when the "fact" of the obligation to perform is determined. * * *

More recently, the courts generally have reached a different conclusion: a taxpayer may deduct the amount of a liability if all the events that fix the liability have occurred and the amount can be determined with reasonable accuracy, even though the activities the taxpayer is obligated to perform are not actually performed until a later year. For example, the Fourth Circuit held that surface mining reclamation costs that could be estimated with reasonable accuracy were properly accrued when the land was stripped although the land was not reclaimed until a subsequent year. Harrold v. Commissioner, 192 F.2d 1002 (4th Cir.1951).

The position of the Fourth Circuit with respect to strip mining reclamation costs has been extended by other courts to certain other situations. For example, the Ninth Circuit held that the fact of the liability under workers' compensation laws is determined in uncontested cases in the year in which injury occurs, even though medical services may be rendered at a future time. Crescent Wharf & Warehouse Co. v. Commissioner, 518 F.2d 772 (9th Cir.1975).

A deduction for a contingent liability generally is not allowed under present or prior law, because all of the events necessary to fix the liability have not yet occurred. * * *

The courts generally have held that the length of time between accrual and performance does not affect whether an amount is properly accruable. However, in Mooney Aircraft, Inc. v. United States, 420 F.2d 400 (5th Cir.1969), [see supra], the court held that a taxpayer, who gave to purchasers of its airplanes a bond redeemable when the plane was permanently retired from service, was not allowed a deduction because the possible interval between accrual and payment was "too long"; the court concluded that the likelihood of payment decreases as the time between accrual and payment increases.

* * *

Reasons for Change

Congress believed that the rules relating to the time for accrual of a deduction by a taxpayer using the accrual method of accounting should be changed to take into account the time value of money and the time the deduction is economically incurred. Recent court decisions in some cases permitted accrual method taxpayers to deduct currently expenses that were not yet economically incurred (i.e., that were attributable to activities to be performed or amounts to be paid in the future). Allowing a taxpayer to take deductions currently for an amount to be paid in the future overstates the true cost of the expense to the extent that the time value of money is not taken into account; the deduction is overstated by the amount by which the face value exceeds the present value of the expense. The longer the period of time involved, the greater is the overstatement.

* * *

Congress recognized that, in the case of noncapital items, a taxpayer, theoretically, should be allowed a deduction for either the full amount of a liability when the liability is satisfied or a discounted amount at an earlier time. However, Congress also recognized that determining the discounted values for all kinds of future expenses would be extraordinarily complex and would be extremely difficult to administer. For instance, a system that allowed current deductions for discounted future expenses would have to include a complex set of rules for recalculating overstated and understated deductions when the future liabilities are reestimated or are actually satisfied at a time, or in an amount, different from that originally projected. Furthermore, in the case of future expenditures, an appropriate discounting system may be equally complex. Therefore, in order to prevent deductions for future expenses in excess of their true cost, while avoiding the complexity of a system of discounted valuation, Congress believed that expenses should be accrued only when economic performance occurs.

Congress recognized that in many ordinary business transactions, economic performance may not occur until the year following the year in which the deduction may be taken under the all events test. Therefore, to avoid disrupting normal business and accounting practices and imposing undue burdens on taxpayers, Congress believed that an exception to the economic performance requirement should be provided for certain recurring items.

Explanation of Provision

In general

The Act provides that, in determining whether an amount has been incurred with respect to any item during the taxable year by a taxpayer using the accrual method of accounting, all the events which establish liability for such amount generally are not to be treated as having occurred any earlier than the time economic performance occurs. * * *

Economic performance

[Section 461(h)] provides a series of principles for determining when economic performance occurs. The principles provided by [section 461(h)(2)(A) and (B)] describe the two most common categories of liabilities: first, cases where the liability arises as a result of another person providing goods and services to the taxpayer and, second, cases where the liability requires the taxpayer to provide goods and services to another person or undertake some activity as a result of its income-producing activities.

With respect to the first category of liabilities, if the liability arises out of the use of property, economic performance occurs as the taxpayer uses the property. If the liability requires a payment for the providing of property, economic performance occurs when the property is provided. * * * If the liability of the taxpayer requires a payment to another person for the providing of services to the taxpayer by another person, economic performance generally occurs when such other person provides the services. With respect to the second category of liabilities, if the liability of the taxpayer requires the taxpayer to provide property or perform services, economic performance occurs as the taxpayer provides the property or performs the services. For this purpose, property does not include money; that is, economic performance generally does not occur as payments are made except as specifically provided in the Code or regulations. For example, if a contractor is engaged by a highway construction company to repair damaged properties, economic performance occurs as the contractor performs the work. Likewise, when the highway construction company itself repairs the damage, economic performance occurs as repairs are made.

Under a special rule for workers' compensation and tort liabilities requiring payments to another person, economic performance occurs as payments are made to that person. In the case of any other liability of the taxpayer, economic performance will occur at the time determined under regulations to be prescribed by the Treasury.

Exception from economic performance requirement for certain recurring items

In general

[Section 461(h)(3)] provides an exception under which certain expenses may be treated as incurred in the taxable year in which the all events test is otherwise met even though economic performance has not yet occurred. This exception applies if four conditions are met: (1) the all events test, without regard to economic performance, is satisfied with respect to the item during the taxable year; (2) economic performance occurs within a reasonable period (but in no event more than 8½ months) after the close of the taxable year; (3) the item is recurring in nature and the taxpayer consistently from year to year treats items of that type as incurred in the taxable year in which the all events test is met; and (4) either (a) the item is not material, or (b) the accrual of the item in the year in which the all events test is met results in a better matching of the item with the income to which it relates than would result from accruing the item in the year in which economic performance occurs. * * *

Matching

In determining whether the accrual of a material item in a particular year results in a better matching of the item with the income to which it relates, generally accepted accounting principles will be an important factor, although not necessarily dispositive. Costs directly associated with the revenue of a period are properly allocable to that period. * * *

Expenses such as insurance or rent generally can be allocated to a period and are best matched to that period. For example, a calendar year taxpayer with a twelve-month insurance contract entered into on July 1, 1984, generally should allocate one-half the expense to 1984 and one-half to 1985. (However, where the expense is an immaterial item, it is accruable in its entirety in 1984). Expenses such as advertising costs that cannot practically be associated with income of a particular period may be assigned to the period in which the costs are incurred (under generally accepted accounting principles). * * *

Modifications and clarifications with respect to economic performance standard

Interest

In the case of interest, economic performance occurs with the passage of time (that is, as the borrower uses, and the lender foregoes [sic] use of, the lender's money) rather than as payments are made. * * *

Contested liabilities

The Act provides that an amount transferred to a section 461(f) trust with respect to a contested liability may not be deducted any earlier than when economic performance with respect to the liability occurs. For example, [section 461(h)(2)(C)] provides that, in the case of workers' compensation or tort liabilities of the taxpayer requiring payments to another person, economic performance occurs as payments are made to that person. Since payment to a section 461(f) trust is not a payment to the claimant, such payment does not satisfy the economic performance test.

* * *

DETAILED ANALYSIS

1.   THE ECONOMIC PERFORMANCE REQUIREMENT IN GENERAL

Section 461(h) eliminates the possibility of accelerating the deduction for estimated future costs in most circumstances by requiring that "economic performance" occur in order for the all events test to be met. That is, in addition to the common law "all events" test, the requirements of § 461(h) must be met as well. If the liability of the taxpayer arises from the providing of services or property by the taxpayer or another, economic performance occurs when the services or property are provided. See Johnson v. Commissioner, 108 T.C. 448 (1997) (where prepayment for services to be rendered to the taxpayer under a multi-year contract was due at the beginning of the contract term, and both the extent and time for performance of services were contingent on facts beyond the control of the parties, a reasonable estimate of the relative amount of services that would be performed in each year was permitted and a deduction for a proportionate amount of the prepayment was allowed). Thus, any possible claim of a deduction based on a reserve for expenses to be incurred in future years to perform services or to purchase services is barred. If the taxpayer incurs a liability for the use of property, the deduction accrues no earlier than when the use occurs. Thus, for example, rent accrues over the term of the lease and interest accrues over the term of the loan.

In certain noncontractual situations, such as workers' compensation and tort liabilities, for which taxpayers previously attempted, sometimes successfully, to claim deductions for a reserve, the statute provides that economic performance does not occur until payment of those liabilities. This reverses the result in cases like Burnham Corp. v. Commissioner, 878 F.2d 86 (2d Cir.1989), which for a year not governed by § 461(h)(3) allowed the taxpayer to deduct the aggregate amount of monthly annuity payments due under a settlement for damages, even though the subsequent death of the annuitant would terminate the obligation.

2.   PAYMENT AS ECONOMIC PERFORMANCE

Although § 461(h) was prompted largely by the problem of reserves, its scope is much broader. Section 461(h)(2)(D) authorizes the Treasury to expand the scope of the economic performance rules by regulation. Based on this authority, the Treasury has promulgated regulations that require treating actual payment as economic performance for a wide variety of payments not specifically covered by the statute. Treas. Reg. § 1.461–4(g) provides that economic performance occurs only upon payment with respect to liabilities for (1) rebates and refunds, (2) awards, prizes, and jackpots, (3) insurance, warranty, and service contracts, (4) taxes, and (5) any liability not specifically covered by another economic performance rule. Thus, for example, in years governed by § 461(h), the deduction allowed in *Hughes Properties,* supra, would not be allowed until the slot machine jackpot paid off. Real estate taxes that the taxpayer has elected under § 461(c) to deduct as they accrue are not subject to this rule. Any expense not specifically exempted from the rules of § 461(h) or specifically treated as economically accruing before payment is treated as accruing only upon payment. Treas. Reg. § 1.461–4(g)(7). The date of payment is determined by applying the principles of cash method accounting. Treas. Reg. § 1.461–4(g)(1)(ii)(A). Treas. Reg. § 1.461–2(e)(2) states that a payment to a trust to provide for satisfaction of a contested claim with respect to which the economic performance rules of § 461(h) require payment to the claimant, such as tort and workers' compensation claims, or warranty claims, will not result in a deduction under § 461(f), discussed above.

3.   RECURRING ITEM EXCEPTION

The economic performance requirement does not apply to certain recurring expenses where economic performance occurs within 8½ months of the close of the year if the all events test is otherwise satisfied. Treas. Reg. § 1.461–5(b)(1) limits use of the recurring item exception to economic performance occurring by the *earlier* of the date the taxpayer files a timely return or 8½ months after the end of the taxable year. In any case where the taxpayer files a return on the normal due date, the period for performance is substantially reduced.

Section 461(h)(3)(C) provides that the recurring item exception does not apply to workers' compensation or tort liabilities. Treas. Reg. § 1.461–5(c) provides that the recurring item exception does not apply to liabilities arising from a violation of law (e.g., fines) or a breach of contract, or to any liability for which payment constitutes economic performance under the regulations because neither payment nor any other event is specifically designated as constituting economic performance. Because payment is specifically treated as economic performance for liabilities relating to (1) rebates and refunds, (2) awards, prizes, and jackpots, (3) insurance, warranty, and service contracts, and (4) taxes, these expenses may be accrued as deductions prior to payment under the recurring item rule.

4. CAPITAL EXPENDITURES

Treas. Reg. § 1.461–4(c)(1) provides that § 461(h) applies to capital expenditures. Thus, until economic performance has occurred, a liability relating to the acquisition of an asset cannot be included in its basis. This rule may affect the timing of depreciation deductions. For example, AmerGen Energy Co., LLC v. United States, 779 F.3d 1368 (Fed. Cir. 2015), applied the economic performance test to deny depreciation deductions for basis claimed by the taxpayer to be attributable to the assumption of future decommissioning costs of nuclear power plants. AmerGen purchased three nuclear power plants for a cash purchase price plus assumption of liabilities for decommissioning costs. The taxpayer included the liabilities in basis and claimed depreciation deductions using that basis. The court pointed to the language of § 461(h)(1), which applies the economic performance requirement for "purposes of this title" and with respect to "any item," to hold that the statutory requirement is not limited to expense deductions.

5. TRANSACTIONS BETWEEN CASH AND ACCRUAL METHOD TAXPAYERS

5.1. *General*

Transactions between cash method and accrual method taxpayers often result in differences in the timing of deduction and income inclusion. Suppose, for example, an accrual method taxpayer is obligated to make a deductible payment to a cash method taxpayer who has performed services but, under the terms of the agreement, the payment is not required to be made until a subsequent year. Since the liability for and amount of the payment are fixed, the accrual method taxpayer would be entitled to a deduction in the year in which the liability arises; on the income side, the cash method taxpayer would not be required to report income until the payment was actually received in the subsequent year. This "mismatching" of income inclusions and deductions generally has been acknowledged to be a problem because it affords taxpayers the opportunity artificially to reduce tax liabilities.

Two techniques are employed to insure the matching of income and deductions. In some situations, the accrual method taxpayer is required to postpone the deduction until the year in which the cash method taxpayer makes a corresponding inclusion in income. In effect, the accrual method taxpayer is put on the cash method in such transactions. This is the solution for compensation for services and most other payments to related parties. In other situations, the cash method taxpayer who is to receive income is required to recognize the income on an accrual method, thus accelerating income inclusion and matching it with the accrual method taxpayer's deduction. Section 1272, discussed in Chapter 32, adopts this technique with respect to interest income in some cases.

5.2. *Compensation for Services Received*

In situations involving services provided to the taxpayer, even economic performance may not give rise to an accrual method deduction. In addition to satisfying the requirements of § 461(h), the taxpayer must satisfy § 404 in order to claim a deduction. Under § 404 any amount due to a cash method taxpayer, whether an employee or an independent contractor, that is not paid until more than 2½ months after the end of the payor-taxpayer's taxable year generally is not deductible until the year that the payment is includable by the payee. If the payee is a cash method taxpayer, this rule can defer the deduction. See Temp. Reg. § 1.404(b)–1T, Q & A 2(a) and (b); Truck and Equipment Corp. of Harrisonburg v. Commissioner, 98 T.C. 141 (1992) (upholding the regulations in face of asserted "impracticality" of paying an employee's bonus prior to an audit of employer's books because the amount of the bonus due was ascertainable at the end of the year). For example, if the taxpayer hires an independent contractor to perform services, and the contractor is to be paid in four equal annual installments beginning in the year services are rendered, the first year's payment is deductible under normal accrual method rules. The amounts owed for years two, three and four are deductible only in those years as the payments are included by the independent contractor. Rev. Rul. 88–68, 1988–2 C.B. 117.

Section 404 applies to control the year for deducting deferred compensation whether the deferral is due to a formal plan, an *ad hoc* agreement, or an arbitrary delay in payment by the employer. See Avon Products, Inc. v. United States, 97 F.3d 1435 (Fed.Cir.1996). In Weaver v. Commissioner, 121 T.C. 273 (2003), an accrual method corporation was denied a deduction for payments for management services to a related cash method corporation where the amounts were not paid within 2½ months after the close of the payor's taxable year. The court indicated that transactions between related parties deserve special scrutiny in determining whether a transaction constituted a method or arrangement to defer the receipt of compensation by the service provider.

Section 404(a)(11) requires that the employee actually receive the compensation income, not merely be required to include it in income, in order for the employer to be entitled to a deduction. According to the legislative history, "actual receipt" does not include income inclusion by the employee under the economic benefit doctrine by virtue of the employer's obligation being secured by a letter of credit, delivery to the employee of a note (whether or not secured or guaranteed by a third party), or the making of a loan, payment of a refundable deposit, or a contingent payment. Furthermore, "[a]mounts set aside in trust for employees generally are not considered to be actually received by the employee." See H. Rep. No. 599, 105th Cong., 2d Sess., 175 (Conf. Rep. 1998). If the language in the Committee Report is broadly construed, § 404(a)(11) might apply to a transfer to an irrevocable trust for the benefit of an employee, even though in such a case § 83 requires current income recognition by the employee if the employee's rights to the trust corpus and income are not subject to a substantial risk of forfeiture. See Chapter 30, Section 2.B. On the other hand, if the employer actually has paid the funds over to the trust and the employee has included the amount pursuant to § 83, a current deduction is warranted and should be allowed under § 83(h) notwithstanding § 404(a)(11).

5.3. *Obligations to Related Cash Method Taxpayers*

Where related parties use different methods of accounting, some limitations are necessary to prevent the parties from avoiding tax by creating deductions that are not matched by a corresponding income inclusion. Suppose that in 2016 a corporation on the accrual method accrues, but does not pay, rent owed to a cash method stockholder-lessor or interest to a cash method stockholder-bondholder. If no limitations applied, the accrual method corporation would be entitled to a deduction in 2016, but the cash method individual would not be required to include the corresponding amount of income until it was received. The income recipient would be willing to postpone receipt because of the indirect benefit resulting from the current deduction taken by the accrual method related party. Section 267(a)(2) deals with this situation by deferring the deduction of the accrual method taxpayer until the year in which the amount is includable in the income of the related person to whom the payment is due. Section 267(b) sets forth the relationships in which the matching of deduction and income inclusion is required. Application of the rules in § 267(b)(2), which treat a shareholder and a corporation as related only if the shareholder directly or indirectly owns more than 50 percent of the corporation's stock, is particularly tricky because under the attribution rules a person is deemed to own stock of related individuals, such as the taxpayer's spouse, ancestors, descendants, and siblings, as well as other related entities. Thus, for example, § 267 applies to an amount owed by a corporation to a grandchild of its 51 percent owner.

(3) LONG-TERM CONTRACTS

INTERNAL REVENUE CODE: Section 460.

Accounting for the income from long-term contracts raises special problems in the context of annual accounting for accrual method taxpayers. Whether a long-term contract ultimately will be profitable or not depends on the relationship of the expenses incurred and the income to be generated over the life of the contract. Section 460(a) and the regulations thereunder permit the use of the "percentage of completion" method of accounting for certain long-term contracts (as defined in § 460(f)(1)) for the manufacture, building, installation, or construction of property. Only contracts for the manufacture of "unique" property not ordinarily carried in the taxpayer's finished goods inventory and property normally requiring more than twelve calendar months to complete qualify. Section 460 does not apply to contracts for the performance of services or the sale of goods regardless of the time required for performance.

Under the percentage of completion method, each year the taxpayer includes a portion of the estimated contract price according to the percentage of the contract completed during each taxable year. The percentage of the contract completed is determined by the ratio of costs incurred during the year to total estimated costs. Expenses are deducted in the year in which they are incurred under normal accounting principles, invariably using the accrual method. Any income not taken into account during the performance of the contract is included in the year after the contract is completed.

The object of the percentage of completion method is to allocate the gross income from the contract in relation to the rate at which the contract is being completed rather than to the year in which the right to payment accrues. This treatment can result in either a substantial benefit or detriment to the taxpayer. To ameliorate the effect of distortions, § 460(b)(2) requires that upon completing the contract the taxpayer must compare the taxes paid using the percentage of completion method and the taxes that would have been paid if the final contract price and expenses had been allocated year by year. If this "look-back" reveals that using the percentage of completion method resulted in accelerating taxable income, then the taxpayer is entitled to interest on the hypothetical loan to the government. Conversely, if the percentage of completion method resulted in deferral, the taxpayer must pay interest to the government. This interest payment provision does not apply to a contract that represents less than one percent of the taxpayer's average annual gross receipts, or, if less, $1,000,000. Taxpayers may elect not to be subject to the look-back rule in *de minimis* cases, instances where for each contract year prior to the year of completion, the cumulative taxable income (or loss) under the contract determined using estimated contract price and costs is within 10 percent of the cumulative taxable income (or loss) determined using actual contract price and costs.

Section 460(e) and Treas. Regs. §§ 1.460–3(b) and –4(d) permit the "completed contract method" to be used for certain "home construction contracts" or with respect to contracts that will be performed within two years by a taxpayer whose average gross receipts do not exceed $10,000,000. Under the completed contract method, income is reported only in the year in which the contract is completed, i.e., the year in which final completion and acceptance of performance have occurred. Costs allocable to the contract are also deductible only in the year in which the contract is completed. Other expenses which are not directly allocable to the contract (so-called "period" costs) are deducted currently. The completed contract method thus provides taxpayers with the opportunity to defer income (since none of the profit from the contract is taken into income until the contract is completed) and accelerate deductions (since many expenses associated with the deferred income may be deducted currently) and hence its use is greatly restricted.

SECTION 4.   INVENTORY ACCOUNTING

INTERNAL REVENUE CODE: Sections 263A(a)–(c), (f); 471; 472(a)–(c).

REGULATIONS: Sections 1.471–1; –2(a)–(c); –3(a)–(b); –4(a)–(c); –11(a).

A taxpayer whose business involves manufacturing or selling goods is not allowed to deduct the cost of manufacturing or purchasing goods when paid or incurred and include the full proceeds of sales in income when received. Rather, "in every case in which the production, purchase, or sale of merchandise is a material income producing factor," the taxpayer must maintain inventories. Treas. Reg. § 1.471–1. This requirement can apply to businesses that are primarily service businesses but which sell goods ancillary to services. See Wilkinson-Beane, Inc. v. Commissioner, 420 F.2d 352 (1st Cir.1970) (funeral home was required to inventory caskets even though they were sold only in conjunction with services); Rev. Rul. 74–279, 1974–1 C.B. 110 (optometrist must inventory glasses). But in RACMP Enterprises, Inc. v. Commissioner, 114 T.C. 211 (2000), the Tax Court held that a construction contracting company that constructed concrete foundations, driveways, and walkways was not required to use the accrual method but could use the cash method to account for its income and expenses for the cost of concrete and other materials. The court held that the taxpayer was in the business of providing services, not of selling merchandise, and that the concrete material was an indispensable and inseparable part of the provision of that service. In Smith v. Commissioner, T.C. Memo 2000–353, the Tax Court found *RACMP Enterprises, Inc.* to be a controlling precedent and held that a flooring contractor who installed custom ordered, and often custom designed, flooring was not required to maintain inventories or use the accrual method. Rather, the taxpayer was a service provider because he installed only floor coverings that were specially ordered from the manufacturer to the customer's specifications and did not maintain a stock of goods to sell to the public (although he did maintain a stock of supplies).

Maintenance of inventories results in capitalizing these costs and recovering them when the items are sold. Treas. Reg. § 1.61–3(a) provides that "in a manufacturing, merchandising, or mining business, 'gross income' means the total sales, less the cost of goods sold." Inventory accounting matches expenses with the income that they produce and is analogous to the rules for prepaid expenses, which are generally not deductible regardless of the accounting method employed. Indeed, the matching principle is so strong that Treas. Reg. § 1.446–1(c)(2) requires the use of the accrual method with respect to inventories. Small nonmanufacturing businesses sometimes may use the cash method for such noninventory items as rent, utilities, interest, and salaries. Treas. Reg. § 1.446–1(c)(1)(iv); Stoller v. United States, 320 F.2d 340 (Ct.Cl.1963).

Inventory costs generally are recovered upon the sale of inventory items. Thus, it is necessary to establish the cost of goods sold during the taxable year. This amount is determined by the use of opening and closing inventories. The opening inventory figure represents goods that are on hand at the beginning of the accounting period. If the taxpayer makes no purchases during the year, the correspondingly smaller closing inventory will reflect those sales made during the year. The difference between opening and closing inventories, the cost of goods sold, is subtracted from the proceeds of sales to determine the income from sales made in the period. If purchases are made during the year, they are added to the opening inventory in order to determine the cost of goods available for sale. If the purchased goods remain on hand at the end of the year, they will be reflected in the closing inventory, which is subtracted from the goods available for sale in arriving at the cost of goods sold for the period. Thus, the beginning inventory of a taxpayer for a taxable period represents costs incurred in earlier years that relate to income that is to be realized in the current year or in a future period. The ending inventory for the period represents the costs of the current or past year periods that relate to income that will be realized in a future taxable period.

The following example illustrates the computation of the cost of goods sold and its role in computing gross income:

Gross Sales		$100,000
Less: Cost of Goods Sold:		
Beginning Inventory	$20,000	
Plus: Purchases	$50,000	
Cost of Goods Available for Sale	$70,000	
Less: Ending Inventory	$30,000	
Cost of Goods Sold		$ 40,000
Gross Income		$ 60,000

In the above example, if the ending inventory were increased by $10,000, the cost of goods sold would decrease by that amount, and gross income thus would increase by $10,000; conversely if the ending inventory were decreased by $10,000, the cost of goods sold would increase by that amount and gross income thus would decrease by that amount.

DETAILED ANALYSIS

1.   COMPONENTS OF INVENTORY "COST"

The allocation of costs to inventory items requires the capitalization of many costs that otherwise would be deductible. Section 263A, discussed in Chapter 13, Section 1.2.3, requires the use of the "full absorption" method for determining which costs must be allocated to inventory. Under the full absorption method, not only must direct material and labor costs, including transportation of raw materials, labor, utilities, depreciation, and repairs with respect to manufacturing plant be included in inventory, but all overhead costs that are incident to and necessary for production or manufacturing operations or processes must also be so allocated. This includes, for example, depreciation, repair expenses, and utility bills on an allocable portion of administrative facilities, state property taxes, employee benefit plan costs, and an allocable portion of salaries for general administration. Some marketing costs may be inventory costs. See Rev. Rul. 89–23, 1989–1 C.B. 85, modified, Rev. Proc. 90–63, 1990–2 C.B. 664 (package design costs). Sales and advertising expenses, however, are not treated as inventory costs.

Interest expense generally is not treated as an inventory cost, even if the interest is on a loan traced to the cost of purchasing or manufacturing inventory. However, interest allocable to producing inventory items that take more than two years to manufacture (one year if the cost exceeds $1,000,000) or tangible property with a class life for depreciation purposes of twenty years or more is an inventory cost. I.R.C. § 263A(f).

Large wholesalers and retailers also must inventory indirect costs, including (1) off-site storage and warehousing costs, (2) wages, salaries, and other expenses incurred to purchase inventory, (3) handling, processing, assembly, repackaging, and similar costs, and (4) general and administrative costs allocable to these functions. However, a taxpayer who purchases inventory for resale and has average gross receipts that do not exceed $10,000,000 is not required to capitalize indirect costs. I.R.C. § 263A(b)(2)(B).

2.   METHODS OF IDENTIFYING INVENTORY COSTS

2.1. *Generally*

Determining the cost of goods sold requires some method to establish which items have been sold during the year and which remain and are thus included in the closing inventory. If the costs of a particular type of inventory item vary, for example, because of changes in the prices of items purchased or in the costs of production, the method adopted will affect calculation of gross income for the year.

In some cases—for example, sales of subdivision homes by a real estate developer or sales of registered property, such as motor vehicles or large boats—this identification is not difficult and the "specific item" method may be used. See Treas. Reg. § 1.471–2(d). Indeed, real estate dealers are required to use the specific identification method. W.C. & A.N. Miller Development Co. v. Commissioner, 81 T.C. 619 (1983); Rev. Rul. 86–149, 1986–2 C.B. 67. For many businesses, however, it is difficult to identify particular items of inventory and relate them to their actual costs. Under these circumstances, two principal methods are authorized for identifying inventory costs.

2.2. *Conventions*

2.2.1. *First-in, First-out (FIFO)*

Under the "first-in, first-out" (FIFO) method, it is assumed that the first items that entered inventory are also the first items to be sold. Assume, for example, that a television dealer had on hand at the beginning of the year five televisions for which it had paid $100 each. In the first half of the year the dealer bought an additional five televisions, paying $120 each, and in the second half of the year the dealer bought yet another five televisions, paying $140 for each television. The dealer sold eleven televisions for $200 each, for gross sales of $2,200. Under the FIFO method, the dealer is treated as having sold the five televisions on hand at the beginning of the year that cost $100 each, the five purchased in the first half of the year that cost $120 each, and one of the televisions that cost $140. Closing inventory consists of four televisions that cost $140 each ($560). The cost of goods sold is computed by adding the opening inventory ($500), the purchases during the year ($1,300) and subtracting the closing inventory ($560); thus the cost of goods sold was $1,240, and the dealer realized gross income of $960.

In a period of stable or falling prices, the FIFO method is acceptable or even beneficial to the taxpayer. On the other hand, when prices are rising, the FIFO method increases profits by relating the lower historical costs to the higher current sales income. Accordingly, an alternative method, the "last-in, first-out" (LIFO) method authorized by § 472 is available at the taxpayer's election. Once a taxpayer has chosen one method or the other, the taxpayer must obtain the consent of the IRS to change. See infra.

2.2.2. *Last-in, First-out (LIFO)*

Under the LIFO method, the last items that entered into inventory are deemed to be disposed of first. Assume that the television dealer in the preceding example used the LIFO method. Under the LIFO method, the dealer sold the five televisions purchased in the last half of the year that cost $140 each, the five purchased in the first half of the year that cost $120 each, and one of the televisions on hand at the beginning of the year that cost $100. Closing inventory consists of four televisions that cost $100 each ($400). The cost of goods sold is computed by adding the opening inventory ($500), the purchases during the year ($1,300), and subtracting the closing inventory ($400); thus the cost of goods sold was $1,400, and the dealer realized gross income of $800 (compared to $960 under FIFO).

In a period of rising prices, the LIFO method thus will relate current costs to current income. On the other hand, if it ever becomes necessary to liquidate all or part of the lower-cost inventory that was acquired first, then there may be a large amount of income realized in the year of liquidation. Taxpayers occasionally try to avoid penetration of lower cost LIFO inventory layers through manipulations, such as purchasing a large amount of purported inventory at year end and reselling it in bulk early the following year. Such items are not properly includable in closing inventory if not actually held for sale to customers. See United States v. Ingredient Technology Corp., 698 F.2d 88 (2d Cir.1983)

Section 472(a) and Treas. Reg. §§ 1.472–2 and 1.472–3 impose various conditions on the taxpayer's right to elect to use the LIFO method. Section 472(c) and (e) require that, if the taxpayer uses the LIFO method for tax purposes, it must likewise use that method for financial reporting purposes. Failure to comply with the conformity rule will result in the termination of the right to use the LIFO method for tax purposes. See Treas. Reg. § 1.472–2(e). Compare Rev. Rul. 88–84, 1988–2 C.B. 124 (use of an inventory method other than LIFO in financial forecasts does not violate the conformity requirement).

The regulations under §§ 471 and 472 seek to provide objective rules to determine beginning and ending inventory values to assure a clear reflection of income. The basic rule is that inventory must be valued at the lower of original cost or current market value. However, if the taxpayer uses the LIFO method, it must value the inventory at cost, rather than at the lower of cost or market.

3. "LOWER OF COST OR MARKET"

Initially, the only method permitted for valuing inventories for tax purposes was the cost method. However, since 1917, regulations (currently Treas. Reg. § 1.471–4) have authorized the use of the lower of cost or market as the method of inventory valuation. Under the regulations, market means the replacement cost of the asset. Thus, in a period of falling prices, the ability to use the lower of cost or market in effect allows the taxpayer a deduction for an unrealized loss. The taxpayer must establish the amount of the loss through objective evidence such as by sales or by actually offering the items for sale at the lower price (followed by actual sales at that price) if the write-down is to be allowed. Thor Power Tool Co. v. Commissioner, 439 U.S. 522 (1979).

In Thomas v. Commissioner, 92 T.C. 206 (1989), the taxpayer adopted an inventory method under which unsold inventory automatically was written-down to zero after two years and nine months. The court upheld the Commissioner's decision that this method did not clearly reflect income. The fact that the taxpayer had consistently used the method for fifty years and it had not been challenged on prior audits did not validate the method.

Rev. Rul. 83–59, 1983–1 C.B. 103, held that purported sales of "excess" inventory to a third party did not allow the taxpayer to reduce its closing inventory. The terms of the "sales" were such that the taxpayer retained dominion and control over the inventory and hence did not meet the tests of *Thor Power Tool*. Accord Paccar, Inc. v. Commissioner, 849 F.2d 393 (9th Cir.1988). In Rexnord, Inc. v. United States, 940 F.2d 1094 (7th Cir.1991), the taxpayer sold inventory of spare parts to another party and claimed a loss. Although the purchaser acquired legal title and the right to resell the inventory, the seller-taxpayer was the only economically viable purchaser because of the unique nature of the parts, which had no value to anyone else. Accordingly, the sale was not respected.

4. ELECTIVE SIMPLIFIED TREATMENT FOR SMALL BUSINESSES

Rev. Proc. 2001–10, 2001–1 C.B. 272, permits any business with average annual gross receipts of $1 million or less to use the cash method, rather than the accrual method, and to use a simplified method of accounting for the purchase and sale of inventory items. A business that adopts the cash method under this revenue procedure treats inventory items as materials and supplies that are not incidental under Treas. Reg. § 1.162–3. This treatment requires the taxpayer to capitalize the cost or actual purchases of goods or materials to be resold or incorporated into manufactured products and to offset the capitalized amounts against the amount realized when the goods are resold, but the taxpayer may deduct currently all other manufacturing and handling costs (including labor, warehousing, and other direct and indirect costs that normally must be capitalized under § 263A).

Subsequently, the IRS granted certain "small business" taxpayers even greater dispensation from the maintenance of inventories and use of the accrual method of accounting. Citing the discretion granted to the IRS in §§ 446 and 471, Rev. Proc. 2002–28, 2002–1 C.B. 815, allows qualifying small business taxpayers with "average annual gross receipts" of more than $1 million but less than $10 million to use the cash receipts and disbursements method of accounting, as described in the revenue procedure, with respect to eligible trades or businesses. Any taxpayer whose principal business is the provision of services—including the provision of property incident to those services—is eligible to use the cash method, as are taxpayers whose principal business activity is the fabrication or modification of tangible personal property upon demand in accordance with customer design or specifications. Other businesses qualify unless they are "ineligible." Ineligible businesses include ones that derive the largest percentage of gross receipts from any of the following activities: (a) mining activities within the meaning of North American Industry Classification System (NAICS) codes 211 and 212; (b) manufacturing within the meaning of NAICS codes 31–33; (c) wholesale trade within the meaning of NAICS code 42; (d) retail trade within the meaning of NAICS codes 44–45; and, (e) information industries within the meaning of NAICS codes 5111 and 5122. Lists of the types of businesses within the various NAICS codes for ineligible businesses can be found on the Census Bureau's website. Among the eligible businesses are those that perform services such as janitorial, medical, veterinary, photo developing, and repairs (including auto repair), as well as restaurants, bars, hotels, and funeral homes.

SECTION 5. CHANGES IN METHOD OF ACCOUNTING OR METHOD OF REPORTING INCOME

INTERNAL REVENUE CODE: Sections 446(e); 481.

REGULATIONS: Section 1.446–1(e)(2), (3).

Section 446(e) provides that a taxpayer who changes a method of accounting must, before computing income for tax purposes under the new method, secure the consent of the IRS to the change. The purpose of this requirement is threefold: (1) from the standpoint of orderly tax administration, the IRS must know of the new method of accounting; (2) notification gives the IRS an opportunity to determine whether the proposed new method will clearly reflect the income of the taxpayer; and (3) notification gives the IRS an opportunity to require adjustments in the year of the change in order that the change in method of accounting will not produce a tax windfall to the taxpayer.

The third aspect has caused the most difficulty. When a taxpayer changes from one method of accounting to another, adjustments may be necessary to prevent an item from being deducted twice or to prevent it from being completely eliminated. Thus, if a taxpayer incorrectly on the cash method changes to the accrual method and uses as the opening inventory figure the cost of goods then on hand, which cost was deducted in earlier years under the cash method, a double deduction will in effect have been taken for those costs. Similarly, if the taxpayer considered existing accounts receivable as having previously accrued though they were not included in income under the cash method, those accounts would never be taxed. Conversely, it may be the taxpayer who desires adjustments. Thus, if a taxpayer erroneously had been treating accounts payable on a cash method, a change to the proper accrual method might eliminate from deductions any accounts paid in the current year but accrued in an earlier year.

Before the enactment of § 481, some cases had held that where the IRS initiated the change in accounting method, adjustments could only be obtained for years in which the statute of limitations was still open. See e.g., Commissioner v. Dwyer, 203 F.2d 522 (2d Cir.1953). Section 481 responded to these cases by requiring that appropriate adjustments be taken into account in the year of the change in order to prevent amounts from being duplicated or omitted.

DETAILED ANALYSIS

1.   TREATMENT OF YEAR OF CHANGE ADJUSTMENTS

A distortion of income could result if the adjustment in income attributable to the year of change had to be taken into account in a single taxable year. Accordingly, mechanisms are available for spreading the adjustment over several years. Rev. Proc. 2015–13, 2015–5 I.R.B. 419, amplified and clarified by Rev. Proc. 2002–54, 2002–2 C.B. 432, deals with situations in which the taxpayer has requested a change of accounting method. In general, a positive adjustment (increasing taxable income) will be taken into account over four years, and a negative adjustment (decreasing taxable income) will be taken into account in the year of the change.

Where the change in accounting method is initiated by the IRS, the adjustment in principle is to be made in the year of change. However, under § 481(c), the taxpayer and the IRS can agree to attribute the adjustment to other taxable years. See Rev. Proc. 2002–18, 2002–1 C.B. 678. In addition, § 481(b) provides special rules that allow for a limited allocation of the adjustment to other years where it is in excess of $3,000.

Section 481 does not authorize voluntary retroactive changes in accounting methods, but the IRS has discretion to permit a retroactive change of method. Rev. Proc. 97–27, supra. At the same time, the IRS may compel a retroactive change from an improper method to a proper method for years not barred by the statute of limitations. Ralston Development Corp. v. United States, 937 F.2d 510 (10th Cir.1991).

2.   WHAT IS A "CHANGE IN ACCOUNTING METHOD?"

The adjustments required by § 446(e) and § 481(a) have important implications for the statute of limitations. Adjustments can be required to be taken into account in the year of change (or the applicable "spread period") even though those adjustments in effect relate to years that are otherwise barred by the statute of limitations. These adjustments occur only if the change constitutes a change in accounting method. If it is simply a change in the treatment of a particular item, no adjustments are permissible in years that are barred by the statute of limitations. See e.g., Witte v. Commissioner, 513 F.2d 391 (D.C.Cir.1975).

Treas. Reg. § 1.446–1(e)(2)(ii)(*a*) provides that a change in the method of accounting includes "a change in the overall plan of accounting for gross income or deductions or a change in the treatment of any material item used in such overall plan." A "material item" is defined as "any item which involves the proper time for the inclusion of the item in income or the taking of a deduction." Thus in the case of the treatment of material items, it is the timing of the inclusion or the deduction that is determinative, not the amount. A change involving the method of valuing inventories has been held to be a change in accounting method. See Fruehauf Corp. v. Commissioner, 356 F.2d 975 (6th Cir.1966) (change in valuation of assets from historical value to lower of cost or market).

Under Treas. Reg. § 1.446–1(e)(2)(ii)(*b*), a change in method of accounting does not include the correction of mathematical errors or errors in the computation of tax liability. See North Carolina Granite Corp. v. Commissioner, 43 T.C. 149 (1964) (correction in method of computing percentage depletion is not a change in method of accounting). Discontinuing an accounting method that results in recurring improper deductions may be a change of accounting method. Copy Data, Inc. v. Commissioner, 91 T.C. 26 (1988) (discontinuance of improper "reserve" for future warranty expenses was a change of accounting resulting in a § 481 adjustment); see also Rev. Rul. 90–38, 1990–1 C.B. 57 (erroneous treatment of a material item on two or more consecutively filed tax returns is a "method of accounting"). Adjustments of items that do not affect timing, but only characterization, i.e., dividend instead of salary, do not constitute changes in method of accounting. See Underhill v. Commissioner, 45 T.C. 489 (1966). The change from immediate expensing of an item to capitalization plus depreciation is treated as a change in the method of accounting. Treas. Regs. §§ 1.167(e)–1(a) and 1.446–1(e)(2)(ii)(a) & (d) provide that any change in depreciation (other than a change in the useful life of an asset depreciated solely under § 167, without reference to § 168) is generally treated as a change of accounting method.

A change from an impermissible method of accounting to a permissible method of accounting requires the consent of the IRS. In Commissioner v. O. Liquidating Corp., 292 F.2d 225 (3d Cir.1961), an accrual method taxpayer could not change its method of accounting for insurance dividends without the Commissioner's consent, even though the taxpayer was accruing dividends for the wrong years and its new method of accounting would have treated the dividends properly. See also Rev. Rul. 75–56, 1975–1 C.B. 98 (taxpayer improperly capitalized taxes and carrying charges without making an election under § 266; held, taxpayer could not file amended returns for open years taking deductions for the expenditures as that constituted a change in accounting method for those years for which no consent had been received).

CHAPTER 29

THE ANNUAL ACCOUNTING CONCEPT

SECTION 1. TRANSACTIONAL PROBLEMS

A. GENERAL PRINCIPLES

Burnet v. Sanford & Brooks Co.

Supreme Court of the United States, 1931.
282 U.S. 359.

■ MR. JUSTICE STONE delivered the opinion of the Court.

* * *

From 1913 to 1915, inclusive, respondent, a Delaware corporation engaged in business for profit, was acting for the Atlantic Dredging Company in carrying out a contract for dredging the Delaware River, entered into by that company with the United States. In making its income tax returns for the years 1913 to 1916, respondent added to gross income for each year the payments made under the contract that year, and deducted its expenses paid that year in performing the contract. The total expenses exceeded the payments received by $176,271.88. The tax returns for 1913, 1915 and 1916 showed net losses. That for 1914 showed net income.

In 1915 work under the contract was abandoned, and in 1916 suit was brought in the Court of Claims to recover for a breach of warranty of the character of the material to be dredged. Judgment for the claimant * * * was affirmed by this Court in 1920. United States v. Atlantic Dredging Co., 253 U.S. 1. It held that the recovery was upon the contract and was "compensatory of the cost of the work, of which the government got the benefit." From the total recovery, [the taxpayer] received in that year the sum of $192,577.59, which included the $176,271.88 by which its expenses under the contract had exceeded receipts from it, and accrued interest amounting to $16,305.71. Respondent having failed to include these amounts as gross income in its tax returns for 1920, the Commissioner made the deficiency assessment here involved, based on the addition of both items to gross income for that year.

The Court of Appeals ruled that * * * the item of $176,271.88 was a return of losses suffered by respondent in earlier years and hence was wrongly assessed as income. Notwithstanding this conclusion, its judgment of reversal and the consequent elimination of this item from gross income for 1920 were made contingent upon the filing by respondent of amended returns for the years 1913 to 1916, from which were to be omitted the deductions of the related items of expenses paid in those years. Respondent insists that as the Sixteenth Amendment and the Revenue Act of 1918, which was in force in 1920, plainly contemplate a tax only on net income or profits, any application of the statute which operates to impose a tax with respect to the present transaction, from which respondent received no profit, cannot be upheld. * * *

If respondent's contention that only gain or profit may be taxed under the Sixteenth Amendment be accepted without qualification * * * the question remains whether the gain or profit which is the subject of the tax may be ascertained, as here, on the basis of fixed accounting periods, or whether, as is pressed upon us, it can only be net profit ascertained on the basis of particular transactions of the taxpayer when they are brought to a conclusion.

All the revenue acts which have been enacted since the adoption of the Sixteenth Amendment have uniformly assessed the tax on the basis of annual returns showing the net result of all the taxpayer's transactions during a fixed accounting period, either the calendar year, or, at the option of the taxpayer, the particular fiscal year which he may adopt. Under §§ 230, 232 and 234(a) of the Revenue Act of 1918* * * , respondent was subject to tax upon its annual net income, arrived at by deducting from gross income for each taxable year all the ordinary and necessary expenses paid during that year in carrying on any trade or business, interest and taxes paid, and losses sustained, during the year. By §§ 233(a) and 213(a) gross income "includes * * * income derived from * * * businesses * * * or the transaction of any business carried on for gain or profit, or gains or profits and income derived from any source whatever." The amount of all such items is required to be included in the gross income for the taxable year in which received by the taxpayer, unless they may be properly accounted for on the accrual basis under § 212(b). * * *

That such receipts from the conduct of a business enterprise are to be included in the taxpayer's return as a part of gross income, regardless of whether the particular transaction results in net profit, sufficiently appears from the quoted words of § 213(a) and from the character of the deductions allowed. Only by including these items of gross income in the 1920 return would it have been possible to ascertain respondent's net income for the period covered by the return, which is what the statute taxes. The excess of gross income over deductions did not any the less constitute net income for the taxable period because respondent, in an earlier period, suffered net losses in the conduct of its business which were in some measure attributable to expenditures made to produce the net income of the later period.

* * *

A taxpayer may be in receipt of net income in one year and not in another. The net result of the two years, if combined in a single taxable period, might still be a loss; but it has never been supposed that fact would relieve him from a tax on the first, or that it affords any reason for postponing the assessment of the tax until the end of a lifetime, or for some other indefinite period, to ascertain more precisely whether the final outcome of the period, or of a given transaction, will be a gain or a loss.

The Sixteenth Amendment was adopted to enable the government to raise revenue by taxation. It is the essence of any system of taxation that it should produce revenue ascertainable, and payable to the government, at regular intervals. Only by such a system is it practicable to produce a regular flow of income and apply methods of accounting, assessment, and collection capable of practical operation. It is not suggested that there has ever been any general scheme for taxing income on any other basis. * * *

The assessment was properly made under the statutes. Relief from their alleged burdensome operation which may not be secured under these provisions, can be afforded only by legislation, not by the courts.

Reversed.

DETAILED ANALYSIS

1. GENERAL

Sanford & Brooks established that each annual accounting period generally is treated as a separate compartment so that the income and deductions of one year have no effect upon other periods. This is an important rule of tax administration. Consider the tax administrative implications of the Court of Appeals holding in *Sanford & Brooks,* reversed by the Supreme Court, that the receipts in 1920 should be accounted for by amending the tax returns for earlier years.

Yet the application of a strict annual accounting period concept as in *Sanford & Brooks* produces serious problems. One general type of problem relates to the effect of the annual accounting period on transactions affecting two or more years. Thus, as in *Sanford & Brooks,* a business may suffer losses on a project or contract in one year but make a profit on that same project in a later year. The loss and profit could be viewed as one transaction so that the separate items should be combined to yield a final net amount. Suppose an employee receives a bonus that she includes in gross income. Several years later it is learned that the bonus was incorrectly computed and a portion must be repaid, raising the question of how to treat these two transactions and whether relief from a strict annual accounting concept should be provided.

The annual accounting concept also causes problems where a taxpayer has bunched or fluctuating income from separate transactions. If the annual accounting concept is rigidly followed, progressive rates will yield a higher tax than that which would have been due if the income had been earned in a more even pattern. This problem arises in many different contexts. An athlete may have a limited period of very high earnings early in his career followed by lower earning years, or a doctor or lawyer may have a high earning period concentrated later in her career. Similarly, a salesman may have an unusually good year in which commissions are extraordinarily high. The fluctuations may result in a loss in one year followed by a profit in a subsequent year. Query whether the taxpayer in *Sanford & Brooks* would have received adequate relief if it could have used the earlier losses to offset the later income.

This Chapter considers a variety of situations in which departures from strict annual accounting have been permitted.

B. INITIAL DEDUCTION FOLLOWED BY LATER RECOVERY: THE TAX BENEFIT DOCTRINE

INTERNAL REVENUE CODE: Section 111(a), (b), (c).

REGULATIONS: Section 1.111–1(a) (first paragraph).

Legislative, judicial and administrative forces have all operated to modify the annual accounting concept in situations in which an item is deducted in one taxable year and then subsequently recovered. Early case law developed the principle that where a deduction in a prior year had reduced the taxpayer's taxable income, a subsequent recovery of the deducted item had to be included in income. As a corollary to this principle, some courts took the position that, where the prior deduction did not result in a tax benefit to the taxpayer, that is, where the deduction in the prior year did not reduce taxable income because of the presence of other deductions, the subsequent recovery of the deducted item would not be taxable.

Sometimes these results were reached on equitable principles: it would be inequitable to allow the taxpayer to reduce the tax in a prior year by means of the deduction and not to pay tax on the recovery received later; conversely, it would be unfair to require inclusion where the item recovered had not previously resulted in a tax benefit. Other cases rest on an analysis of the basis provisions: if the taxpayer obtained a tax benefit from the prior deduction, the basis with respect to that item would be reduced and hence the recovery of the item would be gross income. On the other hand, if there was no tax benefit from the prior deduction, the taxpayer was treated as having maintained a basis for the item and the subsequent recovery not in excess of the basis was simply a return of capital. See Raytheon Production Corp. v. Commissioner, 144 F.2d 110 (1st Cir.1944).

Section 111(a) adopts the exclusionary view of the tax benefit rule by providing an exclusion from gross income for the recovery of an amount previously deducted that did not reduce the tax owed in a prior year.

Hillsboro National Bank v. Commissioner*

Supreme Court of the United States, 1983.
460 U.S. 370.

■ JUSTICE O'CONNOR delivered the opinion of the Court: [In 1972, a bank paid a state property tax imposed on its shareholders and deducted that amount under section 164(e). Because the validity of the tax was uncertain under the state constitution, the amount paid by the bank was placed in escrow. The tax was held unconstitutional and, pursuant to a state court decree, in 1973 the escrowed amount was paid directly to the bank's shareholders. The bank did not amend its 1972 return nor did it include the repaid amount in income in 1973. The Commissioner asserted that the bank was required to include the refunded amount in income in 1973 under the tax benefit rule; the taxpayer argued that the rule was inapplicable because it had not "recovered" any amount.]

The Government * * * relies solely on the tax benefit rule—a judicially developed principle that allays some of the inflexibilities of the annual accounting system. An annual accounting system is a practical necessity if the federal income tax is to produce revenue ascertainable and payable at regular intervals. Burnet v. Sanford & Brooks Co., 282 U.S. 359, 365. Nevertheless, strict adherence to an annual accounting system would create transactional inequities. Often an apparently completed transaction will reopen unexpectedly in a subsequent tax year, rendering the initial reporting improper. For instance, if a taxpayer held a note that became apparently uncollectable early in the taxable year, but the debtor made an unexpected financial recovery before the close of the year and paid the debt, the transaction would have no tax consequences for the taxpayer, for the repayment of the principal would be recovery of capital. If, however, the debtor's financial recovery and the resulting repayment took place after the close of the taxable year, the taxpayer would have a deduction for the apparently bad debt in the first year under § 166(a) of the Code. Without the tax benefit rule, the repayment in the second year, representing a return of capital, would not be taxable. The second transaction, then, although economically identical to the first, could, because of the differences in accounting, yield drastically different tax consequences. The Government, by allowing a deduction that it could not have known to be improper at the time, would be foreclosed from recouping any of the tax saved because of the improper deduction. Recognizing and seeking to avoid the possible distortions of income, the courts have long required the taxpayer to recognize the repayment in the second year as income. * * *

The taxpayers and the Government in these cases propose different formulations of the tax benefit rule. The taxpayers contend that the rule requires the inclusion of amounts *recovered* in later years, and they do

---

*   [Ed.: The Court's discussion of a companion case, United States v. Bliss Dairy, Inc., has been omitted.]

not view the events in these cases as "recoveries." The Government, on the other hand, urges that the tax benefit rule requires the inclusion of amounts previously deducted if later events are inconsistent with the deductions; it insists that no "recovery" is necessary to the application of the rule. Further, it asserts that the events in these cases are inconsistent with the deductions taken by the taxpayers. We are not in complete agreement with either view.

An examination of the purpose and accepted applications of the tax benefit rule reveals that a "recovery" will not always be necessary to invoke the tax benefit rule. The purpose of the rule is not simply to tax "recoveries." On the contrary, it is to approximate the results produced by a tax system based on transactional rather than annual accounting. * * * It has long been accepted that a taxpayer using accrual accounting who accrues and deducts an expense in a tax year before it becomes payable and who for some reason eventually does not have to pay the liability must then take into income the amount of the expense earlier deducted. * * * The bookkeeping entry cancelling the liability, though it increases the balance sheet net worth of the taxpayer, does not fit within any ordinary definition of "recovery." Thus, the taxpayers' formulation of the rule neither serves the purposes of the rule nor accurately reflects the cases that establish the rule. Further, the taxpayers' proposal would introduce an undesirable formalism into the application of the tax benefit rule. Lower courts have been able to stretch the definition of "recovery" to include a great variety of events. For instance, * * * payment to another party may be imputed to the taxpayer, giving rise to a recovery. See First Trust and Savings Bank v. United States, 614 F.2d 1142, 1146 (C.A.7 1980) (alternative holding). Imposition of a requirement that there be a recovery would, in many cases, simply require the Government to cast its argument in different and unnatural terminology, without adding anything to the analysis.

The basic purpose of the tax benefit rule is to achieve rough transactional parity in tax, * * * and to protect the Government and the taxpayer from the adverse effects of reporting a transaction on the basis of assumptions that an event in a subsequent year proves to have been erroneous. Such an event, unforeseen at the time of an earlier deduction, may in many cases require the application of the tax benefit rule. We do not, however, agree that this consequence invariably follows. Not every unforeseen event will require the taxpayer to report income in the amount of his earlier deduction. On the contrary, the tax benefit rule will "cancel out" an earlier deduction only when a careful examination shows that the later event is indeed fundamentally inconsistent with the premise on which the deduction was initially based.[15] That is, if that event had occurred within the same taxable year, it would have

---

[15]   JUSTICE STEVENS accuses us of creating confusion at this point in the analysis by requiring the courts to distinguish "inconsistent events" from "fundamentally inconsistent events." * * * . That line is not the line we draw; rather, we draw the line between merely unexpected events and inconsistent events.

foreclosed the deduction. In some cases, a subsequent recovery by the taxpayer will be the only event that would be fundamentally inconsistent with the provision granting the deduction. In such a case, only actual recovery by the taxpayer would justify application of the tax benefit rule. For example, if a calendar-year taxpayer made a rental payment on December 15 for a 30-day lease deductible in the current year under § 162(a)(3), see Treas. Reg. § 1.461–1(a)(1), (1982); e.g., Zaninovich v. Commissioner, 616 F.2d 429 (C.A.9 1980), the tax benefit rule would not require the recognition of income if the leased premises were destroyed by fire on January 10. The resulting inability of the taxpayer to occupy the building would be an event not fundamentally inconsistent with his prior deduction as an ordinary and necessary business expense under § 162(a). The loss is attributable to the business and therefore is consistent with the deduction of the rental payment as an ordinary and necessary business expense. On the other hand, had the premises not burned and, in January, the taxpayer decided to use them to house his family rather than to continue the operation of his business, he would have converted the leasehold to personal use. This would be an event fundamentally inconsistent with the business use on which the deduction was based. In the case of the fire, only if the lessor—by virtue of some provision in the lease—had refunded the rental payment would the taxpayer be required under the tax benefit rule to recognize income on the subsequent destruction of the building. In other words, the subsequent recovery of the previously deducted rental payment would be the only event inconsistent with the provision allowing the deduction. It therefore is evident that the tax benefit rule must be applied on a case-by-case basis. A court must consider the facts and circumstances of each case in the light of the purpose and function of the provisions granting the deductions.

* * *

The formulation that we endorse today follows clearly from the long development of the tax benefit rule. Justice Stevens' assertion that there is no suggestion in the early cases or from the early commentators that the rule could ever be applied in any case that did not involve a physical recovery * * * is incorrect. The early cases frequently framed the rule in terms consistent with our view and irreconcilable with that of the dissent. See Barnett v. Commissioner, 39 B.T.A. 864, 867 (1939) ("Finally, the present case is analogous to a number of others, where * * * [w]hen some event occurs which is *inconsistent* with a deduction taken in a prior year, adjustment may have to be made by reporting a balancing item in income for the year in which the change occurs.") (emphasis added); Estate of Block v. Commissioner, 39 B.T.A. 338 (1939) ("When recovery *or some other event which is inconsistent* with what has been done in the past occurs, adjustment must be made in reporting income for the year in which the change occurs.") (emphasis added) * * * . The reliance of the dissent on the early commentators is equally misplaced, for the articles cited in the dissent, like the early cases, often stated the rule in terms of inconsistent events.

Justice Stevens also suggests that we err in recognizing transactional equity as the reason for the tax benefit rule. It is difficult to understand why even the clearest recovery should be taxed if not for the concern with transactional equity * * * . Nor does the concern with transactional equity entail a change in our approach to the annual accounting system. Although the tax system relies basically on annual accounting, see Burnet v. Sanford & Brooks Co., 282 U.S. 359 (1931), the tax benefit rule eliminates some of the distortions that would otherwise arise from such a system. * * * The limited nature of the rule and its effect on the annual accounting principle bears repetition: *only* if the occurrence of the event in the earlier year would have resulted in the disallowance of the deduction can the Commissioner require a compensating recognition of income when the event occurs in the later year.

[The majority then went on to hold that the bank was not required to include in its 1973 income the amounts which had been refunded to its shareholders by the state. Curiously, the majority reached this result not by applying its analysis and reformulation of the tax benefit rule, but by a strained interpretation of the legislative history of section 164(e) which it viewed as allowing a deduction to the bank regardless of the use to which the state put the tax paid, i.e., in this case, repaying it to the bank shareholders.]

■ JUSTICE STEVENS, with whom JUSTICE MARSHALL joins, concurring * * * .

Today the Court declares that the purpose of the tax benefit rule is "to approximate the results produced by a tax system based on transactional rather than annual accounting." * * * Whereas the rule has previously been used to determine the character of a current wealth-enhancing event, when viewed in the light of past deductions, the Court now suggests that the rule requires a study of the propriety of earlier deductions, when viewed in the light of later events. The Court states that the rule operates to "cancel out" an earlier deduction if the premise on which it is based is "fundamentally inconsistent" with an event in a later year. * * *

The most striking feature of the rule's history is that from its early formative years, through codification, until the 1960's, Congress, the Internal Revenue Service, courts, and commentators, understood it in essentially the same way. They all saw it as a theory that appropriately characterized certain recoveries of capital as income. Although the rule undeniably helped to accommodate the annual accounting system to multi-year transactions, I have found no suggestion that it was regarded as a generalized method of approximating a transactional accounting system through the fabrication of income at the drop of a fundamentally inconsistent event. An inconsistent event was always a necessary condition, but with the possible exception of the discussion of the Board of Tax Appeals in Barnett v. Commissioner, 39 B.T.A. 864, 867 (1939), inconsistency was never by itself a sufficient reason for applying the rule. Significantly, the first case from this Court dealing with the tax benefit rule emphasized the role of a recovery.[11] And when litigants in this Court suggested that a transactional accounting system would be more equitable, we expressly declined to impose one, stressing the importance of finality and practicability in a tax system.[12]

Today, the Court again has before it a case in which the Commissioner, with the endorsement of some commentators and a closely divided Tax Court, is pushing for a more ambitious tax benefit rule. This time, the Court accepts the invitation. Since there has been no legislation * * * suggesting that our approach over the past half-century has been wrong-headed, * * * the new doctrine that emerges from today's decision is of the Court's own making.

* * *

DETAILED ANALYSIS

1.   THE INCLUSIONARY ASPECT OF THE TAX BENEFIT RULE

1.1. *General*

The tax benefit test propounded by the majority in *Hillsboro* requires that the subsequent "event" be analyzed in terms of the impact it would have had on the initially claimed deduction if it had taken place in the same taxable year in which the deduction was claimed. If the hypothetical conjunction of the deduction and the subsequent event would have resulted in the deduction being disallowed in the earlier year, then income inclusion is required in the subsequent year. The concurring opinion would require the subsequent event to be a "recovery" of the previously taken deduction in order for the tax benefit rule to apply.

Despite the difference in formulations, the two tests produce the same results in most circumstances since generally the inconsistent "event" is in fact a recovery of the previously-taken deduction, e.g., subsequent repayment of a previously written-off debt. It is principally in cases involving the relation between corporations and shareholders (of which *Hillsboro* itself is a peculiar example) that the difference in formulation is consequential. Thus, in United States v. Bliss Dairy, Inc., a companion case to *Hillsboro,* a corporation deducted the cost of feed and subsequently distributed the feed to its shareholders as part of a corporate liquidation. The majority held the

---

[11]   In Dobson v. Commissioner, 320 U.S. 489 (1943), the taxpayer had bought stock, sold it at a loss, and then claimed a deductible loss on his tax return. Eight years later, the taxpayer had sued for rescission of the stock purchase, claiming fraud; he settled the suit and received approximately $30,000 for the stock on which he had sustained the loss. We upheld the Tax Court's determination that the $30,000 recovery did not need to be reported as income, since the earlier deductible losses had not reduced the taxpayer's taxes in the year he had claimed them. * * *

[12]   Burnet v. Sanford & Brooks Co., 282 U.S. 359 (1931), was a mirror image of this case. * * *

tax benefit rule was applicable. It found that the distribution to shareholders of assets for which a deduction had previously been taken was "inconsistent" with the initial deduction since the deduction was "predicated on the consumption of the asset in the trade or business." The dissent would not have applied the tax benefit rule since the distribution of the property in liquidation did not result in a "recovery."

When the inclusionary aspect of the tax benefit rule applies, the subsequent inclusion is subject to the tax rates applicable to the taxpayer in the year of the subsequent event, even though that rate may be higher or lower than the taxpayer's marginal tax rate in the year in which the deduction was taken. Thus, the tax benefit rule may only roughly approximate the results that the transaction would have generated if the two events had taken place in the same year. At one time, the Court of Claims followed a variation of the tax benefit rule under which the amount of recovery was not included in income but the tax for the year of recovery was increased by the amount of tax saved by the deduction in the prior year. See Perry v. United States, 160 F.Supp. 270 (Ct.Cl.1958). This approach, while sound in eliminating the impact of differences in tax rates in the two years, was without support in either the prior case law or the Code. In 1967, the Court of Claims overruled the *Perry* decision and now follows the "normal" rule. Alice Phelan Sullivan Corp. v. United States, 381 F.2d 399 (Ct.Cl.1967).

1.2. *Interaction with the Statute of Limitations*

Where the taxpayer improperly claims a deduction in a prior year for which the statute of limitations has run, some courts have held that the taxpayer is not required to include the recovery in income in the subsequent year even though the deduction resulted in a tax benefit. Streckfus Steamers, Inc. v. Commissioner, 19 T.C. 1 (1952) (Nonacq.); Southern Pacific Transportation Co. v. Commissioner, 75 T.C. 497 (1980). In Canelo v. Commissioner, 53 T.C. 217 (1969) (Nonacq.), aff'd, 447 F.2d 484 (9th Cir.1971), the taxpayer, an attorney, deducted advances to his clients for litigation costs in the years made and, if the advances were subsequently repaid, included the repayment in income. The IRS asserted and the Tax Court agreed that the payments were actually loans and were not deductible in the years made. The court, however, citing *Streckfus Steamers,* held that recoveries of "loans" previously deducted in years now closed by the statute of limitations were not income: "[R]espondent falls back to the 'tax benefit' rule and relies on it. * * * However, the 'tax benefit' rule applies only when the initial deduction was proper; it does not allow the Commissioner to increase a taxpayer's income by the amount of a deduction taken *improperly* in a year now closed by the statute of limitations. * * * We realize that petitioners herein have received a windfall through the improper deductions. But the statute of limitations requires eventual repose. The 'tax benefit' rule disturbs that repose only if respondent had no cause to question the initial deduction, that is, if the deduction was proper at the time it was taken. Here the deduction was improper, and respondent should have challenged it before the years prior to 1960 were closed by the statute of limitations." However, in Mayfair Minerals, Inc. v. Commissioner, 456 F.2d 622 (5th Cir.1972), where the taxpayer's disclosure of improper deductions on its returns was misleading, the fact that the statute of limitations had run did not prevent the application of the tax benefit rule to the subsequent recoveries. The court found the taxpayer estopped by its conduct from claiming the benefit of the *Streckfus Steamers* exception to the tax benefit rule. See also Hughes & Luce, L.L.P. v. Commissioner, 70 F.3d 16 (5th Cir.1995) (requiring a law firm to include reimbursements of amounts advanced to clients in previous years that had been erroneously deducted in the years the advances were made). The improper deduction exception also was rejected in Unvert v. Commissioner, 656 F.2d 483 (9th Cir.1981): "The decisions creating and applying the tax benefit rule make clear that the recovery must be taxed because it previously created a tax benefit, not because of the inherent characteristic of the recovery [as income or the return of capital]. * * * The erroneous deduction exception is also poor public policy. A taxpayer who properly claims a deduction for an expenditure that is recovered in a later year must treat the recovery as income, while one who claims an improper deduction may not be required to include the recovery as income only because of the impropriety of the deduction. * * * [I]mproperly taken tax deductions should not be rewarded." In 885 Investment Co. v. Commissioner, 95 T.C. 156 (1990), the Tax Court, applying the *Golsen* rule, followed *Unvert* in a case appealable to the Ninth Circuit, but indicated that in other circumstances it would continue to follow *Streckfus Steamers*.

2.   THE EXCLUSIONARY ASPECT OF THE TAX BENEFIT RULE

Section 111(a) codifies the tax benefit rule by providing that gross income does not include the recovery of any amount deducted in a prior year to the extent that the deduction did not reduce tax in the prior year. Section 111(a) originally applied on its face only to the recovery of previously deducted bad debts and taxes. In 1984 it was amended to eliminate any limitations on its scope, but this was a mere formality since the courts and regulations had previously taken that step. See e.g., Rosen v. Commissioner, 611 F.2d 942 (1st Cir.1980) (charitable contribution returned to donor). Section 111(b) was added to apply the tax benefit rule to recovered amounts relating to items for which certain tax credits had previously been claimed. Section 111(c) provides that a deduction is treated as having produced a reduction in tax in a prior year if that deduction increased a loss carryover that had not expired at the end of the taxable year in which the recovery occurred. (Loss carryovers are discussed in Section 2 of this chapter.) This rule, coupled with the expansive period for the carryover of net operating losses, significantly diminishes the importance of the exclusionary tax benefit rule as far as profit-seeking deductions are concerned. It remains important, however, with respect to itemized deductions for personal living expenses, such as refunds of home mortgage interest, see Rev. Rul. 92–91, 1992–2 C.B. 49 (refund of erroneously computed excessive interest on adjustable rate home mortgage), and state and local taxes.

The exclusionary aspect also raises a question similar to that presented in *Hillsboro*: Is the later event related to the earlier transaction that gave rise to the deduction or is it a separate transaction whose tax consequences are to be determined independently? In Rev. Rul. 66–320, 1966–2 C.B. 37, the taxpayer received property worth $3,000 in satisfaction of a $5,000 debt and took a $2,000 bad debt deduction for the difference, which generated no tax benefit. In a later year, the property was sold for $5,000 and the issue was whether the subsequent $2,000 gain could be excluded under § 111. The ruling held that a subsequent sale was a separate transaction and the gain was not attributable to the bad debt deducted without tax benefit in the prior year. See also Allen v. Trust Co. of Georgia, 180 F.2d 527 (5th Cir.1950) (same result); Continental Illinois National Bank & Trust Co. of Chicago v. Commissioner, 69 T.C. 357 (1977) (Acq.) (same result even though the stock received for the debt was donated to charity, producing a separate charitable contribution deduction); Waynesboro Knitting Co. v. Commissioner, 225 F.2d 477 (3d Cir.1955) (proceeds from life insurance policy, which had been transferred to taxpayer by an employee in part payment for an embezzlement loss, which the taxpayer had deducted without tax benefit, were not subject to exclusion under the tax benefit rule; the acquisition of the policy was a separate transaction).

The exclusionary aspect of the rule also raises issues not present in the inclusionary aspect. Suppose the taxpayer was tax-exempt in the year of payment but taxable in the year of recovery. In California & Hawaiian Sugar Refining Corp. v. United States, 311 F.2d 235 (Ct.Cl.1962), the taxpayer was required to pay certain processing and other taxes during a period when it was exempt from income taxation as an agricultural marketing cooperative. Subsequent legislation made the taxpayer subject to the income tax. In a year when the cooperative was subject to the income tax, the processing taxes that had been paid in earlier years were found to be unconstitutional and were refunded. The taxpayer argued that the refund was nontaxable since the tax payments had generated no tax benefits in the years made because of the taxpayer's exempt status. The court found the refund nontaxable as a return of capital.

C. INITIAL INCLUSION IN INCOME FOLLOWED BY LATER REPAYMENT

INTERNAL REVENUE CODE: Section 1341.

In cases where the taxpayer has received funds and subsequently is required to repay all or part thereof, the taxpayer nevertheless must include the funds in income in the year received. In accordance with the annual accounting concept, the fact that repayment is subsequently required does not affect the initial inclusion.

Where it applies, § 1341 allows the taxpayer either (1) to deduct repayment of an amount previously included in gross income under the appearance of an unrestricted right to the income or (2) to reduce tax liability for the year of repayment by the amount of the tax increase in the prior year attributable to receipt of the repaid amount. Thus, the basic policy of § 1341 is to adopt a transactional approach for situations involving repayments of amounts originally required to be included in income under "claim of right" principles, if that approach is more favorable to the taxpayer than current deduction of the repayment. In effect, the taxpayer forgoes the deduction for the year of repayment in return for exclusion of the item from income if the latter treatment results in less tax liability.

Prior to the adoption of § 1341, the only remedy was for the taxpayer to claim a deduction for the repayment in the later year. United States v. Lewis, 340 U.S. 590 (1951). In *Lewis*, the taxpayer in 1946 was required to repay a portion of the bonus he had received in 1944 after litigation had determined that the bonus had been improperly computed. The Court held the entire bonus was includable in income in the year of receipt and the taxpayer could not retroactively adjust the prior year's tax results in light of the later repayment.

A deduction in the year of repayment may not reduce the taxpayer's tax liability by the same amount paid as a result of the initial inclusion. If the taxpayer's tax rates are lower in the year of repayment than in the year of inclusion, the taxpayer does not derive a benefit from the deduction equivalent to the burden imposed by inclusion in the year of receipt. Section 1341 was enacted to ameliorate this result by giving the taxpayer a tax credit in the year of repayment equal to the tax liability generated by the initial inclusion. However, if the taxpayer's tax rate is higher in the year of repayment, § 1341 continues to allow the taxpayer to take a deduction of the repayment. Because of § 1341's favorable treatment, taxpayers have argued for an expansive interpretation of its scope.

DETAILED ANALYSIS

1. QUALIFYING CONDITIONS—"APPEARANCE" OF "UNRESTRICTED RIGHT"

Section 1341 deals with situations in which the taxpayer "appeared" to have an "unrestricted right" to an item of income that he is subsequently required to repay. The IRS has attempted to limit the scope of § 1341 to a narrow range of cases by stressing the word "appeared" in the statute. Rev. Rul. 68–153, 1968–1 C.B. 371, distinguished three different situations where, at the end of the year of inclusion the taxpayer had: (1) an "unchallengeable" right to the item of income; (2) a "semblance" of an unrestricted right; and (3) no right at all to the item. The ruling held that only situations falling in the second category are entitled to relief under § 1341. Following these distinctions, the IRS ruled that § 1341 was not applicable to repayments of excessive compensation where the recipients were obligated under a prior agreement to repay any amounts that were found to be excessive as a result of a tax audit. Because the audit that led to the repayments took place in a subsequent year, the taxpayer had more than the "appearance" of an unrestricted right to the items in the year in which they were received and § 1341 relief was therefore not available. Rev. Rul. 67–437, 1967–2 C.B. 296. This restrictive interpretation of § 1341 has been rejected by the courts. In Van Cleave v. United States, 718 F.2d 193 (6th Cir.1983), the taxpayer was required by prior agreement to repay to his employer compensation that was found to be unreasonable in an audit in a subsequent year. The court held that § 1341 was applicable: "[T]he fact that a restriction on a taxpayer's right to income does not arise until the year subsequent to the time of the receipt does not affect the availability of a section 1341 tax adjustment."

This controversy over whether an actual unchallengeable right can trigger the application of § 1341 has been implicated in recent cases involving refund payments by public utilities to their customers. The refunds were the result of tax rate changes that occurred in years after the years of the original payments by customers; the utilities were required by law to make refunds of the amount of tax that they had over-collected. The IRS took the position in these cases that § 1341 did not apply to these refunds because they were triggered by facts that arose after the year in which the customer made the original payments. In Dominion Resources, Inc. v. United States, 219 F.3d 359 (4th Cir. 2000), the court rejected this position. The court reasoned: "[T]hings very often 'appear' to be what they 'actually' are. As a matter of plain meaning, the word 'appeared' generally does not, as the IRS urges, imply only false appearance, and generally does not exclude an appearance that happens to be true." However, in Cinergy Corp. v. United States, 55 Fed. Cl. 489 (2003), the court accepted the IRS's position that § 1341 did not apply to the utility's refunds because the utility's right to the original payment by the customer was absolute in the year of inclusion but was undermined by subsequent facts. But see Pennzoil-Quaker State Co. v. United States, 62 Fed. Cl. 689 (2004) (concluding that the interpretation by *Dominion Resources* is more consistent with Congressional intent than the interpretation by *Cingery* and Rev. Rul. 68–153).

On the other hand, where it is clear that the taxpayer has "no right" to the funds in the year of receipt, the courts have uniformly agreed with the IRS's position that § 1341 is not applicable to the repayment. Culley v. United States, 222 F.3d 1331 (Fed.Cir.2000), involved a deduction claimed for restitution paid by a taxpayer who orchestrated a scheme by which his customers, and ultimately the purchaser of his business, were overcharged through his fraud. Pursuant to a criminal conviction, the taxpayer made partial restitution. Although the taxpayer was allowed a § 165 loss deduction, § 1341 did not apply. The court held that § 1341 applies only if at the time of receipt it appeared to the taxpayer that he had an unrestricted right to the funds subsequently repaid. Thus, a deduction for restitution of funds obtained by fraud is not subject to § 1341, even though it may have appeared to the defrauded parties at the time that they paid him that the taxpayer had an unrestricted right to the funds. See also McKinney v. United States, 574 F.2d 1240 (5th Cir.1978) (§ 1341 did not apply to repayment of embezzled funds); Rev. Rul. 65–254, 1965–2 C.B. 50 (same result; deduction available in year of repayment under § 165(c)(2)).

2.   VOLUNTARY REPAYMENTS

The courts have generally upheld the IRS view that voluntary repayments do not qualify for the election under § 1341. In Pike v. Commissioner, 44 T.C. 787 (1965) (Acq.), the taxpayer paid to a corporation certain profits that he realized from the sale of the corporation's stock because the state insurance commission had investigated the transaction and concluded that the profits properly belonged to the corporation. The court first found that the payments did qualify under § 162(a), the payments being neither personal nor against public policy. Thus, the taxpayer was entitled to a deduction in the year of repayment. However, he was not entitled to the election under § 1341 because the taxpayer did not establish the "probable validity of the adverse claim to the funds repaid." Thus, the repayment was treated as voluntary. But the taxpayer is not always required to contest repayment in order to obtain the benefit of § 1341. Barrett v. Commissioner, 96 T.C. 713 (1991) (Nonacq.), involved facts similar to *Pike*. The taxpayer was a stockbroker who settled a civil suit to recover insider-trading profits, but because the Securities and Exchange Commission was simultaneously conducting an administrative proceeding to suspend his license, he admitted no wrong-doing. The court concluded that the repayment was not voluntary, and held that as long as the repayment was pursuant to a "bona fide, noncollusive, arm's-length settlement" the requirement of § 1341 that it be established that the taxpayer did not have a right to the prior receipt had been met. The taxpayer is not required to prove that he would have lost had the civil suit gone to trial. The court distinguished *Pike* as involving a case in which the repayment was not in settlement of a pending civil action.

3.   RELATION OF SECTION 1341 TO DEDUCTION-GRANTING PROVISIONS

Treas. Reg. § 1.1341–1(a)(1) provides that if the taxpayer is "entitled under other provisions of chapter 1 of the Internal Revenue Code of 1954 to a deduction" because of the repayment, then a current deduction may be available under § 1341. In United States v. Skelly Oil Co., 394 U.S. 678 (1969), the Court made it clear that § 1341 is not itself a deduction-granting section, but rather the deduction must be allowable under some other provision of the Internal Revenue Code: "[T]he use of the words 'a deduction' and the placement of section 1341 in subchapter Q—the subchapter dealing largely with side effects of the annual accounting system—make it clear that it is necessary to refer to other portions of the Code to discover how much of a deduction is allowable." See also Wood v. United States, 863 F.2d 417 (5th Cir.1989) (§ 1341 did not allow a deduction for forfeiture to federal government of proceeds from sale of drugs because on public policy grounds no deduction was allowable under § 165).

Conversely, § 1341 is not necessarily applicable merely because a deduction is allowed for a payment of a disputed amount. In Chernin v. United States, 149 F.3d 805 (8th Cir.1998), the taxpayer was involved in litigation with his former employer regarding the employer's claim that the taxpayer had embezzled funds by authorizing bonuses to be paid to himself. The taxpayer had reported the bonuses as income. While the litigation was pending, the taxpayer's bank account was garnished and the taxpayer claimed a deduction for that year under § 461(f), which was allowed. He was not permitted, however, to apply § 1341. The court held that the § 1341(a)(2) requirement—that it be established that the taxpayer does not have an unrestricted right to the income—requires that the amount actually be repaid to the original payor. The fact that a deduction is allowed under

§ 461(f) because funds to pay a deductible expense have been put in escrow beyond the taxpayer's control is not sufficient to invoke relief under § 1341.

4.   PAYMENTS TO THIRD PARTIES

Section 1341 typically has been applied to instances in which amounts have been returned by the taxpayer either to the person who originally paid them over to the taxpayer (e.g., erroneously computed bonuses) or to the person to whom the amount originally should have been paid (e.g., rents received subject to a title dispute relating to the underlying property). Taxpayers have argued that § 1341 may also apply when payments are made to third parties.

The taxpayer in Reynolds Metal Co. v. United States, 389 F.Supp.2d 692 (E.D.Va. 2005), paid environmental remediation costs to remedy pollution resulting from the manufacture of goods sold by the taxpayer in prior years and claimed that § 1341 applied to the expenditures. Tax rates had dropped significantly between the time the pollution had occurred and the time that the remediation costs were incurred, and the application of § 1341 would provide a credit for the "excess" taxes paid in the earlier high-tax years. The court rejected the argument:

> * * * Reynolds' argument [that § 1341 applies to the payment of remediation expenses] breaks down with regard to the restoration requirement [in Treas. Reg. § 1.1341–1(a)(1)]. * * *

> Reynolds has only demonstrated its obligation to pay for the remediation; it has not demonstrated restoration of an item of income to an entity from whom the income was received or to whom the item of income should have been paid. * * *

> Reynolds has not repaid any funds to anyone. Reynolds was charged, or more accurately held liable, for additional environmental clean-up costs in the face of more stringent standards as a result of its prior manufacturing activities. Reynolds cannot seriously argue that it is restoring its overstated income to any person or entity in the sense contemplated by § 1341.

Alcoa, Inc. v. United States, 509 F.3d 173 (3d Cir.2007), reached a similar result on similar facts. The court held that § 1341 did not apply to environmental remediation expenses incurred in 1993 that related to manufacturing operations for the years 1940–1987, "because Alcoa's expenditure of funds in 1993 was not the restoration of particular moneys to the rightful owner and did not arise from the same circumstances, terms, and conditions as Alcoa's original acquisition of the income." There was no nexus between the income asserted to have been received under a claim of right and the expenditure claimed as a refund of that income. See also Rev. Rul. 2004–17, 2004–1 C.B. 516 (§ 1341 does not apply to environmental remediation costs to remedy pollution resulting from the manufacture of products sold in prior years because the taxpayer had an actual unrestricted right to the proceeds from the sale of its products in the prior years). Pennzoil-Quaker Co. v. United States, 511 F.3d 1365 (Fed.Cir.2008), likewise held that § 1341 did not apply to a payment of anti-trust damages to the taxpayer's suppliers that arose from price fixing because § 1341 applies only to repayments to the original payor.

D. RELATED PROCEDURAL DOCTRINES

(1) MITIGATION OF THE STATUTE OF LIMITATIONS

Sections 1311–1314 provide a partial remedy for the troublesome problems in this area. These sections attempt to provide an equitable solution by applying a transactional approach but on a different basis from the doctrine of estoppel. Instead of freezing the earlier error into permanent acceptability and requiring consistent but incorrect treatment of the item in the later year, which is the basis of estoppel, §§ 1311–1314 operate on the premise that adjustment must be made for the error in the earlier year and that the correct result should be reached in the later year. Thus, in the case described under estoppel, above, the taxpayer who failed to include the $10,000 of stock in 2008 could still claim a $10,000 basis in 2013, but would have to pay, with interest, the additional tax for 2008 that would have resulted from inclusion of the stock in income for that year.

Section 1311 applies to seven specified situations enumerated in § 1312 which, speaking generally, are:

(1) *Double Inclusion of Income.* An item of income is included in one year that erroneously also has been included in the income of another year. Or, an item of income is included in the income of one taxpayer and erroneously also has been included in the income of another taxpayer.

(2) *Double Allowance of Deduction or Credit.* An item of deduction or credit is allowed in one year, or to one taxpayer, which erroneously also has been allowed in another year, or to another taxpayer.[1]

(3) *Double Exclusion of Income.* An item of income is included in one year, or in the income of one taxpayer, so that tax is thus paid on the income, and then the taxpayer obtains, as through refund claim, the exclusion of the item on the ground that it belonged in another year or to another taxpayer, but was simply erroneously excluded from such other year or by such other taxpayer. Or, an item of income is excluded from the gross income of a present year on the similar ground that it properly belonged in a prior year or in the income of another taxpayer and, when the IRS first asserted that it belonged in the present year, it would then

---

[1] In B.C. Cook & Sons, Inc. v. Commissioner, 65 T.C. 422 (1975) (Nonacq.), aff'd per curiam, 584 F.2d 53 (5th Cir.1978), amounts embezzled from the taxpayer were erroneously shown on its books as additional inventory purchases and included in the cost of goods sold. As a result, the taxpayer's gross income was reduced by those amounts. Subsequently, the embezzlement was discovered and the taxpayer claimed a loss for the embezzled amounts. The court held that §§ 1311–1314 were not applicable since the case did not involve a double allowance of a deduction but rather an adjustment to cost of goods sold which was not technically a deduction.

have been timely for him to have proceeded with respect to the proper year or proper taxpayer.[2]

(4) *Double Disallowance of Deduction or Credit.* An item of deduction or credit is disallowed in one year on the ground that it properly was allowable in an earlier year or by or to another taxpayer and, when the taxpayer first claimed that it belonged in the year which turned out to be erroneous, it would then have been timely for him to have proceeded with respect to the proper year or proper taxpayer.

(5) *Trust Items.* An item of trust income or deduction is treated in a manner inconsistent with the correlative treatment of the item in the hands of the fiduciary or beneficiary, as the case may be.

(6) *Corporate Items.* A deduction or credit is treated in a manner inconsistent with the correlative treatment of the item by a related corporation.

(7) *Basis Situations.* The basis of particular property is determined for gain or loss, depreciation, etc., and there has been, with respect to any transaction on which such basis depends, or any transaction which was erroneously treated as affecting the basis, an erroneous treatment of income or deduction or gain or loss with respect to the taxpayer, a predecessor who acquired the property in the transaction, or the donee of a taxpayer who owned the property at the time of the transaction.[3]

In these specified situations, § 1314 permits the error to be corrected by reopening the statute of limitations solely for such purpose. If there are other procedural barriers to the correction of the error, such as res judicata, these are also specially waived. The increase or decrease in tax

---

[2]   Section 1312(3)(A) can apply even though the double exclusion from income is not solely attributable to the actions of the taxpayer. In Chertkof v. Commissioner, 649 F.2d 264 (4th Cir.1981), the taxpayer reported an income item in 1966 which the IRS asserted, by way of deficiency, should have been included in 1965. At the same time, the IRS refunded the tax paid on the amount for 1966. The taxpayer accepted the refund check, paid the 1965 asserted deficiency, sued for refund, and won on the ground that the item was properly includable in 1966. The statute of limitations had then run on 1966. The court held that the statute of limitations was mitigated by § 1312(3)(A) even though the amount was erroneously excluded from the taxpayer's 1966 income by the IRS's own actions and not solely by those of the taxpayer.

[3]   In Chertkof v. United States, 676 F.2d 984 (4th Cir.1982), an estate and revocable inter vivos trust sold assets using the fair market value of the assets as reported in the estate tax return of the decedent as the basis in computing gain. Subsequently, in a Tax Court proceeding, the estate tax values were increased. The taxpayers then sought refunds of income taxes because of the lower gains that would have resulted had the higher estate tax values been utilized as the bases for the assets sold. The court held that the requirements of § 1312(7) had been met; an estate tax determination can be used as the basis for mitigation of the statute of limitations with respect to the income tax. Treas. Reg. § 1.1311(a)–2(b) is to the contrary.

In Gardiner v. United States, 536 F.2d 903 (10th Cir.1976), a taxpayer purchased depreciable property in 1963, claimed no depreciation deductions in 1964–1966, but did claim depreciation deductions in 1967–1970. Upon a sale of the property in 1971, the taxpayer claimed a loss, utilizing as the basis in the property the original cost less the 1967–1970 depreciation actually claimed. The IRS required that gain be reported in 1971 because the basis was required to be reduced by the allowable depreciation deductions in 1964–1966 even though not actually taken. The taxpayer then filed a claim for refund and the court held that § 1312(7) was not applicable to mitigate the running of the statute of limitations since failing to take depreciation deductions was not a "transaction" affecting basis; there must be a "business transaction" such as a sale or exchange to satisfy the requirements of § 1312(7).

that results from correction of the error, together with interest, is then refunded to the taxpayer or paid as a deficiency. However, §§ 1311(a) and 1313 require that there had been an official "determination" of the correct treatment for the closed year in a later year, and under § 1311(b), adjustment of the year of the error is permitted only when a position inconsistent with a previous position is maintained by the party in whose favor the statute of limitations had run. Thus, if the adjustment is by way of refund, the IRS must have urged a position inconsistent with the error[4] and, if by way of deficiency, the taxpayer must have urged the inconsistent position. (Inconsistency is also the justification for waiving the statute of limitations in the adjustments made under § 481 regarding a change in accounting methods.) In the special situations of double exclusion of an item never included in the earlier year and double disallowance of a deduction, an inconsistent position is not required. Here, however, the factor justifying the setting aside of the statute of limitations is that the party made the wrong choice of taxable year at a time when the right taxable year was still open. Where the transaction involves two taxpayers, the above rules apply only if the taxpayers are "related" as defined in § 1313(c). The relationships covered include husband and wife, partners, or members of an affiliated corporate group.

Consideration could be given to the continued expansion of these sections to cover other situations consistent with the principles of the sections. The application of estoppel and recoupment is likely to diminish to the extent that the corrective measures of §§ 1311–1314 are available.[5]

(2) THE JUDICIAL DOCTRINES OF ESTOPPEL AND RECOUPMENT

Suppose that a taxpayer in 2016 receives stock worth $10,000 as compensation for services. The taxpayer fails to include the stock in her income for that year. The taxpayer sells the stock in 2021 for $15,000 and for the first time states that since the taxpayer should have included the stock in income in 2016, the stock has a basis equal to its cost basis, or $10,000, so that the gain in 2021 is only $5,000. The taxpayer's computation of basis is correct if the stock had been properly included in gross income.

But whether the taxpayer can rely on the correct basis upon sale when the taxpayer erroneously failed to include the stock in income upon

---

[4]   See Brigham v. United States, 470 F.2d 571 (Ct.Cl.1972), holding that §§ 1311 through 1314 were not applicable because the Government was not maintaining an "inconsistent position" for purposes of § 1311(b) merely by accepting a taxpayer's contention.

[5]   See Benenson v. United States, 385 F.2d 26 (2d Cir.1967) (court refused to apply equitable recoupment where the taxpayer had a possible remedy under §§ 1311–1314 and suggested that the statutory remedy was exclusive for cases falling within the general scope of the statute); B.C. Cook & Sons, Inc. v. Commissioner, 59 T.C. 516 (1972) (Tax Court allowed the embezzlement loss, indicating that "the Commissioner's recourse is through the correction procedure set forth in §§ 1311–1314"); Stoller v. Commissioner. T.C. Memo. 1990–659 (Tax Court does not have jurisdiction to apply equitable recoupment to overpayment of taxes for a year not before the court, citing Commissioner v. Gooch Milling & Elevator Co., 320 U.S. 418 (1943)), aff'd in part and rev'd in part on other issues, 994 F.2d 855 (D.C.Cir.1993).

acquisition is debatable. The courts have divided on the question, some permitting the taxpayer's claim, others holding that the taxpayer is estopped from claiming the $10,000 basis. Compare Commissioner v. Mellon, 184 F.2d 157 (3d Cir.1950) (no estoppel), with Continental Oil Co. v. Jones, 177 F.2d 508 (10th Cir.1949) (estoppel), and Hess v. United States, 537 F.2d 457 (Ct.Cl.1976) (estate and testamentary trust required to use the fair market value of stock as shown on the estate tax return as basis in computing gain on a subsequent redemption; they were estopped from proving a higher date of death value). The non-estoppel cases argue that a mistake of law is simply a mistake of law and the correct result can always be asserted. The estoppel cases, on the other hand, stress continuity of treatment and the practical necessity, for effective tax administration, of IRS reliance upon the taxpayer's action. This conflict between estoppel and non-estoppel runs through most of the various possible patterns, such as failure to include income in an earlier year only to claim, when the IRS attempts to include it in a later year, that the income correctly belonged in the earlier year. See Ross v. Commissioner, 169 F.2d 483 (1st Cir.1948). However, where a double deduction is attempted, as where a deduction was erroneously taken in an earlier year and claimed again in a correct year, the courts will usually, but not always, deny the second deduction. See Banks v. Commissioner, 345 F.3d 373 (6th Cir.2003), rev'g T.C. Memo. 2001–48, rev'd on other issues, 543 U.S. 426 (2005). Where the IRS is acting erroneously, so as to produce a double inclusion of income, the courts usually hold that estoppel does not apply against the IRS. Generally, all such litigation pivots on the statute of limitations because most corrections are permitted unless barred by the statute of limitations. As a result, the party barred from correcting the earlier error must attempt through estoppel to hold the other party to action consistent with the error.

The IRS has at times successfully resorted to a doctrine of recoupment to avoid the barrier of the statute of limitations. Thus, where a taxpayer is pursuing a refund claim, the IRS has been able in some situations to defeat the refund claim by offsetting against it the tax that was saved by the taxpayer in a related but erroneously treated transaction. See Stone v. White, 301 U.S. 532 (1937), and Lewis v. Reynolds, 284 U.S. 281 (1932), allowing such recoupment, and McEachern v. Rose, 302 U.S. 56 (1937), and Kramer v. United States, 406 F.2d 1363 (Ct.Cl.1969) denying it. Bull v. United States, 295 U.S. 247 (1935), allowed recoupment in favor of the taxpayer where the same item had been subject to both an estate and an income tax and the statute of limitations had run on the estate tax. At the same time, the recoupment doctrine cannot provide an independent basis for a taxpayer seeking a refund after the statute of limitations has expired. United States v. Dalm, 494 U.S. 596 (1990). See also Rothensies v. Electric Storage Battery Co., 329 U.S. 296 (1946), refusing to apply recoupment in favor of the taxpayer, and Wilmington Trust Co. v. United States, 610 F.2d 703

(Ct.Cl.1979), refusing to apply recoupment in favor of the Government where an allowed income tax deduction reduced an allowable deduction for estate tax purposes but the statute of limitations had run on the estate tax.

In these situations, through the doctrines of estoppel or recoupment, the courts in effect may apply a transactional approach and thus depart in a sense from a rigid annual accounting concept. The field abounds with conflicting decisions and questionable distinctions.

(3) RES JUDICATA AND COLLATERAL ESTOPPEL

The general doctrines of res judicata and collateral estoppel apply in the tax field, with some modifications to account for the special nature of tax litigation. For example, the government representative in a tax dispute can either be the IRS or the United States depending on the forum. But for purposes of the application of res judicata or collateral estoppel, the nominal difference in party on the government side is not relevant. I.R.C. § 7422(c); Tait v. Western Md. R. Co., 289 U.S. 620 (1933). In addition, the government is not collaterally estopped from relitigating issues where different taxpayers are involved. A shareholder, for example, may not use collateral estoppel against the government based on previous litigation involving a different shareholder of the same corporation on the same issue. Divine v. Commissioner, 500 F.2d 1041 (2d Cir.1974).

In Commissioner v. Sunnen, 333 U.S. 591 (1948), involving royalty payments as to which there had been a decision in earlier years, the Supreme Court set forth the basic principles regarding the application of res judicata and collateral estoppel in the tax context:

> Income taxes are levied on an annual basis. Each year is the origin of a new liability and of a separate cause of action. Thus if a claim of liability or non-liability relating to a particular tax year is litigated, a judgment on the merits is *res judicata* as to any subsequent proceeding involving the same claim and the same tax year. But if the later proceeding is concerned with a similar or unlike claim relating to a different tax year, the prior judgment acts as a collateral estoppel only as to those matters in the second proceeding which were actually presented and determined in the first suit. Collateral estoppel operates, in other words, to relieve the government and the taxpayer of "redundant litigation of the identical question of the statute's application to the taxpayer's status." Tait v. Western Md. R. Co., 289 U.S. 620, 624.

> But collateral estoppel is a doctrine capable of being applied so as to avoid an undue disparity in the impact of income tax liability. A taxpayer may secure a judicial determination of a particular tax matter, a matter which may recur without substantial variation for some years thereafter. But a

subsequent modification of the significant facts or a change or development in the controlling legal principles may make that determination obsolete or erroneous, at least for future purposes. If such a determination is then perpetuated each succeeding year as to the taxpayer involved in the original litigation, he is accorded a tax treatment different from that given to other taxpayers of the same class. As a result, there are inequalities in the administration of the revenue laws, discriminatory distinctions in tax liability, and a fertile basis for litigious confusion. * * * Such consequences, however, are neither necessitated nor justified by the principle of collateral estoppel. That principle is designed to prevent repetitious lawsuits over matters which have once been decided and which have remained substantially static, factually and legally. It is not meant to create vested rights in decisions that have become obsolete or erroneous with time, thereby causing inequities among taxpayers.

And so where two cases involve income taxes in different taxable years, collateral estoppel must be used with its limitations carefully in mind so as to avoid injustice. It must be confined to situations where the matter raised in the second suit is identical in all respects with that decided in the first proceeding and where the controlling facts and applicable legal rules remain unchanged. If the legal matters determined in the earlier case differ from those raised in the second case, collateral estoppel has no bearing on the situation. * * * And where the situation is vitally altered between the time of the first judgment and the second, the prior determination is not conclusive. * * * [A] judicial declaration intervening between the two proceedings may so change the legal atmosphere as to render the rule of collateral estoppel inapplicable. * * *

Of course, where a question of fact essential to the judgment is actually litigated and determined in the first tax proceeding, the parties are bound by that determination in a subsequent proceeding even though the cause of action is different. * * * And if the very same facts and no others are involved in the second case, a case relating to a different tax year, the prior judgment will be conclusive as to the same legal issues which appear, assuming no intervening doctrinal change. * * *

The *Sunnen* standard was modified in Montana v. United States, 440 U.S. 147 (1979), which involved the applicability of collateral estoppel with regard to a state tax. There the Court articulated the standard as follows: "To determine the appropriate application of collateral estoppel in the instant case necessitates three further inquiries: first, whether the issues presented by this litigation are in substance the same as those resolved [in the first case]; second, whether controlling facts or legal principles have changed significantly since the [first] judgment; and finally, whether other special circumstances warrant an exception to the normal rules of preclusion." Under this standard, direct identity of the issue is not required. This modification of the *Sunnen* criteria since has been applied in federal income tax cases. See ITT Corp. v. United States, 963 F.2d 561 (2d Cir.1992).

SECTION 2.   NET OPERATING LOSS CARRYFORWARD AND CARRYBACK

INTERNAL REVENUE CODE: Section 172(a), (b)(1)(A), (C), (b)(2)–(3), (c), (d)(1)–(4), (e), (f)(1)–(2).

Except in the case of passive activities, see Chapter 35, Section 2, the Code permits current tax losses from one business operation of a taxpayer to offset income from another business operation of that taxpayer in computing income for the year. If business deductions exceed business income in the current year, the net business losses also can be used to offset other income, such as salary and dividends. Suppose, however, that the business deductions exceed all income in the current year. This situation may result from either an economic loss or from tax expenditure deductions that create a tax loss even though the taxpayer has substantial economic income. Rigid application of the annual accounting concept would mean that a taxpayer with income in some years and losses in others would pay more income tax than a taxpayer in the same net income (or loss) position whose income remained constant over the same period of years. This result is aggravated by progressive tax rates.

To provide a type of income "averaging" for the business taxpayer experiencing tax losses in some years and profits in others, since 1918 the Code has provided that operating losses incurred in one year may be carried back and carried forward for a specified period of time. Under current law, the generally applicable carryback period is two years and the carryforward period is 20 years, thus providing a 23-year time span over which fluctuations in income and loss years may be smoothed out.[6]

---

[6]   Section 172(b)(1)(C) and (f) provide a special 10-year carryback period for certain "specified liability" losses.

The carryback period for losses arising from casualties and theft, as well as for net operating losses incurred by a "small business" (a business with average annual receipts of $5,000,000 or less) or a farmer that are "attributable to" a Presidentially declared disaster, is 3 years. I.R.C. § 172(b)(1)(F). Identifying operating losses attributable to the disaster distinctly from other losses can present difficulties in applying this provision.

Section 172(b)(1)(F) provides a special five-year carryback period for "farming losses," as defined in § 172(h)—essentially net operating losses attributable to a farming business. Farming losses are treated as a separate net operating loss from normal net operating losses and are carried over after the normal net operating losses are applied. This ordering rule preserves farming loss net operating losses by first applying to the preceding two years net operating losses that can be carried back only two years, leaving farming losses to be carried back to earlier years.

The net operating loss carryback and carryforward deduction may, however, be used to offset only business income in the years to which carried.

Section 172(b)(3) allows the taxpayer to waive the carryback and thus only to carry forward the net operating loss carryover. This election is useful, for example, if nonrefundable credits have substantially reduced or eliminated the taxpayer's tax liability for the prior year. An election to waive the carryback must be made on a timely filed tax return for the year the net operating loss is incurred. Failure to file a timely return precludes subsequently claiming a net operating loss carryforward without the net operating losses being absorbed, to the extent required, by the carryback year. See Moretti v. Commissioner, 77 F.3d 637 (2d Cir.1996).

Mechanically, if a taxpayer incurs a net operating loss for 2018, it must first carry that loss back to apply against 2016 income and then against 2017. The taxable income in each carryback year is recomputed by utilizing the available carryback loss. The result of the computations is that the taxpayer will receive a refund (without interest) in the year of the loss attributable to the reduction in taxes paid in the preceding 2 years.[7] Any unused losses remaining after the carryback period are then carried forward to the next 20 years, beginning with the first year following the loss year. See Treas. Reg. § 1.172–6.

Two theoretical views of the net operating loss carryforward and carryback provisions exist and have been reflected in the various aspects of § 172. With respect to business deductions, a "taxable income" approach is used. This approach is reflected, for example, in the rule allowing business losses to qualify in full for the carryover even though the taxpayer in the loss year received tax-exempt interest in excess of the business losses sustained for the year. On the other hand, in computing a net operating loss for an individual, an "economic loss" concept has some role. Deductions for personal living expenses are not taken into account to the extent they exceed nonbusiness income.

DETAILED ANALYSIS

1.   TREATMENT OF NONBUSINESS DEDUCTIONS AND INCOME

To qualify for the net operating loss deduction the taxpayer must be engaged in a trade or business. For this purpose, employment has been held to constitute a trade or business. See e.g., Lagreide v. Commissioner, 23 T.C. 508 (1954). On the other hand, a loss was not attributable to a trade or business where the taxpayer, who had never been in the real estate business,

---

[7]   A taxpayer who has a net operating loss carryback can follow normal procedures for filing an amended return for the year to which the loss is carried or apply for a quick refund under § 6411. Section 6411 allows a taxpayer who carries back a net operating loss to apply for a tentative adjustment of the tax liability for the earlier year to which the loss was carried. The request will be processed by the IRS within ninety days. Any such quick refund is provisional, however, and can be adjusted under the normal audit process.

incurred preliminary costs to construct an apartment building but the apartment building was not rented before the taxpayer abandoned the project. Todd v. Commissioner, 77 T.C. 246 (1981), aff'd per curiam, 682 F.2d 207 (9th Cir.1982). See also Rev. Rul. 69–355, 1969–1 C.B. 65 (oil royalties, bonuses, and delay rentals did not constitute business income).

If the taxpayer is in a trade or business, the expenses incurred must relate to the trade or business in order to enter into the net operating loss computation. See Mannette v. Commissioner, 69 T.C. 990 (1978) (loss resulting from repayment of embezzled funds could not be carried back, the court rejecting the taxpayer's argument that the embezzlement was integrally related to the taxpayer's conduct of his trade or business as a securities trader because he used the embezzled funds in that activity). Losses incurred in connection with investment activities that do not constitute a trade or business cannot be utilized in the net operating loss computation. See e.g., Mohr v. Commissioner, 45 T.C. 600 (1966) (taxpayer not in the trade or business of buying or selling auto dealerships could not treat interest, bad debts, or worthless stock losses arising out of such investments as business deductions).

Section 172(d)(4) provides that in computing net operating losses nonbusiness deductions shall be allowed only to the extent of nonbusiness income. For this computation, (1) nonbusiness deductions may not exceed nonbusiness income, and (2) any excess nonbusiness income may offset business deductions. Treas. Reg. § 1.172–3(a)(2)(ii) prohibits the use of nonbusiness capital losses in excess of nonbusiness capital gains in computing the net operating loss computation.

2. ABSORPTION OF NET OPERATION LOSS CARRYOVERS

2.1. *Generally*

The amount of a net operating loss carryover is determined under § 172(c), with the § 172(d) modifications, by applying the law applicable to the year in which the initial loss arose. Thus, the amount of the initial loss remains constant even though the law of the year to which it is carried would have produced a different result. When the loss is carried to another year, the amount of the initial loss that is deductible in the carryover year is determined by § 172(b)(2). Taxable income and the modifications required by § 172(b)(2) for the year against which the deduction may be claimed are determined under the law applicable to that year.

2.2. *Recomputation of Taxable Income*

The effect of the modifications to taxable income of the year to which a net operating loss is carried pursuant to § 172(b)(2) may be to "absorb" an amount of the net operating loss carryover different than the taxable income for the year to which carried as shown before the modifications were made. Assume, for example, that in 2016 an individual taxpayer had taxable income of exactly zero after claiming a personal exemption and the standard deduction. In 2017, the taxpayer had substantial taxable income, but in 2018 the taxpayer had a net operating loss of $5,000. When this net operating loss is carried back to 2016, the taxpayer's 2016 taxable income is modified by ignoring the personal exemption and standard deduction. Thus taxable income against which the 2018 net operating loss is deducted now exceeds $5,000, and the entire NOL is "absorbed." No portion of the net operating loss is carried to 2017 even though the taxpayer in effect received no benefit from carrying the net operating loss back to 2016. This loss of the benefit of the net operating loss carryover might be avoided by electing to waive the carryback period and thus only carrying the deduction forward to 2019.

The net operating loss provisions naturally interact with the statute of limitations. The State Farming Co. v. Commissioner, 40 T.C. 774 (1963), held that the Commissioner could compute the proper amount of income for a closed year in order to determine the correct amount of a net operating loss carryover to an open year. Thus, for example, in computing a NOL carryforward from 2013 that can be applied against income in 2018, the IRS can recompute the taxpayer's taxable income for 2014, even though the statute of limitations on 2014 has run, in determining the amount of the 2013 NOL that was properly absorbed in 2014.

3.   CHANGES IN STATUS

3.1. *Change in Marital Status*

If married taxpayers file joint returns, the net operating losses from the business of one of the spouses can be carried over and deducted against the other spouse's income in carryover years. But in Zeeman v. United States, 395 F.2d 861 (2d Cir.1968), the court held that a net operating loss sustained by a wife after her husband's death could not be carried back and applied against income reported on joint returns filed in a prior year when all of the income in that year had been earned by the husband. The rules are the same for carrybacks arising after divorce. Rev. Rul. 65–140, 1965–1 C.B. 127; Rev. Rul. 71–382, 1971–2 C.B. 156. See also Treas. Reg. § 1.172–7. Similarly, premarital losses of a wife could be carried forward to joint return years only to the extent of the income received by her in those years. Calvin v. United States, 354 F.2d 202 (10th Cir.1965),

3.2. *Death*

A net operating loss sustained in the year of death may not be carried forward to the estate's income tax return or to any subsequent years; the loss can be utilized only in the decedent's final return and as a carryback to the prior year. Rev. Rul. 74–175, 1974–1 C.B. 52.

3.3. *Bankruptcy*

A taxpayer may change legal status, voluntarily or involuntarily, and the net operating loss deduction may be affected. An individual taxpayer's estate in bankruptcy succeeds to the taxpayer's net operating loss carryovers. I.R.C. § 1398(g)(1). Any net operating losses remaining unused after the bankruptcy may be carried forward by the individual taxpayer. I.R.C. § 1398(i). The amount of net operating loss carryovers to which a taxpayer succeeds from the taxpayer's bankruptcy estate may be quite limited, however, because § 108(b) requires that certain tax attributes, including net operating loss carryovers, be reduced by the amount of cancellation of indebtedness income that was realized but was not recognized under § 108(a)(1)(A). See Chapter 10, Section 2. Section 108(b) often results in the elimination of any net operating loss carryovers. See Firsdon v. United States, 95 F.3d 444 (6th Cir.1996).

4.   SPECIFIED LIABILITY LOSSES

Section 172(b)(1)(C) provides a special ten-year carryback for "specified liability losses," as defined in § 172(f). "Specified liability losses" are losses attributable to (1) product liability claims against the taxpayer and (2) certain civil liabilities arising from state or federal law. The second category is limited to liabilities arising under federal or state law requiring (1) land reclamation (excluding deductions for additions to a reclamation reserve under § 468(a)(1)); (2) nuclear power plant decommissioning (excluding deductions for additions to a decommissioning reserve under § 468A(a)); (3) drilling platform dismantlement; (4) environmental remediation; and (5) certain workers' compensation. All product liability losses are subject to the ten-year carryback, but losses attributable to liabilities under state or federal law are entitled to a ten-year carryback only if the act out of which the liability arose occurred more than three years prior to the year in which the loss was incurred. Specified liability losses are treated as separate net operating losses from normal net operating losses and are carried over after the normal net operating losses are applied. I.R.C. § 172(f)(5). This ordering rule preserves specified liability loss carryovers by first applying to the preceding two years net operating losses that can be carried back only two years.

In re Harvard Industries. Inc., 568 F.3d 444 (3d Cir. 2009), involved a bankruptcy proceeding in which the taxpayer claimed income tax refunds based on carrybacks of specified liability losses. The taxpayer had produced defective products. The defects did not result in any physical injuries to persons or property, but the taxpayer suffered monetary losses in suits by distributors who could not resell the defective products. The court concluded that "loss of property" in § 172(f) could refer to the loss of the defective product itself so that losses attributable to settlements with distributors who could not sell the defective product qualified under the definition of specified liability losses.

5.   POLICY ISSUES

An analysis of the policy issues in the net operating loss carryover provisions must begin by differentiating between the situations where deductions in excess of income represent economic losses and where deductions in excess of income result from tax expenditures provided through special exclusion or deduction provisions.

Assume first a world in which only costs of producing income are allowed as deductions and the tax rate is 40 percent. In year 1, A incurs a business expense of $100 but has no income and B has $100 net business income. In year 2, A realizes business net income of $100; B incurs a $100 business expense but has no income. If no carryforwards or carrybacks are allowed, B would pay $40 of tax in year 1 and A would pay $40 of tax in year 2. Yet over the two-year period, both A and B have broken even. Some economists have suggested that the problem ideally should be resolved by having the Treasury make a $40 payment to A in year 1 and a $40 payment to B in year

2; in effect the Treasury should be viewed as a partner in a taxpayer's economic losses as well as in its economic income. The carryover provisions in existing law represent a second-best approach under this view. Although B is entitled to a refund in year 2 by virtue of the loss carryback to year 1, A does not receive a benefit in year 1; A must wait until year 2 when it may offset the $100 of income in year 2 with a $100 loss carryover from year 1.

Existing law concerning carryovers does not distinguish between net operating losses created by costs of producing income and those created by tax expenditures. The issues are conceptually distinct. For example, the excess of MACRS depreciation deductions under § 168 over economic depreciation provides, in effect, an interest-free loan to the taxpayer. If that loan were a direct loan program, its availability would not likely be conditioned upon whether the borrower had positive taxable income in the year of the loan. Thus, as a matter of spending program design, tax losses resulting from the tax expenditure portion of MACRS could be made refundable to the taxpayer so that the results would parallel a direct loan program. This step could be taken even if losses arising from economic depreciation were to continue to be governed by the carryover provisions. Alternatively, the taxpayer could be allowed to sell the tax expenditure benefit to another taxpayer and thus obtain something like the equivalent of refundability. But this procedure in turn creates perceptions of tax inequity.

6.   INCOME AVERAGING

Although § 172 effects a kind of income averaging for business taxpayers by smoothing out loss years and profitable years, the Code provides no general income averaging provisions to ameliorate the effect of graduated rates on taxpayers who have fluctuating incomes or an isolated year with unusually great taxable income. Until 1986, a general averaging device to ease the burden of individual taxpayers who had unusually high incomes in any one year was contained in former §§ 1301–1305. The effect of these provisions was to treat income that was significantly greater than the average income for the preceding three years as if it had been spread over four years, thus reducing the impact of the higher marginal rates. The averaging provisions dealt only with the situation of a series of low-income years followed by a high-income year. They did not ameliorate the effect of the graduated progressive rate structure for taxpayers who had high-income years followed by declining incomes. Corporations never were eligible for income averaging.

The general income averaging provisions for individuals were repealed by the 1986 Act, which reduced the maximum marginal rate from 50 percent to 28 percent and provided only one other rate bracket at 15 percent. Because of the flattening of the rates, income averaging was considered unnecessary. When higher brackets subsequently were added, Congress did not provide for income averaging.

In a limited context, Congress has again recognized the appropriateness of income averaging. Section 1301 permits individuals (but not estates and trusts) engaged in a farming business to average their farm income. If a farmer income averages, the tax is computed as the sum of (1) the tax under

§ 1 on the farmer's nonfarm income, plus (2) the sum of the increases in tax that would have resulted in each of the preceding three years if the taxpayer's income in each of those years had been increased by one-third of his farm income for the current year.

CHAPTER 30

DEFERRED COMPENSATION ARRANGEMENTS

The term "deferred compensation" refers to compensation that is paid after the services giving rise to the right to compensation are performed. Payment is generally deferred until the occurrence of a specified event, such as the death or retirement of the employee, or until a specified time in the future, such as in ten or twenty years.[1]

There are a variety of different types of deferred compensation arrangements. A common type is a simple contractual obligation to pay the employee an amount in a future year in consideration for work performed this year. These deferred compensation arrangements are divided into two categories: qualified plans and nonqualified plans. Qualified plans, such as the well-known § 401(k) plan, have tax consequences analogous to those of traditional IRAs (discussed in Chapter 8, Section 2). The employee does not recognize income when amounts are contributed to the plan by the employer for the employee's benefit, and neither the employee nor the employer recognizes income when the contributed amounts earn an investment yield.[2] When cash is distributed from the plan to the employee, the employee recognizes income in an amount equal to the amount of the distribution. Like IRAs, the significant tax benefit of qualified plans is the effective exemption of the investment yield. See Chapter 8, Section 2. This subsidy is intended to encourage taxpayers to save for retirement. Qualified plans must satisfy a number of highly technical requirements designed to limit the amount of the subsidy and to ensure that the subsidy benefits all employees and not just senior management. For a plan to qualify, it must meet strict limitations on contribution amounts with respect to any particular employee, it must be made available to a broad spectrum of employees, and it cannot discriminate in favor of highly compensated employees.

This Chapter primarily focuses on nonqualified deferred compensation arrangements because most tax practitioners do not give advice with respect to qualified plans, instead leaving this work to qualified plan experts who practice exclusively in the area. The arrangements discussed in this chapter do not qualify as qualified plans

---

[1]   While deferred compensation arrangements can involve an independent contractor, they most commonly involve employees. Accordingly, the text refers to employees, though the rules apply equally to non-employee service providers unless specifically noted.

[2]   When the employer makes a contribution to the plan, the employer gets an immediate deduction equal to the amount contributed. This is consistent with IRA treatment, where the service recipient receives a deduction upon payment of the funds used by the service provider to fund the IRA contribution.

because they fail one or more of the technical requirements. Typically, they are maintained for the exclusive benefit of senior executives or other highly compensated employees.

In designing nonqualified plans, the parties usually strive for the employee to defer including the compensation in income until cash is received.[3] In order to obtain such deferral historically, the parties simply navigated around the cash-method doctrines (constructive receipt, economic benefit, and cash equivalency doctrines) as discussed in Chapter 28. In 2004, however, Congress enacted § 409A, which provides other factors to consider in order to obtain deferral.

In addition to contractual arrangements, some deferred compensation arrangements involve the transfer of property—almost always stock or stock options of the employer—to the employee. The tax consequences of these transfers are discussed in Section 2.

SECTION 1.   NONQUALIFIED DEFERRED COMPENSATION CONTRACTS

A. FUNDED DEFERRED COMPENSATION

United States v. Drescher

United States Court of Appeals, Second Circuit, 1950.
179 F.2d 863.

■ SWAN, CIRCUIT JUDGE.

This appeal brings up for review an action against the United States to recover additional income taxes for the years 1939 and 1940 which the [taxpayer] asserts were illegally assessed and collected. * * *

In 1936 the [Bausch & Lomb] Optical Company inaugurated a plan to provide for the voluntary retirement at the age of 65 of its principal officers then under that age. There were five such, of whom Mr. Drescher was one. * * * Pursuant to this plan and in "recognition of prior services rendered," the Company purchased on December 28, 1939, and on the same date in 1940, a single premium, non-forfeitable annuity contract which named Mr. Drescher as the annuitant. Each policy was issued by Connecticut General Life Insurance Company and was delivered to the Optical Company which retained possession of it. It was the Company's intention, and so understood by the annuitant, that possession of the policy should be retained until the annuitant should reach the age of 65. The premium paid for each policy was $5,000. The amount of such payment was deducted by the Company in its tax return for the year of

---

[3]   When nonqualified deferred compensation is paid, the employer receives its deduction at that time in an amount equal to the amount of the payment. The employer also pays tax on the investment yield generated by the deferred compensation during the period of deferral. This tax on the investment yield is what makes the tax treatment of nonqualified plans less favorable than that of qualified plans, which exempt the yield from tax.

payment as part of the compensation paid to Mr. Drescher during that year. His salary as an officer was not reduced because of the purchase of the annuity contract, and he was not given the option to receive in cash the amounts expended by the Company for the premium payments. * * *

By the terms of the policy the Insurance Company agrees to pay the annuitant, commencing on December 28, 1958, a life income of $54.70 monthly under the 1939 policy and $44.80 monthly under the 1940 policy, with a minimum of 120 monthly payments. If the annuitant dies before receiving 120 monthly payments, the rest of them are payable to the beneficiary named in the policy. Each policy gives the annuitant an option to accelerate the date when monthly payments shall commence, but this option must be exercised by the annuitant in writing and endorsed on the policy. Consequently so long as the Optical Company retains possession of the policy the annuitant cannot exercise the option. If the annuitant dies before December 28, 1958, or before the acceleration date if he has exercised the option to accelerate monthly income payments, a death benefit is payable to the beneficiary designated by him (his wife). The policy reserves to him the right to change the beneficiary. The policy declares that "Neither this contract nor any payment hereunder may be assigned, and the contract and all payments shall be free from the claims of all creditors to the fullest extent permitted by law." The policy has no cash surrender, salable, or loan value, and does not entitle the annuitant to a distribution of surplus.

* * * The [government] contends that the contracts are taxable to the annuitant in the year of purchase by the employer because [§ 61(a)] sweeps into gross income "compensation for personal service, of whatever kind and in whatever form paid, * * * and income derived from any source whatever." The taxpayer * * * cites Treasury rulings to the effect that retirement annuity contracts purchased for an employee gave rise to taxable income only as the annuitant received payments under the contract; and that the entire amount of each annuity payment was includible in gross income for the year of its receipt if he had made no contribution toward the purchase of the annuity * * * .[2]

Whether we should construe the statute in accord with these Treasury rulings if the matter were *res integra,* we need not say.[3] In this court the question of construction is not *res integra* because of our decision in Ward v. Commissioner, 2 Cir., 159 F.2d 502. That case involved a single premium annuity contract delivered to the annuitant and assignable by him. We there held that "the petitioner became taxable in 1941 upon whatever value was, by the delivery of the policy to him in that year, then unconditionally placed at his disposal. * * * This was the

---

[2]   I.T. 1810, II–2 C.B. 70 (1923); I.T. 2891, XIV–1 C.B. 50 (1935); G.C.M. 14593; XIV–1 C.B. 50 (1935); I.T. 2874, XIV–1 C.B. 49 (1935); I.T. 3292, 1939–1 C.B. 84; I.T. 3346, 1940–1 C.B. 62. * * *

[3]   The Treasury rulings were distinguished or rejected in Hackett v. Commissioner, 1 Cir., 159 F.2d 121, 124; Oberwinder v. Commissioner, 8 Cir., 147 F.2d 255, 257.

then assignable value of the policy." 159 F.2d page 504. We then considered whether it was error to value the policy in the amount of the premium paid for it. We recognized that the assignable value of the policy in 1941 might be less than the single premium paid for it, but as the purchaser had offered no proof that it was we held that the Tax Court was right in treating "cost to the purchaser as the assignable value of the policy when received by the taxpayer." 159 F.2d page 505.

As we shall not overrule the *Ward* case, the question is narrowed to determining whether the present case is distinguishable because the plaintiff's policies are non-assignable and were retained in the possession of the employer. We do not think these facts are sufficient to distinguish the cases with respect to taxability of the contracts, although they may affect the value of the rights the respective annuitants acquired. It cannot be doubted that in 1939 the plaintiff received as compensation for prior services something of economic benefit which he had not previously had, namely, the obligation of the insurance company to pay money in the future to him or his designated beneficiaries on the terms stated in the policy. That obligation he acquired in 1939 notwithstanding the employer's retention of possession of the policy and notwithstanding its non-assignability. The perplexing problem is how to measure the value of the annuitant's rights at the date he acquired them. The taxpayer contends that they then had no present value, while the appellant argues that their value was equal to the premium paid by the employer. We are unable to accept either contention.

The prohibition against assignment does not prove complete absence of present value. The right to receive income payments which accrued to the plaintiff when the Optical Company received each contract represented a present economic benefit to him. It may not have been worth to him the amount his employer paid for it; but it cannot be doubted that there is a figure, greater than zero although less than the premium cost, which it would have cost him to acquire identical rights. Likewise, the assurance that any beneficiary named by him at the time the contract was executed, or substituted by him at a later date, would in the event of his death receive the cost of each contract, plus interest after a few years, conferred a present economic benefit on him. Whatever present value the life insurance feature had to him is clearly taxable. See Commissioner of Internal Revenue v. Bonwit, 2 Cir., 87 F.2d 764. * * * Another element of value inheres in the possibility that the annuitant could realize cash by contracting with a putative third person to hold in trust for him any payments to be received under the annuity contract. True, the promisee would run the risk that the annuitant might die before becoming entitled to any payments, in which event they would be payable to the beneficiary designated in the policy, but by exercising the reserved power to change the beneficiary the annuitant could designate his promisee. The power to make such a contract based on the policy may well have had some present value. No proof was offered as to this. For reasons which will be stated later the plaintiff had the burden of proving the amount by which he was overtaxed. On the other hand, it seems clear that the policy was worth less to the annuitant than the premium paid because the employer's retention of possession precluded him from exercising the privilege of accelerating the date of annuity payments since the insurance company's approval had to be endorsed upon the policy. The granting of this privilege must have been one of the factors taken into account in fixing the premium—at least, we may so assume in the absence of evidence. Hence deprivation of ability to exercise the privilege would decrease the value of the policy to the annuitant below its cost to the employer.

None of the authorities relied on by the parties is precisely in point on the issue of valuation. * * * But it is unnecessary on the present appeal to determine the precise valuation of the policies.

As already mentioned the burden of proving by how much he was overtaxed was on the [taxpayer]. He had paid the additional taxes assessed upon the valuation ascribed by the Commissioner to the annuity contracts. * * * Hence the [taxpayer] must show how much was unjustly detained. He relied upon the terms of the contract to prove that it had no present value whatever. But for reasons already stated we are satisfied that the 1939 policy had some present value and since he did not prove that such value was less than $5,000, the judgment in his favor cannot stand.

Judgment reversed and cause remanded.

■ CLARK, CIRCUIT JUDGE (dissenting in part).

I agree that the judgment must be reversed, but do not share in the view that some amount less than the $5,000 expended by the employer for this taxpayer in each of the years in question may be found to be the value of the annuity and hence the amount of additional compensation for which he is to be taxed. * * *

I do not think it is important to discover what reasons impelled the employer to make the slightly differing provisions from those before this court in Ward v. Commissioner, 2 Cir., 159 F.2d 502, 505. * * * In any event the fact is that the employer purchased at the going insurance rate those contracts which for the parties fulfilled the conditions desired.[3] Actually they would return to the annuitant, or to his widow, total amounts at least well in excess of the premiums paid and increasing yet more the longer he lived. The parties got just what they paid for in the insurance market, and its cost price is the additional compensation the executive received. The two features stressed in the opinion, namely, the nonassignability and the present nonaccelerability of the annuities, may

---

[3]   This was a tightly controlled corporation, so much so that the executives receiving the annuities and their families owned approximately 35 percent of the voting stock, while the older officers and directors owned approximately 57 percent. Hence there was never a sharp divergence of interest between these executives and their employer.

add to their usability for the particular purpose, but would seem not to change the basis of value. * * * At least, I do not see what basis we have for thinking they adversely affect values of provisions for a particular purpose, viz., security. * * *

[F]or the reasons I have stated, the fact that the annuities in these cases were assignable should not make their purchase price any more accurate a gauge of their value than is the purchase price here. * * * [I]n the Ward case we spoke of the failure of the taxpayer "to show that the contract was not worth as much as it cost." Surely there is nothing in this record to suggest anything different. * * *

DETAILED ANALYSIS

1. THE STAKES IN *DRESCHER*: THE RELATIONSHIP BETWEEN THE AMOUNT OF INCOME AND THE TIME FOR INCLUDING INCOME

Although *Drescher* may be viewed as dealing with the form of the receipt of income, it also involves the issue of when income must be recognized. Drescher sought to defer tax until he received cash payments from the annuity policy purchased for him by his employer. The government sought to tax Drescher on the purchase price of the policy in the year it was purchased for him. Drescher's argument that deferred taxation might be appropriate was possible only because Drescher's rights currently to enjoy the annuity policy were in some manner restricted. At some point Drescher would be required to pay taxes on the entire amount received. If Drescher had won, he would have been fully taxable on the cash payments when received. As a result of the government's victory, Drescher was required to pay taxes currently on the fair market value of the annuity, which should have been $5,000. When the annuity payments were received, Drescher would pay taxes on the amount received in excess of $5,000.

Before taxes are considered, the purchase price of the annuity (presumably equal to its current fair market value) equaled the discounted present value of the expected aggregate payments, because, as noted in the dissent, the dollar amount of the expected payout on the annuity was far more than its purchase price. Thus, in pure economic terms, as far as Drescher was concerned, the value of the annuity contract equaled the present value of the future payments. A rational person is indifferent between the sums when the discounted present value of an amount of money to be received in the future equals a lesser sum in present value terms. However, Drescher preferred to receive an annuity contract costing $5,000, instead of a $5,000 bonus that he could have used to purchase an annuity, because Drescher hoped to avoid paying taxes currently on the value of the annuity, leaving Drescher with the full $5,000 to invest in the annuity. From a different perspective, to provide Drescher with $5,000 to purchase an annuity, Bausch & Lomb Optical Company would have had to pay Drescher a bonus substantially in excess of $5,000 so that after paying taxes Drescher would have $5,000 left. (Computation of the exact amount of the bonus necessary to leave Drescher the $5,000 is related to the "tax on a tax" question raised by *Old Colony Trust*, see Chapter 2, Section 1.B.)

2. DEFERRED COMPENSATION

Drescher is an example of an early deferred compensation technique. Various devices for setting aside current value to be paid in the future are considered in Rev. Rul. 60–31, 1960–1 C.B. 174 (see Section 1.B. in this Chapter), in the context of rules covering the timing of inclusion of deferred compensation. In addition, Congress has provided for the result that Drescher attempted to achieve (no current taxation to the employee and taxation of the full payment on receipt) by the adoption of multiple forms of qualified deferred compensation arrangements. Broadly, these qualified plans consist of two forms. Under a defined benefit arrangement (a so-called "pension") the employer sets aside money in a trust to provide an annuity payment on retirement that is generally based on the employee's age, years of service, and compensation level at retirement. Under a defined contribution arrangement (such as a so-called "401(k) plan") the employer sets aside a sum of money, sometimes measured by profit share, into an investment account managed on behalf of the employee. The principal difference between the two forms of qualified plan is that the employee in the defined benefit plan is guaranteed an annuity level funded by a trust maintained by the employer, and on which the employer bears market risk. Meanwhile, the retirement income available to the employee with a defined contribution plan depends upon the historic investment performance of the plan, such that the employee not the employer bears the investment risk of the plan. Congress has imposed numerous conditions on the creation of these "qualified" deferred compensation plans, particularly limiting the amounts that may be set aside and excluded by the employee and deducted by the employer, and enacting non-discrimination rules that require similar benefits be made available to all employees, not just officers and highly compensated executives. For this reason, many employers create additional non-qualified deferred compensation plans for higher paid employees. While the intricacies of qualified pension plans are beyond the scope of this work, additional aspects of non-qualified deferred compensation arrangements are discussed below in Sections 1.B. & C. and Section 2.

B. UNFUNDED ARRANGEMENTS BEFORE SECTION 409A

INTERNAL REVENUE CODE: Section 83(a).

TREASURY REGULATIONS: Sections 1.83–3(e); 1.451–2(a).

Revenue Ruling 60–31
1960–1 C.B. 174.

Advice has been requested regarding the taxable year of inclusion in gross income of a taxpayer, using the cash receipts and disbursements method of accounting, of compensation for services received under the circumstances described below.

(1) On January 1, 1958, the taxpayer and corporation X executed an employment contract under which the taxpayer is to be employed by the corporation in an executive capacity for a period of five years. Under the contract, the taxpayer is entitled to a stated annual salary and to additional compensation of $10x$ dollars for each year. The additional compensation will be credited to a bookkeeping reserve account and will be deferred, accumulated, and paid in annual installments equal to one-fifth of the amount in the reserve as of the close of the year immediately preceding the year of first payment. The payments are to begin only upon (a) termination of the taxpayer's employment by the corporation; (b) the taxpayer's becoming a part-time employee of the corporation; or (c) the taxpayer's becoming partially or totally incapacitated. Under the terms of the agreement, corporation X is under a merely contractual obligation to make the payments when due, and the parties did not intend that the amounts in the reserve be held by the corporation in trust for the taxpayer.

The contract further provides that if the taxpayer should fail or refuse to perform his duties, the corporation will be relieved of any obligation to make further credits to the reserve (but not of the obligation to distribute amounts previously contributed); but, if the taxpayer should become incapacitated from performing his duties, then credits to the reserve will continue for one year from the date of the incapacity, but not beyond the expiration of the five-year term of the contract. There is no specific provision in the contract for forfeiture by the taxpayer of his right to distribution from the reserve; and, in the event he should die prior to his receipt in full of the balance in the account, the remaining balance is distributable to his personal representative at the rate of one-fifth per year for five years, beginning three months after his death.

(2) The taxpayer is an officer and director of corporation A, which has a plan for making future payments of additional compensation for current services to certain officers and key employees designated by its board of directors. This plan provides that a percentage of the annual net earnings (before Federal income taxes) in excess of $4,000x$ dollars is to be designated for division among the participants in proportion to their respective salaries. This amount is not currently paid to the participants; but, the corporation has set up on its books a separate account for each participant and each year it credits thereto the dollar amount of his participation for the year, reduced by a proportionate part of the corporation's income taxes attributable to the additional compensation. Each account is also credited with the net amount, if any, realized from investing any portion of the amount in the account.

Distributions are to be made from these accounts annually beginning when the employee (1) reaches age 60, (2) is no longer employed by the company, including cessation of employment due to death, or (3) becomes totally disabled to perform his duties, whichever occurs first. The annual distribution will equal a stated percentage of the balance in the employee's account at the close of the year immediately preceding the year of first payment, and distributions will continue until the account is exhausted. However, the corporation's liability to make these distributions is contingent upon the employee's (1) refraining from engaging in any business competitive to that of the corporation, (2) making himself available to the corporation for consultation and advice after retirement or termination of his services, unless disabled, and (3) retaining unencumbered any interest or benefit under the plan. In the event of his death, either before or after the beginning of payments, amounts in an employee's account are distributable in installments computed in the same way to his designated beneficiaries or heirs-at-law. Under the terms of the compensation plan, corporation A is under a merely contractual obligation to make the payments when due, and the parties did not intend that the amounts in each account be held by the corporation in trust for the participants.

(3) On October 1, 1957, the taxpayer, an author, and corporation Y, a publisher, executed an agreement under which the taxpayer granted to the publisher the exclusive right to print, publish and sell a book he had written. This agreement provides that the publisher will (1) pay the author specified royalties based on the actual cash received from the sale of the published work, (2) render semiannual statements of the sales, and (3) at the time of rendering each statement make settlement for the amount due. On the same day, another agreement was signed by the same parties, mutually agreeing that, in consideration of, and notwithstanding any contrary provisions contained in the first contract, the publisher shall not pay the taxpayer more than $100x$ dollars in any one calendar year. Under this supplemental contract, sums in excess of $100x$ dollars accruing in any one calendar year are to be carried over by the publisher into succeeding accounting periods; and the publisher shall not be required either to pay interest to the taxpayer on any such excess sums or to segregate any such sums in any manner.

(4) In June 1957, the taxpayer, a football player, entered into a two-year standard player's contract with a football club in which he agreed to play football and engage in activities related to football during the two-year term only for the club. In addition to a specified salary for the two-year term, it was mutually agreed that as an inducement for signing the contract the taxpayer would be paid a bonus of $150x$ dollars. The taxpayer could have demanded and received payment of this bonus at the time of signing the contract, but at his suggestion there was added to the standard contract form a paragraph providing substantially as follows:

> The player shall receive the sum of $150x$ dollars upon signing of this contract, contingent upon the payment of this $150x$ dollars to an escrow agent designated by him. The escrow agreement shall be subject to approval by the legal representatives of the player, the Club, and the escrow agent.

  Pursuant to this added provision, an escrow agreement was executed on June 25, 1957, in which the club agreed to pay 150x dollars on that date to the Y bank, as escrow agent; and the escrow agent agreed to pay this amount, plus interest, to the taxpayer in installments over a period of five years. The escrow agreement also provides that the account established by the escrow agent is to bear the taxpayer's name; that payments from such account may be made only in accordance with the terms of the agreement; that the agreement is binding upon the parties thereto and their successors or assigns; and that in the event of the taxpayer's death during the escrow period the balance due will become part of his estate.

* * *

  * * * [T]he question for resolution is whether in each of the situations described the income in question was constructively received in a taxable year prior to the taxable year of actual receipt.

  A mere promise to pay, not represented by notes or secured in any way, is not regarded as a receipt of income within the intendment of the cash receipts and disbursements method. * * * C. Florian Zittel v. Commissioner, 12 B.T.A. 675, in which, holding a salary to be taxable when received, the Board said: "Taxpayers on a receipts and disbursements basis are required to report only income actually received no matter how binding any contracts they may have to receive more."

  This should not be construed to mean that under the cash receipts and disbursements method income may be taxed only when realized in cash. For, under that method a taxpayer is required to include in income that which is received in cash or cash equivalent. W.P. Henritze v. Commissioner, 41 B.T.A. 505. And * * * the "receipt" contemplated by the cash method may be actual or constructive.

  With respect to the constructive receipt of income, section 1.451–2(a) of the Income Tax Regulations (which accords with prior regulations extending back to, and including, Article 53 of Regulations 45 under the Revenue Act of 1918) provides, in part, as follows:

> Income although not actually reduced to a taxpayer's possession is constructively received by him in the taxable year during which it is credited to his account or set apart for him so that he may draw upon it at any time. However, income is not constructively received if the taxpayer's control of its receipt is subject to substantial limitations or restrictions. Thus, if a corporation credits its employees with bonus stock, but the stock is not available to such employees until some future date, the mere crediting on the books of the corporation does not constitute receipt.

  Thus, under the doctrine of constructive receipt, a taxpayer may not deliberately turn his back upon income and thereby select the year for which he will report it. * * * Nor may a taxpayer, by a private agreement, postpone receipt of income from one taxable year to another. James E. Lewis v. Commissioner, 30 B.T.A. 318.

However, the statute cannot be administered by speculating whether the payor would have been willing to agree to an earlier payment. See, for example, J.D. Amend, et ux. v. Commissioner, 13 T.C. 178, Acquiescence, C.B. 1950–1, 1; and C.E. Gullett, et al. v. Commissioner, 31 B.T.A. 1067, in which the court, citing a number of authorities for its holding, stated:

> It is clear that the doctrine of constructive receipt is to be sparingly used; that amounts due from a corporation but unpaid, are not to be included in the income of an individual reporting his income on a cash receipts basis unless it appears that the money was available to him, that the corporation was able and ready to pay him, that his right to receive was not restricted, and that his failure to receive resulted from exercise of his own choice.

Consequently, it seems clear that in each case involving a deferral of compensation a determination of whether the doctrine of constructive receipt is applicable must be made upon the basis of the specific factual situation involved.

Applying the foregoing criteria to the situations described above, the following conclusions have been reached:

(1) The additional compensation to be received by the taxpayer under the employment contract concerned will be includible in his gross income only in the taxable years in which the taxpayer actually receives installment payments in cash or other property previously credited to his account. To hold otherwise would be contrary to the provisions of the regulations and the court decisions mentioned above.

(2) For the reasons in (1) above, it is held that the taxpayer here involved also will be required to include the deferred compensation concerned in his gross income only in the taxable years in which the taxpayer actually receives installment payments in cash or other property previously credited to his account. * * *

(3) Here the principal agreement provided that the royalties were payable substantially as earned, and this agreement was supplemented by a further concurrent agreement which made the royalties payable over a period of years. This supplemental agreement, however, was made before the royalties were earned; in fact, it was made on the same day as the principal agreement and the two agreements were a part of the same transaction. Thus, for all practical purposes, the arrangement from the beginning is similar to that in (1) above. Therefore, it is also held that the author concerned will be required to include the royalties in his gross income only in the taxable years in which they are actually received in cash or other property.

(4)   In arriving at a determination as to the includibility of the $150x$ dollars concerned in the gross income of the football player, under the circumstances described, in addition to the authorities cited above, consideration also has been given to Revenue Ruling 55–727, C.B. 1955–2, 25, and to the decision in E.T. Sproull v. Commissioner, 16 T.C. 244.

In Revenue Ruling 55–727, the taxpayer, a professional baseball player, entered into a contract in 1953 in which he agreed to render services for a baseball club and to refrain from playing baseball for any other club during the term of the contract. In addition to specified compensation, the contract provided for a bonus to the player or his estate, payable one-half in January 1954 and one-half in January 1955, whether or not he was able to render services. The primary question was whether the bonus was capital gain or ordinary income; and, in holding that the bonus payments constituted ordinary income, it was stated that they were taxable for the year in which received by the player. However, under the facts set forth in Revenue Ruling 55–727 there was no arrangement, as here, for placing the amount of the bonus in escrow. Consequently, the instant situation is distinguishable from that considered in Revenue Ruling 55–727.

In E.T. Sproull v. Commissioner, 16 T.C. 244, affirmed, 194 F.2d 541, the petitioner's employer in 1945 transferred in trust for the petitioner the amount of $10,500. The trustee was directed to pay out of principal to the petitioner the sum of $5,250 in 1946 and the balance, including income, in 1947. In the event of the petitioner's prior death, the amounts were to be paid to his administrator, executor, or heirs. The petitioner contended that the Commissioner erred in including the sum of $10,500 in his taxable income for 1945. In this connection, the court stated:

> * * * it is undoubtedly true that the amount which the Commissioner has included in petitioner's income for 1945 was used in that year for his benefit * * * in setting up the trust of which petitioner, or, in the event of his death then his estate, was the sole beneficiary * * * .

> The question then becomes * * * was "any economic or financial benefit conferred on the employee as compensation" in the taxable year. If so, it was taxable to him in that year. This question we must answer in the affirmative. The employer's part of the transaction terminated in 1945. It was then that the amount of the compensation was fixed at $10,500 and irrevocably paid out for petitioner's sole benefit. * * *

Applying the principles stated in the *Sproull* decision to the facts here, it is concluded that the $150x$-dollar bonus is includible in the gross income of the football player concerned in 1957, the year in which the club unconditionally paid such amount to the escrow agent.

* * *

As previously stated, in each case involving a deferral of compensation, a determination of whether the doctrine of constructive receipt is applicable must be made upon the basis of the specific factual situation involved. * * *

DETAILED ANALYSIS

1.   CONSTRUCTIVE RECEIPT

The constructive receipt doctrine provides that if an amount of income is made available to the taxpayer in a taxable year without substantial restriction or limitation, the amount is included in the taxpayer's gross income in that year even if the taxpayer actually receives the amount in a later year. Rev. Rul. 60–31 accepts the principle, in the context of a contractual deferred compensation arrangement, that there is no constructive receipt even though the employer might have been willing to pay cash immediately. The ruling reasons that the tax laws "cannot be administered by speculating whether the payor would have been willing to agree to an earlier payment."

But the question remains as to how early the agreement to defer payment must be made to avoid constructive receipt. In Example (1) of Rev. Rul. 60–31, the deferral arrangement was entered into before the taxpayer began to perform services under the contract. Suppose the payments being deferred were already earned though not yet payable, a situation not addressed in the ruling. The IRS appears to be of the view that constructive receipt would apply in such a situation. See e.g., Rev. Proc. 92–65, 1992–2 C.B. 428 (for advance ruling purposes, contractual agreement to defer must generally be made before related services have been performed to avoid constructive receipt). Some courts have disagreed with this view, though generally on a finding of some business purpose for the arrangement other than the mere postponement of the employee's taxes. In Commissioner v. Oates, 207 F.2d 711 (7th Cir.1953), the taxpayer was entitled to receive commissions on renewal premiums on insurance policies he had sold as a general agent of an insurance company. Under the original agency contract, the renewal commissions were to be paid to the taxpayer after retirement as the premiums were paid by the holders of the policies to the insurance company. As a result, retiring agents received a large amount of renewal commissions in early retirement years which progressively decreased. Dissatisfaction over this arrangement led to a change in company policy under which agents were allowed to amend their employment agreements so as to receive the renewal commissions in level payments. Pursuant to this new arrangement, three days before his retirement the taxpayer and the insurance company amended the employment contract to provide that the company would pay the renewal commissions to the taxpayer at the rate of $1,000 a month. The Court of Appeals held the modification of the original agreement was effective to defer the tax on the renewal commissions until actually received by the taxpayer: "Here the parties were confronted by a situation where inconvenience and resulting dissatisfaction came to the retired agents by reason of the constantly decreasing payments made by the company under the original contract. To relieve the situation, the company and the taxpayer, after full and complete negotiations, before retirement of the agent, agreed to abrogate and annul the old contract, to substitute a new one and thus to improve the unsatisfactory posture of affairs. The taxpayer * * * took no dominion over the accrued commissions other than to agree to receive them in cash installments as they matured under the contract."

Similarly, in an oft-cited case, Veit v. Commissioner, 8 T.C. 809 (1947), the Tax Court held that constructive receipt did not apply. In *Veit*, an employee was owed an amount for past services. Before the date on which the amount was due and payable, the employee and the employer entered into a supplemental agreement to further delay the payment. In concluding that the employee was not in constructive receipt of the amount deferred, the court emphasized that the supplemental agreement was "arm's length" and "bona fide," but, unlike the Seventh Circuit in *Oates*, did not discuss any non-tax business purpose for the second deferral agreement.

2. ECONOMIC BENEFIT

The economic benefit doctrine generally provides that if an employer's contractual obligation to the employee is either secured or "funded," the employer's obligation is immediately taxable to the employee. An obligation to pay is funded when the recipient is no longer relying solely on the employer's financial resources to satisfy the obligation. Funding is usually accomplished through the use of a trust or escrow device. Example (4) of Rev. Rul. 60–31 involves an example of a funded promise. A football player's right to the bonus was funded when the employer contributed the amount to the escrow agent, thereby immunizing the player from the risk of the employer's bankruptcy or insolvency. As such, the player was immediately taxable under the economic benefit doctrine. The economic benefit doctrine is now reflected in the regulations under § 83, discussed in Section 2B, which includes in income the fair market value of all property received as compensation for services except for "unfunded and unsecured promise[s] to pay." Treas. Reg. § 1.83–3(e). Section 83 would require the football player in Example (4) to include the escrow fund in income in the year it is established.

To obtain deferral, the employee must subject the right to unfunded compensation to the risk of the employer's bankruptcy or insolvency. In long-term deferral arrangements, there may be other significant risks. For example, an employee may be concerned that when payment becomes due, the employer might renege on its obligation. This prospect may be particularly worrisome if, prior to payment becoming due, the employer undergoes a change in management or the employee stops working for the employer. To protect the employee from this risk, an arrangement often referred to as a "rabbi trust" was previously used.[4] The employer established the rabbi trust, an irrevocable trust to which money was transferred to pay the deferred compensation when it became due. Pursuant to the terms of the trust, the employee was the primary beneficiary of the trust, but if, and only if, the employer subsequently became insolvent or went bankrupt the assets

---

[4] These trusts are called "rabbi trusts" because the first IRS private letter ruling that ruled favorably on such trusts involved a deferred compensation arrangement for a rabbi. See PLR 8113107.

of the trust became subject to claims of the employer's creditors. Because of the creditors' rights, the economic benefit doctrine did not apply; as a result, the employer remained the owner of the trust assets and the employee was not currently taxed under the economic benefit doctrine. See Rev. Proc. 92–64, 1992–2 C.B. 422 (providing a model form for a rabbi trust). Use of the rabbi trust is affected by § 409A, discussed in the next subsection.

3. CASH EQUIVALENCY

In certain cases, the receipt of even an unfunded and unsecured obligation to pay has triggered immediate taxation based on the rationale that the obligation is so economically similar to cash that it ought to be treated as such. The seminal cash equivalency case, *Cowden* (discussed in Chapter 28, Section 2.2.1), held that a nonnegotiable promissory note was immediately taxable as cash equivalent because the note was, among other things, assignable. To avoid the cash equivalency doctrine, the parties to unfunded deferred compensation arrangements typically make the right to deferred payments unassignable by the employee.

C. SECTION 409A

INTERNAL REVENUE CODE: Section 409A.

House Committee Report, American Jobs Creation Act of 2004*

H.R. Rep. No. 108–548, pt. 1, 108th Cong., 2nd Sess. 317–323 (2004).

REASONS FOR CHANGE

The Committee is aware of the popular use of deferred compensation arrangements by executives to defer current taxation of substantial amounts of income. The Committee believes that many nonqualified deferred compensation arrangements have developed which allow improper deferral of income. Executives often use arrangements that allow deferral of income, but also provide security of future payment and control over amounts deferred. For example, nonqualified deferred compensation arrangements often contain provisions that allow participants to receive distributions upon request, subject to forfeiture of a minimal amount (i.e., a "haircut" provision).

The Committee is aware that since the concept of a rabbi trust was developed, techniques have been used that attempt to protect the assets from creditors despite the terms of the trust. For example, the trust or fund may be located in a foreign jurisdiction, making it difficult or impossible for creditors to reach the assets.

While the general tax principles governing deferred compensation are well established, the determination whether a particular

---

*   [Ed.: The Conference Agreement followed the House bill with some modifications. Language from the Conference Committee Report (H.R. Conf. Rep. No. 108–755) is indicated by brackets.]

arrangement effectively allows deferral of income is generally made on a facts and circumstances basis. There is limited specific guidance with respect to common deferral arrangements. The Committee believes that it is appropriate to provide specific rules regarding whether deferral of income inclusion should be permitted.

The Committee believes that certain arrangements that allow participants inappropriate levels of control or access to amounts deferred should not result in deferral of income inclusion. The Committee also believes that certain arrangements, such as offshore trusts, which effectively protect assets from creditors, should be treated as funded and not result in deferral of income inclusion.

EXPLANATION OF PROVISION

Under [section 409A], all amounts deferred under a nonqualified deferred compensation plan for all taxable years are currently includible in gross income to the extent not subject to a substantial risk of forfeiture and not previously included in gross income, unless certain requirements are satisfied. If the requirements of the provision are not satisfied, in addition to current income inclusion, interest at the underpayment rate plus one percentage point is imposed on the underpayments that would have occurred had the compensation been includible in income when first deferred, or if later, when not subject to a substantial risk of forfeiture. * * * [The amount required to be included in income is also subject to a 20 percent additional tax. I.R.C. § 409A(a)(1)(B)(i)(II).]

Under [section 409A(1)(a)(2)], distributions from a nonqualified deferred compensation plan may be allowed only upon separation from service (as determined by the Secretary), death, a specified time (or pursuant to a fixed schedule), change in control in a corporation (to the extent provided by the Secretary), occurrence of an unforeseeable emergency, or if the participant becomes disabled. A nonqualified deferred compensation plan may not allow distributions other than upon the permissible distribution events and may not permit acceleration of a distribution, except as provided in regulations by the Secretary. [I.R.C. § 409A(a)(3).]

In the case of a specified employee, distributions upon separation from service may not be made earlier than six months after the date of the separation from service. Specified employees are key employees of publicly-traded corporations. [I.R.C. § 409A(a)(2)(B)(i).]

Amounts payable at a specified time or pursuant to a fixed schedule must be specified under the plan at the time of deferral. Amounts payable upon the occurrence of an event are not treated as amounts payable at a specified time. For example, amounts payable when an individual attains age 65 are payable at a specified time, while amounts payable when an individual's child begins college are payable upon the occurrence of an event.

Distributions upon a change in the ownership or effective control of a corporation, or in the ownership of a substantial portion of the assets of a corporation, may only be made to the extent provided by the Secretary. It is intended that the Secretary use a similar, but more restrictive, definition of change in control as is used for purposes of the golden parachute provisions of section 280G consistent with the purposes of the provision. The provision requires the Secretary to issue guidance defining change of control within 90 days after the date of enactment.

An unforeseeable emergency is defined [in section 409A(a)(2)(B)(ii)] as a severe financial hardship to the participant resulting from a sudden and unexpected illness or accident of the participant, the participant's spouse, or a dependent (as defined in 152(a)) of the participant; loss of the participant's property due to casualty; or other similar extraordinary and unforeseeable circumstances arising as a result of events beyond the control of the participant. The amount of the distribution must be limited to the amount needed to satisfy the emergency plus taxes reasonably anticipated as a result of the distribution. Distributions may not be allowed to the extent that the hardship may be relieved through reimbursement or compensation by insurance or otherwise, or by liquidation of the participant's assets (to the extent such liquidation would not itself cause a severe financial hardship).

A participant is considered disabled if he or she (i) is unable to engage in any substantial gainful activity by reason of any medically determinable physical or mental impairment which can be expected to result in death or can be expected to last for a continuous period of not less than 12 months; or (ii) is, by reason on any medically determinable physical or mental impairment which can be expected to result in death or can be expected to last for a continuous period of not less than 12 months, receiving income replacement benefits for a period of not less than three months under an accident and health plan covering employees of the participant's employer. [I.R.C. § 409A(a)(2)(C).]

* * *

[Section 409A(a)(4)(B)] requires that the plan must provide that compensation for services performed during a taxable year may be deferred at the participant's election only if the election to defer is made no later than the close of the preceding taxable year, or at such other time as provided in Treasury regulations.

* * *

The time and form of distributions must be specified at the time of initial deferral. A plan could specify the time and form of payments that are to be made as a result of a distribution event (e.g., a plan could specify that payments upon separation of service will be paid in lump sum within 30 days of separation from service) or could allow participants to elect the time and form of payment at the time of the initial deferral election. If a plan allows participants to elect the time and form of payment, such election is subject to the rules regarding initial deferral elections under the provision. [It is intended that multiple payout events are permissible.] * * *

Under the provision, a plan may allow changes in the time and form of distributions subject to certain requirements. [I.R.C. § 409A(a)(4)(C).] A nonqualified deferred compensation plan may allow a subsequent election to delay the timing or form of distributions only if: (1) the plan requires that such election cannot be effective for at least 12 months after the date on which the election is made; (2) except in the case of elections relating to distributions on account of death, disability or unforeseeable emergency, the plan requires that the additional deferral with respect to which such election is made is for a period of not less than five years from the date such payment would otherwise have been made; and (3) the plan requires that an election related to a distribution to be made upon a specified time may not be made less than 12 months prior to the date of the first scheduled payment. It is expected that in limited cases, the Secretary shall issue guidance, consistent with the purposes of the provision, regarding to what extent elections to change a stream of payments are permissible. [The Secretary may issue regulations regarding elections with respect to payments under nonelective, supplemental retirement plans.]

* * *

Under [section 409A(b)(1)], in the case of assets set aside (directly or indirectly) in a trust (or other arrangement determined by the Secretary) for purposes of paying nonqualified deferred compensation, such assets are treated as property transferred in connection with the performance of services under section 83 (whether or not such assets are available to satisfy the claims of general creditors) at the time set aside if such assets are located outside of the United States or at the time transferred if such assets are subsequently transferred outside of the United States. Any subsequent increases in the value of, or any earnings with respect to, such assets are treated as additional transfers of property. [I.R.C. § 409A(b)(3).] Interest at the underpayment rate plus one percentage point is imposed on the underpayments that would have occurred had the amounts been includible in income for the taxable year in which first deferred or, if later, the first taxable year not subject to a substantial risk of forfeiture. [The amount required to be included in income is also subject to an additional 20-percent tax. I.R.C. § 409A(b)(4)(A)(ii).]

* * *

Under [section 409A(b)(2)], a transfer of property in connection with the performance of services under section 83 also occurs with respect to compensation deferred under a nonqualified deferred compensation plan if the plan provides that upon a change in the employer's financial health, assets will be restricted to the payment of nonqualified deferred compensation. [An amount is treated as restricted even if the assets are available to satisfy the claims of general creditors. For example, the provision applies in the case of a plan that provides that upon a change in financial health, assets will be transferred to a rabbi trust. I.R.C. § 409A(b)(2).]

The transfer of property occurs as of the earlier of when the assets are so restricted or when the plan provides that assets will be restricted. It is intended that the transfer of property occurs to the extent that assets are restricted or will be restricted with respect to such compensation. For example, in the case of a plan that provides that upon a change in the employer's financial health, a trust will become funded to the extent of all deferrals, all amounts deferred under the plan are treated as property transferred under section 83. If a plan provides that deferrals of certain individuals will be funded upon a change in financial health, the transfer of property would occur with respect to compensation deferred by such individuals. [The provision is not intended to apply when assets are restricted for a reason other than a change in financial health (e.g., upon a change in control) or if assets are periodically restricted under a structured schedule and scheduled restrictions happen to coincide with a change in financial status.] Any subsequent increases in the value of, or any earnings with respect to, such assets are treated as additional transfers of property. Interest at the underpayment rate plus one percentage point is imposed on the underpayments that would have occurred had the amounts been includible in income for the taxable year in which first deferred or, if later, the first taxable year not subject to a substantial risk of forfeiture. [The amount required to be included in income is also subject to an additional 20-percent tax. I.R.C. § 409A(b)(4)(A)(ii).]

A nonqualified deferred compensation plan is any plan that provides for the deferral of compensation other than a qualified * * * plan or any bona fide vacation leave, sick leave, compensatory time, disability pay, or death benefit plan. * * *

[For purposes of the provision, it is not intended that the term "nonqualified deferred compensation plan" include an arrangement taxable under section 83 providing for the grant of an option on employer stock with an exercise price that is not less than the fair market value of the underlying stock on the date of grant if such arrangement does not include a deferral feature other than the feature that the option holder has the right to exercise the option in the future. The provision is not intended to change the tax treatment of incentive stock options meeting the requirements of 422 or options granted under an employee stock purchase plan meeting the requirements of section 423.]

DETAILED ANALYSIS

1. LEGISLATIVE STIMULUS

The Joint Committee on Taxation's investigation into the collapse of Enron uncovered a variety of aggressive deferred compensation tactics. The Joint Committee found that, despite the constructive receipt and economic benefit doctrines, Enron executives utilized strategies to maintain security and control over their deferred compensation accounts while still arguably avoiding current inclusion of deferred amounts. For example, a number of Enron executives were contractually permitted to receive accelerated distributions of their deferred compensation accounts, subject only to a 10 percent penalty (commonly known as a "haircut") on the amount of the early distribution. Under the constructive receipt doctrine, this 10 percent haircut would likely constitute a substantial limitation or restriction on the availability of the funds; as a result, the option to receive early distributions was believed not to trigger constructive receipt. The early distribution provisions allowed Enron executives to pull over $50 million of cash out of the company in the months immediately preceding its bankruptcy filing. Staff of the Joint Committee on Taxation, Report of Investigation of Enron Corporation and Related Entities Regarding Federal Tax and Compensation Issues, at pp. 595–637 (2003).

The aggressive tactics uncovered by the Enron investigation were thought to be pervasive among public companies and their senior executives. The restrictions and limitations of § 409A are the Congressional response to these arrangements. In addition to addressing the specific tactics that were discovered by the Joint Committee, § 409A has significantly broader ramifications.

2. SCOPE

Even though the statute appears to apply to all deferred compensation arrangements, the regulations generally limit the scope of § 409A to arrangements between employers and employees. In general, the § 409A restrictions apply to an independent contractor only if the independent contractor does not provide substantial services to at least two unrelated service recipients. Treas. Reg. § 1.409A–1(f)(2). As a result, most deferred compensation arrangements involving independent contractors will need to satisfy only the traditional cash-method rules to obtain deferred inclusion for the service provider

3. INTERACTION WITH TRADITIONAL RULES

Section 409A has significantly changed the tax law governing nonqualified deferred compensation by making it more difficult for the employee to avoid current inclusion in gross income of the deferred amounts. In order for employees to achieve the desired deferral, plans must now satisfy the requirements of § 409A in addition to avoiding immediate taxation under the traditional cash-method doctrines of constructive receipt, economic benefit, and cash equivalency.

The § 409A rules are generally stricter than the traditional rules. For example, consider the constructive receipt case law addressing agreements to further defer compensation that had already been earned but was not yet payable. In *Oates* and *Veit* (see Section 1.B.1. of this Chapter), the courts held that such agreements did not result in current inclusion under their specific facts. Under § 409A, however, elections to extend the distribution date of deferred compensation would not be permissible (thereby triggering immediate income realization and the 20 percent excise tax) unless they meet a number of conditions. Elections to extend the distribution date of deferred compensation generally must (i) not take effect for at least one year after the agreement is made, (ii) defer the payment for at least five years, and (iii) be made at least one year in advance of the date the payment is due. As a result, the liberal rules in *Oates* and *Veit* are effectively superseded by § 409A with respect to deferred compensation arrangements to which the statute applies. *Oates* and *Veit* continue to have relevance in independent contractor arrangements where § 409A is inapplicable.

4.　ACCELERATION OF DISTRIBUTIONS

To comply with § 409A, distributions must generally be made pursuant to a fixed schedule or upon the occurrence of the specified events listed in § 409A(a)(2)(A)(i)–(iii) and (v)–(vi). The statute provides that acceleration of these distributions is not permitted, except as provided by the regulations. I.R.C. § 409A(a)(3). Acting on this delegation of authority, the regulations allow for acceleration in a few extremely limited circumstances. See Treas. Reg. § 1.409A–3(j)(4).

5.　CONSEQUENCES TO THE EMPLOYER

In nonqualified deferred compensation arrangements, the timing of the employer's tax deductions is driven by the timing of the employee's inclusion of the compensation in gross income. I.R.C. § 404(a)(5). If the employee includes gross income in the year in which amounts are paid, then the employer receives the deduction at that time. If the employee includes gross income earlier (e.g., at the time in which it is earned), either because of the traditional cash-method doctrines or § 409A, then the employer's deduction is generally allowed at that earlier time.

SECTION 2.　TRANSFER OF PROPERTY FOR SERVICES

A.　THE SITUATION BEFORE SECTION 83

Commissioner v. LoBue
Supreme Court of the United States, 1956.
351 U.S. 243.

■ MR. JUSTICE BLACK delivered the opinion of the Court.

This case involves the federal income tax liability of respondent LoBue for the years 1946 and 1947. From 1941 to 1947 LoBue was manager of the New York Sales Division of the Michigan Chemical Corporation, a producer and distributor of chemical supplies. In 1944 the company adopted a stock option plan making 10,000 shares of its common stock available for distribution to key employees at $5 per share over a 3-year period. * * *

LoBue's work was so satisfactory that the company in the course of 3 years delivered to him 3 stock options covering 340 shares. He exercised all these $5 per share options in 1946 and in 1947, paying the company only $1,700 for stock having a market value when delivered of $9,930. Thus, at the end of these transactions, LoBue's employer was worth $8,230 less to its stockholders and LoBue was worth $8,230 more than before. The company deducted this sum as an expense in its 1946 and 1947 tax returns but LoBue did not report any part of it as income. Viewing the gain to LoBue as compensation for personal services the Commissioner levied a deficiency assessment against him, relying on [the former version of section 61(a)], which defines gross income as including "gains, profits, and income derived from * * * compensation for personal service * * * of whatever kind and in whatever form paid * * * ."

LoBue petitioned the Tax Court to redetermine the deficiency, urging that "The said options were not intended by the Corporation or the petitioner to constitute additional compensation but were granted to permit the petitioner to acquire a proprietary interest in the Corporation and to provide him with the interest in the successful operation of the Corporation deriving from an ownership interest." The Tax Court held that LoBue had a taxable gain if the options were intended as compensation but not if the options were designed to provide him with "a proprietary interest in the business." Finding after hearings that the options were granted to give LoBue "a proprietary interest in the Corporation, and not as compensation for services" the Tax Court held for LoBue. * * * Relying on this finding the Court of Appeals affirmed, saying: "This was a factual issue which it was the peculiar responsibility of the Tax Court to resolve. From our examination of the evidence we cannot say that its finding was clearly erroneous." 3 Cir., 223 F.2d 367, 371. Disputes over the taxability of stock option transactions such as this are longstanding. We granted certiorari to consider whether the Tax Court and the Court of Appeals had given [the former version of section 61(a)] too narrow an interpretation. * * *

We have repeatedly held that in defining "gross income" as broadly as it did in [the former version of section 61(a)] Congress intended to "tax all gains except those specifically exempted." See, e.g., Commissioner of Internal Revenue v. Glenshaw Glass Co., 348 U.S. 426, 429–430. The only exemption Congress provided from this very comprehensive definition of taxable income that could possibly have application here is the gift exemption of [section 102]. But there was not the slightest indication of the kind of detached and disinterested generosity which might evidence a "gift" in the statutory sense. These transfers of stock bore none of the earmarks of a gift. * * *

Since the employer's transfer of stock to its employee LoBue for much less than the stock's value was not a gift, it seems impossible to say that it was not compensation. The Tax Court held there was no taxable income, however, on the ground that one purpose of the employer was to confer a "proprietary interest."[5] But there is not a word in [the former version of section 61(a)] which indicates that its broad coverage should be narrowed because of an employer's intention to enlist more efficient service from his employees by making them part proprietors of his business. In our view there is no statutory basis for the test established by the courts below. When assets are transferred by an employer to an employee to secure better services they are plainly compensation. It makes no difference that the compensation is paid in stock rather than in money. [The former version of section 61(a)] taxes income derived from compensation "in whatever form paid." And in another stock option case we said that [the former version of section 61(a)] "is broad enough to include in taxable income any economic or financial benefits conferred on the employee as compensation, whatever the form or mode by which it is effected." Commissioner of Internal Revenue v. Smith, 324 U.S. 177. LoBue received a very substantial economic and financial benefit from his employer prompted by the employer's desire to get better work from him. This is "compensation for personal service" within the meaning of [the former version of section 61(a)].

LoBue nonetheless argues that we should treat this transaction as a mere purchase of a proprietary interest on which no taxable gain was "realized" in the year of purchase. It is true that our taxing system has ordinarily treated an arm's length purchase of property even at a bargain price as giving rise to no taxable gain in the year of purchase. * * * But that is not to say that when a transfer which is in reality compensation is given the form of a purchase the Government cannot tax the gain under [the former version of section 61(a)]. The transaction here was unlike a mere purchase. It was not an arm's length transaction between strangers. Instead it was an arrangement by which an employer transferred valuable property to his employees in recognition of their services. We hold that LoBue realized taxable gain when he purchased the stock.

A question remains as to the time when the gain on the shares should be measured. LoBue gave his employer promissory notes for the option price of the first 300 shares but the shares were not delivered until the notes were paid in cash. The market value of the shares was lower when the notes were given than when the cash was paid. The Commissioner measured the taxable gain by the market value of the shares when the cash was paid. LoBue contends that this was wrong, and that the gain should be measured either when the options were granted or when the notes were given.

---

[5]   The Tax Court noted "that in practically all such cases as the one before us, both the element of additional compensation and the granting of a proprietary interest are present." 22 T.C. at page 445. * * *

It is of course possible for the recipient of a stock option to realize an immediate taxable gain. See Commissioner of Internal Revenue v. Smith, 324 U.S. 177. The option might have a readily ascertainable market value and the recipient might be free to sell his option. But this is not such a case. These three options were not transferable and LoBue's right to buy stock under them was contingent upon his remaining an employee of the company until they were exercised. Moreover, the uniform Treasury practice since 1923 has been to measure the compensation to employees given stock options subject to contingencies of this sort by the difference between the option price and the market value of the shares at the time the option is exercised. * * * Under these circumstances there is no reason for departing from the Treasury practice. The taxable gain to LoBue should be measured as of the time the options were exercised and not the time they were granted.

* * *

Reversed and remanded.

* * *

■ MR. JUSTICE HARLAN, whom MR. JUSTICE BURTON joins, concurring in part and dissenting in part.

In my view, the taxable event was the grant of each option, not its exercise. When the respondent received an unconditional option to buy stock at less than the market price, he received an asset of substantial and immediately realizable value, at least equal to the then-existing spread between the option price and the market price. It was at that time that the corporation conferred a benefit upon him. At the exercise of the option, the corporation "gave" the respondent nothing; it simply satisfied a previously-created legal obligation. That transaction, by which the respondent merely converted his asset from an option into stock, should be of no consequence for tax purposes. The option should be taxable as income when given, and any subsequent gain through appreciation of the stock, whether realized by sale of the option, if transferable, or by sale of the stock acquired by its exercise, is attributable to the sale of a capital asset, and, if the other requirements are satisfied, should be taxed as a capital gain. Any other result makes the division of the total gains between ordinary income (compensation) and capital gain (sale of an asset) dependent solely upon the fortuitous circumstance of when the employee exercises his option.[2]

---

[2]   Suppose two employees are given unconditional options to buy stock at $5, the current market value. The first exercises the option immediately and sells the stock a year later at $15. The second holds the option for a year, exercises it, and sells the stock immediately at $15. Admittedly the $10 gain would be taxed to the first as capital gain; under the Court's view, it would be taxed to the second as ordinary income because it is "compensation" for services. I fail to see how the gain can be any more "compensation" to one than it is to the other.

DETAILED ANALYSIS

1.　THE RELATIONSHIP OF VALUATION TO TIMING OF INCLUSION

The majority opinion in *LoBue* observed that the recipient of a stock option as compensation for services might recognize an immediate taxable gain if the option has a readily ascertainable value and the recipient is free to sell the option. The court held, however, that the compensation in the *LoBue* case was includable in income only when the option was exercised because, at the time of the grant and LoBue's purchase of the optioned stock for a promissory note, the options had no readily ascertainable market value, the options "were not transferable and LoBue's right to buy stock under them was contingent upon his remaining an employee of the company until they were exercised." Under this approach, an unrestricted option that has a readily ascertainable fair market value at the time of the grant would be treated as compensation to the employee at that time, which has a number of collateral consequences. The inclusion of that compensation in income transforms the option into an investment. Any subsequent gain or loss upon disposition of the option or the underlying stock will be capital in nature. Also, the subsequent exercise of the option would no longer be a taxable event. The taxpayer's basis for the stock received upon the exercise of the option will equal the sum of the exercise price and the amount included in income at the time of grant. This treatment is an application of the general rule for determining the basis of property received upon the exercise of purchased options, which adds the amount paid for the option to the exercise price. In this case, however, the amount "paid" for the option is the amount included in income as compensation; the transaction is treated as if the employer paid cash to the employee who then used the cash to purchase the option a result mandated by § 83, discussed in the next subsection.

B.　SECTION 83

INTERNAL REVENUE CODE: Section 83(a)–(c), (e), (f), (h).

REGULATIONS: Sections 1.83–1(a); –2(a)–(d); –3; –7.

In a typical "restricted property" arrangement, property (usually shares of the employer corporation) are transferred to the employee subject to the requirement that the employee forfeit the property back to the employer under specified conditions, such as upon leaving the employ of the employer within a certain period of time. Under § 83, property that is subject to substantial risk of forfeiture and nontransferable is not included in income until the restrictions lapse. In addition, § 83(e)(3) provides that the recipient of an option that does not have readily ascertainable fair market value is not subject to tax under § 83. Upon the exercise of the option, however, the transfer of stock would be subject to § 83 and thus result in ordinary income in the amount of the "spread" (i.e., the excess of the fair market value of the stock over the exercise price) at the time of the exercise.

General Explanation of the Tax Reform Act of 1969

Staff of the Joint Committee on Taxation 110–112 (1970).

Explanation of [section 83].—[Section 83] provides that a person who receives a beneficial interest in property, such as stock, by reason of his performance of services must report as income in the taxable period in which received, the value of the property unless his interest in the property is subject to a substantial risk of forfeiture and is nontransferable. The amount included in income is the excess of the fair market value of the property over the amount paid for it. The fair market value of the property is determined without regard to any restrictions, except a restriction which by its terms will never lapse.

If the property is subject to a substantial risk of forfeiture and is nontransferable, the employee is not required to recognize any income with respect to the property until his interest in the property either becomes transferable or no longer is subject to such risk. * * *

An employee is not taxed, either when he receives forfeitable property or when he gives it to another person, if it remains subject to forfeitability in the hands of the donee. However, the employee (and not the donee) is taxable at the time the donee's rights become nonforfeitable. If an employee who has a forfeitable interest in property sells the property in an arm's length transaction, the employee is treated as realizing income at that time.

When a person is allowed to sell property only at a price determined by formula, under a provision which will never lapse, this restriction is taken into account in valuing the property. [Section 83(d)(1)] provides that the formula price is deemed to be the fair market value of the property, unless established to the contrary by the Secretary or his delegate.

If a restriction which was taken into account in valuing an item of property is canceled, the employee must recognize compensation income in the taxable year in which the cancellation occurs. The amount of income recognized is the excess of the fair market value of the property (computed without regard to the restriction) at the time of cancellation over the sum of: (1) the fair market value of such property (computed by taking the restriction into account) immediately before the cancellation, and (2) the amount, if any, paid for the cancellation. It is not necessary to recognize income upon cancellation of a restriction if it can be established that the cancellation is not compensatory and that the person who would be entitled to a deduction if it were compensatory will treat the transaction as not compensatory.

To add flexibility, [section 83(b)] allows employees the option of treating restricted property as compensation in the year it is received, even though it is nontransferable and subject to a substantial risk of forfeiture. If this election is made, the restricted property rules do not apply, and later appreciation in the value of the property is not treated as compensation. * * *

The holding period of restricted property is deemed to begin at the first time the taxpayer's rights in the property are transferable or are not subject to a substantial risk of forfeiture, whichever occurs earlier (i.e., the time he is deemed to receive compensation).

The restricted property rules do not apply to: (1) [statutory incentive stock options]; (2) a transfer to or from a qualified [retirement] trust (described in section 401(a)) or to a transfer under an annuity plan meeting the requirements of section 404(a)(2); * * * (4) the transfer of an option without a readily ascertainable fair market value; or (5) the transfer of property pursuant to the exercise of an option with a readily ascertainable fair market value at date of grant. * * *

[Section 83(h)] allows the employer a deduction equal to the amount which the employee is required to recognize as income. * * *

Alves v. Commissioner
United States Court of Appeals, Ninth Circuit, 1984.
734 F.2d 478.

■ SCHROEDER, CIRCUIT JUDGE.

Lawrence J. Alves appeals a Tax Court decision sustaining the Commissioner's finding of deficiency for 1974 and 1975. * * * The appeal raises an unusual question under section 83 of the Internal Revenue Code * * * . Section 83 requires that an employee who has purchased restricted stock in connection with his "performance of services" must include as ordinary income the stock's appreciation in value between the time of purchase and the time the restrictions lapse, unless at the time he purchased the stock he elected to include as income the difference between the purchase price and the fair market value at that time. The issue here is whether section 83 applies to an employee's purchase of restricted stock when, according to the stipulation of the parties, the amount paid for the stock equaled its full fair market value, without regard to any restrictions. The Tax Court, with two dissenting opinions, held that section 83 applies to all restricted stock that is transferred "in connection with the performance of services," regardless of the amount paid for it. 79 T.C. at 878. We affirm.

FACTS

General Digital Corporation (the company) was formed in April, 1970, to manufacture and market micro-electronic circuits. At its first meeting, the company's board of directors resolved to issue 90,000 shares of its common stock to its company president, and 66,000 shares to the company underwriter. The board also voted to sell an additional 264,000 shares of common stock to seven named individuals, including Alves. All seven became company employees.

Alves joined the company as vice-president for finance and administration. As part of an employment and stock purchase agreement dated May 22, 1970, the company agreed to sell Alves 40,000 shares of common stock at ten cents per share "in order to raise capital for the Company's initial operations while at the same time providing the Employee with an additional interest in the Company. . . ." 79 T.C. at 867. * * * The agreement divided Alves's shares into three categories: one-third were subject to repurchase by the company at ten cents per share if Alves left within four years; one-third were subject to repurchase if he left the company within five years; and one-third were unrestricted. In addition, the company retained an option to repurchase up to one-half of the shares for their fair market value at any time between July 1, 1973 and July 1, 1975.

* * *

On July 1, 1974, when the restrictions on the four-year shares lapsed, Alves still owned 4,667 four-year shares that had a fair market value at that time of $6 per share. On March 24, 1975, the restrictions on the 7,093 remaining five-year shares lapsed with the fair market value at $3.43 per share.

[Alves] * * * did not report the difference between the fair market value of the four and five-year shares when the restrictions ended, and the purchase price paid for the shares. The Commissioner treated the difference as ordinary income in 1974 and 1975, pursuant to section 83(a).

In proceedings before the Tax Court, the parties stipulated that: (1) General Digital's common stock had a fair market value of 10 cents per share on the date Alves entered into the employment and stock purchase agreement; (2) the stock restrictions were imposed to "provide some assurance that key personnel would remain with the company for a number of years;" (3) Alves did not make an election under section 83(b) when the restricted stock was received; (4) the free shares were not includable in gross income under section 83; and (5) the four and five-year restricted shares were subject to a substantial risk of forfeiture until July 1, 1974, and March 24, 1975, respectively.

The Tax Court sustained the Commissioner's deficiency determination. It found as a matter of fact that the stock was transferred to Alves in connection with the performance of services for the company, and, as a matter of law, that section 83(a) applies even where the transferee paid full fair market value for the stock. * * *

DISCUSSION

Resolution of the legal issue presented here requires an understanding of section 83's background and operation. Congress enacted section 83 in 1969 in response to the existing disparity between the tax treatment of restricted stock plans and other types of deferred compensation arrangements. S.Rep. No. 552, 91st Cong., 1st Sess. 120–

21 * * * . Prior to 1969, an individual purchasing restricted stock was taxed either when the restrictions lapsed or when the stock was sold in an arm's length transaction. Tax was imposed upon the difference between the purchase price and the fair market value at the time of transfer or when the restrictions lapsed, whichever was less. See Cohn v. Commissioner, 73 T.C. 443, 446 (1979). This had both tax deferral and tax avoidance advantages over, for example, employer contributions to an employee's pension or profit sharing trust, which were immediately taxable in the year of receipt. H.R.Rep. No. 413, 91st Cong., 1st Sess. 86–87 * * * ; Senate Report at 120–21 * * * .

Section 83 resolved this disparity by requiring the taxpayer either to elect to include the "excess" of the fair market value over the purchase price in the year the stock was transferred, or to be taxed upon the full amount of appreciation when the risk of forfeiture was removed. 26 U.S.C. §§ 83(a), 83(b). * * * By its terms, the statute applies when property is: (1) transferred in connection with the performance of services; (2) subject to a substantial risk of forfeiture; and (3) not disposed of in an arm's length transaction before the property becomes transferable or the risk of forfeiture is removed. In the present case, it is undisputed that the stock in question was subject to a substantial risk of forfeiture, that it was not disposed of before the restrictions lapsed, and that Alves made no section 83(b) election. Alves's contention is that because he paid full fair market value for the shares, they were issued as an investment, rather than in connection with the performance of services.

The Tax Court concluded that Alves obtained the stock "in connection with the performance of services" as company vice-president. To the extent that this conclusion is a finding of fact, it is not clearly erroneous. * * * Although payment of full fair market value may be one indication that stock was not transferred in connection with the performance of services, the record shows that until the company sold stock to TVI, it issued stock only to its officers, directors, and employees, with the exception of the shares sold to the underwriter. Alves purchased the stock when he signed his employment agreement and the stock restrictions were linked explicitly to his tenure with the company. In addition, the parties stipulated that the restricted stock's purpose was to ensure that key personnel would remain with the company. Nothing in the record suggests that Alves could have purchased the stock had he not agreed to join the company.

Alves maintains that, as a matter of law, section 83(a) should not extend to purchases for full fair market value. He argues that "in connection with" means that the employee is receiving compensation for his performance of services. In the unusual situation where the employee pays the same amount for restricted and unrestricted stock, the restriction has no effect on value, and hence, Alves contends, there is no compensation.

The plain language of section 83(a) belies Alves's argument. The statute applies to all property transferred in connection with the performance of services. No reference is made to the term "compensation." Nor is there any statutory requirement that property have a fair market value in excess of the amount paid at the time of transfer. Indeed, if Congress intended section 83(a) to apply solely to restricted stock used to compensate employees, it could have used much narrower language. Instead, Congress made section 83(a) applicable to all restricted "property," not just stock; to property transferred to "any person," not just to employees; and to property transferred "in connection with . . . services" not just compensation for employment. * * * As the Second Circuit has noted, Congress drafted section 83(a) as a "blanket rule" in an effort to create "a workable, practical system of taxing employees' restricted stock options." Sakol v. Commissioner, 574 F.2d 694, 699–700 (2d Cir.) cert. denied, 439 U.S. 859 (1978).

Section 83's legislative history also reveals that while Congress was concerned primarily with the favorable tax treatment afforded restricted stock plans, it also was concerned that such plans were a means of allowing key employees to become shareholders in businesses without adhering to requirements in other sections of the Code. The Senate Report stated:

> To the extent that a restricted stock plan can be considered a means of giving employees a stake in the business, the committee believes the present tax treatment of these plans is inconsistent with the specific rules provided by Congress in the case of qualified stock options, which were considered by Congress as the appropriate means by which an employee could be given a shareholder's interest in the business.

Senate Report at 120–21 * * * . Accord House Report at 90 * * * . The legislative history reveals that Congress perceived restricted stock as more than a problem of deferred compensation. It also demonstrates that Congress intended section 83 to apply to taxpayers like Alves who allege that they purchased restricted stock as an investment.

Alves suggests that the language of section 83(b) indicates that Congress meant for that section to apply only to bargain purchases and that section 83(a) should be interpreted in the same way. Section 83(b) allows taxpayers to elect to include as income in the year of transfer "the excess" of the full fair market value over the purchase price. Alves contends that a taxpayer who pays full fair market value would have "zero excess," and would fall outside the terms of section 83(b).

Section 83(b), however, is not a limitation upon section 83(a). Congress designed section 83(b) merely to add "flexibility," not to condition section 83(a) on the presence or absence of an "excess." Senate Report at 123 * * *

Moreover, nothing in section 83(b) precludes a taxpayer who has paid full market value for restricted stock from making an 83(b) election. Treasury Regulations promulgated in 1978 and made retroactive to 1969 specifically provide that section 83(b) is available in situations of zero excess:

> If property is transferred . . . in connection with the performance of services, the person performing such services may elect to include in gross income under section 83(b) the excess (if any) of the fair market value of the property at the time of transfer . . . over the amount (if any) paid for such property. . . . *The fact that the transferee has paid full value for the property transferred, realizing no bargain element in the transaction, does not preclude the use of the election as provided for in this section.*

26 C.F.R. § 1.83.2(a) (1983) (emphasis supplied). These regulations are consistent with the broad language of section 83 and, as the Tax Court stated, simply make "more explicit a fact which is inherent in the statute itself." 79 T.C. at 877–78 n. 7. * * *

Alves last contends that since every taxpayer who pays full fair market value for restricted stock would, if well informed, choose the section 83(b) election to hedge against any appreciation, applying section 83(a) to the unfortunate taxpayer who made no election is simply a trap for the unwary. The tax laws often make an affirmative election necessary. Section 83(b) is but one example of a provision requiring taxpayers to act or suffer less attractive tax consequences. A taxpayer wishing to avoid treatment of appreciation as ordinary income must make an affirmative election under 83(b) in the year the stock was acquired.

Other courts have considered and rejected even stronger attacks on the broad application of section 83. * * * In the present case, the statutory language, legislative history, applicable regulations and the consistent refusal of courts to create exceptions to the statute's coverage, all compel the conclusion that section 83(a) applies to the income Alves received when the restrictions on his stock lapsed in 1974 and 1975. The decision of the Tax Court is affirmed.

DETAILED ANALYSIS

1. SCOPE OF SECTION 83

1.1. *Generally*

While § 83 was enacted primarily to deal with restricted stock, its application goes well beyond that particular situation. The section applies to all transfers of property made in connection with the performance of services and thus to transfers to independent contractors as well as to employees. For § 83 to be applicable, there must be a "transfer" of "property." Treas. Reg. § 1.83–3(a) states that a transfer takes place only when a person acquires a beneficial interest in the property. Thus, if the transferee does not bear the risk of loss in the value of the property, because, for example, the property is acquired using a nonrecourse obligation to the employer, no "transfer" takes place at the time of the acquisition. As a result, all appreciation in value until the time a transfer occurs (by, for example, paying off the nonrecourse obligation) is ordinary income.

In Rev. Rul. 2004–37, 2004–1 C.B. 583, the IRS responded to a transaction designed to obfuscate the fact that a transfer subject to § 83 had occurred. In that ruling, an employee purchased employer stock by giving the employer a promissory note. The employer and the employee subsequently agreed to reduce the principal amount of the note. The ruling held that the debt reduction constituted a transfer of property subject to § 83 rather than excluded cancellation of indebtedness income under § 108(e)(5), discussed in Chapter 10, Section 2.3.

1.2. *Property*

The meaning of "property" for purposes of § 83 is broad, and includes real property as well as both tangible and intangible personal property. See Treas. Reg. § 1.83–3(e). Rev. Rul. 83–46, 1983–1 C.B. 16, held that a transfer of an overriding royalty interest in an oil and gas property, representing a right to future income as oil and gas were produced, transferred in compensation for services qualified as a transfer of property subject to § 83. See also Zuhone v. Commissioner, 883 F.2d 1317 (7th Cir.1989) (agreeing with the revenue ruling). Mark IV Pictures, Inc. v. Commissioner, 969 F.2d 669 (8th Cir.1992), held that a partnership capital interest received from the partnership in exchange for services constituted a receipt of property under § 83. But see Rev. Proc. 93–27, 1993–2 C.B. 343, clarified by Rev. Proc. 2001–43, 2001–2 C.B. 191 (holding that if certain specified conditions are met, the Service will not treat a partnership interest only in future profits as taxable when received). Montelepre Systemed, Inc. v. Commissioner, T.C. Memo. 1991–46, aff'd, 956 F.2d 496 (5th Cir.1992), held that a right of first refusal to purchase a business, granted to a manager by the owner pursuant to the manager's employment contract, was property. See also Theophilos v. Commissioner, 85 F.3d 440 (9th Cir.1996) (holding that for purposes of § 83, "property" includes a binding executory contract to purchase property).

The definition of "property" expressly excludes "an unfunded and unsecured promise to pay money or property in the future." Treas. Reg. § 1.83–3(e). Thus, § 83 does not apply to deferred compensation arrangements described in Examples (1)–(3) in Rev. Rul. 60–31 (see Section 1.B. of this Chapter). Consistent with the economic benefit doctrine established by case law, however, Treas. Reg. § 1.83–3(e) also provides that the term property includes a beneficial interest in assets set aside from claims of creditors in a trust or escrow account. Thus, for example, the transfer to an escrow agent in Example (4) of Rev. Rul. 60–31, which was ruled taxable under the economic benefit doctrine, would now be covered by § 83 but the tax consequences would remain the same. Grant-Jacoby, Inc. v. Commissioner, 73 T.C. 700 (1980), held that contributions to an educational trust the beneficiaries of which were children of management employees were subject to § 83.

1.3. *Services*

Section 83 applies whenever property is received "in connection with the performance of services." It does not matter whether the taxpayer receiving the property is an employee or independent contractor. Treas. Reg. § 1.83–1(a), –3(f); Cohn v. Commissioner, 73 T.C. 443 (1979). Receipt of property other than in consideration of services, however, is not subject to § 83. Centel Communications Co. v. Commissioner, 920 F.2d 1335 (7th Cir.1990), held that stock warrants issued to a corporation's shareholders in consideration for those shareholders guaranteeing the corporation's debts were not transferred in connection with the performance of services. Rather, the warrants were issued in consideration of a capital contribution to the corporation. See also Kimberlin v. Commissioner, 128 T.C. 163 (2007) (warrants issued to securities underwriter in settlement for breach of contract pursuant to which underwriter was to have performed services were not issued in connection with the performance of services).

2. EFFECT OF RESTRICTIONS

2.1. *Generally*

A substantial risk of forfeiture exists where the right to the property is conditioned on the future performance of substantial services. See Treas. Reg. § 1.83–3(c), which provides examples of restrictions that constitute a substantial risk of forfeiture. If property is transferred subject to a substantial risk of forfeiture at the time of vesting, when the risk of forfeiture lapses the fair market value of the property is included in income as compensation (less the amount, if any, paid by the transferee). An increase in the value of transferred property between the time of the transfer of the property and its vesting is treated as ordinary income rather than capital gain. If the property is subject to a restriction that does not amount to a substantial risk of forfeiture, the property is included in income at the time of the transfer at its full fair market value, disregarding the effect of any restrictions other than restrictions which by their terms will never lapse (such as the requirement that the property may only be sold back to the transferor at a price fixed under a predetermined formula). In Sakol v. Commissioner, 574 F.2d 694 (2d Cir.1978), an employee of Chesebrough-Ponds, Inc. bought 140 shares of Chesebrough-Ponds stock for $21.20 per share pursuant to the Chesebrough-Ponds stock purchase plan. The stock was forfeitable if the employee ceased to be a Chesebrough-Ponds employee within one year after purchase. In addition, under the terms of the plan the stock was not transferable for five years after purchase. On the date the risk of forfeiture lapsed, Chesebrough-Ponds stock was trading on the New York Stock Exchange for $66.50. The Commissioner asserted that the full spread of $45.30 per share was includable under § 83. Sakol argued that it was unconstitutional not to take into account the prohibition on transfer in valuing the stock. After concluding that § 83 would be constitutional if "there is a rational relationship between the criteria set forth in the statutory mandate and a legitimate congressional purpose" the court upheld the constitutionality of § 83:

Applying, then, the rational relationship test to Section 83(a), we note * * * that Congress could legitimately have judged that the law prior to the enactment of Section 83 permitted undue income tax avoidance through the use of restricted stock options. The value received by the employee was not taken into income until the restrictions lapsed, yet such arrangements generally permitted taxpayers to enjoy the voting and dividend benefits of stock ownership, despite restrictions on transfer. Section 83(a) * * * was a congressional attempt to eliminate such tax avoidance, clearly a legitimate governmental purpose. While taxpayer takes exception to the possibly overbroad means utilized to effectuate the congressional purpose, the statutory scheme satisfies constitutional standards of rationality for three reasons.

First, whatever depreciating effect transfer restrictions may have on stock value adversely affects only the taxpayer-employee who wishes to sell his stock during the restriction period and is denied the right to do so by the corporation. Prior to enactment of Section 83 most of these restrictions were cooperatively imposed by the corporation with the aim of providing a tax benefit to the employee rather than advancing purely corporate objectives. Section 83(a) is a reasonably well tailored means of defeating a device the only business purpose of which could be to pay employees with dollars that, because they may be tax-free or tax-favored, may be fewer. Second, the corporation always retains, expressly or by implication of law, the power to waive any restriction. The waiver power thus renders the amount of value depreciation both speculative and dependent upon the subjective intentions of the parties to the plan. Congress was therefore justified in adopting nonindividualistic means * * * because the factual determinations otherwise necessary accurately to value the shares would depend upon matters entirely within the knowledge and control of the corporate employer and its employee. Since a corporation such as Chesebrough could always release its employee from the restrictions, determining share value with any degree of certainty would be most difficult, expensive and, to the tax collector, administratively inordinately inconvenient. * * * Finally, it is not insignificant that those who choose to participate in a restricted stock option purchase plan do so voluntarily, presumably aware of Section 83(a)'s tax consequences. That taxpayers participate in such plans with open eyes minimizes the arbitrariness which flows from the lack of perfect fit between the congressional means and its purpose.

Section 83(a) creates a blanket rule, to be sure, unfair perhaps in an individual case, that transfer restrictions generally are to be given no effect in computing the Section 83(a) inclusion. We nevertheless find the requisite rational relationship between congressional means and the legitimate congressional purpose in curbing tax avoidance from the use of restricted stock options.

* * *

We conclude that a workable, practical system of taxing employees' restricted stock options can overlook, at least temporarily, a speculative decrease in value in ascertaining the amount of compensation received in the form of restricted stock where the employee has obtained both voting power and dividend rights. Absent the statute, some stock restrictions might in the abstract make determination of a fair market value exceedingly difficult or downright impossible. * * * By the statute, Congress has drawn a decisive line between restrictions which either defer taxation or by their own terms affect the fair market value calculation and those restrictions which are not considered in measuring fair market value. Congress is not required to take each and every restriction into account in combating tax-avoidance, or to make equally difficult individual evaluations which depend upon the parties' subjective intentions. Rather, the Sixteenth, and Fifth, Amendments permit the line drawn to be a rough one, in the interest of realistically solving a practical problem, by making a "gross accommodation to the economic reality." Fraser v. Commissioner, 25 F.2d 653, 655 (2d Cir.1928) (L. Hand, J.). * * * Because nonqualified plans have been the vehicles of tax avoidance Congress may clothe the tax incidental to them with a ready-made, rather than a custom-tailored, suit.

In contrast to *Sakol*, Theophilos v. Commissioner, 85 F.3d 440 (9th Cir.1996), held that a minority discount should be taken into account in valuing nonvoting stock in a closely held corporation received in a compensatory bargain purchase subject to § 83. A minority discount is a reduction in the fair market value of stock held by a minority (i.e., less than 50 percent) shareholder to reflect the fact that the owner cannot control the operations of the corporation.

2.2. *Substantial Risk of Forfeiture*

Treas. Reg. § 1.83–3 provides that except as specifically provided in § 83(c)(3) and Treas. Regs. § 1.83–3(j) and (k), a substantial risk of forfeiture may be established only through a service condition or a condition related to the purpose of the transfer. A substantial risk of forfeiture exists where the right to the property is conditioned on the future performance of substantial services. On the other hand, the requirement that the property be returned to the employer on termination of employment for cause is not a substantial risk of forfeiture and, therefore, property subject to such a restriction is includable in income when received. When determining whether a substantial risk of forfeiture exists based on a condition related to the purpose of the transfer, both the likelihood that the forfeiture event will occur and the likelihood that the forfeiture will be enforced must be considered. In Richardson v. Commissioner, 64 T.C. 621 (1975), a nonqualified deferred compensation trust provided that a physician's rights to future payments from the trust would be forfeited if after retirement he refused to provide consulting services to the employer-hospital upon request. Because the evidence indicated that it was unlikely that the hospital would need, or that the taxpayer could provide, the requested services, and because the trust agreement made no provisions for disposition of its assets in the event of forfeiture, the court ignored the forfeiture provision. In addition, transfer restrictions do not create a substantial risk of forfeiture, even if transfer restrictions carry the potential for forfeiture or disgorgement of some or all of the property, or other penalties, if the restriction is violated. Examples illustrate that a substantial risk of forfeiture is not created solely as a result of potential liability under Rule 10b–5 of the Securities Exchange Act of 1934 or an employer-imposed "lock-up" agreement.

A requirement that upon the employee's termination of service stock must be sold back to the employer at the then-existing fair market value of the stock is not a risk of forfeiture. However, other buy-sell agreements may result in a substantial risk of forfeiture. In Robinson v. Commissioner, 805 F.2d 38 (1st Cir.1986), an employee bought stock in his employer at a discount. For the first year after the purchase, the employee's right of resale was restricted to selling back to the corporation at the employee's cost. The court concluded that this restriction created a substantial risk of forfeiture.

2.3. *Restrictions That Will Never Lapse*

Section 83(d) provides that restrictions that will never lapse are taken into account in valuing restricted property that has become nonforfeitable. Treas. Reg. § 1.83–3(h) gives as the primary example of nonlapse restrictions a requirement of resale at a formula-determined price.

Treas. Reg. § 1.83–3(h) also provides that restrictions on resale under securities laws are not nonlapse restrictions. In Pledger v. Commissioner, 641 F.2d 287 (5th Cir.1981), the taxpayer received stock subject to securities law restrictions that prevented the stock from being sold for two years unless there was a registration of the stock during that period (so-called "lettered" stock). The restriction reduced the value of the shares to approximately 65 percent of what it would have been absent the restriction. The court held that the effect of the restriction was to be ignored in determining the value of the stock for purposes of § 83. The court also upheld the constitutionality of this treatment of lapse restrictions in § 83.

3. SECTION 83(b) ELECTION

As discussed in *Alves,* § 83(b) allows the taxpayer to elect current taxation of the value of restricted property in those situations in which taxation would be deferred under the normal rule of § 83(a). This election can be beneficial to the taxpayer if the property has little current value in excess of any consideration paid by the taxpayer and it is anticipated that the property will appreciate substantially in value between the time the property is transferred to the taxpayer and the time the restriction lapses. By including a small amount in ordinary income currently, the taxpayer will be entitled to capital gain treatment on any increase in value that would have been taxed as ordinary income under § 83(a) at the time the restriction lapsed. If, however, the forfeiture condition in fact occurs and the taxpayer is forced to give up the property, no loss deduction is allowed for the amount previously included in income. I.R.C. § 83(b)(1) (last sentence). Any amount actually paid for the forfeited property may be deducted as a loss. Treas. Reg. § 1.83–2(a).

The § 83(b) election is available only if there has been a "transfer" of property under Treas. Reg. § 1.83–3(a), discussed at Section 2.B.1.1 of this Chapter. Section 83(b)(2) provides that the election for current taxation must be made within 30 days of the transfer of the property. *Alves* demonstrates that any transfer in connection with the performance of services brings § 83 into play, even if there is no compensatory element imbued in the transfer.

4. STOCK OPTIONS

Section 83 preserves the general pattern of taxation of nonstatutory stock options that existed under prior law. (Statutory options are discussed in Section 2.C. of this Chapter.) Treas. Reg. § 1.83–7 provides that if an option has a readily ascertainable fair market value, the excess of its value over the amount, if any, paid by the employee to acquire the option will be subject to taxation as ordinary income under § 83 in the year it is granted. The exercise of such an option is excluded from the coverage of § 83 by § 83(e)(4), and the subsequent sale of stock would result in capital gain to the extent the sales proceeds exceed the sum of (1) the amount paid for the option, (2) the amount included under § 83 upon receipt of the option, and (3) the amount paid upon exercise of the option.

If the option does not have a readily ascertainable fair market value, by virtue of § 83(e)(3) receipt of the option is not subject to tax under § 83. Upon the exercise of the option, however, the transfer of the stock would be subject to § 83 and thus result in ordinary income in the amount of the "spread" (i.e., the excess of the fair market value of the stock over the exercise price) at the time of the exercise.

To apply these rules, one must distinguish between options with a readily ascertainable fair market value and options without such a value. Treas. Reg. § 1.83–7(b) tilts the playing field strongly in favor of the latter, making it extremely difficult for options to be considered to have a readily ascertainable fair market value. An option's value is not "readily ascertainable" unless the option is either actively traded in an established market or the value of the option can otherwise be measured with reasonable accuracy. To meet the latter test, the option must be transferable and immediately exercisable. In addition, the value of "option privilege," (i.e., the ability to benefit from any appreciation in the value of the underlying property without risking any capital) must be readily ascertainable. Because of these conditions, it is extremely rare for nonstatutory options to be deemed to have a readily ascertainable fair market value under the regulations. This treatment is consistent with pre-§ 83 case law, which generally found options to lack a readily ascertainable fair market value. See, e.g., *LoBue*, discussed in Section 2.A. of this Chapter); Frank v. Commissioner, 447 F.2d 552 (7th Cir. 1971).

5. IMPACT OF § 409A

Section 409A is generally inapplicable to restricted property subject to § 83 even though the value of the transferred property is not immediately included in the recipient's gross income absent a § 83(b) election. Treas. Reg.

§ 1.409A–1(b)(6). However, § 409A has a potentially significant impact on the taxation of nonstatutory stock options. Section 409A does not apply to nonstatutory options the exercise price of which is at or above the fair market value of the underlying stock at the time the options are granted. Treas. Reg. § 1.409A–1(b)(5). Options whose exercise prices are below this fair market value constitute deferred compensation and are therefore subject to the restrictions in § 409A. Because compensatory stock options are almost always exercisable at the discretion of the transferee after they have vested, these "in-the-money" stock options will inevitably fail to satisfy § 409A's distribution requirements, thus triggering immediate taxation and the 20 percent excise tax. Accordingly, stock options plans are typically designed with fair market value (or greater) exercise prices to avoid this unfavorable result.

6. DEDUCTION BY EMPLOYER

Consistent with § 404(a)(5), § 83(h) generally provides that the employer is allowed a deduction at the same time that the employee includes the compensation in gross income. Treas. Reg. § 1.83–6(a)(4) clarifies the statutory language by providing that § 83(h) does not support a current deduction if the transfer of property represents a capital expenditure, deferred deduction, or inventory cost.

Section 83(h) also limits the amount of employer's deduction to the amount included in the gross income of the employee. Treas. Reg. § 1.83–6(a) provides that an employer's deduction is the amount actually included by the employee on the employee's tax return, not the amount properly includable. The regulation also provides, however, that an amount is deemed to have been "included" by the service provider if the employer (or other service recipient) files with the Service a timely information return (e.g., a Form W-2 or 1099-MISC) reporting the payment to the service provider. But if the employer fails to file an information return and the employee fails to include the amount in income, the employer is not entitled to a deduction. Venture Funding, Ltd. v. Commissioner, 110 T.C. 236 (1998), aff'd by order, 198 F.3d 248 (6th Cir.1999), upheld the validity of the regulation and denied an employer a deduction where the employer did not file an information return and the employee did not report the income on the employee's tax return. However, Robinson v. United States, 335 F.3d 1365 (Fed.Cir.2003), held the regulation to be invalid and allowed a deduction where the employee did not include any income from a bargain purchase of stock and the corporation did not issue a Form W-2 until three years after the year of the transfer, at which time it issued an "amended" Form W-2.

If stock is transferred to the employee as compensation for services by a shareholder of the employer corporation, it is still the corporation that receives the deduction. Treas. Reg. § 1.83–6(d) treats the transaction as if the shareholder had contributed the shares to the capital of the corporation which then subsequently transferred them to the employee. As a result, the shareholder recognizes no gain or loss when the shares are transferred. Tilford v. Commissioner, 705 F.2d 828 (6th Cir.1983), held the regulation valid and disallowed the shareholder's claimed loss deduction when stock that had depreciated in value was transferred to the corporation's employees as compensation.

7. OTHER COMPENSATION DEVICES

Executive compensation structures constantly change as corporations and executives probe for devices that pass muster under corporate law and provide desirable results under tax law. One such technique is the so-called "phantom stock" plan. These plans are essentially contractual deferred compensation arrangements that measure the compensation by assigning to the employee during the period of employment "units" representing shares of the corporate stock at current market values. At a specified time (e.g., five years of continuous employment with the company), the employee is paid an amount based on the dividends paid and the appreciation in value of the corporation's stock since the time the units were assigned. Though economically similar to restricted stock, there are no actual shares outstanding in a phantom stock plan. "Units" are merely hypothetical shares used as a measuring device to determine the amount of the employer's obligation to pay. Because the arrangements constitute unfunded and unsecured promises to pay money in the future, their tax treatment is governed by the traditional cash-method of accounting rules and § 409A. If the prerequisites for deferral are satisfied, the employee is not taxed until receipt the receipt of cash and then at ordinary rates, and the employer receives its deduction at the same time.

While phantom stock rights are analogous to stock ownership, stock appreciation rights (SAR) are economically similar to stock options. The holder of an SAR is entitled to a cash payment equal to the excess of the fair market value of a certain number of shares of stock on the date the SAR is exercised over the value of the stock on the date the SAR was granted. SARs are typically exercisable at the discretion of the holder. Because of this discretion, the constructive receipt doctrine is arguably implicated. However, the IRS has ruled that because upon exercise of the SAR the holder relinquishes a valuable right (specifically, the right to participate in share appreciation without putting any capital at risk), amounts available under a SAR are subject to a substantial restriction or limitation, thus precluding the holder from being deemed in constructive receipt prior to exercise. Rev. Rul. 80–300, 1980–2 C.B. 165. In addition, the regulations under § 409A provide that the section does not apply to SAR plans if, as is typical, amounts payable are determined by reference to the value of the stock at the time of grant and not some lower value. Treas. Reg. § 1.409A–1(b)(5)(i)(B). This rule is analogous to the § 409A safe harbor for stock options with a fair market value at grant exercise price.

C. INCENTIVE STOCK OPTIONS

INTERNAL REVENUE CODE: Sections 421(a)–(b); 422(a)–(b), (d).

Sections 421 and 422 provide special tax rules for "incentive stock options" (ISOs), also known as statutory stock options. If the statutory conditions are met, there are no tax consequences when the ISO is granted or exercised. Upon sale of the underlying stock, the employee recognizes gain to the extent the amount realized exceeds the employee's basis in the stock (i.e., the exercise price of the option). All the gain is characterized as capital gain. The employer corporation is not entitled to a deduction with respect to the ISO at any time.

Summary of H.R. 4242, The Economic Recovery Tax Act of 1981

Staff of Joint Committee on Taxation (Joint Committee Print 31–33, Aug. 5, 1981).

The term "incentive stock option" means an option granted to an individual, for any reason connected with his or her employment, by the employer corporation or by a parent or subsidiary corporation of the employer corporation, to purchase stock of any of such corporations.

To receive incentive stock option treatment, [section 422(a)(1)] provides that the employee must not dispose of the stock within two years after the option is granted, and must hold the stock itself for at least one year. If all requirements other than these holding period rules are met, the tax will be imposed on sale of the stock, but gain will be treated as ordinary income rather than capital gain, and the employer will be allowed a deduction at that time.

In addition, for the entire time from the date of granting the option until three months (12 months if disabled) before the date of exercise, the option holder must be an employee either of the company granting the option, a parent or subsidiary of that corporation, or a successor corporation. This requirement and the holding period requirements are waived in the case of the death of the employee.

For an option to qualify as an "incentive stock option," the following conditions must be met:

1.   The option must be granted under a plan specifying the number of shares of stock to be issued and the employees or class of employees to receive the options. This plan must be approved by the stockholders of the corporation within 12 months before or after the plan is adopted.

2.   The option must be granted within ten years of the date the plan is adopted or the date the plan is approved by the stockholders, whichever is earlier.

3.   The option must by its terms be exercisable only within 10 years of the date it is granted.

4.   The option price must equal or exceed the fair market value of the stock at the time the option is granted. This requirement will be deemed satisfied if there has been a good faith attempt to value the stock accurately, even if the option price is less than the stock value.

5.   The option by its terms must be nontransferable other than at death and must be exercisable during the employee's lifetime only by the employee.

6.   The employee must not, immediately before the option is granted, own stock representing more than 10 percent of the voting power or value of all classes of stock of the employer corporation or its parent or subsidiary. However, the stock ownership limitation will be waived if the option price is at least 110 percent of the fair market value (at the time the option is granted) of the stock subject to the option and the option by its terms is not exercisable more than five years from the date it is granted.

7.   [The aggregate fair market value of stock (determined at the time of grant) subject to options that are first exercisable by an individual in a taxable year cannot exceed $100,000. If this limit is reached, options that exceed this limit are treated as nonstatutory options while options below the limit are treated as incentive stock options.

8.   The terms of the option must not specify that it will not be treated as an incentive stock option.]

[Section 422(c)(5)(A)] provides that stock acquired on exercise of the option may be paid for with stock of the corporation granting the option. The difference between the option price and the fair market value of the stock at the exercise of the option will not be an item of tax preference.

Additional cash or other property may be transferred to the employee at the time the option is exercised, so long as such property is subject to inclusion in income under the provisions of section 83.

An option will not be disqualified because of the inclusion of any condition not inconsistent with the qualification requirements.

DETAILED ANALYSIS

1.   TAX BENEFIT?

From the employee's perspective, ISO's convert ordinary income to capital gain. For example, assume an ISO with a $50 exercise price is exercised when the underlying stock is worth $100. Further assume that the stock is later sold for $125 after the requisite ISO holding period is satisfied. Because of the option's status as an ISO, the entire $75 gain is taxed as a long-term capital gain subject to a maximum rate of 20 percent. If the option had been nonstatutory, $50 of the gain would have been taxed as ordinary income, with only the remaining $25 of gain taxed as a long-term capital gain. Assuming the holder is in the 35 percent tax bracket, the conversion of $50 of ordinary income to capital gain saves the holder $7.50 in tax (($50 × 35%) − ($50 × 20%)).[5] The holder of an ISO also receives a time-value of money benefit because the holder owes no tax until sale of the underlying stock; on the other hand, holders of nonstatutory options must pay tax on the option spread (in this case $50) at the time the option is exercised.

At the same time, from the employer's perspective, ISO's convert a deductible expense to a non-deductible expense. The issuance of an ISO

---

[5]   As discussed in Chapter 39, the alternative minimum tax can have significant ramifications on the holders of ISOs.

results in no deduction at any time. If the option described above had been a nonstatutory option, then the employer would have received a $50 deduction at the time the employee exercised the option. If the employer were subject to the maximum corporate tax rate of 35 percent, the deduction would be worth $17.50 ($50 × 35%). Therefore, the fact that the option constituted an ISO costs the employer $17.50 but only saved the employee $7.50 (plus some time-value of money benefit).

Typically, the benefit of ISO treatment to the employee is outweighed by the cost to the employer (as in the example above, assuming the time-value of money benefit to the employee is less than $10.00). Consequently, ISOs are ordinarily only used by employers who have large net operating losses (like start-up technology companies) or who otherwise expect to be subject to extremely low tax rates in the future. Employers opting out of ISO treatment simply include in the terms of the option the statement that the option is not to be treated as an incentive stock option. This effectively avoids ISO treatment even if all of the other statutory conditions are satisfied. See I.R.C. § 422(b).

2.   EMPLOYEE STOCK PURCHASE PLANS

Section 423 provides special rules for so-called employee stock purchase plans. Like ISOs, no income is realized either upon the grant or the exercise of the purchase option and the entire gain upon disposition qualifies as capital gain, assuming the statutory conditions are satisfied.

Unlike in the case of ISOs, the option price may be as low as 85 percent of the fair market value of the stock at the time the option is granted. In this event, the difference between the fair market value at the date of grant and the option price will be ordinary income upon disposition of the stock to the extent of gain. I.R.C. § 423(c). These plans also differ from incentive stock options in that generally all employees must be covered.

CHAPTER 31

DEFERRED PAYMENT SALES

Section 1001(c) provides that realized gains and losses are to be recognized unless otherwise provided by the Code. This chapter considers deferred recognition of gain on the disposition of property for payments that are received in later taxable years. Deferred recognition of gain may be appropriate when the amount of gain is not reasonably ascertainable, e.g., where the amount realized on disposition of property consists of contingent payments, the present value of which is extremely difficult to estimate. In other cases, Congress has provided rules for deferred recognition of gain to match the receipt of cash payments. Thus, the installment sales rules of § 453 permit deferral of recognized gain in transactions involving deferred payments. Under this provision, a pro rata portion of realized gain is recognized as each deferred payment is received. The timing of recognition under each of these two scenarios produces a very different result for the taxpayer.

SECTION 1.   NONSTATUTORY DEFERRED REPORTING OF GAINS

INTERNAL REVENUE CODE: Section 1001(c).

REGULATIONS: Section 1.1001–1(g).

Burnet v. Logan
Supreme Court of the United States, 1931.
283 U.S. 404.

[The taxpayer had owned stock in an iron company that held a supply contract entitling it to an annual share of iron ore from a certain mine. In 1916, she and the other stockholders sold their stock to the Youngstown Company for cash plus the agreement of the Youngstown Company to pay them annually 60 cents per ton of ore obtained by the Youngstown Company from the mine under the supply contract. The taxpayer's mother had similarly sold her stock and, on her death in 1917, left the taxpayer a portion of her interest in the annual payments to be made by the Youngstown Company. This bequest had been valued at $277,164.50 for estate tax purposes, and became the basis in the taxpayer's hands for the inherited interest. Under the tax law at the time, the basis of the stock sold by the taxpayer for purposes of computing any gain on the sale was the stock's March 1, 1913 value.]

■ Mr. Justice McReynolds delivered the opinion of the Court. * * *

Reports of income for 1918, 1919, and 1920 were made by Mrs. Logan upon the basis of cash receipts and disbursements. They included no part of what she had obtained from annual payments [in those years] by the Youngstown Company. She maintains that until the total amount actually received by her from the sale of her shares equals their value on March 1, 1913, no taxable income will arise from the transaction. Also that, until she actually receives by reason of the right bequeathed to her a sum equal to its appraised value, there will be no taxable income therefrom. * * *

[The Commissioner ruled that the obligation of the Youngstown Company to pay 60 cents per ton had a fair market value in 1916. Since this was less than the March 1, 1913 value of the stock, but more than its cost, he found no taxable profit. He then estimated the number of tons of iron ore in the mine and divided such fair market value by the estimated tons. The resulting amount per ton was regarded as measuring the capital element in each 60 cent payment, and the difference between such return of capital and 60 cents was regarded as the income element for each 60 cent payment. The income element per ton times the number of tons actually mined per year thus became the taxable income. The capital element would not be taxed until the taxpayer recovered the 1916 value of the obligation of the Company and, as respects her inherited interest, the appraised value of the bequest. The Board of Tax Appeals approved this result.]

The Circuit Court of Appeals held that, in the circumstances, it was impossible to determine with fair certainty the market value of the agreement by the Youngstown Company to pay 60 cents per ton. Also that respondent was entitled to the return of her capital—the value of 250 shares on March 1, 1913, and the assessed value of the interest derived from her mother—before she could be charged with any taxable income. As this had not in fact been returned, there was no taxable income.

We agree with the result reached by the Circuit Court of Appeals.

The 1916 transaction was a sale of stock—not an exchange of property. We are not dealing with royalties or deductions from gross income because of depletion of mining property. Nor does the situation demand that an effort be made to place according to the best available data some approximate value upon the contract for future payments. This probably was necessary in order to assess the mother's estate. As annual payments on account of extracted ore come in, they can be readily apportioned first as return of capital and later as profit. The liability for income tax ultimately can be fairly determined without resort to mere estimates, assumptions, and speculation. When the profit, if any, is actually realized, the taxpayer will be required to respond. The consideration for the sale was $2,200,000 in cash and the promise of future money payments wholly contingent upon facts and circumstances not possible to foretell with anything like fair certainty. The promise was in no proper sense equivalent to cash. It had no ascertainable fair market value. The transaction was not a closed one. Respondent might never recoup her capital investment from payments only conditionally promised. Prior to 1921, all receipts from the sale of her shares amounted to less than their value on March 1, 1913. She properly demanded the return of her capital investment before assessment of any taxable profit based on conjecture.

"In order to determine whether there has been gain or loss, and the amount of the gain if any, we must withdraw from the gross proceeds an amount sufficient to restore the capital value that existed at the commencement of the period under consideration." Doyle v. Mitchell Bros. Co., 247 U.S. 179, 184. Ordinarily, at least, a taxpayer may not deduct from gross receipts a supposed loss which in fact is represented by his outstanding note. Eckert v. Burnet, 283 U.S. 140. And, conversely, a promise to pay indeterminate sums of money is not necessarily taxable income. "Generally speaking, the income tax law is concerned only with realized losses, as with realized gains." Lucas v. American Code Co., 280 U.S. 445, 449.

From her mother's estate, Mrs. Logan obtained the right to share in possible proceeds of a contract thereafter to pay indefinite sums. The value of this was assumed to be $277,164.50, and its transfer was so taxed. Some valuation—speculative or otherwise—was necessary in order to close the estate. It may never yield as much, it may yield more. If a sum equal to the value thus ascertained had been invested in an annuity contract, payments thereunder would have been free from income tax until the owner had recouped his capital investment. We think a like rule should be applied here. The statute definitely excepts bequests from receipts which go to make up taxable income. * * *

DETAILED ANALYSIS

1. OTHER JUDICIAL APPROACHES

Burnet v. Logan established the proposition that the right to receive future payments—the purchaser's obligation to pay—may not be treated as an amount realized in the year of sale where the amount and value of the buyer's obligation is not readily ascertainable. The open transaction approach of *Burnet v. Logan,* treating all payments as a recovery of capital until total payments exceed the seller's basis for the property, provides the seller with a significant tax deferral advantage.

Dorsey v. Commissioner, 49 T.C. 606 (1968), is typical of the open transaction cases decided after *Burnet v. Logan.* The taxpayers were stockholders of a corporation that held a patent on automatic pinsetting machines for bowling alleys. The corporation had licensed the patent to a third party in exchange for royalty payments for twenty years based on the sale or lease by the licensee of the pinsetting equipment. When the corporation was liquidated the taxpayers received as a liquidating distribution the right to the future payments to be made under the license agreement. The Tax Court applied the open transaction doctrine "because the value of the rights received by the petitioners * * * depended on numerous uncertainties of such a character as to make any estimate of the fair market value of those rights on that date sheer surmise and speculation."

Warren Jones Co. v. Commissioner, 524 F.2d 788 (9th Cir.1975), reached the opposite conclusion when the buyer's obligation had an ascertainable fair market value. In that case, the taxpayer sold real estate under an assignable contract which was the only evidence of the purchaser's indebtedness. The Tax Court found that the real estate contract had a fair market value but that the price at which the contract could be sold involved a discount of almost 50 percent. The Tax Court held that, in light of the substantial discount, the cash method taxpayer was not required to include the fair market value of the contract in income. The Court of Appeals reversed, holding that if the contract right had a fair market value it was required to be included in income whatever the amount of the discount.

2. THE REGULATORY ANSWER

After these cases were decided the Treasury promulgated Treas. Reg. § 1.1001–1(g), which governs determination of the amount realized on the sale of property and generally forecloses either approach. Under the regulation, if adequate interest is charged, the amount realized generally will be the face amount of the principal obligation. If adequate interest is not charged, the amount realized will be the principal amount of the obligation, which is its face amount minus interest determined under the original issue discount rules, discussed in Chapter 32. The gain so computed will be recognized under § 1001(c). Treas. Reg. § 1.1001–1(g) generally forecloses applying the approach of either *Burnett v. Logan* or *Warren Jones Co.* The regulation is inapplicable "only in rare and extraordinary cases" in which "the fair market value of the contingent payments is not reasonably ascertainable." If § 453, discussed in the next Section, applies, even though Treas. Reg. § 1.1001–1(g) continues to control the amount realized, reporting the realized and recognized gain can be deferred.

SECTION 2. INSTALLMENT REPORTING UNDER SECTION 453

INTERNAL REVENUE CODE: Sections 453(a)–(d), (f)(2)–(4), (i), (*l*)(1); 453A(a), (b), (d); 453B(a)–(c).

REGULATIONS: Temp. Reg. Sections 15a.453–1(a), (b)(1)–(3)(i), (c)(1)–(4), (d)(1)–(3)(i); 1.1001–1(g).

Section 453 generally provides that income from an installment sale is to be taken into account on the installment method. An installment sale is defined as any disposition of property in which all or a portion of the payments are to be received after the close of the taxable year in which the disposition of the property occurs. The installment method is automatic unless the taxpayer elects under § 453(d) not to have the installment method apply.

Under § 453(c), income recognized in any taxable year from an installment sale "is that proportion of the payments received in that year which the gross profit (realized or to be realized when payment is completed) bears to the total contract price." In general, "gross profit" is the "selling price" of the property less its adjusted basis. Temp. Reg. § 15a.453–1(b)(2)(ii) and (v). The "total contract price" is the total amount to be paid for the property, adjusted downward for any indebtedness assumed or taken subject to by the buyer. Temp. Reg. § 15a.453–1(b)(2)(iii). The statutory formula maybe displayed as:

Income/Payments = Gross Profit/Total Contract Price.

Algebraically, this formula may be rearranged to:

Income = (Payments) × (Gross Profit/Total Contract Price).

The operation of the installment method is shown in the following example. Suppose A sells Blackacre to B for $100,000, with $10,000 payable at the closing, and the remainder to be paid in equal installments over the next nine years. The installment obligation is evidenced by a note that bears adequate stated interest. A's basis in Blackacre is $40,000. The "gross profit" in the sale is $60,000 ($100,000 selling price minus $40,000 basis) and the "total contract price" is $100,000. Under § 453(c), a fraction is established, the numerator of which is the gross profit and the denominator of which is the total contract price to be paid. This fraction, the "gross profit ratio," is then applied to each payment received under the contract to determine the amount of gain to be recognized currently. Thus, in the first year ($10,000) × ($60,000/$100,000) = $6,000 is includable in gross income. The remainder of the payment is a recovery of basis. Thus, each $10,000 payment will consist of $6,000 of recognized gain and $4,000 of basis. After all the payments have been received, the taxpayer will have accounted for the initial basis of $40,000 and $60,000 of appreciation. The interest on the installment obligation is taxed as ordinary income.

The example above assumes that the installment note bears an adequate interest rate. If the stated interest rate is below the rate established in §§ 1274 or 483, discussed in Chapter 32, a portion of the $100,000 denominated as the contract price will be recharacterized as interest. The contract price will be reduced by the amount of unstated interest and the determination of the gross profit ratio will be modified accordingly.

DETAILED ANALYSIS

1.   DISQUALIFIED PROPERTY

Section 453 installment reporting automatically applies to all property other than types of property or gain for which installment reporting is specifically disallowed.

1.1. *Inventory or Property Held for Sale to Customers in the Ordinary Course of Business*

Section 453(b)(2) and (*l*) impose the broadest restriction on use of the installment method. In general, sales of inventory or real estate held for sale to customers in the ordinary course of business do not qualify for installment method reporting. In Keith v. Commissioner, 115 T.C. 605 (2000), the taxpayer sold residential real property through contracts for deed, under which the buyers obtained possession, assumed responsibility for taxes, insurance, and maintenance, and agreed to make monthly payments, with interest, of the purchase price. Under the sales contracts, a warranty deed would be delivered to a buyer only upon full payment; any default by a buyer voided the contract. In that event, the taxpayer could retain, as liquidated damages, all amounts previously received, but the buyer was not liable for the remaining unpaid balance. The taxpayer, who reported on the accrual method, did not report any gain attributable to the contracts until the year in which full payment had been received and title was transferred. The Tax Court held that notwithstanding the "nonrecourse" nature of the buyers' obligations, the sales were completed in the year the contracts were executed, because under state law the benefits and burdens of ownership had passed to the buyers upon execution of the contract and transfer of possession. Accordingly, because the sales were dealer dispositions to which § 453 did not apply, the gain from the dispositions was recognized in the year of the sale.

The unavailability of § 453 installment reporting for sales of inventory applies to bulk sales, as well as to sales in the ordinary course of business. See Berger v. Commissioner, T.C. Memo. 1996–76 (sale of inventory as part of the sale of a going business). But in Andrew Crispo Gallery, Inc. v. Commissioner, 86 F.3d 42 (2d Cir.1996), the taxpayer, which operated an art gallery, was permitted to report on the § 453 installment method the sale of its art works that were seized and sold by a creditor (the IRS!) after the owner had been sentenced to prison and the gallery had ceased to conduct business. According to the court, when the gallery went out of business, the art works ceased to be either inventory or property held for sale to customers in the ordinary course of business.

A special rule in § 453(*l*)(2) permits installment reporting for sales of farm property, timeshares, and residential lots, but in these situations § 453(*l*)(3) imposes an interest charge on the deferred tax liability. Thom v. United States, 283 F.3d 939 (8th Cir.2002), held that the exception in § 453(*l*)(2)(A) applies only to the sale of property that has been used in farming by the seller; it does not apply to sales of farm equipment by a non-farmer equipment dealer to a farmer that is "to be used" by the farmer.

Finally, § 453(k)(2) prohibits installment reporting for sales of stock or securities traded on an established securities market.

1.2. *Property Subject to Ordinary Income Recapture*

Section 453(i) denies installment reporting for the portion of the gain (if any) that is depreciation recapture income under §§ 1245 or 1250. Accordingly, depreciation recapture income must be recognized in the year of sale, even if no payments are received. Any gain on the sale of depreciable property that is properly reportable as § 1231 gain (the gain in excess of depreciation recapture), however, is eligible for installment reporting. To avoid taxing depreciation recapture again as payments are received, in computing the gross profit ratio the basis of the property is increased by the recapture income recognized in the year of sale. Suppose, as in the example above, A sold depreciable personal property to B for $100,000, with $10,000 payable at the closing, and the remainder in equal installments over the next nine years (with adequate interest). A's basis in the property is $40,000, but assume in this case that A has claimed $25,000 of depreciation subject to recapture under § 1245. A would be required by § 453(i) to recognize the $25,000 recapture income in the year of sale. As a result, the gross profit for purposes of installment sale reporting is reduced to $35,000 ($100,000 − ($40,000 + $25,000)), and the gross profit ratio is 35 percent ($35,000/$100,000), rather than 60 percent as in the first example. Thus, the income recognized on each payment would be $3,500 ($10,000 × 35 percent).

2.   "PAYMENTS" TO WHICH THE INSTALLMENT METHOD APPLIES

2.1. *In General*

The timing of income recognition under the installment method depends upon when a payment is received, and thus the definition of a "payment" is of paramount importance. The buyer's obligation to make deferred payments does not itself constitute a "payment" requiring the current inclusion of gain. I.R.C. § 453(f)(3). Section 453(f)(3) provides that the purchaser's indebtedness can be guaranteed by a third party without changing this result, and Temp. Reg. § 15a.453–1(b)(3)(i) states that a standby letter of credit issued as security for a deferred payment obligation will be treated as a third-party guarantee. On the other hand, if the security arrangement takes the form of an escrow funded with cash (or a cash equivalent like a certificate of deposit), the regulations provide that the receipt of the secured indebtedness is a "payment." Temp. Reg. § 15a.453–1(b)(3)(i).

Section 453(f)(4)(B) provides a special rule for circumstances when the purchaser's obligation is readily tradable. In that case, receipt of the indebtedness is treated as a payment for purposes of installment reporting.

2.2. *Mortgaged Property*

The assumption by the purchaser of a "qualifying indebtedness" encumbering the property is generally not treated as a payment to the seller. In general, a qualifying indebtedness is a mortgage or other encumbrance on the property that is assumed or incurred by the purchaser as part of the acquisition cost of the property. Temp. Reg. § 15a.453–1(b)(2)(iv).[1] The selling price used in calculating gross profit under § 453 includes the full amount of the mortgage. Total contract price, however, is determined by reducing the selling price by the amount of the mortgage that does not exceed the seller's basis in the property, thus reflecting only the actual cash payments that the seller will receive. In the preceding example, if the

---

[1]   Qualifying indebtedness does not include any indebtedness incurred by the seller incident to the disposition (such as an obligation for attorney's fees) or an indebtedness not related to the property (such as medical bills).

property had been subject to a mortgage of $20,000, B presumably would have paid only $10,000 in cash and given the seller a $70,000 promissory note for the property. The sales price, as defined, would have remained $100,000, but the contract price would have become $80,000. Accordingly, the gross profit ratio would have been ¾ ($60,000 divided by $80,000), and if the $70,000 were due in seven equal installments of $10,000 (plus interest), $7,500 of each payment would have been recognized gain.

If the property is subject to a mortgage in excess of the seller's basis, then in the year of sale the seller's recognized gain is equal to the amount by which the sum of the excess encumbrance and any other payments received in that year exceed the seller's basis. This result is reached because (1) the amount by which the mortgage exceeds the seller's basis is treated as a payment in the year of the sale (Temp. Reg. § 15a.453–1(b)(3)(i)), and (2) the contract price is treated as including the portion of the mortgage in excess of the seller's basis, which invariably results in a gross profit ratio of 100 percent. Assume that in the previous example, the property was subject to a mortgage of $60,000, and the buyer gave the seller $10,000 at the closing and a $30,000 promissory note payable in three installments. The selling price remains $100,000 (including the full amount of the mortgage) and the gross profit remains $60,000 ($100,000 contract price – $40,000 basis). But in this case the contract price is $60,000 – the sum of the $10,000 cash payment, the $30,000 note from the purchaser, and the $20,000 by which the mortgage ($60,000) exceeds the seller's basis ($40,000). Thus, the gross profit ratio is 100 percent ($60,000/$60,000), and the seller must recognize $30,000 in the year of sale, the sum of the $10,000 cash payment and the $20,000 by which the mortgage exceeded basis. As each $10,000 payment on the buyer's note is received, the entire amount is recognized as gain. On receipt of the full principal of B's obligation to A, A will have recognized the full $60,000 of realized gain.

2.3. Like-Kind Exchanges

2.3.1. Installment Treatment of Boot in Like-Kind Exchanges

Section 453(f)(6) applies the installment method to like-kind exchanges under § 1031, discussed in Chapter 26. Section 453(f)(6) defers recognition of gain on the receipt of a note or deferred payment that is treated as boot under § 1031(b). Under § 453(f)(6)(B) gross profit in an installment sale does not include gain that is subject to nonrecognition under § 1031. Thus, the gross profit includes only gain recognized to the extent of boot under § 1031(b). The total contract price for the installment sale does not include the like-kind nonrecognition property. As a consequence, when the boot received in a § 1031 transaction is an installment obligation, the gain recognized under § 1031(b) is taken into account only as payments are received. Assume, for example, the taxpayer exchanged land worth $100,000, with a basis of $90,000, for land worth $80,000 plus a cash payment of $4,000 in the year of sale, and a note requiring payments of $4,000, plus adequate stated interest, in each of the subsequent four years. The taxpayer's realized gain is $10,000. The $4,000 cash payment plus the note for $16,000 of additional payments are boot requiring the taxpayer to recognize $10,000 of gain under § 1031(b). The deferred payments constitute an installment sale. The gross profit under the installment method is the $10,000 of gain recognized under § 1031(b). The total contract price is $100,000 less the $80,000 fair market value of the nonrecognition property, $20,000. Thus, the $4,000 payment in the year of sale requires recognition of $2,000 of gain ($4,000 × $10,000/$20,000). Each subsequent $4,000 payment also results in $2,000 of recognized gain.

Prop. Reg. § 1.453–1(f)(3)(iii) (1984) would reach the same result as § 453(f)(6), but with a slightly different methodology. The proposed regulation would allocate the transferor's basis first to the nonrecognition property to the extent of its fair market value. The remaining basis would be allocated to the deferred payments for purposes of computing installment gain. Under this formulation, in the above example, the taxpayer's basis is allocated first to the land to the extent of its fair market value, $80,000, leaving $10,000 for purposes of computing installment gain. The gross profit is $10,000, the difference between the total contract price of $20,000 and the remaining basis. Thus, each $4,000 payment produces $2,000 of recognized gain ($4,000 × $10,000/$20,000).

2.3.2. *Failed Deferred Section 1031 Like-Kind Exchanges*

If a properly structured deferred § 1031 like-kind exchange, discussed in Chapter 26, ultimately fails to qualify for nonrecognition under § 1031 because the taxpayer receives cash instead of like-kind property, installment reporting under § 453 may be available. This is true even though the buyer's obligation to convey replacement property is secured by cash or a cash equivalent, which would ordinarily preclude installment sale reporting. See Treas. Reg. § 1.1031(k)–1(j)(2). Smalley v. Commissioner, 116 T.C. 450 (2001), involved an interesting application of this rule. In 1994, the taxpayer entered into a deferred exchange agreement under which he relinquished timber-cutting rights on land he owned in fee; the ultimate purchaser paid cash to a qualified escrow account as defined in Treas. Reg. § 1.1031(k)– 1(g)(3). In 1995, within the period required by § 1031(a)(3), the taxpayer received fee simple interests in three parcels of real estate. The IRS asserted that the taxpayer recognized gain in 1994 because the timber cutting rights were personalty and thus not like-kind to a fee simple in timber land. The Tax Court held that regardless of whether the timber cutting rights surrendered and fee land received were of like kind, no income was realized in 1994. At the beginning of the exchange period, the taxpayer had a bona fide intent to enter into a deferred exchange of like-kind property within the meaning of Treas. Reg. § 1.1031(k)–1(j)(2)(iv), and under Treas. Reg. § 1.1031(k)–1(g)(3) he was not in either actual or constructive receipt of property in 1994. Accordingly, under the special rule in Treas. Reg. § 1.1031(k)–1(j)(2), if the transaction was not a like-kind exchange, it would qualify as a § 453 installment sale and, since no payments were received in 1994, the taxpayer would recognize no gain in that year. As a result, the court held for the taxpayer without deciding whether the transaction qualified as a like-kind exchange. While resolution of that issue would affect the taxpayer's basis in the timber land, that issue was not before the court.

3. CONTINGENT PAYMENT SITUATIONS

Section 453(j)(2) authorizes regulations to provide for "ratable basis recovery" in transactions in which the contract price cannot be readily ascertained. Temp. Reg. § 15a.453–1(c) provides rules for several situations.

First, if the contract provides for a maximum selling price, then the stated maximum selling price is treated as the selling price for purposes of the installment sale computations. If the stated maximum selling price is subsequently reduced, the gross profit ratio is accordingly recomputed. If the taxpayer does not in fact receive the maximum selling price and the taxpayer has included in income an amount of gain in excess of the gain actually realized, a loss deduction for the excess is allowable in the final year. Temp. Reg. § 15a.453–1(c)(2).

Second, if the contract does not provide for a maximum selling price, but there is a fixed term in the agreement over which the payments are to be made, the basis is allocated equally over the years in which payments can be received. Temp. Reg. § 15a.453–1(c)(3).

Third, if neither a maximum price nor a fixed term is provided, the basis of the property is allocated over a fifteen-year period commencing on the date of sale. If the payment in any year is less than the basis allocated to that year, the excess basis is reallocated in level amounts over the balance of the fifteen-year term. Any basis not recovered by the end of the fifteenth year is carried forward until the entire basis has been recovered or the installment obligation is determined to be worthless, at which time a loss deduction is taken for any remaining basis. Temp. Reg. § 15a.453–1(c)(4).

Suppose the seller in an installment payment transaction involving a contingent obligation that would otherwise be subject to installment reporting under § 453 elects out of installment method reporting. Temp. Reg. § 15a.453–1(d)(2)(iii) substantially restricts the use of open transaction treatment under *Burnet v. Logan* by providing that only in "rare and extraordinary cases" will a contingent payment obligation be found to have no reasonably ascertainable fair market value. Treas. Reg. § 1.1001–1(g)(2) provides a similar rule for determining the amount realized on a contingent price sale if the taxpayer does not report under § 453, either because § 453 simply does not apply or because the taxpayer elects out. It thus seems unlikely that there will be many situations in which the taxpayer would elect out of the installment method and attempt to use the open transaction approach. The taxpayer who attempts open transaction treatment must give up the certainty of the deferral of tax allowed by the installment method and assume the risk that if the contingent obligation is ultimately found to have a reasonably ascertainable fair market value at the time of sale, the entire amount of the gain will be subject to immediate tax.

4. INTEREST ON DEFERRED TAX LIABILITY

The ability to defer tax liability on realized gains in an installment sale provides an advantage to the installment seller over a seller for cash who is required to pay the tax immediately. In essence, the installment seller receives an interest free loan from the Treasury for the period that recognition of gain is deferred. The imposition of an interest charge under

§ 453A(a)(1) with respect to certain installment sales addresses this issue. Section 453A imposes an interest charge on the tax liability that is deferred under the installment method in the case of the sale of any property if the sales price of the property exceeds $150,000 but only if the amount of outstanding installment obligations owed to the taxpayer that arose during the year, and which are outstanding at the end of the year, exceed $5 million. Thus, for example, if the taxpayer made an installment sale on January 1, 2016 for $5,999,999, with $1,000,000 due on December 31, 2021 and the balance due on December 31, 2071, no interest on deferred tax liability would ever be due under § 453A. But if only $999,999 were due on December 31, 2021, leaving $5,000,001 outstanding until December 31, 2071, compound interest for 50 years of tax deferral would be due. The interest rate used is the tax deficiency rate under § 6621(a)(2), rather than the generally lower Applicable Federal Rate under § 1274, discussed in Chapter 32.

5. DISPOSITION OF INSTALLMENT OBLIGATIONS

5.1. *Gain on Disposition*

When an installment obligation is disposed of, the privilege of tax deferral granted by § 453 is terminated. I.R.C. § 453B(a). As a result, many transactions which would not normally be thought of as taxable events must be carefully examined if installment obligations are involved. Thus, for example, a gift of an installment obligation, either outright or by transfer to a trust, will trigger immediate recognition to the donor of the income postponed under the installment method. Rev. Rul. 67–167, 1967–1 C.B. 107.

Section 453B(a) requires that, on disposition of an installment obligation, gain or loss is recognized in an amount equal to the difference between the amount realized on disposition and the taxpayer's "basis of the obligation." In a disposition other than a sale or exchange, such as a gift, the fair market value of the obligation is used in lieu of amount realized. The taxpayer's basis in an installment obligation is defined as the excess of the unpaid principal of the obligation (face value) over the amount that would be returnable as income if the obligation were paid in full. For example, if A in the example above, were to sell the installment obligation to C for $65,000 after B had made two payments of $10,000, A's recognized gain on the disposition is computed as follows:

Amount Realized		$65,000
Basis of the Obligation		
Unpaid principal	$70,000	
Less Gain if Paid in Full	$42,000	
Remaining Basis		$28,000
Gain Recognized on Disposition		$37,000

5.2. *Installment Notes Pledged as Collateral for a Loan*

Rev. Rul. 65–185, 1965–2 C.B. 153, dealt with an arrangement in which an installment seller assigned its installment obligations to a financing company as collateral for a loan. The finance company made the collections on the installment obligations and, under the terms of the loan agreement, the amounts collected were applied by the finance company in payment of the seller's note, the seller making no payments unless the collections were insufficient to repay the debt. The amounts borrowed were substantially equal to the face amount of the installment obligations. The ruling held that the transaction amounted to a disposition of the installment obligations on the ground that, by receiving the cash from the loan, the taxpayer had the "ability to pay" the tax and the deferral privilege of § 453 was no longer justified. The Tax Court refused to apply this ruling in Town and Country Food Co. Inc. v. Commissioner, 51 T.C. 1049 (1969) (Acq.) and United Surgical Steel Co. v. Commissioner, 54 T.C. 1215 (1970) (Acq.), because in each case it found that the substance of a transaction was a true loan rather than a sale of the installment obligation.

Subsequently, Congress enacted § 453A(d), which generally provides that the proceeds of an indebtedness that is secured by an installment obligation (or an indebtedness that the taxpayer has the option to satisfy by "putting" the installment obligation to the creditor) will be treated as a payment on the installment obligation. Thus, the use of an installment obligation as security for a separate borrowing will trigger recognition of the installment gain. The amount treated as a payment is limited to the total contract price of the installment obligation reduced by payments received. I.R.C. § 453A(d)(2). Section 453A applies only to installment notes derived from a disposition of property for a sales price in excess of $150,000 (regardless of how much of that sales price is paid with installment obligations). There are exceptions for installment obligations arising out of the disposition of certain farm property, timeshares and residential lots. I.R.C. § 453A(b)(3), (4).

5.3. *Other Dispositions*

Section 453B(f) provides that if an installment obligation is canceled or otherwise becomes unenforceable, it will be treated as if it were disposed of, thus triggering gain recognition. However, under § 1038, if an installment note is received in connection with the sale of real property, reacquisition of the property securing the note in satisfaction of the note will not give rise to recognition of either gain or loss to the seller, except to the extent that any payments previously received on the note exceed the amount already reported as gain.

Section 453B(c) provides special rules for installment obligations transferred at death. The death of the owner of an installment obligation does not require the immediate recognition of gain. However, the uncollected installment gain is treated as income in respect of a decedent under § 691(a)(4) and is reported by the decedent's estate or the person acquiring the installment obligation by reason of the death of the decedent as each payment is received using the same gross profit ratio used by the decedent. I.R.C. § 691(a)(3) and (4); Treas. Reg. § 1.691(a)–5(a). Section 1014(c) denies a step up of the basis of the installment by reason of the holder's death. Thus, a transfer of the installment obligation by the decedent's estate or the decedent's heirs will result in recognition of gain in the amount of the difference between the fair market value of the obligation and the basis of the obligation. See I.R.C. § 691(a)(2); Treas. Reg. § 1.691(a)–5(b). If the installment obligation is canceled by reason of the holder's death, or is transferred to the obligor, the estate is required to recognize gain in the amount of the difference between the fair market value of the obligation and the basis of the obligation. I.R.C. § 691(a)(5)(A). See also Frane v. Commissioner, 998 F.2d 567 (8th Cir.1993) (an installment note that by its terms was canceled upon the holder's death was a transmission of the note at death subject to § 453B(c); the deferred gain was taxable to the decedent's estate). If the obligor and the decedent were related persons, gain is computed by using the face amount of the obligation rather than fair market value. I.R.C. § 691(a)(5)(B).

Section 453B(g) permits the transfer of installment obligations between spouses, in which case the transferee spouse will be treated the same as the original holder of the installment obligation. This is consistent with § 1041, discussed in Chapter 38, Section 3.A., which treats all transfers between spouses as nonrecognition events with a transferred basis.

Sections 351 and 721 permit the transfer of an installment obligation to a corporation in exchange for stock and to a partnership in exchange for a partnership interest without immediate recognition of gain if certain qualifying conditions are met. Such transactions are not treated as dispositions for § 453 purposes. See Treas. Reg. § 1.453–9(c)(2) (interpreting prior statutory language identical to § 453B and providing that these transactions did not constitute dispositions).

Pursuant to Treas. Reg. § 1.1001–3, discussed Chapter 6, Section 2.B.2., any material modification of an installment obligation, such as a change in the interest rate, extension of the due date, or adjustment of the principal amount, will be treated as a disposition, thereby triggering recognition under § 453B(a).

6. RELATED-PARTY TRANSACTIONS

6.1. *Subsequent Resale by Related Purchaser*

Special rules apply to installment sales transactions between related parties. These rules are aimed at preventing deferral of income recognition by the related-party seller in circumstances where the related-party buyer within a short period of time after the initial transfer disposes of the property to a third party. Otherwise, the benefit from a disposition of property out of the economic unit (family or related entities as defined in § 267(b)) could be obtained without immediate recognition of gain.

Section 453(e) generally provides that the amount realized on disposition of property acquired in an installment sale from a related party, as defined in § 453(f)(1), through cross references to §§ 267(b) and 318, will be treated as a payment to the original related party seller. Thus, the original seller is required to recognize a pro rata portion of the seller's gain to the extent of payments received on disposition by the related party. For example, if Mother sells land to Son for $4,000 cash plus Son's note for $16,000, and mother's basis in the land is $10,000, mother will recognize only $2,000 of her realized gain of $10,000 in the year of sale ($4,000 $10,000/$20,000) and will defer recognition of the remaining $8,000 gain until payments are made on Son's note. If Son were to then sell the land to another party for $20,000,

§ 453(e)(1) requires Mother to treat the $20,000 received by Son as a payment on Son's note. However, § 453(e)(3)(A) limits the amount treated as a payment to the lesser of the amount realized by Son's disposition or the total contract price for the first sale to a related party, over amounts received as payments (actual or deemed) in prior years. Thus, Mother is treated as receiving a $16,000 payment ($20,000 amount realized by son less the initial $4,000 cash payment). Mother therefore must recognize $8,000 of gain ($16,000 $10,000/$20,000). Subsequent payments on Son's note will not be treated as payments on Mother's installment sale to the extent that the amounts paid by Son do not exceed the amount of the deemed payment under § 453(e). I.R.C. § 453(e)(5).

Section 453(e) only applies to sales by the related-party purchaser within two years of the first installment sale. However, this two-year period is tolled by any arrangement that substantially diminishes the related-party purchaser's risk of ownership such as a put, a call, or a short sale. I.R.C. § 453(e)(2). Section 453(e)(6) provides that a disposition by the related party resulting from involuntary conversion or death will not trigger the deemed payment rule. In addition, § 453(e)(7) provides that § 453(e) will not apply if the taxpayer can demonstrate that neither the initial nor related party's disposition was motivated by tax avoidance.

6.2. *Sale to Controlled Entity*

Section 453(g)(1) denies use of the installment method in the case of a transfer to a "related person" of property that is depreciable in the transferee's hands, see I.R.C. § 453(f)(7). A related person is defined through a cross reference to the § 1239(b) definition of related person, which in turn refers to the definition of a "controlled entity" in § 1239(c), but § 453(g)(3) also includes as related persons two partnerships under common control. Examples of sales to a controlled entity include the sale of property by a majority shareholder (whether an individual or a corporation) to a controlled corporation or the sale of property by a more than 50 percent partner to the partnership. If Congress had not enacted this rule, a transferor could sell depreciable property without currently recognizing gain while the transferee took a stepped-up basis and claimed depreciation deductions with respect to that stepped-up basis in the property. Section 453(g)(2) provides an exception if the transaction did not have tax avoidance as one of its principal purposes, but no case has applied this exception. See Guenther v. Commissioner, T.C. Memo. 1995–280 (the fact that in the absence of § 453(g) a related purchaser would be entitled to claim depreciation on a stepped-up basis is a factor in determining whether the transfer was motivated by tax avoidance).

7.   ELECTING OUT OF SECTION 453

Under § 453(a), income from any installment sale is to be taken into account on the installment method, regardless of the taxpayer's method of accounting. Section 453(d), however, allows the taxpayer to elect out of the application of § 453, thus resulting in recognition of the entire gain in the year of the sale regardless of the taxpayer's method of accounting. Treas. Reg. § 1.1001–1(g) provides that the amount realized on the sale of property is the adjusted issue price of the debt obligation under the original issue discount rules, discussed in Chapter 32. Generally speaking, if adequate interest is charged (i.e., at a rate equal to or in excess of the Applicable Federal Rate), then the adjusted issue price of the debt obligation will be equal to the face amount of the debt. But if adequate interest is not charged, the adjusted issue price is determined by backing out interest using the Applicable Federal Rate to ascertain the principal amount of the obligation, which will constitute the adjusted issue price.

8.   PRIVATE ANNUITIES

8.1. *Unsecured Transactions*

In some situations, a taxpayer may transfer property to a member of the taxpayer's family or to a family trust in exchange for a promise to pay a life annuity (i.e., periodic payments that are made as long as the taxpayer is alive). Where appreciated property is transferred, the proper treatment of the gain element must be determined. In addition, the interest element of the transaction must be considered. Originally, the courts applied the open transaction approach of Burnett v. Logan. See Commissioner v. Kann's Estate, 174 F.2d 357 (3d Cir.1949); Lloyd v. Commissioner, 33 B.T.A. 903 (1936) (Acq.). However, in Rev. Rul. 69–74, 1969–1 C.B. 43, the IRS held that the gain element had to be reported ratably over the property transferor's life expectancy.[2] The approach of Rev. Rul. 69–74 was followed in Garvey, Inc. v. United States, 726 F.2d 1569 (Fed.Cir.1984), which rejected the taxpayer's argument that open transaction treatment should be available for unsecured private annuity transactions.

As to the purchaser of the property, Rev. Rul. 55–119, 1955–1 C.B. 352, prescribes rules for computing basis, depreciation, and gain or loss with respect to property acquired in return for the payment of an annuity. Kaufman's, Inc. v. Commissioner, 28 T.C. 1179 (1957) (Acq.), follows this ruling in requiring capitalization of the present value of the annual annuity payments made by the purchaser. In Dix v. Commissioner, 392 F.2d 313 (4th Cir.1968), the taxpayers' mother transferred appreciated stock to them in exchange for a life annuity; the taxpayers subsequently sold part of the property received. The court held that the taxpayers' cost basis in the property was to be determined by private annuity tables and not by commercial annuity tables (which would have provided a higher basis).

8.2. *Secured Transactions*

In Estate of Bell v. Commissioner, 60 T.C. 469 (1973), a husband and wife transferred their stock in two closely held family farming corporations to their children in exchange for an annuity of $1,000 per month for life. The stock was placed in escrow to secure the agreement and, as further security, the agreement provided for a cognovit judgment (whereby a debtor

---

[2]   In calculating the investment in a contract for purposes of § 72, Rev. Rul. 69–74 uses the taxpayer's cost basis in the property transferred. A portion of the gain recognized under § 72 is treated as gain from the disposition of the property and is capital gain or ordinary income depending on appropriate characterization of gain from the property disposition. Gross income received in excess of the ratable portion of gain from the property is treated as ordinary income. If the annuitant outlives his life expectancy, all of the property gain will have been reported and all subsequent payments are ordinary income.

authorizes a creditor's lawyer to enter a confession in court, usually signed, permitting judgment against the debtor) against the transferees in the event of default. The Tax Court determined that the taxpayers realized an immediate taxable gain at the time of the transfer, measured by the difference between their adjusted basis in the stock and the fair market value of the annuity.

Estate of Bell was followed in 212 Corporation v. Commissioner, 70 T.C. 788 (1978), which required the immediate recognition of gain where the taxpayer transferred real property in exchange for an annuity secured by both the real property and the obligation of the lessee to pay the rentals on the property. A dissent in the case would not have required any immediate gain recognition on the ground that the annuity, while having an ascertainable fair market value, was not equivalent to cash. Five other dissenters would have overruled *Estate of Bell* and allowed the taxpayer to report the gain ratably over the life expectancy of the annuitant, consistent with the approach in Rev. Rul. 69–74 with respect to unsecured private annuities.

8.3. *Other Transactions*

If the taxpayer transfers property to a corporation, trust, fund, or foundation (other than a commercial insurance company), which "from time to time" issues annuity contracts in exchange for an annuity, the taxpayer will realize gain at the time of the transfer to the extent of the excess of the present value of the payments to be received over the basis of the property exchanged. Rev. Rul. 62–136, 1962–2 C.B. 12. See Rev. Rul. 84–162, 1984–2 C.B. 200, for rules used in valuing such annuities.

8.4. *Proposed Regulations*

Proposed regulations would significantly change the treatment of private annuities received in exchange for appreciated property. Prop. Reg. § 1.1001–1(j) (2006) would provide that, if property was exchanged for an annuity, the amount realized attributable to the annuity contract is its fair market value (determined under § 7520) at the time of the exchange. The entire amount of gain or loss realized on the exchange would be recognized in the year of the exchange. However, the preamble to the proposed regulations requested comments from the public "as to the circumstances, if any, in which an exchange of property for an annuity contract should be treated as an installment sale, and as to any changes in the regulations under section 453 that might be advisable with regard to those circumstances."

CHAPTER 32

INTEREST ON DISCOUNT OBLIGATIONS

INTERNAL REVENUE CODE: Sections 163(e); 483; 1272(a)(1)–(5), (7), (b); 1273; 1274; 1274A(a)–(c); 1275(a)(1), (2), (b), (c).

SECTION 1.   INTRODUCTION

In an installment sale, or any other transaction in which a seller agrees to receive deferred payment, the seller expects to receive some compensation for the loss of the immediate use of sales proceeds, just as a lender expects to be compensated for the borrower's use of the lender's funds. In any such transaction, the normal method of compensation for the time value of the use of money is the current payment of interest. Interest, as the cost of borrowed money, often is deductible by the borrower and includable in income by the lender. However, in some deferred payment transactions the interest element may be included as an adjustment to the purchase price of property, with the purchaser paying a higher price to reflect the value of deferred payment thereby increasing the amount realized by the seller, and possibly converting interest into capital gain. At the same time, the purchaser would take a higher basis in the property, but lose the interest deduction. These results do not match economic reality. The amount realized on a disposition of property and the purchaser's basis must be adjusted to account for any interest element hidden in price adjustments that are made to reflect the time-value of deferred payments. Similarly, in a loan transaction interest may be reflected in a payment of nominal principal greater than the amount of proceeds actually received by the borrower. For example, the receipt of $1 in exchange for a promise to repay $1 at the end of one year plus 10 percent stated interest (compounded annually) may also be described as a promise to pay $1.10 at the end of one year in exchange for the present receipt of $1. Likewise, the sale of property for $1 plus 10 percent interest is economically equivalent to the sale of property for $1.10 payable at the end of one year. The increased value of the obligation, from $1 to $1.10 over the period from the date of the loan to maturity is the return to the lender and the cost to the borrower for the use of the borrowed funds, or for the forbearance from collecting the sales price. Accordingly this increment is properly treated as interest. Indeed, at a 10-percent interest rate (compounded annually), the *future value* of $1 at the end of a single one-year term is $1.10.[1] Note

---

[1]   Future value at the end of one period (FV_1) is calculated with the formula $FV_1 = PV + PV(r)$ where PV is the present value of the obligation and r is the interest rate for the period as a percentage. This formula is simplified to $FV_1 = PV(1 + r)$. Thus the future value of $1 due at

also that the *present value* of $1.10 due at the end of a one-year term, again at a 10-percent interest rate, is $1.[2] Proper accounting for interest paid and received requires a method to treat the accrual of interest on an obligation that does not include stated interest, or states interest at a rate below the prevailing market interest rate, in the same manner as the receipt of the stated interest, i.e., to account for the time value of money in a consistent manner. Thus, a device is necessary to identify the growth in the value of an obligation as the due date for repayment becomes nearer in time.

Determining the value of an obligation to pay over multiple periods must include *compounding*. If the creditor holds an obligation with a stated interest rate payable annually, the creditor may be expected to reinvest the annual interest received from the borrower. Therefore, an obligation without stated interest must reflect the interest element earned on unpaid interest. For example, a promise to repay $1 at the end of three years, plus 10-percent interest accruable semiannually (but payable at the end of the term) requires interest accruals of five percent of the outstanding balance, including accrued interest, at the end of each six-month period. Using a 10-percent interest rate compounded semiannually to reflect the obligation to pay interest every six months, the promise is the equivalent of a promise to pay $1.34 at the end of the three-year period. The $1.34 amount is the amount that the creditor would expect to have at the end of the three-year period if $1 is set aside in a savings account that paid 10-percent interest compounded semiannually. The $1 grows to $1.34 as follows:

End of Year	End of Period	Interest For The Period	Annual Interest	Value At End of Period
0				$1.00
	1	$ .05		1.05
1	2	.0525	$0.1025	1.1025
	3	.055125		1.1576
2	4	.057881	0.1130	1.2155
	5	.060775		1.2768
3	6	.063814	0.1246	1.3400

Given the growth rate of $1 over three years, at 10 percent interest compounded semiannually, the borrower can currently sell its promise to pay $1.34 at the end of three years for $1.

---

the end of the year at 10% interest is $1(1 + 0.10)$. For the second period, the formula is $FV_2 = PV(1 + r)(1 + r)$, which is the same as $FV_2 = PV(1 + r)^2$. Thus, the future value for any period is $FV_n = PV(1 + r)^n$.

[2]   The formula for computing present value is $PV_n = FV_n/(1 + r)^n$ which is the converse of the formula described in note 1, supra.

An obligation sold for a price less than its stated principal (or redemption price) is referred to as a discount obligation. The original issue discount is the difference between the amount received at the time the obligation is issued, $1 in our example, and its redemption price, $1.34. Thus the original issue discount in the example is $0.34. This $0.34 difference between the issue price and the redemption price represents interest, or the cost of borrowing $1 for three years. In economic terms, the cost to the borrower of borrowing the $1, and the return on the lender's $1 investment, are the same if the borrower borrowed $1 and agreed to pay 10-percent interest to the lender at the end of each semi-annual period[3] or, alternatively, if the borrower agreed to pay 10-percent interest compounded semiannually at the end of three years when the principal was required to be repaid. However, in the absence of special rules to account for the growth over time of the value of an obligation to pay money, the tax treatment of the interest paid on the obligation may vary depending upon the form of the transaction. Is the interest deductible by the borrower and/or includable in income by the lender only when the obligation is redeemed, or is the interest accounted for as it accrues over the life of the obligation and, if so, at what rate? Furthermore, if an obligation without stated interest is issued in exchange for property, is the full face amount of the obligation to be treated as the purchase price for the property by the seller and the purchaser, or is the purchase price adjusted to reflect an interest element to account for the time value of the deferred payment? Finally, in either case does or should the method of tax accounting employed by either of the parties to the transaction have any impact on the treatment of the transaction?

SECTION 2. ORIGINAL ISSUE DISCOUNT

Tax Reform Act of 1984 General Explanation of the Revenue Provisions

Staff of the Joint Committee on Taxation 108 (1984).

[Pre-1984] Law.

Timing of inclusion and deduction of interest: the OID rules

If, in a lending transaction, the borrower receives less than the amount to be repaid at the loan's maturity, the difference represents "discount." Discount performs the same function as stated interest; that is, it compensates the lender for the use of its money. Sections 1232A and 163(e) of prior law (the "OID rules") generally required the holder of a discount debt obligation to include in income annually a portion of the

---

[3]   This statement assumes that, if current interest were paid, the creditor could reinvest the interest received at the same 10-percent rate and that, if current interest were not paid, the borrower could invest the cash that would otherwise pay the interest at the same 10-percent rate.

original issue discount on the obligation, and allowed the issuer to deduct a corresponding amount, irrespective of whether the cash method or the accrual method of accounting was used.[7]

Original issue discount was defined as the excess of an obligation's stated redemption price at maturity over its issue price. This amount was allocated over the life of the obligation through a series of adjustments to the issue price for each "bond period" (generally, each one-year period beginning on the issue date of the bond and each anniversary). The adjustment to the issue price for each bond period was determined by multiplying the "adjusted issue price" (the issue price increased by adjustments prior to the beginning of the bond period) by the obligation's yield to maturity, and then subtracting the interest payable during the bond period. The adjustment to the issue price for any bond period was the amount of OID allocated to that bond period.

The OID rules did not apply to obligations issued by individuals, obligations with a maturity of one year or less, or obligations issued in exchange for property where neither the obligation nor the property received for it was traded on an established securities exchange.

Measurement of interest in deferred-payment transactions involving property: the imputed interest rules

A deferred-payment sale of property exempt from the OID rules was generally subject to the unstated interest rules of section 483. If the parties to the transaction failed to state a minimum "safe-harbor" rate of interest to be paid on the loan by the purchaser-borrower, section 483 recharacterized a portion of the principal amount as unstated interest.

* * *

If interest was imputed under section 483, a portion of each deferred payment was treated as unstated interest. The allocation between unstated interest and principal was made on the basis of the size of the deferred payment in relation to the total deferred payments. Amounts characterized as unstated interest were included in the income of the lender in the year the deferred payment was received (in the case of a cash method taxpayer) or due (in the case of an accrual method taxpayer). The borrower correspondingly deducted the imputed interest in the year the payment was made or due.

* * *

---

[7]   The premise of the OID rules was that an OID obligation should be treated in the same manner as a nondiscount obligation requiring current payments of interest for tax purposes. To accomplish this result, the rules in essence treated the borrower as having paid the lender the annual unpaid interest accruing on the outstanding principal balance of the loan, which amount the borrower was allowed to deduct as interest expense and the lender was required to include in income. The lender was then deemed to have lent this amount back to the borrower, who in subsequent periods was deemed to pay interest on this amount as well as on the principal balance. This concept of accruing interest on unpaid interest is commonly referred to as the "economic accrual" of interest, or interest "compounding."

Reasons for Change

Mismatching and noneconomic accrual of interest

Enacted in 1969, the OID rules were designed to eliminate the distortions caused by the mismatching of income and deductions by lenders and borrowers in discount lending transactions. Prior to that time, an accrual method borrower could deduct deferred interest payable to a cash method lender prior to the period in which the lender included the interest in income. Although the OID rules prevented mismatching in many situations, the potential for distortion continued to exist where the obligation was excepted from the OID rules. Some taxpayers attempted to exploit these exceptions, particularly the exception relating to nontraded obligations issued for nontraded property, to achieve deferral of tax on interest income and accelerated deductions of interest expense.

For example, in a typical transaction, real estate, machinery, or other depreciable property was purchased for a promissory note providing that interest accrued annually but was not payable until the note matured. The issuer, who used the accrual method of accounting, would claim annual interest deductions for accrued but unpaid interest. The holder, a cash method taxpayer, would defer interest income until it was actually received.

Such a mismatching of income and deductions had serious revenue consequences, since the present value of the income included by the lender in the later period was less than the present value of the deductions claimed by the borrower. The greater the length of time between the borrower's deduction and the lender's inclusion, the greater the loss of tax revenues.

This revenue loss was magnified if the accrual-method purchaser computed its interest deduction using a noneconomic formula such as straight-line amortization, simple interest, or the "Rule of 78's".[13] In Rev. Rul. 83–84, 1983–1 C.B. 97, the IRS stated that interest may be deducted only to the extent it has accrued economically, using a constant yield-to-maturity formula. Some taxpayers, however, took the position that the ruling incorrectly interpreted existing law. Other taxpayers construed the ruling narrowly, as applying only to the precise facts set forth in the ruling.

In light of the significant distortions occurring under prior law, both in the form of mismatching of interest income and deductions and in the form of noneconomic accruals of interest, Congress believed it appropriate to extend the periodic inclusion and deduction rules * * * to nontraded debt instruments issued for nontraded property. The same policy objectives that led to the application of these rules to interest on traded debt instruments or instruments issued for cash—namely, better

---

[13]   The Rule of 78's is a formula for allocating interest over the term of a loan that results in larger deductions in the early years.

compliance by holders and clearer reflection of income—were believed to apply equally in the case of nontraded instruments issued for nontraded property.

The principal obstacle to applying the OID rules to a transaction in which neither side is traded is the difficulty of determining the issue price of the debt instrument directly. Both the issue price and the redemption price of an instrument must be known to compute the amount of OID. In a transaction involving the issuance of an [*sic*] note for cash, the issue price is simply the amount of cash received. Where the issuer receives nontraded property, however, the fair market value of the property determines the obligation's issue price.[14] Using a "facts and circumstances," case-by-case analysis to determine fair market value in these situations was considered impracticable. Congress believed that the valuation problem could best be resolved by incorporating into the OID rules a mechanism for testing the adequacy of interest in a sale of property already present in the Code—the unstated interest rules of section 483—with certain modifications. An approximation of the maximum fair market value of property (and hence the issue price of the obligation issued in exchange for it) could be arrived at by assuming a minimum rate of interest which parties dealing at arm's-length and without tax motivations could be expected to agree upon.

Since individuals frequently issue debt obligations in exchange for property, and these obligations often provide for deferred payments of interest, Congress believed it necessary to eliminate the exception to the OID rules for obligations issued by individuals.

Finally, Congress believed there was no justification for continuing the exemption from the OID rules for holders of obligations not constituting capital assets in the holder's hands. Sales of ordinary income assets may involve deferred interest to the same degree as sales of capital assets, and the timing of income in such sales is as important as its character.

While acknowledging the complexity of the OID rules, Congress believed that the rules could be extended to a broader range of transactions without disrupting the routine, legitimate transactions of individuals or small businesses, which might have difficulty applying the rules. The Act exempts many such routine transactions.

Mismeasurement of interest in transactions involving nontraded property

Congress recognized that, under prior law, it was possible for taxpayers in a sale of nontraded property for nontraded debt to achieve unwarranted tax benefits not only by mismatching interest income and deductions, but by manipulating the principal amount of the debt. This could be accomplished by artificially fixing interest at a below-market

---

[14]   The issue price of the obligation in such a transaction is the value of the property received by the issuer, less any cash down payment made to the holder.

rate. Although economically the parties were in the same position as if interest had been accurately stated, significant tax advantages often resulted from characterizing the transaction as involving a lower rate of interest and a larger loan principal amount. If recognized for tax purposes, this mischaracterization of interest as principal resulted in an overstatement of the sales price and tax basis of the property.[15] In cases where the property was a capital asset in the hands of the seller, the seller was able to convert interest income, which should have been taxable as ordinary income in the year it accrued, into capital gain taxable at lower rates (and, under the installment method provided in sec. 453, generally only as installment payments were made). If the property was depreciable in the hands of the purchaser, the inflated basis enabled the purchaser to claim excessive cost recovery (ACRS) deductions * * * .

These same tax advantages accrued to taxpayers who engaged in low-interest transactions entirely for nontax reasons.

* * *

Explanation of Provisions
a.　Extension of OID rules

Overview

The Act extends the rules for periodic inclusion and deduction of original issue discount by lenders and borrowers to debt instruments that are issued for property that is not publicly traded, and that are themselves not publicly traded. The Act also repeals the exemption for obligations issued by individuals and the exemption from the income accrual requirement for cash-method holders of obligations not constituting capital assets in the holder's hands. Exceptions from the rules are provided to ensure that they will not apply to most routine transactions of individual taxpayers, or to de minimis transactions of individuals and others.

If either the debt instrument or the property for which it is exchanged is publicly traded, the amount of OID is determined as under prior law. The market value of the traded side determines the issue price of the obligation, and the excess of the redemption price over the issue price is original issue discount. Where neither side is traded, the transaction is tested for the adequacy of stated interest in a manner similar to that prescribed in section 483 of [pre-1983] law.

---

[15]　To illustrate, assume a sale of equipment which Seller and Buyer agree is worth $100 in cash, and a market interest rate of 12 percent (compound interest). Buyer agrees to pay, and Seller agrees to accept, a lump sum amount of $176 at the end of five years. From an economic perspective, the $176 lump sum payment is comprised of $100 principal and $76 interest. Under prior law, however, the transaction could be structured as a sale for a $121 note bearing simple interest at 9 percent ($121 grows to approximately $176 in five years at a rate of 9 percent simple interest).

If the stated rate of interest is not equal to or greater than a safe-harbor rate, the issue price is determined by imputing interest to the transaction at a higher rate. The safe-harbor rate and the imputation rate are equal to * * * the "applicable Federal rate," a rate based on the yields of marketable securities of the United States government. [Ed.: The original 1984 legislation imputed interest of 120 percent of the applicable Federal rate if the parties failed to specify interest of at least 110 percent of the applicable federal rate. The 1988 Act adopted the applicable federal rate as both the safe-harbor and imputed interest rate.]

* * *

Applicable Federal rate

The applicable Federal rate for an obligation is a rate based on the average yield for marketable obligations of the United States government with a comparable maturity. Federal rates are periodically computed and published by the Treasury Department. The rates are redetermined at six-month intervals for three categories of obligations: short-term maturity (three years or less); mid-term maturity (more than three years but not in excess of nine years); and long-term maturity (more than nine years). The applicable Federal rate for a transaction is the rate in effect for that category of maturity on the first day there is a binding contract for the sale or exchange. Federal debt obligations with characteristics that result in a yield substantially above or below a market rate of interest are disregarded in computing the applicable Federal rates. Thus, for example, the yield on bonds, the face amount of which may be used to satisfy Federal estate tax obligations (so-called "flower bonds"), is not taken into account. Furthermore, Congress expected that in computing the Federal rates, the Treasury Department will make appropriate adjustments to reflect the tax exemption for interest on an obligation.

* * *

Regulatory authority

The Act authorizes the Treasury Department to issue regulations dealing with the treatment of transactions involving varying interest rates, put or call options, indefinite maturities, contingent payments, assumptions of debt instruments, or other circumstances.

DETAILED ANALYSIS

1.   GENERAL

Section 1272 requires the holder of an original issue discount bond to include in income the daily portion of original issue discount attributable to the obligation. Section 163(e) conversely permits the issuer of an original discount obligation to deduct the aggregate daily portion of original issue discount for the taxable year, to the extent the interest is otherwise deductible. These rules apply to all debt obligations with original issue discount, including bank certificates of deposit that mature in more than one year, with exceptions for tax exempt obligations, U.S. savings bonds, and nonbusiness loans between natural persons if the amount of the loan does not exceed $10,000. I.R.C. § 1272(a)(2).

The holder's basis in the original issue discount obligation is increased to reflect the amount included in income by the holder. I.R.C. § 1272(d)(2). Thus if the obligation is held to maturity, upon redemption its basis equals its stated redemption price and neither gain nor loss will be recognized. If the holder of the obligation disposes of it before maturity, the purchaser steps into the original holder's shoes with respect to the remaining original issue discount attributable to the bond. The original holder treats any amount received in excess of the adjusted basis as gain on disposition; the second owner is entitled to deduct any such excess over the remaining life of the bond from the amount of original issue discount otherwise required to be included in income. I.R.C. § 1272(a)(7).

Original issue discount is defined in § 1273(a)(1) as the difference between the "stated redemption price at maturity" over the "issue price." Thus, original issue discount, the amount that is accounted for over the life of the obligation, is the difference between the amount paid to the issuer for the obligation at its issue (i.e., the borrowed amount available for use by the issuer) over the fixed amount to be repaid at maturity. "Stated redemption price" is defined as the amount to be paid for the obligation at its maturity, including any interest element payable at that time. I.R.C. § 1273(a)(2). Stated redemption price does not include fixed and periodic interest payable at intervals of one year or less during the term of the loan. Fixed and periodic interest is accounted for under the issuer's and holder's normal accounting methods and need not be reflected in the original issue discount allocation. At the same time, one must recognize that an obligation with stated interest may be issued for a price less than the stated redemption price. The annual interest for the obligation thus includes two elements, the stated interest plus the portion of original issue discount allocable to the taxable year.

Determination of the issue price of an obligation under § 1273(b) depends upon the nature of the obligation and the circumstance of its issue. The issue price of an obligation publicly offered for money is the initial offering price to the public at which a substantial amount of the instruments are sold. If publicly traded debt obligations are issued for property other than money, whether or not the property is publicly traded (such as stock of a corporation, either publicly traded or closely held, or real estate), the issue price of the debt obligation is its trading price. See Treas. Reg. § 1.1273–2(b). If a debt obligation that is not publicly traded is issued for property that is regularly traded on an established market, the issue price of the debt obligation is the market price of the property received. For example, if a debt obligation that is not publicly traded is issued in exchange for stock or securities that are traded on an established securities market, under § 1273(b)(3) its issue price is the trading price of the property received. See Treas. Reg. § 1.1273–2(c). The issue price of an obligation issued for property where neither the debt instrument nor the property is traded on an established market is generally determined under § 1274, which imputes original issue discount to most obligations issued for property using the present value of the obligation as the issue price. The present value of an obligation is determined by using the applicable federal rate as the discount rate.

2. ECONOMIC ACCRUAL OF INTEREST

Before 1982, the original issue discount rules required ratable deduction and inclusion of original issue discount over the life of the bond. That approach failed to reflect accurately the economic accrual of the interest. For example, a three-year bond with a face amount of $1,340.00 issued for $1,000.00 reflects an interest rate of 10 percent compounded semiannually (or an effective annual rate of 10.25 percent). Accounting for the $340.00 of original issue discount ratably over the three years would result in a deduction of $113.33 each year for three years. However, in economic terms, the original issue discount transaction is the same as if the borrower had borrowed additional money each year to pay interest. Interest in each period is computed on the original principal plus the borrowed interest. Using a constant interest rate, the amount of the interest should be lower in the early years and then grow as the outstanding "principal" of the loan increases due to the interest which has been "borrowed" back.[4] This calculation allows the interest expense to be compounded.

	Ratable Interest	Economic Interest	"Principal" Outstanding
Year 1	$113.33	$102.50	$1,102.50
Year 2	113.33	113.00	1,215.50
Year 3	113.33	124.50	1,340.00

Current law requires that original issue discount deductions and inclusions be calculated on a compounding or constant interest basis. Under § 1272(a)(3) and (5), original issue discount is calculated by determining the "yield to maturity" based on semiannual compounding (10 percent in the above example).

Original issue discount within an accrual period is ratably allocated to each day of the accrual period. I.R.C. § 1272(a)(3); Treas. Reg. § 1.1272–1(b)(1)(iv). The holder of an original issue discount bond is required to include the daily portions of original issue discount for each day the bond is held. I.R.C. § 1272(a)(1). The issuer deducts original issue discount in the same manner. I.R.C. § 163(e). Treas. Reg. § 1.1272–1(b)(1)(ii) allows the use of any accrual period not exceeding one year. The regulations point out that the computation of yield is simplified if the accrual periods correspond to the intervals between payment dates provided by the terms of the instrument. Under Treas. Reg. § 1.1272–1(b)(1), the original issue discount for any accrual period is calculated first by determining the yield to maturity of the obligation; that is, "the discount rate that, when used in computing the present value of all principal and interest payments to be made under the

---

[4]   This would be the result when a three-year note required annual interest payments but provided that in any year in which interest was not paid, the unpaid interest would be added to principal and would bear interest at the rate stated in the note.

debt instrument, produces an amount equal to the issue price of the debt instrument." The original issue discount allocable to each accrual period is the adjusted issue price of the instrument multiplied by the yield to maturity and reduced by the amount of qualified stated interest allocable to the accrual period. "Adjusted issue price" is the original issue price increased by accrued but unpaid original issue discount and decreased by payments. Treas. Reg. § 1.1275–1(b)(1). "Qualified stated interest" is interest that is unconditionally payable at a fixed rate at least annually. Treas. Reg. § 1.1273–1(c). Thus, in the example above, at the beginning of year 3, the adjusted issue price is $1,215.50, reflecting the original issue price of $1,000 and the accrued interest for years 1 and 2 less stated interest payments of zero. The amount of original issue discount deducted by the borrower and included by the lender for year 3 is $124.50.

3. ORIGINAL ISSUE DISCOUNT OBLIGATIONS ISSUED FOR PROPERTY

3.1. *Introduction*

When A sells property to B in a transaction in which some of the payments for the property are deferred, two separate economic transactions are involved. A is both selling the property to B and loaning B the amount of the unpaid purchase price, while B is correspondingly purchasing the property and simultaneously borrowing the unpaid purchase price from A. Original issue discount is present if the stated principal amount of B's obligation is greater than the fair market value of the transferred property.

3.2. *Publicly Traded Bonds or Property*

Section 1273(b)(3) provides that original issue discount arises in the case of bonds issued for property when either the bonds or the property is traded on an established market and the face amount of the bonds issued exceeds the fair market value of the property received. Treas. Reg. § 1.1273–2(f) provides that property is traded on an established market if it is traded on a recognized exchange, or if the property appears on a system of general circulation that provides a reasonable basis to determine fair market value through dissemination of either price quotations or reports of recent sales.

3.3. *Discount Obligations Issued for Property That Is Not Publicly Traded*

Section 1274 applies original issue discount rules to sales of property for a deferred payment if the stated interest is less than the applicable federal rate compounded semi-annually. For purposes of determining the issue price of the original issue discount obligation, the present value of all payments to be made under the instrument is calculated on the basis of the "applicable federal rate." The resulting difference between the hypothetical issue price and the actual payments to be made under the instrument is original issue discount which must be currently included by the seller and deducted by the buyer using a constant interest rate as described above. Original issue discount is avoided if the debt instrument has a stated annual interest rate equal to or greater than the applicable federal rate.

Section 1274A(a) and (b) provide that the discount rate for purposes of § 1274 is not to exceed 9 percent, compounded semiannually, if the stated principal of the obligation is not in excess of $2.8 million (adjusted for inflation after 1989; $5,664,800 in 2016), and the obligation is not issued as consideration for the sale or exchange of certain tangible personal property used in a trade or business (§ 38 property within the meaning of § 48(b), which, in general, includes depreciable machinery and equipment and certain limited classes of improvements to real property). Section 1274A(a) is of no significance when the applicable federal rate is below 9 percent. In addition, under § 1274A(c), if § 1274 would otherwise apply to a transaction, and the stated principal amount involved does not exceed $2 million (adjusted for inflation after 1989; $4,046,300 in 2016), the parties can elect to have the interest on the debt obligation treated as if both parties were on the cash method of accounting, thus deferring both the deduction and the inclusion of the interest (with the caveat that both the lender and the borrower must elect the cash method and, additionally, that the lender is not a dealer with respect to the property).

The following example illustrates the application of § 1274. Suppose that A agrees to sell property to B for $1,000 on the following terms. Payment for the property will be due three years from the date of the sale and will bear simple interest at 8 percent with all interest to be paid at the end of the third year. Assume that the applicable federal rate is 9 percent. The first question is whether the obligation bears "adequate stated interest." As it turns out, the obligation does not bear adequate stated interest, because (a) the stated rate is only 8 percent, which is less than the applicable federal rate of 9 percent, (b) the interest is not compounded semiannually, and (c) the interest is only payable at the maturity of the obligation. By using a below-market interest rate, A and B have attempted to convert a portion of the financing transaction into a sales transaction. Thus, under § 1274(a)(2), the "imputed principal amount" is treated as the issue price for purposes of determining the original issue discount. The imputed principal amount is defined in § 1274(b) as the present value of all payments due on the debt instrument, using as a discount rate the applicable federal rate. On this basis, the present value of the $1,240 payment to be made in year 3 (the $1,000 principal plus $80 interest per year for three years) is $952.19. This amount is then treated as the issue price of the obligation for purposes of determining the original issue discount on the financing portion of the transaction and as the sales price for the sales portion of the transaction.

Section 1274 thus isolates the unstated interest element in the transaction, using the applicable federal rate as the norm. It indicates that economically A sold the property to B for $952.19 and loaned B that amount in return for a promise to pay $1,240 in three years reflecting a 9 percent interest rate, compounded semiannually. B has a basis of $952.19 in the property for purposes of depreciation and sale. On the financing side of the transaction, A is required to include currently the appropriate amount of the original issue discount income and B is given a deduction for a corresponding amount (if the amount is otherwise deductible), thus matching deduction and inclusion. The original issue discount is $287.81, reported each year as follows:

	Reported OID	Adjusted Issue Price
Year 1	$ 87.62	$1,039.81
Year 2	95.68	1,135.50
Year 3	104.49	1,239.99

If the rate of interest charged and payable under the contract had been equal to the applicable federal rate, the original issue discount rules would not have applied.[5] The agreed price for the property would determine A's gain on the sales portion of the transaction and B's basis for the property. The interest deduction and interest income would likewise be matched because the interest payments must be made currently to prevent the application of the original issue discount rules, thus requiring current inclusion by the cash method seller.

By using the applicable federal rate to identify the interest element of the transaction, § 1274 avoids the necessity of directly valuing non-traded property for purposes of calculating the original issue discount. In effect, it requires the buyer and seller to use at least the appropriate federal rate on the financing portion of the transaction. The remainder of the payments is then considered to be the price paid for the underlying property. The section thus works backward from a given interest rate to calculate the current value of the property.

3.4. *Exceptions to Section 1274 and the Application of Section 483*

Some deferred payment sales are not subject to § 1274, including: sales of a farm by an individual or "small business" for less than $1 million; the sale of a principal residence; any sale or exchange of property if the total amount receivable under the obligation does not exceed $250,000; and certain sales of patents to the extent the sales price is contingent on income from the patent. I.R.C. § 1274(c). Transactions not covered by § 1274 are subject to the imputed interest rules of § 483.

With some exceptions, the amount of imputed interest is calculated for purposes of § 483 in the same manner as under § 1274. Imputed interest under § 483 is the difference between issue price and the present value of the payments required by the obligation using the applicable federal rate, compounded semiannually, as the discount rate. I.R.C. § 483(b). Unlike original issue discount under § 1274, however, imputed interest under § 483 is taken into account by a cash method taxpayer only when payment is received or paid, and by an accrual method taxpayer when payment is due. Treas. Reg. § 1.483–2(a)(1)(ii). Unstated interest must be allocated to each payment using the constant interest method of § 1272(a). I.R.C. § 483(a).

Section 483(e) provides a special rule for sales of a personal residence between related persons. To the extent that the aggregate sales price of all

---

[5]   Section 1274(d)(1)(D) authorizes regulations to permit use of a rate lower than the applicable federal rate if the taxpayer can establish that it would have been possible for the taxpayer to borrow in an arm's length transaction at the lower rate.

such sales does not exceed $500,000, the discount rate for computing unstated interest is not to exceed six percent, compounded semiannually.

Neither § 1274 nor § 483 applies to the borrower with respect to unstated interest on an obligation issued for property purchased for personal use. I.R.C. § 1275(b). Thus, unstated interest incurred for the acquisition of property that is not used in a trade or business or held for investment that is not deductible interest under § 163 will not cause a reduction in the property's basis under § 1272(d)(2). In addition, even if interest on the obligation is deductible under § 163 (for example interest on a home equity loan used to acquire a personal automobile), original issue discount that would be created under § 1274 or imputed interest under § 483 will not be treated as deductible interest. The holder of the obligation remains subject to reporting interest income under § 1274 or § 483.

4.   ORIGINAL ISSUE DISCOUNT AND HYBRID SECURITIES

Corporations sometimes issue hybrid debt obligations that are convertible into stock. Alternatively, corporations can issue debt instruments that are packaged together with warrants that give the holder the right to acquire stock at a specified price. In either case, some portion of the purchase price of the debt instrument is attributable to the value of the conversion feature or the warrant. However, Treas. Reg. § 1.1273–2(j) provides that, in the case of convertible obligations, no original issue discount is created with respect to the option to convert. All of the consideration is deemed to be paid for the debt portion of the transaction.

On the other hand, where debt obligations are issued as part of an investment unit that includes a warrant, the original issue price of the obligation includes only the consideration paid for the debt portion of the unit. Treas. Reg. § 1.1273–2(h).

5.   CONTINGENT INTEREST AND VARIABLE RATE INTEREST

In the case of obligations issued for cash or marketable securities, original issue discount is the difference between the issue price of the obligation and the amount to be paid at maturity. In the case of obligations issued for property that are subject to § 1274, the computation of original issue discount depends upon the present value of all payments under the note. Both of these computations require knowledge of the time and the amount of payments under the obligations. Determining the amount of original issue discount is more complex when either the time or amount of payment under the obligation is contingent on some future event, such as the rate of return from the property transferred in exchange for the obligation, or when the interest rate stated in the obligation is variable in accordance with some outside measure of interest, such as the prime rate of a specified financial institution. Treas. Reg. § 1.1272–1(c) provides detailed rules for determining original issue discount in the case of variable interest rate obligations.

Treas. Reg. § 1.1275–4 applies the OID rules to contingent obligations on the basis of simplifying assumptions. In the case of a publicly traded instrument, generally speaking, the yield on the contingent obligation is determined and a payment schedule to produce that yield is then fixed.

Treas. Reg. § 1.1275–4(b). The yield on the instrument is the yield at which the issuer would issue a fixed rate debt instrument with terms and conditions similar to the contingent payment debt instrument. The issuer's determination of yield and projected payments generally will be respected, but the yield must be reasonable and may not be less than the applicable federal rate (AFR). For market-based payments, projected payments equal the forward price of the payments. For non-market-based payments, projected payments are the expected amount of the payment as of the issue date. Projected payments rather than actual payments are used to determine the adjusted issue price of the debt instrument, the holder's basis in the debt instrument, and the amount of any contingent payment treated as made on the scheduled retirement of the debt instrument. If actual payments are larger or smaller than projected, adjustments—greater accruals, offsets to accruals, or loss deductions—must be made.

Treas. Reg. § 1.1275–4(c) provides special rules applicable to a non-publicly traded debt instrument issued in a purchase or exchange for non-publicly traded property. Noncontingent payments are treated as a separate debt instrument that is subject to the rules applicable to noncontingent debt instruments. Contingent payments are taken into account separately when made. The portion of each contingent payment that is principal is determined by discounting the payment from the payment date to the issue date at the AFR (determined on the instrument's issue date); the remainder of the payment is treated as interest.

Under Treas. Reg. § 1.1274–2(g), the issue price of a contingent payment debt instrument that is issued in exchange for non-publicly traded property, such as real estate, does not include any contingent payments due under the instrument. Thus, in computing the basis of the property, the buyer initially takes into account only the noncontingent payments due under the instrument. As contingent payments treated as principal are made, the buyer increases the basis in the property. See T.D. 8674, 1996–2 C.B. 84, 88. Nevertheless, if such a sale is not reported under the § 453 installment method (see Chapter 31, Section 2), the amount realized by the seller is not the issue price of the instrument determined under Treas. Reg. § 1.1274–2(g), which does not take into account the contingent payments. Rather, the amount realized is the sum of the issue price of the noncontingent payments plus the fair market value of the contingent payments. Treas. Reg. § 1.1001–1(g)(2)(ii).

6. INFLATION-ADJUSTED BONDS

Debt instruments with a principal amount that is indexed for inflation, such as Treasury Inflation Protection Securities, are OID instruments that provide for contingent payments. Treas. Reg. § 1.1275–7 specifically deals with the treatment of inflation-adjusted debt instruments. A simplified "coupon bond" method applies if an inflation-adjusted debt instrument is issued with no more than a *de minimis* difference between its issue price and its stated principal amount and all stated interest is "qualified stated interest" (interest that is unconditionally payable at a fixed rate at least annually). Under the coupon bond method, qualified stated interest is reported under the taxpayer's normal accounting method, and any increase in the inflation-adjusted principal is taken into account as OID. Thus, for a cash method bondholder, the amount of OID attributable to any year is the excess of the inflation-adjusted principal as of January 1 of the following year over the amount of the inflation-adjusted principal on January 1 of the year in question. The more complex "discount bond method" applies if an inflation-adjusted debt instrument is issued at a discount below its stated principal amount, thus creating additional OID over and above the inflation-adjustment. Under this method, no portion of the interest on the bond is treated as qualified stated interest, and the entire amount of OID, after applying a prescribed formula to factor in the inflation-adjusted principal amount, is taken into account under the constant interest method. Under both methods, deflation adjustments are treated as offsets to interest otherwise reportable with respect to the instrument, and as ordinary losses to the extent deflation adjustments exceed interest income, and any excess over the losses allowed is carried over to future years.

7. MARKET DISCOUNT

There is an interest element present on the purchase of a debt obligation in the market for a price below its stated redemption price. From the standpoint of a bondholder, there is no economic difference between original issue discount, which is required to be included in income over the term of the bond, and market discount. Accordingly, §§ 1276–1278 deal with the treatment of market discount and the interest deductions associated with borrowing to finance the purchase of market discount obligations. Under § 1276, gain on the disposition of a market discount bond is treated as ordinary income to the extent of the accrued market discount. Section 1276(b) provides that for this purpose market discount is ratably accrued on a daily basis unless the taxpayer elects to have it accrued on the constant interest rate method of § 1272(a). Section 1276(a)(2) provides that a taxpayer disposing of a market discount bond in a transaction other than a sale, exchange or involuntary conversion is treated as realizing an amount equal to the fair market value of the bond. Thus, a gift of a market discount bond constitutes a realization event with respect to the accrued market discount. Under § 1277, any "net direct interest expense" with respect to a market discount bond is allowed as a deduction for the current taxable year only to the extent that the interest expense exceeds the amount of market discount allocable to the taxable year. Interest that is deferred under § 1277(a) is allowed as a deduction in the year in which the taxpayer disposes of the market discount bond.

Under § 1278(b), a taxpayer may elect to accrue market discount and include it in income on a current basis. If this election is made, the income is accrued under either of the methods specified in § 1276(b). If the taxpayer has made the election, the special rules of §§ 1276(a) and 1277 do not apply.

Section 1282 applies similar rules to interest on debt attributable to purchasing or carrying certain discount obligations that are not within the definition of a market discount bond in § 1278(a)(1).

SECTION 3.   BOND PREMIUM

INTERNAL REVENUE CODE: Sections 171; 249.

REGULATIONS: Sections 1.61–12(c); 1.163–13(a), (c), (d).

DETAILED ANALYSIS

1.   PREMIUM AT ORIGINAL ISSUE

The issuer of a bond with a stated interest rate in excess of prevailing market rates may be in a position to demand a premium for the bond, such as consideration in excess of the stated principal amount of the bond. This premium is not treated as income to the issuer at the time of receipt. Treas. Reg. § 1.61–12(c)(1). Instead, Treas. Regs. §§ 1.61–12(c)(3) and 1.163–13 generally require the issuer to include bond premium over the term of the bond, using the constant interest method, by reducing the issuer's interest deductions.

For the bondholder, § 171 provides an election to amortize premium over the term of the obligation using the constant interest method of § 1272(a). The premium reduces the interest income, although the bondholder also may treat the premium as a deduction. I.R.C. § 171(e). The election is irrevocable absent the consent of the IRS and applies to all bonds held by the taxpayer. See I.R.C. § 171(c). If the bondholder does not make the election, with respect to fully taxable bonds the premium paid is recovered as a loss on redemption of the bond for an amount less than its basis. With respect to tax exempt bonds, the premium must be amortized over the life of the bond as a reduction of tax exempt interest and thereby reduces the creditor's basis. Section 171(b) requires the bondholder to amortize bond premium over the full term to maturity, even though the bond may be callable at an earlier date.

2.   PREMIUM PAID BY THE ISSUER ON REDEMPTION

Bond premium paid by the issuer on redemption of an obligation is deductible by the issuer as additional interest on the obligation. In the case of convertible obligations, § 249 limits the deduction for redemption premium to an amount representing a "normal call premium" on obligations that are not convertible. The balance is a capital transaction. Thus, in the case of bond premium paid to redeem convertible bonds, the bondholder is not allowed to amortize any portion of the premium attributable to the conversion feature, nor is the issuer allowed an interest deduction for that portion of the premium paid upon redemption of its bond that is attributable to the conversion feature. This result presumably corresponds to the parallel treatment of original issue discount between issuer and holder. However, it should be noted that the treatment of the convertibility feature is different as between original issue discount and bond premium in the case of convertible bonds. Treas. Reg. § 1.1273–2(j) adopts the view that in the case of convertible bonds, the conversion feature is not separable from the debt for purposes of determining original issue discount, hence preventing a larger original issue discount from resulting. On the other hand, in the case of bond premiums the conversion feature is deemed under § 249 to be a feature separable from the debt portion of the obligation and hence the amount, if any, attributable to the conversion element is not deductible as interest.

PART IX

TAX-MOTIVATED TRANSACTIONS

CHAPTER 33

TRANSACTIONS INVOLVING LEASED PROPERTY: IS IT A LEASE OR IS IT A SALE AND PURCHASE?

Whether a sale or other disposition of property has occurred is clear in most situations. The transfer of all ownership rights for a fixed price, whether payable at the time of sale or later, is clearly a disposition. But what are the tax consequences where less than all of the incidents of ownership are transferred? This issue commonly arises in transactions characterized as leases in which the holder of legal title either transfers possession of property to another or retains possession of the property but transfers legal title. Where the holder of legal title leases property to another, the transfer of possession does not in itself suggest that ownership for tax purposes has been transferred. But suppose that the lease is for a term that approximates the anticipated useful life of the property and the present value of fixed rental payments approximates the current value of the "leased" property. Or suppose that the lessee has an option to purchase the property at the end of the lease term for a nominal price. Here the rights and obligations under the "lease" may shift the benefits and burdens of ownership to the lessee. Under these conditions, issues arise as to how such transactions be characterized for tax purposes.

Similar issues also arise where the holder of legal title, rather than transferring possession, retains possession but transfers legal title. This transaction, the so-called "sale and leaseback," may be treated as a loan or as a transfer of a future interest depending upon the terms of the lease and any repurchase options.

Classifying a transaction as a "disposition" causes the realization and possible recognition of gain or loss. In addition, if depreciable property is involved, the purchaser will be entitled to deductions under § 167 or 168. The tax consequences are quite different if the transaction is classified as a lease, loan, or transfer of a future interest.

The three cases that follow examine sales and leases in different contexts and reflect three distinct analytical frameworks for classifying sale and lease transactions.

Estate of Starr v. Commissioner

United States Court of Appeals, Ninth Circuit, 1959.
274 F.2d 294.

■ CHAMBERS, CIRCUIT JUDGE.

Yesterday's equities in personal property seem to have become today's leases. This has been generated not a little by the circumstance that one who leases as a lessee usually has less trouble with the federal tax collector. At least taxpayers think so.

But the lease still can go too far and get one into tax trouble. While according to state law the instrument will probably be taken (with the consequent legal incidents) by the name the parties give it, the internal revenue service is not always bound and can often recast it according to what the service may consider the practical realities.[1] We have so held in Oesterreich v. Commissioner, 9 Cir., 226 F.2d 798 * * * . The principal case concerns a fire sprinkler system installed at the taxpayer's plant at Monrovia, California, where Delano T. Starr, now deceased, did business as the Gross Manufacturing Company. The "lessor" was "Automatic" Sprinklers of the Pacific, Inc., a California corporation. The instrument entitled "Lease Form of Contract" (hereafter "contract") is just about perfectly couched in terms of a lease for five years with annual rentals of $1,240. But it is the last paragraph thereof, providing for nominal rental for five years, that has caused the trouble. It reads as follows:

> "28. At the termination of the period of this lease, if Lessee has faithfully performed all of the terms and conditions required of it under this lease, it shall have the privilege of renewing this lease for an additional period of five years at a rental of $32.00 per year. If Lessee does not elect to renew this lease, then the Lessor is hereby granted the period of six months in which to remove the system from the premises of the Lessee."

Obviously, one renewal for a period of five years is provided at $32.00 per year, if Starr so desired. Note, though, that the paragraph is silent as to status of the system beginning with the eleventh year. Likewise the whole contract is similarly silent.

The tax court sustained the commissioner of internal revenue, holding that the five payments of $1,240, or the total of $6,200, were capital expenditures and not pure deductible rental. Depreciation of $269.60 was allowed for each year. Generally, we agree.

* * *

The law in this field for this circuit is established in Oesterreich v. Commissioner, supra, * * * . There we held that for tax purposes form can be disregarded for substance and, where the foreordained practical

---

[1]   Thus it shifts rental payments of a business (fully deductible) to a capital purchase for the business. If the nature of the property is wasting, then depreciation may be taken, but usually not all in one year.

effect of the rent is to produce title eventually, the rental agreement can be treated as a sale.

In this, Starr's case, we do have the troublesome circumstance that the contract does not by its terms ever pass title to the system to the "lessee." Most sprinkler systems have to be tailor-made for a specific piece of property and, if removal is required, the salvageable value is negligible. Also, it stretches credulity to believe that the "lessor" ever intended to or would "come after" the system. And the "lessee" would be an exceedingly careless businessman who would enter into such contract with the practical possibility that the "lessor" would reclaim the installation. He could have believed only that he was getting the system for the rental money. And we think the commissioner was entitled to take into consideration the practical effect rather than the legal, especially when there was a record that on other such installations the "lessor", after the term of the lease was over, had not reclaimed from those who had met their agreed payments. It is obvious that the nominal rental payments after five years of $32.00 per year were just a service charge for inspection.

Recently the Court of Appeals for the Eighth Circuit has decided Western Contracting Corporation v. Commissioner, 1959, 271 F.2d 694, reversing the tax court in its determination that the commissioner could convert leases of contractor's equipment into installment purchases of heavy equipment. The taxpayer believes that case strongly supports him here. We think not.

There are a number of facts there which make a difference. For example, in the contracts of Western there is no evidence that the payments on the substituted basis of rent would produce for the "lessor" the equivalent of his normal sales price plus interest. There was no right to acquire for a nominal amount at the end of the term as in Oesterreich and the value to the "lessor" in the personalty had not been exhausted as in Starr's case. And there was no basis for inferring that Western would just keep the equipment for what it had paid. It appears that Western paid substantial amounts to acquire the equipment at the end of the term. There was just one compelling circumstance against Western in its case: What it had paid as "rent" was apparently always taken into full account in computing the end purchase price. But on the other hand, there was almost a certainty that the "lessor" would come after his property if the purchase was not eventually made for a substantial amount. This was not even much of a possibility in Oesterreich and not a probability in Starr's case.

In Wilshire Holding Corporation v. Commissioner, 9 Cir., 262 F.2d 51, we referred the case back to the tax court to consider interest as a deductible item for the lessee. We think it is clearly called for here. Two yardsticks are present. The first is found in that the normal selling price of the system was $4,960 while the total rental payments for five years were $6,200. The difference could be regarded as interest for the five years on an amortized basis. The second measure is in clause 16 (loss by fire), where the figure of six per cent per annum discount is used. An allowance might be made on either basis, division of the difference (for the five years) between "rental payments" and "normal purchase price" of $1,240, or six per cent per annum on the normal purchase price of $4,960, converting the annual payments into amortization. We do not believe that the "lessee" should suffer the pains of a loss for what really was paid for the use of another's money, even though for tax purposes his lease collapses.

We do not criticize the commissioner. It is his duty to collect the revenue and it is a tough one. If he resolves all questions in favor of the taxpayers, we soon would have little revenue. However, we do suggest that after he has made allowance for depreciation, which he concedes, and an allowance for interest, the attack on many of the "leases" may not be worthwhile in terms of revenue.

Decision reversed for proceedings consistent herewith.

Alstores Realty Corp. v. Commissioner

Tax Court of the United States, 1966.
46 T.C. 363.

[Steinway owned a warehouse part of which it used and part of which was leased to tenants including an affiliate of Alstores. New facilities were being constructed for Steinway but would not be ready for occupancy for several years. Alstores and its affiliates were looking for additional warehouse space. Steinway offered to sell the warehouse for $1 million on the condition that it could lease back a portion of the warehouse until its new facility was ready for occupancy. Steinway ultimately sold the property to Alstores for $750,000, with a space occupancy agreement providing that Steinway could occupy a portion of the warehouse for two and one-half years rent free.]

It is respondent's contention that petitioner realized taxable rent income as a result of the transaction described in our findings. Petitioner contends simply that Steinway's occupancy was expressly made rent free and that petitioner never received any rent payments from Steinway for occupancy of the subject premises in the taxable year in question or any other year.

Steinway & Sons reported the transaction as a sale on which the "amount realized" within the meaning of section 1001(b) was not only the $750,000 cash received, but also included the fair market value of the rent-free space-occupancy agreement; said fair market value was determined to be $253,090.75. This amount was "capitalized" on the books of Steinway and amortized * * * over the 2½ year term of the space-occupancy agreement.

* * *

There are two approaches to analyzing the transaction here involved. One approach is to say that there was a purchase by petitioner of the entire fee interest in the subject premises and at the same time a lease of a portion of the premises back to the seller for a 2½-year term. This is the approach taken by the respondent herein.

* * *

The alternative analysis of the situation looks to the substance of the transaction. Petitioner here argues that, although in form there may have been a sale and leaseback, in substance there was a conveyance of a *future interest* with Steinway reserving to itself, or carving out, a term of 2½ years in a portion of the property. Hence, Steinway in substance retained its right to occupancy not as a lessee of petitioner, but as a legal owner of a reserved term for years. This approach is supported by Kruesel v. United States, an unreported case (D.Minn.1963, 12 A.F.T.R.2d 5701, 63–2 U.S.T.C. par. 9714).

Although at first blush petitioner's argument is an appealing one, we conclude that it must be rejected and we must hold for respondent. Steinway did not in form or substance reserve an estate for years.

An analogous situation was presented in McCulley Ashlock, 18 T.C. 405 (1952). There the building in question was subject to a lease to a third party at the time it was purchased by the taxpayer. The contract of sale provided that the buyer would pay $40,000 cash but the seller was to retain "possession" of the premises and all the rights to the rental income from the lessee until the expiration of the primary term of the existing lease (about 28 months from date of the sale contract). The Commissioner determined that the rent received by the seller subsequent to conveyance of title to the taxpayer purchaser was really taxable income to the taxpayer purchaser. We rejected the Commissioner's approach in that case, holding that the seller had reserved an ownership interest in the property (an estate for years) and that the rents received were income to the seller for occupancy of what was still his property—not income to the purchaser, who did not then have a present legal ownership interest but only a future interest. The essence of our reasoning in the *Ashlock* case was as follows (pp. 411–412).

> Here, the trustees [the sellers of the property] not only retained the rents legally but they also retained control and benefits of ownership. Under the contract of sale on April 18, 1945, the trustees specifically agreed to pay property taxes, insurance premiums, and "all normal maintenance items and expenses," so that the property would be delivered to * * * [the buyer] in the present condition except for normal wear and tear. Furthermore, the June 11, 1945, agreement stated that in the event that the property was damaged or destroyed, and loss of income during the period of repair or reconstruction would be the trustees' loss. It further provided that insurance proceeds

would be devoted to restore and repair the property, except in the event of total destruction petitioner would have the option of rebuilding the premises or compensating the trustees for unpaid rent. Thus the trustee bore the risks of ownership of the rents and managed the property. Larger expenses or a cessation of rents were risks incurred by the trustees. * * *

* * *

The same factors which we looked to in *Ashlock* in deciding in favor of the purchaser, analyzed in the factual posture of the instant case, dictate the opposite result here. Petitioner, the buyer, assumed control of the premises and the benefits of ownership. Petitioner, the buyer, specifically agreed to pay for and supply to Steinway, the seller, heat, electricity, and water. The space-occupancy agreement stated that in the event the property was damaged or destroyed and Steinway's occupancy was thereby destroyed or impaired the burden of loss would be upon *petitioner* (with petitioner agreeing to pay Steinway 6¼ cents per square foot per month for space so affected). It is clear in the instant case that the buyer bore the risks and burdens of ownership during the term of the space-occupancy agreement. Such was not the case in McCulley Ashlock, supra, nor apparently in Kruesel v. United States, supra, relied upon by petitioner.

Furthermore, the rights of Steinway, the seller, as occupant were not those of a holder of a legal estate for years but were specifically limited to those of a lessee. The standard terms and conditions of a New York Real Estate Board form lease were imposed. For example, Steinway could not alter or improve the building nor sublet or assign its interest without the consent of petitioner.

Of key significance in this case is the fact that petitioner was required to pay to Steinway 6¼ cents per square foot per month for space which Steinway was entitled to occupy but which it may have been unable to occupy by reason of an act of God or the fault of petitioner, or which it may have elected to vacate during the last one-half year of the space occupancy agreement. This arrangement is entirely inconsistent with the theory that Steinway had a reserved estate for years; why would petitioner, the alleged remainderman, be required to make payments to Steinway, the alleged owner of an estate for years, as a result of nonoccupancy by the latter? What we really have here is a provision for reimbursement of prepaid rent in the event the tenant is denied (or, during the last one-half year of the term, elects abandonment of) its right of unfettered occupancy, the prepaid rent being in the form of the value of the property received by petitioner in excess of the $750,000 cash paid therefor.

* * *

The president of Steinway testified for respondent that his original asking price for the property was $1,250,000, and later $1 million, and that he agreed to accept $750,000 cash only with the concomitant rent-free space-occupancy agreement, which the evidence indicates had a fair market value of $253,090.75. The parties were both intimately familiar with the property and were dealing at arm's length, and in the absence of evidence to the contrary, it must be concluded that the value of the property conveyed to petitioner was equal to the value of what was received by Steinway as consideration, $1,003,090.75. Petitioner, on whom rests the burden of proof, made no attempt at trial to establish the fair market value of the property.

Possibly the result in the instant case would be different if the parties had in fact *intended* to carve out a reserved term for years in Steinway and had structured their transaction in that form. * * * We do not agree with petitioner, however, that to hold that there was a sale of the fee and a simultaneous leaseback here is to exalt form over substance. The so-called space-occupancy agreement placed the two parties' rights, obligations, and risks as they would be allocated in a typical lease arrangement. Hence, the arrangement was a lease in substance as well as in form.

* * *

Frank Lyon Co. v. United States

Supreme Court of the United States, 1978.
435 U.S. 561.

■ MR. JUSTICE BLACKMUN delivered the opinion of the Court. This case concerns the federal income tax consequences of a sale-and-leaseback in which petitioner Frank Lyon Company (Lyon) took title to a building under construction by Worthen Bank & Trust Company (Worthen) of Little Rock, Ark., and simultaneously leased the building back to Worthen for long-term use as its headquarters and principal banking facility.

I

* * *

A

Lyon is a closely held Arkansas corporation engaged in the distribution of home furnishings, primarily Whirlpool and RCA electrical products. Worthen in 1965 was an Arkansas-chartered bank and a member of the Federal Reserve System. Frank Lyon was Lyon's majority shareholder and board chairman; he also served on Worthen's board. Worthen at that time began to plan the construction of a multi-story bank and office building to replace its existing facility in Little Rock. About the same time Worthen's competitor, Union National Bank of Little Rock, also began to plan a new bank and office building. Adjacent sites on Capitol Avenue, separated only by Spring Street, were acquired by the two banks. It became a matter of competition, for both banking business and tenants, and prestige as to which bank would start and complete its building first.

Worthen initially hoped to finance, to build, and itself to own the proposed facility at a total cost of $9 million for the site, building, and adjoining parking deck. * * * [Worthen] was advised by staff employees of the Federal Reserve System that they would not recommend approval of the plan by the System's Board of Governors.

Worthen therefore was forced to seek an alternative solution that would provide it with the use of the building, satisfy the state and federal regulators, and attract the necessary capital. In September 1967 it proposed a sale-and-leaseback arrangement. The State Bank Department and the Federal Reserve System approved this approach, but the Department required that Worthen possess an option to purchase the leased property at the end of the 15th year of the lease at a set price, and the federal regulator required that the building be owned by an independent third party.

* * *

Worthen then obtained a commitment from New York Life Insurance Company to provide $7,140,000 in permanent mortgage financing on the building, conditioned upon its approval of the title holder. At this point Lyon entered the negotiations and it, too, made a proposal.

* * * Worthen selected Lyon as the investor. * * * In April 1968 the approvals of the state and federal regulators were received.

In the meantime, on September 15, before Lyon was selected, Worthen itself began construction.

B

In May 1968 Worthen, Lyon, City Bank, and New York Life executed complementary and interlocking agreements under which the building was sold by Worthen to Lyon as it was constructed, and Worthen leased the completed building back from Lyon. * * *

Under the ground lease * * * Worthen leased the site to Lyon for 76 years and seven months through November 30, 2044. * * *

Under the sales agreement * * * Worthen agreed to sell the building to Lyon and Lyon agreed to buy it, piece by piece as it was constructed, for a total price not to exceed $7,640,000, in reimbursements to Worthen for its expenditures for the construction of the building.

Under the building lease * * * Lyon leased the building back to Worthen for a primary term of 25 years * * * with options in Worthen to extend the lease for eight additional five-year terms, a total of 65 years. * * * The total rent for the building over the 25-year primary term of the lease * * * was $14,989,767.24. That rent equaled the principal and interest payments that would amortize the $7,140,000 New York Life mortgage loan over the same period. When the mortgage was paid off at the end of the primary term, the annual building rent, if Worthen extended the lease, came down to * * * $300,000. Lyon's net rentals from the building would be further reduced by the increase in ground rent Worthen would receive from Lyon during the extension.[3]

The building lease was a "net lease," under which Worthen was responsible for all expenses usually associated with the maintenance of an office building, including repairs, taxes, utility charges, and insurance, and was to keep the premises in good condition, excluding, however, reasonable wear and tear.

Finally, under the lease, Worthen had the option to repurchase the building at the following times and prices:

> 11/30/80　(after 11 years)—
> $6,325,169.85
>
> 11/30/84　(after 15 years)—
> $5,432,607.32
>
> 11/30/89　(after 20 years)—
> $4,187,328.04
>
> 11/30/94　(after 25 years)—
> $2,145,935.00

These repurchase option prices were the sum of the unpaid balance of the New York Life mortgage, Lyon's $500,000 investment, and 6% interest compounded on that investment.

* * *

C

* * *

On audit of Lyon's 1969 return, the Commissioner of Internal Revenue determined that Lyon was "not the owner for tax purposes of any portion of the Worthen Building," and ruled that "the income and expenses related to this building are not allowable * * * for Federal income tax purposes." * * * [T]he Commissioner determined that the sale-and-leaseback arrangement was a financing transaction in which Lyon loaned Worthen $500,000 and acted as a conduit for the transmission of principal and interest from Worthen to New York Life.

* * *

---

[3]　This, of course, is on the assumption that Worthen exercises its option to extend the building lease. If it does not, Lyon remains liable for the substantial rents prescribed by the ground lease. This possibility brings into sharp focus the fact that Lyon, in a very practical sense, is at least the ultimate owner of the building. If Worthen does not extend, the building lease expires and Lyon may do with the building as it chooses.

The Government would point out, however, that the net amounts payable by Worthen to Lyon during the building lease's extended terms, if all are claimed, would approximate the amount required to repay Lyon's $500,000 investment at 6% compound interest. * * *

II

This Court, almost 50 years ago, observed that "taxation is not so much concerned with the refinements of title as it is with actual command over the property taxed—the actual benefit for which the tax is paid." Corliss v. Bowers, 281 U.S. 376, 378 (1930). In a number of cases, the Court has refused to permit the transfer of formal legal title to shift the incidence of taxation attributable to ownership of property where the transferor continues to retain significant control over the property transferred. E.g., Commissioner of Internal Revenue v. Sunnen, 333 U.S. 591 (1948); Helvering v. Clifford, 309 U.S. 331 (1940). In applying this doctrine of substance over form, the Court has looked to the objective economic realities of a transaction rather than to the particular form the parties employed. The Court has never regarded "the simple expedient of drawing up papers," Commissioner of Internal Revenue v. Tower, 327 U.S. 280, 291 (1946), as controlling for tax purposes when the objective economic realities are to the contrary. "In the field of taxation, administrators of the laws and the courts are concerned with substance and realities, and formal written documents are not rigidly binding." Helvering v. Lazarus & Co., 308 U.S. 252, 255 (1939). * * * Nor is the parties' desire to achieve a particular tax result necessarily relevant. Commissioner of Internal Revenue v. Duberstein, 363 U.S. 278, 286 (1960).

In the light of these general and established principles, the Government takes the position that the Worthen-Lyon transaction in its entirety should be regarded as a sham. The agreement as a whole, it is said, was only an elaborate financing scheme designed to provide economic benefits to Worthen and a guaranteed return to Lyon. The latter was but a conduit used to forward the mortgage payments, made under the guise of rent paid by Worthen to Lyon, on to New York Life as mortgagee. This, the Government claims, is the true substance of the transaction as viewed under the microscope of the tax laws. Although the arrangement was cast in sale-and-leaseback form, in substance it was only a financing transaction, and the terms of the repurchase options and lease renewals so indicate. It is said that Worthen could reacquire the building simply by satisfying the mortgage debt and paying Lyon its $500,000 advance plus interest, regardless of the fair market value of the building at the time; similarly, when the mortgage was paid off, Worthen could extend the lease at drastically reduced bargain rentals that likewise bore no relation to fair rental value but were simply calculated to pay Lyon its $500,000 plus interest over the extended term. Lyon's return on the arrangement in no event could exceed 6% compound interest (although the Government conceded it might well be less, Tr. of Oral Arg. 32). Furthermore, the favorable option and lease renewal terms made it highly unlikely that Worthen would abandon the building after it in effect had "paid off" the mortgage. The Government implies that the arrangement was one of convenience which, if accepted on its face, would enable Worthen to deduct its payments to Lyon as rent and would allow Lyon to claim a deduction for depreciation, based on the cost of construction ultimately borne by Worthen, which Lyon could offset against other income, and to deduct mortgage interest that roughly would offset the inclusion of Worthen's rental payments in Lyon's income. If, however, the Government argues, the arrangement was only a financing transaction under which Worthen was the owner of the building, Worthen's payments would be deductible only to the extent that they represented mortgage interest, and Worthen would be entitled to claim depreciation; Lyon would not be entitled to deductions for either mortgage interest or depreciation and it need not include Worthen's "rent" payments in its income because its function with respect to those payments was that of a conduit between Worthen and New York Life.

The Government places great reliance on Helvering v. Lazarus & Co., supra, and claims it to be precedent that controls this case. The taxpayer there was a department store. The legal title of its three buildings was in a bank as trustee for land-trust certificate holders. When the transfer to the trustee was made, the trustee at the same time leased the buildings back to the taxpayer for 99 years, with option to renew and purchase. The Commissioner, in stark contrast to his posture in the present case, took the position that the statutory right to depreciation followed legal title. The Board of Tax Appeals, however, concluded that the transaction between the taxpayer and the bank in reality was a mortgage loan and allowed the taxpayer depreciation on the buildings. This Court, as had the Court of Appeals, agreed with that conclusion and affirmed. It regarded the "rent" stipulated in the leaseback as a promise to pay interest on the loan, and a "depreciation fund" required by the lease as an amortization fund designed to pay off the loan in the stated period. Thus, said the Court, the Board justifiably concluded that the transaction, although in written form a transfer of ownership with a leaseback, was actually a loan secured by the property involved.

The *Lazarus* case, we feel, is to be distinguished from the present one and is not controlling here. Its transaction was one involving only two (and not multiple) parties, the taxpayer-department store and the trustee-bank. The Court looked closely at the substance of the agreement between those two parties and rightly concluded that depreciation was deductible by the taxpayer despite the nomenclature of the instrument of conveyance and the leaseback.

The present case, in contrast, involves three parties, Worthen, Lyon, and the finance agency. The usual simple two-party arrangement was legally unavailable to Worthen. Independent investors were interested in participating in the alternative available to Worthen and Lyon itself, also independent from Worthen, won the privilege. Despite Frank Lyon's presence on Worthen's board of directors, the transaction, as it ultimately developed, was not a familial one arranged by Worthen, but one compelled by the realities of the restrictions imposed upon the bank. Had Lyon not appeared, another interested investor would have been selected. The ultimate solution would have been essentially the same. Thus, the presence of the third party, in our view, significantly distinguishes this case from *Lazarus* and removes the latter as controlling authority.

III

It is true, of course, that the transaction took shape according to Worthen's needs. As the Government points out, Worthen throughout the negotiations regarded the respective proposals of the independent investors in terms of its own cost of funds. * * * It is also true that both Worthen and the prospective investors compared the various proposals in terms of the return anticipated on the investor's equity. But all this is natural for parties contemplating entering into a transaction of this kind. Worthen needed a building for its banking operations and other purposes and necessarily had to know what its cost would be. The investors were in business to employ their funds in the most remunerative way possible. And, as the Court has said in the past, a transaction must be given its effect in accord with what actually occurred and not in accord with what might have occurred. * * *

There is no simple device available to peel away the form of this transaction and to reveal its substance. The effects of the transaction on all the parties were obviously different from those that would have resulted had Worthen been able simply to make a mortgage agreement with New York Life and to receive a $500,000 loan from Lyon. Then *Lazarus* would apply. Here, however, and most significantly, it was Lyon alone, and not Worthen, who was liable on the notes, first to City Bank, and then to New York Life. Despite the facts that Worthen had agreed to pay rent and that this rent equaled the amounts due from Lyon to New York Life, should anything go awry in the later years of the lease, Lyon was primarily liable.[12] No matter how the transaction could have been devised otherwise, it remains a fact that as the agreements were placed in final form, the obligation on the notes fell squarely on Lyon.[13] Lyon, an ongoing enterprise, exposed its very business well-being to this real and substantial risk.

The effect of this liability on Lyon is not just the abstract possibility that something will go wrong and that Worthen will not be able to make its payments. Lyon has disclosed this liability on its balance sheet for all the world to see. Its financial position is affected substantially by the presence of this long-term debt, despite the offsetting presence of the

---

[12]   New York Life required Lyon, not Worthen, to submit financial statements periodically. * * *

[13]   It may well be that the remedies available to New York Life against Lyon would be far greater than any remedy available to it against Worthen, which, as lessee, is liable to New York Life only through Lyon's assignment of its interest as lessor.

building as an asset. To the extent that Lyon has used its capital in this transaction, it is less able to obtain financing for other business needs.

In concluding that there is this distinct element of economic reality in Lyon's assumption of liability, we are mindful that the characterization of a transaction for financial accounting purposes, on the one hand, and for tax purposes, on the other, need not necessarily be the same. * * * Accounting methods or descriptions, without more, do not lend substance to that which has no substance. But in this case accepted accounting methods, as understood by the several parties to the respective agreements and as applied to the transaction by others, gave the transaction a meaningful character consonant with the form it was given.[14] Worthen was not allowed to enter into the type of transaction which the Government now urges to be the true substance of the arrangement. Lyon and Worthen cannot be said to have entered into the transaction intending that the interests involved were allocated in a way other than that associated with a sale-and-leaseback.

Other factors also reveal that the transaction cannot be viewed as nothing more than a mortgage agreement between Worthen and New York Life and a loan from Lyon to Worthen. There is no legal obligation between Lyon and Worthen representing the $500,000 "loan" extended under the Government's theory. And the assumed 6% return on this putative loan—required by the audit to be recognized in the taxable year in question—will be realized only when and if Worthen exercises its options.

The Court of Appeals acknowledged that the rents alone, due after the primary term of the lease and after the mortgage has been paid, do not provide the simple 6% return which, the Government urges, Lyon is guaranteed, 536 F.2d, at 752. Thus, if Worthen chooses not to exercise its options, Lyon is gambling that the rental value of the building during the last 10 years of the ground lease, during which the ground rent is minimal, will be sufficient to recoup its investment before it must negotiate again with Worthen regarding the ground lease. There are simply too many contingencies, including variations in the value of real estate, in the cost of money, and in the capital structure of Worthen, to permit the conclusion that the parties intended to enter into the transaction as structured in the audit and according to which the Government now urges they be taxed.

It is not inappropriate to note that the Government is likely to lose little revenue, if any, as a result of the shape given the transaction by the parties. No deduction was created that is not either matched by an item of income or that would not have been available to one of the parties if the transaction had been arranged differently. While it is true that Worthen paid Lyon less to induce it to enter into the transaction because

---

[14]   We are aware that accounting standards have changed significantly since 1968 and that the propriety of Worthen's and Lyon's methods of disclosing the transaction in question may be a matter for debate under these new standards. * * *

Lyon anticipated the benefit of the depreciation deductions it would have as the owner of the building, those deductions would have been equally available to Worthen had it retained title to the building. The Government so concedes. * * * The fact that favorable tax consequences were taken into account by Lyon on entering into the transaction is no reason for disallowing those consequences.[15] We cannot ignore the reality that the tax laws affect the shape of nearly every business transaction. * * *

The conclusion that the transaction is not a simple sham to be ignored does not, of course, automatically compel the further conclusion that Lyon is entitled to the items claimed as deductions. Nevertheless, on the facts, this readily follows. As has been noted, the obligations on which Lyon paid interest were its obligations alone and it is entitled to claim deductions therefor, under § 163(a) of the 1954 Code, 26 U.S.C.A. § 163.

As is clear from the facts, none of the parties to this sale-and-leaseback was the owner of the building in any simple sense. But it is equally clear that the facts focus upon Lyon as the one whose capital was committed to the building and as the party, therefore, that was entitled to claim depreciation for the consumption of that capital. The Government has based its contention that Worthen should be treated as the owner on the assumption that throughout the term of the lease Worthen is acquiring an equity in the property. In order to establish the presence of that growing equity, however, the Government is forced to speculate that one of the options will be exercised and that, if it is not, this is only because the rentals for the extended term are a bargain. We cannot indulge in such speculation in view of the District Court's clear finding to the contrary. We therefore conclude that it is Lyon's capital that is invested in the building according to the agreement of the parties, and it is Lyon that is entitled to depreciation deductions, under § 167 of the 1954 Code. * * *

IV

We recognize that the Government's position, and that taken by the Court of Appeals, is not without superficial appeal. One, indeed, may theorize that Frank Lyon's presence on the Worthen board of directors; Lyon's departure from its principal corporate activity into this unusual venture; the parallel between the payments under the building lease and the amounts due from Lyon on the New York Life mortgage; the provisions relating to condemnation or destruction of the property; the nature and presence of the several options available to Worthen; and the tax benefits, such as the use of double declining balance depreciation,

---

[15]   Indeed, it is not inevitable that the transaction, as treated by Lyon and Worthen, will not result in more revenues to the Government rather than less. Lyon is gambling that in the first 11 years of the lease it will have income that will be sheltered by the depreciation deductions, and that it will be able to make sufficiently good use of the tax dollars preserved thereby to make up for the income it will recognize and pay taxes on during the last 14 years of the initial term of the lease and against which it will enjoy no sheltering deduction.

that accrue to Lyon during the initial years of the arrangement, form the basis of an argument that Worthen should be regarded as the owner of the building and as the recipient of nothing more from Lyon than a $500,000 loan.

We however, as did the District Court, find this theorizing incompatible with the substance and economic realities of the transaction: the competitive situation as it existed between Worthen and Union National Bank in 1965 and the years immediately following; Worthen's undercapitalization; Worthen's consequent inability, as a matter of legal restraint, to carry its building plans into effect by a conventional mortgage and other borrowing; the additional barriers imposed by the state and federal regulators; the suggestion, forthcoming from the state regulator, that Worthen possess an option to purchase; the requirement, from the federal regulator, that the building be owned by an independent third party; the presence of several finance organizations seriously interested in participating in the transaction and in the resolution of Worthen's problem; the submission of formal proposals by several of those organizations; the bargaining process and period that ensued; the competitiveness of the bidding; the bona fide character of the negotiations; the three-party aspect of the transaction; Lyon's substantiality[17] and its independence from Worthen; the fact that diversification was Lyon's principal motivation; Lyon's being liable alone on the successive notes to City Bank and New York Life; the reasonableness, as the District Court found, of the rentals and of the option prices; the substantiality of the purchase prices; Lyon's not being engaged generally in the business of financing; the presence of all building depreciation risks on Lyon; the risk borne by Lyon, that Worthen might default or fail, as other banks have failed; the facts that Worthen could "walk away" from the relationship at the end of the 25-year primary term, and probably would do so if the option price were more than the then current worth of the building to Worthen; the inescapable fact that if the building lease were not extended, Lyon would be the full owner of the building, free to do with it as it chose; Lyon's liability for the substantial ground rent if Worthen decides not to exercise any of its options to extend; the absence of any understanding between Lyon and Worthen that Worthen would exercise any of the purchase options; the nonfamily and nonprivate nature of the entire transaction; and the absence of any differential in tax rates and of special tax circumstances for one of the parties—all convince us that Lyon has far the better of the case.[18]

---

[17]   Lyon's consolidated balance sheet on December 31, 1968, showed assets of $12,225,612, and total stockholders' equity of $3,818,671. Of the assets, the sum of $2,674,290 represented its then investment in the Worthen Building.

[18]   Thus, the facts of this case stand in contrast to many others in which the form of the transaction actually created tax advantages that, for one reason or another, could not have been enjoyed had the transaction taken another form. See, e.g., Sun Oil Co. v. Commissioner of Internal Revenue, 562 F.2d 258 (C.A.3 1977) (sale-and-leaseback of land between taxpayer and

In so concluding, we emphasize that we are not condoning manipulation by a taxpayer through arbitrary labels and dealings that have no economic significance. Such, however, has not happened in this case.

In short, we hold that where, as here, there is a genuine multiple-party transaction with economic substance which is compelled or encouraged by business or regulatory realities, is imbued with tax-independent considerations, and is not shaped solely by tax avoidance features that have meaningless labels attached, the Government should honor the allocation of rights and duties effectuated by the parties. Expressed another way, so long as the lessor retains significant and genuine attributes of the traditional lessor status, the form of the transaction adopted by the parties governs for tax purposes. What those attributes are in any particular case will necessarily depend upon its facts. It suffices to say that, as here, a sale-and-leaseback, in and of itself, does not necessarily operate to deny a taxpayer's claim for deductions.

The judgment of the Court of Appeals, accordingly, is reversed. It is so ordered.

* * *

■ MR. JUSTICE STEVENS, dissenting.

In my judgment the controlling issue in this case is the economic relationship between Worthen and petitioner, and matters such as the number of parties, their reasons for structuring the transaction in a particular way, and the tax benefits which may result, are largely irrelevant. The question whether a leasehold has been created should be answered by examining the character and value of the purported lessor's reversionary estate.

For a 25-year period Worthen has the power to acquire full ownership of the bank building by simply repaying the amounts, plus interest, advanced by the New York Life Insurance Company and petitioner. During that period, the economic relationship among the parties parallels exactly the normal relationship between an owner and two lenders, one secured by a first mortgage and the other by a second mortgage.[1] If Worthen repays both loans, it will have unencumbered ownership of the property. What the character of this relationship suggests is confirmed by the economic value that the parties themselves have placed on the reversionary interest.

All rental payments made during the original 25-year term are credited against the option repurchase price, which is exactly equal to

---

tax-exempt trust enabled the taxpayer to amortize, through its rental deductions, the cost of acquiring land not otherwise depreciable). * * *

[1]   "[W]here a fixed price, as in *Frank Lyon Company,* is designed merely to provide the lessor with a predetermined fixed return, the substantive bargain is more akin to the relationship between a debtor and creditor than between a lessor and lessee." Rosenberg and Weinstein, Sale-leasebacks: An Analysis of These Transactions After the Lyon Decision, 45 Journal of Taxation 146, 149 (Sept. 1976).

the unamortized cost of the financing. The value of the repurchase option is thus limited to the cost of the financing, and Worthen's power to exercise the option is cost-free. Conversely, petitioner, the nominal owner of the reversionary estate, is not entitled to receive *any* value for the surrender of its supposed rights of ownership.[2] Nor does it have any power to control Worthen's exercise of the option.[3]

"It is fundamental that 'depreciation is not predicated upon ownership of property *but rather upon an investment in property*.' No such investment exists when payments of the purchase price in accordance with the design of the parties yield no equity to the purchaser." Estate of Franklin v. C.I.R., 544 F.2d 1045, 1049 (C.A.9 1976) (citations omitted and emphasis in original). Here, the petitioner has, in effect, been guaranteed that it will receive its original $500,000 plus accrued interest. But that is all. It incurs neither the risk of depreciation,[4] nor the benefit of possible appreciation. Under the terms of the sale-leaseback, it will stand in no better or worse position after the 11th year of the lease—when Worthen can first exercise its option to repurchase—whether the property has appreciated or depreciated.[5] And this remains true throughout the rest of the 25-year period.

Petitioner has assumed only two significant risks. First, like any other lender, it assumed the risk of Worthen's insolvency. Second, it assumed the risk that Worthen might *not* exercise its option to purchase at or before the end of the original 25-year term.[6] If Worthen should

---

[2]   It is worth noting that the proposals submitted by two other potential investors in the building * * * did contemplate that Worthen would pay a price above the financing costs for acquisition of the leasehold interest. For instance, Goldman, Sachs & Company proposed that, at the end of the lease's primary term, Worthen would have the option to repurchase the property for either its fair market value or 20% of its original cost, whichever was the greater. See Brief for the United States, at 8 n. 7. A repurchase option based on fair market value, since it acknowledges the lessor's equity interest in the property, is consistent with a lessor-lessee relationship. See Breece Veneer & Panel Co. v. Commissioner of Internal Revenue, 232 F.2d 319 (C.A.7 1956); LTV Corp., 63 T.C. 39, 50 (1974) * * * .

[3]   The situation in this case is thus analogous to that in Corliss v. Bowers, 281 U.S. 376 * * * , where the Court held that the grantor of a trust who retains an unrestricted cost-free power of revocation remains the owner of the trust assets for tax purposes. Worthen's power to exercise its repurchase option is similar; the only restraints upon it are those normally associated with the repayment of a loan, such as limitations on the timing of repayment and the amount due at the stated intervals.

[4]   Petitioner argues that it bears the risk of depreciation during the primary term of the lease, because the option price decreases over time. This is clearly incorrect. Petitioner will receive $500,000 plus interest, and no more or less, whether the option is exercised as soon as possible or only at the end of 25 years. Worthen, on the other hand, does bear the risk of depreciation, since its opportunity to make a profit from the exercise of its repurchase option hinges on the value of the building at the time.

[5]   After the 11th year of the lease, there are three ways that the lease might be terminated. The property might be condemned, the building might be destroyed by act of God, or Worthen might exercise its option to purchase. In any such event, if the property had increased in value, the entire benefit would be received by Worthen and petitioner would receive only its $500,000 plus interest.

[6]   The possibility that Worthen might not exercise its option is a risk for petitioner because in that event petitioner's advance would be amortized during the ensuing renewal lease terms, totaling 40 years. Yet there is a possibility that Worthen would choose not to renew for

exercise that right *not* to repay, perhaps it would *then* be appropriate to characterize petitioner as the owner and Worthen as the lessee. But speculation as to what might happen in 25 years cannot justify the *present* characterization of petitioner as the owner of the building. Until Worthen has made a commitment either to exercise or not to exercise its option,[7] I think the Government is correct in its view that petitioner is not the owner of the building for tax purposes. At present, since Worthen has the unrestricted right to control the residual value of the property for a price which does not exceed the cost of its unamortized financing, I would hold, as a matter of law, that it is the owner.

I therefore respectfully dissent.

DETAILED ANALYSIS

1.   DETERMINING THE TAX OWNER OF LEASED PROPERTY

A determination of the ownership of leased property for tax purposes must be made in many different contexts. The traditional analysis focuses on the form of the transaction and the party who would benefit from any increase in the capital value of the property or bear the burden of loss of capital. If the property is anticipated to have significant value at the end of the lease term, and if the lessee either has no option to purchase the property or an option to purchase for the then fair market value of the property, the nominal owner is viewed as benefiting from any capital appreciation or suffering loss of capital and will be considered to be the tax owner of the property.

But it is not clear that this analysis accurately reflects the economics of transactions with leased property. Many situations, including *Frank Lyon,* have involved long-term leases of productive property at fixed rentals on a "net" basis with all expenses are borne by the lessee. If the property goes up in value during the term of the lease, the lessee will likely benefit through greater income. Similarly, if the value of the property decreases, the lessee's income will likely decrease (or expenses increase). This analysis suggests that the courts should focus on whether a temporal division of ownership of leased property has taken place in these types of "lease" transactions. Any increase or decrease in the capital value of the property, the major factor (along with the form of the transaction) under current case law, relates only

---

the full 40 years or that the burdens of owning a building and paying a ground rental of $10,000 during the years 2034 through 2044 would exceed the benefits of ownership.

[7]   In this case, the lessee is not "economically compelled" to exercise its option. See *American Realty Trust v. United States,* 498 F.2d 1194 (C.A.4 1974). Indeed, it may be more advantageous for Worthen to let its option lapse since the present value of the renewal leases is somewhat less than the price of the option to repurchase. * * * But whether or not Worthen is likely to exercise the option, as long as it retains its unrestricted cost-free power to do so, it must be considered the owner of the building. See *Sun Oil Co. v. Commissioner of Internal Revenue,* 562 F.2d 258, 267 (C.A.3 1977) (repurchase option enabling lessees to acquire leased premises by repaying financing costs indicative of lessee's equity interest in those premises).

In effect, Worthen has an option to "put" the building to petitioner if it drops in value below $500,000 plus interest. Even if the "put" appears likely because of bargain lease rates after the primary terms, that would not justify the present characterization of petitioner as the owner of the building.

to the value of the remainder interest. Acknowledging more readily the possible temporal division of property would shift the focus to which party possessed the benefits of ownership during the lease term. Factors such as whether the rents were fixed in amount and which party actually bore expenses during the lease term would become determinative.

2. LEASING TRANSACTIONS

2.1. *General*

In transactions involving elements that in part point to a sale and in part to a lease, the parties involved may seek different tax results because of their own particular tax situations. Thus, some users, such as in *Estate of Starr*, may desire lease characterization because the rental deductions would be greater than the depreciation deductions to which the taxpayer would be entitled as owner. Accelerated capital recovery under MACRS, not available at the time of *Estate of Starr*, makes this result much less likely today in the case of personal property. Lease characterization is attractive if the property is nondepreciable (such as land), buildings subject to 27-year capital recovery, or if the user is not able to benefit directly from the depreciation deductions. For example, users without taxable income will prefer a lease in the hope that, by permitting the owner of the property to retain the tax benefits of ownership, they will indirectly benefit through reduced rental payments.

Transferors also have differing tax goals. Some transferors may desire to have the periodic payments treated as capital gain from the disposition of property (although part will be interest) rather than rent, all of which would be taxable as ordinary income. The price paid for this characterization is that the tax benefits of ownership are shifted to the transferee.[1]

In *Alstores* the transferor/lessee, Steinway, benefited by treating the transaction as a sale of the entire property at capital gains rates and subsequently claiming expense deductions by amortizing the cost of its two-year occupancy. It was attempting to include current income taxable at capital gains rates followed in later years by an offsetting deduction at higher ordinary income rates. Although there is no benefit in recognizing ordinary income in one year that is offset by deductions in future years if both items are subject to the same tax rates, tax savings may be available if the gain is taxed at a lower rate than the income which is offset by the future deduction and the deduction is not too far removed in time from the year in which the gain is recognized.

If Steinway had sold only a remainder interest, presumably it would have determined gain or loss based on an amount realized that did not include the value of the retained possessory interest less the portion of the adjusted basis attributable to the future interest. Where part of a property is sold, and the total basis is known, an "equitable apportionment" is generally required. See Treas. Reg. § 1.61–6(a). The basis of the remainder interest would presumably be the portion of the total basis that the value of the remainder bears to the total value of the property. Thus, if the current

---

[1]   There are numerous non-tax reasons why the parties may prefer leasing to sales transactions as well.

value is $1,000,000, and the value of the remainder is $750,000, 75 percent of the property is being sold for $750,000 and 75 percent of the total basis should be taken into account in determining gain or loss. The remaining basis presumably would be recovered over the period prior to the sale. If the transaction is treated in this manner, as opposed to the way it was treated by Steinway, the result is decreased capital gains on sale of the remainder, and a reduced deduction, limited to the remaining basis, over the period of occupancy.

The sale and long-term leaseback of real estate, as approved in *Frank Lyon,* is a device that enables the owner of property to raise cash without parting with current possession of the property. As such, it can be viewed as a financing transaction coupled with a possible sale of a remainder interest. Under this approach, cash received by the "seller" may be viewed in part as a loan and perhaps in part as proceeds for the sale of the remainder. "Rent" paid by the seller-lessee can thus be viewed as payment of interest and repayment of the principal on that loan. Where the "seller" is given an option to repurchase the property at a predetermined fixed price, such as in *Frank Lyon,* it is unlikely that even the remainder interest has been sold; all of the proceeds could be characterized as a loan.

2.2. *Sale Versus Lease*

In *Estate of Starr,* the court compared the projected rental payments with the potential cost of the property, plus interest, and looked to the lessee's potential retention of the "leased" property. A similar analysis is often found in other cases. In M & W Gear Co. v. Commissioner, 54 T.C. 385 (1970)(A), aff'd in part and rev'd on other issues, 446 F.2d 841 (7th Cir.1971), the taxpayer entered into a contract which provided for the "rental" of a farm for five years for $50,660 per year. The taxpayer was given an option to purchase the property for approximately $173,700 at the end of the lease term. In the aggregate, the rentals plus the option price equaled the fair market value of the property. The court held that the transaction constituted a sale and the taxpayer was not entitled to a deduction for rent. The "rent" was more than double the normal fair market rental of the farm property and the taxpayer was simply building an equity in the property. Economically, it was a forgone conclusion that the taxpayer would exercise its option.

In Highland Farms, Inc. v. Commissioner, 106 T.C. 237 (1996), the taxpayer operated a retirement community in which residents leased land from the taxpayer and purchased cluster homes constructed on the land by the taxpayer. The purchasers were prohibited from reselling the homes to anyone other than the taxpayer, and the taxpayer was unconditionally obligated to repurchase the homes at a price equal to at least 76 percent of the original sales price upon a purchaser's death or at any time any purchaser decided to sell. The transactions all were formalized as sales, and the purchasers were assessed directly for local property taxes. Under agreements with the residents, the taxpayer performed all exterior maintenance. The purchasers were prohibited from altering either the exterior or interior of the homes without the taxpayer's consent. The taxpayer, in essence, attempted to characterize the transactions as leases of homes coupled with characterization of the receipts as loans from the residents, rather than as sales of the homes, but the Commissioner treated the transactions as sales. In holding that the transactions were completed sales, not leases and related borrowing transactions, even though their structure assured that the purchasers never could realize any appreciation in value, the court looked to local law and gave significant weight to the form of the transactions.

In Lester v. Commissioner, 32 T.C. 711 (1959), the taxpayer rented equipment but gave an option to purchase under an agreement whereby, if the lessee exercised the option, the rentals were credited to the purchase price. The court held that the taxpayer realized rental income up to the time of the exercise of the option. The taxpayer had been seeking to treat the entire amount received as long-term capital gain.

3.   SALE AND LEASEBACK VERSUS LOAN

3.1. *Economic Analysis of Frank Lyon*

The Commissioner argued in *Frank Lyon* that the transaction was a loan of $500,000 by Frank Lyon Co. to Worthen Bank from which Frank Lyon Co. could recover no more than the original $500,000 principal plus 6 percent interest. There were no circumstances under which Frank Lyon Co. would share in appreciation in value of the property under which it would receive more than its $500,000 investment plus a 6 percent return. If Worthen exercised one of its options to repurchase the property, Lyon would receive its $500,000 cash investment plus 6 percent interest (plus an amount that would enable Lyon to repay the mortgage). Alternatively, Worthen could choose not to exercise its repurchase options but rather to exercise its option to extend the lease. It appears that the rental rates were calculated so that, if all eight lease extensions were exercised, the payments would "approximate the amount required to repay Lyon's $500,000 investment at 6% compound interest." Footnote 3 of Opinion. Compare footnote 6 of the dissent. The exercise price of the repurchase options and rentals provided in the lease extension options were such that exercise of one of the options would almost certainly occur if the property were worth more than Lyon's investment plus 6 percent. Thus there was a 6 percent cap on the return Lyon could expect to receive.

With respect to the economic risks of the respective parties, Lyon would not be repaid if Worthen became insolvent and Lyon was not otherwise able to realize a return through rental of the building to another tenant. In addition, Lyon ran the risk that Worthen would exercise neither the repurchase options nor the lease extensions. Because of the favorable option terms, however, the building would have to have had very little value for none of these options to be exercised.

The foregoing has assumed that the repurchase options and lease extension options were not at market rates. In this regard the facts of *Frank Lyon* bear some similarity to *Estate of Starr*. Yet the District Court found that these option terms reflected a fair estimate of expected future values. Frank Lyon Company v. United States, 75–2 U.S.T.C. ¶ 9545 (E.D.Ark.1975). The Court of Appeals concluded that this was a finding of fact not subject to review. Footnote 16. It would therefore appear that the result in *Frank Lyon* should not control for transactions where the options do not represent reasonable estimates of fair value.

3.2. *The Frank Lyon Opinion*

The precise test used by the Court to determine who is the owner of property for federal income tax purposes is not clear. The Court stated that substance should control over form, looking to "the objective economic realities of a transaction rather than to the particular form the parties employed." Yet many of the factors cited by the Court to support its conclusion do not appear to relate to economic realities that might distinguish a loan from a sale and leaseback. In distinguishing the *Lazarus* case, for example, the Court noted that *Lazarus* involved only two parties while the *Frank Lyon* transaction involved three, without elaborating on the relevance of that distinction. The Court also noted that because the case involved the determination of which taxpayer was entitled to deductions rather than the creation of a deduction, little revenue was at stake. Even if this statement accurately described the effects of this particular transaction (and the record suggests it does not), such a basis for the decision—i.e., amount of revenue at stake versus sound principles of taxation—lacked reasoned analysis and established poor precedent going forward. In fact, many transactions are structured at least in part to allocate tax benefits to the party who can best utilize them.

The Court also found support in Worthen's nontax motives for the transaction. The Court noted that banking regulations prohibited Worthen from owning the building subject to a long-term mortgage, that there was a competitive bidding among potential investors, and that there was the rivalry between Worthen and another local bank. Which of these factors demonstrate a business purpose? What is the relevance of business purpose in ascertaining the economic realities of the transaction? Indeed, there does not appear to be any good reason that Worthen's business purpose should be taken into account in determining the substance of Frank Lyon's economic position.

3.3. *Refining the Frank Lyon Co. Analysis*

Frank Lyon held that the sale and leaseback should be respected "where * * * there is a genuine multiple-party transaction with economic substance which is compelled or encouraged by business or regulatory realities, is imbued with tax-independent considerations, and is not shaped solely by tax avoidance features that have meaningless labels attached * * * ." This test has been the focal point of subsequent cases involving sale and leaseback transactions. For example, Hilton v. Commissioner, 74 T.C. 305 (1980), aff'd per curiam, 671 F.2d 316 (9th Cir.1982), applied the *Frank Lyon* test to treat the buyer-lessor as a "mere conduit" through which the lessee's payments passed on their way to the lenders. In *Hilton*, Broadway, a large department store chain, undertook construction of a retail department store with financing from insurance companies. Fourth Cavendish was formed to purchase the property from Broadway with funds borrowed from the insurance companies. The property was leased back to Broadway under a "triple net lease" in which Fourth Cavendish had no obligation with respect to the property other than the obligation to make monthly principal and interest payments. Indeed, even the principal and interest payments were structured to be made directly by Broadway to the insurance company lenders. Rental payments were structured to provide Fourth Cavendish with just enough money to meet its principal and interest obligations plus expenses during the 30-year term of the financing. When the loans were paid off, Broadway had an option to renew the lease for reduced rental equal to 1½ percent of the building cost for the first 23-year renewal terms, and 1 percent of the cost for the second and third renewal terms. At the time the sale and leaseback was entered into, Fourth Cavendish transferred its interest to limited partnerships thereby making capital recovery deductions from the property available to partners who invested primarily to obtain the tax benefits.

In applying the test of *Frank Lyon* the Tax Court noted in *Hilton* that from the vantage point of Broadway and the insurance companies, the sale-leaseback transaction followed accepted and widely used business practices and embraced substantial business as well as tax purposes. Thus, the transaction had "significant, economic, nontaxable substance." However, the court added that the seller/lessee sees "a reflection from only one polygon of the prism," and undertook an independent analysis to determine whether "the buyer-lessor's interest [has] substantial legal and economic significance aside from tax considerations, or is that interest simply the purchased tax byproduct of Broadway's economically impelled arrangement with the insurance companies." From the buyer-lessor's vantage point, the court in *Hilton* reformulated the *Frank Lyon* test as follows:

> Under the *Frank Lyon* test, petitioners must show not only that their participation in the sale-leaseback was not motivated or shaped solely by tax avoidance features that have meaningless labels attached, but also that there is economic substance to the transaction independent of the apparent tax shelter potential. Another way of stating the test is suggested by the Ninth Circuit's opinion in Estate of Franklin v. Commissioner, 544 F.2d 1045 (9th Cir.1976), affg. 64 T.C. 752 (1975), to wit: Could the buyer-lessor's method of payment for the property be expected at the outset to rather quickly yield an equity which buyer-lessor could not prudently abandon? An affirmative answer would produce, in the words of the Circuit Court, "the stuff of substance. It meshes with the form of the transaction and constitutes a sale." (544 F.2d at 1098.) Consequently, if the test is not met, the buyer-lessor will not have made an investment in the property, regardless of the form of ownership. And it is fundamental that depreciation is not predicated upon ownership of property but rather upon an investment in property. Estate of Franklin v. Commissioner, supra at 1049; Mayerson v. Commissioner, 47 T.C. 340, 350 (1966).

After reviewing the economics of the buyer/lessor's interest, the court concluded that:

We are * * * persuaded that an objective economic analysis of this transaction from the point of view of the buyer-lessor, and therefore the petitioners [tax shelter investors claiming deductions from the partnerships], should focus on the value of the cash flow derived from the rental payments and that little or no weight should be placed on the speculative possibility that the property will have a substantial residual value at such time, if ever, that Broadway abandons the lease. The low rents and almost nominal cash flow leave little room for doubt that, apart from tax benefits, the value of the interest acquired by the petitioners is substantially less than the amount they paid for it. In terms discussed above, the buyer-lessor would not at any time find it imprudent from an economic point of view to abandon the property. Estate of Franklin v. Commissioner, 544 F.2d 1045 (9th Cir.1976), affg. 64 T.C. 752 (1975). There is thus no justification for the petitioners' participation in this transaction apart from its tax consequences.

The Tax Court in *Hilton* distinguished the buyer-lessor from the buyer-lessor in *Frank Lyon* on a number of grounds: (1) the rent in *Frank Lyon* was sufficient to completely amortize the mortgage principal, whereas in *Hilton* the rent would amortize only 90 percent of the mortgage principal leaving the buyer-lessor responsible for a 10 percent balloon payment (on a nonrecourse basis); (2) the rent in *Hilton* was not based on fair rental value; (3) the buyer-lessor in *Frank Lyon* invested $500,000 of its own funds into acquisition of the property from the seller-lessee where all of the capital invested by the partners in *Hilton* went to compensate the tax-shelter promoters; and (5) the buyer-lessor in *Frank Lyon* was a substantial corporate entity engaged in independent activities. *Hilton* was found to represent a flagrant attempt to sell the tax benefits associated with a building to high-bracket taxpayers to whom they would be the most valuable. These distinctions, while in some respects meaningful, were not necessarily dispositive of "permissible" versus "impermissible" sale-leaseback arrangements. Moreover, they identified factors that future taxpayers could manipulate in structuring transactions in order to look more like the taxpayers in *Frank Lyon* so as to achieve the sought after tax benefits.

4.   SUBSTANCE VERSUS FORM

4.1. *Generally*

The opinions in *Frank Lyon* and *Alstores* give weight to both the substance and the form of the transactions in question. To what extent should the form of the transaction affect its characterization for federal income purposes? The result in *Alstores* likely would have been different if the documents had recited that parties desired to transfer a future interest in the building for $750,000. Likewise, the result in *Frank Lyon* probably would have been different if the documents provided that Lyon loaned $500,000 to Worthen at a 6-percent rate of interest, with prepayment rights corresponding to the repurchase options, that Lyon guaranteed the payment of the mortgage, and that Worthen had the right to "put" the property to Lyon after 25 years with a leaseback at a stipulated rental.

The Court of Appeals opinion in *Frank Lyon,* 536 F.2d 746 (8th Cir.1976)), indicated that intent is relevant in determining the state law relationships between the parties but that the federal income tax characterization is a matter of federal law unrelated to intent: "[T]he asserted 'intent' to effect a sale-leaseback for tax purposes is not a guide to the economic substance of the transaction, but instead appears to be wholly unrelated to the actual allocation of interests."

4.2. *Lease-in-Lease-out (LILO) Transactions*

The tax consequences of a purported leasing transaction involving a lease from the owner of property to another party, coupled with a sublease of the property back to the owner—termed a lease-in-lease-out transaction—is subject to being recast according to its substance where the transaction does not substantively affect the owner's rights to use and possess the property. In BB&T Corp. v. United States, 523 F.3d 461 (4th Cir.2008), the taxpayer was a financial services corporation that in a prearranged transaction (the "head lease") leased equipment from a Swedish wood pulp manufacturer (Sodra) and then re-leased it back to Sodra in a "lease-in-lease-out" (LILO) transaction. BB&T paid Sodra approximately $6 million for its costs and as an incentive to enter into the transaction. All additional payments due to be paid by BB&T to Sodra under the head lease were offset by payment obligation from Sodra to BB&T for the leaseback.

BB&T claimed substantial rental and other deductions flowing from the transaction. The district court granted summary judgment for the government, holding that the form should not be respected for tax purposes, because the taxpayer did not acquire a current leasehold interest in the equipment and incurred no risk of loss. When the reciprocal offsetting obligations were disregarded, the taxpayer in substance acquired only a future interest in the right to use and possess the equipment, and even then only if the owner-sublessee did not exercise its option to buy out taxpayer's interest in the head lease.

The court of appeals affirmed, reasoning:

> First, each right and obligation BB&T obtained under the Head Lease it simultaneously returned to Sodra via the Sublease for the duration of the Basic Lease Term, leaving BB&T only a right to make an annual inspection of the Equipment. Second, although the transaction ostensibly provides for the exchange of tens of millions of dollars in rental payments during the Basic Lease Term, the only money that has (and that may ever) change hands between BB&T and Sodra is the $6,228,702 BB&T provided as Sodra's "incentive for doing the deal." Sodra has therefore not only continued to use the Equipment just as it had before the transaction, it has done so without paying anything to BB&T. Third, Sodra, through the purchase option, can unwind the transaction without ever losing dominion and control over the Equipment or having surrendered any of its own funds to BB&T, and has no economic incentive to do otherwise. BB&T therefore does not expect Sodra to "walk away" from the Equipment. Finally,

regardless of whether Sodra bucks this expectation, the structure of the transaction insulates BB&T from any risk of losing its initial $12,833,846 investment in the government bonds or incurring the obligation to invest additional funds.

In sum, the transaction does not allocate BB&T and Sodra's rights, obligations, and risks in a manner that resembles a traditional lease relationship. * * *

* * * BB&T stands in sharp contrast to the lessor in *Frank Lyon Co.* * * *

Accordingly, we, like the district court, conclude that in substance, the transaction is a financing arrangement, not a genuine lease and sublease. All that BB&T has done is paid Sodra approximately $6 million dollars to sign documents meeting the formal requirements of a lease and sublease, arranged a circular transfer of funds * * *. Sodra, meanwhile, maintains uninterrupted possession and control of the Equipment, and has no economic incentive to cede control to BB&T. Because the funds BB&T provided as the Advance Head Lease Payment do not, in substance, constitute "rental[ ] . . . payments required to be made as a condition to the continued use or possession" of the Equipment, BB&T is not entitled to a deduction under § 162(a)(3).

Courts have considered numerous LILO and SILO transactions (sale-in-lease-out) over the years and repeatedly find grounds for disregarding the form of such transactions and recasting them to reflect their economic reality. John Hancock Life Insurance Co. v. Commissioner, 141 T.C. 1 (2013), is one such case. After detailed fact-findings and an examination of the various courts of appeals opinions in earlier LILO and SILO cases, the Tax Court held for the IRS. In each of four different transactions the substance of the transaction was not consistent with its form. There was only de minimis risk to the taxpayer and the terms of the agreements assured that the taxpayer would receive its expected return on its equity investments. According to the court, "[t]his guaranteed return is not indicative of a leasehold or ownership interest. Rather, it is reflective of what is better described as a very intricate loan from John Hancock to the lessee counterparties." Thus, even though the court found that the transaction had economic substance, it disregarded the LILO (or SILO) form and recast the transaction as a financing arrangement, The result is that the taxpayer, who was recast as a lender, lost its claimed deductions for rent, interest, and depreciation.

5.   "LEVERAGED" OR "FINANCE" EQUIPMENT LEASES

"Leveraged" or "finance" leases are typically three-party transactions in which property is purchased from a manufacturer or dealer by a leasing company that then leases the property to a user. The tax benefits are typically more valuable to the leasing company than to the user although nontax considerations may be present as well. Some of the tax benefits are shifted to the user in the form of reduced rent. Some of the tax benefits also may be captured by the manufacturer who sells the equipment for a higher price—an implicit tax. The leases are "leveraged" in that the leasing company magnifies its tax benefits by borrowing most of the cost of the leased property. Before enactment of the passive activity loss rules of § 469, discussed in Chapter 35, Section 2, the leasing company often would be formed as a limited partnership in order to pass-through the tax advantages of ownership to tax shelter investors. See e.g., American Principals Leasing Corp. v. United States, 904 F.2d 477 (9th Cir.1990), discussed in Chapter 35, Section 1.2. Currently profitable corporations, which generally are not subject to § 469, operate a leasing division (or subsidiary with which they file a consolidated tax return) and lease property to corporations that are unprofitable—at least as far as the calculation of taxable income is concerned.

In Lockhart Leasing Co. v. United States, 446 F.2d 269 (10th Cir.1971), the taxpayer bought machinery as requested by customers and then leased the items under an "Equipment Lease Agreement." The taxpayer claimed the then available investment tax credit with respect to the leased property. Under the lease agreements, the lessor retained title and had the right of repossession in the event of default in performance of the lessee (and in a number of cases this action was in fact taken by the lessor). The lessee, however, had all the risks of loss on the property and was required to pay insurance, taxes and expenses of repair and maintenance. Some, but not all, of the lease agreements contained an option for the lessee to purchase the property and, in the leases in which an option existed, it typically was bargained for on the basis of the actual estimated value of the property at the time of the exercise of the option. The court found that the rentals paid were not disproportionate to the fair rental value of the property, and held that the taxpayer was the owner of the depreciable asset and entitled to the investment credit.

In Northwest Acceptance Corp. v. Commissioner, 58 T.C. 836 (1972), aff'd per curiam 500 F.2d 1222 (9th Cir.1974), the court relied heavily on *Lockhart Leasing Co.* in finding that certain agreements constituted leases and not conditional sales contracts. The taxpayer was a sales finance company which had two methods of providing financing for equipment purchases. In some instances, it purchased "security agreements" from heavy equipment and capital goods dealers covering machinery and equipment which had been placed in the possession of the user. These "security agreements" constituted conditional sales contracts. In other instances, the taxpayer acquired contracts identified as "leases" either by assignment of the original dealer's interest in the lease or by acquiring title to the equipment from the dealer and leasing it to the user. The court rejected the Commissioner's arguments that the "leases" constituted conditional sales contracts (so that the taxpayer would not be entitled to depreciation and the investment credit with respect to the equipment) although (1) the majority of the contracts contained purchase options in which the option prices ranged from 10–50 percent of the original cost of the equipment, (2) the exercise of the options in some of the leases was guaranteed by the dealer, or where there was no repurchase option, the dealer agreed to repurchase the equipment at the end of the lease, (3) the taxpayer for book accounting purposes treated the contracts in many respects as sales contracts, and (4) the sum of rental payments plus the option price closely approximated the amount paid by a purchaser of the equipment under a deferred-payment plan. The court concluded that, although the "factual issue presented here is an extremely close one," the taxpayer did have a residual interest in the equipment and that it bore an economic risk of loss; the contract provisions employed by the taxpayer were merely an attempt to "minimize its business risks." The Tax Court was affirmed per curiam (500 F.2d 1222 (9th Cir.1974)), on the basis that the decision was not clearly erroneous, although the Court of Appeals "might well have decided the case differently notwithstanding the decision in Lockhart Leasing Co. v. United States."

Rev. Proc. 2001–28, 2001–1 C.B. 1156, contains guidelines for obtaining an advance ruling from the IRS regarding a leveraged lease that are stricter than the standards adopted by the courts for identifying a lease. To obtain a favorable ruling the lessor must have a minimum equity investment of at least 20 percent of the cost of the property, which must be maintained throughout the lease term. The lessee cannot be given an option to purchase the leased property at any time for less than the fair market value of the property at the time the option is exercised. Likewise, the lessor cannot have the right to require the lessee to purchase the property. No part of the cost of the property or improvements may be furnished by the lessee (excepting improvements that are readily removable and certain improvements necessary to operation of the property that do not exceed 10 percent of the cost of the property). The lessor must demonstrate that it will derive an overall profit from the lease apart from tax benefits and that it will maintain a positive cash flow from the investment. In addition, the lessor must demonstrate that there will be some residual value inherent in the property at the end of the lease term and that the lease is not for the full useful life of the property.

6. SALE AND LEASEBACK AS A LIKE-KIND EXCHANGE

Century Electric Co. v. Commissioner, 192 F.2d 155 (8th Cir.1951), discussed in Chapter 26, Section 1.4., held that a sale of real estate for cash and a long-term leaseback was a like-kind "exchange" of a fee interest for a long-term leasehold interest. The taxpayer's claimed recognized loss was disallowed. The court in *Century Electric* noted that:

> It is undisputed that the foundry property before the transaction was held by petitioner for productive use in petitioner's business. After the transaction the same property was held by the petitioner for the same use in the same business. Both before and after the transaction the property was necessary to the continued operation of petitioner's business. The only change wrought by the transaction was in the estate or interest of petitioner in the foundry property.

Under the Treasury regulations a 30-year lease is treated as like-kind to real property. See Treas. Reg. § 1.1031(a)–1(c). Thus, the taxpayer's loss was subject to the nonrecognition rules of § 1031, notwithstanding the taxpayer's receipt of boot.

In Jordan Marsh v. Commissioner, 269 F.2d 453 (2d Cir. 1959), the taxpayer transferred its department store property to a bank for $2.3 million of cash, which represented the fair market value of the property, then received a leaseback at a fair rental value. Citing *Century Electric*, the IRS denied the taxpayer's claimed recognized loss under § 1031 on the ground that the taxpayer never gave up possession of the property. The court in *Jordan Marsh* respected the sale and leaseback transactions and allowed recognition of the loss. Where the cash price reflects the full fair market value of the property, the leaseback cannot be treated as part of the consideration realized in exchange for the property. Second, where the rental payments under the leaseback reflect the fair rental value of the property, the lease itself cannot be treated as having an independent capital value. Thus, the sale and leaseback in *Jordan Marsh* were respected as bona fide transactions based on the economics of the pricing for each leg of the transaction.

7.   LEASES TO TAX-EXEMPT ENTITIES

In recent years an increasing number of tax shelters involved leasing to tax exempt entities. Although Congress had acted in 1984 to provide special depreciation rules that apply to property used by tax exempt entities, taxpayers had found ways to structure transactions to avoid the limitations imposed by the 1984 changes. Section 470, enacted in 2004, responds to these concerns largely by limiting deductions attributable to such leased property to the income generated by the property, thus eliminating the sheltering aspect of such transactions. A similar, but not quite as targeted, approach was used in 1986 with the enactment of the passive activity loss provisions of § 469, discussed in Chapter 35, Section 2.

CHAPTER 34

NONRECOURSE DEBT AND LEVERAGED TAX SHELTERS

SECTION 1. ACQUISITION AND DISPOSITION OF PROPERTY SUBJECT TO NONRECOURSE DEBT

INTERNAL REVENUE CODE: Section 1001.

REGULATIONS: Section 1.1001–2.

Chapter 6 considered the fundamentals of the acquisition and disposition of property, including the concept that debt incurred to acquire property is included in basis, and on disposition of property the relief from liability for a debt is included in the amount realized. This chapter addresses the use of debt for which no taxpayer is personally liable—nonrecourse debt. Nonrecourse debt is indebtedness that is secured by property and with respect to which the lender's only recourse in the event of default on repayment of the loan is foreclosing the lien and taking possession of the property. Nonrecourse debt is common in most real estate transactions and in investments through limited partnerships and limited liability companies. Nonrecourse debt provides the backbone for tax shelter investments: for very little cash exposure and low economic risk, the taxpayer can secure a very large loan (the interest on which is tax deductible) to acquire a high-value, high-basis asset (the depreciation of which is also tax deductible).

Liabilities and Basis

A taxpayer's cost basis for purposes of determining gain or loss on disposition, and for purposes of determining allowable cost-recovery deductions, is the purchase price of the property regardless of whether the taxpayer pays the purchase price with cash on hand or by borrowing the necessary funds (see Chapter 6, Section 3.C.). Generally, it does not make any difference that the borrower is not personally liable and the lender's only recourse on default is to the property securing the debt (a nonrecourse debt). As long as the property securing the obligation has a value equal to or in excess of the face amount of the nonrecourse indebtedness, the taxpayer will treat the obligation the same as if it created personal liability. Also, before the borrower can realize economic gain on the transaction, the borrower must realize more than the amount that is required to be paid to the lender before the borrower can dispose of the property and retain the proceeds. As a result, basis, or some alternative accounting device, must include the nonrecourse debt as part of the borrower's "cost" for the property for purposes of determining gain.

While personal liability and nonrecourse debt are similar from the borrower's perspective if the property increases in value, the risk of loss is different between the two types of liability. If the value of the property declines below the amount of a nonrecourse obligation, the borrower can cease to make payments on the indebtedness, and the lender will acquire the property in full satisfaction of the debt. In this case, the lender, rather than the borrower, bears the economic loss if the property declines in value below the outstanding amount of the nonrecourse obligation. In a sense, the borrower invests someone else's money and reaps all the benefits if the investment is economically successful, but walks away from the deal if the property securing the debt should decline in value below the outstanding principal of the debt. Nonetheless, the borrower is allowed to include the nonrecourse obligation in basis.

In Crane v. Commissioner, 331 U.S. 1 (1947), the taxpayer inherited an apartment building from her deceased husband. The fair market value of the building at the time of the husband's death was equal to the amount of a nonrecourse mortgage secured by the building. Mrs. Crane operated the building for several years, reporting the rent as income and deducting depreciation, which reduced her basis under § 1016.[1] Ultimately, Mrs. Crane sold the building subject to the outstanding mortgage for cash, net of expenses, in the amount of $2,500. She claimed that her basis in the property inherited from her late husband was limited to the value of the inherited equity interest, zero, and that her amount realized on the sale was limited to the $2,500 cash received, thereby limiting her gain to $2,500. The Commissioner argued that the full fair market value of the inherited property should be treated as basis under the predecessor to § 1014 (basis equal to the fair market value of "property" acquired in a transfer by death (see Chapter 7, Section 2), that basis is reduced by the depreciation deductions allowable with respect to the property, and that the amount realized on disposition includes the full amount of the debt in addition to the cash received by Mrs. Crane.[2] In what proved to be a very costly victory, the Commissioner prevailed on all three points.

Based on its interpretation of the word "property" in the predecessor to § 1014, the Court concluded that Mrs. Crane's basis was the full fair market value of the whole property at the time of her inheritance, not just her equity interest. Significantly, the Court based its conclusion, in part, on the relationship of basis to depreciation:

---

[1]   As required by § 1016, Mrs. Crane's basis was reduced by the full amount of depreciation allowable for the years she operated the apartment building.

[2]   The fair market value of the property and the amount of the debt inherited by Mrs. Crane was $262,042.50. Of this amount, $55,000.00 was allocable to land and $207,042.50 to the building. Basis in the building was reduced to $178,997.40 by allowable depreciation of $28,045.10. Amount realized including the cash and unpaid principal of the nonrecourse mortgage totaled $257,500.00. The Commissioner allocated $54,471.15 of the amount realized to the land and the remaining $203,028.85 to the building producing a $528.85 loss on the land, which the Commissioner treated as a capital loss, and a gain of $24,031.45 on the building, which the Commissioner treated as ordinary income. 331 U.S. at 4–5.

Section [167] permits deduction from gross income of "a reasonable allowance for the exhaustion, wear and tear of property * * * ." Section [167(c)(1)] declares that the "basis upon which exhaustion, wear and tear . . . are to be allowed" is the basis "provided in section [1011] for the purpose of determining the gain upon the sale" of the property, which is the [section 1011] basis "adjusted . . . for exhaustion, wear and tear . . . to the extent allowed (but not less than the amount allowable). . . ."

Under these provisions, if the mortgagor's equity were the [§ 1011] basis, it would also be the original basis from which depreciation allowances are deducted. If it is, and if the amount of the annual allowances were to be computed on that value, as would then seem to be required, they will represent only a fraction of the cost of the corresponding physical exhaustion, and any recoupment by the mortgagor of the remainder of that cost can be effected only by the reduction of his taxable gain in the year of sale. If, however, the amount of the annual allowances were to be computed on the value of the property, and then deducted from an equity basis, we would in some instances have to accept deductions from a minus basis or deny deductions altogether. The Commissioner also argues that taking the mortgagor's equity as the [§ 1011] basis would require the basis to be changed with each payment on the mortgage, and that the attendant problem of repeatedly recomputing basis and annual allowances would be a tremendous accounting burden on both the Commissioner and the taxpayer. Moreover, the mortgagor would acquire control over the timing of his "depreciation allowances."

Crane v. Commissioner was decided under the predecessor to § 1014. In Mayerson v. Commissioner, 47 T.C. 340 (1966) (Acq.), the Commissioner argued that the reasoning of *Crane* should not apply in the case of a purchase money nonrecourse obligation. Instead, the Commissioner argued, the transaction ought to have been characterized as a long-term lease with an option to purchase the property during the lease term. The Tax Court rejected the Commissioner's argument, holding that the taxpayer's basis in property purchased in exchange for a 99-year nonrecourse note, secured by the property, included the full amount of the liability. The taxpayer in *Mayerson* was thus allowed to claim depreciation deductions using the full amount of this basis. The court explained the decision as follows:

The respondent argues that the *Crane* case should not apply in a purchase situation since the basis in that case started with fair market value and not cost, as in the case of a purchase. The reasoning of the *Crane* case, however, seems equally applicable to a purchase situation and indeed was so applied in the *Blackstone Theatre Co.* case and Parker v. Delaney, 186 F.2d 455 (C.A.1, 1950). It should also be applied here.

The element of the lack of personal liability has little real significance due to common business practices. As we have indicated in our findings it is not at all unusual in current mortgage financing of income-producing properties to limit liability to the property involved. Taxpayers who are not personally liable for encumbrances on property should be allowed depreciation deductions affording competitive equality with taxpayers who are personally liable for encumbrances or taxpayers who own unencumbered property. The effect of such a policy is to give the taxpayer an advance credit for the amount of the mortgage. This appears to be reasonable since it can be assumed that a capital investment in the amount of the mortgage will eventually occur despite the absence of personal liability. The respondent has not suggested any rationale that would reasonably require a contrary conclusion. The lien created by the purchase-money mortgage, like the tax liens in the *Blackstone Theatre* case, should be included in basis for the purpose of computing depreciation.

The IRS indicated in Rev. Rul. 69–77, 1969–1 C.B. 59, that it would follow *Mayerson* only "in situations where it is clear that the property has been acquired at its fair market value in an arm's length transaction creating a bona fide purchase and a bona fide debt obligation."

Depreciation, discussed in Chapter 14, is intended to match income from capital assets with the capital cost of the asset allocated to each of the periods the asset is used to produce income.[3] The holdings of *Crane* and *Mayerson* allow the borrower to acquire property with capital contributed by the lender and recover the lender's capital investment in the form of depreciation deductions even though the borrower is not personally liable to return the full amount of the invested capital to the lender. The absence of personal liability permits the borrower to abandon the property to the lender without satisfying the debt. As a consequence, capital recovered by the borrower through depreciation deductions is capital for which the lender is at-risk. In other words, the holdings of *Crane* and *Mayerson* allow a borrower to claim capital cost recovery deductions for the lender's capital.

Liabilities and Amount Realized

On the question of amount realized, the Court in *Crane* concluded that the relationship of amount realized to basis requires that, if the adjusted basis of property includes the full amount of nonrecourse debt, the amount realized on disposition of the property must also include the unpaid principal of the nonrecourse debt. The Court added:

---

[3]   See Commissioner v. Idaho Power Co., 418 U.S. 1, 10–11 (1974); Massey Motors, Inc. v. United States, 364 U.S. 92, 104 (1960).

[W]e think that a mortgagor, not personally liable on the debt, who sells the property subject to the mortgage and for additional consideration, realizes a benefit in the amount of the mortgage as well as the boot. If a purchaser pays boot [here, the $2,500], it is immaterial as to our problem whether the mortgagor is also to receive money from the purchaser to discharge the mortgage prior to sale, or whether he is merely to transfer subject to the mortgage—it may make a difference to the purchaser and to the mortgagee, but not to the mortgagor. Or put in another way, we are no more concerned with whether the mortgagor is, strictly speaking, a debtor on the mortgage, than we are with whether the benefit to him is, strictly speaking, a receipt of money or property. We are rather concerned with the reality that an owner of property, mortgaged at a figure less than that at which the property will sell, must and will treat the conditions of the mortgage exactly as if they were his personal obligations. If he transfers subject to the mortgage, the benefit to him is as real and substantial as if the mortgage were discharged, or as if a personal debt in an equal amount had been assumed by another.

The Court added in footnote 37:

Obviously, if the value of the property is less than the amount of the mortgage, a mortgagor who is not personally liable cannot realize a benefit equal to the mortgage. Consequently, a different problem might be encountered where a mortgagor abandoned the property or transferred it subject to the mortgage without receiving boot. That is not this case.

This footnote left open the question of amount realized when the value of the property securing nonrecourse debt was less than the amount of the debt. The Court answered that question thirty-six years later.

Commissioner v. Tufts

Supreme Court of the United States, 1983.
461 U.S. 300.

■ JUSTICE BLACKMUN delivered the opinion of the Court.

Over 35 years ago, in Crane v. Commissioner, 331 U.S. 1 (1947), this Court ruled that a taxpayer, who sold property encumbered by a nonrecourse mortgage (the amount of the mortgage being less than the property's value), must include the unpaid balance of the mortgage in the computation of the amount the taxpayer realized on the sale. The case now before us presents the question whether the same rule applies when the unpaid amount of the nonrecourse mortgage exceeds the fair market value of the property sold.

I

On August 1, 1970, respondent Clark Pelt, a builder, and his wholly owned corporation, respondent Clark, Inc., formed a general partnership. The purpose of the partnership was to construct a 120-unit apartment complex in Duncanville, Tex., a Dallas suburb. Neither Pelt nor Clark, Inc., made any capital contribution to the partnership. Six days later, the partnership entered into a mortgage loan agreement with the Farm & Home Savings Association (F & H). Under the agreement, F & H was committed for a $1,851,500 loan for the complex. In return, the partnership executed a note and a deed of trust in favor of F & H. The partnership obtained the loan on a nonrecourse basis: neither the partnership nor its partners assumed any personal liability for repayment of the loan. Pelt later admitted four friends and relatives, respondents Tufts, Steger, Stephens, and Austin, as general partners. None of them contributed capital upon entering the partnership.

The construction of the complex was completed in August 1971. During 1971, each partner made small capital contributions to the partnership; in 1972, however, only Pelt made a contribution. The total of the partners' capital contributions was $44,212. In each tax year, all partners claimed as income tax deductions their allocable shares of ordinary losses and depreciation. The deductions taken by the partners in 1971 and 1972 totaled $439,972. Due to these contributions and deductions, the partnership's adjusted basis in the property in August 1972 was $1,455,740.

In 1971 and 1972, major employers in the Duncanville area laid off significant numbers of workers. As a result, the partnership's rental income was less than expected, and it was unable to make the payments due on the mortgage. Each partner, on August 28, 1972, sold his partnership interest to an unrelated third party, Fred Bayles. As consideration, Bayles agreed to reimburse each partner's sale expenses up to $250; he also assumed the nonrecourse mortgage.

On the date of transfer, the fair market value of the property did not exceed $1,400,000. Each partner reported the sale on his federal income tax return and indicated that a partnership loss of $55,740 had been sustained.[1] The Commissioner of Internal Revenue, on audit, determined that the sale resulted in a partnership capital gain of approximately $400,000. His theory was that the partnership had realized the full amount of the nonrecourse obligation.

Relying on Millar v. Commissioner, 577 F.2d 212, 215 (CA3), cert. denied, 439 U.S. 1046 (1978), the United States Tax Court, in an unreviewed decision, upheld the asserted deficiencies. 70 T.C. 756 (1978). The United States Court of Appeals for the Fifth Circuit reversed. 651

---

[1]   The loss was the difference between the adjusted basis, $1,455,740, and the fair market value of the property, $1,400,000. On their individual tax returns, the partners did not claim deductions for their respective shares of this loss. In their petitions to the Tax Court, however, the partners did claim the loss.

F.2d 1058 (1981). That court expressly disagreed with the *Millar* analysis, and, in limiting *Crane v. Commissioner,* supra, to its facts, questioned the theoretical underpinnings of the *Crane* decision. We granted certiorari to resolve the conflict. 456 U.S. 960 (1982).

II

* * * Section 1001 governs the determination of gains and losses on the disposition of property. Under § 1001(a), the gain or loss from a sale or other disposition of property is defined as the difference between "the amount realized" on the disposition and the property's adjusted basis. Subsection (b) of § 1001 defines "amount realized": "The amount realized from the sale or other disposition of property shall be the sum of any money received plus the fair market value of the property (other than money) received." At issue is the application of the latter provision to the disposition of property encumbered by a nonrecourse mortgage of an amount in excess of the property's fair market value.

A

In *Crane v. Commissioner,* supra, this Court took the first and controlling step toward the resolution of this issue. [Mrs. Crane sold property subject to a nonrecourse mortgage, which she had inherited from her deceased husband, for $3,000 of cash, $500 of which was used to pay the expenses of sale.] * * *

Crane reported a gain of $2,500 on the transaction. She reasoned that her basis in the property was zero (despite her earlier depreciation deductions based on including the amount of the mortgage) and that the amount she realized from the sale was simply the cash she received. The Commissioner disputed this claim. He asserted that Crane's basis in the property, under [§ 1014] was the property's fair market value at the time of her husband's death, adjusted for depreciation in the interim, and that the amount realized was the net cash received plus the amount of the outstanding mortgage assumed by the purchaser.

In upholding the Commissioner's interpretation of [§ 1014], the Court observed that to regard merely the taxpayer's equity in the property as her basis would lead to depreciation deductions less than the actual physical deterioration of the property, and would require the basis to be recomputed with each payment on the mortgage. 331 U.S., at 9–10. The Court rejected Crane's claim that any loss due to depreciation belonged to the mortgagee. The effect of the Court's ruling was that the taxpayer's basis was the value of the property undiminished by the mortgage. Id., at 11.

The Court next proceeded to determine the amount realized under [§ 1001(b)]. In order to avoid the "absurdity," see 331 U.S. 1, at 13, of Crane's realizing only $2,500 on the sale of property worth over a quarter of a million dollars, the Court treated the amount realized as it had treated basis, that is, by including the outstanding value of the mortgage. To do otherwise would have permitted Crane to recognize a tax loss unconnected with any actual economic loss. The Court refused to construe one section of the Revenue Act so as "to frustrate the Act as a whole." Ibid.

Crane, however, insisted that the nonrecourse nature of the mortgage required different treatment. The Court, for two reasons, disagreed. First, excluding the nonrecourse debt from the amount realized would result in the same absurdity and frustration of the Code. Id., at 13–14. Second, the Court concluded that Crane obtained an economic benefit from the purchaser's assumption of the mortgage identical to the benefit conferred by the cancellation of personal debt. Because the value of the property in that case exceeded the amount of the mortgage, it was in Crane's economic interest to treat the mortgage as a personal obligation; only by so doing could she realize upon sale the appreciation in her equity represented by the $2,500 boot. The purchaser's assumption of the liability thus resulted in a taxable economic benefit to her, just as if she had been given, in addition to the boot, a sum of cash sufficient to satisfy the mortgage.

In a footnote, pertinent to the present case, the Court observed:

> "Obviously, if the value of the property is less than the amount of the mortgage, a mortgagor who is not personally liable cannot realize a benefit equal to the mortgage. Consequently, a different problem might be encountered where a mortgagor abandoned the property or transferred it subject to the mortgage without receiving boot. That is not this case." Id., at 14, n. 37.

B

This case presents that unresolved issue. We are disinclined to overrule *Crane,* and we conclude that the same rule applies when the unpaid amount of the nonrecourse mortgage exceeds the value of the property transferred. *Crane* ultimately does not rest on its limited theory of economic benefit; instead, we read *Crane* to have approved the Commissioner's decision to treat a nonrecourse mortgage in this context as a true loan. This approval underlies *Crane*'s holdings that the amount of the nonrecourse liability is to be included in calculating both the basis and the amount realized on disposition. That the amount of the loan exceeds the fair market value of the property thus becomes irrelevant.

When a taxpayer receives a loan, he incurs an obligation to repay that loan at some future date. Because of this obligation, the loan proceeds do not qualify as income to the taxpayer. When he fulfills the obligation, the repayment of the loan likewise has no effect on his tax liability.

Another consequence to the taxpayer from this obligation occurs when the taxpayer applies the loan proceeds to the purchase price of property used to secure the loan. Because of the obligation to repay, the taxpayer is entitled to include the amount of the loan in computing his basis in the property; the loan, under § 1012, is part of the taxpayer's cost of the property. Although a different approach might have been taken with respect to a nonrecourse mortgage loan,[5] the Commissioner has chosen to accord it the same treatment he gives to a recourse mortgage loan. The Court approved that choice in *Crane,* and the respondents do not challenge it here. The choice and its resultant benefits to the taxpayer are predicated on the assumption that the mortgage will be repaid in full. When encumbered property is sold or otherwise disposed of and the purchaser assumes the mortgage, the associated extinguishment of the mortgagor's obligation to repay is accounted for in the computation of the amount realized.[6] See United States v. Hendler, 303 U.S. 564, 566–567 (1938). Because no difference between recourse and nonrecourse obligations is recognized in calculating basis,[7] *Crane* teaches that the Commissioner may ignore the nonrecourse nature of the obligation in determining the amount realized upon disposition of the encumbered property. He thus may include in the amount realized the amount of the nonrecourse mortgage assumed by the purchaser. The rationale for this treatment is that the original inclusion of the amount of the mortgage in basis rested on the assumption that the mortgagor incurred an obligation to repay. Moreover, this treatment balances the fact that the mortgagor originally received the proceeds of the nonrecourse loan tax-free on the same assumption. Unless the outstanding amount of the mortgage is

---

[5]   The Commissioner might have adopted the theory, implicit in *Crane*'s contentions, that a nonrecourse mortgage is not true debt, but, instead, is a form of joint investment by the mortgagor and the mortgagee. On this approach, nonrecourse debt would be considered a contingent liability, under which the mortgagor's payments on the debt gradually increase his interest in the property while decreasing that of the mortgagee. * * * Because the taxpayer's investment in the property would not include the nonrecourse debt, the taxpayer would not be permitted to include that debt in basis. * * *

We express no view as to whether such an approach would be consistent with the statutory structure and, if so, and *Crane* were not on the books, whether that approach would be preferred over *Crane*'s analysis. We note only that the *Crane* Court's resolution of the basis issue presumed that when property is purchased with proceeds from a nonrecourse mortgage, the purchaser becomes the sole owner of the property. 331 U.S., at 6. Under the *Crane* approach, the mortgagee is entitled to no portion of the basis. Id., at 10, n. 28. The nonrecourse mortgage is part of the mortgagor's investment in the property, and does not constitute a coinvestment by the mortgagee. * * *

[6]   In this case, respondents received the face value of their note as loan proceeds. If respondents initially had given their note at a discount, the amount realized on the sale of the securing property might be limited to the funds actually received. See Commissioner v. Rail Joint Co., 61 F.2d 751, 752 (C.A.2 1932) (cancellation of indebtedness); Fashion Park, Inc. v. Commissioner, 21 T.C. 600, 606 (1954) (same). See generally J. Sneed, The Configurations of Gross Income 319 (1967) ("[I]t appears settled that the reacquisition of bonds at a discount by the obligor results in gain only to the extent the issue price, where this is less than par, exceeds the cost of reacquisition").

[7]   The Commissioner's choice in *Crane* "laid the foundation stone of most tax shelters," * * * by permitting taxpayers who bear no risk to take deductions on depreciable property. Congress recently has acted to curb this avoidance device by forbidding a taxpayer to take depreciation deductions in excess of amounts he has at risk in the investment. Pub.L. 94–455, § 204(a), 90 Stat. 1531 (1976), 26 U.S.C. § 465; Pub.L. 95–600, §§ 201–204, 92 Stat. 2814–2817 (1978), 26 U.S.C. § 465(a) (1976 ed., Supp. V). Real estate investments, however, are exempt from this prohibition. § 465(c)(3)(D) (1976 ed., Supp. V). Although this congressional action may foreshadow a day when nonrecourse and recourse debts will be treated differently, neither Congress nor the Commissioner has sought to alter *Crane*'s rule of including nonrecourse liability in both basis and the amount realized.

deemed to be realized, the mortgagor effectively will have received untaxed income at the time the loan was extended and will have received an unwarranted increase in the basis of his property.[8] The Commissioner's interpretation of § 1001(b) in this fashion cannot be said to be unreasonable.

C

The Commissioner in fact has applied this rule even when the fair market value of the property falls below the amount of the nonrecourse obligation. Treas. Reg. § 1.1001–2(b), 26 CFR § 1.1001–2(b) (1982); Rev. Rul. 76–111, 1976–1 Cum.Bull. 214. Because the theory on which the rule is based applies equally in this situation, see Millar v. Commissioner, 67 T.C. 656, 660 (1977), aff'd on this issue, 577 F.2d 212, 215–216 (CA3), cert. denied, 439 U.S. 1046 (1978) * * * , we have no reason, after *Crane,* to question this treatment.[11] Respondents received a mortgage loan with the concomitant obligation to repay by the year 2012. The only difference between that mortgage and one on which the borrower is personally liable is that the mortgagee's remedy is limited to foreclosing on the securing property. This difference does not alter the nature of the obligation; its only effect is to shift from the borrower to the lender any potential loss caused by devaluation of the property. If the fair market value of the property falls below the amount of the outstanding obligation, the mortgagee's ability to protect its interests is impaired, for the mortgagor is free to abandon the property to the mortgagee and be relieved of his obligation.

This, however, does not erase the fact that the mortgagor received the loan proceeds tax-free and included them in his basis on the understanding that he had an obligation to repay the full amount. * * * .

---

[8]   Although the Crane rule has some affinity with the tax benefit rule, * * * the analysis we adopt is different. Our analysis applies even in the situation in which no deductions are taken. It focuses on the obligation to repay and its subsequent extinguishment, not on the taking and recovery of deductions. * * *

[11]   Professor Wayne G. Barnett, as *amicus* in the present case, argues that the liability and property portions of the transaction should be accounted for separately. Under his view, there was a transfer of the property for $1.4 million, and there was a cancellation of the $1.85 million obligation for a payment of $1.4 million. The former resulted in a capital loss of $50,000, and the latter in the realization of $450,000 of ordinary income. Taxation of the ordinary income might be deferred under § 108 by a reduction of respondents' bases in their partnership interests.

Although this indeed could be a justifiable mode of analysis, it has not been adopted by the Commissioner. Nor is there anything to indicate that the Code requires the Commissioner to adopt it. We note that Professor Barnett's approach does assume that recourse and nonrecourse debt may be treated identically.

The Commissioner also has chosen not to characterize the transaction as cancellation of indebtedness. . . .

In the context of a sale or disposition of property under § 1001, the extinguishment of the obligation to repay is not ordinary income; instead, the amount of the canceled debt is included in the amount realized, and enters into the computation of gain or loss on the disposition of property. According to *Crane,* this treatment is no different when the obligation is nonrecourse: the basis is not reduced as in the cancellation-of-indebtedness context, and the full value of the outstanding liability is included in the amount realized. Thus, the problem of negative basis is avoided.

When the obligation is canceled, the mortgagor is relieved of his responsibility to repay the sum he originally received and thus realizes value to that extent within the meaning of § 1001(b). From the mortgagor's point of view, when his obligation is assumed by a third party who purchases the encumbered property, it is as if the mortgagor first had been paid with cash borrowed by the third party from the mortgagee on a nonrecourse basis, and then had used the cash to satisfy his obligation to the mortgagee.

Moreover, this approach avoids the absurdity the Court recognized in *Crane*. Because of the remedy accompanying the mortgage in the nonrecourse situation, the depreciation in the fair market value of the property is relevant economically only to the mortgagee, who by lending on a nonrecourse basis remains at risk. To permit the taxpayer to limit his realization to the fair market value of the property would be to recognize a tax loss for which he has suffered no corresponding economic loss.[13] Such a result would be to construe "one section of the Act . . . so as . . . to defeat the intention of another or to frustrate the Act as a whole." 331 U.S., at 13.

In the specific circumstances of *Crane,* the economic benefit theory did support the Commissioner's treatment of the nonrecourse mortgage as a personal obligation. The footnote in *Crane* acknowledged the limitations of that theory when applied to a different set of facts. *Crane* also stands for the broader proposition, however, that a nonrecourse loan should be treated as a true loan. We therefore hold that a taxpayer must account for the proceeds of obligations he has received tax-free and included in basis. Nothing in either § 1001(b) or in the Court's prior decisions requires the Commissioner to permit a taxpayer to treat a sale of encumbered property asymmetrically, by including the proceeds of the nonrecourse obligation in basis but not accounting for the proceeds upon transfer of the encumbered property. See Estate of Levine v. Commissioner, 634 F.2d 12, 15 (C.A.2 1980).

* * *

■ JUSTICE O'CONNOR, concurring: I concur in the opinion of the Court, accepting the view of the Commissioner. I do not, however, endorse the Commissioner's view. Indeed, were we writing on a slate clean except for the *Crane* decision, I would take quite a different approach—that urged upon us by Professor Barnett as *amicus*.

---

[13]   In the present case, the Government bore the ultimate loss. The nonrecourse mortgage was extended to respondents only after the planned complex was endorsed for mortgage insurance under §§ 221(b) and (d)(4) of the National Housing Act, 12 U.S.C. §§ 17151(b) and (d)(4) (1976 ed. and Supp. V). After acquiring the complex from respondents, Bayles operated it for a few years, but was unable to make it profitable. In 1974, F & H foreclosed, and the Department of Housing and Urban Development paid off the lender to obtain title. In 1976, the Department sold the complex to another developer for $1,502,000. The sale was financed by the Department's taking back a note for $1,314,800 and a nonrecourse mortgage. To fail to recognize the value of the nonrecourse loan in the amount realized, therefore, would permit respondents to compound the Government's loss by claiming the tax benefits of that loss for themselves.

Crane established that a taxpayer could treat property as entirely his own, in spite of the "coinvestment" provided by his mortgagee in the form of a nonrecourse loan. That is, the full basis of the property, with all its tax consequences, belongs to the mortgagor. That rule alone, though, does not in any way tie nonrecourse debt to the cost of property or to the proceeds upon disposition. I see no reason to treat the purchase, ownership, and eventual disposition of property differently because the taxpayer also takes out a mortgage, an independent transaction. In this case, the taxpayer purchased property, using nonrecourse financing, and sold it after it declined in value to a buyer who assumed the mortgage. There is no economic difference between the events in this case and a case in which the taxpayer buys property with cash; later obtains a nonrecourse loan by pledging the property as security; still later, using cash on hand, buys off the mortgage for the market value of the devalued property; and finally sells the property to a third party for its market value.

The logical way to treat both this case and the hypothesized case is to separate the two aspects of these events and to consider, first, the ownership and sale of the property, and, second, the arrangement and retirement of the loan. Under *Crane,* the fair market value of the property on the date of acquisition—the purchase price—represents the taxpayer's basis in the property, and the fair market value on the date of disposition represents the proceeds on sale. The benefit received by the taxpayer in return for the property is the cancellation of a mortgage that is worth no more than the fair market value of the property, for that is all the mortgagee can expect to collect on the mortgage. His gain or loss on the disposition of the property equals the difference between the proceeds and the cost of acquisition. Thus, the taxation of the transaction *in property* reflects the economic fate of the *property*. If the property has declined in value, as was the case here, the taxpayer recognizes a loss on the disposition of the property. The new purchaser then takes as his basis the fair market value as of the date of the sale. See, e.g., United States v. Davis, 370 U.S. 65, 72 (1962) * * * .

In the separate borrowing transaction, the taxpayer acquires cash from the mortgagee. He need not recognize income at that time, of course, because he also incurs an obligation to repay the money. Later, though, when he is able to satisfy the debt by surrendering property that is worth less that the face amount of the debt, we have a classic situation of cancellation of indebtedness, requiring the taxpayer to recognize income in the amount of the difference between the proceeds of the loan and the amount for which he is able to satisfy his creditor. 26 U.S.C. § 61(a)(12). The taxation of the financing transaction then reflects the economic fate of the loan.

The reason that separation of the two aspects of the events in this case is important is, of course, that the Code treats different sorts of income differently. A gain on the sale of the property may qualify for capital gains treatment, §§ 1202, 1221 (1976 ed. and Supp. V), while the cancellation of indebtedness is ordinary income, but income that the taxpayer may be able to defer. §§ 108, 1017 (1976 ed. Supp. V). Not only does Professor Barnett's theory permit us to accord appropriate treatment to each of the two types of income or loss present in these sorts of transactions, it also restores continuity to the system by making the taxpayer-seller's proceeds on the disposition of property equal to the purchaser's basis in the property. Further, and most important, it allows us to tax the events in this case in the same way that we tax the economically identical hypothesized transaction.

Persuaded though I am by the logical coherence and internal consistency of this approach, I agree with the Court's decision not to adopt it judicially. We do not write on a slate marked only by *Crane.* The Commissioner's longstanding position, Rev. Rul. 76–111, 1976–1 C.B. 214, is now reflected in the regulations. Treas. Reg. § 1.1001–2, * * * . In the light of the numerous cases in the lower courts including the amount of the unrepaid proceeds of the mortgage in the proceeds on sale or disposition, see e.g., Estate of Levine v. Commissioner, 634 F.2d 12, 15 (C.A.2 1980); Millar v. Commissioner, 577 F.2d 212 (CA3), cert. denied, 439 U.S. 1046 (1978) * * * , it is difficult to conclude that the Commissioner's interpretation of the statute exceeds the bounds of his discretion. As the Court's opinion demonstrates, his interpretation is defensible. One can reasonably read § 1001(b)'s reference to "the amount realized *from* the sale or other disposition of property" (emphasis added) to permit the Commissioner to collapse the two aspects of the transaction. As long as his view is a reasonable reading of § 1001(b), we should defer to the regulations promulgated by the agency charged with interpretation of the statute. National Muffler Dealers Association v. United States, 440 U.S. 472, 488–489 (1979) * * * . Accordingly, I concur.

DETAILED ANALYSIS

1. THE RELATIONSHIP BETWEEN AMOUNT REALIZED AND BASIS IN ACCOUNTING FOR DEBT UNDER SECTION 1001

1.1. *Acquisition Indebtedness*

Suppose A acquires property worth $100 by giving B $10 in cash and a nonrecourse note for $90.[4] Under the principles discussed Chapter 6, Section 3.C., A has a basis in the property of $100. Assume that A makes a $15 principal payment on the note and then sells the property to C who takes the property subject to the $75 outstanding balance of the note and pays A cash in the amount of $35. *Crane, Tufts* and *Mayerson* together hold that A's basis in the property includes the full amount of the note, and that because basis includes the amount of the note, the full unpaid principal must be included in amount realized on disposition. Thus A's amount realized is $35 cash plus

---

[4]   Assume that all of the notes discussed in the examples in this section state a market interest rate so that the present value of the taxpayer's obligation is equal to the face amount of the note.

the $75 note principal or $110, and A's realized gain is $10 ($110 − $100). The realized gain reflects A's overall economic benefit from the transaction. A invested $10 of cash at the outset, paid an additional $15 of principal on the note, and terminated the investment with $35 of cash in hand ($35 − [$10 + $15] = $10). Under the analysis of *Tufts,* the computation of gain or loss provided in § 1001 compares the amount of after-tax capital that went into the transaction both at acquisition and during the course of A's holding the property, with the amount that was realized at the end of the investment. A's gain on this transaction is the same whether or not A is personally liable on the note.

The above transaction can be analyzed by ignoring the debt and using A's equity investment only. Under this approach, A's initial basis would be $10, increased by $15 to $25 on payment of loan principal. The amount realized on disposition would be the $ 35 in cash that B paid to A. The result is the same $10 of realized gain ($35 less $25). However, as described by the court in *Crane,* this approach would have a significant impact on the way depreciation is calculated.

1.2. *Post-Acquisition Indebtedness*

Relief from post-acquisition debt also is included in the amount realized, thus accounting for borrowed capital removed from the investment subsequent to acquisition. However, post-acquisition mortgage borrowing does not automatically affect basis. For example, assume A purchases property for $100 cash and a $900 nonrecourse note. The property appreciates in value to $2,000, at which time A takes out an additional $800 nonrecourse loan secured by the property. Under Woodsam Associates, Inc. v. Commissioner (see Chapter 6, Section 2.A.), A does not realize gain as the result of the subsequent borrowing. Because the subsequent borrowing was not a cost of acquiring or improving the property it is not included in the basis of the property. Rather, the subsequent borrowing produced $800 of additional cash that A may use for purposes unrelated to the property.[5] Assuming that A has made no principal payments on the note, at disposition A's amount realized will include the full $1700 amount of the outstanding notes. Thus, on disposition of the property to a buyer who takes subject to the mortgage debt but pays no further consideration, A will realize $700 gain. This gain reflects A's overall benefit from the transaction. A invested $100 initially and withdrew $800 tax-free at the time of refinancing, an overall gain of $700.

In the above example, A would realize $700 of gain on the transaction regardless of the absence of personal liability on the note. A would have a $700 accession to wealth on the overall investment even if the value of the property declined to zero and A transferred the property to the lender in a foreclosure proceeding (because of the $800 loan secured by the property that

---

[5]   It might be said that A has a basis of $800 in the cash which in effect includes the full amount of the debt in the property acquired for A's note. If A uses the $800 to acquire other property, A will have an $800 basis in that other property. Similarly, if A had used the $800 to improve the mortgaged property, its basis then would be $1800 and the transfer solely for assumption of the $1700 indebtedness would have resulted in a $100 loss.

A does not have to repay). In this situation, the fair market value of the property is irrelevant to A's overall economic gain on the transaction.

1.3. *Accounting for Capital Recovery from Depreciation and Other Deductions*

The holdings of *Crane* and *Tufts* properly account for the relationship between taxable gain on disposition of property and the recovery of invested capital through depreciation or other capital recovery deductions. Including debt in the basis of depreciable property allows the owner to spread the debt-financed cost of an asset over the periods of its use in an income-producing activity. The annual deduction of capital cost returns a portion of capitalized basis by allowing the taxpayer to recover income from the activity (or, subject to limitations, some other activity) without paying tax on the income. Thus, invested capital is returned in the form of tax-free income as provisions for recovery of basis are intended to do. If the capital being returned in this fashion represents debt, the taxpayer is obtaining a tax-free return of capital on which the taxpayer has yet to pay tax. Including the full amount of unpaid indebtedness in amount realized on disposition accounts for the prior return of this tax-free capital. Determining the amount realized on the disposition of encumbered property thus requires the recognition of gain representing the recovery of debt-financed capital through depreciation deductions just as including liabilities in amount realized accounts for post-acquisition borrowing under *Woodsam Associates*.

To illustrate, assume A acquires income-producing property for a cash payment of $20 and a note in the amount of $80. Each year for three years A receives $10 of income from the property in excess of operating expenses. A also claims $10 of capital cost recovery deductions in each of the three years so that A's net taxable income from the property each year is zero. In effect, the receipt of $10 in cash without tax in each of the first two years returns A's initial $20 out-of-pocket investment. The receipt of $10 in year three returns capital provided by the lender. If the debt is nonrecourse, A is not legally liable for the return of this $10 of the lender's capital. The lender thus bears the risk that this capital will be lost if the value of the property declines below $80. A's adjusted basis in the property is reduced to $70 to reflect recovery of $30 ($10 for each of three years). I.R.C. § 1016.

On disposition of the property at the end of year three, for no consideration other than release from the debt, A's amount realized will include the full amount of the debt and A will realize $10 of gain ($80 − $70). A's realized gain accounts for the fact that A invested $20 of equity and withdrew $30 without tax during the course of the investment. This result is identical with that in *Woodsam Associates*, which recovers on disposition of the encumbered property the tax-free cash obtained in a post-acquisition borrowing. In both cases, "the fair market value of property received on disposition," treated as amount realized, includes the value of debt-financed property received without tax at acquisition, the tax-free capital received in a subsequent borrowing, and the tax-free income received because of capital recovery deductions based on borrowed capital. Including debt in both basis and amount realized is an approach that fully addresses all of these situations.

2.   CONTINGENT LIABILITIES

Revenue Ruling 78–29, 1978–1 C.B. 62, indicates that "an obligation, the payment of which is so speculative as to create a contingent liability, cannot be included in the basis of the property." See also Rev. Rul. 70–110, 1977–1 C.B. 58. The rulings cite three cases for this proposition, Denver & Rio Grande Western Railroad v. United States, 505 F.2d 1266 (Ct.Cl.1974), Columbus & Greenville Railway v. Commissioner, 42 T.C. 834 (1964), aff'd per curiam, 358 F.2d 294 (5th Cir.1966), and Albany Car Wheel Co. v. Commissioner, 40 T.C. 831 (1963), aff'd per curiam, 333 F.2d 653 (2d Cir.1964). In each of these cases factors other than the nonrecourse nature of the debt created contingencies for payment. Redford v. Commissioner, 28 T.C. 773 (1957), reached the same result with respect to recourse indebtedness.

When a contingent obligation related to the acquisition of property is satisfied, however, the amount of the satisfied debt is added to the property's basis. If the property is depreciable, the taxpayer may depreciate the increased basis over the remaining cost-recovery period. See Meredith Corp. v. Commissioner, 102 T.C. 406 (1994). If the property's cost-recovery period has expired prior to payment of the contingent obligation, an ordinary loss deduction is allowable. See Meredith Corp. v. Commissioner, 108 T.C. 89 (1997).

3.   FORECLOSURE   OR   ABANDONMENT   OF   ENCUMBERED PROPERTY

3.1. *Nonrecourse Debt*

One of the consequences of including nonrecourse debt in amount realized is the creation of "phantom" gain on the disposition of property securing a debt that is in excess of basis, even when there is no consideration other than release of debt. In Parker v. Delaney, 186 F.2d 455 (1st Cir.1950), the taxpayer acquired mortgaged properties from a bank in exchange for nonrecourse obligations to finance the acquisition. The taxpayer operated the properties as an owner collecting rents and claiming depreciation deductions on an adjusted basis that included the nonrecourse liabilities. When the taxpayer defaulted on the debt, the bank recovered the properties. The taxpayer claimed that the amount of the mortgages was not part of amount realized on disposition of the properties under § 1001, and attempted to distinguish Crane v. Commissioner on the grounds that unlike the situation in *Crane,* the taxpayer's disposition was to the lender in foreclosure rather than a sale to a third party and the taxpayer received no consideration for the transfer. The court disagreed:

> If the amount of the unassumed mortgage in the Crane case was properly included in the amount realized on the sale, the amounts of the unassumed mortgages should be held to have been realized on the disposition in this case. In both, such amounts had been considered in determining the unadjusted basis. * * * Depreciation had been computed and deducted on such amounts; and their relationship under [§ 1011] to the question of gain under [§ 1001] requires that account be taken of such value or cost in determining

the realization on disposition. Furthermore, the property in the hands of appellant was relieved at the time of disposition of the mortgage liens and obligations. So far as appellant was concerned as owner these were paid even though he was not personally liable for them.

Under *Parker*, when property is subject to a nonrecourse liability, the tax results on the disposition of the property are the same regardless of whether the property is transferred to a third party, as in *Tufts*, or is transferred to the mortgagee through a foreclosure. Thus, in Freeland v. Commissioner, 74 T.C. 970 (1980), the taxpayer purchased property for $9,000 plus a $41,000 nonrecourse mortgage. The property declined in value and was subsequently reconveyed to the seller. The taxpayer realized a capital loss measured by the difference between the original purchase price and the outstanding balance of the mortgage at the time the property was transferred. See also Middleton v. Commissioner, 77 T.C. 310 (1981), aff'd per curiam, 693 F.2d 124 (11th Cir.1982) (abandonment of property subject to a nonrecourse obligation treated as a sale for the amount of the nonrecourse mortgage; a capital loss resulted because the basis in the property was greater than the obligation).

In Yarbro v. Commissioner, 737 F.2d 479 (5th Cir.1984), the taxpayer refused to transfer property to the nonrecourse lender in a foreclosure and abandoned the property to claim that there was no "sale or exchange" of the property. (Sale or exchange treatment is important with respect to limitations on the deduction of losses from the sale or exchange of a capital asset, discussed in Chapter 24, Section 1.3.). The court held:

> Although *Crane* and *Tufts* concerned the *amount* of the gain or loss and not the *character* of the gain or loss, their rationales support the Commissioner's position in the instant case to the extent that the concept of "amount realized" for computing gain or loss may be equated with the concept of consideration for "sale or exchange" purposes.

The court thus concluded that abandonment of property subject to a nonrecourse debt is the equivalent of a sale or exchange of the property for release from the debt. See also Helvering v. Hammel, 311 U.S. 504 (1941) (involuntary foreclosure); Allan v. Commissioner, 856 F.2d 1169 (8th Cir.1988) (accrued and deducted, but unpaid, interest and property taxes which were added to the outstanding principal of the mortgage were included in amount realized on foreclosure). Under § 1234A (see Chapter 24, Section 3), gain or loss attributable to any termination of an interest in property that is a capital asset is now treated as gain or loss from the sale or exchange of a capital asset.

3.2. *Recourse Debt*

The preceding discussion indicates that including the full amount of indebtedness in amount realized on disposition consistently accounts for gains on disposition, post-acquisition indebtedness, and basis reductions attributable to capital recovery of borrowed funds. The majority in *Tufts* based its opinion in part on the ground that the result is consistent with the treatment of recourse liabilities. However, the computation of amount realized in the case of recourse debt can differ where the fair market value of transferred property is less than the debt.

Treas. Reg. § 1.1001–2 provides that the amount realized on the disposition of property that secures a recourse liability does not include any amount treated as cancellation of indebtedness income. The regulations limit amount realized to the fair market value of the property on the transfer of property to the creditor in release of a recourse liability. The excess of the liability over fair market value is treated as cancellation of indebtedness income. See Treas. Reg. § 1.1001–2(c), Ex. (8). Thus, the transaction is bifurcated into two parts: a disposition of the property for a release of the liability to the extent of the fair market value of the property, and a discharge of indebtedness for the remainder of the indebtedness. But if property subject to a recourse mortgage in excess of the fair market value of the property is transferred to a third party who assumes the debt, the entire amount of the debt is treated as amount realized; there is no bifurcation to treat part of the debt as cancelled. Justice O'Connor's concurring opinion in *Tufts* suggests bifurcating the disposition of property subject to a nonrecourse debt. The problem with bifurcating the transaction where the property is transferred to a third party subject to the debt or with an assumption of the debt is that no part of the debt has been cancelled. The creditor still expects the full amount to be repaid and in the case of recourse debt, the creditor can usually realize that expectation.

Distinguishing between property gain and discharge of indebtedness income may be significant because property gain can qualify for capital gain treatment if the asset is a capital asset in the hands of the taxpayer, while cancellation of indebtedness is ordinary income, possibly subject to exclusion under § 108. See Chapter 10.

Whether the disparity in treatment of recourse and nonrecourse debt on transfer of property to the lender in satisfaction of the debt is justified depends in part on how one views the nature of the nonrecourse obligation. The debtor and lender have in effect agreed that the debtor always can fully satisfy the nonrecourse debt by transferring the property to the lender. Obtaining a nonrecourse loan thus can be seen as economically equivalent to an option to sell the property to the lender for the face amount of the loan (a "put" option). Under this view, the entire gain or loss relates to the property disposition. There is, in contrast to the recourse situation, no independent personal liability on the debt to be "canceled" if the value of the property should be less than the face amount of the obligation and cancellation of indebtedness notions do not come into play. On the other hand, the recourse and nonrecourse situations have in common that the taxpayer initially received tax-free cash or valuable property for a note, which subsequent events indicate will not be repaid by the taxpayer. The concept of tax-free receipt of borrowed proceeds is also central to cancellation of indebtedness income. This concept suggests that nonrecourse debt and recourse debt should be treated the same in all dispositions.

SECTION 2.   TAX SHELTERS

The holding of Crane v. Commissioner (see Section 1 of this Chapter), as expanded by Mayerson v. Commissioner (id.) allowing an investor to include nonrecourse debt in basis, was the backbone of the tax shelter phenomenon that began in the 1950s and that reached its zenith between the late 1960s and early 1980s. Tax shelter investments provided a significant portion of the investor's return in the form of tax benefits that not only offset any tax liability that might arise from the investment but also "sheltered" other income, usually from the investor's regular business or professional activities. Investors purchased interests in tax shelter investments, usually in the form of an interest in a limited partnership, and received positive after-tax returns on the purchase price (due to the economic value of the tax attributes) even though the investment was not profitable before taxes.

Virtually all of these tax shelters had three common elements: deferral, conversion, and leverage. Deferral is obtained by accelerating deductions; that is, claiming deductions in excess of economic costs in the early years of an investment, while concentrating income in the later years. These accelerated deductions resulted in taxable income being less than economic income in the years the deductions were claimed. In later years, the investment produces taxable income in excess of economic income.[6] The earlier deductions are offset, but in the interim the taxpayer received what was in effect an interest-free loan from the government equal to the amount of the taxes on the deferred income.

The second element of many tax shelters was conversion of ordinary income to capital gains. Conversion was achieved when the taxpayer claimed a deduction against ordinary income but the income that later offset the deduction was taxed at a lower rate, usually due to the capital gains preference.[7] In some cases, Congress eliminated or limited conversion by "recapture" rules such as § 1245, by requiring a portion of the later income realized on a sale of the investment to be recharacterized as ordinary income. Despite these efforts, the recapture rules were never comprehensive enough to eliminate the advantages of conversion.

Leverage, the use of borrowed money to purchase the tax shelter investment, magnified the effect of the first two elements of the tax shelter, while at the same time providing the normal economic benefit of financial leverage. Whenever an investor uses borrowed money to finance an investment that has a yield rate greater than the interest rate on the loan, the investor receives a before-tax rate of return from invested

---

[6]   This excess income could result from receipts no longer being offset by accelerated depreciation deductions even though the property was still subject to economic depreciation or, in many cases, by the recognition of gain on the disposition of the property, as in *Tufts* (see Section 1 of this Chapter).

[7]   The rate arbitrage (i.e., claiming a deduction at high marginal rates and including income at low marginal rates) that occurs when a taxpayer is in a lower tax bracket at the time the investment generates future income can also be considered a form of conversion.

equity greater than would have been received if the entire investment had been equity financed. In addition, because taxpayers are allowed deductions for expenditures paid with borrowed funds, the tax shelter benefits of the investment are magnified.

Tax shelters were based in part upon Internal Revenue Code provisions, such as accelerated depreciation and expensing of capital investment, that do not accurately measure economic income. In many cases the inaccuracies are the conscious result of Congressional attempts to provide incentives for investment, such as MACRS depreciation (see Chapter 14, Section 1.A.). Tax shelters thus highlight the problems of using the tax system to raise revenues to finance the costs of government while also providing subsidies to encourage certain kinds of behavior, activities, and industries.

DETAILED ANALYSIS

1.   DEFERRAL

The value of deferral is not as obvious as the value of outright tax-exemption. After all, the taxpayer still owes a future tax payment. Even so, the following example illustrates the significant value of deferral.

Suppose A is in the 35 percent marginal tax bracket and incurs expenses of $1,000 to drill an oil well. The well is expected to and does produce $200 a year of income net of current operating expenses (other than cost recovery) for each of the next ten years before going dry. Normally, § 263(a) would require the cost of the well to be capitalized and recovered at the rate of $100 a year. Each year A would receive $200 includable in gross income, but A would also receive an offsetting $100 deduction. Thus, A would pay taxes of $35.00, leaving A with $165.00 of net cash each year. The before-tax internal rate of return[8] is 15.1 percent and the after-tax internal rate of return is 10.3 percent.[9]

In fact, to encourage drilling of oil wells, § 263(c) permits current expensing of most of the costs. Thus, A is permitted to deduct the entire cost of the well in the year the capital expense is incurred. A deduction of $1,000 reduces A's tax liability in that year by $350. One may thus view A's net investment in the well as $650. It is as if A received $350 from the Treasury that A used, along with $650 of A's own money, to drill the well. The $200 of cash profits received annually is subject to $70.00 of tax. The annual after-tax return of $130.00 on A's $650 equity investment represents an internal rate of return of 15.1 percent, which is the same as the before-tax internal rate of return to A. Immediate expensing of the investment through the tax expenditure provision, which might at first seem to provide simply the benefit of deferral, is in fact the equivalent of a tax exemption for the yield.

---

[8]   Internal rate of return analysis is explained in connection with depreciation deductions in Chapter 14, Section 1.C.

[9]   Although one might expect that the after-tax rate of return would be 9.815 percent, exactly 65 percent of the pre-tax rate of return of 15.1 percent, the after-tax rate of return is slightly higher because on the facts even straight-line cost recovery is slightly accelerated relative to economic depreciation.

Admittedly, to obtain the benefit of the immediate expensing of the drilling expense, A must have income from other sources or activities that the deduction offsets in calculating taxable income. During the heyday of individual tax shelters, however, high-income professionals had plenty of income at hand to invest in shelter transactions to offset their salary and other compensation in ways that reduced and even eliminated their tax liability.

Additional examples of the tax benefit of deferral are contained in the discussion of depreciation (see Chapter 14, Section 1.C.), which illustrates the higher rates of return and lower effective rates of tax that result from accelerating capital cost recovery.

2.   LEVERAGE

The advantage of leveraged investment also can be demonstrated by examining the internal rate of return produced by the investment. Reconsider the example at the beginning of Section 1.C. in Chapter 14.

A purchases a machine for $10,000 in cash that will produce $1,500 of income (net of operating expenses) each year for ten years. At the end of the tenth year, A will sell the machine for its $1,000 salvage value. The before-tax internal rate of return for this investment is 9.106 percent. If A were to borrow 80 percent of the cost of the machine, giving a note with nine percent interest requiring annual payments of principal and interest of $1,247, A's return on the investment would be even greater. A's initial cash outlay is reduced to $2,000. Each year, the $1,500 of income from the machine is reduced by principal and interest payments on the note leaving A with an annual before-tax cash flow of $253 in years one through nine, and $1,253 in year ten. A's before-tax internal rate of return is increased to 9.43 percent. The impact on A's after-tax rate of return is more dramatic. Using MACRS depreciation, A's after-tax internal rate of return on the cash purchase of the machine is 6.872 percent (see Table 2 in Chapter 14, Section 1.C.).[10] If A were to finance $8,000 of the purchase price of the machine at 9 percent interest compounded annually, A's return from the investment would be as follows:

---

[10]   As we saw in the earlier discussion of this example, the increased rate of return over the rate that would reflect taxation of income from the machine at the full effective rate of tax is a result of the benefit of deferral.

Debt Financed Acquisition, MACRS Depreciation
Seven Year Recovery Period[1]

Year End	Gross Income	Loan Payments	Interest Payments	Capital Recovery[2]	Remaining Basis	Taxable Income[3]	After Tax Return
0	($2,000)						($2,000)
1	$1,500	$1,247	$720	$1,429	$8,571	($649)	$480
2	$1,500	$1,247	$673	$2,449	$6,122	($1,622)	$821
3	$1,500	$1,247	$621	$1,749	$4,373	($870)	$558
4	$1,500	$1,247	$565	$1,249	$3,124	($314)	$363
5	$1,500	$1,247	$503	$893[4]	$2,231	$104	$217
6	$1,500	$1,247	$436	$892	$1,339	$172	$193
7	$1,500	$1,247	$363	$893	$446	$244	$168
8	$1,500	$1,247	$284	$446	$0	$770	($17)
9	$1,500	$1,247	$197		$0	$1,303	($203)
10	$2,500	$1,247	$103		$0	$2,397[5]	$414
	$16,000			$10,000		$6,000	$3,193

Notes to Table

1. All figures are rounded to the nearest dollar.
2. The depreciation rate is 28.57% (1/7 × 2).
3. Net Cash Flow less taxes of 35% of taxable income.
4. Depreciation shifts to straight line in year 5.
5. Includes $1,000 of gain on disposition of the machine.

The after-tax internal rate of return on the leveraged investment increases to 13.12 percent—191 percent more than the after-tax internal rate of return available from a wholly cash investment (6.87 percent). More importantly, the combination of deferral and leverage results in an after-tax rate of return to this investment that is 144 percent of the before-tax rate of return on a wholly cash investment (13.12%/9.106%). The effective tax rate on the leveraged investment is a negative 44 percent (1 − (13.12%/9.106%)). Thus, not only is the income from the investment tax exempt, but the government pays the taxpayer a 44 percent subsidy to make the investment.

The after-tax benefit of leveraged depreciation is further enhanced by the first-year "bonus depreciation" of 50 percent under § 168(k) (in effect from 2008 and extended through 2019). Recomputing the internal rate of return on the same investment with a first-year capital recovery of $5,000 and reduced MACRS recovery on the smaller remaining basis produces an after-tax internal rate of return of 21.51 percent, which results in an effective tax rate on the leveraged investment of 55.46 percent (1 − (21.51%/9.106%)).

It is clear that the rule allowing capital recovery using an adjusted basis that includes the full amount of nonrecourse debt incurred to acquire property greatly enhances the incentives provided by the capital recovery scheme and demands that capital investment be leveraged as much as possible. The facts of Commissioner v. Tufts (see Section 1 of this Chapter) illustrate the benefit of deferral magnified by leverage, even over a short period of time. The taxpayers invested $44,212 to acquire rental real estate with a basis of almost $1.9 million. The investment produced tax deductions in 1970 and 1971 totaling $440,000. Assuming, not unreasonably for the time, that the taxpayers were in a 50-percent marginal income bracket (the top rate was 70 percent), the deductions saved $220,000 of taxes over the two-year period, an annual return of approximately 225 percent. Even after the taxpayers paid tax on the approximately $396,000 gain realized on disposition of the property in the 1972 taxable year, the *Tufts* investors would have recovered an economic benefit in excess of their original investment attributable to time value of their deferred tax liability. Assuming the investors remained in a 50-percent tax bracket, their collective 1972 tax liability on the gains at ordinary rates would have been $198,000. In the meantime, the investors would have had the use of the of tax savings between the due dates of their 1970 and 1972 tax returns. If the *Tufts* taxpayers collectively deducted $220,000 in each of the two years of the investment, two-years' interest at 10 percent on the $110,000 of tax savings from the first year, $22,000, plus a year's interest on $110,000 saved in the second year, $11,000, plus the additional tax savings caused by the loss of the initial $44,000 investment, $22,000, (which is 50% of the difference between deductions of $440,000 and taxable gain of $396,000), minus the initial investment, $44,200, provides a net return on the investment of approximately $12,800. This represents an after-tax internal rate of return on the cash investment of approximately 10.6 percent. This return is attributable only to the investors' ability to defer taxes that resulted from deductions in 1970 and 1971 that were returned as income in 1972. The value of the deferral increases as the span of time grows between when the taxpayer claims the deductions and disposes of the investment.

While the benefits of leveraged tax shelters are no longer available to the passive investor (see Chapter 35, Section 2), the governmental subsidy for leveraged investment in equipment and machinery is still available to the business taxpayer and corporations. The tax benefits are reduced for some taxpayers due to the alternative minimum tax, which allows capital recovery but at a less accelerated rate (see Chapter 39).

3.   CONVERSION

Conversion of ordinary income into capital gain occurs when the costs of producing capital gain are allowed as deductions against ordinary income on a dollar-for-dollar basis while subsequent gain reflecting those deductions qualifies for preferential capital gain treatment. If gains attributable to depreciation are accorded a preferential tax rate as capital gains, the addition of conversion to the mix of deferral and leverage greatly magnifies the tax benefits of an investment.

Assume, for instance, that in the above example involving the machine the taxpayer's $1,000 gain on the sale of the machine were taxed at 15 percent instead of at 35 percent. The investor's taxes in year 10 would be only $639 ([35% × ($1,500—$103)] + [15% × $1,000]) versus $839. The investor's after-tax cash flow in year 10 would increase to $614 versus $414. The after-tax internal rate of return to the cash investment would increase to 14.16 percent versus 13.12 percent—an increase of 7.95 percent over the after-tax rate of return on the leveraged investment if the gains attributable to depreciation are taxed as ordinary income.

A number of provisions preclude capital gain treatment to the extent various deductions have been claimed. For example, upon the sale of most depreciable personal property, § 1245 (see Chapter 25, Section 1) requires that gain is ordinary income to the extent of the prior depreciation. Real estate is subject to a more lenient rule, however, and benefits from conversion. Under § 1(h), gain on the sale of real estate attributable to prior depreciation remains eligible for a capital gains preference, although such gains are denied the most preferential rates (see Chapter 25, Section 1). Section 1250, a real estate depreciation analog of § 1245, does not apply to recapture as ordinary income depreciation claimed under the straight line method, and instead treats all real estate as depreciable only under the straight-line method.

4. ADMINISTRATIVE AND JUDICIAL RESPONSES TO TAX SHELTERS

One or more of the basic elements of a tax shelter were deployed by tax-shelter promoters in a wide variety of activities, including: real estate, oil and gas drilling, movies, equipment leasing, master recordings, films and video productions, animal breeding and feeding, mining operations, farm crops, vineyards, and many more. Initially, the IRS attacked these tax shelter operations by using one or more statutory or judicially developed approaches. In some cases, the courts would apply § 183 (see Chapter 18, Section 1) to deny deductions, even though that section had been enacted to distinguish personal from profit-seeking activities. In the tax shelter cases, some courts substituted "tax motive" for "personal" in applying § 183. Compare e.g., Karr v. Commissioner, 924 F.2d 1018 (11th Cir.1991) and Smith v. Commissioner, 937 F.2d 1089 (6th Cir.1991). In other cases, the courts disallowed deductions associated with tax shelter investments on the basis that the transactions were "shams" or "lacked economic substance." See e.g., Rose v. Commissioner, 868 F.2d 851 (6th Cir.1989). In still other cases, the courts would allow deductions for any actual cash investment but would disallow those related to noneconomical debt. See e.g., Brannen v. Commissioner, 722 F.2d 695 (11th Cir.1984). Meanwhile, some courts added the element of over-valuation, discussed in the next section, to disallow tax shelter deductions. See e.g., Elliott v. Commissioner, 84 T.C. 227 (1985), aff'd by order, 782 F.2d 1027 (3d Cir.1986).

While the IRS had a number of weapons at its disposal, the possibility of litigation in any given case was unpredictable, and taxpayers ended up prevailing in a significant number of tax shelter cases. See, e.g., Smith v. Commissioner, 937 F.2d 1089 (6th Cir.1991). The expansion of the tax shelter industry led to a series of statutory responses between 1976 and 1986 (discussed in Chapter 38).

SECTION 3. THE VALUATION OF PROPERTY SUBJECT TO DEBT

The investor who purchases property with nonrecourse purchase money debt is not concerned with whether the debt-financed purchase price bears any relation to the value of the acquired property. In fact, the investor is primarily interested in maximizing leverage to create high basis that supports accelerated capital recovery and other deductions. The seller may receive enough cash at closing to satisfy the seller's minimum sale price; anything the seller receives in excess of that amount is a bonus. Furthermore, under the installment sales rules of § 453 (see Chapter 31, Section 2), the seller is not required to report any gain attributable to the receipt of the nonrecourse promissory note until payment is received. Thus, it can be in the interest of both the investor and the seller to inflate the purchase price of property financed with nonrecourse debt. The Commissioner's first line of defense was to challenge the purchase price and the amount of liability claimed as cost basis under the *Crane* doctrine.

Estate of Franklin v. Commissioner

United States Court of Appeals, Ninth Circuit, 1976.
544 F.2d 1045.

■ SNEED, CIRCUIT JUDGE: [Ed.: The taxpayers were limited partners in a partnership ("Associates") that purchased a motel for $1,224,000, giving a nonrecourse note to the sellers ("Romneys") for the full purchase price. Under the partnership rules, the taxpayers were entitled to include their share of the partnership's debt in the basis of their partnership interests. The partnership losses "passed through" the partnership to the taxpayer partners. The partnership prepaid $75,000 of interest and was otherwise obligated to make monthly payments of principal and interest of approximately $9,000 with a balloon payment, forecast to be $975,000, at the end of ten years. The motel was leased back to the Romneys for annual rental in an amount equal to the partnership's obligation to pay principal and interest on the note. Thus, unless the principal payments on the note provided the partnership with an equity interest in the motel property, the taxpayer partners received for their investment only depreciation deductions and a deduction for prepaid interest. In addition, Associates acquired the property subject to the Romneys' pre-existing mortgages for which the Romneys, but not Associates, remained personally liable. Under the terms of the leaseback, the Romneys were entitled to further encumber the property for the purpose of making improvements. The transaction permitted the partnership to abandon the property at any time without risk of losing more than the $75,000 prepaid interest. Quitclaim deeds from the partnership were deposited in escrow to facilitate foreclosure by the sellers. The partnership claimed depreciation deductions based on including the nonrecourse note in its basis for the property.]

In holding that the transaction between Associates and the Romneys more nearly resembled an option than a sale, the Tax Court emphasized that Associates had the power at the end of ten years to walk away from the transaction and merely lose its $75,000 "prepaid interest payment." It also pointed out that a *deed* was never recorded and that the "benefits and burdens of ownership" appeared to remain with the Romneys. Thus, the sale was combined with a leaseback in which no cash would pass; the Romneys remained responsible under the mortgages, which they could increase; and the Romneys could make capital improvements.[2] The Tax Court further justified its option characterization by reference to the nonrecourse nature of the purchase money debt and the nice balance between the rental and purchase money payments. [64 T.C. 752 (1975)]

Our emphasis is different from that of the Tax Court. We believe the characteristics set out above can exist in a situation in which the sale imposes upon the purchaser a genuine indebtedness within the meaning of section 167(a), Internal Revenue Code of 1954, which will support both interest and depreciation deductions. They substantially so existed in Hudspeth v. Commissioner, 509 F.2d 1224 (9th Cir.1975) in which parents entered into sale-leaseback transactions with their children. The children paid for the property by executing nonnegotiable notes and mortgages equal to the fair market value of the property; state law proscribed deficiency judgments in case of default, limiting the parents' remedy to foreclosure of the property. The children had no funds with which to make mortgage payments; instead, the payments were offset in part by the rental payments, with the difference met by gifts from the parents to their children. Despite these characteristics this court held that there was a bona fide indebtedness on which the children, to the extent of the rental payments, could base interest deductions. * * *

In none of these cases, however, did the taxpayer fail to demonstrate that the purchase price was at least approximately equivalent to the fair market value of the property. Just such a failure occurred here. The Tax Court explicitly found that on the basis of the facts before it the value of the property could not be estimated. 64 T.C. at 767–768.[4] In our view this defect in the taxpayers' proof is fatal.

Reason supports our perception. An acquisition * * * at a price approximately equal to the fair market value of the property under ordinary circumstances would rather quickly yield an equity in the property which the purchaser could not prudently abandon. This is the stuff of substance. It meshes with the form of the transaction and constitutes a sale.

---

[2]   There was evidence that not all of the benefits and burdens of ownership remained with the Romneys. Thus, for example, the leaseback agreement appears to provide that any condemnation award will go to Associates. * * *

[4]   The Tax Court found that appellants had "not shown that the purported sales price of $1,224,000 (or any other price) had any relationship to the actual market value of the motel property. * * *"

Petitioners spent a substantial amount of time at trial attempting to establish that, whatever the actual market value of the property, Associates acted in the good faith belief that the market value of the property approximated the selling price. However, this evidence only goes to the issue of sham and does not supply substance to this transaction. "Save in those instances where the statute itself turns on intent, a matter so real as taxation must depend on objective realities, not on the varying subjective beliefs of individual taxpayers." Lynch v. Commissioner, 273 F.2d 867, 872 (2d Cir.1959). * * *

No such meshing occurs when the purchase price exceeds a demonstrably reasonable estimate of the fair market value. Payments on the principal of the purchase price yield no equity so long as the unpaid balance of the purchase price exceeds the then existing fair market value. Under these circumstances the purchaser by abandoning the transaction can lose no more than a mere chance to acquire an equity in the future should the value of the acquired property increase. While this chance undoubtedly influenced the Tax Court's determination that the transaction before us constitutes an option, we need only point out that its existence fails to supply the substance necessary to justify treating the transaction as a sale *ab initio*. It is not necessary to the disposition of this case to decide the tax consequences of a transaction such as that before us if in a subsequent year the fair market value of the property increases to an extent that permits the purchaser to acquire an equity.[5]

Authority also supports our perception. It is fundamental that "depreciation is not predicated upon ownership of property *but rather upon an investment in property*. Gladding Dry Goods Co., 2 BTA 336 (1925)." Mayerson, supra at 350 (italics added). No such investment exists when payments of the purchase price in accordance with the design of the parties yield no equity to the purchaser. * * * In the transaction before us and during the taxable years in question the purchase price payments by Associates have not been shown to constitute an *investment in the property*. Depreciation was properly disallowed. Only the Romneys had an investment in the property.

Authority also supports disallowance of the interest deductions. This is said even though it has long been recognized that the absence of personal liability for the purchase money debt secured by a mortgage on the acquired property does not deprive the debt of its character as a bona fide debt obligation able to support an interest deduction. *Mayerson,* supra at 352. However, this is no longer true when it appears that the debt has economic significance only if the property substantially appreciates in value prior to the date at which a very large portion of the purchase price is to be discharged. Under these circumstances the purchaser has not secured "the use or forbearance of money." See Norton v. Commissioner, 474 F.2d 608, 610 (9th Cir.1973). Nor has the seller advanced money or forborne its use. * * * Prior to the date at which the balloon payment on the purchase price is required, and assuming no substantial increase in the fair market value of the property, the absence of personal liability on the debt reduces the transaction in economic terms to a mere chance that a genuine debt obligation may arise. This is not enough to justify an interest deduction. To justify the deduction the debt must exist; potential existence will not do. For debt to exist, the purchaser, in the absence of personal liability, must confront a situation in which it is presently reasonable from an economic point of view for him

---

[5]   These consequences would include a determination of the proper basis of the acquired property at the date the increments to the purchaser's equity commenced.

to make a capital investment in the amount of the unpaid purchase price. * * * Associates, during the taxable years in question, confronted no such situation. Compare Crane v. Commissioner, 331 U.S. 1, 11–12 (1947).

Our focus on the relationship of the fair market value of the property to the unpaid purchase price should not be read as premised upon the belief that a sale is not a sale if the purchaser pays too much. Bad bargains from the buyer's point of view—as well as sensible bargains from buyer's, but exceptionally good from the seller's point of view—do not thereby cease to be sales. * * * We intend our holding and explanation thereof to be understood as limited to transactions substantially similar to that now before us.

DETAILED ANALYSIS

1.   APPROACHES TO OVERVALUATION SITUATIONS

In Rev. Rul. 69–77, 1969–1 C.B. 59, the IRS indicated it would recognize nonrecourse debt as part of basis only if property were acquired at its fair market value in an arm's-length transaction creating bona fide debt. Restricting the amount of debt to the value of the property given as security provides assurance that the amount claimed as cost for the property reflects an amount of indebtedness that the taxpayer intends to repay to the lender. Thus, quoting from Crane v. Commissioner, the IRS stated that its position was based on " 'the reality that an owner of property, mortgaged at a figure less than that at which property will sell, must and will treat the conditions of the mortgage exactly as if they were his personal obligations.' If the value of the property is less than the amount of the note, however, the owner will not have this economic incentive to treat the obligation as if it were a personal obligation." In Rev. Rul. 77–110, 1977–1 C.B. 58, and Rev. Rul. 78–29, 1978–1 C.B. 62, the IRS ruled that no part of a liability created by a nonrecourse note given as part of the purchase price of depreciable property, the value of which could not be shown to at least approximate the amount of the note, could be included in the property's basis for depreciation purposes (and that no deduction was allowable for interest paid or accrued on the note.)

At the same time, there is no requirement that the taxpayer have any equity in the property at the outset. Bolger v. Commissioner, 59 T.C. 760 (1973) (Acq.), allowed depreciation deductions on the adjusted basis of rental property acquired in full for a nonrecourse note and leased back to the seller. The court in Bolger found that payments of principal on the note from rental income returned to the seller created an equity interest in the property. That finding was supported in part by the court's conclusion that the amounts of the mortgages involved were at least equal to the fair market value of the acquired properties. The court held that the taxpayers' increased equity interest resulting from mortgage payments created a potential benefit in the form of gain on sale or refinancing potential that the taxpayer would seek to protect by paying the mortgage. Also recall that in Crane v. Commissioner itself, the taxpayer had no equity interest in the property at any time.

The courts have taken varied approaches to dealing with the inclusion in basis of nonrecourse debt in excess of the property's value. One approach, applied in *Estate of Franklin*, is similar to the IRS's approach in Rev. Rul. 77–110 and Rev. Rul. 78–29—if the value of the property cannot be shown to approach the amount of the debt, no part of the debt is included in basis. Other cases reached similar conclusions. See e.g., Lukens v. Commissioner, 945 F.2d 92 (5th Cir.1991); Brountas v. Commissioner, 692 F.2d 152 (1st Cir.1982); Segal v. Commissioner, 41 F.3d 1144 (7th Cir.1994). Other courts have followed a different approach. In Pleasant Summit Land Corp. v. Commissioner, 863 F.2d 263 (3d Cir.1988), the court was not willing to disregard completely nonrecourse indebtedness and eliminate all interest and capital cost recovery deductions. The court recognized the nonrecourse debt, but only to the extent of the fair market value of property securing the liability:

> While we realize that a taxpayer holding property subject to a nonrecourse debt in excess of the market value of the property may have no incentive to pay off any portion of the debt, including the amount not exceeding the fair market value of the property, it is equally logical to recognize that the creditor holding the debt has no incentive to take back the property if the taxpayer offers to pay the debt up to the value of the property. For example, if a creditor held a nonrecourse debt for $1,500,000 on a property with a fair market value of $1,000,000, he would have a disincentive to foreclose if his defaulting debtor offered to settle the debt for not less than $1,000,000. Thus, it is appropriate to disregard only the portion of nonrecourse debt in excess of the fair market value of the property when it was acquired for purposes of calculations of the depreciation and interest deductions and to regard the nonrecourse debt as genuine indebtedness to the extent that it is not disregarded.

The court added in a supplemental opinion that recognition of nonrecourse debt up to the fair market value of encumbered property related only to the debt at the time of acquisition. 863 F.2d at 278. Thus, capital recovery and interest deductions are not to be adjusted to reflect appreciation (or depreciation) in the property's fair market value.

2. THE PURCHASER'S BASIS IN *TUFTS*

The purchaser of the property in *Tufts* received property worth $1,400,000 subject to a $1,800,000 liability, presumably in the hope that the property would subsequently increase in value. How should his basis in the property be calculated? While *Tufts* held that the value of the property is irrelevant to the treatment of the nonrecourse liability in amount realized, this result was reached to reflect the fact that the taxpayer had originally included the nonrecourse liability in his basis. It is not appropriate to disregard value to give the purchaser a basis of $1,800,000 where the property was worth substantially less than that. See Brannen v. Commissioner, 722 F.2d 695, 708 n. 4 (11th Cir.1984). If the approach in *Pleasant Summit Land Corp.* were followed, the correct result would seem to be to allow the purchaser to include the nonrecourse liability in basis to the extent of the value of the property at the time of the transfer. If the purchaser were to subsequently default on the mortgage and the property was taken over by the mortgagee, since only a portion of the nonrecourse obligation would have been included in basis, the purchaser should be required to include only $1,400,000 in amount realized. This possibility is recognized in Treas. Reg. § 1.1001–2(a)(3), which excepts from the general rule that liabilities are to be included in the amount realized those liabilities incurred by reason of the acquisition of property that are not taken into account in determining the transferor's basis for the property.

3.   ABSENCE OF AN OWNERSHIP INTEREST

The indebtedness in *Estate of Franklin* was disregarded under the theory that the taxpayer did not acquire ownership of the property for tax purposes. The over-valuation prevented the taxpayer from acquiring an equity interest in the property so that abandonment would be economically imprudent. This rationale was followed in Narver v. Commissioner, 75 T.C. 53 (1980), aff'd per curiam, 670 F.2d 855 (9th Cir.1982), in disallowing depreciation and interest deductions in connection with overvalued real estate.

The Tax Court in *Estate of Franklin* held that the partnership acquired only an option to purchase the property securing the nonrecourse debt. In essence the option to purchase could be exercised by electing to satisfy the nonrecourse obligation. The Tax Court emphasized the facts that the partnership could abandon the transaction at any time, that the lease payments from the sellers/lessees canceled payments of principal and interest, and that the partnership did not appear to possess any of the incidents of ownership. Although this approach to overvaluation cases was not accepted by the Court of Appeals in *Estate of Franklin,* it was applied in Houchins v. Commissioner, 79 T.C. 570 (1982), to disallow deductions for depreciation, interest, and maintenance fees in connection with the purported acquisition of breeding cattle. The option approach has the effect of not only disregarding the purported indebtedness but also of recharacterizing any purported "equity" as an option price. As a consequence, no deductions are available with respect to the "equity" investment until the transaction is terminated.

4.   PENALTIES IN OVERVALUATION CASES

Congress has adopted a penalty provision as one line of defense against abusive situations involving overvaluation. Section 6662(b)(3) imposes an addition to tax in the amount of 20 percent of any underpayment of tax attributable to a substantial valuation misstatement. The substantial valuation misstatement penalty is imposed if the value of any property (or its adjusted basis) claimed on a tax return is 150 percent or more of the true value of the property and the underpayment attributable to the valuation overstatement exceeds $5,000 ($10,000 in the case of corporations other than S corporations and personal holding companies). I.R.C. § 6662(e)(1) and (2). Congress also has enacted a penalty provision for undervaluations pertaining to valuation understatements in the context of the estate and gift tax. I.R.C. § 6662(b)(5).

5.   TAX EXPENDITURE ANALYSIS

Tax expenditure analysis offers another way to view the overvaluation cases. In providing accelerated depreciation deductions for investments in many types of assets, Congress decided that it was appropriate to grant interest-free loans to those who made the qualifying investments. In the overvaluation cases, taxpayers attempted to take out interest-free loans even though they did not make the investment required to generate the loan. Suppose that in *Estate of Franklin*, instead of what amounts to a tax loan program, the government had offered an interest-free loan to investors in real estate. Presumably, in addition to having to return the face value of the loan (with interest), the investors would have been subject to penalty for fraudulently claiming, receiving, and putting to use government funds. By comparison, while the taxpayer-investors in *Estate of Franklin* were denied their claimed deductions for depreciation and interest associated with their purported ownership of the motel, they were never subject to any penalty or sanction for what the court concluded was a "sham" transaction.

CHAPTER 35

STATUTORY LIMITATIONS ON LEVERAGED TAX SHELTERS

The administrative and judicial approaches to overvaluation cases (discussed in Chapter 34, Section 4) proved inadequate to curb the growing number of large-scale tax shelter offerings. Congress entered the anti-shelter effort with a statutory solution to the problems associated with nonrecourse debt. In 1976, lawmakers enacted § 465, limiting deductions in tax-favored investments to the amount that the taxpayer had "at risk" in the investment activity. Although not restricted to overvaluation situations, the primary effect of § 465 was to decrease abuses in such cases. Nevertheless, § 465 proved inadequate to the task of slowing down tax shelter transactions. It was not until 1986, when Congress enacted the passive-activity-loss limitation in § 469, that the government gained the upper hand in the battle against individual tax shelters. Section 469 focused on the degree of the taxpayer's active involvement in an activity, and applied to all activities whether debt financed or equity financed. While § 469 significantly reduced individual participation in tax shelters, leverage and deferral (discussed in Chapter 34) remain important elements in corporate tax planning.

SECTION 1. THE AT-RISK LIMITATION

INTERNAL REVENUE CODE: Section 465 (omitting (c)(4)–(7)).

Senate Finance Committee Report, Tax Reform Act of 1976

S.Rep. No. 94–938, 94th Cong., 2d Sess. 48–51 (1976).

To prevent a situation where the taxpayer may deduct a loss in excess of his economic investment in certain types of activities, [§ 465(a)] provides that the amount of any loss (otherwise allowable for the year under present law) which may be deducted in connection with one of these activities, cannot exceed the aggregate amount with respect to which the taxpayer is at risk in each such activity at the close of the taxable year. This "at risk" limitation applies to the following activities: (1) farming; (2) exploring for, or exploiting, oil and gas resources; (3) the holding, producing, or distributing of motion picture films or video tapes; and (4) equipment leasing. [Ed: § 465(c)(3) enacted in 1978 extends the at risk rules to all other business or investment activities except real estate. The 1986 Act extended the at risk rules to real estate with an exception for "qualified nonrecourse financing," which generally refers to nonrecourse loans from a person actively and regularly engaged in the business of lending money (other than the seller).] The limitation applies to all taxpayers * * * [other than widely held corporations].

The at risk limitation is to apply on the basis of the facts existing at the end of each taxable year.

In applying the at risk limitation, the amount of any loss which is allowable in a particular year reduces the taxpayer's risk investment (but not below zero) as of the end of that year and in all succeeding taxable years with respect to that activity. Thus, if a taxpayer has a loss in excess of his at risk amount, the loss disallowed will not be allowed in a subsequent year unless the taxpayer increases his at risk amount.

Losses which are suspended under this provision with respect to a taxpayer because they are greater than the taxpayer's investment which is "at risk" are to be treated as a deduction with respect to the activity in the following year. Consequently, if a taxpayer's amount at risk increases in later years, he will be able to obtain the benefit of previously suspended losses to the extent that such increases in his amount at risk exceed his losses in later years.

The at risk limitation also applies regardless of the method of accounting used by the taxpayer and regardless of the kind of deductible expenses which contributed to the loss.

The at risk limitation is only intended to limit the extent to which certain losses in connection with the covered activities may be deducted in the year claimed by the taxpayer. The rules of this provision do not apply for other purposes, such as the determination of basis. * * *

For purposes of this provision, a taxpayer is generally to be considered "at risk" with respect to an activity to the extent of his cash and the adjusted basis of other property contributed to the activity, as well as any amount borrowed for use in the activity with respect to which the taxpayer has personal liability for payment from his personal assets. (Also, as discussed further below, a taxpayer is at risk to the extent of his net fair market value of personal assets which secure nonrecourse borrowings.)

A taxpayer is not to be considered at risk with respect to the proceeds from his share of any nonrecourse loan used to finance the activity or the acquisition of property used in the activity. In addition, if the taxpayer borrows money to contribute to the activity and the lender's recourse is either the taxpayer's interest in the activity or property used in the activity, the amount of the proceeds of the borrowing are to be considered amounts financed on a nonrecourse basis and do not increase the taxpayer's amount at risk.

Also, under these rules, a taxpayer's capital is not "at risk" in the business, even as to the equity capital which he has contributed to the extent he is protected against economic loss of all or part of such capital by reason of an agreement or arrangement for compensation or reimbursement to him of any loss which he may suffer. Under this concept, an investor is not "at risk" if he arranges to receive insurance or other compensation for an economic loss after the loss is sustained, or if he is entitled to reimbursement for part or all of any loss by reason of a binding agreement between himself and another person.

* * *

A taxpayer's at risk amount is generally to include amounts borrowed for use in the activity which is secured by property other than property used in the activity. For example, if the taxpayer uses personally-owned real estate to secure nonrecourse indebtedness, the proceeds from which are used in an equipment leasing activity, the proceeds may be considered part of the taxpayer's at risk amount. In such a case, the portion of the proceeds which increases the taxpayer's at risk amount is to be limited by the fair market value of the property used as collateral (determined as of the date the property is pledged as security), less any prior (or superior) claims to which the collateral is subject.

[Section 465(b)(2)] contains a special rule which prevents a taxpayer [from] increasing * * * his at risk amount through collateral in cases where the collateral was financed directly or indirectly by indebtedness which is secured by any property used in the activity. The intent of this rule is to prevent a taxpayer from increasing his at risk amount by cross-collateralizing property used in the activity with other property not used in the activity.

The rules treating a taxpayer as being "at risk" with respect to the net value of pledged property also do not apply to nonrecourse loans if the lender has an interest, other than as a creditor, in the activity or if the lender is related [to a person (other than the taxpayer) who has an interest]*. * * *

The at risk limitation applies only to tax losses produced by expense deductions which are not disallowed by reason of some other provision of the code. For example, if a prepaid interest expense is suspended under the prepaid interest limitation [§ 461(g), see Chapter 16, Part 3.B.], that expense will not enter into the computation of the tax loss subject to the risk limitation. When the interest accrues and becomes deductible, the expense may at that time be deferred under [the at risk rules]. * * *

DETAILED ANALYSIS

1.   COVERED ACTIVITIES

Section 465 applies to any activity conducted as a business or for profit by individuals (including trusts and estates), whether as a proprietor, a partner, or as a shareholder in an S corporation. I.R.C. § 465(c). See Peters v. Commissioner, 77 T.C. 1158 (1981). Nonetheless, § 465 issues are generally encountered in the context of an interest in a partnership. Under §§ 752(b) and 721, a partner's basis in the partnership includes the partner's

---

*   [Ed.: The material in brackets reflects amendments to § 465 in the 1982 Act.]

share of partnership debt, including debt for which no partner is personally liable. Partnership losses are passed through the partnership to the partner who deducts the losses on the partner's individual tax return. The amount of losses that may be deducted by a partner is limited to the partner's basis in the partner's partnership interest. I.R.C. § 704(d). Section 465 applies to limit a partner's loss deductions from a covered activity to the extent that the partner is at risk for partnership liabilities.

The Tax Reform Act of 1986 applied § 465 for the first time to the activity of holding real estate. However, because so many real estate activities are financed through nonrecourse borrowing which meets the definition of "qualified nonrecourse financing" in § 465(b)(6), discussed below, most real estate investments were effectively exempted from the at-risk rules.

The at-risk rules apply separately to each activity conducted by the taxpayer. Section 465(c)(2) specifically provides that certain activities will be treated as separate, but most business activities are subject to the vague rules of § 465(c)(3)(B), which aggregate individual undertakings into a single activity. For example, suppose that a limited partnership operates a hotel and a shopping center located on the same tract of land. It is not clear whether the partnership is engaged in one activity or two activities. The Treasury Department has not promulgated regulations governing this issue. Compare Temp. Reg. § 1.465–1T (permitting partnerships and S corporations to aggregate, by type, activities described in § 465(c)(2)(A)(i) and (iii)–(v) during 1984); Ann. 87–26, 1987 I.R.B. 15, 39 (extending application of Temp. Reg. § 1.465–1T, to certain later taxable years).

2.   THE AT-RISK AMOUNT

2.1. *General*

Under § 465(b), the taxpayer is at risk in an activity for the amount of cash and the adjusted basis of any property contributed to the activity. In addition, the taxpayer is at risk for amounts borrowed for use in an activity to the extent that the taxpayer is personally liable for the indebtedness, and to the extent of the fair market value of property, other than property used in the activity, pledged by the taxpayer as security for the debt. Amounts borrowed from any person with an interest in the activity, or from a person related to a person with an interest in an activity, are not at risk. I.R.C. § 465(b)(3). Section 465(c)(3)(D) provides that, except as provided in the regulations, the § 465(b)(3) limitation applies only to amounts borrowed from an interested or related party for use in one of the activities listed in § 465(c)(1). I.R.C. § 468(c)(3)(D). Treas. Reg. §§ 1.465–8 and 1.465–20 extend the interested party and related party rules to all activities. See Waddell v. Commissioner, 86 T.C. 848 (1986), aff'd per curiam, 841 F.2d 264 (9th Cir.1988). Thus, if Partner A borrows $50,000 from Partner B, with full recourse, to invest with B in the ABC partnership, A is not at risk for the $50,000. Presumably, this result rests on the view that B is the one at risk. But if A has adequate resources to stand behind the liability, as long as the debtor-creditor relationship is not a sham, it is difficult to see how the situation presents the sheltering problem addressed by § 465.

A taxpayer is not at risk for nonrecourse borrowing, unless the debt is "qualified nonrecourse financing" as defined in § 465(b)(6). This term generally includes only nonrecourse borrowing related to the holding of real property, which is borrowed from an unrelated party who is regularly engaged in the lending business, other than the seller of the mortgaged property or the promoter of a partnership. The exception is based on the idea that an institutional lender will not accept over-inflated values for real estate that is given as security for a nonrecourse debt. Borrowing from related parties regularly engaged in the lending business qualifies only if the terms are commercially reasonable and on substantially the same terms as loans from unrelated persons. In addition, borrowing from or indebtedness guaranteed by the federal, state, or local government qualifies.

A taxpayer is not at risk with respect to nonrecourse partnership indebtedness. In the case of borrowing in connection with partnership investments, a partner's at-risk amount is increased by the partner's distributive share of partnership income and is decreased by distributions to the partner and by the partner's share of partnership deductions. See Prop. Reg. § 1.465–22 (1979); Lansburgh v. Commissioner, 92 T.C. 448 (1989). In the case of a partnership, the partner is subject to tax on the partner's share of partnership taxable income. Thus, undistributed partnership income represents an after-tax amount at risk in the activity.

A limited liability company (LLC) is generally treated as a partnership for tax purposes. Under most state LLC acts, a member of an LLC is not liable for the debts of the LLC. Thus, a member of an LLC is not at risk for any amount borrowed by the LLC with full recourse against the LLC unless the member guarantees the debt. Hubert Enterprises, Inc. v. Commissioner, 125 T.C. 72 (2005), vacated and remanded for consideration of other issues, 230 Fed.Appx. 526 (6th Cir. 2007).

2.2. *Devices to Limit the Impact of the At-Risk Rules*

Following the enactment of § 465, transactions were structured to probe the limits of the at-risk rules. For example, in Pritchett v. Commissioner, 827 F.2d 644 (9th Cir.1987), the taxpayers were limited partners in similar limited partnerships formed to conduct oil and gas operations. The partnerships executed fifteen year non-interest bearing recourse notes to finance drilling operations. The notes were payable out of net income available to the partnerships if the drilling operations proved successful. Only the general partners were personally liable for the notes. However, under the partnership agreement, if the notes were not paid off at maturity, each of the limited partners was personally obligated to make additional capital contributions to the partnership if called upon by the general partners to pay off the deficiency. A divided Tax Court, 85 T.C. 580 (1985), held that the limited partners were not at risk with respect to their obligation for future capital contributions because the potential liability was "merely a contingency." In the opinion of the majority, at the time the obligation was incurred, the partners did not know whether income from the drilling activity would be sufficient to satisfy the partnerships' debts or whether the general partners would exercise their discretion to call upon the limited partners' obligation at the end of the fifteen year term of the partnership notes. The Court of Appeals reversed, holding that under § 465(b)(2) a taxpayer is at risk for a debt if the taxpayer is ultimately responsible for repayment. The fact that the liability may flow through another, so that in the end the taxpayer is merely a guarantor of the debt, does not affect the ultimate responsibility of the taxpayer on the obligation. The court determined that the taxpayers' liabilities were not contingent, because if the venture failed to produce sufficient income to satisfy the fifteen-year partnership obligations, "economic reality" would dictate cash calls by the general partners, and the taxpayers' obligations to respond were mandatory. 827 F.2d 644 (9th Cir.1987).

In part, the appellate court in *Pritchett* based its holding on the Tax Court's decision in Melvin v. Commissioner, 88 T.C. 63 (1987), aff'd, 894 F.2d 1072 (9th Cir.1990). In *Melvin,* the taxpayer contributed a $70,000 recourse promissory note to a limited partnership to reflect his obligation to make future capital contributions to the partnership. The partnership borrowed $3,500,000 from an unrelated lender on a recourse basis, pledging partnership property, including the taxpayer's note, to secure the loan. The taxpayer stipulated that the mere contribution of the note did not increase his at-risk amount under § 465(b)(1), and the Tax Court approved the stipulation, noting that the contributed promissory note reflected neither a cash contribution nor a borrowing. Nonetheless, the Tax Court held that the taxpayer was at risk with respect to the $70,000 promissory note even though primary responsibility for repayment of the $3,500,000 recourse note fell to the partnership:

> The relevant question is who, if anyone, will ultimately be obligated to pay the partnership's recourse obligations if the partnership is unable to do so. It is not relevant that the partnership *may* be able to do so. The scenario that controls is the worst-case scenario, not the best case. Furthermore, the fact that the partnership or other partners remain in the "chain of liability" should not detract from the at-risk amount of the parties who do have the ultimate liability. The critical inquiry should be who is the obligor of last resort, and in determining who has the ultimate economic responsibility for the loan, the substance of the transaction controls.

The court also held that under substantive partnership law, each partner had a right to reimbursement from the other partners for any portion of the partnership debt satisfied from the partner's recourse promissory note in excess of the partner's individual share of partnership liabilities. This right of reimbursement protected the taxpayer from any loss in excess of the taxpayer's pro rata share of partnership debt, and thus constituted a stop-loss arrangement under § 465(b)(4). As a consequence, the taxpayer was at risk only to the extent that his personal liability on the bank loan exceeded his pro rata share (or $21,812) of the total partnership debt with respect to the bank loan.

The Ninth Circuit took the application of § 465(b)(4) a step further in American Principals Leasing Corp. v. United States, 904 F.2d 477 (9th Cir.1990). The taxpayers were limited partners in June Properties, a partnership engaged in computer equipment leasing. June Properties acquired an interest in computer equipment in a series of sale and leaseback transactions. Southwestern Bell Telephone Company originally acquired the equipment from IBM for approximately $2.6 million. Southwestern sold the equipment to an entity called Finalco for an amount equal to Southwestern's purchase price. Finalco borrowed the purchase price from a third party lender. Finalco leased the equipment back to Southwestern for a lease payment that was equivalent to Finalco's debt obligations. The indebtedness was secured by Finalco's lease to Southwestern. Finalco sold the equipment, subject to the lease and security agreement, to Softpro for $4.8 million consisting of $20,000 of cash and two recourse notes for the difference. Softpro sold the equipment to June Properties for $4.8 million consisting of $20,000 cash and recourse notes back to Softpro. June Properties leased the equipment to Finalco for rental payments equal to its payment obligation to Softpro. Thus, Finalco's lease payments to June Properties, June Properties' debt obligations on the Softpro note, and Softpro's debt payments to Finalco, were identical. In addition, no party had sufficient resources to make its payments without receiving the payments due it. The parties satisfied the three equal obligations each month by offsetting bookkeeping entries. No cash ever changed hands. The taxpayers were personally liable for $120,000 of June Properties recourse debt and claimed that this amount was at risk. Although the taxpayers were ultimately liable for their share of the partnership's recourse obligation, the court held that they were not at risk under § 465(b)(4):

> We believe that although the * * * analysis of whether a taxpayer would legally be responsible for his debt in a worst-case scenario is proper to determine whether under subsection 465(b)(2) a taxpayer is personally liable for amounts he has borrowed for use in an activity, Pritchett v. Commissioner, 827 F.2d 644, 647 (9th Cir.1987) (quoting Melvin v. Commissioner, 88 T.C. 63, 75 (1987), aff'd, 894 F.2d 1072 (9th Cir.1990)), such analysis is improper to determine whether the taxpayer has engaged in a loss-limiting arrangement prohibited by subsection 465(b)(4). * * * [S]ubsection 465(b)(4)'s use of the term "arrangement" rather than "agreement" indicates that a binding contract is not necessary for this subsection to be applicable. See Melvin at 1075–76, (holding that subsection 465(b)(4) countenances loss protection resulting from California's tort right of contribution among partners); id. at 1074–75 (noting that S.Rep. No. 938's list of examples of 465(b)(4) arrangements, which includes only binding contractual agreements, "does not constitute an exhaustive list of such arrangements"); Capek, 86 T.C. at 50–53.

> Rather, the purpose of subsection 465(b)(4) is to suspend at-risk treatment where a transaction is structured—by whatever method—to remove any realistic possibility that the taxpayer will suffer an economic loss if the transaction turns out to be unprofitable. See Melvin, at 1074. A theoretical possibility that the taxpayer will suffer economic loss is insufficient to avoid the applicability of this subsection. We must be guided by economic

reality. See id. at 1075; Pritchett, 827 F.2d at 647. If at some future date the unexpected occurs and the taxpayer does suffer a loss, or a realistic possibility develops that the taxpayer will suffer a loss, the taxpayer will at that time become at risk and be able to take the deductions for previous years that were suspended under this subsection. I.R.C. § 465(a)(2).

Young v. Commissioner, 926 F.2d 1083 (11th Cir.1991), reached a similar result. Investors in a sale and leaseback transaction with a circular flow of funds effected through bookkeeping entries gave an intermediary a partially recourse note. The investor-partners were not personally liable because the intermediary had purchased the leased equipment on a wholly nonrecourse basis, and "the stated recourse liabilities of the taxpayers were not realistically subject to collection after a discharge of the nonrecourse note." However, in Emershaw v. Commissioner, 949 F.2d 841 (6th Cir.1991), the court reached a contrary result on similar facts. The court in *Emershaw* held that a circular sale and leaseback was not in itself a loss limiting arrangement, because "[a] loss limiting arrangement within the meaning of 465(b)(4) is a *collateral agreement* protecting a taxpayer from loss *after the losses have occurred,* either by excusing him from his obligation to make good on losses or by compensating him for losses he has sustained" (849, emphasis in original). In Martuccio v. Commissioner, 30 F.3d 743 (6th Cir.1994), the Court of Appeals for the Sixth Circuit acknowledged that the majority of circuits have held that circular sale and leaseback transactions represent a stop loss arrangement under § 465(b)(4), but followed its opinion in *Emershaw* to conclude that taxpayers in the Sixth Circuit are at-risk in these transactions. In Levien v. Commissioner, 103 T.C. 120 (1994), aff'd by order, 77 F.3d 497 (11th Cir.1996), the Tax Court followed *Young* and refused to apply the reasoning of *Emershaw* to examine the transaction under a "worst case scenario."

A number of other strategies have been developed to avoid the application of § 465. Rev. Rul. 79–432, 1979–2 C.B. 289, described a widely-marketed "art tax shelter" that provided investors with an original master lithographic plate plus various other rights. The investor was required to provide a "partially recourse" note to the sales promotion corporation in the face amount of $170,000; the investor was purportedly personally liable to the extent of $70,000. The investor could, in the event of default, require the note holder to accept any unsold prints made from the master, thereby reducing the loan balance, based on a formula to determine the value of the prints. The Ruling held the entire note to be nonrecourse.

The ability of ingenious tax shelter promoters to market investments that purported to avoid the at-risk limitations was one of the reasons that the provision did not meet Congress' stated intent to put an end to overvalued transactions.

3.　EFFECT OF THE AT-RISK LIMITATION

3.1. *Deferral of Deductions*

In general, the effect of § 465 is to defer deductions attributable to nonrecourse debt until the debt is repaid. In computing allowable deductions for the year, however, the taxpayer is permitted to treat deductions as being wholly attributable to his at-risk amount—his equity investment or share of recourse debt—until the at-risk amount has been exhausted. Thereafter, deductions in excess of current increases in the taxpayer's at-risk amount are suspended until the taxpayer increases his at-risk amount. A taxpayer's at-risk amount can be increased by an additional contribution to the activity. Most often a taxpayer's at-risk amount is increased when mortgage principal amortization payments in a particular year exceed the depreciation deductions on the property for that year. Upon the sale or other taxable disposition of the activity, deductions that have been deferred under § 465 will be allowable to the extent that the sales proceeds are used to repay the debt, thereby increasing the taxpayer's at-risk amount. Likewise, if the property is transferred subject to the nonrecourse debt, the taxpayer's at-risk amount is increased by the taxpayer's gain from the property, thereby allowing suspended deductions to offset some or all of the gain.

3.2. *Recapture of Amounts Previously At-Risk*

Absent a prophylactic rule, the at-risk limitation might be avoided by the use of recourse liabilities that could be converted into nonrecourse debt after the investment produced the desired losses in the early years of the investment. Section 465(e) requires recapture of previous deductions following a reduction in the taxpayer's amount at risk. Section 465(e) provides that if the taxpayer's amount at risk in an activity is reduced below zero, the taxpayer will recognize gross income to the extent that zero exceeds the amount at risk. For example, if A purchases an investment in an activity for $10,000 cash plus a recourse note for $90,000, then claims $20,000 of deductions from the activity, A's total amount at risk, reduced by the deductions, is $80,000. See I.R.C. § 465(b)(5). If the note is then converted to a nonrecourse note, A's amount at risk becomes a negative $10,000 ($10,000 cash investment minus $20,000 of deductions). Zero exceeds A's at-risk amount by $10,000 requiring A to recognize $10,000 of income. Thus A recaptures $10,000 of deductions as gross income. The amount recaptured into income is treated as a suspended deduction from the activity available in a later year when the taxpayer's amount at risk increases. The amount subject to recapture in any taxable year is limited to the total amount of losses from the activity claimed by the taxpayer in prior years reduced by amounts recaptured in prior years. I.R.C. § 465(e)(2).

4.   RELATION OF AT-RISK TO BASIS

Section 1012 requires the maintenance of a basis account, as adjusted pursuant to § 1016, for each separate asset. Section 465 does not itself affect these "regular basis" rules. It requires the maintenance of an "at-risk account" with respect to each "activity." The regular basis and the at-risk amount may thus differ because of (1) the presence of nonrecourse financing, (2) the presence of deductions that affect the at-risk amount but do not affect basis, and (3) the fact that an "activity" may encompass more than a single asset. For example, a taxpayer acquires an asset with the entire purchase price represented by a $1,000 nonrecourse loan. The taxpayer's regular basis is $1,000, but the at-risk amount is zero. If during the current taxable year the taxpayer's normally allowable depreciation is $200, the regular basis would be reduced to $800, the at-risk amount remains at zero, and the $200 deduction is placed in a suspense account. In the next year, if the asset is sold for $1,000, the taxpayer recognizes $200 gain ($1,000 amount realized less $800 regular basis). However, the $200 in the suspense account is then deductible since the taxpayer has increased the at-risk amount from zero to $200 by realization of the $200 taxable income.

SECTION 2.   PASSIVE-ACTIVITY-LOSS LIMITATION

INTERNAL REVENUE CODE: Section 469.

REGULATIONS: Section 1.469–4.

TEMPORARY REGULATIONS: Sections 1.469–1T(e); –5T(a)–(f).

As Pritchett v. Commissioner (see Section 1.2.2. of this Chapter) and related cases illustrate, taxpayers and their advisors were quick to find ways around the at-risk limitation of § 465, and continued to construct viable tax sheltered investments. Although the IRS had a number of weapons in addition to § 465, the result of litigation in any given case was unpredictable and taxpayers prevailed in a significant number of tax-shelter cases. See e.g., Smith v. Commissioner, 937 F.2d 1089 (6th Cir.1991). As a result, in 1986, Congress enacted a sweeping statutory response to tax shelters (which, it should be noted, Congress had encouraged in the first place by enacting and then condoning the preferential tax provisions on which the shelters were built) contained in § 469, the passive-activity-loss rules.

Senate Finance Committee Report, Tax Reform Act of 1986

S.Rep. No. 99–313, 99th Cong., 2d Sess. 713–718 (1986).

[Pre-1987] Law

In general, no limitations are placed on the ability of a taxpayer to use deductions from a particular activity to offset income from other activities. Similarly, most tax credits may be used to offset tax attributable to income from any of the taxpayer's activities.

* * *

In the absence of more broadly applicable limitations on the use of deductions and credits from one activity to reduce tax liability attributable to other activities, taxpayers with substantial sources of positive income are able to eliminate or sharply reduce tax liability by using deductions and credits from other activities, frequently by investing in tax shelters. Tax shelters commonly offer the opportunity to reduce or avoid tax liability with respect to salary or other positive income, by making available deductions and credits, possibly exceeding real economic costs or losses currently borne by the taxpayer, in excess or in advance of income from the shelters.

Reasons for Change

In recent years, it has become increasingly clear that taxpayers are losing faith in the Federal income tax system. This loss of confidence has resulted in large part from the interaction of two of the system's principal features: its high marginal rates (in 1986, 50 per cent for a single individual with taxable income in excess of $88,270) [or $193,482 in 2016 dollars], and the opportunities it provides for taxpayers to offset income from one source with tax shelter deductions and credits from another.

* * *

Extensive shelter activity contributes to public concerns that the tax system is unfair, and to the belief that tax is paid only by the naive and the unsophisticated. This, in turn, not only undermines compliance, but encourages further expansion of the tax shelter market, in many cases diverting investment capital from productive activities to those principally or exclusively serving tax avoidance goals.

The committee believes that the most important sources of support for the Federal income tax system are the average citizens who simply report their income (typically consisting predominantly of items such as salaries, wages, pensions, interest, and dividends) and pay tax under the general rules. To the extent that these citizens feel that they are bearing a disproportionate burden with regard to the costs of government because of their unwillingness or inability to engage in tax-oriented investment activity, the tax system itself is threatened.

Under these circumstances, the committee believes that decisive action is needed to curb the expansion of tax sheltering and to restore to the tax system the degree of equity that is a necessary precondition to a beneficial and widely desired reduction in rates. So long as tax shelters are permitted to erode the Federal tax base, a low-rate system can provide neither sufficient revenues, nor sufficient progressivity, to satisfy the general public that tax liability bears a fair relationship to the ability to pay. In particular, a provision significantly limiting the use of tax shelter losses is unavoidable if substantial rate reductions are to be provided to high-income taxpayers without disproportionately reducing the share of total liability under the individual income tax that is borne by high-income taxpayers as a group.

The question of how to prevent harmful and excessive tax sheltering is not a simple one. One way to address the problem would be to eliminate substantially all tax preferences in the Internal Revenue Code. For two reasons, however, the committee believes that this course is inappropriate.

* * *

[W]hile the bill reduces or eliminates some tax preference items that the committee believes do not provide social or economic benefits commensurate with their cost, there are many preferences that the committee believes are socially or economically beneficial. This is especially true when such preferences are used primarily to advance the purposes upon which Congress relied in enacting them, rather than to avoid taxation of income from sources unrelated to the preferred activity.

* * *

However, when the tax system, in order to avoid such complexity, permits simpler rules to be applied (e.g., generally not taxing unrealized gain, and allowing depreciation based on broad industry averages), opportunities for manipulation are created. Taxpayers may structure transactions specifically to take advantage of the situations in which the simpler rules lead to undermeasurement or deferral of income.

* * *

In some cases, the availability of tax preferences to nonparticipating investors has even harmed the industries that the preferences were intended to benefit. For example, in the case of farming, credits and favorable deductions have often encouraged investments by wealthy individuals whose principal or only interest in farming is to receive an investment return, largely in the form of tax benefits to offset tax on positive sources of income. Since such investors may not need a positive cash return from farming in order to profit from their investments, they have a substantial competitive advantage in relation to active farmers, who commonly are not in a position to use excess tax benefits to shelter unrelated income. This has significantly contributed to the serious economic difficulties presently being experienced by many active farmers.

The availability of tax benefits to shelter positive sources of income also has harmed the economy generally, by providing a non-economic return on capital for certain investments. This has encouraged a flow of capital away from activities that may provide a higher pre-tax economic return, thus retarding the growth of the sectors of the economy with the greatest potential for expansion.

The committee believes that, in order for tax preferences to function as intended, their benefit must be directed primarily to taxpayers with a substantial and bona fide involvement in the activities to which the preferences relate. The committee also believes that it is appropriate to encourage nonparticipating investors to invest in particular activities, by permitting the use of preferences to reduce the rate of tax on income from those activities; however, such investors should not be permitted to use tax benefits to shelter unrelated income.

There are several reasons why it is appropriate to examine the materiality of a taxpayer's participation in an activity in determining the extent to which such taxpayer should be permitted to use tax benefits from the activity. A taxpayer who materially participates in an activity is more likely than a passive investor to approach the activity with a significant nontax economic profit motive, and to form a sound judgment as to whether the activity has genuine economic significance and value.

* * *

DETAILED ANALYSIS

1. GENERAL

In general, § 469 disallows the use of deductions from "passive" business activities to offset income from other sources, such as salaries, professional fees, interest, dividends, gains from the sale of capital assets, and income from businesses in which the taxpayer actively participates, even if those deductions represent true economic losses. Although § 469 was enacted in response to the particular problem of tax shelters—primarily transactions in which rental real estate was purchased with borrowed money with the resulting accelerated depreciation deductions producing tax losses in excess of economic losses—the provision covers a considerably broader swath of shelter activity. For instance, it can apply to a retail store or restaurant operated as a sole proprietor by a business executive or professional person who, rather than managing the store or restaurant personally, hires a professional manager. If the deductions for the store or restaurant exceed its income, which is highly likely in the start-up phase of a business, then the "excess deductions" cannot be claimed currently against the owner's other income. Thus, it can be said that after 1986, the income tax became "schedular" in that income from different sources gets broken out and taxed without regard to whether the taxpayer realizes net income on a global basis. Because of this schedular nature of § 469 and its broad applicability, every taxpayer engaged in business (except large corporations) must divide the taxpayer's business ventures into separate baskets, termed "activities" for purpose of § 469, and determine whether the taxpayer has been active in each venture; that is, whether the taxpayer "materially participated" in the activity according to the detailed standards developed under § 469. Furthermore, portfolio investments within business ventures must be isolated and separated into yet another basket. After dividing the taxpayer's activities into distinct baskets, the taxpayer can begin computing taxable income for the year with aggregate deductions from all activities placed in a "passive" basket to be claimed currently only to the extent of aggregate income from activities in "passive" baskets.

2. TAXPAYERS SUBJECT TO SECTION 469

Section 469(a)(2) provides that the passive-activity-loss rules apply to individuals, estates, trusts, and certain closely held C corporations. Thus § 469 applies to all taxpayers other than corporations that do not meet the test for being closely held. Partnerships and S corporations (certain corporations the income and losses from which flow through to shareholders in the same manner as partnerships' income and losses flow through to partners) are not expressly subject to § 469 because they are conduits; the individual partners and shareholders report their shares of the entity's income or deductions on their returns, and they are subject to § 469 with respect to their share of income and deductions from any partnership or S corporation in which they do not materially participate.

Personal service corporations and closely held corporations are subject to the passive loss rules, even though their income is taxed at the corporate and not the shareholder level. The purpose of this rule is to prevent individuals from avoiding the impact of § 469 by incorporating their investment assets or personal service businesses and investing retained profits in tax shelters. Nevertheless, the limitations of § 469 applied to closely held C corporations are not as stringent as those applied to other taxpayers.

3.   PASSIVE-ACTIVITY LOSSES

3.1. *Treatment of Passive-Activity Losses*

Section 469(a) disallows any "passive-activity loss." A passive-activity loss is defined in § 469(d)(1) as the aggregate losses from all passive activities for the year in excess of the aggregate income from such activities for the year. In this context, losses means the amount by which all otherwise allowable deductions exceed gross income; and income means the amount by which gross income exceeds deductions. However, casualty losses (as defined for purposes of § 165(c) or (i)) with respect to property used in a passive activity are not treated as passive-activity deductions, and, subject to §§ 165 and 1231, such losses are currently deductible without regard to § 469. Temp. Reg. § 1.469–2T(d)(2)(xi). But where insurance reimbursement exceeds the adjusted basis of the property and § 1033 (see Chapter 27, Section 1) is not applicable, a casualty gain results, and the gain generally is passive-activity gain. Temp. Reg. § 1.469–2T(c)(7)(vi).

Assume, for example, that Passive Activity A generates $1,000 of gross income and $1,200 of deductions, Passive Activity B generates $600 of gross income and $500 of deductions. From Activities A and B, the taxpayer has a $100 passive-activity loss for the year, which will be disallowed. Technically speaking, this is achieved by requiring the taxpayer to include the $1,600 of gross income and allowing only an equal amount of the deductions. The disallowed loss carries over to the next year, where it enters the computation again; and this carry-over continues until the loss is allowed or permanently disallowed. I.R.C. § 469(b). Thus, § 469 generally operates only to defer, and not necessarily disallow, deductions attributable to passive activities. Furthermore, § 469 allows a full current deduction for passive-activity losses to the extent the taxpayer has current passive-activity income from other sources.

Because disallowed passive-activity losses are recovered on disposition of an activity, a taxpayer with multiple passive activities must allocate the total amount of disallowed deductions among the various passive activities that contributed to the overall loss. Temp. Reg. § 1.469–1T(f) provides rules for this allocation and for allocating the total amount of disallowed deductions attributable to each activity among the component deductions.

Passive-activity losses disallowed under § 469 generally are reflected as operating losses of the activity for tax purposes. In St. Charles Investment Co. v. Commissioner, 110 T.C. 46 (1998), rev'd on other issues, 232 F.3d 773

(10th Cir.2000), the Tax Court held that if depreciation deductions are part of a disallowed passive-activity loss, the basis of the depreciable asset is nevertheless reduced by the entire otherwise allowable depreciation deduction. On a subsequent sale of the asset, its basis is not recomputed by adding back disallowed depreciation deductions to reduce gain recognized on the sale of the asset. The fact that the depreciation deductions had not produced a tax benefit, and might never produce a benefit unless the conditions for releasing them from suspension under § 469 are met, is irrelevant.

3.2. *Definition of "Passive Activity" and "Material Participation"*

A "passive activity" generally is any trade or business activity in which the taxpayer does not "materially participate." I.R.C. § 469(c)(1). However, all rental activities except for real estate rental activities of certain persons engaged in the real estate business are deemed to be passive activities regardless of the level of the taxpayer's participation. I.R.C. § 469(c)(2). Temp. Reg. § 1.469–1T(e)(3) defines rental activity in a manner that subjects businesses involving heavy turnover and significant services, such as operation of a motel, short term automobile leasing, or a retail tool rental store, to the material participation test, rather than the per se rental rule. To prevent evasion of the passive-activity-loss limitations by artificially generating passive-activity income, Treas. Reg. § 1.469–2(f)(6) recharacterizes as income from a source other than a passive activity any income derived from leasing property to an activity in which the taxpayer materially participates. Thus, in Schwalbach v. Commissioner, 111 T.C. 215 (1998), rental income received by a taxpayer who leased real property to a professional services corporation through which he conducted a dental practice, and in which he owned one-half of the stock, was recharacterized as other than passive-activity income, and deductions for the taxpayer's passive-activity losses from other sources were disallowed. The same result has been reached in a number of other cases involving similar facts. See Fransen v. United States, 191 F.3d 599 (5th Cir.1999); Sidell v. Commissioner, 225 F.3d 103 (1st Cir.2000); Krukowski v. Commissioner, 279 F.3d 547 (7th Cir.2002).

Section 469(h) defines material participation as regular, continuous, and substantial involvement in the operations of the activity. In addition, § 469(h)(2) specifically provides that, except as provided in regulations, "no interest in a limited partnership as a limited partner shall be treated as an interest with respect to which a taxpayer materially participates." The regulations generally test for material participation by counting the number of hours devoted to the activity by the taxpayer and permit limited partners to be treated as material participants under certain circumstances. Temp. Reg. § 1.469–5T(a). In applying these rules to partners and shareholders in corporations subject to § 469, each taxpayer's individual participation must be tested separately.

Under Temp. Reg. § 1.469–5T(a), a taxpayer materially participates in an activity if any of the following tests are met:

(1)   the taxpayer devotes more than 500 hours to the activity in the year;

(2)   the taxpayer's participation constitutes all of the participation in the activity of any individual;

(3)   the taxpayer participates in the activity for more than 100 hours during the year and his participation is not less than that of any other individual;

(4)   the activity is a trade or business, the taxpayer participates in the activity for more than 100 hours (but not more than 500 hours) during the year, and the taxpayer's total participation in all such trade or business activities during the year exceeds 500 hours;

(5)   the taxpayer materially participated in the activity for five of the preceding ten taxable years;

(6)   the activity is a personal service activity in which the taxpayer materially participated for any three preceding years; or

(7)   based on all the facts and circumstances, the individual participates in the activity on a regular, continuous, and substantial basis.

Work not customarily performed by the owner of a business is not taken into account if one of the principal purposes of performing such work is to meet the material participation requirement. Unless an individual also participates in the day-to-day management or operations of the business, work performed in the capacity of an investor is not counted. Temp. Reg. § 1.469–5T(f)(2). See Lapid v. Commissioner, T.C. Memo 2004–222 (time spent by owners of hotel condominium unit reviewing financial statements and reports provided by condominium complex managers did not count toward hours required to satisfy the material participation test because those hours were "investment activity"). A taxpayer who participates in an activity for 100 hours or less during the year cannot qualify as materially participating under the facts and circumstances test. Temp. Reg. § 1.469–5T(b)(2)(iii). See also Oberle v. Commissioner, T.C. Memo. 1998–156 (taxpayer who owned a charter yacht did not materially participate in chartering activity by cleaning and winterizing the yacht and providing routine maintenance because participation was not more than 100 hours, and even if it did exceed 100 hours, it was not more hours than the yacht broker, who exercised daily management responsibility of chartering the yacht, including routine cleaning and servicing). Management services are taken into account in determining material participation only to a limited extent in applying the facts and circumstances test. Temp. Reg. § 1.469–5T(b)(2)(ii). See Goshorn v. Commissioner, T.C.Memo. 1993–578 (holding that taxpayer did not materially participate in the activity of chartering a boat he owned by performing nominal management services while the marina performed all of the daily work associated with chartering the boat).

In Chapin v. Commissioner, T.C. Memo. 1996–56, the taxpayer's activity of holding a condominium for rental was not a per se passive activity under § 469(c)(2) because the average lease period was seven days or less, but was found to be a passive activity because the taxpayer did not materially participate. The taxpayer thoroughly cleaned the condominium unit after each season, but this work was not regular and continuous because day-to-day management was provided by a rental agent and weekly cleaning was done by a cleaning service. Compare Pohoski v. Commissioner, T.C. Memo. 1998–17 (a taxpayer, who resided in California, presented credible evidence that he spent more than 100 hours during the year managing rentals of a Hawaiian condominium unit, which was rented for average rental periods of less than 7 days, and that he spent more time in the activity than employees of a condominium management company, including front desk staff and maid service, but the taxpayer did not present credible evidence with regard to a second Hawaiian condominium unit).

3.2.1. *Application to Partners and LLC Members*

A general partner does not qualify as a material participant merely because of the partner's status as a general partner. The level of participation in each activity in which the partnership is engaged must be tested separately. A partner may be active as to some partnership activities and passive as to others.

Section 469(h)(2) generally requires that a limited partner be treated as not materially participating in any partnership activity. The definition of a limited partner in Temp. Reg. § 1.469–5T(e)(3)(B), as a partner whose liability is limited to a fixed amount (including the partner's capital contribution), includes a member of a limited liability company (LLC), limited liability partnership (LLP), and other entities that provide all of their owners with limited liability. Temp. Reg. § 1.469–5T(e) provides two exceptions to the rule in § 469(h)(2) that a limited partner (defined as described above) does not materially participate in a partnership activity. First, a limited partner materially participates in a partnership activity if any one of tests (1), (5), or (6) for material participation described above are met. Second, a limited partnership interest held by a general partner is not treated as a limited partnership interest in applying § 469; whether the partner materially participates is determined for the partner's aggregate interest in the partnership under the above described seven tests.

Despite the language in the regulation, Garnett v. Commissioner, 132 T.C. 368 (2009), held that an interest in an LLC (or LLP or other entity in which all members receive the benefit of limited liability) is not treated as a limited partnership interest under § 469(h)(2). Thompson v. United States, 87 Fed. Cl. 728 (2009), reached the same result. Both courts reasoned that § 469(h)(2) treats limited partners differently because of an assumption that limited partners do not materially participate in their limited partnerships. Active participation in a limited partnership would cause a limited partner to lose the benefit of limited liability. In an LLC, on the other hand, all members have limited liability regardless of whether they participate in management. Thus, whether or not the taxpayer is a material participant requires a factual inquiry in which a taxpayer can demonstrate material participation in the activity by using any of the seven tests in Temp. Reg. § 1.469–5T(a). The IRS has acquiesced in *Thompson*, AOD 2010–02 (March 9, 2010), and has proposed regulations that would determine limited partnership status for purposes of § 469(h)(2) by evaluating the partner's right to participate in the management of the entity. Prop. Reg. § 1.469–5(e)(3) (2011).

3.3. *"Significant Participation Activities"*

If a taxpayer's gross income for the year from all significant participation activities exceeds passive-activity deductions from such activities, all of the significant participation activities are aggregated into a single passive activity that did not produce a loss for the year. Temp. Reg. § 1.469–1T(f)(2)(i)(C). Temp. Reg. § 1.469–2T(f)(2) defines as a "significant participation activity" any trade or business activity in which the taxpayer participates for more than 100 hours during the year, but in which he does not materially participate. Since a rental activity is a not a "trade or business activity," as defined in Treas. Reg. § 1.469–4(b)(1), a rental activity cannot be a significant participation activity. In addition, Temp. Reg. § 1.469–2T(f)(2) recharacterizes as active income a portion of the income from any significant participation activity, if all such activities in the aggregate produce net income.

3.4. *Special Rule for Oil and Gas Working Interests*

Section 469(c)(3) provides that any working interest in an oil or gas property is treated as not being a passive activity if the taxpayer holds the interest in a form that does not limit liability, even though the taxpayer does not materially participate. Thus, a general partnership interest qualifies, but a limited partnership interest does not. If any losses from a property are treated as active under this rule, all income from the property in future years must be treated as active income. I.R.C. § 469(c)(3)(B); see Temp. Reg. § 1.469–2T(c)(6).

3.5. *Self-Charged Items*

Section 469(*l*)(2) provides that the Treasury "shall" promulgate regulations "which provide that certain items of gross income will not be taken into account in determining income or loss from any activity (and the treatment of expenses allocable to such income)." Based on this provision, Treas. Reg. § 1.469–7 permits offsetting of "self-charged" interest incurred in lending transactions. This rule permits a taxpayer who realizes portfolio interest income from making a loan to a passive activity, usually a partnership in which the lender-taxpayer is a passive partner, to deduct to some extent otherwise disallowed passive-activity deductions for interest paid. The Treasury has not issued any regulations dealing with self-charged items other than interest.

In Hillman v. Commissioner, 114 T.C. 103 (2000), rev'd 250 F.3d 228 (4th Cir.2001), the taxpayer performed management services for real estate partnerships in which he was a partner. The taxpayer realized nonpassive income from performing the management services and pass-through passive deductions from the partnerships that paid him for those services. Based on § 469(*l*)(2) and its legislative history, under circumstances analogous to but not directly covered by then Prop. Reg. § 1.469–7 (1991), the taxpayer offset the passive management fee deductions against the corresponding nonpassive management fee income. The Commissioner argued that the taxpayer could not set off the deductions and income because the Treasury had not issued any regulations for self-charged items other than interest and that the permitted scope of the offset was thus limited. The Tax Court held that the substantive set-off rule was self-executing and that the taxpayer was entitled to offset the passive management deductions against the nonpassive management income. The court found that such self-charged treatment was congressionally intended not only for interest, but also for other appropriate items, and that there was not any substantial distinction between interest and management fees for this purpose. The court of appeals reversed, finding that "nothing in the plain language of IRC section 469 suggests that an exception to IRC section 469(a)'s general prohibition against a taxpayer's deducting passive-activity losses from nonpassive-activity gains exists where, as in the present case, the taxpayer essentially paid a management fee to himself." The court reasoned that Hillman's argument for ignoring the plain language of the statute could prevail only if one of "two extremely narrow exceptions to the Plain Meaning Rule" applied: (1) "when literal application of the statutory language at issue produces an outcome that is demonstrably at odds with clearly expressed congressional intent to the contrary" or (2) "when literal application of the statutory language at issue 'results in an outcome that can truly be characterized as absurd, i.e., that is so gross as to shock the general moral or common sense.' " In the court of appeal's view, neither of those situations was present.

Absent a prophylactic rule, a taxpayer with an active business conducted through an entity, such as a closely held corporation, could reduce the corporation's income and mitigate the effect of the passive-activity loss limitations by renting property to the entity, thereby generating passive-activity rental income that could be sheltered by passive-activity losses from other sources. Treas. Reg. § 1.469–2(f)(6) prevents this gambit by characterizing as nonpassive any income derived from leasing property to an activity in which the taxpayer materially participates. Beecher v. Commissioner, 481 F.3d 717 (9th Cir. 2007), upheld the application of Treas. Reg. § 1.469–2(f)(6) to treat as active income rentals received with respect to buildings leased to the taxpayer's wholly-owned C corporation for which he worked full-time, and to disallow losses from other rental properties leased to third parties.

4.   APPLICATION ON ACTIVITY-BY-ACTIVITY BASIS

4.1. *General*

Whether a taxpayer's income or loss from a business activity is treated as active or passive is determined by whether the taxpayer personally materially participated in the particular activity that gave rise to the item during the business's taxable year. See Temp. Reg. § 1.469–1T(e)(1). The Code does not provide any guidance for determining the scope of an activity, but such a determination is crucial in applying § 469. Where the taxpayer is engaged in several related activities, a broad definition of "activity" permits a taxpayer to use material participation in one aspect of the grouping to avoid the application of § 469 to losses from another aspect of the grouping. For example, assume that A and B are partners in retail stores located in Louisville and Cincinnati, with A managing the Louisville store and B managing the Cincinnati store. Grouping the stores as one activity would permit A to claim losses from the Cincinnati store and B to claim losses from the Louisville store against their incomes generally. But if they are two different activities, then A is passive with respect to the Cincinnati store and B is passive with respect to the Louisville store, and both A and B could claim losses from the store that they did not manage only against passive income. On the other hand, a narrow definition of an activity can assist a taxpayer in claiming suspended losses under § 469(g) upon the complete disposition of the activity.

4.2. *Scope of "Activity"*

Treas. Reg. § 1.469–4 adopts a facts-and-circumstances approach to identifying separate business activities. Under the regulations, two or more business activities are treated as a single activity "if the activities constitute an appropriate economic unit for the measurement of gain or loss for purposes of section 469." Treas. Reg. § 1.469–4(c)(1). In making this determination, five evidentiary factors are given the greatest weight: (1) similarities and differences in the type of business, (2) the extent of common control, (3) the extent of common ownership, (4) geographical location, and (5) business interdependency, such as the extent to which the activities purchase or sell goods between themselves, involve products or services that are normally provided together, have the same customers, have the same employees, or share a single set of books and records. Treas. Reg. § 1.469–4(c)(2).

A taxpayer may use any reasonable method of applying the relevant facts and circumstances in grouping activities, subject to a consistency requirement. Treas. Reg. § 1.469–4(c)(1). Once a taxpayer has grouped activities, they may not be regrouped unless the original grouping was inappropriate. Furthermore, the taxpayer subsequently must regroup the activities if warranted by a material change in facts and circumstances. Treas. Reg. § 1.469–4(e)(2). Finally, a taxpayer generally may elect to treat the disposition of a substantial part of an activity as a complete disposition of a separate activity, thus allowing suspended losses to be used in that year. Treas. Reg. § 1.469–4(g). The taxpayer's grouping generally is binding on the IRS. It may group activities differently than the taxpayer only if the taxpayer's grouping fails to reflect appropriate economic units *and* one of the primary purposes of the taxpayer's grouping was to circumvent § 469. Treas. Reg. § 1.469–4(f).

Taxpayers have significant flexibility under the regulations. For example, if a taxpayer owns a video arcade and a restaurant at a shopping mall in Sacramento and a video arcade and a restaurant in San Francisco, depending on other relevant facts and circumstances, it may be reasonable to (1) group the video arcades and restaurants into a single activity: (2) group the video arcades and the restaurants into two activities; (3) group the Sacramento video arcade and restaurant into a single activity and the San Francisco video arcade and restaurant into a different activity; or (4) treat each video arcade and restaurant as a separate activity. See Treas. Reg. § 1.469–4(c)(3), Ex. 1.

A rental activity (as defined in Temp. Reg. § 1.469–1T(e)(3)) may not be grouped with a nonrental activity unless one of the activities is insubstantial relative to the other. Treas. Reg. § 1.469–4(d). Thus, for example, if the taxpayer owns a six-story office building, occupying three floors to conduct a business and leases out three floors to tenants, the rental business is a separate activity from the other business. Real property rental activities and personal property rental activities never may be grouped, unless the personal property is provided in connection with the real property, for example, the rental of furnished apartments. Treas. Reg. § 1.469–4(f).

5.   SPECIAL RULES FOR REAL ESTATE ACTIVITIES

5.1. *Special Rule for Rental Real Estate Activities of Persons in the Real Property Business*

Section 469(c)(7) relaxes the passive-activity loss rules for taxpayers who provide more than one-half of their work effort during the year in one or more real estate businesses if (1) the taxpayer materially participates within the meaning of § 469(h), and (2) the taxpayer works more than 750 hours in such activities. If these tests are met, the taxpayer's real estate rental activities are not treated as passive activities under § 469(c)(2). Instead each activity is evaluated using the material participation rules of § 469(h). Any rental activity in which the taxpayer materially participates under that test is not subject to § 469; the losses from that activity are fully deductible against the taxpayer's income from other sources.

Material participation in a rental real estate activity is determined separately with respect to each interest unless the taxpayer elects to aggregate all real estate activities. In Trask v. Commissioner, T.C. Memo. 2010–78, the taxpayer failed to make an explicit election on his return to aggregate rental real estate activities as required by Treas. Reg. § 1.469–9(g). The court held that merely aggregating real estate rental activity losses on his returns was not an effective election. Although the taxpayer established that he was a "real estate professional" as defined in § 469(c)(7), all of the claimed losses were disallowed because he failed to prove that he materially participated in any of the rental activities on an activity-by-activity basis. Rev. Proc. 2010–13, 2010–4 I.R.B. 329, requires taxpayers to report to the IRS their groupings and regroupings of activities and the addition of activities within their existing groupings of activities.

The relief provision of § 469(c)(7) was intended primarily to benefit real estate developers, allowing them to offset income from development activities with losses from rental operations, but because real estate activities are broadly defined, its application is wider. For example, a real estate broker who materially participates in an apartment rental business may deduct losses from the apartment building against commission income from a brokerage business or investment income completely unrelated to real estate activities. Work performed in managing rental real estate, however, is counted as participation in a real estate activity only to the extent it involves management of the taxpayer's own rental real estate. Treas. Reg. § 1.469–9(e)(3)(ii). If married taxpayers file joint returns and one spouse meets the test for being engaged in a real estate business, losses from that spouse's material participation rental real estate activities may be deducted against all income on the joint return, including the other spouse's income. Rental activity losses of the spouse not in the real estate business, however, remain subject to § 469 and may not be deducted other than as passive-activity losses.

To claim the advantage of § 469(c)(7), the taxpayer must document the material participation. In D'Avanzo v. United States, 67 Fed.Cl. 39 (2005), aff'd by order, 215 Fed.Appx. 319 (Fed. Cir. 2007), the taxpayer was denied the benefit of § 469(c)(7) because he did not offer into evidence a contemporaneous written record of the number of hours he spent performing personal services with respect to rental properties. A noncontemporaneous log book of hours claimed to have been devoted to real estate activities and the taxpayer's testimony at trial, standing alone, were held to be inadequate evidence to establish that the taxpayer devoted the requisite number of hours to real estate business activities.

5.2. *Active Participation in Rental Real Estate Activities by Small Investors*

For individuals and some decedents's estates participating in rental real estate activities, § 469(i) allows deduction of up to $25,000 of losses from passive activities with respect to which the taxpayer "actively participates." Under § 469(i)(6) the "active participation" test is met if the taxpayer has a significant and *bona fide* role in managing the real estate. However, no taxpayer with less than a 10 percent interest (by value) in the activity may be considered as actively participating. The $25,000 ceiling is reduced by one-half of the amount by which the taxpayer's adjusted gross income (without taking such losses into account) exceeds $100,000. Active participation real estate losses in excess of the allowable amount are carried over to the subsequent year and continue to be governed by the rental real estate exception, rather than the general rules, only to the extent that the taxpayer continues to qualify for the special rule in the carryover year

6. PORTFOLIO INCOME

Portfolio income is not taken into account as income or loss from a passive activity. Portfolio income is defined generally as all income other than income derived in the ordinary course of a trade or business. I.R.C. § 469(e)(1). Thus, interest, dividends, and gains from the sale of securities, will not be classified as passive-activity income, except in the case of an owner of securities brokerage business or investment banking firm, who does not materially participate. Treas. Reg. § 1.469–1T(e)(6) provides that "an activity of trading personal property for the account of owners of interests in the activity is not a passive activity (without regard to whether such activity is a trade or business activity . . .)." As a result, passive-activity losses cannot be used to reduce portfolio income, and losses from a trade or business of trading stocks and securities are not subject to limitation under § 469. Section 469(e)(1)(B) specifically provides that return on a business's invested working capital is not passive-activity income with respect to an owner who does not materially participate. Thus, for example, the share of partnership interest income of a partner who does not materially participate in the partnership's activities is not passive income. Temp. Reg. § 1.469–2T(c)(3).

In *More v. Commissioner*, 115 T.C. 125 (2000), the taxpayer was an individual Lloyds of London underwriter who pledged stock that he owned to secure a letter of credit posted to show that he could cover insurance claims made against him as an underwriter. When he incurred underwriting losses on claims paid, the issuer of the letter of credit sold the stock. Because the stock had been acquired before underwriting activity began, the gain was portfolio income that could not be offset by the passive-activity losses from the insurance claims. The court noted however, that if the stock had been purchased with premiums for the insurance business and had been acquired and held for the purpose of "showing means" to cover potential losses, the gain might have been passive.

With a similar purpose, that of preventing so-called "positive income sources" from being treated as passive-activity income that might be offset by passive-activity losses, Treas. Reg. § 1.469–2(c)(7)(iv) provides that income from a covenant not to compete cannot be passive-activity income. See *Schaeffer v. Commissioner*, 105 T.C. 227 (1995) (upholding validity of the regulations). See also *Edelberg v. Commissioner*, T.C. Memo. 1995–386, aff'd by order, 111 F.3d 896 (11th Cir.1997) (income received from a third party's trade or business as a contingent sales price on the sale of the goodwill of taxpayer's business, which was not itself a passive activity, was either investment or portfolio income, not passive-activity income that could be offset by passive-activity losses).

7.   EFFECT OF DISPOSITION OF ACTIVITY

7.1. *Fully Taxable Sale or Exchange*

Because § 469 is intended to disallow only "artificial" losses, § 469(g) allows the taxpayer to deduct previously disallowed losses attributable to any activity in the year in which he makes a fully taxable disposition of his entire interest in the activity. Deduction of suspended losses on disposition of an activity is appropriate because artificial losses that were previously suspended will be offset by an equal amount of artificial (phantom) gain on the taxable disposition and only real losses will remain to offset other income.

Generally a sale or taxable exchange to an unrelated taxpayer of all of the assets used in the activity is required. Abandonment, which is a taxable event, also will qualify as a disposition. Tax deferred exchanges, such as like-kind exchanges under § 1031, contribution to a corporation under § 351, or contribution to a partnership under § 721, will not qualify. If the taxpayer disposes of less than his entire interest in a passive activity, disposes of his interest in a nontaxable transaction, or sells the interest to a related party (as defined in either § 267(b) or § 707(b)), any previously disallowed losses continue to be suspended and will be allowed in a future year in which the taxpayer realizes passive-activity income from other sources or upon completion of the disposition. If the initial disposition was a nontaxable transaction, any remaining suspended losses will be allowed upon the fully taxable sale of the property received in the earlier exchange.

Any gain or loss recognized in a fully taxable disposition is treated as passive gain or loss. Temp. Reg. § 1.469–2T(c)(2)(i). The deferred deductions are allowable to the extent of: (1) income from the passive activity, including gain (if any) recognized on the disposition; (2) net income or gain for the year from all other passive activities; (3) other income or gain, including salaries, dividends, etc. If any of the deductions otherwise allowable upon the disposition of the activity are capital losses, either from the disposition or as suspended deductions allowed upon the disposition, § 1211 (see Chapter 24, Section 1.3.) may limit the amount of the deductions currently allowed. If a disposition is an installment sale and gain recognition is deferred under § 453 (see Chapter 31, Section 2) suspended losses are allowed in each year payments are received in proportion to the portion of the total gain reportable in each year.

7.2. *Gifts and Bequests*

Disposition of a passive activity by gift does not permit the donor to claim suspended losses because making a gift is not a realization event. Furthermore, § 469(j)(6) denies the donor the right to carry over to future years the suspended losses and credits attributable to the transferred activity. However, the deferred losses are added to the donor's basis in the transferred activity immediately before the transfer and increase the transferee's basis in the activity under § 1015, unless the limitation of basis to fair market value applies.

Section 469(g)(2) allows suspended deductions to be claimed on a decedent's final return to the extent the deductions exceed the amount by which the basis of the property is stepped-up under § 1014. Any remaining suspended deductions are permanently disallowed because they do not represent a true economic loss.

8. FORMER PASSIVE ACTIVITIES

When a taxpayer materially participates in an activity that was a passive activity for prior years, the activity ceases to be a passive activity. Income and deductions from the activity for any year in which the taxpayer materially participates do not give rise to passive-activity income or loss. Although any suspended deductions attributable to the former passive activity continue to be passive-activity losses, § 469(f)(1) permits those suspended deductions to be claimed against the income from the activity recognized in subsequent years in which the taxpayer materially participates. To the extent that suspended losses from the former passive activity exceed net income from that activity, they remain deductible only against other passive-activity income in the same year (or against net income from that activity in later years).

9. ASSESSMENT OF SECTION 469

To the extent that § 469 acts to deny actual economic losses in certain situations, it goes beyond Congress's stated goal in 1986 to curb the use of tax shelters that create noneconomic losses to reduce or eliminate tax liability on unrelated, positive income. See Senate Finance Committee Report, at Section 2 of this Chapter. If Congress wanted to limit the benefits of tax preferences to persons actively engaged in activities that lawmakers explicitly chose to subsidize, it simply could have provided refundable tax credits to the individuals engaged in the favored activity. The passive investor provides up-front cash to the active real estate developer, movie producer, or oil operator that is not available from deferred tax benefits. Similarly, refundable (and taxable) tax credits can provide immediate cash flow, thereby eliminating the need for passive investors, tax-shelter promoters, and the complex passive-activity-loss rules.

Congress also expressed concern in 1986 that tax-shelter activities drove investment away from its most productive use, thereby creating inefficiencies in the economy. But that argument militates just as forcefully against providing tax subsidies of any kind, which inherently distort behavior and misallocate resources. The argument is similarly overinclusive with respect to which taxpayers are able to take advantage of the subsidy, lumping together tax-favored investments authorized by Congress (or "plain vanilla" transactions) with abusive tax-shelter investments. The only relevant efficiency argument is that syndication expenses were incurred by real estate developers, movie producers, oil operators, and tax-shelter promoters (including lawyers), to sell the tax subsidies to passive investors. But this inefficiency also could be solved by the more targeted mechanism of refundable tax credits.

It is worth pointing out that Congressional justification in 1986 for the passive loss rules based on the need for a proper definition of income also misses the mark. All tax subsidies—intended or unintended by Congress— violate normative income definition rules (see Chapter 11, Tax Expenditures). Thus perhaps the enactment of § 469 simply reflects a recurring theme: that is, Congressional ambivalence over providing government subsidies for certain activities through the tax system while denying such subsidies for other activities. This ambivalence has produced undue complexity and conceptual confusion for the tax system.

Despite these criticisms of the passive-activity-loss rules and how Congress justified them, § 469 has been tremendously effective in frustrating the type of tax-shelter transactions it was intended to target. In conjunction with the at-risk rules in § 465, the passive-activity-loss rules shut down the market for individual, highly leveraged tax shelters. The combination of requiring taxpayers to subject themselves to risk in tax-favored investments while also requiring them to actively participate in the investments prevents taxpayers from claiming noneconomic losses to offset taxable income from compensation.

Nonetheless, as we will see in the next chapter, the ingenuity of tax-shelter promoters whet the insatiable appetite of taxpayers for tax-saving transactions, and subsequently ignited and then fueled the next generation of tax shelters. These new shelter transactions, which largely involved financial transactions, generated artificial losses for wealthy individuals and corporations that dwarfed the size of noneconomic losses in the earlier generation of tax shelters, and that siphoned off tens of billions of dollars in federal and state tax revenues. As you will also see in the next chapter, this later generation of abusive transactions required the government and the courts to update and expand the economic substance and sham transaction doctrines.

CHAPTER 36

ECONOMIC SUBSTANCE DOCTRINE

The deductions from gross income allowed in the Internal Revenue Code are generally intended to reduce gross income to a net figure representing the profit from trade or business operations. Some provisions, however, are intended to provide an incentive or subsidy for a specific activity (e.g., accelerated depreciation). Over the years, tax advisors and investment bankers have designed transactions to take advantage of a literal reading of statutory or regulatory provisions to generate after-tax profits from investments that have little or no economic benefit or purpose apart from tax savings. These tax shelter transactions usually deal with structural provisions of the Code that Congress enacted to measure tax liability accurately rather than to create subsidies for specific investments. Many of the courts that have evaluated these transactions have concluded that while the arrangements may achieve the desired tax result under a literal textual reading of the Code and regulations, they do not necessarily possess sufficient non-tax business purpose to give effect to the sought after tax consequences. Meanwhile, other courts have been less willing to use substance-over-form doctrines (including the economic substance doctrine) to disallow tax transactions that either comport with a literal reading of the tax laws or that possess a modicum of non-tax business purpose. These literalist courts often opine that responsibility for shutting down perceived tax gambits lies with Congress and the IRS, not the courts, and should take the form of targeted statutes and regulations. Thus, the issue becomes whether the words of the Code and Regulations can be used to structure tax shelter transactions in a way never intended by the Congress, or whether the IRS and courts can look to the underlying tax avoidance purpose of a transaction to deny sought-after tax losses not matched by economic losses. The better and generally prevailing view is reflected in the following opinion.

Klamath Strategic Investment Fund v. United States

United States Court of Appeals, Fifth Circuit, 2009.
568 F.3d 537.

■ GARZA, CIRCUIT JUDGE:

In this tax case, Plaintiffs Klamath Strategic Investment Fund (Klamath) and Kinabalu Strategic Investment Fund (Kinabalu) (collectively, the Partnerships) filed suit against defendant the United

States of America for readjustment of partnership items. Both parties appeal various aspects of the district court's readjustment determination. For the following reasons, we affirm in part, vacate in part, and remand.

I

This case involves a highly complex series of financial transactions, which the district court categorized as a tax shelter known as Bond Linked Issue Premium Structure (BLIPS). The transactions were undertaken by two law partners, Cary Patterson and Harold Nix. Patterson and Nix's law firm represented the State of Texas in litigation against the tobacco industry and each partner earned around $30 million between 1998 and 2000. Interested in managing this wealth, Patterson and Nix requested their long-time accounting firm, Pollans & Cohen, to investigate investment opportunities.

[Ed: The BLIPS transaction involved investments in foreign currency trading through three stages. The first stage, which lasted 60 days, involved low risk, low return investments. The risk and return increased in stages two and three, which was used to assert that the transaction ultimately had a profit motive. The investors retained a right to exit the plan at the end of stage I and at each 60 day period thereafter. Each investor formed a limited liability company taxed as a partnership. Each investor contributed $1.5 million to each partnership. In addition, each investor entered into a loan transaction with National Westminster Bank (Nat-West) for $66.7 million divided into a $41.7 million principal amount and $25 million described as a loan premium. Liability for the loan premium varied depending on the time of repayment, starting at about $25 million and decreasing over seven years. After year seven, no prepayment amount would apply. The full $66.7 million remained in a collateral account at Nat-West to secure repayment of the loan. The loan proceeds were contributed to the investors' partnerships, which assumed liability for the loans. Under partnership tax rules, the investor's basis in their partnership interests included the amount of the partnerships' liability for the loans. At the end of stage I, the investors withdrew from the partnerships receiving distributions of cash and foreign currency. Again, under partnership tax rules, each investor's basis in his partnership interests was reduced by the $41.7 million principal loan that remained a partnership liability, but the investors asserted under Treasury regulations in effect at the time that the contingent nature of the $25 million loan premium avoided a reduction in basis for that amount. The District Court agreed with this conclusion. Under partnership tax rules this claimed $25 million basis in each investor's partnership interest transferred to the property distributed to each partner on withdrawal from the partnership, the foreign currency.* Each

---

*   Section 752(a) treats an increase in a partner's share of liability as a contribution to the partnership, which increases the partner's basis in the partnership interest. I.R.C. § 722. Under § 752(b), a decrease in a partner's share of partnership liabilities is treated as a distribution of cash to the partner which is treated as a return to capital to the extent of the

partner thereupon sold the foreign currency and claimed a loss of approximately $25 million on their income tax returns for 2000, 2001, and 2002.]

The IRS disagreed with this basis calculation, and in 2004 issued Final Partnership Administrative Adjustments (FPAAs) to Klamath and Kinabalu stating that under 26 U.S.C. § 752 of the Internal Revenue Code (the Code), the partners should have treated the entire $66.7 million as a liability. Alternatively, the IRS argued that the transactions were shams or lacked economic substance and should be disregarded for tax purposes. The FPAAs also made adjustments to operational expenses reported by the Partnerships and asserted accuracy-related penalties. Patterson and Nix paid the taxes owed based on the FPAAs, and then re-formed the partnerships in order to seek readjustment in the district court.

The Partnerships filed suit against the Government under 26 U.S.C. § 6226 for readjustment of partnership items. * * * [F]ollowing a bench trial the district court held that the loan transactions must nonetheless be disregarded for federal tax purposes because they lacked economic substance. The district court also concluded that * * * the Partnerships' operational expenses were deductible. * * * Finally, the court issued an order holding that * * * Patterson and Nix could deduct the $250,000 management fee paid to their accountants.

* * * The Partnerships [appeal] the district court's bench trial judgment, arguing that the loan transactions had economic substance.

III

We first consider * * * whether the district court erred in determining that the loan transactions lacked economic substance and must be disregarded for tax purposes.

The economic substance doctrine allows courts to enforce the legislative purpose of the Code by preventing taxpayers from reaping tax benefits from transactions lacking in economic reality. See Coltec Indus., Inc. v. United States, 454 F.3d 1340, 1353–54 (Fed.Cir.2006). As the Supreme Court has recognized, taxpayers have the right to decrease or avoid taxes by legally permissible means. See Gregory v. Helvering, 293 U.S. 465, 469 (1935). However, "transactions which do not vary control or change the flow of economic benefits are to be dismissed from consideration." See Higgins v. Smith, 308 U.S. 473, 476 (1940). In a more recent pronouncement, the Supreme Court held that "[w]here. . .there is a genuine multiple-party transaction with economic substance which is compelled or encouraged by business or regulatory realities, is imbued with tax-independent considerations, and is not shaped solely by tax-avoidance features that have meaningless labels attached, the

---

partner's basis (and gain to the extent the distribution exceeds basis), and decreases the partner's basis in the partnership interest. I.R.C. §§ 731(a) and 733.

Government should honor the allocation of rights and duties effectuated by the parties." Frank Lyon, 435 U.S. at 583–84.

The law regarding whether a transaction should be disregarded as lacking economic reality is somewhat unsettled in the Fifth Circuit, and a split exists among other Circuits. The Fourth Circuit applies a rigid two-prong test, where a transaction will only be invalidated if it lacks economic substance and the taxpayer's sole motive is tax avoidance. See Rice's Toyota World, Inc. v. Comm'r, 752 F.2d 89, 91–92 (4th Cir.1985). The majority view, however, is that a lack of economic substance is sufficient to invalidate the transaction regardless of whether the taxpayer has motives other than tax avoidance. See e.g., Coltec, 454 F.3d at 1355; United Parcel Serv. of Am., Inc. v. Comm'r, 254 F.3d 1014, 1018 (11th Cir.2001); ACM Partnership v. Comm'r, 157 F.3d 231, 247 (3d Cir.1998); James v. Comm'r, 899 F.2d 905, 908–09 (10th Cir.1990). We have previously declined to explicitly adopt either approach. See Compaq, 277 F.3d at 781–82 (finding that the transaction in question had both economic substance and a legitimate business purpose, so it would be recognized for tax purposes under either the minority or majority approach).

We conclude that the majority view more accurately interprets the Supreme Court's prescript in Frank Lyon. The Court essentially set up a multi-factor test for when a transaction must be honored as legitimate for tax purposes, with factors including whether the transaction (1) has economic substance compelled by business or regulatory realities, (2) is imbued with tax-independent considerations, and (3) is not shaped totally by tax-avoidance features. See Frank Lyon, 435 U.S. at 583–84. Importantly, these factors are phrased in the conjunctive, meaning that the absence of any one of them will render the transaction void for tax purposes. Thus, if a transaction lacks economic substance compelled by business or regulatory realities, the transaction must be disregarded even if the taxpayers profess a genuine business purpose without tax-avoidance motivations.

The following facts found by the district court are critical to this issue: Presidio [the investment advisory firm that structured the transaction] and NatWest understood that the transactions would not last beyond Stage I, despite the purported seven-year term-meaning that the high risk foreign currency transactions were never intended to occur. If the investors failed to withdraw voluntarily, NatWest could use economic pressure to force them out because the credit agreements required the borrowers to maintain collateral on deposit at NatWest that exceeded the value of the maximum obligations owed to the bank by some varying amount. At the time the loans were issued, this amount was at least 101.25% of the total $66.7 million. NatWest had the discretion to determine whether the ratio was satisfied and could accelerate the ratio to declare a default if the bank wished to force an investor to withdraw. This requirement also meant that none of the $66.7 million loan could ever be used for investments-it had to stay in the accounts at NatWest. NatWest and Presidio understood that the bank would hold the money in relatively risk-free time deposits. Presidio's management fee was calculated as a percentage of the tax losses generated by the investment plan. The district court determined, however, that Patterson and Nix pursued the transactions with a genuine profit motive and were not solely driven by the desire to avoid taxes.

Here, the evidence supports the district court's conclusion that the loan transactions lacked economic substance. Numerous bank documents stated that despite the purported seven-year term, the loans would only be outstanding for about 70 days. NatWest's profit in the loan transactions was calculated based on a 72-day period. In the event that the investors wanted to remain with the plan beyond 72 days, NatWest would force them out. The bank noted in an internal memo that it "had no legal or moral obligation to deal [with the investors] after Day 60." During that 60- to 70-day window the loan funds could not be used to facilitate the investment strategy that Presidio designed. The requirement of keeping at least 101.25% of the $66.7 million in the NatWest account meant, as the Government's expert testified, that the Partnerships could not make any investments without supplying their own funds in excess of the loan amount.

The Partnerships contend that the loan funds were critical to the high-risk foreign currency transactions even if the funding amount could not be spent because the money provided the necessary security for the high-risk transactions. However, the structure of the plan shows that these high-risk transactions could not occur until Stage III, which was never intended to be reached. As the district court found, NatWest would force the investors out long before Stage III, so the loan transactions served no real purpose beyond creating a massive tax benefit for Nix and Patterson.

The Partnerships further argue that the loan transactions had a reasonable possibility of profit, as evidenced by the fact that two small, low-risk investments were actually made in foreign currencies. However, these investments were made using the $1.5 million that Patterson and Nix contributed to the Partnerships, not the funding amounts of the loans. Various courts have held that when applying the economic substance doctrine, the proper focus is on the particular transaction that gives rise to the tax benefit, not collateral transactions that do not produce tax benefits. See Coltec, 454 F.3d at 1356–57; Nicole Rose Corp. v. Comm'r, 320 F.3d 282, 284 (2d Cir.2002). Here, the transactions that provided the tax benefits at issue were the loans from NatWest. Therefore, the proper focus is on whether the loan transactions presented a reasonable possibility of profit, not whether the capital contributions from Patterson and Nix could have produced a profit. The loan transactions could never have been profitable because the funding amount could not actually be used for investments, and the high-risk investments for which the funding amount might have provided security were never intended to occur.

The evidence clearly shows that Presidio and NatWest designed the loan transactions and the investment strategy so that no reasonable possibility of profit existed and so that the funding amount would create massive tax benefits but would never actually be at risk. Regardless of Patterson and Nix's desire to make money, they entered into transactions controlled by Presidio and NatWest that were not structured or implemented to make a profit. This particular situation highlights the logic of following the majority approach to the economic substance doctrine, because the minority approach would allow tax benefits to flow from transactions totally lacking in economic substance as long as the taxpayers offered some conceivable profit motive. In cases such as the instant one, this approach would essentially reward a "head in the sand" defense where taxpayers can profess a profit motive but agree to a scheme structured and controlled by parties with the sole purpose of achieving tax benefits for them. We therefore agree with the district court that since the loan transactions lacked economic substance, they must be disregarded for tax purposes.

IV

* * *

C

The Government also appeals the district court's order that the Partnerships may deduct "operational expenses" associated with the loan and foreign currency transactions. These operational expenses include interest on the loans, a breakage fee, a management fee paid to Presidio, and a $250,000 fee paid to Pollans & Cohen. The Government argues that the district court erred because no deduction may be taken for expenses related to a sham transaction.

* * *

Generally, when a transaction is disregarded for lack of economic substance, deductions for costs expended in furtherance of the transaction are prohibited. See Winn-Dixie Stores, Inc. v. Comm'r, 113 T.C.254, 294 (1999) (observing that "a transaction that lacks economic substance is not recognized for Federal tax purposes" and that "denial of recognition means that such a transaction cannot be the basis for a deductible expense"); * * * This makes sense in light of the fact that the effect of disregarding a transaction for lack of economic substance is that, for taxation purposes, the transaction is viewed to have never occurred at all. * * * However, courts have upheld deductions based on genuine debts, where the debts are elements of a transaction that overall is lacking in economic substance. See Rice's Toyota World, Inc. v. Comm'r, 752 F.2d 89, 95–96 (4th Cir.1985) (allowing deductions based on recourse note debt that was an element of a sham purchase transaction, because the notes represented actual indebtedness).

Here, the district court concluded that the interest payments were deductible because they were real economic losses. However, § 163 does not base the deductibility of interest on whether or not the interest paid was a real economic loss. Rather, the test is simply whether the interest was paid or accrued on indebtedness. See Salley, 464 F.2d at 485 (disallowing interest deductions under § 163 because the taxpayers did not take on actual indebtedness: "[i]n no sense can it be said that taxpayers paid any interest . . . as compensation for the use or forbearance of money . . . which is the standard business test of indebtedness") (internal quotations and citation omitted). Further, "the fact that an enforceable debt exists between the borrower and lender is not dispositive of whether interest arising from that debt is deductible under section 163." Winn-Dixie Stores, 113 T.C. at 279. The overall transaction must have economic substance in order to show genuine indebtedness, otherwise "every tax shelter . . . could qualify for an interest expense deduction as long as there was a real creditor in the transaction that demanded repayment." Id.

In concluding that the loan transactions in this case lacked economic substance, the district court found that "[i]n truth, NatWest did not make any loans" and "[t]he loans . . . were not loans at all." These findings preclude the conclusion that the Partnerships took on actual indebtedness. As we found above, the loan transactions in this case lacked economic substance partly because they were structured such that the Partnerships could never actually spend the loaned funds—101.25% of the funding amount had to stay in the accounts at NatWest to prevent a default. Therefore, despite the appearance of a loan, functionally the Partnerships never took on any actual debt. Since the loans did not constitute indebtedness, the Partnerships may not deduct the interest paid under § 163.

Presumably, though not specified, the district court found the remainder of the operating expenses and fees deductible under § 212 as necessary expenses incurred. This provision requires a profit motive. See Agro Science, 934 F.2d at 576 (noting that an expenditure is deductible under § 212 "only . . . if the facts and circumstances indicate that the taxpayer made them primarily in furtherance of a bona fide profit objective independent of tax consequences"). The Government argues that the profit motive must be determined based on Presidio's subjective intentions because Presidio acted as managing partner when the transactions occurred. The district court, however, determined that the proper focus is on the motives of Patterson and Nix. Having concluded that Patterson and Nix entered into the transactions genuinely seeking to make a profit, the district court allowed the deductions.

The profit motive of a partnership is determined at the partnership level. Id.; Simon v. Comm'r, 830 F.2d 499, 507 (3d Cir.1987). * * * Here, the district court concluded that the partners had different motivations: Nix and Patterson at all times pursued the investment strategy with a genuine profit motive, while Presidio's primary intent was to achieve a tax benefit. The crucial inquiry, then is which partner's intentions should be attributed to the Partnership. Under Agro Science, this answer depends on which partner effectively controlled the partnership's activities. * * *

During the time of the transactions in question, Presidio acted as the managing partner but had less than 10% ownership of Klamath and Kinabalu. Patterson and Nix each had 90% ownership. * * * [T]he LLC agreements state that "the overall management and control of the business and affairs of the Company shall be vested solely in the Managing Member." The district court, however, did not analyze which partner retained control over the partnership. The district court appears to have concluded, with little explanation, that Patterson and Nix's motives must be attributed to the Partnerships because they paid the expenses at issue here and reported them on their individual tax returns. However, for purposes of determining the deductibility of expenses it is the motive of the Partnership that matters, regardless of whether certain operating expenses were borne by one partner or another. None of the arguments articulated by the Partnerships or the district court persuade us that the motives of Patterson and Nix, to whom the overall control and management of the Partnerships was expressly denied under the LLC agreements, should be attributed to the Partnerships. We therefore hold that the district court erred as a matter of law by failing to consider which partners effectively controlled the management of the Partnerships' affairs, at the time the transactions occurred, in determining whether the operating expenses and fees are deductible.

* * *

V

For the foregoing reasons, we AFFIRM the district court's judgment that the loan transactions lacked economic substance and must be disregarded for tax purposes. * * * We VACATE the district court's order allowing the deduction of interest and operating expenses and REMAND for reconsideration in accordance with this opinion. * * *

DETAILED ANALYSIS

1.   ECONOMIC SUBSTANCE AND BUSINESS PURPOSE DOCTRINES

The judicial economic substance and business purpose doctrines are among the government's principal weapons against abusive tax-motivated transactions. Gregory v. Helvering, 293 U.S. 465 (1935), is the seminal business purpose opinion. In that case the taxpayer had structured a multistep corporate reorganization, which complied with the applicable statute in all respects, that had as its principal purpose the reduction of tax on a disposition of stock held by the corporation and a transfer of the proceeds to the corporate shareholder as a dividend. The Supreme Court refused to accept the statutory characterization of the transaction, which it described as, "Simply an operation having no business or corporate purpose—a mere device which put on the form of a corporate reorganization as a disguise for concealing its real character. . . ." In oft quoted dicta, however, the Court said:

> The legal right of a taxpayer to decrease the amount of what otherwise would be his taxes, or altogether avoid them, by means which the law permits, cannot be doubted. [Citations omitted.] But the question for determination is whether what was done, apart from the tax motive, was the thing which the statute intended.

In spite of this sentiment, the court held in *Gregory* that the absence of business purpose justified disregarding the transaction as a sham. The Supreme Court's language in its *Gregory* opinion is similar to the words of Judge Learned Hand in the Court of Appeals opinion in *Helvering v. Gregory*, 69 F.2d 809 (2d Cir.1934).

> [A] transaction, otherwise within an exception of the tax law, does not lose its immunity, because it is actuated by a desire to avoid, or, if one choose, to evade, taxation. Any one may so arrange his affairs that his taxes shall be as low as possible; he is not bound to choose that pattern which will best pay the Treasury; there is not even a patriotic duty to increase one's taxes. * * * Therefore, if what was done here, was what was intended by [the statute], it is of no consequence that it was all an elaborate scheme to get rid of income taxes, as it certainly was. Nevertheless, it does not follow that Congress meant to cover such a transaction, not even though the facts answer the dictionary definitions of each term used in the statutory definition. It is quite true, as the Board [of Tax Appeals] has very well said, that as the articulation of a statute increases, the room for interpretation must contract; but the meaning of a sentence may be more than that of the separate words, as a melody is more than the notes, and no degree of particularity can ever obviate recourse to the setting in which all appear, and which all collectively create. * * * But the underlying presupposition is plain that the readjustment shall be undertaken for reasons germane to the conduct of the venture in hand, not as an ephemeral incident, egregious to its prosecution. To dodge the shareholders' taxes is not one of the transactions contemplated as corporate "reorganizations".

In Knetsch v. United States, 364 U.S. 361 (1960), the Supreme Court again recognized a taxpayer's legal right to structure the taxpayer's affairs in order to minimize taxes, but rejected interest deductions on a life insurance/annuity contract transaction because the taxpayer's "transaction with the insurance company did 'not appreciably affect his beneficial interest except to reduce his tax.'" The court added that "there was nothing of substance to be realized by Knetsch from this transaction beyond a tax deduction." As pointed out by the court in *Klamath*, the Fourth Circuit in Rice's Toyota World v. Commissioner, 752 F.2d 89 (4th Cir.1985), translated the doctrine into a two part test, both of which must be met to void a transaction: "[T]he court must find that the taxpayer was motivated by no business purposes other than obtaining tax benefits in entering the transaction, and that the transaction has no economic substance because no reasonable possibility of a profit exists." The court in In re CM Holdings, Inc., 301 F.3d 96 (3d Cir.2002), indicated that these two inquiries are not discrete prongs of a rigid two-step analysis. See also Black & Decker Corp. v. United States, 436 F.3d 431, 441–43 (4th Cir.2006); Coltec Indus., Inc. v. United States, 454 F.3d 1340, 1353 54 (Fed.Cir.2006). The Fifth Circuit in Compaq Computer Corporation v. Commissioner, 277 F.3d 778 (5th Cir. 2001) declined to opine whether both of these prongs must be satisfied before a transaction can be disregarded for tax purposes, finding in the case before it that the transaction has a profit potential and that the taxpayer had a business purpose. But subsequent case law and the recently codified economic substance doctrine in I.R.C. § 7701(*o*) (see Section 4 of this Chapter) has clearly indicated that a mere "peppercorn" of potential economic profit does not justify respecting comparably large tax benefits generated by tax-favored transactions. See e.g., § 7701(*o*)(2)(A) (considering transactions to possess economic substance "only if the present value of the reasonably expected pre-tax profit from the transaction is substantial in relation to the present value of the expected net tax benefits that would be allowed if the transaction were respected").

1.1. *Judge Learned Hand and Manifestations of Economic Substance and Business Purpose*

Judge Hand had several opportunities to refine his thinking regarding the application of the business purpose doctrine of *Gregory*. In Chisholm v. Commissioner, 79 F.2d 14 (2d Cir.1935), Judge Hand wrote:

> It is important to observe just what the Supreme Court held in that case. It was solicitous to reaffirm the doctrine that a man's motive to avoid taxation will not establish his liability if the transaction does not do so without it. The question always is whether the transaction under scrutiny is in fact what it appears to be in form; a marriage may be a joke; a contract may be intended only to deceive others; an agreement may have a collateral defeasance. In such cases the transaction as a whole is different from its appearance. True, it is always the intent that controls; and we need not for this occasion press the difference between intent and purpose. We may assume that purpose may be the touchstone, but the purpose which counts is one which defeats or contradicts the apparent transaction, not the purpose to escape taxation which the apparent, but not the whole, transaction would realize. In Gregory v. Helvering, supra, 293 U.S. 465, the incorporators adopted the usual form for creating business corporations; but their intent, or purpose, was merely to draught the papers, in fact not to create corporations as the court understood that word. That was the purpose which defeated their exemption, not the accompanying purpose to escape taxation; that purpose was legally neutral. Had they really meant to conduct a business by means of the two reorganized companies, they would have escaped whatever other

aim they might have had, whether to avoid taxes, or to regenerate the world.

One might describe this portrayal of business purpose by saying that the form of a transaction will be recognized if the transaction itself has business or economic substance beyond merely a purpose to escape taxation. To be sure, a transaction with economic substance may be structured in the fashion that best reduces taxes. In this regard, as in *Gregory* itself, the business purpose test may be applied to disregard the existence of a particular transaction or legal status as a "sham" where its existence serves no function apart from its tax-saving function. But a transaction also might be disregarded by the tax law even though it creates binding legal obligations that are not merely transitory in nature, and therefore not a sham arrangement, but nonetheless lacks business reality in the sense that the transaction would not be entered into except for the benefit that results from the expected tax savings. Justice Hand suggested such a consideration in Commissioner v. National Carbide Corporation, 167 F.2d 304 (2d Cir.1948), aff'd 336 U.S. 422 (1949):

> [The *Gregory*] decision has at times been thought to trench upon the doctrine—which courts are never tired of repeating—that the rights resulting from a legal transaction otherwise valid, are not different, vis-à-vis taxation, because it has been undertaken to escape taxation. That is a doctrine essential to industry and commerce in a society like our own, in which, so far as possible, business is always shaped to the form best suited to keep down taxes. Gregory v. Helvering, supra, was no exception, in spite of the fact that it was the purpose for which the taxpayer created the corporation that determined the event; for it is not the presence of an accompanying motive to escape taxation that is ever decisive, but the absence of any motive which brings the corporation within the group of those enterprises which the word ordinarily includes. Indeed, a corporation may be a "sham" and "unreal," when the only reason for its creation was "to deter the creditors of one of the partners," who organized it, for that is not an activity commonly understood to be corporate.

Thus, in Goldstein v. Commissioner 364 F.2d 734 (2d Cir.1966), the court denied an interest deduction to a taxpayer who pre-paid interest on a loan from a bank at 4 percent to invest in Treasury obligations paying 2-percent interest to generate a large tax deduction in the year of the borrowing. The liability created by the debt was real, the taxpayer was liable for the debt and actually purchased the Treasury obligations. Nonetheless, the court disallowed an interest deduction on the ground that the borrowing had not taken place in order to further any "purposive activity" other than obtaining the tax deduction. In *Compaq*, the court made much about the taxpayer engaging in a transaction that included real, arms-length trades of securities on a real public market with real downside risk and exposure. Unlike the *Goldstein* court, however, the *Compaq* court considered the pre-tax profit derived from the activity ($1.9 million) a sufficiently "purposive activity" to justify the tax benefits generated by the transaction (nearly $21 million in tax losses).

2.   THE TRANSACTION IN *COMPAQ v. COMMISSIONER*

2.1. *The Fifth Circuit Decision*

The transaction in Compaq Computer Corporation v. Commissioner, 277 F.3d 778 (5th Cir. 2001), rev'g 113 T.C. 214 (1999) and the Fifth Circuit's decision illustrate the difficulty courts face in applying the economic substance doctrine and identifying whether a transaction is entered into with a bona fide profit motive or merely represents a tax avoidance scheme.

During a period of a little over an hour, Compaq purchased about 450,000 American Depository Receipts (ADR, a form of trading unit representing ownership of stock in a foreign corporation) in Royal Dutch Petroleum Company for $887.6 million and resold the ADRs for $868.4 million, thereby claiming a loss of $20.7 million, including $1.5 million in fees. While Compaq held the Royal Dutch Petroleum ADR's the company paid a dividend of about $22.5 million. The dividend was subject to a $3.4 million Dutch withholding tax, resulting in a net dividend to Compaq of $19.2 million. As illustrated in the next paragraph, in the absence of Netherlands and U.S. tax, Compaq derived a profit on the overall transaction of $1.8 million. Taking into account the liability for the Netherlands withholding tax, which was a certainty when the transaction was entered into, the overall transaction resulted in a loss of $1.5 million. However, with respect to Compaq's U.S. tax liability, the combination of the capital loss deduction against Compaq's capital gains income from other sources and the U.S. foreign tax credit, the overall after-tax return on the transaction was $1,250,000. The issue before the Fifth Circuit was whether to disregard the Netherlands withholding tax to determine that the before-tax profit of $1.8 million (a return of 2 percent on the $887.6 million purchase price of the ADRs), or whether considering that tax, the transaction lacked a profit motive and was motivated by tax avoidance.

The Fifth Circuit first concluded that in determining pre-tax profit, taxes are to be disregarded regardless of whether the tax is imposed by a foreign country or the United States. Thus, the court concluded that, "If the effects of the transaction are computed consistently, Compaq made both a pre-tax profit and an after-tax profit from the ADR transaction." The court further concluded that, "the evidence in the record does not show that Compaq's choice to engage in the ADR transaction was solely motivated by the tax consequences of the transaction. Instead, the evidence shows that Compaq actually and legitimately also sought the (pre-tax) $1.9 million profit it would get from the Royal Dutch dividend of approximately $22.5 million less the $20.7 million or so in capital losses that Compaq would incur from the sale of the ADRs ex dividend." Thus the court held, "Because the Royal Dutch ADR transaction had both economic substance and a non-tax business purpose, it should have been recognized as valid for U.S. income tax purposes."

2.2. *The Economic Substance of the* Compaq *Transaction*

The absence of a non-tax business purpose in *Compaq* is not readily evident unless one focuses on the fact, ignored in the Fifth Circuit's opinion, that from the outset there was an absolute certainty that the transaction would produce a negative cash flow for Compaq before U.S. taxes were taken into account. In other words, if there were no federal corporate income tax, Compaq never would have engaged in the transaction. The transaction is an example of corporate tax accounting departments using tax benefits to produce after-tax profits. Compaq's investment in ADRs produced a pre-tax profit, but only if the Netherlands withholding tax on the dividends is ignored. Indeed, the transactions would not have been undertaken absent the U.S. and Netherlands tax considerations that created the potential for before-tax profit and made realization of an after-tax profit possible. The profit was dependent on the existence of Compaq's capital gain income,[1] the Netherlands' withholding tax, and the availability of the U.S. tax credit for foreign income taxes.

Understanding the transaction in *Compaq* requires knowing a little about the U.S. treatment of foreign income taxes withheld on dividends paid to a U.S. shareholder by a foreign company. Suppose that a foreign corporation (F Corp.) pays a dividend of $100 to a U.S. shareholder, but the foreign country in which F Corp. is located (the Netherlands or "NL") imposes a 15 percent tax on dividends that are remitted to shareholders in another country. The U.S. shareholder is required to include the full $100 dividend in gross income on its U.S. tax return. The United States then grants a tax credit of $15 to account for the withheld income tax paid to the Netherlands. If the U.S. shareholder is in a 35-percent tax bracket for U.S. tax purposes, the net U.S. tax to the shareholder is $20 ($35–$15), and the overall tax on the dividend is $35. The purpose of the foreign tax credit is to avoid double taxation on the dividend income while still requiring taxation at U.S. tax rates on the full amount of the dividend.

Some U.S. taxpayers cannot take advantage of the U.S. foreign tax credit for foreign income taxes, because, for example the U.S. shareholder may be a tax-exempt organization not subject to U.S. tax liability. Assume that a tax-exempt organization (TEO) holds $1,000 of stock in F Corp. which pays a dividend of $100. The dividend is subject to $15 withholding by the Netherlands, leaving TEO with net cash of $85. Also assume that the dividend distribution reduces the value of TEO's F Corp. stock, ex-dividend, to $900. An intermediary will look for a buyer that can utilize the Netherlands tax to generate a U.S. tax credit (Compaq) and which also has a capital gain to offset capital losses generated by the transaction. Assume, therefore, that Compaq has a capital gain of $100 on which it would owe tax of $35. Compaq purchases the stock from TEO for its pre-dividend value net of the withholding tax, $985. A few minutes later, after the record date for the dividend, the TEO will repurchase the F Corp. stock for $900, thereby obtaining the equivalent of the F Corp. dividend net of the Netherlands

---

[1]   Absent capital gains, Compaq's capital loss on the resale of the ADRs would not have been deductible. Section 1211 limits the deduction of capital loss to the taxpayer's capital gains (see Chapter 24, Section 1.3.)

withholding tax. In effect, TEO sells the $100 dividend for $85, the value of the dividend to TEO net of the Netherlands tax. TEO also receives a fee for engaging in the transaction. TEO ends up with its original F Corp. stock worth $900, which would have been the case had it received the dividend directly. The U.S. Treasury has lost nothing on this leg of the transaction because no tax would be due on the F Corp. dividend paid to the tax-exempt entity.

As the holder of F Corp. stock at the moment the dividend becomes payable to shareholders of record, Compaq receives the $100 dividend and can offset its $35 U.S. tax liability on the dividend with a credit for the $15 Netherlands withholding tax. Compaq also generates an $85 capital loss on the resale of the F Corp. stock to TEO ($900–$985), which saves an additional $29.75 of U.S. tax. Compaq has thus received the $85 dividend plus a $29.75 tax saving, a net benefit of $114.75. Overall Compaq acquires the F Corp. stock for a $985 purchase price plus $25 of U.S. tax liability on the dividend ($1,010), and receives back $1,014.75 consisting of the $900 stock sale proceeds, the $85 dividend net of the Netherlands tax, and the $29.75 U.S. tax savings, a net after-tax profit of $4.75. Absent any U.S. tax consequence, the purchase and resale of the F Corp. stock is a wash, and any fees incurred in the transaction create an economic loss. That is exactly what happened in *Compaq*, only the numbers were substantially larger making the transaction worth pursuing. The following table describes the possible different approaches to the Compaq transaction.

Compaq Transaction[1]
(Numbers in 1000's)

Without Tax		With NL Withholding		After U.S. Tax	
Purchase Price	$887,577	Purchase Price	$887,577	Purchase Price	$887,577
Sales Price	$868,412	Sales Price	$868,412	Sales Price	$868,412
Fees	$ 1,486	Fees	$ 1,486	Fees	$ 1,486
Capital Loss	($ 20,651)	Capital Loss	($ 20,651)	Capital Loss	($ 20,651)
Dividend	$ 22,546	Dividend	$ 22,546	Tax Saving 34%	$ 7,021
		–NL Tax Withholding	$ 3,381	Dividend	$ 22,546
				–Tax at 34%	$ 7,666[2]
				–NL Tax Withholding	$ 3,381
				Foreign Tax Credit	$ 3,381
Net Income	$ 1,895	Net Income	($ 1,486)	Net Income	$ 1,250

Notes to the Table

1.   These figures are from Compaq v. Commissioner, 113 T.C. 214 (1999), rounded off to the nearest thousand.

2.   The difference between the value of the tax deduction for Compaq's capital loss and the tax imposed on the dividend represents the additional tax liability asserted by Compaq as supporting the economic substance of the transaction. These figures assume a 34% marginal rate for the deduction and income. The tax court gives the net tax figure as $640,000.

In the absence of any tax whatsoever, Compaq's acquisition and disposition of the Royal Dutch Shell ADRs would have produced a profit of $1.9 million. Viewed apart from tax consequences, and assuming the price would have been the same, which it would not have been, Compaq purchased and sold the ADRs at a loss of $19,165,000, to acquire a dividend of $22,546,000. The difference between the purchase price paid by Compaq for the ADRs and the sum of the selling price plus the amount of the dividend, is $3,381,000 ($887,577,000 – [$868,412,000 + $22,546,000]), the amount of the Netherlands 15 percent withholding tax. The net dividend to a seller who is subject to the Netherlands tax, and who has no opportunity to recover the tax, is $19,165,000, the price of the dividend to Compaq. Thus, Compaq purchased the dividend for its after-tax value to a seller that would not benefit from the foreign tax credit. Compaq, the U.S. taxpayer, was able to utilize the U.S. tax credit to recapture the benefit of the lower selling price of the right to the dividend. Compaq's before-tax profit is the equivalent of the U.S. foreign tax credit, less the $1.4 million of fees to Twenty-First Century Securities Corporation, which marketed the transaction to Compaq.[2] The "economic profit" from the transaction, which is critical to the Court of Appeals' analysis, is entirely the result of the market price of the tax benefit.

Entering the transaction, Compaq knew that the dividend distribution would be subject to the Netherlands withholding tax. The Tax Court took this factor into account in holding that the transaction lacked economic substance. Compaq Computer Corp. v. Commissioner, 113 T.C. 214 (1999). The Tax Court noted that Compaq "would incur a prearranged economic loss from the transaction but for the [U.S.] foreign tax credit." The Tax Court recognized that the transaction was not economically viable in the absence of the U.S. tax consequences of both the deduction for Compaq's capital loss on resale of the ADRs and the U.S. foreign tax credit. The Court of Appeals, on the other hand, held that economic substance cannot be analyzed by "stacking the deck" against the taxpayer by taking into account the Netherlands withholding tax as a cost but refusing to treat the U.S. tax-credit as income in the same amount. The Court of Appeals' reasoning on this point is tautological. It is not self-evident that it is improper to take into account the Netherlands tax as a cost of the transaction but to ignore the U.S. tax benefit of the foreign tax credit in determining whether the transaction should be respected as having economic substance in order to allow the benefit.

Compaq's after-tax profit of $1,250,000 was less than the "cost" of lost revenue to the U.S. Treasury. Absent its ADR investment, Compaq would have been liable for $7,021,000 of tax on its capital gain. Compaq's tax liability of $7,667,000 on the dividend was offset by its $3,381,000 tax credit, leaving a net tax liability of $4,286,000. The loss to the U.S. Treasury was $2,735,000 ($7,021,000–$4,286,000). The burden of the Netherlands' withholding tax, reflected in the price of the ADRs to Compaq, was effectively shifted to the U.S. Treasury to produce an after-tax profit for Compaq.

The Court of Appeals also asserted that Compaq was at risk because the resale transaction took place in the stock market. But the risks were minimal, if not nonexistent. For one thing, although the court does not so state, the transactions all took place at night when the New York Stock Exchange was closed. Even if a third party could have stepped in to buy one of the ADR blocks, Compaq simply could have purchased a replacement block for the same price. The only risk, then, was that Compaq might incur extra

---

2   The Tax Court noted that Twenty-First Century Securities Corporation solicited Compaq's participation in the transaction based on strategies to utilize the benefit of Compaq's capital gain during the year. See Compaq Computer Corp. v. Commissioner, 113 T.C. 214, 215 (1999).

transaction costs; the transaction itself was not at risk. Moreover, it is a logical fallacy to assert that a possible risk of *loss* supports the conclusion that the transaction was entered into to obtain an economic *profit*.

Finally, the case raises the question whether a taxpayer that holds stock in a foreign corporation for as little as a few minutes—and as part of a pre-arranged series of steps over which the taxpayer has no control—should be treated as the owner of the stock for purposes of the foreign tax credit.

While the Fifth Circuit (in *Compaq*) and the Eighth Circuit (in IES Industries, Inc. v. United States, 253 F.3d 350 (8th Cir.2001)) have held that foreign taxes should not be taken into account in evaluating pre-tax profit potential for purposes of the economic substance doctrine, the U.S. Tax Court, not bound by either precedent, continues to maintain its position in *Compaq*—as restated in a more recent foreign tax credit case—that "[e]conomically, foreign taxes are the same as any other transaction cost" and are thus integral in determining pre-tax profit. Bank of New York Mellon Corp. v. Commissioner, 801 F.3d 104 (2d Cir.2015). Similarly, both the Second Circuit and the Federal Circuit have held that foreign taxes should be deducted as a cost in calculating a transaction's overall economic effect. American International Group, Inc. v. United States, No. 1:09–cv–01871 (2d Cir.2013), on appeal in No. 14–765; Salem Financial Inc. v. United States, 786 F.3d 932 (Fed.Cir.2015). The Supreme Court has yet to weigh in on the issue.

2.2. *Statutory Response*

Congress reacted to the *Compaq* transaction, which came to light long before the final court decision, by enacting technical provisions denying or limiting the potential tax benefits relied on by the taxpayer. Section 901(k) disallows the foreign tax credit for withholding taxes on dividends if the stock is held for 15 days or less. The enactment of this provision illustrates the cat and mouse game that is played between tax advisors and the government. As Twenty-First Century Securities did in *Compaq*, accounting firms or other financial advisors develop a "tax product" that is marketed to investors. The tax product is normally accompanied by an opinion from a law firm regarding the merits of the transaction from a tax law perspective. The investor buys into the tax-motivated transaction with the expectation that either the transaction will not be discovered on audit or that, in the event of an audit, courts will reject the government's disallowance of the transaction's tax benefits.

These aggressive tax shelter deals are often marketed with non-disclosure agreements that limit competition for the shelter and attempt to prevent the IRS from learning about the transactions. Ultimately the IRS may learn of particular tax shelter arrangements and seek from Congress specific legislative restrictions on those transactions. But such restrictions are effective only with respect to transactions entered into after the effective date of the legislation. Thus, taxpayers who invest in shelter deals early enough are generally safe from legislative action. In the meantime, financial advisors and tax shelter lawyers develop new iterations of tax-savings transactions.

3.   ADDITIONAL TAX MOTIVATED TRANSACTIONS

The late 1990's and early 2000's saw the development and marketing of numerous transactions similar to the shelters developed in *Klamath* and *Compaq*. Accounting firms, financial advisors, law firms, investment banks, and other members of the tax shelter marketplace actively marketed various forms of tax-motivated transactions to high-income clients. Another widely deployed corporate tax shelter scheme involved the purchase of corporate owned life insurance (COLI plans). In In re CM Holdings, Inc., 301 F.3d 96 (3d Cir. 2002), the court applied the economic substance doctrine to disallow interest deductions on loans incurred by the taxpayer to acquire 1,430 life insurance contracts on employees that were structured to require annual payments in excess of any potential return from the investments. Nonetheless, a substantial after-tax profit was derived from the transactions due to the interest deductions expressly permitted by §§ 163(a) and 264. Interest paid was deductible by the taxpayer while the inside build-up of interest in the life insurance policies was excludable from gross income. The taxpayer also could borrow against the inside build up without realizing gross income. The only reason for buying into the COLI transaction was to take advantage of the tax savings achieved through the interest deduction. Indeed, as the Third Circuit held, the transaction had no net positive economic effect on the taxpayer's financial position apart from tax considerations:

> [The taxpayer's] COLI plan lacked economic substance. It fails the objective prong because, outside of tax considerations, the transaction had no net economic effect on Camelot's financial position. It fails the subjective prong because at the time the plan was under consideration and agreed on, all parties focused solely on the tax benefits the plan provided. Ultimately the most damning piece of evidence against Camelot is that the marketing information presented to its executives showed that, absent tax deductions, the plan would lose money. Camelot agreed to the plan knowing the tax deductions were the only thing that made it worthwhile.

The court in *CM Holdings* also affirmed the imposition of accuracy-related penalties on the taxpayer because of the lack of substantial authority to support the taxpayer's position. Other courts similarly rejected interest deductions under different versions of the COLI plan marketed by other tax planners. See e.g., Winn-Dixie Stores, Inc. v. Commissioner, 254 F.3d 1313 (11th Cir.2001) (life insurance contracts on 36,000 employees); American Electric Power, Inc. v. U.S., 326 F.3d 737 (6th Cir.2003) (20,000 life insurance contracts on employees). As was the case with the *Compaq* transaction, when made aware of these abusive tax shelters, Congress intervened with a statutory response. Thus, since 1995, interest on indebtedness incurred to purchase life insurance contracts on employees or owners generally is not deductible, with certain exceptions with respect to policies on key personnel. See I.R.C. § 264(a)(4) and (e).

Another widely marketed scheme, promoted by Merrill Lynch, involved the use of a combination of rules in Treasury Regulations for allocating basis in contingent installment sales (see Chapter 31, Section 2.3.) and the statutory provisions for taxing partners in a partnership to shift gains to foreign entities not subject to U.S. tax in order to generate huge tax losses for the U.S. taxpayer.[3] In ACM Partnership v. Commissioner, 157 F.3d 231 (3d Cir.1998), the court rejected a version of the Merrill Lynch plan sold to Colgate Palmolive on the grounds that the transaction lacked economic substance. Colgate Palmolive had realized over $104 million of capital gain in a prior year on the sale of a subsidiary. The transaction considered in *ACM Partnership* was designed to produce an $84 million capital loss that Colgate Palmolive could carryback to offset its capital gain. In concluding that the arrangement lacked objective economic effect, the Court of Appeals indicated that:

> [W]e find that ACM's [the partnership's] intervening acquisition and disposition of the Citicorp notes was a mere device to create the appearance of a contingent installment sale despite the transaction's actual character as an investment of $35 million in cash into a roughly equivalent amount of LIBOR notes. Thus, the acquisition and disposition of the qualifying private placement Citicorp notes, based upon which ACM characterized its transactions as a contingent installment sale * * * , had no effect on ACM's net economic position or non-tax business interests and thus, as the Tax Court properly found, did not constitute an economically substantive transaction that may be respected for tax purposes.

The court added:

> Tax losses such as these, which are purely an artifact of tax accounting methods and which do not correspond to any actual economic losses, do not constitute the type of "bona fide" losses that are deductible under the Internal Revenue Code and regulations.

The court also found that the Merrill Lynch strategy failed the subjective aspect of the economic sham analysis. The court concluded that despite explicit statutory language that allowed the claimed deductions and which did not require a business purpose motive, the deductions are not allowable "if they arose from a transaction 'entered into without expectation of economic profit and [with] no purpose beyond creating tax deductions.' " Quoting from United States v. Wexler, 31 F.3d 117, 122 (3d Cir.1994). The court noted:

---

[3]   In a typical transaction, the U.S. taxpayer entered into a partnership with a foreign entity that was not subject to U.S. tax on any capital gains income produced by the transaction. At the outset, the foreign partner held 85 to 90 percent of the partnership interest, with a Merrill Lynch entity holding a nominal partnership interest. The partnership purchased bank notes which it resold within a short period of time for a large up-front cash payment plus notes. Interest on the notes was based on an international index (LIBOR), which made the transaction a contingent installment sale with no maximum selling price. Under the contingent sales regulations the basis in the notes was allocated over the payment period. The basis allocation produced large capital gains in the year that the notes were resold. The bulk of this gain was allocated to the foreign partner and was, therefore, not subject to U.S. tax. Thereafter, the partnership redeemed the foreign partner leaving the U.S. taxpayer holding almost all of the partnership interest. Then, when the notes were disposed of by the partnership the remaining unrecovered basis produced large capital losses that were allocated to the U.S. taxpayer.

ACM's lack of regard for the relative costs and benefits of the contemplated transaction and its failure to conduct a contemporaneous profitability analysis support the Tax Court's conclusion that ACM's transactions were not designed or reasonably anticipated to yield a pre-tax profit, particularly in view of the significant transactions costs involved in exchanging illiquid private placement instruments.

* * *

We find ample support in the record for the Tax Court's conclusion that ACM and its partners did not reasonably anticipate that its contingent installment sale would generate a pre-tax profit. Because ACM's acquisition and disposition of the Citicorp notes in a contingent installment exchange was without objective effect on ACM's net economic position or non-tax objectives, and because its investments in the Citicorp notes and LIBOR notes did not rationally serve ACM's professed non-tax objectives or afford ACM or its partners a reasonable prospect for pre-tax profit, we will affirm the Tax Court's determination that the contingent installment exchange transactions lacked economic substance and its resulting decision providing that the capital gain and loss at issue will not be recognized and thus disallowing deductions arising from the application of the contingent installment sale provisions and the ratable basis recovery rule.

Another version of the Merrill Lynch contingent sale transaction was rejected in ASA Investerings Partnership v. Commissioner, 201 F.3d 505 (D.C.Cir.2000), but on a different theory. Rather than declaring the whole transaction to be without economic substance, as was the case in *ACM Partnership*, the Court of Appeals accepted the conclusion of the Tax Court that Allied Signal, to which the transaction was marketed, and its foreign partner lacked a requisite intent to join together as partners to conduct business activity for a purpose other than tax avoidance. The court thus concluded that the partnership arrangement was not to be respected and that Allied Signal was, therefore, taxable on all of the initial capital gain that the structure attempted to allocate to the foreign partner, thereby defeating the attempted tax avoidance mechanism. In concluding that formation of a partnership requires a nontax business purpose, the court indicated that there is no distinction between the "economic substance" and "business purpose" rules:

> "Both simply state that the Commissioner may look beyond the form of an action to discover its substance. * * * The terminology of one rule may appear in the context of the other because they share the same rationale. Both rules elevate the substance of an action over its form. Although the taxpayer may structure a transaction so that it satisfies the formal requirements of the Internal Revenue Code, the Commissioner may deny legal effect to a transaction if its sole purpose is to evade taxation." [quoting Zmuda v. Commissioner, 731 F.2d 1417, 1420–21 (9th Cir.1984)]

The court in *ASA Investerings* went on to say:

> We note that the "business purpose" doctrine is hazardous. It is uniformly recognized that taxpayers are entitled to structure their transactions in such a way as to minimize tax. When the business purpose doctrine is violated, such structuring is deemed to have gotten out of hand, to have been carried to such extreme lengths that the business purpose is no more than a facade. But there is no absolutely clear line between the two. Yet the doctrine seems essential. A tax system of rather high rates gives a multitude of clever individuals in the private sector powerful incentives to game the system. Even the smartest drafters of legislation and regulation cannot be expected to anticipate every device. The business purpose doctrine reduces the incentive to engage in such essentially wasteful activity, and in addition helps achieve reasonable equity among taxpayers who are similarly situated—in every respect except for differing investments in tax avoidance.

In its concluding paragraph, the *ASA Investerings* court added, "For the deal overall, the most telling evidence is the testimony of AlliedSignal's Chairman and CEO, who could not 'recall any talk or any estimates of how much profit [the transaction] would generate.' The Tax Court concluded that none of the supposed partners had the intent to form a real partnership, a conclusion that undoubtedly encompasses AlliedSignal."

As it did in *ASA Investerings*, the Tax Court in Andantech L.L.C. v. Commissioner, T.C. Memo. 2002–97, aff'd 331 F.3d 972 (D.C.Cir.2003) disregarded the formation of a partnership. That case involved a leasing transaction structured by Comdisco, Inc. (a publicly traded equipment leasing company) and Norwest Equipment Finance, Inc. (now Wells Fargo Equipment Finance, Inc.) that was designed to use a foreign partnership to strip income from a computer leasing transaction by accelerating and allocating rental income to foreign partners, who were not taxable on the income, and saving all of the depreciation deductions for the U.S. participant who would thereby deduct the depreciation without having to report any income.[4] Following its reasoning from *ASA Investerings* the Tax Court in *Andantech* found that the parties did not join together to share the profits and losses of the business activities of a partnership. The court concluded that the partnership "was not created for the purpose of carrying on a trade or business but rather to strip the income from the transaction and avoid U.S. taxation." The court described the economic substance doctrine in the following manner:

> The focus of each party's position, in essence, is in terms of substance over form and related (e.g., sham and step transaction) judicial doctrines. Under these judicial doctrines, although the form of a transaction may literally comply with the provisions of a Code section, the form will not be given effect where it has no

---

[4]   For another example of an income stripping transaction involving a sale and leaseback arrangement that was rejected as lacking economic substance see Nicole Rose Corp. v. Commissioner, 117 T.C. 328 (2001).

business purpose and operates simply as a device to conceal the true character of a transaction. See Gregory v. Helvering, 293 U.S. 465, 469–470 (1935). "To permit the true nature of a transaction to be disguised by mere formalisms, which exist solely to alter tax liabilities, would seriously impair the effective administration of the tax policies of Congress." Commissioner v. Court Holding Co., 324 U.S. 331, 334 (1945). Conversely, if the substance of a transaction accords with its form, then the form will be upheld and given effect for Federal tax purposes. * * * .

A transaction may be treated as a sham where (1) the taxpayer is motivated by no business purpose other than obtaining tax benefits, and (2) the transaction has no economic substance because no reasonable possibility of a profit exists. Rice's Toyota World, Inc. v. Commissioner, 752 F.2d 89, 91–95 (4th Cir.1985) * * * . But a transaction that has a valid business purpose and economic substance may still be recast in order to reflect its true nature.

In Saba Partnership v. Commissioner, 273 F.3d 1135 (D.C.Cir.2001), a Merrill Lynch contingent sale transaction marketed to the Brunswick Corporation was rejected by the Tax Court, T.C. Memo 1999–359, on the grounds that the entire transaction lacked economic substance. The D.C. Circuit Court of Appeals remanded the case for factual findings as to whether the partnership was a sham under the business purpose doctrine following its opinion in *ASA Investerings*. The Court of Appeals indicated that since application of the business purpose doctrine was a question of fact it would not be appropriate for the appellate court to resolve the issue. However, the court signaled its expected result by saying:

> In any case, ASA makes clear that "the absence of a business purpose is fatal" to the argument that the Commissioner should respect an entity for federal tax purposes. ASA, 201 F.3d at 512. Here, the Tax Court specifically found "overwhelming evidence in the record that [the partnerships] were organized solely to generate tax benefits for Brunswick." * * * Arguably, this broader finding subsumes any factual differences that might exist between this case and ASA.

The Merrill Lynch transaction purchased by American Home Products Corporation (now Wyeth) was rejected in Boca Investerings Partnership v. United States, 314 F.3d 625 (D.C.Cir.2003).

In a news release, IR–2001–74 (8/28/2001), the IRS announced that Merrill Lynch had agreed to settle a case brought against it by the IRS under §§ 6700 (promoting abusive tax shelters), 6701 (aiding and abetting understatement of tax liability), 6707 (failure to furnish information regarding tax shelters by persons required to register a tax shelter), and 6708 (failure to maintain lists of investors in abusive tax shelters) with respect to its promotion of the contingent sales scheme.

Another tax shelter based on contingent liabilities, developed by the accounting firm BDO Seidman and the subsequently disbanded law firm

Jenkens & Gilchrist, was held to lack economic substance by the Court of Claims in Jade Trading, LLC v. United States, 80 Fed.Cl. 11 (2007), following the analysis of the court in *Coltec*. This transaction involved the acquisition of offsetting purchase and sales of foreign currency options by U.S. taxpayers with high capital gains and a contribution of the options to a partnership. The taxpayers claimed a high basis in the purchased options, but that the offsetting return on the sold options was contingent and, therefore, did not reduce basis. On liquidating their interests in the partnership, the taxpayers claimed a $15 million basis in the partnership assets, which produced a $15 million loss. The court described the import of the transaction as follows:

> In addition to its inherent lack of potential profitability, the spread transaction was developed as a tax avoidance mechanism and not an investment strategy. The transaction was devised and marketed by a tax accounting group, BDO Seidman's "Tax $ells" Division, a/k/a the Wolf Pack. Although BDO Seidman witnesses claim that Bergmann brought them the idea for the spread transaction, these witnesses acknowledged that BDO Seidman investigated the tax ramifications of the spread transaction, added the spread transaction to its Tax Product Sales Manual, prepared a marketing letter describing the tax benefits of the spread transaction, joined forces with [law firm] Curtis Mallet and sold the spread transaction concept to clients as a tax product, while leaving the execution of the transactions to [hedge fund manager] Sentinel.

The transaction was thus found to lack economic substance under four principles developed by the court in Coltec Industries, Inc. v. United States, 454 F.3d 1340 (Fed.Cir.2006); (i) the law does not permit the taxpayer to reap tax benefits from a transaction that lacks economic reality, (ii) when the taxpayer claims a deduction, it is the taxpayer who bears the burden of proving that the transaction has economic substance, (iii) the economic substance of a transaction must be viewed objectively rather than subjectively, and (iv) the transaction to be analyzed is the one that gave rise to the alleged tax benefit. In addition, the court in *Jade Trading* imposed a 40 percent gross valuation misstatement penalty under § 6662 and, in the alternative, approved a 20 percent accuracy related penalty.

In yet another contingent liability case, New Phoenix Sunrise Corporation v. Commissioner, 132 T.C. 161 (2009), the taxpayer entered into a tax shelter (called a BLISS transaction) that involved the purchase of two pairs of option contracts in a deal designed to eliminate $10 million of capital gain realized on the sale of appreciated assets. The long portion of the options was purchased from Deutsche Bank AG for an initial payment of $10.631 million plus two additional payments of $63 million each. The short option was sold to Deutsche Bank for an initial payment of $10.369 million and two additional payments of $63.066 million. Only the $138,750 difference between the purchase and sales prices changed hands. The options called for offsetting payments based on the U.S. $/Japanese ¥ price with a variance in the options of only 0.00002 (2 Pips). The taxpayer contributed the purchased and sold options to a general partnership for a 99% interest. The 1% partner was a dominant shareholder in the taxpayer. The taxpayer claimed a basis in its partnership interest in the amount of the cost of the purchased long option. It also claimed that its liability on the short position of the sold option was a contingent liability that did not reduce the basis in its partnership interest. Thereafter, the partnership acquired shares of Cisco stock for $149,958. After the options expired, the partnership distributed the Cisco stock to the taxpayer, and the taxpayer claimed that pursuant to § 732 it had a basis in the Cisco stock equal to its partnership interest basis, and as a result realized a $10 million loss on its subsequent sale of the Cisco stock.

The court rejected the claimed loss on several grounds. First, the taxpayer did not suffer a real economic loss. "The loss claimed as a result of the stepped-up basis in the Cisco stock was purely fictional." Second, the transaction had no realistic possibility of earning a profit. Deutsche Bank's control as the calculation agent for the option contracts empowered it to assure that the market rate chosen for the closing of the options would never trigger the so-called "sweet spot" under which the investor would earn substantial profits. Third, the transaction lacked economic substance. The court stated:

> Absent the benefit of the claimed tax loss, there was nothing but a cash flow that was negative for all relevant periods—the "hallmark" of an economic sham as the Court of Appeals for the Sixth Circuit has held. Dow Chem. Co. v. United States, 435 F.3d at 602 (quoting Am. Elec. Power Co. v. United States, 326 F.3d 737, 742 (6th Cir. 2003). Such a deal lacks economic substance. Id. Because we find that the transaction at issue lacked economic substance, we do not consider Mr. Wray's and Capital's profit motive in entering into the transaction. Id. at 605. * * * Pursuant to the aforementioned cases, the BLISS transaction must be ignored for Federal income tax purposes. Accordingly, the overstated loss claimed as a result of the sale of the Cisco stock is disregarded, as is the flowthrough loss from Olentangy Partners.

The court also disallowed a $500,000 deduction for fees paid to a law firm for the tax opinion that purported to legitimize the tax gambit and for structuring the transaction, because the fees were not incurred in the production of taxable income that a deduction could legitimately offset.

In addition, the court sustained a 40-percent gross valuation penalty under § 6662(e) and (h), holding that the undervaluation penalty is applicable to overstated basis. The court indicated that the § 6662(d) substantial understatement of tax and the § 6662(c) negligence penalties were applicable. However, because the penalties are not additive (that is, they cannot be stacked), only the gross-valuation penalty was imposed. In addition, the court rejected the taxpayer's argument that it reasonably relied on its attorney's tax shelter opinion in entering into the transaction, a defense to penalties under § 6664(c). The court found that it was unreasonable for the taxpayer to rely on the advice of attorneys who "actively participated in the development, structuring, promotion, sale, and implementation" of the tax shelter transaction. Id. at 193. The taxpayer could not prove reasonable cause and good faith reliance on its lawyer's tax opinion "in the face of such a conflict of interest." Id.

Over the years, a circuit split developed over whether the substantial-valuation-misstatement penalty under § 6662(e) and the gross valuation penalty under § 6662(h)—both of which were at play in the *New Phoenix* decision—applied to transactions whose tax benefits were ultimately disregarded due to lack of economic substance. See e.g., Keller v. Commissioner, 556 F.3d 1056 (9th Cir.2009); Bemont Investments, LLC v. United States, 679 F.3d 339, 347–48 (5th Cir.2012). The minority of courts that refused to apply valuation penalties to noneconomic substance transactions generally argued—usually with little elaboration and overwrought sympathy for the taxpayer—that "[w]henever the I.R.S. totally disallows a deduction or credit, the I.R.S. may not penalize the taxpayer for a valuation overstatement included in that deduction or credit." Heasley v. Commissioner, 902 F.2d 380, 383 (5th Cir.1990) (reversing the Tax Court's decision to uphold the assessment of both interest and penalties, which the court considered "draconian," id. at 386). In 2013, the Supreme Court addressed the issue with respect to a basis-inflating transaction subsequently disregarded for lack of economic substance. In a unanimous decision, the Court conducted a "straightforward application" of the relevant statute and underlying regulations to find that "the partners underpaid their taxes because they overstated their outside basis, and they overstated their outside basis because the partnerships were shams. We therefore have no difficulty concluding that any underpayment resulting from the * * * tax shelter is attributable to the partners' misrepresentation of outside basis (a valuation misstatement)." United States v. Woods, 134 S. Ct. 557, 566, 568 (2013). As a result, the 40-percent-gross-valuation-misstatement penalty applied to the understatement of tax created by the transaction that had been found lacking in economic substance.

4. CODIFICATION OF THE ECONOMIC SUBSTANCE DOCTRINE

The Health Care and Education Reconciliation Act of 2010 added new § 7701(*o*), codifying the economic substance doctrine. Congress had considered codification of the economic substance doctrine several times prior to the enactment of § 7701(*o*). Some tax practitioners and professional groups had long argued that the Supreme Court never applied the judicial doctrine to deny a taxpayer any tax benefits, and thus other federal courts should act with similar restraint. This argument conveniently omitted Supreme Court decisions in Gregory v. Helvering, 203 U.S. 465 (1935), Higgins v. Smith, 308 U.S. 473 (1940), Commissioner v. Court Holding Co., 324 U.S. 331 (1945), National Carbide Corporation v. Commissioner, 336 U.S. 422 (1949), and Knetsch v. United States, 364 U.S. 361 (1960), in addition to notable Supreme Court denials of certiorari in economic substance cases, as well as dozens of precedential circuit court, district court, and Tax Court cases decided over decades. Nonetheless, congressional concern intensified during the 2000s over inconsistent application of the economic substance doctrine, the variable modes of analysis under the doctrine's so-called subjective and objective prongs, and questions pertaining to the doctrine's continued viability. See Coltec Industries, Inc. v. United

States, 62 Fed. Cl. 716, 756 (2004) (finding that "where a taxpayer has satisfied all statutory requirements established by Congress * * * the use of the 'economic substance' doctrine to trump 'mere compliance with the Code' would violate the separation of powers"), vacated, 454 F.3d 1340 (Fed.Cir.2006). Never mind that on appeal, the Court of Appeals for the Federal Circuit vacated the lower court's decision in *Coltec* explicitly reiterating the validity of the economic substance doctrine, and holding that the transaction in question lacked economic substance.

The codified economic substance doctrine in new § 7701(*o*) clarifies and standardizes some applications of the doctrine, but does not establish when it should be applied. According to the legislative history, "the provision [§ 7701(*o*)(5)(C)] does not change present law standards in determining when to utilize an economic substance analysis." Joint Committee on Taxation (JCT), Technical Explanation of the Revenue Provisions of the "Reconciliation Act of 2010," as amended in combination with the "Patient Protection and Affordable Care Act," 152 (JCX–18–10) (Mar. 21, 2010). Thus, "the fact that a transaction meets the requirements for specific treatment under any provision of the Code is not determinative of whether a transaction or series of transactions of which it is a part has economic substance." Id. at 153. Codification of the economic substance doctrine was not intended to alter or supplant other judicial interpretive doctrines, including the business purpose, substance over form, and step transaction doctrines or any similar rule in the Code, regulations, or guidance thereunder. Instead, § 7701(*o*) merely supplements those rules. Id. at 155.

One of the most important aspects of new § 7701(*o*) is that it requires a *conjunctive* analysis under which a transaction has economic substance only if (1) the transaction changes the taxpayer's economic position in a meaningful way apart from Federal income tax effects *and* (2) the taxpayer has a substantial business purpose, apart from Federal income tax effects, for entering into such a transaction. This conjunctive test resolves the split between the Circuits (and between the Tax Court and certain Circuits) by rejecting the view of those courts that found a transaction to have economic substance if there was *either* (1) a change in the taxpayer's economic position *or* (2) a nontax business purpose for entering into the transaction. See e.g., Rice's Toyota World v. Commissioner, 752 F.2d 89 (4th Cir.1985); IES Industries, Inc. v. United States, 253 F.3d 350, 353 (8th Cir.2001). Section § 7701(*o*)(5)(D) allows the economic substance doctrine to be applied to a single transaction or to a series of transactions. Also, the official explanation of the new provision by the Joint Committee on Taxation further states that the codified doctrine "does not alter the court's ability to aggregate, disaggregate, or otherwise recharacterize a transaction when applying the doctrine." By way of example, the JCT noted courts' continued ability "to bifurcate a transaction in which independent activities with non-tax objectives are combined with an unrelated item having only tax-avoidance objectives in order to disallow those tax-motivated benefits." JCX–18–10 at 153.

Section 7701(*o*)(2) does not require that the taxpayer establish a profit potential to prove that a transaction results in a meaningful change in the taxpayer's economic position or that the taxpayer has a substantial non-Federal-income-tax purpose. Nor does it specify a threshold rate of return if the taxpayer relies on the profit potential to establish economic substance. But, and very importantly, if the taxpayer relies on a claim that the tax shelter investment possessed a profit potential in addition to the tax benefits in order to establish the economic substance of the transaction, then the taxpayer must prove and a court must determine whether "the present value of the reasonably expected pre-tax profit from the transaction is substantial in relation to the present value of the expected net tax benefits that would be allowed if the transaction were respected." I.R.C. § 7701(o)(2)(A). Thus, the analysis of profit potential undertaken by many courts prior to codification—including the analysis conducted by the Court of Federal Claims in Consolidated Edison Co. of New York v. United States, 90 Fed. Cl. 228 (2009), which ignored any present value inquiry—would fail to meet the requirements of the codified doctrine. In addition, transaction costs (including fees paid to lawyers, accountants, investment bankers, and shelter promoters) must be taken into account in determining pre-tax profits. The statute also authorizes the Treasury Department to promulgate regulations requiring foreign taxes to be treated as expenses in determining pre-tax profit in appropriate cases (thereby putting Congress on the side of the government in treating foreign taxes as a cost of shelter investments. I.R.C. § 7701(o)(2)(A). Furthermore, any state or local income tax effect that is related to a Federal income tax effect is treated in the same manner as a Federal income tax effect. Thus, state tax savings that piggyback on Federal income tax savings cannot provide either a profit potential or a business purpose. I.R.C. § 7701(o)(3). Similarly, a financial accounting benefit cannot satisfy the business purpose requirement if the financial accounting benefit originates in a reduction of Federal income tax. I.R.C. § 7701(o)(4).

Section 7701(o)(5)(B) specifically provides that the statutory modifications and clarifications to the economic substance doctrine shall apply to an individual only with respect to "transactions entered into in connection with a trade or business or an activity engaged in for the production of income." As the Joint Committee on Taxation elaborated in the official explanation of the provision, the codified doctrine "is not intended to alter the tax treatment of certain basic business transactions that, under longstanding judicial and administrative practice are respected, merely because the choice between meaningful economic alternatives is largely or entirely based on comparative tax advantages." JCX–18–10 at 152–53. The list of transactions that Congress intended to immunize from application of the codified doctrine includes: (1) the choice between capitalizing a business enterprise with debt or equity; (2) a U.S. person's choice between utilizing a foreign corporation or a domestic corporation to make a foreign investment; (3) the choice to enter a transaction or series of transactions that constitute a corporate organization or reorganization under subchapter C; and (4) the choice to utilize a related-party entity in a transaction, provided that the arm's length standard of section 482 and other applicable concepts are satisfied. Leasing transactions, "like all other types of transactions," will continue to be scrutinized based on all of the facts and circumstances. Id. at 153.

New § 6662(b)(6), in conjunction with new § 6664(c)(2), imposes a strict-liability 20-percent penalty for an underpayment attributable to any disallowance of claimed tax benefits by reason of a transaction lacking economic substance, within the meaning of new § 7701(*o*), "or failing to meet the requirements of any similar rule of law." The penalty is increased to 40 percent if the taxpayer does not adequately disclose the relevant facts on the original return or an amended return filed before the taxpayer has been contacted for audit; an amended return filed thereafter cannot cure the original sin of failing to disclose. I.R.C. § 6662(i). Because the § 6664(c) "reasonable cause and good faith" defense to penalties is unavailable for underpayments of tax attributable to noneconomic substance transactions described in § 6662(b)(6), outside (or in-house) analyses and opinions of counsel or other tax advisors will not insulate a taxpayer from penalty if a transaction is found to lack economic substance. Likewise, new § 6664(d)(2) precludes a reasonable cause defense to imposition of the § 6662A reportable transaction understatement penalty for a transaction lacking in economic substance. (Section 6662A(e)(2) has been amended to provide that the § 6662A penalty with respect to a reportable transaction understatement does not apply to a transaction that lacks economic substance if a 40-percent penalty is imposed under § 6662(i); in other words, the amendment prevents the stacking of penalties in the event the higher noneconomic substance penalty is imposed). A similar no-fault penalty regime applies to excessive erroneous refund claims that are denied on the ground that the transaction on which the refund claim was based lacked economic substance. I.R.C. § 6676(c).

To date, codification of the economic substance doctrine under § 7701(*o*) has had no substantively discernible effect on how courts analyze tax shelter transactions in pre-enactment cases; that is, in cases where taxpayers entered into the transactions prior to the statute's 2010 effective date. Indeed, courts continue to apply longstanding and variable economic substance tests as developed in the different circuits. With the passage of time, it will be interesting to see whether the codified doctrine influences how courts assess the legitimacy of tax-favored transactions. In particular, one wonders if more courts will adopt the conjunctive test as reflected in § 7701(*o*)—and as currently followed in many jurisdictions—that treats a transaction as possessing economic substance only if it changes the taxpayer's economic position "in a meaningful way" (absent tax benefits) *and* the taxpayer entered into the transaction with a "substantial" non-tax purpose.

PART X

THE TAXABLE UNIT

CHAPTER 37

SHIFTING INCOME AMONG TAXABLE UNITS

In most situations, determining who is responsible for paying tax on particular items of income is not difficult. The taxpayer is generally the individual or entity who earns or owns the property that produces the income. Thus, the person who earns a salary should be the one to pay the income tax on that salary and the owner of income-producing property—the landlord who receives rents or the stockholder who receives dividends—is the appropriate taxpayer for that income. That the individual or entity who owns property or provides services is the unit of taxation seems so self-evident that early Revenue Acts did not even address the question. The unit of taxation was the individual, the corporation, and the estate or trust. (Although partnerships are legally separate from their partners, the partnership is not separately taxable.) When other relationships exist among these units, however, the progressive rate structure creates an incentive to shift income among the units. If a mother and daughter are separate units of taxation and the last $10,000 earned by the mother would be taxed at a rate of 28 percent but the first $10,000 received by the daughter would not be taxed at all, the mother has a tax incentive to shift the $10,000 to her daughter, particularly if the mother would use the $10,000 for her daughter's support in any event. The higher the mother's marginal rate, the greater incentive to shift the income.[1]

The simplest way to shift income is for one taxpayer to give income-producing property to another taxpayer. An outright gift of stock, for example, shifts the tax on subsequent dividends on that stock to the donee. But not all taxpayers own property and, even if they do, they may be unwilling to relinquish ownership of the property in order to obtain the attendant income tax saving. Thus, some taxpayers may attempt to shift income from their own personal services to other taxpayers. Other taxpayers attempt to shift the tax while at the same time retaining some control over the income or the property producing it.

The history of this area of the income tax is mainly the record of the successes and failures of various arrangements designed to achieve the objective of shifting income. Although not every plan or device was tax-motivated, the law in this area has developed largely out of tax-motivated transactions. Congress has reacted to particular arrangements by

---

[1]   Legislation has reduced this incentive. As explained in Chapter 38, since 1987 the investment income of children has been taxed at their parent's tax rate, if higher than their own, and since 1948 married people have been treated as one taxpayer for purposes of applying the tax rates.

enacting provisions that preclude income shifting. Nevertheless, over the years it has been the judiciary, urged by the IRS, that has combatted these income-shifting assaults on the progressive tax structure. The result is that determining who should pay tax on an item of income has become the job of courts rather than Congress.

SECTION 1.   INCOME FROM PERSONAL SERVICES

Lucas v. Earl

Supreme Court of the United States, 1930.
281 U.S. 111.

■ MR. JUSTICE HOLMES delivered the opinion of the Court.

Issue ←—   This case presents the question whether the respondent, Earl, could be taxed for the whole of the salary and attorney's fees earned by him in the years 1920 and 1921, or should be taxed for only a half of them in view of a contract with his wife which we shall mention. The Commissioner of Internal Revenue and the Board of Tax Appeals imposed a tax upon the whole, but their decision was reversed by the *Procedural History* ←— Circuit Court of Appeals, 30 F.2d 898. A writ of certiorari was granted by this court.

Contract between them ←— By the contract, made in 1901, Earl and his wife agreed "that any property either of us now has or may hereafter acquire * * * in any way, either by earnings (including salaries, fees, etc.), or any rights by contract or otherwise, during the existence of our marriage, or which we or either of us may receive by gift, bequest, devise, or inheritance, and all the proceeds, issues, and profits of any and all such property shall be treated *FACTS* and considered, and hereby is declared to be received, held, taken, and owned by us as joint tenants, and not otherwise, with the right of survivorship." The validity of the contract is not questioned, and we assume it to be unquestionable under the law of the State of California, in which the parties lived. Nevertheless we are of opinion that the *Holding* ←— Commissioner and Board of Tax Appeals were right.

Rule ←— The Revenue Act of 1918, imposes a tax upon the net income of every individual including "income derived from salaries, wages, or compensation for personal service * * * of whatever kind and in whatever form paid." The provisions of the Revenue Act of 1921, are similar to those of the above. A very forcible argument is presented to the effect that the statute seeks to tax only income beneficially received, and that taking the question more technically the salary and fees became the joint property of Earl and his wife on the very first instant on which they were received. We well might hesitate upon the latter proposition, because however the matter might stand between husband and wife he was the only party to the contracts by which the salary and fees were earned, and it is somewhat hard to say that the last step in the performance of those contracts could be taken by anyone but himself alone. But this case is not to be decided by attenuated subtleties. It turns on the import and reasonable construction of the taxing act. There is no doubt that the statute could tax salaries to those who earned them and provide that the tax could not be escaped by anticipatory arrangements and contracts however skillfully devised to prevent the salary when paid from vesting even for a second in the man who earned it. That seems to us the import of the statute before us and we think that no distinction can be taken according to the motives leading to the arrangement by which the fruits are attributed to a different tree from that on which they grew.

       Judgment reversed.

DETAILED ANALYSIS

1.   EFFECT OF MARRIAGE

       Shortly after the decision in Lucas v. Earl, the Supreme Court held in Poe v. Seaborn, 282 U.S. 101 (1930), that in a community property jurisdiction each spouse is taxable on one-half of the community income regardless of which spouse earns the income. The Court distinguished Lucas v. Earl on the ground that, under the Washington state community property law at issue in *Seaborn*, both spouses had an immediate and vested interest in all community income under state law. See also Commissioner v. Harmon, 323 U.S. 44 (1944) (each spouse's vested interest in income as community property must be dictated by state law as an incident of marriage). The practical effect of the *Seaborn* decision resulted in married couples in community property states enjoying the benefits of "income splitting," which permitted them to reflect half of the community's income on two separate tax returns, while married couples in common law states were forced to aggregate all income on a single return. The disparate treatment, in combination with the progressive rate structure of the federal income tax, meant that married taxpayers in community property states paid less tax (sometimes considerably less) on the same amount of total family income compared to married couples in common law states. For example, if two married couples each had $20,000 in total family income, but one couple resided in a community property state and the other resided in a common law state, the community property couple would pay tax on two $10,000 incomes while the common law couple would pay tax on one $20,000 income that was subject to the higher rates running from $10,001 to, and including, $20,000.

       In response to criticism of the federal tax inequities created by the decision in *Seaborn*, Congress in 1948 extended to married couples nationwide the tax benefits previously reserved for married couples in community property states through enactment of an "income-splitting joint return" for all married couples. The new tax return provided tax brackets that were exactly twice as wide as the existing return for unmarried taxpayers, a structural device that accomplished income splitting by dividing total family income in half, assessing tax on both halves, and then adding the taxes to derive total tax liability. As discussed in Chapter 38, this treatment, though favorable to married couples, resulted in single taxpayers paying significantly higher tax on identical amounts of income compared to married couples. It also created the legal fiction that married couples nationwide owned family income equally—the Supreme Court's legal justification for income splitting in *Seaborn*—at a time when equal ownership of income and property between spouses obtained in only a minority of jurisdictions. For the history and legacy of *Seaborn*, see Dennis J. Ventry, Jr. Saving *Seaborn*: Ownership Not Marriage as the Basis of Family Taxation, 86 Ind. L.J. 1459 (2011).

2.   EARNINGS REFUSED IN FAVOR OF ANOTHER

In Armantrout v. Commissioner, 67 T.C. 996 (1977), aff'd, 570 F.2d 210 (7th Cir.1978), the taxpayer's employer created an education trust fund through a third-party vendor. The trust fund paid tuition, room, and board for the children of key employees. Benefits from the trust fund were paid directly to the educational institution attended by the employees' children. The taxpayer argued that educational benefits provided to his children were not includable in his gross income because the educational benefits were not beneficially received by the taxpayer. The taxpayer had no right under the employer's plan to receive distributions from the fund and thus possessed no ownership interest in the payments. The court concluded, however, that the educational benefits paid for the taxpayer's children were the product of the taxpayer's employment relationship and were thus in the nature of compensation. The court said that, "It is clear that a taxpayer may not avoid taxation by entering into an anticipatory assignment of income; to allow [taxpayers] to enter into such an arrangement through the back door simply by allowing the employer to make the necessary arrangements would be highly anomalous and inconsistent with the rationale of Lucas v. Earl, supra, * * * and United States v. Basye, 410 U.S. 441 (1973)."

In United States v. Basye, 410 U.S. 441 (1973), Permanente, a medical partnership, contracted with Kaiser, a company operating a hospital and medical care program, to provide services in return for monthly payments. In addition, the hospital company made payments to a trust to provide retirement benefits for the doctors. The amounts were irrevocably paid over to the trust, though the rights of individual doctors to the retirement payments were not vested. The Court held that the payments into the retirement trust were includable in gross income by the partnership and were thus taxable to each doctor-partner as their share of partnership earned income:

> There can be no question that Kaiser's payments to the retirement trust were compensation for services rendered by the partnership under the medical service agreement. These payments constituted an integral part of the employment arrangement. The agreement itself called for two forms of "base compensation" to be paid in exchange for services rendered—direct per-member, per-month payments to the partnership and other, similarly computed, payments to the trust. Nor was the receipt of these payments contingent upon any condition other than continuation of the contractual relationship and the performance of the prescribed medical services. Payments to the trust, much like the direct

payments to the partnership, were not forfeitable by the partnership or recoverable by Kaiser upon the happening of any contingency.

> Yet the courts below, focusing on the fact that the retirement fund payments were never actually received by the partnership but were contributed directly to the trust, found that the payments were not includable as income in the partnership's returns. The view of tax accountability upon which this conclusion rests is incompatible with a foundational rule, which this Court has described as "the first principle of income taxation: that income must be taxed to him who earns it." Commissioner v. Culbertson, 337 U.S. 733, 739–740 (1949). The entity earning the income— whether a partnership or an individual taxpayer—cannot avoid taxation by entering into a contractual arrangement whereby that income is diverted to some other person or entity. Such arrangements, known to the tax law as "anticipatory assignments of income," have frequently been held ineffective as means of avoiding tax liability. The seminal precedent, written over 40 years ago, is Mr. Justice Holmes' opinion for a unanimous Court in Lucas v. Earl, 281 U.S. 111 (1930). * * * The principle of Lucas v. Earl, that he who earns income may not avoid taxation through anticipatory arrangements no matter how clever or subtle, has been repeatedly invoked by this Court and stands today as a cornerstone of our graduated income tax system. * * *

In Teschner v. Commissioner, 38 T.C. 1003 (1962) (Nonacq.), the taxpayer successfully shifted to his daughter taxation of income earned from his personal effort. The taxpayer entered a contest and designated his daughter to receive the prize. Persons over the age of seventeen were ineligible for the contest prizes and were required to designate an individual under age 17 as the recipient. When the taxpayer's entry was selected as a prize winner, the taxpayer asserted that he had no gross income because the prize was not payable to him under the contest rules. The court held that the taxpayer's mere power to direct the distribution of the prize to his daughter was not sufficient to tax its value as income to him because the taxpayer did not possess a right to receive the prize under the contest rules.

The court in *Armantrout* (discussed supra) cited § 83 as an alternative holding in addition to assignment of income principles. Under current law, § 83 applies to a transaction like that in *Armantrout* (i.e., an education trust fund established by an employer for the benefit of key employees' children) to tax the employee-parent. See Treas. Reg. § 1.83–3(e).

3. OTHER SITUATIONS INVOLVING REFUSED EARNINGS

3.1. *In General*

Taxpayers who simply refuse to accept compensation for future personal services without designating an alternative recipient are generally not taxable on that compensation.

In Commissioner v. Giannini, 129 F.2d 638 (9th Cir.1942), Mr. Giannini, the president of a bank who was entitled to receive as compensation a percentage of profits, stated that he would not accept further compensation during the year 1927 and suggested that the corporation do something worthwhile with the money. In 1928, the balance of the profits, $1.5 million, was accordingly donated by the corporation to the Regents of the University of California to establish the Giannini Foundation. Mr. Giannini was held not liable on the profits so paid:

> All that he did was to unqualifiedly refuse to accept any further compensation for his services with the suggestion that the money be used for some worth while purpose. So far as the taxpayer was concerned, the corporation could have kept the money. All arrangements with the University of California regarding the donation to the Foundation were made by the corporation, the taxpayer participating therein only as an officer of the corporation. * * *

> To support the Commissioner's argument we should have to hold that only one reasonable inference could be drawn from the evidence, which is that the donation is but a donation of the taxpayer masquerading as a creature of the corporation to save the true donors [taxpayer and his wife] some tax money. The circumstances do not support this contention. In our opinion the inferences drawn by the Board are more reasonable and comport with that presumption of verity that every act of a citizen of good repute should be able to claim and receive.

In Hedrick v. Commissioner, 154 F.2d 90 (2d Cir.1946), the court disagreed with *Giannini* and held that a taxpayer who refused to cash retirement pay checks because he did not want to enter upon the status of pensioner for fear that such a status might prejudice employment elsewhere was nevertheless taxable. As the court explained:

> Perhaps Comm'r v. Giannini, 9 Cir., 129 F.2d 638, may be distinguished on the facts. If, as we understand them, the amount sought to be taxed as income was offered compensation which the taxpayer refused before he performed the services for which he might have been so paid and the bank acquiesced in the taxpayer's insistence that he should serve for the remainder of the year without additional compensation, we agree with it. In so far as it cannot be so distinguished, we are not persuaded that it should be followed.

An executor who intends to perform services gratuitously may waive the right to the compensation to which the executor would otherwise be entitled and avoid having taxable income attributed to the executor. Rev. Rul. 66–167, 1966–1 C.B. 20, discusses the circumstances in which the services will be treated as being provided gratuitously. In general, the executor must waive the right to compensation within six months of the executor's initial appointment.

3.2. *Services Rendered on Behalf of Family Member*

Where one family member performs services for another, assignment of income principles have not been extended to require that income be imputed to the one performing the services. Thus, for example, in Alexander v. Commissioner, 194 F.2d 921 (5th Cir.1952), a rancher gave cattle and grazing land to his 14-year-old daughter, but continued to manage the cattle and land together with his own interests. The court held that the father could not be taxed on the income from the daughter's cattle and land:

> A farmer and ranchman tried to contribute to the training and development of his daughter who had shown interest in farming and had worked on a farm, by giving her cattle and arranging for her to have a farm, and, instead of hiring someone to perform for her what services were required, performed them himself as a matter of paternal interest and affection.

> To say that the profits derived from Frances' land and cattle * * * merely because * * * the father helped his child by attending to necessary business details, were attributable to the [parent and not to the child] is completely specious reasoning. It is to deny the fundamental verities of the traditional parent and child, father and daughter relationship existing in America, and especially in the farming and ranching areas, where individuality, early independence, competence, and self reliance is the rule, and where effective participation in 4-H, F & A Clubs, Fat Stock Shows and County Fairs is the entirely laudable ambition of farmbred boys and girls.

Compare the treatment of interest-free loans between family members, discussed in Section 4 of this Chapter.

3.3. *Other Applications*

The distinction between earnings refused in favor of another and earnings simply refused has been applied in other situations, although the distinction is often an arbitrary one. Treas. Reg. § 1.61–2(c) provides that the "value of services is not includable in gross income when such services are rendered directly and gratuitously" to a charity. But the value of services is includable in the income of the person performing the services where services are rendered to a third party for the benefit of a charity. The Regulation has been applied to "charity day" proceeds of a race track. In Rev. Rul. 72–542, 1972–2 C.B. 37, such proceeds were included in the race track's income where the track was held to be the promoter and not the charity's agent. But in Rev. Rul. 77–121, 1977–1 C.B. 17, the track was not taxed on charity-day proceeds where the track conducted the races but the charity was responsible for advertising and agreed to bear any losses. See also Rev. Rul. 68–503, 1968–2 C.B. 44 (gratuitous services performed for a political fund-raising organization which promoted an event did not result in income to the performer).

4. EARNINGS ACQUIRED UNDER A CLAIMED AGENCY RELATIONSHIP

In general, compensation from third parties has been excluded from the income of a wage-earner acting as an agent of another person in receiving the income. Thus, for example, in Rev. Rul. 74–581, 1974–2 C.B. 25, amounts received as compensation under a law school clinical program and turned over to the law school by a law school faculty member and a student were not taxed to the individuals. The IRS considered the individuals to be acting solely as agents of the school. Likewise, Rev. Rul. 76–479, 1976–2 C.B. 20, held that fees received by physicians from teaching and research patients that were required to be paid over to an educational and research foundation were not includable in the physicians' gross income.

The courts have generally rejected the agency rationale in the case of members of religious orders who work in secular institutions. Thus, in Fogarty v. United States, 780 F.2d 1005 (Fed.Cir.1986), the taxpayer, as a member of the Jesuit Order, had undertaken vows of poverty and obedience that prevented him from receiving or directing the use of moneys for his own benefit. Following the instructions of his religious order, the taxpayer accepted a position as an associate professor at the University of Virginia. The entire amount of the taxpayer's salary was paid to the religious order, which in turn provided the taxpayer with living expenses. The University directed the taxpayer's teaching requirements. Although the University was also aware that the taxpayer was subject to the dictates of his religious superior and to conformance with the religious order's teaching mission, there was no agreement between the University and the taxpayer's religious order. The taxpayer argued that by virtue of his vows of poverty and obedience, wages paid for the taxpayer's services vested immediately in his religious order. The taxpayer relied on Poe v. Seaborn, 282 U.S. 101 (1930), where the Court held in part that the wage earner spouse in a community property state received income under state law as an agent for the marital community. The court in Fogarty distinguished the division of income required under a state's community property law from the ownership rights of a member of a religious order as defined by the member's legal relationship with the religious order, the member's vows, and the canon law of the Catholic Church: "Although such a right may be enforced in law, an enforceable civil right arising from church law is not the same as a right or legal relationship which is created by operation of state law." In addition, the court affirmed the trial court's holding that Fogarty was not in fact acting as an agent of the religious order in the course of his employment with the University of Virginia. The court emphasized the factual nature of the determination and listed several factors to consider including the degree of control over the taxpayer exercised by the third-party employer and the relationship between the employer and the religious order. See also Kircher v. United States, 872 F.2d 1014 (Fed. Cir.1989) (members of the Franciscan Order subject to vows of poverty and obedience were subject to tax on wages derived from employment as chaplains in Federal and State hospitals); Rev. Rul. 77–290, 1977–2 C.B. 26 (earnings of a member of a religious order from the practice of law as an associate in a law firm includable in gross income of the individual even though the earnings were paid directly to the order); Rev. Rul. 84–13, 1984–1 C.B. 21 (earnings of a member of a religious order from the private practice of psychology includable in gross income).

In contrast, the IRS has accepted the agency rationale where the member of the religious order (a nurse) directly furthered the purposes of the order by performing services for the order or an organization affiliated with it (a hospital). The compensation was treated as received by the nurse as agent for the order and was not includable in her income. Rev. Rul. 68–123, 1968–1 C.B. 35, clarified and distinguished by Rev. Rul. 83–127, 1983–2 C.B. 25.

5. PERSONAL SERVICE CORPORATIONS

Differences in the tax rates applicable to corporations and individuals used to make it attractive for certain high-income individuals (typically professional athletes) to form corporations. In Leavell v. Commissioner, 104 T.C. 140 (1995), a professional basketball player formed a corporation and agreed to furnish his services to the corporation, which in turn executed a National Basketball Association Uniform Player Contract with the Houston Rockets to furnish services. The player was also required by the Rockets to personally agree to perform the services called for in the player contract. The court found the player taxable on the salary paid to the corporation because the team had the right to control the manner and means by which the personal services were performed; the player was thus an employee of the team and not of his corporation. The Tax Court declined to follow Sargent v. Commissioner, 929 F.2d 1252 (8th Cir.1991), which found a "bona fide arm's length agreement" between a professional hockey player and his personal service corporation and respected the form of the transaction, and held that a hockey player was an employee of his wholly-owned corporation rather than of the hockey team. Section 11(b)(2), which taxes the income of personal service corporations at a flat rate of 35 percent, the highest rate applicable to corporations, and only 4.6 percentage points lower than the top rate applicable to individuals, mitigates the tax-saving aspects of this technique.

SECTION 2. INCOME FROM PROPERTY

Blair v. Commissioner
Supreme Court of the United States, 1937.
300 U.S. 5.

■ MR. CHIEF JUSTICE HUGHES delivered the opinion of the Court.

This case presents the question of the liability of a beneficiary of a testamentary trust for a tax upon the income which he had assigned to his children prior to the tax years and which the trustees had paid to them accordingly.

The trust was created by the will of William Blair, a resident of Illinois who died in 1899, and was of property located in that State. One-half of the net income was to be paid to the donor's widow during her life. His son, the petitioner Edward Tyler Blair, was to receive the other one-half and, after the death of the widow, the whole of the net income during his life. In 1923, after the widow's death, petitioner assigned to his daughter, Lucy Blair Linn, an interest amounting to $6,000 for the remainder of that calendar year, and to $9,000 in each calendar year thereafter, in the net income which the petitioner was then or might thereafter be entitled to receive during his life. At about the same time, he made like assignments of interests, amounting to $9,000 in each calendar year, in the net income of the trust to his daughter Edith Blair and to his son, Edward Seymour Blair, respectively. In later years, by similar instruments, he assigned to these children additional interests, and to his son William McCormick Blair other specified interests, in the net income. The trustees accepted the assignments and distributed the income directly to the assignees.

* * *

The question of the validity of the assignments is a question of local law. [State courts held that the assignments were valid.] * * *

The question remains whether, treating the assignments as valid, the assignor was still taxable upon the income under the federal income tax act. That is a federal question.

* * *

In the instant case, the tax is upon income as to which, in the general application of the revenue acts, the tax liability attaches to ownership. See Poe v. Seaborn, supra * * * .

The Government points to the provisions of the revenue acts imposing upon the beneficiary of a trust the liability for the tax upon the income distributable to the beneficiary. But the term is merely descriptive of the one entitled to the beneficial interest. These provisions cannot be taken to preclude valid assignments of the beneficial interest, or to affect the duty of the trustee to distribute income to the owner of the beneficial interest, whether he was such initially or becomes such by valid assignment. The one who is to receive the income as the owner of the beneficial interest is to pay the tax. If under the law governing the trust the beneficial interest is assignable, and if it has been assigned without reservation, the assignee thus becomes the beneficiary and is entitled to rights and remedies accordingly. We find nothing in the revenue acts which denies him that status. * * *

The will creating the trust entitled the petitioner during his life to the net income of the property held in trust. He thus became the owner of an equitable interest in the corpus of the property. * * * Irwin v. Gavit, 268 U.S. 161, 167, 168 * * * . By virtue of that interest he was entitled to enforce the trust, to have a breach of trust enjoined and to obtain redress in case of breach. The interest was present property alienable like any other, in the absence of a valid restraint upon alienation. * * * The beneficiary may thus transfer a part of his interest as well as the whole. See Restatement of the Law of Trusts, §§ 130, 132 et seq. The assignment of the beneficial interest is not the assignment of a chose in action but of the "right, title, and estate in and to property." Brown v. Fletcher, supra * * * .

We conclude that the assignments were valid, that the assignees thereby became the owners of the specified beneficial interests in the income, and that as to these interests they and not the petitioner were taxable for the tax years in question. The judgment of the Circuit Court of Appeals is reversed and the cause is remanded with direction to affirm the decision of the Board of Tax Appeals.

Helvering v. Horst

Supreme Court of the United States, 1940.
311 U.S. 112.

■ MR. JUSTICE STONE delivered the opinion of the Court.

The sole question for decision is whether the gift, during the donor's taxable year, of interest coupons detached from the bonds, delivered to the donee and later in the year paid at maturity, is the realization of income taxable to the donor.

→ Issue

In 1934 and 1935 respondent, the owner of negotiable bonds, detached from them negotiable interest coupons shortly before their due date and delivered them as a gift to his son who in the same year collected them at maturity. The Commissioner ruled that under * * * [section of the 1934 Revenue Act, the former version of section 61(a)], the interest payments were taxable, in the years when paid, to the respondent donor who reported his income on the cash receipts basis. The circuit court of appeals reversed the order of the Board of Tax Appeals sustaining the tax. 2 Cir., 107 F.2d 906; 39 B.T.A. 757. We granted certiorari, because of the importance of the question in the administration of the revenue laws and because of an asserted conflict in principle of the decision below with that of Lucas v. Earl, 281 U.S. 111, and with that of decisions by other circuit courts of appeals. * * *

FACTS

→ Procedural History

The court below thought that as the consideration for the coupons had passed to the obligor, the donor had, by the gift, parted with all control over them and their payment, and for that reason the case was distinguishable from Lucas v. Earl, supra, and Burnet v. Leininger, 285 U.S. 136, where the assignment of compensation for services had preceded the rendition of the services, and where the income was held taxable to the donor.

→ What the lower court believed

The holder of a coupon bond is the owner of two independent and separable kinds of right. One is the right to demand and receive at maturity the principal amount of the bond representing capital investment. The other is the right to demand and receive interim payments of interest on the investment in the amounts and on the dates specified by the coupons. Together they are an obligation to pay principal and interest given in exchange for money or property which was presumably the consideration for the obligation of the bond. Here respondent, as owner of the bonds, had acquired the legal right to demand payment at maturity of the interest specified by the coupons and the power to command its payment to others which constituted an economic gain to him.

Admittedly not all economic gain of the taxpayer is taxable income. From the beginning the revenue laws have been interpreted as defining "realization" of income as the taxable event rather than the acquisition of the right to receive it. And "realization" is not deemed to occur until the income is paid. But the decisions and regulations have consistently recognized that receipt in cash or property is not the only characteristic of realization of income to a taxpayer on the cash receipts basis. Where the taxpayer does not receive payment of income in money or property realization may occur when the last step is taken by which he obtains the fruition of the economic gain which has already accrued to him. Old Colony Trust Co. v. Commissioner, 279 U.S. 716 * * * .

In the ordinary case the taxpayer who acquires the right to receive income is taxed when he receives it, regardless of the time when his right to receive payment accrued. But the rule that income is not taxable until realized has never been taken to mean that the taxpayer, even on the cash receipts basis, who has fully enjoyed the benefit of the economic gain represented by his right to receive income, can escape taxation because he has not himself received payment of it from his obligor. The rule, founded on administrative convenience, is only one of postponement of the tax to the final event of enjoyment of the income, usually the receipt of it by the taxpayer, and not one of exemption from taxation where the enjoyment is consummated by some event other than the taxpayer's personal receipt of money or property. * * * This may occur when he has made such use or disposition of his power to receive or control the income as to procure in its place other satisfactions which are of economic worth. The question here is, whether because one who in fact receives payment for services or interest payments is taxable only on his receipt of the payments, he can escape all tax by giving away his right to income in advance of payment. If the taxpayer procures payment directly to his creditors of the items of interest or earnings due him, see Old Colony Trust Co. v. Commissioner, supra * * * , or if he sets up a revocable trust with income payable to the objects of his bounty, [citing the former versions of sections 676, 677], Corliss v. Bowers, supra * * * , he does not escape taxation because he did not actually receive the money. * * *

Underlying the reasoning in these cases is the thought that income is "realized" by the assignor because he, who owns or controls the source of the income, also controls the disposition of that which he could have received himself and diverts the payment from himself to others as the means of procuring the satisfaction of his wants. The taxpayer has equally enjoyed the fruits of his labor or investment and obtained the satisfaction of his desires whether he collects and uses the income to procure those satisfactions, or whether he disposes of his right to collect it as the means of procuring them. * * *

Although the donor here, by the transfer of the coupons, has precluded any possibility of his collecting them himself he has nevertheless, by his act, procured payment of the interest, as a valuable gift to a member of his family. Such a use of his economic gain, the right to receive income, to procure a satisfaction which can be obtained only by the expenditure of money or property, would seem to be the enjoyment of the income whether the satisfaction is the purchase of goods at the corner grocery, the payment of his debt there, or such non-material satisfaction as may result from the payment of a campaign or community chest contribution, or a gift to his favorite son. Even though he never receives the money he derives money's worth from the disposition of the coupons which he has used as money or money's worth in the procuring of a satisfaction which is procurable only by the expenditure of money or money's worth. The enjoyment of the economic benefit accruing to him by virtue of his acquisition of the coupons is realized as completely as it would have been if he had collected the interest in dollars and expended them for any of the purposes named. * * *

The power to dispose of income is the equivalent of ownership of it. The exercise of that power to procure the payment of income to another is the enjoyment and hence the realization of the income by him who exercises it. We have had no difficulty in applying that proposition where the assignment preceded the rendition of the services, Lucas v. Earl, supra * * *, for it was recognized in the Leininger case that in such a case the rendition of the service by the assignor was the means by which the income was controlled by the donor and of making his assignment effective. But it is the assignment by which the disposition of income is controlled when the service precedes the assignment and in both cases it is the exercise of the power of disposition of the interest or compensation with the resulting payment to the donee which is the enjoyment by the donor of income derived from them.

This was emphasized in Blair v. Commissioner, 300 U.S. 5, on which respondent relies, where the distinction was taken between a gift of income derived from an obligation to pay compensation and a gift of income-producing property. In the circumstances of that case the right to income from the trust property was thought to be so identified with the equitable ownership of the property from which alone the beneficiary derived his right to receive the income and his power to command disposition of it that a gift of the income by the beneficiary became effective only as a gift of his ownership of the property producing it. Since the gift was deemed to be a gift of the property the income from it was held to be the income of the owner of the property, who was the donee, not the donor, a refinement which was unnecessary if respondent's contention here is right, but one clearly inapplicable to gifts of interest or wages. Unlike income thus derived from an obligation to pay interest or compensation, the income of the trust was regarded as no more the income of the donor than would be the rent from a lease or a crop raised on a farm after the leasehold or the farm had been given away. Blair v. Commissioner, supra, 300 U.S. at 12, 13, and cases cited. * * * We have held without deviation that where the donor retains control of the trust

→ Holding

property the income is taxable to him although paid to the donee. Corliss v. Bowers, supra. * * *

The dominant purpose of the revenue laws is the taxation of income to those who earn or otherwise create the right to receive it and enjoy the benefit of it when paid. See, Corliss v. Bowers, supra, 281 U.S. 378 * * * . The tax laid by the 1934 Revenue Act upon income "derived from * * * wages, or compensation for personal service, of whatever kind and in whatever form paid * * * ; also from interest * * * " therefore cannot fairly be interpreted as not applying to income derived from interest or compensation when he who is entitled to receive it makes use of his power to dispose of it in procuring satisfactions which he would otherwise procure only by the use of the money when received.

It is the statute which taxes the income to the donor although paid to his donee. Lucas v. Earl, supra; Burnet v. Leininger, supra. True, in those cases the service which created the right to income followed the assignment and it was arguable that in point of legal theory the right to the compensation vested instantaneously in the assignor when paid although he never received it; while here the right of the assignor to receive the income antedated the assignment which transferred the right and thus precluded such an instantaneous vesting. But the statute affords no basis for such "attenuated subtleties." The distinction was explicitly rejected as the basis of decision in Lucas v. Earl. It should be rejected here, for no more than in the Earl case can the purpose of the statute to tax the income to him who earns, or creates and enjoys it be escaped by "anticipatory arrangements * * * however skillfully devised" to prevent the income from vesting even for a second in the donor.

Nor is it perceived that there is any adequate basis for distinguishing between the gift of interest coupons here and a gift of salary or commissions. The owner of a negotiable bond and of the investment which it represents, if not the lender, stands in the place of the lender. When, by the gift of the coupons, he has separated his right to interest payments from his investment and procured the payment of the interest to his donee, he has enjoyed the economic benefits of the income in the same manner and to the same extent as though the transfer were of earnings and in both cases the import of the statute is that the fruit is not to be attributed to a different tree from that on which it grew. See Lucas v. Earl, supra, 281 U.S. 115.

Reversed.

The separate opinion of MR. JUSTICE MCREYNOLDS. * * *

The unmatured coupons given to the son were independent negotiable instruments complete in themselves. Through the gift they became at once the absolute property of the donee, free from the donor's control and in no way dependent upon ownership of the bonds. No question of actual fraud or purpose to defraud the revenue is presented.

Neither Lucas v. Earl, 281 U.S. 111, nor Burnet v. Leininger, 285 U.S. 136, support petitioner's view. Blair v. Commissioner, 300 U.S. 5, 11, 12, shows that neither involved an unrestricted completed transfer of property.

* * *

The general principles approved in Blair v. Commissioner, 300 U.S. 5, are applicable and controlling. The challenged judgment should be affirmed.

■ THE CHIEF JUSTICE and MR. JUSTICE ROBERTS concur in this opinion.

Harrison v. Schaffner

Supreme Court of the United States, 1941.
312 U.S. 579.

■ MR. JUSTICE STONE delivered the opinion of the Court.

In December, 1929, respondent, the life beneficiary of a testamentary trust, "assigned" to certain of her children specified amounts in dollars from the income of the trust for the year following the assignment. She made a like assignment to her children and a son-in-law in November, 1930. The question for decision is whether, under the applicable 1928 Revenue Act, the assigned income, which was paid by the trustees to the several assignees, is taxable as such to the assignor or to the assignees. * * *

Since granting certiorari we have held, following the reasoning of Lucas v. Earl, supra, that one who is entitled to receive at a future date, interest or compensation for services and who makes a gift of it by an anticipatory assignment, realizes taxable income quite as much as if he had collected the income and paid it over to the object of his bounty. Helvering v. Horst, 311 U.S. 112 * * * . Decision in these cases was rested on the principle that the power to dispose of income is the equivalent of ownership of it and that the exercise of the power to procure its payment to another, whether to pay a debt or to make a gift, is within the reach of the statute taxing income "derived from any source whatever". In the light of our opinions in these cases the narrow question presented by this record is whether it makes any difference in the application of the taxing statute that the gift is accomplished by the anticipatory assignment of trust income rather than of interest, dividends, rents and the like which are payable to the donor.

Respondent, recognizing that the practical consequences of a gift by assignment, in advance, of a year's income from the trust, are, so far as the use and enjoyment of the income are concerned, no different from those of the gift by assignment of interest or wages, rests his case on technical distinctions affecting the conveyancing of equitable interests. It is said that since by the assignment of trust income the assignee acquires an equitable right to an accounting by the trustee which, for many purposes, is treated by courts of equity as a present equitable estate in the trust property, it follows that each assignee in the present case is a donee of an interest in the trust property for the term of a year and is thus the recipient of income from his own property which is taxable to him rather than to the donor. See Blair v. Commissioner, 300 U.S. 5. * * *

[The former version of section 61(a) in] the 1928 Revenue Act provides, " 'Gross income' includes gains, profits, and income derived from * * * interest, rent, dividends, securities, or the transaction of any business carried on for gain or profit, or gains or profits and income derived from any source whatever". By [the former versions of sections 641 and 652(a)] the tax is laid upon the income "of any kind of property held in trust", and income of a trust for the taxable year which is to be distributed to the beneficiaries is to be taxed to them "whether distributed to them or not." In construing these and like provisions in other revenue acts we have uniformly held that they are not so much concerned with the refinements of title as with the actual command over the income which is taxed and the actual benefit for which the tax is paid. See Corliss v. Bowers, 281 U.S. 376; Lucas v. Earl, supra; Helvering v. Horst, supra * * * . It was for that reason that in each of those cases it was held that one vested with the right to receive income did not escape the tax by any kind of anticipatory arrangement, however skillfully devised, by which he procures payment of it to another, since, by the exercise of his power to command the income, he enjoys the benefit of the income on which the tax is laid.

Those decisions are controlling here. Taxation is a practical matter and those practical considerations which support the treatment of the disposition of one's income by way of gift as a realization of the income to the donor are the same whether the income be from a trust or from shares of stock or bonds which he owns. It is true, as respondent argues, that where the beneficiary of a trust had assigned a share of the income to another for life without retaining any form of control over the interest assigned, this Court construed the assignment as a transfer in praesenti to the donee, of a life interest in the corpus of the trust property and held in consequence that the income thereafter paid to the donee was taxable to him and not the donor. Blair v. Commissioner, supra. But we think it quite another matter to say that the beneficiary of a trust who makes a single gift of a sum of money payable out of the income of the trust does not realize income when the gift is effectuated by payment, or that he escapes the tax by attempting to clothe the transaction in the guise of a transfer of trust property rather than the transfer of income where that is its obvious purpose and effect. We think that the gift by a beneficiary of a trust of some part of the income derived from the trust property for the period of a day, a month or a year involves no such substantial disposition of the trust property as to camouflage the reality that he is enjoying the benefit of the income from the trust of which he continues to be the beneficiary, quite as much as he enjoys the benefits of interest or wages which he gives away as in the Horst and Eubank cases. Even though the gift of income be in form accomplished by the temporary disposition of the donor's property which produces the income, the donor retaining every other substantial interest in it, we have not allowed the form to obscure the reality. Income which the donor gives away through the medium of a short term trust created for the benefit of the donee is nevertheless income taxable to the donor. Helvering v. Clifford, supra; Hormel v. Helvering, 312 U.S. 552. We perceive no difference, so far as the construction and application of the Revenue Act is concerned, between a gift of income in a specified amount by the creation of a trust for a year, see Hormel v. Helvering, supra, and the assignment by the beneficiary of a trust already created of a like amount from its income for a year.

Nor are we troubled by the logical difficulties of drawing the line between a gift of an equitable interest in property for life effected by a gift for life of a share of the income of the trust and the gift of the income or a part of it for the period of a year as in this case. "Drawing the line" is a recurrent difficulty in those fields of the law where differences in degree produce ultimate differences in kind. See Irwin v. Gavit, 268 U.S. 161, 168. It is enough that we find in the present case that the taxpayer, in point of substance, has parted with no substantial interest in property other than the specified payments of income which, like other gifts of income, are taxable to the donor. Unless in the meantime the difficulty be resolved by statute or treasury regulation, we leave it to future judicial decisions to determine precisely where the line shall be drawn between gifts of income-producing property and gifts of income from property of which the donor remains the owner, for all substantial and practical purposes. * * *

Reversed.

DETAILED ANALYSIS

1.   GENERAL

The Court in *Blair* stated the general proposition that tax liability for income attaches to ownership. Perhaps the Court in *Horst* may be said to have clarified the concept by adding that it is the ownership of the underlying income-producing property, ownership of the tree, that identifies the person who is taxable on the income produced by the property. The opinion in *Horst* distinguishes *Blair* by pointing out that the gift of income in *Blair* became effective only on the transfer of the donor's equitable interest in the income-producing property. This distinction also may explain the different results in *Blair* and *Schaffner*.

The taxpayers in *Blair* and *Schaffner* were both life beneficiaries of testamentary trusts. As such, under the rule of Irwin v. Gavit (see Chapter 7, Section 3), neither was entitled to any exclusion under § 102. All distributions were therefore income and not return of capital. Each assigned a portion of the life estate. The assignment in *Blair* was held effective to shift the tax incidence to the assignee, while the assignment in *Schaffner* was unsuccessful, because, in *Blair,* the assignment of specified annual amounts extended for the entire term of the life estate. Thus, the assignment had the flavor of a transfer of an undivided interest in "property." The assignment in *Schaffner,* on the other hand, was of a fixed amount payable out of only the next year's income. It was the brevity of the assignment that apparently led to a different result: "We think that the gift by a beneficiary of a trust of some part of the income derived by the trust property for the period of a day, a month or a year involves no such substantial disposition of the trust property * * * ." The limited period of the assignment indicates that the transferor retained ownership of the underlying income interest in the trust. Thus, *Blair* may be said to involve a "vertical" slice (or carve-out) of the assignor's interest, in the nature of "property" while the assignment in *Schaffner* consisted of a "horizontal" interest in the nature of income from property. The same may be said of *Horst;* the transfer of the interest coupons was a transfer of the income from the retained property.

2. RELATIONSHIP TO LUCAS v. EARL

An assignment of a percentage of future wages for the life of the earner presumably is not effective for tax purposes under the reasoning of Lucas v. Earl. But such an assignment varies little from that in *Blair*. As in *Horst,* courts have described Lucas v. Earl as providing for taxation of the earner because of the control retained by the earner through the power to deprive the assignee of any income by not working. But where the assignment is for the life of the assignor, it is unlikely that this "control" will be exercised. To continue the analogy to trees and fruits, perhaps the difference is that in cases like *Earl* the individual is the tree that earns the wages, and the individual cannot be divided; that is, the individual tree (or branches of the individual tree) cannot be separated from its fruit. In *Blair* the income interest itself produced the income taxable to Blair; it was, in effect, the tree. Since Blair transferred his complete ownership interest—his entire interest in that which produced the income—he was treated as having transferred the tree.

The distinction between wage and property assignments has the effect of favoring taxpayers who have property they can transfer to a related party. The advantage is particularly significant in cases like *Blair* where zero basis property is available for transfer.

3. TRANSFER OF PROPERTY WITH ACCRUED INCOME: THE "RIPENED FRUIT" DOCTRINE

Generally, the gratuitous transfer of income-producing property (the "tree") is effective in shifting the tax burden on the future income (the "fruit") generated by the property from the donor to the donee. However, the result is different if at the time of the transfer, the property is transferred along with income that has already accrued ("ripened fruit").

In Estate of Smith v. Commissioner, 292 F.2d 478 (3d Cir.1961), the taxpayer transferred stock after a dividend was declared. The corporation declared a dividend on April 7 to be paid to the shareholders of record on

May 10. On May 9, the taxpayers gave stock in the corporation to their children who received the dividends and reported them in their income. The court held that this "ripened fruit" was taxable to the parents. Similarly, in Rev. Rul. 74–562, 1974–2 C.B. 28, a life beneficiary of a trust who assigned her entire interest to a charitable foundation on December 30 was taxable on a dividend on stock held by the trust, declared to stockholders of record on November 27 and payable on December 31. But Caruth Corp. v. United States, 865 F.2d 644 (5th Cir.1989), reached a contrary result where a dividend was paid on stock transferred by a charitable gift after the dividend was declared but before the record date. In holding that the donor was not taxable the court relied on Treas. Reg. § 1.61–9(c), pursuant to which if stock is sold after the dividend declaration date but the purchaser is entitled to the dividend, the dividend is taxed to the purchaser. The court distinguished *Estate of Smith* as turning on a particularity of the relevant state law.

This principle that "ripened fruit" is taxable to the transferor has been applied to accrued interest. In Austin v. Commissioner, 161 F.2d 666 (6th Cir.1947), a wife in 1940 gave to her children a promissory note on which her husband was the obligor. At the time of the transfer, the accumulated but unpaid interest amounted to $43,320.04. The husband was killed in an accident shortly thereafter. In 1940, the executor paid part of the accumulated interest, and then paid the balance in June 1941. The wife was held taxable in 1940 on the interest paid to the children in 1940, but not taxable in 1940 on the balance of the interest paid in 1941.

4. RELATIONSHIP TO CAPITAL GAINS AND *P.G. LAKE*

There is a relationship between capital gains and assignment of income in that each area requires a distinction between property and income from property. See Commissioner v. P. G. Lake (see Chapter 24, Section 2.B.), and compare Hort v. Commissioner (see Chapter 24, Section 2.B.) with *Horst*. In *Hort,* the taxpayer's receipt of payment for future rent may be viewed as the transfer of the income stream from property. It was observed in the capital gains discussion that this distinction is often arbitrary because the value of an asset may always be viewed as the anticipated present value of the receipts generated by that asset. The distinction is no more meaningful where the issue is whether an assignment is effective for tax purposes. If the assignments in *Blair* and *Schaffner* each had the same present value, there appears to be no reason why one should be effective but not the other.

5. TRANSFER OF APPRECIATED PROPERTY

Giving appreciated property to a charity or family member generally allows the donor to avoid including the gain in income. Gifts to family members shift the gain to the donee through the transferred basis mechanism of § 1015(a) or result in no gain for gifts at death (i.e., bequests) through the stepped-up basis mechanism of § 1014(a). Meanwhile, gifts to charity generally result in the gain escaping tax because of the tax-exempt status of the charity. When the charitable contribution deduction is limited to the donor's basis, as is sometimes the case, the result is the equivalent of income inclusion to the donor plus a full charitable contribution deduction. However, some capital assets, such as stock, generally are not subject to these limitations unless donated to a private foundation, which preserves the incentive for gifts prior to realization (see Chapter 21, Section 3.5.).

Gifts of appreciated property immediately prior to realization may cause the gain to be taxed to the donor. This treatment is consistent with the ripened fruit doctrine discussed above in Section 3. Instead of accrued interest or dividends, the ripened fruit in these cases is the built-in gain inherent in the property at the time it is transferred. For example, in Doyle v. Commissioner, 147 F.2d 769 (4th Cir.1945), the taxpayer had purchased an interest in a claim under which he was entitled to obtain some of the proceeds that would be payable if a suit then pending against the Government was successful. After the Government's request for certiorari had been denied in the suit, but before any payment, the taxpayer in 1937 transferred part of his interest to his wife and children. The judgment was paid in 1938. The taxpayer was held liable for tax in 1938 on the amounts paid to the wife and children:

> Counsel for Doyle strenuously insists that Doyle's interest here was property, that it was a capital asset, and that, when Doyle assigned a part of this to his wife and children, he transferred to them property and a capital asset. Ergo, we are told, when this property or capital asset was transferred to the donees, and was realized by them upon its conversion into money, the resultant gain was taxable as income to these same donees and not to Doyle, the donor.

> On the other hand, counsel for the Government takes a firm stand upon the battle-field of realism. Away, they say, with pure jurisprudential concepts; Doyle, after the denial of certiorari and before the transfer to the wife and children, had an enormous profit (he paid $928.75, while he and the wife and children actually received together $34,926.01), which was to all intents and purposes practically assured, and its amount in dollars and cents could be approximated with reasonable certainty, though, before the division of the proceeds of the judgment, the expenses of litigation had to be ascertained and defrayed. Ergo, Doyle's transfer in 1938 to his wife and children, viewed in the fierce light of stark economic reality, was an anticipatory assignment of income and thus taxable to Doyle. With no little intellectual admiration for the astute argument of Doyle's counsel, we yet feel bound to approve this contention of the Government and to affirm the decision of the Tax Court of the United States.

> The problem before us is close and not free from difficulty. No decided case, precisely in point, has been cited to us by counsel; our own independent search has been equally barren. Let us suppose that Spilkins has bought for $1,000 a vacant parcel of realty located in a then residential part of a growing city. The years go by, business edifices crowd all about the Spilkins lot and Spilkins has a bona fide offer of $20,000 for the lot. Spilkins now gives the lot to his son who sells it for $20,000. The resultant gain is clearly taxable to the son and not to Spilkins. The same result would follow if

Spilkins bought for $10 a share 100 shares of stock in the Universal Dirt Corporation and gave them to his son who swiftly sold the shares for $200 a share.

* * *

[In] the supposed realty and corporate shares transfer by Spilkins, an affirmative act was needed on the part of the transferee, as sale by him, before there could be any realization of gain, but, here, there was nothing of this nature required of Doyle's wife and children. They merely had to wait (and that not for long) for the expected benefits to fall (and they did quickly fall) right into their economic laps. They well knew (as did Doyle) that a rare piece of good fortune was "right around the corner" without even the necessity of their going to meet it; or, in a picturesque phrase of the Blue Ridge mountaineers, they could well smile in clear anticipation that "It was about to snow in their hats."

Finally, the equities (if that word be used in its broadest connotation) here can hardly be said to favor Doyle. He has made an extremely fortunate investment. For years he does nothing. Then, when he is confident that a gain of over 2,000 per cent is in the offing, or (to put it more crudely) when a huge profit is practically "in the bag", he assigns (by one assignment on the last day of the tax year, 1937, and another assignment less than two weeks thereafter in a new tax year, 1938) three-fifths of this to his wife and minor sons, to whom he owes both the legal and moral duty of support. The money sent to the sons is deposited in a bank to the credit of the minor sons, but remains absolutely under the control of Doyle, who actually did (until his appointment some years later as guardian) exercise this control. The money deposited to the wife's account could not be withdrawn by Doyle, but the wife could use this money to relieve him pro tanto of his legal duty to support her. And Doyle managed the wife's investments. Certainly, under all these circumstances, the question might well be asked: does not this whole transaction present the stigmata of a deliberate attempt at tax evasion?

A similar issue arises if the appreciated property is transferred subject to an agreement entered into by the transferor to sell the property to a third party. In Malkan v. Commissioner, 54 T.C. 1305 (1970) (Acq.), income from the sale of securities was taxed to the settlor of four trusts, and not to the trusts, where the agreement for sale had already been made prior to any transfer of the securities by the settlor. Similarly, in Salvatore v. Commissioner, T.C. Memo. 1970–30, aff'd, 434 F.2d 600 (2d Cir.1970), the taxpayer made a gift of a one-half interest in a gas station to her children after the taxpayer had contracted to sell the property but before the sale was consummated; the court held the transferor taxable on the gain realized on the sale.

6.   SEPARATION OF INCOME FROM PROPERTY

6.1. *General*

In some situations, an assignment of a right to receive income for a specified period of time can shift taxation of the income to the donee. Where a donor owning property receives income from that property which then is given to the donee, the donor is unquestionably taxed on that income. But our current income tax system for gifts from living donors (no deduction to the donor, no income to the donee and transferred basis for gifted property) allows the unrealized gain from property to be shifted to the donee where the donee is free either to retain or dispose of the property. Assignment-of-income principles help determine how situations in between these extremes should be classified. The issue is often described as distinguishing "income" from "property," perhaps just a shorthand description for the foregoing distinction. From this perspective, rights to receive income for short periods, such as the assignments in *Schaffner* and *Horst,* certainly take on a stronger resemblance to the receipt by the donor followed by a gift of the income, than to the transfer of appreciated property.

A frequent theme in the assignment-of-income cases involving short-term income transfers is that of the power or control retained by the donor. Again, this factor is significant in making an assignment more closely resemble the prior receipt of the income by the donor, rather than the gift of appreciated property.

6.2. *Allocation of Basis*

A strong motivation for taxpayers to separate income from property lies in the various rules for allocating basis. Where a bond and its coupons are owned by one taxpayer, all of the basis is allocated to principal. The receipt of proceeds from the coupons is considered to be income in its entirety; none of the proceeds are treated as return of capital. Where the bond and coupons are owned by one taxpayer, this allocation achieves a correct result.[2] But where the capital and income are severed, application of this rule produces distortions. A bond's value is split between the coupons and the principal. Conceptually, if not practically, the basis ought to be allocated in relation to the relative values of these interests upon severance. Were this allocation to occur, much of the pressure absorbed by the assignment of income rules would be eased. In *Horst,* for example, the redemption of the coupon would have produced virtually no gain to the donee since the proceeds would have been offset almost entirely by basis. Correspondingly, the donor's basis in the retained bond would be reduced, thus producing income to the donor upon disposition or redemption.

In 1982, Congress enacted basis allocation rules specifically governing "stripping" interest coupons from coupon bonds. See I.R.C. § 1286. These rules were adopted in response to taxpayer attempts to create artificial gains or losses by selling either the coupons or the bond principal. For example,

---

[2]   Assume, for example, that a 10-year bond is issued for $1,000 with a 10 percent annual coupon. After one year, the first coupon matures and is paid. If interest rates remain at 10 percent, the present value of the remaining stream of payments is unchanged from the time of issuance. Thus, no cost recovery is indicated.

sale of the principal of a bond recently issued at face value would yield less than face because it would not be paid until years later. Yet, under prior rules, all of the basis would have been allocated to the principal, thus resulting in a loss. Although directed primarily at sales, § 1286 applies to any person who "disposes" of one of more coupons stripped from any bond. Thus, for years after 1984, the holding of *Horst,* on its specific facts, presumably is supplanted by the statutory rule, although the legislative history of § 1286 is silent on this point, (see S. Rep. No. 494 (Vol. 1), 97th Cong., 2d Sess. 215–218 (1982)), and neither the IRS nor the courts have addressed the issue.

Under § 1286, the person who strips and disposes of the coupons recognizes any interest accrued on the coupon prior to disposition; the basis of the bond and the coupons, including both those disposed of and those retained, is increased by the amount of recognized income; and the total basis is allocated among the bond and coupons, including both those retained and those disposed of, relative to their respective fair market values. The transferee of the coupons is treated as having purchased them for an amount equal to the basis allocated to the coupons. The coupons, which invariably have a higher redemption value, thus are OID instruments, subject to the rules discussed in Chapter 32. A similar rule applies to dividend stripping with respect to preferred stock. I.R.C. § 305(e).

The longstanding rules allocating basis to principal or capital continue to apply in situations not specifically governed by statute,[3] thus presenting issues like that in *Horst.* As a consequence of these rules, some taxpayers, wishing to accelerate income into a year in which substantial deductions are available, sell the right to receive dividends and report the entire sales proceeds as income in the year of sale. Thus, in Estate of Stranahan v. Commissioner, 472 F.2d 867 (6th Cir.1973), the right to receive $115,000 of dividends on stock owned by the taxpayer was "sold" to his son. The court upheld the taxpayer's characterization as a "sale," reversing the Tax Court's holding that the transaction was actually a loan. The finding that the Tax Court's holding was "clearly erroneous" is highly questionable. The Tax Court continues to follow the "loan" analysis, as have other courts. See Hydrometals, Inc. v. Commissioner, T.C.Memo. 1972–254, aff'd per curiam, 485 F.2d 1236 (5th Cir.1973); Mapco Inc. v. United States, 556 F.2d 1107 (Ct.Cl.1977).

6.3. *Pass Through of "Income" Characterization*

If basis is not allocated, and the rule of Irwin v. Gavit (see Chapter 7, Section 3) is retained, another approach would be to apply the income versus capital distinction where the income interests and principal are owned by different taxpayers. For example, if basis is not allocated, the income interest should at least retain its character as income and not be assignable for income tax purposes. Under this approach, situations such as *Blair* and *Schaffner* involving income interests would be consistently treated; no assignment of an "income" interest would be respected. Similarly, a sale of

---

[3]　　Special basis allocation rules apply where split interests are created upon the death of the owner of property. See Chapter 7, Section 3.2.

an income interest would never produce a capital gain. While this approach might seem harsh, it must be kept in mind that we are dealing only with the owner of the income interest; the owner of principal has received all the basis and is free to assign that property interest. An arbitrary rule that allocates basis entirely to principal should be expected to have harsh results to some if the results are overly generous to others. The current rule allows more "capital" to be assigned than actually exists.

7.   TIME OF INCOME INCLUSION

Rev. Rul. 69–102, 1969–1 C.B. 32, takes the position that in the *Horst*-type situation gain is included in income by the transferor in the year in which the transferee collects the income. See also Jones v. United States, 395 F.2d 938 (6th Cir.1968) (same conclusion); Friedman v. Commissioner, 41 T.C. 428 (1963)(Acq.), aff'd on another issue, 346 F.2d 506 (6th Cir.1965) (same). This approach to the timing of income inclusion is inconsistent with the reasoning pertaining to realization in the *Horst* case.

SECTION 3.   PROPERTY THAT IS THE PRODUCT OF PERSONAL EFFORTS

Helvering v. Eubank
Supreme Court of the United States, 1940.
311 U.S. 122.

■ MR. JUSTICE STONE delivered the opinion of the Court.

This is a companion case to Helvering v. Horst, 311 U.S. 112, decided this day, and presents issues not distinguishable from those in that case.

Respondent, a general life insurance agent, after the termination of his agency contracts and services as agent, made assignments in 1924 and 1928 respectively of renewal commissions to become payable to him for services which had been rendered in writing policies of insurance under two of his agency contracts. The Commissioner assessed the renewal commissions paid by the companies to the assignees in 1933 as income taxable to the assignor in that year under the provisions of the 1932 Revenue Act, [which do not] differ in any respect now material from [the section] of the 1934 Revenue Act [reference being made to the former version of section 61(a)], involved in the Horst case. * * *

No purpose of the assignments appears other than to confer on the assignees the power to collect the commissions, which they did in the taxable year. The Government and respondent have briefed and argued the case here on the assumption that the assignments were voluntary transfers to the assignees of the right to collect the commissions as and when they become payable, and the record affords no basis for any other.

For the reasons stated at length in the opinion in the Horst case, we hold that the commissions were taxable as income of the assignor in the year when paid. The judgment below is

Reversed.

Revenue Ruling 54–599
1954–2 C.B. 52.

Revenue Ruling 54–409 [1954–2 C.B. 174], holds that copyrights are divisible into separate properties and that a grant of the exclusive right to exploit a copyrighted work in a specific medium such as radio, television, movies or the stage, throughout the life of the copyright transfers a property right. Accordingly, where a taxpayer by deed of gift transfers and divests himself of all rights, title and interest in dramatization rights to his novel necessary for its production in a specific medium, such as radio, television, motion pictures or on stage, he is not liable for Federal income tax with respect to any income deriving from his former interest in these rights. Any income from such dramatization rights would be taxable to the donee to the extent provided by the Internal Revenue Code of 1939. Cf. Edward T. Blair v. Commissioner, 300 U.S. 5 * * * .

DETAILED ANALYSIS

1. ASPECTS OF *EUBANK*

The Court in *Eubank* cites *Horst,* decided the same day, as presenting a similar question and providing rationale for the opinion. If the right to receive renewal commissions is considered property, however, *Blair* would appear to control. *Eubank* can also be analyzed from the perspective of personal services. Lucas v. Earl (see Section 1 of this Chapter) involved future services in which the earner had the power to deprive the donee of the gift by not working, an element of control that is lacking where prior services are involved. Such a distinction is apparently not sufficient to justify a different result.

2. TRANSFERS OF PROPERTY

Transfers of property created by the personal efforts of the owner—an author's book and copyright or an inventor's product and patent—can effectively shift the associated income notwithstanding the personal service flavor of the property. Rev. Rul. 54–599, supra, makes this clear with respect to copyrights as well as certain divisible portions of copyrights. In Rev. Rul. 71–33, 1971–1 C.B. 30, the taxpayer made a gift of his memoirs to a charity which edited and assembled them, subsequently publishing them under a royalty arrangement with the publisher. The ruling held the taxpayer not taxable on the royalties received by the charity since he had transferred "the income producing property" and not merely "the right to the income."

In Wodehouse v. Commissioner, 177 F.2d 881 (2d Cir.1949), an author assigned to his wife an undivided one-half interest in a completed manuscript and its copyright. The author's agent, with notice of the assignment, then arranged for sale of the manuscript under instructions to send one-half of the proceeds to the wife. The court held that the author was taxable on only one-half of the proceeds:

> He assigned to his wife property which is as freely transferable by gift as is real estate or stocks and bonds * * * . Her husband was not the creator of her right to receive royalties. He was the creator of the story but her right to receive royalties arose from a contract negotiated by her agent on her behalf. The situation as we view it is no different than when a husband conveys to his wife a half interest in real estate which is thereafter leased to a tenant.

But, a similar assignment of another manuscript was held not to shift the income to his wife in Wodehouse v. Commissioner, 178 F.2d 987 (4th Cir.1949):

> Apparently, the entire role played by the wife in this little tax drama was that of a receiver of one-half of any pecuniary proceeds received from the sale of the stories or any rights therein. In reality, then, taxpayer, in substance not in form and in spirit not in letter, attempted merely to assign to his wife a share in his future income. And that, for federal income tax purposes, is not permitted. * * * [The court then quotes with approval from a dissent in the Second Circuit case.] "[My] brothers concede, as in the light of Helvering v. Eubank, 311 U.S. 122, they must, that if Wodehouse had given his wife a half-interest in the royalties after he had sold the novel, the income would be taxable to him. To let him escape taxation because the assignment was made *before, rather than after, the assured sale of the novel* seems to me to rely on the kind of nice distinction which the Supreme Court has often told us is not to be permitted to inhibit the taxing power. Our decision seems to me to provide a very easy way around taxes from property, over which in the eyes of the world the taxpayer retains full control" (Italics ours).

The reasoning of the Fourth Circuit's *Wodehouse* opinion contains similarities to the reasoning in cases dealing with assignments of property immediately followed by a pre-arranged sale (see Section 2.5. of this Chapter). But under the current standards applied in those situations, the Fourth Circuit's *Wodehouse* case would probably be decided differently, because when the one-half interest in the manuscript was assigned the manuscript was not subject to an agreement to sell.

3.   ASSIGNMENT OF ROYALTIES

If an author or inventor sells the property for a lump sum and then gives the proceeds to the donee, the donor would, of course, be taxable. Similarly, if the property is sold for a fixed amount to be paid in installments, and the installment obligations are assigned, the donor is immediately taxable. See § 453B at Chapter 31, Section 2.5.1.). Suppose, however, that the author or inventor transfers the property under a royalty arrangement and then transfers the right to the royalties to a donee. Here the courts have generally taxed the donee and not the donor on the assigned royalties. For example, in Commissioner v. Reece, 233 F.2d 30 (1st Cir.1956), in taxing the donee on patent royalties, the court stated that the case did not differ essentially from one in which the patent had first been given to the donee. The same result was reached in Heim v. Fitzpatrick, 262 F.2d 887 (2d Cir.1959).

In Lewis v. Rothensies, 61 F.Supp. 862 (E.D.Pa.1944), aff'd per curiam, 150 F.2d 959 (3d Cir.1945), the District Court described the right to receive royalties as property and not compensation for personal services:

> "When an author writes a book the literary ideas embodied in the manuscript are property. When he sells it in exchange for royalties his interest in the contract by which the royalties are paid is property. Of course, the book came into being by his personal service (a term by no means restricted to services rendered by virtue of an employer-employee relationship), but so do many other kinds of income-producing property. For example, a man might build, entirely by his own labor, a boat or a wagon or a barn. If he did so and rented what he had made to others, it would hardly be contended that the income was income derived from compensation for personal service. Granted that a lawyer who draws a will for a client does not create property and sell it to his client, and, perhaps, that an artist who paints a portrait is paid for his work rather than for the canvas and oils, still a literary work is marketable and has much more than a purely personal or sentimental value. So here, I think that the royalties were derived from income-producing property."

Under the facts of the case, the taxpayer was held taxable on the ground that he had not properly assigned the contract but had merely directed that payment be made to his children.

Thus the royalty situation generally is regarded by the courts as closer to the outright initial gift of the copyright or invention than to its sale for a lump sum and a subsequent gift of the proceeds. An author or inventor selling on a royalty basis is thus not to be forever barred from shifting the income from property sold. This is to be contrasted with situations such as in Townsend v. Commissioner, 37 T.C. 830 (1962), where the taxpayer sold stock based on a percentage of corporate profits for a period of years up to a specified amount. The taxpayer's gift of the sales contract was held not to shift the taxation of the sales proceeds to the donee.

Most of the foregoing cases involved authors or inventors and royalties paid in connection with property they created. Where the property is created by another person, however, and the taxpayer has no interest in the created property, *Eubank* may control. In Strauss v. Commissioner, 168 F.2d 441 (2d Cir.1948), the taxpayer in return for personal services in connection with the financing of the "Kodachrome" camera film developing process, had acquired a right to receive a percentage of royalties paid by the Eastman Kodak Company for the use of the process. The process had been assigned in 1930 to a trustee to collect and pay out such royalties. In 1935 the taxpayer assigned his interest to his wife. Thereafter, the trustee paid the royalties from the share directly to the wife. The taxpayer was held taxable on the annual amounts so paid:

> "The taxpayer did not receive for these services any part of the Kodachrome process itself or any right to control the disposition of

that process. Rather, he obtained the enforceable promise of the owners of the process that he would be paid for his services a definite portion of the royalties they had the right to receive from the Eastman Kodak Company. That is to say, his 'interest in the process' was never greater than a contract right to be paid certain ascertainable sums of money. From first to last his pay for his services was to be only in money determinable in amount by reference to a royalty agreement covering the process. Thus taxpayer's right to receive royalties, we think, is indistinguishable from the right, which was considered in Helvering v. Eubank, supra, to receive part of past earned commissions on insurance contracts."

4.   RELATIONSHIP TO CAPITAL GAINS

Section 1221(a)(3) provides that certain types of property, including copyrights, created by personal efforts are not capital assets. This rule applies to the creator of the property and to the donee of any such property. In contrast to the assignment of income rules described above, the personal service aspect of these types of property controls its character.

SECTION 4.   BELOW-MARKET AND INTEREST-FREE LOANS

INTERNAL REVENUE CODE: Section 7872.

General Explanation of the Revenue Provisions of the Deficit Reduction Act of 1984

Staff of the Joint Committee on Taxation 524–537 (December 31, 1984).

Reasons for Change

A below-market loan is the economic equivalent of a loan bearing a market rate of interest, and a payment by the lender to the borrower to fund the payment of interest by the borrower. The Congress believed that, in many instances, the failure of the tax laws to treat these transactions in accordance with their economic substance provided taxpayers with opportunities to circumvent well-established tax rules.

Under [pre-1984] law, loans between family members (and other similar loans) were being used to avoid the assignment of income rules and the grantor trust rules. A below-market loan to a family member, for example, generally involves a gratuitous transfer of the right to use the proceeds of the borrowing until repayment is demanded (in the case of a demand loan) or until the end of the term of the loan (in the case of a term loan). If the lender had assigned the income from the proceeds to the borrower instead of lending the proceeds to the borrower, the assignment of income doctrine would have taxed the lender (and not the borrower) on the income. If the lender had transferred the principal amount to a trust established for the benefit of the borrower that was revocable at will (similar to a demand loan), or that would terminate at the end of a period of not more than 10 years (similar to a term loan with a term of not more than 10 years), the income earned on trust assets would have been taxed to the lender under the grantor trust provisions set forth in Code secs. 671–679.

In addition, loans from corporations to shareholders were being used to avoid rules requiring the taxation of corporate income at the corporate level. A below-market loan from a corporation to a shareholder is the economic equivalent of a loan by the corporation to the shareholder requiring the payment of interest at a market rate, and a distribution by the corporation to the shareholder with respect to its stock equal to the amount of interest required to be paid under the terms of the loan. If a transaction were structured as a distribution and a loan, the borrower would have dividend income and an offsetting interest deduction. The lender would have interest income. Under prior law, if the transaction was structured as a below-market loan, the lender avoided including in income the interest that would have been paid by the borrower. As a result, the lender was in the same economic position as it would have been if it had deducted amounts distributed as dividends to shareholders.

Finally, loans to persons providing services were being used to avoid rules requiring the payment of employment taxes and rules restricting the deductibility of interest in certain situations by the person providing the services. A below-market loan to a person providing services is the economic equivalent of a loan requiring the payment of interest at a market rate, and a payment in the nature of compensation equal to the amount of interest required to be paid under the terms of the loan. Under prior law, a transaction structured as a loan and a payment in the nature of compensation often did not result in any tax consequences for either the lender or the borrower because each would have offsetting income and deductions. However, there were a number of situations in which the payment of compensation and a loan requiring the payment of interest at a market rate did not offset. For example, if a taxpayer used the proceeds of an arm's-length loan to invest in tax-exempt obligations, the deduction for interest paid on the loan would be disallowed under § 265. Similarly, if a term loan extended beyond the taxable year in which it was made, income and deductions did not offset because the compensation income was includible in the year the loan was made. In such circumstances, substantial tax advantages could have been derived by structuring the transaction as a below-market loan.

Explanation of Provision

Overview

The Act adds to the Code new section 7872 (relating to the tax treatment of loans that, in substance, result in a gift * * * from the lender to the borrower). Loans that are subject to the provision and that do not require payment of interest, or require payment at a rate below the statutory rate (referred to as the "applicable Federal rate"), are recharacterized as an arm's-length transaction in which the lender made a loan to the borrower in exchange for a note requiring the payment of interest at the applicable Federal rate. This rule results in the parties being treated as if:

(1)   The borrower paid interest to the lender that may be deductible to the borrower and is included in income by the lender; and

(2)   The lender * * * made a gift subject to the gift tax * * * .

* * *

Loans subject to the provision

The provision applies to term or demand loans that are gift loans * * * .

Generally, it was intended that the term "loan" be interpreted broadly in light of the purposes of the provision. Thus, any transfer of money that provides the transferor with a right to repayment is a loan. For example, advances and deposits of all kinds are treated as loans.

Demand loans and term loans.—A demand loan is any loan which is payable in full at any time upon the demand of the lender. A term loan is any loan which is not a demand loan.

Gift loans.—A gift loan is any below-market loan where the foregone interest is in the nature of a gift. In general, there is a gift if property (including foregone interest) is transferred for less than full and adequate consideration under circumstances where the transfer is a gift for gift tax purposes. A sale, exchange, or other transfer made in the ordinary course of business (i.e., a transaction which is bona fide, at arm's length and free from any donative intent) generally is considered as made for * * * full and adequate consideration. A loan between unrelated persons can qualify as a gift loan. * * *

DETAILED ANALYSIS

1.   GIFT LOANS

The effect of § 7872 on interest-free gift loans is to require the lender, typically a parent, to include annually in income an amount equal to the applicable Federal interest rate as determined under § 1274(d). The parent is treated as making a gift equal to the foregone interest. This gift generally will have no income tax consequences to either the parent or the child. The child is then treated as paying this foregone interest back to the parent which will be included in the parent's income. The borrower may be entitled to an interest deduction depending on the use to which the borrowed funds are put. The availability of the interest deduction is subject to the limitations generally applicable to interest, such as §§ 163(d) and 265(a)(2) and the limitations on itemized deductions.

If interest is charged, but at a below-market rate, the foregoing rules apply to the difference between the applicable Federal rate and the rate charged for both demand loans and term loans (as discussed in the above excerpted report from the Staff of the Joint Committee on Taxation).

2.   OTHER BELOW-MARKET LOANS

Section 7872 applies to a variety of other below-market loans including compensation-related loans, corporate-shareholder loans, and loans which are motivated by tax avoidance or have a significant effect on the tax liability of the lender or the borrower. These other below-market loans are treated the same as gift loans if they are demand loans. See KTA-Tator, Inc. v. Commissioner, 108 T.C. 100 (1997) (loan advances from a corporation to its to shareholders to finance their construction of real estate projects that were interest free during the construction period were interest-free shareholder loans under § 7872(c)(1)(C), treated as demand loans under § 7872(f)(5) during the construction period, even though upon completion of construction the loans were converted to interest bearing loans with an amortization schedule). Other below-market loans that are term loans are treated as having original issue discount equal to the excess of the amount loaned over the present value of all loan payments required to be made.

The nature of the relationships involved significantly affects the consequences of § 7872. Thus, as described above, gift loans usually result in income to the lender-donor and, perhaps, a deduction to the borrower-donee. Compensation-related demand loans may produce no net income tax consequences. The deemed compensatory transfer creates a deduction to the payor-lender and income to the payee-borrower; this may be offset by the interest income to the lender and the interest deduction to the borrower. Thus, for example, suppose an employer makes an interest-free demand loan of $100,000 to an employee where the annual foregone interest computed under § 7872 is $10,000. The employee invests the loan proceeds in income-producing stocks. The employer will be entitled to a deduction of $10,000 for the deemed payment of compensation (assuming the requirements of § 162 are satisfied) and will have $10,000 of interest income from the deemed payment by the employee. The employee will have $10,000 of income from compensation and will have an offsetting $10,000 deduction for the deemed payment of interest if the employee can satisfy the investment interest limitation of § 163(d).

Where term loans are involved, the analysis is somewhat different. Suppose, for example, that the $100,000 loan of the preceding example is instead a two-year, interest-free term loan. The compensation is the difference between the $100,000 and the present value of the $100,000 repayment in two years—about $17,750 (applying a 10 percent discount rate). This amount would be deductible by the employer and taxable compensation to the employee in the year the loan is made. The interest income and the deduction, if any, would be spread over two years. Also, because the original issue discount rules (discussed in Chapter 32) apply, more interest income and deductions would be allocated to the second year than to the first.

Corporate-shareholder loans differ in one very significant respect from compensation-related loans: the deemed dividend payment by the corporation, unlike the deemed payment of compensation, is not deductible. Corporate-shareholder loans are otherwise treated the same as compensation loans. See Rountree Cotton Co. v. Commissioner, 113 T.C. 422

(1999), aff'd by order, 12 Fed.Appx. 641 (10th Cir.2001) (requiring inclusion of interest by corporation that made interest free loans to its shareholders).

CHAPTER 38

TAXATION OF FAMILIES

As we saw in Chapter 37, the IRS and courts have protected the principle of the individual as the unit of taxation by refusing to recognize anticipatory assignments of income. Given that Lucas v. Earl (see Chapter 37, Section 1), a case involving married couple, established the assignment of income doctrine, it is somewhat ironic that another case involving married taxpayers decided in the same year as *Earl* laid the foundation for the marital unit as an appropriate unit of taxation. By concluding in Poe v. Seaborn (see Chapter 37, Section 1.1.) that a married couple living in a community property state was permitted to achieve the same result via ownership under state property law that the Earls were precluded from achieving via a private law contract, the Supreme Court sparked a longstanding debate over the proper tax treatment of individuals with shared living arrangements and economic interdependency.

SECTION 1.   THE MARRIED COUPLE AS A UNIT OF TAXATION

INTERNAL REVENUE CODE: Sections 1(a), (c), (d); 6013(a); 7703.

Druker v. Commissioner

United States Court of Appeals, Second Circuit, 1982.
697 F.2d 46.

■ FRIENDLY, CIRCUIT JUDGE:

We have here an appeal by taxpayers and a cross-appeal by the Commissioner from a judgment after trial before Chief Judge Tannenwald of the Tax Court, 77 T.C. 867 (1981).

I.

The principal issue on the taxpayers' appeal is the alleged unconstitutionality of the so-called "marriage penalty." The issue relates to the 1975 and 1976 income tax returns of James O. Druker and his wife Joan. During the tax years in question James was employed as a lawyer, first by the United States Attorney for the Eastern District of New York and later by the District Attorney of Nassau County, New York, and Joan was employed as a computer programmer. For each of the two years they filed separate income tax returns, checking the status box entitled "married filing separately". In computing their respective tax liabilities, however, they applied the rates in I.R.C. § 1(c) for "Unmarried individuals" rather than the higher rates prescribed by § 1(d) for "Married individuals filing separate returns". Prior to undertaking this course of action, James consulted with the United States Attorney for the Eastern District and with members of the Intelligence Division of the IRS, explaining that he and his wife wanted to challenge the constitutionality of the "marriage penalty" without incurring liability for fraud or willfulness. Following these conversations they filed their returns as described, attaching to each return a letter explaining that, although married, they were applying the tax tables for single persons because they believed that the "income tax structure unfairly discriminates against working married couples" in violation of the equal protection clause of the fourteenth amendment. The Tax Court rejected this constitutional challenge, sustaining the Commissioner's determination that the Drukers were subject to tax at the rates provided in § 1(d) for married persons filing separately.

Determination of the proper method for federal taxation of the incomes of married and single persons has had a long and stormy history. See generally, Bittker, Federal Income Taxation and the Family, 27 Stan. L. Rev. 1389, 1399–1416 (1975). From the beginning of the income tax in 1913 until 1948 each individual was taxed on his or her own income regardless of marital status. Thus, as a result of the progressive nature of the tax, two married couples with the same aggregate income would often have very different tax liabilities—larger if most of the income belonged to one spouse, smaller as their incomes tended toward equality. The decision in Poe v. Seaborn, 282 U.S. 101 (1930), that a wife was taxable on one half of community income even if this was earned solely by the husband, introduced a further element of geographical inequality, since it gave married couples in community property states a large tax advantage over similarly situated married couples with the same aggregate income in common law states.

After *Poe* the tax status of a married couple in a community property state differed from that of a married couple in a common law state in two significant respects. First, each community property spouse paid the same tax as an unmarried person with one-half the aggregate community income, whereas each common law spouse paid the same tax as an unmarried person with the same individual income. Consequently, marriage usually reduced a couple's tax burden if they resided in a community property state but was a neutral tax event for couples in common law states. Second, in community property states all married couples with the same aggregate income paid the same tax, whereas in common law states a married couple's tax liability depended on the amount of income each spouse earned. * * *

The decision in *Poe* touched off something of a stampede among common law states to introduce community property regimes and thereby qualify their residents for the privilege of income splitting. The Supreme Court's subsequent decision in Commissioner v. Harmon, 323 U.S. 44 (1944), that the income-splitting privileges did not extend to couples in states whose community property systems were elective, slowed but did not halt this movement. The result was considerable confusion and much upsetting of expectations founded on long experience under the common law. Congress responded in 1948 by extending the benefits of "income splitting" to residents of common law as well as community property states. * * * Pursuant to this Act, every married couple was permitted to file a joint return and pay twice the tax that a single individual would pay on one-half of their total income. This in effect taxed a married couple as if they were two single individuals each of whom earned half of the couple's combined income. The Act not only reduced the tax burden on married couples in common law states; it also ensured that all married couples with the same aggregate income paid the same tax regardless of the state in which they lived ("geographical uniformity") and regardless of the relative income contribution of each spouse ("horizontal equity").

While the 1948 Act was good news for married couples, it placed singles at a serious disadvantage. The tax liability of a single person was now sometimes as much as 41% greater than that of a married couple with the same income. S. Rep. No. 552, 91st Cong., 1st Sess. 260 (1969). Although constitutional challenges to the "singles' penalty" were uniformly rejected, see, e.g., Kellems v. Commissioner, 58 T.C. 556 (1972), aff'd per curiam, 474 F.2d 1399 (2 Cir.), cert. denied, 414 U.S. 831 (1973); Faraco v. Commissioner, 261 F.2d 387 (4 Cir.1958), cert. denied, 359 U.S. 925 (1959), the single taxpayer obtained some relief from Congress. The Tax Reform Act of 1969, * * * increased the number of tax schedules from two to four: § 1(a) for marrieds filing jointly; § 1(b) for unmarried heads of households; § 1(c) for unmarried individuals; and § 1(d) for married individuals filing separately. The schedules were set so that a single person's tax liability under § 1(c) would never be more than 120% that of a married couple with the same income filing jointly under § 1(a). See S. Rep. No. 552, supra, at 260–62.

The 1969 reform spawned a new class of aggrieved taxpayers—the two wage-earner married couple whose combined tax burden, whether they chose to file jointly under § 1(a) or separately under § 1(d), was now greater than it would have been if they had remained single and filed under § 1(c). It is this last phenomenon which has been characterized, in somewhat loaded fashion, as the "marriage penalty" or "marriage tax".[2] Here, again, * * * constitutional attack has been unavailing, see Johnson v. United States, 422 F. Supp. 958 (N.D. Ind. 1976), aff'd per curiam sub nom. Barter v. United States, 550 F.2d 1239 (7th Cir.1977), cert. denied, 434 U.S. 1012 (1978); Mapes v. United States, 576 F.2d 896 (Ct. Cl.), cert. denied, 439 U.S. 1046 (1978). * * *

---

[2]   Not all married couples are so "penalized". For the couple whose income is earned primarily or solely by one partner, marriage still offers significant tax savings. * * * As a general rule of thumb, marriage will increase a couple's tax burden as compared with that of two single persons whenever the lesser-earning spouse earns 20% or more of the couple's total income and decrease its tax burden whenever the lesser-earning spouse earns less than 20%. * * *

Subsequent to the decisions in *Johnson* and *Mapes*, the Supreme Court made explicit in Zablocki v. Redhail, 434 U.S. 374 (1978), what had been implicit in earlier decisions, that the right to marry is "fundamental". The Court, however, citing Califano v. Jobst, 434 U.S. 47(1977), took care to explain that it did "not mean to suggest that every state regulation which relates in any way to the incidents of or prerequisites for marriage must be subjected to rigorous scrutiny. To the contrary, reasonable regulations that do not significantly interfere with decisions to enter into the marital relationship may be legitimately imposed." 434 U.S. at 386. Whereas differences in race, religion, and political affiliation are almost always irrelevant for legislative purposes, "a distinction between married persons and unmarried persons is of a different character". *Jobst,* supra, 434 U.S. at 53. "Both tradition and common experience support the conclusion that marriage is an event which normally marks an important change in economic status." Id.

We do not doubt that the "marriage penalty" has some adverse effect on marriage; indeed, James Druker stated at argument that, having failed thus far in the courts, he and his wife had solved their tax problem by divorcing but continuing to live together. The adverse effect of the "marriage penalty", however, like the effect of the termination of social security benefits in *Jobst*, is merely "indirect"; while it may to some extent weight the choice whether to marry, it leaves the ultimate decision to the individual. * * * The tax rate structure of I.R.C. § 1 places "no direct legal obstacle in the path of persons desiring to get married". *Zablocki,* supra, 434 U.S. at n. 12. Nor is anyone "absolutely prevented" by it from getting married, id. at 387. Moreover, the "marriage penalty" is most certainly not "an attempt to interfere with the individual's freedom [to marry]". *Jobst,* supra, 434 U.S. at 54. It would be altogether absurd to suppose that Congress, in fixing the rate schedules in 1969, had any invidious intent to discourage or penalize marriage—an estate enjoyed by the vast majority of its members. Indeed, as has been shown, the sole and express purpose of the 1969 reform was to provide some relief for the single taxpayer. See S. Rep. No. 552, supra, at 260–261. Given this purpose Congress had either to abandon the principle of horizontal equity between married couples, a principle which had been established by the 1948 Act and the constitutionality of which has not been challenged, or to impose a "penalty" on some two-earner married couples. It was put to this hard choice because, as Professor Bittker has shown, supra, 27 Stan. L. Rev. at 1395–96, 1429–31, it is simply impossible to design a progressive tax regime in which all married couples of equal aggregate income are taxed equally and in which an individual's tax liability is unaffected by changes in marital status.[3] See

---

[3]   Professor Bittker puts it thus, 27 Stan. L. Rev. at 1430–31:

Another way to describe this collision of objectives is that the tax paid by a married couple must be (a) greater than they paid before marriage, in which event they are subject to a marriage penalty, (b) less than they paid before marriage, in which event

also Tax Treatment of Single Persons and Married Persons Where Both Spouses Are Working: Hearings Before the House Committee on Ways and Means, 92d Cong., 2d Sess. 78–79 (1972) (Statement of Edwin S. Cohen, Assistant Secretary for Tax Policy) ("No algebraic equation, no matter how sophisticated, can solve this dilemma. Both ends of a seesaw cannot be up at the same time.") Faced with this choice, Congress in 1969 decided to hold fast to horizontal equity, even at the price of imposing a "penalty" on two-earner married couples like the Drukers. There is nothing in the equal protection clause that required a different choice. Since the objectives sought by the 1969 Act—the maintenance of horizontal equity and progressivity, and the reduction of the differential between single and married taxpayers—were clearly compelling, the tax rate schedules in I.R.C. § 1 can survive even the "rigorous scrutiny" reserved by *Zablocki* for measures which "significantly interfere" with the right to marry. * * * Clearly, the alternative favored by the Drukers, that married persons be permitted to file under § 1(c) if they so wish, would entail the loss of horizontal equity.

In the area of family taxation every legislative disposition is "virtually fated to be both over inclusive and under inclusive when judged from one perspective or another". The result, as Professor Bittker has well said, is that there "can be no peace in this area, only an uneasy truce." 27 Stan. L. Rev. at 1443. Congress must be accorded wide latitude in striking the terms of that truce. The history we have reviewed makes clear that Congress has worked persistently to accommodate the competing interests and accomplish fairness. While we could elaborate still further, we think that this, along with the discussion in *Johnson, Mapes*, and in Chief Judge Tannenwald's opinion below, is sufficient to show that what the Drukers choose to call the "marriage penalty" deprived them of no constitutional right. Whether policy considerations warrant a further narrowing of the gap between the schedules applied to married and unmarried persons is for Congress to determine in light of all the relevant legislative considerations.

* * *

DETAILED ANALYSIS

1. MARRIAGE PENALTIES AND BONUSES

1.1. *Rate Schedules, Standard Deduction, Personal Exemptions, and Tax Expenditures*

As the opinion in *Druker* makes clear, the Congressional decision to adopt a joint return based on marital status was a direct reaction to the uniformity problems spawned by the decisions in Lucas v. Earl (see Chapter 37, Section 1) and Poe v. Seaborn (see Chapter 37, Section 1.1.). In adopting the joint return, Congress created the legal fiction that all marital income

---

unmarried persons are subject to a singles penalty, or (c) unchanged by marriage, in which event equal-income married couples are subject to unequal taxes.

was owned equally between spouses even when state law provided otherwise. In addition, the 1948 decision to treat married couples as a unit for federal income tax purposes created its own array of tax inequities between and among different kinds of households.

Between 1948 and 1969, unmarried taxpayers paid significantly higher taxes than married taxpayers. Under the applicable rate structure during those years, married taxpayers enjoyed a "marriage bonus" due to the "income splitting" joint return (see Chapter 37, Section 1). More specifically, married taxpayers used tax brackets that were twice as wide as the brackets for unmarried taxpayers, the effect of which treated married taxpayers as two single taxpayers with combined tax liability twice that on half their income. For example, a married couple with taxable income of $50,000 would be taxed at the same marginal rate as two single individuals each with taxable income of $25,000; in this way, the married couple in our example avoided the progressive rates from $25,001 to (and including) $50,000. Meanwhile, a single taxpayer with taxable income of $50,000—unable to split income in half for purposes of calculating federal income tax liability—paid tax on the full $50,000, subject to the progressive rates from $1 to (and including) $50,000. As the court in *Druker* explained, this tax "penalty" for singles meant that they could pay considerably more in tax than married couples with identical levels of income. It also meant that marrying a person with no, or relatively little, income could result in a substantial tax cut.

In 1969, and as the *Druker* opinion also described, Congress mitigated both the "singles penalty" and the "marriage bonus" by setting tax brackets such that a single taxpayer would never pay tax of more than 120 percent on the same level of income as a married couple. Nonetheless, both the singles penalty and marriage bonus persisted. Moreover, the new rate structure created "marriage penalties" for two-earner married households with similar income levels, who paid more in taxes as a married couple than as two single individuals on the same amounts and ratio of income.

Over the next several decades, Congress addressed these marriage penalties in a variety of ways. In 1981, it enacted a deduction for two-earner married couples equal to 10 percent of the lower earner's qualified earned income up to $30,000 for a maximum deduction of $3,000. The new deduction substantially reduced or eliminated the increased tax liability resulting from marriage in a broad range of cases. But it was short-lived, as Congress repealed the provision as part of the Tax Reform Act of 1986, which significantly reduced marginal tax rates (with a top rate of 28 percent) and widened tax brackets. Lower rates and wider brackets eliminated the marriage penalty in many instances, with combined incomes on a joint return more likely to be applied to one-half of the income of an unmarried taxpayer.

Marriage penalties and marriage bonuses fluctuated in severity over the next 25 years, as tax rates rose (to 39.6 percent in 1993), fell (to 35 percent in 2003), and rose again (to 39.6 percent in 2012), and as Congress expanded the width of some tax brackets (since 2001, the 10-percent and 15-percent brackets have been twice as wide for married taxpayers as for single taxpayers). Higher rates made penalties more expensive and bonuses more lucrative, while wider tax brackets eliminated marriage tax penalties and bonuses (at least those associated with the rate structure) for lower-income and middle-income taxpayers.

Tax rates and brackets are not the only causes of tax penalties and bonuses associated with marriage. For years, the standard deduction created penalties and bonuses, because the dollar amount of the standard deduction for single taxpayers was roughly 60 percent as valuable as that for married taxpayers. Under such a system, two single individuals who subsequently married lost approximately 20 percent of the standard deduction. At the same time, if one of the individuals earned no income, the earning spouse would experience a marriage bonus due to the nearly 70-percent higher standard deduction. In 2001, Congress made the standard deduction amount exactly twice as large for married taxpayers as for single taxpayers, a change that eliminated marriage penalties caused by the standard deduction while increasing the value of marriage bonuses.

The phase-out of the personal exemptions under § 151(d)(3) (discussed in Chapter 22, Section1.B.3.) also produces marriage penalties and bonuses. For single individuals, the phase-out begins at adjusted gross income in excess of $250,000, but for married individuals filing a joint return, the phase-out begins after $300,000 of adjusted gross income (both figures adjusted for inflation; in 2016, they are $259,400 and $311,300, respectively). Thus two unmarried individuals each with $250,000 of adjusted gross income are not subject to the phase-out if they remain unmarried, but, if they decide to marry, their personal exemptions would phase out completely (at $433,800 in 2015). Conversely, if one of the individuals had less than $50,000 of adjusted gross income, the higher phase-out threshold for married couples would produce a bonus.

Yet another source of marriage tax penalties and bonuses involves § 68 (discussed in Chapter 21, Section 7), which effectively creates a higher marginal rate bracket by limiting the value of itemized deductions. Much like the effect of phaseouts for personal exemptions, the limitations on itemized deductions in § 68(a) create both penalties and bonuses, because the amount of income above which the tax benefits begin to phase out are different for single versus married taxpayers; in fact, both § 151(d)(3) and § 68(b) use the same income levels for the beginning and end of the phaseout.

Perhaps the most insidious form of marriage tax penalties and bonuses occurs as low-income individuals phase out of tax credits. Consider the earned income tax credit (EITC), a refundable tax credit for the working poor. Technically, eligibility for the EITC involves a claimant's earned income and number of children, and not necessarily marital status. But the act of marriage can have a profound effect on qualifying for the credit. Consider the following example. An unmarried individual with earned income of $20,000 and two qualifying children is entitled to an EITC payment of $5,191 in 2016 (adjusted for inflation). If two such individuals were to marry, the credit amount for the newly constituted family would drop to $2,845, for a marriage penalty of $7,537; specifically, prior to marriage, both families received an EITC payment of $5,191 for total payments of $10,382, while after marriage they received just $2,845 for a marriage penalty of $7,537, a figure that amounts to 18.85 percent of their total earned income.[1] And while this example appears extreme, it only accounts for one tax credit and does not consider non-tax transfers such as housing subsidies, food stamps, or unemployment benefits, all of which can be reduced and even eliminated by the act of marriage. At the end of the day, any provision—tax or otherwise—that contains income thresholds or phaseouts that are not doubled for married individuals will necessarily impose marriage penalties and might bestow marriage bonuses. At the same time, doubling thresholds and phaseouts is not necessarily the answer: either strategy could raise the cost of programs to prohibitively high levels and subject them to the fatal political charge that they are providing "welfare for the middle class."

2. SAME SEX MARRIED COUPLES

In recent years, one of the stubborn relics of taxing married households differently than other households slipped into history. Until 2013, same-sex couples—whether or not validly married under state law—were prohibited from filing as a marital unit. In United States v. Windsor, 133 S. Ct. 2675 (2013), the Supreme Court held that § 3 of the Defense of Marriage Act (DOMA)—which limited the meaning of the word "marriage" to "a legal union between one man and one woman as husband and wife," and further provided that "the word 'spouse' referred only to a person of the opposite sex who is a husband or wife"—was an unconstitutional denial of equal protection in violation of the Due Process Clause of the Fifth Amendment. Thus, same-sex married couples whose marriages are recognized by local law may file joint returns (and if they do not file a joint return, they must file as married filing separately). The *Windsor* Court limited its holding to the definition of marriage in § 3 of DOMA and did not address § 2, which allows states to refuse to recognize same-sex marriages from other states.

Just two years later, however, the Court in Obergefell v. Hodges, 135 S. Ct. 2584 (2015), held that both the Due Process Clause and the Equal Protection Clause of the Fourteenth Amendment guarantee to same-sex couples the fundamental right to marry, a ruling that requires all states to issue marriage licenses to same-sex couples and to recognize same-sex marriages validly performed in other jurisdictions. Even before *Obergefell* (but after *Windsor*), the IRS ruled that not only would it recognize the marital status of same-sex couples validly married under state laws and that the terms "spouse," "husband and wife," "husband," and "wife" include individuals married to a person of the same sex if the individuals are lawfully married under state law, but also that same-sex marriages validly performed in a state whose laws authorize such marriage would be recognized even if

---

[1]   In 2016, the maximum credit for an individual with two qualifying children was $5,572, or 40 percent of the first $13,930 of earned income. The credit phased out for income above $18,190 at a rate of 21.06 percent (that is, for every dollar above the threshold, the credit declined by $0.2106), and phased out completely at $44,648. Meanwhile, the maximum credit for married individuals filing jointly with two or more qualifying children was $6,269 in 2016, or 45 percent of the first $13,930 of earned income. The credit phased out for income above $23,740 at a rate of 21.06 percent, and phased out completely at $53,505.

the married couple was domiciled in a state that did not recognize the validity of the marriage.[2] Rev. Rul. 2013–17, 2013–38 I.R.B. 201.

In 2016, the Treasury Department finalized regulations defining and describing the marital status of taxpayers as reflected in the holdings of *Obergefell*, *Windsor*, and Rev. Rul. 2013–17. See 81 Fed. Reg. 60609 (Sept. 2, 2016). The regulations provide that for federal tax purposes the terms "spouse," "husband," and "wife" mean an individual lawfully married to another individual, and the term "husband and wife" means two individuals lawfully married to each other. Treas. Reg. § 301.7701–18. These definitions apply regardless of sex. At the same time, the terms "spouse," "husband," and "wife" do not include individuals who have entered into a registered domestic partnership, civil union, or other similar relationship not denominated as a marriage under the law of a state, possession, or territory of the United States. The term "husband and wife" does not include couples entering into such a relationship, and the term "marriage" does not include such relationships.

3. HEADS OF HOUSEHOLD AND MINOR CHILDREN

Although the individual remains the unit of taxation (except for married couples filing joint returns), special rates are provided for two classes of individuals. First, a special rate schedule is provided in § 1(b) for a head of household, defined as any unmarried person who is not a surviving spouse and who maintains a household which includes either a qualifying dependent child (with some exceptions for qualifying children who are not dependents) or any other person whom the taxpayer can claim as a dependent. This rate schedule falls between the schedule for unmarried persons and married persons filing jointly. For example, for tax year 2016, the statutory upper limit of the 10-percent bracket is $18,550 for married individuals filing jointly, $9,275 for single individuals, and $13,250 for heads of households (adjusted for inflation). Second, although § 73 taxes a minor child on his or her income, whether or not the child is emancipated under local law, the unearned income of minor children (and some adult children under age 24), minus a base amount, is subject to tax at the rates the parents would have to pay if the child's unearned income were included in the parents' taxable income. See I.R.C. § 1(g) discussed in Section 2 of this Chapter).

4. POLICY ISSUES IN THE CHOICE OF THE TAXABLE UNIT

The history of the provisions dealing with married couples reveals a complex interaction among competing and inherently conflicting policy objectives: (1) equal treatment of married couples with the same aggregate taxable income, regardless of the proportion of income earned by each spouse; (2) equal treatment of all individuals (married or unmarried) with the same taxable income (in other words, a marriage-neutral system which contains neither penalties nor bonuses for marriage); and (3) a progressive

---

[2]   The IRS ruling also determined that parties who have entered into a registered domestic partnership, civil union, or other similar formal relationship recognized under state law that is not denominated as "marriage" under the laws of the state are not considered married for federal tax purposes, regardless of the substantive similarities between the formal relationship and marriage. This aspect of the Ruling retains its relevance even after *Obergefell*.

rate structure. As it turns out, it is impossible to accomplish all three objectives at the same time.

In order to avoid the marriage penalty while also maintaining progressivity and aggregation of income on joint returns, the rate brackets for married taxpayers must be twice as wide as those for unmarried taxpayers. Moreover, items such as the standard deduction and phase-out thresholds must be twice as generous for married couples as for unmarried individuals. But this approach necessarily creates a marriage bonus, whereby an individual earner who marries a non-earner will experience significant tax savings solely as a result of marriage, while domestic partners, members of civil unions, and others who do not marry will be disadvantaged. Both marriage penalties and bonuses could be avoided if spouses were required to file separate returns using the same rate schedule as unmarried people. Such an approach, however, reintroduces the equally challenging problems that prevailed before 1948 with differences in treatment among married couples depending upon differences in the relative earnings of each spouse and on whether the couple resides in a community-property or common-law state. As long as tax rates remain progressive, policymakers must choose between, on the one hand, equal treatment of married couples with the same aggregate taxable income and, on the other hand, equal treatment of all individuals (married or unmarried) with the same taxable income. Only a pure flat tax—meaning a single-rate tax with no zero bracket amount or exemption for low levels of income—would create a marriage neutral tax system while also taxing all equal-income married couples equally. And since all of the so-called "flat tax" proposals over the last thirty years include a zero bracket amount, the current federal income tax must include one of two evils: (1) a marriage penalty and/or bonus, or (2) a disparity between the tax liabilities of married couples with equal aggregate income.

The principal argument for emphasizing the equal treatment of married couples with equal incomes is based on a view of marriage as an economic partnership. The underlying assumption is that spouses pool and share income jointly, regardless of which spouse earns the income in the traditional market sense of the word. Imposing the same tax burden on couples with equal aggregate incomes requires that married couples be treated as a taxable unit, at which point the choice is between marriage penalties or marriage bonuses. Using a uniform rate schedule that applies both to individuals and married couples would eliminate any rate-induced marriage bonus but would produce an almost universal marriage penalty, while using a rate schedule for married couples exactly double the schedule for individuals would eliminate any rate-induced marriage penalty but would produce an almost universal marriage bonus. Current law reflects an ad hoc compromise between these two extremes, with some married couples enjoying a marriage bonus and others suffering a marriage penalty depending on whether (and to what extent) the couple's aggregate income is earned by one spouse versus the other.

In addition to generating tax penalties and/or bonuses, using the marital unit to determine tax liability reflects a number of longstanding assumptions that increasingly conflict with modern trends in marriage rates, family arrangements, internal family dynamics, and labor demographics. Over the last decade, the marriage rate in the United States dipped to historic lows, with fewer young adults marrying than at any time in history and affirmatively expressing preferences for alternative family living arrangements that do not include marriage. See Wang and Parker, Record Share of Americans Have Never Been Married, PEW Research Center (2014). Moreover, the extent of income pooling and sharing within the marital unit surely varies widely among households, although deriving precise data on income pooling and sharing within households (married or unmarried) is a difficult task. In addition, taxing spouses as a unit can adversely affect the labor-market decision to enter or remain in the workforce for a married household's secondary earner, whose first dollar earned gets taxed at the primary earner's last dollar earned due to income aggregation of joint returns. Meanwhile, the marital unit, in combination with the tax system's failure to tax the imputed income from household services, significantly understates the economic income of one-earner families that receive imputed income in the form of services that two-earner families must purchase with after-tax dollars. For further discussion of these issues, see Motro, A New I Do: Towards a Marriage-Neutral Income Tax, 91 Iowa L. Rev. 1509 (2006); Zelenak, Marriage and the Income Tax, 67 So. Cal. L. Rev. 339 1994); Kornhauser, Love, Money, and the IRS: Family, Income-Sharing, and the Joint Income Tax Return, 45 Hastings L. J. 63 (1993).

SECTION 2.   TAXATION OF CHILDREN AS PART OF THE FAMILY UNIT

INTERNAL REVENUE CODE: Section 1(g).

General Explanation of the Tax Reform Act of 1986
Staff of the Joint Committee on Taxation, 1253–1255 (May 4, 1987).

[Pre-1987] Law

Under both present and [pre-1987] law, if income-producing assets are transferred to a minor child, income earned on those assets generally is taxed to the child. Under [pre-1987] law, that income was taxed at the child's rate.

Reasons for Change

The Congress believed that the [pre-1987] law rules governing the taxation of minor children provided inappropriate tax incentives to shift income-producing assets among family members. In particular, the Congress was aware that the treatment of a child as a separate taxpayer encouraged parents whose income would otherwise be taxed at a high marginal rate bracket to transfer income-producing property to a child to ensure that the income was taxed at the child's lower marginal rates. In order to reduce the opportunities for tax avoidance through transfers of income producing property to minor children, the Congress concluded that it generally is appropriate to tax the unearned income of a minor child under age 14 at the parent's marginal rates.

Explanation of [Section 1(g)]

The net unearned income of a child under 14 years of age is taxed to the child at the top rate of the parents. The provision applies with respect to a child under 14 years of age who has at least one living parent as of the close of the taxable year. The tax payable by a child on the net unearned income is equal to the additional amount of tax that the parent would be required to pay if the child's net unearned income were included in the parent's taxable income. The provision applies to all net unearned income of a child under 14 years of age regardless of the source of the assets creating the child's net unearned income.

Net unearned income means unearned income less the sum of $500 and the greater of: (1) $500 of the standard deduction or $500 of itemized deductions or (2) the amount of allowable deductions which are directly connected with the production of the unearned income. The $500 figures are to be adjusted for inflation beginning in 1989. The Congress expected that the Treasury Department will issue regulations providing for the application of these provisions where either the child or the parent is subject to the alternative minimum tax for the year. * * *

The following examples illustrate the tax consequences of this provision to a dependent child under age 14 in 1988.

Example 1.—If the child has $400 of unearned income and no earned income, the child's standard deduction is $400 which is allocated against the child's unearned income, so that the child has no Federal income tax liability.

Example 2.—If the child has $900 of unearned income and no earned income, the child's standard deduction is $500 which is allocated against the first $500 of unearned income. The child's remaining unearned income is $400. Because the child's net unearned income is less than $500, the remaining unearned income is taxed at the child's rates.

* * *

DETAILED ANALYSIS

1.   GENERAL

Even though minor children are typically part of the family economic unit, they have always been treated as separate taxpayers. The failure to include minor children in the taxable unit led to the use of a variety of devices aimed at splitting the income of the family with minor children to reduce the family's overall tax burden. See Chapter 37. Although the so-called "kiddie tax" of § 1(g) was principally aimed at income-shifting devices and does not tax the child's income to the parents but only at the parent's rate, it can still be viewed as a step toward treating minor children as part of the unit of taxation. See generally, McMahon, Expanding the Taxable Unit: The

Aggregation of the Income of Children and Parents, 56 N.Y.U. L.Rev. 60 (1981).

As explained in the excerpt from the General Explanation of the Tax Reform Act of 1986, since 1987 the unearned income of children under age 14 generally has been taxed at their parents' marginal tax rate. Subsequent legislation has extended the reach of the kiddie tax to apply to unearned income of children who meet one or more of the following conditions as of the end of the taxable year: (1) the child is under the age of 18, (2) the child is at the age of 18 and the child's earned income does not exceed one-half of the amount of the child's support, or (3) the child is under the age of 24, the child's earned income does not exceed one-half of the amount of the child's support, and the child is a full-time student. The kiddie tax does not apply if a child is married and files a joint return. I.R.C. § 1(g)(2)(C).

2. TECHNICAL ISSUES

2.1. *Earned and Unearned Income*

A child's earned income is not taxed at the parent's rate by § 1(g) even though the income might satisfy family needs. The exclusion for earned income is found in the definition of net unearned income in § 1(g)(4)(A). That is, net unearned income is first defined as the portion of adjusted gross income that is not earned income as defined in § 911(d)(2)—wages, salary, or other amounts received as personal compensation.

Net unearned income taxed at the parent's rate is computed by subtracting the standard deduction available under § 63(c)(5)(A) to a person claimed as a dependent on another taxpayer's return ($500; $1,050 in 2015 as adjusted for inflation) *plus* the greater of either the amount allowed by § 63(c)(5)(A) or, if the child itemizes deductions, the child's itemized deductions directly connected to the production of unearned income. As a consequence, a child's unearned income is taxed at the parents' rates only if the unearned income exceeds a minimum of $1,000 ($2,100 in 2015, as adjusted for inflation).

Unearned income subject to tax at the parents' rates includes unearned income from any source. Thus, the fact that the child's unearned income includes interest earned on savings account deposits of income earned from a paper route does not free the interest income from the reach of § 1(g). Temp. Reg. § 1.1(i)–1T, Q & A–8, Ex. 5.

2.2. *Which Parent's Income*

If the child's parents are not married, the child's tax on net unearned income is based upon the income of the custodial parent. If the child's parents are married but file separate returns, the child's tax is based upon the parent with the higher taxable income. I.R.C. § 1(g)(5). The child is required to report the taxpayer identification number (TIN) of the parent upon whose income the child's tax is based, and parents are obligated to provide their TIN to the child. I.R.C. § 1(g)(6). Section 6103(c) authorizes the IRS to disclose to a child or the child's guardian tax return information of the child's parent necessary to prepare a return.

SECTION 3.   TAX ASPECTS OF DIVORCE AND SEPARATION

From a tax perspective, divorce and separation result in three distinct types of cash or property transfers, each of which raise different issues. First, a spouse may make a transfer to effect an equitable division of the marital property. Second, a spouse may make a transfer in the nature of alimony to provide financial support to the other spouse. Finally, a spouse may make a transfer in the nature of child support.

Property divisions or settlements raise important conceptual issues. If the parties are treated as dividing jointly owned marital property, then the division should not be treated as a recognition event since the division of jointly owned property is generally not a taxable event. As discussed below, under current law, property settlements are generally treated as non-events for federal tax purposes, and the technical distinctions among state marital laws have no impact on this treatment. However, if all the assets are not divided equally (e.g., the husband receives asset A while the wife receives asset B) or if the asset is treated under state property law as owned by one spouse subject only to certain claims of the other spouse that are released, the division theoretically could be treated as a taxable exchange. These situations would prompt a consideration of the role for state law characterization of the economic aspects of marriage dissolution in formulating the appropriate tax treatment.

Spousal support (alimony) may be viewed from two different perspectives. First, the parties may be considered as totally distinct taxable units. Under this view, spousal support is a nondeductible personal expense of the payor. Although the payments do not proceed from the detached and disinterested generosity of the payor and therefore do not qualify as gifts for income tax purposes, from the payee's perspective, the payments can be seen as a cash substitute for the normal right to support within the marriage. This treatment raises the question whether the conversion of that right into cash after the marriage is over should result in income. Spousal support also can be analyzed from the point of view of the income-sharing principle, which provides one justification for treating the couple as a single taxable unit during the marriage. When the unit is dissolved, the former partners continue to have an economic relationship in which income is being shared through the mechanism of the spousal support payment. Under this approach, each spouse should be taxed on his or her share of the income arising out of the dissolved marriage. Current law follows this latter approach by generally allowing the payor to deduct alimony payments and requiring the payee to include the payments in gross income. The payor's deduction simply offsets the income the payor realizes upon earning the income that gave rise to the cash used to pay the alimony. The end result is that the payee (and only the payee) is effectively taxed on the payor's earnings that satisfied the payor's alimony obligation (although typically at lower rates than the payor's marginal tax rate).

The proper tax treatment of child support payments is clearer. When a taxpayer makes payments to benefit the taxpayer's children, the payments are generally characterized as nondeductible personal expenses of the payor. This rule ought to apply regardless of whether the payments are made during or after marriage or whether they are made voluntarily or pursuant to court order. Current law is consistent with this view and denies the payor of child support any deduction.

A. PROPERTY SETTLEMENTS

INTERNAL REVENUE CODE: Section 1041.

TEMPORARY REGULATIONS: Section 1.1041–1T, Q & A 1–14.

Balding v. Commissioner

Tax Court of the United States, 1992.
98 T.C. 368.

■ HALPERIN, JUDGE:

Respondent determined deficiencies in petitioner's Federal income tax for the years 1986, 1987, and 1988, in the amounts of $3,605, $3,240, and $1,912, respectively. The sole issue we must decide is whether payments received by petitioner in settlement of her claim to a community property share of her ex-husband's military retirement pay are includible in gross income. * * *

Background

* * *

Petitioner and Joe M. Balding (Balding) were married in 1962, less than 1 year after Balding entered the military. In December 1981, subsequent to Balding's retirement from the military, they were divorced. Among other things, the divorce court ordered a division of their community property and affirmed that Balding's military retirement pay was his sole and separate property. In 1984, because of changes in California's community property law, petitioner asked the divorce court to reopen its judgment of divorce and award her a community property share of Balding's military retirement pay. Before the divorce court could act, petitioner and Balding reached a settlement with regard to the retirement pay, which settlement was stipulated between them and entered as an order by the divorce court. Petitioner relinquished any claim to Balding's military retirement pay (and agreed not to bring any further claims with regard to marital property) in consideration of Balding's promise to pay to her $15,000, $14,000, and $13,000 in 1986, 1987, and 1988, respectively (hereinafter the settlement payments); petitioner also received Balding's promise not to make any future claims with regard to marital property. Petitioner did not include the settlement payments in her original returns for the years in question. * * * We must determine whether any income is recognized to petitioner on account of receipt of such payments. We conclude that no income is recognized to her pursuant to the provisions of section 1041.

Discussion

The settlement payments were received by petitioner on account of her divorce from Balding and in settlement of her claim to a community property interest in property that previously had been determined to be Balding's separate property. Respondent has not argued, nor would we agree, that the settlement payments constitute alimony or separate maintenance taxable to petitioner pursuant to sections 61(a)(8) and 71. Respondent has argued that petitioner's relinquishment of her community property interest in the retirement benefits in question constituted an anticipatory assignment of income such that the consideration she received therefor (i.e., the settlement payments) is immediately taxable to her. Outside of the marital context, we would have little trouble agreeing with respondent. See Commissioner v. P.G. Lake, Inc., 356 U.S. 260 (1958) * * * . Transfers of property, or releases of marital rights, incident to divorce, however, are subject to a special set of rules found in section 1041.

* * *

Prior to the enactment of section 1041, the resolution of property rights incident to a divorce gave rise to differing tax results, depending on how each spouse's entitlements and obligations were viewed for State law purposes. The Supreme Court had ruled that a transfer of separately owned, appreciated property to a spouse (or former spouse) in exchange for the release of marital claims resulted in the recognition of gain to the transferor. United States v. Davis, 370 U.S. 65 (1962).[6] However, in the case of an approximately equal division of community property on divorce, no gain was recognized on the theory that no sale or exchange had occurred but only a nontaxable partition. Carrieres v. Commissioner, 64 T.C. 959, 964 (1975), affd. per curiam 552 F.2d 1350 (9th Cir.1977). * * * Respondent applied a like result to the partition of jointly held property. See Rev. Rul. 74–347, 1974–2 C.B. 26. The tax treatment of divisions of property between spouses involving other various types of ownership under the different State laws was often unclear and resulted in much litigation. See H.Rept. 98–432 (Part 2), at 1941 (1984). Several States had amended their property law in an attempt to avoid the result in the *Davis* case.

Congress was dissatisfied with the aforesaid state of the law and desired to change the tax laws to make them as nonintrusive as possible with respect to relations between spouses. Section 1041 was the result. In part, the Ways and Means Committee explained the new provision as follows:

---

[6]   No gain was recognized to the spouse receiving the property, and she took a tax basis in the asset equal to its fair market value. United States v. Davis, 370 U.S. 65, 73 (1962).

The bill provides that the transfer of property to a spouse incident to a divorce will be treated, for income tax purposes, in the same manner as a gift. Gain (including recapture income) or loss will not be recognized to the transferor, and the transferee will receive the property at the transferor's basis (whether the property has appreciated or depreciated in value). A transfer will be treated as incident to a divorce if the transfer occurs within one year after the parties cease to be married or is related to the divorce. This nonrecognition rule applies whether the transfer is for the relinquishment of marital rights, for cash or other property, for the assumption of liabilities in excess of basis, or for other consideration and is intended to apply to any indebtedness which is discharged. Thus, uniform Federal income tax consequences will apply to these transfers notwithstanding that the property may be subject to differing state property laws. [Id.; fn. ref. omitted.]

The language of section 1041 specifies broad rules of exclusion for both the transferor spouse and the transferee spouse. If the language of the statute leaves any doubt, the relevant legislative history (quoted above) makes clear that, notwithstanding the nature of the consideration received (whether, for instance, the relinquishment of marital rights, cash, property, or "other consideration"), no gain or loss is to be recognized to the transferor spouse on account of any unrealized appreciation or depreciation in the property transferred. Likewise, the transferee spouse is to be viewed as having received the transferred property as if by nontaxable gift. Any doubt that the receipt is nontaxable is answered by the regulations. Sec. 1.1041–1T(d), ("Q–11 How is the transferee of property under section 1041 treated for income tax purposes? A–11 The transferee of property under section 1041 recognizes no gain or loss upon receipt of the transferred property.") It is also clear that, even where the transfer is indisputably not a gift, gift treatment is still appropriate. See sec. 1.1041–1T(d), ("A–11 * * * Even if the transfer is a bona fide *sale,* the transferee does not acquire a basis in the transferred property equal to the transferee's cost (the fair market value).)". (Emphasis added); see Staff of the Joint Comm. on Taxation, General Explanation of the Revenue Provisions of the Deficit Reduction Act of 1984, at 711 (J. Comm. Print 1984) (any transfer of property, "including money", is treated as made by (and acquired by) gift, so that recapture rules do not apply).

Here, petitioner released her claim to a community property share of her ex-husband's military retirement benefits in exchange for the settlement payments. Respondent has not argued, nor could we accept, that such receipt was not incident to the divorce. The state of the law in California with regard to community property was unsettled at the time petitioner and Balding entered into the settlement agreement. Nevertheless, whether we view petitioner's release as constituting (or equivalent to) a transfer of property, or simply a release of marital rights, the transaction whereby she received the settlement payments requires that we analyze her receipt in light of section 1041. The settlement payments having been received from her ex-husband, incident to her divorce (and in consideration of her release of any claim to his military retirement benefits), we must conclude that they constitute nontaxable gifts, pursuant to sections 1041 and 102. Respondent's determination of a deficiency, based on petitioner's failure to include such payments in gross income, cannot be sustained. * * *

DETAILED ANALYSIS

1.   EFFECT OF SECTION 1041

United States v. Davis, 370 U.S. 65 (1962), discussed in *Balding*, required that the taxpayer husband recognize gain on the transfer of appreciated stock to his wife in satisfaction of the wife's marital rights in a divorce under the laws of the State of Delaware, a common law state. The taxpayer argued that the property settlement was comparable to a nontaxable division of property between co-owners. The taxpayer also asserted that "to draw a distinction between a wife's interest in the property of her husband in a common-law jurisdiction such as Delaware and the property interest of a wife in a typical community property jurisdiction would commit a double sin; for such differentiation would depend upon 'elusive and subtle casuistries which * * * possess no relevance for tax purposes,' * * *, and would create disparities between common-law and community property jurisdictions in contradiction to Congress' general policy of equality between the two." The Court rejected the taxpayer's argument by focusing on the nature of marital property rights under Delaware law and thus created the same dynamic as it had over 40 years earlier with its decision in Poe v. Seaborn (see Chapter 37, Section 1.1.)

Like *Seaborn, Davis* generated a great deal of uncertainty and litigation as taxpayers in states other than traditional community property states attempted to claim joint ownership status akin to community property for marital property. What evolved from *Davis* was not only a disparity between common-law and community property states, but a disparity among common law states with virtually identical statutes controlling the division of marital property. See Simmons, Federal Income Taxation of Wealth Transfers on Divorce: A Policy Analysis and Proposal, 37 So. Western L. J. 941, 955–966 (1984).

Section 1041 was enacted in 1984 to resolve the uncertainty and disparate treatment of marital property divisions by providing for nonrecognition of gain or loss on transfers of property between spouses or incident to divorce. Section 1041 thereby altered the treatment under *Davis* of property settlements incident to a divorce in several respects. From the perspective of the party transferring property, no gain or loss is recognized. From the perspective of the party receiving the property, § 1041 codifies prior administrative practice that no gain or loss is recognized on the relinquishment of marital rights in exchange for property. But, in providing for a transferred basis, § 1041 alters prior practice that had allowed the recipient to take a basis equal to the fair market value of the property at the time of transfer. Rev. Rul. 67–221, 1967–2 C.B. 63.

The net effect of the statutory changes has been to shift the tax burden of the unrealized appreciation at the time of the transfer from the transferor to the recipient in the same way that §§ 102 and 1015 operate for gifts. Section 1041 thus reverses the tax considerations previously applicable to property settlements. Under *Davis,* the transferor generally desired to transfer property that had not appreciated in order to avoid gain recognition upon the transfer. The transferee was indifferent because any property received would take a basis equal to fair market value. Under § 1041, the transferor prefers to use appreciated property in order to shift the tax on the appreciation to the transferee. Meanwhile, the transferee prefers not to receive appreciated property because of the associated tax liability. These considerations are but one part of the complex tax negotiations that may be required in a divorce settlement.

2. SCOPE OF SECTION 1041

2.1. *General*

While § 1041 was enacted in response to *Davis,* it applies to all transfers of property between spouses whether or not incident to a divorce. Thus, if a wife sells property to her husband for cash, § 1041 prevents the recognition of gain or loss and provides a transferred basis in the property for the husband. See Godlewski v. Commissioner, 90 T.C. 200 (1988) ($18,000 cash transferred to wife in exchange for transfer of personal residence to husband was not added to husband's basis in the residence).

In the divorce situation, § 1041 applies to a transfer to a former spouse only if the transfer is incident to a divorce. Section 1041(c) treats all transfers within one year after the date on which the marriage ceases as incident to the divorce. Transfers outside the one-year period are covered by § 1041 if they are "related" to the cessation of the marriage. Temp. Reg. § 1.1041–1T, Q & A 7, provides that a transfer is "related" to the cessation of the marriage if it is provided for in a divorce or separation instrument and occurs within six years of the divorce or separation. Any transfers occurring more than six years after the termination of the marriage or that are not pursuant to a divorce or separation instrument are presumed not to be subject to § 1041. This presumption can be overcome by showing that the transfer was made to effect the division of property owned by the parties at the time of the cessation of the marriage.

Transfers that are substitutes for transfers clearly incident to the divorce are also treated as incident to the divorce and subject to § 1041, which can be a mixed blessing. In Young v. Commissioner, 240 F.3d 369 (4th Cir.2001), a former husband defaulted on a $1.5 million promissory note that he had given his former wife in a divorce settlement in 1989. She sued him on the note, obtained a judgment, and in 1992 he satisfied the judgment by transferring to her a parcel of real estate, which she then sold. The court held that the ex-husband's transfer of the real estate was incident to the divorce, which meant that the ex-husband recognized no gain on the transfer, but that also meant that the ex-wife had a transferred basis and recognized a substantial amount of gain on the sale. The court rejected the ex-wife's claim that she was simply a judgment creditor.

Section 1041 applies to a cash payment to a former spouse incident to the divorce only if the payment is not alimony as defined in § 71. Labeling a payment in the divorce instrument as part of the division of marital property does not preclude the payment from being characterized as alimony. In Proctor v. Commissioner, 129 T.C. 92 (2007), pursuant to a divorce decree the taxpayer was required to pay his former wife 25 percent of his disposable retirement pay. When the taxpayer failed to comply, he was ordered to pay his former wife $5,313 relating to her share of the retirement pay he had previously received. The IRS argued that the payment was a division of marital property and did not qualify as alimony because the divorce decree referred to the payments as part of a division of the marital property. However, the Tax Court held that the payments in discharge of the obligation were alimony, because (1) the divorce instrument did not designate the payment as a payment that was not includable in gross income and not allowable as a deduction, and (2) under applicable law the payments were to terminate upon the death of either party. The court rejected the IRS's argument that the payment was not alimony, because "the classification of a payment as part of the division of marital property does not . . . preclude the payment from being alimony."

Although § 1041 eliminates taxation of property transfers between spouses and former spouses incident to a divorce, property transfers between individuals in other closely-related circumstances appear to remain subject to the rules generally applicable prior to the enactment of § 1041. For example, if two unmarried persons have cohabited and if, under state law, one party is deemed to have acquired rights in the other's property, a transfer of property in settlement of those rights would appear to be a recognition event. Since such a transfer is not "incident to a divorce," it is not covered by § 1041.

Transfers of appreciated property prior to marriage or during unmarried cohabitation also do not appear to be covered by § 1041. These situations may require distinguishing taxable transfers from gifts. In Farid-Es-Sultaneh v. Commissioner, 160 F.2d 812 (2d Cir.1947), the court was faced with such a question. Kresge transferred stock to the taxpayer in anticipation of his forthcoming marriage to her. In a subsequently-executed antenuptial agreement, the taxpayer released all dower and other marital rights in consideration of Kresge's promise to marry her and consummate the marriage. The parties were subsequently divorced and the taxpayer retained the stock. Upon a subsequent sale, she contended that her basis in the stock was the fair market value on the date of acquisition, arguing that she had acquired the stock by purchase. The IRS took the position that the transaction constituted a gift and that she was required to use the lower cost basis of her transferor husband. The court found for the taxpayer, concluding that the relinquishment of future marital support rights constituted adequate and full consideration for the stock transfer.

The proper treatment of a transfer like that in *Farid-Es-Sultaneh* under current law would appear to turn on a question of state law: Was the transfer unconditional and therefore effective even if the subsequent marriage did not occur, or was the transfer effective only if the condition subsequent that the marriage occurred was satisfied? If the transferee is legally obligated to return the property to the transferor if the marriage did not occur, for tax purposes the transfer would be treated as occurring at the moment that the parties were married. In that case, § 1041 would apply. On the other hand, if the transfer was unconditional and effective even if the subsequent marriage did not occur, § 1041 would not apply because the parties were not married at the time of the transfer and the transfer was not incident to their divorce.

2.2. *Transfer of Income Items*

Section 1041 applies to a transfer of "property," and, as we saw in connection with the material on assignment of income discussed in Chapter 37, income from property is not considered property. In Gibbs v. Commissioner, T.C. Memo. 1997–196, a former wife received payments pursuant to a court order that required her former husband to pay her a precise amount representing the value of her interest in a jointly-owned business, plus interest. Only the portion of the payments that represented principal (the formers wife's interest in the business property) was property and subject to § 1041; the portion representing interest was income and fully taxable to her.

Income that has accrued to a transferor spouse prior to the transfer will also be taxed to that spouse. Thus, in Rev. Rul. 87–112, 1987–2 C.B. 207, the IRS ruled that the transferor spouse was taxable on accrued but unpaid interest on United States savings bonds transferred as part of a divorce settlement. The transferee spouse is permitted to add the interest income realized by the transferor to the basis of the savings bonds. See Berger v. Commissioner, T.C. Memo. 1996–76.

A somewhat different question arises when one spouse receives a right to be paid income earned by the transferor spouse. In Kochansky v. Commissioner, 92 F.3d 957 (9th Cir.1996), a lawyer who was obligated by a divorce settlement to pay to his former wife a portion of any contingent fee that he might earn in a then-pending medical malpractice action was held to be taxable on the portion of the fee received by his former wife. The fee was compensation for his services.

The IRS has now ruled that it will not apply assignment of income principles to override § 1041 except in cases like *Kochansky*, where the rights to the transferred income are not vested at the time of the transfer. In Rev. Rul. 2002–22, 2002–1 C.B. 9, the IRS held that § 1041 applies to a transfer of interests in nonstatutory stock options and nonqualified deferred compensation benefits pursuant to a divorce. Thus, the former spouse to whom the rights are transferred, and not the transferor-employee spouse, must recognize income upon exercise of the stock options or receipt of the deferred compensation.

In the case of benefits from a qualified pension plan, § 402(e)(1)(A) provides that the spouse or former spouse of a beneficiary who receives distributions from the plan pursuant to a "qualified domestic relations order" ("QDRO") is to be treated as the distributee who is taxable on distributions from the qualified plan under § 402(a).[3] A qualified domestic relations order is necessary both to permit the trustee of a qualified plan to make distributions to the spouse or former spouse of the beneficiary, and to shift income tax liability for distributions to the spouse or former spouse. In general, a qualified domestic relations order, as defined in § 414(p), is a judgment, decree or settlement agreement in a divorce action that assigns rights to distributions from a qualified plan to a spouse, former spouse, child, or other recognized dependent who is entitled to receive benefits payable under a plan.[4] See Hawkins v. Commissioner, 86 F.3d 982 (10th Cir.1996) (to qualify as a QDRO, the divorce instrument is not required to specifically designate the ex-spouse as an "alternate payee" under the qualified plan or specifically evidence intent to affect the tax treatment of plan distributions; it is sufficient that the order or agreement designate the plan as the source of payments). The parties cannot determine who bears income taxes on qualified pension plan distributions pursuant to a QDRO. The alternative payee is taxable on distributions pursuant to a QDRO even though the divorce instrument provides that the plan participant is liable for the income taxes on the distributions. Clawson v. Commissioner, T.C. Memo. 1996–446.

2.3. *Divisions Involving Closely Held Corporations*

Special problems arise when a substantial portion of the assets of a marital community are represented by the stock of a closely held corporation. When husband and wife each own a portion of the stock in the corporation and one of them wants to own all of the stock after the divorce, the transfer can take at least two different forms. First, spouse A can transfer A's stock to spouse B in exchange for cash or other property. Spouse B can then cause the corporation to redeem that stock in exchange for cash (or other property), which effectively replaces the cash or property B transferred to A. After these transactions spouse B will own all of the stock of the corporation while spouse A will own cash or other property. Alternatively, the corporation can redeem all of the stock owned by spouse A in exchange for cash (or other property), thus leaving spouse B as the sole owner of the remaining stock in a corporation that has fewer assets. The end result of these transactions is the same: spouse B ends up with all of the stock of the corporation and spouse A ends up with cash (or other property). Nevertheless, although both forms produce the same result, they can have very different tax consequences.

In the first situation, where spouse A transfers stock to spouse B in exchange for cash or other property, § 1041 would apply to provide for no gain or loss to spouse A on the receipt of the cash or property. Rules of

---

[3]   In Private Letter Ruling 8820076 (2/25/88), the IRS concluded that the transfer of an IRA account to a spouse *during marriage* is a taxable event. In general, distributions from an IRA are taxable. I.R.C. § 408(d). However, § 408(d)(6) provides for the transfer of an IRA to a spouse incident to a divorce without recognition of income. The ruling concludes that § 408(d)(6) would be superfluous if § 1041 permitted transfers of an IRA to a spouse during marriage.

[4]   Plan benefits that are payable to an individual other than a spouse or former spouse are taxable to the beneficiary under § 402(a).

corporate taxation would then apply to the redemption, and in most cases these rules would cause spouse B to be treated as receiving a dividend, fully includable in income (although currently taxed at preferential rates), to the extent of money or corporate property received in the redemption. In the second situation, since the transaction is strictly between the corporation and spouse A, § 1041 would seem to have no application at all, and spouse A would recognize gain (or loss) on the redemption, which would be taxable, though possibly at preferential capital gain rates. For spouse A, then, the difference between the two techniques is no taxation versus full taxation of gain, albeit at capital gains rates if certain formalities are observed. For spouse B the difference is no taxation versus taxation at the rates applicable to dividends (currently taxed between 0 to 20 percent for qualified dividends, 0 to 39.6 percent for non-qualified dividends, and an additional 3.8-percent surtax on net investment income for high-income taxpayers) even though the money or property ends up in the hands of the ex-spouse. If the spouses treat the transaction consistently, one spouse will be taxed while the other will not.

Treas. Reg. § 1.1041–2 allows the couple to determine the tax treatment of the transaction. Under the regulations, a redemption of stock from one spouse generally is treated as a redemption from that spouse, and § 1041 will not apply. Treas. Reg. § 1.1041–2(a)(1). In only two cases will the other spouse, from whom the stock was not redeemed and who continues to be a shareholder, be treated as receiving a constructive distribution from the corporation (taxable to that spouse) that is then used to purchase the redeemed spouse's stock in a transaction subject to § 1041: (1) if the nonredeemed spouse, the continuing shareholder, had a primary and unconditional binding obligation to acquire the redeemed spouse's stock, Treas. Reg. § 1.1041–2(a)(2); or (2) if the divorce or separation instrument or a written agreement between the spouses provides that they will file their tax returns in a manner that reflects such treatment, Treas. Reg. § 1.1041–2(c)(1). The regulations also allow the spouses to agree in the divorce or separation instrument, or other valid written agreement, that the redemption will be taxable to the transferor spouse who receives cash or other property (i.e., not covered by § 1041) even though the nonredeemed spouse had a primary and unconditional binding obligation to acquire the redeemed spouse's stock. See Treas. Reg. § 1.1041–2(c)(2).

B. ALIMONY AND CHILD SUPPORT

INTERNAL REVENUE CODE: Sections 71; 215.

TEMPORARY REGULATIONS: Section 1.71–1T(a)–(c).

General Explanation of the Revenue Provisions of the Deficit Reduction Act of 1984
Staff of the Joint Committee on Taxation 714–716 (Dec. 31, 1984).

[Pre-1984 Law]

Prior to 1942, there was no statutory provision explicitly dealing with alimony payments. In 1917, the Supreme Court held that, under the provisions of the Income Tax Act of 1913, alimony paid to a divorced wife was not taxable income.[15] From 1917 to 1942, the result in the *Gould* case remained unchanged and alimony was neither includible in the recipient's income nor deductible by the payor.

When tax rates were increased significantly in 1942, Congress recognized that the higher tax rates would intensify the hardship of payment of alimony out of after-tax income. Congress, therefore, enacted provisions in the Revenue Act of 1942 to require that certain alimony payments be included in the recipient spouse's income and to permit the payor spouse to deduct those payments as an itemized deduction. These provisions applied to alimony payments made by persons who were divorced or legally separated. In 1954, the alimony provisions were extended to apply to payments made under a decree for support where the parties are physically separated. The Tax Reform Act of 1976 permitted alimony to be deducted in arriving at adjusted gross income so that a taxpayer who does not itemize deductions may nevertheless deduct alimony.

* * *

Payments which were fixed by the decree or agreement as child support were not treated as alimony and therefore were not deductible by the payor or includible in income of the recipient.

Reasons for Change

The Congress believes that the [pre-1984] definition of alimony is not sufficiently objective. Differences in State laws create differences in Federal tax consequences and administrative difficulties for the IRS. The Congress believes that a uniform Federal standard should be set forth to determine what constitutes alimony for Federal tax purposes. This will make it easier for the Internal Revenue Service, the parties to a divorce, and the courts to apply the rules to the facts in any particular case and should lead to less litigation. The Act attempts to define alimony in a way that would conform to general notions of what type of payments

---

[15]   Gould v. Gould, 245 U.S. 151 (1917).

constitute alimony as distinguished from property settlements and to prevent the deduction of large, one-time lump-sum property settlements.

Explanation of Provision

Under [sections 215(a) and 71(a)], alimony payments will continue to be deductible by the payor spouse and includible in income by the recipient spouse. However, [section 71(b) changes] the definition of alimony. The requirement that the payment must be made on account of a marital obligation imposed under local law is repealed and the prior law requirement that the payment be "periodic" is not retained.

Under [section 71(b)], an alimony payment must meet several requirements. The payment must be made in cash and be received by, or on behalf of, the [recipient] spouse (or former spouse). A payment can also qualify as alimony, for example, where a cash payment is made to a third party for the benefit of the payee spouse. As under [pre-1984] law, an alimony payment must be made under a decree of divorce or separate maintenance or under a written instrument incident to the divorce, a written separation agreement, or a decree requiring support or maintenance payments.

Where the parties are divorced or legally separated, they may not be members of the same household at the time the payment is made. The parties are not to be treated as members of the same household where the taxpayer is preparing to shortly depart from the household of the other spouse.

In order to prevent the deduction of amounts which are in effect transfers of property unrelated to the support needs of the recipient, [section 71(b)(1)(D)] provides that a payment qualifies as alimony only if the payor (or any person making a payment on behalf of the payor) has no liability to make any such payment for any period following the death of the payee spouse. * * * A provision for a substitute payment, such as an additional amount to be paid as child support after the death of the payee spouse will prevent a corresponding amount of the payment to the payee spouse from qualifying as alimony. Amounts payable under a life insurance contract on the life of the payee spouse will not be treated as a liability which would affect the status of other payments made by the payor spouse.

The parties, by clearly designating in a written agreement, can provide that otherwise qualifying payments will not be treated as alimony for Federal income tax purposes and therefore will not be deductible or includible in income.

As under [pre-1984] law, amounts fixed as child support will not be treated as alimony. Under [section 71(c)(2)], if any amount specified in the instrument will be reduced on the happening of a contingency relating to a child, then an equal amount will be treated as child support rather than alimony. Thus, for example, if the divorce instrument provides that payments will be reduced by $100 per month when a child reaches age 18 (or in the month the child happens to reach that age), then $100 of each monthly payment will be treated as fixed for child support.

[Section 215(c)] provides that the Internal Revenue Service may require the payor spouse to furnish on his or her tax return the name and social security number of the payee spouse, and that the payee must furnish that number to the payor. * * *

DETAILED ANALYSIS

1.   PAYMENTS QUALIFYING AS ALIMONY

1.1. *General*

Section 71(b)(1)(B) allows divorced spouses significant flexibility in determining which party will be taxable on the alimony payments. Normally, the payments will be deductible by the payor and taxable to the payee. But if the parties stipulate in the agreement that §§ 71 and 215 are not to apply, then no deduction will be allowed for the payments, and they will not be taxable to the recipient. I.R.C. § 71(b)(1)(B). Such a designation does not need to mimic the statutory language of section 71(b)(1)(B); a statement in the divorce instrument that a series of cash payments is intended to be a property settlement payable in installments subject to § 1041 was sufficient to remove the payments from the alimony regime in Estate of Goldman v. Commissioner, 112 T.C. 317 (1999), aff'd by order sub. nom. Schutter v. Commissioner, 242 F.3d 390 (10th Cir.2000).

The relative marginal tax brackets of the payor and the recipient usually will dictate whether the parties will choose to have the payments treated as alimony. For example, assume that spouse A is willing to pay $500 per month (after tax) in support to B. If A is in the 35-percent bracket, qualifying the payment as alimony under § 71 allows A to pay $769 and be out of pocket only $500 after claiming the deduction under § 215. If B is in the 15-percent bracket, B's tax liability on the receipt of $769 is $115.35. B thus receives a net payment after tax of $653.65 per month, and the payment only cost A $500.

1.2. *Disguised Property Settlements*

Although the 1984 amendments to § 71 eliminated the relevance of state law distinctions between support payments and property settlements, the definition of alimony is nonetheless aimed at limiting the taxpayers' ability to disguise nondeductible property settlement transfers as deductible alimony. As described above, spouses will have the motivation to disguise these settlement transfers when the payor spouse is subject to a higher marginal tax rate than the recipient spouse.

Any lump sum property settlement payment can easily be restructured as a series of periodic payments that have the same present value as the lump sum. Recognizing this, Congress required that, for a payment to qualify as alimony, the obligation to make the payment must cease upon the death of the recipient. The rationale is that a recipient who is entitled to a property settlement payment would not allow the payor to avoid making the payment if the recipient were to die prematurely. On the other hand, payments truly in the nature of spousal support would be wholly unnecessary after the recipient's death.

Congress recognized, however, that the cease-upon-death condition alone would not protect against disguised property settlements because the separation agreement could simply provide for a lump sum payment a day or two after the settlement is executed. Even if the payment were conditioned upon the recipient's survival (as would be required to obtain the sought-after alimony characterization), the recipient might be willing to take the small risk to secure a higher payment. To deal with this sort of tax planning, Congress required that, in order to avoid a recapture of the alimony deduction by the payor, alimony payments must be sufficiently spread out over a period of at least three taxable years. These technical "front loading rules" ensure that the recipient must survive at least one year to receive all of the required payments. If the divorce or separation instrument is finalized on December 31 of Year 1, three substantially equal payments made on that day, January 1 of Year 2, and January 1 of Year 3 would pass muster under the front-loading rules. If the parties desire to disguise property settlements in this manner, the front-loading rules effectively require the recipient to assume the risk that the recipient will die within a year (or longer, depending on when during the taxable year the divorce or separation instrument is executed) and not receive full payment. This risk can be ameliorated by the recipient through the purchase of term life insurance.

1.2.1. *Requirement That Payments Terminate on Death*

For payments to qualify as alimony, the liability to make the payments must terminate upon the recipient's death, the time at which any bona fide support obligation would ordinarily terminate. An express provision in the divorce or separation agreement will be determinative with respect to whether the payments terminate on the recipient's death; if the instrument is silent on the issue, local law will determine whether payments terminate upon death. Hoover v. Commissioner, 102 F.3d 842 (6th Cir.1996).

Under § 71(b)(1)(D), if the agreement provides for a substitute payment after the death of the spouse, such as increased child support payments, the initial payment (and its substitute) will not qualify as alimony. Thus, Okerson v. Commissioner, 123 T.C. 258 (2004), held that payments to a former spouse that would terminate upon her death, but which would be replaced by substitute payments of a like amount to her children, did not qualify as alimony.

In general, because of the requirement that payments terminate upon the death of the recipient to qualify as alimony, the payment by one spouse of debts for which the other spouse is liable, whether marital or separate debts, cannot qualify as alimony if, as in the usual case, the payment obligation is not extinguished by the death of the other spouse. In Heffron v. Commissioner, T.C. Memo. 1995–253, aff'd by order sub nom. Murley v. Commissioner, 104 F.3d 361 (6th Cir.1996), the husband's payments of marital debts did not qualify as alimony because neither the divorce decree nor state law unambiguously terminated his obligation to pay the debts if his former wife died. The obligation to pay the debts was labeled as "additional alimony" by the divorce decree, but that did not change the result.

The requirement that payments terminate on death can affect the treatment of payments that could not be disguised property settlements. For example, in many states one spouse must pay an unallocated "family support" allowance while the divorce action is pending; such an allowance could hardly be a substitute property settlement. Nevertheless, if neither the documents nor state law specifically provides that the obligation to pay such an allowance will end upon the recipient's death, the allowance will not be treated as alimony. See Lovejoy v. Commissioner, 293 F.3d 1208 (10th Cir.2002).

1.2.2. *Restrictions on Front-Loading of Alimony*

If support payments in the first year exceed the average of payments in the second and third years by $15,000 and/or the payment in the second year exceeds the third year's payment by $15,000, § 71(f)(1) requires a recapture of deductions by the payor as gross income and provides a deduction to the recipient to offset the payee's prior inclusion. If there are "excess alimony payments" the payor spouse is required to include the excess alimony payments in income in the third calendar year following commencement of alimony payments (the third "post separation year"), and the recipient spouse, who has reported the payments as income, may deduct excess alimony payments in the third post separation year. Under § 71(f)(2), "excess alimony" is the sum of excess alimony payments in the first and second post separation years. Post separation years commence with the calendar year in which the first alimony payment is made. I.R.C. § 71(f)(6). Excess alimony for the second post separation year exists if alimony actually paid during the second post separation year exceeds alimony paid during the third post separation year plus $15,000. Excess alimony paid for the first post separation year exists to the extent that alimony actually paid for the first post separation year exceeds the average of the alimony paid in the second post separation year (less any alimony treated as excess alimony paid in the second post separation year) and third post separation year, plus $15,000. In other words, excess alimony will exist if alimony decreases by more than $15,000 in each of the second and/or third years following separation. Nonetheless, decreases of $15,000 or less do not ensure that the recapture rule will not apply. Section 71(f)(5) provides exceptions for payments that cease by reason of death or remarriage, payments that are required by a decree of separate maintenance which is not a decree of divorce or a separation instrument, and payments that fluctuate as a fixed portion of profits from a business or property or employee compensation.

Suppose, for example, that a separation agreement provides for payment of alimony of $60,000 in the first year, $50,000 in the second year, and $30,000 in the third year. Alimony paid in the second year exceeds the alimony in the third year by $20,000. Thus $5,000 is treated as excess alimony for the second post separation year. The $60,000 of alimony paid in the first post separation year exceeds the average of the alimony paid for the second post separation year reduced by the amount treated as excess alimony for the second post separation year ($45,000) and the alimony paid for the third post separation year, plus $15,000. Thus $7,500 ($60,000 [($45,000 + $30,000)/2 + $15,000]) is excess alimony for the first year. In year three, the payor is required to include $12,500 in income (i.e., $7,500 excess alimony for the first post separation year plus $5,000 excess alimony for the second year) and the recipient may deduct that amount.

The excess alimony recapture rules of § 71(f) may cause double taxation of alimony. Although the recipient is required to include the excess alimony in income, the recipient effectively will be denied a deduction for part of the excess if the deductible excess alimony exceeds the recipient's income in the year of recapture. The unused deduction in the recapture year cannot be carried back to prior years or forward to subsequent years under § 172 (discussed in Chapter 29, Section 2). See I.R.C. § 172(d)(4).

1.3. *Payments "On Behalf Of" a Spouse*

Section 71(b)(1)(A) allows payments to a third party on behalf of a spouse to qualify as alimony. Treas. Reg. § 1.71–1T(b), Q & A 6, provides that payments to maintain property owned by the payor spouse and used by the recipient spouse, including mortgage payments and real estate taxes, do not qualify even if those payments are required under the terms of the divorce or separation agreement. An obligation to pay the other spouse's legal fees incurred in connection with the divorce generally will not qualify as alimony because it is unlikely that the obligation will terminate if the other spouse dies before the fees are paid. Compare Ribera v. Commissioner, T.C. Memo. 1997–38, aff'd by order, 139 F.3d 907 (9th Cir.1998) (husband's payment of wife's legal fees was not deductible alimony because his obligation to pay the fees was fixed by the divorce decree as an absolute obligation that would not terminate upon the wife's death) with Burkes v. Commissioner, T.C. Memo. 1998–61 (husband's payment of wife's legal fees was treated as alimony because under applicable state law the payments were treated as "support alimony" which terminated on the recipient's death).

1.4. *Divorce or Separation Instrument*

Section 71(b)(1)(A) requires that payments be made under a divorce or separation instrument. The agreement need not refer to the separation, if it is clear that the agreement was made "in light of" the separation. Bogard v. Commissioner, 59 T.C. 97 (1972). Treas. Reg. § 1.71–1(b)(2)(i) provides that payments made under a written agreement may qualify as alimony even if the agreement is unenforceable or subsequently found to be invalid. See Richardson v. Commissioner, T.C. Memo. 1995–554, aff'd, 125 F.3d 551 (7th Cir.1997) (prejudgment support payments pursuant to written agreement later found by state court to have been invalid were nevertheless treated as alimony).

1.5. *Requirement of Living Apart*

Where the parties are legally separated under a decree of divorce or separate maintenance, § 71(b)(1)(C) requires that they not be "members of the same household." A related question arose under prior law which required that the parties be "separated." The Tax Court consistently held that a couple could not qualify as "separated" if they occupied the same dwelling even if they shared no common rooms. See e.g., Washington v.

Commissioner, 77 T.C. 601 (1981). Sydnes v. Commissioner, 577 F.2d 60 (8th Cir.1978), refused to follow the Tax Court and held that a couple could in principle be living "separately" in the same residence. Other Courts of Appeals followed the Tax Court's interpretation of the statute. See e.g., Lyddan v. United States, 721 F.2d 873 (2d Cir.1983). Congress enacted § 71(b)(1)(C) to overrule *Sydnes,* and Temp. Reg. § 1.71–1T(b), Q & A 9 specifically provides that spouses residing in the same "dwelling unit" do not have separate households even though they physically segregate themselves.

1.6. *Requirement of "Cash" Payment*

Section 72(b)(1) limits alimony treatment to payments "in cash," a requirement that is strictly construed. Lofstrom v. Commissioner, 125 T.C. 271 (2005), applied Treas. Reg. § 1.71–1T(b), Q & A–5, requiring payment solely in cash, check, or money order, to hold that the transfer of a third-party debt instrument in satisfaction of a state court-ordered alimony payment was not alimony for purposes of § 71, thus denying a § 215 deduction to the transferor, because the payment was not "in cash."

2.   CHILD SUPPORT

2.1. *Treatment of Payments*

Section 71(c) provides that payments "fixed" as child support by the divorce or separation instrument are not treated as alimony. As a result, such payments are not deductible by the payor and are not included in income by the payee. Section 71(c)(2) treats as child support any payments that are reduced on the happening of a contingency relating to a child (reversing Commissioner v. Lester, 366 U.S. 299 (1961), which held that payments that would be made until a child reached majority were not "fixed" as child support unless the instrument expressly indicated that the payments were for the support of the children). Thus, if the agreement provides that certain payments would be made until a child reached majority, the payments would be treated as child support even though not specifically so denominated in the agreement. In addition, in order to prevent taxpayers from avoiding this limitation, if payments are reduced at a time that can be "clearly associated" with an event involving a child, then the payments would likewise be treated as child support payments. Temp. Reg. § 1.71–1T, Q & A 18, states that a contingency will be "clearly associated" with a child if it involves a payment that is reduced not more than 6 months before or after the date that a child attains the age of 18, 21, or the local age of majority, although the presumption may be rebutted by showing that the payments were reduced for reasons unrelated to any child. In Hammond v. Commissioner, T.C. Memo. 1998–53, payments that terminated upon the earlier of the child's eighteenth birthday or the wife's remarriage were treated as child support.

In Israel v. Commissioner, T.C. Memo. 1995–500, one-third of the rent that the husband paid on his former wife's behalf was alimony and two-thirds was treated as child support because the obligation to pay the wife's rent was reduced by two-thirds if the couple's son resided with the husband for more than one-half of the year. In contrast, Ambrose v. Commissioner, T.C. Memo. 1996–128, treated entirely as alimony an unallocated "family support allowance" that provided both spousal and child support. The obligation terminated entirely upon the death of the custodial payee spouse and was not reduced upon the emancipation of the children. In Murphy v. Commissioner, T.C. Memo. 1996–258, none of an unapportioned family support payment that included both child support and spousal support under state law was treated as alimony because the payments did not clearly terminate on the payee wife's death.

2.2. *Dependency Exemptions*

Section 152(e) generally awards the dependency exemption for children of divorced parents to the parent having custody for the greater portion of the calendar year, regardless of the amount of support actually supplied by either parent. However, a noncustodial parent may be entitled to the exemption if the custodial parent waives the exemption in writing and the noncustodial parent attaches the declaration to his or her return. The waiver may pertain to one or more specific years or may be permanent. The right to claim a dependency exemption is controlled exclusively by § 152; a state court decree awarding a dependency exemption inconsistently with the provisions of § 152 is ineffective. White v. Commissioner, T.C. Memo. 1996–438.

In divorce negotiations, the parties should generally allocate the dependency exemption to the parent subject to the higher marginal tax rate, as the exemption is worth more to that parent. However, the phase-out of personal exemptions for higher income taxpayers (discussed in Chapter 21, Section 1.B.3.), which applies equally to dependency exemptions, must also be considered.

SECTION 4.　GRANTOR TRUST RULES

INTERNAL REVENUE CODE: Sections 671–678.

REGULATIONS: Sections 1.671–1; –2(a)–(d), (e)(1), (e)(2)(i), (4); –3(a), (b); 1.672(a)–(c); 1.673(a)–1; 1.672(c)–1; 1.672(d)–1; 1.673(a)–1; 1.674(a)–1; 1.674(b)–1; 1.674(c)–1; 1.674(d)–1; 1.675–1; 1.676(a)–1, (b); 1.677(a)–1, (b); 1.678(a)–1; 1.678(b)–1; 1.678(c)–1.

Trusts are often used to transfer assets among family members. A trust is an arrangement where property is held and managed by one or more trustees for the benefit of identified beneficiaries. The person who creates the trust and contributes property to it is called the grantor. With respect to trusts, the fundamental federal income tax issue is how the income generated by trust property is taxed. Alternative considerations include: ignoring the trust and causing the grantor to be taxed on the income as if the trust was never created; subjecting the trust itself to tax on the income; taxing the beneficiaries on the income that flows through the trust; and, in the event the tax liability flows through the trust to the beneficiaries, determining how to allocate the taxable income among multiple beneficiaries.

In general, under current federal income tax law, grantor trusts are ignored for tax purposes. The result is that the grantor includes any income, gain, loss, deduction, or credit generated by the trust property on the grantor's own income tax return, just as if the trust did not exist. A trust is treated as a grantor trust where the grantor retains a significant relationship with the trust or the trust property. For example, the grantor may reserve a power to revoke the trust and reclaim the trust property.

Alternatively, if the grantor is willing to sever any relationship to the property placed in trust and to have no interest in or control over the trust itself, different rules apply. In the non-grantor trust context, the trust is treated as a separate taxable unit. As a result, the items of income, gain, loss, deduction, and credit generated by the trust property are allocated among the beneficiaries and the trust according to a complex set of rules found in §§ 641–664.

This section will focus on the threshold issue of whether a trust arrangement is subject to the grantor trust rules. The critical tax policy issue is to determine the point at which the grantor has transferred substantial ownership over the trust property for a sufficient period of time to justify treating the trust as a separate taxable unit.

Sections 673 through 677 cover situations in which the grantor of a trust will be treated as the "owner" of the trust and thus, under § 671, required to reflect all income, deductions, and tax credits of the trust on the grantor's own return.[5] Section 678 specifies those situations in which a person other than the grantor will be treated for income tax purposes as the owner of all or a portion of the trust.

Definition of Grantor. Treas. Reg. § 1.671–2(e) defines the term "grantor" to include any person who creates a trust or, directly or indirectly, makes a gratuitous transfer (one for less than fair market value) to a trust. A partnership or a corporation will be treated as the grantor of a trust if the trust is created for a business purpose of the entity. But if the entity creates a trust for the benefit of its partners or shareholders (e.g., to pay education expenses of their children), then the transaction will be treated as a distribution to the partners or shareholders and they, in turn, will be treated as the grantors of such trusts.

Scope of the Grantor Trust Provisions. Pursuant to the last sentence of § 671, subpart E provides the exclusive rules for taxing the grantor "solely on the grounds of his dominion and control over the trust." However, Treas. Reg. § 1.671–1(c) indicates that the following important facts are not considered to involve "dominion and control" and therefore not subject to the exclusivity granted to subpart E: assignments of future income; family partnerships; allowing the grantor deductions for

---

[5]   Note that if the requirements for grantor trust treatment apply only to a portion of a trust, that portion will be treated as a grantor trust. In such a case, the grantor will be treated as the owner of that portion of the trust assets for federal income tax purposes, with the remainder of the trust being taxed according to the non-grantor trust rules.

payments to a trust under a transfer and leaseback arrangement; and trust income used to discharge an obligation of the grantor, so that the grantor is in effect either a beneficiary under the regular trust sections or liable for tax under § 677.

Grantor Reversionary Interest. In the case of a trust with a reversion in the grantor, § 673 taxes the grantor where the grantor has a reversionary interest in either the corpus or income of the trust that at its inception exceeds five percent of the value of the trust. Where a reversion becomes possessory upon only passage of time or the termination of intervening life estates, valuation generally is simple, using actuarial valuation tables promulgated under § 7520. Using reasonable interest rate assumptions, a period exceeding twenty years will be required. But where a reversion is triggered by an event that may occur at a more indeterminate time, valuation of a reversion may be more difficult.

Revocable Trusts and Powers to Control Beneficial Enjoyment. Section 676 taxes the grantor having a power to revest title back to the grantor. The section also applies if the power is possessed by a non-adverse party. Section 674(a) taxes the grantor where the beneficial enjoyment of the corpus or income is subject to a power of disposition exercisable by the grantor or a nonadverse party (or both) without the approval of any adverse party.[6] Section 674(b)–(d) provides important exceptions. The grantor or any other person, including those related or subordinate and subservient to the grantor, are permitted to retain, without taxation of the grantor, certain powers generally involving action under specified standards for the acceleration or postponement of distributions which affect only the share of the distributee. Section 672(c) specifies those persons—spouse, certain relatives, and certain business associates—who are classified as related or subordinate trustees. It further provides those persons are presumed to be subservient unless proven to the contrary by a preponderance of the evidence. Section 674(d) permits related and subordinate trustees, other than the grantor's spouse, to hold a power to allocate income among members of a class of beneficiaries without taxation to the grantor if the power is limited by a "reasonably definite external standard" specified in the trust instrument. Finally, § 674(c) allows independent trustees to apportion income or corpus, to accumulate income, and to pay out corpus in their complete discretion, all without subjecting the grantor to taxation, but they may not add beneficiaries other than after-born or after-adopted children.

---

[6]   Section 674(b)(2) coordinates §§ 674 and 676 with the 5 percent reversionary interest rule of § 673 by excepting powers to revest or control enjoyment if their exercise can only affect the income *after* a period that would not trigger § 673 if the power were a reversion.

Grantor Administrative Control. Section 675 taxes the grantor where the grantor or a nonadverse party, or both, possesses certain specified administrative powers with respect to the trust. Essentially, these powers relate to the ability to borrow or otherwise obtain corpus or income on less than a *quid pro quo* basis unless there is a general lending power to make such loans to any person, or either to vote the trust stock or to control the trust investment policies if the grantor acts in a non-fiduciary capacity. In addition, an actual borrowing of the trust corpus subjects the grantor to tax until the loan is repaid unless there is adequate security and interest. Even if such security and interest exist, the grantor is taxed if the loan is made by a trustee who is the grantor or a related or subordinate person.

Income for Benefit of the Grantor or Spouse. Section 677 provides for taxation of the grantor where the trust income is or can be currently distributed to the grantor or the grantor's spouse, accumulated for future distribution to the grantor or the grantor's spouse, applied to the payment of premiums on insurance on the life of the grantor or the grantor's spouse, or used in satisfaction of a legal obligation of the grantor with respect to a beneficiary of the trust. The grantor is taxed where the power respecting the disposition of the income resides in the grantor, in a non-adverse party, or in both, provided that the approval or consent of any adverse party is not necessary. An "adverse party" is defined in § 672(a) as one having a substantial beneficial interest in the trust which would be adversely affected by the exercise or non-exercise of the power that the party possesses. The concept of adverse interest is thus confined to an economic interest. Section 677 also excepts from this provision those trusts in which the income *may* be used for the support of minor children or others (other than the grantor's spouse), whom the grantor is obligated to support, except to the extent that the income is in fact so applied.

Persons Other than the Grantor. Section 678 taxes the trust income to a person other than the grantor if that person has the power to obtain the trust corpus or income. Section 678(d) provides that the section does not apply if the power is renounced or disclaimed within a reasonable time after the holder first became aware of its existence. There is a possible conflict between §§ 671 and 678. Suppose a six-year trust provides that the income is to be distributed to beneficiary A but third party B has a power to obtain the corpus. In the absence of B's power, the grantor would be taxable on the income under § 671(a) because of the six-year term.[7] Apart from the short term of the trust, B would be taxable under 678 because of the power that B possesses. The problem is to choose between the grantor and B in order to allocate the tax burden. Section 678 provides that if B has the power to obtain the corpus, then B will be taxed and the grantor will not be taxed. But if B's power extends

---

[7]   Under any reasonable assumed interest rate, the value of a reversion at the end of six years exceeds 5 percent of the value of the corpus.

only to income, then the grantor should be taxable in preference to B. Section 678(c) also carries over the restriction respecting support found in § 677(b).

DETAILED ANALYSIS

1.　POWERS AND RIGHTS DEEMED TO BE HELD BY GRANTOR

1.1. *Grantor's Spouse*

Section 672(e) provides that the grantor of a trust is treated as holding any power or interest held by the grantor's spouse. This provision applies to all of the powers and rights described in §§ 673–677, even if the specific provision makes no reference to the grantor's spouse. The grantor is always treated as having a power or right held by the grantor's spouse at the time the trust was created, but if the grantor marries after creation of the trust, the spouse's rights or powers are imputed to the grantor only during the marriage.

1.2. *Non-Adverse Party*

Sections 671–677 generally treat a power held by a party who does not hold an adverse interest in the trust the same as a power held by the grantor. Treas. Reg. § 1.672(a)–1 provides rules amplifying the adverse interest concept. To be adverse the interest must be "substantial" and must be affected by the exercise or nonexercise of the power. For example, interests were held not to be adverse where two grantor-beneficiaries, brother and sister, shared equally in the trust income; any corpus distribution to one required an equal corpus distribution to the other, and the trust could be terminated only by the joint action of both beneficiaries. De Amodio v. Commissioner, 299 F.2d 623 (3d Cir.1962).

In Paxton v. Commissioner, 520 F.2d 923 (9th Cir.1975), the trustees of a trust were an employee of a corporation whose stock was held by the trust and the son of the grantor. The trustees had the power to revoke the trust and to distribute the assets at any time. The court held that the employee had no interest in the trust except as trustee and hence could not be an adverse party. The son had a 3.4-percent interest in the trust and this interest remained unchanged whether he exercised the power to revoke the trust or not. Accordingly, the son was also not an adverse party and the grantor was treated as the owner of the trust under § 676(a).

A remote contingent interest in a trust has been held not to constitute a substantial adverse interest. Chase National Bank of New York v. Commissioner, 225 F.2d 621 (8th Cir.1955); Holt v. United States, 669 F.Supp. 751 (W.D.Va. 1987), aff'd by order, 842 F.2d 1291 (4th Cir.1988).

2.　INCOME FOR BENEFIT OF GRANTOR

2.1. *In General*

Distribution of the income of a trust to the grantor is the most direct benefit in the trust that a grantor may retain. Douglas v. Willcuts, 296 U.S. 1 (1935), held that the predecessor of § 677(a) applied where the trust income could be used to discharge a legal obligation of the grantor, and this rule now is reflected in Treas. Reg. § 1.677(a)–1(d). Under § 677, the *mere possibility* of diversion of income to the grantor or spouse is sufficient to tax the income to the grantor, even if the grantor is an alternative beneficiary and the discretion is held by an independent trustee. Treas. Reg. § 1.677(a)–(1)(c) does not regard the remoteness of the possibility of the diversion as a factor except that, under the last sentence of § 677(a), the interest of the grantor must relate to income accruing within the period that would result in taxation under § 673 if the right were a reversion. If income may be accumulated during that period, the fact that it will not be paid out until after the period has ended will not prevent the current taxation of the income to the grantor. Rev. Rul. 57–363, 1957–2 C.B. 326; Humphrey v. Commissioner, 39 T.C. 199 (1962); Duffy v. United States, 487 F.2d 282 (6th Cir.1973).

A minor can become an "involuntary" grantor of a trust subject to § 677(a). In Rev. Rul. 83–25, 1983–1 C.B. 116, a minor was awarded damages in an action for personal injury. Pursuant to court order the damage award was transferred to a trust for the minor's benefit; the trustee could accumulate or distribute income and corpus for the minor's benefit and, when the minor reached age 21, the corpus would be distributed to him. The IRS ruled that the minor owned the trust under § 677(a).

Rev. Rul. 64–240, 1964–2 C.B. 172, held that trust income required to be paid to a charity in discharge of a charitable pledge made by the grantor was not taxable under § 677. Rev. Rul. 55–410, 1955–1 C.B. 297, held that the charitable pledge was not a "debt" of the grantor. On the other hand, Rev. Rul. 87–127, 1987–2 C.B. 156, dealt with the treatment of income accumulated by a pre-need funeral-trust maintained by a funeral home for customers. If the customer canceled the contract, the original deposit was refundable, but the accumulated income was payable to the funeral home. If the contract was not canceled, the corpus and accumulated income would be paid to the funeral home. The ruling held that the income earned on the accumulated income was currently taxable to the grantor-customer under § 677(a) because it could be used for the benefit of the grantor-customer's estate or spouse. Section 685, enacted in 1997, overrides § 677 with respect to qualified funeral trusts if the trustee elects to treat the trust as a separate entity. Under § 685, the income of the trust is taxed to the trust at the rates prescribed in § 1(e), and no income is recognized by the beneficiary as a result of a distribution.

Taxpayers have attempted to avoid the grantor trust rules by structuring the transfer to the trust as a "sale." In Rev. Rul. 68–183, 1968–1 C.B. 308, the taxpayer sold stock to a trust in return for an obligation to pay him a fixed dollar amount for life with payment of the "purchase price" to be made out of the income that the stock generated. The Ruling held that the transaction was not a sale but a transfer of the stock with a retention of rights to the income, which was taxable to the grantor under § 677. A similar result was reached in Lazarus v. Commissioner, 513 F.2d 824 (9th Cir.1975), which treated a purported sale of property to a trust in exchange for a private annuity as a transfer with a retained income interest, the trust income thus being taxable to the grantor under § 677. But, in La Fargue v. Commissioner,

689 F.2d 845 (9th Cir.1982), sale treatment was upheld in a situation in which the grantor sold assets to a trust of which her daughter was the income beneficiary. The Tax Court, 73 T.C. 40 (1979), followed *Lazarus,* emphasizing among other points that the actuarial value of the annuity was significantly less than the fair market value of the property transferred to the trust and the annuity payments were funded entirely from assets transferred into trust. The Ninth Circuit upheld sale treatment, distinguishing *Lazarus* on the ground that the annuity payments were not tied to the income earned by the trust as was the case in *Lazarus.* On remand, the Tax Court held that the taxpayer's investment in the contract for purposes of § 72 was the fair market value of the annuity and not the fair market value of the property transferred into trust. As a result, almost 50 percent of the annual payments to the grantors were ordinary income. In effect, the Tax Court treated the transfer as a part-sale, part-gift transaction. T.C.Memo. 1985–90.

Suppose that a grantor creates a trust with a reversionary interest having a value of less than 5 percent so that she is not taxable on current income but under the terms of the trust instrument capital gains realized by the trust are allocable to corpus. While § 677(a) speaks of "income," note that § 643(b), defining "income" in terms of local law, does not extend to Subpart E. Thus, "income" in § 677(a) includes capital gains.[8] Treas. Reg. § 1.677(a)–(1)(g), Ex. (2). In Rev. Rul. 66–161, 1966–1 C.B. 164, the grantor transferred property in trust for ten years—which at that time was the minimum term to avoid § 673—with income payable to a named beneficiary. The corpus of the trust was to revert to the grantor with all capital gains to be allocated to corpus; the grantor could require the distribution of the capital gains to the grantor. The Ruling held the grantor taxable on the capital gains realized by the trust under § 677 and on the income attributable to the capital gains allocated to corpus under § 676 since that portion of the corpus could revert to the grantor within the ten-year period.

2.2. *Insurance Trusts*

Section 677(a)(3), the constitutionality of which was sustained in Burnet v. Wells, 289 U.S. 670 (1933), extends only to the part of the trust income which can be used to pay premiums on existing insurance policies on the lives of the grantor or spouse. Weil v. Commissioner, 3 T.C. 579 (1944) (Acq.). If it could be so used, the fact that it actually was not so used will not prevent taxation of the grantor. But for § 677(a)(3) to apply, the trust instrument must itself provide that the income of the trust as such may be used for the prescribed purpose.

In Rev. Rul. 66–313, 1966–2 C.B. 245, trust income used with the consent of the beneficiaries of an irrevocable trust set up by the grantor to pay premiums on life insurance policies on the life of the grantor which were owned by another trust with the same beneficiaries was taxable to the grantor under § 677(a).

---

[8]   Since the grantor is considered as owning the portion of the trust to which the capital gains are attributable, the gains are taxable to the grantor in the taxable year in which realized by the trust and not in the taxable year in which the fiscal year of the trust ends. Scheft v. Commissioner, 59 T.C. 428 (1972).

3.   SUPPORT TRUSTS

3.1.   *Created by Grantor*

The predecessor of § 677(b) was added in 1942 to limit the application of § 677(a)(1) in the case of support trusts. In Helvering v. Stuart, 317 U.S. 154 (1942), the Court applied the predecessors of § 677(a)(1) and (2) to tax the grantor where the trust income could be used by the trustees for the education, support and maintenance of the grantor's minor children, since it thereby would discharge his parental obligation of support. A tax resulted even though no part of the income for the year was actually so used.

The rule of § 677(b) was adopted to limit the *Stuart* doctrine to taxation of only the amount of the trust income actually spent in a support situation, except where the power resides in the grantor or the grantor's spouse individually or jointly. See Estate of Hamiel v. Commissioner, 253 F.2d 787 (6th Cir.1958), construing a trust for the maintenance and education of a minor as providing discretion in the trustee to spend only what was needed for the minor's support and to accumulate the balance, thus bringing the trust under § 677(b). This section also prevents taxation of the grantor under § 61(a). But its scope is limited to the obligation of support, so that the *Stuart* doctrine applies in other areas in which § 677(a)(1) and (2) are applicable. Treas. Reg. § 1.677(b)–1(d).

In Brooke v. United States, 468 F.2d 1155 (9th Cir.1972), the court held that where trust income was used for the support of the grantor's child, the amount taxable to the grantor was limited to the amount which discharged his legal obligation of support under state law. Under Montana law, which was the relevant state law in *Brooke,* payments for private education, music, and swimming lessons were not within the support obligation. Thus the payments were not taxable to the grantor. In other states, however, the support obligation may be broader and thus the ambit of grantor taxation under § 677 is broader. See Braun v. Commissioner, T.C.Memo. 1984–285 (private high school and college tuition for child was within New Jersey support obligation); Stone v. Commissioner, T.C.Memo. 1987–454, aff'd by order, 867 F.2d 613 (9th Cir.1989) (private high school was within California support obligation).

When a grantor personally contracts for the provision to a dependent of luxuries beyond the support obligation and the trust subsequently discharges the debt, § 677(a) is the controlling provision rather than § 677(b), and the grantor is thus taxable. Morrill v. United States, 228 F.Supp. 734 (D.Me. 1964).

3.2.   *Created by Others*

Suppose a grandparent creates a trust with the income to be accumulated during a grandchild's minority but the parent is given a power to use the income for the support of the grandchild. Section 678(c) provides that the parent is taxable to the extent the power is exercised and the income is so applied. Suppose the trust had provided that the trustee, a bank, had to use the income for the grandchild's support. Treas. Reg. § 1.678(c)–1(c) provides that § 678(c) does not apply in that situation. However, Treas. Reg. § 1.662(a)–4 will tax the parent on the income applied to the child's support if under the relevant state law the parent is obligated to support the child even though the child has sufficient resources, such as the beneficial interest of the trust, to provide the necessary support. But if under state law the parent has the power to apply the child's own resources to the child's support (in lieu of the parent's resources), the parent is not so taxed.

4.   GRANTOR CONTROL

4.1. *Power to Revoke*

Section 676 taxes the grantor on the income of a trust if the grantor may revoke the trust. The section also applies whenever any nonadverse party, including an independent trustee, has the power to revest title to all of part of the trust corpus in the grantor. Thus an irrevocable trust, with an independent trustee, of which the grantor is a discretionary beneficiary may be subject to § 676.

In applying § 676, both the specific terms of the trust and state law must be considered. If under state law a trust is revocable unless expressly made irrevocable, the trust income would be taxable to the grantor in the absence of a provision making the trust irrevocable. Gaylord v. Commissioner, 153 F.2d 408 (9th Cir.1946). In Flitcroft v. Commissioner, 328 F.2d 449 (9th Cir.1964), a state court reformation proceeding which amended trust instruments retroactively to make them irrevocable was given effect for federal income tax purposes. Under state law the trusts were revocable unless the trust instrument expressly provided otherwise. The court found the parties intended the trusts to be irrevocable from inception, despite the absence of express reference to irrevocability in the trust instruments.

4.2. *Power to Affect Beneficial Enjoyment*

4.2.1. *Generally*

Section 674(a) taxes the grantor on the income of a portion of a trust with respect to which the grantor or a nonadverse party other than an independent trustee may alter the beneficial enjoyment without the consent of an adverse party. Unlike the other grantor trust provisions, which apply when the income or corpus of the trust may be expended for the benefit of the grantor, § 674(a) applies when the income or corpus cannot be expended for the benefit of the grantor but the grantor retains only the power to alter who will benefit from the trust.

The broad general rule of § 674(a) is deceptive because of the numerous exceptions. Meeting one of these exceptions is crucial in planning a trust where the grantor intends to transfer both the beneficial interest in the trust property and the incidence of taxation on the trust property. First, § 674(b) lists a number of powers to alter beneficial interest that may be retained by the grantor or held by any trustee named by the grantor, including the grantor's spouse or a related or subordinate and subservient trustee. See Treas. Reg. § 1.674(b)–1. Second, § 674(d) allows a trustee other than the grantor or the grantor's spouse to have the power to distribute, apportion, or accumulate income for or among a class of beneficiaries designated in the trust instrument if the power is limited by a "reasonably definite external standard set forth in the trust instrument." Such a power held by a related or subservient trustee does not result in taxation to the grantor. Finally,

§ 674(c) allows an independent trustee to have the power to distribute, apportion, or accumulate income among or for a designated class of beneficiaries or to distribute corpus among the members of the class of beneficiaries without taxation to the grantor. For the trustee to be "independent" neither the grantor nor the grantor's spouse may be a trustee, and no more than one-half of the trustees may be related or subordinate parties. Neither § 674(c) nor (d) applies if any person has the power to add beneficiaries, other than after-born or after-adopted children added to a class. None of these exceptions permits the grantor or the grantor's spouse to have the general power to "sprinkle" income among beneficiaries. See Carson v. Commissioner, 92 T.C. 1134 (1989).

4.2.2. *Effect of Loans to Trust*

In a number of cases taxpayers have attempted to avoid the grantor trust rules by establishing a trust that by its terms was not subject to the grantor trust rules but which was only nominally funded and to which the grantor then made large demand loans. The courts generally have held that the power to demand repayment at any time was sufficient domination and control over the beneficial enjoyment of the trust for § 674(a) to tax the grantor on the trust income earned on the borrowed amounts. See e.g., Kushner v. Commissioner, T.C. Memo. 1991–26, aff'd by order, 955 F.2d 41 (4th Cir.1992).

4.2.3. *Power to Substitute Trustee*

The exceptions in § 674(c) and (d) do not apply if the grantor has the unrestricted ability to remove and replace the trustee. Appointment of a successor trustee in limited circumstances is permitted. Treas. Reg. § 1.674(d)–2. Corning v. Commissioner, 24 T.C. 907 (1955), aff'd per curiam, 239 F.2d 646 (6th Cir.1956), held that where a corporate trustee had discretion to allocate income or corpus among beneficiaries but the grantor had the power to substitute any other corporate trustee without cause, the grantor was taxable on the trust income. In this situation, the trustee's discretion is essentially exercisable with the consent of the grantor, and hence § 674(c) does not apply. But see Estate of Wall v. Commissioner, 101 T.C. 300 (1993) (grantor's power to remove and replace trustee does not result in grantor being deemed to hold trustee's powers for estate tax purposes).

4.3. *Borrowing of Trust Funds*

Section 675(1)–(3) provides that the grantor will be treated as the owner if the grantor retains the power to deal with the trust for less than adequate and full consideration or the power to borrow without adequate interest or security. One issue that may arise is whether the grantor has indirectly borrowed funds where the borrower is an entity controlled by the grantor. In Buehner v. Commissioner, 65 T.C. 723 (1976), the taxpayer created a charitable remainder trust, retaining a life income interest for himself and his wife. Both were also trustees. The trust sold assets to a pension trust of the taxpayer's corporation and then loaned the sale proceeds to the corporation on the basis of 20-year, unsecured notes. The court held that § 675(3) was not applicable even though the taxpayer was the trustee and the sole owner of the corporation. Borrowing by the taxpayer's corporation was not indirect borrowing by the taxpayer as grantor.

Another problem that may arise under § 675 is the determination of the "portion" of the trust of which the grantor is treated as the owner where § 675(2) or § 675(3) is applicable. In Bennett v. Commissioner, 79 T.C. 470 (1982), a father and two sons were general partners in a partnership engaged in farming and construction and leasing of nursing homes. In 1963, they created a trust for the benefit of the children of the sons. Nursing homes were transferred to the trust. The trustees did not distribute all the income from the trusts as required by the trust instruments, but only enough to allow the children to pay income taxes. The balance of the income was loaned to the partnership and a successor corporation or was invested in certificates of deposit in a bank which was owned 51 1/2 percent by the taxpayers. The loans were unsecured and were not repaid until the trusts terminated in 1975. The court held that the loans to the partnership (but not to the corporation) were indirect loans to the grantors under § 675(3). The "portion" of the trusts of which the grantors were owners was determined by multiplying the current year's income by a fraction, the numerator of which was the amount of the loans outstanding at the beginning of the year and the denominator of which was the sum of total trust income for all prior years and the income of the year in question.

5.   REVERSIONARY INTEREST

Section 673 taxes the grantor where the grantor has a reversionary interest or the grantor's spouse has a remainder in either the corpus or income of the trust that at its inception exceeds 5 percent of the value of the trust. The reversion is valued whenever property is transferred to the trust, not when the trust document is executed. See Bibby v. Commissioner, 44 T.C. 638 (1965). Section 673(a) does not apply if a reversion takes effect only upon the death of a beneficiary under 21 years of age who is a lineal descendant of the grantor. Prior to 1986, at a time when use of short term trusts was popular, § 673(a) applied only if the reversionary interest was not postponed beyond ten years. As a result of an amendment in 1986 to § 673(a) extending the minimum term, use of the short-term trust declined dramatically.

Where a reversion becomes possessory upon only passage of time or the termination of intervening life estates, the reversion is valued using actuarial tables promulgated under § 7520. See Treas. Reg. § 1.7520–1. These tables use a discount factor equal to 120 percent of the applicable midterm federal rate for the month in which the valuation occurs. Thus, if the applicable midterm federal rate is 10 percent when the trust is established, the discount factor is 12 percent and the minimum term necessary to avoid § 673 is approximately 26 1/2 years; if the applicable midterm federal rate is 8 percent, the discount factor is 9.6 percent and the minimum term necessary to avoid § 673 is approximately 32 1/2 years. Similarly, if there is an intervening life estate, at 12 percent the life beneficiary must be under 40 years of age at the creation of the trust, while at 9.6 percent the life beneficiary must be under 35 years of age. See Notice 89–60, 1989–1 C.B. 700. The actual expected life expectancy of the holder of an intervening income interest is not taken into account unless the income interest holder is expected to die within a year of the transfer in trust. Treas. Reg. § 1.7520–3(b)(3). Where a reversion is effected by an event that may occur at an indeterminate time because it is conditioned on an event other than mere passage of time or lives, valuation may be very difficult. Presumably, resort should be made to the principles for valuing reversions under § 2037 of the estate tax. In addition, § 673(c) presumes that any discretionary acts by the trustee will be exercised in the grantor's favor, thereby maximizing the value of the reversion to the extent trustee discretion is a factor.

Rev. Rul. 87–127, 1987–2 C.B. 157, held that § 673(a) did not tax the grantor on income of a pre-need funeral trust where the grantor-customer could not revoke the trust (but could change the identity of the funeral home-seller). Because the trust would relieve the grantor's estate of an obligation, the grantor had a reversion, but because the grantor was only 31½ years old, the value of the reversion was not more than 5 percent of the corpus. The ruling further held that if the grantor's spouse were obligated by state law to pay funeral expenses personally, § 677(a) would tax the income to the grantor regardless of the value of the reversion.

6. THE GRANTOR AS "OWNER"

Because the grantor is treated as the "owner" of the portion of the trust over which the grantor maintains the proscribed degree of control, complexities arise in computing the grantor's income. See Treas. Reg. § 1.671–2 for a resolution of some of these problems. Where the grantor is treated as the owner of the property under §§ 671–677, this characterization sometimes also carries over to other Code provisions. Thus, in Rev. Rul. 70–376, 1970–2 C.B. 164, § 1033 applied to defer recognition of gain realized on the involuntary conversion of trust property when the grantor acquired replacement property. Similarly, in Rev. Rul. 88–103, 1988–2 C.B. 304, the grantor was treated as the owner of property purchased by the trust to replace property owned by the grantor that had been involuntarily converted, while § 1033 applied to defer the grantor's gain. See also Treas. Reg. § 1.121–1(c)(3)(i) (treating the grantor as the owner of a principal residence held in trust for purposes of applying the exclusion of gain on the sale of the taxpayer's principal residence under § 121).

A different approach was taken in Rothstein v. United States, 735 F.2d 704 (2d Cir.1984), where the taxpayer transferred stock representing a 50-percent ownership in a real estate corporation to a trust for the benefit of his children. The taxpayer's wife was the trustee. No dividends were ever paid on the stock. Seven years later, the taxpayer purchased the other 50 percent of the stock in the corporation from a third party for $500,000. He then purchased the shares held by the trust for $320,000 with an unsecured 5-percent note. After liquidating the corporation, the taxpayer executed a second mortgage to the trust to secure the note. The IRS disallowed the interest deductions on the note and increased the capital gain realized by the taxpayer on the liquidation of the corporation. In the IRS's view, the taxpayer was not entitled to a $320,000 basis in the stock that he had purchased from the trust since he was the owner of the trust property under § 675(3). There was inadequate security for the loan and there was not an independent trustee. A majority of the court held that the purchase money note was an "indirect" borrowing by the taxpayer covered by § 675(3). But in the majority's view, this meant only that the income, deductions, and credits of the trust were to be included in the grantor's tax return. The characterization of the grantor as "owner" under § 671 did not require recharacterization of the transactions between the grantor and the trust. Hence, the majority concluded that the basis of the stock purchased from the trust was its $320,000 cost and interest deductions were properly allowed to the grantor. As interest payments were made, the grantor would be entitled to a deduction, but, because he was the owner of the trust, that same interest would be taxable income to the grantor; thus the items would be offsetting. Similarly, as the grantor paid off the note, the trust would recognize gain on an installment basis and this gain in turn would be taxable to the grantor. The majority did not find troublesome that the grantor in effect converted an immediate gain (which he would have recognized on the liquidation of the corporation) into a deferred installment gain by virtue of the transaction between himself and the trust. A dissent argued that the taxpayer was not entitled to defer the gain or take interest deductions, because he was the owner of the trust.

Compare Rev. Rul. 85–13, 1985–1 C.B. 184, where a grantor created a reversionary trust with a term that avoided application of § 673. All income was to be payable to the grantor's child with the corpus to be distributed to the child at the termination of the trust. There was no power held by the grantor that would cause him to be the owner under §§ 671–677. The trust was funded with stock having a basis of $20 per share. When the stock was worth $40 per share, the trustee sold it to the grantor for the grantor's unsecured, interest-bearing, 10-year note. The grantor then sold the shares for $50 per share a few weeks later. The Ruling concluded that the grantor was the owner of the entire trust since an unsecured note was used. The grantor was the owner of the sole asset of the trust, the grantor's own note. There was no sale of the stock to the grantor because the grantor was both the maker and owner of the note. Accordingly, the Ruling concluded that the grantor's basis in the stock sold was his original basis of $20 per share.

7.   TAXING PERSONS OTHER THAN THE GRANTOR BECAUSE OF POWER TO OBTAIN INCOME OR CORPUS—SECTION 678

Section 678 essentially adopted the rule established in Mallinckrodt v. Nunan, 146 F.2d 1 (8th Cir.1945). In that case, a son had the power to request that there be paid to him the income of a trust created by his father; in the absence of such request the income was to be added to the corpus. The son could appoint the corpus by will. The son was held taxable on the income under the predecessor to § 61(a). The court said that taxation of the son could not be predicated upon the trust sections, since the income was not currently distributable to him unless he requested it.

In Rev. Rul. 67–268, 1967–2 C.B. 226, the husband was given discretionary power under a trust set up by a third party to distribute income to his wife. The IRS held that the husband was not taxable under § 678 because he had no power to vest income in himself directly. Meanwhile, in Trust No. 3 v. Commissioner, 285 F.2d 102 (7th Cir.1960), the court applied

§ 678 to tax the beneficiary of the trust who had a right to demand at any time a payment of corpus, even though a guardian would have to be appointed for the beneficiary to exercise the right because the beneficiary was a minor. In Koffman v. United States, 300 F.2d 176 (6th Cir.1962), the taxpayer was taxable on the entire amount of income received by a testamentary trust of which the taxpayer was a beneficiary, despite the fact that only a portion of the income was distributed, because under the terms of the trust the taxpayer had the right to demand payment of all the income. Although not at issue in the case, on the facts, the portion of the trust attributable to undistributed income from prior years would constitute a separate grantor trust established by the beneficiary and taxable to the beneficiary under § 677(a).

8.   POLICY ISSUES

The rules in §§ 671–677 offer opportunities for grantors seeking to retain significant control over property while at the same time shifting tax liability on the income from the property. Section 674 permits the grantor to shift income tax liability without having to select the ultimate recipient of the property. In fact, the grantor enjoys at least three choices for shifting tax liability: one, name the grantor or a subservient as trustee, and then exercise powers of allocation among beneficiaries permitted under § 674(b)(4), (5)(A), and (6); two, name a so-called "independent trustee" (such as a lawyer, accountant, or corporate fiduciary), and permit the trustee to exercise still broader powers under § 674(c); or three, appoint close family relatives as trustees under the standard specified in § 674(d). In adopting the first option, the grantor neither selects any particular donee nor alters the family's dependence on the grantor for receipt of future payments of income. In adopting the second and third options, the grantor does not select any particular donee, and only formalistically shifts the family's economic dependence on the grantor to a trustee whose true independence also might be in form only. The advantages over an outright gift are obvious: the ultimate destination of the income and underlying property remain ambiguous while the grantor retains control and enjoyment over the property, but all current tax liability has been shifted from the grantor to another taxpayer.

PART XI

ALTERNATIVE MINIMUM TAX

CHAPTER 39

ALTERNATIVE MINIMUM TAX FOR INDIVIDUALS

INTERNAL REVENUE CODE: Sections 53; 55 (other than 55(b)(1)(B), (b)(4); 55(e)); 56(a)(1)(A), (a)(4), (b)(1), (3), (e)(1), (2); 57(a)(1), (2)(A)–(C), (5)(A), (b).

The Alternative Minimum Tax, or AMT, is an "alternative" income tax regime that operates alongside the "regular" income tax described in the first thirty-eight Chapters of this book. Despite its name, the AMT is not elective. Taxpayers compute their tax liability under the AMT in addition to their tax liability under the "regular" tax, and then pay the higher amount.

The AMT is different from the regular tax system in three significant respects. First, the AMT is imposed on a different and broader tax base than that of the regular tax. Its broader base, termed "alternative minimum taxable income" (AMTI), subjects numerous items to tax that do not constitute a part of taxable income under the regular tax due to "lost" deductions and exclusions. For example, while taxable income under the regular tax generally does not include state or local property taxes paid by an individual thanks to the § 164 deduction, these amounts are included in AMTI. Second, the AMT's tax rate structure (found in § 55(b)(1)(A)) is markedly different from the regular tax brackets in § 1. Third, many of the credits that can reduce a taxpayer's regular tax liability are unavailable under the AMT.

Congress enacted the predecessor to the current AMT in 1969 as a reaction to learning that 155 high-income households with gross income exceeding $200,000 (or roughly $1.5 million in 2016) had paid zero federal income tax in tax year 1966. Motivated to ensure that high-income earners paid their "fair share" of federal income taxes, Congress chartered the new "minimum tax" with a specific objective:

> to ensure that no taxpayer with substantial economic income can avoid significant tax liability by using exclusions, deductions, and credits. Although these provisions may provide incentives for worthy goals, they become counterproductive when taxpayers are allowed to use them to avoid virtually all tax liability. The ability of high-income taxpayers to pay little or no tax undermines respect for the entire tax system and, thus, for the incentive provisions themselves. In addition, even aside from public perceptions, Congress concluded that it is inherently unfair for high-income taxpayers to pay little or no tax due to their ability to utilize tax preferences.

Joint Committee on Taxation, General Explanation of the Tax Reform Act of 1986, 429 (1987).

Over the years, Congress's initial motivation to enact a supplement to the regular income tax targeted at high-income taxpayers receded as a result of numerous statutory amendments and Congress's failure to index for inflation the AMT exemptions, rate brackets, and phaseouts. As late at 1987, the AMT applied to only 0.1 percent of tax returns (generating less than $2 billion in annual revenue). Joint Committee on Taxation, Present Law and Background Relating to the Individual Alternative Minimum Tax (2007). By 2012—and before Congress permanently "patched" the AMT by raising and indexing its exemption levels, brackets, and phaseouts in that year's American Taxpayer Relief Act (see Section 1.1 in the DETAILED ANALYSIS below)—more than 34 million taxpayers (or 25 percent of all taxpayers) were scheduled to pay $85 billion in AMT liability. Even after the 2012 restructuring of the AMT, it continues to subject nearly four million taxpayers to higher income taxes every year. Williams, How the New Tax Act Affects the Alternative Minimum Tax, Tax Policy Center (2013). This Chapter describes the structure of the current AMT, illustrates its effect on tax liability, and discusses its transformation from a strictly class tax to a near mass tax.

Present Law and Background Relating to the Individual Alternative Minimum Tax

Staff of the Joint Committee on Taxation, 2–5 (2007).

* * *

I. Individual Alternative Minimum Tax

A. Present Law and Legislative Background

In general

An alternative minimum tax ("AMT") is imposed on an individual, estate, or trust in an amount by which the tentative minimum tax exceeds the regular income tax for the taxable year. The tentative minimum tax is the sum of (1) 26 percent of so much of the taxable excess as does not exceed $175,000 ($87,500 in the case of a married individual filing a separate return) [adjusted for inflation, and equaling $186,300 and $93,150, respectively, for 2016] and (2) 28 percent of the remaining taxable excess. The taxable excess is so much of the alternative minimum taxable income ("AMTI") as exceeds the exemption amount. The maximum tax rates on net capital gain and dividends used in computing the regular tax are used in computing the tentative minimum tax.

The exemption amounts are: (1) [$83,800 for 2016] in the case of married individuals filing a joint return and surviving spouses; (2) [$53,900] in the case of other unmarried individuals; (3) [$41,900] in the case of married individuals filing separate returns; and (4) [$23,900] in the case of an estate or trust. The exemption amounts are phased out by an amount equal to 25 percent of the amount by which the individual's AMTI exceeds (1) [$159,700 for 2016] in the case of married individuals filing a joint return and surviving spouses, (2) [$119,700] in the case of other unmarried individuals, and (3) [$79,850] in the case of married individuals filing separate returns or an estate or a trust. These amounts are * * * indexed for inflation [since 2012].

Alternative minimum taxable income is the individual's regular taxable income increased by certain adjustments and preference items. In the case of items that involve the timing of deductions, the AMTI treatment negates the deferral of income resulting from the regular tax treatment of these items.

Adjustments and preferences

The adjustments [listed in section 56] and preferences [listed in section 57] that individuals must take into account to compute AMTI are:

1. Depreciation on property placed in service after 1986 and before January 1, 1999, is computed by using the generally longer class lives prescribed by the alternative depreciation system of section 168(g) and either (a) the straight-line method in the case of property subject to the straight-line method under the regular tax or (b) the 150-percent declining balance method in the case of other property. Depreciation on property placed in service after December 31, 1998, is computed by using the regular tax recovery periods and the AMT methods described in the previous sentence. * * *

2. Mining exploration and development costs are capitalized and amortized over a 10-year period.

3. Taxable income from a long-term contract (other than a home construction contract) is computed using the percentage of completion method of accounting.

* * *

5. Miscellaneous itemized deductions are not allowed.

6. Deductions for State, local, and foreign real property taxes; State and local personal property taxes; State, local, and foreign income, war profits, and excess profits taxes; and State and local sales taxes are not allowed.

7. Medical expenses are allowed only to the extent they exceed ten percent of the taxpayer's adjusted gross income.

8. The standard deduction and personal exemptions are not allowed.

* * *

10. The amount allowable as a deduction for research and experimentation expenditures from passive activities are capitalized and amortized over a 10-year period.

11. The regular tax rules relating to incentive stock options do not apply.

12. The excess of the deduction for percentage depletion over the adjusted basis of each mineral property (other than oil and gas properties) at the end of the taxable year is not allowed.

13. The amount by which excess intangible drilling costs (i.e., expenses in excess of the amount that would have been allowable if amortized over a 10-year period) exceed 65 percent of the net income from oil, gas, and geothermal properties is not allowed. This preference applies to independent producers only to the extent it reduces the producer's AMTI (determined without regard to this preference and the net operating loss deduction) by more than 40 percent.

14. Tax-exempt interest income on private activity bonds (other than qualified 501(c)(3) bonds) issued after August 7, 1986, is included in AMTI.

* * *

17. Losses from any tax shelter farm activity or passive activities are not taken into account in computing AMTI.

[18. The deduction for interest paid on home equity indebtedness is not allowed. Eds.]

Other rules

Net operating loss deduction

The taxpayer's net operating loss deduction cannot reduce the taxpayer's AMTI by more than 90 percent of the AMTI (determined without the net operating loss deduction).

Nonrefundable tax credits

Except as otherwise described below, nonrefundable tax credits may not exceed the excess of the individual's regular tax liability over the tentative minimum tax, meaning they are not allowed against the alternative minimum tax. Thus, credits such as the general business credit, the alternative motor vehicle credit, and the alternative fuel vehicle refueling credit generally are not allowed against the AMT.

Several exceptions apply to the general rule denying credits against the AMT.

The alternative minimum tax foreign tax credit reduces the tentative minimum tax.

* * *

[T]he nonrefundable personal credits * * * are allowed.] * * *

If an individual is subject to AMT in any year, the amount of tax exceeding the taxpayer's regular tax liability is allowed as a credit (the "AMT credit") in any subsequent taxable year to the extent the taxpayer's regular tax liability exceeds his or her tentative minimum tax liability in such subsequent year. For individuals, the AMT credit is allowed only to the extent that the taxpayer's AMT liability is the result of adjustments that are timing in nature. The individual AMT adjustments relating to itemized deductions and personal exemptions are not timing in nature, and no minimum tax credit is allowed with respect to these items. * * *

Klaassen v. Commissioner*

United States Court of Appeals, Tenth Circuit, 1999.
83 A.F.T.R.2d 99–1750.

■ ANDERSON (CIRCUIT JUDGE):

* * *

David R. and Margaret J. Klaassen appeal from the Tax Court's ruling that they are liable for an alternative minimum tax (AMT) in the amount of $1,085 for the 1994 tax year. The Klaassens contend that the tax court erred (1) by applying the AMT provisions, I.R.C. §§ 55–59 (1988 & Supp. 1994), to them in violation of congressional intent; or, alternatively (2) by applying the AMT provisions to them in violation of their First and Fifth Amendment rights. We affirm.

BACKGROUND

The facts are undisputed. During the 1994 tax year, the Klaassens were the parents of ten dependent children. According to their 1994 joint tax return, they earned an adjusted gross income (AGI) of $83,056.42. On Schedule A, the Klaassens claimed deductions for medical expenses and for state and local taxes in the respective amounts of $4,767.13 and $3,263.56. Including their claimed deductions for interest and charitable contributions, their total Schedule A itemized deductions equaled $19,563.95. Therefore, they subtracted that amount from their AGI, and on line 35 of their Form 1040, they showed a balance of $63,492.47. On line 36, they entered a total of $29,400 for twelve personal exemptions— one each for themselves and their ten children. After subtracting that amount, they showed a taxable income of $34,092.47 on line 37 of their Form 1040, and a resulting regular tax of $5,111.00 on line 38. They did not provide any computations for AMT liability.

Following an audit, the IRS issued a notice of deficiency, advising the Klaassens that they were liable for a $1,085.43 AMT pursuant to I.R.C. §§ 55–59. Specifically, the IRS concluded that, in the Klaassens' case, I.R.C. §§ 55–56 required three specific adjustments, or increases, to the taxable income which they showed on line 37 of their Form 1040. According to the IRS's interpretation, subsection 56(b)(1)(A)(ii) required the entire $3,263.56 deduction for state and local taxes to be added back. Next, subsection 56(b)(1)(B) reduced the deduction allowable for medical expenses by setting a 10% floor in lieu of the 7.5% floor normally allowed under § 213(a)—resulting in a net adjustment of $2,076.41. Finally, § 56(b)(1)(E) deprived the Klaassens of the entire $29,400 deduction they claimed on line 36 of their Form 1040. After adjusting the taxable income

---

* Ed.: The Court of Appeals affirmed the Tax Court, T.C. Memo 1998–241, by order, 182 F.3d 932 (10th Cir.1999), which under the rules of the 10th Circuit is not binding precedent.

by these three amounts, the IRS set the alternative minimum taxable income at $68,832.44. After deducting the $45,000 exemption, the tentative minimum tax was computed on the excess: 26% × $23,832.44 = $6,196.43. The difference between that figure and the Klaassens' regular tax was $1,085.43. The Tax Court upheld the IRS's position, see Klaassen v. Commissioner, T.C. Memo 1998–241, and the Klaassens brought this appeal.

DISCUSSION

The Klaassens do not dispute the numbers or the mechanics used to calculate the AMT deficiency. Rather, they claim that, as a matter of law, the AMT provisions should not apply to them. * * *

A.

I.R.C. § 56(b)(1)(E) plainly states that, in computing the alternative minimum taxable income, "the deduction for personal exemptions under section 151 . . . shall not be allowed." Nonetheless, the Klaassens argue that Congress intended the AMT to apply only to very wealthy persons who claim the types of tax preferences described in I.R.C. § 57. Essentially, the Klaassens contend that Congress did not intend to disallow personal exemptions for taxpayers at their income level when no § 57 preferences are involved. Although they cite no legislative history to support their contention, the Klaassens argue that their entitlement to their personal exemptions is mandated by I.R.C. §§ 151–153. In particular, they note that for 1994, I.R.C. § 151(d) allowed taxpayers filing joint returns to claim the full exemption so long as their AGI was less than $167,700. Appellant's Br. at 6. They then argue that the § 151(d) threshold amount should be interpolated as a threshold for the AMT provisions. We disagree.

In the absence of exceptional circumstances, where a statute is clear and unambiguous our inquiry is complete. Burlington Northern R.R. Co. v. Oklahoma Tax Comm'n, 481 U.S. 454, 461 (1987); * * * . The AMT framework establishes a precise method for taxing income which the regular tax does not reach. In creating this framework, Congress included several provisions, "marked by a high degree of specificity," by which deductions or advantages which are allowed in computing the regular tax are specifically disallowed for purposes of computing the AMT. Huntsberry v. Commissioner, 83 T.C. 742, 747–48 (1984) * * * . Instead of permitting those separate "regular tax" deductions, Congress specifically substituted the $45,000 fixed exemption for purposes of AMT computations. I.R.C. § 55(d)(1). If, as the Klaassens claim, Congress had intended the AMT to apply only to taxpayers whose incomes reached a certain threshold, or only to taxpayers with § 57 tax preferences, it could have easily drafted the statute to achieve that result. Instead, as the tax court correctly held, the statute's plain language unequivocally reaches the Klaassens, and our inquiry is therefore complete. While the law may result in some unintended consequences, in the absence of any ambiguity, it must be applied as written. It is therefore from Congress that the Klaassens should seek relief.

B.

As their second, alternative, point of error, the Klaassens contend that applying the AMT provisions to them violates their First Amendment rights, as well as their equal protection and due process rights. First, the Klaassens contend that, by disallowing the personal exemptions for their children, the statute impermissibly burdens their free exercise of religion.[4] Second, they contend that their equal protection and due process rights are violated, because the statute deprives them of full deductions for medical and local taxes, whereas those deductions are allowed for families with similar incomes, but fewer than eight children.

[The court denied all of the constitutional claims.]

AFFIRMED.

■ KELLY, CIRCUIT JUDGE, concurring.

Although I agree with the court that the taxpayers cannot prevail on the theories advanced, we are not precluded from examining the legislative history of the alternative minimum tax (AMT), despite the clarity of the statute. See Train v. Colorado Public Interest Research Group, 426 U.S. 1, 10 (1976), * * * . The legislative history supports an argument that the original purpose of the AMT, one of the more complex parts of the Internal Revenue Code, was to insure that taxpayers with substantial economic income pay a minimum amount of tax on it. See S. Rep. No. 97–494 (1982), reprinted in 1982 U.S.C.C.A.N. 781, 876; S. Rep. No. 99–313, at 518 reprinted in 1986–3 C.B. 518. The regular income tax may be insufficient to achieve that objective because it favors certain types of income and allows deductions, exclusions and credits for certain types of expenses.

For a variety of reasons, the number of moderate income taxpayers subject to the AMT has been steadily increasing. From a tax compliance and administration perspective, many of these taxpayers simply are unaware of their AMT obligations. If aware, they probably would need the assistance of a tax professional to comply with the separate rules and computations (apart from regular tax) and additional record keeping essential for the AMT. From a fairness perspective, many of these taxpayers have not utilized I.R.C. § 57 preferences (or other more arcane AMT adjustment items) to reduce regular taxable income but are caught up in the AMT's attempt to impose fairness. That certainly seems to be the case here. In the interest of progressivity, the regular tax already reduces or phases out itemized deductions and personal exemptions based upon income, see e.g., I.R.C. § 67(a) (miscellaneous itemized deductions), § 68 (overall reduction of itemized deductions), § 151(d)(3)

---

4   The Klaassens are members of the Reformed Presbyterian Church of North America. As part of their religious beliefs, they are opposed to any form of birth control. See Appellant's Br. at 10–11.

(phaseout of personal exemptions); § 213(a) (medical and dental expenses deduction only for amounts beyond 7.5% floor); surely Congress never intended a family of twelve that still qualified for these items under the regular tax to partly forfeit them under the AMT.

That said, we must apply the law as it is plainly written, despite what appears to be the original intent behind the AMT. As the tax court has explained, neither the statutory language nor unequivocal legislative history support the argument that the AMT is limited to individuals with tax preferences. See Huntsberry v. Commissioner, 83 T.C. 742, 747–48 (1984). This is particularly true given the Congressional power to raise revenue. See Okin v. Commissioner, 808 F.2d 1338, 1341–42 (9th Cir.1987). The solution to this inequity, whether it be (1) eliminating itemized deductions and personal exemptions as adjustments to regular taxable income in arriving at alternative minimum taxable income, (2) exempting low and moderate income taxpayers from the AMT, (3) raising and indexing the AMT exemption amount, or (4) some other measure, must come from Congress, as the tax court rightly concluded. See Klaassen v. Commissioner (T.C. Memo. 1998–241).

DETAILED ANALYSIS

1. STRUCTURE OF THE ALTERNATIVE MINIMUM TAX

1.1. *General*

As described by the Joint Committee on Taxation, the AMT tax rates are imposed on the excess of AMTI over an exemption amount. I.R.C. § 55(b)(1)(A). The first $175,000 (adjusted for inflation, $186,300 for 2016), of such excess is taxed at 26 percent with any remaining amount of the excess taxed at 28 percent. The statutory exemption amounts are $78,750 ($83,800 for 2016) for married taxpayers filing jointly and $50,600 ($53,900 for 2016) for unmarried individuals. I.R.C. § 55(d)(1).

The American Taxpayer Relief Act of 2012 permanently "patched" the AMT exemption by raising it to $78,750 for married couples filing jointly and $50,600 for unmarried individuals. Beginning in 2013, the Act also indexed for inflation the exemption amounts (by 2016, those amounts were $83,800 and $53,900, respectively), the $175,000 bracket breakpoint between the 26-percent and 28-percent AMT tax brackets ($186,300 in 2016), and the exemption phaseout thresholds (discussed below).

The exemption amounts gradually phase out once a taxpayer's AMTI reaches certain inflation-adjusted levels. I.R.C. § 55(d)(3). The exemption amount is reduced by 25 percent of the amount by which AMTI exceeds statutory thresholds of (1) $150,000 in the case of married individuals filing a joint return and surviving spouses ($159,700 for 2016), (2) $112,500 in the case of other unmarried individuals ($119,700 for 2016), and (3) $75,000 in the case of married individuals filing separate returns or an estate or a trust ($79,850 for 2016).

Even though the AMT uses different tax rate brackets than those found in § 1 of the Internal Revenue Code, it still retains the preferential rates for long-term capitals gains and qualified dividends found in § 1(h). I.R.C. § 55(b)(3).

In form, the AMT is payable only to the extent that the AMT liability exceeds the regular tax liability (defined in § 26(b)), which is due in any event. In substance, the AMT is a complete, separate alternative tax system, because in any year the taxpayer's actual tax liability is either the regular tax liability, or if higher, the AMT liability.

1.2. *Computation of AMTI*

The starting point in computing AMTI is regular taxable income as determined under § 63(a) for taxpayers who itemize their deductions and § 63(b) for taxpayers who elect to take the standard deduction. Certain modifications, set forth in §§ 56 and 57, are then taken into account to arrive at AMTI. These modifications can be split into two categories: permanent adjustments and timing adjustments.

1.2.1. *Permanent Adjustments*

Permanent adjustments are those that permanently negate the benefit of a deduction or exclusion granted under the regular tax by adding back the amount deducted or excluded in arriving at AMTI. The most significant of these adjustments in terms of revenue generation (as determined in the above Joint Committee on Taxation report) are described below.

Under § 56(b)(1)(A)(ii), amounts paid for state and local property, income, and sales taxes are not deductible for AMT purposes; therefore, the amounts deducted under § 164 for regular tax purposes are added back to AMTI.

Pursuant § 56(b)(1)(E), personal exemptions for the taxpayer, the taxpayer's spouse, and the taxpayer's dependents are not allowed for AMT purposes. These amounts, which are generally[1] deductible under § 151 for regular tax purposes, must also be added back to AMTI.

Section 56(b)(1)(A)(i) disallows for AMT purposes "miscellaneous itemized deductions" as that term is defined in § 67(b). Accordingly, any miscellaneous itemized deductions taken for regular tax purposes are added back to AMTI.[2] The most common miscellaneous itemized deductions are unreimbursed employee business expenses (e.g., union dues, uniform maintenance expenses) and investment expenses described in § 212 (e.g., fees for investment advice).

The AMT's harsh treatment of miscellaneous itemized deductions sometimes leads to a role reversal in which the taxpayer claims that investment-related costs are capital expenditures while the IRS argues that the costs are deductible § 212 expenses. See e.g., Dye v. United States, 121

---

[1]   For high-income individuals, § 151(d)(3) phases out the personal exemption deduction for higher income taxpayers under the regular tax. See Chapter 22, Section 1.B.3. Accordingly, the personal exemption amounts are not fully deductible in all instances under the regular tax.

[2]   Under the regular income tax, miscellaneous itemized deductions are allowed only to the extent that they in the aggregate exceed two percent of the taxpayer's adjusted gross income. I.R.C. § 67(a). This two-percent floor means that most taxpayers get little or no benefit from these deductions under the regular income tax. See Chapter 21, Section 7. As a result, disallowing the deduction for AMT has no significant adverse effect on these taxpayers.

F.3d 1399 (10th Cir.1997) (applying origin of the claim test, and permitting taxpayer to characterize as capital expenses only a portion of legal fees incurred in a suit against stock broker for engaging in unauthorized transactions on taxpayer's margin account). Typically, taxpayers argue for an immediate deduction, while the IRS argues for capitalization, due to the time value of money.

Under § 56(b)(1)(E), the standard deduction found in § 63(c) is disallowed for AMT purposes. Accordingly, for any taxpayer who takes the standard deduction, it is added back to AMTI. Concomitantly, any itemized deductions that the taxpayer eschewed for regular tax purposes in favor of the standard deduction (and that are allowed for AMT purposes) will reduce AMTI. However, because the amount of unused itemized deductions will be less than the amount of the standard deduction (otherwise the taxpayer would have itemized deductions in the first instance instead of taking the standard deduction), the net adjustments to AMTI relating to the standard deduction will almost always be positive.[3]

Other permanent adjustments involve the inclusion in AMTI of certain tax-exempt bond income (excluded under the regular income tax pursuant to § 103) under § 57(a)(5), and the disallowance for AMTI purposes of the home equity interest deduction (allowed under the regular income tax pursuant to § 163(h)(2)(D) and (h)(3)(C)) as reflected in § 56(b)(1)(C).

1.2.2. *Timing Adjustments*

The adjustments described above involve the permanent disallowance of deductions. Other AMTI adjustments defer deductions by moving them from an earlier year to a later year or accelerate gains by moving them from a later year to an earlier year. For example, the adjustments in § 56(a) require the use of slower rates of cost recovery than under the regular income tax for tangible personal property with a cost recovery period of three, five, seven, and ten years. These adjustments will be positive (thus increasing AMTI) early in an asset's life, when cost recovery under the regular tax is accelerated, and negative (decreasing AMTI) in later years of the asset's life, when greater cost recovery remains under the AMT's decelerated method.

Another timing adjustment is found in § 56(b)(3) relating to compensatory stock options that qualify as incentive stock options (ISOs). Under the regular income tax, ISOs generally result in no gain when they are exercised.[4] See I.R.C. § 421(a)(1), discussed in Chapter 30, Section 2.C. This deferral of income recognition beyond exercise of the options is not

---

[3]   We say "almost" because in rare cases the net adjustments will be negative because of the § 68 overall limitation on itemized deductions, which generally reduces itemized deductions by an amount equal to 3 percent of the taxpayer's adjusted gross income for high income taxpayers, I.R.C. § 68(a), but which does not apply for AMT purposes. I.R.C. § 56(b)(1)(F). Thus, for example, if a taxpayer with no state or local tax deductions or miscellaneous itemized deductions chose to take the standard deduction strictly because of the impact of the § 68 limitation, the disallowance of the standard deduction combined with the inapplicability of the § 68 limitation would result in a net negative adjustment to AMTI.

[4]   If certain holding period requirements are met, the gain on the sale of the stock underlying the ISO will be long-term capital gain for regular tax purposes. Because of the minimum tax credit in § 53, described below, the AMT does not undo this preferential treatment.

available with respect to other compensatory options. Under the AMT, the deferral benefit of ISOs is negated and the taxpayer recognizes income upon exercise of the ISO, resulting in a positive adjustment to AMTI in the year of exercise. This is a timing adjustment (rather than a permanent adjustment), because when the stock is sold the taxpayer will subsequently realize less gain for AMT purposes than for regular tax purposes since the taxpayer's AMT basis in the stock will be higher than the taxpayer's regular tax basis in the stock. This higher basis reflects the fact that the taxpayer has already realized gain for AMT purposes (but not for regular tax purposes) upon exercise of the ISO.

Timing adjustments result in additional complexity and record-keeping because the taxpayer must keep two different sets of tax books, one reflecting the regular income tax basis of affected assets and the other reflecting the AMT basis of these assets. This is true even in years in which no AMT is due, because the adjustments in those years may affect later years when AMT is due.

In addition, timing adjustments create the need for § 53, which allows a credit against *regular taxes* for minimum taxes paid in prior years, to prevent the whipsawing of the taxpayer. Without such a credit mechanism, a taxpayer could effectively lose deductions that are intended only to be accelerated under the AMT. For example, in the early years of a depreciable asset's life the taxpayer could be subject to the AMT and thus receive slower cost recovery. Then in the later years of the asset's life, the taxpayer could be subject to the regular tax and receive only the small remaining portion of cost recovery under the accelerated depreciation system. The end result is that the taxpayer never gets the benefit of full cost recovery because some of the depreciation deductions are lost in the taxpayer's transition from the AMT to the regular tax.[5]

The minimum tax credit in § 53 is designed to ameliorate this problem. Section 53 allows the taxpayer to claim a tax credit to reduce regular taxes for minimum tax previously paid as a result of timing adjustments. The amount of the credit is generally equal to the amount of extra tax owed in the earlier year as a result of the AMT. However, the amount of the credit cannot bring the taxpayer's regular tax liability below the taxpayer's AMT liability for the year in which the credit is claimed. The effect of the minimum tax credit is to ensure that the timing adjustments negate only the time value of accelerated deductions (or the time value of deferred gain in the case of ISOs) instead of negating the deduction entirely (or double taxing ISO gains).[6]

1.3. *Availability of Tax Credits Against AMT Liability*

After the AMT tax rates are applied to the excess of the AMTI over the appropriate exemption amount, the resulting amount constitutes the amount of tentative AMT liability. The next step is to determine whether

---

[5]   For this reason many taxpayers regularly subject to the AMT will elect to use the 150 percent declining balance method of depreciation for regular tax purposes in order to harmonize regular tax accounting with AMT tax accounting.

[6]   In general, the minimum tax credit is not refundable, and any portion that is unused because of this rule is effectively carried over to subsequent years. I.R.C. § 53(c).

any of the credits that reduce regular tax liability also apply to reduce AMT liability. While the nonrefundable personal credits (in §§ 21–26) and refundable personal credits (in §§ 31–36 and 36B) serve to reduce AMT liability, the various other nonrefundable credits (such as the general business credit in § 38) typically do not.

After the appropriate credits are applied to each of the taxpayer's tentative regular tax liability and tentative AMT liability, the taxpayer compares the two resulting liabilities and pays the greater amount.

1.4. *Exemption Levels, Tax Rates, and the Taxable Unit*

The AMT adjusts tax liability to reflect the size of the taxable unit only to a limited extent. The exemption amount takes into account only filing status, such as single versus married, and provides no additional exemptions for dependents. Combined with the disallowance of the personal exemption deduction for dependents, the AMT is less favorable than the regular tax for taxpayers with children.

In addition, the rate schedules for the AMT are also unlike the regular tax, and do not differentiate between different taxable units. Under the AMT, the top 28-percent marginal rate applies to both single and married taxpayers with AMTI in excess of the exemption amount. Moreover, the exemption amount allowed for single taxpayers ($53,900 in 2016) is 64 percent (rather than 50 percent) of the exemption amount allowed for married taxpayers ($83,800). Likewise, the exemption begins to phase out for single taxpayers at an adjusted gross income level that is 75 percent (rather than 50 percent) of the level for married taxpayers. As a result, married two-earner couples often face a significant "marriage penalty" under the AMT.

2.   TAX PREFERENCES IN THE AMT

As Congress creates new tax preferences, it must determine whether to extend the preferential treatment to the AMT. For example, when Congress enacted the controversial deduction for "qualified production activities" in the 2004 Jobs Act, it chose not to add back the tax offset to AMTI, thus extending the preferential treatment for these activities to the AMT. Similarly the election to deduct the capital cost of § 179 property does not require an addition to AMTI notwithstanding the acceleration of deductions that would otherwise be subject to depreciation.

Historically, the preferential rate for long-term capital gains under the regular tax did not apply to the AMT. However, in 1997, Congress enacted § 55(b)(3), which extends the preferential treatment of long-term capital gains to the AMT. At the same time, and unlike the regular tax, the AMT does not provide any specific preferential rate for collectibles. Gains on collectibles are taxed at the normal AMT rates of 26 or 28 percent.

The preferential treatment of qualified dividends, enacted in 2003, has also been extended to the AMT. Qualified dividends received by taxpayers other than corporations generally are taxed at the same rate as long-term capital gains (discussed in Chapter 24): 20 percent for income otherwise in the 39.6-percent bracket, 15 percent for income otherwise in the 25 percent or higher bracket (but below the 39.6-percent bracket), and zero for income otherwise in the 10- or 15-percent bracket. See Chapter 8, Section 3 and I.R.C. § 1(h)(11). The same preferential rate applies for AMT purposes. I.R.C. §§ 55(b)(3)(B) and (C), 1(h)(11).

Given the historic purpose of the AMT to reduce potential tax preferences for the wealthy, extending the preferential capital gains and dividend rate to the AMT appears anomalous, particularly when one considers that the most significant "preferences" captured by the AMT amount to ability-to-pay deductions (that is, the state and local tax deduction and the personal exemption deduction). The inconsistent scope and application of the modern AMT is discussed in the following section.

3.　THE GROWTH OF THE AMT—FROM CLASS TAX TO MASS TAX

3.1. *Illustrations of Middle-Class AMT Taxpayers*

In Holly v. Commissioner, T. C. Memo 1998–55, the taxpayer was a retired government employee and self-employed consultant. He reported adjusted gross income of $49,379 and claimed itemized deductions totaling $33,002, including real estate taxes, charitable contributions, and moving and job related legal expenses. These deductions left him with taxable income of $13,927, and a total regular tax liability of $1,850. Because some of the taxpayer's itemized deductions, such as real estate taxes and job related legal expenses were not deductible for AMT purposes, the IRS determined that the taxpayer owed an additional $1,675 in AMT. The IRS also initially assessed an accuracy-related penalty of $335, despite not challenging the propriety of any of the taxpayer's itemized or other deductions (the penalty issue was eventually conceded by the IRS). Meanwhile, the taxpayer "argue[d] that since the AMT was intended to apply only to wealthier individuals, it should not apply to him in this instance." As in *Klaassen* (the principal case earlier in this Chapter), the court concluded that it could "find no fault with respondent's application of the AMT provisions or the method by which respondent computed petitioner's AMT liability. The plain meaning of the AMT provisions is that the amounts claimed by petitioner on Schedule A of his return for legal expenses and real estate taxes paid are not deductible for purposes of calculating AMTI. Section 56(b)(1)(A). Although the results may seem harsh to petitioner in this case, Congress created the AMT by enacting the applicable statutory provisions, and we do not have the authority to disregard a legislative mandate."

A similar case, Kamara v. Commissioner, T.C. Summary Opinion 2007–103, involved a taxpayer employed as a nurse with $121,309 of wages. He claimed head of household filing status and claimed his parents as dependents. The taxpayer also claimed $35,017 of itemized deductions: $6,450 of medical expenses, $10,298 of state and local income taxes, $4,203 of other state and local taxes, $7,680 of charitable contributions, $13,762 of unreimbursed employee business expenses, $250 of tax preparation fees, and $1,250 of attorney and accounting fees. Strictly as a result of the AMT, which the taxpayer neglected to compute on his tax return, the IRS assessed a deficiency of $4,176. All of the taxpayer's claimed itemized deductions, except charitable contributions, were disallowed for AMT purposes, as well as the taxpayer's personal exemptions for himself and his dependent parents. The court explained the taxpayer's argument as follows:

> [P]etitioner does not challenge respondent's calculation of his AMT liability and agrees that the calculation was in accordance with the Internal Revenue Code. Petitioner's objection is simply that respondent erred in applying the AMT to petitioner. He asserts that Congress did not intend for the AMT to apply to taxpayers like him, who are in the nonwealthy working class. He believes he should not be subject to the AMT since he works two jobs, night shifts, weekends, and overtime to support his family.

While the Tax Court "was not unsympathetic to petitioner's concerns about the AMT's reach," it rejected his arguments, citing *Holly* in concluding that "Congress enacted the AMT provisions, and we have no authority to disregard them."

3.2. *Policy Concerns*

3.2.1. *Equity*

The Joint Committee on Taxation has described some of the equitable concerns of the expansion of the AMT from class tax to mass tax as follows:

> The AMT raises particular equity issues with respect to preference items that are personal in nature. For example, some believe that it is fair that families with many dependents pay less tax than families with fewer dependents and support the regular-tax allowance of personal exemptions . . . to further this goal. Additionally, many believe that the regular tax permits a deduction for State and local taxes because such payments impact ability to pay Federal income tax, and therefore they believe that a similar deduction for AMT purposes should be allowed. The AMT, in disallowing these exemptions [and] deductions . . . may frustrate this view of fairness. Also, under present law, as a result of the lack of indexing the AMT exemption levels [a structural flaw that Congress rectified in 2012], the reach of the AMT will increasingly extend further down the income distribution and thus make the tax system less progressive. . . .

Joint Committee on Taxation, Present Law and Background Relating to the Individual Alternative Minimum Tax 19 (2007).

While the AMT disallows deductions such as the personal exemption, the state and local tax deduction, and the home equity indebtedness interest deduction, it does not currently disallow many of the significant preferences that benefit primarily high-income taxpayers. The capital gains preference, which was disallowed for AMT purposes until 1997, is the most glaring example. Another example is the charitable contribution deduction for the fair market value of appreciated assets, even though the appreciation has never been taxed, which was disallowed for AMT purposes between 1986 and 1993.

3.2.2. *Complexity*

The AMT makes tax compliance and administration more complex. It requires taxpayers, tax professionals, and the IRS to make a second calculation of the tax base and a second set of tax computations. Taxpayers who do not currently owe AMT must make these calculations in order to confirm that they have no AMT liability. Furthermore, because of the temporary adjustments described above, taxpayers not currently subject to the AMT may be required to compute their AMT bases in depreciable property because they may be subject to the AMT in subsequent years.

In addition, consider the impact of the AMT's disallowance of the standard deduction. Taxpayers who know that they will have an amount of itemized deductions below the standard deduction amount would ordinarily not have to worry about keeping track of and substantiating itemized deductions because these taxpayers will simply take the standard deduction. However, if these taxpayers might be subject to the AMT, such record-keeping is necessary, thus undoing the simplification benefit of the standard deduction.

Furthermore, the AMT makes legitimate tax planning more complicated. For example, it may be difficult to predict whether a taxpayer will be subject to the AMT in future years. As a result, the future tax consequences of activities that are favored by the regular tax but not under the AMT (e.g., buying private activity tax-exempt bonds or taking out a home equity loan) are unclear.

Another decision that is complicated by the AMT is the decision to pay an investment adviser on an annual fee basis (which is deductible under § 212, subject to the § 68 two-percent floor) or on a commission basis (not deductible, but added to the basis of the asset purchased). While paying an investment advisor on an annual fee basis may be preferable under the regular income tax in certain circumstances, it will never be preferable under the AMT because the § 212 deduction is denied in its entirety.

4.   TAX PLANNING UNDER THE AMT

The AMT offers some planning opportunities for sophisticated taxpayers who are aware (either personally or through their advisors) of its impact. For example, taxpayers who know that they will be subject to the AMT can avoid purchasing private activity tax-exempt bonds or taking out home equity loans. Moreover, they can transmute disfavored deductions into capital expenditures, as described above with respect to the decision as to how to compensate investment advisors.

In addition, taxpayers who know that they will be subject to the AMT in a particular year but subject to the regular tax in a previous or subsequent year can attempt to defer or accelerate disfavored deductions away from the year that the AMT applies. Also, taxpayers subject to marginal rates in excess of 28 percent under the regular income tax can attempt to move income from a regular tax year into an AMT year. As a result, the shifted income will be subject to the lower 28-percent marginal tax rate of the AMT. For example, if a taxpayer in the 39.6-percent bracket knows that the AMT will apply in the current year but the regular tax will apply in the next year (due to, for example, large miscellaneous itemized deductions in the current year), the taxpayer should attempt to accelerate income items and defer deductions for the current year. The effect is to push income from the regular tax year, during which the taxpayer will be subject to a 39.6-percent marginal tax rate, to the AMT year, during which the taxpayer will be subject to a 28-percent marginal rate.

While sophisticated taxpayers adjust their affairs to best manage (and even avoid) being on the AMT tax rolls, unsophisticated taxpayers are typically unaware of the AMT until it is too late; that is, until they incur the higher AMT liability after computing and filing their returns or after their tax preparers inform them of the additional tax owed.

INDEX

References are to Pages